HANDBOOK OF DIGITAL IMAGE SYNTHESIS

SCIENTIFIC FOUNDATIONS OF RENDERING

HANDBOOK OF DIGITAL IMAGE SYNTHESIS

SCIENTIFIC FOUNDATIONS OF RENDERING

VINCENT PEGORARO

CRC Press is an imprint of the
Taylor & Francis Group, an informa business
AN A K PETERS BOOK

CRC Press
Taylor & Francis Group
6000 Broken Sound Parkway NW, Suite 300
Boca Raton, FL 33487-2742

Printed on acid-free paper
Version Date: 20161019

International Standard Book Number-13: 978-1-4987-7424-6 (Hardback)

Visit the Taylor & Francis Web site at
http://www.taylorandfrancis.com

and the CRC Press Web site at
http://www.crcpress.com

Table of Contents

Part IV Computational Foundations

Part Appendices

List of Figures

List of Tables

List of Algorithms

Preface

MOTIVATION

While its history only dates back to the second half of the twentieth century, the field of computer graphics has undergone a rapid development, not only by adapting techniques from other well-established scientific disciplines, but also by devising alternative approaches to tackle both interdisciplinary and domain-specific challenges. Nowadays, computer graphics is taught at universities and used in industries across continents, so much so that computer-generated imagery has become ubiquitous in modern society, with notable applications including the movie and gaming industries, digital marketing, computer-aided industrial design, architectural design, virtual-environment simulators, and medical imaging.

The technical contributions made by the graphics community over the last few decades have led to the publication of a vast number of scholarly articles and numerous scientific books. The latter range, on the one hand, from general primers gently introducing elementary notions to advanced monographs highly focused in scope, and, on the other hand, from theory-driven treatises to practice-oriented guides putting a greater emphasis on platform-specific implementations. Nevertheless, looking up relevant formulas can still be a rather tedious process, with the derivation of various reported research results remaining hard to find, which may make it daunting for field practitioners to distill and leverage the material disseminated across the substantial amount of published work.

OBJECTIVES

Motivated by the incentive to create a consolidated reference guide, this handbook provides an extensive, yet concise, treatment of the basic principles and advanced concepts underpinning digital image synthesis, while covering a broad range of scientific topics as diverse as pure and applied mathematics, geometric surfaces and data structures, the physics of light interaction and propagation, analytical and numerical simulation schemes, and optical perception and imaging. The presentation of the material is substantiated by numerous figures and computer-generated images illustrating the core ideas, several tables synthesizing results and industry standards, and platform-independent pseudocode highlighting the core algorithms, in addition to a large (though non-exhaustive) collection of bibliographic references to the literature and an index of the standard scientific terms defined therein. Moreover, the foundations that this book rests upon are laid from the ground up, including a compilation of the theoretical formulas relevant for practical implementation in an actual rendering system, along with their step-by-step derivation following a deductive (rather than inductive) reasoning approach.

Besides allowing the reader to fully grasp their underlying assumptions and limitations, the derivations additionally illustrate the methodologies necessary to adapt the results to new problems. To this end, this book explicitly discusses how the latter apply to various instances of algebraic *transformations*, *variance-reduction techniques*, low-pass *filters*, geometric surfaces, *indexing structures*, *phase functions*, *surface reflectance* models, *light transport* simulation techniques, and color spaces, among others. Furthermore, the derivations

102
152
201
356
444
472
563

provide a means of verifying that the presented results are consistent. Because the formulas reported in original publications may occasionally contain typos or rely on under-appreciated assumptions, it is not uncommon for such inaccuracies to appear in subsequent material. By providing a step-by-step derivation of the formulas, this book offers the reader the opportunity to verify the correctness of the results for themselves, which can be used with confidence by practitioners in the field.

STRUCTURE

Instead of providing a predetermined syllabus and sets of exercises like a classical textbook would, the content of this handbook is hierarchically organized by field of study with the intent of shedding light on various issues while simultaneously raising and addressing related problems. The non-sequential access of isolated subsets is further supported by systematic cross-references to sectioning units, equations, figures, tables and algorithms (with the corresponding page number appearing in the margin), as well as to bibliographic citations and indexed terms.

While the book's overall structure follows a logical layout, its design aims at facilitating the navigation through the material in any alternative order. For instance, an instructor may choose to start with a theoretical discussion of the interaction of light with refractive surfaces
647 before introducing *image-forming optical systems*, or conversely consider the practical implementation of a virtual camera model to be a prerequisite for rendering scenes containing
494 *dielectric* materials, both approaches being equally sensible.

AUDIENCE

The content of this handbook not only aims at assisting course instructors in the design of customized syllabi and assignments tailored to the academic background of specific attendees, but also at providing a pedagogical resource allowing the reader to rapidly harness fundamental concepts and experimental trends. The broad scope of the material contained therein is intended to serve as a reference guide for graduate/upper-undergraduate students, professors, faculty members, research scientists, software developers and engineers, and other practitioners in the field of computer graphics, across academia and industry alike. Secondary target audiences additionally include practitioners in the fields of scientific visualization and visual computing as a whole, as well as in other scientific disciplines at a broader scale.

From a theoretical standpoint, the reader is assumed to be familiar with basic notions of algebra and calculus, geometry, physics, algorithms, and biology. In order to implement the results in a rendering system, a prior knowledge of (object-oriented) programming languages and a preliminary understanding of the software architecture of a rendering engine (either based on rasterization, or, more suitably, on ray tracing) will also be necessary.

ACKNOWLEDGMENTS

First and foremost, I would like to acknowledge all members of the graphics community who have contributed to the advancement of the field, either through pioneering research or pedagogical resources. Writing this book would have never been possible without standing on the shoulders of giants, and the material presented therein is merely a synthesis of these original contributions, to which the reader is readily referred for further details.

I am also grateful to Philipp Slusallek for giving me the opportunity to co-instruct the courses on computer graphics and realistic image synthesis while at Saarland University. This experience sparked my incentive to create content that would facilitate the process of customarily selecting material to redesign the lectures. His interest and support of my initiative further encouraged me to undertake this endeavor as a spare-time project, which I subsequently expanded into the more comprehensive resource that this handbook constitutes, with parts of my own dissertation (written at the University of Utah under the supervision of Steve Parker and the former members of my PhD committee) serving as a stepping-stone for some of the chapters within.

Finally, I wish to thank my friends, for being a constant source of inspiration, as well as my parents and family, for their invaluable moral support and continuous encouragements. Last but not least, I am deeply indebted to Hanieh, for attempting to share my life, and for bearing with me throughout those hectic years.

CREDITS

The "Tangle Box" scene, used in *Figure 13.2*, *Chapter 16*, *Figure 17.1*, *Figure 17.2* and 568
Figure 18.21, is modeled after the Cornell Box,[1] hosted by the Program of Computer Graphics 597 629
at Cornell University. 634

The light probe of the Uffizi Gallery, used with permission in *Figure 11.16*, *Chapter 12*, 670
Figure 16.7, *Figure 16.8* and *Figure 18.25*, belongs to the Light Probe Image Gallery[2] and 469 472
High-Resolution Light Probe Image Gallery,[3] courtesy of Paul Debevec from the Institute 607
for Creative Technologies at the University of Southern California. 609 673

[1] `http://www.graphics.cornell.edu/online/box/`.
[2] `http://www.pauldebevec.com/Probes/`.
[3] `http://gl.ict.usc.edu/Data/HighResProbes/`.

Prologue

CHAPTER 1

Introduction

TABLE OF CONTENTS

1.1 HISTORY

From early technological advances made during the 1940s and 1950s [Perez Molina, 2014], to pioneering research carried out during the 1960s and 1970s at the University of Utah [Gaboury, 2014], the Massachusetts Institute of Technology (MIT) and various other institutions [Machover, 1978], computer graphics has undergone a rapid development during the first four decades of the field [Machover, 1994], counting a seminal series of academic publications [Wolfe, 1998b, Wolfe, 1998a]. While a comprehensive account of the notable contributing individuals, companies and events could be an object of study on its own, a time line highlighting key milestones may include:

1950 By deviating the electron beams of an oscilloscope, Ben Laposky creates art pieces that may be regarded as the first form of electronically generated graphic images.

1951 Initially envisioning a flight simulation system to train military pilots, Jay Forrester and Robert Everett of the MIT publicly unveil the *Whirlwind*, a mainframe computer that displays blips representing radar-detected aircrafts on a CRT-based vectorscope.

1955 Based on multiple Whirlwind computers, the *SAGE* (Semi-Automatic Ground Equipment) air defense system is designed at MIT's Lincoln Laboratory [Hurst *et al.*, 1989b, Hurst *et al.*, 1989a] using a CRT-based radar screen to display a scanned region as wireframe vector graphics, and introducing the light pen as an input device for operators to select on-screen targets.

1959 General Motors [Krull, 1994] and IBM develop the *DAC-1* (Design Augmented by Computers), the first industrial computer-aided design (CAD) system, which allows the user to manipulate and visualize the 3-D geometry of a car from various viewpoints.

1960 The term "computer graphics" is coined by William A. Fetter of Boeing to describe the new design methods for his human factors and ergonomics (HF&E) cockpit simulations. Two years later, he creates the "first man," a virtual 3-D model of a human being used for cockpit studies.

1961 The first public video game, *Spacewar!*, is developed by MIT student Steve Russell for the DEC (Digital Equipment Corporation) PDP-1 minicomputer.

1963 Developed for his doctoral thesis at MIT's Lincoln Laboratory, Ivan Sutherland publicly unveils *Sketchpad* [Sutherland, 1963a, Sutherland, 1963b], the first computer-aided drafting and design (CADD) package that allows geometry to be interactively drawn on a vector-graphics display screen using a light pen, whose position is determined by timing the signal emitted by the photoelectric cell at its tip when swept by the electron beam.

1963 Larry Roberts develops the first effective hidden-line removal algorithm, the precursor to various subsequent hidden-line and hidden-surface algorithms.

1963 Doug Englebart of the Stanford Research Institute (SRI) invents a new input device: the computer mouse.

1965 Jack Bresenham of IBM publishes the digital line drawing algorithm for raster devices he had developed three years earlier [Bresenham, 1965].

1966 Ivan Sutherland of MIT's Lincoln Laboratory creates the first head-mounted display (HMD), the *Sword of Damocles* [Sutherland, 1968, Sutherland, 1998], which enabled stereoscopic 3-D depth perception by presenting distinct wireframe images to each eye.

1966 Dave Evans is hired by the University of Utah to form a program in computer science, and creates a group in computer graphics.

1967 Gyorgy Kepes founds the MIT Center for Advanced Visual Studies.

1967 Don Greenberg starts a program at Cornell.

1968 Dave Evans recruits Ivan Sutherland to join his program at the University of Utah, and together found their own company, Evans & Sutherland (E&S), specialized in the development of graphics hardware.

1968 Intel is founded.

1968 Arthur Appel of IBM introduces ray casting/*ray tracing* [Appel, 1968], a technique 598
for hidden-surface removal that may be augmented with a shadow algorithm.

1969 Under the initiative of Sam Matsa and Andy van Dam, the Association for Computing Machinery (ACM) creates a special interest group on graphics, SIGGRAPH [Brown and Cunningham, 2007], whose first conference is held in Boulder in 1973 and counts about 1,200 attendees, compared to over 30,000 nowadays.

1969 Utah alumnus Alan Kay develops the concept of graphical user interface (GUI) at the Palo Alto Research Center (PARC) of Xerox.

1969 Bell Labs build the first framebuffer using 3 bits per pixel, thereby initiating the transition from vector graphics (i.e., drawing lines between coordinates) to raster images containing a value for each picture element (pixel) on the screen.

1971 Utah student Henri Gouraud develops a shading model, that, unlike flat shading, continuously interpolates the color values computed at the vertices of a polygonal mesh [Gouraud, 1971b, Gouraud, 1971a].

1973 The entertainment feature film *Westworld* makes the first use of 2-D computer animation, while 3-D wireframe CGI is first used 3 years later in its 1976 sequel *Futureworld*, featuring an animation of a human hand [Catmull, 1972] and face [Parke, 1972] created in 1972 at the University of Utah by Ed Catmull and Fred Parke, respectively.

1974 Doctoral student Ed Catmull (now president of Pixar Animation Studios), who had returned to the University of Utah and joined Ivan Sutherland's group after working as a computer programmer at Boeing, develops both the Z-buffer hidden-surface algorithm and texture mapping [Catmull, 1974].

1974 Alex Schure, founder of the New York Institute of Technology (NYIT), creates the Computer Graphics Lab (CGL) and names Ed Catmull as director. Joined by Alvy Ray Smith and others, the team produces what could have been the first feature-length CGI film, *The Works*, but which was never completed due to the lack of artistic direction and computational resources.

1975 Utah student Bùi Tuòng Phong develops a specular illumination model, as well as a shading model, that, unlike Gouraud shading, continuously interpolates the normals at the vertices of a polygonal mesh [Phong, 1973, Phong, 1975, Phong and Crow, 1975].

1975 Mathematician Benoît Mandelbrot of IBM introduces "fractals," which are geometric entities of fractional dimension used in computer graphics to create mountainous terrains and textured patterns of various other natural phenomena [Mandelbrot, 1975].

326 **1975** Using *Bézier patches*, Utah student Martin Newell creates a virtual 3-D model of a physical teapot (now on display at the Computer Museum in Boston), which has since been used as a standard model by practitioners in the field and has become an icon of computer graphics [Crow, 1987].

1975 Nineteen-year-old undergraduate student Bill Gates drops out of Harvard and, together with Paul Allen, founds Microsoft.

1976 Inspired by their visit of Xerox's PARC, Steve Jobs and Steve Wozniak found Apple, and release the Macintosh in 1984, which is the first personal computer equipped with a GUI.

1977 Utah alumnus Frank Crow develops anti-aliasing techniques [Crow, 1977].

1977 The Academy of Motion Picture Arts and Sciences (AMPAS) introduces an Oscar category for "Visual Effects," and the "Best Animated Feature Film" award in 2001.

1977 After presenting environment mapping the year before, Utah student Jim Blinn (now at Microsoft Research) introduces a Phong-like specular illumination model expressed in terms of the normal distribution of surface micro-geometry [Blinn, 1977], as well as bump-mapping a year later [Blinn, 1978b, Blinn, 1978a].

1979 After realizing the potential of CGI for special effects, George Lucas recruits Ed Catmull, Alvy Ray Smith and others from the NYIT to form Lucasfilm's computer graphics division.

598 **1980** Turner Whitted of Bell Labs introduces a recursive form of *ray tracing* to simulate specular reflections and refractions [Whitted, 1979, Whitted, 1980].

1980 The European Association for Computer Graphics is created, and the first Eurographics conference is held in Geneva.

1980 The computer-animation production studios Pacific Data Images (PDI) are founded by Carl Rosendahl.

1981 After some work on fractals while at Boeing in 1980, Loren Carpenter joins Lucasfilm and, in collaboration with Rob Cook and Ed Catmull, develops *Reyes* (an acronym for "Renders Everything You Ever Saw," and a pun on Point Reyes, CA) [Cook *et al.*, 1987], which will ultimately become Renderman's rendering engine.

1981 The IEEE Computer Society starts publishing the *Computer Graphics and Applications* (CG&A) journal.

1982 The ACM starts publishing the *Transactions on Graphics* (TOG) journal.

1982 Utah alumnus Jim Clark founds *Silicon Graphics Incorporated* (SGI), which specializes in manufacturing high-end graphics computers.

1982 Utah alumnus John Warnock founds Adobe Systems, and subsequently invents the PostScript page description language (PDL).

1982 Autodesk is founded and the computer-aided design application *AutoCAD* is released.

1982 Within Lucasfilm's CG division, a programming team led by Bill Reeves, develops particle systems [Reeves, 1983] and creates the "genesis" effect for a one-minute shot of *Star Trek II: The Wrath of Khan.*

1982 Disney releases *Tron*, the first film with over 20 minutes of fully computer-generated 3-D shots, including the famous "light cycle" sequence set within a video game. Despite its box-office failure, the movie is now recognized as a landmark, and its sequel, *Tron: Legacy*, is released in 2010.

1984 *The Last Starfighter* is released, which is the first movie to include realistic CGI composited with live-action footage.

1984 Cornell student Michael Cohen creates a virtual 3-D model of a physical box, which has since been used as a standard model by practitioners and has become an icon of global illumination.

1984 Based on techniques from the heat-transfer literature, Cindy Goral and colleagues of
Cornell University introduce the *radiosity method* [Goral *et al.*, 1984] to realistically 593
simulate light propagation between diffuse surfaces.

1984 Cornell alumnus Rob Cook of Lucasfilm introduces distribution *ray tracing* [Cook *et* 598
al., 1984, Cook, 1989] to realistically simulate motion blur, *depth of field*, penumbrae, 662
gloss and translucency.

1984 Lucasfilm's CG division releases *The Adventures of André and Wally B.*, the first fully computer-animated short film, followed by Pixar's *Luxo Jr.* in 1985.

1985 Ken Perlin introduces procedural noise as a means of generating natural patterns such as clouds, fire, marble, wood and terrain height maps [Perlin, 1985].

1986 Utah alumnus Jim Kajiya (now at Microsoft Research) introduces the "rendering equation" [Kajiya, 1986], which mathematically describes the interaction of light with arbitrarily reflecting surfaces, together with *path tracing* to realistically simulate light 613
propagation between such surfaces.

1986 Lucasfilm's CG division becomes Pixar, an independent company that focuses on computer-animated films, which is bought by Steve Jobs and headed by Ed Catmull as president and Alvy Ray Smith as executive vice president.

1986 The special effects division of Lucasfilm, Industrial Light and Magic (ILM), starts a CG group.

1989 The Reyes-based RenderMan system is released by Pixar, and its shading language is published a year later by Pat Hanrahan and Jim Lawson [Hanrahan and Lawson, 1990], who lead the project.

1991 Disney releases *Beauty and the Beast*, which is the first animation to feature computer-generated 3-D scenes (such as an entire ballroom) that were shaded so as to match the appearance of hand-drawn characters blended in together.

1992 SGI releases the specification for the Open Graphics Library (OpenGL), which defines a standard cross-platform graphics API.

1993 Nvidia is founded.

1995 Pixar Animation Studios release *Toy Story*, the first full-length computer-animated film.

1996 Under the supervision of John Carmack as lead programmer, ID Software produces *Quake*, which, unlike its predecessor *Doom*, is the first video game to use fully 3-D geometry.

2001 *Final Fantasy – The Spirits Within* is released, which is the first film featuring virtual actors, but whose realism had reached the rim of the *uncanny valley* [Tinwell, 2014], which is a dip in the subjective comfort towards robots as they become more and more human-like, causing a feeling of revulsion presumed to be one of the key reasons for the movie's box-office failure.

1.2 WORLDWIDE

Over the years, computer graphics has progressively drawn interest from the international research community around the world [Cameron, 1996a, Marcos, 1998], not only in America (e.g., the United States [Machover, 1969, Green, 1969, Machover, 1996, Henderson, 1996, McConnell, 1996] and Brazil [Zuffo, 1996, Netto, 1998]), but also in Asia (e.g., Russia [Paltashev, 1996, Bayakovsky, 1996], Japan [Nakamae *et al.*, 1984, Kunii *et al.*, 1996, Inakage and Inakage, 1996, Suzuki, 1997], Korea [Kim *et al.*, 2002], China [Shi and Pan, 1996b, Shi and Pan, 1996a, Shi and Pan, 2001], Hong Kong [Pan *et al.*, 2000], Singapore [Seah and Lee, 1998], India [Mudur *et al.*, 1999], Israel [Gotsman, 1996, Adler, 1996] and Turkey [Özgüç, 1996b, Özgüç, 1996a]) as well as in Europe [Brunetti, 1998] (e.g., Portugal [Teixeira, 1996], Spain [Brunet and Navazo, 1996], Italy [Valle, 1996, Falcidieno, 1996], France [Chenais, 1996, Wennberg, 1996, Sillion, 1996, Welker, 2013], Germany [Encarnação, 1994, Encarnação and Felger, 1996, Hansmann, 1996, Saupe and Alexa, 2001], former Czechoslovakia [Slavik, 1992], the Czech Republic [Slavik, 1996], the United Kingdom [Jones and Lansdown, 1996, Brodlie and Mumford, 1996], Sweden [Kjelldahl, 1996] and Scandinavia [Kjelldahl and Jern, 1996, Kjelldahl, 1999]), in Oceania (e.g., Australia [Robertson, 1996, Cottingham, 1996]) and in Africa [Asare *et al.*, 2002].

Since then, the pedagogical value of the field has been increasingly recognized, not only as a supporting tool to teach other topics in higher education [Brown, 1992], but also as an integral discipline of its own [Mair and Owen, 1993, Cameron, 1996b, Bailey and Cunningham, 2005].

1.3 TERMINOLOGY

In the field of computer science, *visual computing* is concerned with the computational acquisition, processing, analysis, and/or synthesis of visual data. To this end, visual computing draws upon many other scientific domains such as mathematics, statistics, signal theory, geometry, physics, algorithmics, numerical analysis, optics, photography, physiology, psychophysics and perception. The realm of visual computing in turn encompasses various disciplines, including:

- *3-D modeling*: the digital acquisition, representation, processing and manipulation of geometry and material properties for visual purposes
- *computer animation*: the time-dependent capture, animation and simulation of rigid/soft-body motion and fluid-flow dynamics for visual purposes
- *rendering*: the digital synthesis of 2-D images from 2-D or 3-D virtual content
- *scientific visualization* and *information visualization*: the digital synthesis of informative images from scientific data

- *virtual reality* (*VR*) and *augmented reality* (*AR*): the visual immersion into a virtual environment, and the combination of elements from both real and virtual environments, respectively
- *human–computer interaction* (*HCI*): the design of ergonomic user interfaces via tactile, visual or auditory input-output devices
- *computational photography*: the computational acquisition of digital images from real-world environments
- *image processing*: the computerized enhancement of image (or video) data
- *computer vision*: the extraction, analysis and semantic interpretation of visual content from images via inverse rendering

The field of *computer graphics* is then broadly defined as the set of disciplines involved in digitally synthesizing and manipulating images or visual content, thereby consensually including rendering, 3-D modeling and computer animation, as well as to a lesser extent scientific/information visualization, VR/AR, HCI (especially in the context of *graphical user interfaces* (*GUI*)) and imaging.

Within rendering, different specializations may be further distinguished:

- *non-photorealistic rendering* (*NPR*): the digital synthesis of artistically/aesthetically stylized images such as paintings, drawings, illustrations and cartoons
- *real-time rendering*: the digital synthesis of images at highly interactive frame rates
- *(photo-)realistic rendering*: the digital synthesis of images that are qualitatively as realistic as an actual photograph
- *physically based rendering*: the digital synthesis of images based on the laws of physics
- *predictive rendering*: the digital synthesis of images whose content is quantitatively predictive of real-world phenomena

1.4 APPLICATIONS

Computer graphics is now ubiquitous in modern societies, and the field has come to span a broad range of applications. Within the realm of the entertainment industry, those encompass realistic visual effects in movies [Aitken *et al.*, 2004, Hiebert *et al.*, 2006] (and motion pictures in the larger sense, including television programs and commercials) as well as visually pleasing renderings for animated films [Adamson *et al.*, 2001, Christensen *et al.*, 2006, Shah *et al.*, 2007, Bredow *et al.*, 2007], both being commonly referred to as *computer-generated imagery* (*CGI*) as opposed to live-action footage and hand-drawn images, respectively. In contrast, video games are, by definition, computer-generated, and while the industry still strives for aesthetically appealing visuals, interactivity is paramount in ray-traced video games [Schmittler *et al.*, 2004, Schmittler *et al.*, 2005, Friedrich *et al.*, 2006, Bikker, 2007], and even more so in real-time video games [Tatarchuk *et al.*, 2006, Tatarchuk *et al.*, 2007, Tatarchuk *et al.*, 2008, Tatarchuk, 2009, Tatarchuk, 2011].

Physical accuracy is typically of greater importance in virtual reality and industrial design [Wald *et al.*, 2006], be it for the *computer-aided design* (*CAD*) of car interiors and paints in the automotive industry [Benthin *et al.*, 2002], or for the design of the cabin and fuselage of aircrafts in the aerospace industry [Dietrich *et al.*, 2006]. The trade-offs between visual quality and interactive feedback are also of concern in engineering applications such as driving simulators [Wang *et al.*, 2007, Slob, 2008], as well as in the context of medical imaging and virtual surgery planning [Ezquerra *et al.*, 1999, Bartz, 2003, Vidal *et al.*, 2004, Klein *et al.*, 2008].

Likewise, high-fidelity rendering provides predictive tools for stage lighting [Dorsey *et al.*, 1991], and lighting design in general [Ward Larson, 1996], as well as for interior/architectural design [Dorsey and McMillan, 1998] and building science [Inanici, 2001, Ochoa *et al.*, 2011]. Larger-scale applications not only include urban [Vanegas *et al.*, 2009] and landscape planning [Dietrich *et al.*, 2005], but also means of unveiling the past, as in the context of virtual archaeological reconstruction [Happa *et al.*, 2010, Stanco *et al.*, 2011].

1.5 FURTHER READING

Additional material may be found in books dedicated to the history of computer graphics [Ryan, 2011].

I

Mathematical Foundations

CHAPTER 2

Elementary Algebra & Calculus

TABLE OF CONTENTS

2.1 SERIES

2.1.1 Triangular and Tetrahedral Numbers

As illustrated in *Figure 2.1*, the nth *triangular number* t_n is defined as the number of elements 15
forming a triangle of height n

$$t_n \triangleq \sum_{i=0}^{n} i = 0+1+2+3+\ldots+n = \frac{\sum_{i=0}^{n} i + \sum_{i=0}^{n} n-i}{2} = \frac{\sum_{i=0}^{n} n}{2} = \frac{n(n+1)}{2} = \binom{n+1}{2} \tag{2.1}$$

from which follow the identities

$$\begin{aligned} t_{m\times n} &= t_m t_n + t_{m-1}t_{n-1} &(2.2)\\ t_{m+n} &= t_m + t_n + mn &(2.3)\\ t_{2n} &= 3t_n + t_{n-1} &(2.4)\\ t_{2n+1} &= 3t_n + t_{n+1} &(2.5)\\ t_n + t_{n-1} &= (t_n - t_{n-1})^2 &(2.6)\end{aligned}$$

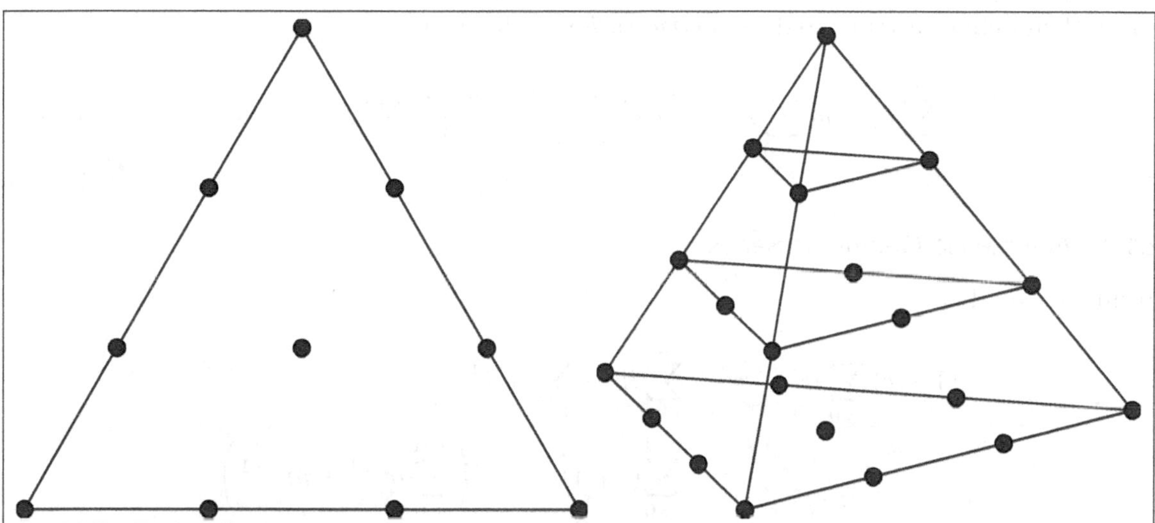

Figure 2.1: Triangular and Tetrahedral Numbers: Illustration of the triangular (left) and tetrahedral (right) numbers, corresponding to the number of elements forming a triangle and tetrahedron, respectively, of given height.

Similarly, the nth *tetrahedral number* T_n is defined as the number of elements forming a tetrahedron of height n

$$T_n \triangleq \sum_{i=0}^{n} t_i \overset{(2.1)}{=} 0+1+3+6+\ldots+t_n = \frac{n(n+1)(n+2)}{6} = \binom{n+2}{3} \tag{2.7}$$ 15

2.1.2 Arithmetic Series

Given an *arithmetic sequence* $a_i \triangleq a_0 + id$ with *common difference* d, the sum of its first $n+1$ terms defines a truncated *arithmetic series* of the form

$$\begin{aligned} \sum_{i=0}^{n} a_i &= \sum_{i=0}^{n} a_0 + d\sum_{i=0}^{n} i \overset{(2.1)}{=} (n+1)a_0 + d\frac{n(n+1)}{2} \\ &= \frac{(n+1)(2a_0+nd)}{2} = \frac{(n+1)(a_0+a_n)}{2} \end{aligned} \tag{2.8}$$ 15

2.1.3 Geometric Series

From the equality

$$(1-r)\sum_{i=0}^{n} r^i = \sum_{i=0}^{n} r^i - \sum_{i=0}^{n} r^{i+1} = \left(1 + \sum_{i=1}^{n} r^i\right) - \left(\sum_{i=1}^{n} r^i + r^{n+1}\right) = 1 - r^{n+1} \tag{2.9}$$

follows the identity

$$\sum_{i=0}^{n} r^i = 1 + r + r^2 + r^3 + \ldots + r^n = \frac{1-r^{n+1}}{1-r}, \quad \forall r \neq 1 \tag{2.10}$$

whose limit as $n \to \infty$, whenever $|r| < 1$, reduces to

$$\sum_{i=0}^{\infty} r^i = \frac{1}{1-r}, \quad \forall |r| < 1 \tag{2.11}$$

Given a *geometric sequence* $a_i = a_0 r^i$ with *common ratio* r, the sum of its first $n+1$ terms then defines a truncated *geometric series* of the form

16

$$\sum_{i=0}^{n} a_i = a_0 \sum_{i=0}^{n} r^i \overset{(2.10)}{=} a_0 \frac{1-r^{n+1}}{1-r} = \frac{a_0 - a_{n+1}}{1-r}, \quad \forall r \neq 1 \tag{2.12}$$

2.1.4 Arithmetico-Geometric Series

From the equality

16

$$\begin{aligned}
(1-r)\sum_{i=0}^{n} i r^i &= \sum_{i=1}^{n} i r^i - \sum_{i=0}^{n} i r^{i+1} \\
&= \sum_{i=0}^{n-1} (i+1) r^{i+1} - \left(\sum_{i=0}^{n-1} i r^{i+1} + n r^{n+1}\right) \\
&= \sum_{i=0}^{n-1} r^{i+1} - n r^{n+1} \\
&\overset{(2.10)}{=} r\frac{1-r^n}{1-r} - n r^{n+1}, \quad \forall r \neq 1
\end{aligned} \tag{2.13}$$

follows the identity

$$\sum_{i=0}^{n} i r^i = 0 + r + 2r^2 + 3r^3 + \ldots + n r^n = \frac{r - r^{n+1}}{(1-r)^2} - \frac{n r^{n+1}}{1-r}, \quad \forall r \neq 1 \tag{2.14}$$

whose limit as $n \to \infty$, whenever $|r| < 1$, reduces to

$$\sum_{i=0}^{\infty} i r^i = \frac{r}{(1-r)^2}, \quad \forall |r| < 1 \tag{2.15}$$

Given an *arithmetico-geometric sequence* $a_i = (a_0 + id) r^i$ with common difference d and common ratio r, the sum of its first $n+1$ terms then defines a truncated *arithmetico-geometric series* of the form

$$\begin{aligned}
\sum_{i=0}^{n} a_i &= a_0 \sum_{i=0}^{n} r^i + d \sum_{i=0}^{n} i r^i \\
&\overset{(2.10)}{\underset{(2.14)}{=}} a_0 \frac{1-r^{n+1}}{1-r} + d\left(\frac{r-r^{n+1}}{(1-r)^2} - \frac{n r^{n+1}}{1-r}\right) \\
&= \frac{a_0 - a_0 r^{n+1}}{1-r} + d\left(\frac{r-r^{n+1}}{(1-r)^2} - \frac{(n+1) r^{n+1}}{1-r} + \frac{(1-r) r^{n+1}}{(1-r)^2}\right) \\
&= \frac{a_0 - a_{n+1}}{1-r} + d\frac{r-r^{n+2}}{(1-r)^2}, \quad \forall r \neq 1 \qquad (2.16)
\end{aligned}$$

16

16

2.2 POLYNOMIAL ANALYSIS

2.2.1 Polynomial Interpolation

2.2.1.1 Definition

Given a set of $n+1$ distinct pairs of coordinates $[x_i, y_i], \forall i \in [0, n]$, the *unisolvence theorem* states that there exists a unique polynomial $f(x)$ of degree n that interpolates all data points such that

$$f(x_i) = y_i, \quad \forall i \in [0, n] \tag{2.17}$$

More generally, given a set of $n+1$ distinct tuples of coordinates $[x_i, y_i, y_i^{(1)}, \ldots, y_i^{(m-1)}], \forall i \in [0, n]$ containing the ordinates y_i and the values of the $m-1$ first derivatives $y_i^{(j)}$ at abscissa x_i, there exists a unique polynomial $f(x)$ of degree $(n+1)m-1$ that interpolates all data points such that

$$f^{(j)}(x_i) = y_i^{(j)}, \quad \forall i \in [0, n], \forall j \in [0, m-1] \tag{2.18}$$

2.2.1.2 Monomial Form

Given a set of $n+1$ distinct pairs of coordinates $[x_i, y_i], \forall i \in [0, n]$, an interpolating polynomial may be expressed in *monomial form*

$$f(x) \triangleq \sum_{i=0}^{n} c_i x^i \tag{2.19}$$

as a linear combination of the *monomial basis functions* x^i.

The coefficients are then given as the solution of the system of linear equations defined by the *Vandermonde matrix*

$$\begin{bmatrix} 1 & x_0 & \cdots & x_0^{n-1} & x_0^n \\ 1 & x_1 & \cdots & x_1^{n-1} & x_1^n \\ \vdots & \vdots & \ddots & \vdots & \vdots \\ 1 & x_{n-1} & \cdots & x_{n-1}^{n-1} & x_{n-1}^n \\ 1 & x_n & \cdots & x_n^{n-1} & x_n^n \end{bmatrix} \begin{bmatrix} c_0 \\ c_1 \\ \vdots \\ c_{n-1} \\ c_n \end{bmatrix} = \begin{bmatrix} y_0 \\ y_1 \\ \vdots \\ y_{n-1} \\ y_n \end{bmatrix} \tag{2.20}$$

As an alternative, the polynomial can also be recursively formulated via *Horner's method* as

$$f(x) = b_0(x) \tag{2.21}$$

where

$$b_i(x) \triangleq \begin{cases} c_n & \text{if } i = n \\ c_i + b_{i+1}(x)x & \text{if } i < n \end{cases} \tag{2.22}$$

which may be efficiently evaluated in order of decreasing index via backward recursion.

2.2.1.3 Lagrange Form

Given a set of $n+1$ distinct pairs of coordinates $[x_i, y_i], \forall i \in [0, n]$, an interpolating polynomial may be expressed in the form of a *Lagrange polynomial*, so-called *Lagrange form*,

$$f(x) \triangleq \sum_{i=0}^{n} y_i l_i(x) \tag{2.23}$$

as a linear combination of the *Lagrange basis polynomials*

$$l_i(x) \triangleq \prod_{\substack{j=0 \\ j \neq i}}^{n} \frac{x - x_j}{x_i - x_j}, \quad \forall i \in [0, n] \tag{2.24}$$

44 which satisfy the identity expressed in terms of the Kronecker *delta function*

$$l_i(x_k) = \delta[i - k] \tag{2.25}$$

such that

18
18
46

$$f(x_k) \overset{(2.23)}{=} \sum_{i=0}^{n} y_i l_i(x_k) \overset{(2.25)}{=} \sum_{i=0}^{n} y_i \delta[i - k] \overset{(2.223)}{=} y_k \tag{2.26}$$

In order to reduce the asymptotic cost of the evaluation process from $O(n^2)$ to $O(n)$, the basis polynomials can alternatively be formulated in barycentric form as

18

$$l_i(x) \overset{(2.24)}{=} \frac{\prod_{\substack{j=0 \\ j \neq i}}^{n} (x - x_j)}{\prod_{\substack{j=0 \\ j \neq i}}^{n} (x_i - x_j)} = \frac{l(x)}{x - x_i} w_i, \quad \forall x \neq x_i \tag{2.27}$$

with the *generating function*

$$l(x) \triangleq \prod_{j=0}^{n} (x - x_j) \tag{2.28}$$

and precomputed weights

$$w_i \triangleq \frac{1}{\prod_{\substack{j=0 \\ j \neq i}}^{n} (x_i - x_j)} \tag{2.29}$$

such that the formulation of the polynomial becomes

18
18

$$f(x) \overset{(2.23)}{\underset{(2.27)}{=}} l(x) \sum_{i=0}^{n} y_i \frac{w_i}{x - x_i} = \frac{l(x) \sum_{i=0}^{n} y_i \frac{w_i}{x - x_i}}{l(x) \sum_{i=0}^{n} 1 \frac{w_i}{x - x_i}} = \frac{\sum_{i=0}^{n} y_i \frac{w_i}{x - x_i}}{\sum_{i=0}^{n} \frac{w_i}{x - x_i}}, \quad \forall x \neq x_i \tag{2.30}$$

2.2.1.4 Newton Form

Given a set of $n+1$ distinct pairs of coordinates $[x_i, y_i], \forall i \in [0, n]$, an interpolating polynomial may be expressed in the form of a *Newton polynomial*, so-called *Newton form*,

$$f(x) \triangleq \sum_{i=0}^{n} a_i n_i(x) \tag{2.31}$$

as a linear combination of the *Newton basis polynomials*

$$n_i(x) \triangleq \prod_{j=0}^{i-1}(x - x_j), \quad \forall i \in [0, n] \tag{2.32}$$

$$= \begin{cases} 1 & \text{if } i = 0 \\ (x - x_{i-1}) \prod_{j=0}^{i-2}(x - x_j) = (x - x_{i-1}) n_{i-1}(x) & \text{if } i \geq 1 \end{cases} \tag{2.33}$$

which satisfy

$$n_i(x_k) = 0, \quad \forall i \in [k+1, n] \tag{2.34}$$

such that

$$f(x_k) \overset{(2.31)}{=} \sum_{i=0}^{n} a_i n_i(x_k) \overset{(2.34)}{=} \sum_{i=0}^{k} a_i n_i(x_k) \tag{2.35}$$ 19 19

The coefficients are then given as the solution of the system of linear equations $f(x_k) = y_k$ defined by the lower triangular matrix

$$\begin{bmatrix} 1 & 0 & \dots & 0 & 0 \\ 1 & n_1(x_1) & \dots & 0 & 0 \\ \vdots & \vdots & \ddots & \vdots & \vdots \\ 1 & n_1(x_{n-1}) & \dots & n_{n-1}(x_{n-1}) & 0 \\ 1 & n_1(x_n) & \dots & n_{n-1}(x_n) & n_n(x_n) \end{bmatrix} \begin{bmatrix} a_0 \\ a_1 \\ \vdots \\ a_{n-1} \\ a_n \end{bmatrix} = \begin{bmatrix} y_0 \\ y_1 \\ \vdots \\ y_{n-1} \\ y_n \end{bmatrix} \tag{2.36}$$

which can be iteratively solved in order of increasing index k as

$$f(x_k) \overset{(2.35)}{=} a_k n_k(x_k) + \sum_{i=0}^{k-1} a_i n_i(x_k) = y_k \iff a_k = \frac{y_k - \sum_{i=0}^{k-1} a_i n_i(x_k)}{n_k(x_k)} \tag{2.37}$$ 19

with an asymptotic cost of $O(n^2)$, instead of $O(n^3)$, by recursively evaluating the basis polynomials using *Equation 2.33* rather than *Equation 2.32*. 19

As an alternative, the coefficients may be equivalently expressed as 19

$$a_k = [y_0, \dots, y_k] \tag{2.38}$$

in terms of forward *divided differences* (reducing to forward finite differences in the case of uniformly spaced intervals)

$$[y_m, \dots, y_n] \triangleq \begin{cases} y_m & \text{if } n = m \\ \frac{[y_{m+1}, \dots, y_n] - [y_m, \dots, y_{n-1}]}{x_n - x_m} & \text{if } n > m \end{cases} \tag{2.39}$$

$$= \frac{[y_{m+2}, \dots, y_n] - [y_{m+1}, \dots, y_{n-1}]}{(x_n - x_{m+1})(x_n - x_m)} + \frac{[y_{m+1}, \dots, y_{n-1}] - [y_m, \dots, y_{n-2}]}{(x_{n-1} - x_m)(x_m - x_n)}, \quad \forall n > m+1$$

$$= \dots$$

$$= \sum_{i=m}^{n} \frac{y_i}{\prod_{\substack{j=m \\ j \neq i}}^{n} (x_i - x_j)} \tag{2.40}$$

such that all coefficients can be computed in-place by evaluating the divided differences in order of decreasing index successively on each level of the tree from the leaves to the root

$$
\begin{array}{cccccc}
x_0 & y_0 = [y_0] & & & & \\
 & & [y_0, y_1] & & & \\
x_1 & y_1 = [y_1] & & [y_0, \ldots, y_2] & & \\
\vdots & \vdots & \vdots & \vdots & \ddots & \\
x_i & y_i = [y_i] & & [y_{i-1}, \ldots, y_{i+1}] & & \\
 & & [y_i, y_{i+1}] & & \cdots & [y_0, \ldots, y_n] \\
x_{i+1} & y_{i+1} = [y_{i+1}] & & [y_i, \ldots, y_{i+2}] & & \\
\vdots & \vdots & \vdots & \vdots & \iddots & \\
x_{n-1} & y_{n-1} = [y_{n-1}] & & [y_{n-2}, \ldots, y_n] & & \\
 & & [y_{n-1}, y_n] & & & \\
x_n & y_n = [y_n] & & & &
\end{array}
\tag{2.41}
$$

Similarly, the interpolating polynomial may be expressed recursively by means of *Neville's algorithm*

$$f(x) = p_{0,n}(x) \tag{2.42}$$

where

$$p_{i,j}(x) \triangleq \begin{cases} y_i & \text{if } 0 \leq i = j \leq n \\ \frac{(x_j - x)p_{i,j-1}(x) + (x - x_i)p_{i+1,j}(x)}{x_j - x_i} & \text{if } 0 \leq i < j \leq n \end{cases} \tag{2.43}$$

2.2.1.5 Hermite Interpolation

Given a set of $n+1$ distinct tuples of coordinates $[x_i, y_i, y_i^{(1)}, \ldots, y_i^{(m-1)}], \forall i \in [0, n]$, *Hermite interpolation* (in contrast to *Birkhoff interpolation*, which allows the values of lower deriva-
19 tives to be omitted) expresses the interpolating polynomial in a generalized *Newton form*

$$f(x) \triangleq \sum_{i=0}^{(n+1)m-1} a_i n_i(x) \tag{2.44}$$

as a linear combination of the generalized basis polynomials

$$n_i(x) \triangleq \prod_{j=0}^{i-1} (x - x_{\lfloor j/m \rfloor}) \tag{2.45}$$

The coefficients are then defined as

$$a_i \triangleq [y_0, \ldots, y_i] \tag{2.46}$$

in terms of generalized divided differences where the leaves of the tree are duplicated m times and all internal nodes $[y_i, \ldots, y_j]$ for which $\lfloor i/m \rfloor = \ldots = \lfloor j/m \rfloor$ are substituted by

$$\frac{y_{\lfloor i/m \rfloor}^{(k)}}{k!} = \ldots = \frac{y_{\lfloor j/m \rfloor}^{(k)}}{k!} \tag{2.47}$$

such that, for $m = 3$, the tree of coefficients reads

$$
\begin{array}{lllllll}
x_0 & y_0 = [y_0] & & & & & \\
 & & \frac{y_0'}{1!} = [y_0, y_1] & & & & \\
x_0 & y_0 = [y_1] & & \frac{y_0''}{2!} = [y_0, y_1, y_2] & & & \\
 & & \frac{y_0'}{1!} = [y_1, y_2] & & [y_0, \ldots, y_3] & & \\
x_0 & y_0 = [y_2] & & [y_1, y_2, y_3] & & & \\
 & & [y_2, y_3] & & [y_1, \ldots, y_4] & & \\
x_1 & y_1 = [y_3] & & [y_2, y_3, y_4] & & & \\
 & & \frac{y_1'}{1!} = [y_3, y_4] & & [y_2, \ldots, y_5] & & \\
x_1 & y_1 = [y_4] & & \frac{y_1''}{2!} = [y_3, y_4, y_5] & & & \\
 & & \frac{y_1'}{1!} = [y_4, y_5] & & [y_3, \ldots, y_6] & & \\
x_1 & y_1 = [y_5] & & [y_4, y_5, y_6] & & & \\
\vdots & \vdots & \vdots & \vdots & \vdots & \ddots & \\
x_i & y_i = [y_{3i}] & & [y_{3i-1}, y_{3i}, y_{3i+1}] & & & \\
 & & \frac{y_i'}{1!} = [y_{3i}, y_{3i+1}] & & [y_{3i-1}, \ldots, y_{3i+2}] & & \\
x_i & y_i = [y_{3i+1}] & & \frac{y_i''}{2!} = [y_{3i}, y_{3i+1}, y_{3i+2}] & & & \\
 & & \frac{y_i'}{1!} = [y_{3i+1}, y_{3i+2}] & & [y_{3i}, \ldots, y_{3i+3}] & & \\
x_i & y_i = [y_{3i+2}] & & [y_{3i+1}, y_{3i+2}, y_{3i+3}] & & & \\
 & & [y_{3i+2}, y_{3i+3}] & & [y_{3i+1}, \ldots, y_{3i+4}] & \cdots & [y_0, \ldots, y_{3n+2}] \\
x_{i+1} & y_{i+1} = [y_{3i+3}] & & [y_{3i+2}, y_{3i+3}, y_{3i+4}] & & & \\
 & & \frac{y_{i+1}'}{1!} = [y_{3i+3}, y_{3i+4}] & & [y_{3i+2}, \ldots, y_{3i+5}] & & \\
x_{i+1} & y_{i+1} = [y_{3i+4}] & & \frac{y_{i+1}''}{2!} = [y_{3i+3}, y_{3i+4}, y_{3i+5}] & & & \\
 & & \frac{y_{i+1}'}{1!} = [y_{3i+4}, y_{3i+5}] & & [y_{3i+3}, \ldots, y_{3i+6}] & & \\
x_{i+1} & y_{i+1} = [y_{3i+5}] & & [y_{3i+4}, y_{3i+5}, y_{3i+6}] & & & \\
\vdots & \vdots & \vdots & \vdots & \vdots & \iddots & \\
x_{n-1} & y_{n-1} = [y_{3n-3}] & & [y_{3n-4}, y_{3n-3}, y_{3n-2}] & & & \\
 & & \frac{y_{n-1}'}{1!} = [y_{3n-3}, y_{3n-2}] & & [y_{3n-4}, \ldots, y_{3n-1}] & & \\
x_{n-1} & y_{n-1} = [y_{3n-2}] & & \frac{y_{n-1}''}{2!} = [y_{3n-3}, y_{3n-2}, y_{3n-1}] & & & \\
 & & \frac{y_{n-1}'}{1!} = [y_{3n-2}, y_{3n-1}] & & [y_{3n-3}, \ldots, y_{3n}] & & \\
x_{n-1} & y_{n-1} = [y_{3n-1}] & & [y_{3n-2}, y_{3n-1}, y_{3n}] & & & \\
 & & [y_{3n-1}, y_{3n}] & & [y_{3n-2}, \ldots, y_{3n+1}] & & \\
x_n & y_n = [y_{3n}] & & [y_{3n-1}, y_{3n}, y_{3n+1}] & & & \\
 & & \frac{y_n'}{1!} = [y_{3n}, y_{3n+1}] & & [y_{3n-1}, \ldots, y_{3n+2}] & & \\
x_n & y_n = [y_{3n+1}] & & \frac{y_n''}{2!} = [y_{3n}, y_{3n+1}, y_{3n+2}] & & & \\
 & & \frac{y_n'}{1!} = [y_{3n+1}, y_{3n+2}] & & & & \\
x_n & y_n = [y_{3n+2}] & & & & &
\end{array}
\tag{2.48}
$$

2.2.1.6 Approximation Error

Subsequently generalized into the *Stone–Weierstrass theorem*, the *Weierstrass approximation theorem* states that for every continuous function $f(x)$ defined on an interval $[a, b]$, there exists a sequence of uniformly convergent polynomials $f_n(x)$ of degree n such that

$$\lim_{n \to \infty} \sup_{x \in [a,b]} \{|f_n(x) - f(x)|\} = 0 \tag{2.49}$$

Shall $f(x)$ be approximated by a polynomial $f_n(x)$ that interpolates $n+1$ pairs of coordinates, the error term reads

$$f_n(x) - f(x) = \frac{f^{(n+1)}(\xi)}{(n+1)!} \prod_{i=0}^{n} (x - x_i) \tag{2.50}$$

for some $\xi \in [a, b]$. However, when using equidistant sample points within the interval, uniform convergence is not guaranteed, and $f_n(x)$ becomes increasingly oscillatory as n grows,
22 a property known as *Runge's phenomenon* and illustrated in *Figure 2.2*. Runge's phenomenon can be minimized by using non-equally spaced data points instead, such as the *Chebyshev nodes*, which are distributed more densely towards the periphery of the interval so as to minimize $\max_{x\in[a,b]} |\prod_{i=0}^{n}(x - x_i)|$.

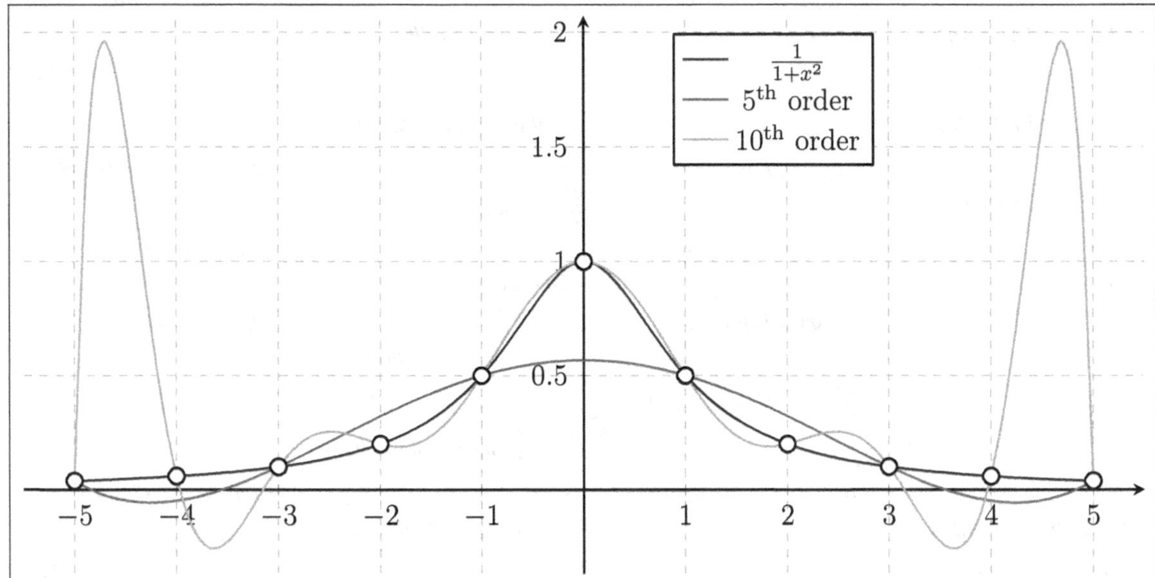

Figure 2.2: Runge's Phenomenon: Illustration of Runge's phenomenon exhibited by polynomials of different orders interpolating equally spaced data points of the Runge function.

More generally, if $f(x)$ is approximated by a higher-degree polynomial that also matches the first $m-1$ derivatives at the $n+1$ data points, the error term becomes

$$f_n(x) - f(x) = \frac{f^{((n+1)m)}(\xi)}{((n+1)m)!} \prod_{i=0}^{n} (x - x_i)^m \tag{2.51}$$

2.2.2 Polynomial Integration

2.2.2.1 Definition

The *fundamental theorem of calculus* states that the *definite integral* of a given *integrand* $f(x)$ can be expressed in closed form in terms of its *indefinite integral*, so-called *antiderivative*, $f^{(-1)}(x) \triangleq \int f(x)\mathrm{d}x$ as

$$\int_a^b f(x)\mathrm{d}x = \left[f^{(-1)}(x)\right]_a^b = f^{(-1)}(b) - f^{(-1)}(a) \tag{2.52}$$

54 Shall the integral involve a *special function* or infinite series, the antiderivative be unknown or the integrand be represented by point samples rather than by an analytical expression, the definite integral instead ought to be numerically evaluated.

Given a set of $n+1$ sample coordinates $x_i \in [a, b], \forall i \in [0, n]$, approximating the integrand via *polynomial interpolation* using a polynomial in *Lagrange form* 17
18

18

$$f(x) \overset{(2.23)}{\approx} \sum_{i=0}^{n} f(x_i) l_i(x) \tag{2.53}$$

yields a scheme known in numerical analysis as *quadrature* in the one-dimensional case, and as *cubature* in higher dimensions

$$\int_a^b f(x)\mathrm{d}x \approx \int_a^b \sum_{i=0}^{n} f(x_i) l_i(x)\mathrm{d}x = \sum_{i=0}^{n} w_i f(x_i) \tag{2.54}$$

with weights $w_i \triangleq \int_a^b l_i(x)\mathrm{d}x, \forall i \in [0, n]$. The scheme is then said to be of *closed type* if the sample coordinates x_i include the endpoints a and b of the integration domain, and of *open type* if the latter are excluded, while the approximation error can be derived from the *mean value theorem* for some $\xi \in [a, b]$

$$f(\xi) = \frac{f^{(-1)}(b) - f^{(-1)}(a)}{b - a} \tag{2.55}$$

Assuming equally spaced data points with step size $x_i - x_{i-1} = \Delta x \triangleq \frac{x_n - x_0}{n}$ then yields the *Newton–Cotes formulas*, whose error bound for a one-dimensional quadrature based on a pth-degree polynomial is proportional to $(\Delta x)^{k+1} f^{(k)}(\xi) = \left(\frac{x_n - x_0}{n}\right)^{k+1} f^{(k)}(\xi)$ (here assuming a closed-type scheme) with $k = 2 + 2\lfloor p/2 \rfloor$. The scheme is therefore exact for any polynomial f of degree strictly less than k, as may be illustrated by considering a 0th-degree polynomial reconstructing a linear function at its midpoint, the integral of both being equal.

To limit the impact of Runge's phenomenon as the number of data points increases though, *Gaussian quadrature* instead relies on non-uniformly spaced data points, typically distributed more densely towards the periphery of the integration domain. As an alternative, the integral may be formulated as a *Riemann sum* by subdividing the domain of integration into n intervals $[a = x_0 < x_1 < \ldots < x_n = b]$ of equal size $x_i - x_{i-1} = \Delta x \triangleq \frac{x_n - x_0}{n}$ with boundaries $x_i = x_0 + i\Delta x$ and midpoints $\frac{x_{i-1} + x_i}{2} = x_0 + (i - 1/2)\Delta x$

$$\int_{x_0}^{x_n} f(x)\mathrm{d}x = \sum_{i=1}^{n} \int_{x_{i-1}}^{x_i} f(x)\mathrm{d}x \tag{2.56}$$

within each of which a low-order Newton–Cotes formula of degree m is applied separately, thereby yielding a *composite rule* with an error bound proportional to $n\left(\frac{x_n - x_0}{mn}\right)^{k+1} f^{(k)}(\xi) \propto \frac{f^{(k)}(\xi)}{n^k}$ (the expression on the left-hand side here assuming a closed-type scheme). The one-dimensional quadrature thus exhibits a convergence rate of $O(n^{-k})$ whenever the integrand is C_k-continuous. For a d-dimensional cubature, the multiple integral can be repeatedly formulated as one-dimensional *iterated integrals* by means of *Fubini's theorem*, and the convergence rate becomes $O(n^{-\frac{k}{d}})$, while the asymptotic cost of the evaluation process (i.e., the number of d-dimensional data points, and therefore of function evaluations) increases exponentially as $O(n^d)$, a phenomenon known as the *curse of dimensionality*.

2.2.2.2 Rectangle Rule

Given the midpoint $\frac{a+b}{2}$ of the integration domain as illustrated in *Figure 2.3*, approximating the integrand by a 0th-degree polynomial of the form 24

$$f(x) \approx f\left(\frac{a+b}{2}\right) \tag{2.57}$$

yields an open-type scheme known as the *rectangle rule* or *midpoint rule*

$$\int_a^b f(x)\mathrm{d}x \approx (b-a)f\left(\frac{a+b}{2}\right) \tag{2.58}$$

with error bound $\frac{(b-a)^3}{24}f''(\xi)$ for some $\xi \in [a,b]$.

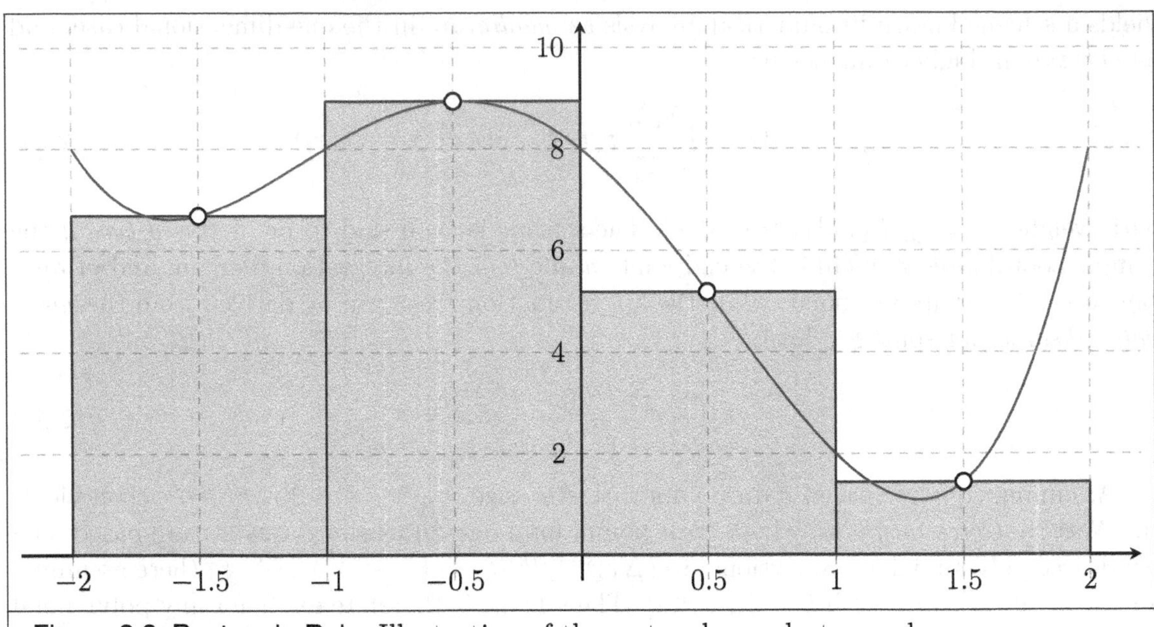

Figure 2.3: Rectangle Rule: Illustration of the rectangle quadrature rule.

The corresponding composite rule is then readily given as

23

$$\int_{x_0}^{x_n} f(x)\mathrm{d}x \overset{(2.56)}{\underset{(2.58)}{\approx}} \sum_{i=1}^{n}(x_i - x_{i-1})f\left(\frac{x_{i-1}+x_i}{2}\right)$$

24

which, in the case of equally spaced intervals, reduces to the composite Newton–Cotes formula

$$\int_{x_0}^{x_n} f(x)\mathrm{d}x \approx \Delta x \sum_{i=1}^{n} f\left(\frac{x_{i-1}+x_i}{2}\right) \tag{2.59}$$

with error bound $\frac{n}{24}\left(\frac{x_n-x_0}{n}\right)^3 f''(\xi)$ for some $\xi \in [x_0, x_n]$.

2.2.2.3 Trapezoidal Rule

25 As illustrated in *Figure 2.4*, approximating the integrand by a first-degree polynomial of the form

$$f(x) \approx \mathrm{lerp}\left(\frac{x-a}{b-a}, f(a), f(b)\right) \tag{2.60}$$

yields a closed-type scheme known as the *trapezoidal rule*

$$\int_a^b f(x)\mathrm{d}x \approx (b-a)\frac{f(a)+f(b)}{2} \tag{2.61}$$

with error bound $-\frac{(b-a)^3}{12}f''(\xi)$ for some $\xi \in [a,b]$.

The corresponding composite rule is then readily given as

23

$$\int_{x_0}^{x_n} f(x)\mathrm{d}x \overset{(2.56)}{\underset{(2.61)}{\approx}} \frac{1}{2}\sum_{i=1}^{n}(x_i - x_{i-1})(f(x_{i-1}) + f(x_i)) \tag{2.62}$$

24

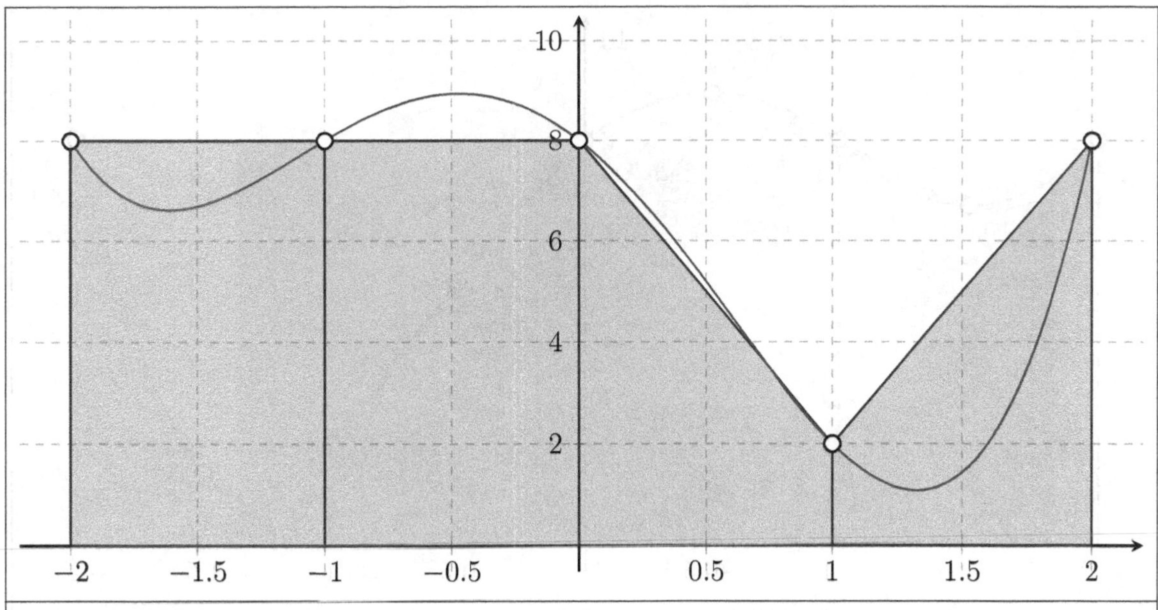

Figure 2.4: Trapezoidal Rule: Illustration of the trapezoidal quadrature rule.

which, in the case of equally spaced intervals, reduces to the composite Newton–Cotes formula

$$\int_{x_0}^{x_n} f(x)\mathrm{d}x \approx \Delta x \left(\frac{f(x_0) + f(x_n)}{2} + \sum_{i=1}^{n-1} f(x_i) \right) \tag{2.63}$$

with error bound $-\frac{n}{12}\left(\frac{x_n - x_0}{n}\right)^3 f''(\xi)$ for some $\xi \in [x_0, x_n]$.

2.2.2.4 Simpson's Rule

Given the midpoint $m \triangleq \frac{a+b}{2}$ of the integration domain as illustrated in *Figure 2.5*, approxi- 26
mating the integrand by a second-degree polynomial expressed in *Lagrange form* 18

18

$$f(x) \overset{(2.23)}{\approx} f(a)\frac{(x-m)(x-b)}{(a-m)(a-b)} + f(m)\frac{(x-a)(x-b)}{(m-a)(m-b)} + f(b)\frac{(x-a)(x-m)}{(b-a)(b-m)} \tag{2.64}$$

yields a closed-type scheme known as *Simpson's rule*, corresponding to a convex combination of the *trapezoidal rule* and *rectangle rule* with weights 1/3 and 2/3, respectively 24 23

$$\int_a^b f(x)\mathrm{d}x \approx \frac{b-a}{3}\left(\frac{f(a)+f(b)}{2} + 2f\left(\frac{a+b}{2}\right)\right) \tag{2.65}$$

with error bound $-\frac{1}{90}\left(\frac{b-a}{2}\right)^5 f^{(4)}(\xi)$ for some $\xi \in [a, b]$.

The corresponding composite rule is then readily given as

23

$$\int_{x_0}^{x_n} f(x)\mathrm{d}x \underset{(2.65)}{\overset{(2.56)}{\approx}} \frac{1}{3}\sum_{i=1}^{n}(x_i - x_{i-1})\left(\frac{f(x_{i-1}) + f(x_i)}{2} + 2f\left(\frac{x_{i-1}+x_i}{2}\right)\right) \tag{2.66}$$

25

which, in the case of equally spaced intervals, reduces to the composite Newton–Cotes formula

$$\int_{x_0}^{x_n} f(x)\mathrm{d}x \approx \frac{\Delta x}{3}\left(\frac{f(x_0)+f(x_n)}{2} + \sum_{i=1}^{n-1} f(x_i) + 2\sum_{i=1}^{n} f\left(\frac{x_{i-1}+x_i}{2}\right)\right) \tag{2.67}$$

with error bound $-\frac{n}{90}\left(\frac{x_n - x_0}{2n}\right)^5 f^{(4)}(\xi)$ for some $\xi \in [x_0, x_n]$.

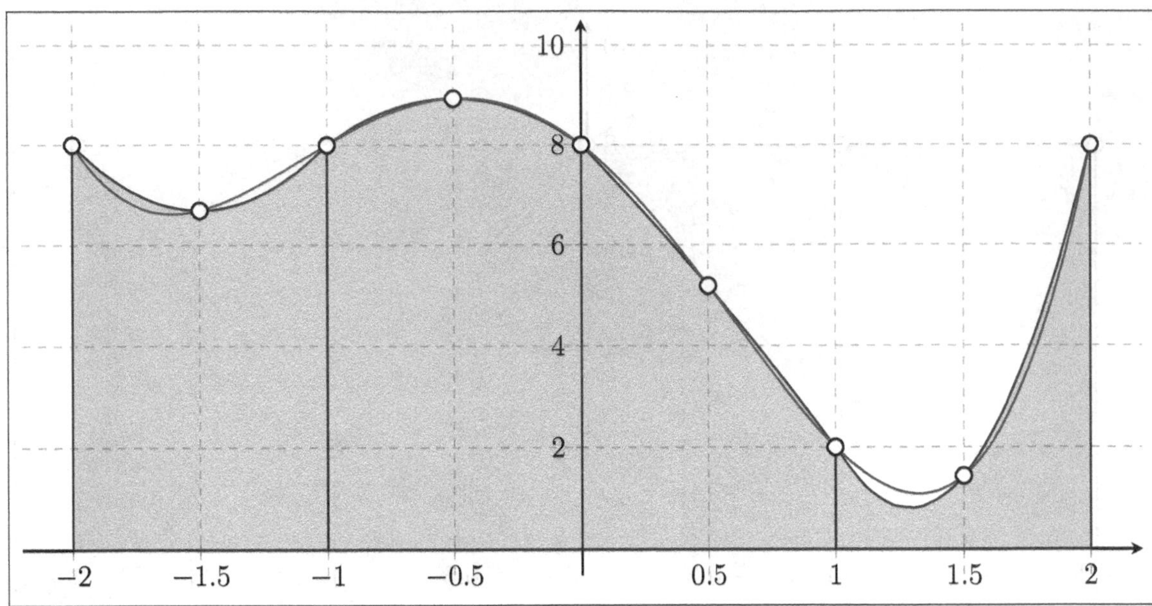

Figure 2.5: Simpson's Rule: Illustration of Simpson's quadrature rule.

2.2.2.5 *Higher-Order Rules*

Approximating the integrand by a third-degree polynomial yields a closed-type scheme known as *Simpson's 3/8 rule*

$$\int_a^b f(x)\mathrm{d}x \approx \frac{b-a}{8}\left(f(a) + 3f\left(\frac{2a+b}{3}\right) + 3f\left(\frac{a+2b}{3}\right) + f(b)\right) \tag{2.68}$$

with error bound $-\frac{3}{80}(\frac{b-a}{3})^5 f^{(4)}(\xi)$ for some $\xi \in [a, b]$.

Likewise, approximating the integrand by a fourth-degree polynomial yields a closed-type scheme known as *Boole's rule*

$$\int_a^b f(x)\mathrm{d}x \approx \frac{b-a}{90}\left(7f(a) + 32f\left(\frac{3a+b}{4}\right) + 12f\left(\frac{2a+2b}{4}\right) + 32f\left(\frac{a+3b}{4}\right) + 7f(b)\right) \tag{2.69}$$

with error bound $-\frac{8}{945}\left(\frac{b-a}{4}\right)^7 f^{(6)}(\xi)$ for some $\xi \in [a, b]$.

2.2.3 Polynomial Equation

2.2.3.1 *Definition*

A univariate *polynomial* of degree n with coefficients c_i is an algebraic expression of the form

$$p_n(x) \triangleq \sum_{i=0}^{n} c_i x^i, \quad \forall c_n \neq 0 \tag{2.70}$$

whose roots are, according to the *fundamental theorem of algebra*, the n (not necessarily distinct) real-valued or complex-valued solutions x_i of the *polynomial equation*

$$p_n(x) = 0 \tag{2.71}$$

The expression of the polynomial can then be factored into

$$p_n(x) = c_n \prod_{i=1}^{n}(x - x_i) \tag{2.72}$$

such that expanding the product and matching the coefficients to those of *Equation 2.70* 26
yields *Vieta's formula*, which relates the sums and products of the roots to the polynomial coefficients as

$$+\frac{c_n}{c_n} = 1 \tag{2.73}$$

$$-\frac{c_{n-1}}{c_n} = \sum_{i=1}^{n} x_i \tag{2.74}$$

$$+\frac{c_{n-2}}{c_n} = \sum_{i=1}^{n-1} x_i \sum_{j=i+1}^{n} x_j \tag{2.75}$$

$$-\frac{c_{n-3}}{c_n} = \sum_{i=1}^{n-2} x_i \sum_{j=i+1}^{n-1} x_j \sum_{k=j+1}^{n} x_k \tag{2.76}$$

$$\vdots = \vdots$$

$$(-1)^n \frac{c_0}{c_n} = \prod_{i=1}^{n} x_i \tag{2.77}$$

Dividing all coefficients of the polynomial equation by c_n yields a *monic polynomial equation*, whose term of highest degree has a unit coefficient. Instead, applying the *Tschirnhaus transformation* by substituting

$$t \triangleq x + \frac{c_{n-1}}{nc_n} \tag{2.78}$$

yields a *depressed polynomial equation* in t with no $n-1$-degree term, and whose real-valued or complex-valued solutions t_i define the roots x_i of the original polynomial.

2.2.3.2 Linear Equation

A *linear equation* is a first-degree algebraic expression of the form

$$c_1 x + c_0 = 0, \quad \forall c_1 \neq 0 \tag{2.79}$$

which may be formulated as a *depressed linear equation* with no constant term by means of
the substitution $x \overset{(2.78)}{=} t - \alpha$ with $\alpha \triangleq \frac{c_0}{c_1}$ 27

$$0 \overset{(2.79)}{=} c_1(t-\alpha) + c_0 = d_1 t + d_0 \tag{2.80}$$ 27

where

$$d_1 \triangleq c_1 \tag{2.81}$$

$$d_0 \triangleq c_0 - c_1\alpha = 0 \tag{2.82}$$

The solution $t_1 = 0$ of the depressed linear equation then readily yields the unique root
of *Equation 2.79* 27

$$x_1 = t_1 - \alpha = -\frac{c_0}{c_1} \tag{2.83}$$

which satisfies Vieta's formula given in *Equation 2.74* and *Equation 2.77.* 27 27

2.2.3.3 Quadratic Equation

A *quadratic equation* is a second-degree algebraic expression of the form

$$c_2 x^2 + c_1 x + c_0 = 0, \quad \forall c_2 \neq 0 \tag{2.84}$$

which may be formulated as a *depressed quadratic equation* with no linear term by means of
27 the substitution $x \overset{(2.78)}{=} t - \alpha$ with $\alpha \triangleq \frac{c_1}{2c_2}$

28

$$c_2(t-\alpha)^2 + c_1(t-\alpha) + c_0 = c_2(t^2 - 2t\alpha + \alpha^2) + c_1(t-\alpha) + c_0 = d_2 t^2 + d_1 t + d_0 \overset{(2.84)}{=} 0 \tag{2.85}$$

where

$$\begin{aligned} d_2 &\triangleq c_2 & (2.86)\\ d_1 &\triangleq c_1 - 2c_2\alpha = 0 & (2.87)\\ d_0 &\triangleq c_2\alpha^2 - c_1\alpha + c_0 = -\frac{c_1\alpha}{2} + c_0 & (2.88)\\ &= -\frac{c_1^2}{4c_2} + c_0 = \frac{-c_1^2 + 4c_2c_0}{4c_2} & (2.89) \end{aligned}$$

Rearranging the terms then yields

28
28
28

$$t^2 \overset{(2.85)}{=} -\frac{d_0}{d_2} \underset{(2.86)}{\overset{(2.89)}{=}} -\frac{4c_2c_0 - c_1^2}{4c_2^2} = \frac{\Delta}{(2c_2)^2} \tag{2.90}$$

with the *discriminant* defined as

$$\Delta \triangleq c_1^2 - 4c_2c_0 \tag{2.91}$$

As an alternative, rearranging the terms of the original quadratic equation and multiplying both sides by $4c_2$ yields

28

$$4c_2^2x^2 + 4c_2c_1x \overset{(2.84)}{=} -4c_2c_0 \tag{2.92}$$

while completing the square equivalently gives

28

$$4c_2^2x^2 + 4c_2c_1x + c_1^2 = (2c_2x + c_1)^2 = -4c_2c_0 + c_1^2 \overset{(2.91)}{=} \Delta \tag{2.93}$$

Whenever $\Delta > 0$, the equation has two distinct real-valued roots

28

$$x_{1|2} = t_{1|2} - \frac{c_1}{2c_2} \overset{(2.90)}{=} \pm\sqrt{\frac{\Delta}{(2c_2)^2}} - \frac{c_1}{2c_2} = \frac{-c_1 \pm \sqrt{\Delta}}{2c_2} \in \mathbb{R} \tag{2.94}$$

which, when $\Delta = 0$, reduce to the double root

28

$$x_{1|2} = t_{1|2} - \frac{c_1}{2c_2} \overset{(2.90)}{=} 0 - \frac{c_1}{2c_2} = -\frac{c_1}{2c_2} \in \mathbb{R} \tag{2.95}$$

whereas if $\Delta < 0$, which can only occur if $c_2c_0 > 0$, the equation has instead two mutually
87 *complex conjugate* roots

28

$$x_{1|2} = t_{1|2} - \frac{c_1}{2c_2} \overset{(2.90)}{=} \pm\sqrt{\frac{-\imath^2\Delta}{(2c_2)^2}} - \frac{c_1}{2c_2} = \frac{-c_1 \pm \imath\sqrt{-\Delta}}{2c_2} \in \mathbb{C} \tag{2.96}$$

whose *polar coordinates* read 86

$$|x_{1|2}| \overset{(3.147)}{=} \sqrt{\left(\frac{-c_1}{2c_2}\right)^2 + \left(\pm\frac{\sqrt{-\Delta}}{2c_2}\right)^2} = \sqrt{\frac{c_1^2 - \Delta}{4c_2^2}} \overset{(2.91)}{=} \sqrt{\frac{c_0}{c_2}} \tag{2.97}$$ 86 28

$$\arg(x_{1|2}) \overset{(3.148)}{=} \operatorname{arctan2}\left(\pm\frac{\sqrt{-\Delta}}{2c_2}, \frac{-c_1}{2c_2}\right) \overset{(2.91)}{=} \pm\arccos\left(\frac{-c_1}{2\sqrt{c_2 c_0}}\right) \tag{2.98}$$ 86 28

In accordance with Vieta's formula given in *Equation 2.74* and *Equation 2.77*, the sum 27
and the product of the roots, respectively, evaluate to 27

$$x_1 + x_2 \overset{\substack{(2.94)\\(2.95)\\(2.96)}}{=} \frac{-c_1 + D}{2c_2} + \frac{-c_1 - D}{2c_2} = \frac{-2c_1}{2c_2} = -\frac{c_1}{c_2} \tag{2.99}$$ 28 28 28

$$x_1 \times x_2 \overset{\substack{(2.94)\\(2.95)\\(2.96)}}{=} \frac{(-c_1)^2 - D^2}{4c_2^2} = \frac{c_1^2 - \Delta}{4c_2^2} \overset{(2.91)}{=} \frac{4c_2c_0}{4c_2^2} = \frac{c_0}{c_2} \tag{2.100}$$ 28 28 28 28

where $D \triangleq \sqrt{\Delta}$, $D \triangleq 0$ or $D \triangleq \imath\sqrt{-\Delta}$ when $\Delta > 0$, $\Delta = 0$ or $\Delta < 0$, respectively.

In order to avoid the numerical precision issues that arise when subtracting nearly equal quantities, the real-valued roots may alternatively be computed by means of a numerically stable floating-point scheme of the form [Press *et al.*, 1992, §5.6]

$$x_1 \overset{(2.94)}{=} \frac{-c_1 - \operatorname{sgn}(c_1)\sqrt{\Delta}}{2c_2} \tag{2.101}$$ 28

$$x_2 \overset{(2.100)}{=} \frac{c_0}{c_2 x_1} = \frac{c_0}{c_2}\frac{2c_2}{-c_1 - \operatorname{sgn}(c_1)\sqrt{\Delta}} = \frac{2c_0}{-c_1 - \operatorname{sgn}(c_1)\sqrt{\Delta}} \tag{2.102}$$ 29

In the special case of an even linear coefficient $c_1 \triangleq 2c_1'$, the discriminant can alternatively be reduced to

$$\Delta' \triangleq \frac{\Delta}{4} \overset{(2.91)}{=} \frac{4c_1'^2 - 4c_2c_0}{4} = c_1'^2 - c_2c_0 \tag{2.103}$$ 28

such that the real-valued roots of the polynomial simplify into

$$x_{1|2} \overset{(2.94)}{=} \frac{-2c_1' \pm \sqrt{4\Delta'}}{2c_2} = \frac{-2c_1' \pm 2\sqrt{\Delta'}}{2c_2} = \frac{-c_1' \pm \sqrt{\Delta'}}{c_2} \tag{2.104}$$ 28

2.2.3.4 Cubic Equation

A *cubic equation* is a third-degree algebraic expression of the form

$$c_3x^3 + c_2x^2 + c_1x + c_0 = 0, \quad \forall c_3 \neq 0 \tag{2.105}$$

which may be formulated as a *depressed cubic equation* with no quadratic term by means of the substitution $x \overset{(2.78)}{=} t - \alpha$ with $\alpha \triangleq \frac{c_2}{3c_3}$ 27

$$\begin{aligned} 0 &\overset{(2.105)}{=} c_3(t-\alpha)^3 + c_2(t-\alpha)^2 + c_1(t-\alpha) + c_0 \\ &= c_3(t^3 - 3t^2\alpha + 3t\alpha^2 - \alpha^3) + c_2(t^2 - 2t\alpha + \alpha^2) + c_1(t-\alpha) + c_0 \\ &= d_3t^3 + d_2t^2 + d_1t + d_0 \end{aligned} \tag{2.106}$$ 29

where

$$
\begin{aligned}
d_3 &\triangleq c_3 && (2.107)\\
d_2 &\triangleq -3c_3\alpha + c_2 = 0 && (2.108)\\
d_1 &\triangleq 3c_3\alpha^2 - 2c_2\alpha + c_1 = -c_2\alpha + c_1 && (2.109)\\
&= -\frac{c_2^2}{3c_3} + c_1 = \frac{-c_2^2 + 3c_3c_1}{3c_3} && (2.110)\\
d_0 &\triangleq -c_3\alpha^3 + c_2\alpha^2 - c_1\alpha + c_0 = \frac{2c_2\alpha^2}{3} - c_1\alpha + c_0 && (2.111)\\
&= \frac{2c_2^3}{27c_3^2} - \frac{c_2c_1}{3c_3} + c_0 = \frac{2c_2^3 - 9c_3c_2c_1 + 27c_3^2c_0}{27c_3^2} && (2.112)
\end{aligned}
$$

Defining the auxiliary variables u and v such that $t \triangleq u + v$ as per *Cardano's method* (originally introduced by del Ferro and Tartaglia) then yields

29

$$
\begin{aligned}
0 &\overset{(2.106)}{=} d_3(u+v)^3 + d_1(u+v) + d_0\\
&= d_3(u^3 + 3u^2v + 3uv^2 + v^3) + d_1(u+v) + d_0\\
&= d_3(u^3 + v^3) + 3d_3uv(u+v) + d_1(u+v) + d_0\\
&= d_3(u^3 + v^3) + (3d_3uv + d_1)(u+v) + d_0 && (2.113)
\end{aligned}
$$

which, with the additional constraint $uv \triangleq -\frac{d_1}{3d_3}$, becomes

$$
\begin{aligned}
0 &= d_3\left(u^3 + \left(-\frac{d_1}{3d_3u}\right)^3\right) + \cancel{\left(-3d_3\frac{d_1}{3d_3} + d_1\right)}\left(u - \frac{d_1}{3d_3u}\right) + d_0\\
&= d_3u^3 - \frac{d_1^3}{27d_3^2u^3} + d_0 && (2.114)
\end{aligned}
$$

29 as may be directly obtained from *Equation 2.106* by applying *Vieta's substitution*

$$
t = u - \frac{d_1}{3d_3u} \qquad (2.115)
$$

28 Multiplying both sides by $w \triangleq u^3$ then yields the *quadratic equation*

30

$$
0 \overset{(2.114)}{=} d_3u^6 + d_0u^3 - \frac{d_1^3}{27d_3^2} = d_3w^2 + d_0w - \frac{d_1^3}{27d_3^2} \qquad (2.116)
$$

whose roots satisfy

29

$$
w_1 + w_2 \overset{(2.99)}{=} -\frac{d_0}{d_3} \qquad (2.117)
$$

29

$$
w_1 \times w_2 \overset{(2.100)}{=} -\frac{d_1^3}{27d_3^3} = \left(-\frac{d_1}{3d_3}\right)^3 \qquad (2.118)
$$

and whose discriminant reads

$$\Delta \overset{(2.91)}{=} d_0^2 + \frac{4d_1^3}{27d_3} \tag{2.119}$$ 28

$$= (2d_3)^2 \left(\left(\frac{d_0}{2d_3} \right)^2 + \left(\frac{d_1}{3d_3} \right)^3 \right) \tag{2.120}$$

$$\overset{(2.107)}{\underset{(2.111)}{\overset{(2.109)}{=}}} 4c_3^2 \left(\left(\frac{2c_2^3 - 9c_3c_2c_1 + 27c_3^2c_0}{54c_3^3} \right)^2 + \left(\frac{3c_3c_1 - c_2^2}{9c_3^2} \right)^3 \right)$$ 30 30 30

$$= \frac{-c_2^2c_1^2 + 4c_2^3c_0 - 18c_3c_2c_1c_0 + 27c_3^2c_0^2 + 4c_3c_1^3}{27c_3^2} \tag{2.121}$$

Given the roots $w_{1|2} = u_{1|2}^3$ of *Equation 2.116* with real-valued or otherwise principal cube roots $\sqrt[3]{w_{1|2}}$, substituting the latter and complex-valued cube roots 30

$$u_{1|2} \overset{(3.172)}{=} \sqrt[3]{w_{1|2}} e^{\pm \imath k \frac{2\pi}{3}}, \quad \forall k \in [0, 2] \tag{2.122}$$ 88

into Vieta's substitution formula while exploiting the identity

$$\sqrt[3]{w_1}\sqrt[3]{w_2} \overset{(2.118)}{=} -\frac{d_1}{3d_3} \tag{2.123}$$ 30

then yields the following general expressions for the roots of the depressed cubic [Schwarze, 1990]

$$t_1 \underset{(2.122)}{\overset{(2.115)}{=}} \sqrt[3]{w_1} - \frac{d_1}{3d_3} \frac{1}{\sqrt[3]{w_1}}$$ 30 31

$$\overset{(2.123)}{=} \sqrt[3]{w_1} + \sqrt[3]{w_2} \tag{2.124}$$ 31

$$t_2 \underset{(2.122)}{\overset{(2.115)}{=}} e^{\imath \frac{2\pi}{3}} \sqrt[3]{w_1} - \frac{d_1}{3d_3} \frac{1}{e^{\imath \frac{2\pi}{3}} \sqrt[3]{w_1}}$$ 30 31

$$\overset{(2.123)}{=} e^{\imath \frac{2\pi}{3}} \sqrt[3]{w_1} + e^{-\imath \frac{2\pi}{3}} \sqrt[3]{w_2} \tag{2.125}$$ 31

$$= \left(-\frac{1}{2} + \imath \frac{\sqrt{3}}{2} \right) \sqrt[3]{w_1} + \left(-\frac{1}{2} - \imath \frac{\sqrt{3}}{2} \right) \sqrt[3]{w_2}$$

$$= -\frac{1}{2}(\sqrt[3]{w_1} + \sqrt[3]{w_2}) + \imath \frac{\sqrt{3}}{2}(\sqrt[3]{w_1} - \sqrt[3]{w_2}) \tag{2.126}$$

$$t_3 \underset{(2.122)}{\overset{(2.115)}{=}} e^{-\imath \frac{2\pi}{3}} \sqrt[3]{w_1} - \frac{d_1}{3d_3} \frac{1}{e^{-\imath \frac{2\pi}{3}} \sqrt[3]{w_1}}$$ 30 31

$$\overset{(2.123)}{=} e^{-\imath \frac{2\pi}{3}} \sqrt[3]{w_1} + e^{\imath \frac{2\pi}{3}} \sqrt[3]{w_2} \tag{2.127}$$ 31

$$= \left(-\frac{1}{2} - \imath \frac{\sqrt{3}}{2} \right) \sqrt[3]{w_1} + \left(-\frac{1}{2} + \imath \frac{\sqrt{3}}{2} \right) \sqrt[3]{w_2}$$

$$= -\frac{1}{2}(\sqrt[3]{w_1} + \sqrt[3]{w_2}) - \imath \frac{\sqrt{3}}{2}(\sqrt[3]{w_1} - \sqrt[3]{w_2}) \tag{2.128}$$

30 Whenever $\Delta > 0$, the real-valued roots of *Equation 2.116* read

28 31
$$w_{1|2} \overset{(2.94)}{=} \frac{-d_0 \pm \sqrt{\Delta}}{2d_3} = -\frac{d_0}{2d_3} \pm \sqrt{\frac{\Delta}{(2d_3)^2}} \overset{(2.120)}{=} -\frac{d_0}{2d_3} \pm \sqrt{\left(\frac{d_0}{2d_3}\right)^2 + \left(\frac{d_1}{3d_3}\right)^3} \tag{2.129}$$

whose real-valued cube roots may be evaluated by means of the following numerically stable floating-point scheme [Press *et al.*, 1992, §5.6] [Herbison-Evans, 1995]

$$\sqrt[3]{w_1} = \sqrt[3]{-\frac{d_0}{2d_3} - \operatorname{sgn}\left(\frac{d_0}{2d_3}\right)\sqrt{\left(\frac{d_0}{2d_3}\right)^2 + \left(\frac{d_1}{3d_3}\right)^3}} \tag{2.130}$$

31
$$\sqrt[3]{w_2} \overset{(2.123)}{=} -\frac{d_1}{3d_3}\frac{1}{\sqrt[3]{w_1}} \tag{2.131}$$

31 and the depressed cubic has a single real-valued root $t_1 \in \mathbb{R}$, readily given by *Equation 2.124*, and two complex-valued roots $t_2, t_3 \in \mathbb{C}$.

30 If $\Delta = 0$ instead, the real-valued double root of *Equation 2.116* reads

28
$$w_1 = w_2 \overset{(2.95)}{=} -\frac{d_0}{2d_3} \tag{2.132}$$

and the depressed cubic has a real-valued single root $t_1 \in \mathbb{R}$ and a real-valued double root $t_2 = t_3 \in \mathbb{R}$

31
$$t_1 \overset{(2.124)}{=} 2\sqrt[3]{w_{1|2}} \tag{2.133}$$

31 31
$$t_{2|3} \underset{(2.128)}{\overset{(2.126)}{=}} -\sqrt[3]{w_{1|2}} \tag{2.134}$$

30 In contrast, when $\Delta < 0$, the complex-valued roots of *Equation 2.116* read

28
$$w_{1|2} \overset{(2.96)}{=} \frac{-d_0 \pm \imath\sqrt{-\Delta}}{2d_3} = re^{\pm\imath\varphi} \tag{2.135}$$

86 whose *polar coordinates* are given by

29
$$r \overset{(2.97)}{=} \sqrt{-\frac{d_1^3}{27d_3^3}} = \left(\sqrt{-\frac{d_1}{3d_3}}\right)^3 \tag{2.136}$$

29
$$\varphi \overset{(2.98)}{=} \arccos\left(-\frac{d_0}{2d_3}\frac{1}{r}\right) \tag{2.137}$$

It then follows that $\sqrt[3]{r} = \sqrt{-\frac{d_1}{3d_3}}$ while the principal value of the cube roots satisfy

$$\sqrt[3]{w_1} + \sqrt[3]{w_2} = \sqrt[3]{r}e^{\imath\frac{\varphi}{3}} + \sqrt[3]{r}e^{-\imath\frac{\varphi}{3}} = \sqrt[3]{r}\left(e^{\imath\frac{\varphi}{3}} + e^{-\imath\frac{\varphi}{3}}\right) = 2\sqrt[3]{r}\cos\left(\frac{\varphi}{3}\right) \tag{2.138}$$

$$\sqrt[3]{w_1} - \sqrt[3]{w_2} = \sqrt[3]{r}e^{\imath\frac{\varphi}{3}} - \sqrt[3]{r}e^{-\imath\frac{\varphi}{3}} = \sqrt[3]{r}\left(e^{\imath\frac{\varphi}{3}} - e^{-\imath\frac{\varphi}{3}}\right) = \imath 2\sqrt[3]{r}\sin\left(\frac{\varphi}{3}\right) \tag{2.139}$$

such that the depressed cubic has three distinct real-valued roots

$$t_1 \overset{(2.124)}{=} 2\sqrt[3]{r}\cos\left(\frac{\varphi}{3}\right) \tag{2.140}$$ 31

$$\begin{aligned} t_2 &\overset{(2.125)}{=} e^{\imath\frac{2\pi}{3}}\sqrt[3]{r}e^{\imath\frac{\varphi}{3}} + e^{-\imath\frac{2\pi}{3}}\sqrt[3]{r}e^{-\imath\frac{\varphi}{3}} = \sqrt[3]{r}\left(e^{\imath\frac{\varphi+2\pi}{3}} + e^{-\imath\frac{\varphi+2\pi}{3}}\right) \\ &= 2\sqrt[3]{r}\cos\left(\frac{\varphi+2\pi}{3}\right) = -2\sqrt[3]{r}\cos\left(\frac{\varphi+2\pi}{3} - \pi\right) = -2\sqrt[3]{r}\cos\left(\frac{\varphi-\pi}{3}\right) \quad (2.141) \end{aligned}$$ 31

$$\overset{(2.126)}{=} -\frac{1}{2}\sqrt[3]{r}2\cos\left(\frac{\varphi}{3}\right) + \imath\frac{\sqrt{3}}{2}\sqrt[3]{r}2\imath\sin\left(\frac{\varphi}{3}\right) = \sqrt[3]{r}\left(-\cos\left(\frac{\varphi}{3}\right) - \sqrt{3}\sin\left(\frac{\varphi}{3}\right)\right) \tag{2.142}$$ 31

$$\begin{aligned} t_3 &\overset{(2.127)}{=} e^{-\imath\frac{2\pi}{3}}\sqrt[3]{r}e^{\imath\frac{\varphi}{3}} + e^{\imath\frac{2\pi}{3}}\sqrt[3]{r}e^{-\imath\frac{\varphi}{3}} = \sqrt[3]{r}\left(e^{\imath\frac{\varphi-2\pi}{3}} + e^{-\imath\frac{\varphi-2\pi}{3}}\right) \\ &= 2\sqrt[3]{r}\cos\left(\frac{\varphi-2\pi}{3}\right) = -2\sqrt[3]{r}\cos\left(\frac{\varphi-2\pi}{3} + \pi\right) = -2\sqrt[3]{r}\cos\left(\frac{\varphi+\pi}{3}\right) \quad (2.143) \end{aligned}$$ 31

$$\overset{(2.128)}{=} -\frac{1}{2}\sqrt[3]{r}2\cos\left(\frac{\varphi}{3}\right) - \imath\frac{\sqrt{3}}{2}\sqrt[3]{r}2\imath\sin\left(\frac{\varphi}{3}\right) = \sqrt[3]{r}\left(-\cos\left(\frac{\varphi}{3}\right) + \sqrt{3}\sin\left(\frac{\varphi}{3}\right)\right) \tag{2.144}$$ 31

According to Vieta's formula, the sums and products of the roots are then related to the polynomial coefficients by

$$-\frac{c_2}{c_3} \overset{(2.74)}{=} x_1 + x_2 + x_3 \tag{2.145}$$ 27

$$+\frac{c_1}{c_3} \overset{(2.75)}{=} x_1(x_2 + x_3) + x_2 x_3 \tag{2.146}$$ 27

$$-\frac{c_0}{c_3} \overset{(2.77)}{=} x_1 x_2 x_3 \tag{2.147}$$ 27

2.2.3.5 Quartic Equation

A *quartic equation* is a fourth-degree algebraic expression of the form

$$c_4 x^4 + c_3 x^3 + c_2 x^2 + c_1 x + c_0 = 0, \quad \forall c_4 \neq 0 \tag{2.148}$$

which may be formulated as a *depressed quartic equation* with no cubic term by means of the substitution $x \overset{(2.78)}{=} t - \alpha$ with $\alpha \triangleq \frac{c_3}{4c_4}$ 27

$$\begin{aligned} 0 &\overset{(2.148)}{=} c_4(t-\alpha)^4 + c_3(t-\alpha)^3 + c_2(t-\alpha)^2 + c_1(t-\alpha) + c_0 \\ &= c_4(t^4 - 4t^3\alpha + 6t^2\alpha^2 - 4t\alpha^3 + \alpha^4) + c_3(t^3 - 3t^2\alpha + 3t\alpha^2 - \alpha^3) \\ &\quad + c_2(t^2 - 2t\alpha + \alpha^2) + c_1(t - \alpha) + c_0 \\ &= d_4 t^4 + d_3 t^3 + d_2 t^2 + d_1 t + d_0 \end{aligned} \tag{2.149}$$ 33

where

$$\begin{aligned}
d_4 &\triangleq c_4 && (2.150)\\
d_3 &\triangleq -4c_4\alpha + c_3 = 0 && (2.151)\\
d_2 &\triangleq 6c_4\alpha^2 - 3c_3\alpha + c_2 = -\frac{3c_3\alpha}{2} + c_2 && (2.152)\\
&= -\frac{3c_3^2}{8c_4} + c_2 = \frac{8c_4c_2 - 3c_3^2}{8c_4} && (2.153)\\
d_1 &\triangleq -4c_4\alpha^3 + 3c_3\alpha^2 - 2c_2\alpha + c_1 = 2c_3\alpha^2 - 2c_2\alpha + c_1 && (2.154)\\
&= \frac{c_3^3}{8c_4^2} - \frac{c_3c_2}{2c_4} + c_1 = \frac{c_3^3 - 4c_4c_3c_2 + 8c_4^2c_1}{8c_4^2} && (2.155)\\
d_0 &\triangleq c_4\alpha^4 - c_3\alpha^3 + c_2\alpha^2 - c_1\alpha + c_0 = -\frac{3c_3\alpha^3}{4} + c_2\alpha^2 - c_1\alpha + c_0 && (2.156)\\
&= -\frac{3c_3^4}{256c_4^3} + \frac{c_3^2c_2}{16c_4^2} - \frac{c_3c_1}{4c_4} + c_0 = \frac{16c_4c_3^2c_2 - 3c_3^4 - 64c_4^2c_3c_1 + 256c_4^3c_0}{256c_4^3} && (2.157)
\end{aligned}$$

Moreover, according to Vieta's formula, the sums and products of the roots are related to the polynomial coefficients by

27 $$-\frac{c_3}{c_4} \overset{(2.74)}{=} x_1 + x_2 + x_3 + x_4 \quad (2.158)$$

27 $$+\frac{c_2}{c_4} \overset{(2.75)}{=} x_1(x_2 + x_3 + x_4) + x_2(x_3 + x_4) + x_3x_4 \quad (2.159)$$

27 $$-\frac{c_1}{c_4} \overset{(2.76)}{=} x_1(x_2(x_3 + x_4) + x_3x_4) + x_2x_3x_4 \quad (2.160)$$

27 $$+\frac{c_0}{c_4} \overset{(2.77)}{=} x_1x_2x_3x_4 \quad (2.161)$$

Ferrari's Method Assuming that $d_4 \triangleq 1$ such that the depressed quartic is in monic form, *Ferrari's method* (subsequently published by Cardano) starts by rearranging the latter as

33 $$-d_2t^2 - d_1t - d_0 \overset{(2.149)}{=} t^4 \quad (2.162)$$

and completing the square on the right-hand side, with the auxiliary variable u, by adding $2t^2u + u^2$ to both sides yields

$$(2u - d_2)t^2 - d_1t + (u^2 - d_0) = t^4 + 2t^2u + u^2 = (t^2 + u)^2 \quad (2.163)$$

The discriminant of the quadratic term on the left-hand side is zero whenever u is a root
29 u_1 of the *cubic equation* [Schwarze, 1990]

28 $$\begin{aligned}
0 &\overset{(2.91)}{=} d_1^2 - 4(2u - d_2)(u^2 - d_0)\\
&= d_1^2 - 4(2u^3 - 2ud_0 - d_2u^2 + d_2d_0)\\
&= -8u^3 + 4d_2u^2 + 8d_0u + d_1^2 - 4d_2d_0 && (2.164)
\end{aligned}$$

whose number of roots corresponds to the number of permutations in which the quartic can be factored as the product of two quadratics. Its discriminant Δ is therefore indicative of whether the quartic has either two real and two complex conjugate roots ($\Delta < 0$), four real or four complex roots ($\Delta > 0$) or a multiple root ($\Delta = 0$).

Given the first real-valued root u_1 of *Equation 2.164*, and the double root 34

$$t_0 \overset{(2.95)}{=} \frac{d_1}{2(2u_1 - d_2)} \overset{(2.100)}{=} \operatorname{sgn}(d_1)\sqrt{\frac{u_1^2 - d_0}{2u_1 - d_2}} \tag{2.165}$$ 28 29

of the corresponding *quadratic equation* given by the left-hand side of *Equation 2.163*, factoring the latter as per *Equation 2.72* yields 28 34 26

$$(2u_1 - d_2)(t - t_0)^2 = \left(t\sqrt{2u_1 - d_2} - t_0\sqrt{2u_1 - d_2}\right)^2 = (t^2 + u_1)^2 \tag{2.166}$$

The above may then be equivalently factorized into two *quadratic equations* 28

$$\begin{aligned} 0 &= (t^2 + u_1)^2 - (\alpha_1 t - \alpha_0)^2 && (2.167) \\ &= (t^2 + u_1 + \alpha_1 t - \alpha_0)(t^2 + u_1 - \alpha_1 t + \alpha_0) && (2.168) \end{aligned}$$

whose roots are the solutions of the depressed quartic equation, and where the intermediate terms

$$\begin{aligned} \alpha_0 &\triangleq t_0\sqrt{2u_1 - d_2} \overset{(2.165)}{=} \frac{d_1}{2\sqrt{2u_1 - d_2}} \overset{(2.165)}{=} \operatorname{sgn}(d_1)\sqrt{u_1^2 - d_0} && (2.169) \\ \alpha_1 &\triangleq \sqrt{2u_1 - d_2} && (2.170) \end{aligned}$$ 35 35

can be computed as formulated on the right-hand side whenever the minuend and subtrahend under the square root have opposite signs, whereas the identity $\alpha_0\alpha_1 = \frac{d_1}{2}$ instead ought to be exploited to compute one of the terms from the other via a numerically stable floating-point scheme shall it be prone to the numerical precision issues that arise when subtracting nearly equal quantities.

It is finally worth noting that multiple variants of the solution hereby presented may be readily obtained via a mapping of the form $u \mapsto \alpha u + \beta$, where α and β are constant with respect to both t and u. These alternative formulations thereby provide a means of mitigating the numerical characteristics of the computation scheme with respect to overflow and round-off errors [Herbison-Evans, 1995].

Descartes's Method *Descartes's method* starts by factorizing the monic form of a quartic as the product of two monic quadratics

$$\begin{aligned} 0 &= (x^2 + p_1 x + p_0)(x^2 + q_1 x + q_0) && (2.171) \\ &= x^4 + d_3 x^3 + d_2 x^2 + d_1 x + d_0 && (2.172) \end{aligned}$$

where

$$\begin{aligned} d_3 &\triangleq p_1 + q_1 && (2.173) \\ d_2 &\triangleq p_0 + q_0 + p_1 q_1 && (2.174) \\ d_1 &\triangleq p_0 q_1 + p_1 q_0 && (2.175) \\ d_0 &\triangleq p_0 q_0 && (2.176) \end{aligned}$$

In the case of a depressed quartic, it holds that $d_3 \overset{(2.151)}{=} 0$, and substituting $q_1 \overset{(2.173)}{=} -p_1$ yields 34 35

$$\begin{aligned} d_2 &\overset{(2.174)}{=} p_0 + q_0 - p_1^2 \iff p_0 + q_0 = d_2 + p_1^2 \\ d_1 &\overset{(2.175)}{=} -(p_0 - q_0)p_1 \iff p_0 - q_0 = -\frac{d_1}{p_1} \end{aligned} \tag{2.177}$$ 35 35

Eliminating p_0 and q_0 then gives

$$(d_2 + p_1^2)^2 p_1^2 - d_1^2 = (d_2^2 + 2d_2p_1^2 + p_1^4)p_1^2 - d_1^2 = d_2^2p_1^2 + 2d_2p_1^4 + p_1^6 - d_1^2 \quad (2.178)$$

35 35

$$\overset{(2.177)}{=} (p_0 + q_0)^2 p_1^2 - (p_0 - q_0)^2 p_1^2 = 4p_0q_0p_1^2 \overset{(2.176)}{=} 4d_0p_1^2 \quad (2.179)$$

29 from which follows that p_1^2 is the root of the resolvent *cubic equation*

36

$$0 \overset{(2.178)}{=} p_1^6 + 2d_2p_1^4 + (d_2^2 - 4d_0)p_1^2 - d_1^2$$

36

$$\overset{(2.179)}{=} (p_1^2)^3 + 2d_2(p_1^2)^2 + (d_2^2 - 4d_0)p_1^2 - d_1^2 \quad (2.180)$$

35 Instead, adding or subtracting both sides of the right-hand equalities in *Equation 2.177* yields an expression of the remaining coefficients

35

$$2p_0 \overset{(2.177)}{=} d_2 + p_1^2 - \frac{d_1}{p_1} \quad (2.181)$$

35

$$2q_0 \overset{(2.177)}{=} d_2 + p_1^2 + \frac{d_1}{p_1} \quad (2.182)$$

28 of the two *quadratic equations* from *Equation 2.171*, whose roots are the solutions of the
35 depressed quartic equation.

2.2.3.6 Quintic Equation

Polynomial equations of degree five or greater can similarly be reduced to a depressed equation, some specific instances of which then being analytically solvable. However, *Abel's impossibility theorem*, also known as the *Abel–Ruffini theorem*, states that the existence of a general algebraic solution is impossible in such a case. Determining the roots of quintic or
36 higher-degree polynomials thus generally requires the use of a numerical *root finding* algorithm.

The roots of a quintic polynomial f may be bracketed by first determining the roots of its
33 derivative. Solving for the resulting *quartic equation* yields the (at most 4) *stationary points* of the quintic, each being either a *local minimum*, a *local maximum* or an *inflection point* if the second derivative at the point is positive, negative or zero, respectively. Together with the limits $-\infty$ and $+\infty$ (or the bounds of a pre-determined region of interest), the stationary points x_i then define up to 5 intervals, within each of which the quintic is monotonic, such that each interval $[x_i, x_{i+1}]$ is guaranteed to contain a single real-valued root if $f(x_i)f(x_{i+1}) \leq 0$, and no root otherwise. Assuming the roots are computed with sufficient numerical accuracy, the approach might also be recursively extended to higher-degree polynomial equations, such as sextic or septic equations.

2.2.3.7 Root Finding

Bracketing Method Given an initial interval $[l_0, h_0]$ encompassing a root of a (not necessarily polynomial) function f that is continuous over this interval, the *bracketing method* iteratively evaluates the root r_i of a low-degree polynomial approximation to f within the interval, which is then defined at each subsequent iteration as

$$[l_{i+1}, h_{i+1}] \triangleq \begin{cases} [l_i, r_i] & \text{if } \operatorname{sgn}(f(r_i)) = \operatorname{sgn}(f(h_i)) \\ [r_i, r_i] & \text{if } \operatorname{sgn}(f(r_i)) = 0 \\ [r_i, h_i] & \text{if } \operatorname{sgn}(f(r_i)) = \operatorname{sgn}(f(l_i)) \end{cases} \quad (2.183)$$

It follows that $\operatorname{sgn}(f(l_i)) = -\operatorname{sgn}(f(h_i)), \forall i \in \mathbb{N}$, which, according to *Bolzano's theorem* (a special case of the *intermediate value theorem*), guarantees the existence of a root within the successive intervals. The iterative process then terminates whenever the size of the interval is sufficiently small relative to $|r_i|$, or when $r_i \leq l_i \vee r_i \geq h_i$ once the limited numerical precision of the given floating-point representation has been reached.

As illustrated in *Figure 2.6*, the *bisection method* uses a piecewise-constant approximation 37
to f, thereby defining the approximate root r_i as the midpoint of the interval

$$r_i \triangleq \frac{l_i + h_i}{2} \tag{2.184}$$

The method essentially performs a binary search and is guaranteed to converge to the root, but exhibits a linear convergence rate, thereby halving the absolute error (i.e., gaining only one bit of accuracy) with each iteration.

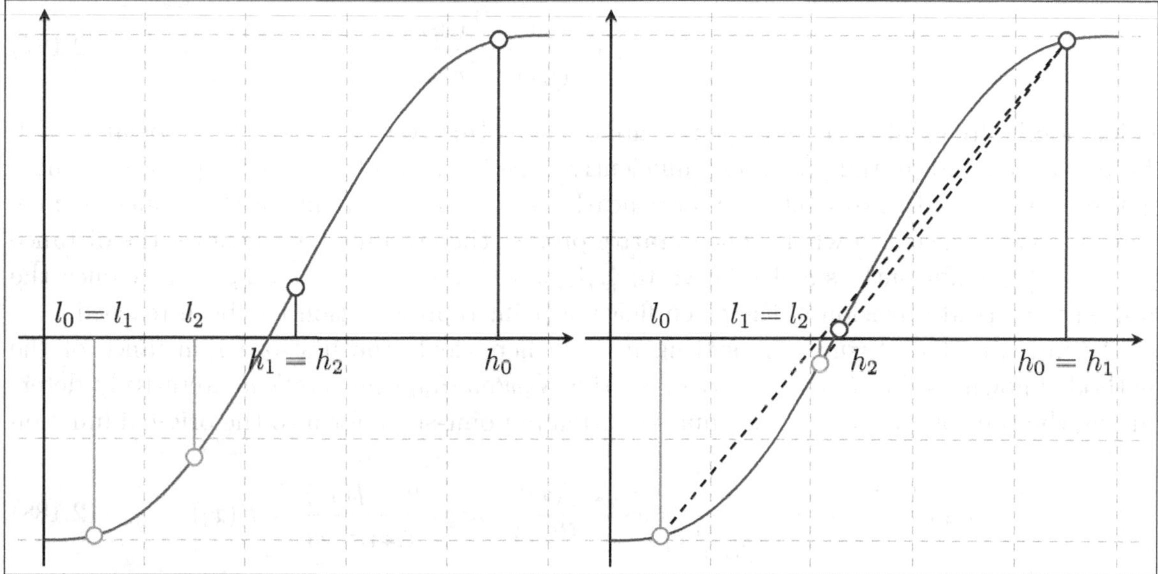

Figure 2.6: Bracketing Method: Illustration of successive iterations of various bracketing methods, including the bisection method (left) and the regula falsi method (right).

Instead, the *regula falsi method*, also known as the *false position method*, uses a linear approximation to f, thereby defining the false position r_i as the root of the line equation in two-point form

$$\begin{aligned} \frac{0 - f(l_i)}{r_i - l_i} = \frac{f(h_i) - f(l_i)}{h_i - l_i} \iff r_i &\triangleq l_i - f(l_i)\frac{h_i - l_i}{f(h_i) - f(l_i)} \\ &= \frac{l_i(f(h_i) - f(l_i)) - f(l_i)(h_i - l_i)}{f(h_i) - f(l_i)} \\ &= \frac{f(h_i)l_i - f(l_i)h_i}{f(h_i) - f(l_i)} \end{aligned} \tag{2.185}$$

When f does not contain any inflection point within an interval, such that the function is either convex or concave over that interval (i.e., the sign of its second derivative is constant), the endpoint at which f has the same sign as its second derivative will remain fixed for all subsequent iterations while the other endpoint of the interval will converge to the root, thereby causing the width of the interval to tend to a non-zero finite value. To address this problem, the *Illinois algorithm* defines the false position r_i as the weighted combination

$$r_i \triangleq \frac{w_l f(h_i) l_i - w_h f(l_i) h_i}{w_l f(h_i) - w_h f(l_i)} \tag{2.186}$$

where the weights are such that $w_l = 2w_h$ whenever l_i has already remained fixed twice in a row, and such that $w_h = 2w_l$ whenever the h_i has already remained fixed twice in a row instead, thereby yielding supra-linear convergence in the order of $\approx \sqrt{2}$.

In order to obtain greater convergence rates, a higher-degree polynomial approximation to f may alternatively be used.

Householder's Method Given an initial guess x_0 to a root of a $d+1$-times continuously differentiable function f, *Householder's method* of order d iteratively evaluates the approximations x_i to the root of f in terms of the derivatives of the reciprocal of f as

$$x_{i+1} \triangleq x_i + d\frac{\left({}^1\!/\!_f\right)^{(d-1)}(x_i)}{\left({}^1\!/\!_f\right)^{(d)}(x_i)} \tag{2.187}$$

which nominally exhibits a convergence rate of $d+1$. However, degeneracies associated with the points (e.g., an initial guess not sufficiently close to the root or a cyclic point sequence) or the derivative (e.g., discontinuity or a nearly zero value at a point in the sequence) may prevent convergence as a whole. The iterative process then terminates whenever the distance $|x_{i+1} - x_i|$ is sufficiently small relative to $|x_i|$, or when $x_{i+1} = x_i \vee x_{i+1} = x_{i-1}$ once the limited numerical precision of the given floating-point representation has been reached.

39 As illustrated in *Figure 2.7*, setting $d = 1$ then yields the first-order instance of the method, known as *Newton's method* or as the *Newton–Raphson method*, iteratively determining the root of a locally linear approximation in point-slope form to the original function

38

$$x_{i+1} \overset{(2.187)}{=} x_i + \frac{\frac{1}{f(x_i)}}{-\frac{f'(x_i)}{f(x_i)^2}} = x_i - \frac{f(x_i)}{f'(x_i)} \iff \frac{0 - f(x_i)}{x_{i+1} - x_i} = f'(x_i) \tag{2.188}$$

which converges quadratically, thereby squaring the absolute error (i.e., doubling the number of accurate digits) with each iteration. On the other hand, approximating the derivative with a finite difference via the line secant to the last two points in the sequence yields the *secant method*

38

$$\begin{aligned} x_{i+1} &\overset{(2.188)}{\approx} x_i - \frac{f(x_i)}{\frac{f(x_i)-f(x_{i-1})}{x_i - x_{i-1}}} \\ &= \frac{x_i(f(x_i) - f(x_{i-1})) - (x_i - x_{i-1})f(x_i)}{f(x_i) - f(x_{i-1})} \\ &= \frac{x_{i-1}f(x_i) - x_i f(x_{i-1})}{f(x_i) - f(x_{i-1})} \end{aligned} \tag{2.189}$$

which reduces the order of convergence to the golden ratio $\varphi \approx 1.618$.

Instead, setting $d = 2$ yields the second-order instance of the method, known as *Halley's method*

38

$$x_{i+1} \overset{(2.187)}{=} x_i + 2\frac{-\frac{f'(x_i)}{f(x_i)^2}}{2\frac{f'(x_i)^2}{f(x_i)^3} - \frac{f''(x_i)}{f(x_i)^2}} = x_i - \frac{f(x_i)f'(x_i)}{f'(x_i)^2 - {}^1\!/\!_2 f(x_i)f''(x_i)} \tag{2.190}$$

which exhibits a cubic convergence rate.

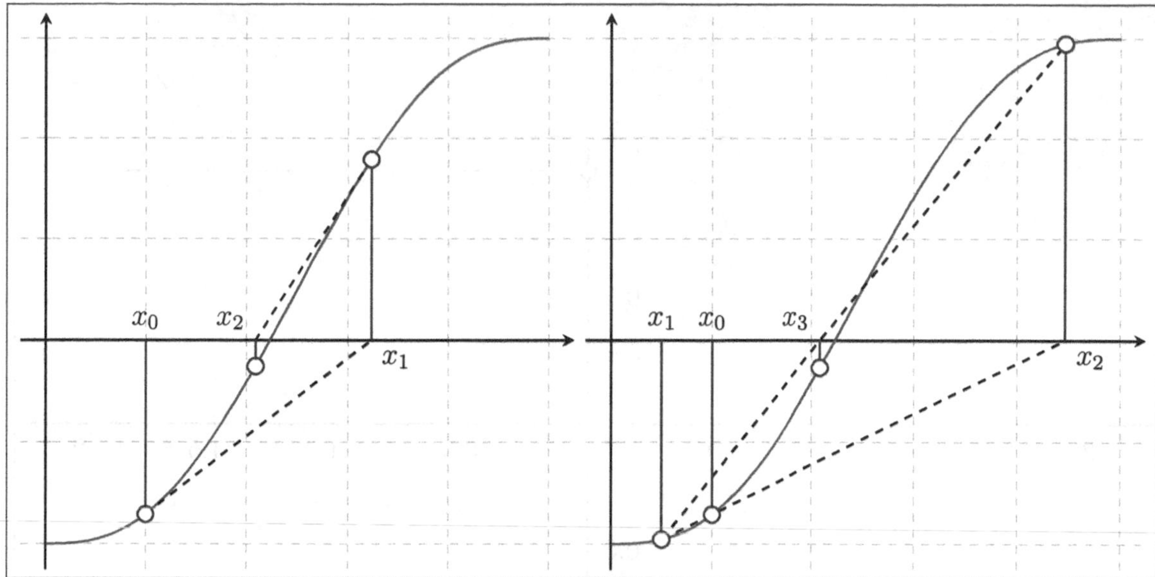

Figure 2.7: Newton's Method: Illustration of successive iterations of Newton's method (left), compared to those of the secant method (right).

2.3 CANONICAL FUNCTIONS

2.3.1 Compressive Function

2.3.1.1 Signum Function

As illustrated in *Figure 2.8*, the *signum function* is an odd function defined as 40

$$\operatorname{sgn}(x) \triangleq \frac{\mathrm{d}|x|}{\mathrm{d}x} = \frac{x}{|x|} = \frac{|x|}{x}, \quad \forall x \neq 0 \tag{2.191}$$

$$= \begin{cases} -1 & \text{if } x < 0 \\ 0 & \text{if } x = 0 \\ +1 & \text{if } x > 0 \end{cases} \tag{2.192}$$

2.3.1.2 Clamp Function

As illustrated in *Figure 2.9*, the *clamp function*, also known as the *symmetric saturating linear function*, is defined as 40

$$C(x) \triangleq \min\{\max\{-1, x\}, +1\} = \begin{cases} -1 & \text{if } x \leq -1 \\ x & \text{if } x \in [-1, +1] \\ +1 & \text{if } x \geq +1 \end{cases} \tag{2.193}$$

while a generalization of the latter to a given interval $[a, b]$ reads

$$C_{[a,b]}(x) \triangleq \min\{\max\{a, x\}, b\} = \begin{cases} a & \text{if } x \leq a \\ x & \text{if } x \in [a, b] \\ b & \text{if } x \geq b \end{cases} \tag{2.194}$$

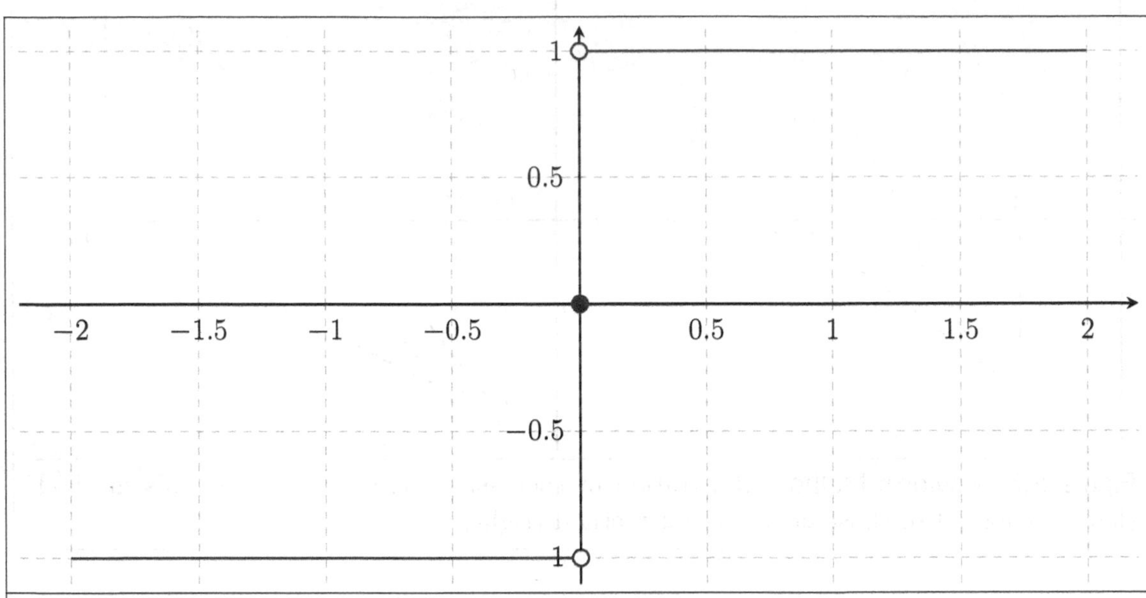

Figure 2.8: Signum Function: Plot of the signum function.

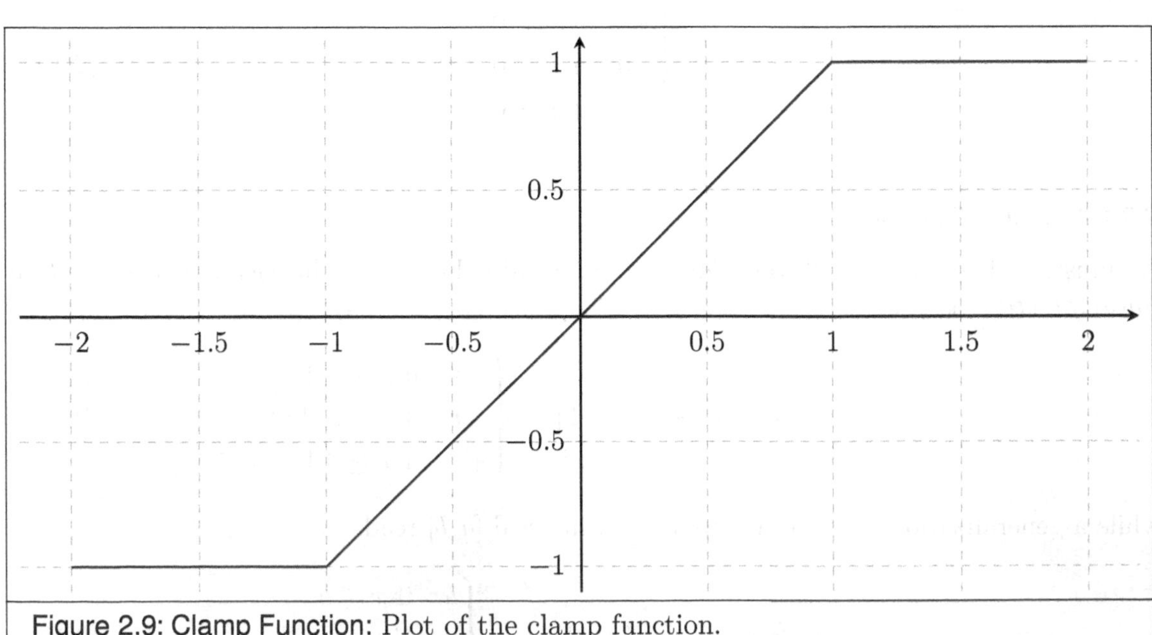

Figure 2.9: Clamp Function: Plot of the clamp function.

2.3.1.3 Sigmoid Function

A *sigmoid function* is an S-shaped odd monotonic function $S(x)$ satisfying $S(0) = 0$ and
$\lim_{x\to\pm\infty} S(x) = \pm 1$, as well as $S'(0) = 1$. As illustrated in *Figure 2.10*, an algebraic sigmoid 41
function and its inverse are readily given as

$$\frac{x}{\sqrt[n]{1+|x|^n}} \quad \rightleftharpoons \quad \frac{x}{\sqrt[n]{1-|x|^n}} \tag{2.195}$$

where $n \geq 1$ is such that the sigmoid approaches the *clamp function* in the limit as $n \to \infty$. 39
Instances of transcendental sigmoid functions and their inverse include

$$\frac{2}{\pi}\arctan\left(\frac{\pi}{2}x\right) \quad \rightleftharpoons \quad \frac{2}{\pi}\tan\left(\frac{\pi}{2}x\right) \tag{2.196}$$

$$\operatorname{sgn}(x)(1-e^{-|x|}) \quad \rightleftharpoons \quad -\operatorname{sgn}(x)\ln(1-|x|) \tag{2.197}$$

$$\frac{2}{\pi}\operatorname{gd}\left(\frac{\pi}{2}x\right) \quad \rightleftharpoons \quad \frac{2}{\pi}\operatorname{gd}^{-1}\left(\frac{\pi}{2}x\right) \tag{2.198}$$

$$\tanh(x) \quad \rightleftharpoons \quad \operatorname{arctanh}(x) \tag{2.199}$$

$$\operatorname{erf}\left(\frac{\sqrt{\pi}}{2}x\right) \quad \rightleftharpoons \quad \frac{2}{\sqrt{\pi}}\operatorname{erf}^{-1}(x) \tag{2.200}$$

where *Equation 2.200* is expressed in terms of the *error function*, and *Equation 2.199* is a 41
scaled and shifted instance of the *logistic function*. Instead, *Equation 2.198* is expressed in 55 41
terms of the *Gudermannian function* 41

$$\operatorname{gd}(x) \triangleq \int_0^x \frac{1}{\cosh(t)}dt = \arcsin(\tanh(x)) = \arctan(\sinh(x)) = 2\arctan(\tanh(x \div 2)) \tag{2.201}$$

and its inverse $\forall x \in [-\pi/2, \pi/2]$

$$\operatorname{gd}^{-1}(x) \triangleq \int_0^x \frac{1}{\cos(t)}dt = \operatorname{arctanh}(\sin(x)) = \operatorname{arcsinh}(\tan(x)) = 2\operatorname{arctanh}(\tan(x \div 2)) \tag{2.202}$$

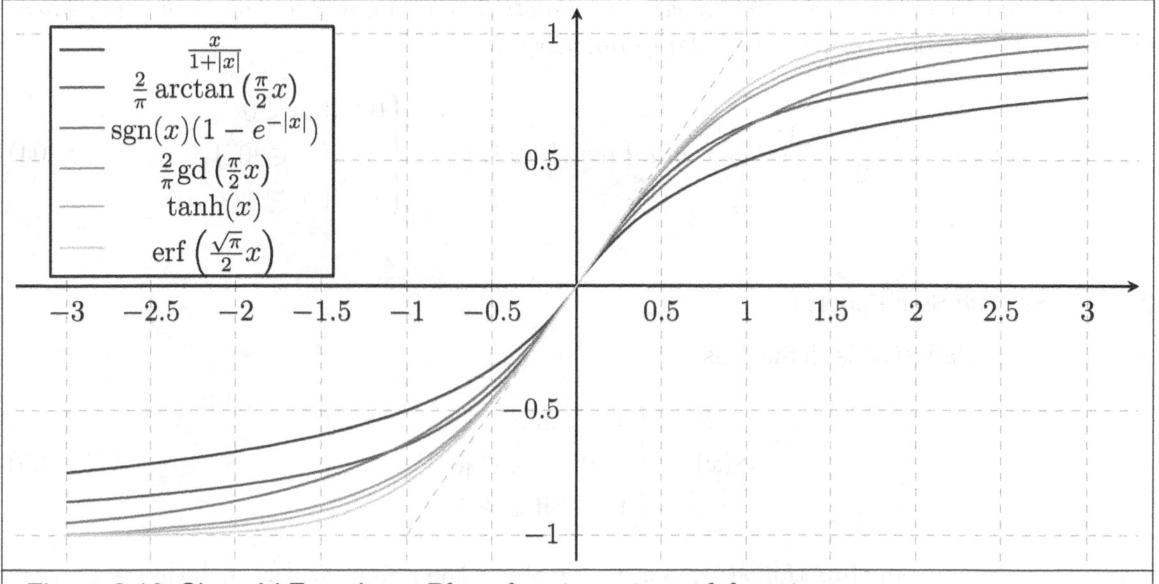

Figure 2.10: Sigmoid Functions: Plot of various sigmoid functions.

2.3.2 Step Function

2.3.2.1 Heaviside Step Function

42 As illustrated in *Figure 2.11*, the *Heaviside step function* is defined in terms of the Dirac
44 *delta function* and *signum function* as
39

39

$$H(x) \triangleq \int_{-\infty}^{x} \delta(s) \mathrm{d}s = \frac{1+\operatorname{sgn}(x)}{2} \stackrel{(2.192)}{=} \begin{cases} 0 & \text{if } x < 0 \\ \frac{1}{2} & \text{if } x = 0 \\ 1 & \text{if } x > 0 \end{cases} \tag{2.203}$$

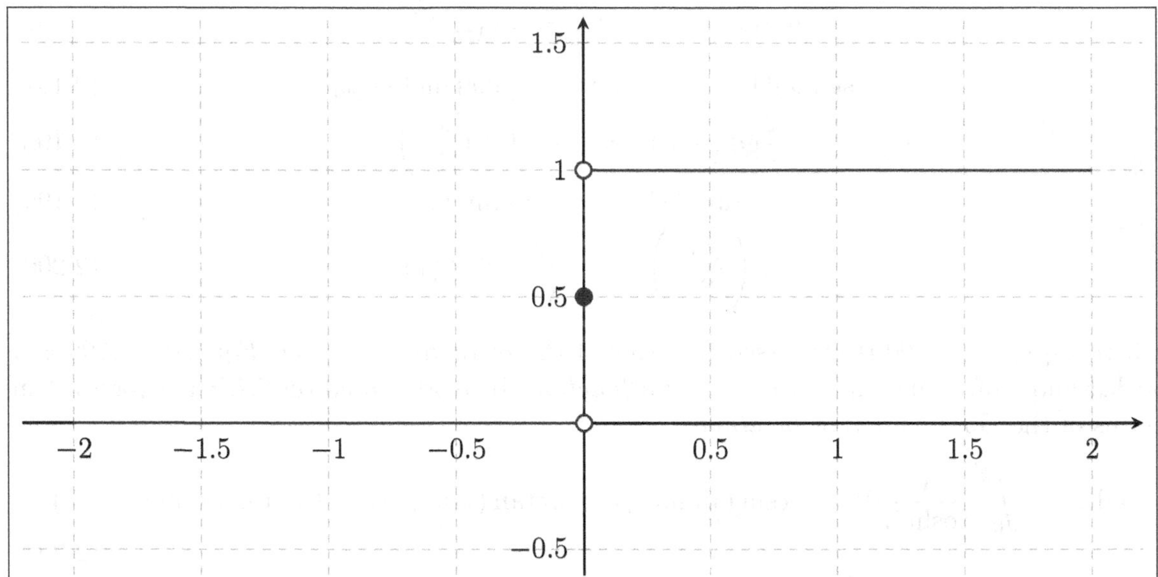

Figure 2.11: Heaviside Step Function: Plot of the Heaviside step function.

2.3.2.2 Linear Step Function

43 As illustrated in *Figure 2.12*, the *linear step function*, also known as the *saturating linear*
39 *function*, is defined in terms of the *clamp function* as

39

$$L(x) \triangleq \frac{1+C(2x-1)}{2} \stackrel{(2.193)}{=} \min\{\max\{0,x\},1\} = \begin{cases} 0 & \text{if } x \leq 0 \\ x & \text{if } x \in [0,1] \\ 1 & \text{if } x \geq 1 \end{cases} \tag{2.204}$$

2.3.2.3 Smooth Step Function

A *smooth step function* is defined as

$$S(x) \triangleq \begin{cases} 0 & \text{if } x \leq 0 \\ s(x) & \text{if } x \in [0,1] \\ 1 & \text{if } x \geq 1 \end{cases} \tag{2.205}$$

in terms of a monotonic function $s(x)$, symmetric about the point $[{}^1/_2, {}^1/_2]$ such that $s(1-x) = 1 - s(x), \forall x \in [0,1]$, and satisfying $s(0) = 0$, $s({}^1/_2) = {}^1/_2$ and $s(1) = 1$ as well as $s'(0) = 0$ and $s'(1) = 0$.

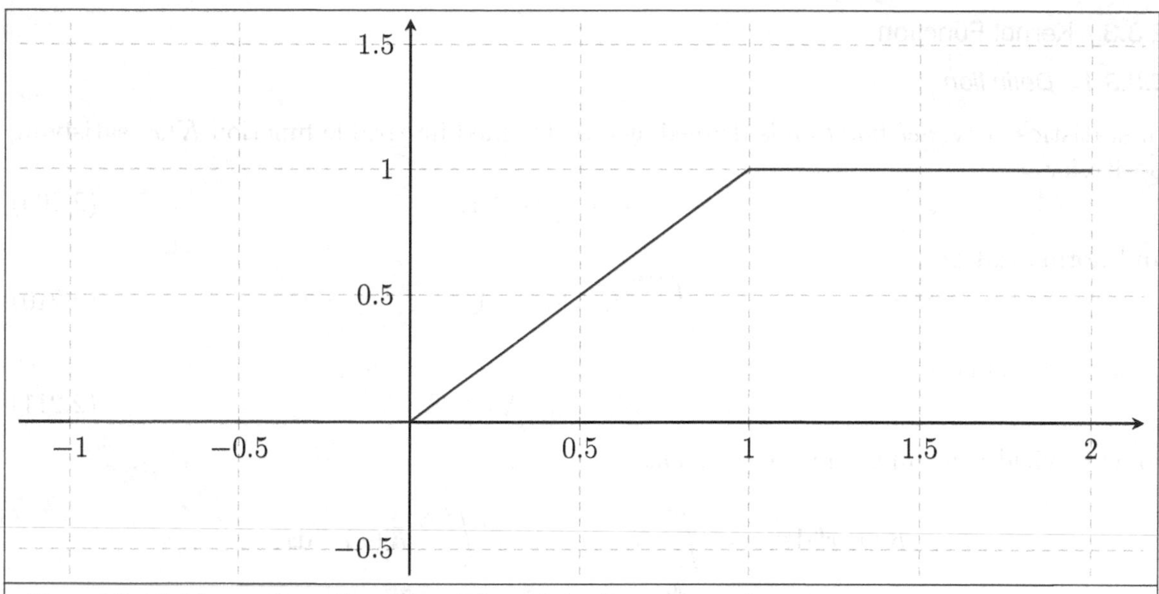

Figure 2.12: Linear Step Function: Plot of the linear step function.

As illustrated in *Figure 2.13*, instances of smooth step functions include 43

$$s(x) \triangleq h_{p1}(x) \implies s'(1/2) \overset{(8.165)}{=} 3/2 = 1.5 \tag{2.206}$$ 344

$$s(x) \triangleq \frac{1-\cos(\pi x)}{2} \implies s'(1/2) = \pi/2 \approx 1.570796 \tag{2.207}$$

$$s(x) \triangleq 6x^5 - 15x^4 + 10x^3 \implies s'(1/2) = 15/8 = 1.875 \tag{2.208}$$

where *Equation 2.206* corresponds to a cubic *Hermite basis function*, while *Equation 2.208* 43
similarly follows from quintic *Hermite interpolation* by constraining the coefficients of a 343 43
general fifth-degree polynomial such that its first and second derivatives are both zero at 20
$x = 0$ and $x = 1$, in addition to yielding the predefined value of the function at those points.

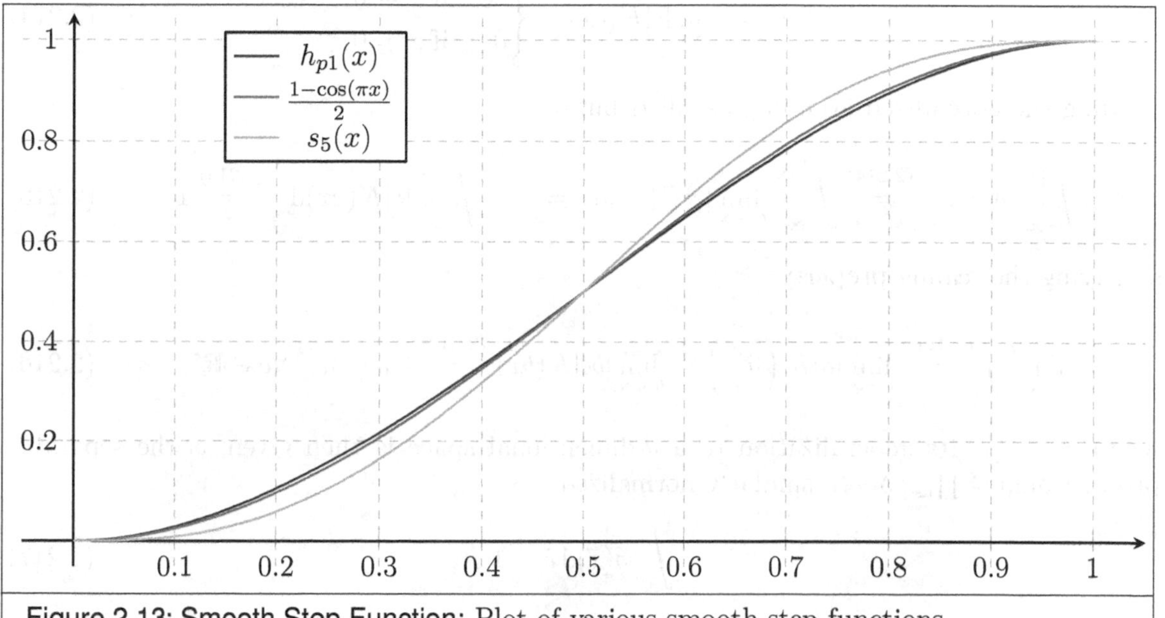

Figure 2.13: Smooth Step Function: Plot of various smooth step functions.

2.3.3 Kernel Function

2.3.3.1 *Definition*

In statistics, a *kernel function* is defined as a real-valued integrable function $K(x)$ satisfying positivity

$$K(x) \geq 0, \quad \forall x \in \mathbb{R} \tag{2.209}$$

and normalization

$$\int_{-\infty}^{+\infty} K(x)\mathrm{d}x = 1 \tag{2.210}$$

as well as evenness

$$K(x) = K(-x), \quad \forall x \in \mathbb{R} \tag{2.211}$$

140 so as to yield vanishing odd raw *moments*

$$\begin{aligned}\int_{-\infty}^{+\infty} K(x)x^n\mathrm{d}x &= \int_{-\infty}^{0} K(x)x^n\mathrm{d}x + \int_{0}^{+\infty} K(x)x^n\mathrm{d}x \\ &= \int_{-\infty}^{0} K(-x)x^n\mathrm{d}x - \int_{0}^{-\infty} K(-x)(-x)^n\mathrm{d}x \\ &= 0, \quad \forall n \in \text{odd } \mathbb{Z}\end{aligned} \tag{2.212}$$

Scaling of the bandwidth of a kernel function by a factor c is then readily given by

$$\int_{-\infty}^{+\infty} K(cx)|c|\mathrm{d}x = 1 \tag{2.213}$$

such that $|c|K(cx)$ is a normalized kernel function as well.

2.3.3.2 *Delta Function*

45 As illustrated in *Figure 2.14*, the *Dirac delta function* is defined $\forall x \in \mathbb{R}$ as the limit of a scaled arbitrary kernel

$$\delta(x) \triangleq \lim_{c\to\infty} |c|K(cx) = \begin{cases} \infty & \text{if } x = 0 \\ 0 & \text{if } x \neq 0 \end{cases} \tag{2.214}$$

yielding the normalized even impulse distribution

44
44

$$\int_{-\infty}^{+\infty} \delta(x)\mathrm{d}x \overset{(2.214)}{=} \int_{-\infty}^{+\infty} \lim_{c\to\infty} |c|K(cx)\mathrm{d}x = \lim_{c\to\infty} \int_{-\infty}^{+\infty} |c|K(cx)\mathrm{d}x \overset{(2.213)}{=} 1 \tag{2.215}$$

satisfying the scaling property

44
44

$$\delta\left(\frac{x}{c}\right) \overset{(2.214)}{=} \lim_{a\to\infty} |a|K\left(a\frac{x}{c}\right) = \lim_{b\to\infty} |bc|K(bx) \overset{(2.214)}{=} |c|\delta(x), \quad \forall c \in \mathbb{R}^* \tag{2.216}$$

where $b \triangleq a/c$. Its generalization to a d-dimensional space is then given as the separable product $\delta(\vec{x}) \triangleq \prod_{i=1}^{d} \delta(x_i)$, similarly normalized

$$\int_{\mathbb{R}^d} \delta(\vec{x})\mathrm{d}\vec{x} = 1 \tag{2.217}$$

and satisfying the scaling property $\delta(\vec{x} \div c) = |c|^d \delta(\vec{x})$. It also holds that $x\delta(x) = 0$, while the integral of a function multiplied by a time-delayed Dirac delta is given by the *sifting property*, also called *sampling property*

$$\int_{-\infty}^{+\infty} f(x)\frac{1}{|c|}\delta\left(\frac{x-x_0}{c}\right)\mathrm{d}x \overset{(2.216)}{=} \int_{-\infty}^{+\infty} f(x)\delta(x-x_0)\mathrm{d}x$$ 44

$$\overset{(2.214)}{=} \lim_{c\to\infty}\int_{-\infty}^{+\infty} f(x)|c|K(c(x-x_0))\mathrm{d}x$$ 44

$$= f(x_0)\lim_{c\to\infty}\int_{-\infty}^{+\infty}|c|K(c(x-x_0))\mathrm{d}x$$

$$\overset{(2.213)}{=} f(x_0) \qquad (2.218)$$ 44

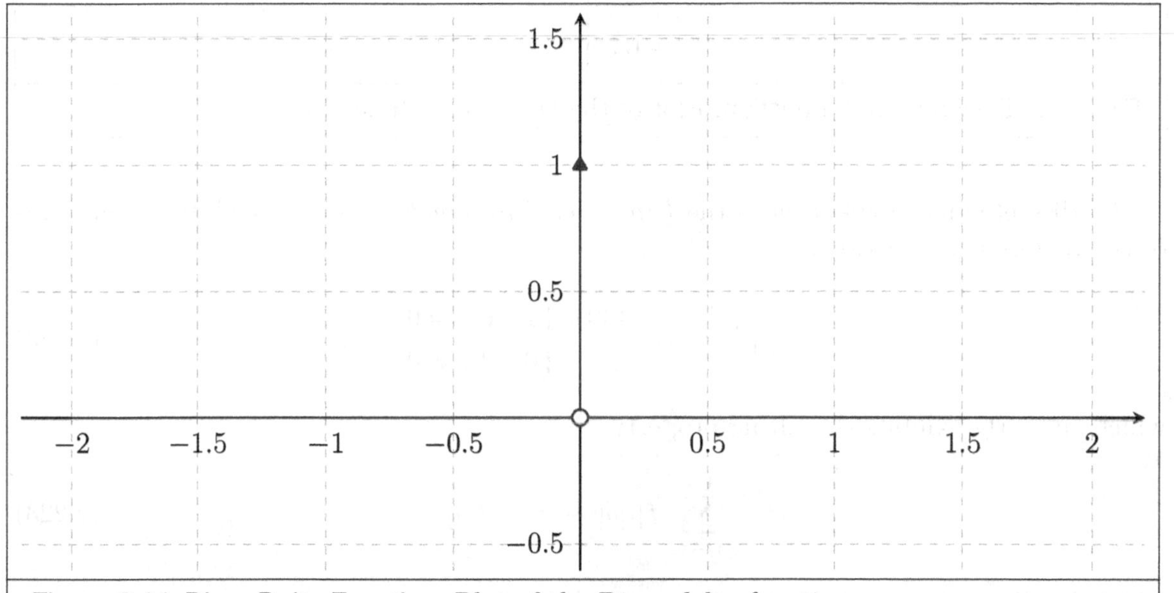

Figure 2.14: Dirac Delta Function: Plot of the Dirac delta function.

As illustrated in *Figure 2.15*, the *Dirac comb function*, also called *Shah function*, is then defined as a periodic impulse train of Dirac delta functions 46

$$\mathrm{III}(x) \triangleq \sum_{n=-\infty}^{+\infty}\delta(x\pm n) \qquad (2.219)$$

from which similarly follows the scaling property

$$\frac{1}{|c|}\mathrm{III}\left(\frac{x}{c}\right) \overset{(2.219)}{=} \frac{1}{|c|}\sum_{n=-\infty}^{+\infty}\delta\left(\frac{x}{c}\pm n\right) \overset{(2.216)}{=} \sum_{n=-\infty}^{+\infty}\delta(x\pm nc) \qquad (2.220)$$ 45 44

while the integral of a function multiplied by a time-delayed Dirac comb reads

$$\int_{-\infty}^{+\infty} f(x)\frac{1}{|c|}\mathrm{III}\left(\frac{x-x_0}{c}\right)\mathrm{d}x \overset{(2.220)}{=} \int_{-\infty}^{+\infty} f(x)\sum_{n=-\infty}^{+\infty}\delta(x-x_0\pm nc)\mathrm{d}x$$ 45

$$= \sum_{n=-\infty}^{+\infty}\int_{-\infty}^{+\infty} f(x)\delta(x-x_0\pm nc)\mathrm{d}x$$

$$\overset{(2.218)}{=} \sum_{n=-\infty}^{+\infty} f(x_0\mp nc) \qquad (2.221)$$ 45

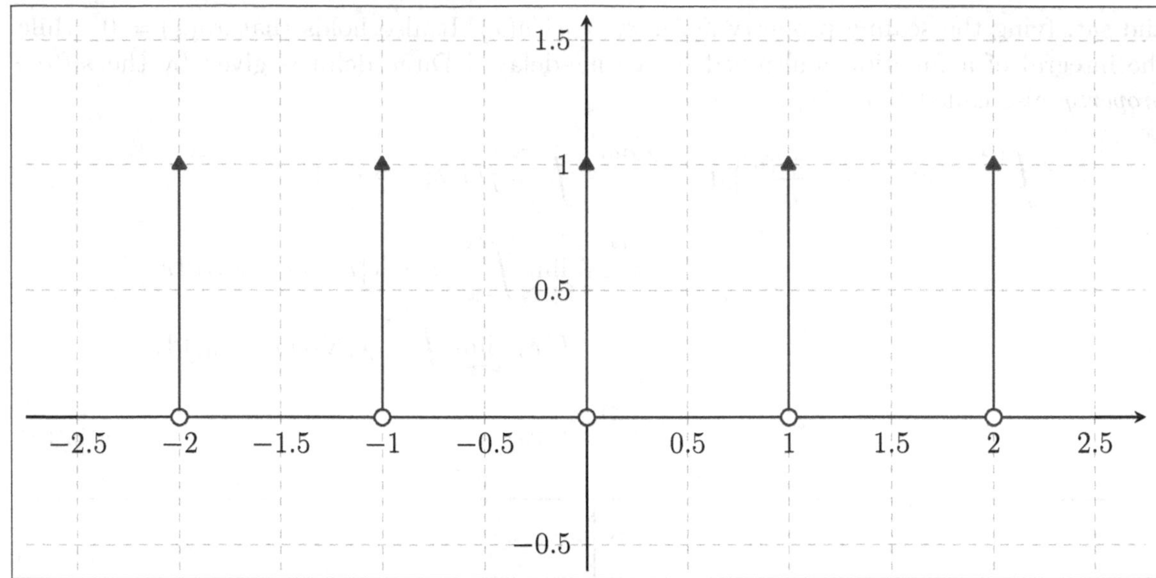

Figure 2.15: Dirac Comb Function: Plot of the Dirac comb function.

Its discrete analog is known as the *Kronecker delta function* and defined $\forall i \in \mathbb{Z}$ in terms
46 of the *rectangular function* as

46
$$\delta[i] \triangleq \sqcap(i) \overset{(2.225)}{=} \begin{cases} 1 & \text{if } i = 0 \\ 0 & \text{if } i \neq 0 \end{cases} \tag{2.222}$$

which similarly exhibits the sifting property

$$\sum_{i=-\infty}^{+\infty} f[i]\delta[i-j] = f[j] \tag{2.223}$$

while the *Kronecker comb function* is in turn defined as

$$\text{III}[i] \triangleq \sum_{n=-\infty}^{+\infty} \delta[i \pm n] \tag{2.224}$$

2.3.3.3 Rectangular Function

47 As illustrated in *Figure 2.16*, the *rectangular function* is defined in terms of the *Heaviside*
42 *step function*

42
$$\sqcap(x) \triangleq H\left(\frac{1}{2} - |x|\right) = H\left(x + \frac{1}{2}\right) - H\left(x - \frac{1}{2}\right) \overset{(2.203)}{=} \begin{cases} 1 & \text{if } |x| < 1/2 \\ 1/2 & \text{if } |x| = 1/2 \\ 0 & \text{if } |x| > 1/2 \end{cases} \tag{2.225}$$

as a normalized distribution

46
$$\int_{-\infty}^{+\infty} \sqcap(x)\mathrm{d}x \overset{(2.225)}{=} \int_{-1/2}^{+1/2} \mathrm{d}x = [x]_{-1/2}^{+1/2} = 1 \tag{2.226}$$

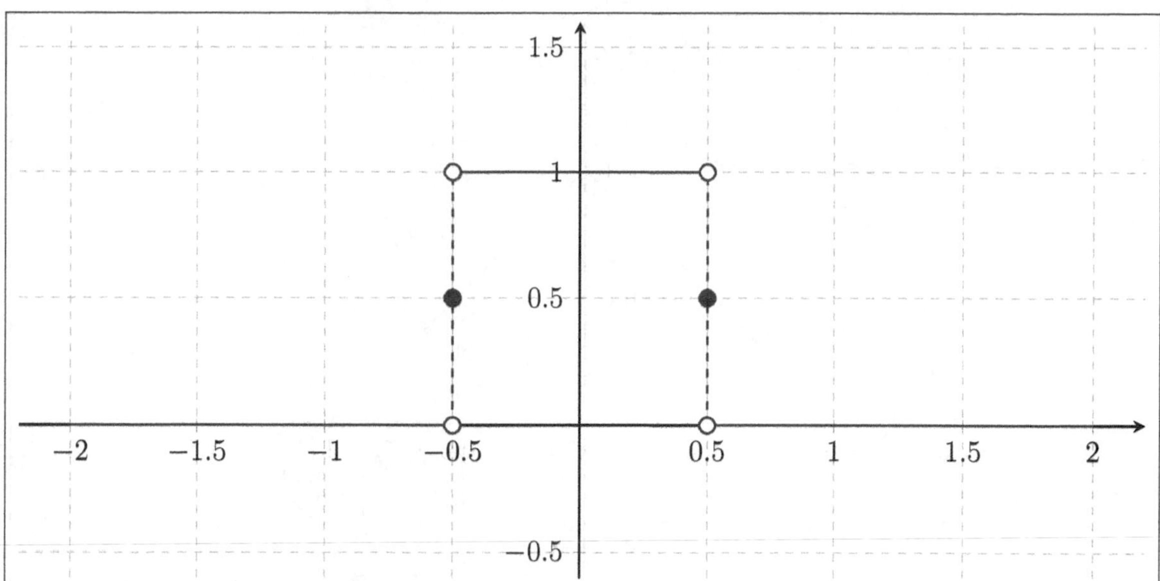

Figure 2.16: Rectangular Function: Plot of the rectangular function.

The *indicator function*, also called *characteristic function*, is then defined as

$$\chi_{[a,b]}(x) \triangleq \sqcap\left(\frac{x-a}{b-a}-\frac{1}{2}\right) = \sqcap\left(\frac{1}{2}-\frac{b-x}{b-a}\right) = \sqcap\left(\frac{x-\frac{a+b}{2}}{b-a}\right) \tag{2.227}$$

$$\overset{(2.225)}{=} \begin{cases} 1 & \text{if } x \in (a,b) \\ 1/2 & \text{if } x = a \vee x = b \\ 0 & \text{if } x \notin [a,b] \end{cases} \tag{2.228}$$ 46

2.3.3.4 Triangular Function

As illustrated in *Figure 2.17*, the *triangular function* is defined in terms of the *linear step* 48
function and *rectangular function* 42
46

$$\wedge(x) \triangleq L(1-|x|) = L(x+1) - L(x) \tag{2.229}$$

$$= \sqcap(x) * \sqcap(x) = \sqcap(x \div 2)(1-|x|) \tag{2.230}$$

$$\underset{(2.225)}{\overset{(2.204)}{=}} \max\{0, 1-|x|\} = \begin{cases} 1-|x| & \text{if } |x| \leq 1 \\ 0 & \text{if } |x| \geq 1 \end{cases} \tag{2.231}$$ 42 46

as a normalized distribution

$$\begin{aligned} \int_{-\infty}^{+\infty} \wedge(x)\mathrm{d}x &\overset{(2.229)}{=} \int_{-1}^{0}(1+x)\mathrm{d}x + \int_{0}^{1}(1-x)\mathrm{d}x \\ &= 2\int_{0}^{1}(1-x)\mathrm{d}x \\ &= 2\left[x-\frac{x^2}{2}\right]_0^1 \\ &= 2\left(1-\frac{1}{2}\right) \\ &= 1 \end{aligned} \tag{2.232}$$ 47

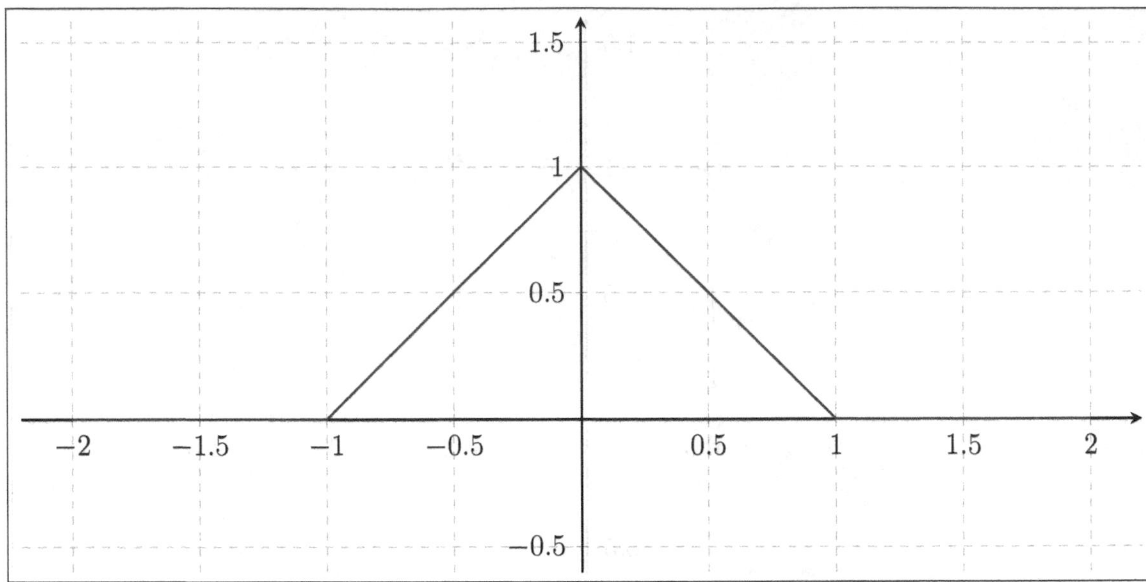

Figure 2.17: Triangular Function: Plot of the triangular function.

2.3.3.5 *Multiweight Function*

49 As illustrated in *Figure 2.18*, the multiweight function

$$W_n(x) \triangleq c_n \max\{0, 1 - x^2\}^n = \begin{cases} c_n(1-x^2)^n & \text{if } |x| \leq 1 \\ 0 & \text{if } |x| \geq 1 \end{cases} \tag{2.233}$$

is defined as a normalized distribution by means of the binomial theorem

48

$$\begin{aligned} \int_{-\infty}^{+\infty} W_n(x)\mathrm{d}x &\overset{(2.233)}{=} c_n \int_{-1}^{+1} (1-x^2)^n \mathrm{d}x \\ &= c_n \int_{-1}^{+1} \sum_{k=0}^{n} \binom{n}{k} (-x^2)^k \mathrm{d}x \\ &= c_n \sum_{k=0}^{n} \binom{n}{k} (-1)^k \int_{-1}^{+1} x^{2k} \mathrm{d}x \\ &= c_n \sum_{k=0}^{n} \binom{n}{k} (-1)^k \left[\frac{x^{2k+1}}{2k+1} \right]_{-1}^{+1} \\ &= c_n \sum_{k=0}^{n} \binom{n}{k} (-1)^k \left(\frac{1}{2k+1} - \frac{(-1)^{2k+1}}{2k+1} \right) \\ &= 2c_n \sum_{k=0}^{n} \binom{n}{k} \frac{(-1)^k}{2k+1} \\ &= 1 \end{aligned} \tag{2.234}$$

with the normalization constant

$$c_n \triangleq \frac{1}{2\sum_{k=0}^{n} \binom{n}{k} \frac{(-1)^k}{2k+1}} \tag{2.235}$$

whose values for the *Epanechnikov function* ($n = 1$), *biweight function* ($n = 2$) and *triweight function* ($n = 3$), respectively, read

$$c_1 = \frac{3}{4} \quad (2.236)$$

$$c_2 = \frac{15}{16} \quad (2.237)$$

$$c_3 = \frac{35}{32} \quad (2.238)$$

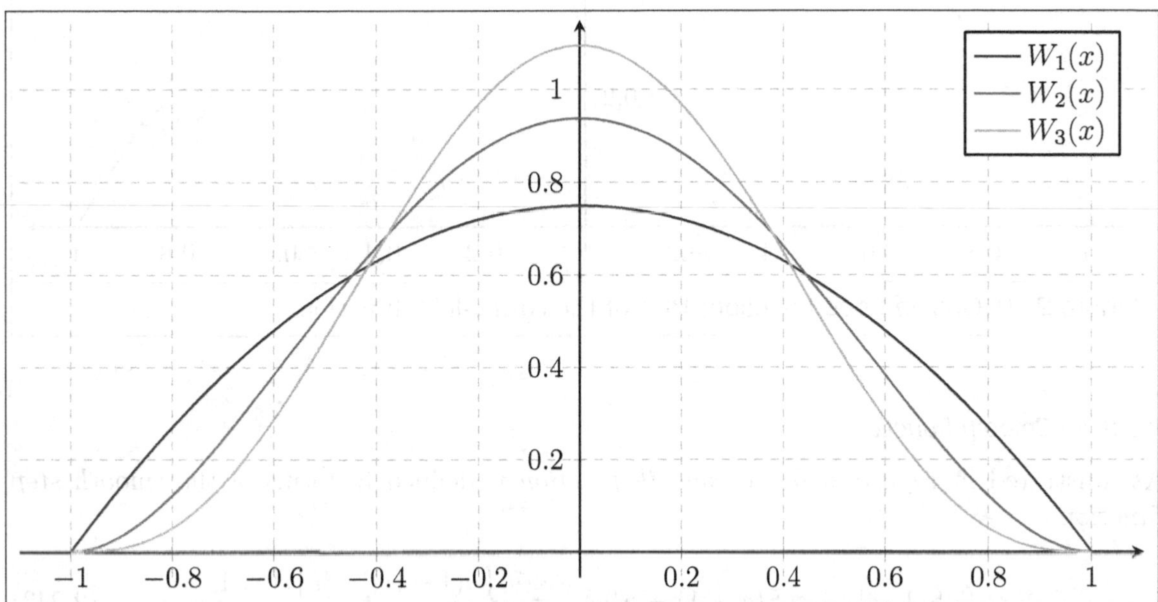

Figure 2.18: Multiweight Function: Plot of various multiweight kernels including the Epanechnikov, biweight and triweight functions.

Instead, the radial kernel is defined as the normalized distribution

$$\int_0^{\infty} W_n(\rho)\rho \mathrm{d}\rho \overset{(2.233)}{=} c_n \int_0^1 (1-\rho^2)^n \rho \mathrm{d}\rho = c_n \left[-\frac{(1-\rho^2)^{n+1}}{2n+2}\right]_0^1 = \frac{c_n}{2n+2} = 1 \quad (2.239)$$ 48

with the normalization constant

$$c_n \triangleq 2n + 2 \quad (2.240)$$

2.3.3.6 Cosine-Lobe Function

As illustrated in *Figure 2.19*, the *cosine-lobe function* 50

$$C(x) \triangleq \begin{cases} \frac{\pi}{4}\cos\left(\frac{\pi}{2}x\right) & \text{if } |x| \leq 1 \\ 0 & \text{if } |x| \geq 1 \end{cases} \quad (2.241)$$

is defined as a normalized distribution

$$\begin{aligned} \int_{-\infty}^{+\infty} C(x)\mathrm{d}x &\overset{(2.241)}{=} \frac{\pi}{4}\int_{-1}^{+1} \cos\left(\frac{\pi}{2}x\right)\mathrm{d}x \\ &= \frac{\pi}{4}\left[\frac{2}{\pi}\sin\left(\frac{\pi}{2}x\right)\right]_{-1}^{+1} \\ &= \frac{1}{2}\left(\sin\left(\frac{\pi}{2}\right) - \sin\left(-\frac{\pi}{2}\right)\right) \\ &= 1 \end{aligned} \quad (2.242)$$ 49

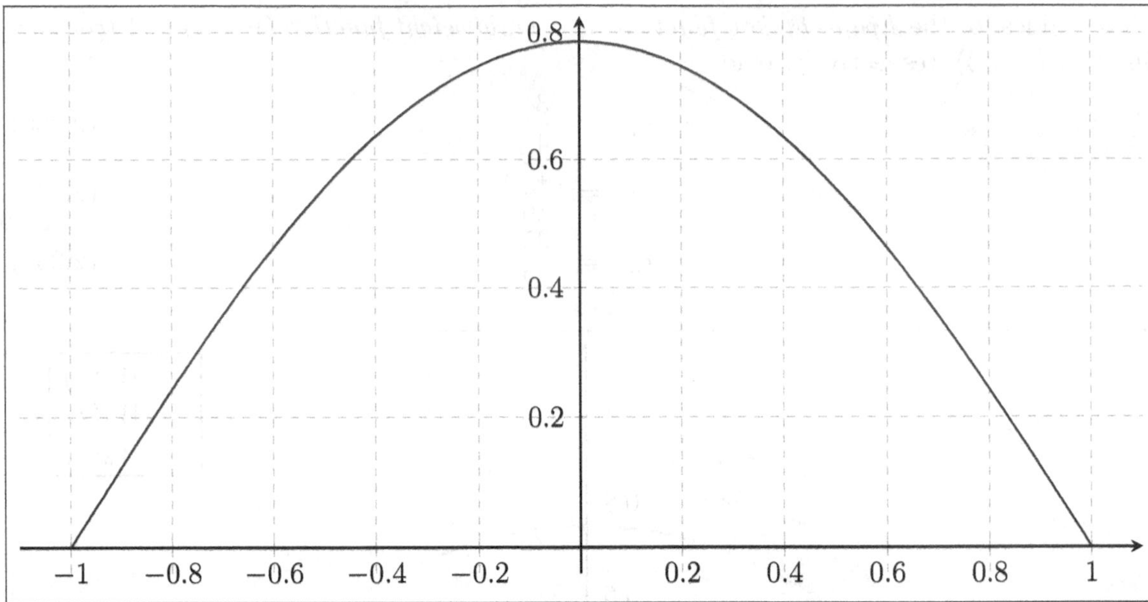

Figure 2.19: Cosine-Lobe Function: Plot of the cosine-lobe function.

2.3.3.7 Smooth Function

51 As illustrated in *Figure 2.20*, the *smooth function* is defined in terms of the *smooth step*
42 *function*

42
$$\cap(x) \triangleq S(1-|x|) = S(x+1) - S(x) \overset{(2.205)}{=} \begin{cases} s(1-|x|) & \text{if } |x| \leq 1 \\ 0 & \text{if } |x| \geq 1 \end{cases} \tag{2.243}$$

as a normalized distribution

50
$$\begin{aligned} \int_{-\infty}^{+\infty} \cap(x)\mathrm{d}x &\overset{(2.243)}{=} \int_{-1}^{0} s(1+x)\mathrm{d}x + \int_{0}^{1} s(1-x)\mathrm{d}x \\ &= \int_{0}^{1} s(x) + s(1-x)\mathrm{d}x \\ &= \int_{0}^{1} \mathrm{d}x \\ &= [x]_0^1 \\ &= 1 \end{aligned} \tag{2.244}$$

42 In the case of the cubic *smooth step function*, the kernel actually simplifies into

43
$$\cap(x) \underset{(8.177)}{\overset{(2.206)}{=}} \begin{cases} h_{p0}(|x|) & \text{if } |x| \leq 1 \\ 0 & \text{if } |x| \geq 1 \end{cases} \tag{2.245}$$
345

42 while in the case of the cosine-based *smooth step function*, it reduces to

50
$$\cap(x) \underset{(2.207)}{\overset{(2.243)}{=}} \begin{cases} \frac{1+\cos(\pi x)}{2} & \text{if } |x| \leq 1 \\ 0 & \text{if } |x| \geq 1 \end{cases} \tag{2.246}$$
43

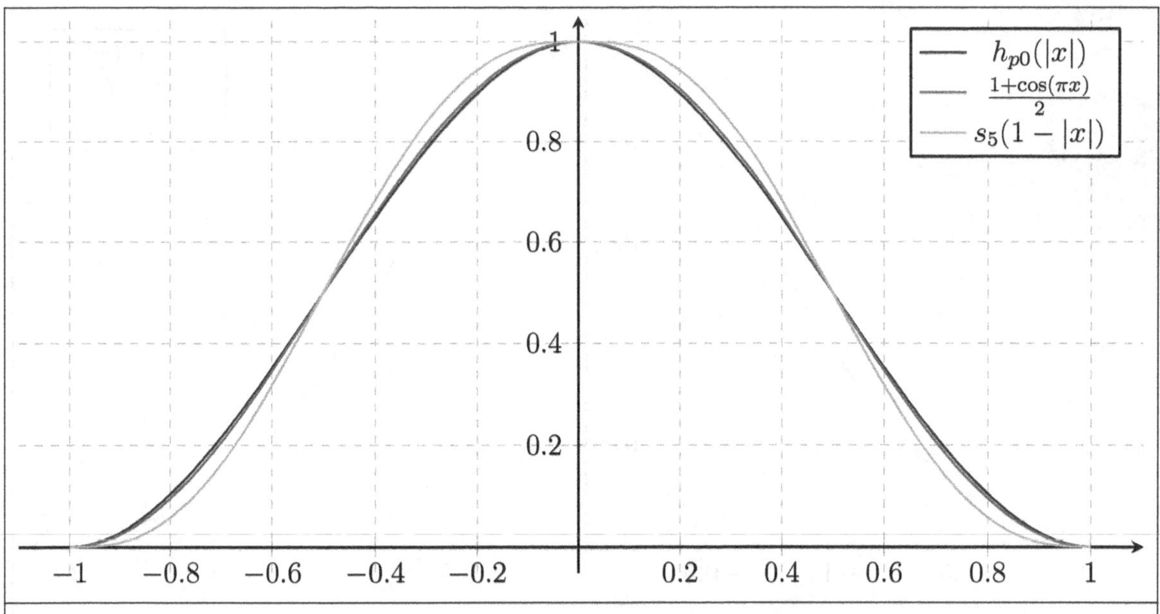

Figure 2.20: Smooth Function: Plot of various smooth functions.

2.3.3.8 Gaussian

As illustrated in *Figure 2.21*, the *Gaussian function* 52

$$G(x) \triangleq e^{-x^2} \tag{2.247}$$

with inflection points at $x = \pm\sqrt{1/2}$, is defined as a normalized distribution expressed in terms of the *error function* as 55

$$\int_{-\infty}^{+\infty} G(\sqrt{\pi}x)\mathrm{d}x \overset{(2.270)}{=} \left[\frac{\mathrm{erf}(\sqrt{\pi}x)}{2}\right]_{-\infty}^{+\infty} = \frac{\mathrm{erf}(+\infty) - \mathrm{erf}(-\infty)}{2} \overset{(2.272)}{=} \frac{1+1}{2} = 1 \tag{2.248}$$ 55 55

The standard *normal distribution* is then defined as 51

$$G_N(x) \triangleq \frac{1}{\sqrt{2\pi}} G\left(\sqrt{\pi}\frac{x}{\sqrt{2\pi}}\right) \overset{(2.247)}{=} \frac{1}{\sqrt{2\pi}} e^{-\frac{x^2}{2}} \tag{2.249}$$

such that the *probability density* function of a normally distributed *random variable* with 131 129
expected value μ and *standard deviation* σ reads 141 146 51

$$\frac{1}{\sigma} G_N\left(\frac{x-\mu}{\sigma}\right) \overset{(2.249)}{=} \frac{1}{\sqrt{2\pi}\sigma} e^{-\frac{(x-\mu)^2}{2\sigma^2}} \tag{2.250}$$

while the extension to two dimensions is readily given as the separable product of two one-dimensional Gaussian functions 51

$$\frac{1}{\sigma_x} G_N\left(\frac{x-\mu_x}{\sigma_x}\right) \frac{1}{\sigma_y} G_N\left(\frac{y-\mu_y}{\sigma_y}\right) \overset{(2.249)}{=} \frac{1}{2\pi\sigma_x\sigma_y} e^{-\left(\frac{(x-\mu_x)^2}{2\sigma_x^2} + \frac{(y-\mu_y)^2}{2\sigma_y^2}\right)} \tag{2.251}$$

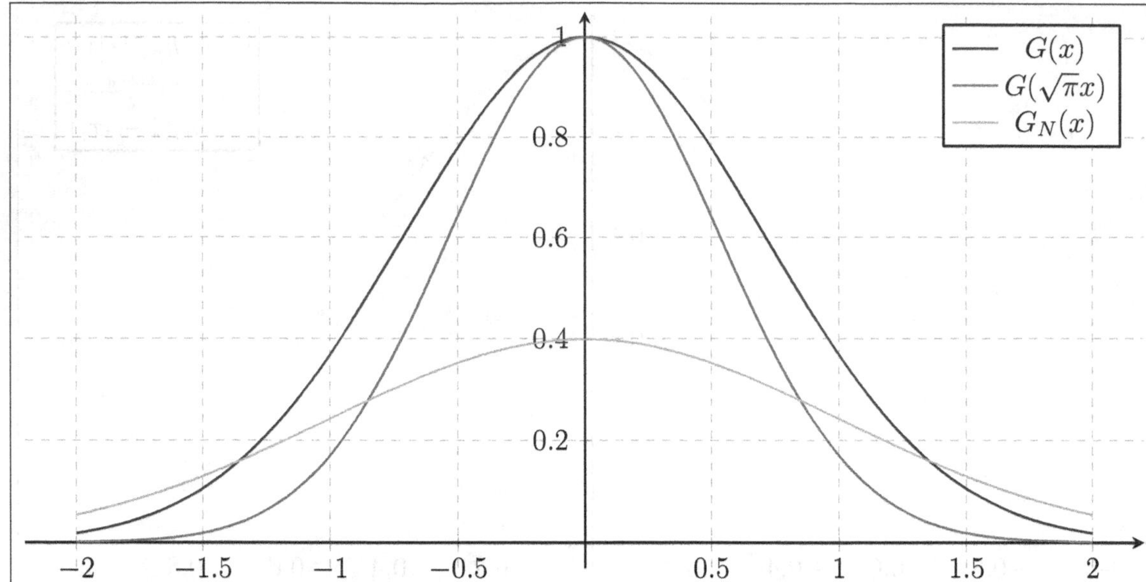

Figure 2.21: Gaussian Function: Plot of the unnormalized and normalized Gaussian function and of the normal distribution.

2.3.4 Oscillatory Function

2.3.4.1 *Sinc Function*

53 As illustrated in *Figure 2.22*, the *cardinal sine function*, often abbreviated *sinc function*,

$$\operatorname{sinc}(x) \triangleq \begin{cases} \frac{\sin(x)}{x} & \text{if } x \neq 0 \\ 1 & \text{if } x = 0 \end{cases} \tag{2.252}$$

58 is defined in terms of the *sine integral* function as a normalized distribution

58
58

$$\int_{-\infty}^{+\infty} \operatorname{sinc}(\pi x) \mathrm{d}x \overset{(2.298)}{=} \left[\frac{\operatorname{Si}(\pi x)}{\pi}\right]_{-\infty}^{+\infty} = \frac{\operatorname{Si}(+\infty) - \operatorname{Si}(-\infty)}{\pi} \overset{(2.300)}{=} \frac{{}^{\pi}/_{2} + {}^{\pi}/_{2}}{\pi} = 1 \tag{2.253}$$

Given the derivative of the function

$$\frac{\mathrm{d}\operatorname{sinc}(x)}{\mathrm{d}x} = \frac{x\cos(x) - \sin(x)}{x^2} \tag{2.254}$$

it follows that the local extrema occur at the solutions of $\operatorname{sinc}(x) = \cos(x)$, which may be
36 determined using a numerical *root finding* algorithm.

2.3.4.2 *Jinc Function*

53 As illustrated in *Figure 2.23*, the *jinc function*, also called *besinc function* or *sombrero func-*
54 *tion*, is defined in terms of the first-order *Bessel function* of the first kind as

$$\operatorname{jinc}(x) \triangleq \begin{cases} \frac{J_1(x)}{x} & \text{if } x \neq 0 \\ {}^{1}/_{2} & \text{if } x = 0 \end{cases} \tag{2.255}$$

54 while its derivative is given by the second-order *Bessel function* of the first kind as

54

$$\frac{\mathrm{d}\operatorname{jinc}(x)}{\mathrm{d}x} \overset{(2.268)}{=} \begin{cases} \frac{\frac{J_1(x)}{x} - J_2(x)}{x} - \frac{J_1(x)}{x^2} = -\frac{J_2(x)}{x} & \text{if } x \neq 0 \\ 0 & \text{if } x = 0 \end{cases} \tag{2.256}$$

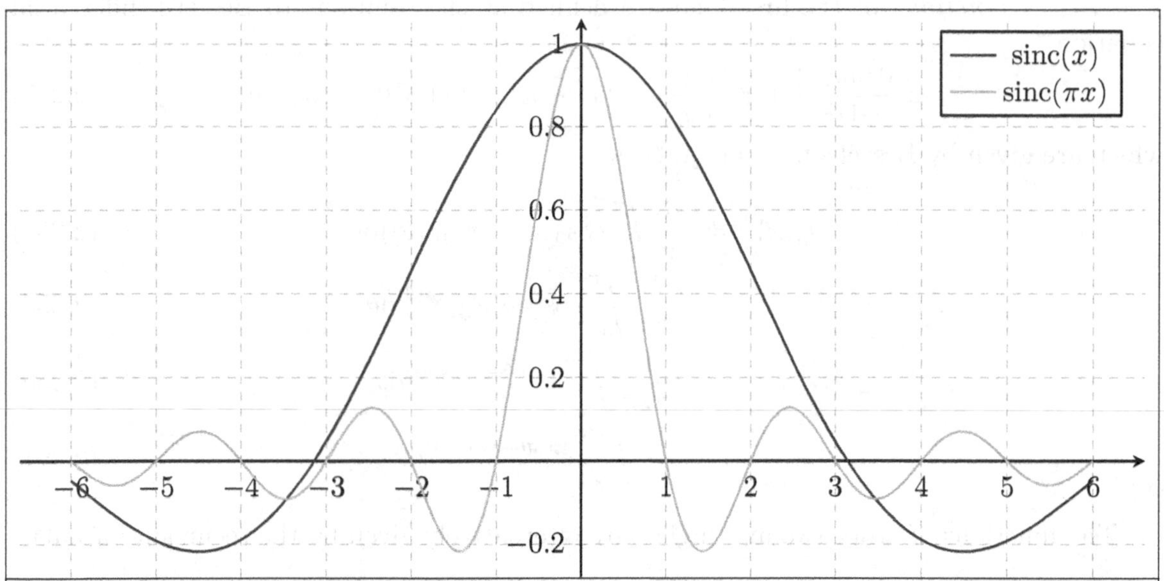

Figure 2.22: Sinc Function: Plot of the unnormalized and normalized cardinal sine function.

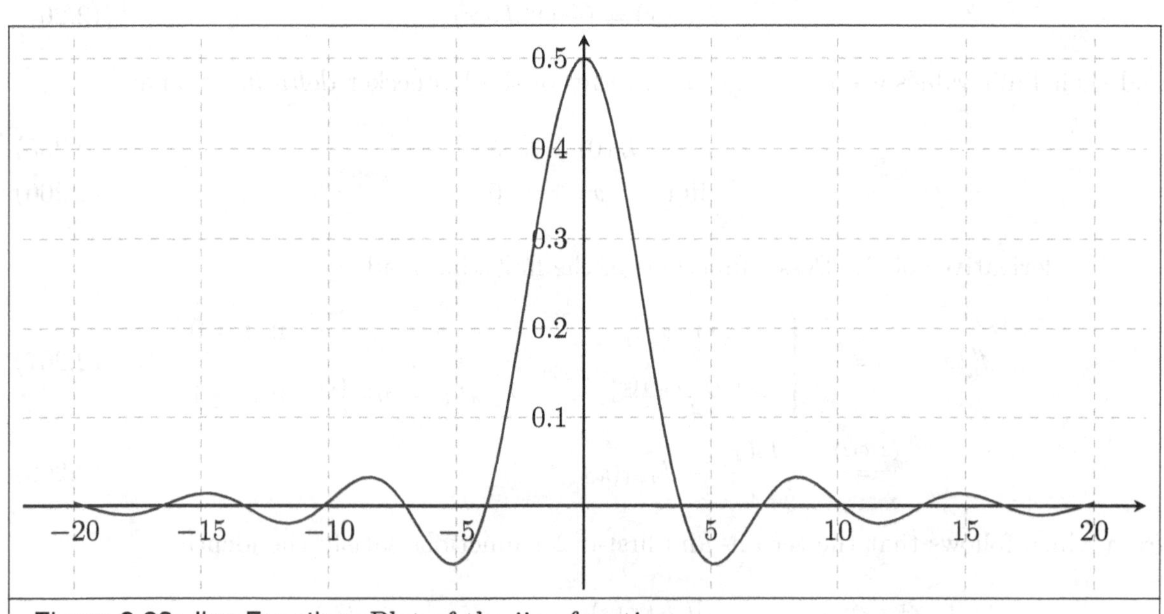

Figure 2.23: Jinc Function: Plot of the jinc function.

2.3.5 Special Function

2.3.5.1 Bessel Function

The *Bessel functions* of the first kind are defined as the solutions to Bessel's differential equation

$$x^2\frac{\mathrm{d}^2 J_n(x)}{\mathrm{d}x^2} + x\frac{\mathrm{d}J_n(x)}{\mathrm{d}x} + (x^2 - n^2)J_n(x) = 0, \quad \forall n \geq 0 \tag{2.257}$$

which are given by Bessel's first integrals as

$$J_n(x) \triangleq \frac{1}{\pi}\int_0^{\pi} \cos\left(n\theta - x\sin(\theta)\right)\mathrm{d}\theta \tag{2.258}$$

$$= \frac{1}{\imath^n \pi}\int_0^{\pi} \cos(n\theta)e^{\imath x\cos(\theta)}\mathrm{d}\theta \tag{2.259}$$

$$= \frac{1}{\imath^n 2\pi}\int_0^{2\pi} e^{\imath(n\theta + x\cos(\theta))}\mathrm{d}\theta \tag{2.260}$$

$$= \frac{1}{2\pi}\int_{-\pi}^{+\pi} e^{\imath(n\theta - x\sin(\theta))}\mathrm{d}\theta \tag{2.261}$$

The functions of order two and higher are alternatively given by the recursion formula

$$J_{n+1}(x) = 2n\frac{J_n(x)}{x} - J_{n-1}(x), \quad \forall n \geq 1 \tag{2.262}$$

while all functions are normalized such that

$$\int_0^{\infty} J_n(x)\mathrm{d}x = 1 \tag{2.263}$$

55 As illustrated in *Figure 2.24*, the Bessel functions of the first kind are alternatively even and odd, depending on the parity of the order n

$$J_n(-x) = (-1)^n J_n(x) \tag{2.264}$$

44 and their limit values are readily given in terms of the Kronecker *delta function* as

$$J_n(0) = \delta[n] \tag{2.265}$$

$$\lim_{x\to\pm\infty} J_n(x) = 0 \tag{2.266}$$

The derivatives of the Bessel functions of the first kind read

54

$$J_n'(x) = \begin{cases} -J_1(x) & \text{if } n = 0 \\ \frac{J_{n-1}(x) - J_{n+1}(x)}{2} \overset{(2.262)}{=} J_{n-1}(x) - n\frac{J_n(x)}{x} & \text{if } n \geq 1 \end{cases} \tag{2.267}$$

54

$$\overset{(2.262)}{=} n\frac{J_n(x)}{x} - J_{n+1}(x) \tag{2.268}$$

from which follows that the zeroth- and first-order functions satisfy the identity

54

$$J_1(x) = \frac{1}{x}\int_0^x J_0(t)t\mathrm{d}t \implies \frac{\mathrm{d}(J_1(x)x)}{\mathrm{d}x} = J_1'(x)x + J_1(x) \overset{(2.267)}{=} J_0(x)x \tag{2.269}$$

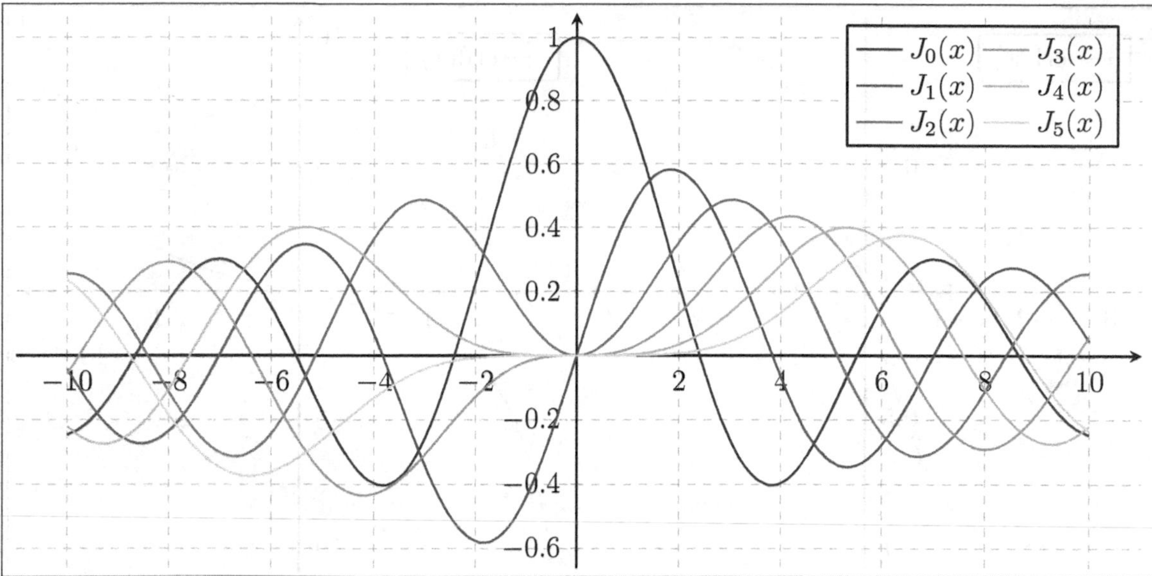

Figure 2.24: Bessel Functions: Plot of the first few orders of the Bessel functions of the first kind.

2.3.5.2 *Error Function*

As illustrated in *Figure 2.25*, the complex-valued *error function* and the *imaginary error* 56
function are odd monotonous functions defined in terms of the *Gaussian* function as 51

51

$$\operatorname{erf}(z) \triangleq 2\int_0^z \frac{1}{\sqrt{\pi}} G\left(\sqrt{\pi}\frac{t}{\sqrt{\pi}}\right) \mathrm{d}t \overset{(2.247)}{=} \frac{2}{\sqrt{\pi}} \int_0^z e^{-t^2} \mathrm{d}t \tag{2.270}$$

$$\operatorname{erfi}(z) \triangleq \frac{2}{\sqrt{\pi}} \int_0^z e^{t^2} \mathrm{d}t \tag{2.271}$$

with limit values on the real axis

$$\lim_{x \to \pm\infty} \operatorname{erf}(x) = \pm 1 \tag{2.272}$$

$$\lim_{x \to \pm\infty} \operatorname{erfi}(x) = \pm\infty \tag{2.273}$$

The two functions are related by

$$\imath \operatorname{erfi}(z) = \operatorname{erf}(\imath z) \iff \operatorname{erfi}(z) = \frac{\operatorname{erf}(\imath z)}{\imath} = -\imath \operatorname{erf}(\imath z) \tag{2.274}$$

while it also holds that

$$\operatorname{erf}(-z) = -\operatorname{erf}(z) \tag{2.275}$$

$$\operatorname{erf}(\bar{z}) = \overline{\operatorname{erf}(z)} \tag{2.276}$$

The antiderivatives of the error function and imaginary error function read

$$\int \operatorname{erf}(z) \mathrm{d}z = z \operatorname{erf}(z) + \frac{e^{-z^2}}{\sqrt{\pi}} \tag{2.277}$$

$$\int \operatorname{erfi}(z) \mathrm{d}z = z \operatorname{erfi}(z) - \frac{e^{z^2}}{\sqrt{\pi}} \tag{2.278}$$

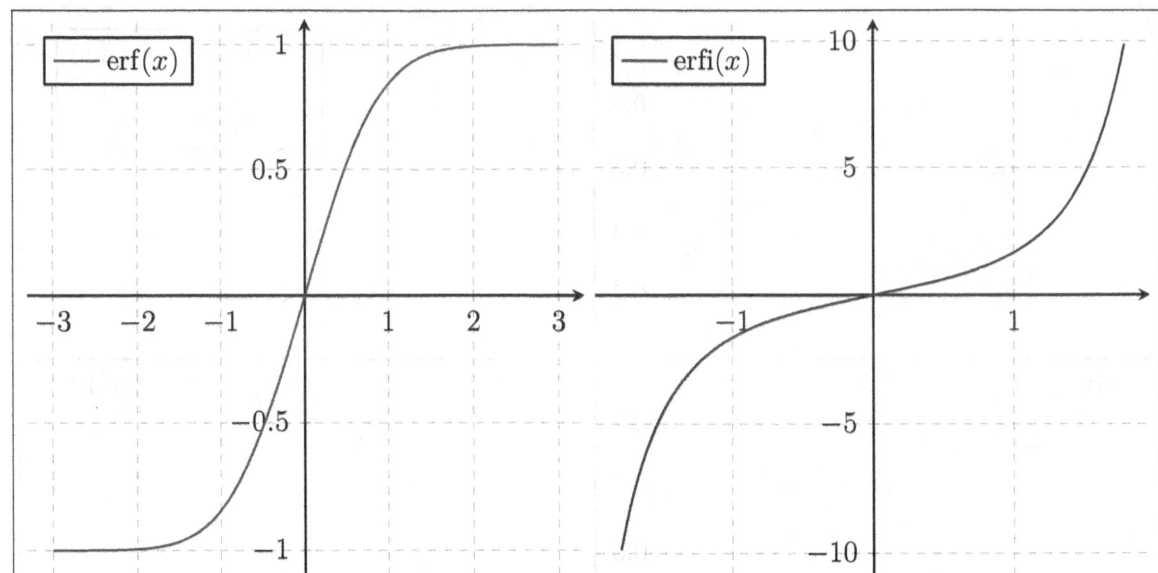

Figure 2.25: Error Function: Plots of the real-valued error function and imaginary error function.

while that of the exponential of a quadratic polynomial is readily given as [Gradshteyn and Ryzhik, 2007, §2.3]

$$\int e^{c_2x^2+c_1x+c_0}\mathrm{d}x = e^{c_0} \times \begin{cases} \frac{e^{-\frac{c_1^2}{4c_2}}}{\sqrt{-c_2}}\frac{\sqrt{\pi}}{2}\operatorname{erf}\left(\sqrt{-c_2}\left(x+\frac{c_1}{2c_2}\right)\right) & \text{if } c_2 < 0 \\ \frac{e^{c_1x}}{c_1} & \text{if } c_2 = 0 \\ \frac{e^{-\frac{c_1^2}{4c_2}}}{\sqrt{c_2}}\frac{\sqrt{\pi}}{2}\operatorname{erfi}\left(\sqrt{c_2}\left(x+\frac{c_1}{2c_2}\right)\right) & \text{if } c_2 > 0 \end{cases} \tag{2.279}$$

2.3.5.3 Exponential Integral

The complex-valued *exponential integral function* is defined as

$$\operatorname{Ei}(z) \triangleq -\int_{-z}^{\infty}\frac{e^{-t}}{t}\mathrm{d}t, \quad |\arg(z)| < \pi \tag{2.280}$$

while its restriction to the real axis may be formulated in terms of the *Cauchy principal value* $⨍$ of the singular integral (with singularity at $t = 0$)

$$\operatorname{Ei}(x) = -⨍_{-x}^{\infty}\frac{e^{-t}}{t}\mathrm{d}t = -⨍_{x}^{-\infty}\frac{e^{t}}{-t}(-1)\mathrm{d}t = ⨍_{-\infty}^{x}\frac{e^{t}}{t}\mathrm{d}t \tag{2.281}$$

with limit values

$$\lim_{x\to-\infty}\operatorname{Ei}(x) = 0 \tag{2.282}$$

$$\lim_{x\to\pm 0}\operatorname{Ei}(x) = -\infty \tag{2.283}$$

$$\lim_{x\to+\infty}\operatorname{Ei}(x) = +\infty \tag{2.284}$$

57 As illustrated in *Figure 2.26*, the complex-valued function verifies the identity $\operatorname{Ei}(\bar{z}) = \overline{\operatorname{Ei}(z)}$, and presents a branch-cut discontinuity on both the positive and negative imaginary
42 sides of the negative real axis, which can be expressed in terms of the *Heaviside step function*

and *signum function* as 39

$$\lim_{y \to 0} \mathrm{Ei}(x + \imath y) = \mathrm{Ei}(x) + \imath\pi H(-x)\,\mathrm{sgn}(y) \tag{2.285}$$

while its derivative is readily given as

$$\frac{\mathrm{d}\,\mathrm{Ei}(z)}{\mathrm{d}z} = \frac{e^z}{z} \tag{2.286}$$

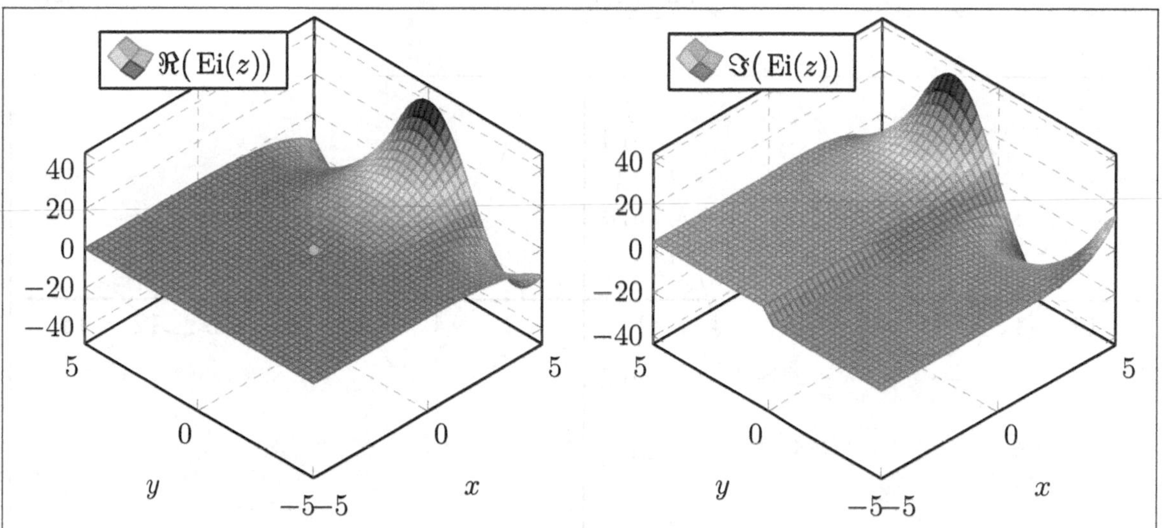

Figure 2.26: Exponential Integral: Plots of the real and imaginary parts of the complex-valued exponential integral.

The exponential integral is related to the *Theis well function* E_1 by [Pegoraro and Slusallek, 2011]

$$\mathrm{Ei}(z) = -\,\mathrm{E}_1(-z) + \frac{1}{2}\left(\ln(z) - \ln\left(\frac{1}{z}\right)\right) - \ln(-z) \tag{2.287}$$

$$\overset{(3.170)}{=} -\,\mathrm{E}_1(-z) - \imath\pi\,\mathrm{sgn}\left(\arg(-z)\right) \tag{2.288}$$ 88

$$= \begin{cases} -\,\mathrm{E}_1(-z) + \imath\pi & \text{if } \Im(z) > 0 \\ -\,\mathrm{E}_1(-z) - \imath\pi & \text{if } \Im(z) < 0 \\ -\,\mathrm{E}_1(-z) - \imath\pi & \text{if } \Im(z) = 0 \wedge \Re(z) > 0 \\ -\,\mathrm{E}_1(-z) & \text{if } \Im(z) = 0 \wedge \Re(z) \leq 0 \end{cases} \tag{2.289}$$

while being related to the *cosine integral* and *sine integral* functions by 58 58

$$\mathrm{Ei}(\imath y) \overset{(2.289)}{=} -\,\mathrm{E}_1(-\imath y) + \imath\pi\,\mathrm{sgn}(y) = \mathrm{Ci}(y) + \imath\left(\mathrm{Si}(y) + \frac{\pi}{2}\,\mathrm{sgn}(y)\right) \tag{2.290}$$ 57

where

$$\mathrm{E}_1(\imath y) = -\,\mathrm{Ci}(y) + \imath\left(\mathrm{Si}(y) - \frac{\pi}{2}\,\mathrm{sgn}(y)\right) \tag{2.291}$$

2.3.5.4 *Cosine Integral*

58 As illustrated in *Figure 2.27*, the *cosine integral function* is an even function defined as

$$\mathrm{Ci}(x) \triangleq -\int_x^\infty \frac{\cos(t)}{t}\mathrm{d}t \tag{2.292}$$

with limit values

$$\lim_{x\to\pm 0} \mathrm{Ci}(x) = -\infty \tag{2.293}$$

$$\lim_{x\to\pm\infty} \mathrm{Ci}(x) = 0 \tag{2.294}$$

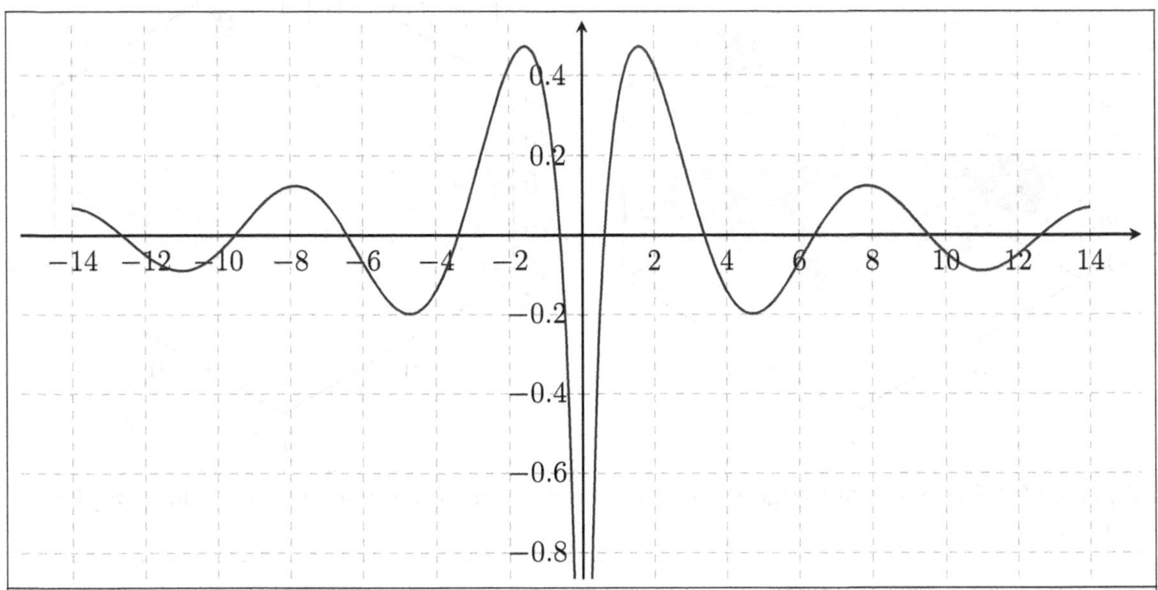

Figure 2.27: Cosine Integral: Plot of the cosine integral function.

Its derivative reads

$$\frac{\mathrm{d}\,\mathrm{Ci}(x)}{\mathrm{d}x} = \frac{\cos(x)}{x} \tag{2.295}$$

while its antiderivative is readily given as

$$\int \mathrm{Ci}(x)\mathrm{d}x = x\,\mathrm{Ci}(x) - \sin(x) \tag{2.296}$$

56 The cosine integral is related to the *exponential integral* and Theis well functions by

57
57

$$\mathrm{Ci}(y) \overset{(2.290)}{=} \Re(\mathrm{Ei}(\imath y)) \overset{(2.291)}{=} -\Re(\mathrm{E}_1(\imath y)) \tag{2.297}$$

2.3.5.5 *Sine Integral*

59 As illustrated in *Figure 2.28*, the *sine integral function* is an odd function defined as

52

$$\mathrm{Si}(x) \triangleq \int_0^x \mathrm{sinc}(t)\mathrm{d}t \overset{(2.252)}{=} \int_0^x \frac{\sin(t)}{t}\mathrm{d}t = \frac{\pi}{2} - \int_x^\infty \frac{\sin(t)}{t}\mathrm{d}t \tag{2.298}$$

with limit values

$$\mathrm{Si}(0) = 0 \tag{2.299}$$

$$\lim_{x\to\pm\infty} \mathrm{Si}(x) = \pm\frac{\pi}{2} \tag{2.300}$$

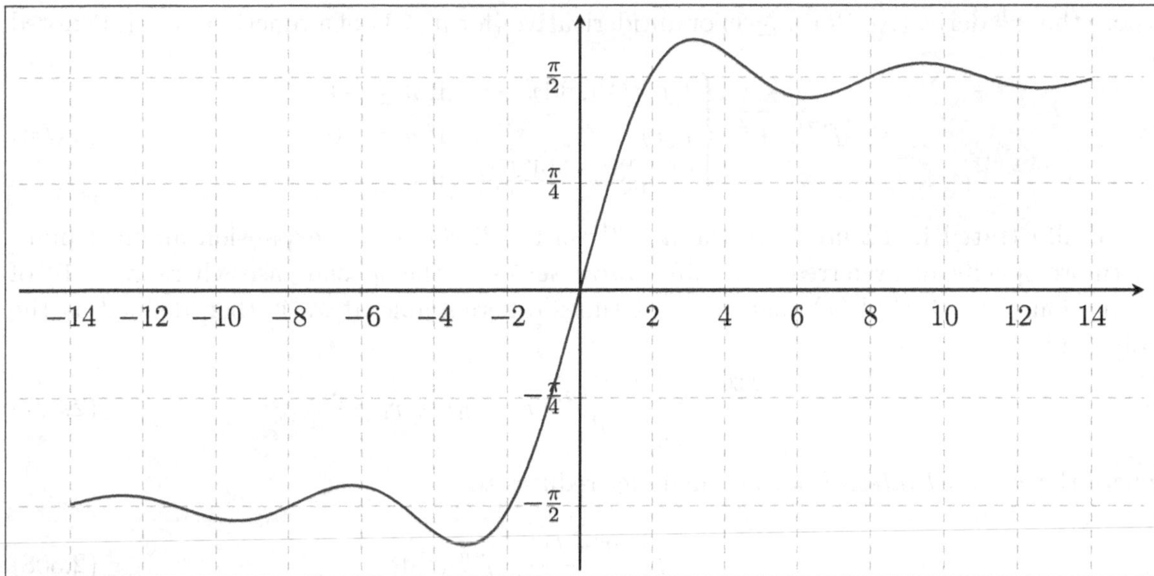

Figure 2.28: Sine Integral: Plot of the sine integral function.

Its derivative reads

$$\frac{\mathrm{d}\,\mathrm{Si}(x)}{\mathrm{d}x} = \frac{\sin(x)}{x} \tag{2.301}$$

while its antiderivative is readily given as

$$\int \mathrm{Si}(x)\mathrm{d}x = \cos(x) + x\,\mathrm{Si}(x) \tag{2.302}$$

The sine integral is related to the *exponential integral* and Theis well functions by 56

$$\mathrm{Si}(y) \overset{(2.290)}{=} \Im(\,\mathrm{Ei}(\imath y)) - \frac{\pi}{2}\,\mathrm{sgn}(y) \overset{(2.291)}{=} \Im(\,\mathrm{E}_1(\imath y)) + \frac{\pi}{2}\,\mathrm{sgn}(y) \tag{2.303}$$ 57 57

2.4 FUNCTIONAL APPROXIMATIONS

2.4.1 Taylor Series

Given an n-time integrable function $g(x)$, a sequence defined as

$$r_n(x) \triangleq \begin{cases} g(x) & \text{if } n = 0 \\ \int_{x_0}^{x} r_{n-1}(t)\mathrm{d}t & \text{if } n \geq 1 \end{cases} \tag{2.304}$$

can be expanded out to

$$\begin{aligned}
r_0(x) &= g^{(-0)}(x) \\
r_1(x) &= g^{(-1)}(x) - g^{(-1)}(x_0) \\
r_2(x) &= g^{(-2)}(x) - g^{(-2)}(x_0) - (x - x_0)g^{(-1)}(x_0) \\
r_3(x) &= g^{(-3)}(x) - g^{(-3)}(x_0) - (x - x_0)g^{(-2)}(x_0) - \frac{(x - x_0)^2}{2}g^{(-1)}(x_0) \\
\cdots &= \cdots \\
r_n(x) &= g^{(-n)}(x) - \sum_{i=0}^{n-1} \frac{(x - x_0)^i}{i!} g^{(i-n)}(x_0)
\end{aligned} \tag{2.305}$$

where the nth derivative (for $n \geq 1$) or antiderivative (for $n \leq 1$) of a function $f(x)$ is denoted as

$$f^{(n)}(x) \triangleq \begin{cases} \int f^{(n+1)}(x)\mathrm{d}x & \text{if } n \leq -1 \\ f(x) & \text{if } n = \quad 0 \\ \frac{\mathrm{d}f^{(n-1)}(x)}{\mathrm{d}x} = \frac{\mathrm{d}^n f(x)}{\mathrm{d}x^n} & \text{if } n \geq +1 \end{cases} \tag{2.306}$$

60 As illustrated in *Figure 2.29*, the $n-1^{\text{th}}$-order *Taylor series* expansion about a point x_0 (more specifically referred to as *Maclaurin series* in the special case where $x_0 = 0$) of a function $f(x) \triangleq g^{(-n)}(x)$ that is $n-1$ times differentiable at x_0 is then defined as the polynomial

59
$$f(x) \overset{(2.305)}{=} \sum_{i=0}^{n-1} \frac{f^{(i)}(x_0)}{i!}(x - x_0)^i + r_n(x) \tag{2.307}$$

where the *repeated integral* of the remainder reduces to

$$r_n(x) = \int_{x_0}^{x} \frac{(x-t)^{n-1}}{(n-1)!} f^{(n)}(t)\mathrm{d}t \tag{2.308}$$

such that $\lim_{n\to\infty} r_n(x) = 0$, yielding the *power series*

$$f(x) = \sum_{i=0}^{\infty} a_i (x - x_0)^i \tag{2.309}$$

with coefficients

$$a_i \triangleq \frac{f^{(i)}(x_0)}{i!} \tag{2.310}$$

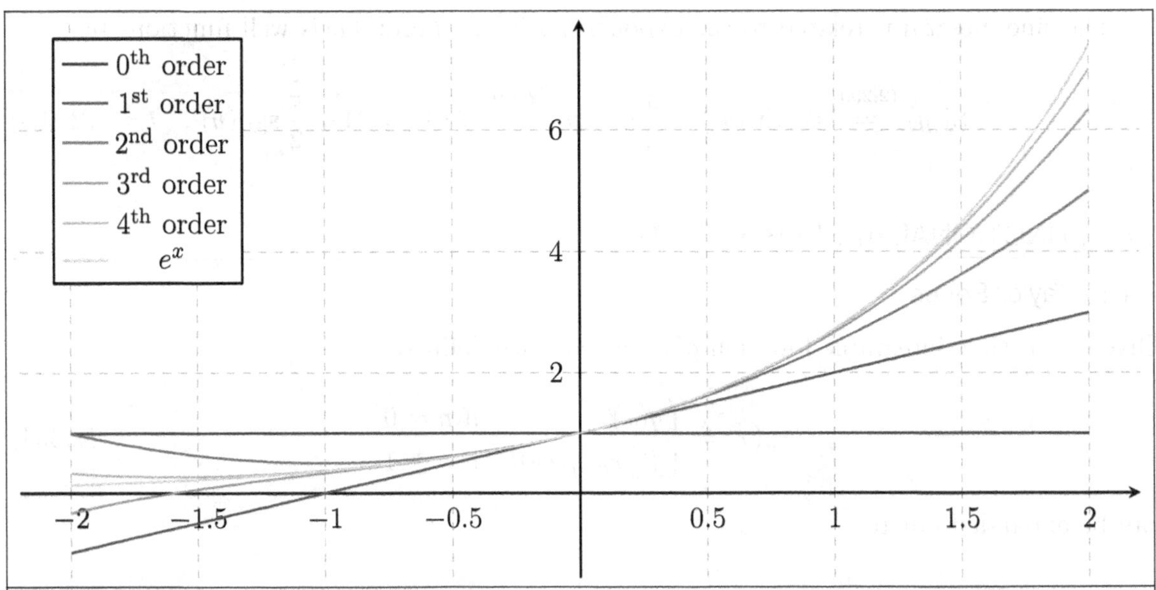

Figure 2.29: Taylor Series: Illustration of the truncated Taylor series of a sample function.

The degree-n approximation of $f(x)$ given by its truncated series may alternatively be reformulated in a monomial basis by use of the binomial theorem as

$$\begin{aligned} f(x) &\approx \sum_{i=0}^{n} \frac{f^{(i)}(x_0)}{i!}(x-x_0)^i \\ &= \sum_{i=0}^{n} \frac{f^{(i)}(x_0)}{i!} \sum_{k=0}^{i} \frac{i!}{k!(i-k)!} x^k (-x_0)^{i-k} \\ &= \sum_{k=0}^{n} \frac{x^k}{k!} \sum_{i=k}^{n} \frac{f^{(i)}(x_0)}{(i-k)!}(-x_0)^{i-k} \\ &= \sum_{k=0}^{n} \frac{g_k(x_0)}{k!} x^k \end{aligned} \tag{2.311}$$

where the monomial coefficients can be computed in-place in order of increasing index k from the values of the derivatives at x_0 as

$$g_k(x_0) \triangleq \sum_{i=0}^{n-k} \frac{f^{(i+k)}(x_0)}{i!}(-x_0)^i \tag{2.312}$$

2.4.2 Orthogonal Basis Functions

The functions Ψ_n of an $N+1$-dimensional set are referred to as *orthogonal basis functions* over a domain $\mathcal{D}$ if their *inner product* over $\mathcal{D}$ is defined in terms of non-zero coefficients b_n 76
and of the Kronecker *delta function* as 44

$$\langle \Psi_m(x), \Psi_n(x) \rangle_{\mathcal{D}} = \int_{\mathcal{D}} \Psi_m(x)\Psi_n(x)\mathrm{d}x = b_n\delta[m-n] \tag{2.313}$$

while they are additionally referred to as *orthonormal basis functions* if $b_n = 1, \forall n \in [0, N]$.

Given a function $f(x)$, its projection into the basis may then be expressed as a truncated series of the form

$$f(x) = \sum_{n=0}^{N} a_n \Psi_n(x) \tag{2.314}$$

which, when multiplied on both sides by Ψ_m and integrated over $\mathcal{D}$, yields

$$\begin{aligned} \int_{\mathcal{D}} \Psi_m(x) f(x)\mathrm{d}x &= \int_{\mathcal{D}} \Psi_m(x) \sum_{n=0}^{N} a_n \Psi_n(x)\mathrm{d}x \\ &= \sum_{n=0}^{N} a_n \int_{\mathcal{D}} \Psi_m(x)\Psi_n(x)\mathrm{d}x \\ &\overset{(2.313)}{=} \sum_{n=0}^{N} a_n b_n \delta[m-n] \\ &\overset{(2.223)}{=} a_m b_m \end{aligned} \tag{2.315}$$

61

46

from which follows that the projection coefficients of $f(x)$ read

$$a_n = \frac{1}{b_n}\int_{\mathcal{D}} \Psi_n(x) f(x)\mathrm{d}x \tag{2.316}$$

2.4.3 Legendre Polynomial

The *Legendre functions* of the first kind, also known as *Legendre polynomials*, are defined as the solutions to Legendre's differential equation

$$\frac{\mathrm{d}}{\mathrm{d}x}\left[(1-x^2)\frac{\mathrm{d}P_n(x)}{\mathrm{d}x}\right] + n(n+1)P_n(x) = 0, \quad \forall n \geq 0 \tag{2.317}$$

which are given by *Rodrigues's formula* as

$$P_n(x) \triangleq \frac{1}{2^n n!}\frac{\mathrm{d}^n(x^2-1)^n}{\mathrm{d}x^n} \tag{2.318}$$

Alternatively, the polynomials may be expressed in an iterative form as

$$P_n(x) = \sum_{k=0}^{n}\binom{n}{k}^2\left(\frac{x+1}{2}\right)^{n-k}\left(\frac{x-1}{2}\right)^k \tag{2.319}$$

$$= \frac{1}{2^n}\sum_{k=0}^{n}(-1)^k\binom{n}{k}^2(1+x)^{n-k}(1-x)^k$$

$$= \frac{1}{2^n}\sum_{k=0}^{\lfloor\frac{n}{2}\rfloor}(-1)^k\binom{n}{k}\binom{2n-2k}{n}x^{n-2k} \tag{2.320}$$

$$= \frac{1}{2^n}\sum_{k=0}^{\lfloor\frac{n}{2}\rfloor}(-1)^k\frac{(2n-2k)!}{k!(n-k)!(n-2k)!}x^{n-2k}$$

$$= \sum_{\substack{m=n\\ m-=2}}^{\geq 0} b_{mn}x^m \tag{2.321}$$

where the coefficients read

$$b_{mn} \triangleq \frac{(-1)^{\frac{n-m}{2}}}{2^n}\frac{(n+m)!}{\left(\frac{n-m}{2}\right)!\left(\frac{n+m}{2}\right)!\, m!} \tag{2.322}$$

Expanding the polynomials of the first few degrees then yields the explicit formulations

$$P_0(x) = 1 \tag{2.323}$$

$$P_1(x) = x \tag{2.324}$$

$$P_2(x) = \frac{3x^2-1}{2} \tag{2.325}$$

$$P_3(x) = \frac{5x^3-3x}{2} \tag{2.326}$$

$$P_4(x) = \frac{35x^4-30x^2+3}{8} \tag{2.327}$$

$$P_5(x) = \frac{63x^5-70x^3+15x}{8} \tag{2.328}$$

$$P_6(x) = \frac{231x^6-315x^4+105x^2-5}{16} \tag{2.329}$$

$$P_7(x) = \frac{429x^7-693x^5+315x^3-35x}{16} \tag{2.330}$$

$$P_8(x) = \frac{6435x^8 - 12012x^6 + 6930x^4 - 1260x^2 + 35}{128} \tag{2.331}$$

$$P_9(x) = \frac{12155x^9 - 25740x^7 + 18018x^5 - 4620x^3 + 315x}{128} \tag{2.332}$$

$$P_{10}(x) = \frac{46189x^{10} - 109395x^8 + 90090x^6 - 30030x^4 + 3465x^2 - 63}{256} \tag{2.333}$$

while the polynomials of degree two and higher are recursively given by *Bonnet's recursion formula*

$$(n+1)P_{n+1}(x) = (2n+1)xP_n(x) - nP_{n-1}(x), \quad \forall n \geq 1 \tag{2.334}$$

which can be most efficiently evaluated via backward recursion by iteratively evaluating the next term in the sequence from the last two.

As illustrated in *Figure 2.30*, Legendre polynomials are alternatively even and odd, depending on the parity of the degree n 63

$$P_n(-x) = (-1)^n P_n(x) \tag{2.335}$$

and their values at the endpoints of the interval $[-1, +1]$ are readily given by

$$P_n(+1) = (+1)^n = 1 \tag{2.336}$$

$$P_n(-1) = (-1)^n \tag{2.337}$$

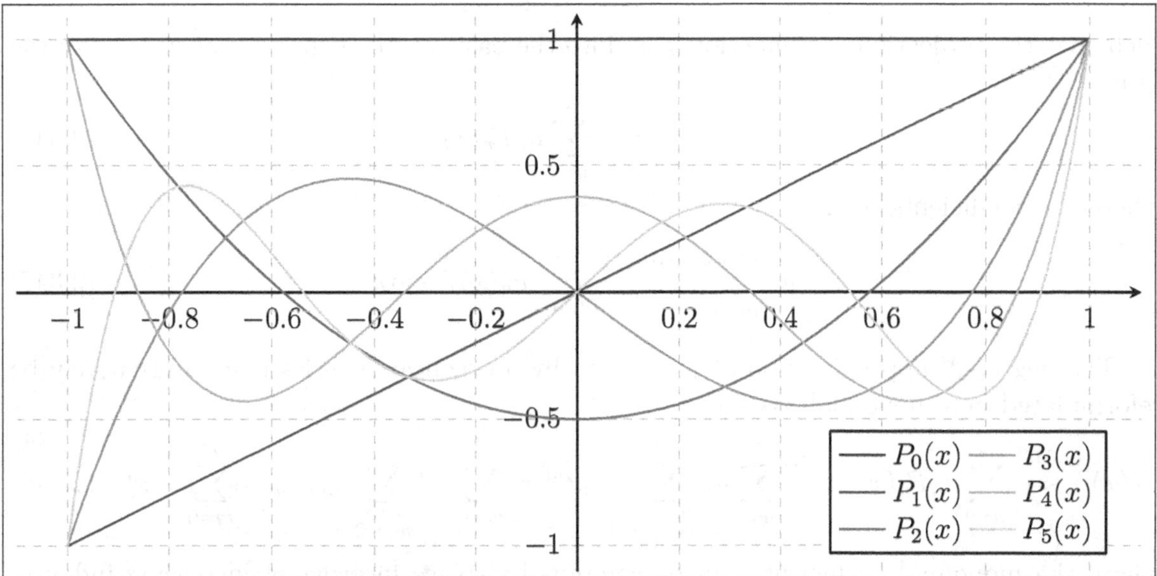

Figure 2.30: Legendre Polynomials: Plot of the first few Legendre polynomials on the interval $[-1, +1]$.

Moreover, *Turán's inequality* states that

$$P_n(x)^2 > P_{n-1}(x)P_{n+1}(x), \quad \forall x \in [-1, +1] \tag{2.338}$$

while the *Askey–Gasper inequality* gives

$$\sum_{n=0}^{N} P_n(x) \geq 0, \quad \forall x \in [-1, +1] \tag{2.339}$$

The derivatives of the Legendre polynomials read

63

$$\frac{\mathrm{d}P_n(x)}{\mathrm{d}x} = \begin{cases} 0 & \text{if } n = 0 \\ \frac{n(n+1)}{2n+1} \frac{P_{n+1}(x) - P_{n-1}(x)}{x^2 - 1} \overset{(2.334)}{=} n \frac{xP_n(x) - P_{n-1}(x)}{x^2 - 1} & \text{if } n \geq 1 \end{cases} \tag{2.340}$$

63

$$\overset{(2.334)}{=} (n+1) \frac{P_{n+1}(x) - xP_n(x)}{x^2 - 1} \tag{2.341}$$

such that $P_n'(1) = \frac{n(n+1)}{2}$, while their antiderivatives are readily given as

63

$$\int P_n(x)\mathrm{d}x = \begin{cases} P_1(x) & \text{if } n = 0 \\ \frac{P_{n+1}(x) - P_{n-1}(x)}{2n+1} \overset{(2.334)}{=} \frac{xP_n(x) - P_{n-1}(x)}{n+1} & \text{if } n \geq 1 \end{cases} \tag{2.342}$$

63

$$\overset{(2.334)}{=} \frac{P_{n+1}(x) - xP_n(x)}{n} \tag{2.343}$$

44 and their definite integrals are formulated in terms of the Kronecker *delta function* as

$$\int_{-1}^{+1} P_n(x)\mathrm{d}x = 2\delta[n] \tag{2.344}$$

61 Legendre polynomials form a complete system of *orthogonal basis functions* over the interval $[-1, +1]$

$$\int_{-1}^{+1} P_m(x)P_n(x)\mathrm{d}x = \frac{2}{2n+1}\delta[m-n] \tag{2.345}$$

such that the projection of a function $f(x)$ into the basis can be expressed as a series of the form

61

$$f(x) \overset{(2.314)}{=} \sum_{n=0}^{\infty} a_n P_n(x) \tag{2.346}$$

where the coefficients read

61

64

$$a_n \underset{(2.345)}{\overset{(2.316)}{=}} \frac{2n+1}{2} \int_{-1}^{+1} P_n(x) f(x)\mathrm{d}x \tag{2.347}$$

The degree-N approximation of $f(x)$ given by its truncated series may alternatively be reformulated in a monomial basis as

64

62

$$f(x) \overset{(2.346)}{\approx} \sum_{n=0}^{N} a_n P_n(x) \overset{(2.321)}{=} \sum_{n=0}^{N} a_n \sum_{\substack{m=n \\ m-=2}}^{\geq 0} b_{mn} x^m = \sum_{m=0}^{N} x^m \sum_{\substack{n=m \\ n+=2}}^{\leq N} a_n b_{mn} = \sum_{m=0}^{N} c_m x^m \tag{2.348}$$

where the monomial coefficients can be computed in-place in order of increasing index m from the Legendre coefficients a_n as

$$c_m \triangleq \sum_{\substack{n=m \\ n+=2}}^{\leq N} a_n b_{mn} \tag{2.349}$$

2.5 FURTHER READING

Additional material may be found in books dedicated to mathematical functions [Abramowitz and Stegun, 1972], integrals and series [Gradshteyn and Ryzhik, 2007, Gradshteyn and Ryzhik, 2014], scientific computing [Press *et al.*, 1992] and calculus for computer graphics [Vince, 2013a].

CHAPTER 3

Linear Algebra

TABLE OF CONTENTS

3.1 COORDINATE SYSTEMS

3.1.1 Cartesian Coordinates

As illustrated in *Figure 3.1*, a three-dimensional *Cartesian coordinate system* is parameterized 67
by the *abscissa coordinate* $x \in (-\infty, +\infty)$, the *ordinate coordinate* $y \in (-\infty, +\infty)$ and the *applicate coordinate* $z \in (-\infty, +\infty)$. The coordinates correspond to the signed distances of a point $\vec{p}$ to the principal planes formed by each pair of coordinate axes, so-called *number lines*, or equivalently to the signed distances between the origin $\vec{o}$ and the orthogonal projections of $\vec{p}$ onto the coordinate axes.

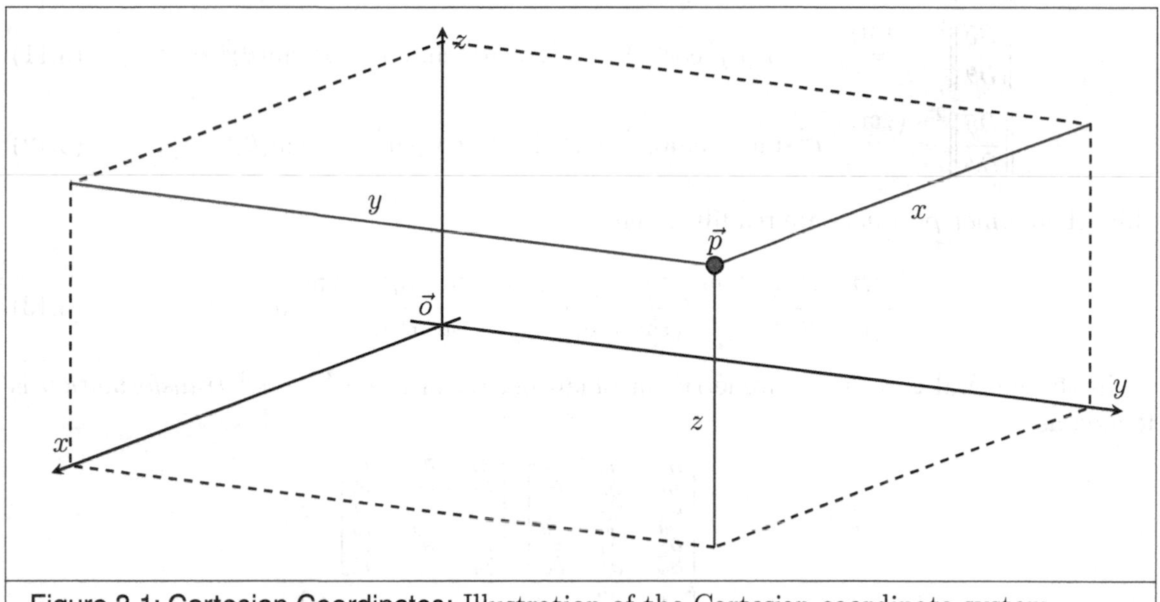

Figure 3.1: Cartesian Coordinates: Illustration of the Cartesian coordinate system.

Cartesian coordinates are related to *cylindrical coordinates* via the *transformation* 69
$[x, y, z]^T = T(\rho, \phi, z)$ defined as 102

$$x = \rho\cos(\phi) \tag{3.1}$$

$$y = \rho\sin(\phi) \tag{3.2}$$

$$z = z \tag{3.3}$$

whose Jacobian matrix reads

$$J_T \triangleq \begin{bmatrix} \frac{\partial x}{\partial \rho} & \frac{\partial x}{\partial \phi} & \frac{\partial x}{\partial z} \\ \frac{\partial y}{\partial \rho} & \frac{\partial y}{\partial \phi} & \frac{\partial y}{\partial z} \\ \frac{\partial z}{\partial \rho} & \frac{\partial z}{\partial \phi} & \frac{\partial z}{\partial z} \end{bmatrix} = \begin{bmatrix} \cos(\phi) & -\rho\sin(\phi) & 0 \\ \sin(\phi) & \rho\cos(\phi) & 0 \\ 0 & 0 & 1 \end{bmatrix} \tag{3.4}$$

with Jacobian *determinant* 98

$$\det(J_T) \overset{(3.308)}{=} \cos(\phi)\ \rho\cos(\phi) + \sin(\phi)\ \rho\sin(\phi) = \rho\left(\cos(\phi)^2 + \sin(\phi)^2\right) = \rho \tag{3.5}$$ 100

Instead, Cartesian coordinates are related to *spherical coordinates* via the *transformation* 70
$\vec{v} \triangleq [x, y, z]^T = T(r, \theta, \phi)$ defined as 102

$$x = r\sin(\theta)\cos(\phi) \tag{3.6}$$

$$y = r\sin(\theta)\sin(\phi) \tag{3.7}$$

$$z = r\cos(\theta) \tag{3.8}$$

whose Jacobian matrix reads

$$J_T \triangleq \left[\frac{\partial\vec{v}}{\partial r}, \frac{\partial\vec{v}}{\partial\theta}, \frac{\partial\vec{v}}{\partial\phi}\right] = \begin{bmatrix} \frac{\partial x}{\partial r} & \frac{\partial x}{\partial\theta} & \frac{\partial x}{\partial\phi} \\ \frac{\partial y}{\partial r} & \frac{\partial y}{\partial\theta} & \frac{\partial y}{\partial\phi} \\ \frac{\partial z}{\partial r} & \frac{\partial z}{\partial\theta} & \frac{\partial z}{\partial\phi} \end{bmatrix} = \begin{bmatrix} \sin(\theta)\cos(\phi) & r\cos(\theta)\cos(\phi) & -r\sin(\theta)\sin(\phi) \\ \sin(\theta)\sin(\phi) & r\cos(\theta)\sin(\phi) & r\sin(\theta)\cos(\phi) \\ \cos(\theta) & -r\sin(\theta) & 0 \end{bmatrix} \tag{3.9}$$

where the 2-norms of the column vectors read

74

$$\left\|\frac{\partial\vec{v}}{\partial r}\right\|^2 \overset{(3.61)}{=} \sin(\theta)^2\cos(\phi)^2 + \sin(\theta)^2\sin(\phi)^2 + \cos(\theta)^2 = 1 \tag{3.10}$$

74

$$\left\|\frac{\partial\vec{v}}{\partial\theta}\right\|^2 \overset{(3.61)}{=} r^2\cos(\theta)^2\cos(\phi)^2 + r^2\cos(\theta)^2\sin(\phi)^2 + r^2\sin(\theta)^2 = r^2 \tag{3.11}$$

74

$$\left\|\frac{\partial\vec{v}}{\partial\phi}\right\|^2 \overset{(3.61)}{=} r^2\sin(\theta)^2\sin(\phi)^2 + r^2\sin(\theta)^2\cos(\phi)^2 = r^2\sin(\theta)^2 \tag{3.12}$$

76 while their *inner products* are readily given as

76
76
76

$$\left\langle\frac{\partial\vec{v}}{\partial r}, \frac{\partial\vec{v}}{\partial\theta}\right\rangle \overset{(3.70)}{=} \left\langle\frac{\partial\vec{v}}{\partial r}, \frac{\partial\vec{v}}{\partial\phi}\right\rangle \overset{(3.70)}{=} \left\langle\frac{\partial\vec{v}}{\partial\theta}, \frac{\partial\vec{v}}{\partial\phi}\right\rangle \overset{(3.70)}{=} 0 \tag{3.13}$$

102 In the general case, the symmetric Jacobian matrix of the $\mathbb{R}^3 \to \mathbb{R}^3$ *transformation* is defined as

68
76
76
68
68
68
68

$$\begin{aligned} J_T^T J_T &\overset{(3.9)}{=} \begin{bmatrix} \frac{\partial x}{\partial r} & \frac{\partial y}{\partial r} & \frac{\partial z}{\partial r} \\ \frac{\partial x}{\partial\theta} & \frac{\partial y}{\partial\theta} & \frac{\partial z}{\partial\theta} \\ \frac{\partial x}{\partial\phi} & \frac{\partial y}{\partial\phi} & \frac{\partial z}{\partial\phi} \end{bmatrix} \begin{bmatrix} \frac{\partial x}{\partial r} & \frac{\partial x}{\partial\theta} & \frac{\partial x}{\partial\phi} \\ \frac{\partial y}{\partial r} & \frac{\partial y}{\partial\theta} & \frac{\partial y}{\partial\phi} \\ \frac{\partial z}{\partial r} & \frac{\partial z}{\partial\theta} & \frac{\partial z}{\partial\phi} \end{bmatrix} \\ &\underset{(3.75)}{\overset{(3.70)}{=}} \begin{bmatrix} \left\|\frac{\partial\vec{v}}{\partial r}\right\|^2 & \left\langle\frac{\partial\vec{v}}{\partial r}, \frac{\partial\vec{v}}{\partial\theta}\right\rangle & \left\langle\frac{\partial\vec{v}}{\partial r}, \frac{\partial\vec{v}}{\partial\phi}\right\rangle \\ \left\langle\frac{\partial\vec{v}}{\partial r}, \frac{\partial\vec{v}}{\partial\theta}\right\rangle & \left\|\frac{\partial\vec{v}}{\partial\theta}\right\|^2 & \left\langle\frac{\partial\vec{v}}{\partial\theta}, \frac{\partial\vec{v}}{\partial\phi}\right\rangle \\ \left\langle\frac{\partial\vec{v}}{\partial r}, \frac{\partial\vec{v}}{\partial\phi}\right\rangle & \left\langle\frac{\partial\vec{v}}{\partial\theta}, \frac{\partial\vec{v}}{\partial\phi}\right\rangle & \left\|\frac{\partial\vec{v}}{\partial\phi}\right\|^2 \end{bmatrix} \\ &\underset{(3.12)\,(3.13)}{\overset{(3.10)\,(3.11)}{=}} \begin{bmatrix} 1 & 0 & 0 \\ 0 & r^2 & 0 \\ 0 & 0 & r^2\sin(\theta)^2 \end{bmatrix} \end{aligned} \tag{3.14}$$

98 whose associated Jacobian *determinant* reads

98
98
100

$$|\det(J_T)| \overset{(3.286)}{=} \sqrt{\det(J_T^T)\det(J_T)} \overset{(3.284)}{=} \sqrt{\det(J_T^T J_T)} \overset{(3.308)}{=} \sqrt{r^4\sin(\theta)^2} = r^2\sin(\theta) \tag{3.15}$$

Whenever the radial coordinate is constant though, the symmetric Jacobian matrix of
102 the $\mathbb{R}^2 \to \mathbb{R}^3$ *transformation* is instead defined as

68
76
68
76
68

$$J_T^T J_T \triangleq \begin{bmatrix} \frac{\partial x}{\partial\theta} & \frac{\partial y}{\partial\theta} & \frac{\partial z}{\partial\theta} \\ \frac{\partial x}{\partial\phi} & \frac{\partial y}{\partial\phi} & \frac{\partial z}{\partial\phi} \end{bmatrix} \begin{bmatrix} \frac{\partial x}{\partial\theta} & \frac{\partial x}{\partial\phi} \\ \frac{\partial y}{\partial\theta} & \frac{\partial y}{\partial\phi} \\ \frac{\partial z}{\partial\theta} & \frac{\partial z}{\partial\phi} \end{bmatrix} \underset{(3.75)}{\overset{(3.70)}{=}} \begin{bmatrix} \left\|\frac{\partial\vec{v}}{\partial\theta}\right\|^2 & \left\langle\frac{\partial\vec{v}}{\partial\theta}, \frac{\partial\vec{v}}{\partial\phi}\right\rangle \\ \left\langle\frac{\partial\vec{v}}{\partial\theta}, \frac{\partial\vec{v}}{\partial\phi}\right\rangle & \left\|\frac{\partial\vec{v}}{\partial\phi}\right\|^2 \end{bmatrix} \underset{(3.13)}{\overset{(3.11)\,(3.12)}{=}} \begin{bmatrix} r^2 & 0 \\ 0 & r^2\sin(\theta)^2 \end{bmatrix} \tag{3.16}$$

98 whose associated Jacobian *determinant* reads

100

$$\sqrt{\det(J_T^T J_T)} \overset{(3.306)}{=} \sqrt{r^4\sin(\theta)^2} = r^2\sin(\theta) \tag{3.17}$$

On the other hand, if the polar coordinate is constant, the symmetric Jacobian matrix of the $\mathbb{R}^2 \to \mathbb{R}^3$ *transformation* is then defined as 102

$$J_T^T J_T \triangleq \begin{bmatrix} \frac{\partial x}{\partial r} & \frac{\partial y}{\partial r} & \frac{\partial z}{\partial r} \\ \frac{\partial x}{\partial \phi} & \frac{\partial y}{\partial \phi} & \frac{\partial z}{\partial \phi} \end{bmatrix} \begin{bmatrix} \frac{\partial x}{\partial r} & \frac{\partial x}{\partial \phi} \\ \frac{\partial y}{\partial r} & \frac{\partial y}{\partial \phi} \\ \frac{\partial z}{\partial r} & \frac{\partial z}{\partial \phi} \end{bmatrix} \overset{(3.70)}{\underset{(3.75)}{=}} \begin{bmatrix} \left\|\frac{\partial \vec{v}}{\partial r}\right\|^2 & \left\langle \frac{\partial \vec{v}}{\partial r}, \frac{\partial \vec{v}}{\partial \phi} \right\rangle \\ \left\langle \frac{\partial \vec{v}}{\partial r}, \frac{\partial \vec{v}}{\partial \phi} \right\rangle & \left\|\frac{\partial \vec{v}}{\partial \phi}\right\|^2 \end{bmatrix} \overset{(3.10)}{\overset{(3.12)}{\underset{(3.13)}{=}}} \begin{bmatrix} 1 & 0 \\ 0 & r^2 \sin(\theta)^2 \end{bmatrix} \quad (3.18)$$

68 76 68 76 68

whose associated Jacobian *determinant* reads 98

$$\sqrt{\det(J_T^T J_T)} \overset{(3.306)}{=} \sqrt{r^2 \sin(\theta)^2} = r \sin(\theta) \quad (3.19)$$

100

In contrast, when the azimuthal coordinate is held constant instead, the symmetric Jacobian matrix of the $\mathbb{R}^2 \to \mathbb{R}^3$ *transformation* is defined as 102

$$J_T^T J_T \triangleq \begin{bmatrix} \frac{\partial x}{\partial r} & \frac{\partial y}{\partial r} & \frac{\partial z}{\partial r} \\ \frac{\partial x}{\partial \theta} & \frac{\partial y}{\partial \theta} & \frac{\partial z}{\partial \theta} \end{bmatrix} \begin{bmatrix} \frac{\partial x}{\partial r} & \frac{\partial x}{\partial \theta} \\ \frac{\partial y}{\partial r} & \frac{\partial y}{\partial \theta} \\ \frac{\partial z}{\partial r} & \frac{\partial z}{\partial \theta} \end{bmatrix} \overset{(3.70)}{\underset{(3.75)}{=}} \begin{bmatrix} \left\|\frac{\partial \vec{v}}{\partial r}\right\|^2 & \left\langle \frac{\partial \vec{v}}{\partial r}, \frac{\partial \vec{v}}{\partial \theta} \right\rangle \\ \left\langle \frac{\partial \vec{v}}{\partial r}, \frac{\partial \vec{v}}{\partial \theta} \right\rangle & \left\|\frac{\partial \vec{v}}{\partial \theta}\right\|^2 \end{bmatrix} \overset{(3.10)}{\overset{(3.11)}{\underset{(3.13)}{=}}} \begin{bmatrix} 1 & 0 \\ 0 & r^2 \end{bmatrix} \quad (3.20)$$

68 76 68 76 68

whose associated Jacobian *determinant* reads 98

$$\sqrt{\det(J_T^T J_T)} \overset{(3.306)}{=} \sqrt{r^2} = r \quad (3.21)$$

100

3.1.2 Cylindrical Coordinates

As illustrated in *Figure 3.2*, a three-dimensional *cylindrical coordinate system* is parameterized by the *radial distance* $\rho \in [0, \infty)$ of a point $\vec{p}$ to the longitudinal axis, the *azimuthal angle* $\phi \in (-\pi, +\pi]$ (or $\phi \in [0, 2\pi)$) between the azimuthal axis and the vector from the origin $\vec{o}$ to the projection of $\vec{p}$ onto the principal plane orthogonal to the longitudinal axis, and the *longitudinal coordinate* $z \in (-\infty, +\infty)$ corresponding to the signed distance of $\vec{p}$ to the principal plane orthogonal to the longitudinal axis, or equivalently to the signed distance between $\vec{o}$ and the orthogonal projection of $\vec{p}$ onto the longitudinal axis. 69

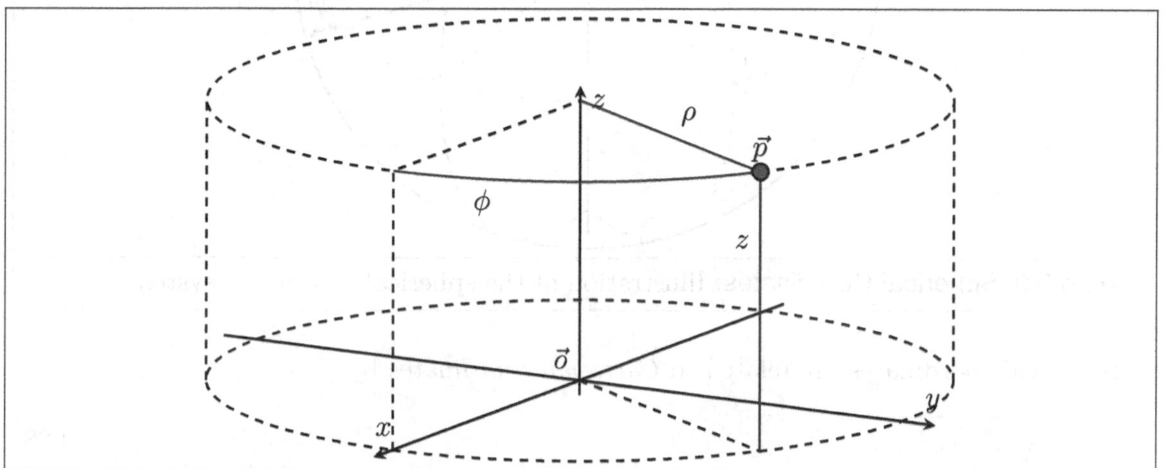

Figure 3.2: Cylindrical Coordinates: Illustration of the cylindrical coordinate system.

67 Cylindrical coordinates are related to *Cartesian coordinates* by expressing the first two coordinates within a two-dimensional *polar coordinate system*

$$\rho = \sqrt{x^2 + y^2} \tag{3.22}$$
$$\phi = \text{arctan2}(y, x) \tag{3.23}$$
$$z = z \tag{3.24}$$

70 and to *spherical coordinates* by

$$\rho = r\sin(\theta) \tag{3.25}$$
$$\phi = \phi \tag{3.26}$$
$$z = r\cos(\theta) \tag{3.27}$$

3.1.3 Spherical Coordinates

70 As illustrated in *Figure 3.3*, a three-dimensional *spherical coordinate system* is parameterized by the *radial distance* $r \in [0, \infty)$ of a point $\vec{p}$ to the origin $\vec{o}$, the *polar angle* (also called *zenith angle* or *inclination angle*) $\theta \in [0, \pi]$ between the zenith axis and the vector from $\vec{o}$ to $\vec{p}$ (in contrast to the *elevation angle* $\theta \in [-\pi/2, +\pi/2]$ between the vector and the principal plane) and the *azimuthal angle* $\phi \in (-\pi, +\pi]$ (or $\phi \in [0, 2\pi)$) between the azimuthal axis and the vector from $\vec{o}$ to the projection of $\vec{p}$ onto the principal plane orthogonal to the zenith axis.

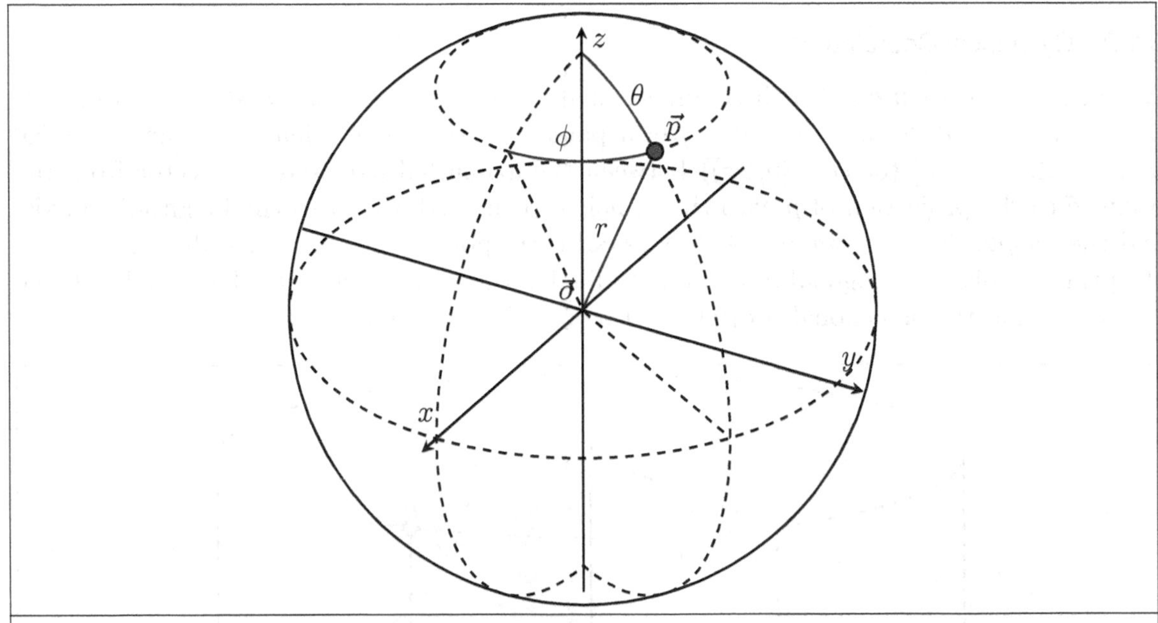

Figure 3.3: Spherical Coordinates: Illustration of the spherical coordinate system.

67 Spherical coordinates are related to *Cartesian coordinates* by

$$r = \sqrt{x^2 + y^2 + z^2} \tag{3.28}$$
$$\theta = \text{arctan2}(\sqrt{x^2 + y^2}, z) = \arccos\left(\frac{1}{\sqrt{1 + (\sqrt{x^2 + y^2} \div z)^2}}\right) = \arccos(z \div r) \tag{3.29}$$
$$\phi = \text{arctan2}(y, x) \tag{3.30}$$

and to *cylindrical coordinates* by expressing the first two coordinates in polar form 69

$$r = \sqrt{\rho^2 + z^2} \tag{3.31}$$

$$\theta = \operatorname{arctan2}(\rho, z) = \arccos\left(\frac{1}{\sqrt{1 + (\rho \div z)^2}}\right) = \arccos(z \div r) \tag{3.32}$$

$$\phi = \phi \tag{3.33}$$

3.2 VECTOR ALGEBRA

3.2.1 Vector Space

An n-dimensional *vector space* over a scalar field F is defined as a set of *vectors* $V(F)$ (each representing a *direction* in Euclidean space) whose entries are defined by the n coordinates of their terminal point, their initial point being necessarily bound to the origin. The elements of the set support the two operations of componentwise vector addition (and subtraction)

$$(\vec{u} \pm \vec{v})_i \triangleq \vec{u}_i \pm \vec{v}_i, \quad \forall i \in [1, n] \tag{3.34}$$

satisfying the following axioms $\forall \vec{u}, \vec{v}, \vec{w} \in V$

- commutativity: $$\vec{u} + \vec{v} = \vec{v} + \vec{u} \tag{3.35}$$
- associativity: $$\vec{u} + (\vec{v} + \vec{w}) = (\vec{u} + \vec{v}) + \vec{w} \tag{3.36}$$
- zero vector: $$\vec{v} + \vec{0} = \vec{v} \tag{3.37}$$
- additive inverse: $$\vec{v} + (-\vec{v}) = \vec{0} \tag{3.38}$$

and scalar multiplication and division (i.e., by a 1×1 scalar matrix)

$$(\vec{u} \stackrel{\times}{\div} c)_i \triangleq (\vec{u})_i \stackrel{\times}{\div} c, \quad \forall i \in [1, n] \tag{3.39}$$

satisfying the following axioms

- associativity: $$c(d\vec{v}) = (cd)\vec{v} \tag{3.40}$$
- distributivity: $$c(\vec{u} + \vec{v}) = c\vec{u} + c\vec{v} \tag{3.41}$$
- distributivity: $$(c + d)\vec{v} = c\vec{v} + d\vec{v} \tag{3.42}$$
- identity scalar: $$1\vec{v} = \vec{v} \tag{3.43}$$

The vectors of a linear space may be combined by means of a *linear combination* of the form

$$\vec{v} = \sum_{i=1}^{n} c_i \vec{v}_i \tag{3.44}$$

while the set of all linear combinations of vectors in a given set S is called the *linear hull*, or *linear span*, of S. If $c_i \geq 0, \forall i \in [1, n]$, then the linear combination is referred to as a *conical combination*, and the set of all conical combinations of vectors in S is called the *conical hull* of S.

A subset of n vectors from a vector space is said to be *linearly dependent* if there exist coefficients c_i, not all zero, such that

$$\sum_{i=1}^{n} c_i \vec{v}_i = \vec{0} \tag{3.45}$$

in which case a vector of the subset can be written as a linear combination of the other vectors

$$\vec{v}_j = -\frac{1}{c_j} \sum_{i=1, i \neq j}^{n} c_i \vec{v}_i \tag{3.46}$$

whereas the subset is conversely said to be *linearly independent* if

$$\sum_{i=1}^{n} c_i \vec{v}_i = \vec{0} \iff c_i = 0, \forall i \in [1, n] \tag{3.47}$$

A *basis* of a vector space V of dimension n is then defined as a subset $B \subset V$ of n linearly independent vectors $\vec{b}_i$ of V that span the vector space V, such that any vector $\vec{v} \in V$ can be uniquely represented as a linear combination of the basis elements by means of its coordinates c_i with respect to the basis B

$$\vec{v} = \sum_{i=1}^{n} c_i \vec{b}_i \tag{3.48}$$

A canonical instance is given by the *standard basis* $(\hat{e}_i)_j \triangleq \delta[i-j]$ within which any vector
67 is readily represented by its *Cartesian coordinates*.

3.2.2 Affine Space

Rather than distinguishing a specific origin, an *affine space* over a scalar field F is defined as a set of *points* $A(F)$ whose elements (each representing a *position* in Euclidean space) can be bijectively translated into other points by means of componentwise addition (or subtraction)
71 of the elements of a *vector space* V

$$A \times V \to A, (\vec{a}, \vec{v}) \mapsto \vec{a} \pm \vec{v} \tag{3.49}$$

satisfying the following properties $\forall \vec{u}, \vec{v} \in V$ and $\forall \vec{a} \in A$

- associativity: $$(\vec{a} + \vec{u}) + \vec{v} = \vec{a} + (\vec{u} + \vec{v}) \tag{3.50}$$
- uniqueness: $$\exists! \vec{b} \in A \mid \vec{a} + \vec{v} = \vec{b} \tag{3.51}$$
- identity: $$\vec{a} + \vec{0} = \vec{a} \tag{3.52}$$

Rather than adding a vector to a point to yield another point, an affine space may equivalently be defined by means of a subtraction map subtracting two points to yield a vector

$$A \times A \to V, (\vec{a}, \vec{b}) \mapsto \vec{b} - \vec{a} = \vec{ab} \tag{3.53}$$

with the vector between an arbitrary reference origin $\vec{o}$ and a point $\vec{a}$ being referred to as the *position vector* $\vec{oa}$ of that point.

An n-dimensional affine space over the field of real numbers is then known as an n-dimensional *Euclidean space* E^n (also denoted by $\mathbb{R}^n$), and subtracting a point $\vec{a}$ of the latter space from another point $\vec{b}$ yields a vector accordingly referred to as a *Euclidean vector* $\vec{ab} = \vec{b} - \vec{a}$.

The points of an affine space may be combined by means of an *affine combination*, i.e., a linear combination whose coefficients sum up to one (other arbitrary linear combinations being meaningless), of the form

$$\vec{a} = \sum_{i=1}^{n} \alpha_i \vec{a}_i, \quad \forall \alpha_i \mid \sum_{i=1}^{n} \alpha_i = 1 \tag{3.54}$$

while the set of all affine combinations of points in a given set S is called the *affine hull* of S. If the combination also is a conical combination such that $\alpha_i \in [0,1], \forall i \in [1,n]$, the affine combination is referred to as a *convex combination*, and the set of all convex combinations of points in S is called the *convex hull* of S.

A subset of points from an affine space is then said to be *affinely dependent* if there exist coefficients such that a point of the subset can be written as an affine combination of the other points, whereas the subset is conversely said to be *affinely independent* otherwise. In the latter case, the coefficients of the affine combination are referred to as *barycentric coordinates*, and the polytope representing the convex hull of the points forms a so-called *simplex* of the space (i.e., a point in 0-D, a line segment in 1-D, a triangle in 2-D, and a tetrahedron in 3-D).

Due to the unit sum of the coefficients, any affine combination is independent of the origin $\vec{o}$ of the space and of the *affine coordinate system*

$$\sum_{i=1}^{n} \alpha_i \vec{a}_i = \vec{o} - \sum_{i=1}^{n} \alpha_i \vec{o} + \sum_{i=1}^{n} \alpha_i \vec{a}_i = \vec{o} + \sum_{i=1}^{n} \alpha_i (\vec{a}_i - \vec{o}), \forall \vec{o} \in A \tag{3.55}$$

By selecting instead one of the points of the set as the origin $\vec{a}_0$, an n-dimensional affine space A^n with $n+1$ points may be converted into an n-dimensional *vector space* V^n with 71 the explicitly specified origin $\vec{a}_0$

$$\begin{aligned} \vec{a} &= \sum_{i=0}^{n} \alpha_i \vec{a}_i = \alpha_0 \vec{a}_0 + \sum_{i=1}^{n} \alpha_i \vec{a}_i = \left(1 - \sum_{i=1}^{n} \alpha_i\right) \vec{a}_0 + \sum_{i=1}^{n} \alpha_i \vec{a}_i \\ &= \vec{a}_0 + \sum_{i=1}^{n} \alpha_i (\vec{a}_i - \vec{a}_0) = \vec{a}_0 + \sum_{i=1}^{n} \alpha_i \vec{b}_i \end{aligned} \tag{3.56}$$

thereby defining a coordinate *frame* with origin $\vec{a}_0$ and basis vectors $\vec{b}_i \triangleq \vec{a}_i - \vec{a}_0$ that span the space of vectors whose initial point is $\vec{a}_0$. A canonical instance is given by the *standard frame* with origin $\vec{0}$ and standard basis vectors $\hat{e}_i$, within which any point is readily represented by its *Cartesian coordinates*. 67

The affine span of a set of n points corresponds to the $n-1$-dimensional flat manifold containing the points, such as the line joining 2 points or the plane containing 3 non-collinear points. Under the assumption of non-negative coefficients, the affine span actually corresponds to the convex hull of the points, and the coefficient of a given point represents, as illustrated in *Figure 3.4*, the ratio of the $n-1$-dimensional hypervolume (e.g., length, area, 73 volume) of the opposite partition to the hypervolume of the convex hull.

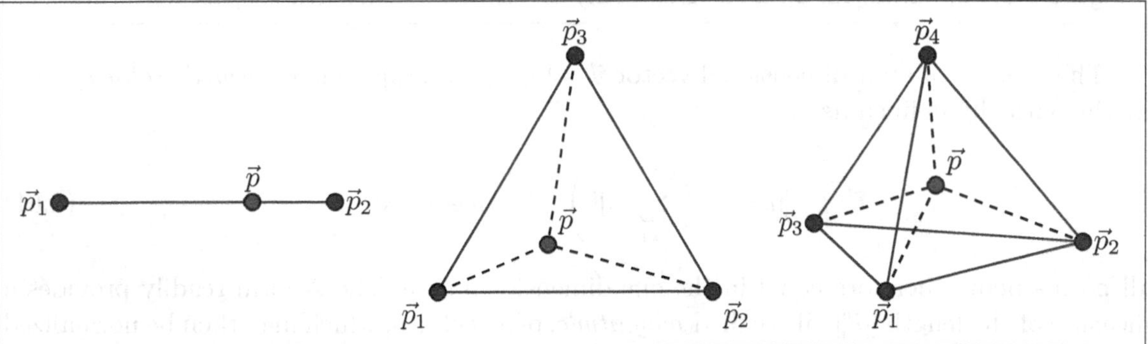

Figure 3.4: Affine Combination: Illustration of an affine combination of two, three and four points.

3.2.3 Metric and Norm

72 A *metric space* M is an *affine space* equipped with a *distance* metric $d\colon M \times M \to \mathbb{R}$ between two points $\vec{a} \in M$ and $\vec{b} \in M$ satisfying the following properties

- non-negativity: $$d(\vec{a}, \vec{b}) \geq 0 \tag{3.57}$$
- identity: $$d(\vec{a}, \vec{b}) = 0 \iff \vec{a} = \vec{b} \tag{3.58}$$
- symmetry: $$d(\vec{a}, \vec{b}) = d(\vec{b}, \vec{a}) \tag{3.59}$$
- triangle inequality: $$d(\vec{a}, \vec{c}) \leq d(\vec{a}, \vec{b}) + d(\vec{b}, \vec{c}) \tag{3.60}$$

74 As illustrated in *Figure 3.5*, a distance metric between two points $\vec{a} \in M$ and $\vec{b} \in M$
may be defined as the norm of their difference vector $d(\vec{a}, \vec{b}) = \|\vec{b} - \vec{a}\|_p$. As illustrated in
75 *Figure 3.6* and *Figure 3.7*, widely used metrics include the *Manhattan distance* $\|\vec{b} - \vec{a}\|_1$
75 (commonly referred to as the *city-block distance* or *taxicab distance* as it corresponds to the
distance a taxicab would effectively travel when driving around the city blocks on the island of Manhattan), the *Euclidean distance* $\|\vec{b} - \vec{a}\|_2$ (corresponding to the length of the Euclidean vector $\vec{ab} = \vec{b} - \vec{a}$), as well as the *Chebyshev distance* $\|\vec{b} - \vec{a}\|_\infty$ (commonly referred to as the *chessboard distance* as it corresponds to the minimum number of moves required for a king to go from one square to another on a chessboard).

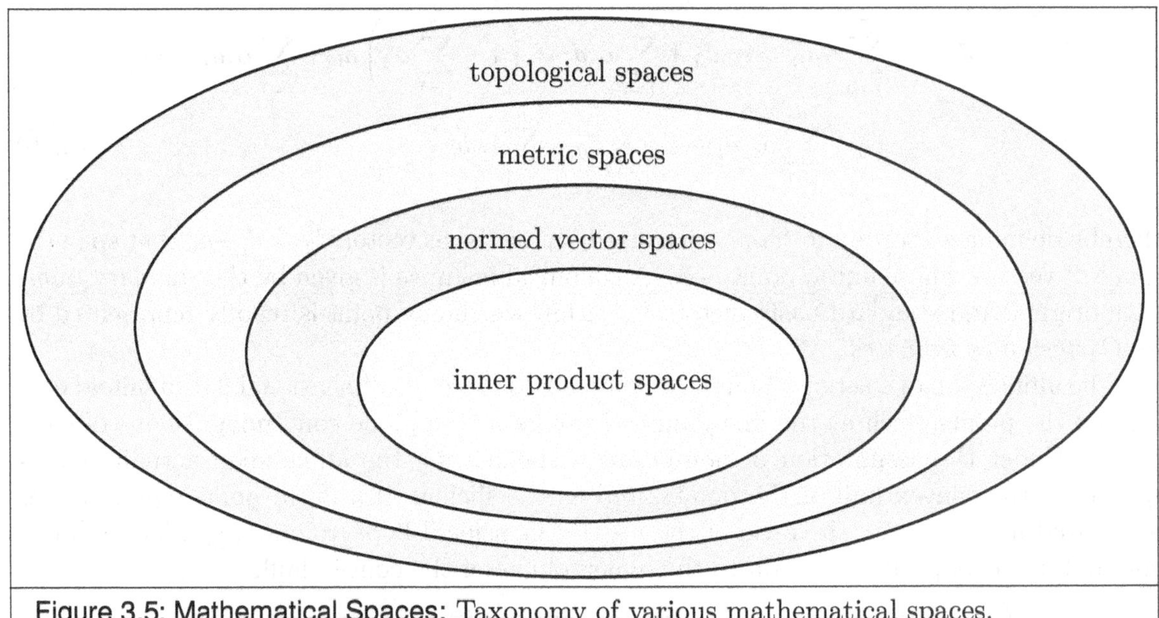

Figure 3.5: Mathematical Spaces: Taxonomy of various mathematical spaces.

The *p-norm* of an n-dimensional vector $\vec{v} = [v_1, v_2, \ldots, v_n]$ from a *normed vector space* is mathematically defined as

$$\|\vec{v}\|_p \triangleq \left(\sum_{i=1}^{n} |v_i|^p\right)^{\frac{1}{p}}, \quad \forall p \in [1, \infty) \tag{3.61}$$

all norms being therefore equal in the one-dimensional case. The 2-norm readily provides a measure of the length $\|\vec{v}\|$, also called *magnitude*, of a vector $\vec{v}$, which may then be normalized to yield the identically oriented *unit vector* $\hat{v} = \vec{v} \div \|\vec{v}\|, \forall \vec{v} \neq \vec{0}$, such that $\|\hat{v}\| = 1$. In the limit as $p \to \infty$, the infinity norm is given as

$$\|\vec{v}\|_\infty \triangleq \max\{|v_1|, |v_2|, \ldots, |v_n|\} \tag{3.62}$$

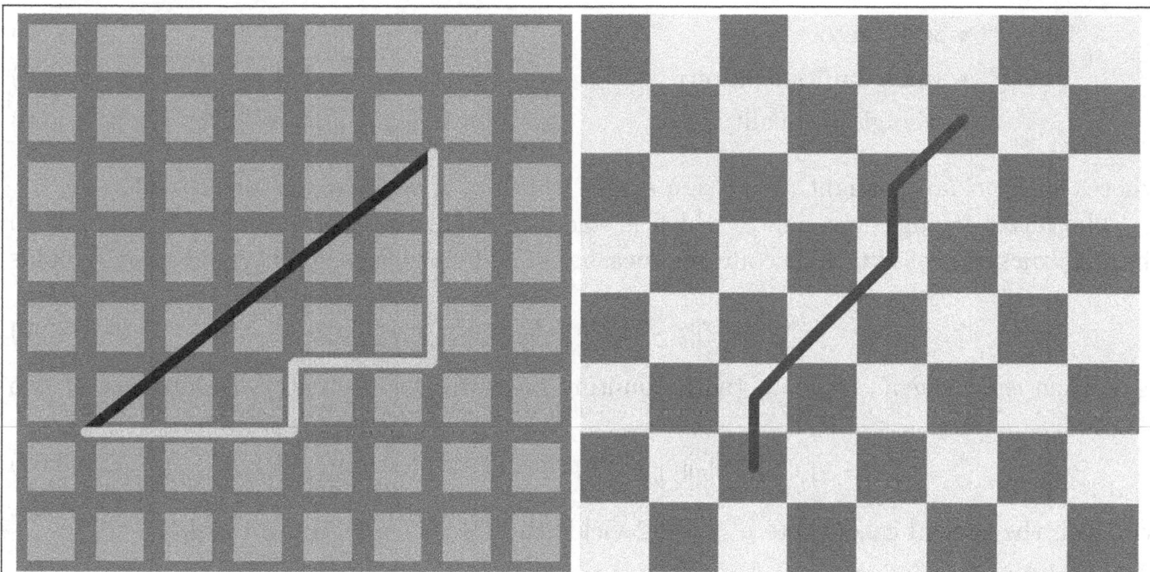

Figure 3.6: Distance Metrics: Illustration of various distance metrics including the Manhattan distance of a taxicab and the distance as the crow flies (left), as well as the chessboard distance (right).

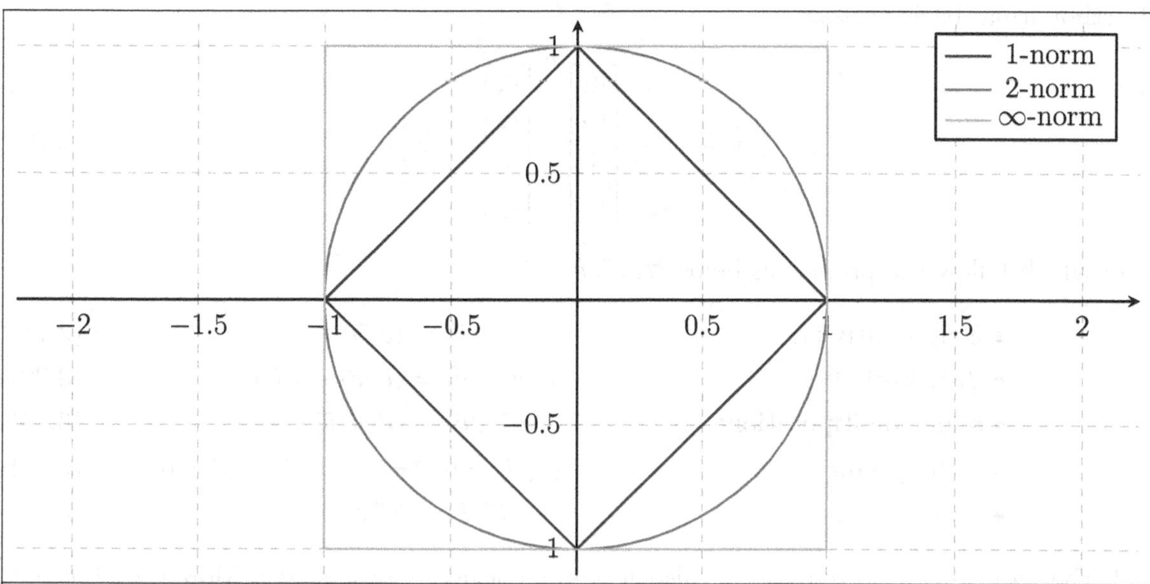

Figure 3.7: Vector Norms: Illustration of a circle whose unit-radius is defined according to different norms.

thereby satisfying the following axioms

- non-negativity: $$\|\vec{v}\|_p \geq 0 \tag{3.63}$$
- zero vector: $$\|\vec{v}\|_p = 0 \iff \vec{v} = \vec{0} \tag{3.64}$$
- scalar multiplication: $$\|c\vec{v}\|_p = |c|\|\vec{v}\|_p \tag{3.65}$$
- triangle inequality: $$\|\vec{u} + \vec{v}\|_p \leq \|\vec{u}\|_p + \|\vec{v}\|_p \tag{3.66}$$

whereas a *semi-norm* might also assign a zero length to a non-zero vector instead.

The latter triangle inequality, which is solely fulfilled if $p \geq 1$, actually corresponds to the *Minkowski inequality* with counting measure. The following inequality additionally holds

$$\|\vec{v}\|_p \leq \|\vec{v}\|_q \leq n^{\frac{1}{q}-\frac{1}{p}}\|\vec{v}\|_p, \quad \forall p \geq q > 0 \tag{3.67}$$

as well as the *Hölder inequality* (with counting measure) for the entrywise product of two vectors

$$\|\vec{u} \circ \vec{v}\|_1 \leq \|\vec{u}\|_p\|\vec{v}\|_q, \quad \forall p, q \in (1, \infty) \mid \frac{1}{p} + \frac{1}{q} = 1 \tag{3.68}$$

which in the special case where $p = q = 2$ yields the *Cauchy–Schwarz inequality*

$$\|\vec{u} \circ \vec{v}\|_1 \leq \|\vec{u}\|\|\vec{v}\| \iff \left(\sum_{i=1}^{n} |u_i v_i|\right)^2 \leq \left(\sum_{i=1}^{n} u_i^2\right)\left(\sum_{i=1}^{n} v_i^2\right) \tag{3.69}$$

3.2.4 Inner Product

71 The *inner product* of two n-dimensional vectors from a *vector space*, then referred to as an *inner product space*, is defined as the product of the conjugate transpose of the first vector with the second, which, in the special case of a Euclidean space, reduces to a scalar quantity referred to as the *dot product* or *scalar product* between vectors expressed in terms of orthonormal basis vectors

$$\langle \vec{u}, \vec{v} \rangle \triangleq \vec{u} \cdot \vec{v} = \begin{bmatrix} u_1 \\ u_2 \\ \vdots \\ u_n \end{bmatrix}^T \begin{bmatrix} v_1 \\ v_2 \\ \vdots \\ v_n \end{bmatrix} = \sum_{i=1}^{n} u_i v_i \tag{3.70}$$

from which follow the properties below $\forall \vec{u}, \vec{v}, \vec{w} \in V$

- commutativity: $$\langle \vec{u}, \vec{v} \rangle = \langle \vec{v}, \vec{u} \rangle \tag{3.71}$$
- distributivity: $$\langle \vec{u}, \vec{v} + \vec{w} \rangle = \langle \vec{u}, \vec{v} \rangle + \langle \vec{u}, \vec{w} \rangle \tag{3.72}$$
- scalar multiplication: $$\langle c\vec{u}, d\vec{v} \rangle = cd\langle \vec{u}, \vec{v} \rangle \tag{3.73}$$
- orthogonality: $$\langle \vec{u}, \vec{v} \rangle = 0 \iff \vec{u} \perp \vec{v}, \forall \vec{u}, \vec{v} \neq \vec{0} \tag{3.74}$$
- norm: $$\langle \vec{v}, \vec{v} \rangle = \|\vec{v}\|^2 \tag{3.75}$$

71 such that any inner product space also forms a normed *vector space*. Moreover, the dot product does not obey the cancellation law in the sense that

$$\langle \vec{u}, \vec{v} \rangle = \langle \vec{u}, \vec{w} \rangle \implies \langle \vec{u}, \vec{v} - \vec{w} \rangle = 0 \tag{3.76}$$

which does not necessarily imply that $\vec{v} = \vec{w}$.

As illustrated in *Figure 3.8*, the inner product additionally provides a measure of the angle between two Euclidean vectors 77

$$\langle\vec{u},\vec{v}\rangle = \|\vec{u}\|\|\vec{v}\|\cos\left(\angle(\vec{u},\vec{v})\right) \tag{3.77}$$

and thereby of the projection of a vector onto another

$$\|\vec{v}\|\cos\left(\angle(\vec{u},\vec{v})\right) = \frac{\langle\vec{u},\vec{v}\rangle}{\|\vec{u}\|} = \left\langle\frac{\vec{u}}{\|\vec{u}\|},\vec{v}\right\rangle = \langle\hat{u},\vec{v}\rangle \tag{3.78}$$

The *law of cosines* in a *triangle* with edge vectors $\vec{u}$ and $\vec{v}$ then states that 250

$$\|\vec{u}\pm\vec{v}\|^2 \overset{(3.75)}{=} \langle\vec{u}\pm\vec{v},\vec{u}\pm\vec{v}\rangle \overset{(3.72)}{=} \langle\vec{u},\vec{u}\rangle\pm\langle\vec{u},\vec{v}\rangle\pm\langle\vec{v},\vec{u}\rangle+\langle\vec{v},\vec{v}\rangle \overset{(3.75)}{=} \|\vec{u}\|^2\pm2\langle\vec{u},\vec{v}\rangle+\|\vec{v}\|^2 \tag{3.79}$$

76 76 76

from which follows the parallelogram equality

$$\|\vec{u}+\vec{v}\|^2+\|\vec{u}-\vec{v}\|^2 = (\|\vec{u}\|^2+2\langle\vec{u},\vec{v}\rangle+\|\vec{v}\|^2)+(\|\vec{u}\|^2-2\langle\vec{u},\vec{v}\rangle+\|\vec{v}\|^2) = 2(\|\vec{u}\|^2+\|\vec{v}\|^2) \tag{3.80}$$

as well as the triangle inequality

$$\|\vec{u}+\vec{v}\|^2 \leq \|\vec{u}\|^2+2|\langle\vec{u},\vec{v}\rangle|+\|\vec{v}\|^2 \overset{(3.77)}{\leq} \|\vec{u}\|^2+2\|\vec{u}\|\|\vec{v}\|+\|\vec{v}\|^2 = (\|\vec{u}\|+\|\vec{v}\|)^2 \tag{3.81}$$

77

An upper bound on the absolute value of the dot product is also given by the entrywise vector product

$$|\langle\vec{u},\vec{v}\rangle| \leq \|\vec{u}\circ\vec{v}\|_1 \iff \left(\sum_{i=1}^{n}u_iv_i\right)^2 \leq \left(\sum_{i=1}^{n}|u_iv_i|\right)^2 \tag{3.82}$$

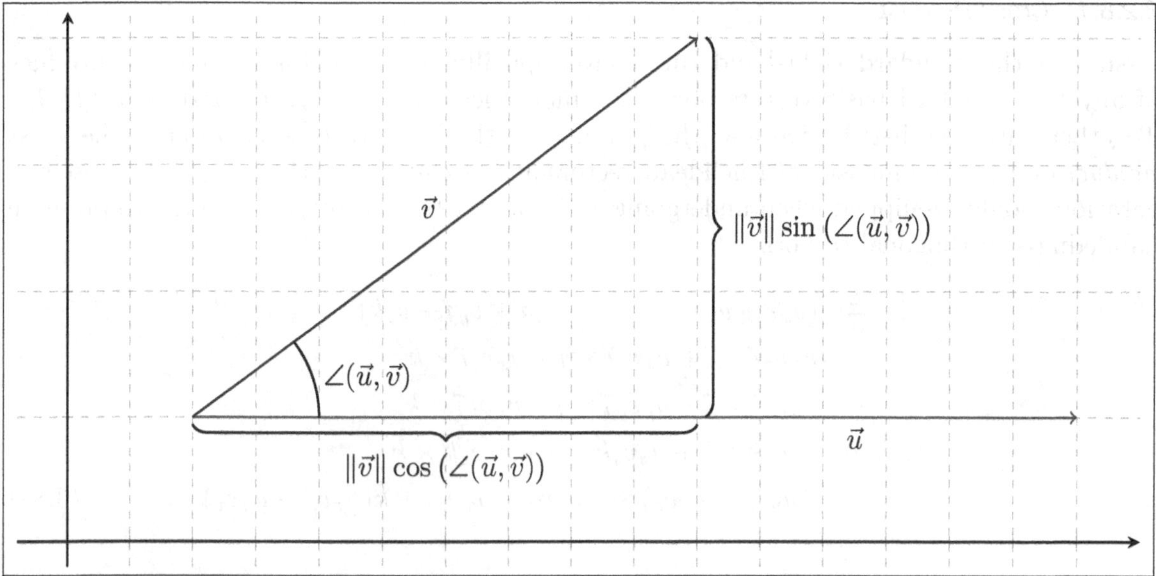

Figure 3.8: Vector Projection: Illustration of the projection of a vector onto another by means of their dot and cross products.

3.2.5 Outer Product

The *outer product* of an m-dimensional vector $\vec{u}$ with an n-dimensional vector $\vec{v}$ is defined as the second-order *tensor product* yielding a (two-dimensional array) $m \times n$ matrix of the form

$$\vec{u} \otimes \vec{v} \triangleq \begin{bmatrix} u_1 \\ u_2 \\ \vdots \\ u_m \end{bmatrix} \begin{bmatrix} v_1 \\ v_2 \\ \vdots \\ v_n \end{bmatrix}^T = \begin{bmatrix} u_1v_1 & u_1v_2 & \cdots & u_1v_n \\ u_2v_1 & u_2v_2 & \cdots & u_2v_n \\ \vdots & \vdots & \ddots & \vdots \\ u_mv_1 & u_mv_2 & \cdots & u_mv_n \end{bmatrix} \tag{3.83}$$

whose elements are defined as $(\vec{u} \otimes \vec{v})_{ij} = u_iv_j, \forall i \in [1, m], \forall j \in [1, n]$. In the special case
95 where $m = n$, the trace of the *square matrix* actually corresponds to the *inner product* of
76 the two vectors.

It then follows the properties below $\forall \vec{u}, \vec{v}, \vec{w} \in V$

- right distributivity: $$(\vec{u} + \vec{v}) \otimes \vec{w} = \vec{u} \otimes \vec{w} + \vec{v} \otimes \vec{w} \tag{3.84}$$
- left distributivity: $$\vec{w} \otimes (\vec{u} + \vec{v}) = \vec{w} \otimes \vec{u} + \vec{w} \otimes \vec{v} \tag{3.85}$$
- scalar multiplication: $$c(\vec{u} \otimes \vec{v}) = (c\vec{u}) \otimes \vec{v} = \vec{u} \otimes (c\vec{v}) \tag{3.86}$$

76 as well as the identity with the *inner product*

76 78

$$\vec{u}\langle\vec{v}, \vec{w}\rangle \overset{(3.70)}{=} \begin{bmatrix} u_1 \\ u_2 \\ \vdots \\ u_m \end{bmatrix} \begin{bmatrix} v_1 \\ v_2 \\ \vdots \\ v_n \end{bmatrix}^T \begin{bmatrix} w_1 \\ w_2 \\ \vdots \\ w_n \end{bmatrix} \overset{(3.83)}{=} [\vec{u} \otimes \vec{v}]\vec{w} \tag{3.87}$$

3.2.6 Three-Dimensional Vector Space

3.2.6.1 Cross Product

79 Assuming the standard right-hand rule convention illustrated in *Figure 3.9*, the product
79 of any two standard basis vectors obeys the multiplication rules synthesized in *Table 3.1*.
Together with the distributive law, the products of the basis vectors then define the *cross product* of 2 three-dimensional Euclidean vectors as a *pseudovector* (i.e., a vector whose orientation should be flipped when undergoing an improper transformation in order to preserve handedness) orthogonal to both

$$\begin{aligned} \vec{u} \times \vec{v} &\triangleq (u_x\vec{\imath} + u_y\vec{\jmath} + u_z\vec{k}) \times (v_x\vec{\imath} + v_y\vec{\jmath} + v_z\vec{k}) \\ &= u_xv_x\vec{\imath} \times \vec{\imath} + u_xv_y\vec{\imath} \times \vec{\jmath} + u_xv_z\vec{\imath} \times \vec{k} \\ &+ u_yv_x\vec{\jmath} \times \vec{\imath} + u_yv_y\vec{\jmath} \times \vec{\jmath} + u_yv_z\vec{\jmath} \times \vec{k} \\ &+ u_zv_x\vec{k} \times \vec{\imath} + u_zv_y\vec{k} \times \vec{\jmath} + u_zv_z\vec{k} \times \vec{k} \\ &= \vec{\imath}(u_yv_z - u_zv_y) + \vec{\jmath}(u_zv_x - u_xv_z) + \vec{k}(u_xv_y - u_yv_x) \end{aligned} \tag{3.88}$$

which in a skew-symmetric matrix form reads

$$\vec{u} \times \vec{v} = \begin{bmatrix} u_x \\ u_y \\ u_z \end{bmatrix} \times \begin{bmatrix} v_x \\ v_y \\ v_z \end{bmatrix} = \begin{bmatrix} 0 & -u_z & u_y \\ u_z & 0 & -u_x \\ -u_y & u_x & 0 \end{bmatrix} \begin{bmatrix} v_x \\ v_y \\ v_z \end{bmatrix} = \begin{bmatrix} \begin{vmatrix} u_y & v_y \\ u_z & v_z \end{vmatrix} \\ \\ \begin{vmatrix} u_z & v_z \\ u_x & v_x \end{vmatrix} \\ \\ \begin{vmatrix} u_x & v_x \\ u_y & v_y \end{vmatrix} \end{bmatrix} \tag{3.89}$$

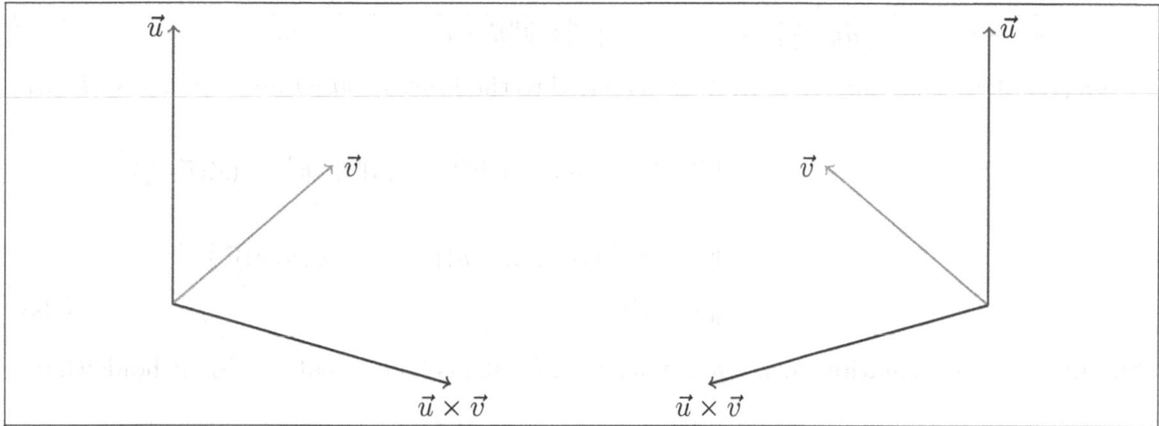

Figure 3.9: Handedness: Illustration of the orientation of the cross product according to the left-hand (left) and right-hand (right) rules, where the vectors $\vec{u}$, $\vec{v}$ and $\vec{u} \times \vec{v}$ are oriented along the thumb, index and middle finger, respectively, of the corresponding hand.

Table 3.1: Vector Multiplication: Multiplication rules for the product of a basis vector from the left-most column as a left operand with a basis vector from the topmost row as a right operand.

$\times$	$\vec{\imath}$	$\vec{\jmath}$	$\vec{k}$
$\vec{\imath}$	$\vec{0}$	$\vec{k}$	$-\vec{\jmath}$
$\vec{\jmath}$	$-\vec{k}$	$\vec{0}$	$\vec{\imath}$
$\vec{k}$	$\vec{\jmath}$	$-\vec{\imath}$	$\vec{0}$

It then follows the properties below $\forall \vec{u}, \vec{v}, \vec{w} \in V$

- anti-commutativity: $$\vec{u} \times \vec{v} = -\vec{v} \times \vec{u} \tag{3.90}$$
- distributivity: $$\vec{u} \times (\vec{v} + \vec{w}) = \vec{u} \times \vec{v} + \vec{u} \times \vec{w} \tag{3.91}$$
- scalar multiplication: $$(c\vec{u}) \times (d\vec{v}) = (cd)(\vec{u} \times \vec{v}) \tag{3.92}$$
- collinearity: $$\vec{u} \times \vec{v} = \vec{0} \iff \vec{u} \parallel \vec{v}, \forall \vec{u}, \vec{v} \neq \vec{0} \tag{3.93}$$

Moreover, the cross product does not obey the cancellation law in the sense that

$$\vec{u} \times \vec{v} = \vec{u} \times \vec{w} \iff \vec{u} \times (\vec{v} - \vec{w}) = 0 \tag{3.94}$$

which does not necessarily imply that $\vec{v} = \vec{w}$.

77 As illustrated in *Figure 3.8*, the norm of the cross product additionally provides a measure of the angle between 2 three-dimensional Euclidean vectors

$$\|\vec{u} \times \vec{v}\| = \|\vec{u}\|\|\vec{v}\| \sin\left(\angle(\vec{u}, \vec{v})\right) \tag{3.95}$$

and thereby of the distance from a point to an axis

$$\|\vec{v}\| \sin\left(\angle(\vec{u}, \vec{v})\right) = \frac{\|\vec{u} \times \vec{v}\|}{\|\vec{u}\|} = \left\|\frac{\vec{u}}{\|\vec{u}\|} \times \vec{v}\right\| = \|\hat{u} \times \vec{v}\| \tag{3.96}$$

258 in turn determining the area of the *parallelogram* defined by the two vectors, as illustrated
80 in *Figure 3.10*. The *law of sines* in a *triangle* with edge vectors $\vec{u}$ and $\vec{v}$ then states that
250

79

$$\frac{\sin\left(\angle(\vec{u}, \vec{v})\right)}{\|\vec{u} - \vec{v}\|} = \frac{\|\vec{u} \times \vec{v}\|}{\|\vec{u}\|\|\vec{v}\|\|\vec{u} - \vec{v}\|} \overset{(3.93)}{=} \frac{\|\vec{u} \times (\vec{u} - \vec{v})\|}{\|\vec{u}\|\|\vec{v}\|\|\vec{u} - \vec{v}\|} = \frac{\sin\left(\angle(\vec{u}, \vec{u} - \vec{v})\right)}{\|\vec{v}\|} \tag{3.97}$$

76 It also follows that the cross product is related to the *inner product* by *Lagrange's identity*

77
80

$$\begin{aligned} \langle \vec{u}, \vec{v}\rangle^2 + \|\vec{u} \times \vec{v}\|^2 &\underset{(3.95)}{\overset{(3.77)}{=}} \|\vec{u}\|^2\|\vec{v}\|^2 \cos\left(\angle(\vec{u}, \vec{v})\right)^2 + \|\vec{u}\|^2\|\vec{v}\|^2 \sin\left(\angle(\vec{u}, \vec{v})\right)^2 \\ &= \|\vec{u}\|^2\|\vec{v}\|^2 \left(\cos\left(\angle(\vec{u}, \vec{v})\right)^2 + \sin\left(\angle(\vec{u}, \vec{v})\right)^2\right) \\ &= \|\vec{u}\|^2\|\vec{v}\|^2 \end{aligned} \tag{3.98}$$

95 while under transformation by a *square matrix* M with cofactor matrix C_M, it holds that

99

$$(M\vec{u}) \times (M\vec{v}) = \det(M) M^{-T} (\vec{u} \times \vec{v}) \overset{(3.303)}{=} C_M (\vec{u} \times \vec{v}) \tag{3.99}$$

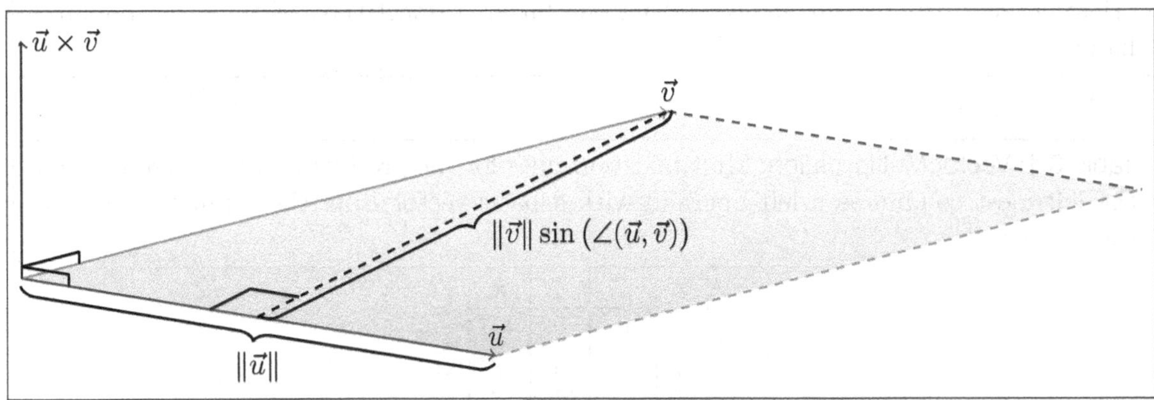

Figure 3.10: Cross Product: Illustration of the geometric interpretation of the magnitude of the cross product as the area of the parallelogram defined by two vectors.

3.2.6.2 Scalar Triple Product

81 As illustrated in *Figure 3.11*, the *scalar triple product* of 3 three-dimensional Euclidean vectors $\vec{v}_1$, $\vec{v}_2$ and $\vec{v}_3$ is a *pseudoscalar* (i.e., a scalar whose sign should be flipped when undergoing an improper transformation) representing the signed volume of the parallelepiped defined by the three vectors, and it may be expressed as the determinant of the associated matrix

$$|\vec{v}_1, \vec{v}_2, \vec{v}_3| \triangleq \begin{vmatrix} x_1 & x_2 & x_3 \\ y_1 & y_2 & y_3 \\ z_1 & z_2 & z_3 \end{vmatrix} = \langle \vec{v}_1, \vec{v}_2 \times \vec{v}_3 \rangle \tag{3.100}$$

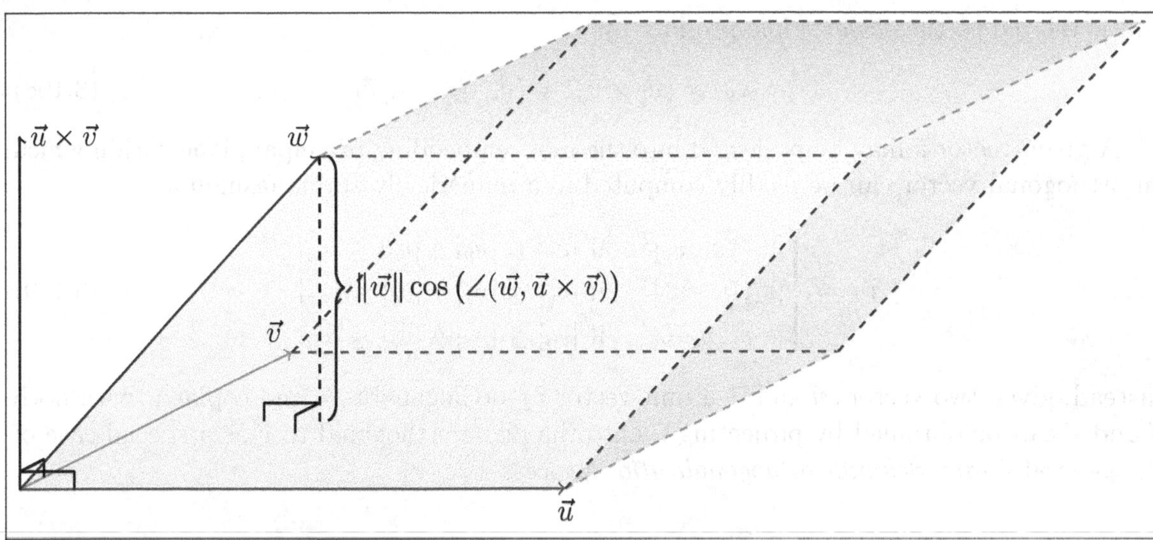

Figure 3.11: Scalar Triple Product: Illustration of the geometric interpretation of the scalar triple product as the signed volume of the parallelepiped defined by three vectors.

It then follows the properties below $\forall \vec{v}_1, \vec{v}_2, \vec{v}_3 \in V$

- shift invariance: $$|\vec{v}_1, \vec{v}_2, \vec{v}_3| = |\vec{v}_2, \vec{v}_3, \vec{v}_1| = |\vec{v}_3, \vec{v}_1, \vec{v}_2| \tag{3.101}$$
- anti-commutativity: $$|\vec{v}_1, \vec{v}_2, \vec{v}_3| = -|\vec{v}_1, \vec{v}_3, \vec{v}_2| \tag{3.102}$$
- distributivity: $$|\vec{v}_1 + \vec{v}_1', \vec{v}_2, \vec{v}_3| = |\vec{v}_1, \vec{v}_2, \vec{v}_3| + |\vec{v}_1', \vec{v}_2, \vec{v}_3| \tag{3.103}$$
- coplanarity: $$|a\vec{v}_1 + b\vec{v}_2, \vec{v}_1, \vec{v}_2| = 0 \tag{3.104}$$

while the *Binet–Cauchy identity* states that

$$\langle \vec{v}_1 \times \vec{v}_2, \vec{v}_3 \times \vec{v}_4 \rangle = \langle \vec{v}_1, \vec{v}_3 \rangle \langle \vec{v}_2, \vec{v}_4 \rangle - \langle \vec{v}_1, \vec{v}_4 \rangle \langle \vec{v}_2, \vec{v}_3 \rangle \tag{3.105}$$

3.2.6.3 Vector Triple Product

The *vector triple product* of 3 three-dimensional Euclidean vectors $\vec{v}_1$, $\vec{v}_2$ and $\vec{v}_3$ may be expanded in terms of *inner products* by means of *Lagrange's formula* 76

78

$$\begin{aligned}
\vec{v}_1 \times (\vec{v}_2 \times \vec{v}_3) &\overset{(3.88)}{=} \begin{bmatrix} y_1(x_2y_3 - y_2x_3) - z_1(z_2x_3 - x_2z_3) \\ z_1(y_2z_3 - z_2y_3) - x_1(x_2y_3 - y_2x_3) \\ x_1(z_2x_3 - x_2z_3) - y_1(y_2z_3 - z_2y_3) \end{bmatrix} \\
&= \begin{bmatrix} (y_1y_3 + z_1z_3)x_2 - (y_1y_2 + z_1z_2)x_3 \\ (z_1z_3 + x_1x_3)y_2 - (z_1z_2 + x_1x_2)y_3 \\ (x_1x_3 + y_1y_3)z_2 - (x_1x_2 + y_1y_2)z_3 \end{bmatrix} \\
&= \begin{bmatrix} (x_1x_3 + y_1y_3 + z_1z_3)x_2 - (x_1x_2 + y_1y_2 + z_1z_2)x_3 \\ (x_1x_3 + y_1y_3 + z_1z_3)y_2 - (x_1x_2 + y_1y_2 + z_1z_2)y_3 \\ (x_1x_3 + y_1y_3 + z_1z_3)z_2 - (x_1x_2 + y_1y_2 + z_1z_2)z_3 \end{bmatrix} \\
&\overset{(3.70)}{=} \langle \vec{v}_1, \vec{v}_3 \rangle \vec{v}_2 - \langle \vec{v}_1, \vec{v}_2 \rangle \vec{v}_3
\end{aligned} \tag{3.106}$$

76

Despite the non-associativity of the *cross product*, the vector triple product satisfies the *Jacobi identity* 78

$$\vec{v}_1 \times (\vec{v}_2 \times \vec{v}_3) + \vec{v}_2 \times (\vec{v}_3 \times \vec{v}_1) + \vec{v}_3 \times (\vec{v}_1 \times \vec{v}_2) = \vec{0} \tag{3.107}$$

80 and is related to the *scalar triple product* by

$$(\vec{v}_1 \times \vec{v}_2) \times (\vec{v}_1 \times \vec{v}_3) = \langle \vec{v}_1, \vec{v}_2 \times \vec{v}_3 \rangle \vec{v}_1 \tag{3.108}$$

A given vector $\vec{v}$ may be projected into the most embedding principal plane within which an orthogonal vector can be readily computed in a numerically stable fashion as

$$\vec{v}_\perp \triangleq \begin{cases} [0, -v_z, v_y]^T & \text{if } |v_x| \leq |v_y| \wedge |v_x| \leq |v_z| \\ [v_z, 0, -v_x]^T & \text{if } |v_y| \leq |v_z| \wedge |v_y| \leq |v_x| \\ [-v_y, v_x, 0]^T & \text{if } |v_z| \leq |v_x| \wedge |v_z| \leq |v_y| \end{cases} \tag{3.109}$$

Instead, given two vectors $\vec{u}$ and $\vec{v}$, a unit vector $\hat{v}_\perp$ orthogonal to $\vec{v}$ and coplanar with both $\vec{u}$ and $\vec{v}$ can be obtained by projecting $\vec{u}$ onto the plane orthogonal to $\vec{v}$ as a special case of the general *Gram–Schmidt orthogonalization* process

79
81
76
80

$$\hat{v}_\perp \triangleq \frac{(\vec{v} \times \vec{u}) \times \vec{v}}{\|(\vec{v} \times \vec{u}) \times \vec{v}\|} \underset{(3.95)}{\overset{(3.90)\,(3.106)}{=}} \frac{\langle \vec{v}, \vec{v} \rangle \vec{u} - \langle \vec{v}, \vec{u} \rangle \vec{v}}{\|\vec{v}\|^2 \|\vec{u}\| \sin(\angle(\vec{v}, \vec{u}))} \overset{(3.75)}{=} \frac{\hat{u} - \langle \hat{v}, \hat{u} \rangle \hat{v}}{\sqrt{1 - \langle \hat{v}, \hat{u} \rangle^2}} \tag{3.110}$$

83 As illustrated in *Figure 3.12*, the *spherical linear interpolation* of two unit vectors $\hat{v}_0$ and $\hat{v}_1$,
77 separated by an angle $\theta \triangleq \angle(\hat{v}_0, \hat{v}_1) \overset{(3.77)}{=} \arccos(\langle \hat{v}_0, \hat{v}_1 \rangle)$, with a parameter $t \in [0, 1]$, is then
82 defined in terms of an orthonormal vector $\hat{v}_{0\perp} \overset{(3.110)}{=} ((\hat{v}_0 \times \hat{v}_1) \times \hat{v}_0) \div \|(\hat{v}_0 \times \hat{v}_1) \times \hat{v}_0\|$ as

82

$$\begin{aligned} \text{slerp}(t, \hat{v}_0, \hat{v}_1) &\triangleq \cos(t\theta)\hat{v}_0 + \sin(t\theta)\hat{v}_{0\perp} \\ &\overset{(3.110)}{=} \cos(t\theta)\hat{v}_0 + \sin(t\theta)\frac{\hat{v}_1 - \cos(\theta)\hat{v}_0}{\sin(\theta)} \\ &= \left(\cos(t\theta) - \frac{\sin(t\theta)}{\sin(\theta)}\cos(\theta)\right)\hat{v}_0 + \frac{\sin(t\theta)}{\sin(\theta)}\hat{v}_1 && (3.111) \\ &= \frac{\cos(t\theta)\sin(\theta) - \sin(t\theta)\cos(\theta)}{\sin(\theta)}\hat{v}_0 + \frac{\sin(t\theta)}{\sin(\theta)}\hat{v}_1 \\ &= \frac{\sin((1-t)\theta)}{\sin(\theta)}\hat{v}_0 + \frac{\sin(t\theta)}{\sin(\theta)}\hat{v}_1 && (3.112) \end{aligned}$$

3.2.7 Vector Operator

67 In n-dimensional *Cartesian coordinates* $\mathbb{R}^n$, the *Del* differential operator is defined in terms of the first partial derivatives as

$$\nabla \triangleq \left[\frac{\partial}{\partial x_1}, \ldots, \frac{\partial}{\partial x_n}\right]^T \tag{3.113}$$

The *gradient* of a scalar field $f(x_1, \ldots, x_n)$ is then defined as the vector field whose direction is that of greatest increase of f and whose magnitude corresponds to the rate of increase along that direction

$$\nabla f(x_1, \ldots, x_n) = \left[\frac{\partial f(x_1, \ldots, x_n)}{\partial x_1}, \ldots, \frac{\partial f(x_1, \ldots, x_n)}{\partial x_n}\right]^T \tag{3.114}$$

which satisfies

$$\nabla(fg) = (\nabla f)g + (\nabla g)f \tag{3.115}$$

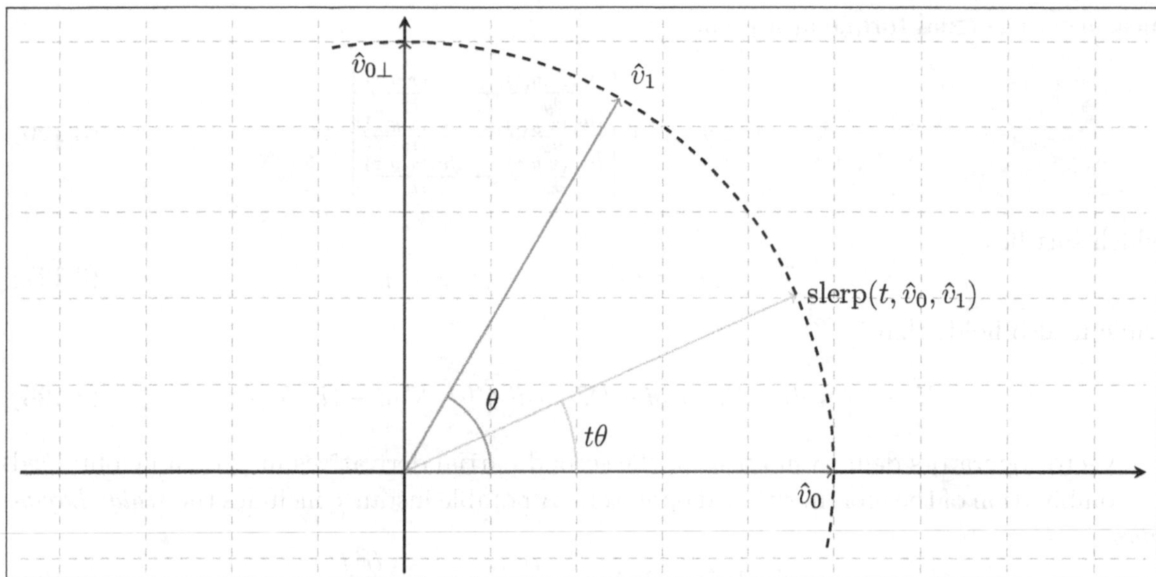

Figure 3.12: Spherical Linear Interpolation: Illustration of the geometric terms involved in the spherical linear interpolation of two unit vectors.

Instead, the rate of change along a given direction $\hat{u}$ is readily given by the *directional derivative*

$$\nabla_{\hat{u}} f(x_1, \ldots, x_n) \triangleq (\hat{u} \cdot \nabla) f(x_1, \ldots, x_n) = \hat{u} \cdot \nabla f(x_1, \ldots, x_n) \tag{3.116}$$

which, given a constant c, a 1-D function h, and two scalar fields f and g, satisfies

$$\nabla_{\hat{u}}(f+g) = \nabla_{\hat{u}} f + \nabla_{\hat{u}} g \tag{3.117}$$
$$\nabla_{\hat{u}}(cf) = c\nabla_{\hat{u}} f \tag{3.118}$$
$$\nabla_{\hat{u}}(fg) = (\nabla_{\hat{u}} f)g + (\nabla_{\hat{u}} g)f \tag{3.119}$$
$$\nabla_{\hat{u}}(h \circ g) = h'(g)\nabla_{\hat{u}} g \tag{3.120}$$

Analogously, the gradient of a vector field $\vec{v}$ is defined as the dyadic tensor

$$\nabla \vec{v}(x_1, \ldots, x_n) = [\nabla v_1(x_1, \ldots, x_n), \ldots, \nabla v_n(x_1, \ldots, x_n)] \tag{3.121}$$

which satisfies

$$\vec{u} \cdot \nabla \vec{v} = [\vec{u} \cdot \nabla \vec{v}_1, \ldots, \vec{u} \cdot \nabla \vec{v}_n] \tag{3.122}$$

Instead, the *divergence* of a vector field $\vec{v}(x_1, \ldots, x_n)$ is defined as the scalar field measuring the convergence or divergence of $\vec{v}$ at a point

$$\nabla \cdot \vec{v}(x_1, \ldots, x_n) = \frac{\partial v_1(x_1, \ldots, x_n)}{\partial x_1} + \ldots + \frac{\partial v_n(x_1, \ldots, x_n)}{\partial x_n} \tag{3.123}$$

which satisfies

$$\nabla \cdot (f\vec{v}) = (\nabla f) \cdot \vec{v} + (\nabla \cdot \vec{v}) f \tag{3.124}$$

while in $\mathbb{R}^3$, it also holds that

$$\nabla \cdot (\vec{u} \times \vec{v}) = (\nabla \times \vec{u}) \cdot \vec{v} - (\nabla \times \vec{v}) \cdot \vec{u} \tag{3.125}$$

The *curl* of a three-dimensional vector field $\vec{v}(x, y, z)$ is then defined as the vector field measuring the axial torque at a point

$$\nabla \times \vec{v}(x, y, z) = \begin{bmatrix} \frac{\partial v_z(x,y,z)}{\partial y} - \frac{\partial v_y(x,y,z)}{\partial z} \\ \frac{\partial v_x(x,y,z)}{\partial z} - \frac{\partial v_z(x,y,z)}{\partial x} \\ \frac{\partial v_y(x,y,z)}{\partial x} - \frac{\partial v_x(x,y,z)}{\partial y} \end{bmatrix} \tag{3.126}$$

which satisfies

$$\nabla \times (f\vec{v}) = (\nabla f) \times \vec{v} + (\nabla \times \vec{v})f \tag{3.127}$$

while it also holds that

$$\nabla \times (\vec{u} \times \vec{v}) = (\nabla \cdot \vec{v})\vec{u} - (\nabla \cdot \vec{u})\vec{v} + (\vec{v} \cdot \nabla)\vec{u} - (\vec{u} \cdot \nabla)\vec{v} \tag{3.128}$$

Vector operators defined in terms of the second partial derivatives may then be obtained by combination of the aforementioned operators. A notable instance includes the *scalar Laplacian*

$$\Delta f \triangleq \nabla^2 f = \nabla \cdot \nabla f = \frac{\partial^2 f}{\partial x_1^2} + \ldots + \frac{\partial^2 f}{\partial x_n^2} \tag{3.129}$$

as well as the *vector Laplacian*

$$\Delta \vec{v} \triangleq \nabla^2 \vec{v} = \nabla \cdot \nabla \vec{v} = \left[\nabla^2 v_1, \ldots, \nabla^2 v_n\right] \tag{3.130}$$

while in $\mathbb{R}^3$ it also holds that

$$\nabla \times \nabla f = \vec{0} \tag{3.131}$$

$$\nabla \cdot (\nabla \times \vec{v}) = 0 \tag{3.132}$$

$$\nabla \times (\nabla \times \vec{v}) = \nabla(\nabla \cdot \vec{v}) - \nabla^2 \vec{v} \tag{3.133}$$

81 where the last identity is analogous to the *vector triple product*.

It is also worth noting that despite its vector-like notation, Del is an operator, which, unlike vectors, doesn't generally commute, such that $(\nabla \cdot \vec{v})f \neq (\vec{v} \cdot \nabla)f$.

3.2.8 Further Reading

Additional material may be found in books dedicated to vector analysis [Vince, 2007].

3.3 HYPERCOMPLEX ALGEBRA

3.3.1 Overview

71 An *algebra* over a scalar field F is a *vector space* V over F equipped with a bilinear product $V \times V \rightarrow V$ such that vector multiplication and addition as well as scalar multiplication by elements of F satisfy the following axioms

- right distributivity: $(\vec{u} + \vec{v}) \times \vec{w} = \vec{u} \times \vec{w} + \vec{v} \times \vec{w}$ (3.134)
- left distributivity: $\vec{w} \times (\vec{u} + \vec{v}) = \vec{w} \times \vec{u} + \vec{w} \times \vec{v}$ (3.135)
- scalar multiplication: $(c\vec{u}) \times (d\vec{v}) = cd(\vec{u} \times \vec{v})$ (3.136)

3.3.2 Scalar Number

3.3.2.1 *Cartesian Coordinates*

Scalar numbers form a one-dimensional *inner product* space over the field of real numbers. A 76
scalar number $x \in \mathbb{R}$ defined in *Cartesian coordinates* is related to its *polar coordinates* by 67 85

$$x = |x| \operatorname{sgn}(x) \tag{3.137}$$

3.3.2.2 *Polar Coordinates*

A scalar number $x = |x| \operatorname{sgn}(x) \in \mathbb{R}$ can alternatively be defined in polar coordinates by
its *absolute value* $|x| \in [0, \infty)$ and its *sign* $\operatorname{sgn}(x) \in \{-1, 0, +1\}$, which are related to its
Cartesian coordinates by 85

$$|x| = \sqrt{x^2} = \sqrt{\langle x, x \rangle} \tag{3.138}$$

$$\operatorname{sgn}(x) = \frac{x}{|x|} \tag{3.139}$$

3.3.3 Complex Number

3.3.3.1 *Cartesian Coordinates*

As illustrated in *Figure 3.13*, complex numbers form a two-dimensional *inner product* space 85
over the field of real numbers. Noting the *imaginary unit* $\imath^2 = -1$, a *complex number* $z \triangleq$ 76
$x + \imath y \in \mathbb{C}$ is defined in *Cartesian coordinates* by its *real part* $x = \Re(z) \in \mathbb{R}$ and its *imaginary* 67
part $y = \Im(z) \in \mathbb{R}$, which are related to its *polar coordinates* by 86

$$x = r \cos(\varphi) \tag{3.140}$$

$$y = r \sin(\varphi) \tag{3.141}$$

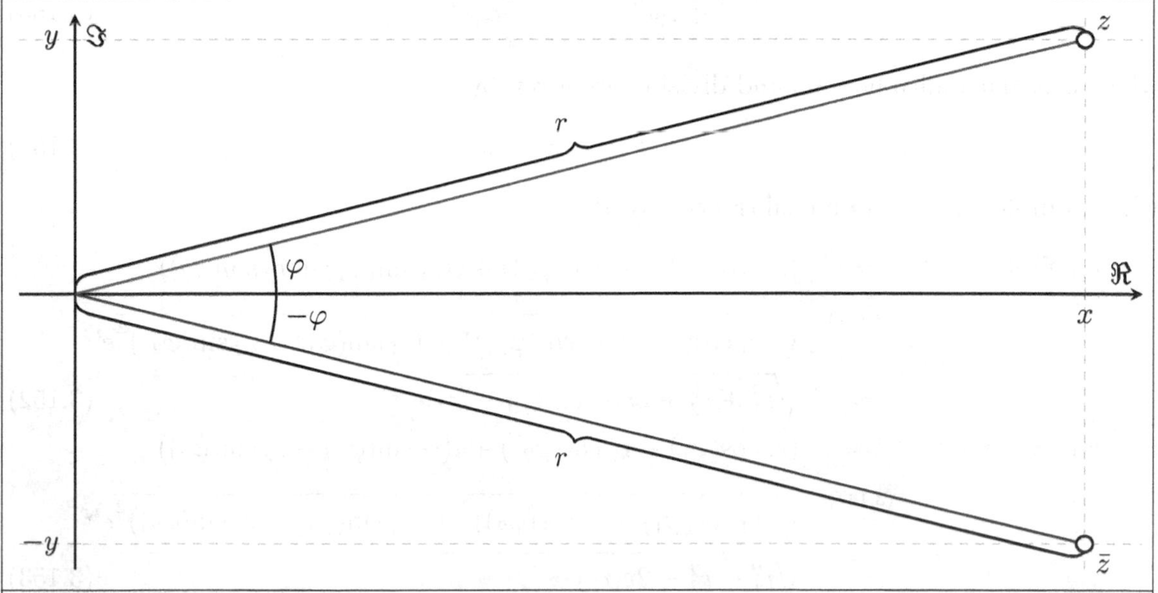

Figure 3.13: Complex Number: Illustration of a complex number and of its complex conjugate, expressed both in Cartesian and in polar coordinates.

Complex addition and subtraction are then defined as

$$(x_1 + \imath y_1) + (x_2 + \imath y_2) = (x_1 + x_2) + \imath(y_1 + y_2) \tag{3.142}$$

$$(x_1 + \imath y_1) - (x_2 + \imath y_2) = (x_1 - x_2) + \imath(y_1 - y_2) \tag{3.143}$$

whereas complex multiplication and division are given by

$$\begin{aligned}(x_1+\imath y_1)\times(x_2+\imath y_2) &= x_1x_2+\imath y_1x_2+\imath x_1y_2+\imath^2 y_1y_2 \\ &= (x_1x_2-y_1y_2)+\imath(y_1x_2+x_1y_2) \qquad (3.144)\\ (x_1+\imath y_1)\div(x_2+\imath y_2) &= \frac{(x_1+\imath y_1)\times(x_2-\imath y_2)}{(x_2+\imath y_2)\times(x_2-\imath y_2)} \\ &= \frac{x_1x_2+y_1y_2}{x_2^2+y_2^2}+\imath\frac{y_1x_2-x_1y_2}{x_2^2+y_2^2} \qquad (3.145)\end{aligned}$$

while scalar multiplication and division (i.e., by a complex number whose imaginary part is zero) read

$$z \overset{\times}{\div} c = (x+\imath y)\overset{\times}{\div} c = (x \overset{\times}{\div} c)+\imath(y \overset{\times}{\div} c) \qquad (3.146)$$

3.3.3.2 Polar Coordinates

Based on *Euler's formula* $e^{\imath\varphi} \triangleq \cos(\varphi)+\imath\sin(\varphi)$, a complex number $z = re^{\imath\varphi} \in \mathbb{C}$ can alternatively be defined in polar coordinates by its *modulus* $r = |z| \in [0,\infty)$ and its sign $\operatorname{sgn}(z) = e^{\imath \arg(z)}$ with the *principal value* of its *argument* $\varphi = \arg(z) \in (-\pi,\pi]$, which are
85 related to its *Cartesian coordinates* by

$$r = \sqrt{x^2+y^2} = \sqrt{\langle z,z\rangle} \qquad (3.147)$$

$$\varphi = \operatorname{arctan2}(y,x) = \operatorname{sgn}(y)\arccos\left(\frac{\operatorname{sgn}(x)}{\sqrt{1+(y\div x)^2}}\right) = \operatorname{sgn}(y)\arccos\left(\frac{x}{|z|}\right) \qquad (3.148)$$

Complex multiplication and division are then defined as

$$r_1e^{\imath\varphi_1}\times r_2e^{\imath\varphi_2} = r_1r_2e^{\imath(\varphi_1+\varphi_2)} \qquad (3.149)$$

$$r_1e^{\imath\varphi_1}\div r_2e^{\imath\varphi_2} = \frac{r_1}{r_2}e^{\imath(\varphi_1-\varphi_2)} \qquad (3.150)$$

whereas scalar multiplication and division are given by

$$re^{\imath\varphi}\overset{\times}{\div} c = (r \overset{\times}{\div} c)e^{\imath\varphi} \qquad (3.151)$$

while complex addition and subtraction read

$$r_1e^{\imath\varphi_1}+r_2e^{\imath\varphi_2} = (r_1\cos(\varphi_1)+r_2\cos(\varphi_2))+\imath(r_1\sin(\varphi_1)+r_2\sin(\varphi_2))$$

86
$$\overset{(3.147)}{=} \sqrt{(r_1\cos(\varphi_1)+r_2\cos(\varphi_2))^2+(r_1\sin(\varphi_1)+r_2\sin(\varphi_2))^2}e^{\imath\varphi^+}$$

$$= \sqrt{r_1^2+r_2^2+2r_1r_2\cos(\varphi_1-\varphi_2)}e^{\imath\varphi^+} \qquad (3.152)$$

$$r_1e^{\imath\varphi_1}-r_2e^{\imath\varphi_2} = (r_1\cos(\varphi_1)-r_2\cos(\varphi_2))+\imath(r_1\sin(\varphi_1)-r_2\sin(\varphi_2))$$

86
$$\overset{(3.147)}{=} \sqrt{(r_1\cos(\varphi_1)-r_2\cos(\varphi_2))^2+(r_1\sin(\varphi_1)-r_2\sin(\varphi_2))^2}e^{\imath\varphi^-}$$

$$= \sqrt{r_1^2+r_2^2-2r_1r_2\cos(\varphi_1-\varphi_2)}e^{\imath\varphi^-} \qquad (3.153)$$

where

86
$$\varphi^+ \overset{(3.148)}{=} \operatorname{arctan2}\left(r_1\sin(\varphi_1)+r_2\sin(\varphi_2), r_1\cos(\varphi_1)+r_2\cos(\varphi_2)\right) \qquad (3.154)$$

86
$$\varphi^- \overset{(3.148)}{=} \operatorname{arctan2}\left(r_1\sin(\varphi_1)-r_2\sin(\varphi_2), r_1\cos(\varphi_1)-r_2\cos(\varphi_2)\right) \qquad (3.155)$$

3.3.3.3 Complex Conjugate

As illustrated in *Figure 3.13*, the *complex conjugate* of a complex number z is defined in 85
Cartesian coordinates as $\bar{z} \triangleq x - \imath y$ such that 85

$$\Re(z) = \frac{z+\bar{z}}{2} \tag{3.156}$$

$$\imath\Im(z) = \frac{z-\bar{z}}{2} \tag{3.157}$$

while in *polar coordinates* it reads $\bar{z} = re^{-\imath\varphi}$ such that 86

$$|z| = \sqrt{z \times \bar{z}} \tag{3.158}$$

$$\imath \arg(z) = \frac{\ln(z \div \bar{z})}{2} \tag{3.159}$$

It then follows the identities

$$\bar{\bar{z}} = z \tag{3.160}$$

$$\overline{-z} = -\bar{z} \tag{3.161}$$

$$\frac{1}{z} = \frac{\bar{z}}{z\bar{z}} = \frac{\bar{z}}{|z|^2} \tag{3.162}$$

as well as the addition and subtraction identities

$$\overline{z_1 + z_2} = \overline{z_1} + \overline{z_2} \tag{3.163}$$

$$\overline{z_1 - z_2} = \overline{z_1} - \overline{z_2} \tag{3.164}$$

and the multiplication and division identities

$$\overline{z_1 \times z_2} = \overline{z_1} \times \overline{z_2} \tag{3.165}$$

$$\overline{z_1 \div z_2} = \overline{z_1} \div \overline{z_2} \tag{3.166}$$

Finally, the product of the complex conjugate of $z_1 = x_1 + \imath y_1$ with a complex number
$z_2 = x_2 + \imath y_2$ may be related to the *inner product* and the *cross product* of the three- 76
dimensional Euclidean vectors $\vec{v}_{1|2} = [x_{1|2}, y_{1|2}, 0]^T$ by 78

$$\bar{z}_1 z_2 \overset{(3.144)}{=} (x_1x_2 + y_1y_2) + \imath(-y_1x_2 + x_1y_2) \underset{(3.88)}{\overset{(3.70)}{=}} \langle \vec{v}_1, \vec{v}_2 \rangle + \imath(\vec{v}_1 \times \vec{v}_2)_z \tag{3.167}$$

86 76 78

where the last subscript denotes the z coordinate of the resulting vector.

More generally, if f is a holomorphic function whose restriction to the real numbers is real-valued, it holds that

$$f(\bar{z}) = \overline{f(z)} \tag{3.168}$$

whereas a complex-valued function whose real part is even and imaginary part is odd such that $f(-x) = \overline{f(x)}$ is referred to as a *Hermitian function*.

3.3.3.4 Complex Functions

The complex exponential is defined as a generalization of Euler's formula

$$e^z = e^{\Re(z)}\Big(\cos\left(\Im(z)\right) + \imath \sin\left(\Im(z)\right)\Big) \tag{3.169}$$

while the definition of the complex logarithm directly follows from the polar form

$$\ln(z) = \ln\left(|z|e^{\imath \arg(z)}\right) = \ln(|z|) + \imath \arg(z) \tag{3.170}$$

Additionally, exponentiation is given by *de Moivre's formula*

$$z^n = (re^{\imath\varphi})^n = r^n e^{\imath n\varphi} \tag{3.171}$$

and the nth root similarly reads

$$\sqrt[n]{z} = z^{\frac{1}{n}} = \left(re^{\imath(\varphi \pm k2\pi)}\right)^{\frac{1}{n}} = r^{\frac{1}{n}} e^{\imath\frac{\varphi \pm k2\pi}{n}} = \sqrt[n]{r} e^{\imath\frac{\varphi}{n}} e^{\pm\imath k\frac{2\pi}{n}}, \quad \forall k \in [0, n-1] \tag{3.172}$$

whose *principal value* is obtained for $k = 0$ whereas the real-valued root of a negative real number (for which $\varphi = \pi$) is given for odd values of n by $k = \pm\frac{n-1}{2}$, while the principal
85 square root can be readily formulated in *Cartesian coordinates* as

$$\sqrt{z} = \sqrt{\frac{|z| + \Re(z)}{2}} + \imath\,\mathrm{sgn}\left(\Im(z)\right)\sqrt{\frac{|z| - \Re(z)}{2}} \tag{3.173}$$

where the inequality $|z| \pm \Re(z) \geq 0$ always holds since $|z| \geq |\Re(z)|$.

3.3.4 Triplex Number

3.3.4.1 *Cartesian Coordinates*

Studied by Daniel White and Paul Nylander,[1] triplex numbers are defined as hyper-complex
76 numbers forming a three-dimensional *inner product* space over the field of real numbers whose basis elements satisfy

$$\imath^2 = \jmath^2 = -1 \tag{3.174}$$

and $\imath\jmath = -\jmath\imath$. No canonical three-dimensional extension forming a complete algebra analog to
85 the two-dimensional *complex numbers* exists though, and other formulations might therefore be encountered in the literature.

67 A *triplex number* $p \triangleq x + \imath y + \jmath z \in \mathbb{R}^3$ can be defined in *Cartesian coordinates* by its
89 parts $x, y, z \in \mathbb{R}$, which are related to its *spherical coordinates* by

$$x = \rho\cos(\theta)\cos(\phi) \tag{3.175}$$
$$y = \rho\cos(\theta)\sin(\phi) \tag{3.176}$$
$$z = \rho\sin(\theta) \tag{3.177}$$

It then follows the addition and subtraction identities

$$(x_1 + \imath y_1 + \jmath z_1) + (x_2 + \imath y_2 + \jmath z_2) = (x_1 + x_2) + \imath(y_1 + y_2) + \jmath(z_1 + z_2) \tag{3.178}$$
$$(x_1 + \imath y_1 + \jmath z_1) - (x_2 + \imath y_2 + \jmath z_2) = (x_1 - x_2) + \imath(y_1 - y_2) + \jmath(z_1 - z_2) \tag{3.179}$$

[1] **http://www.fractalforums.com/theory/triplex-algebra/**.

as well as the multiplication and division identities

$$\begin{aligned}
&(x_1 + \imath y_1 + \jmath z_1) \times (x_2 + \imath y_2 + \jmath z_2) \\
&= (x_1 x_2 - y_1 y_2)\left(1 - \frac{z_1 z_2}{\sqrt{x_1^2 + y_1^2}\sqrt{x_2^2 + y_2^2}}\right) \\
&+ \imath(y_1 x_2 + x_1 y_2)\left(1 - \frac{z_1 z_2}{\sqrt{x_1^2 + y_1^2}\sqrt{x_2^2 + y_2^2}}\right) \\
&+ \jmath\left(\sqrt{x_2^2 + y_2^2} z_1 + \sqrt{x_1^2 + y_1^2} z_2\right) \qquad (3.180)
\end{aligned}$$

$$\begin{aligned}
&(x_1 + \imath y_1 + \jmath z_1) \div (x_2 + \imath y_2 + \jmath z_2) \\
&= (x_1 + \imath y_1 + \jmath z_1) \times \overline{(x_2 + \imath y_2 + \jmath z_2)} \div \|x_2 + \imath y_2 + \jmath z_2\|^2 \\
&= (x_1 x_2 + y_1 y_2)\left(1 + \frac{z_1 z_2}{\sqrt{x_1^2 + y_1^2}\sqrt{x_2^2 + y_2^2}}\right) \div \|x_2 + \imath y_2 + \jmath z_2\|^2 \\
&+ \imath(y_1 x_2 - x_1 y_2)\left(1 + \frac{z_1 z_2}{\sqrt{x_1^2 + y_1^2}\sqrt{x_2^2 + y_2^2}}\right) \div \|x_2 + \imath y_2 + \jmath z_2\|^2 \\
&+ \jmath\left(\sqrt{x_2^2 + y_2^2} z_1 - \sqrt{x_1^2 + y_1^2} z_2\right) \div \|x_2 + \imath y_2 + \jmath z_2\|^2 \qquad (3.181)
\end{aligned}$$

with the following properties

- commutativity: $$p_2 p_1 = p_1 p_2 \qquad (3.182)$$
- non-associativity: $$p_1(p_2 p_3) \neq (p_1 p_2) p_3 \qquad (3.183)$$

whereas scalar multiplication and division is given as

$$p \overset{\times}{\div} c = (x + \imath y + \jmath z) \overset{\times}{\div} c = (x \overset{\times}{\div} c) + \imath(y \overset{\times}{\div} c) + \jmath(z \overset{\times}{\div} c) \qquad (3.184)$$

3.3.4.2 Spherical Coordinates

A triplex number $p = [\rho, \theta, \phi] \in \mathbb{R}^3$ can alternatively be defined in *spherical coordinates* by 70
its radius $\rho = \|p\| \in [0, \infty)$, its elevation angle $\theta \in [-\pi/2, \pi/2]$ (which yields a more consistent
formulation of the triplex exponentiation than using the inclination angle $\theta \in [0, \pi]$) and its
azimuthal angle $\phi \in (-\pi, \pi]$, which are related to its *Cartesian coordinates* by 88

$$\rho = \sqrt{x^2 + y^2 + z^2} = \sqrt{\langle p, p \rangle} \qquad (3.185)$$

$$\theta = \operatorname{arctan2}(z, \sqrt{x^2 + y^2}) = \arcsin\left(\frac{z \div \sqrt{x^2 + y^2}}{\sqrt{1 + (z \div \sqrt{x^2 + y^2})^2}}\right) = \arcsin\left(\frac{z}{\|p\|}\right) \qquad (3.186)$$

$$\phi = \operatorname{arctan2}(y, x) \qquad (3.187)$$

It then follows the multiplication and division identities

$$[\rho_1, \theta_1, \phi_1] \times [\rho_2, \theta_2, \phi_2] = [\rho_1 \times \rho_2, \theta_1 + \theta_2, \phi_1 + \phi_2] \qquad (3.188)$$

$$[\rho_1, \theta_1, \phi_1] \div [\rho_2, \theta_2, \phi_2] = [\rho_1 \div \rho_2, \theta_1 - \theta_2, \phi_1 - \phi_2] \qquad (3.189)$$

3.3.4.3 Triplex Conjugate

88 The *triplex conjugate* of a triplex number p is defined in *Cartesian coordinates* as $\bar{p} \triangleq$
$x - \imath y - \jmath z$ such that

$$\begin{aligned} x &= \frac{p+\bar{p}}{2} && (3.190) \\ \imath y + \jmath z &= \frac{p-\bar{p}}{2} && (3.191) \end{aligned}$$

89 while its *spherical coordinates* are such that

$$||p|| = \sqrt{p\bar{p}} \tag{3.192}$$

It then follows the identities

$$\begin{aligned} \bar{\bar{p}} &= p && (3.193) \\ \frac{1}{p} &= \frac{\bar{p}}{p\bar{p}} = \frac{\bar{p}}{||p||^2} && (3.194) \end{aligned}$$

3.3.4.4 Triplex Functions

The triplex exponentiation is given by

$$p^n = [\rho^n, n\theta, n\phi] \tag{3.195}$$

which yields the consistent results $p^0 = 1$ and $p^1 = p$.

3.3.5 Quaternion

3.3.5.1 Cartesian Coordinates

First introduced by William Rowan Hamilton in 1843, quaternions [Vince, 2011a] are defined
as complex-valued two-dimensional vectors $q = (x + \imath y)1 + (z + \imath w)\jmath$, i.e., as hyper-complex
76 numbers forming a four-dimensional *inner product* space over the field of real numbers whose
basis elements satisfy

$$\imath^2 = \jmath^2 = k^2 = \imath\jmath k = -1 \tag{3.196}$$

67 A *quaternion* $q \triangleq x + \imath y + \jmath z + kw = (x, \vec{v}) \in \mathbb{H}$ is defined in *Cartesian coordinates* by its
scalar part $x \in \mathbb{R}$ and its *vector part* $\vec{v} = \imath y + \jmath z + kw \in \mathbb{R}^3$, which are related to its *polar*
91 *coordinates* by

$$\begin{aligned} x &= r\cos(\varphi) && (3.197) \\ ||\vec{v}|| &= r\sin(\varphi) && (3.198) \\ \vec{v} &= ||\vec{v}||\hat{n} && (3.199) \end{aligned}$$

It then follows the addition and subtraction identities

$$\begin{aligned} q_1 \pm q_2 &= (x_1 + \imath y_1 + \jmath z_1 + kw_1) \pm (x_2 + \imath y_2 + \jmath z_2 + kw_2) \\ &= (x_1 \pm x_2) + \imath(y_1 \pm y_2) + \jmath(z_1 \pm z_2) + k(w_1 \pm w_2) \\ &= (x_1 \pm x_2, \vec{v}_1 \pm \vec{v}_2) && (3.200) \end{aligned}$$

whereas scalar multiplication and division (i.e., by a quaternion whose vector part is zero) is given as

$$q \divideontimes c = (x + \imath y + \jmath z + kw) \divideontimes c = (x \divideontimes c) + \imath(y \divideontimes c) + \jmath(z \divideontimes c) + k(w \divideontimes c) \tag{3.201}$$

By left/right multiplying both sides of the identity $\imath\jmath k = -1$ by a given basis element, the product of any two basis elements may then be derived to yield the multiplication rules synthesized in *Table 3.2*. Together with the distributive law, the products of the basis elements 91
then define the *Hamilton product* of two quaternions as

$$
\begin{aligned}
q_1 \times q_2 &= (x_1 + \imath y_1 + \jmath z_1 + k w_1) \times (x_2 + \imath y_2 + \jmath z_2 + k w_2) \\
&= x_1 x_2 + \imath x_1 y_2 + \jmath x_1 z_2 + k x_1 w_2 \\
&+ \imath y_1 x_2 + \imath^2 y_1 y_2 + \imath\jmath y_1 z_2 + \imath k y_1 w_2 \\
&+ \jmath z_1 x_2 + \jmath\imath z_1 y_2 + \jmath^2 z_1 z_2 + \jmath k z_1 w_2 \\
&+ k w_1 x_2 + k\imath w_1 y_2 + k\jmath w_1 z_2 + k^2 w_1 w_2 \\
&= (x_1 x_2 - y_1 y_2 - z_1 z_2 - w_1 w_2) \\
&+ \imath(y_1 x_2 + x_1 y_2 - w_1 z_2 + z_1 w_2) \\
&+ \jmath(z_1 x_2 + w_1 y_2 + x_1 z_2 - y_1 w_2) \\
&+ k(w_1 x_2 - z_1 y_2 + y_1 z_2 + x_1 w_2) \\
&= (x_1 x_2 - \langle \vec{v}_1, \vec{v}_2 \rangle, x_2 \vec{v}_1 + x_1 \vec{v}_2 + \vec{v}_1 \times \vec{v}_2) \qquad (3.202)
\end{aligned}
$$

which is only commutative if the vector parts are collinear such that their *cross product* is 78
zero, and with the following general properties

- non-commutativity: $q_1 q_2 \neq q_2 q_1 = q_1 q_2 - (0, 2\vec{v}_1 \times \vec{v}_2)$ (3.203)
- distributivity: $q_1(q_2 + q_3) = q_1 q_2 + q_1 q_3$ (3.204)
- associativity: $q_1(q_2 q_3) = (q_1 q_2) q_3$ (3.205)

whereas division is defined as

$$q_1 \div q_2 = q_1 \times q_2^{-1} \overset{(3.218)}{=} q_1 \times \frac{\bar{q}_2}{\|q_2\|^2} \overset{(3.202)}{=} \frac{x_1 x_2 + \langle \vec{v}_1, \vec{v}_2 \rangle, x_2 \vec{v}_1 - x_1 \vec{v}_2 - \vec{v}_1 \times \vec{v}_2}{\|q_2\|^2} \qquad (3.206)$$ 92 91

where $q_1 \times q_2^{-1} \neq q_2^{-1} \times q_1$, therefore making the notation $\frac{q_1}{q_2}$ ambiguous as it does not specify whether the reciprocal acts as a left or as a right operand.

Table 3.2: Quaternion Multiplication: Multiplication rules for the product of a basis element from the left-most column as a left operand with a basis element from the topmost row as a right operand.

$\times$	1	$\imath$	$\jmath$	k
1	1	$\imath$	$\jmath$	k
$\imath$	$\imath$	-1	k	$-\jmath$
$\jmath$	$\jmath$	$-k$	-1	$\imath$
k	k	$\jmath$	$-\imath$	-1

3.3.5.2 Polar Coordinates

Based on the extension of Euler's formula $e^{\hat{n}\varphi} = \cos(\varphi) + \hat{n}\sin(\varphi)$, a quaternion $q = re^{\hat{n}\varphi} \in \mathbb{H}$ can alternatively be defined in polar coordinates by its norm $r = \|q\| \in [0, \infty)$ and its axis–angle argument $\hat{n}\varphi$, which are related to its *Cartesian coordinates* by 90

$$
\begin{aligned}
r &= \sqrt{x^2 + y^2 + z^2 + w^2} = \sqrt{x^2 + \|\vec{v}\|^2} = \sqrt{\langle q, q \rangle} && (3.207) \\
\hat{n} &= \vec{v} \div \|\vec{v}\| && (3.208) \\
\varphi &= \operatorname{arctan2}(\|\vec{v}\|, x) = \arccos\left(\frac{\operatorname{sgn}(x)}{\sqrt{1 + (\|\vec{v}\| \div x)^2}}\right) = \arccos\left(\frac{x}{\|q\|}\right) && (3.209)
\end{aligned}
$$

Quaternion multiplication and division are then defined as

$$r_1 e^{\hat{n}_1\varphi_1} \times r_2 e^{\hat{n}_2\varphi_2} = r_1 r_2 e^{\hat{n}_1\varphi_1 + \hat{n}_2\varphi_2} \tag{3.210}$$

$$r_1 e^{\hat{n}_1\varphi_1} \div r_2 e^{\hat{n}_2\varphi_2} = \frac{r_1}{r_2} e^{\hat{n}_1\varphi_1 - \hat{n}_2\varphi_2} \tag{3.211}$$

whereas scalar multiplication and division are given by

$$r e^{\hat{n}\varphi} \overset{\times}{\div} c = (r \overset{\times}{\div} c) e^{\hat{n}\varphi} \tag{3.212}$$

3.3.5.3 Quaternion Conjugate

90 The *quaternion conjugate* of a quaternion q is defined in *Cartesian coordinates* as $\bar{q} \triangleq x - \imath y - \jmath z - kw = (x, -\vec{v})$ such that

$$x = \frac{q + \bar{q}}{2} \tag{3.213}$$

$$\vec{v} = \frac{q - \bar{q}}{2} \tag{3.214}$$

91 while in *polar coordinates* it reads $\bar{q} = re^{-\hat{n}\varphi}$ such that

$$r = \sqrt{q \times \bar{q}} = \sqrt{\bar{q} \times q} \tag{3.215}$$

$$\hat{n}\varphi = \frac{\ln(q \div \bar{q})}{2} \tag{3.216}$$

It then follows the identities

$$\bar{\bar{q}} = q \tag{3.217}$$

$$\frac{1}{q} = \frac{\bar{q}}{q\bar{q}} = \frac{\bar{q}}{\|q\|^2} \tag{3.218}$$

as well as the addition and subtraction identities

$$\overline{q_1 + q_2} = \overline{q_1} + \overline{q_2} \tag{3.219}$$

$$\overline{q_1 - q_2} = \overline{q_1} - \overline{q_2} \tag{3.220}$$

and the multiplication and division identities

$$\overline{q_1 \times q_2} = \overline{q_2} \times \overline{q_1} \tag{3.221}$$

$$\overline{q_1 \div q_2} = \overline{q_2^{-1}} \times \overline{q_1} \tag{3.222}$$

3.3.5.4 Quaternion Functions

The exponential function is defined as a generalization of the extension of Euler's formula

$$e^q = e^x \left(\cos(\|\vec{v}\|) + \frac{\vec{v}}{\|\vec{v}\|} \sin(\|\vec{v}\|) \right) \tag{3.223}$$

while the definition of the logarithm directly follows from the polar form

$$\ln(q) = \ln(re^{\hat{n}\varphi}) = \ln(r) + \hat{n}\varphi \tag{3.224}$$

Additionally, exponentiation is given by

$$q^n = (re^{\hat{n}\varphi})^n = r^n e^{\hat{n}n\varphi} \tag{3.225}$$

3.4 MATRIX ALGEBRA

3.4.1 Arbitrary Matrix

3.4.1.1 Definition

An $m \times n$ *matrix* is a 2-D array of elements a_{ij} comprising m rows and n columns

$$A \triangleq \begin{bmatrix} a_{11} & a_{12} & \cdots & a_{1n} \\ a_{21} & a_{22} & \cdots & a_{2n} \\ \vdots & \vdots & \ddots & \vdots \\ a_{m1} & a_{m2} & \cdots & a_{mn} \end{bmatrix} \tag{3.226}$$

which is referred to as a *row vector* whenever $m = 1$ and as a *column vector* instead whenever $n = 1$, yielding a *scalar* in the special case where $m = n = 1$.

Addition and subtraction of two $m \times n$ matrices are then defined as

$$(A \pm B)_{ij} \triangleq (A)_{ij} \pm (B)_{ij}, \quad \forall i \in [1, m], \forall j \in [1, n] \tag{3.227}$$

with the following properties

- commutativity: $$A + B = B + A \tag{3.228}$$
- associativity: $$A + (B + C) = (A + B) + C \tag{3.229}$$

while the entrywise product, known as the *Hadamard product* or *Schur product*, similarly reads

$$(A \circ B)_{ij} \triangleq (A)_{ij}(B)_{ij}, \quad \forall i \in [1, m], \forall j \in [1, n] \tag{3.230}$$

with the properties below

- commutativity: $$A \circ B = B \circ A \tag{3.231}$$
- associativity: $$A \circ (B \circ C) = (A \circ B) \circ C \tag{3.232}$$
- distributivity: $$A \circ (B + C) = A \circ B + A \circ C \tag{3.233}$$

As illustrated in *Figure 3.14*, the product of an $m \times l$ matrix A with an $l \times n$ matrix B 94
is instead an $m \times n$ matrix whose entries are given by the dot products of the ith row vector of A with the jth column vector of B

$$(AB)_{ij} \triangleq \sum_{k=1}^{l} (A)_{ik}(B)_{kj}, \quad \forall i \in [1, m], \forall j \in [1, n] \tag{3.234}$$

while scalar multiplication and division of an $m \times n$ matrix read

$$(A \overset{\times}{\div} c)_{ij} \triangleq (A)_{ij} \overset{\times}{\div} c, \quad \forall i \in [1, m], \forall j \in [1, n] \tag{3.235}$$

It then follows the properties below

- non-commutativity: $$AB \neq BA \tag{3.236}$$
- associativity: $$A(BC) = (AB)C \tag{3.237}$$
- distributivity: $$A(B + C) = AB + AC \tag{3.238}$$
- scalar multiplication: $$(cA)B = c(AB) \tag{3.239}$$

The above rule of matrix multiplication more generally extends to that of a *block matrix* whose elements are represented as blockwise subsets. Minding the proper multiplicative ordering of the blocks, the product of two matrices with compatible block sizes is then readily given as

$$\begin{bmatrix} A_{11} & A_{12} \\ A_{21} & A_{22} \end{bmatrix} \begin{bmatrix} B_{11} & B_{12} \\ B_{21} & B_{22} \end{bmatrix} = \begin{bmatrix} A_{11}B_{11} + A_{12}B_{21} & A_{11}B_{12} + A_{12}B_{22} \\ A_{21}B_{11} + A_{22}B_{21} & A_{21}B_{12} + A_{22}B_{22} \end{bmatrix} \tag{3.240}$$

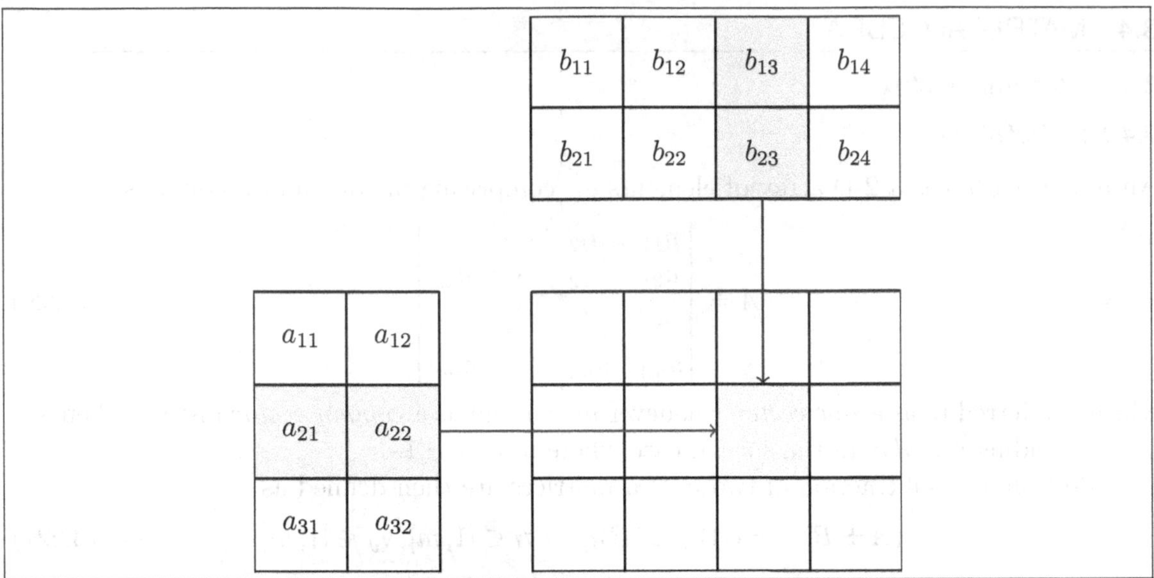

Figure 3.14: Matrix Multiplication: Illustration of the product of two matrices of compatible sizes.

3.4.1.2 Transposition

The *transpose matrix* of an $m \times n$ matrix is an $n \times m$ matrix whose entries are defined by

$$(A^T)_{ji} \triangleq (A)_{ij}, \quad \forall i \in [1, m], \forall j \in [1, n] \tag{3.241}$$

from which follow the properties below

$$(A^T)^T = A \tag{3.242}$$
$$(A+B)^T = A^T + B^T \tag{3.243}$$
$$(cA)^T = cA^T \tag{3.244}$$
$$(AB)^T = B^T A^T \tag{3.245}$$

3.4.1.3 Rank

The column rank of a matrix is defined as the dimensionality of the space spanned by the
column vectors of the matrix (i.e., its total number of linearly independent column vectors),
while its row rank is similarly defined as the dimensionality of the space spanned by its row
vectors (i.e., its total number of linearly independent row vectors). Since the column rank
and row rank of a matrix are necessarily equal, the (column/row) *rank* of a matrix defines
102 the dimensionality of the image space of the *linear transformation* encoded by the matrix.

Given an $m \times n$ matrix A, it follows that $0 \leq \text{rank}(A) \leq \min\{m, n\}$, such that the
matrix is said to have *full rank* whenever $\text{rank}(A) = \min\{m, n\}$ and to be *rank deficient*
whenever $\text{rank}(A) < \min\{m, n\}$. A matrix is similarly said to have full row rank whenever
102 $\text{rank}(A) = m \leq n$, in which case A defines a surjective *linear transformation*, whereas the
matrix is said to have full column rank whenever $\text{rank}(A) = n \leq m$, in which case A defines
95 an injection. Conversely, a *square matrix* has full rank $\text{rank}(A) = m = n$ if and only if it
102 is invertible, i.e., if and only if $\det(A) \neq 0$, so as to define a bijective *linear transformation*.

The properties below additionally follow

$$\begin{aligned} \text{rank}(0) &= 0 & (3.246) \\ \text{rank}(I) &= n & (3.247) \\ \text{rank}(AB) &\leq \min\{\text{rank}(A), \text{rank}(B)\} & (3.248) \\ \text{rank}(A+B) &\leq \text{rank}(A) + \text{rank}(B) & (3.249) \\ \text{rank}(A^T) &= \text{rank}(A) = \text{rank}(A^T A) = \text{rank}(AA^T) & (3.250) \end{aligned}$$

3.4.2 Square Matrix

3.4.2.1 Definition

An $m \times n$ matrix is referred to as a *square matrix* whenever $m = n$. It is then said to be an

- *upper triangular matrix* if $(A)_{ij} = 0, \forall i > j$
- *lower triangular matrix* if $(A)_{ij} = 0, \forall i < j$ (3.251)
- *diagonal matrix* if $(A)_{ij} = 0, \forall i \neq j$

A diagonal matrix whose diagonal elements are all ones forms a so-called *identity matrix* I, which maps any matrix or vector to itself such that $AI = IA = A$. Moreover, the following properties hold

- symmetry: $I^T = I$ (3.252)
- orthogonality: $I^T I = I$ (3.253)
- involution: $I^{-1} = I$ (3.254)

whereas a diagonal matrix whose elements are equal to the same scalar value is referred to as a *scalar matrix*.

A matrix is additionally referred to as a *symmetric matrix* whenever $A^T = A$ such that

$$(A)_{ij} = (A)_{ji}, \quad \forall i \in [1, m], \forall j \in [1, n] \tag{3.255}$$

and as a *skew-symmetric matrix*, also called *antisymmetric matrix*, whenever $A^T = -A$ such that

$$(A)_{ij} = -(A)_{ji}, \quad \forall i \in [1, m], \forall j \in [1, n] \tag{3.256}$$

whose diagonal elements are therefore necessarily zero. It then follows that any square matrix A may be decomposed into the sum of a symmetric and an antisymmetric matrix

$$A = \frac{1}{2}(A + A^T) + \frac{1}{2}(A - A^T) \tag{3.257}$$

Defining the quadratic form $Q(\vec{v}) \triangleq \vec{v}^T A \vec{v}$ associating an arbitrary non-zero vector $\vec{v}$ to an $n \times n$ symmetric matrix A, the latter is said to be a

- *positive-definite matrix* if $Q(\vec{v}) > 0, \forall \vec{v} \in \mathbb{R}^n \mid \vec{v} \neq \vec{0}$
- *negative-definite matrix* if $Q(\vec{v}) < 0, \forall \vec{v} \in \mathbb{R}^n \mid \vec{v} \neq \vec{0}$
- *positive-semidefinite matrix* if $Q(\vec{v}) \geq 0, \forall \vec{v} \in \mathbb{R}^n \mid \vec{v} \neq \vec{0}$ (3.258)
- *negative-semidefinite matrix* if $Q(\vec{v}) \leq 0, \forall \vec{v} \in \mathbb{R}^n \mid \vec{v} \neq \vec{0}$
- *indefinite matrix* otherwise

from which follows that a square matrix A is positive semidefinite if and only if there exists a unique positive semidefinite matrix $A^{\frac{1}{2}}$, so-called square root of A, such that $A^{\frac{1}{2}}A^{\frac{1}{2}} = A$. Conversely, the exponentiation of a square matrix A is readily defined as

$$A^k \triangleq \prod_{i=1}^{k} A, \quad \forall k \in \mathbb{N} \tag{3.259}$$

such that

$$A^0 = I \tag{3.260}$$

$$(cA)^n = c^n A^n \tag{3.261}$$

Additionally, the *trace* of an $n \times n$ matrix is defined as the sum of the elements on its main diagonal

$$\text{tr}(A) \triangleq \sum_{i=1}^{n} (A)_{ii} \tag{3.262}$$

whose properties read

$$\text{tr}(I) = n \tag{3.263}$$

$$\text{tr}(cA) = c\,\text{tr}(A) \tag{3.264}$$

$$\text{tr}(A+B) = \text{tr}(A) + \text{tr}(B) \tag{3.265}$$

$$\text{tr}(AB) = \text{tr}(BA) \tag{3.266}$$

$$\text{tr}(A^T) = \text{tr}(A) \tag{3.267}$$

3.4.2.2 Orthogonality

Given an $m \times n$ matrix A, the product $A^T A$ defines a positive-semidefinite matrix since its associated quadratic form reads

94 76

$$Q(\vec{v}) = \vec{v}^T (A^T A)\vec{v} \overset{(3.245)}{=} (A\vec{v})^T (A\vec{v}) \overset{(3.70)}{=} \langle A\vec{v}, A\vec{v} \rangle = \|A\vec{v}\|^2 \tag{3.268}$$

from which follows that the transformation defined by A preserves vector length if and only
76 if $Q(\vec{v}) = \|\vec{v}\|^2 \overset{(3.70)}{=} \vec{v}^T\vec{v} \iff A^T A = I$.

By representing A as n column vectors of size m, the following symmetric matrix may then be defined

$$A^T A = \begin{bmatrix} \vec{v}_1^T \\ \vec{v}_2^T \\ \vdots \\ \vec{v}_n^T \end{bmatrix} [\vec{v}_1, \vec{v}_2, \ldots, \vec{v}_n] = \begin{bmatrix} \langle \vec{v}_1, \vec{v}_1 \rangle & \langle \vec{v}_1, \vec{v}_2 \rangle & \cdots & \langle \vec{v}_1, \vec{v}_n \rangle \\ \langle \vec{v}_2, \vec{v}_1 \rangle & \langle \vec{v}_2, \vec{v}_2 \rangle & \cdots & \langle \vec{v}_2, \vec{v}_n \rangle \\ \vdots & \vdots & \ddots & \vdots \\ \langle \vec{v}_n, \vec{v}_1 \rangle & \langle \vec{v}_n, \vec{v}_2 \rangle & \cdots & \langle \vec{v}_n, \vec{v}_n \rangle \end{bmatrix} \tag{3.269}$$

A square matrix A whose columns form orthonormal vectors (i.e., orthogonal unit vectors) such that $A^T A = I$ is then referred to as an *orthogonal matrix*, from which follows that a square matrix A is orthogonal if and only if it is invertible with inverse $A^{-1} = A^T$. Transposing both sides of the latter equation then yields $(A^{-1})^T = (A^T)^{-1} = (A^T)^T$, from which additionally follows that the transpose of an orthogonal matrix A is also orthogonal such that $(A^T)^T A^T = AA^T = I$, and that the rows of A also form orthonormal vectors. The
98 value of the *determinant* is then given by

98 98 98

$$\det(A)^2 \overset{(3.286)}{=} \det(A^T)\det(A) \overset{(3.284)}{=} \det(A^T A) = \det(I) \overset{(3.282)}{=} 1 \implies \det(A) = \pm 1 \tag{3.270}$$

whereas $|\det(A)| = 1$ conversely does not necessarily imply orthogonality. Similarly, orthogonal matrices preserve vector length since

$$\|A\vec{v}\|^2 = \langle A\vec{v}, A\vec{v}\rangle \overset{(3.70)}{=} (A\vec{v})^T(A\vec{v}) \overset{(3.245)}{=} \vec{v}^T A^T A\vec{v} = \vec{v}^T\vec{v} \overset{(3.70)}{=} \langle \vec{v}, \vec{v}\rangle = \|\vec{v}\|^2 \qquad (3.271)$$ 76 94 76

3.4.2.3 Eigenvalues and Eigenvectors

An *eigenvector* of a square matrix A is defined as a non-zero vector $\vec{v} \in V$ whose multiplication by A yields $\vec{v}$ scaled by its corresponding scalar *eigenvalue* $\lambda \in \mathbb{R}$

$$A\vec{v} = \lambda\vec{v} \qquad (3.272)$$

whose length is

$$\begin{array}{ll} \bullet \text{ increased} & \text{if } \|\lambda\| > 1 \\ \bullet \text{ equal} & \text{if } \|\lambda\| = 1 \\ \bullet \text{ decreased} & \text{if } \|\lambda\| < 1 \end{array} \qquad (3.273)$$

while its direction is

$$\begin{array}{ll} \bullet \text{ preserved} & \text{if } \lambda > 0 \\ \bullet \text{ undefined} & \text{if } \lambda = 0 \\ \bullet \text{ reversed} & \text{if } \lambda < 0 \end{array} \qquad (3.274)$$

The eigenvalue equation may alternatively be reformulated as

$$0 \overset{(3.272)}{=} A\vec{v} - \lambda\vec{v} = (A - \lambda I)\vec{v} \qquad (3.275)$$ 97

which has a non-zero solution vector $\vec{v}$ if and only if $\det(A - \lambda I) = 0$. It then follows that the eigenvalues of an $n \times n$ matrix A are given by the at-most n real roots, or by the exactly n complex roots, of the *characteristic polynomial* $\det(A - \lambda I)$ of order n.

The multiset of the eigenvalues of a square matrix defines the so-called *spectrum* of the matrix, while the maximum of their absolute values defines its *spectral radius* ρ. Moreover, the sum of the eigenvalues corresponds to the trace of the matrix, whereas their product corresponds to its *determinant* 98

$$\rho(A) \triangleq \max\{|\lambda_1|, \dots, |\lambda_n|\} \qquad (3.276)$$

$$\mathrm{tr}(A) = \sum_{i=1}^{n} \lambda_i \qquad (3.277)$$

$$\det(A) = \prod_{i=1}^{n} \lambda_i \qquad (3.278)$$

from which follows that a matrix is invertible if and only if all of its eigenvalues are non-zero, with the eigenvalues of its inverse defined as $1 \div \lambda_i$, while the eigenvalues of A^k are more generally given by λ_i^k. For any matrix norm, it also holds that $\|A^k\| \geq \rho(A)^k$, while *Gelfand's formula* additionally states that

$$\lim_{k\to\infty} \|A^k\| = \rho(A)^k \qquad (3.279)$$

Once an eigenvalue is known, the associated eigenvectors (possibly infinitely many as in the case of a scalar matrix, but all being linearly independent of the vectors associated with another eigenvalue) may then be computed by explicitly solving the above reformulation of the eigenvalue equation with the given eigenvalue. Together with their associated eigenvalues, the set of all eigenvectors then defines the *eigensystem* of the matrix, whereas the set of all eigenvectors (which are defined within a scaling factor) associated to the same eigenvalue defines an *eigenspace* of the matrix.

In the specific case of a symmetric matrix, every eigenvalue is real, and all of them are positive, negative, non-negative or non-positive if the matrix additionally is positive-definite, negative-definite, positive-semidefinite or negative-semidefinite, respectively. Every symmetric matrix is actually guaranteed to possess an *eigenbasis*, i.e., a basis that consists of linearly independent eigenvectors such that the matrix may be transformed into a diagonal matrix relative to that basis and whose entries are defined by the eigenvalues. It follows that the eigenvalues of a diagonal matrix are readily given by the elements of its main diagonal, each having for corresponding eigenvector the basis vector whose single non-zero coordinate lies on the same row as the given eigenvalue.

3.4.2.4 Determinant

Defining S_{ij} as the $n-1 \times n-1$ submatrix obtained by removing the ith row and j^{th} column from A, as well as the *minor* $m_{ij} \triangleq \det(S_{ij})$ and the *cofactor* $c_{ij} \triangleq (-1)^{i+j} m_{ij}$, the *determinant* of a square matrix A may be recursively formulated as a *Laplace expansion* of the form

$$\det(A) \triangleq |A| \triangleq \sum_{i=1}^{n} (A)_{ij} c_{ij}, \quad \forall j \in [1, n] \tag{3.280}$$

$$= \sum_{j=1}^{n} (A)_{ij} c_{ij}, \quad \forall i \in [1, n] \tag{3.281}$$

which for an $n \times n$ matrix A expands into a sum of $n!$ products of n elements of A, while the determinants of the resulting 1×1 matrices is trivially given by the value of their single element.

The (absolute value of the) determinant actually represents the factor by which a hyper-
102 volume (i.e., area in 2-D or volume 3-D) is scaled when undergoing the *linear transformation* defined by a given matrix, while a positive or negative sign, respectively, corresponds to a *direct transformation* or *indirect transformation*, also called *proper transformation* or *improper transformation*, that, respectively, preserve or reverse orientation (i.e., the winding for a 2-D surface). The identities below additionally hold

$$\det(I) = 1 \tag{3.282}$$

$$\det(cA) = c^n \det(A) \tag{3.283}$$

$$\det(AB) = \det(A)\det(B) \tag{3.284}$$

$$\det(A^k) = \det(A)^k \tag{3.285}$$

$$\det(A^T) = \det(A) \tag{3.286}$$

$$\det\left(\operatorname{adj}(A)\right) = \det(A)^{n-1} \tag{3.287}$$

$$\det(A^{-1}) = \det(A)^{-1} \tag{3.288}$$

where the last equality stems from the fact that

$$\det(A^{-1})\det(A) = \det(A^{-1}A) = \det(I) = 1 \tag{3.289}$$

3.4.2.5 Inverse

Defining the *cofactor matrix* of a square matrix A as the matrix C of cofactors $(C)_{ij} \triangleq c_{ij}$, its transpose is referred to as the *adjugate matrix* (also called classical *adjoint matrix*) $\operatorname{adj}(A) \triangleq$

C^T. The latter verifies

$$A\,\mathrm{adj}(A) = \mathrm{adj}(A)A = \det(A)I \tag{3.290}$$

while it additionally holds that

$$\begin{aligned}
\mathrm{adj}(I) &= I && (3.291)\\
\mathrm{adj}(cA) &= c^{n-1}\,\mathrm{adj}(A) && (3.292)\\
\mathrm{adj}(AB) &= \mathrm{adj}(B)\,\mathrm{adj}(A) && (3.293)\\
\mathrm{adj}(A^k) &= \mathrm{adj}(A)^k && (3.294)\\
\mathrm{adj}(A^T) &= \mathrm{adj}(A)^T && (3.295)\\
\mathrm{adj}\left(\mathrm{adj}(A)\right) &= \det(A)^{n-2}A && (3.296)
\end{aligned}$$

It follows that a square matrix A is invertible (as opposed to being a *singular matrix*, also called *degenerate matrix*) if and only if $\det(A) \neq 0$, i.e., if and only if its column/row vectors are linearly independent such that the matrix has full rank, and the *inverse matrix* of A, which represents an isomorphism allowing the explicit formulation of the solution to a *system of linear equations* (also called *linear system*) with the elements of a vector $\vec{v}$ as unknown variables

$$A\vec{v} = \vec{v}_b \implies \vec{v} = A^{-1}\vec{v}_b \tag{3.297}$$

is then defined as

$$A^{-1} \overset{(3.290)}{=} \frac{1}{\det(A)}\,\mathrm{adj}(A) \tag{3.298}$$ 99

such that $A^{-1}A = AA^{-1} = I$. The following properties then hold

$$\begin{aligned}
(A^{-1})^{-1} &= A && (3.299)\\
(A^T)^{-1} &= (A^{-1})^T \triangleq A^{-T} && (3.300)\\
(cA)^{-1} &= c^{-1}A^{-1} && (3.301)\\
(AB)^{-1} &= B^{-1}A^{-1} && (3.302)
\end{aligned}$$

where the entity on the second line is known as the *inverse transpose matrix*, from which follows that

$$C \overset{(3.242)}{=} \mathrm{adj}(A)^T \overset{(3.298)}{=} \left(\det(A)A^{-1}\right)^T \overset{(3.244)}{=} \det(A)A^{-T} \tag{3.303}$$ 94 99 94

In particular, a matrix A that is its own inverse $A^{-1} = A$ is said to form an *involution*. Shall the matrix be orthogonal instead, it then holds that $A^{-1} = A^T$, from which follows that $C = \det(A)A$.

The inverse of a block matrix is readily given as

$$\begin{bmatrix} A & B \\ C & D \end{bmatrix}^{-1} = \begin{bmatrix} S_D^{-1} & -A^{-1}BS_A^{-1} \\ -D^{-1}CS_D^{-1} & S_A^{-1} \end{bmatrix} = \begin{bmatrix} S_D^{-1} & -S_D^{-1}BD^{-1} \\ -S_A^{-1}CA^{-1} & S_A^{-1} \end{bmatrix} \tag{3.304}$$

where $S_A = D - CA^{-1}B$ and $S_D = A - BD^{-1}C$ are the *Schur complements* of blocks A and D, respectively.

More specifically, the inverse of a 2×2 matrix reads

$$\begin{bmatrix} a_{11} & a_{12} \\ a_{21} & a_{22} \end{bmatrix}^{-1} = \frac{1}{d_2}\begin{bmatrix} +a_{22} & -a_{21} \\ -a_{12} & +a_{11} \end{bmatrix}^T \tag{3.305}$$

with *determinant* 98

98 $$d_2 \overset{(3.280)}{=} a_{11}a_{22} - a_{12}a_{21} \tag{3.306}$$

and each line of the system of linear equations $A\vec{v} = \vec{v}_b$ represents the equation of a 2-D line, while the solution $\vec{v}$ gives the locus of their geometric intersection, as illustrated in
100 *Figure 3.15.*

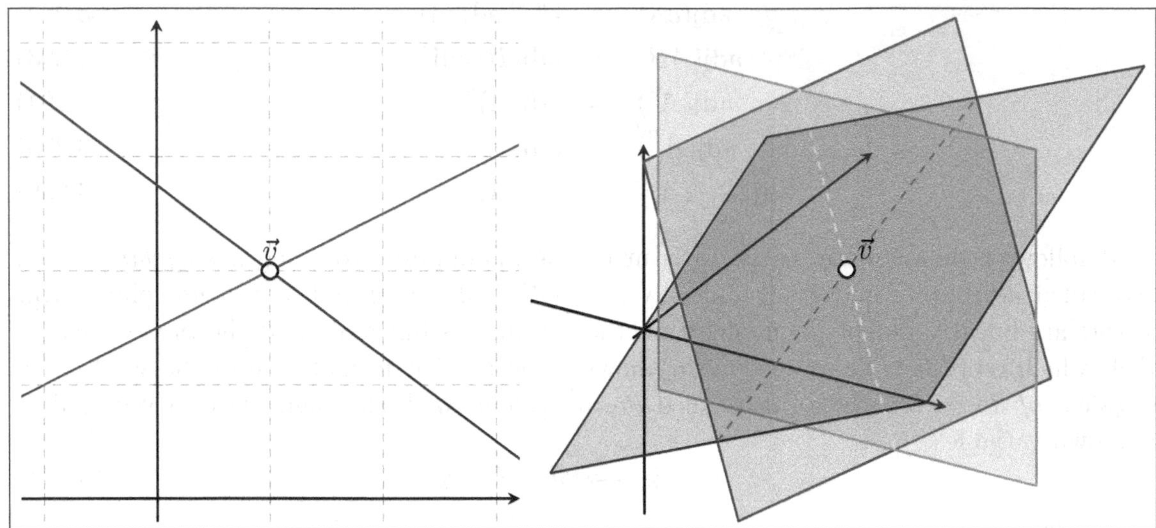

Figure 3.15: System of Linear Equations: Geometric interpretation of the solution to a 2×2 and to a 3×3 system of linear equations.

Similarly, the inverse of a 3×3 matrix is defined as

$$\begin{bmatrix} a_{11} & a_{12} & a_{13} \\ a_{21} & a_{22} & a_{23} \\ a_{31} & a_{32} & a_{33} \end{bmatrix}^{-1} = \frac{1}{d_3} \begin{bmatrix} +(a_{22}a_{33} - a_{32}a_{23}) & -(a_{21}a_{33} - a_{31}a_{23}) & +(a_{21}a_{32} - a_{31}a_{22}) \\ -(a_{12}a_{33} - a_{32}a_{13}) & +(a_{11}a_{33} - a_{31}a_{13}) & -(a_{11}a_{32} - a_{31}a_{12}) \\ +(a_{12}a_{23} - a_{22}a_{13}) & -(a_{11}a_{23} - a_{21}a_{13}) & +(a_{11}a_{22} - a_{21}a_{12}) \end{bmatrix}^T \tag{3.307}$$

101 where, as illustrated in *Figure 3.16*, the *determinant* may be expressed by means of *Sarrus's*
98 *rule* as the sum of the products of the diagonals minus the sum of the products of the anti-diagonals of the matrix obtained by duplicating the first two columns to the right of the third one

98 $$d_3 \overset{(3.280)}{=} a_{11}a_{22}a_{33} + a_{12}a_{23}a_{31} + a_{13}a_{21}a_{32} - a_{31}a_{22}a_{13} - a_{32}a_{23}a_{11} - a_{33}a_{21}a_{12} \tag{3.308}$$

Each line of the system of linear equations $A\vec{v} = \vec{v}_b$ then represents the equation of a 3-D plane, while the solution $\vec{v}$ gives the locus of their geometric intersection, as illustrated in
100 *Figure 3.15.*

3.4.2.6 Cramer's Rule

Given a 3×3 matrix composed of 3 three-dimensional Euclidean column vectors

$$A = [\vec{v}_1, \vec{v}_2, \vec{v}_3] = \begin{bmatrix} x_1 & x_2 & x_3 \\ y_1 & y_2 & y_3 \\ z_1 & z_2 & z_3 \end{bmatrix} \tag{3.309}$$

98 its *determinant* is readily given by the *scalar triple product*
80

$$\det(A) = |A| = |\vec{v}_1, \vec{v}_2, \vec{v}_3| \tag{3.310}$$

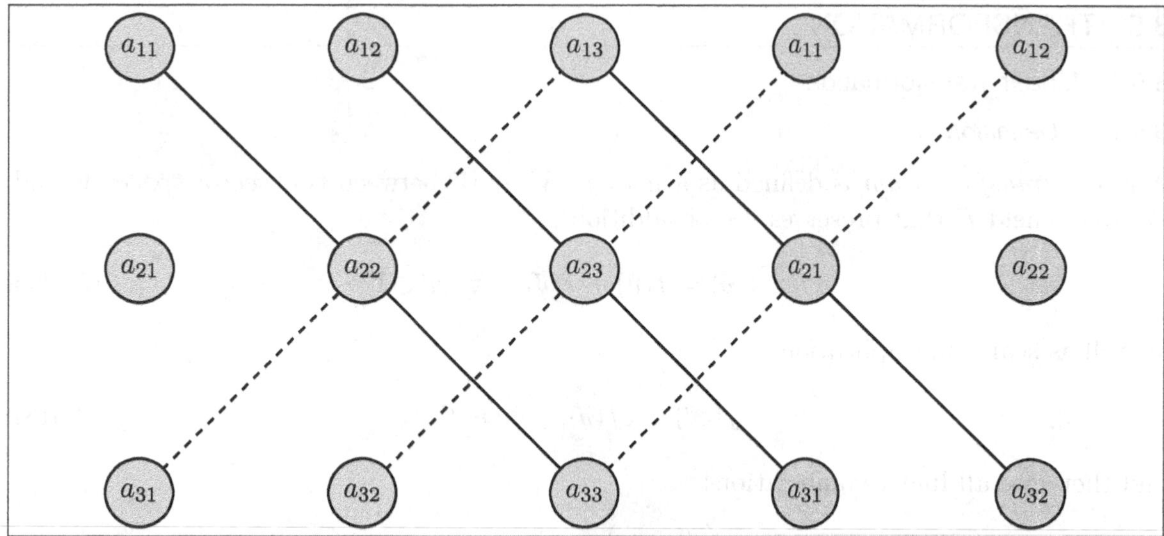

Figure 3.16: Sarrus's Rule: Illustration of Sarrus's rule for computing the determinant of a 3 × 3 matrix.

and its cofactor matrix may be expressed in terms of *cross products* as 78

$$C = [\vec{v}_2 \times \vec{v}_3, \vec{v}_3 \times \vec{v}_1, \vec{v}_1 \times \vec{v}_2] \tag{3.311}$$

Defining the unknowns as the entries of a vector $\vec{v} = [x, y, z]^T$, a system of linear equations $A\vec{v} = \vec{v}_b$ may then be solved by means of *Cramer's rule*, whose three-dimensional form reads 99

$$\vec{v} = A^{-1}\vec{v}_b \overset{(3.298)}{=} \frac{1}{|\vec{v}_1, \vec{v}_2, \vec{v}_3|} \begin{bmatrix} (\vec{v}_2 \times \vec{v}_3)^T \\ (\vec{v}_3 \times \vec{v}_1)^T \\ (\vec{v}_1 \times \vec{v}_2)^T \end{bmatrix} \vec{v}_b \tag{3.312}$$

$$= \frac{1}{|\vec{v}_1, \vec{v}_2, \vec{v}_3|} \begin{bmatrix} \langle \vec{v}_b, \vec{v}_2 \times \vec{v}_3 \rangle \\ \langle \vec{v}_b, \vec{v}_3 \times \vec{v}_1 \rangle \\ \langle \vec{v}_b, \vec{v}_1 \times \vec{v}_2 \rangle \end{bmatrix}$$

$$= \frac{1}{|\vec{v}_1, \vec{v}_2, \vec{v}_3|} \begin{bmatrix} |\vec{v}_b, \vec{v}_2, \vec{v}_3| \\ |\vec{v}_1, \vec{v}_b, \vec{v}_3| \\ |\vec{v}_1, \vec{v}_2, \vec{v}_b| \end{bmatrix} \tag{3.313}$$

Equivalently, given a 3×3 matrix composed of 3 three-dimensional Euclidean row vectors

$$A^T = \begin{bmatrix} \vec{v}_1^T \\ \vec{v}_2^T \\ \vec{v}_3^T \end{bmatrix} = \begin{bmatrix} x_1 & y_1 & z_1 \\ x_2 & y_2 & z_2 \\ x_3 & y_3 & z_3 \end{bmatrix} \tag{3.314}$$

its *determinant* is identically given by the *scalar triple product* 98 80

$$\det(A^T) = |A^T| = |\vec{v}_1, \vec{v}_2, \vec{v}_3| \tag{3.315}$$

whereas, by exploiting the fact that the adjugate/cofactor matrix of a transposed matrix A^T is the transpose of the adjugate/cofactor matrix of A, its cofactor matrix may be expressed in terms of *cross products* as 78

$$C = \begin{bmatrix} (\vec{v}_2 \times \vec{v}_3)^T \\ (\vec{v}_3 \times \vec{v}_1)^T \\ (\vec{v}_1 \times \vec{v}_2)^T \end{bmatrix} \tag{3.316}$$

3.5 TRANSFORMATION

3.5.1 Linear Transformation

3.5.1.1 Definition

71 A *linear transformation* is defined as a map $f : V \to W$ between two *vector spaces* V and W over a field F that preserves vector addition

$$f(\vec{u} + \vec{v}) = f(\vec{u}) + f(\vec{v}), \quad \forall \vec{u}, \vec{v} \in V \tag{3.317}$$

as well as scalar multiplication

$$f(c\vec{v}) = cf(\vec{v}), \quad \forall c \in F \tag{3.318}$$

and therefore all linear combinations

$$f\left(\sum_{i=1}^{n} c_i \vec{v}_i\right) = \sum_{i=1}^{n} c_i f(\vec{v}_i) \tag{3.319}$$

102 As illustrated in *Figure 3.17*, a linear transformation $f : V \to W$ is said to be *injective* (one-to-one), or to form a *monomorphism*, if every element of W is mapped to by at most one element of V, i.e., if and only if $f(\vec{u}) = f(\vec{v}) \implies \vec{u} = \vec{v}, \forall \vec{u}, \vec{v} \in V$, such that f is left-invertible and there exists a map $g : W \to V$ for which $g(f(\vec{v})) = \vec{v}, \forall \vec{v} \in V$. Conversely, a linear transformation is said to be *surjective* (onto), or to form an *epimorphism*, if every element of W is mapped to by at least one element of V, i.e., if and only if $\exists \vec{v} \in V \mid f(\vec{v}) = \vec{w}, \forall \vec{w} \in W$, such that f is right-invertible and there exists a map $g : W \to V$ for which $f(g(\vec{w})) = \vec{w}, \forall \vec{w} \in W$. Finally, a linear transformation is said to be *bijective* (one-to-one and onto), or to form an *isomorphism*, if every element of W is mapped to by exactly one element of V, i.e., if and only if $\exists! \vec{v} \in V \mid f(\vec{v}) = \vec{w}, \forall \vec{w} \in W$, such that f is both left- and right-invertible and there exists an inverse transformation $f^{-1} : W \to V$ for which $f^{-1}(f(\vec{v})) = \vec{v}, \forall \vec{v} \in V$ and $f(f^{-1}(\vec{w})) = \vec{w}, \forall \vec{w} \in W$.

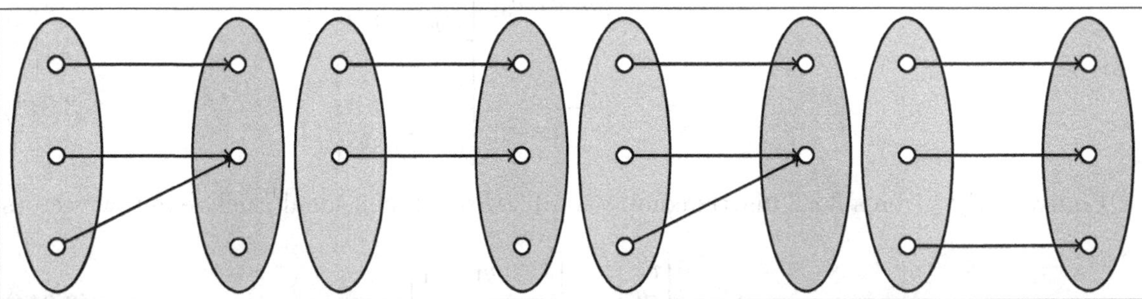

Figure 3.17: Classification of Transformations: Illustration of various types of transformations, including a projection (non-injective and non-surjective), an injection (injective and non-surjective), a surjection (non-injective and surjective) and a bijection (injective and surjective) (from left to right, respectively).

71 Given a basis $\vec{v}_j$ in an n-dimensional *vector space* V and a basis $\vec{w}_i$ in an m-dimensional
71 *vector space* W, a linear transformation $f : V \to W, \vec{v} \mapsto A\vec{v}$ between the two spaces can be
71 solely specified by the images of the basis vectors, since any other element of the *vector spaces*
is uniquely defined as a linear combination of the latter. Defining a vector $\vec{v} \triangleq \sum_{j=1}^{n} c_j \vec{v}_j \in V$

with coefficients c_j, the map may then be represented as an $m \times n$ transformation matrix

$$f(\vec{v}) = f\left(\sum_{j=1}^{n} c_j \vec{v}_j\right) \overset{(3.319)}{=} \sum_{j=1}^{n} c_j f(\vec{v}_j) \overset{(3.70)}{=} \begin{bmatrix} f(\vec{v}_1) & f(\vec{v}_2) & \cdots & f(\vec{v}_n) \end{bmatrix} \vec{v} \tag{3.320}$$ 102 76

whose j^{th} column vector represents the image $f(\vec{v}_j) \in W$ of the basis vector $\vec{v}_j \in V$
transformed into W, while its *determinant* corresponds to the area/volume of the paral- 98
lelogram/parallelepiped formed by their image, as illustrated in *Figure 3.18*. 103

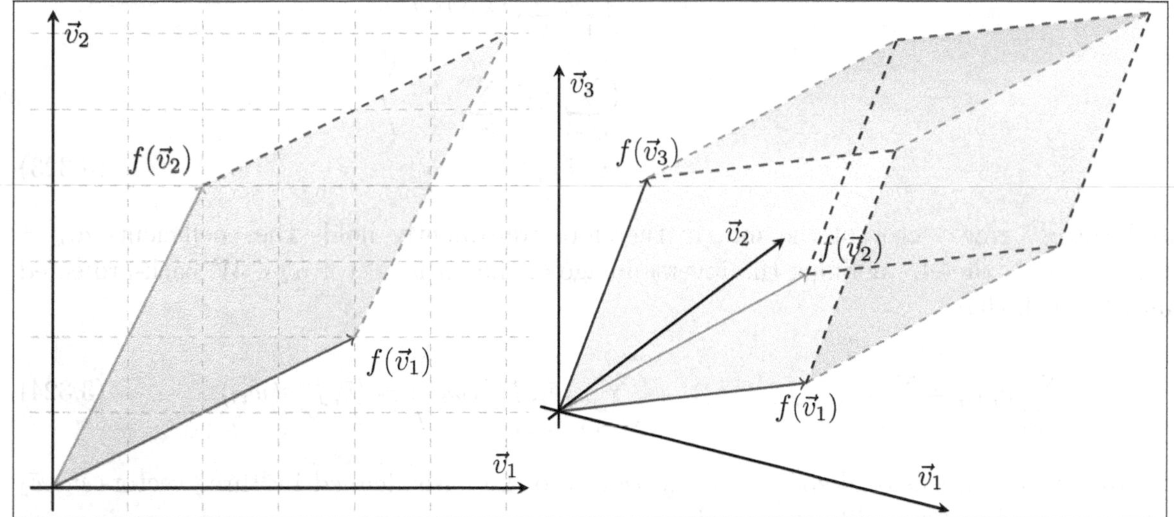

Figure 3.18: Basis Vectors: Illustration of the geometric interpretation of the determinant as the area/volume of the parallelogram/parallelepiped defined by the transformed basis vectors.

Expanding each jth column vector $f(\vec{v}_j) \triangleq \sum_{i=1}^{m} a_{ij} \vec{w}_i$ into its individual coordinates a_{ij} equivalently yields

$$f(\vec{v}) \overset{(3.320)}{=} \begin{bmatrix} a_{11} & a_{12} & \cdots & a_{1n} \\ a_{21} & a_{22} & \cdots & a_{2n} \\ \vdots & \vdots & \ddots & \vdots \\ a_{m1} & a_{m2} & \cdots & a_{mn} \end{bmatrix} \begin{bmatrix} c_1 \\ c_2 \\ \vdots \\ c_n \end{bmatrix} = \sum_{j=1}^{n} c_j \sum_{i=1}^{m} a_{ij} \vec{w}_i = \sum_{i=1}^{m} \vec{w}_i \sum_{j=1}^{n} c_j a_{ij} \tag{3.321}$$ 103

where, in the case of orthonormal basis vectors $\vec{w}_i$ such that $a_{ij} = \langle f(\vec{v}_j), \vec{w}_i \rangle$, the projection coordinates of vector $\vec{v} \in V$ transformed into W read

$$\sum_{j=1}^{n} c_j a_{ij} = \sum_{j=1}^{n} c_j \langle f(\vec{v}_j), \vec{w}_i \rangle = \left\langle \sum_{j=1}^{n} c_j f(\vec{v}_j), \vec{w}_i \right\rangle \overset{(3.320)}{=} \langle f(\vec{v}), \vec{w}_i \rangle \tag{3.322}$$ 103

Shall the basis vectors $\vec{v}_j$ and their images be orthonormal such that $c_j = \langle \vec{v}, \vec{v}_j \rangle$, and the associated matrix therefore be orthogonal, the linear transformation then preserves the *inner*
product 76

103

$$\begin{aligned}
\langle f(\vec{v}), f(\vec{v}')\rangle &\overset{(3.320)}{=} \left\langle \sum_{j=1}^{n} c_j f(\vec{v}_j), \sum_{k=1}^{n} c'_k f(\vec{v}_k)\right\rangle \\
&= \sum_{j=1}^{n} c_j \sum_{k=1}^{n} c'_k \langle f(\vec{v}_j), f(\vec{v}_k)\rangle \\
&= \sum_{j=1}^{n} c_j \sum_{k=1}^{n} c'_k \delta_{jk} \\
&= \sum_{j=1}^{n} c_j \sum_{k=1}^{n} c'_k \langle \vec{v}_j, \vec{v}_k\rangle \\
&= \left\langle \sum_{j=1}^{n} c_j \vec{v}_j, \sum_{k=1}^{n} c'_k \vec{v}_k\right\rangle \\
&= \langle \vec{v}, \vec{v}'\rangle
\end{aligned} \tag{3.323}$$

and the ith row vector of the matrix therefore equivalently holds the coefficients $a_{ij} = \langle \vec{v}_j, f^{-1}(\vec{w}_i)\rangle$, thereby defining the inverse image of the basis vector $\vec{w}_i \in W$ back-projected into V, such that

$$\sum_{j=1}^{n} c_j a_{ij} = \sum_{j=1}^{n} c_j \langle \vec{v}_j, f^{-1}(\vec{w}_i)\rangle = \left\langle \sum_{j=1}^{n} c_j \vec{v}_j, f^{-1}(\vec{w}_i)\right\rangle = \langle \vec{v}, f^{-1}(\vec{w}_i)\rangle \tag{3.324}$$

In a three-dimensional space, a projection into the basis defined by three vectors $\vec{v}_1$, $\vec{v}_2$ and $\vec{v}_3$ may then be readily expressed as

$$[\hat{e}_1, \hat{e}_2, \hat{e}_3]\vec{v} = [\vec{v}_1, \vec{v}_2, \vec{v}_3] M \vec{v} \tag{3.325}$$

with the matrix

$$M = [\vec{v}_1, \vec{v}_2, \vec{v}_3]^{-1}[\hat{e}_1, \hat{e}_2, \hat{e}_3] = [\vec{v}_1, \vec{v}_2, \vec{v}_3]^{-1} \tag{3.326}$$

which, when the vectors are orthogonal, and so is M, yields

$$M\vec{v} = [\vec{v}_1, \vec{v}_2, \vec{v}_3]^T \vec{v} = \begin{bmatrix} \vec{v}_1^T \\ \vec{v}_2^T \\ \vec{v}_3^T \end{bmatrix} \vec{v} = \begin{bmatrix} \langle \vec{v}_1, \vec{v}\rangle \\ \langle \vec{v}_2, \vec{v}\rangle \\ \langle \vec{v}_3, \vec{v}\rangle \end{bmatrix} \tag{3.327}$$

3.5.1.2 Scaling

A *scaling transformation* may be expressed as a diagonal matrix of the form

$$S(s_x, s_y, s_z)\vec{v} \triangleq \begin{bmatrix} s_x & 0 & 0 \\ 0 & s_y & 0 \\ 0 & 0 & s_z \end{bmatrix} \begin{bmatrix} v_x \\ v_y \\ v_z \end{bmatrix} = \begin{bmatrix} s_x v_x \\ s_y v_y \\ s_z v_z \end{bmatrix} \tag{3.328}$$

whose positive scaling factors correspond to the eigenvalues associated with the major axes, which form the eigenvectors of the matrix.

105 As illustrated in *Figure 3.19*, the transformation is then referred to as a *dilation* whenever $s_{x|y|z} > 1$ and as a *contraction* whenever $0 < s_{x|y|z} < 1$. Moreover, the transformation results in a *uniform scaling transformation* by a scalar matrix whenever $s_x = s_y = s_z$, or in a *squeeze mapping transformation* whenever $s_x s_y s_z = 1$ so as to preserve volumes by maintaining a
98 unit *determinant*.

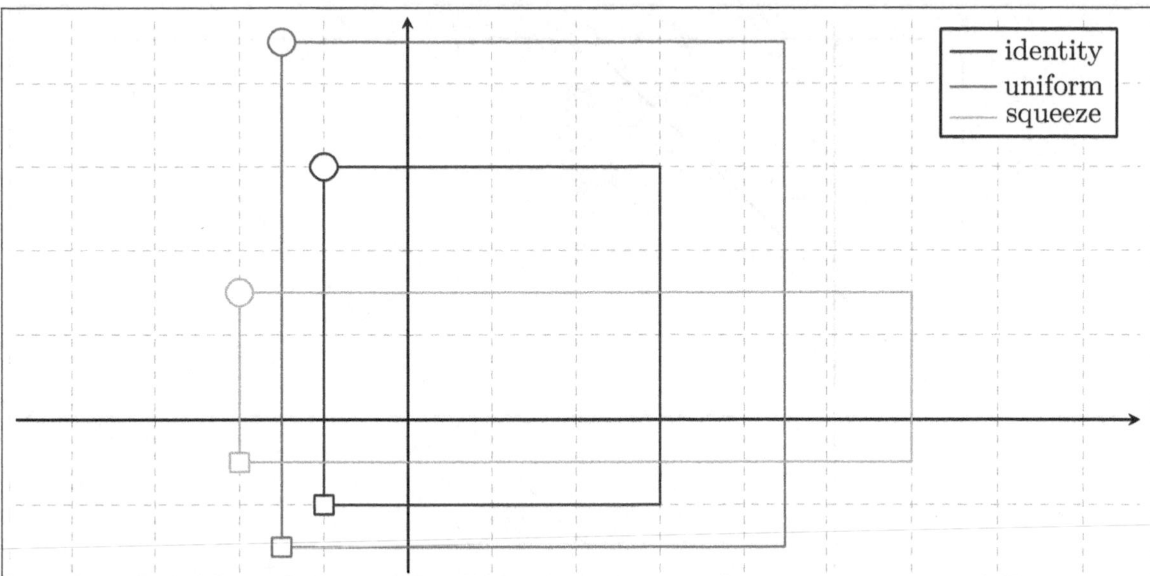

Figure 3.19: Scaling Transformation: Illustration of a uniform scaling and of a squeeze mapping transformation.

Moreover, the following properties hold

- identity: $$S(1,1,1) = I \tag{3.329}$$
- composition: $$S(s_x s'_x, s_y s'_y, s_z s'_z) = S(s_x, s_y, s_z) S(s'_x, s'_y, s'_z) \tag{3.330}$$
- commutativity: $$S(s_x, s_y, s_z) S(s'_x, s'_y, s'_z) = S(s'_x, s'_y, s'_z) S(s_x, s_y, s_z) \tag{3.331}$$
- inverse: $$S^{-1}(s_x, s_y, s_z) = S\left(1 \div s_x, 1 \div s_y, 1 \div s_z\right) \tag{3.332}$$

3.5.1.3 Shearing

As illustrated in *Figure 3.20*, a *shearing transformation* by some angles $\phi_{x|y|z}^{x|y|z}$ may be ex- 106
pressed in matrix form as

$$\begin{aligned} S(\phi_x^y, \phi_x^z, \phi_y^z, \phi_y^x, \phi_z^x, \phi_z^y)\vec{v} &\triangleq \begin{bmatrix} 1 & \tan(\phi_x^y) & \tan(\phi_x^z) \\ \tan(\phi_y^x) & 1 & \tan(\phi_y^z) \\ \tan(\phi_z^x) & \tan(\phi_z^y) & 1 \end{bmatrix} \begin{bmatrix} v_x \\ v_y \\ v_z \end{bmatrix} \\ &= \begin{bmatrix} v_x + \tan(\phi_x^y) v_y + \tan(\phi_x^z) v_z \\ \tan(\phi_y^x) v_x + v_y + \tan(\phi_y^z) v_z \\ \tan(\phi_z^x) v_x + \tan(\phi_z^y) v_y + v_z \end{bmatrix} \end{aligned} \tag{3.333}$$

whose *determinant* reads 98

100

$$\begin{aligned} \det\left(S(\phi_x^y, \phi_x^z, \phi_y^z, \phi_y^x, \phi_z^x, \phi_z^y)\right) &\overset{(3.308)}{=} 1 - \tan(\phi_y^z)\tan(\phi_z^y) - \tan(\phi_x^y)\tan(\phi_y^x) - \tan(\phi_x^z)\tan(\phi_z^x) \\ &\quad + \tan(\phi_x^y)\tan(\phi_y^z)\tan(\phi_z^x) + \tan(\phi_x^z)\tan(\phi_y^x)\tan(\phi_z^y) \end{aligned} \tag{3.334}$$

Letting only the two shear angles of a single column take on non-zero values then yields a planar shearing, where each point is displaced in a direction parallel to a principal plane by an amount proportional to its signed distance to that plane. Letting only the two shear angles of a single row take on non-zero values instead yields an axial shearing, where each point is displaced in a direction parallel to a principal axis by an amount proportional to

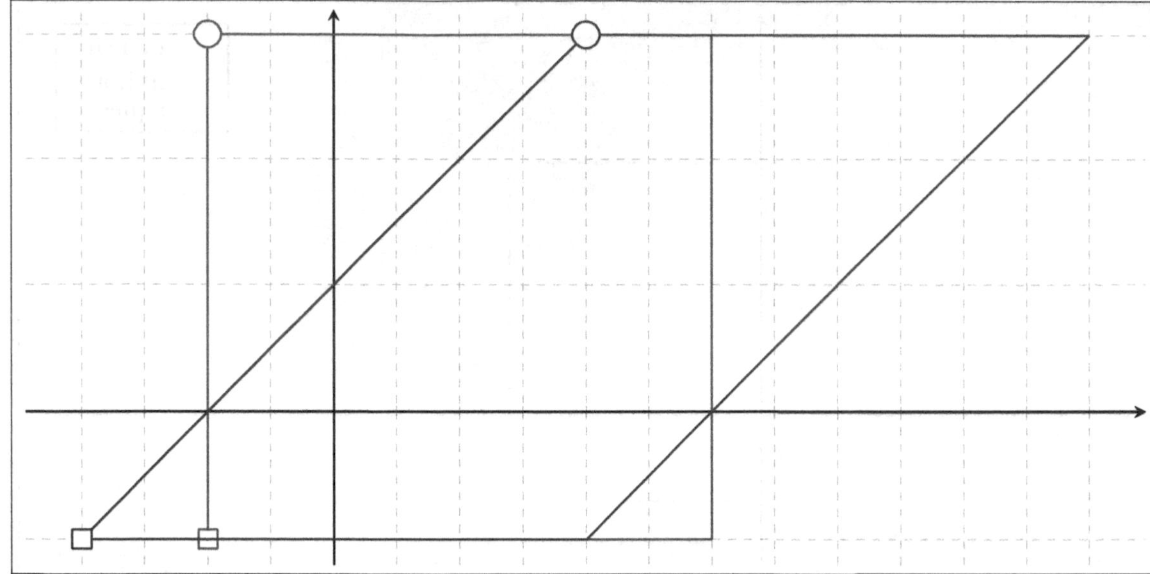

Figure 3.20: Shearing Transformation: Illustration of a shearing transformation.

98 its signed distance to that axis. In both cases, the matrix has a unit *determinant* and the
transformation preserves volumes.

Moreover, the following properties hold

- identity: $$S(0,0,0,0,0,0) = I \tag{3.335}$$

3.5.1.4 Reflection

107 As illustrated in *Figure 3.21*, a *reflection transformation* through a plane orthogonal to
$\hat{n} = [n_x, n_y, n_z]^T$ is defined by the *Householder transformation*

$$R(\hat{n})\vec{v} \triangleq \vec{v} - 2\langle\hat{n}, \vec{v}\rangle\hat{n} = [I - 2\hat{n}\langle\hat{n}, \cdot\rangle]\,\vec{v} \tag{3.336}$$

which may be expressed as a symmetric and orthogonal matrix of the form

$$\begin{aligned} R(\hat{n}) &= \begin{bmatrix} 1 & 0 & 0 \\ 0 & 1 & 0 \\ 0 & 0 & 1 \end{bmatrix} - 2 \begin{bmatrix} n_x \\ n_y \\ n_z \end{bmatrix} \begin{bmatrix} n_x \\ n_y \\ n_z \end{bmatrix}^T \\ &= \begin{bmatrix} 1 & 0 & 0 \\ 0 & 1 & 0 \\ 0 & 0 & 1 \end{bmatrix} - 2 \begin{bmatrix} n_x n_x & n_x n_y & n_x n_z \\ n_y n_x & n_y n_y & n_y n_z \\ n_z n_x & n_z n_y & n_z n_z \end{bmatrix} \\ &= \begin{bmatrix} 1 - 2n_x^2 & -2n_x n_y & -2n_x n_z \\ -2n_y n_x & 1 - 2n_y^2 & -2n_y n_z \\ -2n_z n_x & -2n_z n_y & 1 - 2n_z^2 \end{bmatrix} \end{aligned} \tag{3.337}$$

98 with eigenvalues $\{1, 1, -1\}$ and *determinant* -1. It then follows that each reflection reverses
handedness, such that a series of an even/odd number of successive reflections is equivalent to
a proper/improper rotation preserving/reversing handedness. More specifically, a reflection
104 through a plane orthogonal to one of the major axes degenerates into a non-uniform *scaling*
with a single negative scale factor, whereas two negative scale factors correspond to an axial
98 reflection with eigenvalues $\{1, -1, -1\}$ and *determinant* 1, and setting all three scale factors

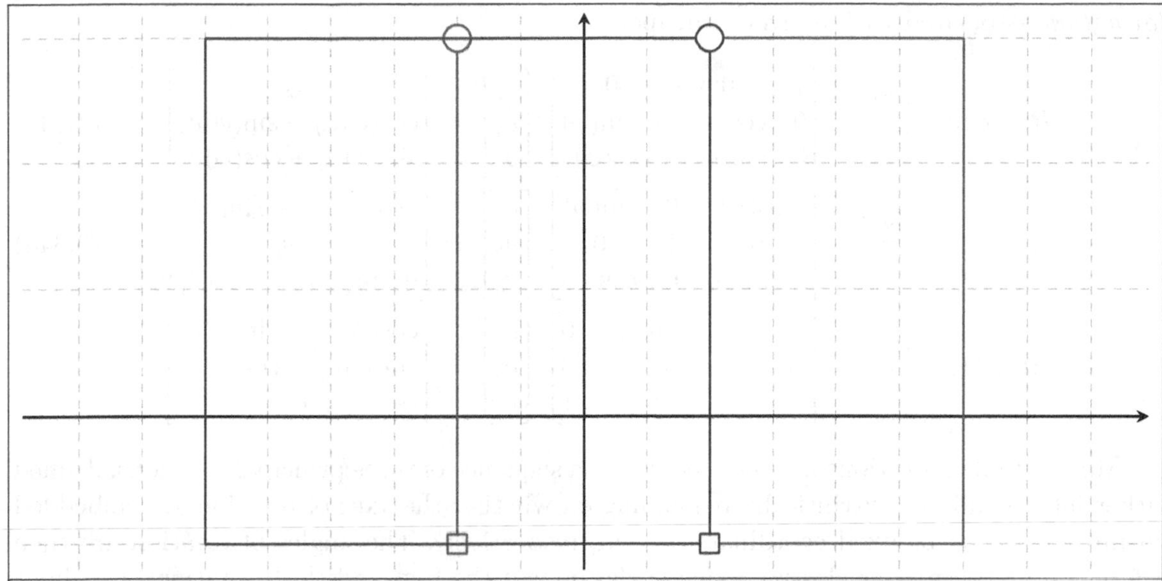

Figure 3.21: Reflection Transformation: Illustration of a reflection transformation.

to -1 would result in a central reflection, also called a *point inversion transformation*, about the origin with eigenvalues $\{-1, -1, -1\}$ and *determinant* -1. 98

Moreover, the following properties hold

- identity: $$R(\vec{0}) = I \quad (3.338)$$
- symmetry: $$R^T(\hat{n}) = R(\hat{n}) \quad (3.339)$$
- orthogonality: $$R^{-1}(\hat{n}) = R^T(\hat{n}) \quad (3.340)$$
- involution: $$R^{-1}(\hat{n}) = R(\hat{n}) \quad (3.341)$$

3.5.1.5 Rotation

Euler Angles By representing the two coordinates embedded in the plane orthogonal to one of the principal axes by means of a single *complex number* $z = x + \imath y = re^{\imath\varphi}$, a *rotation* 85
transformation by an angle ϕ around the axis may be readily formulated in terms of the *rotor* $e^{\imath\phi}$ as

$$\begin{aligned} re^{\imath(\varphi+\phi)} &= r\cos(\varphi+\phi) + \imath r\sin(\varphi+\phi) \\ &= (r\cos(\varphi)\cos(\phi) - r\sin(\varphi)\sin(\phi)) + \imath(r\cos(\varphi)\sin(\phi) + r\sin(\varphi)\cos(\phi)) \\ &= (x\cos(\phi) - y\sin(\phi)) + \imath(x\sin(\phi) + y\cos(\phi)) && (3.342) \\ &\overset{(3.144)}{=} (x + \imath y) \times (\cos(\phi) + \imath\sin(\phi)) \\ &= ze^{\imath\phi} && (3.343) \end{aligned}$$

86

Expressing the complex-valued rotor in matrix form then yields the *Givens rotation trans-*

formation associated with a given principal plane

107
$$R(\hat{x},\phi)\vec{v} \overset{(3.342)}{=} \begin{bmatrix} 1 & 0 & 0 \\ 0 & \cos(\phi) & -\sin(\phi) \\ 0 & \sin(\phi) & \cos(\phi) \end{bmatrix} \begin{bmatrix} v_x \\ v_y \\ v_z \end{bmatrix} = \begin{bmatrix} v_x \\ \cos(\phi)v_y - \sin(\phi)v_z \\ \sin(\phi)v_y + \cos(\phi)v_z \end{bmatrix} \quad (3.344)$$

107
$$R(\hat{y},\phi)\vec{v} \overset{(3.342)}{=} \begin{bmatrix} \cos(\phi) & 0 & \sin(\phi) \\ 0 & 1 & 0 \\ -\sin(\phi) & 0 & \cos(\phi) \end{bmatrix} \begin{bmatrix} v_x \\ v_y \\ v_z \end{bmatrix} = \begin{bmatrix} \cos(\phi)v_x + \sin(\phi)v_z \\ v_y \\ -\sin(\phi)v_x + \cos(\phi)v_z \end{bmatrix} \quad (3.345)$$

107
$$R(\hat{z},\phi)\vec{v} \overset{(3.342)}{=} \begin{bmatrix} \cos(\phi) & -\sin(\phi) & 0 \\ \sin(\phi) & \cos(\phi) & 0 \\ 0 & 0 & 1 \end{bmatrix} \begin{bmatrix} v_x \\ v_y \\ v_z \end{bmatrix} = \begin{bmatrix} \cos(\phi)v_x - \sin(\phi)v_y \\ \sin(\phi)v_x + \cos(\phi)v_y \\ v_z \end{bmatrix} \quad (3.346)$$

More complex rotations may be modeled as a sequence of three principal rotations, defined either intrinsically or extrinsically depending on whether the axes of rotation are embedded within a rotating or fixed coordinate system, respectively. The angles of rotation are then referred to as (proper or classic) *Euler angles* in case the first and third rotations are about the same axis (i.e., x-y-x, x-z-x, y-x-y, y-z-y, z-x-z, z-y-z), or more specifically as *Tait–Bryan angles*, also called *nautical angles*, shall all three rotations be about different axes (i.e., x-
108 y-z, x-z-y, y-x-z, y-z-x, z-x-y, z-y-x). As illustrated in *Figure 3.22*, the latter angles allow the control of the extrinsically defined *yaw* $\phi_z \in (-\pi, \pi]$, *pitch* $\phi_y \in [-\pi/2, \pi/2]$ and *roll* $\phi_x \in (-\pi, \pi]$ of a rigid body, which in matrix form reads

$$\begin{aligned} R(\phi_z,\phi_y,\phi_x) &\triangleq R(\hat{z},\phi_z)R(\hat{y},\phi_y)R(\hat{x},\phi_x) && (3.347) \\ &= \begin{bmatrix} \cos(\phi_z)\cos(\phi_y) & -\sin(\phi_z) & \cos(\phi_z)\sin(\phi_y) \\ \sin(\phi_z)\cos(\phi_y) & \cos(\phi_z) & \sin(\phi_z)\sin(\phi_y) \\ -\sin(\phi_y) & 0 & \cos(\phi_y) \end{bmatrix} \begin{bmatrix} 1 & 0 & 0 \\ 0 & \cos(\phi_x) & -\sin(\phi_x) \\ 0 & \sin(\phi_x) & \cos(\phi_x) \end{bmatrix} \\ &= \begin{bmatrix} c_z c_y & -s_z c_x + c_z s_y s_x & s_z s_x + c_z s_y c_x \\ s_z c_y & c_z c_x + s_z s_y s_x & -c_z s_x + s_z s_y c_x \\ -s_y & c_y s_x & c_y c_x \end{bmatrix} && (3.348) \end{aligned}$$

where $c_{x|y|z} \triangleq \cos(\phi_{x|y|z})$ and $s_{x|y|z} \triangleq \sin(\phi_{x|y|z})$.

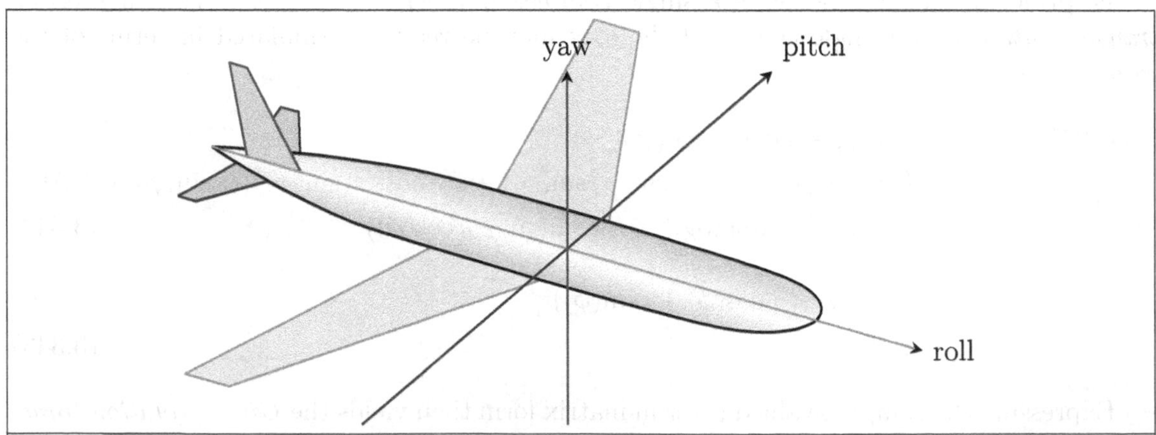

Figure 3.22: Yaw, Pitch and Roll: Illustration of the yaw, pitch and roll principal axes of an aircraft.

Conversely, the corresponding principal angles may be readily retrieved from the resulting matrix [Shoemake, 1994] by means of the following identities whenever $\phi_y \neq \pm\pi/2$ such that

$\cos(\phi_y) \neq 0$

$$\frac{\left(R(\phi_z, \phi_y, \phi_x)\right)_{21}}{\left(R(\phi_z, \phi_y, \phi_x)\right)_{11}} \overset{(3.348)}{=} \tan(\phi_z) \tag{3.349}$$ 108

$$\left(R(\phi_z, \phi_y, \phi_x)\right)_{31} \overset{(3.348)}{=} -\sin(\phi_y) \tag{3.350}$$ 108

$$\frac{\left(R(\phi_z, \phi_y, \phi_x)\right)_{32}}{\left(R(\phi_z, \phi_y, \phi_x)\right)_{33}} \overset{(3.348)}{=} \tan(\phi_x) \tag{3.351}$$ 108

and by means of the following identities whenever $\phi_y = {}^{\pi}/_{2}$ such that $\sin(\phi_y) = 1$

$$-\left(R(\phi_z, \phi_y, \phi_x)\right)_{12} = \left(R(\phi_z, \phi_y, \phi_x)\right)_{23} \overset{(3.348)}{=} \sin(\phi_z - \phi_x) \tag{3.352}$$ 108

$$\left(R(\phi_z, \phi_y, \phi_x)\right)_{22} = \left(R(\phi_z, \phi_y, \phi_x)\right)_{13} \overset{(3.348)}{=} \cos(\phi_z - \phi_x) \tag{3.353}$$ 108

while the following identities hold whenever $\phi_y = -{}^{\pi}/_{2}$ such that $\sin(\phi_y) = -1$

$$\left(R(\phi_z, \phi_y, \phi_x)\right)_{12} = \left(R(\phi_z, \phi_y, \phi_x)\right)_{23} \overset{(3.348)}{=} -\sin(\phi_z + \phi_x) \tag{3.354}$$ 108

$$\left(R(\phi_z, \phi_y, \phi_x)\right)_{22} = \left(R(\phi_z, \phi_y, \phi_x)\right)_{13} \overset{(3.348)}{=} \cos(\phi_z + \phi_x) \tag{3.355}$$ 108

As illustrated in *Figure 3.23*, such a parameterization is, however, prone to a degeneracy 109
known as *gimbal lock* whenever the pitch angle $\phi_y = \pm{}^{\pi}/_{2}$, causing the yaw ϕ_z and roll ϕ_x axes to coincide, in turn leading to the loss of one of the two other degrees of freedom.

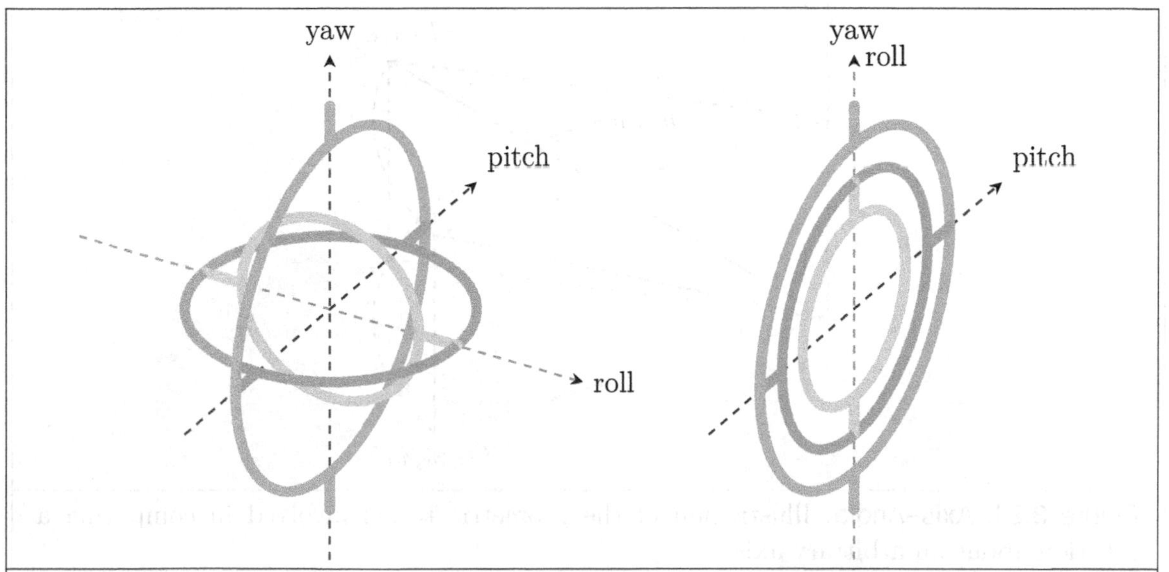

Figure 3.23: Euler Angles: Illustration of the yaw, pitch or roll angles of three nested gimbals.

Axis–Angle General rotations may alternatively be specified using an *axis–angle* representation in which the axis of rotation is described by a unit three-dimensional vector and the angle of rotation by a scalar value. As an equivalent alternative, both may be more compactly represented as a single unnormalized *rotation vector*, so-called *Euler vector*, whose direction and magnitude describe the axis and angle of rotation, respectively. It then follows that any rotation reduces in essence to a total of three degrees of freedom, each corresponding to an angle of the three principal rotations into which any rotation may be decomposed.

82
80 By defining a basis $[\hat{u}, \vec{v} - \langle \hat{u}, \vec{v} \rangle \hat{u}, \hat{u} \times \vec{v}]$ where $\|\vec{v} - \langle \hat{u}, \vec{v} \rangle \hat{u}\| \overset{(3.110)}{=} \|\hat{u} \times \vec{v}\| \overset{(3.96)}{=}$
110 $\|\vec{v}\| \sin(\angle(\hat{u}, \vec{v}))$ as illustrated in *Figure 3.24*, a rotation about an arbitrary unit axis $\hat{u}$ may be expressed in terms of *Rodrigues's rotation formula* as

$$\begin{aligned} R(\hat{u}, \phi)\vec{v} &\triangleq \langle \hat{u}, \vec{v} \rangle \hat{u} + \cos(\phi)(\vec{v} - \langle \hat{u}, \vec{v} \rangle \hat{u}) + \sin(\phi)\hat{u} \times \vec{v} & (3.356) \\ &= (1 - \cos(\phi))\langle \hat{u}, \vec{v} \rangle \hat{u} + \cos(\phi)\vec{v} + \sin(\phi)\hat{u} \times \vec{v} & (3.357) \\ &= [(1 - \cos(\phi))\hat{u}\langle \hat{u}, \cdot \rangle + \cos(\phi) I + \sin(\phi)\hat{u} \times \cdot]\,\vec{v} & (3.358) \end{aligned}$$

which in matrix form reads [Pique, 1990]

78
79

$$\begin{aligned} R(\hat{u}, \phi) &\underset{(3.89)}{\overset{(3.87)}{=}} (1 - \cos(\phi)) \begin{bmatrix} u_x \\ u_y \\ u_z \end{bmatrix} \begin{bmatrix} u_x \\ u_y \\ u_z \end{bmatrix}^T + \cos(\phi) \begin{bmatrix} 1 & 0 & 0 \\ 0 & 1 & 0 \\ 0 & 0 & 1 \end{bmatrix} + \sin(\phi) \begin{bmatrix} 0 & -u_z & u_y \\ u_z & 0 & -u_x \\ -u_y & u_x & 0 \end{bmatrix} \\ &= (1 - c) \begin{bmatrix} u_x u_x & u_x u_y & u_x u_z \\ u_y u_x & u_y u_y & u_y u_z \\ u_z u_x & u_z u_y & u_z u_z \end{bmatrix} + \begin{bmatrix} c & -u_z s & u_y s \\ u_z s & c & -u_x s \\ -u_y s & u_x s & c \end{bmatrix} & (3.359) \\ &= \begin{bmatrix} u_x^2(1-c) + c & u_x u_y(1-c) - u_z s & u_x u_z(1-c) + u_y s \\ u_y u_x(1-c) + u_z s & u_y^2(1-c) + c & u_y u_z(1-c) - u_x s \\ u_z u_x(1-c) - u_y s & u_z u_y(1-c) + u_x s & u_z^2(1-c) + c \end{bmatrix} & (3.360) \end{aligned}$$

where $c \triangleq \cos(\phi)$ and $s \triangleq \sin(\phi)$.

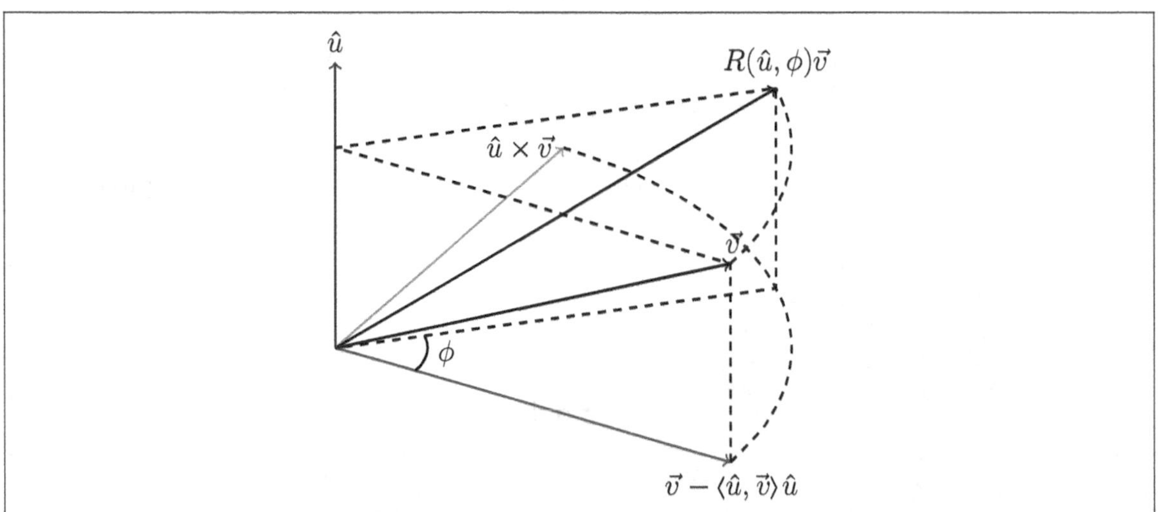

Figure 3.24: Axis–Angle: Illustration of the geometric terms involved in computing a rotation about an arbitrary axis.

Alternatively, the rotation about the unit axis $\hat{u}$ can be equivalently formulated by means
81
81 of the *vector triple product* expansion $\hat{u} \times (\hat{u} \times \vec{v}) \overset{(3.106)}{=} \langle \hat{u}, \vec{v} \rangle \hat{u} - \|\hat{u}\|^2 \vec{v}$ to yield

110

$$\begin{aligned} R(\hat{u}, \phi)\vec{v} &\overset{(3.357)}{=} (1 - \cos(\phi))(\hat{u} \times (\hat{u} \times \vec{v}) + \vec{v}) + \cos(\phi)\vec{v} + \sin(\phi)\hat{u} \times \vec{v} \\ &= (1 - \cos(\phi))\hat{u} \times (\hat{u} \times \vec{v}) + \vec{v} + \sin(\phi)\hat{u} \times \vec{v} & (3.361) \\ &= [(1 - \cos(\phi))\hat{u} \times (\hat{u} \times \cdot) + I + \sin(\phi)\hat{u} \times \cdot]\vec{v} & (3.362) \end{aligned}$$

which in matrix form reads

$$R(\hat{u},\phi) \overset{(3.89)}{=} (1-\cos(\phi))\begin{bmatrix}0 & -u_z & u_y\\ u_z & 0 & -u_x\\ -u_y & u_x & 0\end{bmatrix}^2 + \begin{bmatrix}1&0&0\\0&1&0\\0&0&1\end{bmatrix} + \sin(\phi)\begin{bmatrix}0 & -u_z & u_y\\ u_z & 0 & -u_x\\ -u_y & u_x & 0\end{bmatrix}$$ 79

$$= (1-c)\begin{bmatrix}-u_z^2-u_y^2 & u_y u_x & u_z u_x\\ u_x u_y & -u_z^2-u_x^2 & u_z u_y\\ u_x u_z & u_y u_z & -u_y^2-u_x^2\end{bmatrix} + \begin{bmatrix}1 & -u_z s & u_y s\\ u_z s & 1 & -u_x s\\ -u_y s & u_x s & 1\end{bmatrix}$$

$$= \begin{bmatrix}u_x^2+(u_z^2+u_y^2)c & u_y u_x(1-c)-u_z s & u_z u_x(1-c)+u_y s\\ u_x u_y(1-c)+u_z s & u_y^2+(u_z^2+u_x^2)c & u_z u_y(1-c)-u_x s\\ u_x u_z(1-c)-u_y s & u_y u_z(1-c)+u_x s & u_z^2+(u_y^2+u_x^2)c\end{bmatrix} \quad (3.363)$$

where $c \triangleq \cos(\phi)$ and $s \triangleq \sin(\phi)$.

Conversely, the corresponding axis–angle representation may be readily retrieved from the resulting matrix by means of the following identities [Goldman, 1991b]

$$\mathrm{tr}\,(R(\hat{u},\phi)) \overset{(3.360)}{=} (u_x^2+u_y^2+u_z^2)(1-\cos(\phi))+3\cos(\phi)$$ 110

$$\overset{(3.363)}{=} (u_x^2+u_y^2+u_z^2)+2(u_x^2+u_y^2+u_z^2)\cos(\phi)$$ 111

$$= 1+2\cos(\phi) \quad (3.364)$$

and whenever $\phi \neq 0 \wedge \phi \neq \pm\pi$ such that $\sin(\phi) \neq 0$

$$\begin{bmatrix}(R(\hat{u},\phi))_{32}-(R(\hat{u},\phi))_{23}\\ (R(\hat{u},\phi))_{13}-(R(\hat{u},\phi))_{31}\\ (R(\hat{u},\phi))_{21}-(R(\hat{u},\phi))_{12}\end{bmatrix} \overset{(3.360)}{\underset{(3.363)}{=}} \begin{bmatrix}2u_x\sin(\phi)\\ 2u_y\sin(\phi)\\ 2u_z\sin(\phi)\end{bmatrix} = 2\sin(\phi)\begin{bmatrix}u_x\\u_y\\u_z\end{bmatrix} \quad (3.365)$$ 110 111

In the case where $\phi = 0$, there is no rotation, while whenever $\phi = \pm\pi$ instead such that $\sin(\phi) = 0$, the matrix reduces to

$$R(\hat{u},\phi) \overset{(3.360)}{=} \begin{bmatrix}2u_x^2-1 & 2u_x u_y & 2u_x u_z\\ 2u_y u_x & 2u_y^2-1 & 2u_y u_z\\ 2u_z u_x & 2u_z u_y & 2u_z^2-1\end{bmatrix} \quad (3.366)$$ 110

and the numerical stability issues associated with divisions by small numbers can be avoided by extracting one of the axis coordinates from the greatest component of the diagonal, and computing the remaining coordinates by dividing the non-diagonal terms by it.

According to *Euler's rotation theorem*, any sequence of rotations about a fixed point in three-dimensional space reduces to a single equivalent rotation by a given angle about a given axis, so-called *Euler axis*, running through the fixed point, from which follows that the product of two rotation matrices is itself a rotation matrix. However, computing the angle and Euler axis describing an arbitrary sequence of rotations directly without conversion into another representation is generally non-trivial, and may instead be more effectively handled by means of a *quaternion* representation. 111

Quaternion Given an *axis–angle* representation, a rotation by an angle ϕ about an arbitrary 109
unit vector $\hat{u}$ can be equivalently encoded as a unit *quaternion*, then referred to as *versor* 90
[Maillot, 1990], expressed in *polar coordinates* as $q \triangleq e^{\hat{u}\frac{\phi}{2}} = \cos\left(\frac{\phi}{2}\right) + \hat{u}\sin\left(\frac{\phi}{2}\right) = (q_s, \vec{q_v})$. 91
By letting an ordinary 3-D vector $\vec{v}$ define the vector part of a *quaternion* $p \triangleq (0, \vec{v})$ with a 90

zero scalar part, Rodrigues's rotation formula may be reformulated as the vector part of the *conjugation* of p by the *rotor* q

110 $$R(\hat{u},\phi)\vec{v} \overset{(3.357)}{=} 2\sin\left(\frac{\phi}{2}\right)^2\langle\hat{u},\vec{v}\rangle\hat{u} + \left(\cos\left(\frac{\phi}{2}\right)^2 - \sin\left(\frac{\phi}{2}\right)^2\right)\vec{v} + 2\cos\left(\frac{\phi}{2}\right)\sin\left(\frac{\phi}{2}\right)\hat{u}\times\vec{v}$$

$$= 2\langle\vec{q_v},\vec{v}\rangle\vec{q_v} + (q_s^2 - \|\vec{q_v}\|^2)\vec{v} + 2q_s\vec{q_v}\times\vec{v} \quad (3.367)$$

91 $$\overset{(3.202)}{=} (q_s,\vec{q_v})(0,\vec{v})(q_s,-\vec{q_v})$$

92 $$\overset{(3.218)}{=} qpq^{-1} \quad (3.368)$$

whose scalar part is necessarily zero. It is also worth noting that $R(\hat{u},\phi\pm 2\pi) = e^{\hat{u}(\frac{\phi}{2}\pm\pi)} = -q$, from which follows that both q and $-q$ describe the same rotation. The inverse rotation
92 $q^{-1} \overset{(3.218)}{=} \bar{q} = e^{-\hat{u}\frac{\phi}{2}}$ is then equivalently defined either by the opposite angle along the same axis or by the same angle along the opposite axis.

Conversely, the angle and unit axis vector corresponding to the rotation described by a versor $q = (q_s,\vec{q_v})$ can be readily extracted as

$$\phi = 2\arccos(q_s) = 2\arcsin(\|\vec{q_v}\|) = 2\,\mathrm{arctan2}(\|\vec{q_v}\|, q_s) \quad (3.369)$$

$$\hat{u} = \vec{q_v} \div \|\vec{q_v}\| \quad (3.370)$$

The composition of successive rotations may then be readily expressed as the conjugation by the product of their corresponding versors

112 $$R(\hat{u}_2,\phi_2)R(\hat{u}_1,\phi_1)\vec{v} \overset{(3.368)}{=} q_2(q_1pq_1^{-1})q_2^{-1} = (q_2q_1)p(q_1^{-1}q_2^{-1}) = (q_2q_1)p(q_2q_1)^{-1} \quad (3.371)$$

By noting that exponentiation corresponds to a multiplication of the angle of rotation, *spherical linear interpolation* between an initial rotation state q_0 and a final rotation state q_1 can additionally be formulated as the application of the initial rotation followed by a fraction t of its inverse combined with the final rotation

$$\mathrm{slerp}(t,q_0,q_1) \triangleq (q_1q_0^{-1})^tq_0 = q_0(q_0^{-1}q_1)^t = (q_0q_1^{-1})^{1-t}q_1 = q_1(q_1^{-1}q_0)^{1-t} \quad (3.372)$$

with q_0 potentially being defined as the identity, while interpolation through the shortest
76 path may be guaranteed by negating one of the two versors shall their *inner product* be negative. Alternatively, the interpolation may be equivalently carried by adapting the vector formulation into

82 $$\mathrm{slerp}(t,q_0,q_1) \overset{(3.112)}{=} \frac{\sin((1-t)\theta)}{\sin(\theta)}q_0 + \frac{\sin(t\theta)}{\sin(\theta)}q_1 \quad (3.373)$$

where $\theta \triangleq \arccos(\langle q_0,q_1\rangle)$. Higher-order interpolation is similarly given by an adaptation of
343 cubic *Hermite spline* interpolation to *quaternions*. Given four rotation states q_{i-1}, q_i, q_{i+1}
90 and q_{i+2}, *spherical quadrangle interpolation* is then readily defined as

$$\mathrm{squad}(t,q_i,q_{i+1},d_i,d_{i+1}) \triangleq \mathrm{slerp}\left(2t(1-t), \mathrm{slerp}(t,q_i,q_{i+1}), \mathrm{slerp}(t,d_i,d_{i+1})\right) \quad (3.374)$$

90 with the tangential *quaternions* given by

$$d_i \triangleq q_i\exp\left(-\frac{\ln(q_i^{-1}q_{i-1}) + \ln(q_i^{-1}q_{i+1})}{4}\right) \quad (3.375)$$

Due to numerical errors occurring in computations with fixed-precision floating-point
representations, the product of several versors might in practice yield a *quaternion* that is 90
no longer normalized, in which case renormalization can be readily carried, whereas directly
reestablishing the orthogonality of the corresponding rotation matrix is generally more complex [Raible, 1990]. Furthermore, *quaternions* provide a more compact representation and 90
more effective concatenation than matrices, but at the cost of a more computationally expensive vector rotation.

Given a versor $q = (q_s, \vec{q}_v) = q_s + \imath q_x + \jmath q_y + k q_z$, the rotated vector may also be reformulated as

112

$$R(\hat{u}, \phi)\vec{v} \overset{(3.367)}{=} [2\vec{q}_v\langle\vec{q}_v, \cdot\rangle + (q_s^2 - \|\vec{q}_v\|^2)I + 2q_s\vec{q}_v \times \cdot]\vec{v} \tag{3.376}$$

which in matrix form reads [Shoemake, 1991]

78 79

$$\begin{aligned} R(\hat{u}, \phi) &\underset{(3.89)}{\overset{(3.87)}{=}} 2\begin{bmatrix} q_x \\ q_y \\ q_z \end{bmatrix}\begin{bmatrix} q_x \\ q_y \\ q_z \end{bmatrix}^T + (q_s^2 - \|\vec{q}_v\|^2)\begin{bmatrix} 1 & 0 & 0 \\ 0 & 1 & 0 \\ 0 & 0 & 1 \end{bmatrix} + 2q_s\begin{bmatrix} 0 & -q_z & q_y \\ q_z & 0 & -q_x \\ -q_y & q_x & 0 \end{bmatrix} \\ &= 2\begin{bmatrix} q_xq_x & q_xq_y & q_xq_z \\ q_yq_x & q_yq_y & q_yq_z \\ q_zq_x & q_zq_y & q_zq_z \end{bmatrix} + \begin{bmatrix} q_s^2 - \|\vec{q}_v\|^2 & -2q_sq_z & 2q_sq_y \\ 2q_sq_z & q_s^2 - \|\vec{q}_v\|^2 & -2q_sq_x \\ -2q_sq_y & 2q_sq_x & q_s^2 - \|\vec{q}_v\|^2 \end{bmatrix} \\ &= \begin{bmatrix} d_x(q) & 2(q_xq_y - q_sq_z) & 2(q_xq_z + q_sq_y) \\ 2(q_yq_x + q_sq_z) & d_y(q) & 2(q_yq_z - q_sq_x) \\ 2(q_zq_x - q_sq_y) & 2(q_zq_y + q_sq_x) & d_z(q) \end{bmatrix} \end{aligned} \tag{3.377}$$

with the diagonal terms defined using the identity $1 \overset{(3.207)}{=} q_s^2 + \|\vec{q}_v\|^2$ 91

$$d_x(q) \triangleq 2(q_x^2 + q_s^2) - 1 = q_s^2 + q_x^2 - q_y^2 - q_z^2 = 1 - 2(q_y^2 + q_z^2) \tag{3.378}$$

$$d_y(q) \triangleq 2(q_y^2 + q_s^2) - 1 = q_s^2 - q_x^2 + q_y^2 - q_z^2 = 1 - 2(q_z^2 + q_x^2) \tag{3.379}$$

$$d_z(q) \triangleq 2(q_z^2 + q_s^2) - 1 = q_s^2 - q_x^2 - q_y^2 + q_z^2 = 1 - 2(q_x^2 + q_y^2) \tag{3.380}$$

where the second formulation, known as the *Euler–Rodrigues formula* as it was initially
presented by Euler prior to the introduction of *quaternions* by Hamilton, is expressed in 90
homogeneous form so as to yield an orthogonal matrix scaled by $\|q\|^2$ shall the *quaternion* 90
not be normalized, whereas the latter inhomogeneous expressions stem from alternatively
formulating the rotation about the unit axis $\hat{u}$ by means of the *vector triple product* expansion 81
$\vec{q}_v \times (\vec{q}_v \times \vec{v}) \overset{(3.106)}{=} \langle\vec{q}_v, \vec{v}\rangle\vec{q}_v - \|\vec{q}_v\|^2\vec{v}$ to yield 81

112

$$\begin{aligned} R(\hat{u}, \phi)\vec{v} &\overset{(3.367)}{=} 2(\vec{q}_v \times (\vec{q}_v \times \vec{v}) + \|\vec{q}_v\|^2\vec{v}) + (q_s^2 - \|\vec{q}_v\|^2)\vec{v} + 2q_s\vec{q}_v \times \vec{v} \\ &= 2\vec{q}_v \times (\vec{q}_v \times \vec{v}) + (q_s^2 + \|\vec{q}_v\|^2)\vec{v} + 2q_s\vec{q}_v \times \vec{v} \\ &= 2\vec{q}_v \times (\vec{q}_v \times \vec{v} + q_s\vec{v}) + \vec{v} \end{aligned} \tag{3.381}$$

Conversely, the corresponding versor can be readily retrieved from the resulting matrix while avoiding the numerical stability issues associated with divisions by small numbers by means of the following identities

113 $$\operatorname{tr}(R(\hat{u},\phi)) \overset{(3.377)}{=} (q_s^2 - q_x^2 - q_y^2 - q_z^2) + 2q_s^2 \tag{3.382}$$

113 $$(R(\hat{u},\phi))_{11} \overset{(3.377)}{=} (q_s^2 - q_x^2 - q_y^2 - q_z^2) + 2q_x^2 \tag{3.383}$$

113 $$(R(\hat{u},\phi))_{22} \overset{(3.377)}{=} (q_s^2 - q_x^2 - q_y^2 - q_z^2) + 2q_y^2 \tag{3.384}$$

113 $$(R(\hat{u},\phi))_{33} \overset{(3.377)}{=} (q_s^2 - q_x^2 - q_y^2 - q_z^2) + 2q_z^2 \tag{3.385}$$

and if $\operatorname{tr}(R(\hat{u},\phi)) = \max\{\operatorname{tr}(R(\hat{u},\phi)), (R(\hat{u},\phi))_{11}, (R(\hat{u},\phi))_{22}, (R(\hat{u},\phi))_{33}\}$

113 $$\operatorname{tr}(R(\hat{u},\phi)) \overset{(3.377)}{=} 3q_s^2 - q_x^2 - q_y^2 - q_z^2 = 4q_s^2 - 1 \tag{3.386}$$

113 $$\begin{bmatrix} (R(\hat{u},\phi))_{32} - (R(\hat{u},\phi))_{23} \\ (R(\hat{u},\phi))_{13} - (R(\hat{u},\phi))_{31} \\ (R(\hat{u},\phi))_{21} - (R(\hat{u},\phi))_{12} \end{bmatrix} \overset{(3.377)}{=} \begin{bmatrix} 4q_sq_x \\ 4q_sq_y \\ 4q_sq_z \end{bmatrix} = 4q_s \begin{bmatrix} q_x \\ q_y \\ q_z \end{bmatrix} \tag{3.387}$$

or if $(R(\hat{u},\phi))_{11} = \max\{\operatorname{tr}(R(\hat{u},\phi)), (R(\hat{u},\phi))_{11}, (R(\hat{u},\phi))_{22}, (R(\hat{u},\phi))_{33}\}$

113 $$+(R(\hat{u},\phi))_{11} - (R(\hat{u},\phi))_{22} - (R(\hat{u},\phi))_{33} \overset{(3.377)}{=} -q_s^2 + 3q_x^2 - q_y^2 - q_z^2 = 4q_x^2 - 1 \tag{3.388}$$

113 $$\begin{bmatrix} (R(\hat{u},\phi))_{32} - (R(\hat{u},\phi))_{23} \\ (R(\hat{u},\phi))_{13} + (R(\hat{u},\phi))_{31} \\ (R(\hat{u},\phi))_{21} + (R(\hat{u},\phi))_{12} \end{bmatrix} \overset{(3.377)}{=} \begin{bmatrix} 4q_xq_s \\ 4q_xq_z \\ 4q_xq_y \end{bmatrix} = 4q_x \begin{bmatrix} q_s \\ q_z \\ q_y \end{bmatrix} \tag{3.389}$$

or if $(R(\hat{u},\phi))_{22} = \max\{\operatorname{tr}(R(\hat{u},\phi)), (R(\hat{u},\phi))_{11}, (R(\hat{u},\phi))_{22}, (R(\hat{u},\phi))_{33}\}$

113 $$-(R(\hat{u},\phi))_{11} + (R(\hat{u},\phi))_{22} - (R(\hat{u},\phi))_{33} \overset{(3.377)}{=} -q_s^2 - q_x^2 + 3q_y^2 - q_z^2 = 4q_y^2 - 1 \tag{3.390}$$

113 $$\begin{bmatrix} (R(\hat{u},\phi))_{32} + (R(\hat{u},\phi))_{23} \\ (R(\hat{u},\phi))_{13} - (R(\hat{u},\phi))_{31} \\ (R(\hat{u},\phi))_{21} + (R(\hat{u},\phi))_{12} \end{bmatrix} \overset{(3.377)}{=} \begin{bmatrix} 4q_yq_z \\ 4q_yq_s \\ 4q_yq_x \end{bmatrix} = 4q_y \begin{bmatrix} q_z \\ q_s \\ q_x \end{bmatrix} \tag{3.391}$$

or if $(R(\hat{u},\phi))_{33} = \max\{\operatorname{tr}(R(\hat{u},\phi)), (R(\hat{u},\phi))_{11}, (R(\hat{u},\phi))_{22}, (R(\hat{u},\phi))_{33}\}$

113 $$-(R(\hat{u},\phi))_{11} - (R(\hat{u},\phi))_{22} + (R(\hat{u},\phi))_{33} \overset{(3.377)}{=} -q_s^2 - q_x^2 - q_y^2 + 3q_z^2 = 4q_z^2 - 1 \tag{3.392}$$

113 $$\begin{bmatrix} (R(\hat{u},\phi))_{32} + (R(\hat{u},\phi))_{23} \\ (R(\hat{u},\phi))_{13} + (R(\hat{u},\phi))_{31} \\ (R(\hat{u},\phi))_{21} - (R(\hat{u},\phi))_{12} \end{bmatrix} \overset{(3.377)}{=} \begin{bmatrix} 4q_zq_y \\ 4q_zq_x \\ 4q_zq_s \end{bmatrix} = 4q_z \begin{bmatrix} q_y \\ q_x \\ q_s \end{bmatrix} \tag{3.393}$$

107 Alternatively, the versor corresponding to a given set of *Euler angles* is readily given by the product of the versors corresponding to each of the yaw, pitch and roll rotations

$$\begin{aligned} &\big(\cos(\phi_z/2) + k\sin(\phi_z/2)\big)\big(\cos(\phi_y/2) + \jmath\sin(\phi_y/2)\big)\big(\cos(\phi_x/2) + \imath\sin(\phi_x/2)\big) \\ &= \big(\cos(\phi_z/2)\cos(\phi_y/2)\cos(\phi_x/2) + \sin(\phi_z/2)\sin(\phi_y/2)\sin(\phi_x/2)\big) \\ &+ \imath\big(\cos(\phi_z/2)\cos(\phi_y/2)\sin(\phi_x/2) - \sin(\phi_z/2)\sin(\phi_y/2)\cos(\phi_x/2)\big) \\ &+ \jmath\big(\cos(\phi_z/2)\sin(\phi_y/2)\cos(\phi_x/2) + \sin(\phi_z/2)\cos(\phi_y/2)\sin(\phi_x/2)\big) \\ &+ k\big(\sin(\phi_z/2)\cos(\phi_y/2)\cos(\phi_x/2) - \cos(\phi_z/2)\sin(\phi_y/2)\sin(\phi_x/2)\big) \end{aligned} \tag{3.394}$$

while the three angles may conversely be retrieved from a given versor by associating the elements of their respective matrices to yield

$$\frac{2(q_y q_x + q_s q_z)}{d_x(q)} \overset{(3.349)}{=} \tan(\phi_z) \tag{3.395}$$ 109

$$2(q_z q_x - q_s q_y) \overset{(3.350)}{=} -\sin(\phi_y) \tag{3.396}$$ 109

$$\frac{2(q_z q_y + q_s q_x)}{d_z(q)} \overset{(3.351)}{=} \tan(\phi_x) \tag{3.397}$$ 109

Properties As illustrated in *Figure 3.25*, a rotation matrix is necessarily an orthogonal 115
matrix with eigenvalues $\{1, e^{\imath\phi}, e^{-\imath\phi}\}$ and *determinant* +1, and whose eigenvector associated 98
to the eigenvalue 1 is defined by the axis of rotation. Moreover, the following properties hold

- identity: $$R(\hat{u}, 0) = I \tag{3.398}$$
- composition: $$R(\hat{u}, \phi + \phi') = R(\hat{u}, \phi)R(\hat{u}, \phi') \tag{3.399}$$
- commutativity: $$R(\hat{u}, \phi)R(\hat{u}, \phi') = R(\hat{u}, \phi')R(\hat{u}, \phi) \tag{3.400}$$
- non-commutativity: $$R(\hat{u}, \phi)R(\hat{v}, \phi') \neq R(\hat{v}, \phi')R(\hat{u}, \phi) \tag{3.401}$$
- orthogonality: $$R^{-1}(\hat{u}, \phi) = R^T(\hat{u}, \phi) \tag{3.402}$$
- inverse: $$R^{-1}(\hat{u}, \phi) = R(\hat{u}, -\phi) = R(-\hat{u}, \phi) \tag{3.403}$$

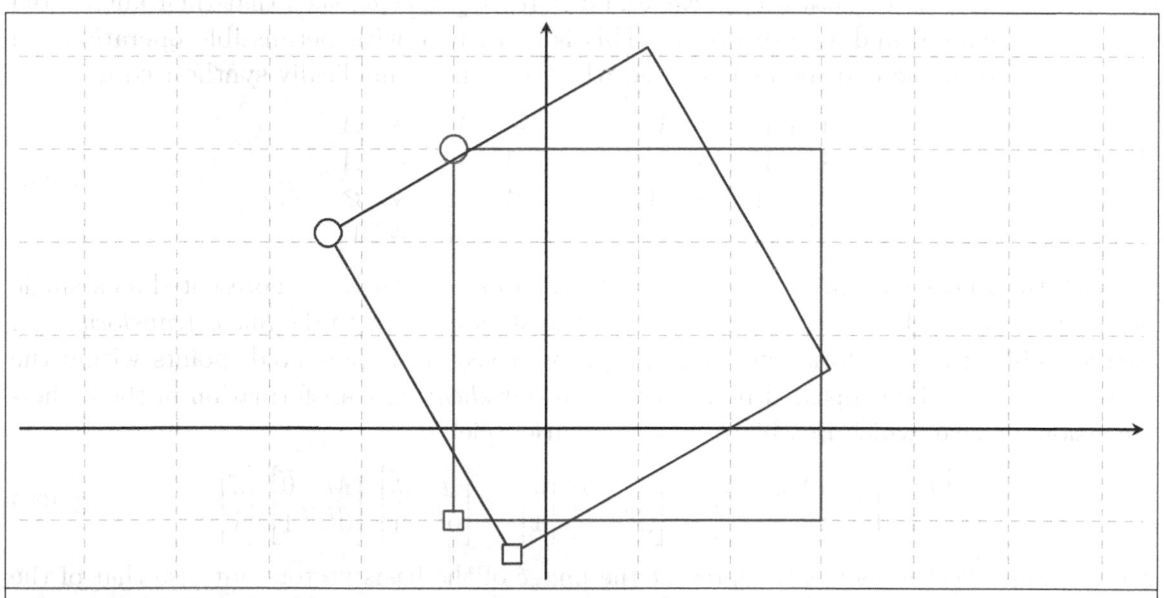

Figure 3.25: Rotation Transformation: Illustration of a rotation transformation.

Further Reading Additional material may be found in books dedicated to rotation transforms [Vince, 2011b].

3.5.2 Affine Transformation

3.5.2.1 Definition

An *affine transformation* is defined as a map $f : A \to B$ between two *affine spaces* A and B 72 that preserves all affine combinations

$$f\left(\sum_{i=1}^{n} \alpha_i \vec{a}_i\right) = \sum_{i=1}^{n} \alpha_i f(\vec{a}_i), \quad \forall \alpha_i \mid \sum_{i=1}^{n} \alpha_i = 1 \tag{3.404}$$

102 such that the map on the points determines a *linear transformation* l on the vectors between
72 points of the *affine space* A

$$\overrightarrow{f(\vec{a})f(\vec{b})} = l(\vec{ab}), \quad \forall \vec{a}, \vec{b} \in A \tag{3.405}$$

102 An affine transformation is therefore composed of a *linear transformation* (of position
117 vectors) and a *translation* (thereby allowing the origin to be not necessarily preserved at the
zero point), the vector from the initial position of a point $\vec{a}$ to its image $f(\vec{a})$ being known
102 as the *displacement vector* $\overrightarrow{\vec{a}f(\vec{a})}$. It follows that every *linear transformation* is affine, but
not all affine transformations are linear, although an affine transformation acts linearly on
vectors expressed as the difference between two points.

An affine transformation is uniquely defined by the mapping of a non-degenerated simplex
(e.g., a triangle in 2-D or a tetrahedron in 3-D) into another. By representing the *linear*
102 *transformation* as a matrix multiplication M on A and the *translation* as a vector addition
117 $\vec{b}$ in B, the affine map may be formulated as $f(\vec{a}) = M\vec{a} + \vec{b}$.

In order to unify the transformation of points and vectors, both can be represented by
71 means of *augmented coordinates*, thereby embedding the n-dimensional *vector space* as a
71 slice of fixed augmented coordinate through an $n+1$-dimensional *vector space*. By treating
the origin of the affine frame as an additional basis vector, the expressions for a vector and
a point then become $\vec{v} = 0\vec{b}_0 + \sum_{i=1}^{n} c_i \vec{b}_i$ and $\vec{a} = 1\vec{b}_0 + \sum_{i=1}^{n} c_i \vec{b}_i$, such that their augmented
coordinate equals 0 and 1, respectively. This is consistent with permissible operations on
elements between the two spaces V and A, which may be symbolically synthesized as

$$\begin{array}{lcl} V+V & \rightarrow & V \\ V-V & \rightarrow & V \\ V+A & \rightarrow & A \\ V-A & \rightarrow & \varnothing \end{array} \qquad \begin{array}{lcl} A+V & \rightarrow & A \\ A-V & \rightarrow & A \\ A+A & \rightarrow & \varnothing \\ A-A & \rightarrow & V \end{array} \tag{3.406}$$

102 Both the *linear transformation* and the *translation* may then be represented as a single
117 *augmented matrix* obtained by appending the *translation* vector to the *linear transformation*
117
102 matrix. While the translation-invariant property of vectors is preserved, points within the
105 original space can be translated by means of a linear *shearing* transformation in the higher-
dimensional space, which in a block matrix notation yields

$$\begin{bmatrix} f(\vec{a}) \\ 1 \end{bmatrix} = \begin{bmatrix} M\vec{a}+\vec{b} \\ 1 \end{bmatrix} = \begin{bmatrix} M & \vec{b} \\ \vec{0}^T & 1 \end{bmatrix} \begin{bmatrix} \vec{a} \\ 1 \end{bmatrix} = \begin{bmatrix} I & \vec{b} \\ \vec{0}^T & 1 \end{bmatrix} \begin{bmatrix} M & \vec{0} \\ \vec{0}^T & 1 \end{bmatrix} \begin{bmatrix} \vec{a} \\ 1 \end{bmatrix} \tag{3.407}$$

whose column vectors not only represent the image of the basis vectors but also that of the origin of the coordinate system

$$\begin{bmatrix} [\vec{v}_1, \vec{v}_2, \vec{v}_3] & \vec{o} \\ \vec{0}^T & 1 \end{bmatrix} [1,0,0,0]^T = \begin{bmatrix} \vec{v}_1 \\ 0 \end{bmatrix} \tag{3.408}$$

$$\begin{bmatrix} [\vec{v}_1, \vec{v}_2, \vec{v}_3] & \vec{o} \\ \vec{0}^T & 1 \end{bmatrix} [0,1,0,0]^T = \begin{bmatrix} \vec{v}_2 \\ 0 \end{bmatrix} \tag{3.409}$$

$$\begin{bmatrix} [\vec{v}_1, \vec{v}_2, \vec{v}_3] & \vec{o} \\ \vec{0}^T & 1 \end{bmatrix} [0,0,1,0]^T = \begin{bmatrix} \vec{v}_3 \\ 0 \end{bmatrix} \tag{3.410}$$

$$\begin{bmatrix} [\vec{v}_1, \vec{v}_2, \vec{v}_3] & \vec{o} \\ \vec{0}^T & 1 \end{bmatrix} [0,0,0,1]^T = \begin{bmatrix} \vec{o} \\ 1 \end{bmatrix} \tag{3.411}$$

In a three-dimensional space, a projection into the frame defined by three vectors $\vec{v}_1$, $\vec{v}_2$ and $\vec{v}_3$ and origin $\vec{o}$ can then be readily expressed as

$$\begin{bmatrix} \hat{e}_1 & \hat{e}_2 & \hat{e}_3 & \vec{0} \\ 0 & 0 & 0 & 1 \end{bmatrix} \begin{bmatrix} \vec{a} \\ 1 \end{bmatrix} = \begin{bmatrix} \vec{v}_1 & \vec{v}_2 & \vec{v}_3 & \vec{o} \\ 0 & 0 & 0 & 1 \end{bmatrix} M \begin{bmatrix} \vec{a} \\ 1 \end{bmatrix} \tag{3.412}$$

with the matrix

$$M = \begin{bmatrix} \vec{v}_1 & \vec{v}_2 & \vec{v}_3 & \vec{o} \\ 0 & 0 & 0 & 1 \end{bmatrix}^{-1} \begin{bmatrix} \hat{e}_1 & \hat{e}_2 & \hat{e}_3 & \vec{0} \\ 0 & 0 & 0 & 1 \end{bmatrix} = \begin{bmatrix} \vec{v}_1 & \vec{v}_2 & \vec{v}_3 & \vec{o} \\ 0 & 0 & 0 & 1 \end{bmatrix}^{-1} \tag{3.413}$$

which, when the vectors are orthogonal, and so is the submatrix, yields

$$M \begin{bmatrix} \vec{a} \\ 1 \end{bmatrix} = \begin{bmatrix} [\vec{v}_1, \vec{v}_2, \vec{v}_3]^T & -[\vec{v}_1, \vec{v}_2, \vec{v}_3]^T \vec{o} \\ \vec{0}^T & 1 \end{bmatrix} \begin{bmatrix} \vec{a} \\ 1 \end{bmatrix} = \begin{bmatrix} \vec{v}_1^T & -\langle \vec{v}_1, \vec{o} \rangle \\ \vec{v}_2^T & -\langle \vec{v}_2, \vec{o} \rangle \\ \vec{v}_3^T & -\langle \vec{v}_3, \vec{o} \rangle \\ \vec{0}^T & 1 \end{bmatrix} \begin{bmatrix} \vec{a} \\ 1 \end{bmatrix} = \begin{bmatrix} \langle \vec{v}_1, \vec{a} - \vec{o} \rangle \\ \langle \vec{v}_2, \vec{a} - \vec{o} \rangle \\ \langle \vec{v}_3, \vec{a} - \vec{o} \rangle \\ 1 \end{bmatrix} \tag{3.414}$$

3.5.2.2 Translation

As illustrated in *Figure 3.26*, a *translation transformation* may be expressed as an upper-triangular matrix of the form 117

$$T(t_x, t_y, t_z)\vec{v} \triangleq \begin{bmatrix} 1 & 0 & 0 & t_x \\ 0 & 1 & 0 & t_y \\ 0 & 0 & 1 & t_z \\ 0 & 0 & 0 & 1 \end{bmatrix} \begin{bmatrix} v_x \\ v_y \\ v_z \\ v_w \end{bmatrix} = \begin{bmatrix} v_x + v_w t_x \\ v_y + v_w t_y \\ v_z + v_w t_z \\ v_w \end{bmatrix} \tag{3.415}$$

thereby resulting in the same displacement vector for all points while leaving vectors unaffected.

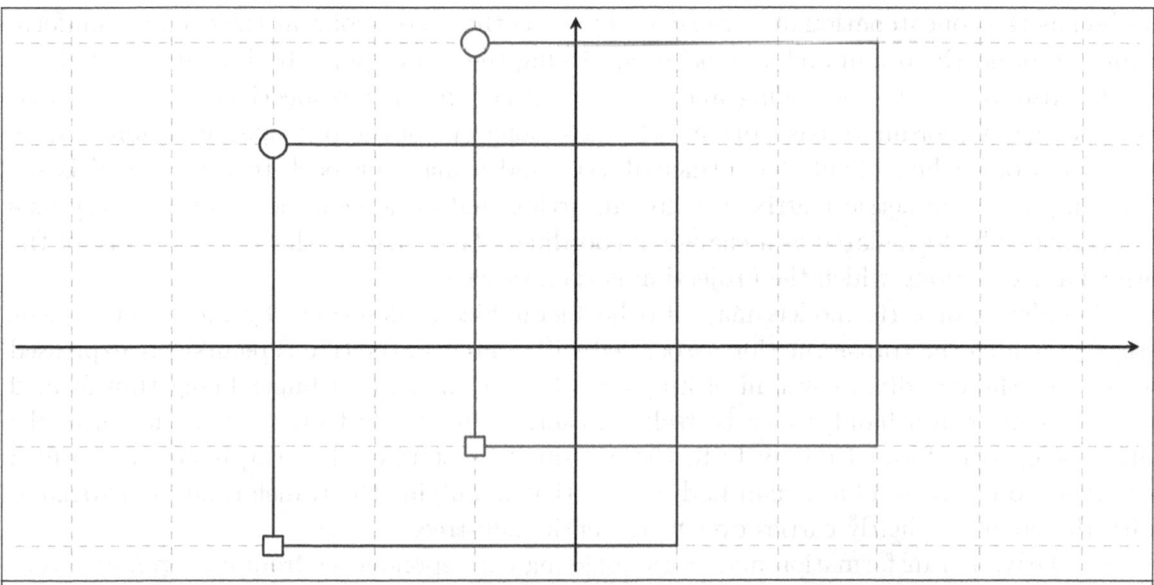

Figure 3.26: Translation Transformation: Illustration of a translation transformation.

Moreover, the following properties hold

- identity: $$T(0,0,0) = I \tag{3.416}$$
- composition: $$T(t_x + t'_x, t_y + t'_y, t_z + t'_z) = T(t_x, t_y, t_z)T(t'_x, t'_y, t'_z) \tag{3.417}$$
- commutativity: $$T(t_x, t_y, t_z)T(t'_x, t'_y, t'_z) = T(t'_x, t'_y, t'_z)T(t_x, t_y, t_z) \tag{3.418}$$
- inverse: $$T^{-1}(t_x, t_y, t_z) = T(-t_x, -t_y, -t_z) \tag{3.419}$$

3.5.3 Composite Transformation

3.5.3.1 Overview

By exploiting the properties of linear maps, a series of elementary transformations can be combined into a single *composite transformation*. As such, the sum of two linear maps $f : V \to W$ and $g : V \to W$ also is a linear map $(f+g)(\vec{v}) = f(\vec{v})+g(\vec{v})$, expressed as the addition of the respective transformation matrices. Similarly, the product of a linear map $f : V \to W$ with a scalar c is again a linear map $(cf)(\vec{v}) = cf(\vec{v})$, expressed as the multiplication of the associated transformation matrix with the scalar. Also, the composition of two linear maps $f : U \to V$ and $g : V \to W$ is a linear map $(g \circ f)(\vec{v}) = g(f(\vec{v}))$, expressed as the product of the respective transformation matrices by means of the associative property of matrix multiplication

$$A_g(A_f\vec{v}) = (A_gA_f)\vec{v} \tag{3.420}$$

106 117 For instance, the combination of a *reflection* across a plane and a *translation* along that
107 plane results in a so-called *glide reflection transformation*, while the combination of a *rotation*
106 with a (planar) *reflection* or with a point inversion is known as a *roto-reflection transforma-*
107 *tion* or *roto-inversion transformation*, respectively. A *rotation* about an arbitrary point may
117 also be described as the concatenation of a *translation* placing the point at the origin, a
107 117 *rotation* around the origin, and a *translation* placing the point back to its original location
[Goldman, 1990, Goldman, 1991a].

Similarly, a *homothetic transformation*, i.e., a dilation about a center point, can be de-
117 scribed as the concatenation of a *translation* placing the center point at the origin, a uniform
104 117 *scaling* around the origin and a *translation* placing the center point back to its original po-
107 104 sition. Also, a *rotation* or *scaling* about an arbitrary axis may, respectively, be formulated
as a change of coordinate basis placing the axis along one of the principal axes, followed by
107 104 a *rotation* or *scaling* about that principal axis, and a mapping back to the original basis,
resulting in a symmetric matrix. Finally, an orthogonal projection along an arbitrary axis can similarly be formulated as a change of coordinate basis placing the axis along one of the principal axes, along which the projection is then carried.

Complex geometric models may also be hierarchically described by means of a *scene graph*, in which the transformation associated with a node of the tree is recursively expressed relative to the coordinate system of its parent (e.g., a model of a finger being transformed relative to that of a hand, which is itself transformed relatively to that of the forearm, the latter being transformed relatively to the coordinate system of the arm, itself transformed relatively to the torso of a human body), such that modifying the transformation associated with the latter implicitly carries over to the entire sub-tree.

Similarly, a transformation matrix establishing correspondences from a *coordinate space* to another can be effectively represented as the concatenation of the transformations between each pair of intermediate spaces, whose canonical instances include

- *surface coordinate space*: defined by the normal, tangent and bitangent at a given surface point, which is the intrinsic coordinate system of a BRDF.

- *object coordinate space*: representing the intrinsic coordinate system of a given object in which the positions of its vertices lie, and which is related to world space by means of the so-called "model" transformation, the latter being possibly expressed hierarchically as in a scene graph or in a time-dependent manner for animated objects.

- *world coordinate space*: representing the reference system of the whole scene in which the roots of all hierarchical models lie, and which is related to camera space by means of the so-called "view" transformation.

- *camera coordinate space*: representing the intrinsic coordinate system of a given camera based on its world-space position and orientation, which may be related to the various *image-plane coordinate spaces* by means of a *projective transformation*. 668 121

3.5.3.2 Forward Transformation

The composition of two general *affine transformations* may be explicitly formulated as 115
$f_2(f_1(\vec{a})) = M_2(M_1\vec{a} + \vec{b}_1) + \vec{b}_2 = (M_2M_1)\vec{a} + (M_2\vec{b}_1 + \vec{b}_2)$, which in matrix form reads

$$A_2A_1 = \begin{bmatrix} M_2 & \vec{b}_2 \\ \vec{0}^T & 1 \end{bmatrix} \begin{bmatrix} M_1 & \vec{b}_1 \\ \vec{0}^T & 1 \end{bmatrix} = \begin{bmatrix} M_2M_1 & M_2\vec{b}_1 + \vec{b}_2 \\ \vec{0}^T & 1 \end{bmatrix} \tag{3.421}$$

Simplified expressions [Thompson, 1990, Cychosz, 1990] can then be readily obtained by substituting $M_1 = I$ or $M_2 = I$ in case one of the transformations is a pure *translation* 117

$$T(t_x, t_y, t_z)A \overset{(3.415)}{=} \begin{bmatrix} I & \vec{t} \\ \vec{0}^T & 1 \end{bmatrix} \begin{bmatrix} M & \vec{b} \\ \vec{0}^T & 1 \end{bmatrix} = \begin{bmatrix} M & \vec{b} + \vec{t} \\ \vec{0}^T & 1 \end{bmatrix} \tag{3.422}$$ 117

$$AT(t_x, t_y, t_z) \overset{(3.415)}{=} \begin{bmatrix} M & \vec{b} \\ \vec{0}^T & 1 \end{bmatrix} \begin{bmatrix} I & \vec{t} \\ \vec{0}^T & 1 \end{bmatrix} = \begin{bmatrix} M & M\vec{t} + \vec{b} \\ \vec{0}^T & 1 \end{bmatrix} \tag{3.423}$$ 117

or by substituting $\vec{b}_1 = \vec{0}$ or $\vec{b}_2 = \vec{0}$ shall one of the *affine transformations* be a pure *linear* 115
transformation instead such as a *shearing*, a *reflection* or a *rotation* 102 105 106 107 105 106

$$RA \underset{(3.337)}{\overset{(3.333)}{=}} \begin{bmatrix} L & \vec{0} \\ \vec{0}^T & 1 \end{bmatrix} \begin{bmatrix} M & \vec{b} \\ \vec{0}^T & 1 \end{bmatrix} = \begin{bmatrix} LM & L\vec{b} \\ \vec{0}^T & 1 \end{bmatrix} \tag{3.424}$$

$$AR \underset{(3.337)}{\overset{(3.333)}{=}} \begin{bmatrix} M & \vec{b} \\ \vec{0}^T & 1 \end{bmatrix} \begin{bmatrix} L & \vec{0} \\ \vec{0}^T & 1 \end{bmatrix} = \begin{bmatrix} ML & \vec{b} \\ \vec{0}^T & 1 \end{bmatrix} \tag{3.425}$$ 105 106

whereas in the special case where one of the transformations is a pure *scaling*, the expressions 104
reduce to

$$\begin{aligned} S(s_x, s_y, s_z)A &\overset{(3.328)}{=} \begin{bmatrix} s_x & 0 & 0 & 0 \\ 0 & s_y & 0 & 0 \\ 0 & 0 & s_z & 0 \\ 0 & 0 & 0 & 1 \end{bmatrix} \begin{bmatrix} m_{11} & m_{12} & m_{13} & b_1 \\ m_{21} & m_{22} & m_{23} & b_2 \\ m_{31} & m_{32} & m_{33} & b_3 \\ 0 & 0 & 0 & 1 \end{bmatrix} \\ &= \begin{bmatrix} s_xm_{11} & s_xm_{12} & s_xm_{13} & s_xb_1 \\ s_ym_{21} & s_ym_{22} & s_ym_{23} & s_yb_2 \\ s_zm_{31} & s_zm_{32} & s_zm_{33} & s_zb_3 \\ 0 & 0 & 0 & 1 \end{bmatrix} \end{aligned} \tag{3.426}$$ 104

104

$$\begin{aligned} AS(s_x, s_y, s_z) &\overset{(3.328)}{=} \begin{bmatrix} m_{11} & m_{12} & m_{13} & b_1 \\ m_{21} & m_{22} & m_{23} & b_2 \\ m_{31} & m_{32} & m_{33} & b_3 \\ 0 & 0 & 0 & 1 \end{bmatrix} \begin{bmatrix} s_x & 0 & 0 & 0 \\ 0 & s_y & 0 & 0 \\ 0 & 0 & s_z & 0 \\ 0 & 0 & 0 & 1 \end{bmatrix} \\ &= \begin{bmatrix} s_x m_{11} & s_y m_{12} & s_z m_{13} & b_1 \\ s_x m_{21} & s_y m_{22} & s_z m_{23} & b_2 \\ s_x m_{31} & s_y m_{32} & s_z m_{33} & b_3 \\ 0 & 0 & 0 & 1 \end{bmatrix} \end{aligned} \tag{3.427}$$

In order to remain orthogonal to the transformations of the surface tangents $\vec{t}$ and bitangents $\vec{b}$, surface normals $\vec{n}$ instead ought to be transformed by the cofactor matrix C_M of M [Turkowski, 1990b]

240 80 99

$$\vec{n}' \overset{(6.27)}{=} \vec{t}' \times \vec{b}' = (M\vec{t}) \times (M\vec{b}) \overset{(3.99)}{=} \det(M)M^{-T}(\vec{t} \times \vec{b}) \overset{(3.303)}{=} C_M\vec{n} \tag{3.428}$$

120 as illustrated in *Figure 3.27*, such that

76 94 99 76 76

$$\begin{aligned} \langle \vec{n}', \vec{t}' \rangle &\overset{(3.70)}{=} \vec{n}'^T \vec{t}' = (C_M\vec{n})^T(M\vec{t}) \overset{(3.245)}{=} \vec{n}^T C_M^T M\vec{t} = \vec{n}^T \operatorname{adj}(M) M\vec{t} \\ &\overset{(3.290)}{=} \vec{n}^T \det(M) I\vec{t} = \det(M)\vec{n}^T\vec{t} \overset{(3.70)}{=} \det(M)\langle \vec{n}, \vec{t} \rangle \overset{(3.74)}{=} 0 \end{aligned} \tag{3.429}$$

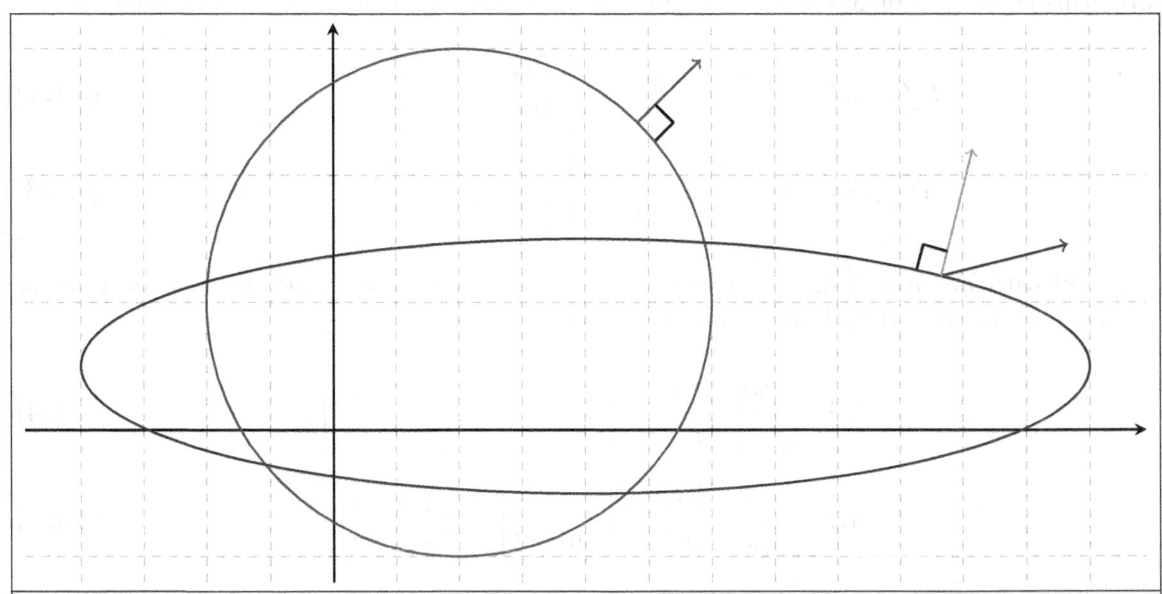

Figure 3.27: Normal Transformation: Illustration of the special treatment required to properly transform surface normals.

3.5.3.3 *Backward Transformation*

Rather than explicitly transforming all of the components of a non-trivially complex geometric model for evaluation against a simple range query such as a *ray* of origin $\vec{o} = [x_o, y_o, z_o]^T$ and direction $\vec{d} = [x_d, y_d, z_d]^T$ parameterized by the distance t

$$\vec{r}(t) = \vec{o} + t\vec{d} = \begin{bmatrix} x(t) \\ y(t) \\ z(t) \end{bmatrix} = \begin{bmatrix} x_o + tx_d \\ y_o + ty_d \\ z_o + tz_d \end{bmatrix} \tag{3.430}$$

a geometric range search on a transformed instance of the object may alternatively be equivalently carried directly in object coordinate space. Doing so entails applying the *inverse transformation*, which is also a linear map, to the origin and direction of the ray, the length of which might need to be scaled by its reciprocal to yield a unit vector in object-space, followed by a transformation of the intersection point and associated normal back into world coordinate space, where the distance to the intersection point shall conversely be scaled by the same normalization factor.

Assuming the *linear transformation* M is invertible, the inverse of an *affine transformation* is then readily given as $f^{-1}(\vec{a}) = M^{-1}(\vec{a} - \vec{b}) = M^{-1}\vec{a} - M^{-1}\vec{b}$, which in matrix form yields a special case of the block matrix inversion 102 115

$$\begin{bmatrix} f^{-1}(\vec{a}) \\ 1 \end{bmatrix} = \begin{bmatrix} M^{-1}\vec{a} - M^{-1}\vec{b} \\ 1 \end{bmatrix} = \begin{bmatrix} M^{-1} & -M^{-1}\vec{b} \\ \vec{0}^T & 1 \end{bmatrix} \begin{bmatrix} \vec{a} \\ 1 \end{bmatrix} = \begin{bmatrix} I & -M^{-1}\vec{b} \\ \vec{0}^T & 1 \end{bmatrix} \begin{bmatrix} M^{-1} & \vec{0} \\ \vec{0}^T & 1 \end{bmatrix} \begin{bmatrix} \vec{a} \\ 1 \end{bmatrix} \quad (3.431)$$

3.5.4 Projective Transformation

3.5.4.1 Orthographic Projection

As illustrated in *Figure 3.28*, a *parallel projection* is defined as a projection in which all lines of projection are parallel. Whenever the projective lines are orthogonal to the plane of projection, the projection is then referred to as an *orthographic projection*, whereas it is otherwise referred to as an *oblique projection* in which the projected coordinates along the plane axis most aligned with the projective lines are stretched by the reciprocal of the cosine between the optical axis and the lines of projection. 121

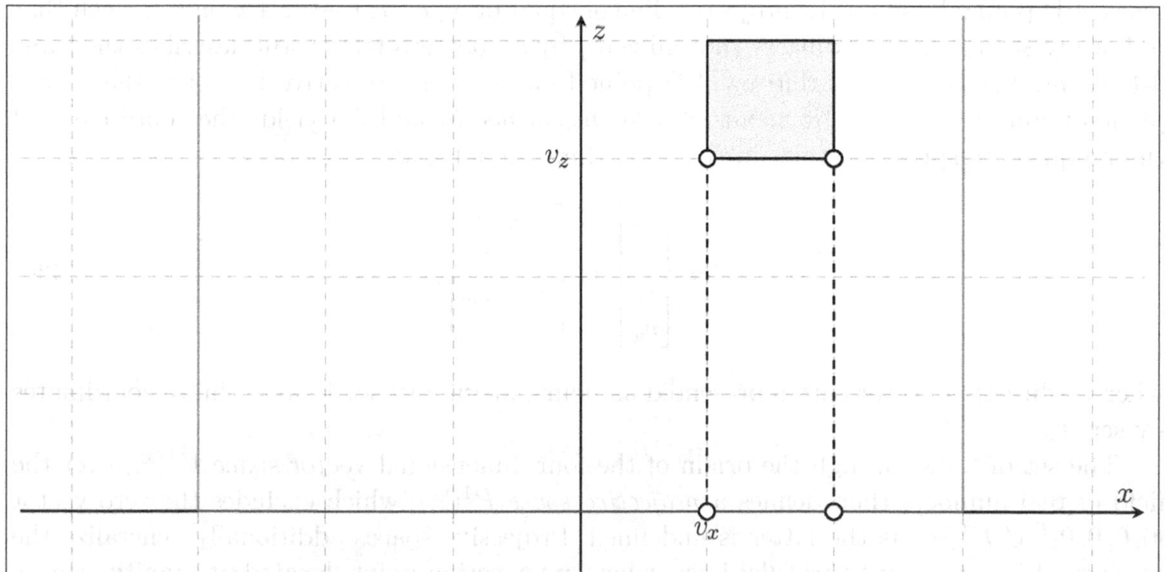

Figure 3.28: Orthographic Transformation: Illustration of a transformation defining an orthographic projection.

An orthographic projection can be regarded as a singular *scaling* transformation in which one of the scaling factors equals zero 104

$$P\vec{v} \triangleq \begin{bmatrix} 1 & 0 & 0 & 0 \\ 0 & 1 & 0 & 0 \\ 0 & 0 & 0 & 0 \\ 0 & 0 & 0 & 1 \end{bmatrix} \begin{bmatrix} v_x \\ v_y \\ v_z \\ v_w \end{bmatrix} = \begin{bmatrix} v_x \\ v_y \\ 0 \\ v_w \end{bmatrix} \quad (3.432)$$

whereas setting two scaling factors to zero would degenerate into an orthogonal projection onto the corresponding axis. It then follows that a projection forms an *idempotent transformation* as repeatedly applying the transformation yields the same result as applying it a single time, i.e., $P^n = P, \forall n \in \mathbb{N}^*$.

117 The projection may also be preceded by a *translation* centering the left, right, bottom, top, near and far coordinates of the viewing cuboid $[l, r] \times [b, t] \times [n, f]$ around the origin,
104 and a *scaling* of the result to the unit cube

$$\begin{bmatrix} \frac{2}{r-l} & 0 & 0 & 0 \\ 0 & \frac{2}{t-b} & 0 & 0 \\ 0 & 0 & \frac{2}{f-n} & 0 \\ 0 & 0 & 0 & 1 \end{bmatrix} \begin{bmatrix} 1 & 0 & 0 & -\frac{r+l}{2} \\ 0 & 1 & 0 & -\frac{t+b}{2} \\ 0 & 0 & 1 & -\frac{f+n}{2} \\ 0 & 0 & 0 & 1 \end{bmatrix} = \begin{bmatrix} \frac{2}{r-l} & 0 & 0 & -\frac{r+l}{r-l} \\ 0 & \frac{2}{t-b} & 0 & -\frac{t+b}{t-b} \\ 0 & 0 & \frac{2}{f-n} & -\frac{f+n}{f-n} \\ 0 & 0 & 0 & 1 \end{bmatrix} \tag{3.433}$$

which maps

$$[l, b, n, 1]^T \mapsto [-1, -1, -1, 1]^T \tag{3.434}$$
$$[r, t, f, 1]^T \mapsto [1, 1, 1, 1]^T \tag{3.435}$$

3.5.4.2 Perspective Projection

102 In order to express more general perspective projections as a *linear transformation*, the concept of augmented coordinates can be generalized to that of *homogeneous coordinates* by lifting the requirement that the additional coordinate be constant. As illustrated in *Fig-*
123 *ure 3.29*, a point in 3-D space may then be equivalently embedded as any of the infinitely many 4-D points lying on the projective line of equation $v_x x + v_y y + v_z z + v_w w = 0$, such that uniformly scaling all coordinates (not all zero) by a non-zero factor still describes the same 3-D point. Projecting an arbitrary 4-D point from a given projective line onto the hyperplane of equation $v_w = 1$ by means of a *homogeneous divide* then yields the coordinates of the unique corresponding point in the lower-dimensional space

$$\vec{v} = \begin{bmatrix} v_x \\ v_y \\ v_z \\ v_w \end{bmatrix} \triangleq \begin{bmatrix} v_x \div v_w \\ v_y \div v_w \\ v_z \div v_w \\ 1 \end{bmatrix} \tag{3.436}$$

whereas direction vectors are represented as points at infinity solely using finite coordinates by setting $v_w = 0$.

71 The set of lines through the origin of the four-dimensional *vector space* $V^4(\mathbb{R})$ over the field of real numbers then defines a *projective space* $P^4(\mathbb{R})$, which excludes the zero vector $[0, 0, 0, 0]^T \notin P^4(\mathbb{R})$ as the latter is undefined. Projective spaces additionally generalize the concept of intersection to parallel lines, whose intersection point, located at infinity, can be computed similarly to any other intersection point.

123 As illustrated in *Figure 3.30*, a *perspective transformation* using the origin as the *center of projection* and the plane of equation $z = p$ as the image plane may then be expressed in matrix form as

$$\begin{bmatrix} 1 & 0 & 0 & 0 \\ 0 & 1 & 0 & 0 \\ 0 & 0 & 0 & 1 \\ 0 & 0 & \frac{1}{p} & 0 \end{bmatrix} \begin{bmatrix} v_x \\ v_y \\ v_z \\ v_w \end{bmatrix} = \begin{bmatrix} v_x \\ v_y \\ v_w \\ \frac{v_z}{p} \end{bmatrix} = \begin{bmatrix} p\frac{v_x}{v_z} \\ p\frac{v_y}{v_z} \\ p\frac{v_w}{v_z} \\ 1 \end{bmatrix} \tag{3.437}$$

where the last step is referred to as the *perspective divide*. Concatenating the perspective

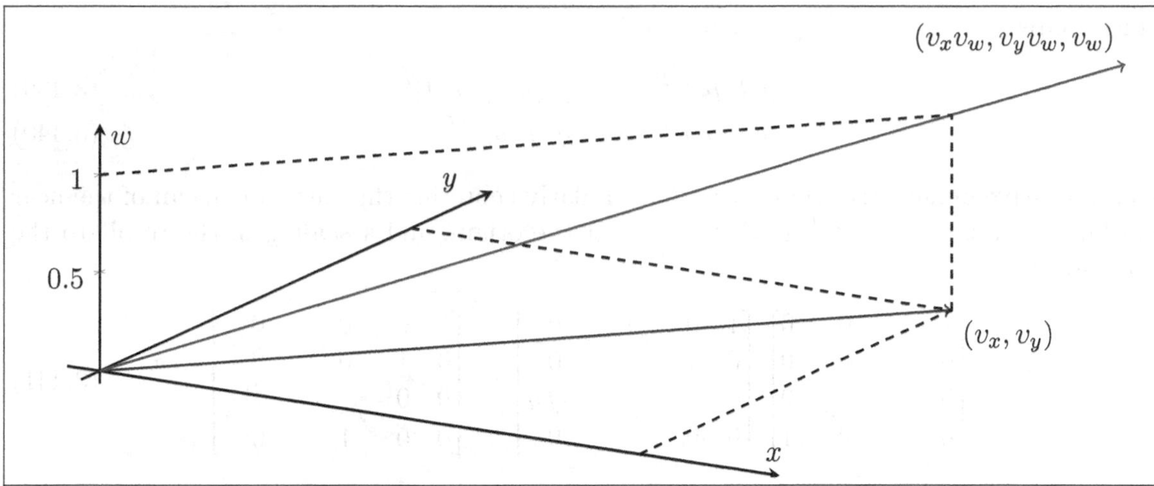

Figure 3.29: Homogeneous Coordinates: Illustration of the embedding of a 2-D space into a 3-D space by means of homogeneous coordinates.

transformation with an orthogonal projection to reduce the dimensionality of the *vector space* then readily yields a *perspective projection*. 71

The projection may also be preceded by a *shearing* centering the left, right, bottom and 105
top coordinates of the rectangle $[l, r] \times [b, t]$ at depth $z = p$ around the optical axis, and a
scaling of the result to a 90° angle of view 104

$$\begin{bmatrix} \frac{2p}{r-l} & 0 & 0 & 0 \\ 0 & \frac{2p}{t-b} & 0 & 0 \\ 0 & 0 & 1 & 0 \\ 0 & 0 & 0 & 1 \end{bmatrix} \begin{bmatrix} 1 & 0 & -\frac{r+l}{2p} & 0 \\ 0 & 1 & -\frac{t+b}{2p} & 0 \\ 0 & 0 & 1 & 0 \\ 0 & 0 & 0 & 1 \end{bmatrix} = \begin{bmatrix} \frac{2p}{r-l} & 0 & -\frac{r+l}{r-l} & 0 \\ 0 & \frac{2p}{t-b} & -\frac{t+b}{t-b} & 0 \\ 0 & 0 & 1 & 0 \\ 0 & 0 & 0 & 1 \end{bmatrix} \tag{3.438}$$

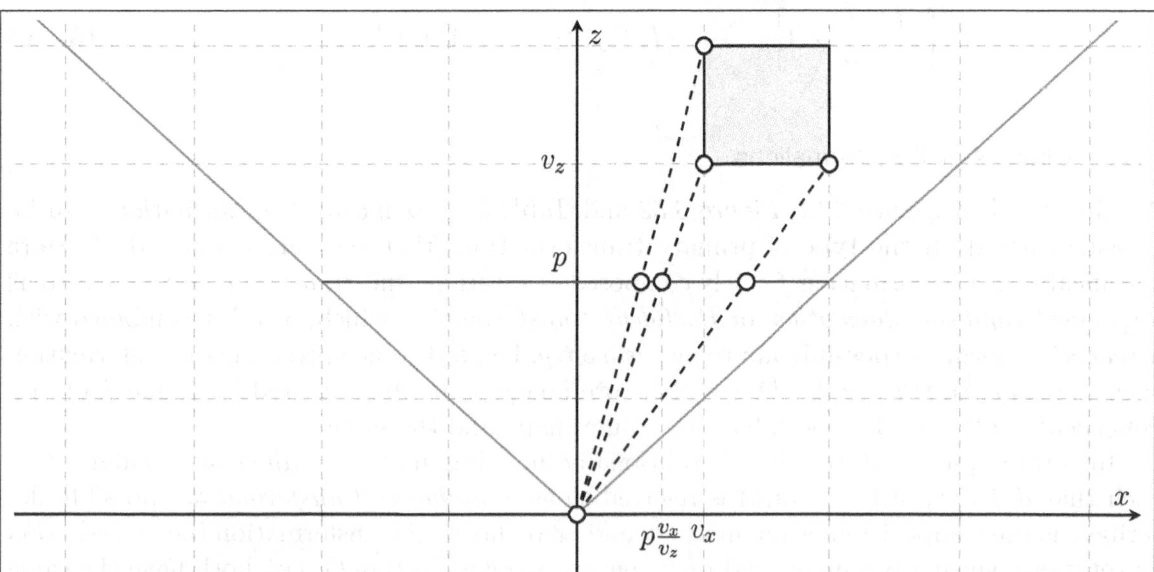

Figure 3.30: Perspective Transformation: Illustration of the geometric terms involved in the transformation defining a perspective projection.

which maps

$$[l, b, p, 1]^T \mapsto [-p, -p, p, 1]^T \quad (3.439)$$
$$[r, t, p, 1]^T \mapsto [p, p, p, 1]^T \quad (3.440)$$

An alternative perspective transformation similarly centering the harmonic mean of the near
104 and far coordinates $z = 2(\frac{1}{n} + \frac{1}{f})^{-1} = \frac{2fn}{f+n}$ at the origin, and a *scaling* of the result to the unit interval

$$\begin{bmatrix} 1 & 0 & 0 & 0 \\ 0 & 1 & 0 & 0 \\ 0 & 0 & \frac{2}{f-n} & 0 \\ 0 & 0 & 0 & 1 \end{bmatrix} \begin{bmatrix} 1 & 0 & 0 & 0 \\ 0 & 1 & 0 & 0 \\ 0 & 0 & \frac{f+n}{2} & -fn \\ 0 & 0 & 1 & 0 \end{bmatrix} = \begin{bmatrix} 1 & 0 & 0 & 0 \\ 0 & 1 & 0 & 0 \\ 0 & 0 & \frac{f+n}{f-n} & -\frac{2fn}{f-n} \\ 0 & 0 & 1 & 0 \end{bmatrix} \quad (3.441)$$

then maps

$$[x, y, n, 1]^T \mapsto [x, y, -n, n]^T \quad (3.442)$$
$$[x, y, f, 1]^T \mapsto [x, y, f, f]^T \quad (3.443)$$

Together, they yield an overall normalization of the viewing frustum to the unit cube

$$\begin{bmatrix} 1 & 0 & 0 & 0 \\ 0 & 1 & 0 & 0 \\ 0 & 0 & \frac{f+n}{f-n} & -\frac{2fn}{f-n} \\ 0 & 0 & 1 & 0 \end{bmatrix} \begin{bmatrix} \frac{2p}{r-l} & 0 & -\frac{r+l}{r-l} & 0 \\ 0 & \frac{2p}{t-b} & -\frac{t+b}{t-b} & 0 \\ 0 & 0 & 1 & 0 \\ 0 & 0 & 0 & 1 \end{bmatrix} = \begin{bmatrix} \frac{2p}{r-l} & 0 & -\frac{r+l}{r-l} & 0 \\ 0 & \frac{2p}{t-b} & -\frac{t+b}{t-b} & 0 \\ 0 & 0 & \frac{f+n}{f-n} & -\frac{2fn}{f-n} \\ 0 & 0 & 1 & 0 \end{bmatrix} \quad (3.444)$$

which maps

$$\left[l\frac{n}{p}, b\frac{n}{p}, n, 1\right]^T \mapsto [-n, -n, -n, n]^T = [-1, -1, -1, 1]^T \quad (3.445)$$
$$\left[r\frac{f}{p}, t\frac{f}{p}, f, 1\right]^T \mapsto [f, f, f, f]^T = [1, 1, 1, 1]^T \quad (3.446)$$

3.5.5 Classes of Transformations

125 125 As illustrated in *Figure 3.31*, *Figure 3.32* and *Table 3.3*, *composite transformations* can be
125 classified based on the type of primary transformations that they are composed of. More
118 specifically, a transformation f solely composed of *rotations* and *translations* is referred to as
107 117 a (proper) *rigid transformation*, or *Euclidean transformation*, which, possibly combined with
106 a *reflection*, forms a (possibly improper) *isometry*, i.e., a distance-preserving transformation such that $d(f(\vec{a}), f(\vec{b})) = d(\vec{a}, \vec{b})$, since the pre-image of an object O and its image $f(O)$ are *congruent* $f(O) \cong O$, i.e., both have the same shape and the same size.

104 In contrast, a transformation f additionally including uniform *scaling* by a scalar $s \in \mathbb{R}$ such that $d(f(\vec{a}), f(\vec{b})) = sd(\vec{a}, \vec{b})$ is referred to as a *similarity transformation*, possibly de-
106 scribed as the composition of a homothety and an orthogonal transformation (i.e., a *reflection*
107 or *rotation*), since a pre-image and its image are *similar* $f(O) \sim O$, i.e., both have the same shape but possibly different sizes, whereas *equivalent* images $f(O) \equiv O$ would conversely have the same size but possibly different shapes.

3.5.6 Further Reading

Additional material may be found in books dedicated to matrix transforms [Vince, 2012].

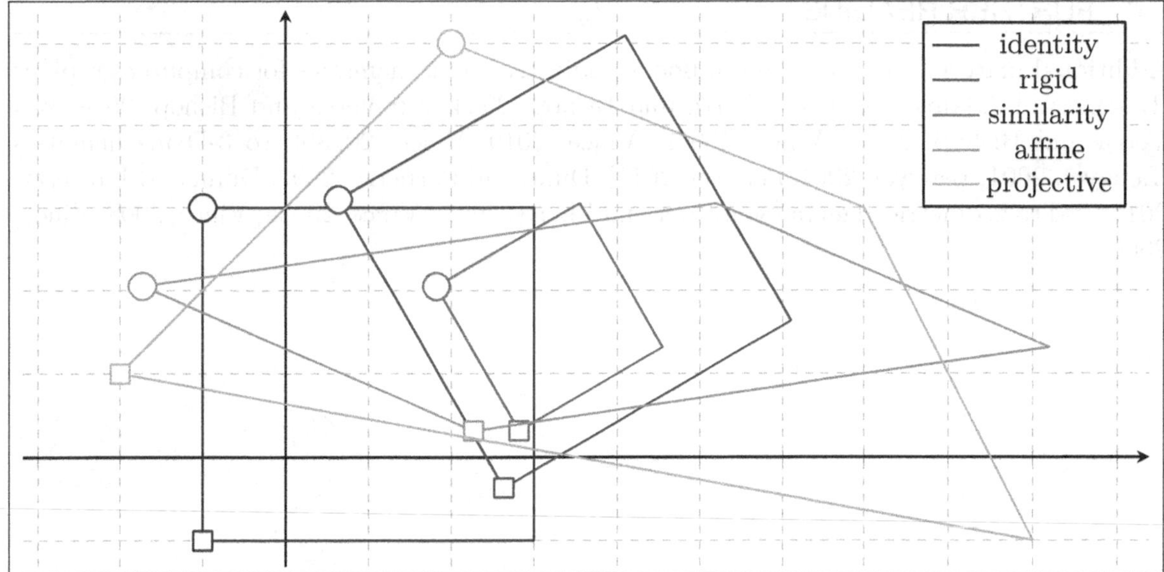

Figure 3.31: Transformations Classes: Illustration of the invariant properties of various classes of transformations.

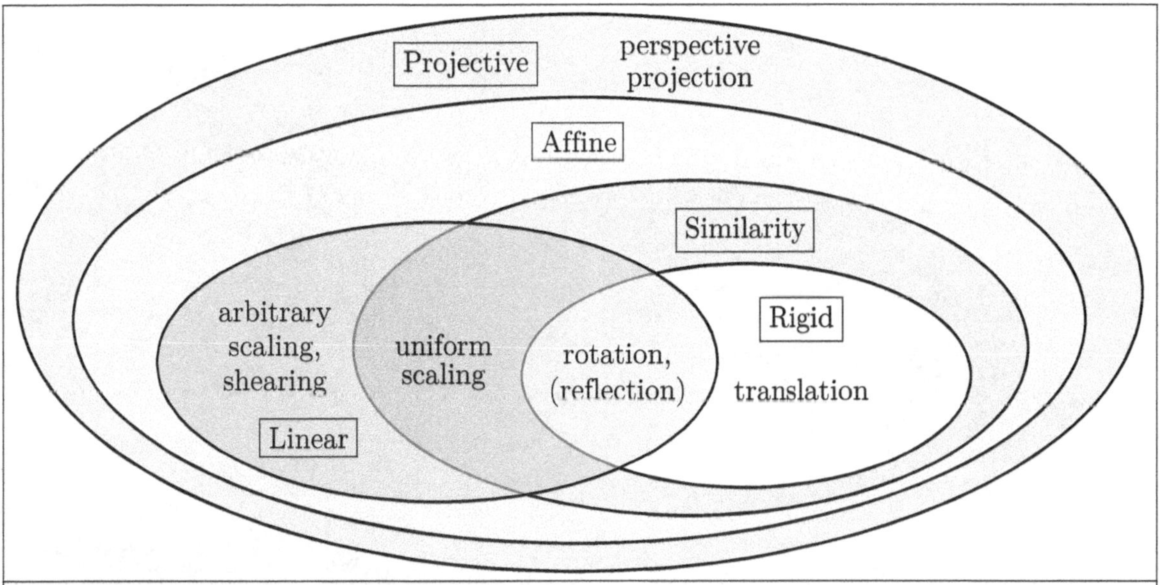

Figure 3.32: Transformations Taxonomy: Taxonomy of the various types of transformations.

Table 3.3: Transformations Nomenclature: Nomenclature of transformations, where each transformation forms a subset of the one above, such that each set of corresponding operations includes all of the ones below, whereas each set of corresponding invariants includes all of the ones above.

Transformation	Operations	Invariants
projective	↓, projection	collinearity
affine	↓, arbitrary scaling, shearing	↑, parallelism, barycenter, ratio of areas/volumes
similarity	↓, uniform scaling	↑, angle, ratio of lengths
rigid	translation, rotation, (reflection)	↑, distance, length, area, volume

3.6 FURTHER READING

Additional material may be found in books dedicated to mathematics for computer graphics [Rogers and Adams, 1989] [van Verth and Bishop, 2004, van Verth and Bishop, 2008, van Verth and Bishop, 2015] [Vince, 2005b, Vince, 2010, Vince, 2013b], to 3-D mathematics [Lengyel, 2001, Lengyel, 2004, Lengyel, 2011] [Dunn and Parberry, 2002, Dunn and Parberry, 2011] and to geometric algebra [Schneider and Eberly, 2002] [Vince, 2005a, Vince, 2008, Vince, 2009].

CHAPTER 4

Monte Carlo Methods

TABLE OF CONTENTS

4.1 HISTORY

Monte Carlo methods are a class of computational algorithms that estimate a result based on repeated stochastic sampling. The earliest documented instance of such a method dates back to 1777, when Georges-Louis Leclerc, Comte de Buffon, performed an experiment consisting in dropping a needle at random onto a plane marked with equally spaced parallel lines to
infer the *probability* of the needle lying across one of the lines, the latter *probability* being 129
actually directly related to the value of π. Inspired by the famous casino of Monte Carlo in 129
Monaco, the name of the methods was then coined in the 1940s by physicists working on nuclear weapon projects at the Los Alamos National Laboratory.

4.2 PROBABILITY THEORY

In mathematics, *probability theory* is concerned with the analysis of random phenomena, stochastic processes and statistical patterns. As such, it provides conceptual models and logical abstractions for the formal study of non-deterministic events.

More specifically, discrete/continuous probability theory deals with events that occur in a countable/continuous sample space, while a measure-theory treatment of probability covers both the discrete and continuous case or any mix of the two. Although most of the concepts from continuous probability theory are directly applicable to the discrete case by dividing the continuous space into a finite number of subsets with constant properties, the material to follow will essentially focus on the theoretical concepts relating to the former.

4.2.1 Random Variable

A continuous *random variable* X is a variable that may probabilistically take any actually observable value over a certain domain. A single sample outcome x randomly generated
according to the *probability density* of X is called a *realization* or *observation* of the random 131
variable. A specific instance of such a variable is the canonical *uniform random variable* U, which is uniformly distributed on $[0, 1]$. In computer simulations, realizations of the latter variable may be obtained via a pseudo-*random number generator* (*RNG*) algorithm, such as the *linear congruential generator* or the *Mersenne twister generator*.

4.2.2 Event

The infinite set of all possible outcomes $x \in \Omega$ is referred to as the *sample space* Ω of X. In contrast, the *empty set* $\emptyset$ defines the set of no outcomes, while an *event* A is a subset of the sample space such that $\emptyset \subseteq A \subseteq \Omega$. The intersection $A \cap B$ is then defined as the event that both A and B occur, and the events A and B are said to be *mutually exclusive* or *disjoint* if $A \cap B = \emptyset$. Conversely, the union $A \cup B$ is defined as the event that either A or B or both occur, and the events A and B are said to be *exhaustive* if $A \cup B = \Omega$. Finally, the *complement* $A' = \Omega \setminus A$ of A is defined as the complementary event that A does not occur, and the events A and A' are both mutually exclusive and exhaustive.

4.2.3 Probability

A *probability* is a measure of the likelihood of occurrence of a potential event. Assuming an n-dimensional space, likelihood can be thought of as a volume of proportional size, as
illustrated by the Venn diagram shown in *Figure 4.1*. The probability $\Pr(A)$ of an event A 130
is then defined as the ratio of the volume of A to the volume of the entire sample space Ω.

It follows that a probability is a non-negative real-valued number such that

$$\Pr(\emptyset) \triangleq 0 \tag{4.1}$$
$$\Pr(A) \in [0,1] \tag{4.2}$$
$$\Pr(\Omega) \triangleq 1 \tag{4.3}$$

Therefore, an impossible event has a probability of 0 and a certain event has a probability of 1. However, the converses are not always true: events with probability 0 are not always impossible, nor are events with probability 1 certain. Indeed, for any continuous *probability*
131 *density*, the infinitesimal probability of any single elementary event is 0, yet the event is not logically impossible, as would, for instance, be one outside the sample space.

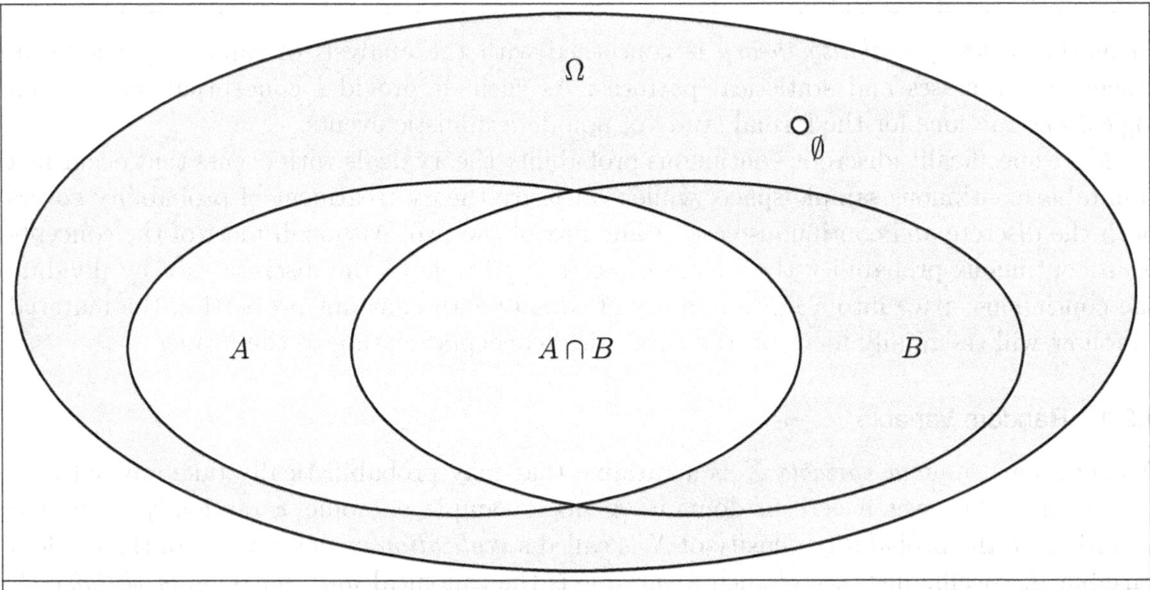

Figure 4.1: Venn Diagram: Illustration of a Venn diagram.

Considering two events A and B, their *joint probability* is related to the probability of their union by

$$\Pr(A \cap B) + \Pr(A \cup B) \triangleq \Pr(A) + \Pr(B) \tag{4.4}$$

If the events A and B are mutually exclusive, it therefore holds that

130
$$\Pr(A \cap B) = \Pr(\emptyset) \overset{(4.1)}{=} 0 \tag{4.5}$$
130
$$\Pr(A \cup B) \overset{(4.4)}{=} \Pr(A) + \Pr(B) \tag{4.6}$$

while if they are exhaustive, then

130
$$\Pr(A \cup B) = \Pr(\Omega) \overset{(4.3)}{=} 1 \tag{4.7}$$
130
$$\Pr(A \cap B) \overset{(4.4)}{=} \Pr(A) + \Pr(B) - 1 \tag{4.8}$$

Since A and its complement A' are both mutually exclusive and exhaustive, it also follows that

$$\Pr(A) + \Pr(A') = 1 \tag{4.9}$$

Given the a priori occurrence of an event B that may then be virtually considered as a local sample space, the probability of event A is given by the *conditional probability* $\Pr(A \mid B)$. The latter is defined as the ratio of the remaining volume $\Pr(A \cap B)$ of A to the volume $\Pr(B)$ of the virtual sample space B, such that the joint probability reads

$$\Pr(A \cap B) \triangleq \Pr(A \mid B)\Pr(B) = \Pr(B \mid A)\Pr(A) \tag{4.10}$$

Whenever $\Pr(B) = 0$, then $\Pr(A \cap B) = 0$ and $\Pr(A \mid B)$ is undefined.

By definition, the events of a collection are called mutually *independent events* if and only if for any finite subset $A_1, \ldots, A_n$ of the collection, the following multiplication rule holds

$$\Pr\left(\bigcap_{i=1}^{n} A_i\right) = \prod_{i=1}^{n} \Pr(A_i) \tag{4.11}$$

It follows that if two events A and B are independent, the conditional probability of A given B reduces to the unconditional probability, also called *marginal probability*, of A

$$\Pr(A \mid B) \overset{(4.10)}{=} \frac{\Pr(A \cap B)}{\Pr(B)} \overset{(4.11)}{=} \frac{\Pr(A)\Pr(B)}{\Pr(B)} = \Pr(A) \tag{4.12}$$ 131 131

and the occurrence of one event makes it neither more nor less probable that the other occurs.

4.2.4 Probability Density

The distribution of the observations of a *random variable* X over a given domain is described 129
by its *probability density function* (*PDF*) $p(x)$, which represents the infinitesimal *probability* 129
per unit length of the outcome of X being the realization x (the discrete equivalent being
referred to as *probability mass function* (*PMF*)). The *random variable* $X \sim p(x)$ is then said 129
to be distributed according to $p(x)$, while it is said to be uniformly distributed if $p(x)$ is
constant. Integrating the PDF over a given subdomain $\mathcal{D}$ consequently yields the *probability* 129
of a random sample to lie within that subdomain

$$\Pr(X \in \mathcal{D}) \triangleq \int_{\mathcal{D}} p(x)\mathrm{d}x \tag{4.13}$$

In order for the *probability* to be non-negative on any subset of the sample space Ω, the 129
PDF must satisfy

$$p(x) \geq 0, \quad \forall x \in \Omega \tag{4.14}$$

and it must additionally be normalized to ensure that the *probability* of all possible outcomes 129
integrates to one

$$\Pr(X \in \Omega) \overset{(4.13)}{=} \int_{\Omega} p(x)\mathrm{d}x \overset{(4.3)}{=} 1 \tag{4.15}$$ 131 130

whereas the probability density is said to be a *sub-critical PDF* whenever

$$\int_{\Omega} p(x)\mathrm{d}x < 1 \tag{4.16}$$

As illustrated in *Figure 4.2*, the probability density function in an n-dimensional space is 132
referred to as the *joint PDF* and defined as a function $p_{x_1,\ldots,x_n}(x_1, \ldots, x_n)$ of the n variables. Considering a joint PDF $p(x, y)$ parameterized by the pair $[x, y] \in \Omega$ with $\Omega = \Omega_x \times \Omega_y$ and where $x \in \Omega_x$ and $y \in \Omega_y$, the *marginal PDF* $p(x)$ is defined as

$$p(x) \triangleq \int_{\Omega_y} p(x, y)\mathrm{d}y \tag{4.17}$$

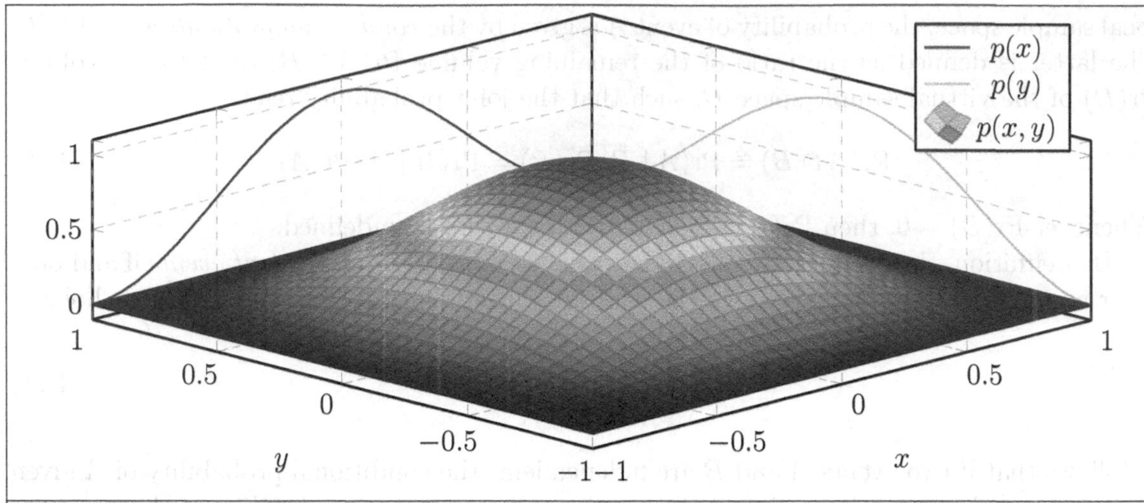

Figure 4.2: Joint PDF: Illustration of a joint probability density.

131 satisfying $\int_{\Omega_x} p(x)\mathrm{d}x = \int_{\Omega_x}\int_{\Omega_y} p(x,y)\mathrm{d}y\mathrm{d}x \overset{(4.15)}{=} 1$, while the *conditional PDFs* are defined such that

$$p(x,y) \triangleq p(x \mid y)p(y) = p(y \mid x)p(x) \tag{4.18}$$

129 A finite collection of continuous *random variables* $X_1, \dots, X_n$ is then said to be a collection of *independent random variables* if and only if for any finite set of subdomains $\mathcal{D}_1, \dots, \mathcal{D}_n$ the events $X_1 \in \mathcal{D}_1, \dots, X_n \in \mathcal{D}_n$ are independent events. In other words, given the proba-
129 bility densities $p_{x_1}(x_1), \dots, p_{x_n}(x_n)$, the *random variables* are independent if and only if the
129 combined *random variable* $[X_1, \dots, X_n]$ has a separable joint density

$$p_{x_1,\dots,x_n}(x_1, \dots, x_n) = \prod_{i=1}^{n} p_{x_i}(x_i) \tag{4.19}$$

129 It follows that if two continuous *random variables* X and Y are independent, the conditional
131 *probability density* of either given the observed value of the other is the same as if the other's value had not been observed

132
132

$$p(x \mid y) \overset{(4.18)}{=} \frac{p(x,y)}{p(y)} \overset{(4.19)}{=} \frac{p(x)p(y)}{p(y)} = p(x) \tag{4.20}$$

4.2.5 Cumulative Distribution

131 Given a *probability density* satisfying $p(x) = 0, \forall x \notin \Omega$, its *cumulative distribution function*
129 (*CDF*) defines the *probability* of a random sample to take a value less than or equal to x

131

$$P(x) \triangleq \int_{-\infty}^{x} p(x')\mathrm{d}x' \overset{(4.13)}{=} \Pr(X \le x) \tag{4.21}$$

while the *joint CDF* of the multidimensional variable $x = [x_1, \dots, x_n]$ similarly reads

131

$$P(x) \triangleq \int_{-\infty}^{x_1} \cdots \int_{-\infty}^{x_n} p(x_1', \dots x_n')\mathrm{d}x_1' \dots \mathrm{d}x_n' \overset{(4.13)}{=} \Pr(X_1 \le x_1, \dots, X_n \le x_n) \tag{4.22}$$

It then directly follows that the derivative of the CDF is precisely defined by the *proba-*
131 *bility density*

$$\frac{\mathrm{d}P(x)}{\mathrm{d}x} \overset{(4.21)}{=} p(x) \tag{4.23}$$ 132

and that the *probability* of a random sample to belong to the interval $[x_a, x_b]$ is readily given 129
by

$$\Pr(x_a \leq X \leq x_b) \overset{(4.13)}{=} \int_{x_a}^{x_b} p(x)\mathrm{d}x \overset{(4.21)}{=} P(x_b) - P(x_a) \tag{4.24}$$ 131 132

Due to the non-negativity of the *probability density*, the CDF is a monotonically non- 131
decreasing function which additionally satisfies

$$\lim_{x \to -\infty} P(x) \overset{(4.14)}{=} \lim_{[x_1,\ldots,x_n] \to -\infty} P(x_1, \ldots, x_n) = 0 \tag{4.25}$$ 131

$$\lim_{x \to +\infty} P(x) \overset{(4.15)}{=} \lim_{[x_1,\ldots,x_n] \to +\infty} P(x_1, \ldots, x_n) = 1 \tag{4.26}$$ 131

so that the integral of the *probability density* over the whole domain fulfills normalization 131

$$\lim_{x \to +\infty} P(x) - \lim_{x \to -\infty} P(x) = 1 \tag{4.27}$$

Finally, whenever the joint density of a multidimensional *random variable* is separable, 129
due to the independence of its components along each individual axis, the joint CDF is also
separable and may be written as

$$P(x) \underset{(4.19)}{\overset{(4.22)}{=}} \int_{-\infty}^{x_1} \ldots \int_{-\infty}^{x_n} \prod_{i=1}^{n} p_{x_i}(x'_i)\mathrm{d}x'_1 \ldots \mathrm{d}x'_n = \prod_{i=1}^{n} \int_{-\infty}^{x_i} p_{x_i}(x'_i)\mathrm{d}x'_i \overset{(4.21)}{=} \prod_{i=1}^{n} P_{x_i}(x_i) \tag{4.28}$$ 132 132 132

4.2.6 Transformed Probability Density

Given a continuous *random variable* X distributed according to the *probability density* $p_x(x)$ 129
on an initial space Ω_x, the (multidimensional) *transformation* $T(x)$ into the target space Ω_y 131 102
defines another continuous *random variable* $Y = T(X)$ whose *probability density* $p_y(y)$ is 129
related for any subdomain $\mathcal{D}_y = T(\mathcal{D}_x)$ to that of X by 131

$$\Pr(X \in \mathcal{D}_x) = \Pr(Y \in \mathcal{D}_y) \tag{4.29}$$

Defining the inverse *transformation* $T^{-1}(y)$, the above expression may then be rewritten 102

$$\begin{aligned} \int_{\mathcal{D}_x} p_x(x)\mathrm{d}x &= \int_{\mathcal{D}_y} p_x(T^{-1}(y)) \left|\det\left(J_{T^{-1}}(y)\right)\right| \mathrm{d}y = \\ \int_{\mathcal{D}_y} p_y(y)\mathrm{d}y &= \int_{\mathcal{D}_x} p_y(T(x)) \left|\det\left(J_T(x)\right)\right| \mathrm{d}x \end{aligned} \tag{4.30}$$

from which follows that

$$p_x(x) = p_y(T(x)) \left|\det\left(J_T(x)\right)\right| \tag{4.31}$$

as well as the identity

$$p_y(y) = p_x(T^{-1}(y)) \left|\det\left(J_{T^{-1}}(y)\right)\right| = \frac{p_x(T^{-1}(y))}{\left|\det\left(J_T(T^{-1}(y))\right)\right|} \tag{4.32}$$

where $\det(J)$ is the Jacobian *determinant* of the *transformation*. 98 102

The relationship between the PDFs in the initial and the target space similarly extends
132 to their associated *cumulative distributions*, and two samples x and y are therefore probabilistically equivalent if they identically divide their corresponding distributions

132 133 132

$$P_x(x) \overset{(4.21)}{=} \Pr(X \leq x) \overset{(4.29)}{=} \Pr(Y \leq y) \overset{(4.21)}{=} P_y(y) \tag{4.33}$$

132 Without loss of generality, assuming that $X = U$, whose *cumulative distribution* is the
identity function $P_x(x) = x$, then leads to the *probability integral transform* rule, which
132 states that applying the *cumulative distribution* of a given continuous *random variable* to
129 129 that variable yields the continuous canonical uniform *random variable*

$$P_x(X) = P_y(Y) = U \tag{4.34}$$

4.3 SAMPLING SCHEMES

4.3.1 Inverse-Transform Sampling

132 Given an invertible *cumulative distribution*, random samples may be generated according to
131 the target *probability density* using a method referred to as *inverse-transform sampling*, also
known as the inverse probability integral transform or the inverse transformation method.
129 Considering two 1-D continuous *random variables* X and Y with distinct *cumulative*
132 *distributions* $P_x(x)$ and $P_y(y)$, the method entails transforming a sample x into a sample
132 y by solving the *cumulative distribution* equality established for a *transformed probability*
133 *density*. If the *cumulative distribution* is continuous and strictly monotonically increasing, it
132 132 is invertible, with its inverse given by the *cumulative distribution* called the *quantile function*,
and the variable Y may therefore be generated as follows

134

$$Y \overset{(4.33)}{=} P_y^{-1}(P_x(X)) \tag{4.35}$$

135 As illustrated in *Figure 4.3*, samples distributed according to the target distribution can
129 similarly be generated from the continuous canonical uniform *random variable* by letting
$X = U$, which then yields

$$Y = P_y^{-1}(P_x(U)) = P_y^{-1}(U) \tag{4.36}$$

132 In a multidimensional space, the *cumulative distribution* inversion entails iteratively computing the marginal distributions along each dimension but the first by integrating the previous distribution in the iteration against the current dimension. The inverse *cumulative*
132 *distribution* of the resulting 1-D *probability density* may then be used to draw a random
131 sample coordinate along that first dimension. Holding the first coordinate fixed, the conditional distribution of the previous variable in the series can in turn be used to draw a
random sample coordinate along the second dimension, and the process is repeated until all
132 coordinates have been sampled, therefore processing the marginal *cumulative distributions* in
reverse order so as to draw samples distributed according to the multidimensional *probability*
131 *density*.
131 Given a 2-D joint *probability density* $p(x, y)$ such that $\int_{\Omega_x} \int_{\Omega_y} p(x, y)\mathrm{d}y\mathrm{d}x = 1$, a random
131 131 coordinate x_i may be sampled from the marginal *probability density* $p(x) \overset{(4.17)}{=} \int_{\Omega_y} p(x, y)\mathrm{d}y$
since $\int_{\Omega_x} p(x)\mathrm{d}x = 1$, and a random coordinate y_i can then be sampled from the conditional
132 131 *probability density* $p(y \mid x_i) \overset{(4.18)}{=} p(x_i, y) \div p(x_i)$ since $\int_{\Omega_y} p(y \mid x_i)\mathrm{d}y = \int_{\Omega_y} p(x_i, y)\mathrm{d}y \div$

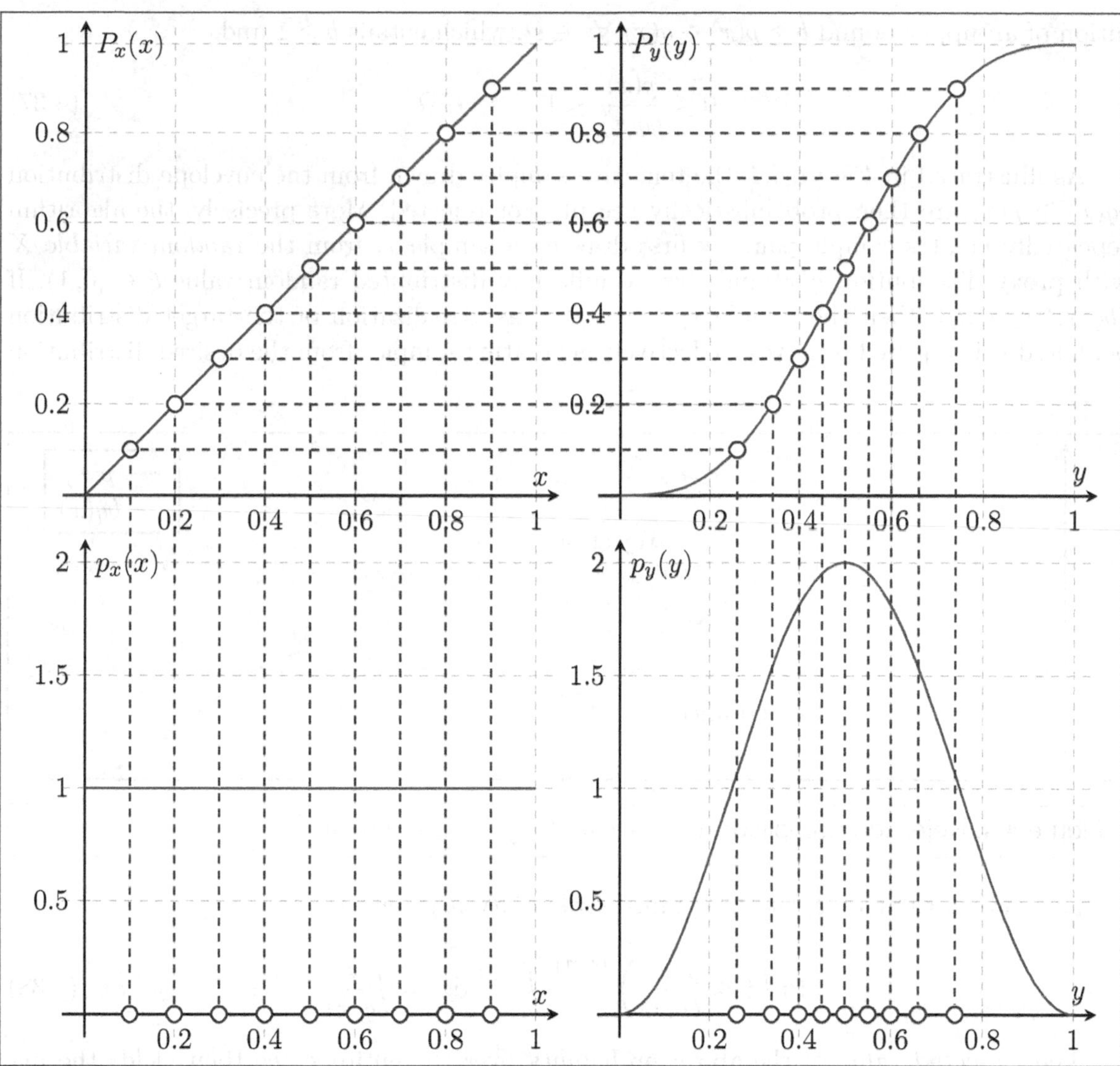

Figure 4.3: Inverse-Transform Sampling: Illustration of the transformation of samples between two PDFs (bottom row) using their respective CDFs (top row).

$p(x_i) \overset{(4.17)}{=} 1$. If the joint *probability density* is separable though, e.g., if it is constant along some dimension, the random sample coordinates may instead be drawn independently since 131 131

$\int\int p(x,y)\mathrm{d}y\mathrm{d}x \overset{(4.19)}{=} \int\int p_x(x)p_y(y)\mathrm{d}y\mathrm{d}x \overset{(4.21)}{=} \int p_x(x)\mathrm{d}x \int p_y(y)\mathrm{d}y$. 132 132

4.3.2 Acceptance–Rejection Sampling

In cases where it is not possible to invert the *cumulative distribution*, or if its inverse is too 132
computationally expensive to evaluate in practice, an alternative is to use *rejection sampling*, also commonly referred to as the acceptance–rejection method or as the accept–reject algorithm. This technique may be used to generate observations from an arbitrary *probability density* even if it cannot be analytically integrated. 131

Assuming an instrumental *probability density* $q(x) \neq 0, \forall x \in \Omega$ that can be easily sam- 131
pled, e.g., via *inverse-transform sampling*, the technique has for its only restriction the defi- 134

nition of an upper bound $b \geq p(x) \div q(x), \forall x \in \Omega$, which entails $b \geq 1$ and

$$0 \leq \frac{p(x)}{bq(x)} \leq 1, \quad \forall x \in \Omega \tag{4.37}$$

136 As illustrated in *Figure 4.4*, the tentative samples drawn from the envelope distribution
$bq(x) \geq p(x)$ are then probabilistically accepted or rejected. More precisely, the algorithm
129 repeatedly creates sample pairs by first drawing a sample x_i from the *random variable* X
with proxy distribution $q(x)$ and then a uniformly distributed random value $\xi \in [0, 1)$. If $\xi bq(x_i) \leq p(x_i)$, then the sample x_i is accepted as a realization of the target distribution $p(x)$, and it is rejected otherwise, effectively generating samples from the desired distribution $p(x)$.

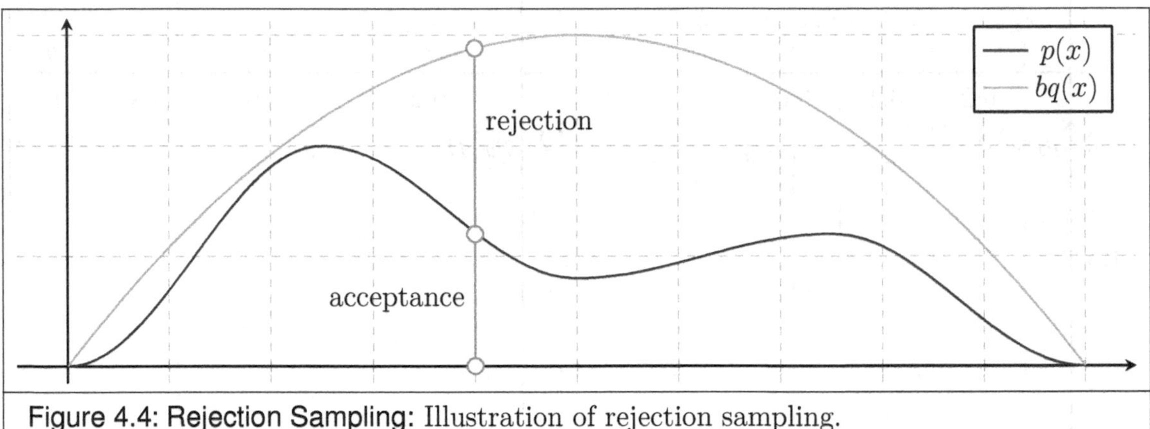

Figure 4.4: Rejection Sampling: Illustration of rejection sampling.

129 For a given value of x, the acceptance *probability* is given as

132

$$\Pr\left(\xi \leq \frac{p(x)}{bq(x)}\right) \overset{(4.21)}{=} \int_0^{\frac{p(x)}{bq(x)}} \mathrm{d}x' = \frac{p(x)}{bq(x)} \tag{4.38}$$

141 The *expected value* of the above *probability* over the entire space then yields the un-
129 conditional *acceptance probability*, i.e., the overall proportion of proposed samples that are
accepted

141

$$\mathrm{E}\left[\frac{p(X)}{bq(X)}\right] \overset{(4.65)}{=} \int_\Omega \frac{p(x)}{bq(x)} q(x)\mathrm{d}x = \frac{1}{b}\int_\Omega p(x)\mathrm{d}x = \frac{1}{b} \tag{4.39}$$

It follows that b samples must be taken in average before one sample is accepted. Therefore, if b is low, fewer samples are rejected and the required number of samples for the target distribution is obtained more quickly. Because b must be no less than the maximum
129 of $p(x) \div q(x)$, the unconditional acceptance *probability* is higher the lower that maximum
is. In the limit, setting $b = 1$ and $q(x) = p(x)$ would yield an acceptance ratio of one, such that no sample is ever rejected. On the other hand, the rejection probability tends to grow exponentially with the number of dimensions, thereby making rejection sampling prone to the curse of dimensionality.

4.3.3 Metropolis–Hastings Sampling

131 Rather than being drawn independently from a given *probability density*, a sequence of
samples may instead be constructed in a correlated fashion based on the PDF $p(x_0)$ of an initial sample x_0, so-called "seed," and the conditional PDF $p(x_i \mid x_0, \ldots, x_{i-1})$ of the subsequent samples x_i. The sequence of samples is then said to form a *random walk* through the sample space Ω.

Defining the sample coordinates as states from a continuous *state space* Ω, the walk is said to form a *Markov chain* (and the technique called a *Markov chain Monte Carlo* (*MCMC*) method) if the conditional *transition density* to the next sample x_i is solely linked to the current state x_{i-1} and independent of the previous states in the sequence, a condition known as the *Markov property*

$$p(x_i \mid x_0, \ldots, x_{i-1}) = p(x_i \mid x_{i-1}) \tag{4.40}$$

The chain is more specifically referred to as a *reversible Markov chain* if it additionally satisfies the *detailed balance* property

$$p(x_{i-1})p(x_i \mid x_{i-1}) = p(x_i)p(x_{i-1} \mid x_i) \tag{4.41}$$

which, in the case of a bounded domain, may for instance be preserved by assuming that the latter is periodic, thereby wrapping the sample coordinate associated with each state around the ends of the domain.

Given a non-negative target function f, *Metropolis–Hastings sampling* [Metropolis *et al.*, 1953, Hastings, 1970], also known as the M(RT)^2 algorithm, is a Markov chain Monte Carlo method generating observations from the *probability density* 131

$$p(x) = \frac{f(x)}{\int_\Omega f(y)\mathrm{d}y} \tag{4.42}$$

by solely evaluating the relative ratio of f at two sample states rather than the absolute value of p. As such, the technique doesn't require f to be normalized or even integrable, while providing a more robust alternative to *acceptance–rejection sampling* in high-dimensional 135 spaces.

The method consists in generating a sample state x_i by randomly mutating the previous state x_{i-1} in the sequence based on a normalized transition density

$$\int_\Omega p_t(x_{i-1} \to x_i)\mathrm{d}x_i = 1, \quad \forall x_{i-1} \in \Omega \tag{4.43}$$

Given the *probability density* p_0 of the initial state x_0, the *probability density* of the subse- 131
quent states reads 131

$$p_i(x_i) = \int_\Omega p_{i-1}(x_{i-1})p_t(x_{i-1} \to x_i)\mathrm{d}x_{i-1}, \quad \forall i \geq 1 \tag{4.44}$$

which, if $p_t(x_{i-1} \to x_i) = p_t(x_i - x_{i-1})$ is homogeneous, reduces to the *convolution* 176

$$p_i(x_i) = \int_\Omega p_{i-1}(x_{i-1})p_t(x_i - x_{i-1})\mathrm{d}x_{i-1} \overset{(5.5)}{=} (p_{i-1} * p_t)(x_i) \tag{4.45}$$ 176

A sufficient though not necessary condition for the densities to converge to a *stationary distribution* $\pi(x) = \lim_{i\to\infty} p_i(x)$ is given by the detailed balance property

$$p_\infty(x_{i-1})p_t(x_{i-1} \to x_i) \overset{(4.41)}{=} p_\infty(x_i)p_t(x_i \to x_{i-1}) \tag{4.46}$$ 137

from which follows that if $p_{i-1}(x) = p_\infty(x)$, then equilibrium is preserved

$$\begin{aligned} p_i(x_i) &\overset{(4.44)}{=} \int_\Omega p_\infty(x_{i-1})p_t(x_{i-1} \to x_i)\mathrm{d}x_{i-1} \\ &\overset{(4.46)}{=} \int_\Omega p_\infty(x_i)p_t(x_i \to x_{i-1})\mathrm{d}x_{i-1} \\ &= p_\infty(x_i)\int_\Omega p_t(x_i \to x_{i-1})\mathrm{d}x_{i-1} \\ &\overset{(4.43)}{=} p_\infty(x_i) \end{aligned} \tag{4.47}$$ 137 137 137

138 As illustrated in *Algorithm 4.1*, the transition density can be defined such that the stationary distribution equates the given target distribution $p_\infty(x) = p(x)$ by generating a sample candidate x_i with normalized *proposal density*

$$\int_\Omega p_p(x_i \mid x_{i-1})\mathrm{d}x_i = 1, \quad \forall x_{i-1} \in \Omega \tag{4.48}$$

and then accepting or rejecting it with *acceptance probability* $a(x_{i-1} \to x_i) \in [0,1], \forall x_{i-1}, x_i \in \Omega$, yielding

$$p_t(x_{i-1} \to x_i) \geq p_p(x_i \mid x_{i-1})a(x_{i-1} \to x_i) \tag{4.49}$$

thereby reformulating the detailed balance as

137 $$\frac{a(x_{i-1} \to x_i)}{a(x_i \to x_{i-1})} \overset{(4.46)}{=} \frac{p_\infty(x_i)p_p(x_{i-1} \mid x_i)}{p_\infty(x_{i-1})p_p(x_i \mid x_{i-1})} = \frac{p(x_i)p_p(x_{i-1} \mid x_i)}{p(x_{i-1})p_p(x_i \mid x_{i-1})} \tag{4.50}$$

Algorithm 4.1: Metropolis Sampling: Pseudocode for Metropolis sampling.

Data: Target density f
Result: A set of samples distributed according to f

```
x0 ← StartUpSample();
for i ← 1 to n do
    x ← Mutate(x_{i-1});
    a ← Accept(f(x), f(x_{i-1}));
    if ξ < a then
        x_i ← x;
    else
        x_i ← x_{i-1};
    end
end
return {x_1, ..., x_n}
```

The rate at which the distribution reaches equilibrium may then be maximized by maximizing the acceptance probability within the constraints of the detailed balance

$$a(x_{i-1} \to x_i) \triangleq \min\left\{\frac{p(x_i)p_p(x_{i-1} \mid x_i)}{p(x_{i-1})p_p(x_i \mid x_{i-1})}, 1\right\} = \min\left\{\frac{f(x_i)p_p(x_{i-1} \mid x_i)}{f(x_{i-1})p_p(x_i \mid x_{i-1})}, 1\right\} \tag{4.51}$$

which, in the case of the original Metropolis sampling scheme where the proposal distribution $p_p(x_{i-1} \mid x_i) = p_p(x_i \mid x_{i-1})$ is assumed to be symmetric, reduces to

138 $$a(x_{i-1} \to x_i) \overset{(4.51)}{=} \min\left\{\frac{f(x_i)}{f(x_{i-1})}, 1\right\} \tag{4.52}$$

such that the tentative sample is systematically accepted if $f(x_i) \geq f(x_{i-1})$, and probabilisti-
143 cally rejected otherwise. When used as part of an estimation scheme, *variance* can be further
152 reduced via the *use of expected values* by scoring the contributions of both the accepted and
the rejected samples with weights a and $1 - a$, respectively, prior to acceptance/rejection of
the next state.

Instead, the proposal distribution may be defined arbitrarily, possibly in a way that is independent of the current state x_{i-1}, in which case the acceptance probability can be increased by setting $p_p(x_i \mid x_{i-1}) \approx p(x_i)$. In fact, if $p_p(x_i \mid x_{i-1}) = p(x_i)$, it holds that

$$a(x_{i-1} \to x_i) \overset{(4.51)}{=} \min\left\{\frac{f(x_i)}{f(x_{i-1})}\frac{p(x_{i-1})}{p(x_i)}, 1\right\} = \min\{1, 1\} = 1 \tag{4.53}$$ 138

and no mutation is ever rejected. In the more general case, it is desirable for the mutation
strategy to frequently yield small scale perturbations, while periodically generating large scale
perturbations ensures that all states $x \in \Omega \mid f(x) > 0$ are reachable with non-zero probability, a property known as *ergodicity*. A sufficient but non-necessary condition to guarantee
ergodicity is given by $p_p(x_i \mid x_{i-1}) > 0, \forall x_{i-1}, x_i \mid f(x_{i-1}) > 0 \wedge f(x_i) > 0$, for which a shifted
Gaussian distribution is a typical choice. More complex proposal distributions can also be 51
defined as a convex combination of simpler mutation strategies, probabilistically selected
based on their given weights.

Because the *probability density* p_i of each sample x_i only approaches the stationary 131
distribution in the limit as $i \to \infty$, the algorithm is prone to so-called *start-up bias* [Szirmay-
Kalos *et al.*, 1999], which may be mitigated by discarding the samples generated during a
preliminary *burn-in* phase, until their distribution is believed to be sufficiently close to the
stationary distribution. Given one or more estimators of the form

$$\tilde{E} \overset{(4.158)}{=} \frac{1}{n}\sum_{i=1}^{n}\frac{g(X_i)}{p(X_i)} \overset{(4.42)}{=} \frac{\int_\Omega f(y)\mathrm{d}y}{n}\sum_{i=1}^{n}\frac{g(X_i)}{f(X_i)} \tag{4.54}$$ 156 137

the introduction of start-up bias can alternatively be eliminated [Veach and Guibas, 1997,
Veach, 1997, Ch. 11] by estimating the normalization factor of the target distribution (which
is an absolute scaling factor common to the possibly many relative estimates) by means of
the initial *probability density* p_0 as 131

$$\int_\Omega f(y)\mathrm{d}y \overset{(4.156)}{=} \mathrm{E}\left[\frac{f(Y)}{p_0(Y)}\right] \overset{(4.158)}{\approx} \frac{1}{m}\sum_{i=1}^{m}\frac{f(Y_i)}{p_0(Y_i)} \tag{4.55}$$ 155 156

either using a single sample y_0, yielding the initial chain sample $x_0 = y_0$, or, in order to minimize the likelihood of the estimate being zero, using $m > 1$ samples y_i, referred to as seeds, in which case the initial chain sample x_0 is probabilistically drawn from the seeds y_i using the ratios $\frac{f(y_i)}{p_0(y_i)}$ as the weights of the probability mass function.

The *correlation* between successive samples may be similarly reduced by discarding all 147
but every n^{th} sample, where n depends on the autocorrelation between adjacent samples. The
autocorrelation is itself a function of the proposal distribution, as exceedingly large jumps will
be more likely to yield samples having a low PDF value and therefore a low acceptance ratio,
while exceedingly small jumps will yield a greater acceptance ratio but generate samples that
explore the state space too slowly, both cases resulting in a *slow-mixing Markov chain* whose
samples are highly correlated, thereby being representative of the stationary distribution
in the limit of a large number of samples, while limiting the reduction in *variance* as per 143
Equation 4.96 where $\lim_{k\to\infty} R_k = 0$. 144

4.4 STATISTICAL ANALYSIS

4.4.1 Estimator

An *estimator* is a function of a collection of *random variables* X_i (which are not necessarily 129
independent or identically distributed) whose purpose is to estimate an unknown parameter

129 called the *estimand*. An estimator is therefore a *random variable* of the form

$$\tilde{S}_n \triangleq f(X_1, X_2, \ldots, X_n) \tag{4.56}$$

A distinction is often made between a *primary estimator* $\tilde{S}(X_i)$, which is expressed in terms of
129 a single *random variable*, and a *secondary estimator* built by averaging several such primary
estimators

$$\tilde{S}_n = \frac{1}{n}\sum_{i=1}^{n} \tilde{S}(X_i) \tag{4.57}$$

In practice, the function is actually applied to a particular observable sample set of data
to yield an *estimate*. The observations $\{x_1, x_2, \ldots, x_n\}$ may then be viewed either as a single
sample vector of sample size n, or as n individual samples. An estimator yielding estimates
that are systematically guaranteed to equal the estimand, i.e., an unbiased estimator with
143 zero *variance*, is called a *perfect estimator*.

4.4.2 Convergence

129 Mathematically, a sequence S_n of *random variables* is said to converge in *probability* towards
129 a parameter S if

$$\lim_{n\to\infty} \Pr(|S_n - S| < \varepsilon) = 1, \quad \forall \varepsilon > 0 \tag{4.58}$$

noted $S_n \xrightarrow{\Pr} S$, while it is said to converge almost surely towards S if

$$\Pr\left(\lim_{n\to\infty} S_n = S\right) = 1 \tag{4.59}$$

noted $S_n \xrightarrow{\text{a.s.}} S$, with *almost sure convergence* implying *convergence in probability*.
139 An *estimator* for a given parameter is then said to be (asymptotically) *consistent* if it
is guaranteed to converge to the value of the parameter. Intuitively, it means that as the
number of samples n increases, each subsequent estimate in the sequence is more likely to
be somewhere in the vicinity of the parameter being estimated, and in the limit the estimate
129 will be arbitrarily close to the parameter with *probability* one. A sufficient condition for an
139 *estimator* to be consistent is that its bias goes to zero as the sample size increases (i.e., it
143 is asymptotically unbiased) and so does its *variance*. More specifically, the *estimator* $\tilde{S}_n$ is a
139 139 *weakly consistent estimator* for parameter S if and only if the sequence $S_n = \tilde{S}_n$ converges
in probability to that parameter, i.e., $\tilde{S}_n \xrightarrow{\Pr} S$, while it is said to be *strongly consistent* if it
converges almost surely to the estimand, i.e., $\tilde{S}_n \xrightarrow{\text{a.s.}} S$.

4.4.3 Moment

By definition, the nth *moment* about the value c of a real-valued function $f(x)$ over the space Ω is the constant

$$\int_{\Omega} (x - c)^n f(x) \mathrm{d}x \tag{4.60}$$

131 Given a *probability density* $p(x)$ of a continuous *random variable* X, it follows that the
129 n^{th} moment about the origin, i.e., with $c = 0$, also called *raw moment* or *crude moment*, of
the distribution is given by

$$\mathrm{E}[X^n] \triangleq \int_{\Omega} x^n p(x) \mathrm{d}x \tag{4.61}$$

Similarly, the nth moment about the mean, i.e., with $c = \mathrm{E}[X]$, also called *central moment*,
131 of the *probability density* reads

$$\mathrm{E}\left[(X-\mathrm{E}[X])^n\right] \triangleq \int_\Omega (x-\mathrm{E}[X])^n p(x)\mathrm{d}x \tag{4.62}$$

and the first central moment thus is

$$\mathrm{E}\left[X-\mathrm{E}[X]\right] = \int_\Omega (x-\mathrm{E}[X])p(x)\mathrm{d}x = \int_\Omega xp(x)\mathrm{d}x - \mathrm{E}[X]\int_\Omega p(x)\mathrm{d}x \overset{(4.61)}{=} \mathrm{E}[X]-\mathrm{E}[X] = 0 \tag{4.63}$$ 140

4.4.4 Expected Value

The first raw moment of a continuous *random variable* X distributed according to a *probabil-* 129
ity density $p(x)$ over a space Ω_x is referred to as the *expected value*, also called mathematical 131
expectation or *mean*, of the *probability density* of X, and is defined as 131

$$\mathrm{E}[X] \overset{(4.61)}{=} \int_{\Omega_x} xp(x)\mathrm{d}x \tag{4.64}$$ 140

and that of a function $y = f(x)$ as

$$\mathrm{E}[f(X)] \overset{(4.61)}{=} \int_{\Omega_y} yp_y(y)\mathrm{d}y = \int_{\Omega_x} f(x)p_y(f(x))\left|\det\left(J_f(x)\right)\right|\mathrm{d}x \overset{(4.31)}{=} \int_{\Omega_x} f(x)p(x)\mathrm{d}x \tag{4.65}$$ 140 133

Given two continuous *random variables* X and Y and the non-random constants a and 129
b, it directly follows from the definition that

$$\begin{aligned}
\mathrm{E}[a] &= a && (4.66)\\
\mathrm{E}[aX+b] &= a\,\mathrm{E}[X]+b && (4.67)\\
\mathrm{E}[aX+bY] &= a\,\mathrm{E}[X]+b\,\mathrm{E}[Y] && (4.68)
\end{aligned}$$

while if X and Y are independent, then it additionally holds that

$$\begin{aligned}
\mathrm{E}[XY] &\triangleq \int_{\Omega_x}\int_{\Omega_y} xyp(x,y)\mathrm{d}x\mathrm{d}y\\
&\overset{(4.19)}{=} \int_{\Omega_x}\int_{\Omega_y} xyp(x)p(y)\mathrm{d}x\mathrm{d}y\\
&= \int_{\Omega_x} xp(x)\mathrm{d}x \int_{\Omega_y} yp(y)\mathrm{d}y\\
&\overset{(4.64)}{=} \mathrm{E}[X]\,\mathrm{E}[Y] && (4.69)
\end{aligned}$$ 132 141

In a multidimensional space, the *conditional expectation* of a *random variable* $Z =$ 129
$f(X,Y)$ with joint *probability density* $p(x,y)$ then reads 131

$$\mathrm{E}[Z \mid x] \triangleq \int_{\Omega_y} f(x,y)p(y\mid x)\mathrm{d}y \overset{(4.18)}{=} \frac{1}{p(x)}\int_{\Omega_y} f(x,y)p(x,y)\mathrm{d}y \tag{4.70}$$ 132

from which follows that

$$\begin{aligned}
\mathrm{E}[Z] &= \int_{\Omega_x}\int_{\Omega_y} f(x,y)p(x,y)\mathrm{d}y\mathrm{d}x\\
&= \int_{\Omega_x}\frac{1}{p(x)}\int_{\Omega_y} f(x,y)p(x,y)\mathrm{d}yp(x)\mathrm{d}x\\
&\overset{(4.70)}{=} \int_{\Omega_x} \mathrm{E}[Z\mid x]p(x)\mathrm{d}x\\
&\overset{(4.64)}{=} \mathrm{E}_X\left[\mathrm{E}[Z\mid x]\right] && (4.71)
\end{aligned}$$ 141 141

129 Given a random sample $[x_1, \ldots, x_n]$ from an n-dimensional *random variable* X (i.e., a
129 realization of a set of n independent and identically distributed (i.i.d.) *random variables* X_i with the same distribution as X), the expected value may in practice be estimated via the *sample mean*

$$\tilde{\mathrm{E}}_n[X] \triangleq \frac{1}{n}\sum_{i=1}^{n} x_i \tag{4.72}$$

which can be incrementally updated after i samples as follows

$$\tilde{\mathrm{E}}_i[X] = \frac{(i-1)\tilde{\mathrm{E}}_{i-1}[X] + x_i}{i} \tag{4.73}$$

139 The sample mean is an unbiased *estimator* of the expected value since its own expected value reads

142 141 141

$$\mathrm{E}\left[\tilde{\mathrm{E}}_n[X]\right] \overset{(4.72)}{=} \mathrm{E}\left[\frac{1}{n}\sum_{i=1}^{n} X_i\right] \overset{(4.67)}{=} \frac{1}{n}\mathrm{E}\left[\sum_{i=1}^{n} X_i\right] \overset{(4.68)}{=} \frac{1}{n}\sum_{i=1}^{n}\mathrm{E}[X_i] = \frac{1}{n} n\,\mathrm{E}[X] = \mathrm{E}[X] \tag{4.74}$$

Moreover, according to the *strong law of large numbers*, the sequence $S_n = \frac{1}{n}\sum_{i=1}^{n} X_i$ converges almost surely to the expected value $\mathrm{E}[X]$, provided that the latter exists, even if the
143 *variance* of each estimate is infinite, i.e., $\tilde{\mathrm{E}}_n[X] \xrightarrow{\text{a.s.}} \mathrm{E}[X]$. As more and more samples are taken, the sample mean is consequently guaranteed to converge to the expected value.

4.4.5 Covariance

129 Mathematically, the extent to which two real-valued *random variables* X and Y vary together is measured by the *covariance* between the two variables

141 141

$$\begin{aligned} \mathrm{C}[X,Y] &\triangleq \mathrm{E}\left[(X - \mathrm{E}[X])(Y - \mathrm{E}[Y])\right] \qquad (4.75) \\ &= \mathrm{E}\left[XY - X\,\mathrm{E}[Y] - Y\,\mathrm{E}[X] + \mathrm{E}[X]\,\mathrm{E}[Y]\right] \\ &\overset{(4.68)}{=} \mathrm{E}[XY] - \mathrm{E}\left[X\,\mathrm{E}[Y]\right] - \mathrm{E}\left[Y\,\mathrm{E}[X]\right] + \mathrm{E}\left[\mathrm{E}[X]\,\mathrm{E}[Y]\right] \\ &\overset{(4.67)}{=} \mathrm{E}[XY] - \mathrm{E}[X]\,\mathrm{E}[Y] - \mathrm{E}[Y]\,\mathrm{E}[X] + \mathrm{E}[X]\,\mathrm{E}[Y] \\ &= \mathrm{E}[XY] - \mathrm{E}[X]\,\mathrm{E}[Y] \qquad (4.76) \end{aligned}$$

That is, if when one variable is above its expected value the other variable tends to be also above its expected value, then their covariance will be positive. On the other hand, if one variable tends to be above its expected value when the other variable is below its expected
147 value, then their covariance will be negative. If the covariance is zero, then the *correlation* of the variables is also zero, and the latter are said to be uncorrelated.

129 Given three continuous *random variable* X, Y and Z and the non-random constants a and b, it directly follows from the definition that

$$\begin{aligned} \mathrm{C}[a,Z] &= 0 \qquad (4.77) \\ \mathrm{C}[X,Y] &= \mathrm{C}[Y,X] \qquad (4.78) \\ \mathrm{C}[aX+bY,Z] &= a\,\mathrm{C}[X,Z] + b\,\mathrm{C}[Y,Z] \qquad (4.79) \end{aligned}$$

while if X and Y are independent, then it additionally holds that their covariance is zero

142 141

$$\mathrm{C}[X,Y] \underset{(4.69)}{\overset{(4.76)}{=}} \mathrm{E}[X]\,\mathrm{E}[Y] - \mathrm{E}[X]\,\mathrm{E}[Y] = 0 \tag{4.80}$$

If X is an m-dimensional vector and Y an n-dimensional vector of real-valued *random variables*, assuming column vectors, then the definition of covariance generalizes into the 129
$m \times n$ *covariance matrix* $\mathrm{C}[X, Y] = \mathrm{E}\left[(X - E[X])(Y - E[Y])^T\right]$, from which follows that $\mathrm{C}[X, Y]$ and $\mathrm{C}[Y, X]$ are each other's transposes.

Given a set of random samples, the covariance may in practice be estimated via the *sample covariance*

$$\tilde{\mathrm{C}}[X, Y] \triangleq \frac{1}{n}\sum_{i=1}^{n}(X_i - \mathrm{E}[X])(Y_i - \mathrm{E}[Y]) \tag{4.81}$$

4.4.6 Variance

The second central moment of a continuous *random variable* X is referred to as the *variance*, which is a special case of covariance with the two variables being identical, and it is 129
mathematically defined as

$$\begin{aligned}
\mathrm{V}[X] &\triangleq \mathrm{C}[X, X] && (4.82)\\
&\overset{(4.75)}{=} \mathrm{E}\left[(X - \mathrm{E}[X])^2\right] && (4.83)\\
&= \mathrm{E}\left[X^2 - 2X\,\mathrm{E}[X] + \mathrm{E}[X]^2\right] &&\\
&\overset{(4.68)}{=} \mathrm{E}[X^2] - \mathrm{E}\left[2X\,\mathrm{E}[X]\right] + \mathrm{E}\left[\mathrm{E}[X]^2\right] &&\\
&\overset{(4.67)}{=} \mathrm{E}[X^2] - 2\,\mathrm{E}[X]\,\mathrm{E}[X] + \mathrm{E}[X]^2 &&\\
&= \mathrm{E}[X^2] - \mathrm{E}[X]^2 && (4.84)
\end{aligned}$$

142
141
141

such that

$$\mathrm{V}[X] \underset{(4.64)}{\overset{(4.83)}{=}} \int_\Omega (x - \mathrm{E}[X])^2 p(x)\mathrm{d}x \underset{(4.64)}{\overset{(4.84)}{=}} \int_\Omega x^2 p(x)\mathrm{d}x - \left(\int_\Omega x p(x)\mathrm{d}x\right)^2 \tag{4.85}$$

143
143
141
141

while the variance of a function $f(x)$ similarly reads

$$\begin{aligned}
\mathrm{V}[f(X)] &\underset{(4.65)}{\overset{(4.83)}{=}} \int_\Omega \left(f(x) - \mathrm{E}[f(X)]\right)^2 p(x)\mathrm{d}x && (4.86)\\
&\underset{(4.65)}{\overset{(4.84)}{=}} \int_\Omega f(x)^2 p(x)\mathrm{d}x - \left(\int_\Omega f(x)p(x)\mathrm{d}x\right)^2 && (4.87)
\end{aligned}$$

143
141
143
141

which measures the average squared deviation between the sample data and the mean of the distribution.

Given two continuous *random variables* X and Y and the non-random constants a and 129
b, it directly follows from the definition that

$$\begin{aligned}
\mathrm{V}[a] &= 0 && (4.88)\\
\mathrm{V}[aX + b] &= a^2\,\mathrm{V}[X] && (4.89)\\
\mathrm{V}[aX + bY] &= a^2\,\mathrm{V}[X] + b^2\,\mathrm{V}[Y] + 2ab\,\mathrm{C}[X, Y] && (4.90)
\end{aligned}$$

where the generalization of the latter expression to n *random variables* reads 129

143 $$\mathrm{V}\left[\sum_{i=1}^{n} a_i X_i\right] \overset{(4.82)}{=} \mathrm{C}\left[\sum_{i=1}^{n} a_i X_i, \sum_{j=1}^{n} a_j X_j\right]$$

142 $$\overset{(4.79)}{=} \sum_{i=1}^{n} a_i \,\mathrm{C}\left[X_i, \sum_{j=1}^{n} a_j X_j\right]$$

142 $$\overset{(4.79)}{=} \sum_{i=1}^{n}\sum_{j=1}^{n} a_i a_j \,\mathrm{C}[X_i, X_j]$$

$$= \sum_{i=1}^{n}\left(a_i^2 \,\mathrm{C}[X_i, X_i] + \sum_{j=1}^{i-1} a_i a_j \,\mathrm{C}[X_i, X_j] + \sum_{j=i+1}^{n} a_i a_j \,\mathrm{C}[X_i, X_j]\right)$$

143 $$\overset{(4.82)}{=} \sum_{i=1}^{n} a_i^2 \,\mathrm{V}[X_i] + \sum_{j=1}^{n}\sum_{i=j+1}^{n} a_i a_j \,\mathrm{C}[X_i, X_j] + \sum_{i=1}^{n}\sum_{j=i+1}^{n} a_i a_j \,\mathrm{C}[X_i, X_j]$$

142 $$\overset{(4.78)}{=} \sum_{i=1}^{n} a_i^2 \,\mathrm{V}[X_i] + 2\sum_{i=1}^{n}\sum_{j=i+1}^{n} a_i a_j \,\mathrm{C}[X_i, X_j] \tag{4.91}$$

which, in the case of uncorrelated variables, i.e., $\mathrm{C}[X_i, X_j] = 0, \forall i, j \in [1, n]$, reduces to

$$\mathrm{V}\left[\sum_{i=1}^{n} a_i X_i\right] = \sum_{i=1}^{n} a_i^2 \,\mathrm{V}[X_i] \tag{4.92}$$

while for independent variables X and Y, it also holds that

$$\mathrm{V}[XY] = \mathrm{E}[X]^2\,\mathrm{V}[Y] + \mathrm{E}[Y]^2\,\mathrm{V}[X] + \mathrm{V}[X]\,\mathrm{V}[Y] \tag{4.93}$$

$$= \mathrm{E}[X^2]\,\mathrm{E}[Y^2] - \mathrm{E}[X]^2\,\mathrm{E}[Y]^2 \tag{4.94}$$

The variance of the sample mean consequently decreases with a factor n with respect to
139 that of the primary *estimator*

142 $$\mathrm{V}\left[\tilde{\mathrm{E}}[X]\right] \overset{(4.72)}{=} \mathrm{V}\left[\frac{1}{n}\sum_{i=1}^{n} X_i\right]$$

143 $$\overset{(4.89)}{=} \frac{1}{n^2}\mathrm{V}\left[\sum_{i=1}^{n} X_i\right]$$

144 $$\overset{(4.91)}{=} \frac{\sum_{i=1}^{n}\mathrm{V}[X_i] + 2\sum_{i=1}^{n}\sum_{j=i+1}^{n}\mathrm{C}[X_i, X_j]}{n^2}$$

$$= \frac{\mathrm{V}[X]}{n} + 2\frac{\sum_{i=1}^{n}\sum_{j=i+1}^{n}\mathrm{C}[X_i, X_j]}{n^2} \tag{4.95}$$

which, in the case where the covariance between X_i and X_j is stationary and only depends on $j - i$ such that $\mathrm{C}[X_i, X_j] = R_{j-i}$, reduces to

$$\mathrm{V}\left[\tilde{\mathrm{E}}[X]\right] = \frac{\mathrm{V}[X]}{n} + 2\frac{\sum_{i=1}^{n}\sum_{j=i+1}^{n} R_{j-i}}{n^2} = \frac{\mathrm{V}[X]}{n} + 2\frac{\sum_{k=1}^{n-1}(n-k)R_k}{n^2} \leq \frac{\mathrm{V}[X] + 2\sum_{k=1}^{n-1} R_k}{n} \tag{4.96}$$

and, in the case of uncorrelated variables, reduces further to

$$\mathrm{V}\left[\tilde{\mathrm{E}}[X]\right] = \frac{\mathrm{V}[X]}{n} \tag{4.97}$$

In case of an n-dimensional column vector X of real-valued *random variables*, the definition of variance generalizes into a positive semidefinite square matrix, also commonly referred to as the covariance matrix $\mathrm{E}\left[(X - \mathrm{E}[X])(X - \mathrm{E}[X])^T\right]$. 129

In a multidimensional space, the *conditional variance* of a *random variable* $Z = f(X, Y)$ then reads 129

$$\mathrm{V}[Z \mid x] \triangleq \mathrm{E}[Z^2 \mid x] - \mathrm{E}[Z \mid x]^2 \tag{4.98}$$

from which follows that

$$\mathrm{V}[Z] \overset{(4.84)}{=} \mathrm{E}[Z^2] - \mathrm{E}[Z]^2$$ 143

$$\overset{(4.71)}{=} \mathrm{E}_X\left[\mathrm{E}[Z^2 \mid x]\right] - \mathrm{E}_X\left[\mathrm{E}[Z \mid x]\right]^2$$ 141

$$= \mathrm{E}_X\left[\mathrm{E}[Z^2 \mid x] - \mathrm{E}[Z \mid x]^2 + \mathrm{E}[Z \mid x]^2\right] - \mathrm{E}_X\left[\mathrm{E}[Z \mid x]\right]^2$$

$$\overset{(4.68)}{=} \mathrm{E}_X\left[\mathrm{E}[Z^2 \mid x] - \mathrm{E}[Z \mid x]^2\right] + \mathrm{E}_X\left[\mathrm{E}[Z \mid x]^2\right] - \mathrm{E}_X\left[\mathrm{E}[Z \mid x]\right]^2$$ 141

$$\underset{(4.84)}{\overset{(4.98)}{=}} \mathrm{E}_X\left[\mathrm{V}[Z \mid x]\right] + \mathrm{V}_X\left[\mathrm{E}[Z \mid x]\right] \tag{4.99}$$ 145 143

Given a set of random samples, the variance may in practice be estimated via the *sample variance*

$$\tilde{\mathrm{V}}[X] \triangleq \frac{1}{n}\sum_{i=1}^{n}(X_i - \mathrm{E}[X])^2 \tag{4.100}$$

However, because the sample mean is usually used instead as an estimate of the true expectation, the latter being typically unknown, it is necessary to adjust the leading constant using *Bessel's correction factor*

$$\begin{aligned}
\tilde{\mathrm{V}}[X] &\triangleq \frac{1}{n-1}\sum_{i=1}^{n}(X_i - \tilde{\mathrm{E}}[X])^2 && (4.101)\\
&= \frac{1}{n-1}\sum_{i=1}^{n}(X_i^2 - 2X_i\tilde{\mathrm{E}}[X] + \tilde{\mathrm{E}}[X]^2)\\
&= \frac{1}{n-1}\left(\sum_{i=1}^{n}X_i^2 - 2\tilde{\mathrm{E}}[X]\sum_{i=1}^{n}X_i + \sum_{i=1}^{n}\tilde{\mathrm{E}}[X]^2\right)
\end{aligned}$$

$$\overset{(4.72)}{=} \frac{1}{n-1}\left(\sum_{i=1}^{n}X_i^2 - 2\tilde{\mathrm{E}}[X]n\tilde{\mathrm{E}}[X] + n\tilde{\mathrm{E}}[X]^2\right)$$ 142

$$= \frac{1}{n-1}\left(\sum_{i=1}^{n}X_i^2 - n\tilde{\mathrm{E}}[X]^2\right) \tag{4.102}$$

in order for the *estimator* to be unbiased 139

145 $$\mathrm{E}\left[\tilde{\mathrm{V}}[X]\right] \overset{(4.102)}{=} \mathrm{E}\left[\frac{1}{n-1}\left(\sum_{i=1}^{n} X_i^2 - n\tilde{\mathrm{E}}[X]^2\right)\right]$$

141 $$\overset{(4.68)}{=} \frac{1}{n-1}\left(\sum_{i=1}^{n} \mathrm{E}\left[X_i^2\right] - \mathrm{E}\left[n\tilde{\mathrm{E}}[X]^2\right]\right)$$

141 $$\overset{(4.67)}{=} \frac{n}{n-1}\left(\mathrm{E}\left[X^2\right] - \mathrm{E}\left[\tilde{\mathrm{E}}[X]^2\right]\right)$$

143 $$\overset{(4.84)}{=} \frac{n}{n-1}\left(\mathrm{V}[X] + \mathrm{E}[X]^2 - \mathrm{V}\left[\tilde{\mathrm{E}}[X]\right] - \mathrm{E}\left[\tilde{\mathrm{E}}[X]\right]^2\right)$$

144 142 $$\underset{(4.74)}{\overset{(4.97)}{=}} \frac{n}{n-1}\left(\mathrm{V}[X] + \mathrm{E}[X]^2 - \frac{1}{n}\mathrm{V}[X] - \mathrm{E}[X]^2\right)$$

$$= \frac{n}{n-1}\left(1 - \frac{1}{n}\right)\mathrm{V}[X]$$

$$= \mathrm{V}[X] \tag{4.103}$$

4.4.7 Standard Deviation

143 Mathematically, *standard deviation* is defined as the square root of *variance*

$$\sigma[X] \triangleq \sqrt{\mathrm{V}[X]} \tag{4.104}$$

and is therefore a non-negative measure of the statistical dispersion, or variability, of a
131 *probability density*. A low standard deviation indicates that the data points tend to be very close to the mean, while high standard deviation indicates that the data are spread out over a large range of values. Sample sets with lower standard deviation are generally more efficient as they typically require fewer random samples before the sample mean is a good estimate of the true mean of the underlying distribution.

129 Given a continuous *random variable* X and the non-random constants a and b, it directly follows from the definition that

$$\sigma[a] = 0 \tag{4.105}$$
$$\sigma[aX + b] = |a|\sigma[X] \tag{4.106}$$

Standard deviation may in practice be estimated via the *sample standard deviation*

$$\tilde{\sigma}[X] \triangleq \sqrt{\tilde{\mathrm{V}}[X]} \tag{4.107}$$

139 which is a biased *estimator* as it tends to underestimate the standard deviation of the distribution due to the non-linearity of the square-root operator.

129 141 143 Given a *random variable* $\tilde{S} = \tilde{\mathrm{E}}[X]$ with finite *expected value* and *variance*, a probabilistic

bound on the absolute error can be derived using *Chebyshev's inequality*

$$\begin{aligned}
\Pr\left(\frac{|\tilde{S}-\mathrm{E}[\tilde{S}]|}{\sigma[\tilde{S}]} \geq k\right) &\overset{(4.72)}{\underset{(4.97)}{\overset{(4.74)}{=}}} \Pr\left(\left|\frac{1}{n}\sum_{i=1}^{n} X_i - \mathrm{E}[X]\right| \geq k\frac{\sigma[X]}{\sqrt{n}}\right) \\
&= \mathrm{E}\left[\chi_{[k,\infty]}\left(\frac{|\tilde{S}-\mathrm{E}[\tilde{S}]|}{\sigma[\tilde{S}]}\right)\right] \\
&= \mathrm{E}\left[\chi_{[1,\infty]}\left(\frac{|\tilde{S}-\mathrm{E}[\tilde{S}]|}{k\sigma[\tilde{S}]}\right)\right] \\
&= \mathrm{E}\left[\chi_{[1,\infty]}\left(\left(\frac{|\tilde{S}-\mathrm{E}[\tilde{S}]|}{k\sigma[\tilde{S}]}\right)^2\right)\right] \\
&\leq \mathrm{E}\left[\left(\frac{|\tilde{S}-\mathrm{E}[\tilde{S}]|}{k\sigma[\tilde{S}]}\right)^2\right] \\
&\overset{(4.67)}{\underset{(4.104)}{=}} \frac{\mathrm{E}\left[(|\tilde{S}-\mathrm{E}[\tilde{S}]|)^2\right]}{k^2\,\mathrm{V}[\tilde{S}]} \\
&\overset{(4.83)}{=} \frac{1}{k^2}, \quad \forall k > 0
\end{aligned} \tag{4.108}$$

142 142 144 141 146 143

As an alternative, a bound on the absolute error may also be obtained from the *central limit theorem*, which states that the distribution of the average of independent samples of a *random variable* X with finite *expected value* and *variance* is given by the *convolution* 129
of their individual *probability density* functions, and asymptotically converges to a normal 141
Gaussian distribution 143 176 131 51

$$\frac{\tilde{S}-\mathrm{E}[\tilde{S}]}{\sigma[\tilde{S}]} \overset{(4.72)}{\underset{(4.97)}{\overset{(4.74)}{=}}} \frac{\sqrt{n}}{\sigma[X]}\left(\frac{1}{n}\sum_{i=1}^{n} X_i - \mathrm{E}[X]\right) \overset{n\to\infty}{\approx} G_N(t) \tag{4.109}$$

142 142 144

whose *cumulative distribution* yields 132

$$\begin{aligned}
\lim_{n\to\infty} \Pr\left(\frac{\tilde{S}-\mathrm{E}[\tilde{S}]}{\sigma[\tilde{S}]} \leq k\right) &\overset{(4.72)}{\underset{(4.97)}{\overset{(4.74)}{=}}} \lim_{n\to\infty} \Pr\left(\frac{1}{n}\sum_{i=1}^{n} X_i - \mathrm{E}[X] \leq k\frac{\sigma[X]}{\sqrt{n}}\right) \\
&\overset{(4.21)}{=} \int_{-\infty}^{k} G_N(t)\mathrm{d}t
\end{aligned} \tag{4.110}$$

142 142 144 132

4.4.8 Correlation

Given two *random variables* X and Y with *covariance* $\mathrm{C}[X,Y]$ and with finite and non- 129
zero *standard deviations* $\sigma[X]$ and $\sigma[Y]$, the strength and direction of a linear relationship 142 146
between them is measured by their *correlation*

$$\rho[X,Y] \triangleq \frac{\mathrm{C}[X,Y]}{\sigma[X]\sigma[Y]} \in [-1,+1] \tag{4.111}$$

In case of an increasing linear relationship, the correlation is +1 while it is −1 in case of a decreasing linear relationship. In all other cases, the correlation takes some intermediate value while its absolute value increases with the degree of linear dependence between the variables. Given that the covariance of independent variables is zero, so is their correlation and the variables are then said to be uncorrelated, but the converse is generally not true because the correlation coefficient is only an indicator of linear dependencies between two variables. For
129 instance, assuming a continuous *random variable* X uniformly distributed on the interval
$[-1, +1]$ and another variable defined as $Y = X^2$, X and Y are obviously dependent since Y is completely determined by X, but they are nonetheless uncorrelated since their correlation is zero.

More general measures, such as *total correlation*, which is based on entropy, are better indicators of how cohesive or related the variables of a group are. A near-zero total correlation indicates that the variables in the group are essentially statistically independent, i.e., they are completely unrelated, in the sense that knowing the value of one variable does not provide any clue as to the values of the other variables. It is important to note, though, that establishing a correlation between two variables is not a sufficient condition to formally infer a causal relationship between them in either direction; in other words, correlation does not necessarily imply causation.

Correlation may in practice be estimated via the *sample correlation* coefficient, also known as the *Pearson product-moment correlation* coefficient

$$\tilde{\rho}[X, Y] \triangleq \frac{\tilde{\mathrm{C}}[X, Y]}{\tilde{\sigma}[X]\tilde{\sigma}[Y]} \tag{4.112}$$

4.4.9 Error

139 Given an *estimator* $\tilde{S}$, the *error* of the estimation is defined as the difference between the
140 estimate and the actual value of the estimand S. The first raw *moment* of the error is then
139 referred to as the *systematic error*, also commonly known as the *bias*, of the *estimator*

141
141

$$\mathrm{B}[\tilde{S}] \triangleq \mathrm{E}[\tilde{S} - S] \overset{(4.67)}{=} \mathrm{E}[\tilde{S}] - \mathrm{E}[S] \overset{(4.66)}{=} \mathrm{E}[\tilde{S}] - S \tag{4.113}$$

139 An *estimator* $\tilde{S}$ is said to be unbiased if and only if $\mathrm{B}[\tilde{S}] = 0$ for any estimand S, while it is
141 said to be biased if its *expected value* differs from S. Also, an *estimator* is said to be *asymp-*
139 *totically unbiased* if it is unbiased as the sample size tends to infinity, i.e., $\lim_{n\to\infty} \mathrm{B}[\tilde{S}_n] = 0$.
139 It follows that all unbiased *estimators* are asymptotically unbiased, while only some but not
139 all biased *estimators* are asymptotically unbiased.
140 Similarly, the second raw *moment* of the error is referred to as the *mean squared error*
(*MSE*), which corresponds to the expected value of the squared errors

$$\mathrm{MSE}[\tilde{S}] \triangleq \mathrm{E}[(\tilde{S} - S)^2] \tag{4.114}$$

$$= \mathrm{E}[\tilde{S}^2 - 2\tilde{S}S + S^2]$$

141

$$\overset{(4.68)}{=} \mathrm{E}[\tilde{S}^2] - \mathrm{E}[2\tilde{S}S] + \mathrm{E}[S^2]$$

141

$$\overset{(4.67)}{=} \mathrm{E}[\tilde{S}^2] - \mathrm{E}[\tilde{S}]^2 + \mathrm{E}[\tilde{S}]^2 - 2\,\mathrm{E}[\tilde{S}]S + S^2$$

141

$$\underset{(4.66)}{=} \mathrm{E}[\tilde{S}^2] - \mathrm{E}[\tilde{S}]^2 + (\mathrm{E}[\tilde{S}] - S)^2$$

143
148

$$\overset{(4.84)}{\underset{(4.113)}{=}} \mathrm{V}[\tilde{S}] + \mathrm{B}[\tilde{S}]^2 \tag{4.115}$$

from which follows that the MSE assesses the quality of an *estimator* in terms of both its 139
variance and squared bias, and it is therefore an indicator of the amount by which the 143
collection of estimates differs overall from the true value of the estimand.

Except for some ideal cases, it is usually impossible in practice to design a perfect *estimator*. Depending on the application, a biased *estimator* with low *variance* might be more 139
desirable than an unbiased one with higher *variance*, while the inverse is preferable in other 139 143
cases. Like *variance*, the mean squared error has the disadvantage of heavily weighting out- 143
liers due to the squaring of the terms, effectively weighting large errors more heavily than 143
small ones. In applications where this property is undesirable, the *mean absolute error* can be used instead as an alternative.

The square root of the MSE is then called the *root mean squared error* (*RMSE*)

$$\mathrm{RMSE}[\tilde{S}] = \sqrt{\mathrm{MSE}[\tilde{S}]} \tag{4.116}$$

Like *variance*, MSE has the same unit of measurement as the square of the estimand, while 143
similarly to *standard deviation*, RMSE has the same units as the estimand. For an unbi- 146
ased *estimator*, the MSE is the *variance* of (the sampling distribution associated with) the 139
estimator, while the RMSE is its *standard deviation*, also known as the *standard error*. 143 139

In the case of an estimand $S(t)$ defined as a function of a continuous parameter t, the 146
aggregate error of the *estimator* over the entire domain is given by the *mean integrated* 139
squared error (*MISE*)

$$\mathrm{MISE}[\tilde{S}] \triangleq \mathrm{E}\left[\int_{\mathcal{D}} \left(\tilde{S}(t) - S(t)\right)^2 \mathrm{d}t\right] \stackrel{(4.68)}{=} \int_{\mathcal{D}} \mathrm{E}\left[\left(\tilde{S}(t) - S(t)\right)^2\right] \mathrm{d}t \stackrel{(4.114)}{=} \int_{\mathcal{D}} \mathrm{MSE}[\tilde{S}(t)]\mathrm{d}t \tag{4.117}$$
141 148

While the *variance* of an estimate may be reduced by increasing the sample size, the 143
running time $\mathrm{T}[\tilde{S}]$ required to evaluate the estimate will typically increase as a counterpart. The trade-off between the quality of an unbiased Monte Carlo *estimator* and its cost can 139
then be measured by its *efficiency*

$$\epsilon[\tilde{S}] \triangleq \frac{1}{\mathrm{V}[\tilde{S}]\,\mathrm{T}[\tilde{S}]} \tag{4.118}$$

Assuming that the cost of the sample mean is proportional to the number of samples, its efficiency is consequently constant given that its *variance* decreases linearly with the number 143
of samples.

4.5 MONTE CARLO INTEGRATION

Monte Carlo integration is a numerical method for the stochastic estimation of definite integrals. Unlike deterministic *polynomial integration* schemes, the convergence rate and sta- 22
tistical error of the technique are independent of the dimensionality of the integral and of its continuity properties, and so is the number of function samples required by the evaluation process, thereby making the method robust and particularly well suited for estimating general multidimensional integrals.

4.5.1 Integral Estimation

Assuming a constant *probability density* $p(x) = 1 \div \|\mathcal{D}\|$ over a domain $\mathcal{D}$ as in the crude 131
Monte Carlo algorithm, the expectation of a function $f(x)$ reduces to its mean

$$\bar{f} \triangleq \frac{1}{\|\mathcal{D}\|} \int_{\mathcal{D}} f(x)\mathrm{d}x \stackrel{(4.65)}{=} \mathrm{E}[f(X)] \tag{4.119}$$
141

and rearranging the terms leads to the following formulation of the definite integral

$$F \triangleq \int_{\mathcal{D}} f(x)\mathrm{d}x = \|\mathcal{D}\|\bar{f} = \|\mathcal{D}\|\,\mathrm{E}[f(X)] \tag{4.120}$$

In practice, the expectation of the integrand may be estimated using the sample mean of n random sample points x_i uniformly distributed according to $p(x)$ in the integration volume defined by the hypercube $\mathcal{D}$

142 $$\tilde{F} \triangleq \|\mathcal{D}\|\tilde{\mathrm{E}}[f(X)] \overset{(4.72)}{=} \frac{\|\mathcal{D}\|}{n}\sum_{i=1}^{n} f(X_i) \tag{4.121}$$

139 which is an unbiased *estimator* as its expected value equals the true value of the integral

150 141 142 150 $$\mathrm{E}[\tilde{F}] \overset{(4.121)}{=} \mathrm{E}\left[\|\mathcal{D}\|\tilde{\mathrm{E}}[f(X)]\right] \overset{(4.67)}{=} \|\mathcal{D}\|\,\mathrm{E}\left[\tilde{\mathrm{E}}[f(X)]\right] \overset{(4.74)}{=} \|\mathcal{D}\|\,\mathrm{E}[f(X)] \overset{(4.120)}{=} F \tag{4.122}$$

143 Also, the *variance* of the function simplifies into

143 143 $$\mathrm{V}[f(X)] \overset{(4.86)}{=} \frac{1}{\|\mathcal{D}\|}\int_{\mathcal{D}} (f(x) - \bar{f})^2 \mathrm{d}x \overset{(4.87)}{=} \frac{1}{\|\mathcal{D}\|}\int_{\mathcal{D}} f(x)^2 \mathrm{d}x - \bar{f}^2 \tag{4.123}$$

143 139 such that, assuming uncorrelated variables, the *variance* of the *estimator* evaluates to

150 143 144 $$\mathrm{V}[\tilde{F}] \overset{(4.121)}{=} \mathrm{V}\left[\|\mathcal{D}\|\tilde{\mathrm{E}}[f(X)]\right] \overset{(4.89)}{=} \|\mathcal{D}\|^2\,\mathrm{V}\left[\tilde{\mathrm{E}}[f(X)]\right] \overset{(4.97)}{=} \frac{\|\mathcal{D}\|^2}{n}\mathrm{V}[f(X)] \tag{4.124}$$

150 150 $$\overset{(4.123)}{=} \frac{\|\mathcal{D}\|}{n}\int_{\mathcal{D}} (f(x) - \bar{f})^2 \mathrm{d}x \overset{(4.123)}{=} \frac{1}{n}\left(\|\mathcal{D}\|\int_{\mathcal{D}} f(x)^2 \mathrm{d}x - F^2\right) \tag{4.125}$$

which decreases to zero as the function tends towards a constant value.

146 139 The *standard deviation* of the *estimator* consequently reads

146 150 146 $$\sigma[\tilde{F}] \overset{(4.104)}{=} \sqrt{\mathrm{V}[\tilde{F}]} \overset{(4.124)}{=} \sqrt{\frac{\|\mathcal{D}\|^2}{n}\mathrm{V}[f(X)]} \overset{(4.104)}{=} \frac{\|\mathcal{D}\|}{n^{\frac{1}{2}}}\sigma[f(X)] \tag{4.126}$$

from which follows that the *convergence rate* of the method is $1/2$, a property often referred to as *diminishing return* since an n^2-fold increase in the number of sample points is needed to reduce the expected error by a factor of $1/n$.

4.5.2 Integral Equation

Given an unknown function $f(x)$, a known function $g(x)$ and a kernel function $K(x, y)$, a *Fredholm integral equation* of the second kind is an equation of the form

150 $$f(x) = g(x) + \int_{\mathcal{D}} K(x, y) f(y)\mathrm{d}y \overset{(4.129)}{=} g(x) + (\mathcal{T}f)(x) = (\mathcal{S}g)(x) \tag{4.127}$$

where the solution operator

16 $$\mathcal{S} \triangleq 1 + \mathcal{T}\mathcal{S} = \sum_{i=0}^{\infty} \mathcal{T}^i \overset{(2.11)}{=} (1 - \mathcal{T})^{-1}, \quad \exists i \geq 1 \mid |\mathcal{T}^i| < 1 \tag{4.128}$$

is defined in terms of the integral operator

$$(\mathcal{T}f)(x) \triangleq \int_{\mathcal{D}} K(x, y) f(y)\mathrm{d}y \tag{4.129}$$

Expanding the solution into a Neumann series yields

$$\begin{aligned}
f(x_0) &\stackrel{(4.127)}{=} g(x_0) + \int_{\mathcal{D}} K(x_0, x_1) f(x_1) \mathrm{d}x_1 \\
&\stackrel{(4.127)}{=} g(x_0) + \int_{\mathcal{D}} K(x_0, x_1) \left(g(x_1) + \int_{\mathcal{D}} K(x_1, x_2) f(x_2) \mathrm{d}x_2 \right) \mathrm{d}x_1 \\
&= g(x_0) + \int_{\mathcal{D}} K(x_0, x_1) g(x_1) \mathrm{d}x_1 + \int_{\mathcal{D}} \int_{\mathcal{D}} K(x_0, x_1) K(x_1, x_2) f(x_2) \mathrm{d}x_2 \mathrm{d}x_1 \\
&= \ldots \\
&= g(x_0) + \sum_{i=1}^{\infty} \int_{\mathcal{D}} \cdots \int_{\mathcal{D}} T(x_0, \ldots, x_i) g(x_i) \mathrm{d}x_i \ldots \mathrm{d}x_1 \qquad (4.130)
\end{aligned}$$

150

150

where the throughput is defined as

$$T(x_0, \ldots, x_i) \triangleq \prod_{j=1}^{i} K(x_{j-1}, x_j) \qquad (4.131)$$

The sum of multidimensional integrals

$$\begin{aligned}
f(x) &\stackrel{(2.218)}{=} \int_{\mathcal{D}} \delta(x - x_0) f(x_0) \mathrm{d}x_0 \\
&= \sum_{i=0}^{\infty} \int_{\mathcal{D}} \cdots \int_{\mathcal{D}} \delta(x - x_0) T(x_0, \ldots, x_i) g(x_i) \mathrm{d}x_i \ldots \mathrm{d}x_0 \qquad (4.132)
\end{aligned}$$

45

may then be evaluated using *estimators* of the form 139

$$\tilde{f}(x) \stackrel{(4.158)}{=} \sum_{i=0}^{\infty} \frac{\delta(x - x_0) T(x_0, \ldots, x_i) g(x_i)}{p(x_0, \ldots, x_i)} \qquad (4.133)$$

156

While drawing the multidimensional sample $[x_0, \ldots, x_i]$ of each summand independently would avoid any form of correlation, efficiency may generally be increased by incrementally constructing the latter by extending the sample of the previous summand in the sequence with an additional step x_i. Doing so results in a random walk through the (continuous) domain $\mathcal{D}$, effectively estimating the nested integral recursively with a single sample at each step of the walk. Given the PDF $p(x_0)$ of the initial state x_0 and the transition PDF $p(x_i \mid x_0, \ldots, x_{i-1}) = p(x_i \mid x_{i-1})$ of the subsequent states x_i, the joint *probability density* 131
reads

$$p(x_0, \ldots, x_i) = p(x_0) \prod_{j=1}^{i} p(x_j \mid x_{j-1}) \qquad (4.134)$$

When carrying *importance sampling* by defining the transition PDF in terms of the kernel 155
function $p(x_i \mid x_{i-1}) = K(x_{i-1}, x_i)$ and $p(x_0) = \delta(x - x_0)$, the estimator reduces to

$$\tilde{f}(x) \stackrel{(4.133)}{=} \sum_{i=0}^{\infty} \frac{\delta(x - x_0) T(x_0, \ldots, x_i) g(x_i)}{p(x_0) \prod_{j=1}^{i} K(x_{j-1}, x_j)} \stackrel{(4.131)}{=} \sum_{i=0}^{\infty} g(x_i) \qquad (4.135)$$

151
151

While the PDF of the initial state $p(x_0)$ ought to be normalized, the transition PDFs can be sub-critical $\int_{\mathcal{D}} p(x_i \mid x_{i-1}) \mathrm{d}x_i < 1$. Absorption may then occur and the walk be terminated at x_i using *Russian roulette* with probability $1 - \int_{\mathcal{D}} p(x_i \mid x_{i-1}) \mathrm{d}x_i$. As an alternative, the 163
latter integral can be used as a partial propagation factor, allowing the sub-critical PDFs to be renormalized via the *use of expected values*, a technique known as *absorption suppression*. 152

4.6 VARIANCE-REDUCTION TECHNIQUES

143 Variance-reduction techniques focus on decreasing the *variance* of an *estimator* in order to
139 improve the quality of the resulting Monte Carlo estimate, potentially leading to an increase
in the efficiency of the estimation scheme for a given number of samples.

4.6.1 Use of Expected Values

The *use of expected values* consists in reducing the dimensionality of the sample space by integrating analytically with respect to one or several variables. Considering the potentially multidimensional vectors x and y and assuming that the function

150

$$g(x) \triangleq \int_{\mathcal{D}_y} f(x,y)\mathrm{d}y \overset{(4.120)}{=} \|\mathcal{D}_y\| \operatorname{E}[f(X,Y) \mid x] \tag{4.136}$$

can be integrated by means other than stochastic methods, the integral of interest may then be rewritten as

$$F \triangleq \int_{\mathcal{D}_x} \int_{\mathcal{D}_y} f(x,y)\mathrm{d}y\mathrm{d}x = \int_{\mathcal{D}_x} g(x)\mathrm{d}x \tag{4.137}$$

131 Defining the constant *probability density* $p(x,y) = \frac{1}{\|\mathcal{D}_x\|\|\mathcal{D}_y\|}$, the crude Monte Carlo
139 *estimator* reads
150

$$\tilde{F}_0 \overset{(4.121)}{=} \frac{\|\mathcal{D}_x\|\|\mathcal{D}_y\|}{n} \sum_{i=1}^{n} f(X_i, Y_i) \tag{4.138}$$

143 and its *variance* is

144

$$\operatorname{V}[\tilde{F}_0] \overset{(4.92)}{=} \frac{\|\mathcal{D}_x\|^2\|\mathcal{D}_y\|^2}{n^2} \sum_{i=1}^{n} \operatorname{V}[f(X_i, Y_i)] = \frac{\|\mathcal{D}_x\|^2\|\mathcal{D}_y\|^2}{n} \operatorname{V}[f(X,Y)] \tag{4.139}$$

131 Defining the constant *probability density* $p(x) = \frac{1}{\|\mathcal{D}_x\|}$ instead, the new *estimator* can be
139
139 expressed as the conditional expected value of the crude *estimator*

150
152

$$\tilde{F} \overset{(4.121)}{=} \frac{\|\mathcal{D}_x\|}{n} \sum_{i=1}^{n} g(X_i) \overset{(4.136)}{=} \frac{\|\mathcal{D}_x\|\|\mathcal{D}_y\|}{n} \sum_{i=1}^{n} \operatorname{E}[f(X_i, Y) \mid X_i] \tag{4.140}$$

143 whose *variance*, assuming uncorrelated variables, then reads

144
145
152

$$\begin{aligned}
\operatorname{V}[\tilde{F}] &\overset{(4.92)}{=} \frac{\|\mathcal{D}_x\|^2\|\mathcal{D}_y\|^2}{n^2} \sum_{i=1}^{n} \operatorname{V}_X\left[\operatorname{E}[f(X_i, Y) \mid X_i]\right] \\
&= \frac{\|\mathcal{D}_x\|^2\|\mathcal{D}_y\|^2}{n} \operatorname{V}_X\left[\operatorname{E}[f(X,Y) \mid X]\right] \\
&\overset{(4.99)}{=} \frac{\|\mathcal{D}_x\|^2\|\mathcal{D}_y\|^2}{n} \left(\operatorname{V}[f(X,Y)] - \operatorname{E}_X\left[\operatorname{V}[f(X,Y) \mid X]\right]\right) \\
&\overset{(4.139)}{=} \operatorname{V}[\tilde{F}_0] - \operatorname{E}_X\left[\operatorname{V}[\tilde{F}_0 \mid X]\right]
\end{aligned} \tag{4.141}$$

143 where the latter term represents the component of the *variance* of $\tilde{F}_0$ caused by the random
143 sampling of Y. Because this term is always non-negative, the *variance* of the new *estimator*
139
139 is consequently guaranteed to be no greater than that of the crude *estimator*.

4.6.2 Stratified Sampling

Based on the idea that a function generally tends to vary less over a smaller domain, *stratified sampling* consists in dividing an initial domain of integration into a set of exhaustive and mutually exclusive strata and in generating random samples so that at least one sample lies in each stratum. Considering the 1-D case where $\|\mathcal{D}\| \triangleq x_b - x_a$ with m non-overlapping intervals such that $x_a = x_0 < x_1 < \ldots < x_{m-1} < x_m = x_b$, the integral is rewritten

$$F \triangleq \int_{x_a}^{x_b} f(x)\mathrm{d}x = \sum_{j=1}^{m} F_j \tag{4.142}$$

where $F_j \triangleq \int_{x_{j-1}}^{x_j} f(x)\mathrm{d}x$, and the estimator becomes 139

$$\tilde{F} \overset{(4.121)}{=} \sum_{j=1}^{m} \frac{x_j - x_{j-1}}{n_j} \sum_{i=1}^{n_j} f(X_{ij}) \tag{4.143}$$
150

where $X_{ij} \in [x_{j-1}, x_j)$ is defined as $X_{ij} \triangleq x_{j-1} + (x_j - x_{j-1})\xi_{ij}$ with $\xi_{ij} \in [0, 1)$ being a newly chosen random number for every combination of $[i, j]$. The sample mean for the jth stratum is estimated using n_j samples and then multiplied by the size of the interval, which
is an unbiased generalization of the deterministic rectangle rule for integration based on the 23
midpoint of the intervals. It is also worth noting that if all strata use the same number of samples $n_j = n$, the offsets may alternatively be correlated by instead choosing a new random number $\xi_{ij} = \xi_i$ for every i only.

Assuming uncorrelated variables, the variance of the stratified estimator reads 143 139

$$\begin{aligned}
\mathrm{V}[\tilde{F}] &\overset{(4.92)}{=} \sum_{j=1}^{m} \frac{(x_j - x_{j-1})^2}{n_j^2} \sum_{i=1}^{n_j} \mathrm{V}[f(X_{ij})] \\
&= \sum_{j=1}^{m} \frac{(x_j - x_{j-1})^2}{n_j} \mathrm{V}[f(X_j)] \\
&\overset{(4.87)}{=} \sum_{j=1}^{m} \frac{1}{n_j} \left((x_j - x_{j-1}) \int_{x_{j-1}}^{x_j} f(x)^2 \mathrm{d}x - F_j^2 \right)
\end{aligned} \tag{4.144}$$
144 143

which might be less than that of the crude Monte Carlo estimator depending on how strati- 139
fication is carried, i.e., depending on the interplay between the interval boundaries and the ratio of samples $\alpha_j \triangleq n_j \div n$ in the jth stratum, where $0 \leq \alpha_j \leq 1, \forall j$ and $\sum_{j=1}^{m} \alpha_j = 1$, with the total number of samples defined as

$$n \triangleq \sum_{j=1}^{m} n_j = n \sum_{j=1}^{m} \alpha_j \tag{4.145}$$

For instance, if the number of samples in each stratum is proportional to the size of the
interval, i.e., $\alpha_j = (x_j - x_{j-1}) \div (x_b - x_a)$, then the estimator becomes 139

$$\tilde{F} \overset{(4.143)}{=} \frac{x_b - x_a}{n} \sum_{j=1}^{m} \sum_{i=1}^{n_j} f(X_{ij}) \tag{4.146}$$
153

and its variance reads 143

153

$$\mathrm{V}[\tilde{F}] \overset{(4.144)}{=} \sum_{j=1}^{m}\left(\frac{x_b - x_a}{n}\int_{x_{j-1}}^{x_j} f(x)^2 \mathrm{d}x - \frac{F_j^2}{n_j}\right)$$

$$= \frac{x_b - x_a}{n}\sum_{j=1}^{m}\int_{x_{j-1}}^{x_j} f(x)^2 \mathrm{d}x - \sum_{j=1}^{m}\frac{F_j^2}{n_j}$$

$$= \frac{x_b - x_a}{n}\int_{x_a}^{x_b} f(x)^2 \mathrm{d}x - \sum_{j=1}^{m}\frac{F_j^2}{n_j}$$

150

$$\overset{(4.120)}{=} \frac{x_b - x_a}{n}(x_b - x_a)\,\mathrm{E}[f(X)^2] - \sum_{j=1}^{m}\frac{F_j^2}{n_j}$$

143

$$\overset{(4.84)}{=} \frac{\|\mathcal{D}\|^2}{n}\left(\mathrm{V}[f(X)] + \mathrm{E}[f(X)]^2\right) - \sum_{j=1}^{m}\frac{F_j^2}{n_j}$$

141

$$\overset{(4.65)}{=} \frac{\|\mathcal{D}\|^2}{n}\mathrm{V}[f(X)] + \frac{\|\mathcal{D}\|^2}{n}\left(\frac{1}{x_b - x_a}\int_{x_a}^{x_b} f(x)\mathrm{d}x\right)^2 - \sum_{j=1}^{m}\frac{F_j^2}{n_j}$$

153

$$\overset{(4.142)}{=} \frac{\|\mathcal{D}\|^2}{n}\mathrm{V}[f(X)] + \frac{1}{n}\left(\left(\sum_{j=1}^{m} F_j\right)^2 - n\sum_{j=1}^{m}\frac{F_j^2}{n_j}\right)$$

153

$$\overset{(4.145)}{=} \frac{\|\mathcal{D}\|^2}{n}\mathrm{V}[f(X)] + \frac{1}{n}\left(\left(\sum_{j=1}^{m}\sqrt{n_j}\frac{F_j}{\sqrt{n_j}}\right)^2 - \sum_{j=1}^{m}\sqrt{n_j}^2\sum_{j=1}^{m}\left(\frac{F_j}{\sqrt{n_j}}\right)^2\right)$$

76

$$\overset{(3.69)}{\leq} \frac{\|\mathcal{D}\|^2}{n}\mathrm{V}[f(X)] \tag{4.147}$$

from which follows that integral estimates from such stratified samples can be probabilistically no worse than estimates from the crude approach for the same number of samples.

More generally, the optimal ratio of samples per stratum may actually be derived by
143 reformulating the *variance* of the stratified-sampling *estimator* as
139
153

$$\mathrm{V}[\tilde{F}] \overset{(4.144)}{=} \sum_{j=1}^{m}\frac{a_j}{n_j} = \frac{1}{n}\sum_{j=1}^{m}\frac{a_j}{\alpha_j} \tag{4.148}$$

where

$$a_j \triangleq (x_j - x_{j-1})^2\,\mathrm{V}[f(X_j)] \geq 0, \quad \forall j \tag{4.149}$$

143 For a given number of samples n, minimizing the above *variance* is consequently equivalent to minimizing the sum

$$S \triangleq \sum_{j=1}^{m}\frac{a_j}{\alpha_j} = \frac{a_k}{\alpha_k} + \frac{a_l}{\alpha_l} + \sum_{\substack{j=1\\ j\neq k, j\neq l}}^{m}\frac{a_j}{\alpha_j} = \frac{a_k}{\alpha_k} + \frac{a_l}{1-\beta-\alpha_k} + \sum_{\substack{j=1\\ j\neq k, j\neq l}}^{m}\frac{a_j}{\alpha_j} \tag{4.150}$$

where $\beta \triangleq 1 - \alpha_k - \alpha_l = \sum^{m}{}_{\substack{j=1\\ j\neq k, j\neq l}} \alpha_j$, and whose extrema belong to the set of points where all first-order partial derivatives of the multivariate function vanish, leading to

$$\frac{\mathrm{d}S}{\mathrm{d}\alpha_k} = -\frac{a_k}{\alpha_k^2} + \frac{a_l}{(1-\beta-\alpha_k)^2} + 0 = -\frac{a_k}{\alpha_k^2} + \frac{a_l}{(1-\beta)^2 - 2\alpha_k(1-\beta) + \alpha_k^2} = 0 \tag{4.151}$$

28 yielding the *quadratic equation*

$$(a_l - a_k)\alpha_k^2 + 2a_k(1-\beta)\alpha_k - a_k(1-\beta)^2 = 0 \tag{4.152}$$

with discriminant

$$\Delta \overset{(2.91)}{=} 4a_k^2(1-\beta)^2 + 4(a_l - a_k)a_k(1-\beta)^2 = 4a_l a_k(1-\beta)^2 \geq 0 \tag{4.153}$$ 28

and whose solution reads

$$\begin{aligned}
\alpha_k &\overset{(2.94)}{=} \frac{-2a_k(1-\beta) + 2(1-\beta)\sqrt{a_l a_k}}{2(a_l - a_k)} = (1-\beta)\frac{\sqrt{a_l a_k} - a_k}{a_l - a_k} \\
&= (\alpha_k + \alpha_l)\frac{\sqrt{a_l a_k} - a_k}{a_l - a_k} = \frac{\alpha_l}{\frac{a_l - a_k}{\sqrt{a_l a_k} - a_k} - 1} = \alpha_l \frac{\sqrt{a_l a_k} - a_k}{(a_l - a_k) - (\sqrt{a_l a_k} - a_k)} \\
&= -\alpha_l \frac{\sqrt{a_l a_k} - a_k}{\sqrt{a_l a_k} - a_l} = -\alpha_l \frac{\sqrt{a_k}\,\sqrt{a_l} - \sqrt{a_k}}{\sqrt{a_l}\,\sqrt{a_k} - \sqrt{a_l}} = \alpha_l \frac{\sqrt{a_k}}{\sqrt{a_l}}
\end{aligned} \tag{4.154}$$ 28

to finally yield

$$\alpha_l = 1 - \sum_{\substack{j=1 \\ j \neq l}}^{m} \alpha_j = 1 - \sum_{\substack{j=1 \\ j \neq l}}^{m} \alpha_l \frac{\sqrt{a_j}}{\sqrt{a_l}} = \frac{1}{1 + \sum_{\substack{j=1 \\ j \neq l}}^{m} \frac{\sqrt{a_j}}{\sqrt{a_l}}} = \frac{1}{\sum_{j=1}^{m} \frac{\sqrt{a_j}}{\sqrt{a_l}}} = \frac{\sqrt{a_l}}{\sum_{j=1}^{m} \sqrt{a_j}} \tag{4.155}$$

Instead of adapting the sampling rate to the size of the intervals, a predefined number of samples can alternatively be taken in each subinterval whose size is then determined such that the variation of the integrand is the same on each interval, i.e., having large intervals where the function is nearly constant and smaller intervals where it is rapidly changing, such that the differences between the mean values of the function in the various strata are greater than its variations within them. For instance, if each interval has the same number of samples such that $\alpha_l = 1 \div m, \forall l$, then the optimal partitioning is obtained if $a_j = a_l, \forall j, l$ holds.

Although the technique may additionally yield a higher convergence rate as the number of strata increases, the generalization of the method to d-dimensional integrals leads to an exponential growth in the sampling rate due to the necessity of sampling in each of the n^d cells, in which case stratifying only the dimensions that carry the majority of the variation
is preferable. This is equally problematic in recursive estimations where *splitting* is required 166
to draw the n samples needed for the computation of an estimate. As an alternative, given a number n of samples, *N-rooks sampling*, or more generally, *Latin hypercube sampling*, subdivides the multidimensional domain into n subintervals along each dimension and proceeds to a permutation to ensure that one sample lies in each subinterval along each dimension, as
illustrated in *Figure 4.5*. Generalizing the technique yields *orthogonal array sampling* where 156
rather than stratifying all the one-dimensional projections of the samples, stratification is done for all of the d-dimensional projections for $d \geq 2$.

4.6.3 Importance Sampling

The goal of *importance sampling* is to concentrate the distribution of the sample points in the regions of the integration domain that are of most importance instead of spreading them out evenly. This effectively translates into taking more random samples in regions where the integrand has higher values and fewer samples where it has smaller values. Given a continuous
random variable X distributed according to a *probability density* $p(x)$ over a domain $\mathcal{D}$ such 129
that $p(x) \neq 0$ whenever $f(x) \neq 0$, the integral of $f(x)$ can be written as 131

$$F \triangleq \int_{\mathcal{D}} f(x)\mathrm{d}x = \int_{\mathcal{D}} \frac{f(x)}{p(x)} p(x)\mathrm{d}x \overset{(4.65)}{=} \mathrm{E}\left[\frac{f(X)}{p(X)}\right] \tag{4.156}$$ 141

or, alternatively, defining the *cumulative distribution* $P(x)$ and the change of variable 132

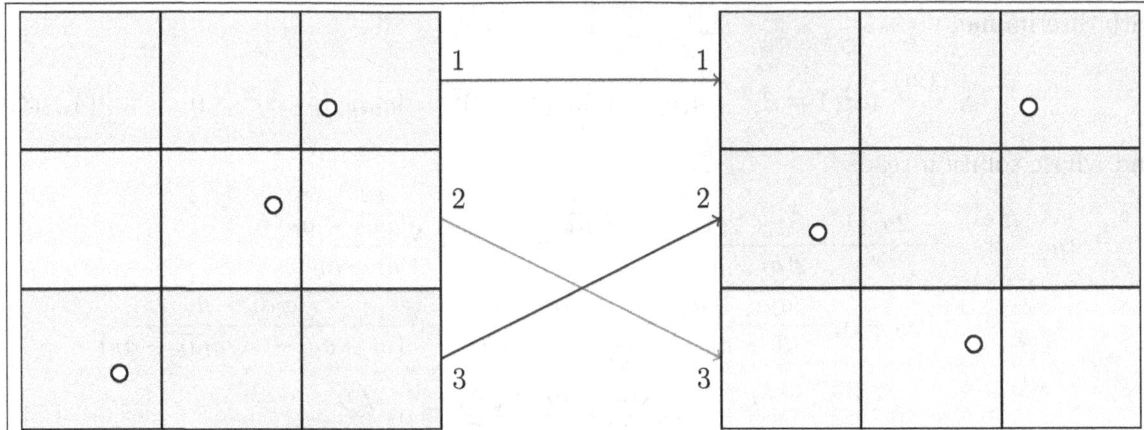

Figure 4.5: N-Rooks Sampling: Illustration of Latin hypercube sampling with the rooks defined by the permutation [1, 3, 2].

$y = P(x) \in [0, 1]$, i.e., finding a transformation with appropriate Jacobian determinant for multidimensional integrals, yields

$$F = \int_{\mathcal{D}} f(x)\mathrm{d}x = \int_0^1 f(P^{-1}(y))\frac{\mathrm{d}y}{p(P^{-1}(y))} = \int_0^1 \frac{f(P^{-1}(y))}{p(P^{-1}(y))}\mathrm{d}y \tag{4.157}$$

139 The corresponding *estimator* then reads

150
$$\tilde{F} \overset{(4.121)}{=} \frac{1}{n}\sum_{i=1}^{n} \frac{f(X_i)}{p(X_i)} \tag{4.158}$$

where although samples for which $p(x) = 0$ might seem problematic due to the induced
129 division by zero, the *probability* of generating such samples is conveniently null, and so
143 no such samples shall be generated. Assuming uncorrelated variables, the *variance* of the
139 *estimator* evaluates to

144
$$\mathrm{V}[\tilde{F}] = \mathrm{V}\left[\frac{1}{n}\sum_{i=1}^{n}\frac{f(X_i)}{p(X_i)}\right] \overset{(4.92)}{=} \frac{1}{n^2}\sum_{i=1}^{n}\mathrm{V}\left[\frac{f(X_i)}{p(X_i)}\right] = \frac{1}{n}\mathrm{V}\left[\frac{f(X)}{p(X)}\right] \tag{4.159}$$

143 from which follows that if the ratio $f(x) \div p(x)$ is nearly constant, the *variance* will decrease.
In fact, if $p(x) \propto f(x)$, i.e., $p(x) = f(x) \div F$, which requires knowing the value of F in
143 advance, then $f(x) \div p(x)$ is constant and its *variance* reduces to zero, leading to a perfect
139 *estimator*.

In order to better match the integrand, a complex distribution may actually be built as a mixture of simpler distributions, a technique known as *mixture importance sampling*.
131 Defining the *probability density* as a convex combination of m base PDFs, with weights
$w_j \geq 0$ satisfying $\sum_{j=1}^{m} w_j = 1$ such that $p(x)$ is normalized, yields

$$p(x) = \sum_{j=1}^{m} w_j p_j(x) \tag{4.160}$$

139 and the importance sampling *estimator* becomes

156
$$\tilde{F} \overset{(4.158)}{=} \frac{1}{n}\sum_{i=1}^{n}\frac{f(X_i)}{\sum_{j=1}^{m} w_j p_j(X_i)} \tag{4.161}$$

Viewed as a special case of *combined sampling*, such a distribution can be efficiently sampled 157
in practice by first stochastically selecting one of the PDFs with *probability* w_j, and then 129
drawing a sample according to its distribution, effectively drawing a sample from the combined *probability density* $p(x)$. As an alternative, the number of samples $n_j \triangleq w_j n$ drawn 131
from each distribution may be deterministically determined from the total number of samples $n = \sum_{j=1}^{m} n_j$, a technique known as *deterministic mixture sampling*

$$\tilde{F} = \sum_{j=1}^{m} \frac{w_j}{n_j} \sum_{i=1}^{n_j} \frac{f(X_{ij})}{p_j(X_{ij})} = \frac{1}{n} \sum_{j=1}^{m} \sum_{i=1}^{n_j} \frac{f(X_{ij})}{p_j(X_{ij})} \tag{4.162}$$

Importance sampling might be more difficult to apply when the integrand changes sign, since by definition $p(x) \geq 0$, in which case an alternative is to correlate $p(x)$ with $|f(x)|$ rather
than $f(x)$ [Bekaert, 1999], although the resulting *variance* is no longer zero. Another alter- 143
native is to use positivisation [Owen and Zhou, 2000], which entails dividing the integrand into its non-negative and non-positive constituents and integrating each separately.

A well-known problem of importance sampling occurs when the integrand has much heav-
ier tails than the *probability density*. In such a case, the sample value $f(x) \div p(x)$ may be 131
orders of magnitude larger than typical samples, which will greatly skew the sample mean
away from the true mean while increasing the sample *variance*. Such a sample will require 143
many more samples to cancel out its effect. This can be avoided by artificially bounding the minimal value of $p(x)$, which as a countereffect might substantially limit the potential benefits of the overall importance sampling strategy. Other techniques such as *defensive importance sampling* [Hesterberg, 1988], or alternatively *defensive mixture sampling* [Hesterberg, 1995], address this problem by preventing the distribution to be much smaller than the integrand when the latter has low values while still qualitatively matching it in regions of higher importance.

4.6.4 Combined Sampling

4.6.4.1 Definition

Given several potentially good estimation strategies, the goal of *combined sampling* is to combine the resulting sample estimates into one that preserves the strengths of each in a way that is provably good. Defining the weight functions $\sum_{j=1}^{m} w_j(x) = 1, \forall x \in \mathcal{D}$, the integrand is rewritten as an affine combination of the form

$$F \triangleq \int_{\mathcal{D}} f(x)\mathrm{d}x = \int_{\mathcal{D}} \sum_{j=1}^{m} w_j(x) f(x)\mathrm{d}x = \sum_{j=1}^{m} \int_{\mathcal{D}} w_j(x) f(x)\mathrm{d}x = \sum_{j=1}^{m} W_j \tag{4.163}$$

Evaluating each of the m integrals $W_j \triangleq \int_{\mathcal{D}} w_j(x) f(x)\mathrm{d}x$ with a different *estimator* $\tilde{W}_j(X_j)$ 139
and combining the results then yields the following combined *estimator* 139

140

$$\tilde{F} \overset{(4.57)}{=} \sum_{j=1}^{m} \frac{1}{n_j} \sum_{i=1}^{n_j} \tilde{W}_j(X_{ij}) \tag{4.164}$$

where the X_{ij} are independent samples with the underlying distribution assumed by $\tilde{W}_j(X_j)$.
This *estimator* is unbiased as long as $\mathrm{E}[\tilde{W}_j(X_j)] = W_j$ 139

141
157

$$\mathrm{E}[\tilde{F}] \overset{(4.68)}{=} \sum_{j=1}^{m} \frac{1}{n_j} \sum_{i=1}^{n_j} \mathrm{E}[\tilde{W}_j(X_{ij})] = \sum_{j=1}^{m} \mathrm{E}[\tilde{W}_j(X_j)] = \sum_{j=1}^{m} W_j \overset{(4.163)}{=} F \tag{4.165}$$

and its *variance* reads 143

144
143

$$\mathrm{V}[\tilde{F}] \overset{(4.92)}{=} \sum_{j=1}^{m} \frac{1}{n_j^2} \sum_{i=1}^{n_j} \mathrm{V}[\tilde{W}_j(X_{ij})] = \sum_{j=1}^{m} \frac{\mathrm{V}[\tilde{W}_j(X_j)]}{n_j} \overset{(4.84)}{=} \sum_{j=1}^{m} \frac{\mathrm{E}[\tilde{W}_j(X_j)^2] - \mathrm{E}[\tilde{W}_j(X_j)]^2}{n_j} \tag{4.166}$$

In the special case where the weights are constant, i.e., $w_j(x) = w_j$, the integral simplifies into

157
157

$$F \overset{(4.163)}{=} \sum_{j=1}^{m} w_j \int_{\mathcal{D}} f(x)\mathrm{d}x \overset{(4.163)}{=} \sum_{j=1}^{m} w_j F \tag{4.167}$$

139 and, defining the *estimators* $\tilde{F}_j(X_j) \triangleq \tilde{W}_j(X_j) \div w_j$ that all evaluate the same quantity F,
139 the combined *estimator* becomes

157

$$\tilde{F} \overset{(4.164)}{=} \sum_{j=1}^{m} \frac{w_j}{n_j} \sum_{i=1}^{n_j} \tilde{F}_j(X_{ij}) \tag{4.168}$$

139 which, in case of individual *estimators* based on *importance sampling* with weights $w_j =$
155 $n_j \div n$ where $n = \sum_{j=1}^{m} n_j$ is the total number of samples, yields the deterministic mixture
139 sampling *estimator*. For instance, given two *estimators* $\tilde{S}_1$ and $\tilde{S}_2$ for the estimand S (the
139 generalization to many more *estimators* being provided elsewhere [Bekaert, 1999]) and the
139 constant weights $w_1 + w_2 = 1$ with a single sample per *estimator*, the combined *estimator* $\tilde{S}$
139 is defined as the linear combination

$$\tilde{S} \triangleq w_1\tilde{S}_1 + w_2\tilde{S}_2 \tag{4.169}$$

143 whose *variance* reads

143

$$\begin{aligned} \mathrm{V}[\tilde{S}] &\overset{(4.90)}{=} w_1^2\,\mathrm{V}[\tilde{S}_1] + w_2^2\,\mathrm{V}[\tilde{S}_2] + 2w_1w_2\,\mathrm{C}[\tilde{S}_1, \tilde{S}_2] & (4.170)\\ &= w_1^2\,\mathrm{V}[\tilde{S}_1] + (1 - w_1)^2\,\mathrm{V}[\tilde{S}_2] + 2w_1(1 - w_1)\,\mathrm{C}[\tilde{S}_1, \tilde{S}_2] \\ &= w_1^2\,\mathrm{V}[\tilde{S}_1] + (1 - 2w_1 + w_1^2)\,\mathrm{V}[\tilde{S}_2] + (2w_1 - 2w_1^2)\,\mathrm{C}[\tilde{S}_1, \tilde{S}_2] \\ &= w_1^2(\mathrm{V}[\tilde{S}_1] + \mathrm{V}[\tilde{S}_2] - 2\,\mathrm{C}[\tilde{S}_1, \tilde{S}_2]) + w_1 2(\mathrm{C}[\tilde{S}_1, \tilde{S}_2] - \mathrm{V}[\tilde{S}_2]) + \mathrm{V}[\tilde{S}_2] & (4.171) \end{aligned}$$

143 Minimizing the *variance* then requires solving the *linear equation*
27

$$\frac{\mathrm{d}\,\mathrm{V}[\tilde{S}]}{\mathrm{d}w_1} = 2w_1(\mathrm{V}[\tilde{S}_1] + \mathrm{V}[\tilde{S}_2] - 2\,\mathrm{C}[\tilde{S}_1, \tilde{S}_2]) + 2(\mathrm{C}[\tilde{S}_1, \tilde{S}_2] - \mathrm{V}[\tilde{S}_2]) = 0 \tag{4.172}$$

whose root reads

$$w_1 = \frac{\mathrm{V}[\tilde{S}_2] - \mathrm{C}[\tilde{S}_1, \tilde{S}_2]}{\mathrm{V}[\tilde{S}_1] + \mathrm{V}[\tilde{S}_2] - 2\,\mathrm{C}[\tilde{S}_1, \tilde{S}_2]} \tag{4.173}$$

139 which, if the *estimators* are uncorrelated, simplifies into

$$w_1 = \frac{\mathrm{V}[\tilde{S}_2]}{\mathrm{V}[\tilde{S}_1] + \mathrm{V}[\tilde{S}_2]} = 1 - \frac{\mathrm{V}[\tilde{S}_1]}{\mathrm{V}[\tilde{S}_1] + \mathrm{V}[\tilde{S}_2]} \tag{4.174}$$

4.6.4.2 Multiple Importance Sampling

In the general case of spatially varying weighting functions, the method is referred to as *multiple importance sampling* [Veach and Guibas, 1995, Veach, 1997, Ch. 9] whenever the
139 individual *estimators*
156

$$\tilde{W}_j(X_j) \overset{(4.158)}{=} w_j(X_j)\frac{f(X_j)}{p_j(X_j)} \tag{4.175}$$

are based on *importance sampling*. The combined *estimator* then becomes 155 139

$$\tilde{F} \overset{(4.164)}{=} \sum_{j=1}^{m} \frac{1}{n_j} \sum_{i=1}^{n_j} w_j(X_{ij}) \frac{f(X_{ij})}{p_j(X_{ij})} \tag{4.176}$$ 157

and, assuming each of the PDFs is in some sense optimal in capturing some of the features of the original integrand as aimed at by *importance sampling*, the extra degree of freedom 155 provided by the weighting functions can be used to in turn make the individual integrands better match their respective PDFs.

To this end, the variance of the *estimator* may be formulated as 139

$$\begin{aligned} \mathrm{V}[\tilde{F}] &\underset{(4.175)}{\overset{(4.166)}{=}} \sum_{j=1}^{m} \frac{1}{n_j} \left(\mathrm{E}\left[\left(w_j(X_j) \frac{f(X_j)}{p_j(X_j)} \right)^2 \right] - \mathrm{E}\left[w_j(X_j) \frac{f(X_j)}{p_j(X_j)} \right]^2 \right) \\ &\overset{(4.65)}{=} \sum_{j=1}^{m} \frac{1}{n_j} \left(\int_{\Omega} \left(w_j(x) \frac{f(x)}{p_j(x)} \right)^2 p_j(x) \mathrm{d}x - \left(\int_{\Omega} w_j(x) \frac{f(x)}{p_j(x)} p_j(x) \mathrm{d}x \right)^2 \right) \\ &= \int_{\Omega} \sum_{j=1}^{m} \frac{w_j(x)^2 f(x)^2}{n_j p_j(x)} \mathrm{d}x - \sum_{j=1}^{m} \frac{1}{n_j} \left(\int_{\Omega} w_j(x) f(x) \mathrm{d}x \right)^2 \end{aligned} \tag{4.177}$$ 158 158 141

and minimizing the first integrand independently at each point x using the method of Lagrange multipliers then yields the *balance heuristic*, which defines each weighting function to be proportional to its associated *probability density* 131

$$w_j(x) = \frac{\frac{n_j p_j(x)}{f(x)^2}}{\sum_{k=1}^{m} \frac{n_k p_k(x)}{f(x)^2}} = \frac{n_j p_j(x)}{\sum_{k=1}^{m} n_k p_k(x)} = \frac{1}{\sum_{k=1}^{m} \frac{n_k p_k(x)}{n_j p_j(x)}} = \left(1 + \sum_{\substack{k=1 \\ k \neq j}}^{m} \frac{n_k p_k(x)}{n_j p_j(x)} \right)^{-1} \tag{4.178}$$

where the latter formulation seamlessly handles Dirac *delta function* distributions. The *estimator*, whose variance can be proven to be within some bounds of the optimal combination, 44 139 then becomes

$$\tilde{F} \overset{(4.176)}{=} \sum_{j=1}^{m} \frac{1}{n_j} \sum_{i=1}^{n_j} \frac{n_j p_j(X_{ij})}{\sum_{k=1}^{m} n_k p_k(X_{ij})} \frac{f(X_{ij})}{p_j(X_{ij})} = \frac{1}{n} \sum_{j=1}^{m} \sum_{i=1}^{n_j} \frac{f(X_{ij})}{\sum_{k=1}^{m} (n_k \div n) p_k(X_{ij})} \tag{4.179}$$ 159

yielding the mixture *importance sampling estimator* with mixture coefficients $n_k \div n$, which 155 139 may consequently be regarded as a special case of multiple importance sampling. Because the weights of the linear combination depend on the positions of the samples, the technique allows not only to give more importance to more reliable *estimators*, but also to take into 139 account the fact that some *estimators* might have different qualities in different regions of 139 the integration domain.

More aggressive generalizations may additionally be derived by exponentiation, yielding the so-called *power heuristic*

$$w_j(x) = \frac{(n_j p_j(x))^{\beta}}{\sum_{k=1}^{m} (n_k p_k(x))^{\beta}} = \frac{1}{\sum_{k=1}^{m} \left(\frac{n_k p_k(x)}{n_j p_j(x)} \right)^{\beta}} = \left(1 + \sum_{\substack{k=1 \\ k \neq j}}^{m} \left(\frac{n_k p_k(x)}{n_j p_j(x)} \right)^{\beta} \right)^{-1} \tag{4.180}$$

which allows more emphasis to be placed on an individual *estimator* as the latter appears 139 to be more optimal in a given region of the domain. Considering the limit case where the exponent is set to infinity then yields the so-called *maximum heuristic*

$$w_j(x) = \begin{cases} 1 & \text{if } n_j p_j(x) \geq n_i p_i(x), \forall i \\ 0 & \text{otherwise} \end{cases} \tag{4.181}$$

thereby avoiding the need to evaluate the estimator j and the PDFs of the other estimators whenever $\exists i \mid n_j p_j(x) < n_i p_i(x)$.

45 When extending the integral $\int_{\mathcal{D}_x} f(x)\mathrm{d}x \overset{(2.218)}{=} \int_{\mathcal{D}_x}\int_{\mathcal{D}_y} f(y)\delta(y-x)\mathrm{d}x\mathrm{d}y \approx$
176 $\int_{\mathcal{D}_x}\int_{\mathcal{D}_y} f(y)K(y-x)\mathrm{d}x\mathrm{d}y$ over an additional dimension y by introducing a *convolution* over
44 the extent of a *kernel function* K (e.g., by resorting to *non-parametric density estimation*),
168 the variance of the *estimator* becomes [Křivánek *et al.*, 2014, §6]
167
139

$$\begin{aligned} \mathrm{V}[\tilde{F}] &= \sum_{j=1}^{m} \frac{1}{n_j}\left(\mathrm{E}\left[\left(w_j(X_j)\frac{f(Y_j)K(Y_j-X_j)}{p_j(X_j,Y_j)}\right)^2\right] - \mathrm{E}\left[w_j(X_j)\frac{f(Y_j)K(Y_j-X_j)}{p_j(X_j,Y_j)}\right]^2\right) \\ &= \sum_{j=1}^{m} \frac{1}{n_j}\left(\int_{\Omega_x}\int_{\Omega_y}\left(w_j(x)\frac{f(y)K(y-x)}{p_j(x,y)}\right)^2 p_j(x,y)\mathrm{d}x\mathrm{d}y\right. \\ &\quad \left. -\left(\int_{\Omega_x}\int_{\Omega_y} w_j(x)\frac{f(y)K(y-x)}{p_j(x,y)}p_j(x,y)\mathrm{d}x\mathrm{d}y\right)^2\right) \\ &= \int_{\Omega_x}\sum_{j=1}^{m}\frac{w_j(x)^2}{n_j}\left(\int_{\Omega_y}\frac{f(y)^2K(y-x)^2}{p_j(x,y)}\mathrm{d}y\right)\mathrm{d}x \\ &\quad -\sum_{j=1}^{m}\frac{1}{n_j}\left(\int_{\Omega_x}\int_{\Omega_y} w_j(x)f(y)K(y-x)\mathrm{d}x\mathrm{d}y\right)^2 \end{aligned} \tag{4.182}$$

and similarly minimizing the first integrand independently at each point x using the method of Lagrange multipliers then yields the *extended balance heuristic*

$$\begin{aligned} w_j(x) &= \frac{n_j\left(\int_{\Omega_y}\frac{f(y)^2K(y-x)^2}{p_j(x,y)}\mathrm{d}y\right)^{-1}}{\sum_{k=1}^{m} n_k\left(\int_{\Omega_y}\frac{f(y)^2K(y-x)^2}{p_k(x,y)}\mathrm{d}y\right)^{-1}} \\ &\approx \frac{n_j\left(\frac{f(y')^2}{p_j(x,y')}\int_{\Omega_y}K(y-x)^2\mathrm{d}y\right)^{-1}}{\sum_{k=1}^{m} n_k\left(\frac{f(y')^2}{p_k(x,y')}\int_{\Omega_y}K(y-x)^2\mathrm{d}y\right)^{-1}} \\ &= \frac{n_j p_j(x,y')\left(\int_{\Omega_y}K(y)^2\mathrm{d}y\right)^{-1}}{\sum_{k=1}^{m} n_k p_k(x,y')\left(\int_{\Omega_y}K(y)^2\mathrm{d}y\right)^{-1}} \end{aligned} \tag{4.183}$$

where $\frac{f(y)^2}{p_j(x,y)}$ is assumed to be approximately constant within the support of the kernel and y' is a y coordinate within it, which yields extended weights whose numerators and denominators have the same dimensions as non extended weights, thereby allowing the different estimators to be readily combined with one-another via the generalized weights

$$w_j(x) \triangleq \frac{n_j p'_j(x,y')}{\sum_{k=1}^{m} n_k p'_k(x,y')} \tag{4.184}$$

where

$$p'_j(x,y') = \begin{cases} p_j(x) & \text{if } j \text{ is a non-extended estimator} \\ p_j(x,y')\left(\int_{\Omega_y}K(y)^2\mathrm{d}y\right)^{-1} & \text{if } j \text{ is an extended estimator} \end{cases} \tag{4.185}$$

4.6.4.3 Discussion

Because the approach cannot produce a good *estimator* out of several bad estimators, each 139
individual estimator should have the potential of yielding good estimates for parts of the
integrand in order for the combined estimator to be efficient. In general, though, there is no
guarantee that the *variance* of a combination of many estimators will be better than that of 143
many samples from a single of the estimators. This is especially true if one of the primary
estimators is perfect or nearly perfect, in which case additional estimators will only increase 139
the *variance* of the result. 143

On the other hand, it is also worth noting that in cases where the PDFs are too complex to evaluate, the heuristics can instead rely on approximations to the latter, as long as the weighting functions satisfy normalization over the whole integration domain and are consistently used within the combined estimation framework. Finally, the sum of the different *estimators* may itself be estimated in a probabilistic fashion by means of a PMF whose 139
weights are proportional to the associated number of samples n_i, thereby avoiding the use of
splitting in recursive evaluations. 166

4.6.5 Control Variates

Assuming a function $g(x)$ whose integral $G \triangleq \int_{\mathcal{D}} g(x)\mathrm{d}x$ can be analytically computed, the *control variates* method reformulates the original integral as

$$F \triangleq \int_{\mathcal{D}} f(x)\mathrm{d}x = \int_{\mathcal{D}} g(x)\mathrm{d}x + \int_{\mathcal{D}} f(x) - g(x)\mathrm{d}x = G + \int_{\mathcal{D}} f(x) - g(x)\mathrm{d}x \tag{4.186}$$

The corresponding *estimator* then reads 139

150
$$\tilde{F} \overset{(4.121)}{=} G + \frac{\|\mathcal{D}\|}{n}\sum_{i=1}^{n}(f(X_i) - g(X_i)) \tag{4.187}$$

whose *variance*, assuming uncorrelated variables, evaluates to 143

144
143
$$\mathrm{V}[\tilde{F}] \overset{(4.92)}{=} \mathrm{V}[G] + \frac{\|\mathcal{D}\|^2}{n^2}\sum_{i=1}^{n}\mathrm{V}[f(X_i) - g(X_i)] \overset{(4.88)}{=} \frac{\|\mathcal{D}\|^2}{n}\mathrm{V}[f(X) - g(X)] \tag{4.188}$$

from which follows that a reduction in *variance* occurs if $\mathrm{V}[f(X) - g(X)] < \mathrm{V}[f(X)]$, i.e., 143
if the difference $f(x) - g(x)$ is nearly constant. In fact, if the difference equals a constant
$c \triangleq f(x) - g(x)$, then the *variance* reduces to zero, leading to the perfect *estimator* 143
139

161
161
$$\begin{aligned}\tilde{F} &\overset{(4.187)}{=} \int_{\mathcal{D}} f(x) - c\,\mathrm{d}x + \frac{\|\mathcal{D}\|}{n}\sum_{i=1}^{n}c = \int_{\mathcal{D}} f(x)\mathrm{d}x - \int_{\mathcal{D}} c\mathrm{d}x + \frac{\|\mathcal{D}\|}{n}nc \\ &\overset{(4.186)}{=} F - \|\mathcal{D}\|c + \|\mathcal{D}\|c = F\end{aligned} \tag{4.189}$$

It is worth noting, though, that when $g(x) = g$ is constant, the *estimator* reduces to the 139
crude MC *estimator* 139

161
$$\begin{aligned}\tilde{F} &\overset{(4.187)}{=} G + \frac{\|\mathcal{D}\|}{n}\sum_{i=1}^{n}(f(X_i) - g) = G + \frac{\|\mathcal{D}\|}{n}\sum_{i=1}^{n}f(X_i) - \frac{\|\mathcal{D}\|}{n}\sum_{i=1}^{n}g \\ &= \|\mathcal{D}\|g + \frac{\|\mathcal{D}\|}{n}\sum_{i=1}^{n}f(X_i) - \frac{\|\mathcal{D}\|}{n}ng = \frac{\|\mathcal{D}\|}{n}\sum_{i=1}^{n}f(X_i)\end{aligned} \tag{4.190}$$

and due to the translation-invariant property of *variance*, the latter remains unchanged. 143

4.6.6 Antithetic Variates

129 The method of *antithetic variates* exploits the negative correlation of *random variables* to
143 reduce *variance*. By matching overestimating samples with underestimating samples, their
143 average is likely to be a better estimate of the actual mean with lower *variance* than if
the two variables were independent. Considering the one-dimensional case over the domain
$\|\mathcal{D}\| \triangleq b - a$ and defining $y \triangleq a + b - x$, the integral may be rewritten as

$$F \triangleq \int_a^b f(x)\mathrm{d}x = -\int_b^a f(a+b-y)\mathrm{d}y = \int_a^b f(a+b-y)\mathrm{d}y \tag{4.191}$$

which, defining $\alpha \in [0, 1]$, leads to

$$F = \alpha \int_a^b f(x)\mathrm{d}x + (1-\alpha)\int_a^b f(a+b-x)\mathrm{d}x = \int_a^b \alpha f(x) + (1-\alpha) f(a+b-x)\mathrm{d}x \tag{4.192}$$

139 The corresponding *estimator* then reads

150

$$\tilde{F} \overset{(4.121)}{=} \frac{\|\mathcal{D}\|}{n}\sum_{i=1}^{n}(\alpha f(X_i) + (1-\alpha) f(a+b-X_i)) \tag{4.193}$$

143 whose *variance* evaluates to

144

$$\begin{aligned} \mathrm{V}[\tilde{F}] &\overset{(4.92)}{=} \frac{\|\mathcal{D}\|^2}{n^2}\sum_{i=1}^{n}\mathrm{V}[\alpha f(X_i) + (1-\alpha) f(a+b-X_i)] \\ &= \frac{\|\mathcal{D}\|^2}{n}\mathrm{V}[\alpha f(X) + (1-\alpha) f(a+b-X)] \end{aligned} \tag{4.194}$$

139 such that a perfect *estimator* is obtained for a symmetric integrand verifying $f(x) = (\bar{f} -$
$(1-\alpha) f(a+b-x)) \div \alpha$.

The domain can alternatively be subdivided to exploit correlation between the resulting subsets by rewriting the integral as

162

$$F \overset{(4.191)}{=} \int_a^{a+\alpha(b-a)} f(x)\mathrm{d}x + \int_{a+\alpha(b-a)}^b f(x)\mathrm{d}x \tag{4.195}$$

139 leading to the *estimator*

150

$$\tilde{F} \overset{(4.121)}{=} \frac{\|\mathcal{D}\|}{n}\sum_{i=1}^{n}\Big(\alpha f(a + U_i\alpha(b-a)) + (1-\alpha) f(b - (1-U_i)(1-\alpha)(b-a))\Big) \tag{4.196}$$

or by rewriting the integral as

162

$$F \overset{(4.191)}{=} \int_a^{a+\alpha(b-a)} f(x)\mathrm{d}x + \int_{a+\alpha(b-a)}^b f(a + \alpha(b-a) + b - x)\mathrm{d}x \tag{4.197}$$

139 leading to the *estimator*

150

$$\tilde{F} \overset{(4.121)}{=} \frac{\|\mathcal{D}\|}{n}\sum_{i=1}^{n}\Big(\alpha f(a + U_i\alpha(b-a)) + (1-\alpha) f(b - U_i(1-\alpha)(b-a))\Big) \tag{4.198}$$

The major drawback of the method is that two samples need to be drawn in order to
166 compute a single estimate. In recursive estimations, this requires the use of *splitting*, which
leads to an exponential growth in the number of evaluations.

Generalizing the concept of exploiting correlation to m unknown estimands S_i and a set
139 of n *estimators* $\tilde{S}_j$ with $m \leq n$, *regression methods* assume the knowledge of constants α_{ij}
such that $\mathrm{E}[\tilde{S}_j] = \sum_{i=1}^{m} \alpha_{ij} S_i, \forall j \leq n$. Applying standard linear regression techniques to a
139 linear combination involving the variance-covariance matrix of the *estimators*, the minimum-
143 *variance estimator* of the set of estimands may then be determined.
139

4.6.7 Adaptive Sampling

As the number of samples increases, the *variance* of the estimate decreases and the latter 143
converges towards the mean. In order to determine how many samples are needed to reach
a given accuracy, *adaptive sampling* iteratively generates a new sample and recalculates the
sample mean and sample *variance*, which are used as estimates of the true mean and true 143
variance of the underlying distribution, until the sample *variance* falls below a given threshold 143
so that the sample mean is likely to be a good estimate of the true mean. This allows the 143
number of samples to be adapted to the variations of the integrand, and more samples to be
taken for integrals or parts of an integral that have higher *variance*. 143

One of the main drawbacks of the method is that it can introduce bias if not carefully designed. Also, defining a relevant threshold for a given problem might be non-trivial. Moreover, due to the stochastic nature of the process, there is no guarantee that the sample mean is a good estimate once the sampling process stops. Nevertheless, adaptive sampling is very effective in practice as it allows the number of samples to be adapted to the complexity of accurately estimating a given integral.

4.6.8 Russian Roulette

Russian roulette consists in conditionally evaluating an integral based on the outcome of a
probabilistic process. For a given number of samples and a given integral, the estimation
process tends to increase *variance* and the method may consequently not be regarded as a 143
variance reduction technique per se. However, for a given computation time and a given set
of integrals, the technique allows a better allocation of the computational efforts by reducing
the time spent evaluating integrals with minor contributions, and can therefore yield a lower
overall *variance*. 143

Considering the one-dimensional case on the domain $\|\mathcal{D}\| \triangleq b - a$ and defining $y \triangleq$
$a + p(x - a)$ as well as the constant c and the *probability* $p \in [0, 1]$, the integral may be 129
rewritten in terms of the indicator function as

$$\begin{aligned} F &\triangleq \int_a^b f(x)\mathrm{d}x \\ &= \int_a^b c\mathrm{d}x + \int_a^b f(x) - c\mathrm{d}x \\ &= \int_a^b c\mathrm{d}x + \int_a^{a+p(b-a)} f\left(a + \frac{y-a}{p}\right) - c\frac{\mathrm{d}y}{p} \\ &= \int_a^b c\mathrm{d}y + \int_a^b \chi_{[a,a+p(b-a)]}(y)\frac{f\left(a + \frac{y-a}{p}\right) - c}{p}\mathrm{d}y \\ &= \int_a^b c + \chi_{[a,a+p(b-a)]}(y)\frac{f\left(a + \frac{y-a}{p}\right) - c}{p}\mathrm{d}y \end{aligned} \tag{4.199}$$

Sampling $y_i = a + \xi_i(b - a)$ with the uniformly distributed *random variable* $\xi \in [0, 1)$, 129
the corresponding *estimator* reads 139

150

$$\tilde{F} \overset{(4.121)}{=} \frac{b-a}{n}\sum_{i=1}^{n} c + \chi_{[a,a+p(b-a)]}(y_i)\frac{f\left(a+\frac{y_i-a}{p}\right)-c}{p}$$

$$\begin{aligned}
&= \frac{b-a}{n}\sum_{i=1}^{n}\begin{cases} c+\frac{f\left(a+\frac{y_i-a}{p}\right)-c}{p} & \text{if } y_i < a+p(b-a)\\ c & \text{otherwise}\end{cases}\\
&= \frac{1}{n}\sum_{i=1}^{n}\begin{cases} (b-a)c+\frac{(b-a)f\left(a+\frac{\xi_i}{p}(b-a)\right)-(b-a)c}{p} & \text{if } \xi_i < p\\ (b-a)c & \text{otherwise}\end{cases}\\
&= \frac{1}{n}\sum_{i=1}^{n}\begin{cases} C+\frac{\tilde{F}'-C}{p} & \text{if } \xi_i < p\\ C & \text{otherwise}\end{cases} \qquad (4.200)
\end{aligned}$$

139 where $C \triangleq (b-a)c$ and $\tilde{F}'$ is an *estimator* of F.

139 This *estimator* is unbiased as long as $\mathrm{E}[\tilde{F}'] = F$ (unless $p = 0$ and $C \neq F$)

$$\mathrm{E}[\tilde{F}] = \frac{1}{n}\sum_{i=1}^{n}\left(p\,\mathrm{E}\left[C+\frac{\tilde{F}'-C}{p}\right]+(1-p)\,\mathrm{E}[C]\right)$$

141

141

$$\begin{aligned}
&\underset{(4.66)}{\overset{(4.67)}{=}} p\left(C+\frac{\mathrm{E}[\tilde{F}']-C}{p}\right)+(1-p)C\\
&= pC+\mathrm{E}[\tilde{F}']-C+C-pC\\
&= F \qquad (4.201)
\end{aligned}$$

143 and its *variance* reads

144

143

$$\mathrm{V}[\tilde{F}] \underset{(4.84)}{\overset{(4.92)}{=}} \frac{1}{n^2}\sum_{i=1}^{n}\left(p\,\mathrm{E}\left[\left(C+\frac{\tilde{F}'-C}{p}\right)^2\right]+(1-p)\,\mathrm{E}[C^2]-\mathrm{E}[\tilde{F}]^2\right)$$

$$= \frac{1}{n}\left(p\,\mathrm{E}\left[C^2+2C\frac{\tilde{F}'-C}{p}+\frac{\tilde{F}'^2-2\tilde{F}'C+C^2}{p^2}\right]+(1-p)\,\mathrm{E}[C^2]-F^2\right)$$

141

141

$$\begin{aligned}
&\underset{(4.66)}{\overset{(4.68)}{=}} \frac{1}{n}\left(pC^2+2C(\mathrm{E}[\tilde{F}']-C)+\frac{\mathrm{E}[\tilde{F}'^2]-2\,\mathrm{E}[\tilde{F}']C+C^2}{p}+(1-p)C^2-F^2\right)\\
&= \frac{1}{n}\left(2CF+\frac{\mathrm{E}[\tilde{F}'^2]-2FC+C^2}{p}-C^2-F^2\right)\\
&= \frac{1}{n}\frac{\mathrm{E}[\tilde{F}'^2]+(1-p)(-2FC+C^2)-pF^2}{p}\\
&= \frac{1}{n}\frac{\mathrm{E}[\tilde{F}'^2]-\mathrm{E}[\tilde{F}']^2+(1-p)(F^2-2FC+C^2)}{p}
\end{aligned}$$

143

$$\begin{aligned}
&\overset{(4.84)}{=} \frac{\mathrm{V}[\tilde{F}']+(1-p)(F-C)^2}{np} \qquad (4.202)\\
&\geq \frac{\mathrm{V}[\tilde{F}']}{np}\\
&\geq \frac{\mathrm{V}[\tilde{F}']}{n} \qquad (4.203)
\end{aligned}$$

or equivalently

$$\mathrm{V}[\tilde{F}] \overset{(4.125)}{=} \frac{1}{n}\left(\|\mathcal{D}\|\int_a^b\left(c+\chi_{[a,a+p(b-a)]}(y)\frac{f\left(a+\frac{y-a}{p}\right)-c}{p}\right)^2\mathrm{d}y-F^2\right)$$ 150

$$\begin{aligned}
&= \frac{1}{n}\left(\|\mathcal{D}\|\int_a^{a+p(b-a)}\left(c+\frac{f\left(a+\frac{y-a}{p}\right)-c}{p}\right)^2\mathrm{d}y+\|\mathcal{D}\|\int_{a+p(b-a)}^b c^2\mathrm{d}y-F^2\right)\\
&= \frac{1}{n}\left(\|\mathcal{D}\|\int_a^b\left(\frac{cp+f(x)-c}{p}\right)^2 p\mathrm{d}x+\|\mathcal{D}\|c^2(b-a-p(b-a))-F^2\right)\\
&= \frac{1}{n}\left(\frac{\|\mathcal{D}\|}{p}\int_a^b\left(f(x)-c(1-p)\right)^2\mathrm{d}x+\|\mathcal{D}\|c^2(b-a)(1-p)-F^2\right)\\
&= \frac{1}{n}\left(\frac{\|\mathcal{D}\|}{p}\int_a^b f(x)^2-2f(x)c(1-p)+c^2(1-p)^2\mathrm{d}x+\|\mathcal{D}\|^2c^2(1-p)-F^2\right)\\
&= \frac{1}{n}\left(\frac{\|\mathcal{D}\|}{p}\left(\int_a^b f(x)^2\mathrm{d}x-2c(1-p)\int_a^b f(x)\mathrm{d}x+c^2(1-p)^2\int_a^b\mathrm{d}x\right)\right.\\
&\qquad\left.+\|\mathcal{D}\|^2c^2(1-p)-F^2\right)\\
&= \frac{1}{n}\left(\frac{\|\mathcal{D}\|}{p}\left(\int_a^b f(x)^2\mathrm{d}x-2c(1-p)F+c^2(1-p)^2\|\mathcal{D}\|\right)+\|\mathcal{D}\|^2c^2(1-p)-F^2\right)\\
&= \frac{1}{n}\left(\frac{\|\mathcal{D}\|}{p}\int_a^b f(x)^2\mathrm{d}x-2C\frac{1-p}{p}F+C^2\frac{(1-p)^2}{p}+C^2(1-p)-F^2\right)\\
&= \frac{1}{n}\left(\frac{\|\mathcal{D}\|}{p}\int_a^b f(x)^2\mathrm{d}x+\left(-2CF+C^2(1-p)+C^2p\right)\frac{1-p}{p}-\left(\frac{1}{p}+1-\frac{1}{p}\right)F^2\right)\\
&= \frac{1}{n}\left(\frac{1}{p}\left(\|\mathcal{D}\|\int_a^b f(x)^2\mathrm{d}x-F^2\right)+(-2CF+C^2)\frac{1-p}{p}+\frac{1-p}{p}F^2\right)
\end{aligned}$$

$$\overset{(4.120)}{=} \frac{1}{n}\left(\frac{\|\mathcal{D}\|^2}{p}\left(\frac{1}{\|\mathcal{D}\|}\int_a^b f(x)^2\mathrm{d}x-\bar{f}^2\right)+\frac{1-p}{p}(-2CF+C^2+F^2)\right)$$ 150

$$\overset{(4.123)}{=} \frac{\|\mathcal{D}\|^2\,\mathrm{V}[f(X)]+(1-p)(F-C)^2}{np} \tag{4.204}$$ 150

$$\begin{aligned}
&\geq \frac{\|\mathcal{D}\|^2\,\mathrm{V}[f(X)]}{np}\\
&\geq \frac{\|\mathcal{D}\|^2\,\mathrm{V}[f(X)]}{n}
\end{aligned} \tag{4.205}$$

which is consequently greater than that of the crude MC *estimator*. The increase in *variance* 139
can, however, be minimized if $C = F$, although this value is in practice commonly set to 143
$C = 0$ since F itself is unknown.

While resorting to a constant *probability* is mathematically valid, a more effective strat- 129
egy entails accounting for the expected contribution k of $\tilde{F}'$ (typically, based on a subset of
its constitutive terms) with a *probability* of the form $p = \min\{1, k \div t\}$, thereby evaluating 129
all contributions greater than a predefined threshold t and probabilistically skipping lower contributions, such that low values of t yield a low variance but high computational cost, while high values result in a lower computational cost but higher variance. In order to deter-

mine the threshold maximizing the trade-off between computational cost and variance, an estimate of both quantities may then be evaluated, a technique known as *efficiency-optimized Russian roulette* [Veach, 1997, §10.4].

4.6.9 Splitting

163 Conversely to *Russian roulette*, which probabilistically avoids sampling the integrand if the
estimated contribution is low, *splitting* provides an unbiased means of taking several independent samples if the estimated importance of the next step in a path sequence is high by
139 increasing the splitting factor n. An *estimator* is then constructed as a function of several
139 individual *estimators* $\tilde{S}_i$, which might happen to be identical

$$\tilde{S} = \frac{1}{n}\sum_{i=1}^{n} \tilde{S}_i \tag{4.206}$$

Given the current state $x_0, x_1, \ldots, x_n$ of a random walk, any function of the sequence of random steps may be used to estimate the potential contribution of the next step x_{n+1}. However, the main drawback of the method occurs when solving integral equations since the splitting process leads to an exponential growth of the number of branches in the tree of recursive evaluations.

4.6.10 Composite Techniques

143 Several variance reduction techniques can be combined in order to reduce *variance* more effectively. For instance, *stratified importance sampling* consists in dividing the domain of inte-
132 gration by partitioning the $[0, 1]$ domain resulting from the *cumulative distribution* transform
131 of the given *probability density* $p(x)$ so as to reflect some measure of importance. Assuming
that the integrand is more likely to fluctuate over an interval as both the magnitude of the
integrand and the size of the interval increase, the fraction of samples per stratum may then
be determined based on the importance of each stratum

131

$$\alpha_j \triangleq \frac{\int_{x_{j-1}}^{x_j} p(x)\mathrm{d}x}{\int_{x_a}^{x_b} p(x)\mathrm{d}x} \overset{(4.15)}{=} \int_{x_{j-1}}^{x_j} p(x)\mathrm{d}x \tag{4.207}$$

132 such that equally dividing the *cumulative distribution*'s domain results in an identical number
of samples per stratum.

167 As illustrated in *Figure 4.6*, it is also possible to estimate the integral term appearing in
161 the *control variates* formulation using *importance sampling* rather than a crude MC *estima-*
155
139 *tor*. Given a continuous *random variable* X distributed according to the *probability density*
129 $p(x)$ over the domain $\mathcal{D}$, the integral of the function $f(x)$ is therefore rewritten as [Owen and
131 Zhou, 2000]

161
155

$$F \overset{(4.186)}{=} G + \int_{\mathcal{D}} f(x) - g(x)\mathrm{d}x = G + \int_{\mathcal{D}} \frac{f(x) - g(x)}{p(x)} p(x)\mathrm{d}x \overset{(4.156)}{=} G + \mathrm{E}\left[\frac{f(X) - g(X)}{p(X)}\right] \tag{4.208}$$

139 The corresponding *estimator* then reads

150

$$\tilde{F} \overset{(4.121)}{=} G + \frac{1}{n}\sum_{i=1}^{n} \frac{f(X_i) - g(X_i)}{p(X_i)} \tag{4.209}$$

which is unbiased since

141
141
166

$$\mathrm{E}[\tilde{F}] \overset{(4.68)}{=} \mathrm{E}[G] + \frac{1}{n}\sum_{i=1}^{n} \mathrm{E}\left[\frac{f(X_i) - g(X_i)}{p(X_i)}\right] \overset{(4.66)}{=} G + \mathrm{E}\left[\frac{f(X) - g(X)}{p(X)}\right] \overset{(4.208)}{=} F \tag{4.210}$$

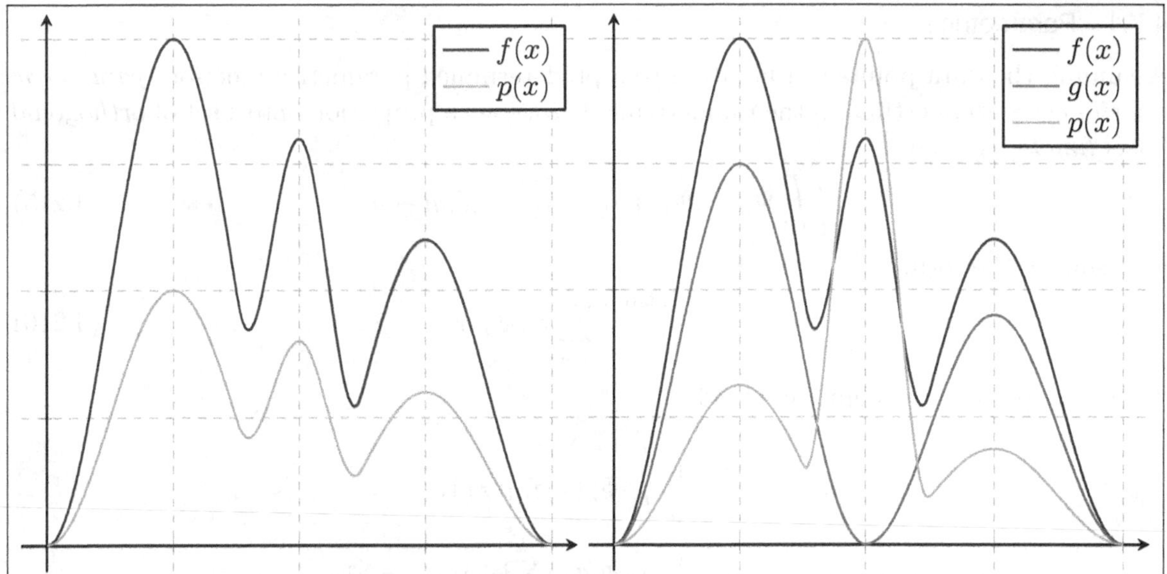

Figure 4.6: Composite Variance Reduction: Illustration of the integration of a sample function using importance sampling, and a combination of control variates with importance sampling.

Assuming uncorrelated variables, its *variance* evaluates to 143

$$\mathrm{V}[\tilde{F}] \overset{(4.92)}{=} \mathrm{V}[G] + \frac{1}{n^2}\sum_{i=1}^{n}\mathrm{V}\left[\frac{f(X_i)-g(X_i)}{p(X_i)}\right] \overset{(4.88)}{=} \frac{1}{n}\mathrm{V}\left[\frac{f(X)-g(X)}{p(X)}\right] \quad (4.211)$$ 144 143

while its *standard deviation* reads 146

$$\sigma[\tilde{F}] \overset{(4.104)}{=} \frac{1}{n^{\frac{1}{2}}}\sigma\left[\frac{f(X)-g(X)}{p(X)}\right] \quad (4.212)$$ 146

It follows that $p(x)$ should now resemble $f(x)-g(x)$ rather than $f(x)$. As the sign of the integrand $f(x)-g(x)$ might here vary while $p(x) \geq 0$ must hold, $p(x)$ may be correlated with $|f(x)-g(x)|$ instead. It is also important to note that if $g(x) \propto p(x)$, though, for instance if $g(x) = kp(x)$, then $G = \int_{\mathcal{D}} kp(x)\mathrm{d}x = k\int_{\mathcal{D}} p(x)\mathrm{d}x = k$ and the *estimator* is identical to the 139
one with *importance sampling* alone 155

$$\tilde{F} \overset{(4.209)}{=} G + \frac{1}{n}\sum_{i=1}^{n}\frac{f(X_i)-kp(X_i)}{p(X_i)} = k + \frac{1}{n}\sum_{i=1}^{n}\frac{f(X_i)}{p(X_i)} - \frac{1}{n}\sum_{i=1}^{n}k = \frac{1}{n}\sum_{i=1}^{n}\frac{f(X_i)}{p(X_i)} \quad (4.213)$$ 166

This implies that if a function is used for *importance sampling*, using it as a control variate 155
as well (up to a constant of proportionality) will not yield any further *variance* reduction. 143

4.7 DENSITY ESTIMATION

Given a density function $f(x)$ defined over a domain $\mathcal{D}$, *density estimation* techniques are concerned with computing an estimate $\tilde{f}(x)$ from a discrete set of k observations y_i at coordinates x_i. Formulating the discrete observations by means of Dirac *delta function* then 44
yields

$$f_{\text{III}}(x) = \sum_{i=1}^{k} y_i\delta(x-x_i) \quad (4.214)$$

where the observations satisfy $\sum_{i=1}^{k} y_i = 1$ if the function f is a normalized *probability density*, thereby yielding $y_i = {}^1\!/_k$ in the case of equally weighted observations. 131

4.7.1 Parametric

Assuming the data points can be fitted to a predetermined parametric function, *parametric density estimation* estimates their underlying density via a projection onto a set of *orthogonal*
61 *basis functions*

61

$$\int_{\mathcal{D}} \Psi_m(x)\Psi_n(x)\mathrm{d}x \overset{(2.313)}{=} b_m\delta[m-n] \tag{4.215}$$

as a sum of the form

61

$$\tilde{f}(x) \overset{(2.314)}{=} \sum_{n=0}^{N} a_n\Psi_n(x) \tag{4.216}$$

where the projection coefficients read

61
167
45

$$\begin{aligned} a_n &\overset{(2.316)}{=} \frac{1}{b_n}\int_{\mathcal{D}} \Psi_n(x) f_{\text{III}}(x)\mathrm{d}x \\ &\overset{(4.214)}{=} \frac{1}{b_n}\int_{\mathcal{D}} \Psi_n(x) \sum_{i=1}^{k} y_i\delta(x-x_i)\mathrm{d}x \\ &= \frac{1}{b_n}\sum_{i=1}^{k} y_i \int_{\mathcal{D}} \Psi_n(x)\delta(x-x_i)\mathrm{d}x \\ &\overset{(2.218)}{=} \frac{1}{b_n}\sum_{i=1}^{k} y_i\Psi_n(x_i) \end{aligned} \tag{4.217}$$

46 Shall the basis functions $\Psi_n(x) = \chi_{[x_n,x_{n+1}]}(x)$ be defined as *rectangular functions* over the domain $\mathcal{D} = [x_0, \ldots, x_{N+1}]$ such that $b_n = x_{n+1} - x_n$, the projection coefficients a_n then reduce to the sum of the observations y_i whose coordinate x_i lies within the sub-interval $[x_n, x_{n+1}]$, essentially generating a histogram. In contrast, higher-order basis functions might in some instances result in a density function that can be negative and/or un-normalized.

4.7.2 Non-Parametric

Without any a priori knowledge about the underlying density function, *non-parametric den-*
201 176 44 *sity estimation* relies on a form of non-interpolative *reconstruction* via a *convolution* of the non-uniform discrete observations with a given *kernel function* K

201
176
167
45

$$\begin{aligned} \tilde{f}(x) &\overset{(5.175)}{=} (f_{\text{III}} * K)(x) \\ &\overset{(5.5)}{\underset{(4.214)}{=}} \int_{-\infty}^{+\infty} \sum_{i=1}^{k} y_i\delta(\tau - x_i)K(x-\tau)\mathrm{d}\tau \\ &= \sum_{i=1}^{k} y_i \int_{-\infty}^{+\infty} \delta(\tau - x_i)K(x-\tau)\mathrm{d}\tau \\ &\overset{(2.218)}{=} \sum_{i=1}^{k} y_i K(x - x_i) \end{aligned} \tag{4.218}$$

which may either be interpreted as gathering the contributions of the observations weighted by the kernel centered at x, or as splatting onto x the contributions of each observation with a distribution K centered at x_i.

In the case of equally weighted observations distributed according to a normalized *prob-*
131 141 44 *ability density* f, the *expected value* of the shifted *kernel function* can then be formulated

as

$$\mathrm{E}[K(x-X)] \overset{(4.65)}{=} \int_{-\infty}^{+\infty} K(x-\tau)f(\tau)\mathrm{d}\tau$$ 141

$$\overset{(5.5)}{=} (f * K)(x) \tag{4.219}$$ 176

$$\overset{(5.5)}{=} \int_{-\infty}^{+\infty} K(\tau)f(x-\tau)\mathrm{d}\tau$$ 176

$$\overset{(2.309)}{=} \int_{-\infty}^{+\infty} K(\tau)\sum_{n=0}^{\infty}\frac{f^{(n)}(x)}{n!}(-\tau)^n\mathrm{d}\tau$$ 60

$$= \sum_{n=0}^{\infty}\frac{f^{(n)}(x)}{n!}\int_{-\infty}^{+\infty} K(\tau)(-\tau)^n\mathrm{d}\tau$$

$$\overset{(2.212)}{=} \sum_{\substack{n=0\\n+=2}}^{\infty}\frac{f^{(n)}(x)}{n!}\int_{-\infty}^{+\infty} K(\tau)\tau^n\mathrm{d}\tau - \cancel{\sum_{\substack{n=1\\n+=2}}^{\infty}\frac{f^{(n)}(x)}{n!}\int_{-\infty}^{+\infty} K(\tau)\tau^n\mathrm{d}\tau} \tag{4.220}$$ 44

$$\overset{(2.210)}{\approx} f(x) + \frac{f''(x)}{2}\int_{-\infty}^{+\infty} K(\tau)\tau^2\mathrm{d}\tau \tag{4.221}$$ 44

while its second raw *moment* similarly reads 140

$$\mathrm{E}[K(x-X)^2] \overset{(4.61)}{=} \int_{-\infty}^{+\infty} K(x-\tau)^2 f(\tau)\mathrm{d}\tau$$ 140

$$\overset{(5.5)}{=} (f * K^2)(x) \tag{4.222}$$ 176

$$\overset{(5.5)}{=} \int_{-\infty}^{+\infty} K(\tau)^2 f(x-\tau)\mathrm{d}\tau$$ 176

$$\overset{(2.309)}{=} \int_{-\infty}^{+\infty} K(\tau)^2\sum_{n=0}^{\infty}\frac{f^{(n)}(x)}{n!}(-\tau)^n\mathrm{d}\tau$$ 60

$$= \sum_{n=0}^{\infty}\frac{f^{(n)}(x)}{n!}\int_{-\infty}^{+\infty} K(\tau)^2(-\tau)^n\mathrm{d}\tau$$

$$\approx f(x)\int_{-\infty}^{+\infty} K(\tau)^2\mathrm{d}\tau \tag{4.223}$$

It follows that the *expected value* of the *estimator* is readily given as 141 139

$$\mathrm{E}[\tilde{f}(x)] \overset{(4.218)}{=} \mathrm{E}\left[\sum_{i=1}^{k}\frac{1}{k}K(x-X)\right] \overset{(4.68)}{=} \frac{1}{k}\sum_{i=1}^{k}\mathrm{E}[K(x-X)] = \mathrm{E}[K(x-X)] \tag{4.224}$$ 168 141

such that its bias reads

148 $$\mathrm{B}[\tilde{f}(x)] \overset{(4.113)}{=} \mathrm{E}[\tilde{f}(x)] - f(x)$$

169 $$\overset{(4.224)}{=} \mathrm{E}[K(x-X)] - f(x) \tag{4.225}$$

169 $$\overset{(4.220)}{=} \sum_{\substack{n=0\\ n+=2}}^{\infty} \frac{f^{(n)}(x)}{n!} \int_{-\infty}^{+\infty} K(\tau)\tau^n \mathrm{d}\tau - f(x)$$

$$= f(x)\int_{-\infty}^{+\infty} K(\tau)\mathrm{d}\tau + \sum_{\substack{n=2\\ n+=2}}^{\infty} \frac{f^{(n)}(x)}{n!} \int_{-\infty}^{+\infty} K(\tau)\tau^n \mathrm{d}\tau - f(x)$$

44 $$\overset{(2.210)}{=} \sum_{\substack{n=2\\ n+=2}}^{\infty} \frac{f^{(n)}(x)}{n!} \int_{-\infty}^{+\infty} K(\tau)\tau^n \mathrm{d}\tau \tag{4.226}$$

$$\approx \frac{f''(x)}{2} \int_{-\infty}^{+\infty} K(\tau)\tau^2 \mathrm{d}\tau \tag{4.227}$$

143 while its *variance* is given as

168 $$\mathrm{V}[\tilde{f}(x)] \overset{(4.218)}{=} \mathrm{V}\left[\sum_{i=1}^{k} \frac{1}{k} K(x-X)\right]$$

144 $$\overset{(4.92)}{=} \frac{1}{k^2}\sum_{i=1}^{k} \mathrm{V}\left[K(x-X)\right]$$

$$= \frac{1}{k}\mathrm{V}\left[K(x-X)\right]$$

143 $$\overset{(4.84)}{=} \frac{\mathrm{E}[K(x-X)^2] - \mathrm{E}[K(x-X)]^2}{k} \tag{4.228}$$

169 169 $$\underset{(4.221)}{\overset{(4.223)}{\approx}} \frac{f(x)\int_{-\infty}^{+\infty} K(\tau)^2\mathrm{d}\tau - \left(f(x) + \frac{f''(x)}{2}\int_{-\infty}^{+\infty} K(\tau)\tau^2\mathrm{d}\tau\right)^2}{k} \tag{4.229}$$

$$\approx \frac{f(x)}{k}\int_{-\infty}^{+\infty} K(\tau)^2 \mathrm{d}\tau \tag{4.230}$$

143 For a predetermined *variance* $\int_{-\infty}^{+\infty} K(\tau)\tau^2\mathrm{d}\tau$ of the kernel distribution, minimizing the
148 139 mean squared *error* of the *estimator* therefore entails minimizing $\int_{-\infty}^{+\infty} K(\tau)^2\mathrm{d}\tau$, the optimal
48 solution of which is given by the Epanechnikov *multiweight function*, although other *kernel*
44 *functions* tend to exhibit rather similar efficiency characteristics.

143 In contrast, the *variance* of the kernel distribution, or equivalently its *standard deviation*
146 or its spectral bandwidth, typically has a substantial impact on both the quantitative and
148 the qualitative nature of the *error*. Reformulating the bias and *variance* by expressing the
143 44 143 variable-bandwidth kernel in terms of a canonical *kernel function* with fixed *variance* $\sigma_K^2 \triangleq$

$\int_{-\infty}^{+\infty} K(t)^2 \mathrm{d}t$ then yields

$$\mathrm{B}[\tilde{f}(x)] \overset{(4.227)}{\underset{(2.213)}{\approx}} \frac{f''(x)}{2} \int_{-\infty}^{+\infty} \frac{1}{h} K\left(\frac{\tau}{h}\right) \tau^2 \mathrm{d}\tau$$ 170 44

$$= \frac{f''(x)}{2} \int_{-\infty}^{+\infty} \frac{1}{h} K(t)(ht)^2 h \mathrm{d}t$$

$$= \frac{f''(x)h^2}{2} \int_{-\infty}^{+\infty} K(t)t^2 \mathrm{d}t \tag{4.231}$$

$$\mathrm{V}[\tilde{f}(x)] \overset{(4.230)}{\underset{(2.213)}{\approx}} \frac{f(x)}{k} \int_{-\infty}^{+\infty} \frac{1}{h^2} K\left(\frac{\tau}{h}\right)^2 \mathrm{d}\tau$$ 170 44

$$= \frac{f(x)}{k} \int_{-\infty}^{+\infty} \frac{1}{h^2} K(t)^2 h \mathrm{d}t$$

$$= \frac{f(x)}{kh} \int_{-\infty}^{+\infty} K(t)^2 \mathrm{d}t \tag{4.232}$$

from which follows that the bias of the *estimator* increases with the spatial footprint of the 139
kernel, whereas its *variance* decreases instead. Defining the constant $c_K \triangleq \int_{-\infty}^{+\infty} K(t)t^2 \mathrm{d}t$, 143
minimizing the mean squared *error* 148

$$\mathrm{MSE}[\tilde{f}(x)] \overset{(4.115)}{=} \mathrm{V}[\tilde{f}(x)] + \mathrm{B}[\tilde{f}(x)]^2 \approx \frac{f(x)}{kh}\sigma_K^2 + \frac{f''(x)^2 h^4}{4} c_K^2 \tag{4.233}$$ 148

therefore entails finding the optimal trade-off between the two types of artifacts, which is obtained for

$$\frac{\mathrm{d}\,\mathrm{MSE}[\tilde{f}(x)]}{\mathrm{d}h} \approx -\frac{f(x)}{kh^2}\sigma_K^2 + f''(x)^2 h^3 c_K^2 = 0 \iff h = \sqrt[5]{\frac{f(x)\sigma_K^2}{k f''(x)^2 c_K^2}} \tag{4.234}$$

Instead, in order for sparsely populated regions to be blurred more heavily while capturing finer details in highly populated ones, the bandwidth of the kernel can be locally adapted based on an estimate of the local density. In the case of a gathering approach, the kernel $K = K_x$ may then be adapted for each estimation x based on the average distance of the neighboring observations or on the distance to the kth nearest neighbor (k-NN), which can, however, yield an estimated function exhibiting a discontinuous first derivative regardless of the order of continuity of the kernel. In the case of a splatting approach, the kernel $K = K_i$ may instead be adapted for each observation i based on the proximity of the surrounding observations or on the distance to the kth nearest neighbor, which allows the estimated function to preserve the differential properties of the kernel and tends to better capture details in regions of high gradient magnitude.

In both cases, the k nearest neighbors can be efficiently queried by means of a spatial
indexing scheme such as a *k-D tree*. Given a search radius, each observation lying within the 381
latter may then be stored in an array of length k, which, when full, is reordered by distance as a heap so as to reduce the search radius to the distance of the most distant observation in the array, and efficiently substitute it with any necessarily closer, subsequently found observation, while repeating the process with a larger radius if less than k observations have been found. As an alternative, the tree can be traversed using a priority queue in which the priority of each node is negatively correlated with the shortest distance of its *bounding
volume* to the query point, such that the search terminates whenever the distance to the kth 357
nearest observation is smaller than that of the queued node with highest priority.

46 In the literature, defining the kernel as the *rectangular function* is commonly referred to
as *naïve density estimation* in the case of a fixed kernel bandwidth, and as *nearest-neighbor
density estimation* in the case of a k-NN bandwidth. Similarly, the use of a more general
44 *kernel function* is commonly referred to as *kernel density estimation* in the case of a fixed
bandwidth, and as *generalized nearest-neighbor density estimation* or *variable-kernel density
estimation* in the case of a variable bandwidth per estimation or per observation, respectively.

4.7.3 Further Reading

Additional material may be found in books dedicated to density estimation [Silverman, 1986] and kernel smoothing [Wand and Jones, 1995].

4.8 FURTHER READING

Additional material may be found in books dedicated to Monte Carlo methods [Hammersley and Handscomb, 1964, Kalos and Whitlock, 1986].

CHAPTER 5

Signal Theory

TABLE OF CONTENTS

5.1 CROSS-INTEGRATION

5.1.1 Correlation

As illustrated in *Figure 5.1*, the *cross correlation* of two real-valued functions f and g is 175
defined as the integral of the product of one function with a shifted instance of the other

$$(f \star g)(t) \triangleq \int_{-\infty}^{+\infty} f(\tau)g(t+\tau)\mathrm{d}\tau = \int_{-\infty}^{+\infty} f(\tau - t)g(\tau)\mathrm{d}\tau \tag{5.1}$$

thereby providing a measure of the similarity of two signals as a function of the time-delay t, and whose maximum (or minimum if the signals are negatively correlated) yields optimal alignment between the two functions.

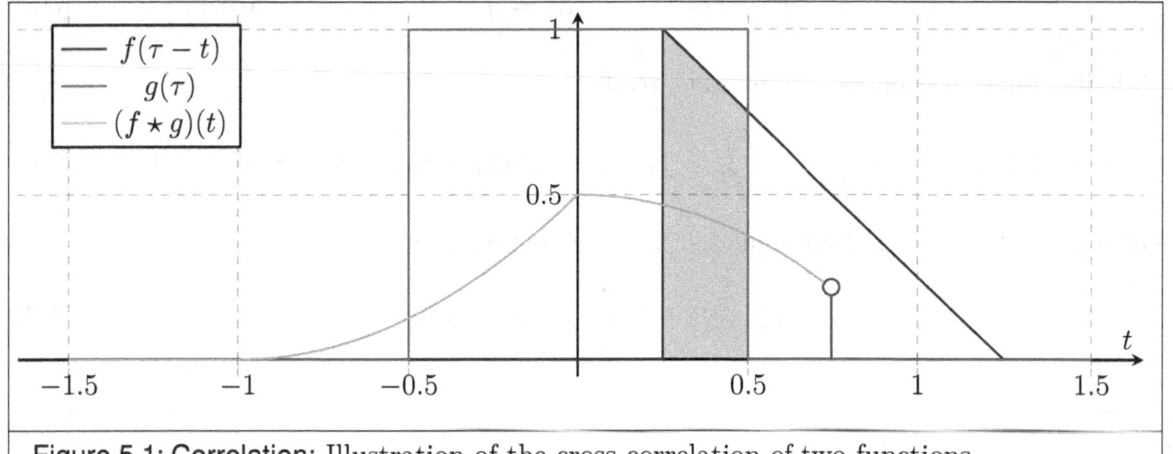

Figure 5.1: Correlation: Illustration of the cross correlation of two functions.

The cross correlation of a function with a Dirac *delta function* yields a time-reversed 44
instance of the function

$$f(t) \star \frac{1}{|c|}\delta\left(\frac{t}{c}\right) \overset{(5.1)}{=} \int_{-\infty}^{+\infty} f(\tau)\frac{1}{|c|}\delta\left(\frac{t+\tau}{c}\right)\mathrm{d}\tau \overset{(2.216)}{=} \int_{-\infty}^{+\infty} f(\tau)\delta(t+\tau)\mathrm{d}\tau \overset{(2.218)}{=} f(-t) \tag{5.2}$$

175 44 45

while the cross correlation of a function with a Dirac comb results in a summation of an infinite number of time-reversed instances of the function offset by integer multiples of the scaling factor c

$$\begin{aligned} f(t) \star \frac{1}{|c|}\mathrm{III}\left(\frac{t}{c}\right) &\overset{(5.1)}{=} \int_{-\infty}^{+\infty} f(\tau)\frac{1}{|c|}\mathrm{III}\left(\frac{t+\tau}{c}\right)\mathrm{d}\tau \\ &\overset{(2.220)}{=} \int_{-\infty}^{+\infty} f(\tau)\sum_{n=-\infty}^{+\infty}\delta(t+\tau \pm nc)\mathrm{d}\tau \\ &= \sum_{n=-\infty}^{+\infty}\int_{-\infty}^{+\infty} f(\tau)\delta(t+\tau \pm nc)\mathrm{d}\tau \\ &\overset{(2.218)}{=} \sum_{n=-\infty}^{+\infty} f(-t \mp nc) \end{aligned} \tag{5.3}$$

175 45 45

The cross correlation of a signal f with itself is instead referred to as *autocorrelation* $(f \star f)(t)$. The latter yields an even function with maximum at zero delay that similarly provides a means of identifying periodic patterns in a given signal.

The generalization of correlation to complex-valued signals entails conjugating the first of the two functions, while the discrete form is readily given as

$$(f \star g)[n] \triangleq \sum_{m=-\infty}^{+\infty} f[m]g[n+m] \tag{5.4}$$

5.1.2 Convolution

176 As illustrated in *Figure 5.2*, the *convolution* of two functions f and g is defined as the integral of the product of one function with a reversed and shifted instance of the other

$$(f * g)(t) \triangleq \int_{-\infty}^{+\infty} f(\tau)g(t-\tau)\mathrm{d}\tau = \int_{-\infty}^{+\infty} f(-\tau)g(t+\tau)\mathrm{d}\tau \tag{5.5}$$

while its generalization to d dimensions reads

$$(f * g)(t_1, \ldots, t_d) \triangleq \int_{-\infty}^{+\infty} \cdots \int_{-\infty}^{+\infty} f(\tau_1, \ldots, \tau_d)g(t_1 - \tau_1, \ldots, t_d - \tau_d)\mathrm{d}\tau_1 \ldots \mathrm{d}\tau_d \tag{5.6}$$

which may alternatively be formulated in vector notation as

$$(f * g)(\vec{t}) \triangleq \int_{\mathbb{R}^d} f(\vec{\tau})g(\vec{t} - \vec{\tau})\mathrm{d}\vec{\tau} \tag{5.7}$$

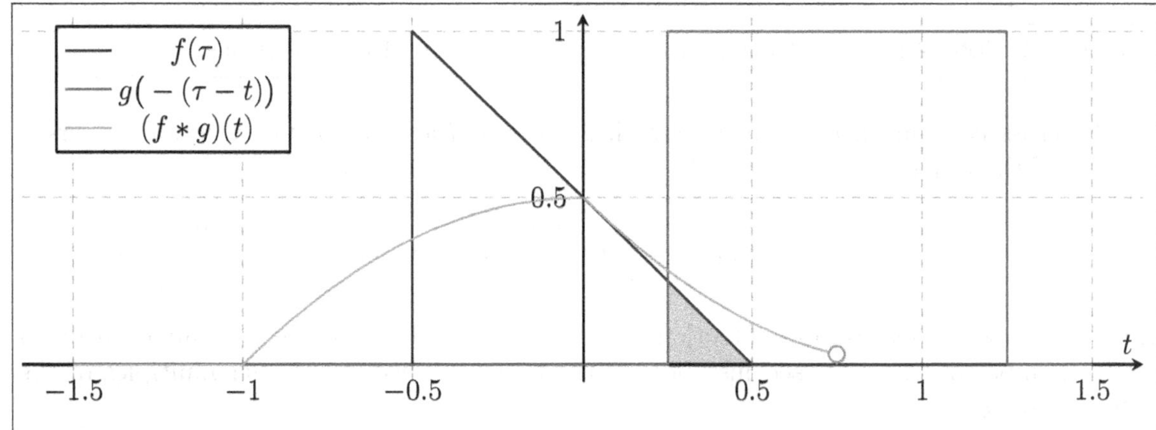

Figure 5.2: Convolution: Illustration of the convolution of two functions.

Convolution satisfies the following properties

- commutativity: $$f * g = g * f \tag{5.8}$$
- associativity: $$f * (g * h) = (f * g) * h \tag{5.9}$$
- distributivity: $$f * (g + h) = f * g + f * h \tag{5.10}$$
- scalar multiplication: $$(cf) * g = c(f * g) \tag{5.11}$$
- identity: $$f * \delta = f \tag{5.12}$$

while in the case of an even function f it also holds that

176
175

$$(f * g)(t) \overset{(5.5)}{=} \int_{-\infty}^{+\infty} f(\tau)g(t+\tau)\mathrm{d}\tau \overset{(5.1)}{=} (f \star g)(t) \tag{5.13}$$

The integral of the convolution of two functions reads

$$\int_{-\infty}^{+\infty}(f*g)(t)\mathrm{d}t = \int_{-\infty}^{+\infty} f(t)\mathrm{d}t \int_{-\infty}^{+\infty} g(t)\mathrm{d}t \tag{5.14}$$

while its derivative is given by

$$\frac{\mathrm{d}(f*g)(t)}{\mathrm{d}t} = \frac{\mathrm{d}f(t)}{\mathrm{d}t} * g(t) \tag{5.15}$$

The identity property directly stems from the sifting property of the Dirac *delta function* 44

$$f(t) * \frac{1}{|c|}\delta\left(\frac{t}{c}\right) \overset{(5.5)}{=} \int_{-\infty}^{+\infty} f(\tau)\frac{1}{|c|}\delta\left(\frac{t-\tau}{c}\right)\mathrm{d}\tau \overset{(2.216)}{=} \int_{-\infty}^{+\infty} f(\tau)\delta(t-\tau)\mathrm{d}\tau \overset{(2.218)}{=} f(t) \tag{5.16}$$

176 44 45

while the convolution of a function with a Dirac comb results in a *periodic summation* of the function

$$\begin{aligned} f(t) * \frac{1}{|c|}\mathrm{III}\left(\frac{t}{c}\right) &\overset{(5.5)}{=} \int_{-\infty}^{+\infty} f(\tau)\frac{1}{|c|}\mathrm{III}\left(\frac{t-\tau}{c}\right)\mathrm{d}\tau \\ &\overset{(2.220)}{=} \int_{-\infty}^{+\infty} f(\tau)\sum_{n=-\infty}^{+\infty}\delta(t-\tau\pm nc)\mathrm{d}\tau \\ &= \sum_{n=-\infty}^{+\infty}\int_{-\infty}^{+\infty} f(\tau)\delta(t-\tau\pm nc)\mathrm{d}\tau \\ &\overset{(2.218)}{=} \sum_{n=-\infty}^{+\infty} f(t\pm nc) \end{aligned} \tag{5.17}$$

176 45 45

such that any periodic function of period c can be represented as a periodic summation of an infinite number of instances of an aperiodic function f offset by integer multiples of the period.

The *circular convolution*, also called *cyclic convolution*, of two aperiodic functions f and g defining the periodic summations of period P

$$f_P(t) \overset{(5.17)}{=} \sum_{n=-\infty}^{+\infty} f(t+nP) \tag{5.18}$$

177

$$g_P(t) \overset{(5.17)}{=} \sum_{n=-\infty}^{+\infty} g(t+nP) \tag{5.19}$$

177

is then given by the *periodic convolution* of f_P and g_P

$$\begin{aligned} (f*g_P)(t) &\overset{(5.5)}{=} \int_{-\infty}^{+\infty} f(\tau)g_P(t-\tau)\mathrm{d}\tau \\ &= \sum_{n=-\infty}^{+\infty}\int_{t_0+nP}^{t_0+(n+1)P} f(\tau)g_P(t-\tau)\mathrm{d}\tau \\ &= \int_{t_0}^{t_0+P}\sum_{n=-\infty}^{+\infty} f(\tau+nP)g_P(t-\tau-nP)\mathrm{d}\tau \\ &\underset{(5.19)}{\overset{(5.18)}{=}} \int_P f_P(\tau)g_P(t-\tau)\mathrm{d}\tau \end{aligned} \tag{5.20}$$

176 177 177

Considering the case of piecewise-constant functions and replacing the integral by a Riemann sum alternatively leads to the *discrete convolution* of two sequences of coefficients f and g

$$(f * g)[n] \triangleq \sum_{m=-\infty}^{+\infty} f[m]g[n-m] \tag{5.21}$$

while their *circular discrete convolution*, also called *cyclic discrete convolution*, based on the periodic sequences of coefficients of period N

$$f_N[n] \triangleq \sum_{k=-\infty}^{+\infty} f[n+kN] \tag{5.22}$$

$$g_N[n] \triangleq \sum_{k=-\infty}^{+\infty} g[n+kN] \tag{5.23}$$

is similarly defined by the *periodic discrete convolution* of f_N and g_N

178

$$\begin{aligned}(f * g_N)[n] &\overset{(5.21)}{=} \sum_{m=-\infty}^{+\infty} f[m]g_N[n-m] \\ &= \sum_{k=-\infty}^{+\infty} \sum_{m=m_0+kN}^{m_0+(k+1)N} f[m]g_N[n-m] \\ &= \sum_{m=m_0}^{m_0+N} \sum_{k=-\infty}^{+\infty} f[m+kN]g_N[n-m-kN]\end{aligned}$$

178

178

$$\overset{(5.22)}{\underset{(5.23)}{=}} \sum_{m \in N} f_N[m]g_N[n-m] \tag{5.24}$$

5.2 FOURIER ANALYSIS

5.2.1 History

Fourier analysis is concerned with the study of the frequency content of a signal, representing a given time-varying or spatially varying physical quantity, and with its mathematical decomposition into individual spectral components. Conversely, the process of reconstructing the original signal from its spectral representation is known as *Fourier synthesis*.

The techniques are named after the French mathematician and physicist Jean-Baptiste Joseph Fourier who introduced the concepts while investigating heat transfer in metal plates [Fourier, 1808, Fourier, 1822]. Starting from solutions to the heat equation only known at the time in the special case of a sinusoidal source, Fourier proposed to solve the partial differential equation in the general case by modeling complex heat sources as a series of sine and cosine waves, and to express the full solution as a linear combination of the individual results.

5.2.2 Fourier Transform

5.2.2.1 *Forward Transform*

A real-valued signal s can be decomposed into the sum of its even part $\mathfrak{E}$ and its odd part $\mathfrak{O}$

$$s(t) = \mathfrak{E}(s(t)) + \mathfrak{O}(s(t)) \tag{5.25}$$

which are defined as

$$\mathfrak{E}(s(t)) \triangleq \frac{s(t)+s(-t)}{2} \tag{5.26}$$

$$\mathfrak{O}(s(t)) \triangleq \frac{s(t)-s(-t)}{2} \tag{5.27}$$

such that

$$\mathfrak{E}(s(-t)) = \frac{s(-t)+s(t)}{2} = \frac{s(t)+s(-t)}{2} = \mathfrak{E}(s(t)) \tag{5.28}$$

$$\mathfrak{O}(s(-t)) = \frac{s(-t)-s(t)}{2} = -\frac{s(t)-s(-t)}{2} = -\mathfrak{O}(s(t)) \tag{5.29}$$

As illustrated in *Figure 5.3*, the *Fourier transform* of a signal is then defined as the complex-valued function 179

$$S(\nu) \triangleq \mathcal{F}\{s(t)\} \triangleq \int_{-\infty}^{+\infty} s(t)e^{-\imath 2\pi\nu t}\mathrm{d}t \tag{5.30}$$

$$= \int_{-\infty}^{+\infty} s(t)\big(\cos(2\pi\nu t) - \imath\sin(2\pi\nu t)\big)\mathrm{d}t$$

$$= \Re(S(\nu)) + \imath\Im(S(\nu)) \tag{5.31}$$

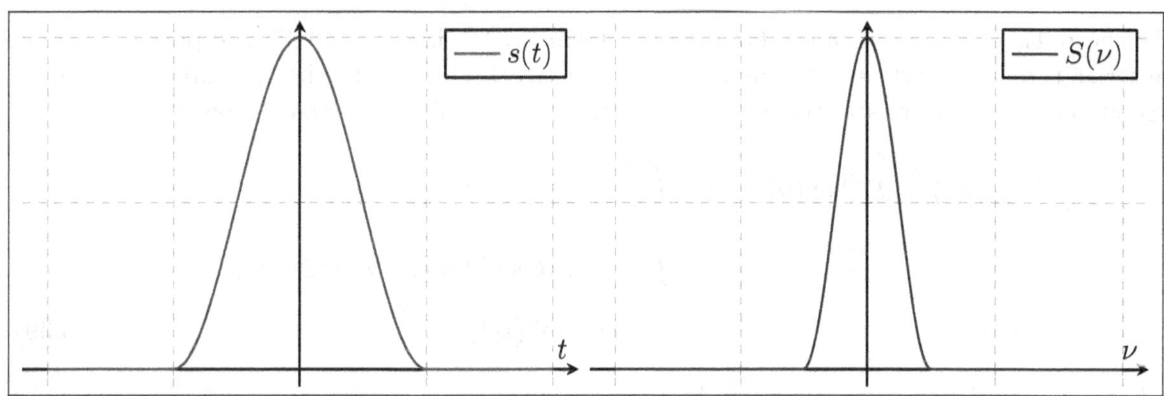

Figure 5.3: Fourier Transform: Schematic illustration of the Fourier transform of a continuous aperiodic signal.

It then holds that $S(0) = \int_{-\infty}^{+\infty} s(t)\mathrm{d}t$, while the real and imaginary parts are given by

$$\Re(S(\nu)) = \int_{-\infty}^{+\infty} s(t)\cos(2\pi\nu t)\mathrm{d}t \tag{5.32}$$

$$\overset{(5.25)}{=} \int_{-\infty}^{+\infty} \mathfrak{E}(s(t))\cos(2\pi\nu t)\mathrm{d}t + \cancel{\int_{-\infty}^{+\infty} \mathfrak{O}(s(t))\cos(2\pi\nu t)\mathrm{d}t}$$ 178

$$\overset{(5.29)}{=} \int_{-\infty}^{+\infty} \mathfrak{E}(s(t))\cos(2\pi\nu t)\mathrm{d}t \tag{5.33}$$ 179

$$\Im(S(\nu)) = -\int_{-\infty}^{+\infty} s(t)\sin(2\pi\nu t)\mathrm{d}t \tag{5.34}$$

$$\overset{(5.25)}{=} -\cancel{\int_{-\infty}^{+\infty} \mathfrak{E}(s(t))\sin(2\pi\nu t)\mathrm{d}t} - \int_{-\infty}^{+\infty} \mathfrak{O}(s(t))\sin(2\pi\nu t)\mathrm{d}t$$ 178

$$\overset{(5.28)}{=} -\int_{-\infty}^{+\infty} \mathfrak{O}(s(t))\sin(2\pi\nu t)\mathrm{d}t \tag{5.35}$$ 179

It follows that $\Re(S(0)) = S(0)$ and $\Im(S(0)) = 0$, while $\Re(S(\nu)) = \mathfrak{E}(s(t)) = 0$ if the time-domain signal is odd, and $\Im(S(\nu)) = \mathfrak{O}(s(t)) = 0$ if the time-domain signal is even instead. It also holds that the real and imaginary parts are, respectively, even and odd

179

$$\Re(S(-\nu)) \overset{(5.33)}{=} \int_{-\infty}^{+\infty} \mathfrak{E}(s(t)) \cos(-2\pi\nu t)\mathrm{d}t = \int_{-\infty}^{+\infty} \mathfrak{E}(s(t)) \cos(2\pi\nu t)\mathrm{d}t$$

179

$$\overset{(5.33)}{=} \Re(S(\nu)) \tag{5.36}$$

179

$$\Im(S(-\nu)) \overset{(5.35)}{=} -\int_{-\infty}^{+\infty} \mathfrak{O}(s(t)) \sin(-2\pi\nu t)\mathrm{d}t = \int_{-\infty}^{+\infty} \mathfrak{O}(s(t)) \sin(2\pi\nu t)\mathrm{d}t$$

179

$$\overset{(5.35)}{=} -\Im(S(\nu)) \tag{5.37}$$

from which follows that $S(-\nu) = \overline{S(\nu)}$, and $S(\nu)$ is therefore a Hermitian function.

5.2.2.2 Inverse Transform

86 As the *polar coordinates* of the Fourier transform $S(\nu) = |S(\nu)|e^{\imath \arg(S(\nu))}$, respectively, characterize the magnitude and the phase of the constitutive sinusoids, the original signal can be reconstructed from its spectral representation by means of the *inverse Fourier transform*

$$s(t) = \mathcal{F}^{-1}\{S(\nu)\} \triangleq \int_{-\infty}^{+\infty} S(\nu)e^{\imath 2\pi\nu t}\mathrm{d}\nu \tag{5.38}$$

$$= \int_{-\infty}^{+\infty} S(\nu)\big(\cos(2\pi\nu t) + \imath\sin(2\pi\nu t)\big)\mathrm{d}\nu = \mathfrak{E}(s(t)) + \mathfrak{O}(s(t)) \tag{5.39}$$

whose even and odd parts are given by

$$\mathfrak{E}(s(t)) = \int_{-\infty}^{+\infty} S(\nu)\cos(2\pi\nu t)\mathrm{d}\nu \tag{5.40}$$

179

$$\overset{(5.31)}{=} \int_{-\infty}^{+\infty} \Re(S(\nu))\cos(2\pi\nu t)\mathrm{d}\nu + \cancel{\imath\int_{-\infty}^{+\infty} \Im(S(\nu))\cos(2\pi\nu t)\mathrm{d}\nu}$$

180

$$\overset{(5.37)}{=} \int_{-\infty}^{+\infty} \Re(S(\nu))\cos(2\pi\nu t)\mathrm{d}\nu \tag{5.41}$$

$$\mathfrak{O}(s(t)) = \imath\int_{-\infty}^{+\infty} S(\nu)\sin(2\pi\nu t)\mathrm{d}\nu \tag{5.42}$$

179

$$\overset{(5.31)}{=} \cancel{\imath\int_{-\infty}^{+\infty} \Re(S(\nu))\sin(2\pi\nu t)\mathrm{d}\nu} + \imath^2\int_{-\infty}^{+\infty} \Im(S(\nu))\sin(2\pi\nu t)\mathrm{d}\nu$$

180

$$\overset{(5.36)}{=} -\int_{-\infty}^{+\infty} \Im(S(\nu))\sin(2\pi\nu t)\mathrm{d}\nu \tag{5.43}$$

which do satisfy

$$\mathfrak{E}(s(-t)) \overset{(5.41)}{=} \int_{-\infty}^{+\infty} \Re(S(\nu))\cos(-2\pi\nu t)\mathrm{d}\nu$$ 180

$$= \int_{-\infty}^{+\infty} \Re(S(\nu))\cos(2\pi\nu t)\mathrm{d}\nu$$

$$\overset{(5.41)}{=} \mathfrak{E}(s(t)) \tag{5.44}$$ 180

$$\mathfrak{O}(s(-t)) \overset{(5.43)}{=} -\int_{-\infty}^{+\infty} \Im(S(\nu))\sin(-2\pi\nu t)\mathrm{d}\nu$$ 180

$$= \int_{-\infty}^{+\infty} \Im(S(\nu))\sin(2\pi\nu t)\mathrm{d}\nu$$

$$\overset{(5.43)}{=} -\mathfrak{O}(s(t)) \tag{5.45}$$ 180

More generally, the *Fourier inversion theorem* states that

$$s(t) = \mathcal{F}^{-1}\{\mathcal{F}\{s(t)\}\} \tag{5.46}$$

$$S(\nu) = \mathcal{F}\{\mathcal{F}^{-1}\{S(\nu)\}\} \tag{5.47}$$

from which follows the *Fourier integral theorem*

$$s(t) \underset{(5.38)}{\overset{(5.30)}{=}} \int_{-\infty}^{+\infty}\left(\int_{-\infty}^{+\infty} s(t')e^{-\imath 2\pi\nu t'}\mathrm{d}t'\right)e^{\imath 2\pi\nu t}\mathrm{d}\nu$$ 179 180

$$= \int_{-\infty}^{+\infty}\int_{-\infty}^{+\infty} s(t')e^{\imath 2\pi\nu(t-t')}\mathrm{d}t'\mathrm{d}\nu$$

$$= \Re\left(\int_{-\infty}^{+\infty}\int_{-\infty}^{+\infty} s(t')e^{\imath 2\pi\nu(t-t')}\mathrm{d}t'\mathrm{d}\nu\right)$$

$$= \int_{-\infty}^{+\infty}\int_{-\infty}^{+\infty} s(t')\cos\left(2\pi\nu(t-t')\right)\mathrm{d}t'\mathrm{d}\nu \tag{5.48}$$

where the previous-to-last equality must hold true for any real-valued signal.

5.2.2.3 Multidimensional Transform

The extension of the transform to a complex-valued signal directly follows from the definition

$$S(\nu) \overset{(5.30)}{=} \int_{-\infty}^{+\infty}\left(\Re(s(t)) + \imath\Im(s(t))\right)e^{-\imath 2\pi\nu t}\mathrm{d}t \tag{5.49}$$ 179

$$= \int_{-\infty}^{+\infty} \Re(s(t))e^{-\imath 2\pi\nu t}\mathrm{d}t + \imath\int_{-\infty}^{+\infty} \Im(s(t))e^{-\imath 2\pi\nu t}\mathrm{d}t \tag{5.50}$$

$$= \int_{-\infty}^{+\infty} \Re(s(t))\cos(2\pi\nu t) + \Im(s(t))\sin(2\pi\nu t)\mathrm{d}t$$

$$+ \quad \imath\int_{-\infty}^{+\infty} \Im(s(t))\cos(2\pi\nu t) - \Re(s(t))\sin(2\pi\nu t)\mathrm{d}t \tag{5.51}$$

such that $\mathcal{F}\{\overline{s(t)}\} = \overline{S(-\nu)}$, and its generalization to d dimensions is equivalent to successively applying the one-dimensional transform in turn along each individual dimension in any order

$$S(\nu_1,\ldots,\nu_d) \triangleq \int_{-\infty}^{+\infty}\cdots\int_{-\infty}^{+\infty} s(t_1,\ldots,t_d)e^{-\imath 2\pi(\nu_1 t_1+\ldots+\nu_d t_d)}\mathrm{d}t_1\ldots\mathrm{d}t_d \tag{5.52}$$

$$= \int_{-\infty}^{+\infty}\cdots\left(\int_{-\infty}^{+\infty} s(t_1,\ldots,t_d)e^{-\imath 2\pi\nu_1 t_1}\mathrm{d}t_1\right)\ldots e^{-\imath 2\pi\nu_d t_d}\mathrm{d}t_d \tag{5.53}$$

while the corresponding multidimensional inverse similarly reads

$$s(t_1,\ldots,t_d) \triangleq \int_{-\infty}^{+\infty}\cdots\int_{-\infty}^{+\infty} S(\nu_1,\ldots,\nu_d)e^{\imath 2\pi(\nu_1 t_1+\ldots+\nu_d t_d)}\mathrm{d}\nu_1\ldots\mathrm{d}\nu_d \tag{5.54}$$

$$= \int_{-\infty}^{+\infty}\cdots\left(\int_{-\infty}^{+\infty} S(\nu_1,\ldots,\nu_d)e^{\imath 2\pi\nu_1 t_1}\mathrm{d}\nu_1\right)\ldots e^{\imath 2\pi\nu_d t_d}\mathrm{d}\nu_d \tag{5.55}$$

Representing the variables of integration as the components of a d-dimensional vector,
76 the above formulation may be more compactly written using *inner products* as

$$S(\vec{\nu}) = \int_{\mathbb{R}^d} s(\vec{t})e^{-\imath 2\pi\langle\vec{\nu},\vec{t}\rangle}\mathrm{d}\vec{t} \tag{5.56}$$

$$s(\vec{t}) = \int_{\mathbb{R}^d} S(\vec{\nu})e^{\imath 2\pi\langle\vec{\nu},\vec{t}\rangle}\mathrm{d}\vec{\nu} \tag{5.57}$$

which might alternatively be expressed in terms of angular frequencies $\omega \triangleq 2\pi\nu$

$$S(\vec{\omega}) = \int_{\mathbb{R}^d} s(\vec{t})e^{-\imath\langle\vec{\omega},\vec{t}\rangle}\mathrm{d}\vec{t} \tag{5.58}$$

$$s(\vec{t}) = \frac{1}{(2\pi)^d}\int_{\mathbb{R}^d} S(\vec{\omega})e^{\imath\langle\vec{\omega},\vec{t}\rangle}\mathrm{d}\vec{\omega} \tag{5.59}$$

In the case of a radially symmetric two-dimensional signal $s(t_x,t_y) = s(r)$, the Fourier transform $S(\nu_x,\nu_y) = S(\rho)$ is also radially symmetric and can be formulated by expressing the vectors $\vec{t}$ and $\vec{\nu}$ in polar coordinates $(r = \sqrt{t_x^2+t_y^2}, \varphi)$ and $(\rho = \sqrt{\nu_x^2+\nu_y^2}, \phi)$, respectively, which yields a *zero-order Hankel transform* of the form

182

$$S(\nu_x,\nu_y) \overset{(5.52)}{=} \int_{-\infty}^{+\infty}\int_{-\infty}^{+\infty} s(t_x,t_y)e^{-\imath 2\pi(\nu_x t_x+\nu_y t_y)}\mathrm{d}t_x\mathrm{d}t_y$$

77

$$\overset{(3.77)}{=} \int_0^{2\pi}\int_0^{\infty} s(r)e^{-\imath 2\pi r\rho\cos(\varphi-\phi)}r\mathrm{d}r\mathrm{d}\varphi$$

$$= \int_0^{\infty} s(r)\int_{-\phi}^{2\pi-\phi} e^{-\imath 2\pi r\rho\cos(\theta)}\mathrm{d}\theta r\mathrm{d}r$$

$$= \int_0^{\infty} s(r)\int_0^{2\pi} e^{-\imath 2\pi r\rho\cos(\theta)}\mathrm{d}\theta r\mathrm{d}r$$

54
54

$$\underset{(2.264)}{\overset{(2.260)}{=}} 2\pi\int_0^{\infty} s(r)J_0(2\pi r\rho)r\mathrm{d}r \tag{5.60}$$

54 with $\theta \triangleq \varphi - \phi$, and where J_0 is the zero-order *Bessel function* of the first kind.

5.2.2.4 Properties

The Fourier transform satisfies the following properties

- linearity: $$c_1 s_1(t) + c_2 s_2(t) \underset{\mathcal{F}^{-1}}{\overset{\mathcal{F}}{\rightleftharpoons}} c_1 S_1(\nu) + c_2 S_2(\nu) \tag{5.61}$$
- time-shift: $$s(t - t_0) \underset{\mathcal{F}^{-1}}{\overset{\mathcal{F}}{\rightleftharpoons}} e^{-\imath 2\pi\nu t_0} S(\nu) \tag{5.62}$$
- frequency-shift: $$e^{\imath 2\pi\nu_0 t} s(t) \underset{\mathcal{F}^{-1}}{\overset{\mathcal{F}}{\rightleftharpoons}} S(\nu - \nu_0) \tag{5.63}$$
- scaling: $$|c| s(ct) \underset{\mathcal{F}^{-1}}{\overset{\mathcal{F}}{\rightleftharpoons}} S\left(\frac{\nu}{c}\right) \tag{5.64}$$
- inverse: $$S(t) \underset{\mathcal{F}^{-1}}{\overset{\mathcal{F}}{\rightleftharpoons}} s(-\nu) \tag{5.65}$$
- time-derivative: $$\frac{\mathrm{d}^n s(t)}{\mathrm{d}t^n} \underset{\mathcal{F}^{-1}}{\overset{\mathcal{F}}{\rightleftharpoons}} (\imath 2\pi\nu)^n S(\nu) \tag{5.66}$$
- frequency-derivative: $$(-\imath 2\pi t)^n s(t) \underset{\mathcal{F}^{-1}}{\overset{\mathcal{F}}{\rightleftharpoons}} \frac{\mathrm{d}^n S(\nu)}{\mathrm{d}\nu^n} \tag{5.67}$$
- correlation theorem: $$(s_1 \star s_2)(t) \underset{\mathcal{F}^{-1}}{\overset{\mathcal{F}}{\rightleftharpoons}} \overline{S_1(\nu)} S_2(\nu) \tag{5.68}$$
- time-convolution: $$(s_1 * s_2)(t) \underset{\mathcal{F}^{-1}}{\overset{\mathcal{F}}{\rightleftharpoons}} S_1(\nu) S_2(\nu) \tag{5.69}$$
- frequency-convolution: $$s_1(t) s_2(t) \underset{\mathcal{F}^{-1}}{\overset{\mathcal{F}}{\rightleftharpoons}} (S_1 * S_2)(\nu) \tag{5.70}$$

where a scaling by $c = -1$ yields the time-reversal property. Also, the inverse property states that the Fourier transform is its own inverse for any even input signal, while in the general case, successively applying the Fourier transform three or four times yields the inverse Fourier transform or the identity transform, respectively.

The scaling property is a direct manifestation of the *Fourier uncertainty principle* underpinning the time-frequency duality of support compactness, as a given signal cannot be both time limited and band limited. Although the concept of a band-limited signal is valuable for the sake of theoretical analysis, real-world signals are in practice necessarily limited in their time span, and, as such, are consequently never band limited.

The time-convolution and frequency-convolution identities then readily stem from the *convolution theorem*

$$\mathcal{F}\{(s_1 * s_2)(t)\} \overset{(5.5)}{\underset{(5.30)}{=}} \int_{-\infty}^{+\infty} \left(\int_{-\infty}^{+\infty} s_1(u) s_2(t-u) \mathrm{d}u \right) e^{-\imath 2\pi\nu t} \mathrm{d}t$$ 176 179

$$= \int_{-\infty}^{+\infty} s_1(u) \int_{-\infty}^{+\infty} s_2(t-u) e^{-\imath 2\pi\nu t} \mathrm{d}t \mathrm{d}u$$

$$= \int_{-\infty}^{+\infty} s_1(u) \int_{-\infty}^{+\infty} s_2(v) e^{-\imath 2\pi\nu(u+v)} \mathrm{d}v \mathrm{d}u$$

$$= \int_{-\infty}^{+\infty} s_1(u) e^{-\imath 2\pi\nu u} \mathrm{d}u \int_{-\infty}^{+\infty} s_2(v) e^{-\imath 2\pi\nu v} \mathrm{d}v$$

$$\overset{(5.30)}{=} \mathcal{F}\{s_1(t)\} \mathcal{F}\{s_2(t)\} \tag{5.71}$$ 179

with the change of variable $v \triangleq t - u$.

Also, *Parseval's theorem* states that

183
176

$$\begin{aligned}\int_{-\infty}^{+\infty} s_1(t)s_2(t)\mathrm{d}t &= \mathcal{F}\{s_1(t)s_2(t)\}(0)\\ &\overset{(5.70)}{=} (S_1 * S_2)(0)\\ &\overset{(5.5)}{=} \int_{-\infty}^{+\infty} S_1(\nu)S_2(0-\nu)\mathrm{d}\nu\\ &= \int_{-\infty}^{+\infty} S_1(\nu)\overline{S_2(\nu)}\mathrm{d}\nu \end{aligned} \tag{5.72}$$

from which follows that the *energy spectral density* of a signal can be expressed by means of *Plancherel's theorem* as

87

$$\int_{-\infty}^{+\infty} s(t)^2\mathrm{d}t = \int_{-\infty}^{+\infty} S(\nu)\overline{S(\nu)}\mathrm{d}\nu \overset{(3.158)}{=} \int_{-\infty}^{+\infty} |S(\nu)|^2\mathrm{d}\nu \tag{5.73}$$

5.2.2.5 Canonical Transforms

44 The Fourier transforms of canonical *kernel functions* include

$$\sqcap(t) \underset{\mathcal{F}^{-1}}{\overset{\mathcal{F}}{\rightleftharpoons}} \mathrm{sinc}(\pi\nu) \tag{5.74}$$

$$\mathrm{sinc}(\pi t) \underset{\mathcal{F}^{-1}}{\overset{\mathcal{F}}{\rightleftharpoons}} \sqcap(\nu) \tag{5.75}$$

$$\wedge(t) \underset{\mathcal{F}^{-1}}{\overset{\mathcal{F}}{\rightleftharpoons}} \mathrm{sinc}(\pi\nu)^2 \tag{5.76}$$

$$\mathrm{sinc}(\pi t)^2 \underset{\mathcal{F}^{-1}}{\overset{\mathcal{F}}{\rightleftharpoons}} \wedge(\nu) \tag{5.77}$$

$$G(\sqrt{\pi}t) \underset{\mathcal{F}^{-1}}{\overset{\mathcal{F}}{\rightleftharpoons}} G(\sqrt{\pi}\nu) \tag{5.78}$$

184 where *Equation 5.76* stems from the fact that

47
183
184

$$\mathcal{F}\{\wedge(t)\} \overset{(2.230)}{=} \mathcal{F}\{\sqcap(t) * \sqcap(t)\} \overset{(5.71)}{=} \mathcal{F}\{\sqcap(t)\}^2 \overset{(5.74)}{=} \mathrm{sinc}(\pi\nu)^2 \tag{5.79}$$

184 *Equation 5.78* illustrates the fact that the *Gaussian* function lies precisely at the frontier
51 of the time-frequency duality of support compactness. Given that the product of two normal
51 distributions G_1 and G_2 with means $\mu_{1|2}$ and standard deviations $\sigma_{1|2}$ yields another *Gaussian* with mean $\frac{\mu_2\sigma_1^2+\mu_1\sigma_2^2}{\sigma_1^2+\sigma_2^2}$ and standard deviation $\sqrt{\frac{\sigma_1^2\sigma_2^2}{\sigma_1^2+\sigma_2^2}}$, it additionally follows that so does their convolution, with mean $\mu_1 + \mu_2$ and standard deviation $\sqrt{\sigma_1^2 + \sigma_2^2}$.

5.2.3 Fourier Series

5.2.3.1 Poisson Summation

192 Based on the relationship between the Dirac comb and its *discrete Fourier transform*

$$\mathrm{III}(t) \overset{(2.219)}{=} \sum_{n=-\infty}^{+\infty} \delta(t \pm n)$$ 45

$$\overset{(5.163)}{=} \mathcal{F}^{-1}\{\mathrm{III}(\nu)\}$$ 196

$$\overset{(2.219)}{=} \mathcal{F}^{-1}\left\{\sum_{k=-\infty}^{+\infty} \delta(\nu \pm k)\right\}$$ 45

$$= \sum_{k=-\infty}^{+\infty} \mathcal{F}^{-1}\{\delta(\nu \pm k)\}$$

$$\underset{(5.63)}{\overset{(5.105)}{=}} \sum_{k=-\infty}^{+\infty} e^{\mp\imath 2\pi k t} \tag{5.80}$$ 189 183

the *Poisson summation formula* relates a signal $s(t)$ to its *Fourier transform* $S(\nu) \overset{(5.30)}{=}$ 179 178
$\mathcal{F}\{s(t)\}$ as

$$\sum_{k=-\infty}^{+\infty} S(k) \overset{(5.30)}{=} \sum_{k=-\infty}^{+\infty} \int_{-\infty}^{+\infty} s(t) e^{-\imath 2\pi k t} \mathrm{d}t$$ 179

$$= \int_{-\infty}^{+\infty} s(t) \sum_{k=-\infty}^{+\infty} e^{-\imath 2\pi k t} \mathrm{d}t$$

$$\overset{(5.80)}{=} \int_{-\infty}^{+\infty} s(t) \sum_{n=-\infty}^{+\infty} \delta(t-n) \mathrm{d}t$$ 185

$$= \sum_{n=-\infty}^{+\infty} \int_{-\infty}^{+\infty} s(t)\delta(t-n) \mathrm{d}t$$

$$\overset{(2.218)}{=} \sum_{n=-\infty}^{+\infty} s(n) \tag{5.81}$$ 45

5.2.3.2 *Forward Transform*

By applying the time shift and scaling *properties* of the *Fourier transform* to the *Poisson* 183
summation formula with $P > 0$, a real-valued time-periodic signal s_P of period P repre- 178 184
sented as a periodic summation can be reformulated as a discretization of the inverse *Fourier*
transform into a Riemann sum (at intervals $\Delta\nu = {}^1\!/_P$) 178

$$s_P(t) \overset{(5.17)}{=} \sum_{n=-\infty}^{+\infty} s(t+nP) \underset{(5.64)}{\overset{(5.81)}{\overset{(5.62)}{=}}} \frac{1}{P} \sum_{k=-\infty}^{+\infty} S\left(\frac{k}{P}\right) e^{\imath 2\pi \frac{k}{P} t} = \sum_{k=-\infty}^{+\infty} S(k\Delta\nu) e^{\imath 2\pi k \Delta\nu t} \Delta\nu \tag{5.82}$$ 185 177 183 183

As illustrated in *Figure 5.4*, the *Fourier transform* of the signal is then defined as a 186 178 discrete-frequency impulse train of period $1/P$

$$S_P(\nu) \triangleq \mathcal{F}\{s_P(t)\} \quad (5.83)$$

186

$$\overset{(5.85)}{=} \mathcal{F}\left\{\sum_{k=-\infty}^{+\infty} S[k] e^{\imath 2\pi \frac{k}{P} t}\right\}$$

$$= \sum_{k=-\infty}^{+\infty} S[k] \mathcal{F}\left\{e^{\imath 2\pi \frac{k}{P} t}\right\}$$

189
183

$$\underset{(5.63)}{\overset{(5.105)}{=}} \sum_{k=-\infty}^{+\infty} S[k] \delta\left(\nu - \frac{k}{P}\right) \quad (5.84)$$

modulated by the complex-valued coefficients

$$S[k] \triangleq \frac{1}{P} S\left(\frac{k}{P}\right) \quad (5.85)$$

179

$$\overset{(5.30)}{=} \frac{1}{P} \int_{-\infty}^{+\infty} s(t) e^{-\imath 2\pi \frac{k}{P} t} \mathrm{d}t$$

$$= \frac{1}{P} \sum_{n=-\infty}^{+\infty} \int_{t_0+nP}^{t_0+(n+1)P} s(t) e^{-\imath 2\pi \frac{k}{P} t} \mathrm{d}t$$

$$= \frac{1}{P} \sum_{n=-\infty}^{+\infty} \int_{t_0}^{t_0+P} s(t+nP) e^{-\imath 2\pi \frac{k}{P}(t+nP)} \mathrm{d}t$$

$$= \frac{1}{P} \int_{t_0}^{t_0+P} \sum_{n=-\infty}^{+\infty} s(t+nP) e^{-\imath 2\pi \frac{k}{P} t} \cancel{e^{-\imath 2\pi k n}} \mathrm{d}t$$

185

$$\overset{(5.82)}{=} \frac{1}{P} \int_P s_P(t) e^{-\imath 2\pi \frac{k}{P} t} \mathrm{d}t \quad (5.86)$$

$$= \frac{1}{P} \int_P s_P(t) \left(\cos\left(2\pi \frac{k}{P} t\right) - \imath \sin\left(2\pi \frac{k}{P} t\right)\right) \mathrm{d}t$$

$$= \Re(S[k]) + \imath \Im(S[k]) \quad (5.87)$$

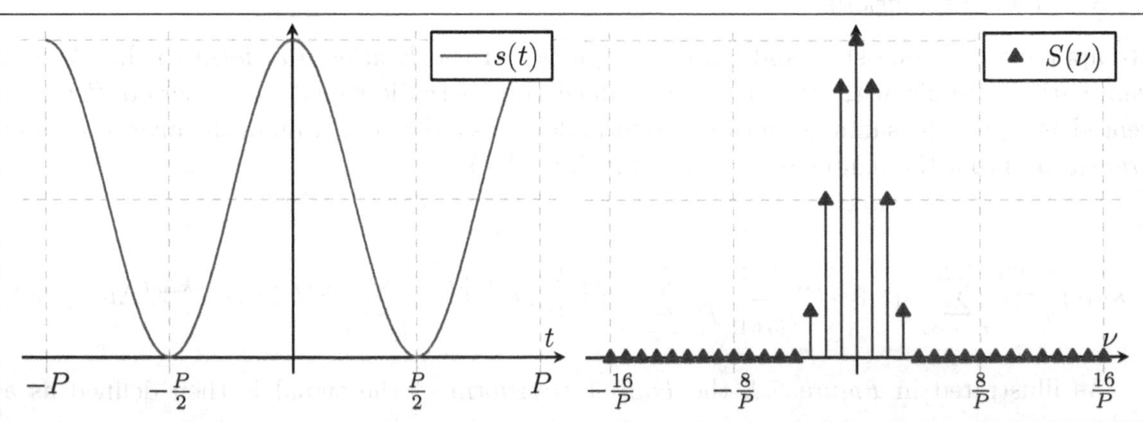

Figure 5.4: Fourier Series: Schematic illustration of the Fourier series of a continuous periodic signal.

It then holds that $S[0] = \frac{1}{P}\int_P s_P(t)\mathrm{d}t$, while the real and imaginary parts are given by

$$\Re(S[k]) = \frac{1}{P}\int_P s_P(t)\cos\left(2\pi\frac{k}{P}t\right)\mathrm{d}t \tag{5.88}$$

$$\overset{(5.94)}{=} \frac{1}{P}\int_P \mathfrak{E}(s_P(t))\cos\left(2\pi\frac{k}{P}t\right)\mathrm{d}t + \cancel{\frac{1}{P}\int_P \mathfrak{O}(s_P(t))\cos\left(2\pi\frac{k}{P}t\right)\mathrm{d}t}$$ 187

$$= \frac{1}{P}\int_P \mathfrak{E}(s_P(t))\cos\left(2\pi\frac{k}{P}t\right)\mathrm{d}t \tag{5.89}$$

$$\Im(S[k]) = -\frac{1}{P}\int_P s_P(t)\sin\left(2\pi\frac{k}{P}t\right)\mathrm{d}t \tag{5.90}$$

$$\overset{(5.94)}{=} \cancel{-\frac{1}{P}\int_P \mathfrak{E}(s_P(t))\sin\left(2\pi\frac{k}{P}t\right)\mathrm{d}t} - \frac{1}{P}\int_P \mathfrak{O}(s_P(t))\sin\left(2\pi\frac{k}{P}t\right)\mathrm{d}t$$ 187

$$= -\frac{1}{P}\int_P \mathfrak{O}(s_P(t))\sin\left(2\pi\frac{k}{P}t\right)\mathrm{d}t \tag{5.91}$$

It follows that $\Re(S[0]) = S[0]$ and $\Im(S[0]) = 0$, while $\Re(S[k]) = \mathfrak{E}(s_P(t)) = 0$ if the time-domain signal is odd, and $\Im(S[k]) = \mathfrak{O}(s_P(t)) = 0$ if the time-domain signal is even instead. It also holds that the real and imaginary parts are, respectively, even and odd since $\Re(S[-k]) = \Re(S[k])$ and $\Im(S[-k]) = -\Im(S[k])$, from which follows that $S[-k] = \overline{S[k]}$.

5.2.3.3 *Inverse Transform*

The original signal can be reconstructed from its spectral representation by means of the inverse *Fourier transform*, which yields the time-domain *Fourier series* 178

$$s_P(t) = \mathcal{F}^{-1}\{S_P(\nu)\} \tag{5.92}$$

$$\overset{(5.38)}{=} \int_{-\infty}^{+\infty} S_P(\nu)e^{\imath 2\pi\nu t}\mathrm{d}\nu$$ 180

$$\overset{(5.84)}{=} \int_{-\infty}^{+\infty}\sum_{k=-\infty}^{+\infty} S[k]\delta\left(\nu - \frac{k}{P}\right)e^{\imath 2\pi\nu t}\mathrm{d}\nu$$ 186

$$\overset{(2.218)}{=} \sum_{k=-\infty}^{+\infty} S[k]e^{\imath 2\pi\frac{k}{P}t} \tag{5.93}$$ 45

$$= \sum_{k=-\infty}^{+\infty} S[k]\left(\cos\left(2\pi\frac{k}{P}t\right) + \imath\sin\left(2\pi\frac{k}{P}t\right)\right)$$

$$= \mathfrak{E}(s_P(t)) + \mathfrak{O}(s_P(t)) \tag{5.94}$$

whose even and odd parts are given by

$$\mathfrak{E}(s_P(t)) = \sum_{k=-\infty}^{+\infty} S[k]\cos\left(2\pi\frac{k}{P}t\right) \tag{5.95}$$

$$= \sum_{k=-\infty}^{-1} S[k]\cos\left(2\pi\frac{k}{P}t\right) + S[0] + \sum_{k=1}^{+\infty} S[k]\cos\left(2\pi\frac{k}{P}t\right)$$

$$= S[0] + \sum_{k=1}^{\infty} S[k]\cos\left(2\pi\frac{k}{P}t\right) + S[-k]\cos\left(-2\pi\frac{k}{P}t\right)$$

$$= S[0] + \sum_{k=1}^{\infty} (S[k] + \overline{S[k]})\cos\left(2\pi\frac{k}{P}t\right)$$

87
$$\overset{(3.156)}{=} \Re(S[0]) + 2\sum_{k=1}^{\infty} \Re(S[k])\cos\left(2\pi\frac{k}{P}t\right) \tag{5.96}$$

$$\mathfrak{O}(s_P(t)) = \imath\sum_{k=-\infty}^{+\infty} S[k]\sin\left(2\pi\frac{k}{P}t\right) \tag{5.97}$$

$$= \imath\left(\sum_{k=-\infty}^{-1} S[k]\sin\left(2\pi\frac{k}{P}t\right) + 0 + \sum_{k=1}^{+\infty} S[k]\sin\left(2\pi\frac{k}{P}t\right)\right)$$

$$= \imath\sum_{k=1}^{\infty} S[k]\sin\left(2\pi\frac{k}{P}t\right) + S[-k]\sin\left(-2\pi\frac{k}{P}t\right)$$

$$= \imath\sum_{k=1}^{\infty} (S[k] - \overline{S[k]})\sin\left(2\pi\frac{k}{P}t\right)$$

87
$$\overset{(3.157)}{=} -2\sum_{k=1}^{\infty} \Im(S[k])\sin\left(2\pi\frac{k}{P}t\right) \tag{5.98}$$

which do satisfy $\mathfrak{E}(s_P(-t)) = \mathfrak{E}(s_P(t))$ and $\mathfrak{O}(s_P(-t)) = -\mathfrak{O}(s_P(t))$.

5.2.3.4 Multidimensional Transform

The extension of the Fourier coefficients to a complex-valued signal directly follows from the definition

186
$$S[k] \overset{(5.86)}{=} \frac{1}{P}\int_P \left(\Re(s_P(t)) + \imath\Im(s_P(t))\right) e^{-\imath 2\pi\frac{k}{P}t}\mathrm{d}t \tag{5.99}$$

$$= \frac{1}{P}\int_P \Re(s_P(t)) e^{-\imath 2\pi\frac{k}{P}t}\mathrm{d}t + \imath\frac{1}{P}\int_P \Im(s_P(t)) e^{-\imath 2\pi\frac{k}{P}t}\mathrm{d}t \tag{5.100}$$

such that its generalization to d dimensions is equivalent to successively applying the one-dimensional transform in turn along each individual dimension in any order

$$S[k_1,\ldots,k_d] \triangleq \frac{1}{P_d\ldots P_1}\int_{P_d}\cdots\int_{P_1} s(t_1,\ldots,t_d)e^{-\imath 2\pi\left(\frac{k_1}{P_1}t_1+\cdots+\frac{k_d}{P_d}t_d\right)}\mathrm{d}t_1\ldots\mathrm{d}t_d \tag{5.101}$$

$$= \frac{1}{P_d}\int_{P_d}\cdots\left(\frac{1}{P_1}\int_{P_1} s(t_1,\ldots,t_d)e^{-\imath 2\pi\frac{k_1}{P_1}t_1}\mathrm{d}t_1\right)\ldots e^{-\imath 2\pi\frac{k_d}{P_d}t_d}\mathrm{d}t_d \tag{5.102}$$

while the corresponding multidimensional Fourier series similarly reads

$$s_{P_1,\ldots,P_d}(t_1,\ldots,t_d) \triangleq \sum_{k_d=-\infty}^{+\infty}\cdots\sum_{k_1=-\infty}^{+\infty} S[k_1,\ldots,k_d]e^{\imath 2\pi\left(\frac{k_1}{P_1}t_1+\ldots+\frac{k_d}{P_d}t_d\right)} \tag{5.103}$$

$$= \sum_{k_d=-\infty}^{+\infty}\cdots\left(\sum_{k_1=-\infty}^{+\infty} S[k_1,\ldots,k_d]e^{\imath 2\pi\frac{k_1}{P_1}t_1}\right)\ldots e^{\imath 2\pi\frac{k_d}{P_d}t_d} \tag{5.104}$$

5.2.3.5 Canonical Transforms

The Fourier series of canonical functions include

$$1 \underset{\mathcal{F}^{-1}}{\overset{\mathcal{F}}{\rightleftharpoons}} \delta(\nu) \tag{5.105}$$

$$e^{\imath t} \underset{\mathcal{F}^{-1}}{\overset{\mathcal{F}}{\rightleftharpoons}} \delta\left(\nu - \frac{1}{2\pi}\right) \tag{5.106}$$

$$e^{-\imath t} \underset{\mathcal{F}^{-1}}{\overset{\mathcal{F}}{\rightleftharpoons}} \delta\left(\nu + \frac{1}{2\pi}\right) \tag{5.107}$$

$$\cos(t) \underset{\mathcal{F}^{-1}}{\overset{\mathcal{F}}{\rightleftharpoons}} \frac{\delta\left(\nu - \frac{1}{2\pi}\right) + \delta\left(\nu + \frac{1}{2\pi}\right)}{2} \tag{5.108}$$

$$\sin(t) \underset{\mathcal{F}^{-1}}{\overset{\mathcal{F}}{\rightleftharpoons}} \frac{\delta\left(\nu - \frac{1}{2\pi}\right) - \delta\left(\nu + \frac{1}{2\pi}\right)}{2\imath} \tag{5.109}$$

5.2.4 Discrete-Time Fourier Transform

5.2.4.1 Forward Transform

As illustrated in *Figure 5.5*, the *discrete-time Fourier transform* (*DTFT*) of a real-valued 190
discrete-time signal $s_{1/T}$, represented as an impulse train of period T

$$s_{1/T}(t) \triangleq \sum_{n=-\infty}^{+\infty} s[n]\delta(t - nT) \tag{5.110}$$

modulated by the real-valued coefficients $s[n] \triangleq Ts(nT)$, is defined as a complex-valued frequency-periodic function $S_{1/T}$ of period $1/T$

$$\begin{aligned} S_{1/T}(\nu) &\triangleq \mathcal{F}\left\{s_{1/T}(t)\right\} &(5.111)\\ &= \mathcal{F}\left\{\sum_{n=-\infty}^{+\infty} s[n]\delta(t - nT)\right\}\\ &= \sum_{n=-\infty}^{+\infty} s[n]\mathcal{F}\{\delta(t - nT)\}\\ &\overset{(5.132)}{\underset{(5.62)}{=}} \sum_{n=-\infty}^{+\infty} s[n]e^{-\imath 2\pi\nu nT} &(5.112)\\ &= \sum_{n=-\infty}^{+\infty} s[n]\left(\cos(2\pi\nu nT) - \imath\sin(2\pi\nu nT)\right)\\ &= \Re(S_{1/T}(\nu)) + \imath\Im(S_{1/T}(\nu)) &(5.113) \end{aligned}$$

192 183

The result actually corresponds to a discretization of the *Fourier transform* into a Riemann 178
sum (at intervals $\Delta t = T$), which, by applying the frequency shift and scaling *properties* of 183
the *Fourier transform* to the *Poisson summation* formula with $T > 0$, can alternatively be 178
reformulated as a periodic summation of period T 184

$$S_{1/T}(\nu) \overset{(5.112)}{=} \sum_{n=-\infty}^{+\infty} s(n\Delta t)e^{-\imath 2\pi\nu n\Delta t}\Delta t = T\sum_{n=-\infty}^{+\infty} s(nT)e^{-\imath 2\pi\nu nT} \overset{(5.81)\,(5.63)}{\underset{(5.64)}{=}} \sum_{k=-\infty}^{+\infty} S\left(\nu + \frac{k}{T}\right) \tag{5.114}$$

185 189 183 183

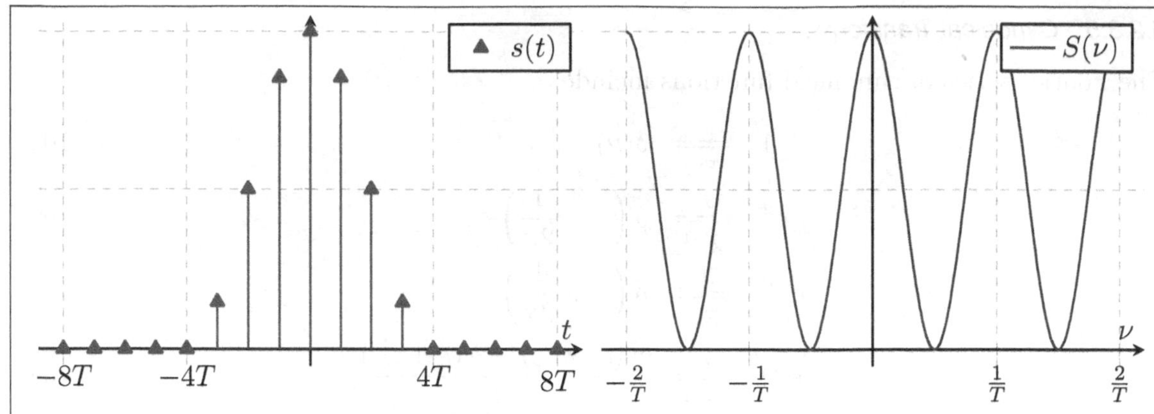

Figure 5.5: Discrete-Time Fourier Transform: Schematic illustration of the discrete-time Fourier transform of a discrete aperiodic signal.

It then holds that $S_{1/T}(0) = \sum_{n=-\infty}^{+\infty} s[n]$, while the real and imaginary parts are given by

$$\begin{aligned}
\Re(S_{1/T}(\nu)) &= \sum_{n=-\infty}^{+\infty} s[n]\cos(2\pi\nu nT) && (5.115)\\
&= \sum_{n=-\infty}^{-1} s[n]\cos(2\pi\nu nT) + s[0] + \sum_{n=1}^{+\infty} s[n]\cos(2\pi\nu nT)\\
&= s[0] + \sum_{n=1}^{\infty} s[n]\cos(2\pi\nu nT) + s[-n]\cos(-2\pi\nu nT)\\
&= s[0] + \sum_{n=1}^{\infty} (s[n] + s[-n])\cos(2\pi\nu nT)
\end{aligned}$$

179

$$\begin{aligned}
&\overset{(5.26)}{=} s[0] + 2\sum_{n=1}^{\infty} \mathfrak{E}(s[n])\cos(2\pi\nu nT) && (5.116)\\
\Im(S_{1/T}(\nu)) &= -\sum_{n=-\infty}^{+\infty} s[n]\sin(2\pi\nu nT) && (5.117)\\
&= -\sum_{n=-\infty}^{-1} s[n]\sin(2\pi\nu nT) - 0 - \sum_{n=1}^{+\infty} s[n]\sin(2\pi\nu nT)\\
&= -\sum_{n=1}^{\infty} s[n]\sin(2\pi\nu nT) + s[-n]\sin(-2\pi\nu nT)\\
&= -\sum_{n=1}^{\infty} (s[n] - s[-n])\sin(2\pi\nu nT)
\end{aligned}$$

179

$$\overset{(5.27)}{=} -2\sum_{n=1}^{\infty} \mathfrak{O}(s[n])\sin(2\pi\nu nT) \qquad (5.118)$$

It follows that $\Re(S_{1/T}(0)) = S_{1/T}(0)$ and $\Im(S_{1/T}(0)) = 0$, while $\Re(S_{1/T}(\nu)) = \mathfrak{E}(s[n]) = 0$ if the time-domain signal is odd, and $\Im(S_{1/T}(\nu)) = \mathfrak{O}(s[n]) = 0$ if the time-domain signal is even instead. It also holds that the real and imaginary parts are, respectively, even and odd since $\Re(S_{1/T}(-\nu)) = \Re(S_{1/T}(\nu))$ and $\Im(S_{1/T}(-\nu)) = -\Im(S_{1/T}(\nu))$, from which follows that $S_{1/T}(-\nu) = \overline{S_{1/T}(\nu)}$, and $S_{1/T}(\nu)$ is therefore a Hermitian function.

5.2.4.2 *Inverse Transform*

The coefficients of the original signal can be reconstructed from its spectral representation by means of the inverse *Fourier transform* 178

$$
\begin{aligned}
s[n] &= Ts(nT) && (5.119)\\
&\overset{(5.38)}{=} T\int_{-\infty}^{+\infty} S(\nu)e^{\imath 2\pi\nu nT}\mathrm{d}\nu && 180\\
&= T\sum_{k=-\infty}^{+\infty}\int_{\nu_0+\frac{k}{T}}^{\nu_0+\frac{k+1}{T}} S(\nu)e^{\imath 2\pi\nu nT}\mathrm{d}\nu\\
&= T\sum_{k=-\infty}^{+\infty}\int_{\nu_0}^{\nu_0+\frac{1}{T}} S\left(\nu+\frac{k}{T}\right)e^{\imath 2\pi\left(\nu+\frac{k}{T}\right)nT}\mathrm{d}\nu\\
&= T\int_{\nu_0}^{\nu_0+\frac{1}{T}}\sum_{k=-\infty}^{+\infty} S\left(\nu+\frac{k}{T}\right)e^{\imath 2\pi\nu nT}\cancel{e^{\imath 2\pi kn}}\mathrm{d}\nu\\
&\overset{(5.114)}{=} T\int_{1/T} S_{1/T}(\nu)e^{\imath 2\pi\nu nT}\mathrm{d}\nu && (5.120)\quad 189\\
&= T\int_{1/T} S_{1/T}(\nu)\left(\cos(2\pi\nu nT)+\imath\sin(2\pi\nu nT)\right)\mathrm{d}\nu\\
&= \mathfrak{E}(s[n])+\mathfrak{O}(s[n]) && (5.121)
\end{aligned}
$$

whose even and odd parts are given by

$$
\begin{aligned}
\mathfrak{E}(s[n]) &= T\int_{1/T} S_{1/T}(\nu)\cos(2\pi\nu nT)\mathrm{d}\nu && (5.122)\\
&\overset{(5.113)}{=} T\int_{1/T}\Re(S_{1/T}(\nu))\cos(2\pi\nu nT)\mathrm{d}\nu + \cancel{\imath T\int_{1/T}\Im(S_{1/T}(\nu))\cos(2\pi\nu nT)\mathrm{d}\nu} && 189\\
&= T\int_{1/T}\Re(S_{1/T}(\nu))\cos(2\pi\nu nT)\mathrm{d}\nu && (5.123)\\
\mathfrak{O}(s[n]) &= \imath T\int_{1/T} S_{1/T}(\nu)\sin(2\pi\nu nT)\mathrm{d}\nu && (5.124)\\
&\overset{(5.113)}{=} \cancel{\imath T\int_{1/T}\Re(S_{1/T}(\nu))\sin(2\pi\nu nT)\mathrm{d}\nu} + \imath^2 T\int_{1/T}\Im(S_{1/T}(\nu))\sin(2\pi\nu nT)\mathrm{d}\nu && 189\\
&= -T\int_{1/T}\Im(S_{1/T}(\nu))\sin(2\pi\nu nT)\mathrm{d}\nu && (5.125)
\end{aligned}
$$

which do satisfy $\mathfrak{E}(s[-n]) = \mathfrak{E}(s[n])$ and $\mathfrak{O}(s[-n]) = -\mathfrak{O}(s[n])$.

5.2.4.3 *Multidimensional Transform*

The extension of the discrete-time Fourier transform to a complex-valued signal directly follows from the definition

$$
\begin{aligned}
S_{1/T}(\nu) &\overset{(5.112)}{=} \sum_{n=-\infty}^{+\infty}\left(\Re(s[n])+\imath\Im(s[n])\right)e^{-\imath 2\pi\nu nT} && (5.126)\quad 189\\
&= \sum_{n=-\infty}^{+\infty}\Re(s[n])e^{-\imath 2\pi\nu nT} + \imath\sum_{n=-\infty}^{+\infty}\Im(s[n])e^{-\imath 2\pi\nu nT} && (5.127)
\end{aligned}
$$

such that its generalization to d dimensions is equivalent to successively applying the one-dimensional transform in turn along each individual dimension in any order

$$S_{1/T_1,\ldots,1/T_d}(\nu_1,\ldots,\nu_d) \triangleq \sum_{n_d=-\infty}^{+\infty} \cdots \sum_{n_1=-\infty}^{+\infty} s[n_1,\ldots,n_d]e^{-\imath 2\pi(\nu_1 n_1 T_1+\ldots+\nu_d n_d T_d)} \tag{5.128}$$

$$= \sum_{n_d=-\infty}^{+\infty} \cdots \left(\sum_{n_1=-\infty}^{+\infty} s[n_1,\ldots,n_d]e^{-\imath 2\pi\nu_1 n_1 T_1} \right) \ldots e^{-\imath 2\pi\nu_d n_d T_d} \tag{5.129}$$

while the corresponding multidimensional inverse similarly reads

$$s[n_1,\ldots,n_d] \triangleq T_d \ldots T_1 \int_{1/T_d} \cdots \int_{1/T_1} S_{1/T_1,\ldots,1/T_d}(\nu_1,\ldots,\nu_d)e^{\imath 2\pi(\nu_1 n_1 T_1+\ldots+\nu_d n_d T_d)} \mathrm{d}\nu_1 \ldots \mathrm{d}\nu_d \tag{5.130}$$

$$= T_d \int_{1/T_d} \cdots \left(T_1 \int_{1/T_1} S_{1/T_1,\ldots,1/T_d}(\nu_1,\ldots,\nu_d)e^{\imath 2\pi\nu_1 n_1 T_1} \mathrm{d}\nu_1 \right) \ldots e^{\imath 2\pi\nu_d n_d T_d} \mathrm{d}\nu_d \tag{5.131}$$

5.2.4.4 Canonical Transforms

The discrete-time Fourier transform of canonical functions include

$$\delta(t) \underset{\mathcal{F}^{-1}}{\overset{\mathcal{F}}{\rightleftharpoons}} 1 \tag{5.132}$$

$$\delta\left(t+\frac{1}{2\pi}\right) \underset{\mathcal{F}^{-1}}{\overset{\mathcal{F}}{\rightleftharpoons}} e^{\imath\nu} \tag{5.133}$$

$$\delta\left(t-\frac{1}{2\pi}\right) \underset{\mathcal{F}^{-1}}{\overset{\mathcal{F}}{\rightleftharpoons}} e^{-\imath\nu} \tag{5.134}$$

5.2.5 Discrete Fourier Transform

5.2.5.1 Forward Transform

A real-valued time-periodic signal s_N of period P represented as a periodic summation of a real-valued discrete-time signal $s_{1/T}$

177

$$s_N(t) \overset{(5.17)}{=} \sum_{k=-\infty}^{+\infty} s_{1/T}(t+kP)$$

189

$$\begin{aligned} &\overset{(5.110)}{=} \sum_{k=-\infty}^{+\infty} \sum_{n=-\infty}^{+\infty} s[n]\delta(t+kP-nT) \\ &= \sum_{k=-\infty}^{+\infty} \sum_{n=-\infty}^{+\infty} s[n]\delta(t-(n-kN)T) \\ &= \sum_{n=-\infty}^{+\infty} \sum_{k=-\infty}^{+\infty} s[n+kN]\delta(t-nT) \end{aligned}$$

192

$$\overset{(5.137)}{=} \sum_{n=-\infty}^{+\infty} s_N[n]\delta(t-nT) \tag{5.136}$$

yields an impulse train of period T modulated by the real-valued time-periodic sequence of coefficients s_N of period $N = \frac{P}{T}$ represented by the periodic summation

$$s_N[n] \triangleq \sum_{k=-\infty}^{+\infty} s[n+kN] \tag{5.137}$$

By applying the time shift and scaling *properties* of the *Fourier transform* to the *Poisson* 183
summation formula with $P > 0$, the signal can be reformulated as 178 184

$$s_N(t) \overset{(5.135)}{=} \sum_{n=-\infty}^{+\infty} s_{1/T}(t+nP) \overset{(5.81)}{\underset{(5.63)}{\overset{(5.62)}{=}}} \frac{1}{P} \sum_{k=-\infty}^{+\infty} S_{1/T}\left(\frac{k}{P}\right) e^{\imath 2\pi \frac{k}{P} t} \tag{5.138}$$

185 192 183 183

As illustrated in *Figure 5.6*, the *discrete Fourier transform* (*DFT*) of the signal is then 194
defined as a discrete-frequency impulse train of period $1/P$

$$\begin{aligned} S_N(\nu) &\triangleq \mathcal{F}\{s_N(t)\} && (5.139) \\ &\overset{(5.141)}{=} \mathcal{F}\left\{\sum_{k=-\infty}^{+\infty} S_N[k] e^{\imath 2\pi \frac{k}{P} t}\right\} \\ &= \sum_{k=-\infty}^{+\infty} S_N[k] \mathcal{F}\left\{e^{\imath 2\pi \frac{k}{P} t}\right\} \\ &\overset{(5.105)}{\underset{(5.63)}{=}} \sum_{k=-\infty}^{+\infty} S_N[k] \delta\left(\nu - \frac{k}{P}\right) && (5.140) \end{aligned}$$

193 189 183

modulated by the complex-valued frequency-periodic sequence of coefficients

$$\begin{aligned} S_N[k] &\triangleq \frac{1}{P} S_{1/T}\left(\frac{k}{P}\right) && (5.141) \\ &\overset{(5.112)}{=} \frac{1}{P} \sum_{n=-\infty}^{+\infty} s[n] e^{-\imath 2\pi \frac{k}{P} nT} \\ &= \frac{1}{P} \sum_{k=-\infty}^{+\infty} \sum_{n=n_0+kN}^{n_0+(k+1)N-1} s[n] e^{-\imath 2\pi \frac{kn}{N}} \\ &= \frac{1}{P} \sum_{k=-\infty}^{+\infty} \sum_{n=n_0}^{n_0+N-1} s[n+kN] e^{-\imath 2\pi \frac{k(n+kN)}{N}} \\ &= \frac{1}{P} \sum_{n=n_0}^{n_0+N-1} \sum_{k=-\infty}^{+\infty} s[n+kN] e^{-\imath 2\pi \frac{kn}{N}} \cancel{e^{-\imath 2\pi k^2}} \\ &\overset{(5.137)}{=} \frac{1}{P} \sum_{n \in N} s_N[n] e^{-\imath 2\pi \frac{kn}{N}} && (5.142) \\ &= \frac{1}{P} \sum_{n \in N} s_N[n] \left(\cos\left(2\pi \frac{kn}{N}\right) - \imath \sin\left(2\pi \frac{kn}{N}\right)\right) \\ &= \Re(S_N[k]) + \imath \Im(S_N[k]) && (5.143) \end{aligned}$$

189 192

which can alternatively be expressed as a periodic summation

$$S_N[k] = \sum_{n=-\infty}^{+\infty} S[k+nN] \tag{5.144}$$

of period N

193
$$S_N[k+N] \overset{(5.142)}{=} \frac{1}{P}\sum_{n\in N} s_N[n] e^{-\imath 2\pi \frac{(k+N)n}{N}}$$
$$= \frac{1}{P}\sum_{n\in N} s_N[n] e^{-\imath 2\pi \frac{kn}{N}} \cancel{e^{-\imath 2\pi n}}$$
$$= \frac{1}{P}\sum_{n\in N} s_N[n] e^{-\imath 2\pi \frac{kn}{N}}$$
193
$$\overset{(5.142)}{=} S_N[k] \tag{5.145}$$

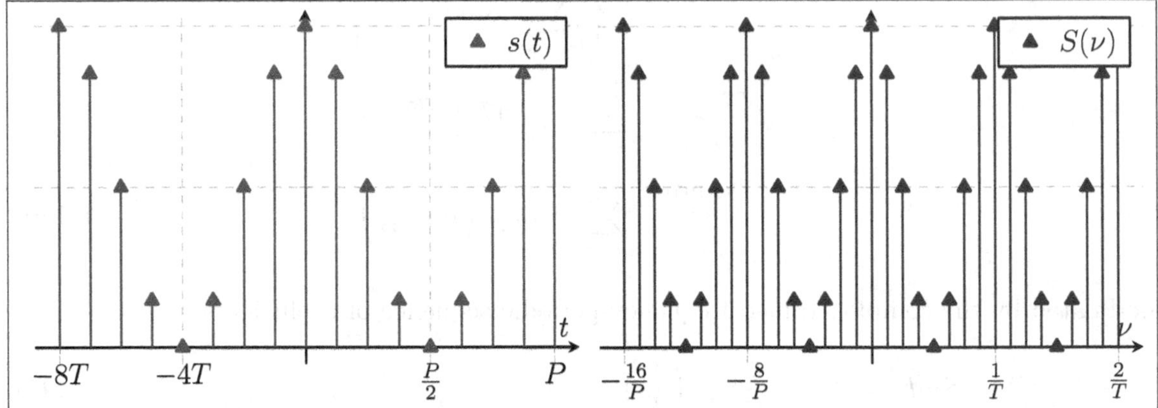

Figure 5.6: Discrete Fourier Transform: Schematic illustration of the discrete Fourier transform of a discrete periodic signal.

It then holds that $S_N[0] = \frac{1}{P}\sum_{n\in N} s_N[n]$, while the real and imaginary parts are given by

$$\Re(S_N[k]) = \frac{1}{P}\sum_{n\in N} s_N[n]\cos\left(2\pi\frac{kn}{N}\right) \tag{5.146}$$
195
$$\overset{(5.152)}{=} \frac{1}{P}\sum_{n\in N} \mathfrak{E}(s_N[n])\cos\left(2\pi\frac{kn}{N}\right) + \cancel{\frac{1}{P}\sum_{n\in N} \mathfrak{O}(s_N[n])\cos\left(2\pi\frac{kn}{N}\right)}$$
$$= \frac{1}{P}\sum_{n\in N} \mathfrak{E}(s_N[n])\cos\left(2\pi\frac{kn}{N}\right) \tag{5.147}$$
$$\Im(S_N[k]) = -\frac{1}{P}\sum_{n\in N} s_N[n]\sin\left(2\pi\frac{kn}{N}\right) \tag{5.148}$$
195
$$\overset{(5.152)}{=} \cancel{-\frac{1}{P}\sum_{n\in N} \mathfrak{E}(s_N[n])\sin\left(2\pi\frac{kn}{N}\right)} - \frac{1}{P}\sum_{n\in N} \mathfrak{O}(s_N[n])\sin\left(2\pi\frac{kn}{N}\right)$$
$$= -\frac{1}{P}\sum_{n\in N} \mathfrak{O}(s_N[n])\sin\left(2\pi\frac{kn}{N}\right) \tag{5.149}$$

It follows that $\Re(S_N[0]) = S_N[0]$ and $\Im(S_N[0]) = 0$, while $\Re(S_N[k]) = \mathfrak{E}(s_N[n]) = 0$ if the time-domain signal is odd, and $\Im(S_N[k]) = \mathfrak{O}(s_N[n]) = 0$ if the time-domain signal is even instead. It also holds that the real and imaginary parts are, respectively, even and odd since $\Re(S_N[-k]) = \Re(S_N[k])$ and $\Im(S_N[-k]) = -\Im(S_N[k])$, from which follows that $S_N[-k] = \overline{S_N[k]}$.

Because each of the N individual coefficients evaluates to a sum of N terms, the complexity of naively evaluating the DFT is therefore $O(N^2)$, whereas the asymptotic cost can be reduced to $O(N\log(N))$ by means of a *fast Fourier transform* (*FFT*) algorithm, such as the Cooley–Tukey FFT algorithm, typically bearing some requirements on the size of the input data.

5.2.5.2 Inverse Transform

The coefficients of the original signal can be reconstructed from its spectral representation by means of the inverse *Fourier transform* 178

$$s_N[n] \overset{(5.137)}{=} Ts_P(nT) \tag{5.150}$$ 192

$$\overset{(5.93)}{=} T\sum_{k=-\infty}^{+\infty} S[k]e^{\imath 2\pi\frac{k}{P}nT}$$ 187

$$\begin{aligned}
&= T\sum_{n=-\infty}^{+\infty}\sum_{k=k_0+nN}^{k_0+(n+1)N-1} S[k]e^{\imath 2\pi\frac{kn}{N}} \\
&= T\sum_{n=-\infty}^{+\infty}\sum_{k=k_0}^{k_0+N-1} S[k+nN]e^{\imath 2\pi\frac{(k+nN)n}{N}} \\
&= T\sum_{k=k_0}^{k_0+N-1}\sum_{n=-\infty}^{+\infty} S[k+nN]e^{\imath 2\pi\frac{kn}{N}}\cancel{e^{\imath 2\pi n^2}}
\end{aligned}$$

$$\overset{(5.144)}{=} T\sum_{k\in N} S_N[k]e^{\imath 2\pi\frac{kn}{N}} \tag{5.151}$$ 193

$$= T\sum_{k\in N} S_N[k]\left(\cos\left(2\pi\frac{kn}{N}\right)+\imath\sin\left(2\pi\frac{kn}{N}\right)\right)$$

$$= \mathfrak{E}(s_N[n])+\mathfrak{O}(s_N[n]) \tag{5.152}$$

whose even and odd parts are given by

$$\mathfrak{E}(s_N[n]) = T\sum_{k\in N} S_N[k]\cos\left(2\pi\frac{kn}{N}\right) \tag{5.153}$$

$$\overset{(5.143)}{=} T\sum_{k\in N}\Re(S_N[k])\cos\left(2\pi\frac{kn}{N}\right)+\imath T\cancel{\sum_{k\in N}\Im(S_N[k])\cos\left(2\pi\frac{kn}{N}\right)}$$ 193

$$= T\sum_{k\in N}\Re(S_N[k])\cos\left(2\pi\frac{kn}{N}\right) \tag{5.154}$$

$$\mathfrak{O}(s_N[n]) = \imath T\sum_{k\in N} S_N[k]\sin\left(2\pi\frac{kn}{N}\right) \tag{5.155}$$

$$\overset{(5.143)}{=} \imath T\cancel{\sum_{k\in N}\Re(S_N[k])\sin\left(2\pi\frac{kn}{N}\right)}+\imath^2 T\sum_{k\in N}\Im(S_N[k])\sin\left(2\pi\frac{kn}{N}\right)$$ 193

$$= -T\sum_{k\in N}\Im(S_N[k])\sin\left(2\pi\frac{kn}{N}\right) \tag{5.156}$$

which do satisfy $\mathfrak{E}(s_N[-n]) = \mathfrak{E}(s_N[n])$ and $\mathfrak{O}(s_N[-n]) = -\mathfrak{O}(s_N[n])$.

Shall the time-domain and frequency-domain periods not be known, setting the normalization factors to $\frac{1}{P} = T = \frac{1}{\sqrt{N}}$ then yields a unitary transform.

5.2.5.3 Multidimensional Transform

The extension of the discrete Fourier transform to a complex-valued signal directly follows from the definition

193
$$S_N[k] \overset{(5.142)}{=} \frac{1}{P}\sum_{n\in N}\left(\Re(s_N[n]) + \imath\Im(s_N[n])\right)e^{-\imath 2\pi\frac{kn}{N}} \tag{5.157}$$

$$= \frac{1}{P}\sum_{n\in N}\Re(s_N[n])e^{-\imath 2\pi\frac{kn}{N}} + \imath\frac{1}{P}\sum_{n\in N}\Im(s_N[n])e^{-\imath 2\pi\frac{kn}{N}} \tag{5.158}$$

such that its generalization to d dimensions is equivalent to successively applying the one-dimensional transform in turn along each individual dimension in any order, an approach known as the *row-column algorithm*

$$S_{N_1,\ldots,N_d}[k_1,\ldots,k_d] \triangleq \frac{1}{P_d\ldots P_1}\sum_{n_d\in N_d}\cdots\sum_{n_1\in N_1} s_{N_1,\ldots,N_d}[n_1,\ldots,n_d]e^{-\imath 2\pi\left(\frac{k_1n_1}{N_1}+\ldots+\frac{k_dn_d}{N_d}\right)} \tag{5.159}$$

$$= \frac{1}{P_d}\sum_{n_d\in N_d}\cdots\left(\frac{1}{P_1}\sum_{n_1\in N_1} s_{N_1,\ldots,N_d}[n_1,\ldots,n_d]e^{-\imath 2\pi\frac{k_1n_1}{N_1}}\right)\ldots e^{-\imath 2\pi\frac{k_dn_d}{N_d}} \tag{5.160}$$

while the corresponding multidimensional inverse similarly reads

$$s_{N_1,\ldots,N_d}[n_1,\ldots,n_d] \triangleq T_d\ldots T_1\sum_{k_d\in N_d}\cdots\sum_{k_1\in N_1} S_{N_1,\ldots,N_d}[k_1,\ldots,k_d]e^{\imath 2\pi\left(\frac{k_1n_1}{N_1}+\ldots+\frac{k_dn_d}{N_d}\right)} \tag{5.161}$$

$$= T_d\sum_{k_d\in N_d}\cdots\left(T_1\sum_{k_1\in N_1} S_{N_1,\ldots,N_d}[k_1,\ldots,k_d]e^{\imath 2\pi\frac{k_1n_1}{N_1}}\right)\ldots e^{\imath 2\pi\frac{k_dn_d}{N_d}} \tag{5.162}$$

5.2.5.4 Canonical Transforms

The discrete Fourier transforms of canonical functions include

$$\text{III}(t) \underset{\mathcal{F}^{-1}}{\overset{\mathcal{F}}{\rightleftharpoons}} \text{III}(\nu) \tag{5.163}$$

5.3 SIGNAL PROCESSING

5.3.1 Sampling

197
As illustrated in *Figure 5.7*, sampling a continuous signal s at a frequency ν_s mathematically corresponds to evaluating its product with a Dirac comb of sampling interval $T_s = \frac{1}{\nu_s}$

45
$$s(t)\,\text{III}\left(\frac{t}{T_s}\right) \overset{(2.220)}{=} s(t)T_s\sum_{n=-\infty}^{+\infty}\delta(t-nT_s) = \sum_{n=-\infty}^{+\infty} s[n]\delta(t-nT_s) \tag{5.164}$$

where the coefficients read $s[n] \triangleq T_s s(nT_s)$.

178
The *Fourier transform* of the sampled signal is then readily given by the convolution
183
178
theorem and scaling *properties* of the *Fourier transform*, and corresponds to a periodic sum-

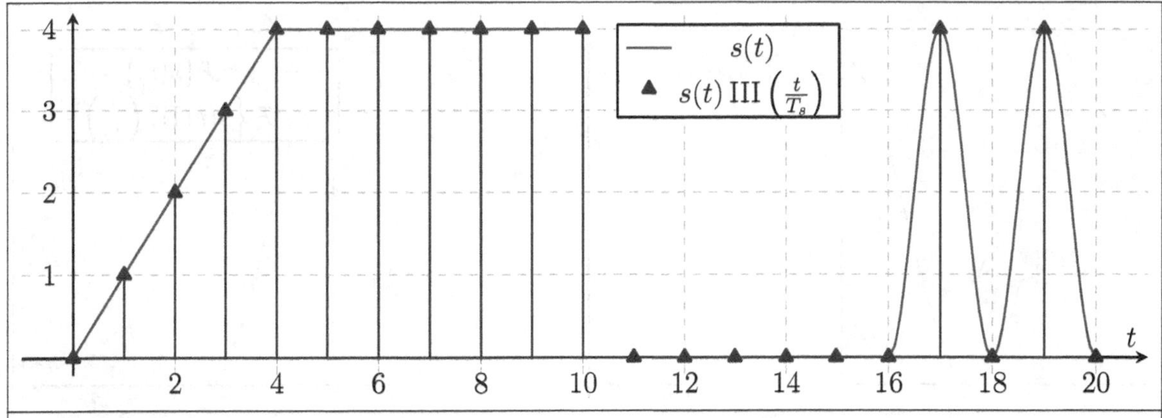

Figure 5.7: Discrete Sampling: Illustration of the discrete sampling of a continuous signal.

mation of the spectral response of the original signal, i.e., to a replication of the latter with a period determined by the sampling rate ν_s

$$\mathcal{F}\left\{s(t)\,\text{III}\left(\frac{t}{T_s}\right)\right\} \overset{(5.71)}{\underset{(5.64)}{=}} S(\nu) * T_s\,\text{III}(T_s\nu)$$ 183 183

$$\overset{(5.5)}{=} \int_{-\infty}^{+\infty} S(u) T_s\,\text{III}\,(T_s(\nu - u))\mathrm{d}u$$ 176

$$\overset{(2.220)}{=} \int_{-\infty}^{+\infty} S(u) \sum_{k=-\infty}^{+\infty} \delta\left(\nu - u \pm \frac{k}{T_s}\right) \mathrm{d}u$$ 45

$$= \sum_{k=-\infty}^{+\infty} \int_{-\infty}^{+\infty} S(u)\delta\left(\nu - u \pm \frac{k}{T_s}\right) \mathrm{d}u$$

$$\overset{(2.218)}{=} \sum_{k=-\infty}^{+\infty} S\left(\nu \pm \frac{k}{T_s}\right) \tag{5.165}$$ 45

Considering a band-limited signal $S(\nu) = 0, \forall|\nu| > \nu_b$ with band-limit ν_b (i.e., the maximal frequency of non-negligible magnitude contained in the signal), the *Nyquist–Shannon sampling theorem* states that the original spectral response can be exactly isolated from the periodic spectrum, and the original signal therefore perfectly reconstructed from its sampled representation, whenever the *Nyquist criterion* $\frac{\nu_s}{\nu_b} > 2$ is satisfied, that is, whenever the sampling frequency ν_s is greater than the *Nyquist rate* $2\nu_b$, or equivalently whenever the band-limit ν_b is less than the *Nyquist frequency* $\frac{\nu_s}{2}$.

The size of the intermediate band between successive copies may consequently be increased by *oversampling* the signal by a factor of $N > 1$ such that $\frac{\nu_s}{\nu_b} = 2N$, thereby relaxing
the bandwidth requirements on the transition band of anti-aliasing *filters*. While the Nyquist 201
criterion represents a sufficient rather than necessary condition for bandpass signals as illustrated in *Figure 5.8*, *undersampling* a baseband signal by a factor of $N \leq 1$ will in contrast 198
result in a partial overlap of the spectral replicas as illustrated in *Figure 5.9*, in which case 198
the original frequency response may no longer be recovered from the periodic spectrum. As
shown in *Figure 5.10*, there exist indeed multiple continuous signals, so-called “aliases,” with 198
strictly identical sampled representations and corresponding spectral responses. Any attempt to recover the original signal will then lead to *aliasing* artifacts characterized by originally
high-frequency features interpreted as low-frequency content during *reconstruction*, as illus- 201
trated in *Figure 5.11*. 199

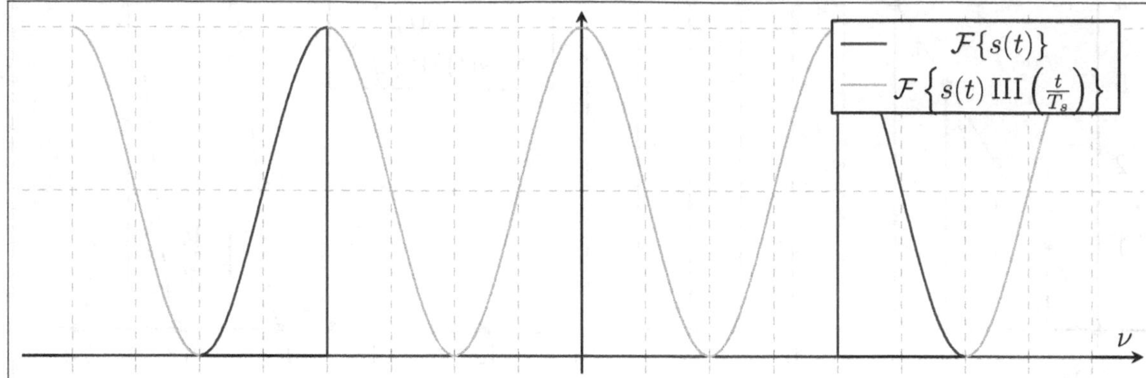

Figure 5.8: Bandpass Sampling: Schematic illustration of the undersampling of a bandpass signal without spectral aliasing.

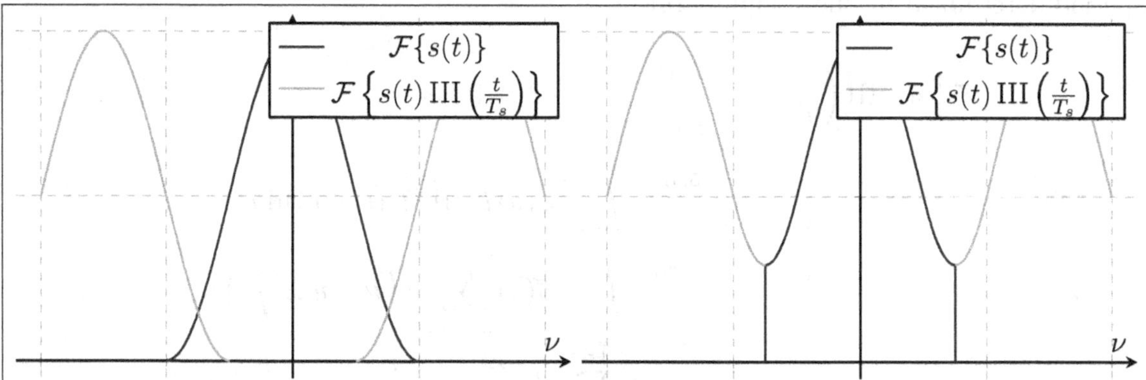

Figure 5.9: Aliased Spectrum: Schematic illustration of the spectral response of aliased discrete signals.

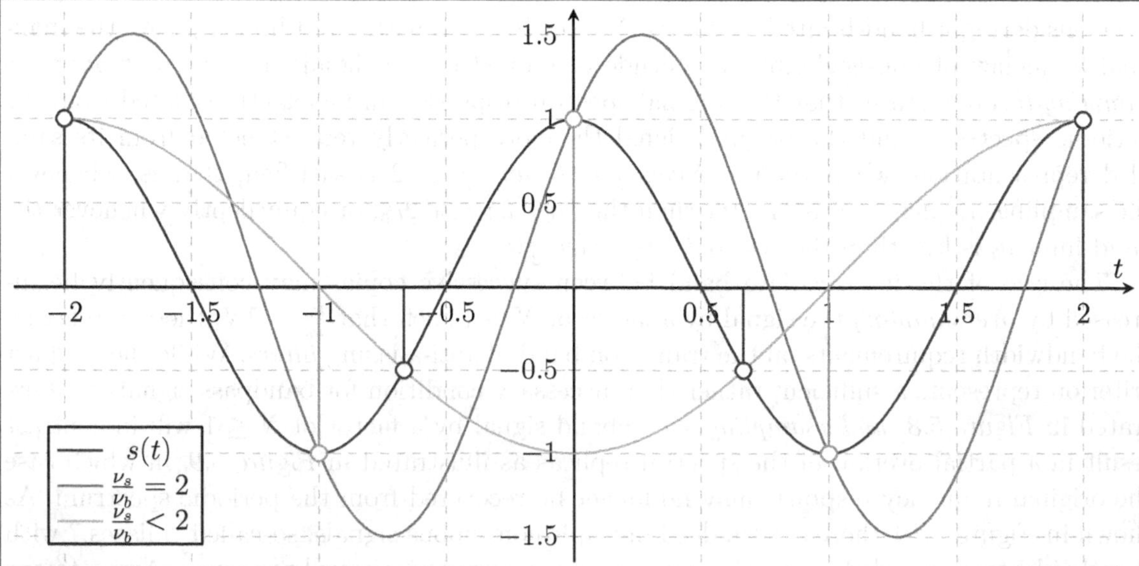

Figure 5.10: Aliased Signal: Illustration of the time-domain representation of aliased discrete signals at and below the Nyquist frequency.

Figure 5.11: Aliasing Artifacts: Illustration of ghosting artifacts in undersampled regions and of jagged edges in a wave (left) and a tile (right) pattern.

Similar artifacts can actually be readily observed in real-life whenever a hatched structure (such as a chain-link fence or a netted fabric) is superimposed before a pattern of more than half the hatching frequency, resulting in a so-called *moiré pattern*. Notable instances of temporal aliasing also include the *wagon-wheel effect* iconically observed in Western films, whereby the limited frame rate of the video camera may induce a stroboscopic effect causing the spoked wheels of stagecoaches to appear as if they were rotating more slowly, stationary or in the reverse direction than they actually are.

Given a pre-determined sampling frequency, the amount of aliasing introduced by the
sampling process, so-called *pre-aliasing*, may be effectively reduced by lossilly dampening
the high-frequency content of the original signal via a time-domain *convolution* of the latter 176
with a low-pass *filter* f_l prior to sampling, a process know as *anti-aliasing*. The sampled 201
representation of the filtered signal then reads

45

$$(s * f_l)(t) \operatorname{III}\left(\frac{t}{T_s}\right) \overset{(2.220)}{=} (s * f_l)(t) T_s \sum_{n=-\infty}^{+\infty} \delta(t - nT_s) = \sum_{n=-\infty}^{+\infty} s_l[n] \delta(t - nT_s) \tag{5.166}$$

thereby reducing the continuous *convolution* to a discrete set of integrals via the evaluation 176
of the coefficients

176

$$s_l[n] \triangleq T_s (s * f_l)(nT_s) \overset{(5.5)}{=} T_s \int_{-\infty}^{+\infty} s(u) f_l(nT_s - u) \mathrm{d}u \tag{5.167}$$

which may be estimated by means of *super-sampling* using *importance sampling* via the 155
unbiased *estimator* 139

156
$$\tilde{s}_l[n] \overset{(4.158)}{=} \frac{T_s}{N} \sum_{i=1}^{N} \frac{s(X_i) f_l(nT_s - X_i)}{p(X_i)} \tag{5.168}$$

201 If the *filter* is instead defined in terms of an unnormalized kernel f_u

$$f_l(t) \triangleq \frac{f_u(t)}{\int_{-\infty}^{+\infty} f_u(u) \mathrm{d}u} \tag{5.169}$$

the filtering integral then generalizes to

199
$$s_l[n] \overset{(5.167)}{=} \frac{T_s \int_{-\infty}^{+\infty} s(u) f_u(nT_s - u) \mathrm{d}u}{\int_{-\infty}^{+\infty} f_u(u) \mathrm{d}u} = T_s \frac{\int_{-\infty}^{+\infty} s(u) f_u(nT_s - u) \mathrm{d}u}{\int_{-\infty}^{+\infty} f_u(nT_s - u) \mathrm{d}u} \tag{5.170}$$

155 139 which may be estimated using *importance sampling* via the biased but consistent *estimator*

156
$$\tilde{s}_l[n] \overset{(4.158)}{=} T_s \frac{\frac{1}{N} \sum_{i=1}^{N} \frac{s(X_i) f_u(nT_s - X_i)}{p(X_i)}}{\frac{1}{N} \sum_{i=1}^{N} \frac{f_u(nT_s - X_i)}{p(X_i)}} = T_s \frac{\sum_{i=1}^{N} \frac{s(X_i) f_u(nT_s - X_i)}{p(X_i)}}{\sum_{i=1}^{N} \frac{f_u(nT_s - X_i)}{p(X_i)}} \tag{5.171}$$

as both its numerator and denominator are, respectively, unbiased. In the case of a normalized
201 131 *filter* $f_u = f_l$ with *probability density* $p(X_i) = f_l(nT_s - X_i)$, carrying *importance sampling*
155 139 with $X \sim p$ reduces the consistent *estimator* to

200
$$\tilde{s}_l[n] \overset{(5.171)}{=} T_s \frac{\sum_{i=1}^{N} \frac{s(X_i) f_l(nT_s - X_i)}{f_l(nT_s - X_i)}}{\sum_{i=1}^{N} \frac{f_l(nT_s - X_i)}{f_l(nT_s - X_i)}} = T_s \frac{\sum_{i=1}^{N} s(X_i)}{\sum_{i=1}^{N} 1} = \frac{T_s}{N} \sum_{i=1}^{N} s(X_i) \tag{5.172}$$

139 and so does the previous unbiased *estimator*, such that both are identical and unbiased.
139 Aside from handling unnormalized kernels, the consistent *estimator* may also be preferred
201 when dealing with normalized *filters* for which ideal *importance sampling* is not achievable as
155 143 the weighted average results in lower *variance* while the introduced bias is often less visually
139 objectionable than the noise artifacts of the unbiased *estimator*.

201 In contrast, *post-aliasing* refers to aliasing introduced by an imperfect *reconstruction*
kernel, such as the blocky pixels of computer monitors used to visualize raster images, whose
pixels represent point samples of the signal to be reconstructed [Smith, 1995, Blinn, 2005].
By smoothing out otherwise blocky edges between adjacent pixels, anti-aliasing additionally
provides an effective means of reducing *jaggies* caused by the limited resolution of display
devices, despite the possible loss in contrast incurred by the fuzzy edges.

From a theoretical standpoint, converting the sampling rate of a discrete-time signal to a
204 different rate first entails interpolating the discrete data by means of a *reconstruction filter*
tailored to the original rate. Given the resulting representation of the underlying continuous-
201 time signal, *re-sampling* may then be carried by means of a low-pass *filter* (such as a *blurring*
220 176 *filter*) tailored to the target rate. Due to the associative property of *convolution*, both operations can actually be performed in a single step whereby the values of the new samples are
201 obtained by convolving the original discrete data with a single *filter* resulting from the *con-*
176 *volution* of the *reconstruction filter* with the low-pass filter. In practice, though, the impact
204 204 of the *reconstruction filter* is mostly preponderant when increasing the sampling rate, a process known as *up-sampling*, while the process of decreasing the sampling rate, also known as
down-sampling or "decimation," is predominantly impacted by the band-limiting properties
201 of the low-pass *filter*.

5.3.2 Reconstruction

As illustrated in *Figure 5.12*, the continuous filtered signal can be reconstructed from its 202
discrete sampled representation by isolating its spectral response from the periodic spectrum
via a frequency-domain multiplication with the spectral response F_r of a *reconstruction filter* 204

$$S_r(\nu) \triangleq \mathcal{F}\left\{(s * f_l)(t)\,\mathrm{III}\left(\frac{t}{T_s}\right)\right\} F_r\left(\frac{\nu}{\nu_s}\right) \tag{5.173}$$

$$\overset{(5.166)}{=} \mathcal{F}\left\{\sum_{n=-\infty}^{+\infty} s_l[n]\delta(t - nT_s)\right\} F_r\left(\frac{\nu}{\nu_s}\right)$$ 199

$$\underset{(5.62)}{\overset{(5.132)}{=}} \sum_{n=-\infty}^{+\infty} s_l[n] e^{-\imath 2\pi\nu n T_s} F_r(T_s\nu)$$ 192 183

$$\overset{(5.167)}{=} \sum_{n=-\infty}^{+\infty} (s * f_l)(nT_s) T_s F_r(T_s\nu) e^{-\imath 2\pi\nu n T_s}$$ 199

$$\underset{(5.64)}{\overset{(5.62)}{=}} \sum_{n=-\infty}^{+\infty} (s * f_l)(nT_s) \mathcal{F}\left\{f_r\left(\frac{t}{T_s} - n\right)\right\} \tag{5.174}$$ 183 183

or equivalently via a time-domain *convolution* of the discrete signal with the *reconstruction* 176
filter f_r 204

$$s_r(t) \triangleq \mathcal{F}^{-1}\{S_r(\nu)\} \tag{5.175}$$

$$\overset{(5.173)}{=} \left(\sum_{n=-\infty}^{+\infty} s_l[n]\delta(t - nT_s)\right) * \frac{1}{T_s} f_r\left(\frac{t}{T_s}\right) \tag{5.176}$$ 201

$$\overset{(5.5)}{=} \int_{-\infty}^{+\infty} \sum_{n=-\infty}^{+\infty} s_l[n]\delta(u - nT_s) \frac{1}{T_s} f_r\left(\frac{t-u}{T_s}\right) du$$ 176

$$= \sum_{n=-\infty}^{+\infty} \frac{s_l[n]}{T_s} \int_{-\infty}^{+\infty} \delta(u - nT_s) f_r\left(\frac{t-u}{T_s}\right) du$$

$$\underset{(2.218)}{\overset{(5.167)}{=}} \sum_{n=-\infty}^{+\infty} (s * f_l)(nT_s) f_r\left(\frac{t}{T_s} - n\right) \tag{5.177}$$ 199 45

If the *reconstruction filter* has finite support $f_r(t) = 0, \forall |t| \geq t_m$, *interpolation* between the 204
sample points then reduces to a linear combination of instances of f_r centered at those points

$$s_r(t) = \sum_{n=\left\lceil \frac{t}{T_s} - t_m \right\rceil}^{\left\lfloor \frac{t}{T_s} + t_m \right\rfloor} (s * f_l)(nT_s) f_r\left(\frac{t}{T_s} - n\right) \tag{5.178}$$

which, if f_r forms a partition of unity, may conversely be regarded as an affine combination of the sample values.

5.4 FILTER

5.4.1 Definition

5.4.1.1 Terminology

In the *time domain*, a *filter* [Turkowski, 1990a] is readily characterized by the amplitude of
its *kernel function*, also known as the *impulse response* as it corresponds to the *convolution* 44 176

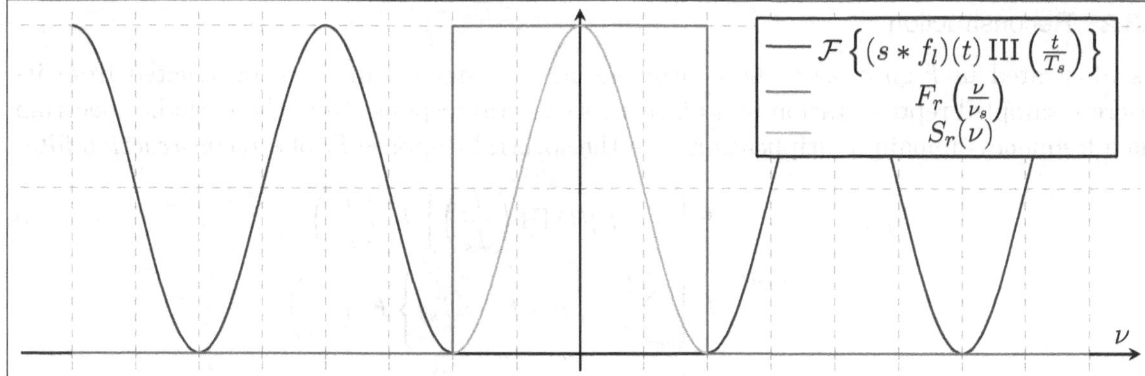

Figure 5.12: Signal Reconstruction: Schematic illustration of the reconstruction of a band-limited signal from its sampled representation by isolating its spectral response from the periodic spectrum.

44 of the kernel with a Dirac *delta function*. Alternatively, the filter may also be characterized
by any other *transient response*, which induces a change from a steady state at equilibrium,
42 such as its *step response* to a *Heaviside step function*.

In the *frequency domain*, the *frequency response* of a filter is characterized by the band
of frequencies within which magnitude and phase are preserved, so-called *pass band*, the
band of frequencies that are attenuated, so-called *stop band*, as well as any intermediate
202 band, so-called *transition band*. As illustrated in *Figure 5.13*, a filter mostly preserving all
frequencies below a given *cut-off frequency* is then referred to as a *low-pass filter*, whereas a filter conversely preserving all frequencies above it is referred to as a *high-pass filter*, while a filter solely preserving a given band of frequencies is referred to as a *band-pass filter*. A signal is then said to be *band-limited* if the band of frequencies that it contains has finite support, the width of the band between the upper and lower frequencies being referred to as the *bandwidth*, while the band itself is called *base band* shall the lower frequency be zero.

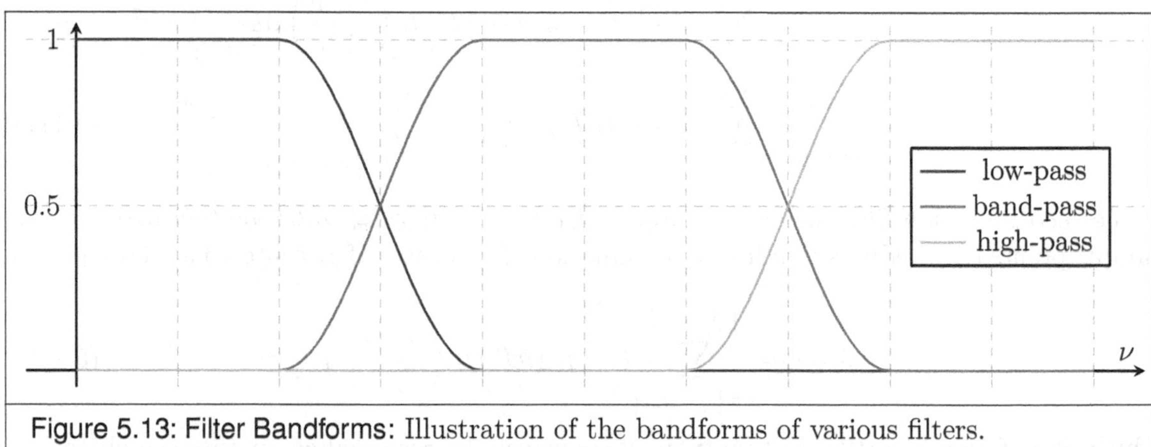

Figure 5.13: Filter Bandforms: Illustration of the bandforms of various filters.

In contrast to the perfectly sharp cut-off of an ideal filter, actual filters exhibit transition bands of finite width. The resulting loss of in-spectrum energy then manifests itself by the blurring of otherwise sharp features, while the excess of out-of-spectrum energy conversely introduces aliasing artifacts.

5.4.1.2 Polynomial Filter

A filter may be designed as a time-domain piecewise *polynomial filter* of the form

$$f_n(t) \triangleq \begin{cases} k_n(t) & \text{if } |t| < \frac{n+1}{2} \\ 0 & \text{otherwise} \end{cases} \tag{5.179}$$

where

$$k_n(t) \triangleq \sum_{i=0}^{n} c_{ij} t^i, \quad \forall t \in [j - o, j - o + 1], j = \lfloor t + o \rfloor \tag{5.180}$$

with

$$o \triangleq \frac{(n+1) \bmod 2}{2} = \begin{cases} 1/2 & \text{if } n \text{ is even} \\ 0 & \text{if } n \text{ is odd} \end{cases} \tag{5.181}$$

thereby defining an nth-order polynomial over each of the $n+1$ unit-length segments into which the support domain $[-\frac{n+1}{2}, \frac{n+1}{2}]$ (spanning the $n+1$ nearest data points) is subdivided.

5.4.1.3 Separable Filter

Given a rectangular sampling lattice, a normalized two-dimensional *separable filter* may be expressed in *Cartesian coordinates* as the product of two normalized 1-D functions 67

$$f(x, y) \triangleq f(x) f(y) \tag{5.182}$$

such that the time-domain *convolution* of the discrete signal with a *reconstruction filter* is 176
equivalent to successively applying a one-dimensional *convolution* in turn along each indi- 204
vidual dimension 176

$$\begin{aligned} s_r(x, y) &\overset{(5.178)}{=} \sum_{n_y = \lceil \frac{y}{T_y} - t_m \rceil}^{\lfloor \frac{y}{T_y} + t_m \rfloor} \sum_{n_x = \lceil \frac{x}{T_x} - t_m \rceil}^{\lfloor \frac{x}{T_x} + t_m \rfloor} (s * f_l)(n_x T_x, n_y T_y) f_r\left(\frac{x}{T_x} - n_x, \frac{y}{T_y} - n_y\right) \\ &= \sum_{n_y = \lceil \frac{y}{T_y} - t_m \rceil}^{\lfloor \frac{y}{T_y} + t_m \rfloor} \left(\sum_{n_x = \lceil \frac{x}{T_x} - t_m \rceil}^{\lfloor \frac{x}{T_x} + t_m \rfloor} (s * f_l)(n_x T_x, n_y T_y) f_r\left(\frac{x}{T_x} - n_x\right) \right) f_r\left(\frac{y}{T_y} - n_y\right) \end{aligned} \tag{5.183}$$ 201

Its *cumulative distribution* can then be expressed in a separable form over each quadrant 132
as

$$4 \int_0^{y_s} \int_0^{x_s} f(x, y) \mathrm{d}x \mathrm{d}y = \left(2 \int_0^{x_s} f(x) \mathrm{d}x\right) \left(2 \int_0^{y_s} f(y) \mathrm{d}y\right) \tag{5.184}$$

and carrying the integral over the whole domain by substituting $x_s = \infty$ and $y_s = \infty$ then ensures normalization, while applying *inverse-transform sampling* allows *importance* 134
sampling to be readily carried. 155

Horizontal scaling of a normalized linear distribution $f(t)$ may be readily obtained by means of the normalization factor

$$2 \int_0^{t_s} \frac{1}{|T|} f\left(\frac{t}{T}\right) \mathrm{d}t = 2 \int_0^{\frac{t_s}{T}} f(t) \mathrm{d}t \tag{5.185}$$

and carrying the integral over the whole domain by substituting $t_s = \infty$ similarly ensures
normalization, while applying *inverse-transform sampling* allows *importance sampling* to be 134
carried by scaling the coordinate drawn from the original distribution by T. 155

5.4.1.4 Radial Filter

Given a continuous 2-D function, a normalized two-dimensional rotationally symmetric *radial*
69 *filter* may be expressed in *cylindrical coordinates* as a 1-D function parameterized by the
radial distance

$$f(\rho,\phi) \triangleq \frac{f(\rho)}{2\pi c} \tag{5.186}$$

132 Its *cumulative distribution* can then be expressed in a separable form as

$$\int_0^{\phi_s}\int_0^{\rho_s} f(\rho,\phi)\rho \mathrm{d}\rho \mathrm{d}\phi = \int_0^{\phi_s}\frac{1}{2\pi}\mathrm{d}\phi \int_0^{\rho_s}\frac{1}{c}f(\rho)\rho \mathrm{d}\rho \tag{5.187}$$

and carrying the integral over the whole domain by substituting $\phi_s = 2\pi$ and $\rho_s = \infty$ then yields the normalization constant

$$c \triangleq \int_0^{\infty} f(\rho)\rho \mathrm{d}\rho \tag{5.188}$$

134 155 while applying *inverse-transform sampling* allows *importance sampling* to be readily carried.
Horizontal scaling of a normalized radial distribution $\frac{1}{c}f(\rho)$ may be readily obtained by means of the normalization factor

$$\int_0^{\rho_s}\frac{1}{T|T|}\frac{1}{c}f\left(\frac{\rho}{T}\right)\rho \mathrm{d}\rho = \int_0^{\frac{\rho_s}{T}}\frac{1}{c}f(\rho)\rho \mathrm{d}\rho \tag{5.189}$$

and carrying the integral over the whole domain by substituting $\rho_s = \infty$ similarly ensures
134 155 normalization, while applying *inverse-transform sampling* allows *importance sampling* to be
carried by scaling the coordinate drawn from the original distribution by T.

5.4.2 Reconstruction Filter

5.4.2.1 Overview

A *reconstruction filter* is defined as a filter satisfying $f(i) = \delta[i], \forall i \in \mathbb{Z}$, thereby yielding a reconstructed signal that interpolates the original sample points. For quadratic polynomial orders and beyond, such filters exhibit features similar to those of a second-order differential Laplacian operator, whose negative lobes enhance contrast along edges, thereby increasing overall *acutance* (i.e., the gradient of the signal) as well as *perceived sharpness* (i.e., the gradient magnitude, or maximum slope). Besides ringing artifacts, the negative lobes of the
176 *convolution* kernel may conversely introduce negative values in an originally non-negative
signal as well as overshoots in the reconstruction process.

5.4.2.2 Box Filter

203 **Definition** The *box filter* is a time-domain piecewise constant *polynomial filter* defined in
46 terms of the *rectangular function* as

$$f(t) \triangleq \sqcap(t) \tag{5.190}$$

52 whose spectral response is a normalized *sinc function*

184

$$F(\nu) \overset{(5.74)}{=} \mathrm{sinc}(\pi\nu) \tag{5.191}$$

205 with the anti-aliasing properties illustrated in *Figure 5.14*.

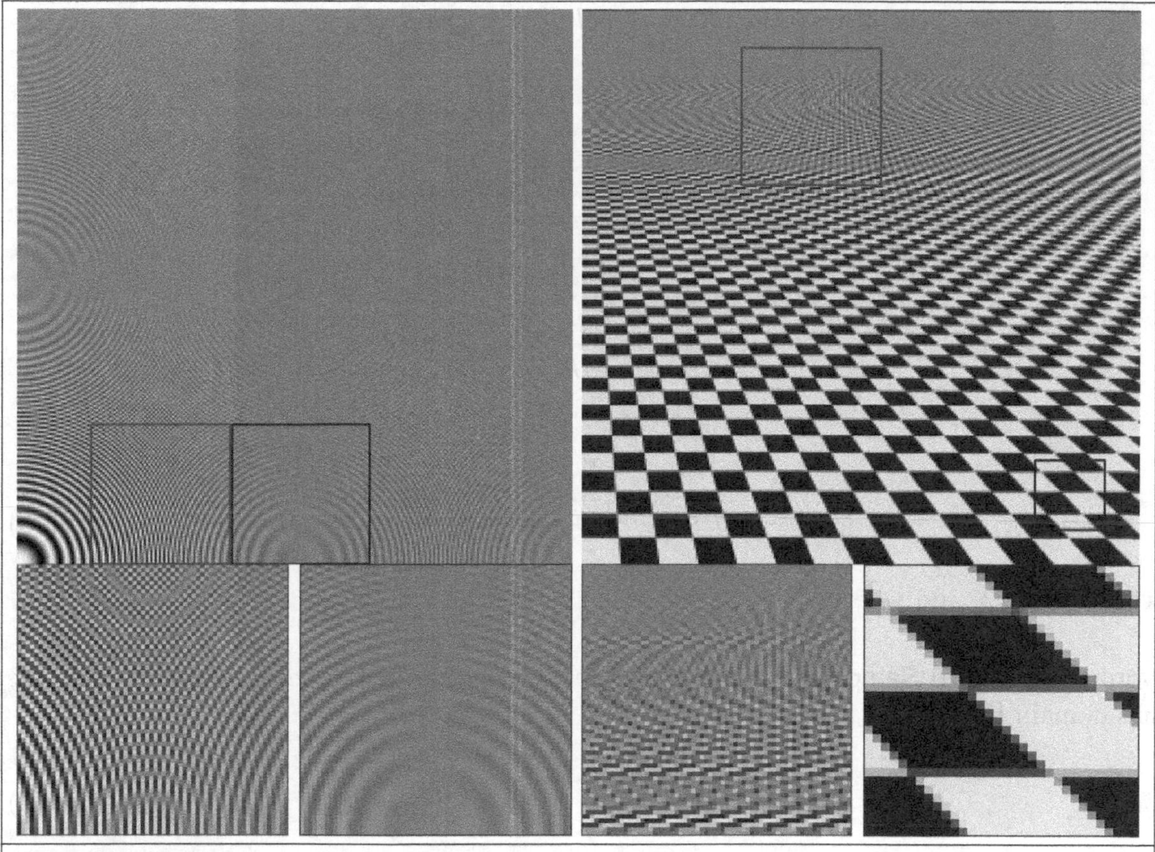

Figure 5.14: Box Anti-Aliasing: Illustration of the anti-aliasing properties of the box filter.

The functions $f(t-i), \forall i \in \mathbb{Z}$ actually form a partition of unity $\forall t \in \mathbb{R}$ by translation of the periodic summation

$$\sum_{i=0}^{0} f(t-i) \overset{(2.225)}{=} 1, \quad \forall t \in [-1/2, 1/2] \tag{5.192}$$ 46

and the corresponding reconstruction scheme illustrated in *Figure 5.15* is known as *nearest-neighbor interpolation*. 205

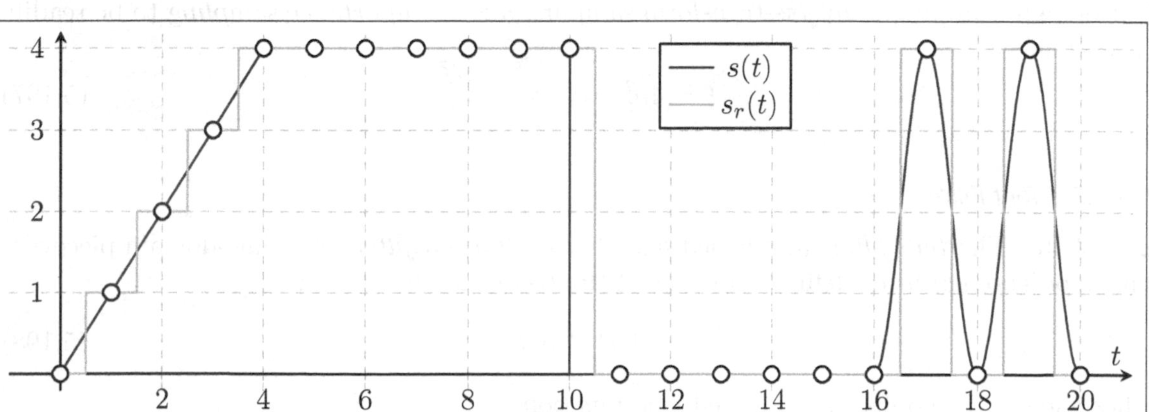

Figure 5.15: Nearest-Neighbor Reconstruction: Illustration of a reconstructed signal using a piecewise-constant interpolation kernel.

204 Instead, the spectral response of the *radial filter* is given as

182
46
54
52

$$\begin{aligned}\mathcal{F}\left(\sqcap\left(\frac{r}{c}\right)\right) &\overset{(5.60)}{=} 2\pi\int_0^{\infty}\sqcap\left(\frac{r}{c}\right)J_0(2\pi r\rho)r\mathrm{d}r\\ &\overset{(2.225)}{=} 2\pi\int_0^{\frac{c}{2}}J_0(2\pi r\rho)r\mathrm{d}r\\ &= 2\pi\int_0^{c\pi\rho}J_0(\tau)\frac{\tau}{2\pi\rho}\frac{\mathrm{d}\tau}{2\pi\rho}\\ &= \frac{1}{2\pi\rho^2}\int_0^{c\pi\rho}J_0(\tau)\tau\mathrm{d}\tau\\ &\overset{(2.269)}{=} \frac{c}{2\rho}J_1(c\pi\rho)\\ &\overset{(2.255)}{=} \frac{c^2\pi}{2}\operatorname{jinc}(c\pi\rho)\end{aligned} \tag{5.193}$$

54 with $\tau \triangleq 2\pi r\rho$, and where J_1 is the first-order *Bessel function* of the first kind.

132
203 **Normalization and Sampling** The *cumulative distribution* of the *separable filter* over the sub-domain $[0, t_s]$ reads

46

$$2\int_0^{t_s}\sqcap(t)\mathrm{d}t \overset{(2.225)}{=} 2\int_0^{t_s}\mathrm{d}t = 2[t]_0^{t_s} = 2t_s \tag{5.194}$$

and carrying the integral over the whole domain by substituting $t_s = \frac{1}{2}$ then ensures normal-
134 ization, while applying *inverse-transform sampling* allows *importance sampling* to be readily
155 carried as

$$\xi = 2t_s \implies t_s = \frac{\xi}{2} \tag{5.195}$$

132 Similarly, the *cumulative distribution* of the *radial filter* over the sub-domain $[0, \rho_s]$ reads
204

46

$$\int_0^{\rho_s}8\sqcap(\rho)\rho\mathrm{d}\rho \overset{(2.225)}{=} 8\int_0^{\rho_s}\rho\mathrm{d}\rho = 8\left[\frac{\rho^2}{2}\right]_0^{\rho_s} = 4\rho_s^2 \tag{5.196}$$

and carrying the integral over the whole domain by substituting $\rho_s = \frac{1}{2}$ then ensures normal-
134 ization, while applying *inverse-transform sampling* allows *importance sampling* to be readily
155 carried as

$$\xi = 4\rho_s^2 \implies \rho_s = \frac{\sqrt{\xi}}{2} \tag{5.197}$$

5.4.2.3 Tent Filter

Definition The *tent filter*, also called *hat filter* or *Bartlett filter*, is a time-domain piecewise
203 linear *polynomial filter* defined in terms of the *triangular function* as
47

$$f(t) \triangleq \wedge(t) \tag{5.198}$$

52 whose spectral response is a squared *sinc function*

184

$$F(\nu) \overset{(5.76)}{=} \operatorname{sinc}(\pi\nu)^2 \tag{5.199}$$

207 with the anti-aliasing properties illustrated in *Figure 5.16*.

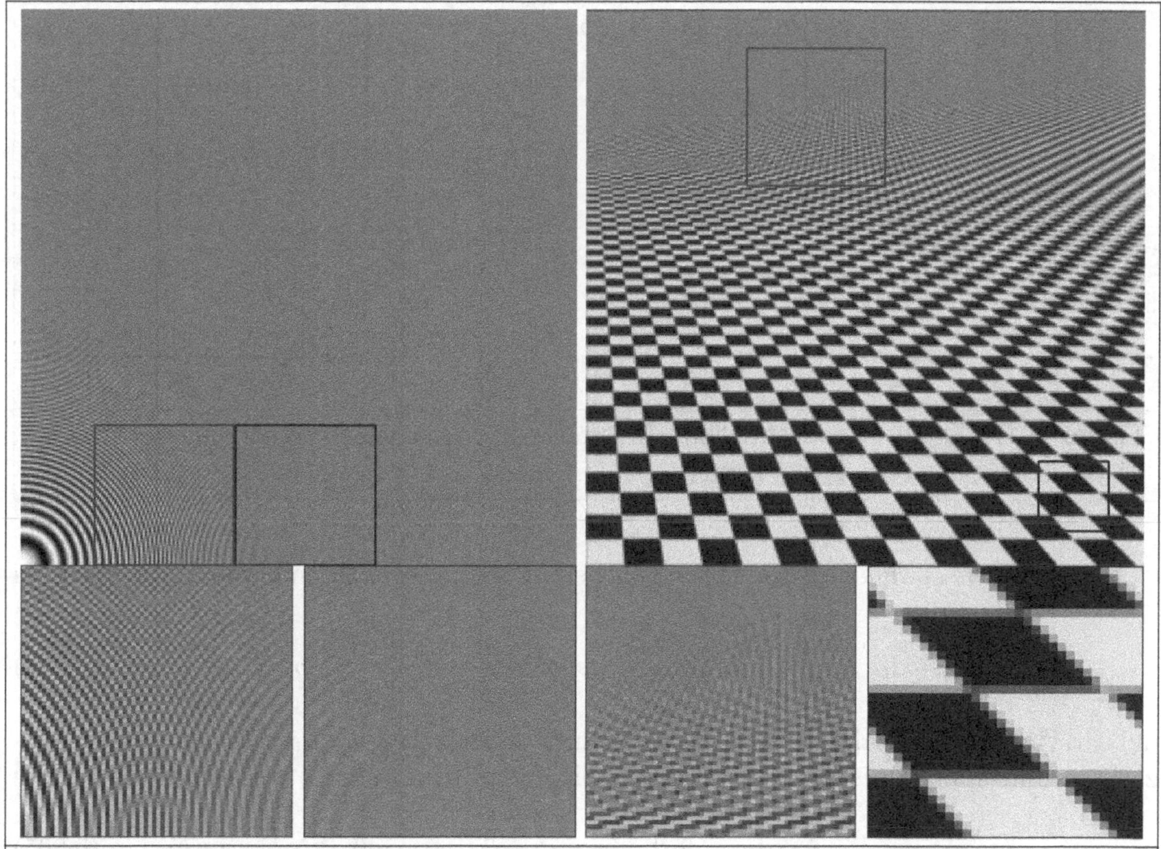

Figure 5.16: Tent Anti-Aliasing: Illustration of the anti-aliasing properties of the tent filter.

The functions $f(t-i), \forall i \in \mathbb{Z}$ actually form a partition of unity $\forall t \in \mathbb{R}$ by translation of the periodic summation

$$\sum_{i=0}^{1} f(t-i) \overset{(2.231)}{=} (1-t) + (1+(t-1)) = 1, \quad \forall t \in [0,1] \tag{5.200}$$ 47

and the corresponding reconstruction scheme illustrated in *Figure 5.17* is known as *lin-* 208
ear interpolation. The latter is readily given between two sample values y_0 and y_1 as $\text{lerp}\left(\frac{x-x_0}{x_1-x_0}, y_0, y_1\right), \forall x \in [x_0, x_1]$ with the function

$$\text{lerp}(t, y_0, y_1) \triangleq (1-t) \times y_0 + t \times y_1 = y_0 + t(y_1 - y_0), \quad \forall t \in [0,1] \tag{5.201}$$

where the second form, although computationally cheaper, does not guarantee $y_1 = \text{lerp}(1, y_0, y_1)$ due to the limited numerical precision of floating-point representations.

Normalization and Sampling The *cumulative distribution* of the *separable filter* over the 132
sub-domain $[0, t_s]$ reads 203

$$2\int_0^{t_s} \wedge(t)\mathrm{d}t \overset{(2.231)}{=} 2\int_0^{t_s} 1 - |t|\mathrm{d}t = 2\left[t - \frac{t^2}{2}\right]_0^{t_s} = t_s(2-t_s) \tag{5.202}$$ 47

and carrying the integral over the whole domain by substituting $t_s = 1$ then ensures normalization, while applying *inverse-transform sampling* allows *importance sampling* to be readily 134
carried as 155

$$\xi = t_s(2-t_s) \implies t_s = 1 - \sqrt{1-\xi} \tag{5.203}$$

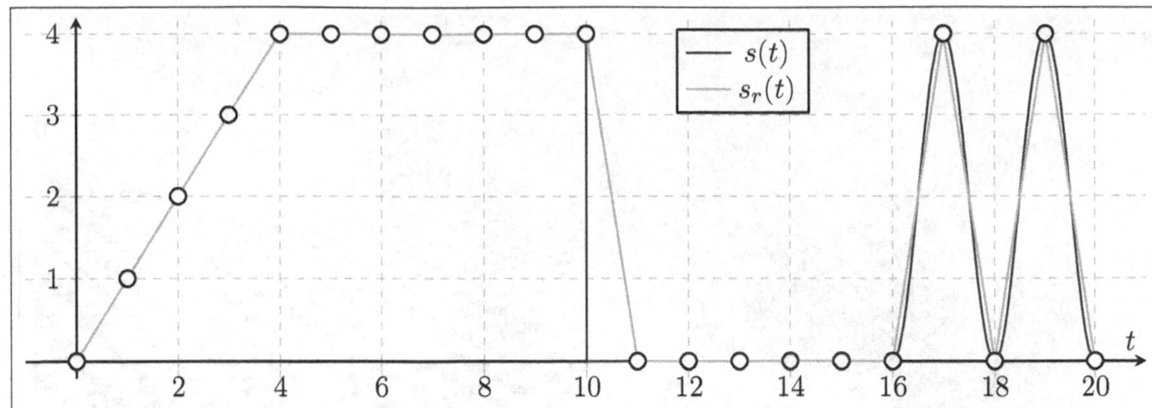

Figure 5.17: Linear Reconstruction: Illustration of a reconstructed signal using a piecewise-linear interpolation kernel.

132 204 Similarly, the *cumulative distribution* of the *radial filter* over the sub-domain $[0, \rho_s]$ reads

47

$$\int_0^{\rho_s} 6 \wedge (\rho)\rho \mathrm{d}\rho \overset{(2.231)}{=} 6 \int_0^{\rho_s} (1 - |\rho|)\rho \mathrm{d}\rho = 6 \left[\frac{\rho^2}{2} - \frac{\rho^3}{3} \right]_0^{\rho_s} = 3\rho_s^2 - 2\rho_s^3 \tag{5.204}$$

and carrying the integral over the whole domain by substituting $\rho_s = 1$ then ensures normal-
134 155 ization, while applying *inverse-transform sampling* allows *importance sampling* to be readily carried as

$$\xi = 3\rho_s^2 - 2\rho_s^3 \implies 2\rho_s^3 - 3\rho_s^2 + \xi = 0 \tag{5.205}$$

29 where the sample coordinate $\rho_s \in [0, 1]$ is the third solution of the *cubic equation* with discriminant

31

$$\Delta \overset{(2.119)}{=} \xi^2 - \xi = \xi(\xi - 1) \leq 0, \quad \forall \xi \in [0, 1] \tag{5.206}$$

5.4.2.4 *Quadratic Filter*

209 203 **Definition** As illustrated in *Figure 5.18*, the *quadratic filter* [Dodgson, 1992, Dodgson, 1997] is a C0-continuous time-domain piecewise quadratic *polynomial filter* defined as

$$f(t) \triangleq \begin{cases} -2|t|^2 + 1 & \text{if } |t| \in [0, 1/2] \\ |t|^2 - 5/2|t| + 3/2 & \text{if } |t| \in [1/2, 3/2] \\ 0 & \text{otherwise} \end{cases} \tag{5.207}$$

whose minimum is $f(\pm 5/4) = -1/16$, and with the anti-aliasing properties illustrated in *Fig-*
209 *ure 5.19*.

The functions $f(t - i), \forall i \in \mathbb{Z}$ actually form a partition of unity $\forall t \in \mathbb{R}$ by translation of the periodic summation

208

$$\begin{aligned} \sum_{i=-1}^{1} f(t - i) &\overset{(5.207)}{=} \left((t + 1)^2 - \frac{5}{2}(t + 1) + \frac{3}{2} \right) \\ &+ \left(-2t^2 + 1 \right) \\ &+ \left((t - 1)^2 + \frac{5}{2}(t - 1) + \frac{3}{2} \right) \\ &= 1, \quad \forall t \in [-1/2, 1/2] \end{aligned} \tag{5.208}$$

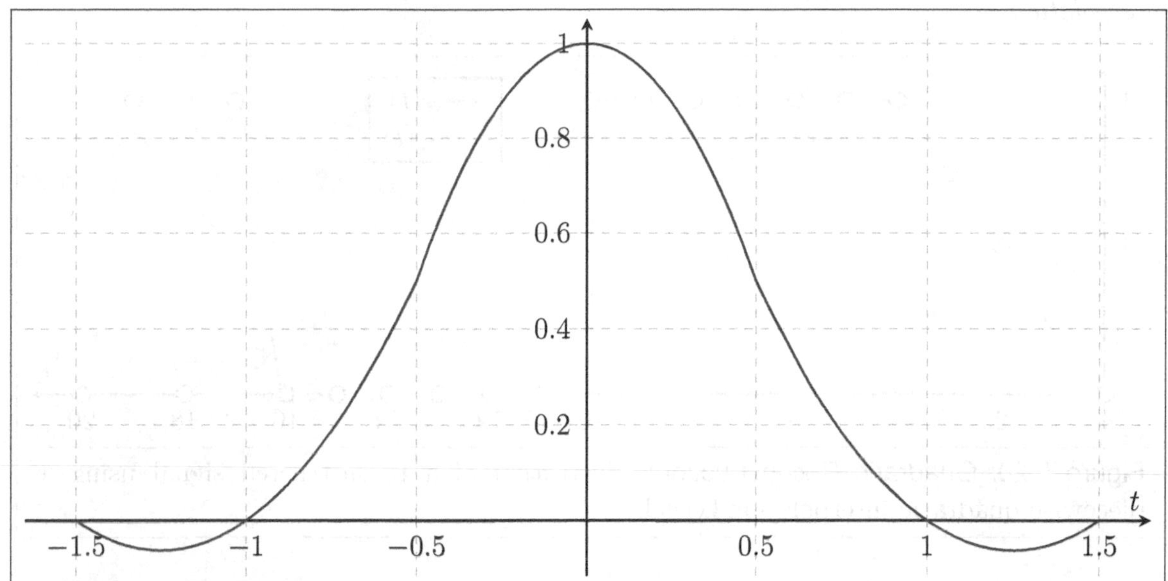

Figure 5.18: Quadratic Filter: Plot of the quadratic filter.

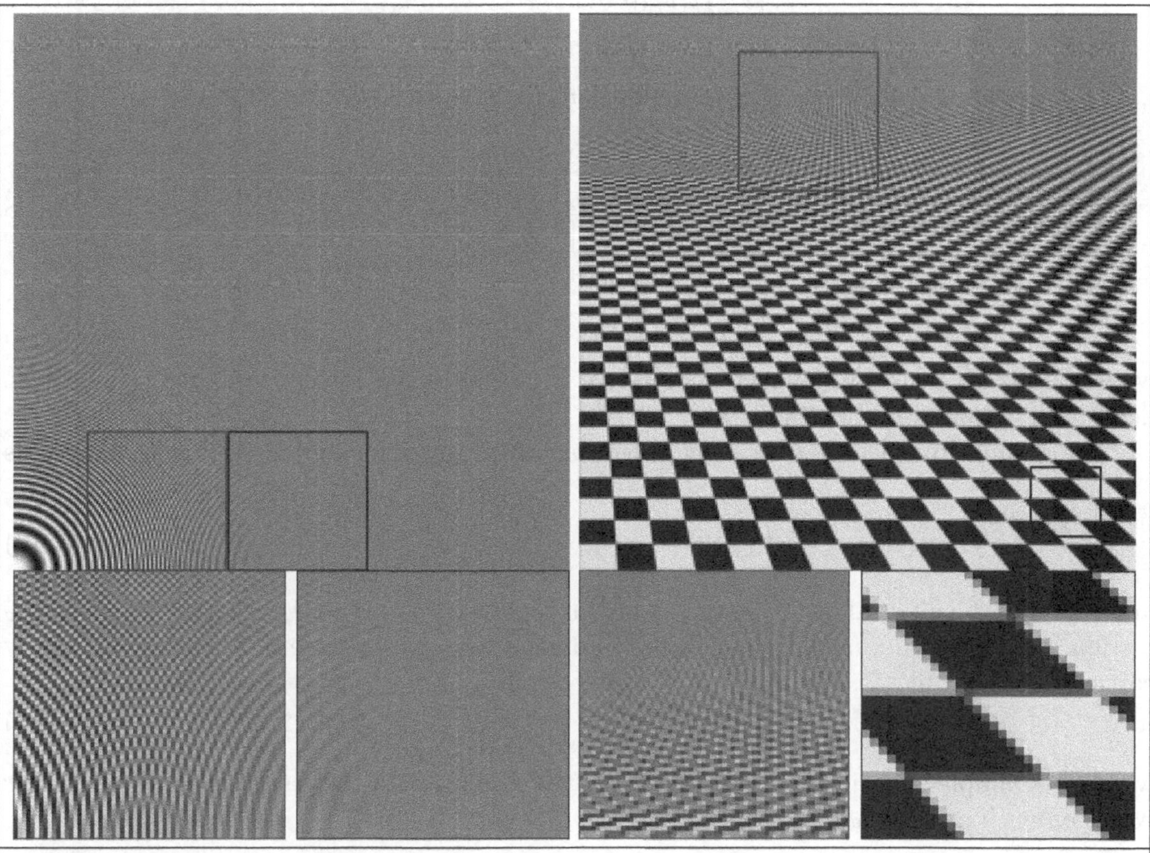

Figure 5.19: Quadratic Anti-Aliasing: Illustration of the anti-aliasing properties of the quadratic filter.

210 and the corresponding reconstruction scheme illustrated in *Figure 5.20* is known as *quadratic interpolation*.

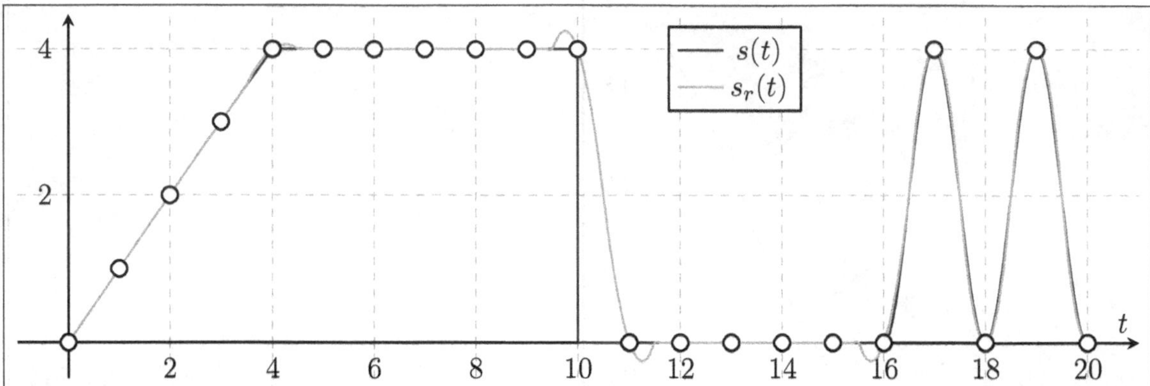

Figure 5.20: Quadratic Reconstruction: Illustration of a reconstructed signal using a piecewise-quadratic interpolation kernel.

131 **Normalization and Sampling** Defining the *probability density* as being proportional to the absolute value of the filter yields

$$
\begin{aligned}
p(t) &\triangleq \frac{|f(t)|}{\int_{-\infty}^{+\infty}|f(t)|\mathrm{d}t} \\
&= \frac{|f(t)|}{2\left(\left|\int_0^{1/2} f(t)\mathrm{d}t\right| + \left|\int_{1/2}^{1} f(t)\mathrm{d}t\right| + \left|\int_1^{3/2} f(t)\mathrm{d}t\right|\right)}
\end{aligned}
$$

210 211 211

$$
\begin{aligned}
&\overset{(5.210)}{\underset{(5.215)}{\overset{(5.213)}{=}}} \frac{|f(t)|}{2\left(\left|\frac{5}{12}\right| + \left|\frac{5}{48}\right| + \left|-\frac{1}{48}\right|\right)} \\
&= \frac{12}{13}|f(t)| \qquad (5.209)
\end{aligned}
$$

where the PMF of sampling each subinterval is readily given by the absolute value of the definite integrals over those intervals.

132 203 The *cumulative distribution* of the *separable filter* over the sub-domain $[0, t_s]$ then reads

208

$$\frac{12}{5}\int_0^{t_s} f(t)\mathrm{d}t \overset{(5.207)}{=} \frac{12}{5}\int_0^{t_s} -2|t|^2 + 1\mathrm{d}t = \frac{12}{5}\left[-\frac{2}{3}t^3 + t\right]_0^{t_s} = \frac{12}{5}t_s - \frac{8}{5}t_s^3 \qquad (5.210)$$

134 155 and carrying the integral over the whole domain by substituting $t_s = 1/2$ then ensures normalization, while applying *inverse-transform sampling* allows *importance sampling* to be readily carried as

$$\xi = \frac{12}{5}t_s - \frac{8}{5}t_s^3 \implies 8t_s^3 - 12t_s + 5\xi = 0 \qquad (5.211)$$

29 where the sample coordinate $t_s \in [0, 1/2]$ is the third solution of the resulting depressed *cubic equation* with discriminant

31

$$\Delta \overset{(2.119)}{=} \frac{25}{144}\xi^2 - \frac{2}{9} = \frac{25\xi^2 - 32}{144} < 0, \quad \forall \xi \in [0, 1] \qquad (5.212)$$

132 203 Instead, the *cumulative distribution* of the *separable filter* over the sub-domain $[1/2, t_s]$

reads

$$\frac{48}{5}\int_0^{\tau_s} f(\tau+1/2)\mathrm{d}\tau \overset{(5.207)}{=} \frac{48}{5}\int_0^{\tau_s} \tau^2-\frac{3}{2}\tau+\frac{1}{2}\mathrm{d}\tau = \frac{48}{5}\left[\frac{\tau^3}{3}-\frac{3}{4}\tau^2+\frac{\tau}{2}\right]_0^{\tau_s} = \frac{16}{5}\tau_s^3-\frac{36}{5}\tau_s^2+\frac{24}{5}\tau_s \quad (5.213)$$ 208

with the change of variable $\tau \triangleq |t| - 1/2$, and carrying the integral over the whole domain by substituting $t_s = 1$ then ensures normalization, while applying *inverse-transform sampling* 134
allows *importance sampling* to be readily carried as 155

$$\xi = \frac{16}{5}\tau_s^3 - \frac{36}{5}\tau_s^2 + \frac{24}{5}\tau_s \implies 16\tau_s^3 - 36\tau_s^2 + 24\tau_s - 5\xi = 0 \quad (5.214)$$

where the sample coordinate $t_s = 1/2 + \tau_s \in [1/2, 1]$ is given by the unique solution of the resulting *cubic equation* when the discriminant is positive, and by the second solution when 29
it is negative.

Finally, the *cumulative distribution* of the *separable filter* over the sub-domain $[1, t_s]$ 132
reads 203

$$-48\int_0^{\tau_s} f(\tau+1)\mathrm{d}\tau \overset{(5.207)}{=} -48\int_0^{\tau_s} \tau^2 - \frac{\tau}{2}\mathrm{d}t = -48\left[\frac{\tau^3}{3} - \frac{\tau^2}{4}\right]_0^{\tau_s} = 12\tau_s^2 - 16\tau_s^3 \quad (5.215)$$ 208

with the change of variable $\tau \triangleq |t| - 1$, and carrying the integral over the whole domain by substituting $t_s = 3/2$ then ensures normalization, while applying *inverse-transform sampling* 134
allows *importance sampling* to be readily carried as 155

$$\xi = 12\tau_s^2 - 16\tau_s^3 \implies 16\tau_s^3 - 12\tau_s^2 + \xi = 0 \quad (5.216)$$

where the sample coordinate $t_s = 1+\tau_s \in [1, 3/2]$ is given by the third solution of the resulting *cubic equation* with discriminant 29

$$\Delta \overset{(2.119)}{=} -\frac{(1-\xi)\xi}{48^2} \leq 0, \quad \forall \xi \in [0, 1] \quad (5.217)$$ 31

5.4.2.5 Cubic Filter

Definition As illustrated in *Figure 5.21*, the *cubic filter* is a time-domain piecewise cubic 212
polynomial filter defined as a uniform Catmull–Rom *cardinal spline* 203 348 349

$$f(t) \triangleq \begin{cases} h_{p0}(|t|) - 1/2 h_{d1}(|t|) \overset{(8.207)}{=} 3/2|t|^3 - 5/2|t|^2 + 1 & \text{if } |t| \in [0, 1] \\ -1/2 h_{d0}(|t| - 1) \overset{(8.206)}{=} -1/2|t|^3 + 5/2|t|^2 - 4|t| + 2 & \text{if } |t| \in [1, 2] \\ 0 & \text{otherwise} \end{cases} \quad (5.218)$$ 349

whose minimum is $f(\pm 4/3) = -2/27$, and with the anti-aliasing properties illustrated in *Figure 5.22*. 212

The functions $f(t-i), \forall i \in \mathbb{Z}$ actually form a partition of unity $\forall t \in \mathbb{R}$ by translation of the periodic summation

$$\begin{aligned} \sum_{i=-1}^{2} f(t-i) &\overset{(5.218)}{=} -\frac{h_{d0}(t)}{2} + \left(h_{p0}(t) - \frac{h_{d1}(t)}{2}\right) + \left(h_{p0}(1-t) - \frac{h_{d1}(1-t)}{2}\right) - \frac{h_{d0}(1-t)}{2} \\ &\overset{(8.177)}{\underset{(8.178)}{=}} -\frac{h_{d0}(t)}{2} + h_{p0}(t) - \frac{h_{d1}(t)}{2} + h_{p1}(t) + \frac{h_{d0}(t)}{2} + \frac{h_{d1}(t)}{2} \\ &= h_{p0}(t) + h_{p1}(t) \\ &\overset{(8.179)}{=} 1, \quad \forall t \in [0, 1] \end{aligned} \quad (5.219)$$ 211 345 345 345

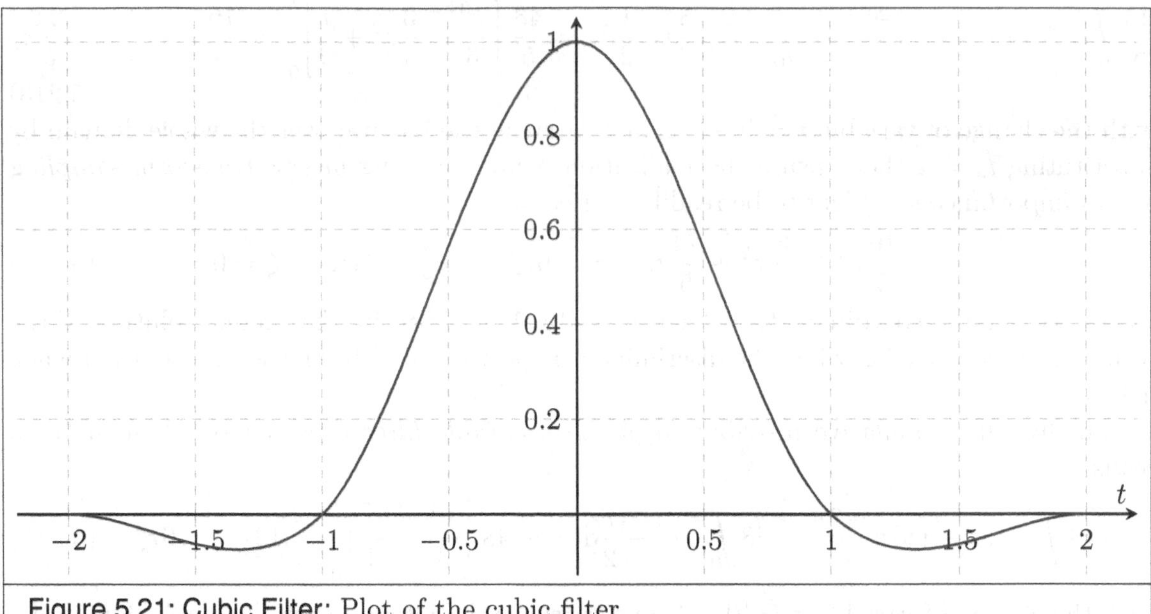

Figure 5.21: Cubic Filter: Plot of the cubic filter.

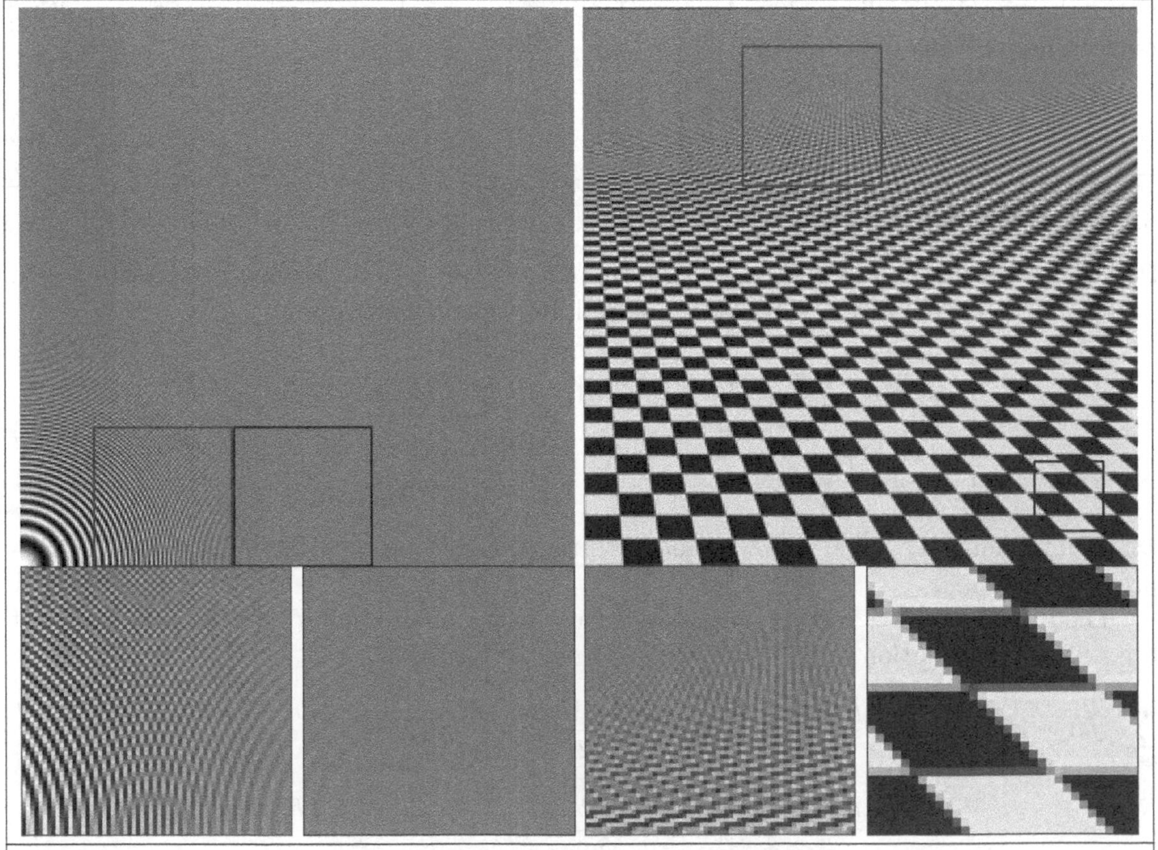

Figure 5.22: Cubic Anti-Aliasing: Illustration of the anti-aliasing properties of the cubic filter.

and the corresponding reconstruction scheme illustrated in *Figure 5.23* is known as *cubic interpolation.* 213

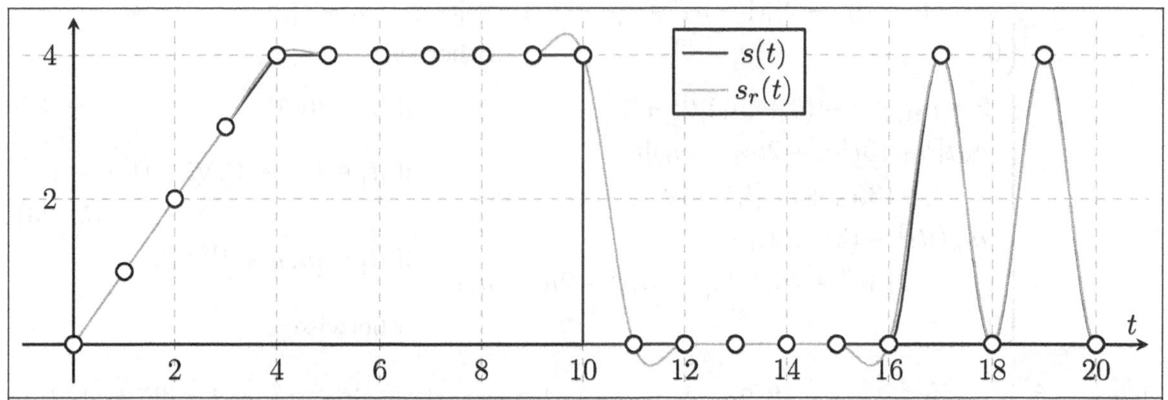

Figure 5.23: Cubic Reconstruction: Illustration of a reconstructed signal using a piecewise-cubic interpolation kernel.

Normalization and Sampling Carrying the integral over the whole domain ensures normalization of the *separable filter* 203

$$\int_{-\infty}^{+\infty} f(t)\mathrm{d}t \overset{(5.218)}{=} 2\left(\int_0^1 h_{p0}(t) - \frac{h_{d1}(t)}{2}\mathrm{d}t - \int_1^2 \frac{h_{d0}(t-1)}{2}\mathrm{d}t\right)$$ 211

$$= 2\left(\int_0^1 h_{p0}(t)\mathrm{d}t - \frac{1}{2}\int_0^1 h_{d1}(t)\mathrm{d}t + \frac{1}{2}\int_0^1 h_{d0}(t)\mathrm{d}t\right)$$

345
345
$$\overset{(8.180)}{\underset{(8.181)}{\overset{(8.183)}{=}}} 2\left(\frac{1}{2} - \frac{1}{2}\frac{1}{12} + \frac{1}{2}\frac{1}{12}\right)$$
345

$$= 1 \tag{5.220}$$

where the PMF of sampling each subinterval is readily defined by the absolute value of the definite integrals over those intervals, while applying *inverse-transform sampling* allows 134
importance sampling to be readily carried as a special case of the *extended cubic filter*. 155 213

5.4.2.6 Extended Cubic Filter

Definition As illustrated in *Figure 5.24*, time-domain piecewise *polynomial filters* of higher 214
order may be approximated by a generalization of the *cubic filter* parametrized by the slopes 203 211
m_i at $t = \pm i$, with $\mathrm{sgn}(m_i) = (-1)^i, \forall i \leq n \in \mathbb{N}$ and $m_i = 0, \forall i > n \in \mathbb{N}$

$$f_n(t) \triangleq \begin{cases} h_{p0}(|t|) + m_1 h_{d1}(|t|) & \text{if } |t| \in [0,1] \\ m_i h_{d0}(|t|-i) + m_{i+1} h_{d1}(|t|-i) & \text{if } |t| \in [i, i+1], \forall i \in [1, n-1] \\ m_n h_{d0}(|t|-n) & \text{if } |t| \in [n, n+1] \\ 0 & \text{otherwise} \end{cases} \tag{5.221}$$

344

$$\overset{(8.165)}{=} \begin{cases} (2+m_1)|t|^3 - (3+m_1)|t|^2 + 1 & \text{if } |t| \in [0,1] \\ c_3(|t|-i)^3 - c_2(|t|-i)^2 + m_i(|t|-i) & \text{if } |t| \in [i,i+1], \forall i \in [1,n-1] \\ m_n((|t|-n)^3 - 2(|t|-n)^2 + (|t|-n)) & \text{if } |t| \in [n,n+1] \\ 0 & \text{otherwise} \end{cases} \tag{5.222}$$

$$= \begin{cases} (2+m_1)|t|^3 - (3+m_1)|t|^2 + 1 & \text{if } |t| \in [0,1] \\ c_3|t|^3 + (3i^2c_3 + 2ic_2 + m_i)|t| \\ \quad - (3ic_3 + c_2)|t|^2 - (i^3c_3 + i^2c_2 + im_i) & \text{if } |t| \in [i,i+1], \forall i \in [1,n-1] \\ m_n(|t|^3 - (3n+2)|t|^2 \\ \quad + (3n^2+4n+1)|t| - (n^3+2n^2+n)) & \text{if } |t| \in [n,n+1] \\ 0 & \text{otherwise} \end{cases} \tag{5.223}$$

where $c_3 \triangleq m_i + m_{i+1}$ and $c_2 \triangleq 2m_i + m_{i+1}$, with the anti-aliasing properties illustrated in
215 *Figure 5.25.*

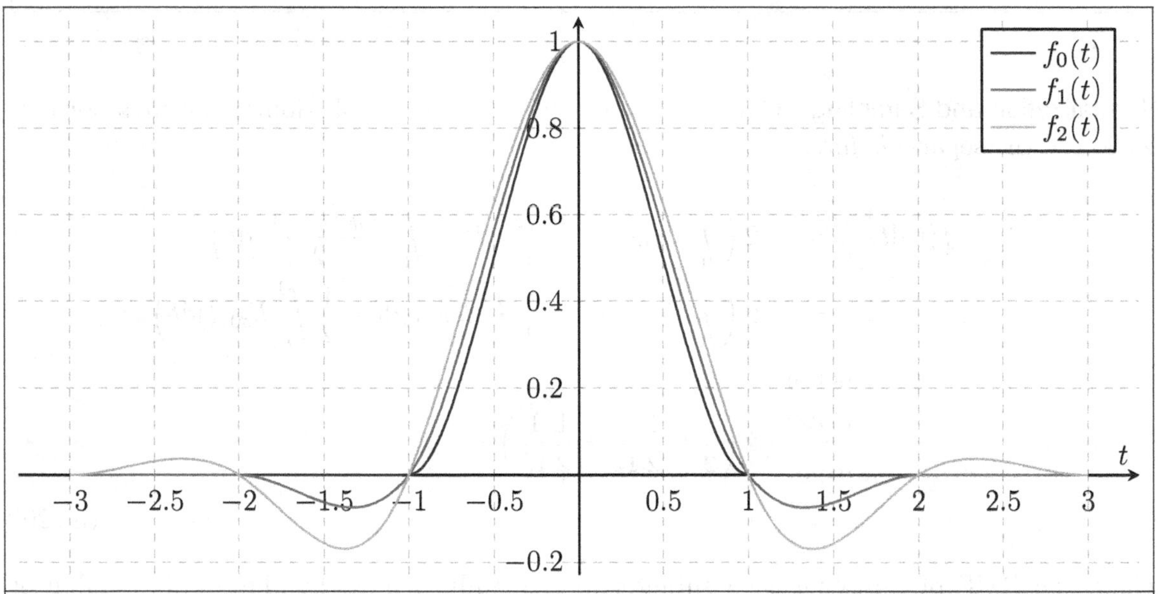

Figure 5.24: Extended Cubic Filter: Plot of the extended cubic filter for various support sizes.

Setting $m_i = \frac{(-1)^i}{i}$ then yields a filter whose slopes at $t = \pm i$ match those of the *sinc*
217 *filter*, whereas the parameters ought to be related by $2m_1 + 4m_2 = -1$ in order for the filter f_2 to perfectly reconstruct straight lines. Instead, the filter

213

$$f_1(t) \overset{(5.221)}{=} \begin{cases} (2+m_1)|t|^3 - (3+m_1)|t|^2 + 1 & \text{if } |t| \in [0,1] \\ m_1(|t|^3 - 5|t|^2 + 8|t| - 4) & \text{if } |t| \in [1,2] \\ 0 & \text{otherwise} \end{cases} \tag{5.224}$$

348 corresponds to the uniform cubic *cardinal spline* solely parametrized by the slope m_1 at
211 $t = \pm 1$, which reduces to the *cubic filter* whenever $m_1 = -1/2$.

Figure 5.25: Extended Cubic Anti-Aliasing: Illustration of the anti-aliasing properties of the extended cubic filter f_2.

The functions $f_n(t-i), \forall i \in \mathbb{Z}$ actually form a partition of unity $\forall t \in \mathbb{R}$ by translation of the periodic summation

$$
\begin{aligned}
\sum_{i=-n}^{n+1} f_n(t-i) &\overset{(5.221)}{=} m_n h_{d0}(t) + \left(\sum_{i=1}^{n-1} m_i h_{d0}(t) + m_{i+1} h_{d1}(t) \right) && 213 \\
&+ \quad (h_{p0}(t) + m_1 h_{d1}(t)) + (h_{p0}(1-t) + m_1 h_{d1}(1-t)) \\
&+ \quad \left(\sum_{i=1}^{n-1} m_i h_{d0}(1-t) + m_{i+1} h_{d1}(1-t) \right) + m_n h_{d0}(1-t) \\
&\overset{(8.177)}{\underset{(8.178)}{=}} m_n h_{d0}(t) + \left(\sum_{i=1}^{n-1} m_i h_{d0}(t) + \sum_{i=2}^{n} m_i h_{d1}(t) \right) + h_{p0}(t) + m_1 h_{d1}(t) && 345 \; 345 \\
&+ \quad h_{p1}(t) - m_1 h_{d0}(t) - \left(\sum_{i=1}^{n-1} m_i h_{d1}(t) + \sum_{i=2}^{n} m_i h_{d0}(t) \right) - m_n h_{d1}(t) \\
&= \quad \sum_{i=1}^{n} m_i h_{d0}(t) + \sum_{i=1}^{n} m_i h_{d1}(t) + h_{p0}(t) \\
&+ \quad h_{p1}(t) - \sum_{i=1}^{n} m_i h_{d1}(t) - \sum_{i=1}^{n} m_i h_{d0}(t) \\
&= \quad h_{p0}(t) + h_{p1}(t) \\
&\overset{(8.179)}{=} 1, \quad \forall t \in [0,1] \qquad (5.225) && 345
\end{aligned}
$$

216 and the corresponding reconstruction scheme is illustrated in *Figure 5.26*.

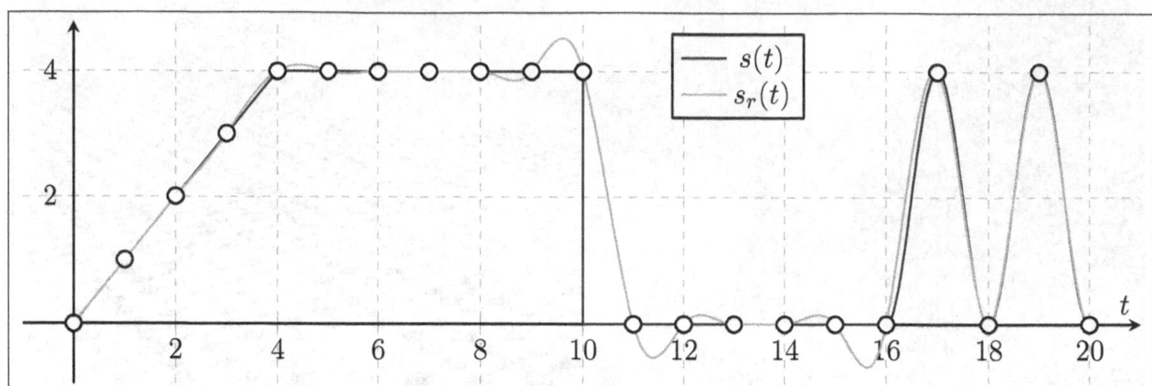

Figure 5.26: Extended Cubic Reconstruction: Illustration of a reconstructed signal using an extended piecewise-cubic interpolation kernel.

131 **Normalization and Sampling** Defining the *probability density* as being proportional to the absolute value of the filter yields

$$\begin{aligned} p(t) &\triangleq \frac{|f_n(t)|}{\int_{-\infty}^{+\infty}|f_n(t)|\mathrm{d}t} \\ &= \frac{|f_n(t)|}{2\left(\left|\int_0^1 f_n(t)\mathrm{d}t\right| + \sum_{i=1}^{n-1}\left|\int_i^{i+1} f_n(t)\mathrm{d}t\right| + \left|\int_n^{n+1} f_n(t)\mathrm{d}t\right|\right)} \end{aligned}$$

216 (5.228)

217 (5.230)

217 (5.232)

$$\begin{aligned} &\overset{(5.228)}{\underset{(5.232)}{\overset{(5.230)}{=}}} \frac{|f_n(t)|}{2\left(\left|\frac{1}{2} - m_1\frac{1}{12}\right| + \sum_{i=1}^{n-1}\left|m_i\frac{1}{12} - m_{i+1}\frac{1}{12}\right| + \left|m_n\frac{1}{12}\right|\right)} && (5.226) \\ &= \frac{6|f_n(t)|}{|6 - m_1| + \sum_{i=1}^{n-1}|m_i - m_{i+1}| + |m_n|} \\ &= \frac{3|f_n(t)|}{3 + \sum_{i=1}^{n}|m_i|} && (5.227) \end{aligned}$$

where the PMF of sampling each subinterval is readily defined by the absolute value of the definite integrals over those intervals.

132 The *cumulative distribution* of the *separable filter* over the sub-domain $[0, t_s]$ then reads
203
213

$$\begin{aligned} \frac{12}{6 - m_1}\int_0^{t_s} f_n(t)\mathrm{d}t &\overset{(5.221)}{=} \frac{12}{6 - m_1}\int_0^{t_s}(2 + m_1)|t|^3 - (3 + m_1)|t|^2 + 1\mathrm{d}t \\ &= \frac{12}{6 - m_1}\left[\frac{2 + m_1}{4}t^4 - \frac{3 + m_1}{3}t^3 + t\right]_0^{t_s} \\ &= \frac{(6 + 3m_1)t_s^4 - (12 + 4m_1)t_s^3 + 12t_s}{6 - m_1} && (5.228) \end{aligned}$$

and carrying the integral over the whole domain by substituting $t_s = 1$ then ensures normal-
134 ization, while applying *inverse-transform sampling* allows *importance sampling* to be readily
155 carried as

$$\begin{aligned} \xi &= \frac{(6 + 3m_1)t_s^4 - (12 + 4m_1)t_s^3 + 12t_s}{6 - m_1} \\ &\implies (6 + 3m_1)t_s^4 - (12 + 4m_1)t_s^3 + 12t_s - (6 - m_1)\xi = 0 && (5.229) \end{aligned}$$

where the sample coordinate $t_s \in [0, 1]$ is the second solution of the resulting *quartic equation.* 33

Instead, the *cumulative distribution* of the *separable filter* over the sub-domain $[i, t_s]$ 132
reads 203

$$\begin{aligned}
\frac{12}{m_i - m_{i+1}} \int_0^{\tau_s} f_n(\tau + i)\mathrm{d}\tau &\overset{(5.221)}{=} \frac{12}{m_i - m_{i+1}} \int_0^{\tau_s} (m_i + m_{i+1})\tau^3 - (2m_i + m_{i+1})\tau^2 + m_i\tau \mathrm{d}\tau \\
&= \frac{12}{m_i - m_{i+1}} \left[\frac{m_i + m_{i+1}}{4}\tau^4 - \frac{2m_i + m_{i+1}}{3}\tau^3 + \frac{m_i}{2}\tau^2 \right]_0^{\tau_s} \\
&= \frac{3(m_i + m_{i+1})\tau_s^4 - (8m_i + 4m_{i+1})\tau_s^3 + 6m_i\tau_s^2}{m_i - m_{i+1}} \qquad (5.230)
\end{aligned}$$
213

with the change of variable $\tau \triangleq |t| - i$, and carrying the integral over the whole domain by
substituting $t_s = i+1$ then ensures normalization, while applying *inverse-transform sampling* 134
allows *importance sampling* to be readily carried as 155

$$\begin{aligned}
\xi &= \frac{3(m_i + m_{i+1})\tau_s^4 - (8m_i + 4m_{i+1})\tau_s^3 + 6m_i\tau_s^2}{m_i - m_{i+1}} \\
&\implies 3(m_i + m_{i+1})\tau_s^4 - (8m_i + 4m_{i+1})\tau_s^3 + 6m_i\tau_s^2 - (m_i - m_{i+1})\xi = 0 \qquad (5.231)
\end{aligned}$$

where the sample coordinate $t_s = i + \tau_s \in [i, i + 1]$ is given by the second solution of the
resulting *quartic equation.* 33

Finally, the *cumulative distribution* of the *separable filter* over the sub-domain $[n, t_s]$ 132
reads 203

$$\begin{aligned}
\frac{12}{m_n} \int_0^{\tau_s} f_n(\tau + n)\mathrm{d}\tau &\overset{(5.221)}{=} \frac{12}{m_n} \int_0^{\tau_s} m_n(\tau^3 - 2\tau^2 + \tau)\mathrm{d}\tau \\
&= 12 \left[\frac{\tau^4}{4} - \frac{2}{3}\tau^3 + \frac{\tau^2}{2} \right]_0^{\tau_s} \\
&= 3\tau_s^4 - 8\tau_s^3 + 6\tau_s^2 \qquad (5.232)
\end{aligned}$$
213

with the change of variable $\tau \triangleq |t| - n$, and carrying the integral over the whole domain by substituting $t_s = n + 1$ then ensures normalization, while applying *inverse-transform*
sampling allows *importance sampling* to be readily carried as 134 155

$$\xi = 3\tau_s^4 - 8\tau_s^3 + 6\tau_s^2 \implies 3\tau_s^4 - 8\tau_s^3 + 6\tau_s^2 - \xi = 0 \qquad (5.233)$$

where the sample coordinate $t_s = n + \tau_s \in [n, n + 1]$ is given by the second solution of the
resulting *quartic equation.* 33

5.4.2.7 *Sinc Filter*

Definition The *sinc filter* is a time-domain kernel defined in terms of the normalized *sinc*
function as 52

$$f(t) \triangleq \mathrm{sinc}(\pi t) \qquad (5.234)$$

whose spectral response is a *rectangular function* 46

184

$$F(\nu) \overset{(5.75)}{=} \sqcap(\nu) \qquad (5.235)$$

The functions $f(t-i), \forall i \in \mathbb{Z}$ actually form an orthonormal basis, as well as a partition of unity by means of the periodic summation

52

$$\sum_{i=-\infty}^{+\infty} f(t-i) \overset{(2.252)}{=} 1, \quad \forall t \in \mathbb{R} \tag{5.236}$$

and the corresponding reconstruction scheme is known as *Whittaker–Shannon interpolation*.

From a theoretical standpoint, optimal anti-aliasing entails band-limiting the original signal by eliminating all content in the band of frequencies above the Nyquist frequency while preserving all content in the band of frequencies below it. Similarly, optimal reconstruction entails isolating the spectral response of the filtered signal from the periodic spectrum by eliminating all frequency content above the Nyquist frequency while leaving its lower frequency content unaffected. The sinc filter is therefore a mathematically ideal low-pass and reconstruction filter.

176 In practice, though, *convolution* with a sinc filter entails carrying an integral over an infinite domain, and the negative lobes of the kernel may introduce negative values in an originally non-negative signal as well as *overshoots* in the reconstruction process. As illustrated
218 in *Figure 5.27*, the oscillatory nature of the ripples additionally induces *ringing artifacts*,
176 canonically depicted as the step response of the filter whose *convolution* with a *Heaviside*
42 *step function* yields a sine-integral function, or by truncating the *Fourier series* of a periodic
184 square wave, both cases exhibiting the *Gibbs phenomenon* whereby a higher cutoff frequency decreases the period of the oscillations but not their amplitude. In compressed digital audio signals, the oscillations similarly manifest themselves as echoes both before (so-called pre-echo) and after (though generally masked by the causing transient) transients such as impulses from percussions.

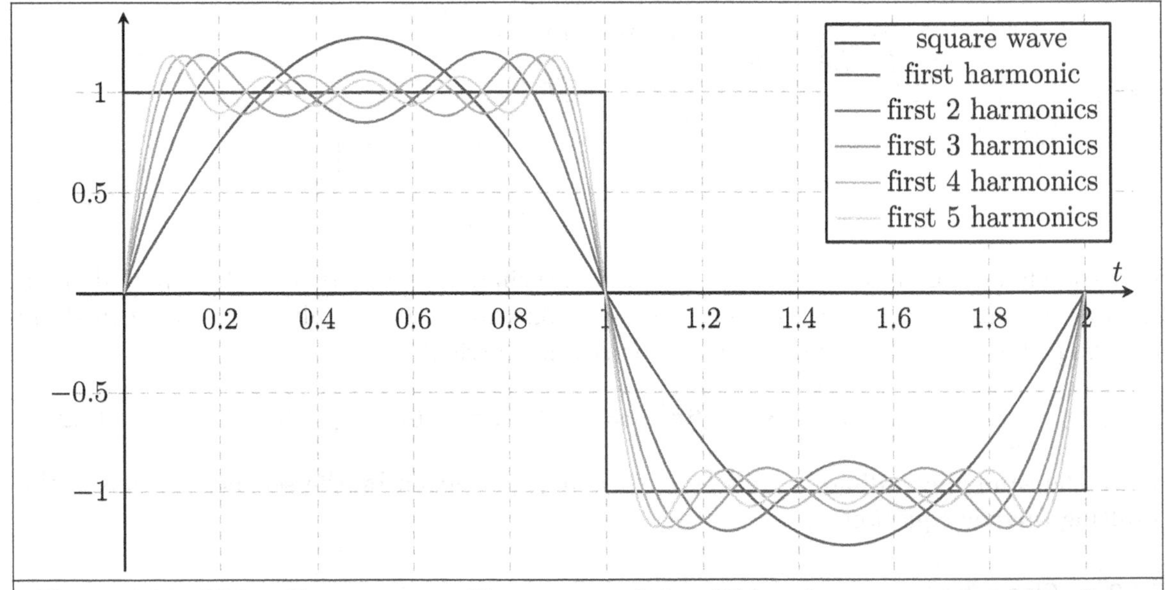

Figure 5.27: Gibbs Phenomenon: Illustration of the Gibbs phenomenon resulting from applying a low-pass filter with various band-limits to a periodic square wave.

203 **Normalization and Sampling** The integral of the *separable filter* over the sub-domain $[0, t_s]$
58 is given in terms of the *sine integral* function as

52
58
58

$$2\int_0^{t_s} \operatorname{sinc}(\pi t)\mathrm{d}t \overset{(2.252)}{=} 2\int_0^{t_s} \frac{\sin(\pi t)}{\pi t}\mathrm{d}t \overset{(2.298)}{=} 2\left[\frac{\operatorname{Si}(\pi t)}{\pi}\right]_0^{t_s} \overset{(2.299)}{=} \frac{2}{\pi}\operatorname{Si}(\pi t_s) \tag{5.237}$$

and carrying the integral over the whole domain by substituting $t_s = \infty$ then ensures normalization.

Similarly, the integral of the *radial filter* over the sub-domain $[0, \rho_s]$ reads 204

$$\int_0^{\rho_s} \frac{1}{c} \operatorname{sinc}(\pi\rho)\rho \mathrm{d}\rho \overset{(2.252)}{=} \frac{1}{c} \int_0^{\rho_s} \frac{\sin(\pi\rho)}{\pi\rho} \rho \mathrm{d}\rho = \frac{1}{c} \left[-\frac{\cos(\pi\rho)}{\pi^2} \right]_0^{\rho_s} = \frac{1 - \cos(\pi\rho_s)}{c\pi^2} \tag{5.238}$$ 52

and carrying the integral over the whole domain by substituting $\rho_s = \infty$ then shows that the normalization constant is divergent

$$c \triangleq \lim_{\rho_s \to \infty} \frac{1 - \cos(\pi\rho_s)}{\pi^2} \tag{5.239}$$

as the inverse *Fourier transform* of a radially symmetric frequency-domain *rectangular func-* 178
tion is defined by the *jinc function* instead. 46 52

5.4.2.8 Lanczos Filter

Definition As illustrated in *Figure 5.28*, the *Lanczos filter* is a time-domain kernel defined in 219
terms of a normalized *sinc function* windowed by the central lobe of a dilated *sinc function*, 52
so-called *Lanczos window*, as 52

$$f_n(t) \triangleq \begin{cases} \operatorname{sinc}(\pi t) \operatorname{sinc}\left(\frac{\pi}{n} t\right) & \text{if } |t| < n \in \mathbb{N}^* \\ 0 & \text{otherwise} \end{cases} \tag{5.240}$$

whose spectral response is a *rectangular function* convolved with the frequency response of 46
the window.

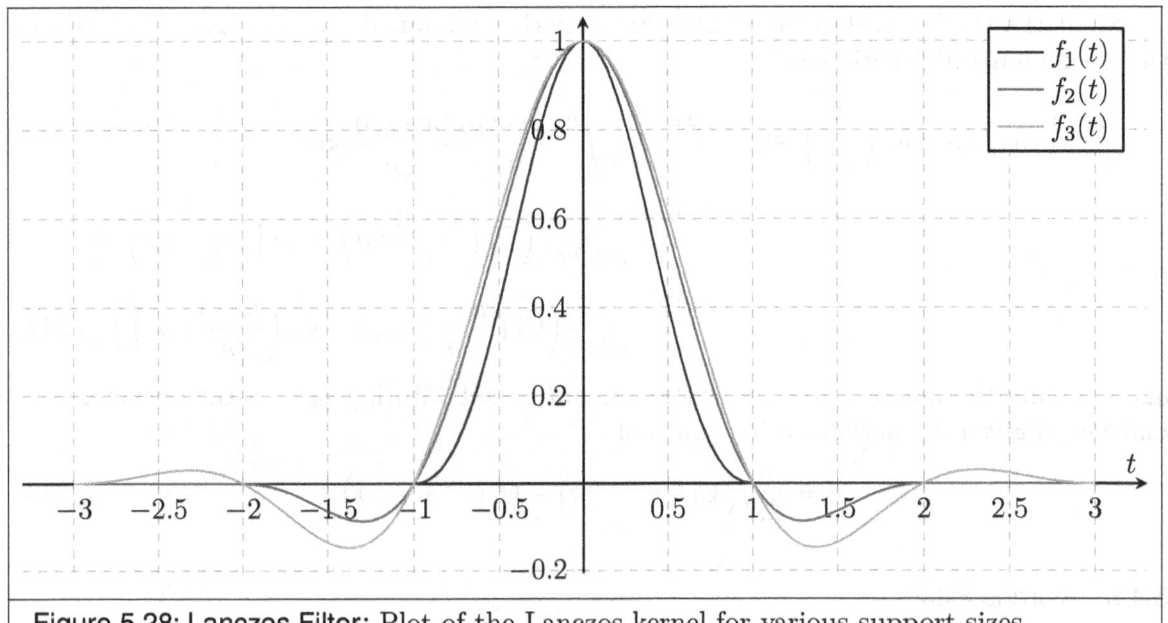

Figure 5.28: Lanczos Filter: Plot of the Lanczos kernel for various support sizes.

The corresponding reconstruction scheme illustrated in *Figure 5.29* is known as *Lanczos* 220
interpolation.

Normalization and Sampling The integral of the *separable filter* over the sub-domain $[0, t_s]$ 203
is given in terms of the *sine integral* function as 58

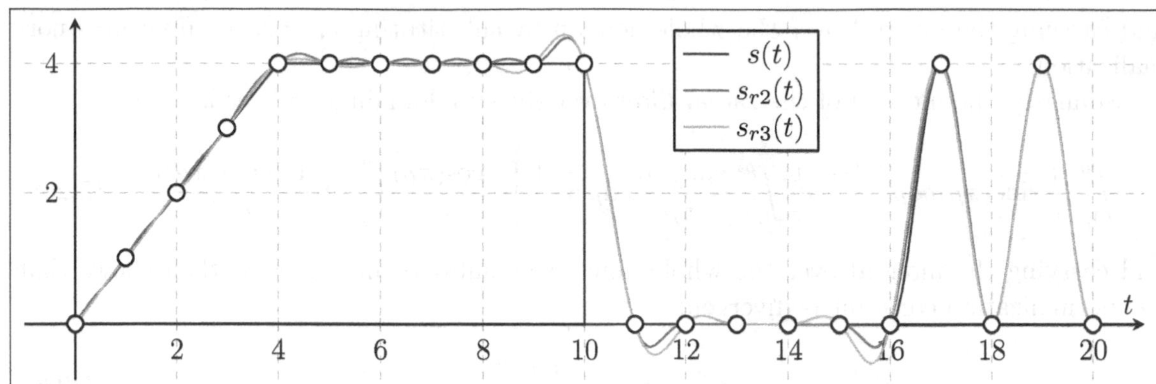

Figure 5.29: Lanczos Reconstruction: Illustration of a reconstructed signal using a Lanczos interpolation kernel with various support sizes.

$$2\int_0^{t_s} \operatorname{sinc}(\pi t)\operatorname{sinc}\left(\frac{\pi}{n}t\right)\mathrm{d}t$$

52 $$\stackrel{(2.252)}{=} 2\int_0^{t_s} \frac{\sin(\pi t)}{\pi t}\frac{\sin\left(\frac{\pi}{n}t\right)}{\frac{\pi}{n}t}\mathrm{d}t$$

58 $$\stackrel{(2.298)}{=} 2\left[\frac{n+1}{2\pi}\operatorname{Si}\left(\frac{n+1}{n}\pi t\right) - \frac{n-1}{2\pi}\operatorname{Si}\left(\frac{n-1}{n}\pi t\right) - t\operatorname{sinc}(\pi t)\operatorname{sinc}\left(\frac{\pi}{n}t\right)\right]_0^{t_s}$$

58 $$\stackrel{(2.299)}{=} \frac{n+1}{\pi}\operatorname{Si}\left(\frac{n+1}{n}\pi t_s\right) - \frac{n-1}{\pi}\operatorname{Si}\left(\frac{n-1}{n}\pi t_s\right) - 2t_s\operatorname{sinc}(\pi t_s)\operatorname{sinc}\left(\frac{\pi}{n}t_s\right) \quad (5.241)$$

and carrying the integral over the whole domain by substituting $t_s = n$ then ensures normalization as $n \to \infty$.

204 Similarly, the integral of the *radial filter* over the sub-domain $[0, \rho_s]$ is given in terms of
58 the *cosine integral* function as

52 $$\int_0^{\rho_s} \frac{1}{c}\operatorname{sinc}(\pi\rho)\operatorname{sinc}\left(\frac{\pi}{n}\rho\right)\rho\mathrm{d}\rho \stackrel{(2.252)}{=} \frac{1}{c}\int_0^{\rho_s} \frac{\sin(\pi\rho)}{\pi\rho}\frac{\sin\left(\frac{\pi}{n}\rho\right)}{\frac{\pi}{n}\rho}\rho\mathrm{d}\rho$$

58 $$\stackrel{(2.292)}{=} \frac{1}{c}\left[\frac{n}{2\pi^2}\left(\operatorname{Ci}\left(\frac{n-1}{n}\pi\rho\right) - \operatorname{Ci}\left(\frac{n+1}{n}\pi\rho\right)\right)\right]_0^{\rho_s}$$

58 $$\stackrel{(2.293)}{=} \frac{n}{c2\pi^2}\left(\operatorname{Ci}\left(\frac{n-1}{n}\pi\rho_s\right) - \operatorname{Ci}\left(\frac{n+1}{n}\pi\rho_s\right)\right) \quad (5.242)$$

and carrying the integral over the whole domain by substituting $\rho_s = n$ then ensures normalization given the normalization constant

$$c \triangleq \frac{n}{2\pi^2}\Big(\operatorname{Ci}\left((n-1)\pi\right) - \operatorname{Ci}\left((n+1)\pi\right)\Big) \quad (5.243)$$

5.4.3 Blurring Filter

5.4.3.1 Overview

A *blurring filter* is defined as a low-pass filter that takes strictly positive values over its support domain, thereby generally dampening high-frequency content more aggressively.

5.4.3.2 B-Spline Filter

203 **Definition** The *B-spline filter* is a time-domain piecewise *polynomial filter* defined in terms

of a centered uniform *B-spline* as 333

$$f_n(t) \triangleq U_n\left(t + \frac{n+1}{2}\right) \tag{5.244}$$

which corresponds to n successive *convolutions* of the *rectangular function* with itself, and 176
whose spectral response is an exponentiated *sinc function* 46 52

184

$$F(\nu) \overset{(5.74)}{\underset{(5.71)}{=}} \operatorname{sinc}(\pi\nu)^{n+1} \tag{5.245}$$

183

The functions $f_n(t-i), \forall i \in \mathbb{Z}$ actually form a partition of unity $\forall t \in \mathbb{R}$ by translation of the periodic summation

221 335

$$\sum_{i=-n}^{0} f_n\left(t - i - \frac{n+1}{2}\right) \overset{(5.244)}{=} \sum_{i=-n}^{0} U_n(t-i) \overset{(8.109)}{\underset{(8.108)}{=}} 1, \quad \forall t \in [0,1] \tag{5.246}$$

334

As illustrated in *Figure 5.30*, the instance of order 0 actually corresponds to the one- 222
piecewise constant *box filter* 204

221

$$f_0(t) \overset{(5.244)}{\underset{(8.115)}{=}} \begin{cases} 1 & \text{if } |t| \in [0, 1/2] \\ 0 & \text{otherwise} \end{cases} \tag{5.247}$$

337

and the first order to the two-piecewise linear *tent filter* 206

221

$$f_1(t) \overset{(5.244)}{\underset{(8.116)}{=}} \begin{cases} 1 - |t| & \text{if } |t| \in [0, 1] \\ 0 & \text{otherwise} \end{cases} \tag{5.248}$$

337

The second-order instance is then given as a C1-continuous three-piecewise quadratic filter of the form

221

$$f_2(t) \overset{(5.244)}{\underset{(8.120)}{=}} \begin{cases} -|t|^2 + 3/4 & \text{if } |t| \in [0, 1/2] \\ 1/2|t|^2 - 3/2|t| + 9/8 & \text{if } |t| \in [1/2, 3/2] \\ 0 & \text{otherwise} \end{cases} \tag{5.249}$$

337

with the anti-aliasing properties illustrated in *Figure 5.31*, and the third order as the four- 222
piecewise cubic polynomial

221

$$f_3(t) \overset{(5.244)}{\underset{(8.121)}{=}} \begin{cases} 1/2|t|^3 - |t|^2 + 2/3 & \text{if } |t| \in [0, 1] \\ -1/6|t|^3 + |t|^2 - 2|t| + 4/3 & \text{if } |t| \in [1, 2] \\ 0 & \text{otherwise} \end{cases} \tag{5.250}$$

337

with the anti-aliasing properties illustrated in *Figure 5.32*. 223

Normalization and Sampling The *cumulative distribution* of the second-order *separable filter* 132
over the sub-domain $[0, t_s]$ reads 203

221

$$3\int_0^{t_s} f_2(t)\mathrm{d}t \overset{(5.249)}{=} 3\int_0^{t_s} -|t|^2 + \frac{3}{4}\mathrm{d}t = 3\left[-\frac{t^3}{3} + \frac{3}{4}t\right]_0^{t_s} = \frac{9}{4}t_s - t_s^3 \tag{5.251}$$

and carrying the integral over the whole domain by substituting $t_s = 1/2$ then ensures normalization, while applying *inverse-transform sampling* allows *importance sampling* to be readily 134 155

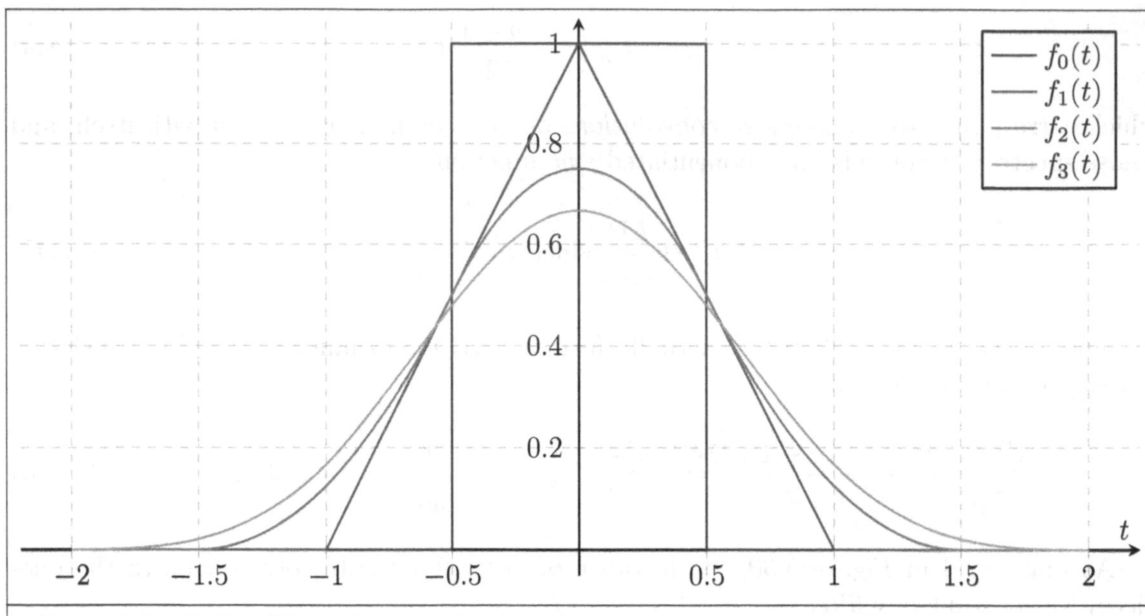

Figure 5.30: Spline Filter: Plot of the first few orders of the spline filter.

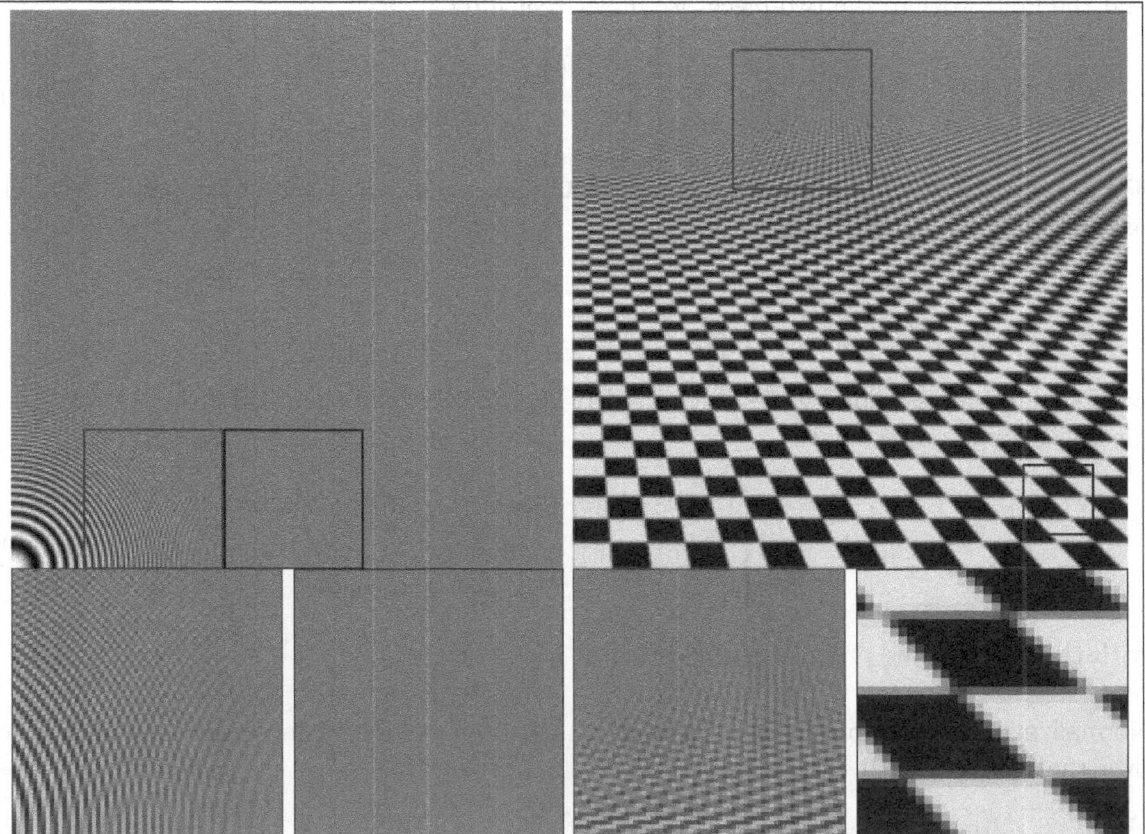

Figure 5.31: Second-Order Spline Anti-Aliasing: Illustration of the anti-aliasing properties of the second-order spline filter.

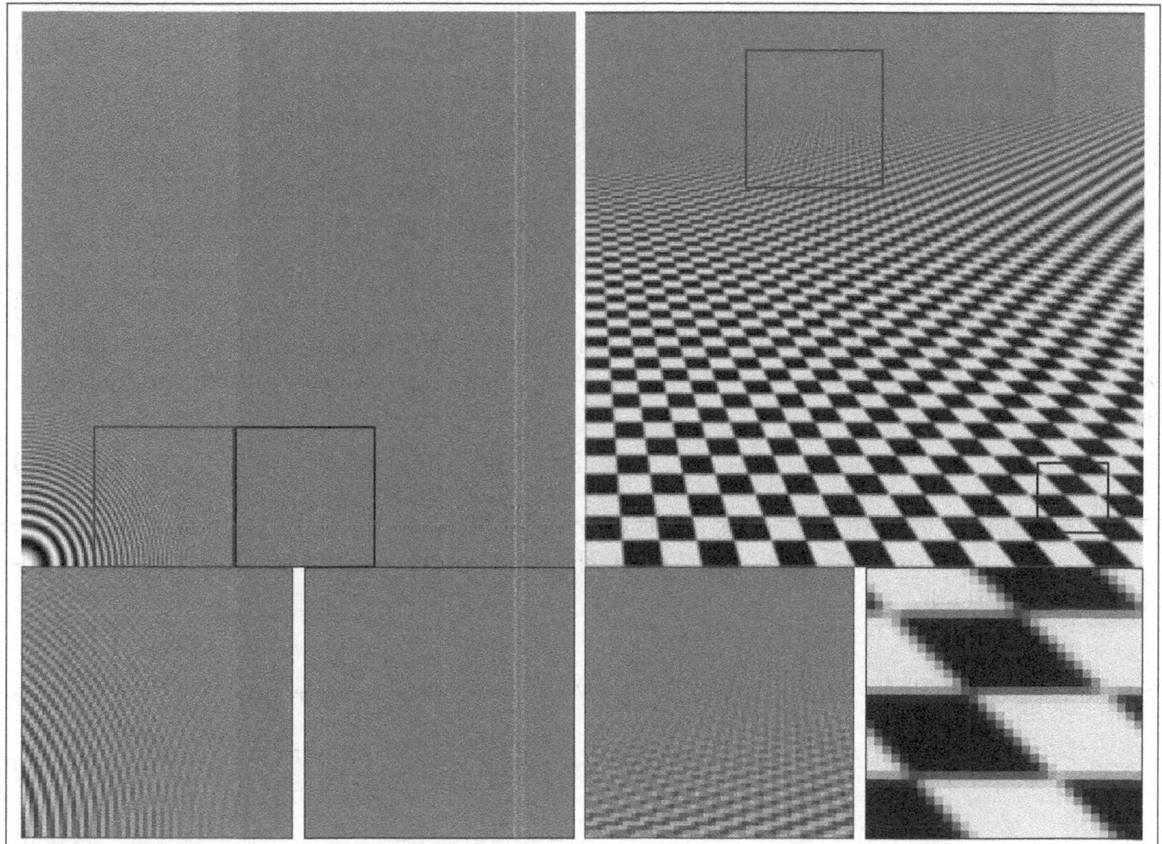

Figure 5.32: Third-Order Spline Anti-Aliasing: Illustration of the anti-aliasing properties of the third-order spline filter.

carried as

$$\xi = \frac{9}{4}t_s - t_s^3 \implies 4t_s^3 - 9t_s + 4\xi = 0 \tag{5.252}$$

where the sample coordinate $t_s \in [0, 1/2]$ is the third solution of the resulting depressed *cubic*
equation with discriminant 29

31

$$\Delta \overset{(2.119)}{=} \frac{\xi^2}{9} - \frac{3}{16} = \frac{16\xi^2 - 27}{144} < 0, \quad \forall \xi \in [0, 1] \tag{5.253}$$

Instead, the *cumulative distribution* of the second-order *separable filter* over the sub- 132
domain $[1/2, t_s]$ reads 203

221

$$6\int_0^{\tau_s} f_2(\tau + 1/2)\mathrm{d}\tau \overset{(5.249)}{=} 6\int_0^{\tau_s} \frac{\tau^2}{2} - \tau + \frac{1}{2}\mathrm{d}\tau = 6\left[\frac{\tau^3}{6} - \frac{\tau^2}{2} + \frac{\tau}{2}\right]_0^{\tau_s} = \tau_s^3 - 3\tau_s^2 + 3\tau_s \tag{5.254}$$

with the change of variable $\tau \triangleq |t| - 1/2$, and carrying the integral over the whole domain by
substituting $t_s = 3/2$ then ensures normalization, while applying *inverse-transform sampling* 134
allows *importance sampling* to be readily carried as 155

$$\xi = \tau_s^3 - 3\tau_s^2 + 3\tau_s \implies \tau_s^3 - 3\tau_s^2 + 3\tau_s - \xi = 0 \tag{5.255}$$

where the sample coordinate $t_s = 1/2 + \tau_s \in [1/2, 3/2]$ is given by the unique solution of the
resulting *cubic equation* with discriminant 29

31

$$\Delta \overset{(2.119)}{=} -\frac{1+2\xi}{12} < 0, \quad \forall \xi \in [0,1] \tag{5.256}$$

132 Similarly, the *cumulative distribution* of the third-order *separable filter* over the sub-
203 domain $[0, t_s]$ reads

221

$$\frac{24}{11}\int_0^{t_s} f_3(t)\mathrm{d}t \overset{(5.250)}{=} \frac{24}{11}\int_0^{t_s} \frac{|t|^3}{2} - |t|^2 + \frac{2}{3}\mathrm{d}t = \frac{24}{11}\left[\frac{t^4}{8} - \frac{t^3}{3} + \frac{2}{3}t\right]_0^{t_s} = \frac{3t_s^4 - 8t_s^3 + 16t_s}{11} \tag{5.257}$$

and carrying the integral over the whole domain by substituting $t_s = 1$ then ensures normal-
134 ization, while applying *inverse-transform sampling* allows *importance sampling* to be readily
155 carried as

$$\xi = \frac{3t_s^4 - 8t_s^3 + 16t_s}{11} \implies 3t_s^4 - 8t_s^3 + 16t_s - 11\xi = 0 \tag{5.258}$$

33 where the sample coordinate $t_s \in [0,1]$ is the second solution of the resulting *quartic equation*.
132 Instead, the *cumulative distribution* of the third-order *separable filter* over the sub-
203 domain $[1, t_s]$ reads

221

$$\begin{aligned} 24\int_0^{\tau_s} f_3(\tau+1)\mathrm{d}\tau &\overset{(5.250)}{=} 24\int_0^{\tau_s} -\frac{\tau^3}{6} + \frac{\tau^2}{2} - \frac{\tau}{2} + \frac{1}{6}\mathrm{d}\tau \\ &= 24\left[-\frac{\tau^4}{24} + \frac{\tau^3}{6} - \frac{\tau^2}{4} + \frac{\tau}{6}\right]_0^{\tau_s} \\ &= -\tau_s^4 + 4\tau_s^3 - 6\tau_s^2 + 4\tau_s \end{aligned} \tag{5.259}$$

with the change of variable $\tau \triangleq |t| - 1$, and carrying the integral over the whole domain by
134 substituting $t_s = 2$ then ensures normalization, while applying *inverse-transform sampling*
155 allows *importance sampling* to be readily carried as

$$\xi = -\tau_s^4 + 4\tau_s^3 - 6\tau_s^2 + 4\tau_s \implies \tau_s^4 - 4\tau_s^3 + 6\tau_s^2 - 4\tau_s + \xi = 0 \tag{5.260}$$

where the sample coordinate $t_s = 1 + \tau_s \in [1,2]$ is given by the first solution of the resulting
33 *quartic equation*.

5.4.3.3 Gaussian Filter

51 **Definition** The *Gaussian filter* is a time-domain kernel defined in terms of a *Gaussian* as

$$f(t) \triangleq G(\sqrt{\pi}t) \tag{5.261}$$

51 whose spectral response is also a *Gaussian*

184

$$F(\nu) \overset{(5.78)}{=} G(\sqrt{\pi}\nu) \tag{5.262}$$

225 with the anti-aliasing properties illustrated in *Figure 5.33*.

132 **Normalization and Sampling** The *cumulative distribution* of the *separable filter* over the
203 sub-domain $[0, t_s]$ is given in terms of the *error function* function as
55

51
55

$$2\int_0^{t_s} G(\sqrt{\pi}t)\mathrm{d}t \overset{(2.247)}{=} 2\int_0^{t_s} e^{-\pi t^2}\mathrm{d}t \overset{(2.270)}{=} 2\left[\frac{\mathrm{erf}(\sqrt{\pi}t)}{2}\right]_0^{t_s} = \mathrm{erf}(\sqrt{\pi}t_s) \tag{5.263}$$

Figure 5.33: Gaussian Anti-Aliasing: Illustration of the anti-aliasing properties of the Gaussian filter.

and carrying the integral over the whole domain by substituting $t_s = \infty$ then ensures normalization, while applying *inverse-transform sampling* allows *importance sampling* to be readily 134
carried as 155

$$\xi = \operatorname{erf}(\sqrt{\pi} t_s) \implies t_s = \frac{\operatorname{erf}^{-1}(\xi)}{\sqrt{\pi}} \tag{5.264}$$

Similarly, the *cumulative distribution* of the *radial filter* over the sub-domain $[0, \rho_s]$ reads 132
204

51

$$\int_0^{\rho_s} 2\pi G(\sqrt{\pi}\rho)\rho \mathrm{d}\rho \overset{(2.247)}{=} 2\pi \int_0^{\rho_s} e^{-\pi\rho^2}\rho \mathrm{d}\rho = 2\pi \left[-\frac{e^{-\pi\rho^2}}{2\pi}\right]_0^{\rho_s} = 1 - e^{-\pi\rho_s^2} \tag{5.265}$$

and carrying the integral over the whole domain by substituting $\rho_s = \infty$ then ensures normalization, while applying *inverse-transform sampling* allows *importance sampling* to be readily 134
carried as 155

$$\xi = 1 - e^{-\pi\rho_s^2} \implies \rho_s = \sqrt{-\frac{\ln(1-\xi)}{\pi}} \tag{5.266}$$

Due to the multiplicative property of *Gaussians*, the two-dimensional *separable filter* and 51
radial filter are actually identical with *Fourier transform* 203
204
178

$$G(\sqrt{\pi}r) \underset{\mathcal{F}^{-1}}{\overset{\mathcal{F}}{\rightleftharpoons}} G(\sqrt{\pi}\rho) \tag{5.267}$$

such that the distinction between the two representations merely provides two different means of sampling the same distribution.

5.4.4 Composite Filter

5.4.4.1 Overview

Definition More complex filters may be modeled as an affine combination of simpler filters

$$f(t) \triangleq \sum_{j=1}^{n} w_j f_j(t) \tag{5.268}$$

with weights $\sum_{j=1}^{n} w_j = 1$.

Whenever the property holds for each of the individual base filters, the functions $f(t-i), \forall i \in \mathbb{Z}$ actually form a partition of unity

226

$$\sum_{i=-\infty}^{+\infty} f(t-i) \overset{(5.268)}{=} \sum_{i=-\infty}^{+\infty} \sum_{j=1}^{n} w_j f_j(t-i) = \sum_{j=1}^{n} w_j \cancel{\sum_{i=-\infty}^{+\infty} f_j(t-i)} = \sum_{j=1}^{n} w_j = 1, \quad \forall t \in \mathbb{R} \tag{5.269}$$

131 **Normalization and Sampling** Defining the *probability density* as an affine combination of the associated PDFs

$$p(t) \triangleq \sum_{j=1}^{n} w_j p_j(t) \tag{5.270}$$

132 the *cumulative distribution* may be expressed as

$$\int_{-\infty}^{t_s} p(t)\mathrm{d}t = \int_{-\infty}^{t_s} \sum_{j=1}^{n} w_j p_j(t)\mathrm{d}t = \sum_{j=1}^{n} w_j \int_{-\infty}^{t_s} p_j(t)\mathrm{d}t \tag{5.271}$$

Integrating over the whole domain by substituting $t_s = +\infty$ then ensures normalization

$$\int_{-\infty}^{+\infty} p(t)\mathrm{d}t = \sum_{j=1}^{n} w_j \cancel{\int_{-\infty}^{+\infty} p_j(t)\mathrm{d}t} = \sum_{j=1}^{n} w_j = 1 \tag{5.272}$$

while drawing random samples from the mixture of distributions may be readily carried by
155 means of mixture *importance sampling*.

5.4.4.2 Dodgson Filter

227 **Definition** As illustrated in *Figure 5.34*, the *Dodgson filter* [Dodgson, 1992, Dodgson, 1997]
203 is a time-domain piecewise quadratic *polynomial filter* defined as the convex combination of
208 220 the *quadratic filter* and the second-order *B-spline filter*

208 221

$$\begin{aligned} f(t) &\overset{(5.207)}{\underset{(5.249)}{=}} \begin{cases} \alpha(-2|t|^2+1)+(1-\alpha)(-|t|^2+3/4) & \text{if } |t| \in [0, 1/2] \\ \alpha(|t|^2-5/2|t|+3/2)+(1-\alpha)(1/2|t|^2-3/2|t|+9/8) & \text{if } |t| \in [1/2, 3/2] \\ 0 & \text{otherwise} \end{cases} \\ &= \begin{cases} -(\alpha+1)|t|^2+\frac{\alpha+3}{4} & \text{if } |t| \in [0, 1/2] \\ \frac{\alpha+1}{2}|t|^2-(\alpha+\frac{3}{2})|t|+\frac{3\alpha+9}{8} & \text{if } |t| \in [1/2, 3/2] \\ 0 & \text{otherwise} \end{cases} \end{aligned} \tag{5.273}$$

$$= \begin{cases} -2r|t|^2+\frac{r+1}{2} & \text{if } |t| \in [0, 1/2] \\ r|t|^2-\left(2r+\frac{1}{2}\right)|t|+\frac{3}{4}(r+1) & \text{if } |t| \in [1/2, 3/2] \\ 0 & \text{otherwise} \end{cases} \tag{5.274}$$

with $r \triangleq \frac{\alpha+1}{2}$ and the fixed point $f(\pm^1\!/_2) = {}^1\!/_2$, and with the anti-aliasing properties illustrated in *Figure 5.35*. Setting $\alpha = 1$ or $r = 1$ then yields the *quadratic filter*, and setting 227
$\alpha = 0$ or $r = {}^1\!/_2$ yields the second-order *B-spline filter*, while setting $\alpha \approx {}^3\!/_5$ or $r \approx {}^4\!/_5$ 208
provides an adequate trade-off between ringing and blurring artifacts. 220

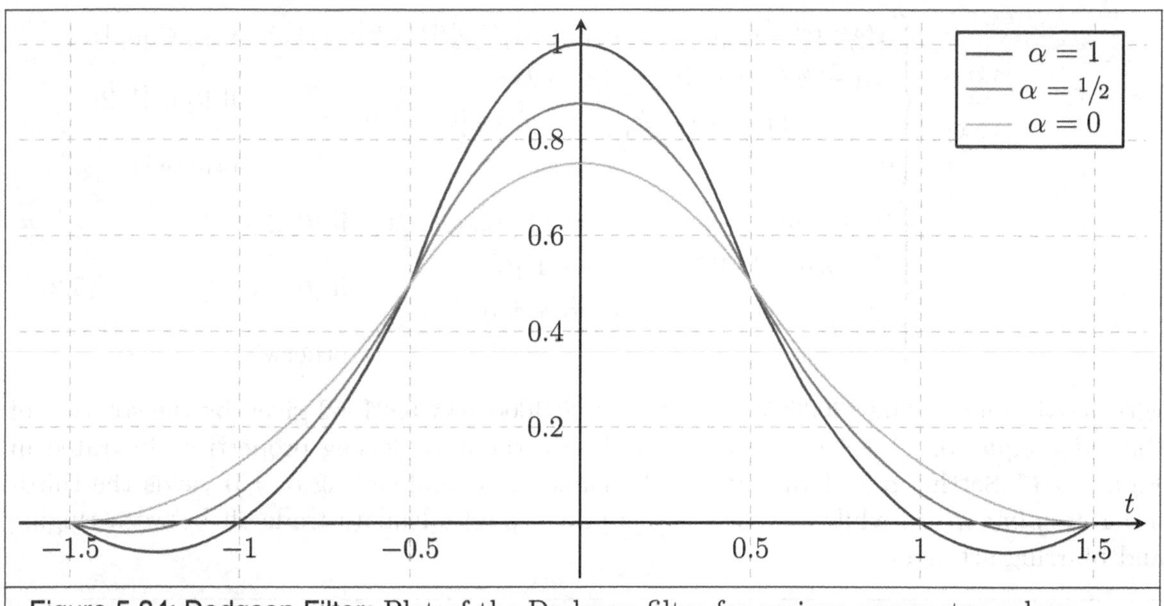

Figure 5.34: Dodgson Filter: Plot of the Dodgson filter for various parameter values.

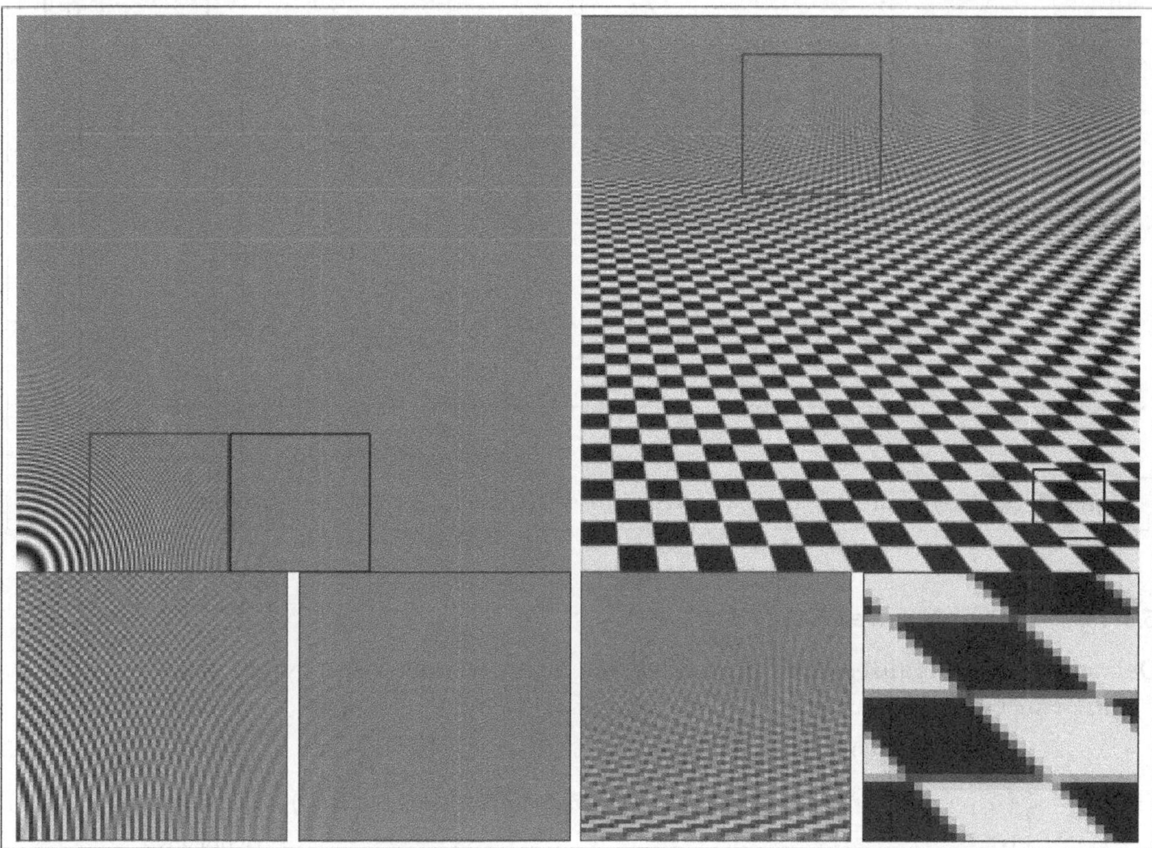

Figure 5.35: Dodgson Anti-Aliasing: Illustration of the anti-aliasing properties of the Dodgson filter.

5.4.4.3 *Keys Filter*

228 **Definition** As illustrated in *Figure 5.36*, the *Keys filter* [Keys, 1981] is a time-domain piece-
203 wise cubic *polynomial filter* defined as the convex combination of the *cubic filter* and the
211 220 third-order *B-spline filter*

211 221

$$f(t) \overset{(5.218)}{\underset{(5.250)}{=}} \begin{cases} \alpha(3/2|t|^3 - 5/2|t|^2 + 1) + (1-\alpha)(1/2|t|^3 - |t|^2 + 2/3) & \text{if } |t| \in [0,1] \\ \alpha(-1/2|t|^3 + 5/2|t|^2 - 4|t| + 2) \\ \quad + (1-\alpha)(-1/6|t|^3 + |t|^2 - 2|t| + 4/3) & \text{if } |t| \in [1,2] \\ 0 & \text{otherwise} \end{cases}$$

$$= \begin{cases} (\alpha + 1/2)|t|^3 - (3/2\alpha + 1)|t|^2 + (1/3\alpha + 2/3) & \text{if } |t| \in [0,1] \\ -(1/3\alpha + 1/6)|t|^3 + (3/2\alpha + 1)|t|^2 \\ \quad - (2\alpha + 2)|t| + (2/3\alpha + 4/3) & \text{if } |t| \in [1,2] \\ 0 & \text{otherwise} \end{cases} \tag{5.275}$$

with fixed point $f(\pm 0.613036856894604\ldots) \approx 0.4060464530221962$ given by the solution of
29 the *cubic equation* $t^3 - 3/2t^2 + 1/3 = 0$, and with the anti-aliasing properties illustrated in
229 *Figure 5.37*. Setting $\alpha = 1$ then yields the *cubic filter*, and setting $\alpha = 0$ yields the third-
211 220 order *B-spline filter*, while setting $\alpha \approx 2/3$ provides an adequate trade-off between ringing and blurring artifacts.

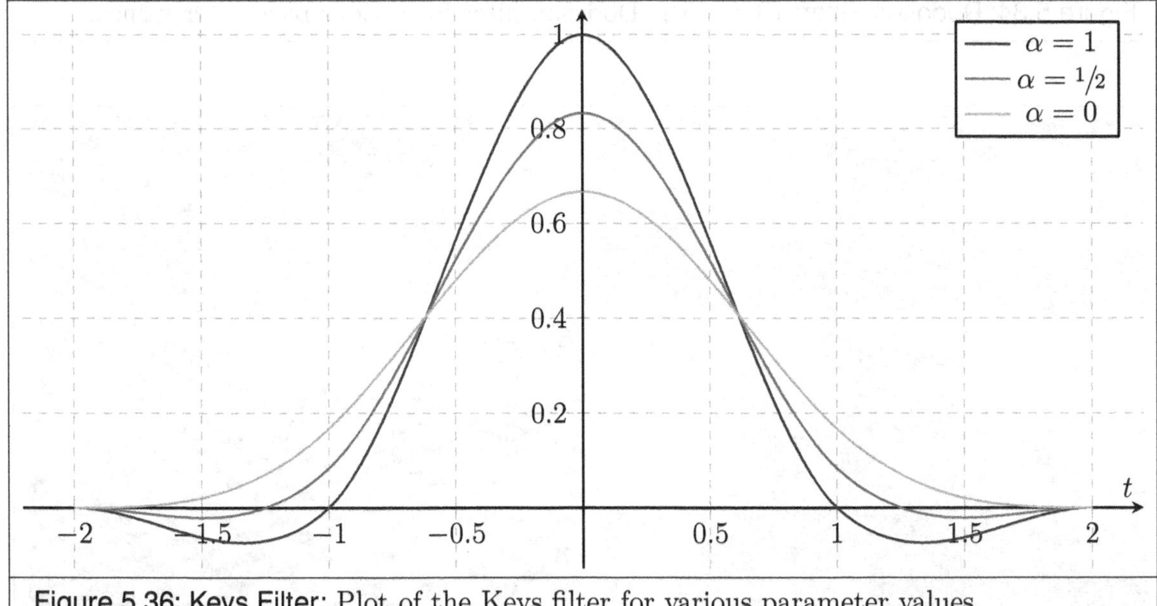

Figure 5.36: Keys Filter: Plot of the Keys filter for various parameter values.

5.4.4.4 *Mitchell–Netravali Filter*

220 **Definition** A generalized third-order *B-spline filter* parameterized by the slope $m_1 - 1/2$ at $t = \pm 1$ can be defined as

$$f_3(t) \triangleq \begin{cases} (1/2 + m_1)|t|^3 - (m_1 + 1)|t|^2 + 2/3 & \text{if } |t| \in [0,1] \\ (m_1 - 1/6)|t|^3 + (1 - 5m_1)|t|^2 + (8m_1 - 2)|t| + (4/3 - 4m_1) & \text{if } |t| \in [1,2] \\ 0 & \text{otherwise} \end{cases} \tag{5.276}$$

with fixed point $f_3(\pm 1) = 1/6$, such that setting $m_1 = 0$ yields the original third-order
220 221 229 *B-spline filter* given in *Equation 5.250*, as illustrated in *Figure 5.38*.

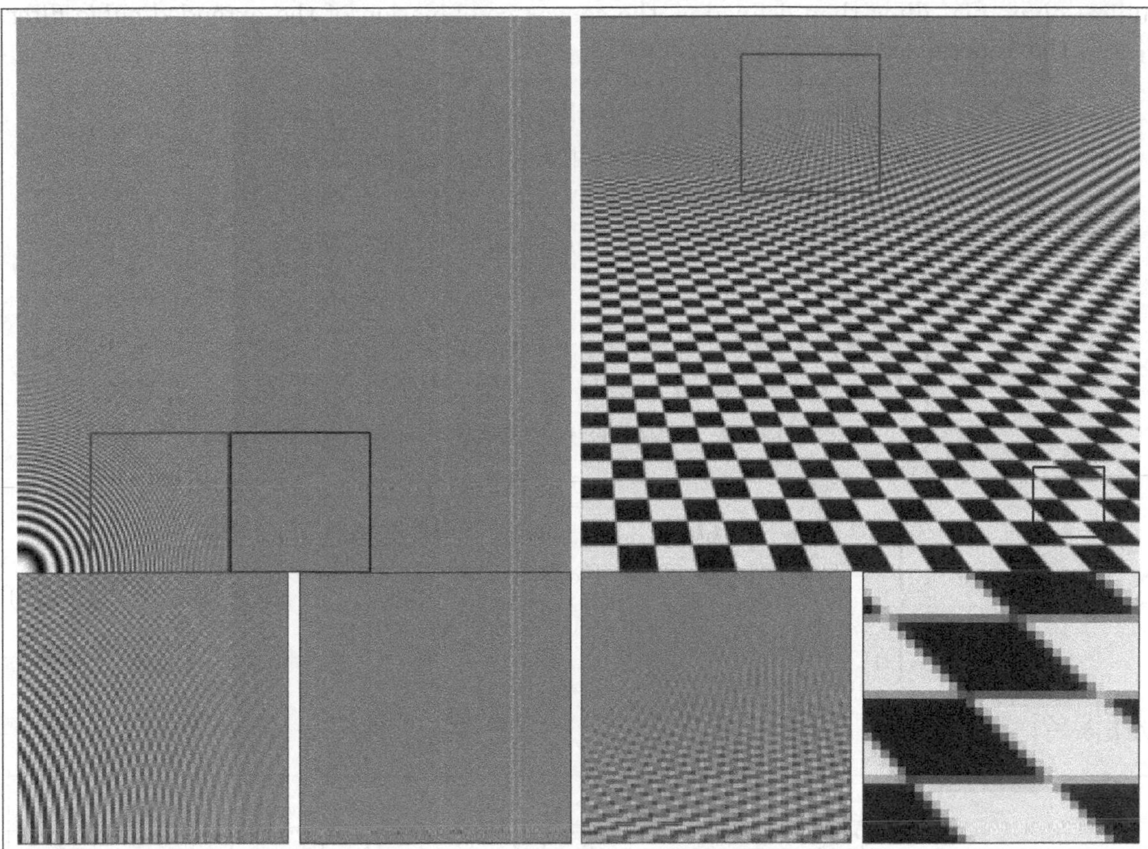

Figure 5.37: Keys Anti-Aliasing: Illustration of the anti-aliasing properties of the Keys filter.

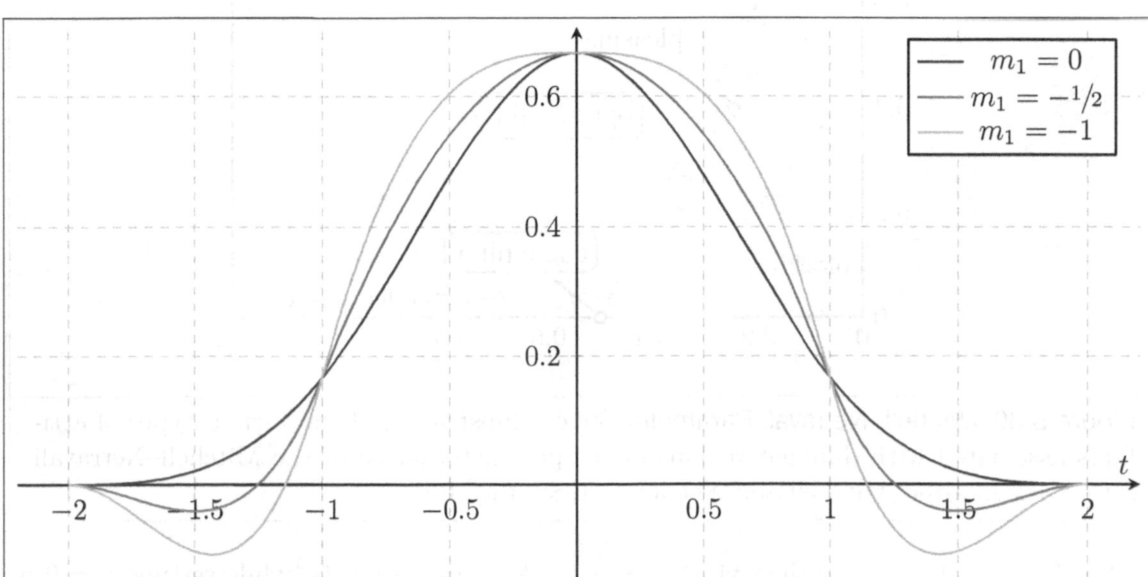

Figure 5.38: Mitchell–Netravali Filter: Plot of the generalized third-order B-spline forming the Mitchell–Netravali filter for various parameter values.

The *Mitchell–Netravali filter* [Mitchell and Netravali, 1988] is a time-domain piecewise
203 213 cubic *polynomial filter* then defined as the convex combination of the *extended cubic filter* f_1 and the generalized third-order B-spline f_3

214 228

$$f(t) \overset{(5.224)}{\underset{(5.276)}{=}} \begin{cases} \alpha((2+m_1)|t|^3 - (3+m_1)|t|^2 + 1) \\ \quad + (1-\alpha)((1/2+m_1)|t|^3 - (m_1+1)|t|^2 + 2/3) & \text{if } |t| \in [0,1] \\ \alpha m_1(|t|^3 - 5|t|^2 + 8|t| - 4) + (1-\alpha)((m_1 - 1/6)|t|^3 \\ \quad + (1-5m_1)|t|^2 + (8m_1 - 2)|t| + (4/3 - 4m_1)) & \text{if } |t| \in [1,2] \\ 0 & \text{otherwise} \end{cases}$$

$$= \begin{cases} (m_1 + 1/2 + 3/2\alpha)|t|^3 - (2\alpha + 1 + m_1)|t|^2 + (2/3 + 1/3\alpha) & \text{if } |t| \in [0,1] \\ (m_1 - 1/6 + 1/6\alpha)|t|^3 + (1 - \alpha - 5m_1)|t|^2 \\ \quad + (8m_1 - 2 + 2\alpha)|t| + (4/3 - 4/3\alpha - 4m_1) & \text{if } |t| \in [1,2] \\ 0 & \text{otherwise} \end{cases}$$

$$= \frac{1}{6} \begin{cases} (12 - 9b - 6c)|t|^3 + (12b + 6c - 18)|t|^2 + (6 - 2b) & \text{if } |t| \in [0,1] \\ -(b + 6c)|t|^3 + (6b + 30c)|t|^2 \\ \quad - (12b + 48c)|t| + (8b + 24c) & \text{if } |t| \in [1,2] \\ 0 & \text{otherwise} \end{cases} \quad (5.277)$$

with $b \triangleq 1 - \alpha$ and $c \triangleq -m_1$.

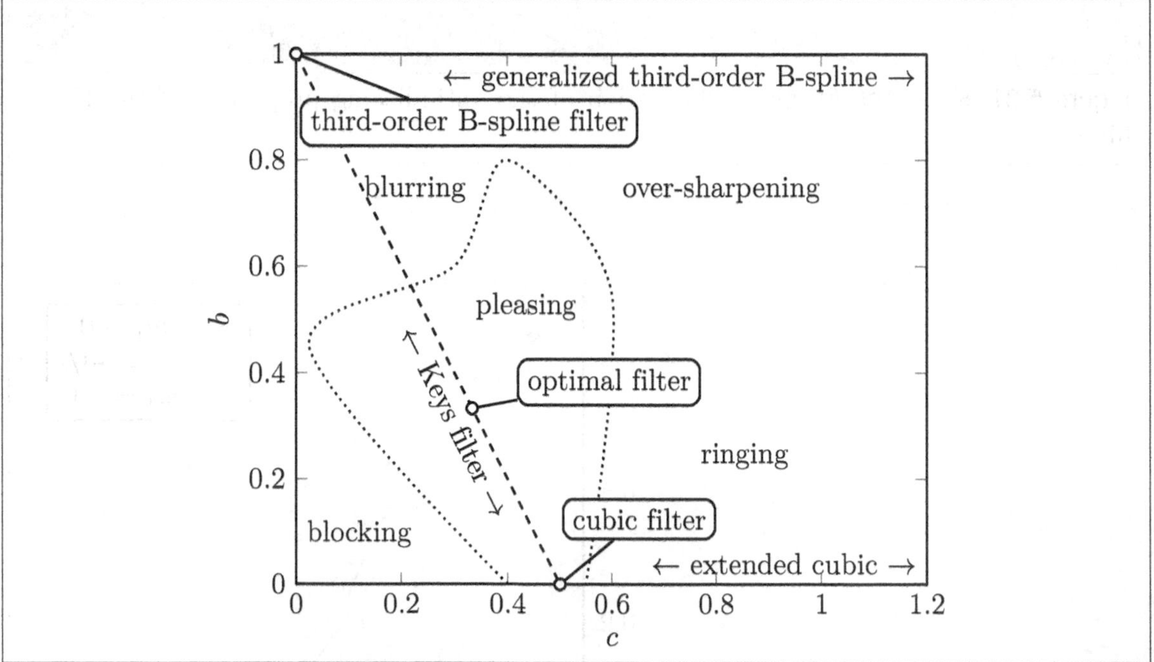

Figure 5.39: Mitchell–Netravali Parameter Space: Illustration of the various types of artifacts associated with different regions of the parameter space of the Mitchell–Netravali filter (drawn after [Mitchell and Netravali, 1988, Fig. 13]).

213 Setting $\alpha = 1$ or $b = 0$ then yields the *extended cubic filter* f_1, while setting $\alpha = 0$ or
220 $b = 1$ and $m_1 = c = 0$ yields the third-order *B-spline filter*. As illustrated in *Figure 5.39*, the
230 228 *Keys filter*, which is described by the line of equation $b + 2c = 1$, has been experimentally
shown (by means of surveyed results from a user study) to provide an adequate trade-off
between the different types of visual artifacts. More specifically, the locus $b = c = 1/3$ (which

corresponds to the *Keys filter* with $\alpha = {}^2\!/\!_3$) is generally agreed to yield the best perceptual 228
compromise and is typically used as the default set of parameters.

Normalization and Sampling The integral of the generalized third-order B-spline reads

228

$$
\begin{aligned}
\int_0^2 f_3(t)\mathrm{d}t \overset{(5.276)}{=} & \int_0^1 ({}^1\!/\!_2 + m_1)t^3 - (m_1+1)t^2 + {}^2\!/\!_3\mathrm{d}t \\
+ & \int_1^2 (m_1 - {}^1\!/\!_6)t^3 + (1-5m_1)t^2 + (8m_1-2)t + ({}^4\!/\!_3 - 4m_1)\mathrm{d}t \\
= & \left[\frac{{}^1\!/\!_2 + m_1}{4}t^4 - \frac{m_1+1}{3}t^3 + \frac{2}{3}t\right]_0^1 \\
+ & \left[\frac{m_1 - {}^1\!/\!_6}{4}t^4 + \frac{1-5m_1}{3}t^3 + \frac{8m_1-2}{2}t^2 + \left(\frac{4}{3} - 4m_1\right)t\right]_1^2 \\
= & \frac{1}{2} \qquad (5.278)
\end{aligned}
$$

which ensures normalization, while defining the *probability density* $p(t) \propto |f_3(t)|$ as being 131
proportional to the absolute value of the filter for *importance sampling* purposes requires 155
partitioning the domain at the root of the *cubic equation* $f_3(t) = 0$ with $t \in [1, 2]$. 29

5.5 FURTHER READING

Additional material may be found in books dedicated to digital image processing [Gonzalez and Woods, 2002, Gonzalez and Woods, 2008] [Pratt, 2001, Pratt, 2006, Pratt, 2013].

II

Geometrical Foundations

CHAPTER 6

Analytic Surfaces

TABLE OF CONTENTS

6.1 SURFACE PROPERTIES

6.1.1 Surface Representation

6.1.1.1 Explicit Form

A surface may be mathematically defined as a height field, expressing one of the coordinates in terms of every pair of the other two coordinates, yielding an *explicit representation* of the form

$$z = f(x, y) \tag{6.1}$$

An *implicit form* can equivalently be obtained by converting the explicit representation 239
to the scalar field

$$f(x, y, z) \triangleq z - f(x, y) \tag{6.2}$$

whose gradient, expressed in terms of the slopes $\frac{\partial f(x,y)}{\partial x}$ and $\frac{\partial f(x,y)}{\partial y}$, yields a field of vectors orthogonal to the surface

$$\nabla f(x, y, z) \overset{(6.20)}{=} \begin{bmatrix} -\frac{\partial f(x,y)}{\partial x} \\ -\frac{\partial f(x,y)}{\partial y} \\ 1 \end{bmatrix} \tag{6.3}$$ 239

Substituting the ray equation $\vec{r}(t) \triangleq \vec{o} + t\vec{d}$, the values of the scalar field along the ray are then defined as

$$f(t) \overset{(6.21)}{=} z_o + tz_d - f(x_o + tx_d, y_o + ty_d) \tag{6.4}$$ 239

and the intersections of the ray with the isosurface $f(x, y, z) = v$ for the given isovalue $v = 0$ are determined by the solutions of the equation $f(t) = v$. Conversely, the silhouette of the surface projected along a direction $\vec{v}$ is the set of points satisfying $\langle \vec{v}, \nabla f(x, y, z) \rangle = 0$, while the point of the surface at which the gradient is collinear with a given vector $\vec{n}$ ought to satisfy

$$\vec{n} \times \nabla f(x, y, z) \overset{(3.88)}{=} \begin{bmatrix} n_y + n_z \frac{\partial f(x,y)}{\partial y} \\ -n_z \frac{\partial f(x,y)}{\partial x} - n_x \\ -n_x \frac{\partial f(x,y)}{\partial y} + n_y \frac{\partial f(x,y)}{\partial x} \end{bmatrix} \overset{(3.93)}{=} \vec{0} \tag{6.5}$$ 78 79

and solving for the slopes in the first two equations

$$\frac{\partial f(x, y)}{\partial x} = -\frac{n_x}{n_z} \tag{6.6}$$

$$\frac{\partial f(x, y)}{\partial y} = -\frac{n_y}{n_z} \tag{6.7}$$

necessarily guarantees that the third equality holds, as can be easily verified by substituting the above expressions.

Alternatively, the explicit representation may instead be converted into a *parametric form* 239
called *Monge patch*

$$\vec{p}(x, y) \triangleq \begin{bmatrix} x \\ y \\ f(x, y) \end{bmatrix} \tag{6.8}$$

whose first partial derivatives

237
$$\frac{\partial \vec{p}(x,y)}{\partial x} \overset{(6.8)}{=} \begin{bmatrix} 1 \\ 0 \\ \frac{\partial f(x,y)}{\partial x} \end{bmatrix} \tag{6.9}$$

237
$$\frac{\partial \vec{p}(x,y)}{\partial y} \overset{(6.8)}{=} \begin{bmatrix} 0 \\ 1 \\ \frac{\partial f(x,y)}{\partial y} \end{bmatrix} \tag{6.10}$$

yield a formulation of the non-unit surface normal expressed in terms of the slopes $\frac{\partial f(x,y)}{\partial x}$ and $\frac{\partial f(x,y)}{\partial y}$

240
78
$$\vec{n}(x,y) \overset{(6.27)}{=} \begin{bmatrix} 1 \\ 0 \\ \frac{\partial f(x,y)}{\partial x} \end{bmatrix} \times \begin{bmatrix} 0 \\ 1 \\ \frac{\partial f(x,y)}{\partial y} \end{bmatrix} \overset{(3.88)}{=} \begin{bmatrix} -\frac{\partial f(x,y)}{\partial x} \\ -\frac{\partial f(x,y)}{\partial y} \\ 1 \end{bmatrix} \tag{6.11}$$

In turn, the second partial derivatives

238
$$\frac{\partial^2 \vec{p}(x,y)}{\partial x^2} \overset{(6.9)}{=} \begin{bmatrix} 0 \\ 0 \\ \frac{\partial^2 f(x,y)}{\partial x^2} \end{bmatrix} \tag{6.12}$$

238
238
$$\frac{\partial^2 \vec{p}(x,y)}{\partial x \partial y} \underset{(6.10)}{\overset{(6.9)}{=}} \begin{bmatrix} 0 \\ 0 \\ \frac{\partial^2 f(x,y)}{\partial x \partial y} \end{bmatrix} \tag{6.13}$$

238
$$\frac{\partial^2 \vec{p}(x,y)}{\partial y^2} \overset{(6.10)}{=} \begin{bmatrix} 0 \\ 0 \\ \frac{\partial^2 f(x,y)}{\partial y^2} \end{bmatrix} \tag{6.14}$$

yield the Gaussian curvature

243
$$K \overset{(6.56)}{=} \frac{\frac{\partial^2 f(x,y)}{\partial x^2}\frac{\partial^2 f(x,y)}{\partial y^2} - \left(\frac{\partial^2 f(x,y)}{\partial x \partial y}\right)^2}{\left(\left(\frac{\partial f(x,y)}{\partial x}\right)^2 + \left(\frac{\partial f(x,y)}{\partial y}\right)^2 + 1\right)^2} \tag{6.15}$$

Equivalently, the Gaussian curvature can also be obtained by considering a composite transformation mapping parametric coordinates $[x, y]$ first to the slopes $[u, v]$ and then to the coordinates $[n_x, n_y]$ of the unit normal vector $\hat{n}$

$$T(x,y) \triangleq \left\{[n_x, n_y] = \left[\frac{-u}{\|\vec{n}(x,y)\|}, \frac{-v}{\|\vec{n}(x,y)\|}\right]\right\} \circ \left\{[u,v] = \left[\frac{\partial f(x,y)}{\partial x}, \frac{\partial f(x,y)}{\partial y}\right]\right\} \tag{6.16}$$

with Jacobian matrix

$$\begin{aligned} J_T &= \begin{bmatrix} \frac{\partial n_x}{\partial u} & \frac{\partial n_y}{\partial u} \\ \frac{\partial n_x}{\partial v} & \frac{\partial n_y}{\partial v} \end{bmatrix} \begin{bmatrix} \frac{\partial u}{\partial x} & \frac{\partial v}{\partial x} \\ \frac{\partial u}{\partial y} & \frac{\partial v}{\partial y} \end{bmatrix} \\ &= \frac{1}{\|\vec{n}(x,y)\|^2} \begin{bmatrix} \frac{u^2}{\|\vec{n}(x,y)\|} - \|\vec{n}(x,y)\| & \frac{uv}{\|\vec{n}(x,y)\|} \\ \frac{uv}{\|\vec{n}(x,y)\|} & \frac{v^2}{\|\vec{n}(x,y)\|} - \|\vec{n}(x,y)\| \end{bmatrix} \begin{bmatrix} \frac{\partial^2 f(x,y)}{\partial x^2} & \frac{\partial^2 f(x,y)}{\partial x \partial y} \\ \frac{\partial^2 f(x,y)}{\partial x \partial y} & \frac{\partial^2 f(x,y)}{\partial y^2} \end{bmatrix} \end{aligned} \tag{6.17}$$

98 whose Jacobian *determinant* reads

238
$$\det(J_T) = \frac{\cancel{\|\vec{n}(x,y)\|^2 - u^2 - v^2}}{\|\vec{n}(x,y)\|^4}\left(\frac{\partial^2 f(x,y)}{\partial x^2}\frac{\partial^2 f(x,y)}{\partial y^2} - \left(\frac{\partial^2 f(x,y)}{\partial x \partial y}\right)^2\right) \overset{(6.15)}{=} K \tag{6.18}$$

6.1.1.2 Implicit Form

As an alternative, a surface may be more generally defined as an *isosurface*, also called *level-set*, i.e., as the set of points at which a scalar field f equals a given *isovalue* v, yielding an *implicit representation* of the form

$$f(x, y, z) = v \tag{6.19}$$

intrinsically defining the interior and exterior volumes of the surface as the sets of points for which the function evaluation is strictly greater or smaller, respectively, than the given isovalue.

The gradient ∇f of such a scalar field then defines a vector field that, at any given point, is always orthogonal to the isosurface defined by the isovalue at that point

$$\nabla f(x, y, z) \overset{(3.114)}{=} \begin{bmatrix} \frac{\partial f(x,y,z)}{\partial x} \\ \frac{\partial f(x,y,z)}{\partial y} \\ \frac{\partial f(x,y,z)}{\partial z} \end{bmatrix} \tag{6.20}$$ 82

Substituting the ray equation $\vec{r}(t) \triangleq \vec{o} + t\vec{d}$, the values of the scalar field along the ray are then defined as

$$f(t) \triangleq f(x_o + tx_d, y_o + ty_d, z_o + tz_d) \tag{6.21}$$

while the gradient of the scalar field along the ray is similarly obtained

$$\nabla f(t) \triangleq \nabla f(x_o + tx_d, y_o + ty_d, z_o + tz_d) \tag{6.22}$$

The intersection of the ray with the implicit surface $f(x, y, z) = v$ defined by the isovalue v can then be determined by solving for the value of t satisfying $f(t) = v$, while a normal vector orthogonal to the isosurface at the intersection point is readily given by $\nabla f(t)$.

Given a vector $\vec{n}$, the points of the field at which the gradient is collinear with $\vec{n}$ conversely ought to satisfy

$$\vec{n} \times \nabla f(x, y, z) \overset{(3.88)}{=} \begin{bmatrix} n_y \frac{\partial f(x,y,z)}{\partial z} - n_z \frac{\partial f(x,y,z)}{\partial y} \\ n_z \frac{\partial f(x,y,z)}{\partial x} - n_x \frac{\partial f(x,y,z)}{\partial z} \\ n_x \frac{\partial f(x,y,z)}{\partial y} - n_y \frac{\partial f(x,y,z)}{\partial x} \end{bmatrix} \overset{(3.93)}{=} \vec{0} \tag{6.23}$$ 78 79

and solving for any two coordinates then guarantees that the equation for the third one also holds.

6.1.1.3 Parametric Form

A surface may also be mathematically defined via a *parametric representation* by expressing the *Cartesian coordinates* of its points $\vec{p} = \vec{p}(u, v)$ in terms of the parametric coordinates 67
$u \in [0, 1]$ and $v \in [0, 1]$

$$\vec{p}(u, v) = \begin{bmatrix} p_x(u, v) \\ p_y(u, v) \\ p_z(u, v) \end{bmatrix} \tag{6.24}$$

whose tangent and bitangent are given by the first partial derivatives

$$\frac{\partial \vec{p}(u, v)}{\partial u} = \begin{bmatrix} \frac{\partial p_x(u,v)}{\partial u} & \frac{\partial p_y(u,v)}{\partial u} & \frac{\partial p_z(u,v)}{\partial u} \end{bmatrix}^T \tag{6.25}$$

$$\frac{\partial \vec{p}(u, v)}{\partial v} = \begin{bmatrix} \frac{\partial p_x(u,v)}{\partial v} & \frac{\partial p_y(u,v)}{\partial v} & \frac{\partial p_z(u,v)}{\partial v} \end{bmatrix}^T \tag{6.26}$$

The cross product of the tangent and bi-tangent then yields the non-unit surface normal

$$\vec{n}(u,v) \triangleq \frac{\partial \vec{p}(u,v)}{\partial u} \times \frac{\partial \vec{p}(u,v)}{\partial v} \tag{6.27}$$

whose partial derivatives can be computed using the extension of the product rule to *cross*
78 *products* of vector functions

$$\begin{aligned}\frac{\partial \vec{n}(u,v)}{\partial u} &= \frac{\partial}{\partial u}\left(\frac{\partial \vec{p}(u,v)}{\partial u} \times \frac{\partial \vec{p}(u,v)}{\partial v}\right)\\ &= \frac{\partial^2 \vec{p}(u,v)}{\partial u^2} \times \frac{\partial \vec{p}(u,v)}{\partial v} + \frac{\partial \vec{p}(u,v)}{\partial u} \times \frac{\partial^2 \vec{p}(u,v)}{\partial u \partial v} \qquad (6.28)\\ \frac{\partial \vec{n}(u,v)}{\partial v} &= \frac{\partial}{\partial v}\left(\frac{\partial \vec{p}(u,v)}{\partial u} \times \frac{\partial \vec{p}(u,v)}{\partial v}\right)\\ &= \frac{\partial^2 \vec{p}(u,v)}{\partial u \partial v} \times \frac{\partial \vec{p}(u,v)}{\partial v} + \frac{\partial \vec{p}(u,v)}{\partial u} \times \frac{\partial^2 \vec{p}(u,v)}{\partial v^2} \qquad (6.29)\end{aligned}$$

while the partial derivatives of its norm are readily given as

$$\begin{aligned}\frac{\partial \|\vec{n}(u,v)\|}{\partial u} &= \frac{\partial \sqrt{\langle \vec{n}(u,v), \vec{n}(u,v)\rangle}}{\partial u} = \frac{\frac{\partial \langle \vec{n}(u,v), \vec{n}(u,v)\rangle}{\partial u}}{2\sqrt{\langle \vec{n}(u,v), \vec{n}(u,v)\rangle}}\\ &= \frac{2\left\langle \frac{\partial \vec{n}(u,v)}{\partial u}, \vec{n}(u,v)\right\rangle}{2\|\vec{n}(u,v)\|} = \left\langle \frac{\partial \vec{n}(u,v)}{\partial u}, \frac{\vec{n}(u,v)}{\|\vec{n}(u,v)\|}\right\rangle \qquad (6.30)\\ \frac{\partial \|\vec{n}(u,v)\|}{\partial v} &= \frac{\partial \sqrt{\langle \vec{n}(u,v), \vec{n}(u,v)\rangle}}{\partial v} = \frac{\frac{\partial \langle \vec{n}(u,v), \vec{n}(u,v)\rangle}{\partial v}}{2\sqrt{\langle \vec{n}(u,v), \vec{n}(u,v)\rangle}}\\ &= \frac{2\left\langle \frac{\partial \vec{n}(u,v)}{\partial v}, \vec{n}(u,v)\right\rangle}{2\|\vec{n}(u,v)\|} = \left\langle \frac{\partial \vec{n}(u,v)}{\partial v}, \frac{\vec{n}(u,v)}{\|\vec{n}(u,v)\|}\right\rangle \qquad (6.31)\end{aligned}$$

In the field of differential geometry, the coefficients of the *first fundamental form*

$$\mathrm{I} \triangleq \begin{bmatrix} \mathrm{d}u \\ \mathrm{d}v \end{bmatrix}^T M_I \begin{bmatrix} \mathrm{d}u \\ \mathrm{d}v \end{bmatrix} = E\mathrm{d}u^2 + 2F\mathrm{d}u\mathrm{d}v + G\mathrm{d}v^2 \tag{6.32}$$

are defined by the symmetric matrix

$$M_I \triangleq \begin{bmatrix} E & F \\ F & G \end{bmatrix} \triangleq \begin{bmatrix} \left\|\frac{\partial \vec{p}(u,v)}{\partial u}\right\|^2 & \left\langle \frac{\partial \vec{p}(u,v)}{\partial u}, \frac{\partial \vec{p}(u,v)}{\partial v}\right\rangle \\ \left\langle \frac{\partial \vec{p}(u,v)}{\partial v}, \frac{\partial \vec{p}(u,v)}{\partial u}\right\rangle & \left\|\frac{\partial \vec{p}(u,v)}{\partial v}\right\|^2 \end{bmatrix} \tag{6.33}$$

98 with *determinant*

240

$$\begin{aligned}\det(M_I) &\overset{(6.33)}{=} EG - F^2 \qquad (6.34)\\ &= \left\|\frac{\partial \vec{p}(u,v)}{\partial u}\right\|^2 \left\|\frac{\partial \vec{p}(u,v)}{\partial v}\right\|^2 - \left\langle \frac{\partial \vec{p}(u,v)}{\partial u}, \frac{\partial \vec{p}(u,v)}{\partial v}\right\rangle^2\end{aligned}$$

80

$$\begin{aligned}&\overset{(3.98)}{=} \left\|\frac{\partial \vec{p}(u,v)}{\partial u} \times \frac{\partial \vec{p}(u,v)}{\partial v}\right\|^2\\ &= \|\vec{n}(u,v)\|^2 \qquad (6.35)\\ &> 0 \qquad (6.36)\end{aligned}$$

from which the arc length (called "spatium" in Latin) of a curve $\vec{p}(t) = [u(t), v(t)]$ is given by

$$\begin{aligned}
s &= \int_S \mathrm{d}s \\
&= \int_S \sqrt{(\mathrm{d}x)^2 + (\mathrm{d}y)^2 + (\mathrm{d}z)^2} \\
&= \int_S \sqrt{\left(\frac{\mathrm{d}x}{\mathrm{d}t}\right)^2 + \left(\frac{\mathrm{d}y}{\mathrm{d}t}\right)^2 + \left(\frac{\mathrm{d}z}{\mathrm{d}t}\right)^2}\,\mathrm{d}t && (6.37) \\
&= \int_S \left\| \frac{\mathrm{d}\vec{p}(t)}{\mathrm{d}t} \right\| \mathrm{d}t && (6.38) \\
&= \int_S \sqrt{\left(\frac{\mathrm{d}x}{\mathrm{d}u}\frac{\mathrm{d}u}{\mathrm{d}t} + \frac{\mathrm{d}x}{\mathrm{d}v}\frac{\mathrm{d}v}{\mathrm{d}t}\right)^2 + \left(\frac{\mathrm{d}y}{\mathrm{d}u}\frac{\mathrm{d}u}{\mathrm{d}t} + \frac{\mathrm{d}y}{\mathrm{d}v}\frac{\mathrm{d}v}{\mathrm{d}t}\right)^2 + \left(\frac{\mathrm{d}z}{\mathrm{d}u}\frac{\mathrm{d}u}{\mathrm{d}t} + \frac{\mathrm{d}z}{\mathrm{d}v}\frac{\mathrm{d}v}{\mathrm{d}t}\right)^2}\,\mathrm{d}t \\
&= \int_S \sqrt{\left(\left(\frac{\mathrm{d}x}{\mathrm{d}u}\right)^2 + \left(\frac{\mathrm{d}y}{\mathrm{d}u}\right)^2 + \left(\frac{\mathrm{d}z}{\mathrm{d}u}\right)^2\right)\left(\frac{\mathrm{d}u}{\mathrm{d}t}\right)^2 + 2\left(\frac{\mathrm{d}x}{\mathrm{d}u}\frac{\mathrm{d}x}{\mathrm{d}v} + \frac{\mathrm{d}y}{\mathrm{d}u}\frac{\mathrm{d}y}{\mathrm{d}v} + \frac{\mathrm{d}z}{\mathrm{d}u}\frac{\mathrm{d}z}{\mathrm{d}v}\right)\frac{\mathrm{d}u}{\mathrm{d}t}\frac{\mathrm{d}v}{\mathrm{d}t}} \\
&\qquad \overline{+\left(\left(\frac{\mathrm{d}x}{\mathrm{d}v}\right)^2 + \left(\frac{\mathrm{d}y}{\mathrm{d}v}\right)^2 + \left(\frac{\mathrm{d}z}{\mathrm{d}v}\right)^2\right)\left(\frac{\mathrm{d}v}{\mathrm{d}t}\right)^2}\,\mathrm{d}t \\
&\overset{(6.33)}{=} \int_S \sqrt{Eu'(t)^2 + 2Fu'(t)v'(t) + Gv'(t)^2}\mathrm{d}t && (6.39)
\end{aligned}$$ 240

and the surface area by

$$A = \int_{\mathcal{D}_u}\int_{\mathcal{D}_v} \|\vec{n}(u,v)\|\mathrm{d}u\mathrm{d}v \overset{(6.35)}{=} \int_{\mathcal{D}_u}\int_{\mathcal{D}_v} \sqrt{\det(M_I)}\mathrm{d}u\mathrm{d}v \qquad (6.40)$$ 240

Similarly, the coefficients of the *second fundamental form*

$$\mathrm{II} \triangleq \begin{bmatrix}\mathrm{d}u \\ \mathrm{d}v\end{bmatrix}^T M_{II} \begin{bmatrix}\mathrm{d}u \\ \mathrm{d}v\end{bmatrix} = L\mathrm{d}u^2 + 2M\mathrm{d}u\mathrm{d}v + N\mathrm{d}v^2 \qquad (6.41)$$

are defined by the symmetric matrix

$$\begin{aligned}
M_{II} \triangleq \begin{bmatrix} L & M \\ M & N \end{bmatrix} &\triangleq \begin{bmatrix} \left\langle \hat{n}(u,v), \frac{\partial^2 \vec{p}(u,v)}{\partial u^2} \right\rangle & \left\langle \hat{n}(u,v), \frac{\partial^2 \vec{p}(u,v)}{\partial u \partial v} \right\rangle \\ \left\langle \hat{n}(u,v), \frac{\partial^2 \vec{p}(u,v)}{\partial v \partial u} \right\rangle & \left\langle \hat{n}(u,v), \frac{\partial^2 \vec{p}(u,v)}{\partial v^2} \right\rangle \end{bmatrix} && (6.42) \\
&= -\begin{bmatrix} \left\langle \frac{\partial \hat{n}(u,v)}{\partial u}, \frac{\partial \vec{p}(u,v)}{\partial u} \right\rangle & \left\langle \frac{\partial \hat{n}(u,v)}{\partial u}, \frac{\partial \vec{p}(u,v)}{\partial v} \right\rangle \\ \left\langle \frac{\partial \hat{n}(u,v)}{\partial v}, \frac{\partial \vec{p}(u,v)}{\partial u} \right\rangle & \left\langle \frac{\partial \hat{n}(u,v)}{\partial v}, \frac{\partial \vec{p}(u,v)}{\partial v} \right\rangle \end{bmatrix} && (6.43)
\end{aligned}$$

with *determinant* 98

$$\begin{aligned}
\det(M_{II}) &\overset{(6.42)}{=} LN - M^2 && (6.44) \\
&= \frac{\left\langle \vec{n}(u,v), \frac{\partial^2 \vec{p}(u,v)}{\partial u^2} \right\rangle \left\langle \vec{n}(u,v), \frac{\partial^2 \vec{p}(u,v)}{\partial v^2} \right\rangle - \left\langle \vec{n}(u,v), \frac{\partial^2 \vec{p}(u,v)}{\partial u \partial v} \right\rangle^2}{\|\vec{n}(u,v)\|^2} && (6.45)
\end{aligned}$$ 241

The partial derivatives of the unit normal vector $\hat{n}(u,v) = \frac{\vec{n}(u,v)}{\|\vec{n}(u,v)\|}$ may be explicitly formulated as the scaled orthogonal projections

$$\frac{\partial \hat{n}(u,v)}{\partial u} = \frac{\partial \frac{\vec{n}(u,v)}{\|\vec{n}(u,v)\|}}{\partial u} = \frac{\frac{\partial \vec{n}(u,v)}{\partial u}\|\vec{n}(u,v)\| - \frac{\partial \|\vec{n}(u,v)\|}{\partial u}\vec{n}(u,v)}{\|\vec{n}(u,v)\|^2}$$

240

$$\overset{(6.30)}{=} \frac{\frac{\partial \vec{n}(u,v)}{\partial u} - \left\langle \frac{\partial \vec{n}(u,v)}{\partial u}, \frac{\vec{n}(u,v)}{\|\vec{n}(u,v)\|} \right\rangle \frac{\vec{n}(u,v)}{\|\vec{n}(u,v)\|}}{\|\vec{n}(u,v)\|} \quad (6.46)$$

$$\frac{\partial \hat{n}(u,v)}{\partial v} = \frac{\partial \frac{\vec{n}(u,v)}{\|\vec{n}(u,v)\|}}{\partial v} = \frac{\frac{\partial \vec{n}(u,v)}{\partial v}\|\vec{n}(u,v)\| - \frac{\partial \|\vec{n}(u,v)\|}{\partial v}\vec{n}(u,v)}{\|\vec{n}(u,v)\|^2}$$

240

$$\overset{(6.31)}{=} \frac{\frac{\partial \vec{n}(u,v)}{\partial v} - \left\langle \frac{\partial \vec{n}(u,v)}{\partial v}, \frac{\vec{n}(u,v)}{\|\vec{n}(u,v)\|} \right\rangle \frac{\vec{n}(u,v)}{\|\vec{n}(u,v)\|}}{\|\vec{n}(u,v)\|} \quad (6.47)$$

or by the *Weingarten equations*

$$\left[\frac{\partial \hat{n}(u,v)}{\partial u}, \frac{\partial \hat{n}(u,v)}{\partial v}\right] = \left[\frac{\partial \vec{p}(u,v)}{\partial u}, \frac{\partial \vec{p}(u,v)}{\partial v}\right](-S) \quad (6.48)$$

where the *shape operator*, also called *Weingarten map*, reads

$$S \triangleq M_I^{-1} M_{II} \quad (6.49)$$

240
241

$$\underset{(6.42)}{\overset{(6.33)}{=}} \frac{1}{EG - F^2}\begin{bmatrix} G & -F \\ -F & E \end{bmatrix}\begin{bmatrix} L & M \\ M & N \end{bmatrix}$$

$$= \frac{1}{EG - F^2}\begin{bmatrix} GL - FM & GM - FN \\ EM - FL & EN - FM \end{bmatrix} \quad (6.50)$$

The symmetric Jacobian matrix of the $\mathbb{R}^2 \to \mathbb{R}^3$ transformation is then defined as

$$J_T^T J_T = \begin{bmatrix} \left(\frac{\partial \hat{n}(u,v)}{\partial u}\right)^T \\ \left(\frac{\partial \hat{n}(u,v)}{\partial v}\right)^T \end{bmatrix} \begin{bmatrix} \frac{\partial \hat{n}(u,v)}{\partial u} & \frac{\partial \hat{n}(u,v)}{\partial v} \end{bmatrix}$$

242

$$\overset{(6.48)}{=} (-S^T) \begin{bmatrix} \left(\frac{\partial \vec{p}(u,v)}{\partial u}\right)^T \\ \left(\frac{\partial \vec{p}(u,v)}{\partial v}\right)^T \end{bmatrix} \begin{bmatrix} \frac{\partial \vec{p}(u,v)}{\partial u} & \frac{\partial \vec{p}(u,v)}{\partial v} \end{bmatrix}(-S)$$

240

$$\overset{(6.33)}{=} (-S^T) M_I (-S) \quad (6.51)$$

98 with Jacobian *determinant*

98
240
98

$$\sqrt{\det(J_T^T J_T)} \overset{(3.284)}{=} \sqrt{\det(-S^T)\det(M_I)\det(-S)} \underset{(3.286)}{\overset{(6.35)}{=}} \|\vec{n}(u,v)\| |\det(S)| \quad (6.52)$$

Considering a *normal plane* (i.e., a plane containing the normal vector $\hat{n}$ and a given tangent direction) at a point $\vec{p}$ on the surface, the parametrization-independent *curvature* is defined as the signed reciprocal radius, so-called *radius of curvature*, of the *osculating circle* (with center $\vec{c}$) of the *normal section* (i.e., the curve resulting from the intersection of the surface and the normal plane), where the sign of the curvature $\text{sgn}(\langle \vec{c} - \vec{p}, \hat{n} \rangle)$ is negative whenever the curve is convex, and positive if it is concave. The *principal directions* (given as the eigenvectors of the shape operator) are defined as the two orthogonal directions along which the curvature reaches a maximum and a minimum, so-called *principal curvatures* (which correspond to the eigenvalues of the shape operator), or equivalently as the solutions κ_1 and κ_2 of the *quadratic equation* 28

$$
\begin{aligned}
\det(M_{II} - \kappa M_I) &\underset{(6.33)}{\overset{(6.42)}{=}} \begin{vmatrix} L-\kappa E & M-\kappa F \\ M-\kappa F & N-\kappa G \end{vmatrix} \\
&= (L-\kappa E)(N-\kappa G) - (M-\kappa F)^2 \\
&= (LN - \kappa LG - \kappa EN + \kappa^2 EG) - (M^2 - 2\kappa MF + \kappa^2 F^2) \\
&= (LN - M^2) + \kappa(2MF - LG - EN) + \kappa^2(EG - F^2) \\
&= 0 \qquad (6.53)
\end{aligned}
$$

241 240

from which the *mean curvature* H and the *Gaussian curvature* K are, respectively, defined as

$$2H \triangleq \kappa_1 + \kappa_2 \overset{(2.99)}{=} \frac{EN + LG - 2MF}{EG - F^2} \overset{(6.50)}{=} \operatorname{tr}(S) \qquad (6.54)$$

29 242

$$K \triangleq \kappa_1 \times \kappa_2 \overset{(2.100)}{=} \frac{LN - M^2}{EG - F^2} \underset{(6.34)}{\overset{(6.44)}{=}} \frac{\det(M_{II})}{\det(M_I)} \underset{(3.288)}{\overset{(6.49)}{=}} \det(S) \qquad (6.55)$$

29 241 242 240 98

$$\underset{(6.35)}{\overset{(6.45)}{=}} \frac{\left\langle \vec{n}(u,v), \frac{\partial^2 \vec{p}(u,v)}{\partial u^2} \right\rangle \left\langle \vec{n}(u,v), \frac{\partial^2 \vec{p}(u,v)}{\partial v^2} \right\rangle - \left\langle \vec{n}(u,v), \frac{\partial^2 \vec{p}(u,v)}{\partial u \partial v} \right\rangle^2}{\|\vec{n}(u,v)\|^4} \qquad (6.56)$$

241 240

Equivalently rewriting the *quadratic equation* as 28

$$K - 2H\kappa + \kappa^2 \overset{(6.53)}{=} 0 \qquad (6.57)$$

243

additionally yields

$$\kappa_{1|2} \overset{(2.104)}{=} H \pm \sqrt{H^2 - K} \qquad (6.58)$$

29

where

$$H^2 - K \underset{(6.55)}{\overset{(6.54)}{=}} \left(\frac{\kappa_1 + \kappa_2}{2}\right)^2 - \kappa_1\kappa_2 = \frac{\kappa_1^2 + 2\kappa_1\kappa_2 + \kappa_2^2}{4} - \frac{4\kappa_1\kappa_2}{4} = \left(\frac{\kappa_1 - \kappa_2}{2}\right)^2 \geq 0 \qquad (6.59)$$

243 243

As illustrated in *Figure 6.1*, several cases are then distinguished depending on the value of 244

$$\operatorname{sgn}(K) \overset{(6.55)}{=} \operatorname{sgn}(\kappa_1) \times \operatorname{sgn}(\kappa_2) \underset{(6.36)}{\overset{(6.55)}{=}} \operatorname{sgn}\left(\det(M_{II})\right) \overset{(6.55)}{=} \operatorname{sgn}\left(\det(S)\right) \qquad (6.60)$$

243 243 243 240

and a point on the surface is said to be an:

- *umbilic point* if $K = \kappa_1^2 = \kappa_2^2$, i.e., $\kappa_1 = \kappa_2$, such that any tangent vector of the surface is a principal direction
- *elliptic point* if $K > 0$, i.e., κ_1 and κ_2 have the same sign, such that the surface is either locally convex or locally concave along both principal directions
- *parabolic point* if $K = 0$, i.e., κ_1 or κ_2 is zero, such that the surface is locally flat along one principal direction
- *hyperbolic point* if $K < 0$, i.e., κ_1 and κ_2 have different signs, such that the saddle-shaped surface is locally convex along one principal direction and locally concave along the other

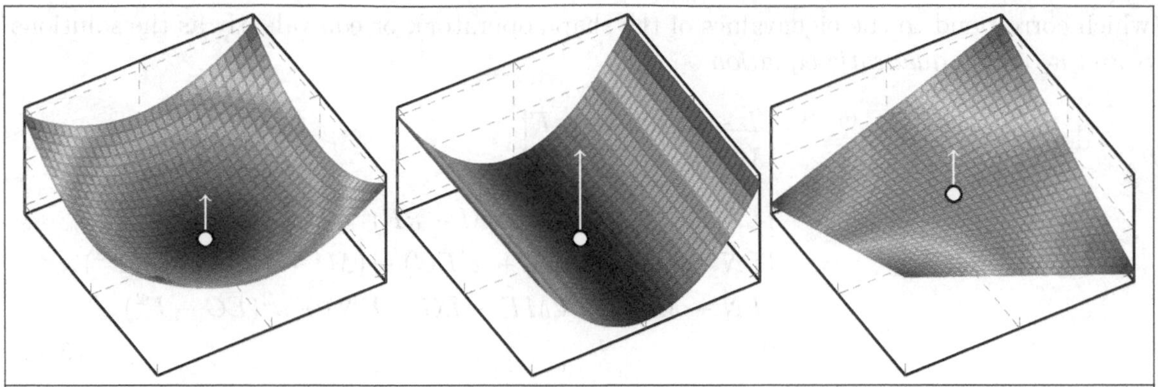

Figure 6.1: Gaussian Curvature: Illustration of an elliptic, a parabolic and a hyperbolic point (from left to right, respectively).

6.1.2 Spherical Geometry

6.1.2.1 Solid Angle

A *solid angle* is a dimensionless quantity ($\text{m}^2{\cdot}\text{m}^{-2}$) expressed in units of steradian (sr) (from the Greek "stereos" meaning "solid" and the Latin "radius" meaning "ray/beam") that measures a two-dimensional angle in three-dimensional space, i.e., the area of a patch on the
269 surface of a unit *sphere* encompassing the given set of unit-length directions $\hat{\omega}$

$$\Omega = \int_{\Omega} \mathrm{d}\hat{\omega} \tag{6.61}$$

An integral over solid angles is defined as a double integral over two of the *Cartesian*
67 *coordinates* $\hat{\omega} = [x, y, z]^T$, the magnitude of the third coordinate being determined by the
74 245 unit-length constraint $\|\hat{\omega}\| \overset{(3.61)}{=} x^2 + y^2 + z^2 = 1$. As illustrated in *Figure 6.2*, by dividing
98 the Jacobian *determinant* of the *transformation* between *spherical coordinates* and *Cartesian*
102 70 *coordinates* for a constant radius by the square of the radius, the differential solid angle may
67 be related to the differential polar and azimuthal angles by

68

$$\mathrm{d}\hat{\omega} \overset{(3.17)}{=} \sin(\theta)\mathrm{d}\theta\mathrm{d}\phi \tag{6.62}$$

It follows that the integral of a function $f(\hat{\omega})$ over a solid angle $\Omega \triangleq [\theta_l, \theta_h] \times [\phi_l, \phi_h]$ can be
70 69 equivalently reformulated as an integral over *spherical coordinates* or *cylindrical coordinates*

244

$$\int_{\Omega} f(\hat{\omega})\mathrm{d}\hat{\omega} \overset{(6.62)}{=} \int_{\phi_l}^{\phi_h} \int_{\theta_l}^{\theta_h} f(\theta, \phi) \sin(\theta)\mathrm{d}\theta\mathrm{d}\phi \tag{6.63}$$

$$= \int_{\phi_l}^{\phi_h} \int_{\cos(\theta_h)}^{\cos(\theta_l)} f\big(\arccos(\mu), \phi\big)\mathrm{d}\mu\mathrm{d}\phi \tag{6.64}$$

$$= \int_{\phi_l}^{\phi_h} \int_{\sin(\theta_l)}^{\sin(\theta_h)} f\big(\arcsin(\rho), \phi\big)\frac{\rho}{\sqrt{1-\rho^2}}\mathrm{d}\rho\mathrm{d}\phi \tag{6.65}$$

77 70 where $\mu \triangleq \langle \hat{z}, \hat{\omega} \rangle \overset{(3.77)}{=} \cos(\theta) = \sqrt{1 - \sin(\theta)^2} \overset{(3.25)}{=} \sqrt{1-\rho^2}$. Carrying the integral of a unit
269 function $f(\hat{\omega}) = 1$ over the whole *sphere* by letting $\Omega = [0, \pi] \times [0, 2\pi]$ then yields a solid angle of 4π sr, while that of a hemisphere, for which $\Omega = [0, \pi/2] \times [0, 2\pi]$ instead, is 2π sr.

246 As illustrated in *Figure 6.3*, both the angle and the solid angle subtended by an object at a point $\vec{p}$ are measures of the relative apparent size of the object as seen from $\vec{p}$. In two

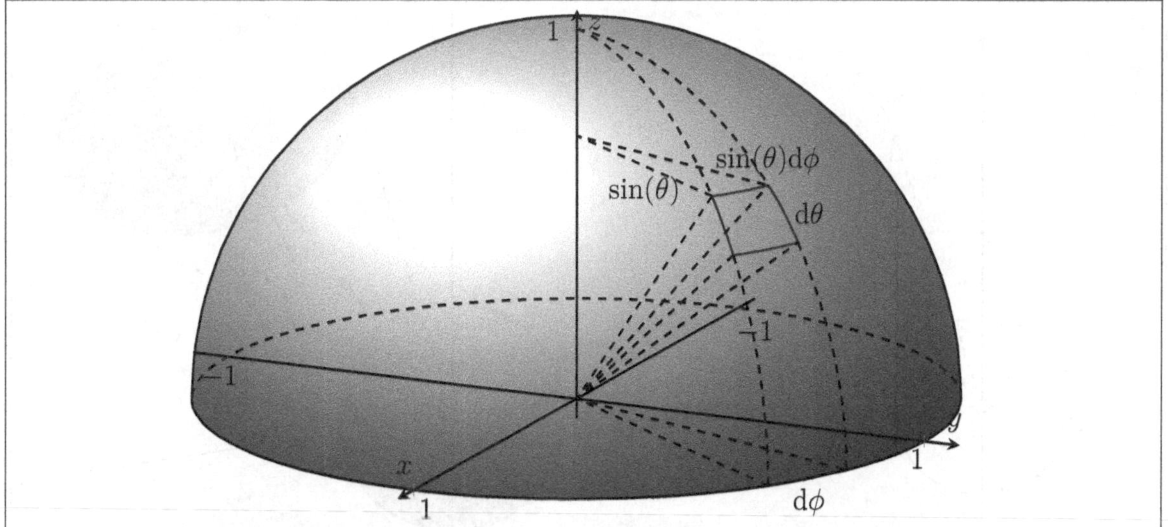

Figure 6.2: Solid Angle: Illustration of differential solid angle in terms of differential spherical coordinates.

dimensions, the angle subtended by an object represents the length of its projection onto a unit circle centered in $\vec{p}$. Similarly, a solid angle corresponds to the projected area of a 3-D object onto a unit *sphere* centered at $\vec{p}$, which is a function of both the orientation of the 269
object's surface normal $\hat{n}_q$ at each point $\vec{q} \triangleq \vec{p} + \|\vec{q} - \vec{p}\|\hat{\omega}$, such that $\widehat{pq} = \hat{\omega}$, and its distance to $\vec{p}$, yielding the identity

$$\mathrm{d}\hat{\omega} = \frac{T(\vec{p}, \vec{q})}{\|\vec{q} - \vec{p}\|^2} \langle \hat{n}_q, -\widehat{pq} \rangle \mathrm{d}A(\vec{q}) = \frac{T(\vec{p}, \vec{q})}{\|\vec{p} - \vec{q}\|^3} \langle \hat{n}_q, \vec{p} - \vec{q} \rangle \mathrm{d}A(\vec{q}) \tag{6.66}$$

where $T(\vec{p}, \vec{q})$ is the transmittance between $\vec{p}$ and $\vec{q}$, such that $T(\vec{p}, \vec{q}) = 1$ if $\vec{q}$ belongs to the set S_v of surfaces fully visible from $\vec{p}$, as defined by the visibility operator $\vec{q} = v(\vec{p}, \hat{\omega})$, and $T(\vec{p}, \vec{q}) = 0$ if $\vec{p}$ and $\vec{q}$ are mutually occluded. It follows that the integral of a function $f(\hat{\omega})$ over a projected solid angle Ω can be equivalently reformulated as an integral over the points $\vec{q}$ on the surface S of the object as

$$\int_\Omega f(\hat{\omega}) \mathrm{d}\hat{\omega} \overset{(6.66)}{=} \int_S f(\widehat{pq}) \frac{T(\vec{p}, \vec{q})}{\|\vec{q} - \vec{p}\|^2} \langle \hat{n}_q, -\widehat{pq} \rangle \mathrm{d}A(\vec{q}) = \int_S f(\widehat{pq}) \frac{T(\vec{p}, \vec{q})}{\|\vec{p} - \vec{q}\|^3} \langle \hat{n}_q, \vec{p} - \vec{q} \rangle \mathrm{d}A(\vec{q}) \tag{6.67}$$ 245

From the property of a *transformed probability density*, a PDF $p(\vec{p}, \hat{\omega})$ expressed over 133
solid angles can then be reformulated as a *probability density* $p(\vec{q})$ over surface area via the 131
identity

$$\int_\Omega p(\vec{p}, \hat{\omega}) \mathrm{d}\hat{\omega} \overset{(6.67)}{=} \int_S p(\vec{p}, \widehat{pq}) \frac{T(\vec{p}, \vec{q})}{\|\vec{q} - \vec{p}\|^2} \langle \hat{n}_q, -\widehat{pq} \rangle \mathrm{d}A(\vec{q}) \overset{(4.30)}{=} \int_S p(\vec{q}) \mathrm{d}A(\vec{q}) \tag{6.68}$$ 245 133

which must hold for any domain of integration, and from which follows the identity based on the Jacobian *determinant* of the *transformation* 98 102

$$p(\vec{q}) \overset{(4.31)}{=} p(\vec{p}, \widehat{pq}) \frac{T(\vec{p}, \vec{q})}{\|\vec{q} - \vec{p}\|^2} \langle \hat{n}_q, -\widehat{pq} \rangle \tag{6.69}$$ 133

Likewise, the differential solid angle projected onto the underlying unit disk is readily

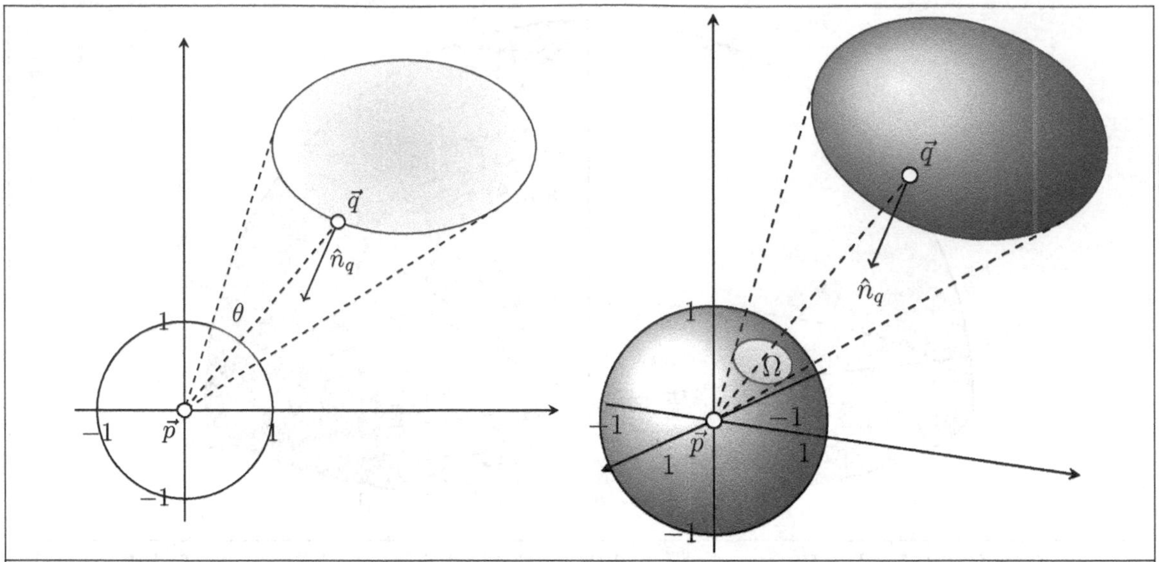

Figure 6.3: Subtended Solid Angle: Illustration of the angle and solid angle subtended at a point by the visible surface of an arbitrary object.

given as

245
246 $$\langle \hat{n}_p, \hat{\omega} \rangle \mathrm{d}\hat{\omega} \overset{(6.66)}{=} \langle \hat{n}_p, \widehat{pq} \rangle \frac{T(\vec{p}, \vec{q})}{\|\vec{q} - \vec{p}\|^2} \langle \hat{n}_q, -\widehat{pq} \rangle \mathrm{d}A(\vec{q}) \overset{(6.71)}{=} G(\vec{p}, \vec{q}) \mathrm{d}A(\vec{q}) \tag{6.70}$$

where the *geometric term* is defined as

$$\begin{aligned} G(\vec{p}, \vec{q}) &\triangleq \langle \hat{n}_p, \widehat{pq} \rangle \frac{T(\vec{p}, \vec{q})}{\|\vec{q} - \vec{p}\|^2} \langle \hat{n}_q, -\widehat{pq} \rangle & (6.71) \\ &= \left\langle \hat{n}_p, \frac{\vec{q} - \vec{p}}{\|\vec{q} - \vec{p}\|} \right\rangle \frac{T(\vec{p}, \vec{q})}{\|\vec{q} - \vec{p}\|^2} \left\langle \hat{n}_q, -\frac{\vec{q} - \vec{p}}{\|\vec{q} - \vec{p}\|} \right\rangle \\ &= \langle \hat{n}_p, \vec{q} - \vec{p} \rangle \frac{T(\vec{p}, \vec{q})}{\|\vec{q} - \vec{p}\|^4} \langle \hat{n}_q, \vec{p} - \vec{q} \rangle & (6.72) \end{aligned}$$

6.1.2.2 Axial Moment

By means of the generalized *Stokes theorem*, the nth *axial moment* [Arvo, 1995b, Arvo, 1995a, Ch. 4] of a spherical domain Ω about an axis $\vec{a}$ may be recursively expressed in terms of a boundary integral as

$$\int_\Omega \langle \vec{a}, \hat{\omega} \rangle^n \mathrm{d}\hat{\omega} = \begin{cases} 0 & \text{if } n \leq -1 \\ \Omega & \text{if } n = \ \ 0 \\ \frac{1}{n+1} \left((n-1)\|\vec{a}\|^2 \int_\Omega \langle \vec{a}, \hat{\omega} \rangle^{n-2} \mathrm{d}\hat{\omega} - \int_{\partial\Omega} \langle \vec{a}, \hat{\omega}(s) \rangle^{n-1} \langle \vec{a}, \vec{b}(s) \rangle \mathrm{d}s \right) & \text{if } n \geq +1 \end{cases} \tag{6.73}$$

where $\vec{b}(s)$ is the outward binormal to the boundary curve $\partial\Omega$ of the domain at arc length
247 s, as illustrated in *Figure 6.4*, while expanding the recursion yields

$$\int_\Omega \langle \vec{a}, \hat{\omega} \rangle^n \mathrm{d}\hat{\omega} = \frac{1}{n+1} \left(((n+1) \bmod 2)\Omega - \sum_{\substack{k=(n+1) \bmod 2 \\ k+=2}}^{n-1} \int_{\partial\Omega} \langle \vec{a}, \hat{\omega}(s) \rangle^k \langle \vec{a}, \vec{b}(s) \rangle \mathrm{d}s \right) \tag{6.74}$$

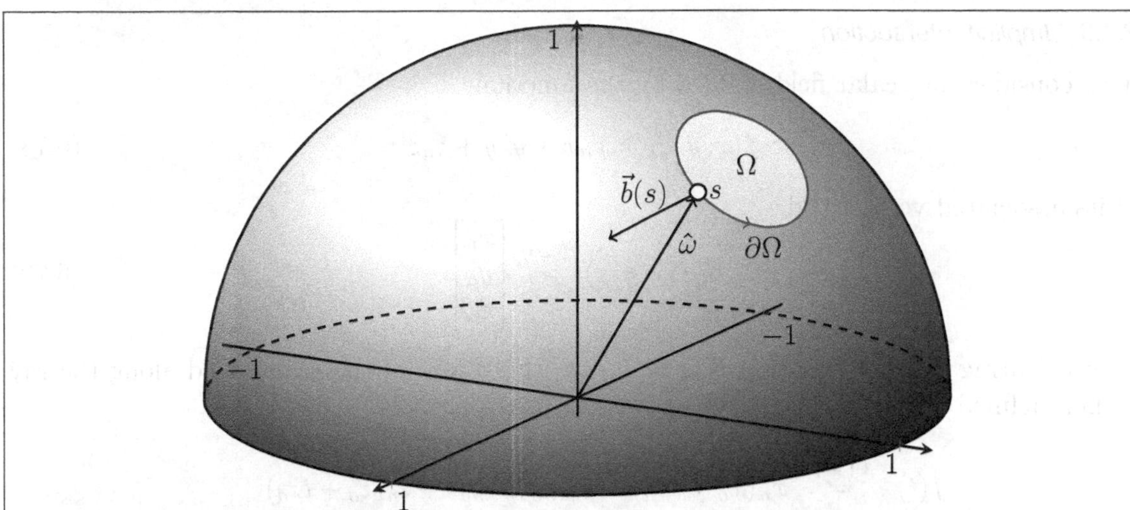

Figure 6.4: Axial Moment: Illustration of the axial moment of a projected spherical domain expressed as a boundary integral (drawn after [Arvo, 1995b, Fig. 1] and [Arvo, 1995a, Fig. 4.7 and 4.8]).

where the *solid angle* ought to be signed in order to match the orientation of the boundary 244
integral.

The *double-axis moment* about two axes $\vec{a}_1$ and $\vec{a}_2$ can similarly be expressed in terms of a single-axis moment and a boundary integral as

$$\int_\Omega \langle \vec{a}_1, \hat{\omega} \rangle^n \langle \vec{a}_2, \hat{\omega} \rangle \mathrm{d}\hat{\omega} = \frac{n \langle \vec{a}_1, \vec{a}_2 \rangle \int_\Omega \langle \vec{a}_1, \hat{\omega} \rangle^{n-1} \mathrm{d}\hat{\omega} - \int_{\partial\Omega} \langle \vec{a}_1, \hat{\omega}(s) \rangle^n \langle \vec{a}_2, \vec{b}(s) \rangle \mathrm{d}s}{n+2} \tag{6.75}$$

6.2 FIRST-ORDER SURFACES

6.2.1 Plane

6.2.1.1 *Algebraic Intersection*

A *plane* of center $\vec{c}$ orthogonal to a vector $\vec{n}$ is defined as the set of points $\vec{p}$ such that
$\langle \vec{p}-\vec{c}, \vec{n} \rangle \overset{(3.74)}{=} 0$. Substituting $\vec{p}$ with the set of points defined by the ray equation $\vec{r}(t) \triangleq \vec{o}+t\vec{d}$ 76
then yields the *linear equation* 27

$$\langle \vec{o}+t\vec{d}-\vec{c}, \vec{n} \rangle = \langle t\vec{d}+(\vec{o}-\vec{c}), \vec{n} \rangle \underset{(3.73)}{\overset{(3.72)}{=}} t\langle \vec{d}, \vec{n} \rangle + \langle \vec{o}-\vec{c}, \vec{n} \rangle = 0 \tag{6.76}$$ 76 76

whose solution determines the point of intersection along the ray, while a vector orthogonal to the surface at that point is readily given by $\vec{n}$.

6.2.1.2 *Distance Estimation*

The distance from a point $\vec{p}$ to a plane of center $\vec{c}$ orthogonal to a vector $\vec{n}$ reads [Georgiades, 1992]

$$f(\vec{p}) \overset{(3.78)}{=} \left\langle \vec{p}-\vec{c}, \frac{\vec{n}}{\|\vec{n}\|} \right\rangle \overset{(3.72)}{=} \frac{\langle \vec{p}, \vec{n} \rangle - \langle \vec{c}, \vec{n} \rangle}{\|\vec{n}\|} \tag{6.77}$$ 77 76

6.2.1.3 *Implicit Intersection*

Let us consider the scalar field defined by the function

$$f(x,y,z) \triangleq x_n x + y_n y + z_n z \tag{6.78}$$

and its associated vector field

239 $$\nabla f(x,y,z) \overset{(6.20)}{=} \begin{bmatrix} x_n \\ y_n \\ z_n \end{bmatrix} \tag{6.79}$$

Substituting the ray equation $\vec{r}(t) \triangleq \vec{o} + t\vec{d}$, the values of the scalar field along the ray are then defined as

239
248
$$\begin{aligned} f(t) &\overset{(6.21)}{\underset{(6.78)}{=}} x_n(x_o + tx_d) + y_n(y_o + ty_d) + z_n(z_o + tz_d) \\ &= (x_n x_o + y_n y_o + z_n z_o) + (x_n x_d + y_n y_d + z_n z_d)t \end{aligned} \tag{6.80}$$

A plane may then be defined as the set of points satisfying $f(x,y,z) = v$ for a given isovalue v. A geometric interpretation of the various parameters can actually be readily provided by making a parallel with the previous algebraic formulation, thereby defining the plane of center $\vec{c}$ orthogonal to a vector $\vec{n} = [x_n, y_n, z_n]^T$ as the set of points $\vec{p} = [x,y,z]^T$
248 such that $f(\vec{p}) \overset{(6.78)}{=} \langle \vec{n}, \vec{p} \rangle = v$, while substituting $\vec{p}$ with the set of points defined by the ray
27 equation $\vec{r}(t) = \vec{o} + t\vec{d}$ yields the geometric equivalent of the *linear equation* to be solved $f(t) = f(\vec{o} + t\vec{d}) = \langle \vec{n}, \vec{o} + t\vec{d} \rangle = \langle \vec{n}, \vec{o} \rangle + \langle \vec{n}, \vec{d} \rangle t = v$, where $v = \langle \vec{n}, \vec{c} \rangle$.

6.2.2 Annulus

6.2.2.1 *Plane-Based Intersection*

248 As illustrated in *Figure 6.5*, an *annulus* of inner radius ρ_i and outer radius ρ_o may be
247 carved out of an infinite *plane* by discarding all intersection points for which the distance $\|\vec{p} - \vec{c}\| \notin [\rho_i, \rho_o]$.

Figure 6.5: Annulus: Illustration of an annulus.

6.2.2.2 Surface Parameterization

As illustrated in *Figure 6.6*, an *annular patch* of extent $[\rho_l, \rho_h] \times [\phi_l, \phi_h]$ centered at the 249
origin and contained within the x-y plane of a given coordinate system may alternatively be
represented in *cylindrical coordinates* as a parametric surface of the form 69

$$\vec{p}(u,v) = \begin{bmatrix} \operatorname{lerp}(u,\rho_l,\rho_h)\cos\left(\operatorname{lerp}(v,\phi_l,\phi_h)\right) \\ \operatorname{lerp}(u,\rho_l,\rho_h)\sin\left(\operatorname{lerp}(v,\phi_l,\phi_h)\right) \\ 0 \end{bmatrix} \tag{6.81}$$

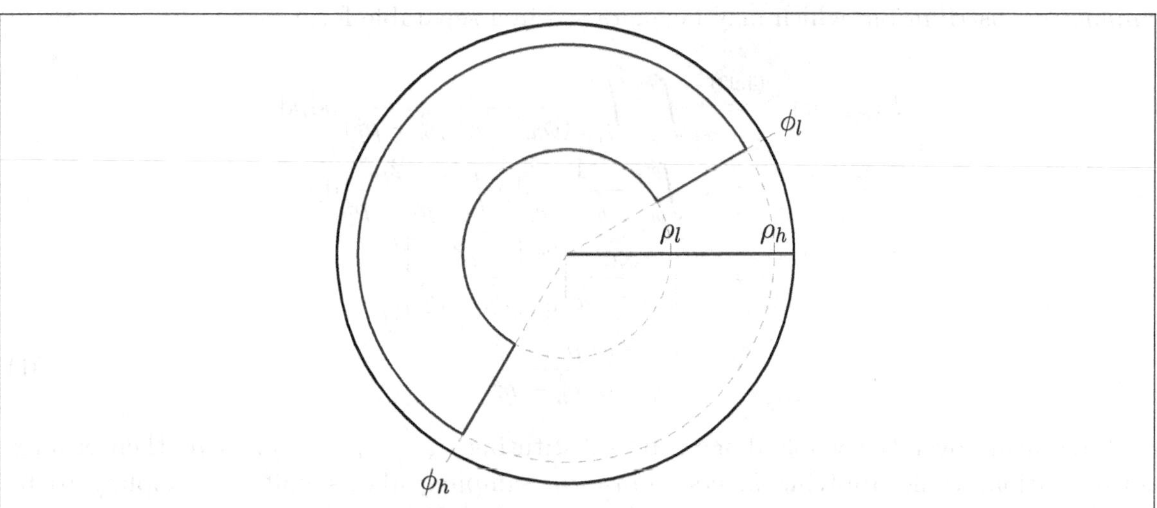

Figure 6.6: Annulus Parameterization: Illustration of the parametric representation of the surface of an annulus.

The first partial derivatives are then given by

$$\frac{\partial \vec{p}(u,v)}{\partial u} = \begin{bmatrix} (\rho_h - \rho_l)\cos\left(\operatorname{lerp}(v,\phi_l,\phi_h)\right) \\ (\rho_h - \rho_l)\sin\left(\operatorname{lerp}(v,\phi_l,\phi_h)\right) \\ 0 \end{bmatrix} \tag{6.82}$$

$$= (\rho_h - \rho_l)\vec{p}(u,v) \div \operatorname{lerp}(u,\rho_l,\rho_h) \tag{6.83}$$

$$\frac{\partial \vec{p}(u,v)}{\partial v} = \begin{bmatrix} -(\phi_h - \phi_l)\operatorname{lerp}(u,\rho_l,\rho_h)\sin\left(\operatorname{lerp}(v,\phi_l,\phi_h)\right) \\ (\phi_h - \phi_l)\operatorname{lerp}(u,\rho_l,\rho_h)\cos\left(\operatorname{lerp}(v,\phi_l,\phi_h)\right) \\ 0 \end{bmatrix} \tag{6.84}$$

$$= (\phi_h - \phi_l)\begin{bmatrix} -p_y(u,v) \\ p_x(u,v) \\ 0 \end{bmatrix} \tag{6.85}$$

while the second partial derivatives read

$$\frac{\partial^2 \vec{p}(u,v)}{\partial u^2} = \vec{0} \tag{6.86}$$

$$\frac{\partial^2 \vec{p}(u,v)}{\partial u \partial v} = \begin{bmatrix} -(\phi_h - \phi_l)(\rho_h - \rho_l)\sin\left(\operatorname{lerp}(v,\phi_l,\phi_h)\right) \\ (\phi_h - \phi_l)(\rho_h - \rho_l)\cos\left(\operatorname{lerp}(v,\phi_l,\phi_h)\right) \\ 0 \end{bmatrix} \tag{6.87}$$

$$= (\phi_h - \phi_l)(\rho_h - \rho_l)\begin{bmatrix} -p_y(u,v) \\ p_x(u,v) \\ 0 \end{bmatrix} \div \operatorname{lerp}(u,\rho_l,\rho_h) \tag{6.88}$$

$$\begin{aligned}\frac{\partial^2\vec{p}(u,v)}{\partial v^2} &= \begin{bmatrix}-(\phi_h-\phi_l)^2\,\mathrm{lerp}(u,\rho_l,\rho_h)\cos\big(\mathrm{lerp}(v,\phi_l,\phi_h)\big)\\ -(\phi_h-\phi_l)^2\,\mathrm{lerp}(u,\rho_l,\rho_h)\sin\big(\mathrm{lerp}(v,\phi_l,\phi_h)\big)\\ 0\end{bmatrix} && (6.89)\\ &= -(\phi_h-\phi_l)^2\vec{p}(u,v) && (6.90)\end{aligned}$$

6.2.2.3 Area and Sampling

Given the surface area $A \triangleq (\phi_h-\phi_l)(\rho_h^2-\rho_l^2) \div 2$ of the annular patch, the integral of the
131 uniform joint *probability density* $p(\rho,\phi) \triangleq 1 \div A$ over a subdomain A_s yields the associated
132 *cumulative distribution*, which may be expressed in a separable form as

132

$$\begin{aligned}P(\rho_s,\phi_s) &\overset{(4.22)}{=} \int_{\phi_l}^{\phi_s}\int_{\rho_l}^{\rho_s} \frac{2}{(\phi_h-\phi_l)(\rho_h^2-\rho_l^2)}\rho\mathrm{d}\rho\mathrm{d}\phi\\ &= \int_{\phi_l}^{\phi_s}\frac{1}{\phi_h-\phi_l}\mathrm{d}\phi\int_{\rho_l}^{\rho_s}\frac{2\rho}{\rho_h^2-\rho_l^2}\mathrm{d}\rho\\ &= \left[\frac{\phi}{\phi_h-\phi_l}\right]_{\phi_l}^{\phi_s}\left[\frac{\rho^2}{\rho_h^2-\rho_l^2}\right]_{\rho_l}^{\rho_s}\\ &= \frac{\phi_s-\phi_l}{\phi_h-\phi_l}\frac{\rho_s^2-\rho_l^2}{\rho_h^2-\rho_l^2} && (6.91)\end{aligned}$$

Integrating over the whole domain by substituting $\phi_s = \phi_h$ and $\rho_s = \rho_h$ then ensures
134 normalization, while applying *inverse-transform sampling* allows uniform sampling to be
readily carried as

$$\begin{aligned}\xi_\phi &= \frac{\phi_s-\phi_l}{\phi_h-\phi_l} &&\Longrightarrow\quad \phi_s = \mathrm{lerp}(\xi_\phi,\phi_l,\phi_h) && (6.92)\\ \xi_\rho &= \frac{\rho_s^2-\rho_l^2}{\rho_h^2-\rho_l^2} &&\Longrightarrow\quad \rho_s = \sqrt{\mathrm{lerp}(\xi_\rho,\rho_l^2,\rho_h^2)} && (6.93)\end{aligned}$$

6.2.3 Triangle

6.2.3.1 Plane-Based Intersection

251 As illustrated in *Figure 6.7*, a *triangle* may be carved out of an infinite *plane* by discarding
247 all intersection points that lie outside of three auxiliary half-spaces. A plane passing through
the vertices $\vec{p}_0$, $\vec{p}_1$ and $\vec{p}_2$ can be defined as the set of points $\vec{p}$ for which the three vectors
joining $\vec{p}$ to each of the vertices are all coplanar, consequently equating the following *scalar*
80 *triple product* to zero

81

$$|\vec{p}-\vec{p}_0,\vec{p}-\vec{p}_1,\vec{p}-\vec{p}_2| \overset{(3.103)}{=} |\vec{p},\vec{p}_1,\vec{p}_2| + |\vec{p},\vec{p}_2,\vec{p}_0| + |\vec{p},\vec{p}_0,\vec{p}_1| - |\vec{p}_0,\vec{p}_1,\vec{p}_2|$$

81

$$\overset{(3.104)}{+} \cancel{|\vec{p}-\vec{p}_0-\vec{p}_1-\vec{p}_2,\vec{p},\vec{p}|}$$

80

$$\overset{(3.100)}{=} \langle\vec{p},\vec{p}_1\times\vec{p}_2+\vec{p}_2\times\vec{p}_0+\vec{p}_0\times\vec{p}_1\rangle - \langle\vec{p}_0,\vec{p}_1\times\vec{p}_2\rangle$$

$$= \langle\vec{p},\vec{n}\rangle - v$$

81

$$\overset{(3.104)}{=} 0 \qquad (6.94)$$

247 which readily corresponds to the *plane* equation $f(\vec{p}) = \langle\vec{n},\vec{p}\rangle = v$ with

78

$$\vec{n} \triangleq \vec{p}_1 \times \vec{p}_2 + \vec{p}_2 \times \vec{p}_0 + \vec{p}_0 \times \vec{p}_1 \overset{(3.88)}{=} (\vec{p}_1 - \vec{p}_0) \times (\vec{p}_2 - \vec{p}_0) \triangleq \vec{n}_{012} \tag{6.95}$$

$$v \triangleq \langle \vec{p}_0, \vec{p}_1 \times \vec{p}_2 \rangle \tag{6.96}$$

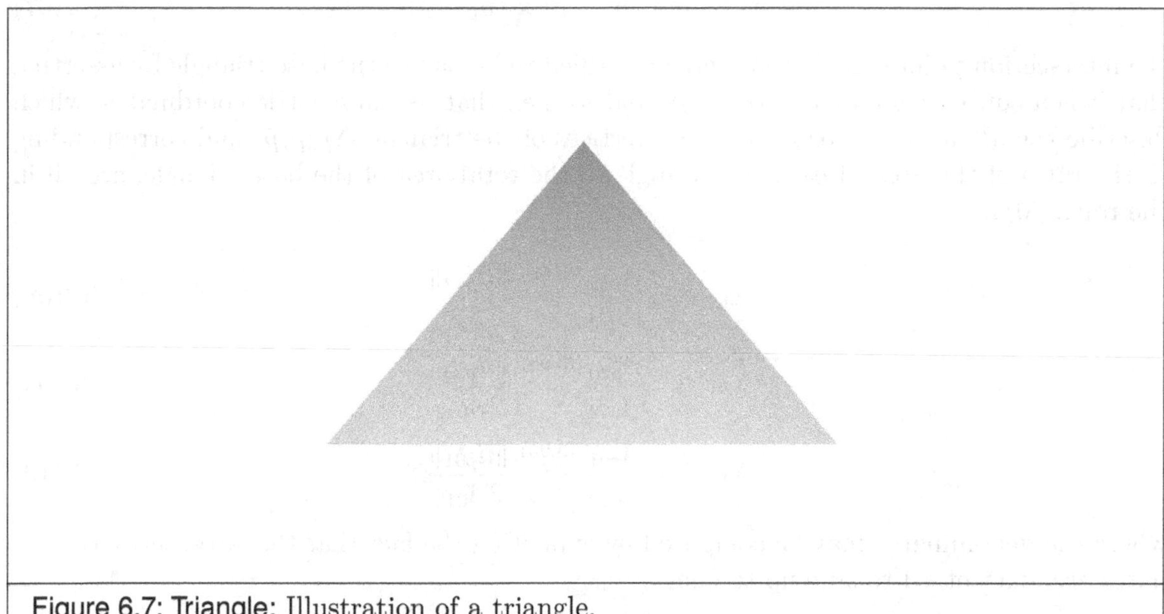

Figure 6.7: **Triangle:** Illustration of a triangle.

Recalling that the four vectors orthogonal to the four faces of a general tetrahedron sum up to zero, provided that each vector has a magnitude equal to the area of the corresponding face and that all vectors point inward/outward, the above expression of $\hat{n}$ may be geometrically interpreted as the sum of the normals of the triangles $\Delta\vec{0}\vec{p}_1\vec{p}_2$, $\Delta\vec{0}\vec{p}_2\vec{p}_0$ and $\Delta\vec{0}\vec{p}_0\vec{p}_1$.

Given a ray of equation $\vec{r}(t) \triangleq \vec{o} + t\vec{d}$, discarding intersection points lying outside of the convex hull of the three triangle vertices can then be achieved by computing the normals of the triangles $\Delta\vec{o}\vec{p}_1\vec{p}_2$, $\Delta\vec{o}\vec{p}_2\vec{p}_0$ and $\Delta\vec{o}\vec{p}_0\vec{p}_1$

$$\vec{n}_{o12} \triangleq (\vec{p}_1 - \vec{o}) \times (\vec{p}_2 - \vec{o}) \tag{6.97}$$

$$\vec{n}_{o20} \triangleq (\vec{p}_2 - \vec{o}) \times (\vec{p}_0 - \vec{o}) \tag{6.98}$$

$$\vec{n}_{o01} \triangleq (\vec{p}_0 - \vec{o}) \times (\vec{p}_1 - \vec{o}) \tag{6.99}$$

and asserting that their dot products with the ray direction

$$d_{o12} \triangleq \langle \vec{d}, \vec{n}_{o12} \rangle \tag{6.100}$$

$$d_{o20} \triangleq \langle \vec{d}, \vec{n}_{o20} \rangle \tag{6.101}$$

$$d_{o01} \triangleq \langle \vec{d}, \vec{n}_{o01} \rangle \tag{6.102}$$

all have the same sign, that is, that the ray direction points towards all three inner/outer half-spaces, hence asserting that the intersection point $\vec{p} = \vec{o} + t\vec{d}$ lies within the convex hull of interest. Based on the aforementioned property of the four face normals of a tetrahedron, the normal of the base triangle $\Delta\vec{p}_0\vec{p}_1\vec{p}_2$ may equivalently be computed as follows

$$\vec{n} = -\vec{n}_{210} = \vec{n}_{o12} + \vec{n}_{o20} + \vec{n}_{o01} \tag{6.103}$$

and therefore

$$\langle \vec{d}, \vec{n} \rangle = \langle \vec{d}, \vec{n}_{o12} + \vec{n}_{o20} + \vec{n}_{o01} \rangle = d_{o12} + d_{o20} + d_{o01} \tag{6.104}$$

Defining the normals of the sub-triangles $\Delta\vec{p}\vec{p}_1\vec{p}_2$, $\Delta\vec{p}\vec{p}_2\vec{p}_0$ and $\Delta\vec{p}\vec{p}_0\vec{p}_1$ as

$$\vec{n}_{p12} \triangleq (\vec{p}_1 - \vec{p}) \times (\vec{p}_2 - \vec{p}) \tag{6.105}$$

$$\vec{n}_{p20} \triangleq (\vec{p}_2 - \vec{p}) \times (\vec{p}_0 - \vec{p}) \tag{6.106}$$

$$\vec{n}_{p01} \triangleq (\vec{p}_0 - \vec{p}) \times (\vec{p}_1 - \vec{p}) \tag{6.107}$$

the intersection point can alternatively be verified to belong to the base triangle by asserting that it is a convex combination of $\vec{p}_0$, $\vec{p}_1$ and $\vec{p}_2$, i.e., that its barycentric coordinates, which
72 describe the *affine space* spanned by the vertices of the triangle $\Delta\vec{p}_0\vec{p}_1\vec{p}_2$ and corresponding to the ratio of the area of each sub-triangle to the total area of the base triangle, are all in the range $[0, 1]$

80

$$\lambda_0 \triangleq \frac{A_{p12}}{A_{012}} \overset{(3.95)}{=} \frac{\|\vec{n}_{p12}\|}{2A_{012}} \tag{6.108}$$

80

$$\lambda_1 \triangleq \frac{A_{p20}}{A_{012}} \overset{(3.95)}{=} \frac{\|\vec{n}_{p20}\|}{2A_{012}} \tag{6.109}$$

80

$$\lambda_2 \triangleq \frac{A_{p01}}{A_{012}} \overset{(3.95)}{=} \frac{\|\vec{n}_{p01}\|}{2A_{012}} \tag{6.110}$$

where the denominator may be computed by exploiting the fact that the barycentric coordinates are guaranteed to sum up to one

$$\lambda_0 + \lambda_1 + \lambda_2 = \frac{\|\vec{n}_{p12}\| + \|\vec{n}_{p20}\| + \|\vec{n}_{p01}\|}{2A_{012}} = 1 \tag{6.111}$$

from which follows that

$$2A_{012} = \|\vec{n}_{p12}\| + \|\vec{n}_{p20}\| + \|\vec{n}_{p01}\| \tag{6.112}$$

6.2.3.2 *Geometric Intersection*

A more computationally efficient alternative consists in computing the barycentric coordinates of the intersection point within the triangle. Expressing the areas of the three triangles $\Delta\vec{o}\vec{p}_1\vec{p}_2$, $\Delta\vec{o}\vec{p}_2\vec{p}_0$ and $\Delta\vec{o}\vec{p}_0\vec{p}_1$ in terms of the magnitudes of their respective normals

251
80

$$A_{o12} \underset{(3.95)}{\overset{(6.97)}{=}} \frac{\|\vec{n}_{o12}\|}{2} \tag{6.113}$$

251
80

$$A_{o20} \underset{(3.95)}{\overset{(6.98)}{=}} \frac{\|\vec{n}_{o20}\|}{2} \tag{6.114}$$

251
80

$$A_{o01} \underset{(3.95)}{\overset{(6.99)}{=}} \frac{\|\vec{n}_{o01}\|}{2} \tag{6.115}$$

the signed volumes of the tetrahedra formed by joining the triangles to a point $\vec{p} = \vec{o} + t\vec{d}$ on the surface are then given as a third of the product of their base area times their height

$$V_{o12p} \triangleq \left\langle \vec{p} - \vec{o}, \frac{\vec{n}_{o12}}{\|\vec{n}_{o12}\|} \right\rangle \frac{A_{o12}}{3} = \frac{\langle \vec{p} - \vec{o}, \vec{n}_{o12} \rangle}{6} = \frac{t}{6}\langle \vec{d}, \vec{n}_{o12} \rangle \tag{6.116}$$

$$V_{o20p} \triangleq \left\langle \vec{p} - \vec{o}, \frac{\vec{n}_{o20}}{\|\vec{n}_{o20}\|} \right\rangle \frac{A_{o20}}{3} = \frac{\langle \vec{p} - \vec{o}, \vec{n}_{o20} \rangle}{6} = \frac{t}{6}\langle \vec{d}, \vec{n}_{o20} \rangle \tag{6.117}$$

$$V_{o01p} \triangleq \left\langle \vec{p} - \vec{o}, \frac{\vec{n}_{o01}}{\|\vec{n}_{o01}\|} \right\rangle \frac{A_{o01}}{3} = \frac{\langle \vec{p} - \vec{o}, \vec{n}_{o01} \rangle}{6} = \frac{t}{6}\langle \vec{d}, \vec{n}_{o01} \rangle \tag{6.118}$$

Observing that the area of each sub-triangle $\triangle\vec{p}\vec{p}_1\vec{p}_2$, $\triangle\vec{p}\vec{p}_2\vec{p}_0$ and $\triangle\vec{p}\vec{p}_0\vec{p}_1$ is similarly proportional to the volume of the corresponding tetrahedron

$$V_{o12p} = h_o\frac{A_{p12}}{3} \quad (6.119)$$

$$V_{o20p} = h_o\frac{A_{p20}}{3} \quad (6.120)$$

$$V_{o01p} = h_o\frac{A_{p01}}{3} \quad (6.121)$$

where the height h_o of the tetrahedron is the orthogonal distance from the ray origin to the base triangle $\triangle\vec{p}_0\vec{p}_1\vec{p}_2$, the barycentric coordinates are then given as

$$\lambda_0 \triangleq \frac{A_{p12}}{A_{012}} = \frac{3\ V_{o12p}}{h_o\ A_{012}} = \frac{t}{2h_o}\frac{\langle\vec{d},\vec{n}_{o12}\rangle}{A_{012}} = \frac{\langle\vec{d},\vec{n}_{o12}\rangle}{C_{012}} \quad (6.122)$$

$$\lambda_1 \triangleq \frac{A_{p20}}{A_{012}} = \frac{3\ V_{o20p}}{h_o\ A_{012}} = \frac{t}{2h_o}\frac{\langle\vec{d},\vec{n}_{o20}\rangle}{A_{012}} = \frac{\langle\vec{d},\vec{n}_{o20}\rangle}{C_{012}} \quad (6.123)$$

$$\lambda_2 \triangleq \frac{A_{p01}}{A_{012}} = \frac{3\ V_{o01p}}{h_o\ A_{012}} = \frac{t}{2h_o}\frac{\langle\vec{d},\vec{n}_{o01}\rangle}{A_{012}} = \frac{\langle\vec{d},\vec{n}_{o01}\rangle}{C_{012}} \quad (6.124)$$

with $C_{012} = \frac{2h_o}{t}A_{012}$.

Exploiting the fact that the barycentric coordinates are guaranteed to sum up to one, the constant of proportionality may be computed by writing

$$\lambda_0 + \lambda_1 + \lambda_2 = \frac{\langle\vec{d},\vec{n}_{o12}\rangle + \langle\vec{d},\vec{n}_{o20}\rangle + \langle\vec{d},\vec{n}_{o01}\rangle}{C_{012}} = 1 \quad (6.125)$$

from which follows that

$$C_{012} = \langle\vec{d},\vec{n}_{o12}\rangle + \langle\vec{d},\vec{n}_{o20}\rangle + \langle\vec{d},\vec{n}_{o01}\rangle \quad (6.126)$$

If all three barycentric coordinates are positive, the intersection point

$$\vec{p} = \lambda_0\vec{p}_0 + \lambda_1\vec{p}_1 + \lambda_2\vec{p}_2 \quad (6.127)$$

lies within the convex hull defined by the vertices of the base triangle, whereas it lies outside otherwise, while the intersection parameter can be derived as $t = \langle\vec{d}, \vec{p} - \vec{o}\rangle$.

6.2.3.3 Surface Parameterization

A triangle with vertices $\vec{p}_0$, $\vec{p}_1$ and $\vec{p}_2$ may alternatively be represented in *Cartesian coordinates* as a parametric surface of the form 67

$$\vec{p}(u,v) \triangleq (1-u-v)\vec{p}_0 + u\vec{p}_1 + v\vec{p}_2 = \vec{p}_0 + u(\vec{p}_1 - \vec{p}_0) + v(\vec{p}_2 - \vec{p}_0) \quad (6.128)$$

The first partial derivatives are then given by

$$\frac{\partial\vec{p}(u,v)}{\partial u} = \vec{p}_1 - \vec{p}_0 \quad (6.129)$$

$$\frac{\partial\vec{p}(u,v)}{\partial v} = \vec{p}_2 - \vec{p}_0 \quad (6.130)$$

while the second partial derivatives read

$$\frac{\partial^2\vec{p}(u,v)}{\partial u^2} = \vec{0} \quad (6.131)$$

$$\frac{\partial^2\vec{p}(u,v)}{\partial u\partial v} = \vec{0} \quad (6.132)$$

$$\frac{\partial^2\vec{p}(u,v)}{\partial v^2} = \vec{0} \quad (6.133)$$

6.2.3.4 Parametric Intersection

Equating the parametric representation $\vec{p}(u, v)$ with the set of points $\vec{p}$ defined by the ray equation $\vec{r}(t) \triangleq \vec{o} + t\vec{d}$ and rearranging the terms yields [Möller and Trumbore, 1997]

253

$$-t\vec{d} + u(\vec{p}_1 - \vec{p}_0) + v(\vec{p}_2 - \vec{p}_0) \overset{(6.128)}{=} \vec{o} - \vec{p}_0 \tag{6.134}$$

The above equation can then be expressed as a system of linear equations

$$\begin{bmatrix} -x_d & x_1 - x_0 & x_2 - x_0 \\ -y_d & y_1 - y_0 & y_2 - y_0 \\ -z_d & z_1 - z_0 & z_2 - z_0 \end{bmatrix} \begin{bmatrix} t \\ u \\ v \end{bmatrix} = \begin{bmatrix} x_o - x_0 \\ y_o - y_0 \\ z_o - z_0 \end{bmatrix} \tag{6.135}$$

100 which may be solved using *Cramer's rule*, such that the resulting intersection belongs to the triangle if both $0 \leq u$ and $0 \leq v$ hold as well as $u + v \leq 1$.

6.2.3.5 Area and Sampling

Given the surface area $A \triangleq \frac{bh}{2} = \frac{\|(\vec{p}_1 - \vec{p}_0) \times (\vec{p}_2 - \vec{p}_0)\|}{2}$ of a triangle of base b and height h,
131 the integral of the uniform joint *probability density* $p(x, y) \triangleq 1 \div A$ over a subdomain A_s
132 yields the associated *cumulative distribution*. As illustrated in *Figure 6.8*, the latter can be
254 expressed, without loss of generality, for a right triangle as

132

$$P(x_s, y_s) \overset{(4.22)}{=} \int_0^{x_s} \int_0^{y_s} \frac{2}{bh} \mathrm{d}y\mathrm{d}x \tag{6.136}$$

such that carrying the integral over the whole domain by substituting $x_s = b$ and $y_s = h\frac{b-x}{b}$ ensures normalization.

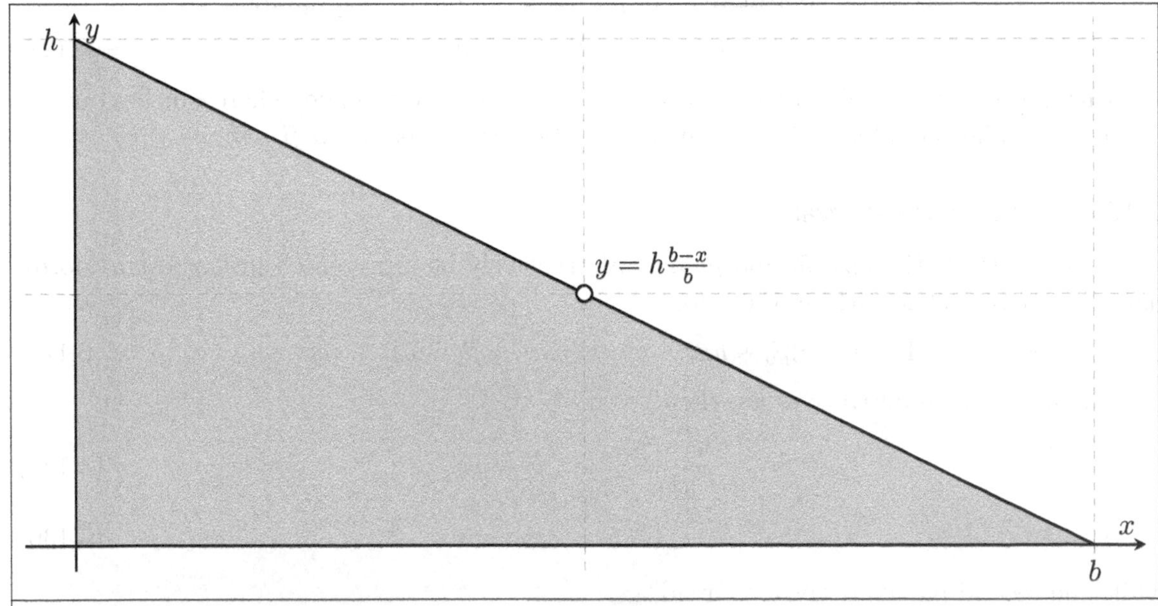

Figure 6.8: Triangle Sampling: Coordinate system used to draw a uniformly distributed random sample position on the surface of a triangle.

131 Integrating the joint *probability density* along the y axis then yields the marginal density in x

$$p(x) \triangleq \int_0^{h\frac{b-x}{b}} p(x, y)\mathrm{d}y = \int_0^{h\frac{b-x}{b}} \frac{2}{bh} \mathrm{d}y = \frac{2}{b} \frac{b - x}{b} \tag{6.137}$$

while applying *inverse-transform sampling* allows uniform sampling to be readily carried 134
from the respective marginal and conditional densities as

$$\begin{aligned}
\xi_x &= \int_0^{x_s} p(x)\mathrm{d}x = \int_0^{x_s} \frac{2}{b}\frac{b-x}{b}\mathrm{d}x = \frac{2}{b^2}\left[bx - \frac{x^2}{2}\right]_0^{x_s} = \frac{2bx_s - x_s^2}{b^2} \\
&\implies x_s = b\left(1 - \sqrt{1-\xi_x}\right) & (6.138) \\
\xi_y &= \int_0^{y_s} p(y \mid x_s)\mathrm{d}y \overset{(4.18)}{=} \int_0^{y_s} \frac{p(x_s, y)}{p(x_s)}\mathrm{d}y = \int_0^{y_s} \frac{\frac{2}{bh}}{\frac{2}{b}\frac{b-x_s}{b}}\mathrm{d}y = \frac{y_s}{h}\frac{b}{b-x_s} \\
&\implies y_s = h\frac{b-x_s}{b}\xi_y = h\frac{b - b\left(1-\sqrt{1-\xi_x}\right)}{b}\xi_y = h\xi_y\sqrt{1-\xi_x} & (6.139)
\end{aligned}$$

132

The sample position may finally be expressed in terms of barycentric coordinates to yield [Turk, 1990]

$$\begin{aligned}
\lambda_0 &\triangleq 1 - \lambda_1 - \lambda_2 &= (1-\xi_y)\sqrt{1-\xi_x} \\
\lambda_1 &\triangleq \frac{x_s}{b} &= 1 - \sqrt{1-\xi_x} \\
\lambda_2 &\triangleq \frac{y_s}{h} &= \xi_y\sqrt{1-\xi_x}
\end{aligned} \quad (6.140)$$

As an alternative, a similar distribution can instead be obtained by uniformly sampling
the extended *parallelogram* spanned by the two edge vectors. As illustrated in *Figure 6.9*, 258
a realization is directly accepted as a valid sample point on the triangle's surface whenever 255
$\xi_x + \xi_y \leq 1$. Otherwise, the sample point belongs to the complementary triangle, and it ought
to be either rejected, or reflected about the *parallelogram*'s center back into the original 258
triangle by substituting ξ_x with $1 - \xi_x$ and ξ_y with $1 - \xi_y$, although such an approach might
admittedly be less optimal for stratification purposes.

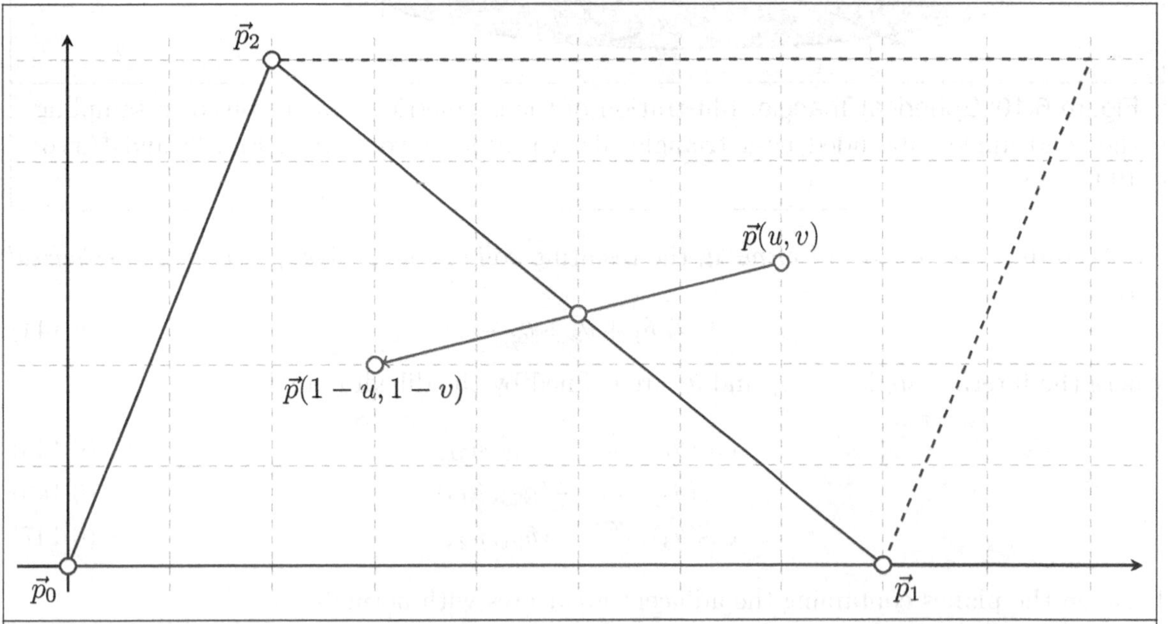

Figure 6.9: Triangle Resampling: Coordinate system used to remap a uniformly distributed random sample position drawn from the surface of a parallelogram onto the surface of an enclosed triangle.

6.2.3.6 Spherical Triangle

As illustrated in *Figure 6.10*, the projection of a triangle with vertices $\vec{p}_1$, $\vec{p}_2$ and $\vec{p}_3$, onto 256

269 a *sphere* of unit radius centered at a point $\vec{p}$, defines a *spherical triangle* that is delimited by the three adjacent great arcs (i.e., segments of great circles) connecting the three apex directions

$$\hat{\omega}_1 \triangleq \frac{\vec{p}_1 - \vec{p}}{||\vec{p}_1 - \vec{p}||} \tag{6.141}$$

$$\hat{\omega}_2 \triangleq \frac{\vec{p}_2 - \vec{p}}{||\vec{p}_2 - \vec{p}||} \tag{6.142}$$

$$\hat{\omega}_3 \triangleq \frac{\vec{p}_3 - \vec{p}}{||\vec{p}_3 - \vec{p}||} \tag{6.143}$$

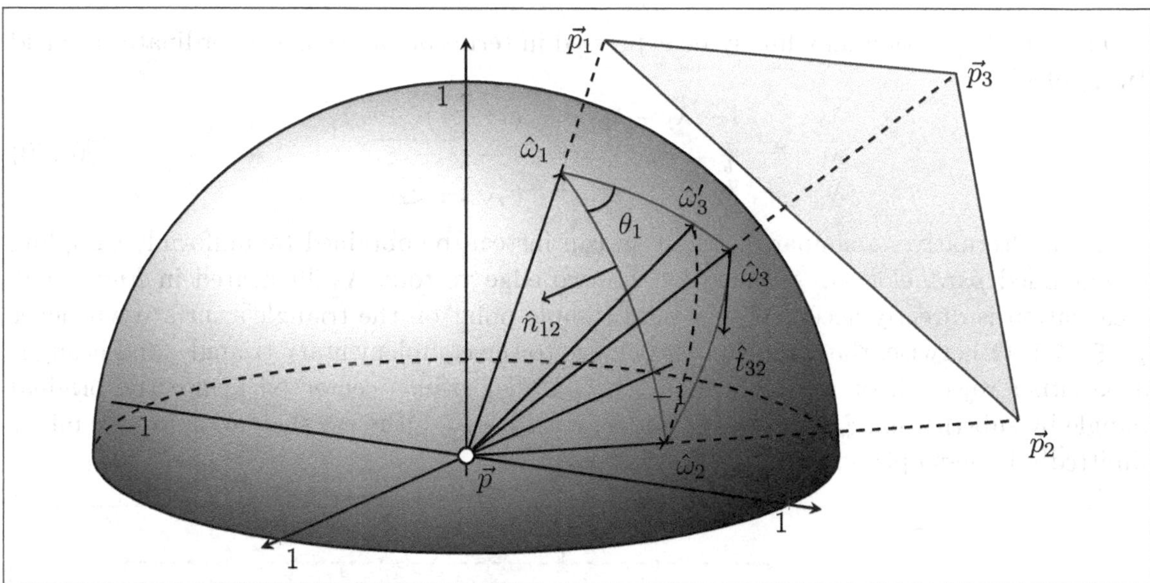

Figure 6.10: Spherical Triangle: Illustration of the geometric terms involved in sampling the solid angle subtended by a triangle (drawn after [Arvo, 1995b, Fig. 3] and [Arvo, 1995a, Fig. 4.11]).

244 According to the *Girard formula*, the resulting *solid angle* is then given by the *spherical excess*

$$\Omega \triangleq \theta_1 + \theta_2 + \theta_3 - \pi \tag{6.144}$$

where the internal angles θ_1, θ_2 and θ_3 are defined by the dihedral angles

$$\cos(\theta_1) \triangleq -\langle \hat{n}_{12}, \hat{n}_{31} \rangle \tag{6.145}$$

$$\cos(\theta_2) \triangleq -\langle \hat{n}_{23}, \hat{n}_{12} \rangle \tag{6.146}$$

$$\cos(\theta_3) \triangleq -\langle \hat{n}_{31}, \hat{n}_{23} \rangle \tag{6.147}$$

between the planes containing the adjacent great arcs with normals

$$\hat{n}_{12} \triangleq \frac{\hat{\omega}_1 \times \hat{\omega}_2}{||\hat{\omega}_1 \times \hat{\omega}_2||} \tag{6.148}$$

$$\hat{n}_{23} \triangleq \frac{\hat{\omega}_2 \times \hat{\omega}_3}{||\hat{\omega}_2 \times \hat{\omega}_3||} \tag{6.149}$$

$$\hat{n}_{31} \triangleq \frac{\hat{\omega}_3 \times \hat{\omega}_1}{||\hat{\omega}_3 \times \hat{\omega}_1||} \tag{6.150}$$

Alternatively, the cosine angles may be equivalently expressed in terms of the planes' tangents as

$$\cos(\theta_1) = \langle \hat{t}_{12}, \hat{t}_{13} \rangle \quad (6.151)$$
$$\cos(\theta_2) = \langle \hat{t}_{23}, \hat{t}_{21} \rangle \quad (6.152)$$
$$\cos(\theta_3) = \langle \hat{t}_{31}, \hat{t}_{32} \rangle \quad (6.153)$$

yielding the *spherical law of cosines for sides*

$$\langle \hat{t}_{ij}, \hat{t}_{ik} \rangle \triangleq \left\langle \frac{(\hat{\omega}_i \times \hat{\omega}_j) \times \hat{\omega}_i}{\|(\hat{\omega}_i \times \hat{\omega}_j) \times \hat{\omega}_i\|}, \frac{(\hat{\omega}_i \times \hat{\omega}_k) \times \hat{\omega}_i}{\|(\hat{\omega}_i \times \hat{\omega}_k) \times \hat{\omega}_i\|} \right\rangle$$
$$\overset{(3.110)}{=} \left\langle \frac{\hat{\omega}_j - \langle \hat{\omega}_i, \hat{\omega}_j \rangle \hat{\omega}_i}{\sqrt{1 - \langle \hat{\omega}_i, \hat{\omega}_j \rangle^2}}, \frac{\hat{\omega}_k - \langle \hat{\omega}_i, \hat{\omega}_k \rangle \hat{\omega}_i}{\sqrt{1 - \langle \hat{\omega}_i, \hat{\omega}_k \rangle^2}} \right\rangle$$ 82
$$\overset{(3.72)}{=} \frac{\langle \hat{\omega}_j, \hat{\omega}_k \rangle - \langle \hat{\omega}_i, \hat{\omega}_j \rangle \langle \hat{\omega}_i, \hat{\omega}_k \rangle}{\sqrt{1 - \langle \hat{\omega}_i, \hat{\omega}_j \rangle^2} \sqrt{1 - \langle \hat{\omega}_i, \hat{\omega}_k \rangle^2}} \quad (6.154)$$ 76

whereas the *spherical law of cosines for angles* reads

$$\langle \hat{\omega}_1, \hat{\omega}_2 \rangle = \frac{\cos(\theta_3) + \cos(\theta_1)\cos(\theta_2)}{\sin(\theta_1)\sin(\theta_2)} \quad (6.155)$$
$$\langle \hat{\omega}_2, \hat{\omega}_3 \rangle = \frac{\cos(\theta_1) + \cos(\theta_2)\cos(\theta_3)}{\sin(\theta_2)\sin(\theta_3)} \quad (6.156)$$
$$\langle \hat{\omega}_3, \hat{\omega}_1 \rangle = \frac{\cos(\theta_2) + \cos(\theta_3)\cos(\theta_1)}{\sin(\theta_3)\sin(\theta_1)} \quad (6.157)$$

Uniform sampling of the resulting *solid angle* may then be carried with joint *probability* 244
density $p(\hat{\omega}) \triangleq 1 \div \Omega$ by sampling a spherical sub-triangle with apex direction $\hat{\omega}'_3$, and 131
drawing a sample direction along the arc defined by $\hat{\omega}_2$ and $\hat{\omega}'_3$, according to the following
cumulative distributions [Arvo, 1995c, Arvo, 1995a, Ch. 5] 132

$$P(\hat{\omega}'_3) \triangleq \frac{\Omega'}{\Omega} \quad (6.158)$$
$$P(\hat{\omega}_s \mid \hat{\omega}'_3) \triangleq \frac{1 - \langle \hat{\omega}_2, \hat{\omega}_s \rangle}{1 - \langle \hat{\omega}_2, \hat{\omega}'_3 \rangle} \quad (6.159)$$

Applying *inverse-transform sampling* to the first *cumulative distribution* allows a sample 134
area to be uniformly drawn as 132

$$\xi_\Omega \overset{(6.158)}{=} \frac{\Omega'}{\Omega} \implies \Omega' = \xi_\Omega \Omega \quad (6.160)$$ 257

with the internal angles of the spherical sub-triangle being related by $\theta'_3 \overset{(6.144)}{=} \Omega' - \theta_1 - \theta'_2 + \pi$. 256
Substituting θ'_2 and the expression of θ'_3 into the spherical law of cosines for angles then yields

$$\langle \hat{\omega}_1, \hat{\omega}_2 \rangle \overset{(6.155)}{=} \frac{\cos(\Omega' - \theta_1 - \theta'_2 + \pi) + \cos(\theta_1)\cos(\theta'_2)}{\sin(\theta_1)\sin(\theta'_2)}$$ 257
$$= \frac{\cos(\theta_1)\cos(\theta'_2) - \cos(\Omega' - \theta_1 - \theta'_2)}{\sin(\theta_1)\sin(\theta'_2)}$$
$$= \frac{\cos(\theta_1)\cos(\theta'_2) - \left(\cos(\Omega' - \theta_1)\cos(\theta'_2) + \sin(\Omega' - \theta_1)\sin(\theta'_2)\right)}{\sin(\theta_1)\sin(\theta'_2)}$$
$$= \frac{\cos(\theta_1) - \cos(\Omega' - \theta_1) - \sin(\Omega' - \theta_1)\tan(\theta'_2)}{\sin(\theta_1)\tan(\theta'_2)} \quad (6.161)$$

such that

$$\tan(\theta_2') = \frac{\cos(\theta_1) - \cos(\Omega' - \theta_1)}{\langle\hat{\omega}_1, \hat{\omega}_2\rangle \sin(\theta_1) + \sin(\Omega' - \theta_1)} \tag{6.162}$$

while carrying a similar substitution eventually leads to

257

$$\begin{aligned}
\langle\hat{\omega}_3', \hat{\omega}_1\rangle &\overset{(6.157)}{=} \frac{\cos(\theta_2') + \cos(\Omega' - \theta_1 - \theta_2' + \pi)\cos(\theta_1)}{\sin(\Omega' - \theta_1 - \theta_2' + \pi)\sin(\theta_1)} \\
&= \frac{\cos(\Omega' - \theta_1 - \theta_2')\cos(\theta_1) - \cos(\theta_2')}{\sin(\Omega' - \theta_1 - \theta_2')\sin(\theta_1)} \\
&= \frac{\big(\cos(\Omega' - \theta_1)\cos(\theta_2') + \sin(\Omega' - \theta_1)\sin(\theta_2')\big)\cos(\theta_1) - \cos(\theta_2')}{\big(\sin(\Omega' - \theta_1)\cos(\theta_2') - \cos(\Omega' - \theta_1)\sin(\theta_2')\big)\sin(\theta_1)} \\
&= \frac{\big(\cos(\Omega' - \theta_1) + \sin(\Omega' - \theta_1)\tan(\theta_2')\big)\cos(\theta_1) - 1}{\big(\sin(\Omega' - \theta_1) - \cos(\Omega' - \theta_1)\tan(\theta_2')\big)\sin(\theta_1)} \qquad (6.163)
\end{aligned}$$

258

$$\begin{aligned}
&\overset{(6.162)}{=} \frac{\Big(\cos(\Omega' - \theta_1) + \sin(\Omega' - \theta_1)\frac{\cos(\theta_1) - \cos(\Omega' - \theta_1)}{\langle\hat{\omega}_1, \hat{\omega}_2\rangle\sin(\theta_1) + \sin(\Omega' - \theta_1)}\Big)\cos(\theta_1) - 1}{\Big(\sin(\Omega' - \theta_1) - \cos(\Omega' - \theta_1)\frac{\cos(\theta_1) - \cos(\Omega' - \theta_1)}{\langle\hat{\omega}_1, \hat{\omega}_2\rangle\sin(\theta_1) + \sin(\Omega' - \theta_1)}\Big)\sin(\theta_1)} \\
&= \frac{\langle\hat{\omega}_1, \hat{\omega}_2\rangle\big(\cos(\Omega' - \theta_1)\cos(\theta_1) - 1\big) - \sin(\Omega' - \theta_1)\sin(\theta_1)}{\langle\hat{\omega}_1, \hat{\omega}_2\rangle\sin(\Omega' - \theta_1)\sin(\theta_1) - \big(\cos(\Omega' - \theta_1)\cos(\theta_1) - 1\big)} \qquad (6.164)
\end{aligned}$$

Given $\hat{\omega}_3'$ by means of a form of spherical linear interpolation between $\hat{\omega}_1$ and $\hat{\omega}_3$, apply-
134 ing *inverse-transform sampling* to the second conditional distribution then allows a sample direction to be uniformly drawn as

257

$$\xi_\omega \overset{(6.159)}{=} \frac{1 - \langle\hat{\omega}_2, \hat{\omega}_s\rangle}{1 - \langle\hat{\omega}_2, \hat{\omega}_3'\rangle} \implies \langle\hat{\omega}_2, \hat{\omega}_s\rangle = 1 - \xi_\omega(1 - \langle\hat{\omega}_2, \hat{\omega}_3'\rangle) \tag{6.165}$$

6.2.3.7 Axial Moment

246 255 262 An *axial moment* defined over the domain of a *spherical triangle* can be readily evaluated as a special case of one defined over a *spherical polygon* with three vertices.

6.2.3.8 Further Reading

Additional material may be found in surveys dedicated to the comparison of ray–triangle intersection tests [Segura and Feito, 2001, Löfstedt and Möller, 2005, Kensler and Shirley, 2006].

6.2.4 Parallelogram

6.2.4.1 Plane-Based Intersection

259 As illustrated in *Figure 6.11*, a *parallelogram* of apex vertex $\vec{c}$ and edge vectors $\vec{e}_1$ and $\vec{e}_2$
247 may be carved out of an infinite *plane* by discarding all intersection points that lie outside
247 either of the two slabs defined by the edge vectors. A point $\vec{p}$ on the surface of the *plane* belongs to a slab if it belongs to the half plane containing the second edge vector

$$\begin{aligned}
\langle(\vec{p} - \vec{c}) \times \vec{e}_2, \vec{e}_1 \times \vec{e}_2\rangle &\geq 0 \qquad (6.166) \\
\langle(\vec{p} - \vec{c}) \times \vec{e}_1, \vec{e}_2 \times \vec{e}_1\rangle &\geq 0 \qquad (6.167)
\end{aligned}$$

and if its distance to the corresponding edge vector is less than the width of the slab

$$\frac{\|(\vec{p}-\vec{c})\times\vec{e}_2\|}{\|\vec{e}_2\|} \le \frac{\|\vec{e}_1\times\vec{e}_2\|}{\|\vec{e}_2\|} \tag{6.168}$$

$$\frac{\|(\vec{p}-\vec{c})\times\vec{e}_1\|}{\|\vec{e}_1\|} \le \frac{\|\vec{e}_2\times\vec{e}_1\|}{\|\vec{e}_1\|} \tag{6.169}$$

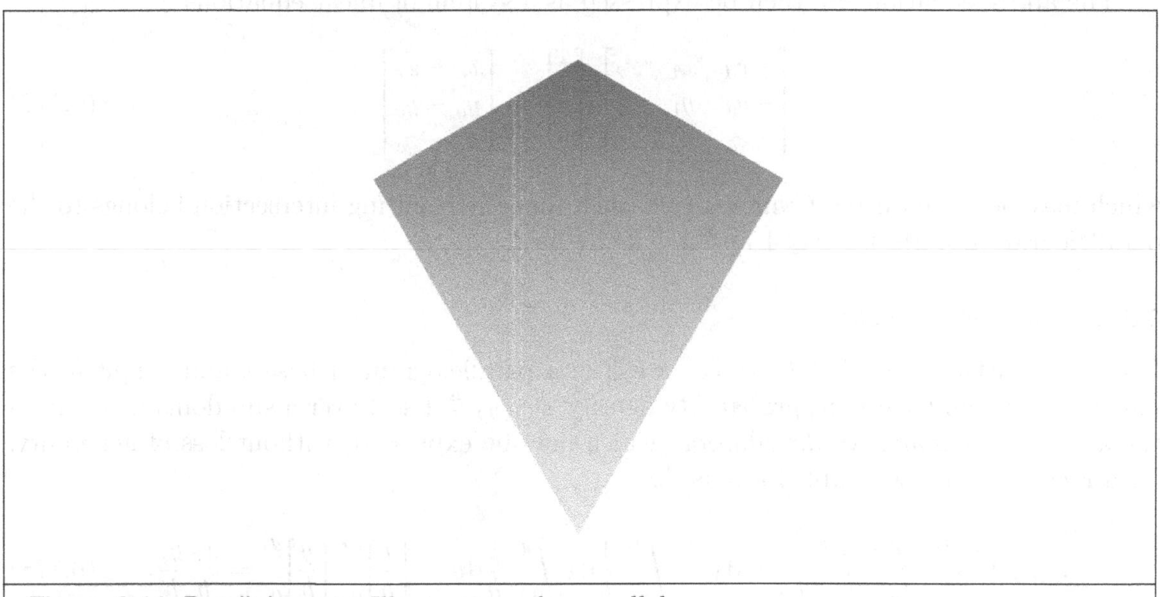

Figure 6.11: Parallelogram: Illustration of a parallelogram.

6.2.4.2 *Surface Parameterization*

A parallelogram of apex vertex $\vec{c}$ and edge vectors $\vec{e}_1$ and $\vec{e}_2$ may alternatively be represented
in *Cartesian coordinates* as a parametric surface of the form 67

$$\vec{p}(u,v) \triangleq \vec{c} + u\vec{e}_1 + v\vec{e}_2 \tag{6.170}$$

The first partial derivatives are then given by

$$\frac{\partial\vec{p}(u,v)}{\partial u} = \vec{e}_1 \tag{6.171}$$

$$\frac{\partial\vec{p}(u,v)}{\partial v} = \vec{e}_2 \tag{6.172}$$

while the second partial derivatives read

$$\frac{\partial^2\vec{p}(u,v)}{\partial u^2} = \vec{0} \tag{6.173}$$

$$\frac{\partial^2\vec{p}(u,v)}{\partial u\partial v} = \vec{0} \tag{6.174}$$

$$\frac{\partial^2\vec{p}(u,v)}{\partial v^2} = \vec{0} \tag{6.175}$$

6.2.4.3 *Parametric Intersection*

Equating the parametric representation $\vec{p}(u, v)$ with the set of points $\vec{p}$ defined by the ray equation $\vec{r}(t) \triangleq \vec{o} + t\vec{d}$ and rearranging the terms yields

259
$$-t\vec{d} + u\vec{e}_1 + v\vec{e}_2 \overset{(6.170)}{=} \vec{o} - \vec{c} \tag{6.176}$$

The above equation can then be expressed as a system of linear equations

$$\begin{bmatrix} -x_d & x_1 & x_2 \\ -y_d & y_1 & y_2 \\ -z_d & z_1 & z_2 \end{bmatrix} \begin{bmatrix} t \\ u \\ v \end{bmatrix} = \begin{bmatrix} x_o - x_c \\ y_o - y_c \\ z_o - z_c \end{bmatrix} \tag{6.177}$$

100 which may be solved using *Cramer's rule*, such that the resulting intersection belongs to the parallelogram if both $0 \le u \le 1$ and $0 \le v \le 1$ hold.

6.2.4.4 *Area and Sampling*

Given the surface area $A \triangleq bh = \|\vec{e}_1 \times \vec{e}_2\|$ of a parallelogram of base b and height h, the
131 integral of the uniform joint *probability density* $p(x, y) \triangleq 1 \div A$ over a sub-domain A_s yields
132 the associated *cumulative distribution*, which may be expressed, without loss of generality, for a rectangle in a separable form as

132
$$P(x_s, y_s) \overset{(4.22)}{=} \int_0^{x_s} \int_0^{y_s} \frac{1}{bh} \mathrm{d}y\mathrm{d}x = \int_0^{x_s} \frac{1}{b} \mathrm{d}x \int_0^{y_s} \frac{1}{h} \mathrm{d}y = \left[\frac{x}{b}\right]_0^{x_s} \left[\frac{y}{h}\right]_0^{y_s} = \frac{x_s}{b}\frac{y_s}{h} \tag{6.178}$$

Integrating over the whole domain by substituting $x_s = b$ and $y_s = h$ then ensures
134 normalization, while applying *inverse-transform sampling* allows uniform sampling to be readily carried as

$$\xi_x = \frac{x_s}{b} \implies x_s = \xi_x b \tag{6.179}$$

$$\xi_y = \frac{y_s}{h} \implies y_s = \xi_y h \tag{6.180}$$

6.2.4.5 *Spherical Rectangle*

261 As illustrated in *Figure 6.12*, the projection of a rectangular parallelogram, onto a *sphere*
269 of unit radius centered at a point $\vec{p}$, defines a *spherical rectangle* whose *solid angle* can be
244 readily evaluated by defining a local coordinate frame centered in $\vec{p}$ such that the rectangle lies in the z-plane with extent $[x_l, x_h] \times [y_l, y_h]$. Substituting $\vec{p} = [0, 0, 0]^T$, $\vec{q} = [x, y, z]^T$ and

$\hat{n}_q = [0, 0, -1]^T$ then yields

$$\begin{aligned}
\Omega &\overset{(6.61)}{\underset{(6.67)}{=}} \int_S \frac{\langle \hat{n}_q, \vec{p} - \vec{q} \rangle}{\|\vec{p} - \vec{q}\|^3} \mathrm{d}A(\vec{q}) \\
&\overset{(3.70)}{\underset{(3.61)}{=}} \int_{y_l}^{y_h} \int_{x_l}^{x_h} \frac{z}{(x^2 + y^2 + z^2)^{\frac{3}{2}}} \mathrm{d}x\mathrm{d}y \\
&= \int_{y_l}^{y_h} \left[\frac{xz}{(y^2 + z^2)\sqrt{x^2 + y^2 + z^2}} \right]_{x_l}^{x_h} \mathrm{d}y \\
&= \left[\left[\arctan\left(\frac{xy}{z\sqrt{x^2 + y^2 + z^2}} \right) \right]_{x_l}^{x_h} \right]_{y_l}^{y_h} \\
&\overset{(6.183)}{=} \arctan(\alpha_{hh}) - \arctan(\alpha_{lh}) - \arctan(\alpha_{hl}) + \arctan(\alpha_{ll}) && (6.181) \\
&= \arctan\left(\frac{\alpha_{hh} + \alpha_{ll}}{1 - \alpha_{hh}\alpha_{ll}} \right) - \arctan\left(\frac{\alpha_{lh} + \alpha_{hl}}{1 - \alpha_{lh}\alpha_{hl}} \right) \\
&= \arctan\left(\frac{\frac{\alpha_{hh}+\alpha_{ll}}{1-\alpha_{hh}\alpha_{ll}} - \frac{\alpha_{lh}+\alpha_{hl}}{1-\alpha_{lh}\alpha_{hl}}}{1 + \frac{\alpha_{hh}+\alpha_{ll}}{1-\alpha_{hh}\alpha_{ll}} \frac{\alpha_{lh}+\alpha_{hl}}{1-\alpha_{lh}\alpha_{hl}}} \right) \\
&= \arctan\left(\frac{(\alpha_{hh} + \alpha_{ll})(1 - \alpha_{lh}\alpha_{hl}) - (\alpha_{lh} + \alpha_{hl})(1 - \alpha_{hh}\alpha_{ll})}{(1 - \alpha_{hh}\alpha_{ll})(1 - \alpha_{lh}\alpha_{hl}) + (\alpha_{hh} + \alpha_{ll})(\alpha_{lh} + \alpha_{hl})} \right) && (6.182)
\end{aligned}$$

244 245 76 74 261

where

$$\alpha_{ij} \triangleq \frac{x_i y_j}{z\sqrt{x_i^2 + y_j^2 + z^2}} = \frac{\frac{x_i}{z}\frac{y_j}{z}}{\sqrt{\left(\frac{x_i}{z}\right)^2 + \left(\frac{y_j}{z}\right)^2 + 1}} \tag{6.183}$$

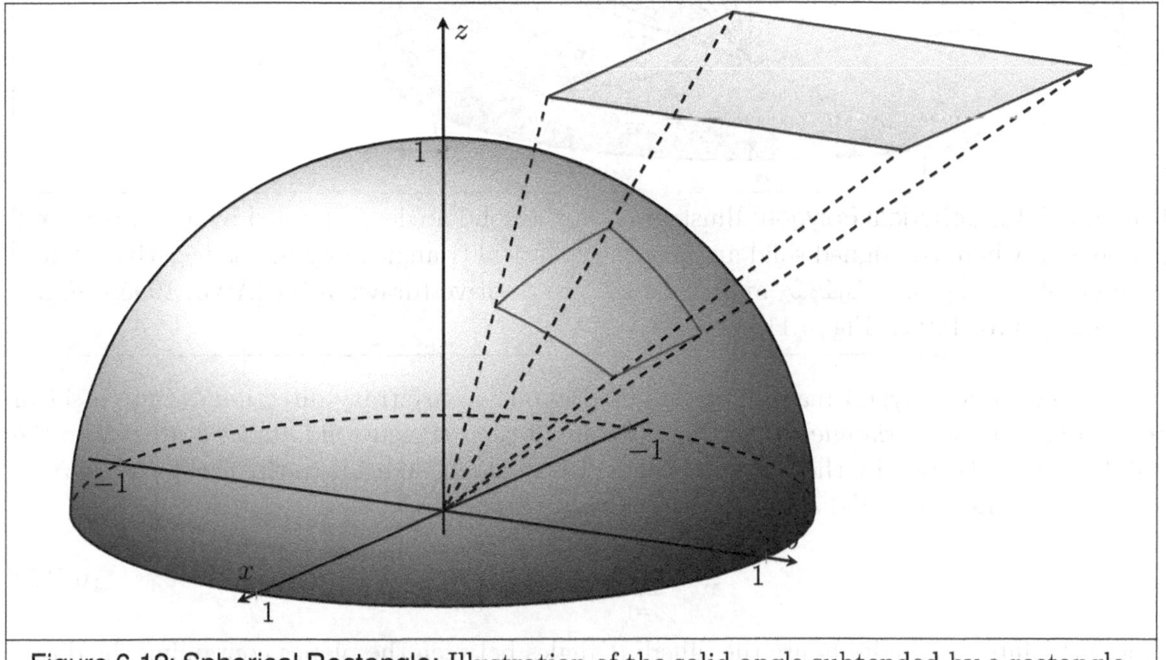

Figure 6.12: Spherical Rectangle: Illustration of the solid angle subtended by a rectangle.

Uniform sampling of the resulting *solid angle* may then be readily carried by decomposing 244
the spherical rectangle into two adjacent *spherical triangles*. 255

6.2.4.6 Axial Moment

246 An *axial moment* defined over the domain of a *spherical rectangle* can be readily evaluated
260 262 as a special case of one defined over a *spherical polygon* with four vertices.

6.2.5 Polygon

6.2.5.1 Spherical Polygon

262 As illustrated in *Figure 6.13*, the projection of an arbitrary (i.e., convex or concave) polygon
269 with n vertices $\vec{p}_i$, onto a *sphere* of unit radius centered at a point $\vec{p}$, defines a *spherical polygon*
that is delimited by the adjacent great arcs (i.e., segments of great circles) connecting the
apex directions

$$\hat{\omega}_i = \frac{\vec{p}_i - \vec{p}}{\|\vec{p}_i - \vec{p}\|} \tag{6.184}$$

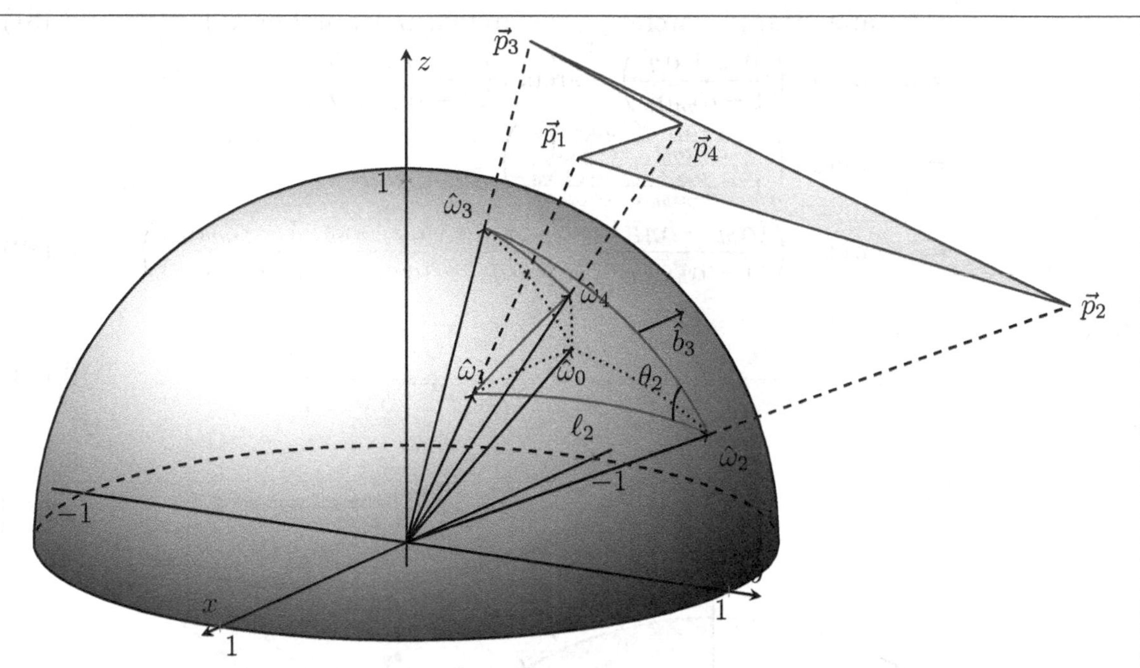

Figure 6.13: Spherical Polygon: Illustration of the solid angle subtended by a non-convex polygon, where the signed solid angle of the spherical triangle $\Delta\hat{\omega}_0\hat{\omega}_3\hat{\omega}_4$ is negative while those of $\Delta\hat{\omega}_0\hat{\omega}_1\hat{\omega}_2$, $\Delta\hat{\omega}_0\hat{\omega}_2\hat{\omega}_3$ and $\Delta\hat{\omega}_0\hat{\omega}_4\hat{\omega}_1$ are positive (drawn after [Arvo, 1995b, Fig. 3] and [Arvo, 1995a, Fig. 4.11]).

The geodesic polygon may be decomposed about an arbitrary direction $\hat{\omega}_0$ into a set of
255 individual *spherical triangles*, such that the sum of their signed *solid angles* evaluates to the
244 244 *solid angle* subtended by the polygon [Miller, 1994]. Doing so leads to the *generalized Girard*
244 *formula*, defining the *solid angle* as the *generalized spherical excess*

$$\Omega \triangleq \sum_{i=1}^{n} \theta_i - (n-2)\pi \tag{6.185}$$

where the internal angles θ_i are the dihedral angles between the planes containing the direction $\hat{\omega}_i$ and the adjacent directions $\hat{\omega}_{i-1}$ and $\hat{\omega}_{i+1}$, respectively.

6.2.5.2 Axial Moment

262 246 262 As illustrated in *Figure 6.13*, an *axial moment* defined over the domain of a *spherical polygon*

can be evaluated by reducing the boundary integral, whose sign depends on the orientation of the polygon, to a discrete sum of the integrals along the great arcs $\ell_k \triangleq [s_{k-1}, s_k]$ delineating the *spherical polygon*, along which the binormal $\hat{b}_k \triangleq (\vec{s}_{k-1} \times \vec{s}_k) \div \|\vec{s}_{k-1} \times \vec{s}_k\|$ is constant 262

$$\int_{\partial\Omega} \langle \vec{a}_1, \hat{\omega}(s)\rangle^n \langle \vec{a}_2, \vec{b}(s)\rangle \mathrm{d}s = \sum_{\ell_k \in \partial\Omega} \langle \vec{a}_2, \hat{b}_k\rangle \int_{s_{k-1}}^{s_k} \langle \vec{a}_1, \hat{\omega}(s)\rangle^n \mathrm{d}s \tag{6.186}$$

Parameterizing the direction $\hat{\omega}(s) = \cos(s)\hat{u} + \sin(s)\hat{v}$ in terms of the arc length s and two orthonormal vectors $\hat{u}$ and $\hat{v}$ forming a basis embedded within the corresponding great circle, the great arc integral then becomes

$$\begin{aligned}
\int_{s_{k-1}}^{s_k} \langle \vec{a}, \hat{\omega}(s)\rangle^n \mathrm{d}s &\overset{(3.72)}{=} \int_{s_{k-1}}^{s_k} \big(\cos(s)\langle \vec{a}, \hat{u}\rangle + \sin(s)\langle \vec{a}, \hat{v}\rangle\big)^n \mathrm{d}s \\
&= \int_{s_{k-1}}^{s_k} \big(\rho\cos(s)\cos(\phi) + \rho\sin(s)\sin(\phi)\big)^n \mathrm{d}s \\
&= \rho^n \int_{s_{k-1}}^{s_k} \cos(s-\phi)^n \mathrm{d}s \\
&= \rho^n \int_{s_{k-1}-\phi}^{s_k-\phi} \cos(s')^n \mathrm{d}s' \qquad (6.187)
\end{aligned}$$

76

where $\rho \triangleq \sqrt{\langle \vec{a}, \hat{u}\rangle^2 + \langle \vec{a}, \hat{v}\rangle^2}$ and $\phi \triangleq \operatorname{arctan2}(\langle \vec{a}, \hat{v}\rangle, \langle \vec{a}, \hat{u}\rangle)$.

The resulting integral may finally be evaluated in closed form by integrating the integrand by parts to yield the following antiderivative [Gradshteyn and Ryzhik, 2007]

$$\begin{aligned}
\int \cos(x)^n \mathrm{d}x &= \int \cos(x)\cos(x)^{n-1}\mathrm{d}x \\
&= \sin(x)\cos(x)^{n-1} + (n-1)\int \sin(x)\cos(x)^{n-2}\sin(x)\mathrm{d}x \\
&= \sin(x)\cos(x)^{n-1} + (n-1)\int \big(1-\cos(x)^2\big)\cos(x)^{n-2}\mathrm{d}x \\
&= \sin(x)\cos(x)^{n-1} + (n-1)\int \cos(x)^{n-2}\mathrm{d}x - (n-1)\int \cos(x)^n \mathrm{d}x \\
&= \frac{\sin(x)\cos(x)^{n-1} + (n-1)\int \cos(x)^{n-2}\mathrm{d}x}{n} \qquad (6.188) \\
&= \dots \\
&= \frac{\sin(x)}{n} \sum_{\substack{k=1 \\ k+=2}}^{\leq n-1} \left(\prod_{\substack{l=1 \\ l+=2}}^{\leq k-2} \frac{n-l}{n-l-1} \right) \cos(x)^{n-k} \qquad (6.189) \\
&+ \frac{(n \bmod 2)+1}{n} \left(\prod_{\substack{l=1 \\ l+=2}}^{\leq n-3} \frac{n-l}{n-l-1} \right) \times \begin{cases} x & \text{if } n \bmod 2 = 0 \\ \sin(x) & \text{if } n \bmod 2 = 1 \end{cases}
\end{aligned}$$

From an algorithmic standpoint, the summation that appears in *Equation 6.74* may 246
actually be folded into the one of the above antiderivative, allowing the computational cost to be reduced from $O(kn^2)$ to $O(kn)$, where k represents the number of edges of the polygon and n is the degree of the axial moment [Arvo, 1995b].

6.3 SECOND-ORDER SURFACES

6.3.1 Bilinear Patch

6.3.1.1 Explicit Form

Given sample values $s[i, j]$ at coordinates $[x_i, y_j]$ with sampling periods $T_x = x_1 - x_0$ and $T_y = y_1 - y_0$, a *bilinear patch* [Mehra and Kumar, 2008] may be explicitly defined as the
201 *reconstruction* of a height field $z = f(x, y)$ within the cell $[x_0, x_1] \times [y_0, y_1]$ using a *separable*
203 *filter* defined as the tensor product of two *tent filters*. As illustrated in *Figure 6.14*, substi-
206 265 tuting the semi-extent $t_m = 1$ of the filter and defining $[x_0, y_0]$ as the origin of the coordinate system then yields

203
$$\begin{aligned}
f(x, y) &\overset{(5.183)}{=} \sum_{n_y=\left\lceil \frac{y-y_0}{T_y}-1 \right\rceil}^{\left\lfloor \frac{y-y_0}{T_y}+1 \right\rfloor} \sum_{n_x=\left\lceil \frac{x-x_0}{T_x}-1 \right\rceil}^{\left\lfloor \frac{x-x_0}{T_x}+1 \right\rfloor} s[n_x, n_y] \left(1 - \left|\frac{x - x_0}{T_x} - n_x\right|\right) \left(1 - \left|\frac{y - y_0}{T_y} - n_y\right|\right) \\
&= \sum_{n_y=0}^{1} \sum_{n_x=0}^{1} s[n_x, n_y] (-1)^{1-n_x} \frac{x - x_{1-n_x}}{T_x} (-1)^{1-n_y} \frac{y - y_{1-n_y}}{T_y} \\
&= \frac{1}{T_x T_y} \sum_{n_x=0}^{1} (-1)^{n_x} (x - x_{1-n_x}) \sum_{n_y=0}^{1} (-1)^{n_y} (y - y_{1-n_y}) s[n_x, n_y] && (6.190) \\
&= \sum_{i=0}^{1} \sum_{j=0}^{1} d_{ij} x^i y^j && (6.191)
\end{aligned}$$

where

$$\begin{aligned}
d_{11} &\triangleq \frac{1}{T_x T_y} \sum_{n_x=0}^{1} \sum_{n_y=0}^{1} (-1)^{n_x+n_y} s[n_x, n_y] && (6.192) \\
&= \frac{(s[1, 1] + s[0, 0]) - (s[1, 0] + s[0, 1])}{T_x T_y} && (6.193) \\
d_{10} &\triangleq \frac{-1}{T_x T_y} \sum_{n_x=0}^{1} \sum_{n_y=0}^{1} (-1)^{n_x+n_y} y_{1-n_y} s[n_x, n_y] && (6.194) \\
&= \frac{y_1(s[1, 0] - s[0, 0]) - y_0(s[1, 1] - s[0, 1])}{T_x T_y} && (6.195) \\
d_{01} &\triangleq \frac{-1}{T_x T_y} \sum_{n_x=0}^{1} \sum_{n_y=0}^{1} (-1)^{n_x+n_y} x_{1-n_x} s[n_x, n_y] && (6.196) \\
&= \frac{x_1(s[0, 1] - s[0, 0]) - x_0(s[1, 1] - s[1, 0])}{T_x T_y} && (6.197) \\
d_{00} &\triangleq \frac{1}{T_x T_y} \sum_{n_x=0}^{1} \sum_{n_y=0}^{1} (-1)^{n_x+n_y} x_{1-n_x} y_{1-n_y} s[n_x, n_y] && (6.198) \\
&= \frac{(x_0 y_0 s[1, 1] + x_1 y_1 s[0, 0]) - (x_0 y_1 s[1, 0] + x_1 y_0 s[0, 1])}{T_x T_y} && (6.199)
\end{aligned}$$

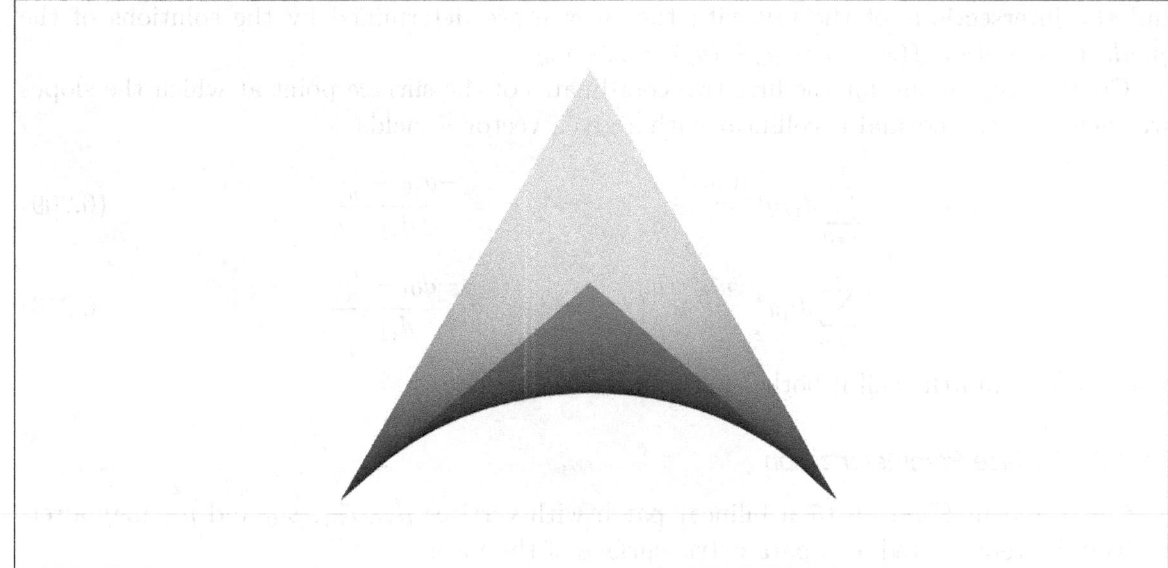

Figure 6.14: Bilinear Patch: Illustration of a bilinear patch.

The first partial derivatives are then given by

$$\frac{\partial f(x,y)}{\partial x} = \sum_{j=0}^{1} d_{1j} y^j = d_{10} + d_{11} y \tag{6.200}$$

$$\frac{\partial f(x,y)}{\partial y} = \sum_{i=0}^{1} d_{i1} x^i = d_{01} + d_{11} x \tag{6.201}$$

while the second partial derivatives read

$$\frac{\partial^2 f(x,y)}{\partial x^2} = 0 \tag{6.202}$$

$$\frac{\partial^2 f(x,y)}{\partial x \partial y} = d_{11} \tag{6.203}$$

$$\frac{\partial^2 f(x,y)}{\partial y^2} = 0 \tag{6.204}$$

Substituting the ray equation $\vec{r}(t) \triangleq \vec{o} + t\vec{d}$, the values of the height field under the ray are then defined as

264

$$\begin{aligned} f(x_o + tx_d, y_o + ty_d) &\overset{(6.191)}{=} \sum_{i=0}^{1}\sum_{j=0}^{1} d_{ij}(x_o + tx_d)^i (y_o + ty_d)^j \\ &= c_0 + c_1 t + c_2 t^2 \end{aligned} \tag{6.205}$$

where

$$c_0 \triangleq \sum_{i=0}^{1}\sum_{j=0}^{1} d_{ij} x_o^i y_o^j = d_{00} + d_{01} y_o + d_{10} x_o + d_{11} x_o y_o \tag{6.206}$$

$$c_1 \triangleq y_d \sum_{i=0}^{1} d_{i1} x_o^i + x_d \sum_{j=0}^{1} d_{1j} y_o^j = y_d(d_{01} + d_{11} x_o) + x_d(d_{10} + d_{11} y_o) \tag{6.207}$$

$$c_2 \triangleq x_d y_d d_{11} \tag{6.208}$$

and the intersections of the ray with the surface are determined by the solutions of the
28 quadratic equation $f(x_o + tx_d, y_o + ty_d) = z_o + tz_d$.

Conversely, solving for the first two coordinates of the surface point at which the slopes are such that the normal is collinear with a given vector $\vec{n}$ yields

237
$$\sum_{j=0}^{1} d_{1j} y^j \overset{(6.6)}{=} -\frac{n_x}{n_z} \implies y = \frac{-d_{10} - \frac{n_x}{n_z}}{d_{11}} \tag{6.209}$$

237
$$\sum_{i=0}^{1} d_{i1} x^i \overset{(6.7)}{=} -\frac{n_y}{n_z} \implies x = \frac{-d_{01} - \frac{n_y}{n_z}}{d_{11}} \tag{6.210}$$

which lies within the cell if both x and y are within range.

6.3.1.2 Surface Parameterization

266 As illustrated in *Figure 6.15*, a bilinear patch with vertices $\vec{p}_{00}$, $\vec{p}_{01}$, $\vec{p}_{10}$ and $\vec{p}_{11}$ may alternatively be represented as a parametric surface of the form

$$\begin{aligned} \vec{p}(u, v) &\triangleq uv\vec{p}_{11} + u(1 - v)\vec{p}_{10} + (1 - u)v\vec{p}_{01} + (1 - u)(1 - v)\vec{p}_{00} \\ &= uv\vec{d}_{11} + u\vec{d}_{10} + v\vec{d}_{01} + \vec{d}_{00} \end{aligned} \tag{6.211}$$

where

$$\vec{d}_{11} \triangleq \vec{p}_{11} - \vec{p}_{10} - \vec{p}_{01} + \vec{p}_{00} \tag{6.212}$$
$$\vec{d}_{10} \triangleq \vec{p}_{10} - \vec{p}_{00} \tag{6.213}$$
$$\vec{d}_{01} \triangleq \vec{p}_{01} - \vec{p}_{00} \tag{6.214}$$
$$\vec{d}_{00} \triangleq \vec{p}_{00} \tag{6.215}$$

and whose normal is readily given as

240
$$\vec{n}(u, v) \overset{(6.27)}{=} u\vec{d}_{10} \times \vec{d}_{11} + v\vec{d}_{11} \times \vec{d}_{01} + \vec{d}_{10} \times \vec{d}_{01} \tag{6.216}$$

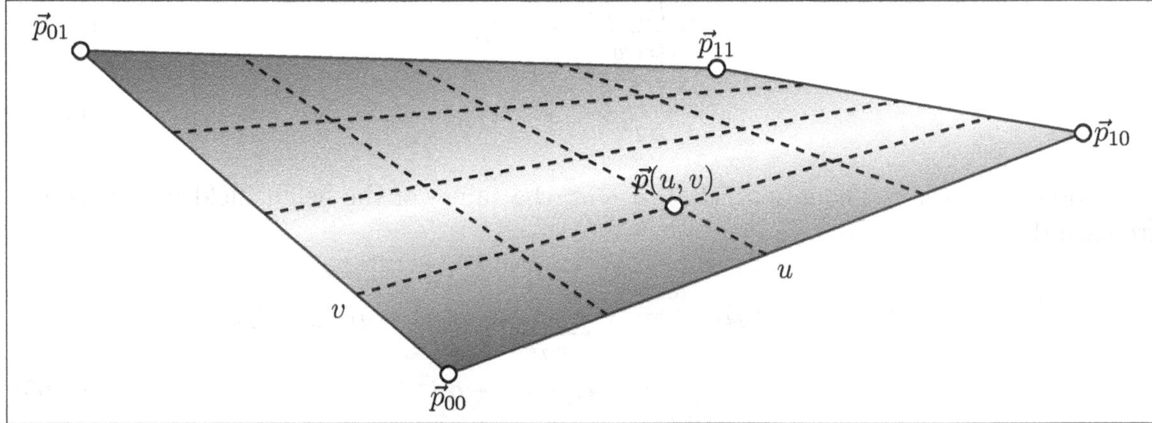

Figure 6.15: Bilinear Patch Parameterization: Illustration of the parametric representation of the surface of a bilinear patch.

The first partial derivatives are then given by

$$\frac{\partial \vec{p}(u, v)}{\partial u} = v\vec{d}_{11} + \vec{d}_{10} \tag{6.217}$$
$$\frac{\partial \vec{p}(u, v)}{\partial v} = u\vec{d}_{11} + \vec{d}_{01} \tag{6.218}$$

while the second partial derivatives read

$$\frac{\partial^2 \vec{p}(u,v)}{\partial u^2} = \vec{0} \tag{6.219}$$

$$\frac{\partial^2 \vec{p}(u,v)}{\partial u \partial v} = \vec{d}_{11} \tag{6.220}$$

$$\frac{\partial^2 \vec{p}(u,v)}{\partial v^2} = \vec{0} \tag{6.221}$$

Substituting the above expressions into the formulation of the Gaussian curvature then yields

$$K \overset{(6.56)}{=} \frac{\cancel{\langle \vec{n}(u,v), \vec{0}\rangle \langle \vec{n}(u,v), \vec{0}\rangle} - \langle \vec{n}(u,v), \vec{d}_{11}\rangle^2}{\|\vec{n}(u,v)\|^4}$$ 243

$$\overset{(6.224)}{=} -\frac{\langle u\vec{d}_{10} \times \vec{d}_{11} + v\vec{d}_{11} \times \vec{d}_{01} + \vec{d}_{10} \times \vec{d}_{01}, \vec{d}_{11}\rangle^2}{\|\vec{n}(u,v)\|^4}$$ 267

$$\overset{(3.74)}{=} -\frac{(u\cancel{\langle \vec{d}_{10} \times \vec{d}_{11}, \vec{d}_{11}\rangle} + v\cancel{\langle \vec{d}_{11} \times \vec{d}_{01}, \vec{d}_{11}\rangle} + \langle \vec{d}_{10} \times \vec{d}_{01}, \vec{d}_{11}\rangle)^2}{\|\vec{n}(u,v)\|^4}$$ 76

$$\overset{(3.100)}{=} -\frac{|\vec{d}_{11}, \vec{d}_{10}, \vec{d}_{01}|^2}{\|\vec{n}(u,v)\|^4} \tag{6.222}$$ 80

$$\leq 0 \tag{6.223}$$

Given a vector $\vec{n}$, the point of the patch at which the normal

$$\vec{n}(u,v) \overset{(6.27)}{=} (v\vec{d}_{11} + \vec{d}_{10}) \times (u\vec{d}_{11} + \vec{d}_{01})$$ 240

$$= uv\cancel{\vec{d}_{11} \times \vec{d}_{11}} + u\vec{d}_{10} \times \vec{d}_{11} + v\vec{d}_{11} \times \vec{d}_{01} + \vec{d}_{10} \times \vec{d}_{01}$$

$$\overset{(3.93)}{=} \begin{bmatrix} \vec{d}_{10} \times \vec{d}_{11} & \vec{d}_{11} \times \vec{d}_{01} & \vec{d}_{10} \times \vec{d}_{01} \end{bmatrix} \begin{bmatrix} u \\ v \\ 1 \end{bmatrix} \tag{6.224}$$ 79

is collinear with $\vec{n}$ conversely ought to satisfy

$$\begin{aligned} \vec{n} \times \vec{n}(u,v) &= \vec{n} \times \left(\begin{bmatrix} \vec{d}_{10} \times \vec{d}_{11} & \vec{d}_{11} \times \vec{d}_{01} & \vec{d}_{10} \times \vec{d}_{01} \end{bmatrix} \begin{bmatrix} u \\ v \\ 1 \end{bmatrix} \right) \\ &= M \begin{bmatrix} u \\ v \\ 1 \end{bmatrix} = \begin{bmatrix} m_{00}u + m_{01}v + m_{02} \\ m_{10}u + m_{11}v + m_{12} \\ m_{20}u + m_{21}v + m_{22} \end{bmatrix} = \vec{0} \end{aligned} \tag{6.225}$$

where

$$M \triangleq \begin{bmatrix} m_{00} & m_{01} & m_{02} \\ m_{10} & m_{11} & m_{12} \\ m_{20} & m_{21} & m_{22} \end{bmatrix} \triangleq \vec{n} \times \begin{bmatrix} \vec{d}_{10} \times \vec{d}_{11} & \vec{d}_{11} \times \vec{d}_{01} & \vec{d}_{10} \times \vec{d}_{01} \end{bmatrix} \tag{6.226}$$

and with the *cross product* being applied componentwise to the column vectors of the matrix. 78
Solving for the parametric coordinates by substituting the terms from the third equation into the first two then yields

$$m_{00}u - m_{01}\frac{m_{20}u + m_{22}}{m_{21}} + m_{02} = 0 \implies u = \frac{m_{01}m_{22} - m_{02}m_{21}}{m_{00}m_{21} - m_{01}m_{20}} \tag{6.227}$$

$$-m_{10}\frac{m_{21}v + m_{22}}{m_{20}} + m_{11}v + m_{12} = 0 \implies v = \frac{m_{10}m_{22} - m_{12}m_{20}}{m_{11}m_{20} - m_{10}m_{21}} \tag{6.228}$$

which lies within the patch if $u, v \in [0,1]$.

6.3.1.3 Parametric Intersection

Equating the parametric representation $\vec{p}(u, v)$ with the set of points $\vec{p}$ defined by the ray equation $\vec{r}(t) \triangleq \vec{o} + t\vec{d}$ and rearranging the terms yields [Ramsey *et al.*, 2004]

266

$$uv\vec{e}_{11} + u\vec{e}_{10} + v\vec{e}_{01} + \vec{e}_{00} \overset{(6.211)}{=} t\vec{d} \tag{6.229}$$

where

$$\begin{aligned}\vec{e}_{11} &\triangleq \vec{d}_{11} && (6.230)\\ \vec{e}_{10} &\triangleq \vec{d}_{10} && (6.231)\\ \vec{e}_{01} &\triangleq \vec{d}_{01} && (6.232)\\ \vec{e}_{00} &\triangleq \vec{d}_{00} - \vec{o} && (6.233)\end{aligned}$$

Expanding the vector form of the equation into its individual coordinates

$$\begin{aligned}\frac{uvx_{11} + ux_{10} + vx_{01} + x_{00}}{x_d} &= t && (6.234)\\ \frac{uvy_{11} + uy_{10} + vy_{01} + y_{00}}{y_d} &= t && (6.235)\\ \frac{uvz_{11} + uz_{10} + vz_{01} + z_{00}}{z_d} &= t && (6.236)\end{aligned}$$

and equating the expressions in x and y to the one in z yields

$$\begin{aligned}(uvx_{11} + ux_{10} + vx_{01} + x_{00})z_d &= (uvz_{11} + uz_{10} + vz_{01} + z_{00})x_d && (6.237)\\ (uvy_{11} + uy_{10} + vy_{01} + y_{00})z_d &= (uvz_{11} + uz_{10} + vz_{01} + z_{00})y_d && (6.238)\end{aligned}$$

such that rearranging the terms gives

$$\begin{aligned}uvc_{11} + uc_{10} + vc_{01} + c_{00} &= 0 && (6.239)\\ uvd_{11} + ud_{10} + vd_{01} + d_{00} &= 0 && (6.240)\end{aligned}$$

where

$$\begin{aligned}c_{11} &\triangleq x_{11}z_d - z_{11}x_d & d_{11} &\triangleq y_{11}z_d - z_{11}y_d\\ c_{10} &\triangleq x_{10}z_d - z_{10}x_d & d_{10} &\triangleq y_{10}z_d - z_{10}y_d\\ c_{01} &\triangleq x_{01}z_d - z_{01}x_d & d_{01} &\triangleq y_{01}z_d - z_{01}y_d\\ c_{00} &\triangleq x_{00}z_d - z_{00}x_d & d_{00} &\triangleq y_{00}z_d - z_{00}y_d\end{aligned} \tag{6.241}$$

Rearranging the equations into

$$\begin{aligned}u &= -\frac{vc_{01} + c_{00}}{vc_{11} + c_{10}} && (6.242)\\ u &= -\frac{vd_{01} + d_{00}}{vd_{11} + d_{10}} && (6.243)\end{aligned}$$

and equating the resulting expressions of u then yields

$$(vc_{01} + c_{00})(vd_{11} + d_{10}) = (vd_{01} + d_{00})(vc_{11} + c_{10}) \tag{6.244}$$

28 and thereby the *quadratic equation*

$$v^2(c_{01}d_{11} - d_{01}c_{11}) + v(c_{01}d_{10} + c_{00}d_{11} - d_{01}c_{10} - d_{00}c_{11}) + (c_{00}d_{10} - d_{00}c_{10}) = 0 \tag{6.245}$$

whose solutions give the values of v at the intersection points, in turn allowing the corresponding values of u and t to be computed via any of the above expressions.

6.3.2 Sphere

6.3.2.1 *Algebraic Intersection*

As illustrated in *Figure 6.16*, a *sphere* [Hultquist, 1990] of center $\vec{c}$ and radius r is defined 269
as the set of points $\vec{p}$ such that $\|\vec{p}-\vec{c}\| = r$. Substituting $\vec{p}$ with the set of points defined by
the ray equation $\vec{r}(t) \triangleq \vec{o} + t\vec{d}$ and squaring the result then yields the *quadratic equation* 28

$$\begin{aligned} \|\vec{o}+t\vec{d}-\vec{c}\|^2 &= \|t\vec{d}+(\vec{o}-\vec{c})\|^2 \\ &\overset{(3.75)}{=} \langle t\vec{d}+(\vec{o}-\vec{c}), t\vec{d}+(\vec{o}-\vec{c})\rangle \\ &\overset{(3.72)}{=} t^2\|\vec{d}\|^2 + 2t\langle\vec{d}, \vec{o}-\vec{c}\rangle + \|\vec{o}-\vec{c}\|^2 \\ &\overset{(3.75)}{=} r^2 \end{aligned} \quad (6.246)$$

76 76 76

whose solutions determine the points of intersection along the ray, while a vector orthogonal to the surface at that point is readily given by $\vec{n} = \vec{p} - \vec{c}$.

Figure 6.16: Sphere: Illustration of a sphere.

6.3.2.2 *Geometric Intersection*

As illustrated in *Figure 6.17*, the intersection of a ray with a sphere may also be determined 270
geometrically by first computing the parametric coordinate of the projection of its center $\vec{c}$ along the ray of origin $\vec{o}$ and direction $\vec{d}$ as

$$t_c \triangleq \langle\vec{d}, \vec{c}-\vec{o}\rangle \quad (6.247)$$

while the square of the distance between $\vec{c}$ and its projection is given by the Pythagorean theorem as

$$d_c^2 \triangleq \|\vec{c}-\vec{o}\|^2 - t_c^2 \quad (6.248)$$

Whenever $d_c^2 \leq r^2$, the distance between the projection of $\vec{c}$ and the points of intersection is similarly given by the Pythagorean theorem as

$$t_d \triangleq \sqrt{r^2 - d_c^2} \quad (6.249)$$

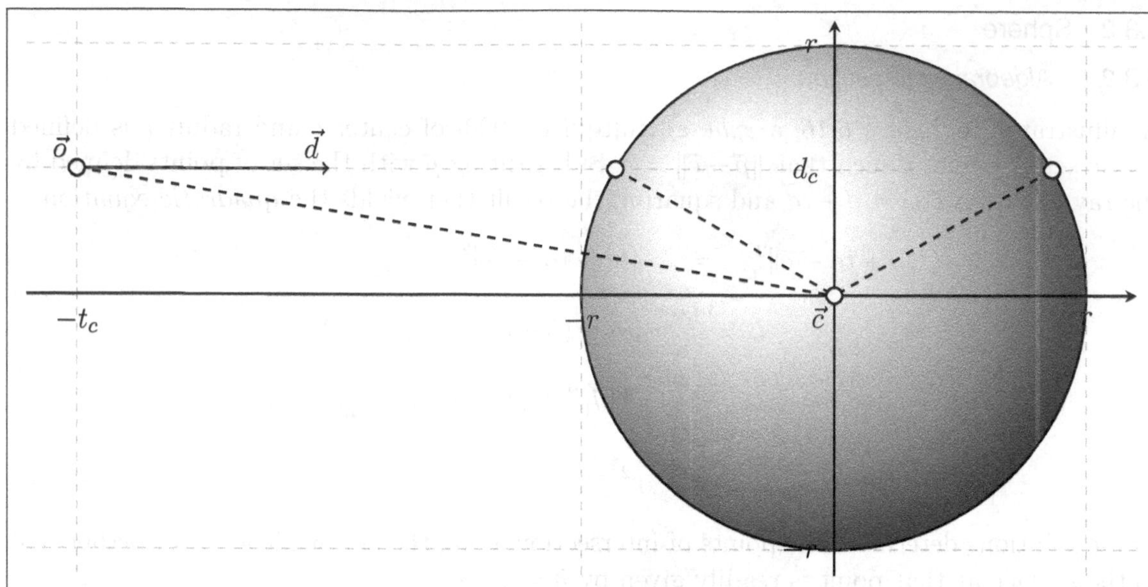

Figure 6.17: Sphere Intersection: Illustration of the terms involved in geometrically computing the intersection of a ray with a sphere.

such that the parametric coordinates of the intersection points read $t_c \pm t_d$, whereas no solutions exist shall $d_c^2 > r^2$.

6.3.2.3 Distance Estimation

The distance from a point $\vec{p}$ to a sphere of center $\vec{c}$ and radius r reads

$$f(\vec{p}) \triangleq \|\vec{p} - \vec{c}\| - r \tag{6.250}$$

6.3.2.4 Surface Parameterization

271 As illustrated in *Figure 6.18*, a *spherical patch* of radius r and extent $[\theta_l, \theta_h] \times [\phi_l, \phi_h]$ centered at the origin of a given coordinate system may alternatively be represented in *spherical*
70 *coordinates* as a parametric surface of the form

$$\vec{p}(u, v) \triangleq \begin{bmatrix} r \sin\left(\operatorname{lerp}(u, \theta_l, \theta_h)\right) \cos\left(\operatorname{lerp}(v, \phi_l, \phi_h)\right) \\ r \sin\left(\operatorname{lerp}(u, \theta_l, \theta_h)\right) \sin\left(\operatorname{lerp}(v, \phi_l, \phi_h)\right) \\ r \cos\left(\operatorname{lerp}(u, \theta_l, \theta_h)\right) \end{bmatrix} \tag{6.251}$$

whose unit normal is readily given as

240

$$\hat{n}(u, v) \overset{(6.27)}{=} \begin{bmatrix} \sin\left(\operatorname{lerp}(u, \theta_l, \theta_h)\right) \cos\left(\operatorname{lerp}(v, \phi_l, \phi_h)\right) \\ \sin\left(\operatorname{lerp}(u, \theta_l, \theta_h)\right) \sin\left(\operatorname{lerp}(v, \phi_l, \phi_h)\right) \\ \cos\left(\operatorname{lerp}(u, \theta_l, \theta_h)\right) \end{bmatrix} = \frac{\vec{p}(u, v)}{r} \tag{6.252}$$

The first partial derivatives are then given by

$$\frac{\partial \vec{p}(u, v)}{\partial u} = \begin{bmatrix} (\theta_h - \theta_l) r \cos\left(\operatorname{lerp}(u, \theta_l, \theta_h)\right) \cos\left(\operatorname{lerp}(v, \phi_l, \phi_h)\right) \\ (\theta_h - \theta_l) r \cos\left(\operatorname{lerp}(u, \theta_l, \theta_h)\right) \sin\left(\operatorname{lerp}(v, \phi_l, \phi_h)\right) \\ -(\theta_h - \theta_l) r \sin\left(\operatorname{lerp}(u, \theta_l, \theta_h)\right) \end{bmatrix} \tag{6.253}$$

$$= (\theta_h - \theta_l) \begin{bmatrix} p_z(u, v) \cos\left(\operatorname{lerp}(v, \phi_l, \phi_h)\right) \\ p_z(u, v) \sin\left(\operatorname{lerp}(v, \phi_l, \phi_h)\right) \\ -\sqrt{r^2 - p_z(u, v)^2} \end{bmatrix} \tag{6.254}$$

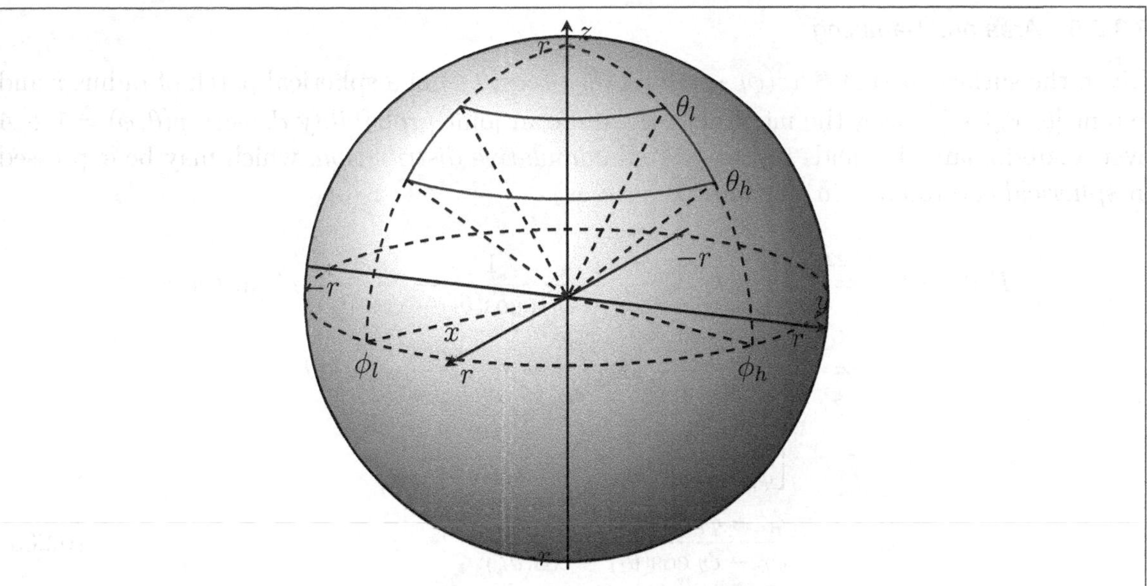

Figure 6.18: Sphere Parameterization: Illustration of the parametric representation of the surface of a sphere.

$$\frac{\partial \vec{p}(u,v)}{\partial v} = \begin{bmatrix} -(\phi_h - \phi_l) r \sin\left(\operatorname{lerp}(u, \theta_l, \theta_h)\right) \sin\left(\operatorname{lerp}(v, \phi_l, \phi_h)\right) \\ (\phi_h - \phi_l) r \sin\left(\operatorname{lerp}(u, \theta_l, \theta_h)\right) \cos\left(\operatorname{lerp}(v, \phi_l, \phi_h)\right) \\ 0 \end{bmatrix} \tag{6.255}$$

$$= (\phi_h - \phi_l) \begin{bmatrix} -p_y(u,v) \\ p_x(u,v) \\ 0 \end{bmatrix} \tag{6.256}$$

while the second partial derivatives read

$$\frac{\partial^2 \vec{p}(u,v)}{\partial u^2} = \begin{bmatrix} -(\theta_h - \theta_l)^2 r \sin\left(\operatorname{lerp}(u, \theta_l, \theta_h)\right) \cos\left(\operatorname{lerp}(v, \phi_l, \phi_h)\right) \\ -(\theta_h - \theta_l)^2 r \sin\left(\operatorname{lerp}(u, \theta_l, \theta_h)\right) \sin\left(\operatorname{lerp}(v, \phi_l, \phi_h)\right) \\ -(\theta_h - \theta_l)^2 r \cos\left(\operatorname{lerp}(u, \theta_l, \theta_h)\right) \end{bmatrix} \tag{6.257}$$

$$= -(\theta_h - \theta_l)^2 \vec{p}(u,v) \tag{6.258}$$

$$\frac{\partial^2 \vec{p}(u,v)}{\partial u \partial v} = \begin{bmatrix} -(\theta_h - \theta_l)(\phi_h - \phi_l) r \cos\left(\operatorname{lerp}(u, \theta_l, \theta_h)\right) \sin\left(\operatorname{lerp}(v, \phi_l, \phi_h)\right) \\ (\theta_h - \theta_l)(\phi_h - \phi_l) r \cos\left(\operatorname{lerp}(u, \theta_l, \theta_h)\right) \cos\left(\operatorname{lerp}(v, \phi_l, \phi_h)\right) \\ 0 \end{bmatrix} \tag{6.259}$$

$$= (\theta_h - \theta_l)(\phi_h - \phi_l) \begin{bmatrix} -p_z(u,v) \sin\left(\operatorname{lerp}(v, \phi_l, \phi_h)\right) \\ p_z(u,v) \cos\left(\operatorname{lerp}(v, \phi_l, \phi_h)\right) \\ 0 \end{bmatrix} \tag{6.260}$$

$$\frac{\partial^2 \vec{p}(u,v)}{\partial v^2} = \begin{bmatrix} -(\phi_h - \phi_l)^2 r \sin\left(\operatorname{lerp}(u, \theta_l, \theta_h)\right) \cos\left(\operatorname{lerp}(v, \phi_l, \phi_h)\right) \\ -(\phi_h - \phi_l)^2 r \sin\left(\operatorname{lerp}(u, \theta_l, \theta_h)\right) \sin\left(\operatorname{lerp}(v, \phi_l, \phi_h)\right) \\ 0 \end{bmatrix} \tag{6.261}$$

$$= -(\phi_h - \phi_l)^2 \begin{bmatrix} p_x(u,v) \\ p_y(u,v) \\ 0 \end{bmatrix} \tag{6.262}$$

6.3.2.5 Area and Sampling

Given the surface area $A \triangleq r^2(\phi_h - \phi_l)(\cos(\theta_l) - \cos(\theta_h))$ of a spherical patch of radius r and
131 extent $[\theta_l, \theta_h] \times [\phi_l, \phi_h]$, the integral of the uniform joint *probability density* $p(\theta, \phi) \triangleq 1 \div A$
132 over a subdomain A_s yields the associated *cumulative distribution*, which may be expressed
70 in *spherical coordinates* in a separable form as

132

$$\begin{aligned}
P(\theta_s, \phi_s) &\overset{(4.22)}{=} \int_{\phi_l}^{\phi_s} \int_{\theta_l}^{\theta_s} \frac{1}{r^2(\phi_h - \phi_l)(\cos(\theta_l) - \cos(\theta_h))} r^2 \sin(\theta) \mathrm{d}\theta \mathrm{d}\phi \\
&= \int_{\phi_l}^{\phi_s} \frac{1}{\phi_h - \phi_l} \mathrm{d}\phi \int_{\theta_l}^{\theta_s} \frac{\sin(\theta)}{\cos(\theta_l) - \cos(\theta_h)} \mathrm{d}\theta \\
&= \left[\frac{\phi}{\phi_h - \phi_l}\right]_{\phi_l}^{\phi_s} \left[\frac{-\cos(\theta)}{\cos(\theta_l) - \cos(\theta_h)}\right]_{\theta_l}^{\theta_s} \\
&= \frac{\phi_s - \phi_l}{\phi_h - \phi_l} \frac{\cos(\theta_l) - \cos(\theta_s)}{\cos(\theta_l) - \cos(\theta_h)} \qquad (6.263)
\end{aligned}$$

Integrating over the whole domain by substituting $\phi_s = \phi_h$ and $\theta_s = \theta_h$ then ensures
134 normalization, while applying *inverse-transform sampling* allows uniform sampling to be readily carried as

$$\xi_\phi = \frac{\phi_s - \phi_l}{\phi_h - \phi_l} \implies \phi_s = \operatorname{lerp}(\xi_\phi, \phi_l, \phi_h) \qquad (6.264)$$

$$\xi_\theta = \frac{\cos(\theta_l) - \cos(\theta_s)}{\cos(\theta_l) - \cos(\theta_h)} \implies \theta_s = \arccos\Big(\operatorname{lerp}\left(\xi_\theta, \cos(\theta_l), \cos(\theta_h)\right)\Big) \qquad (6.265)$$

6.3.2.6 Spherical Cap

273 As illustrated in *Figure 6.19*, the projection of a sphere of radius r centered at a point $\vec{c}$, onto a sphere of unit radius centered at a point $\vec{p}$, defines a *spherical cap* with apex angle θ_a whose cosine reads

$$\cos(\theta_a) = \sqrt{1 - \sin(\theta_a)^2} = \sqrt{1 - \frac{r^2}{\|\vec{c} - \vec{p}\|^2}} \qquad (6.266)$$

244 while the resulting *solid angle* is readily given by

244

$$\Omega \underset{(6.63)}{\overset{(6.61)}{=}} \int_0^{2\pi} \mathrm{d}\phi \int_0^{\theta_a} \sin(\theta)\mathrm{d}\theta = [\phi]_0^{2\pi}[-\cos(\theta)]_0^{\theta_a} = 2\pi(1 - \cos(\theta_a)) \qquad (6.267)$$

244

244 Uniform sampling of the resulting *solid angle* may then be readily carried by drawing a random direction within an oriented patch from the surface of a sphere of radius $r = 1$ with extent $[0, \theta_a] \times [0, 2\pi]$.

6.3.3 Cylinder

6.3.3.1 Algebraic Intersection

274 As illustrated in *Figure 6.20*, a circular *cylinder* [Shene, 1994, Cychosz and Waggenspack,
80 1994] of center $\vec{c}$, axis $\hat{u}$ and radius r is defined as the set of points $\vec{p}$ such that $\|(\vec{p} - \vec{c}) \times \hat{u}\| \overset{(3.96)}{=} r$. Substituting $\vec{p}$ with the set of points defined by the ray equation $\vec{r}(t) \triangleq \vec{o} + t\vec{d}$ and squaring
28 the result then yields the *quadratic equation*

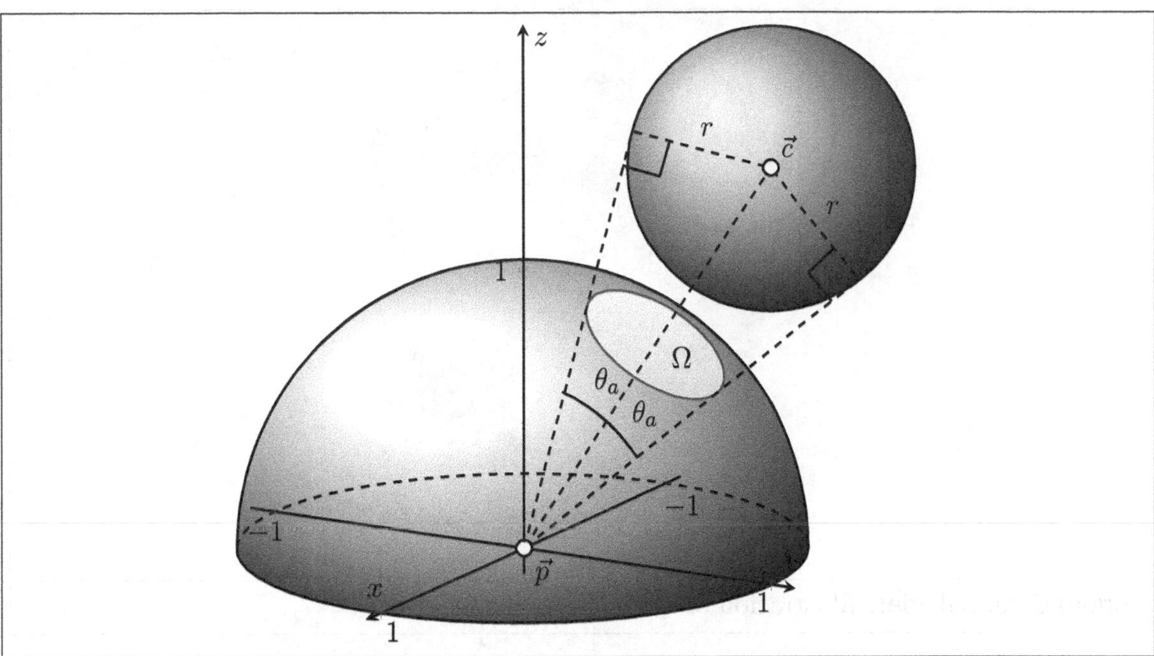

Figure 6.19: Spherical Cap: Illustration of the geometric terms involved in evaluating the solid angle subtended by a sphere.

$$\begin{aligned}
\|(\vec{o}+t\vec{d}-\vec{c})\times\hat{u}\|^2 &\overset{(3.91)}{=} \|t\vec{d}\times\hat{u}+(\vec{o}-\vec{c})\times\hat{u}\|^2 \\
&\overset{(3.75)}{=} \langle t\vec{d}\times\hat{u}+(\vec{o}-\vec{c})\times\hat{u}, t\vec{d}\times\hat{u}+(\vec{o}-\vec{c})\times\hat{u}\rangle \\
&\overset{(3.72)}{=} t^2\|\vec{d}\times\hat{u}\|^2+2t\langle\vec{d}\times\hat{u},(\vec{o}-\vec{c})\times\hat{u}\rangle+\|(\vec{o}-\vec{c})\times\hat{u}\|^2 \\
&\overset{(3.75)}{=} r^2
\end{aligned} \tag{6.268}$$

79 76 76 76

whose solutions determine the points of intersection along the ray, while a vector orthogonal to the surface at that point is readily given by $\vec{n} = (\hat{u}\times(\vec{p}-\vec{c}))\times\hat{u} = (\vec{p}-\vec{c}) - \langle\hat{u},\vec{p}-\vec{c}\rangle\hat{u}$.

6.3.3.2 Distance Estimation

The distance from a point $\vec{p}$ to a circular cylinder of center $\vec{c}$, axis $\hat{u}$ and radius r reads

$$f(\vec{p}) \overset{(3.96)}{=} \|(\vec{p}-\vec{c})\times\hat{u}\| - r \tag{6.269}$$ 80

6.3.3.3 Surface Parameterization

As illustrated in *Figure 6.21*, a *cylindrical patch* of radius ρ and extent $[\phi_l, \phi_h] \times [z_l, z_h]$ 274
centered at the origin and oriented along the z axis of a given coordinate system may alternatively be represented in *cylindrical coordinates* as a parametric surface of the form 69

$$\vec{p}(u,v) \triangleq \begin{bmatrix} \rho\cos(\operatorname{lerp}(u,\phi_l,\phi_h)) \\ \rho\sin(\operatorname{lerp}(u,\phi_l,\phi_h)) \\ \operatorname{lerp}(v,z_l,z_h) \end{bmatrix} \tag{6.270}$$

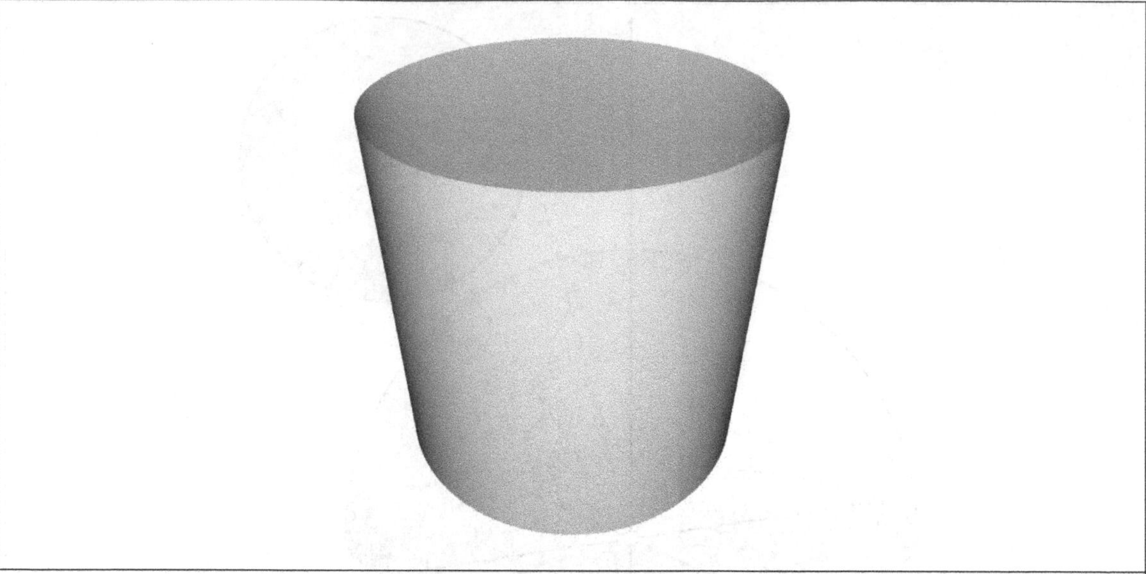

Figure 6.20: Cylinder: Illustration of a circular cylinder.

whose unit normal is readily given as

240

$$\hat{n}(u,v) \stackrel{(6.27)}{=} \begin{bmatrix} \cos\left(\operatorname{lerp}(u,\phi_l,\phi_h)\right) \\ \sin\left(\operatorname{lerp}(u,\phi_l,\phi_h)\right) \\ 0 \end{bmatrix} \tag{6.271}$$

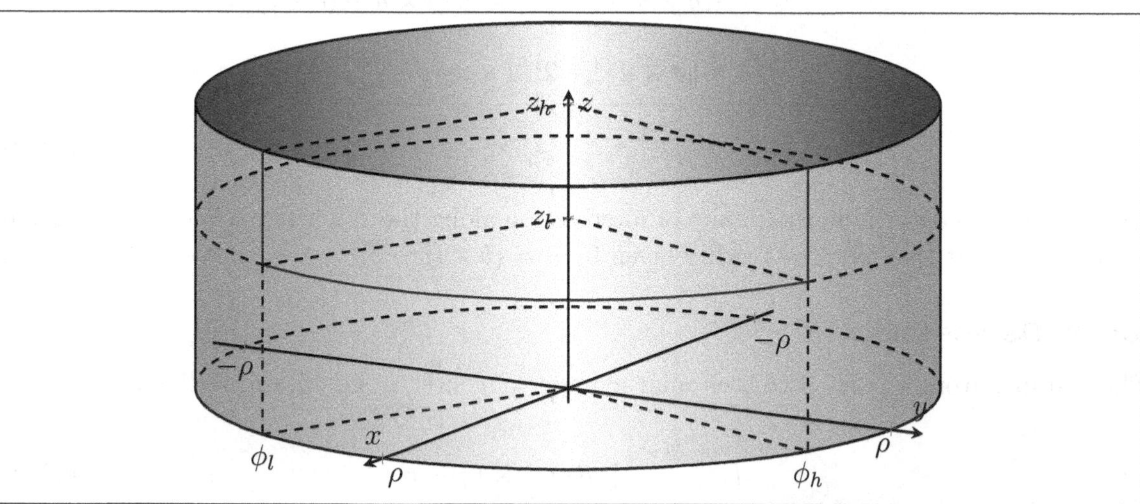

Figure 6.21: Cylinder Parameterization: Illustration of the parametric representation of the surface of a circular cylinder.

The first partial derivatives are then given by

$$\frac{\partial\vec{p}(u,v)}{\partial u} = \begin{bmatrix} -(\phi_h-\phi_l)\rho\sin\left(\operatorname{lerp}(u,\phi_l,\phi_h)\right) \\ (\phi_h-\phi_l)\rho\cos\left(\operatorname{lerp}(u,\phi_l,\phi_h)\right) \\ 0 \end{bmatrix} = (\phi_h-\phi_l)\begin{bmatrix} -p_y(u,v) \\ p_x(u,v) \\ 0 \end{bmatrix} \tag{6.272}$$

$$\frac{\partial\vec{p}(u,v)}{\partial v} = \begin{bmatrix} 0 \\ 0 \\ z_h-z_l \end{bmatrix} = (z_h-z_l)\begin{bmatrix} 0 \\ 0 \\ 1 \end{bmatrix} \tag{6.273}$$

while the second partial derivatives read

$$\frac{\partial^2 \vec{p}(u,v)}{\partial u^2} = \begin{bmatrix} -(\phi_h - \phi_l)^2 \rho \cos\left(\operatorname{lerp}(u, \phi_l, \phi_h)\right) \\ -(\phi_h - \phi_l)^2 \rho \sin\left(\operatorname{lerp}(u, \phi_l, \phi_h)\right) \\ 0 \end{bmatrix} = -(\phi_h - \phi_l)^2 \begin{bmatrix} p_x(u,v) \\ p_y(u,v) \\ 0 \end{bmatrix} \quad (6.274)$$

$$\frac{\partial^2 \vec{p}(u,v)}{\partial u \partial v} = \vec{0} \quad (6.275)$$

$$\frac{\partial^2 \vec{p}(u,v)}{\partial v^2} = \vec{0} \quad (6.276)$$

6.3.3.4 *Area and Sampling*

Given the surface area $A \triangleq (\phi_h - \phi_l)\rho(z_h - z_l)$ of the cylindrical patch, the integral of the uniform joint *probability density* $p(\phi, z) \triangleq 1 \div A$ over a subdomain A_s yields the associated 131
cumulative distribution, which may be expressed in a separable form as 132

$$\begin{aligned} P(\phi_s, z_s) &\overset{(4.22)}{=} \int_{\phi_l}^{\phi_s} \int_{z_l}^{z_s} \frac{1}{(\phi_h - \phi_l)\rho(z_h - z_l)} \rho \mathrm{d}z \mathrm{d}\phi \\ &= \int_{\phi_l}^{\phi_s} \frac{1}{\phi_h - \phi_l} \mathrm{d}\phi \int_{z_l}^{z_s} \frac{1}{z_h - z_l} \mathrm{d}z \\ &= \left[\frac{\phi}{\phi_h - \phi_l}\right]_{\phi_l}^{\phi_s} \left[\frac{z}{z_h - z_l}\right]_{z_l}^{z_s} \\ &= \frac{\phi_s - \phi_l}{\phi_h - \phi_l} \frac{z_s - z_l}{z_h - z_l} \quad (6.277) \end{aligned}$$ 132

Integrating over the whole domain by substituting $\phi_s = \phi_h$ and $z_s = z_h$ then ensures normalization, while applying *inverse-transform sampling* allows uniform sampling to be 134
readily carried as

$$\xi_\phi = \frac{\phi_s - \phi_l}{\phi_h - \phi_l} \implies \phi_s = \operatorname{lerp}(\xi_\phi, \phi_l, \phi_h) \quad (6.278)$$

$$\xi_z = \frac{z_s - z_l}{z_h - z_l} \implies z_s = \operatorname{lerp}(\xi_z, z_l, z_h) \quad (6.279)$$

6.3.4 Cone

6.3.4.1 *Algebraic Intersection*

As illustrated in *Figure 6.22*, a circular *cone* [Shene, 1995] of center $\vec{c}$, axis $\hat{u}$ and cosine angle 276
$\mu \triangleq \cos(\theta)$ is defined as the set of points $\vec{p}$ such that $\langle \vec{p} - \vec{c}, \hat{u} \rangle \div \|\vec{p} - \vec{c}\| \overset{(3.77)}{=} \mu$. Substituting 77
$\vec{p}$ with the set of points defined by the ray equation $\vec{r}(t) \triangleq \vec{o} + t\vec{d}$ and squaring the result then yields

$$\begin{aligned} \frac{\langle \vec{o} + t\vec{d} - \vec{c}, \hat{u} \rangle^2}{\|\vec{o} + t\vec{d} - \vec{c}\|^2} &= \frac{\langle t\vec{d} + (\vec{o} - \vec{c}), \hat{u} \rangle^2}{\|t\vec{d} + (\vec{o} - \vec{c})\|^2} \\ &\overset{(3.72)}{\underset{(3.75)}{=}} \frac{(t\langle \vec{d}, \hat{u} \rangle + \langle \vec{o} - \vec{c}, \hat{u} \rangle)^2}{\langle t\vec{d} + (\vec{o} - \vec{c}), t\vec{d} + (\vec{o} - \vec{c}) \rangle} \\ &\overset{(3.72)}{\underset{(3.75)}{=}} \frac{t^2 \langle \vec{d}, \hat{u} \rangle^2 + 2t\langle \vec{d}, \hat{u} \rangle \langle \vec{o} - \vec{c}, \hat{u} \rangle + \langle \vec{o} - \vec{c}, \hat{u} \rangle^2}{t^2 \|\vec{d}\|^2 + 2t\langle \vec{d}, \vec{o} - \vec{c} \rangle + \|\vec{o} - \vec{c}\|^2} \\ &= \mu^2 \quad (6.280) \end{aligned}$$ 76 76 76 76

28 leading to the *quadratic equation*

$$t^2(\langle\vec{d},\hat{u}\rangle^2-\|\vec{d}\|^2\mu^2)+2t(\langle\vec{d},\hat{u}\rangle\langle\vec{o}-\vec{c},\hat{u}\rangle-\langle\vec{d},\vec{o}-\vec{c}\rangle\mu^2)+(\langle\vec{o}-\vec{c},\hat{u}\rangle^2-\|\vec{o}-\vec{c}\|^2\mu^2)=0 \quad (6.281)$$

whose solutions determine the points of intersection along the ray, while a vector orthogonal
81 to the surface at that point is readily given by the *vector triple product*

$$\begin{aligned}\vec{n} &\triangleq -((\vec{p}-\vec{c})\times\hat{u})\times(\vec{p}-\vec{c})\\ &\overset{(3.110)}{=} \langle\vec{p}-\vec{c},\hat{u}\rangle(\vec{p}-\vec{c})-\|\vec{p}-\vec{c}\|^2\hat{u}\\ &= \|\vec{p}-\vec{c}\|\mu(\vec{p}-\vec{c})-\|\vec{p}-\vec{c}\|^2\hat{u} \qquad (6.282)\end{aligned}$$

82

Figure 6.22: Cone: Illustration of a circular cone.

6.3.4.2 *Distance Estimation*

The distance from a point $\vec{p}$ to a circular cone of center $\vec{c}$, axis $\hat{u}$ and half-opening angle θ reads

$$\begin{aligned}f(\vec{p}) &\triangleq \|\vec{p}-\vec{c}\|\sin(\angle(\vec{p}-\vec{c},\hat{u})-\theta)\\ &= \|\vec{p}-\vec{c}\|\Big(\sin(\angle(\vec{p}-\vec{c},\hat{u}))\cos(\theta)-\cos(\angle(\vec{p}-\vec{c},\hat{u}))\sin(\theta)\Big)\\ &= \|\vec{p}-\vec{c}\|\sin(\angle(\vec{p}-\vec{c},\hat{u}))\cos(\theta)-\|\vec{p}-\vec{c}\|\cos(\angle(\vec{p}-\vec{c},\hat{u}))\sin(\theta)\\ &\underset{(3.78)}{\overset{(3.96)}{=}} \|(\vec{p}-\vec{c})\times\hat{u}\|\cos(\theta)-|\langle\vec{p}-\vec{c},\hat{u}\rangle|\sin(\theta) \qquad (6.283)\end{aligned}$$

80

77

6.3.4.3 *Surface Parameterization*

277 As illustrated in *Figure 6.23*, a *conical patch* of apex angle θ and extent $[r_l, r_h]\times[\phi_l,\phi_h]$ centered at the origin and oriented along the z axis of a given coordinate system may alter-
70 natively be represented in *spherical coordinates* as a parametric surface of the form

$$\vec{p}(u, v) \triangleq \begin{bmatrix} \operatorname{lerp}(u, r_l, r_h) \sin(\theta) \cos\left(\operatorname{lerp}(v, \phi_l, \phi_h)\right) \\ \operatorname{lerp}(u, r_l, r_h) \sin(\theta) \sin\left(\operatorname{lerp}(v, \phi_l, \phi_h)\right) \\ \operatorname{lerp}(u, r_l, r_h) \cos(\theta) \end{bmatrix} \tag{6.284}$$

whose unit normal is readily given as

$$\hat{n}(u, v) \overset{(6.27)}{=} \begin{bmatrix} -\cos(\theta) \cos\left(\operatorname{lerp}(v, \phi_l, \phi_h)\right) \\ -\cos(\theta) \sin\left(\operatorname{lerp}(v, \phi_l, \phi_h)\right) \\ \sin(\theta) \end{bmatrix} \tag{6.285}$$ 240

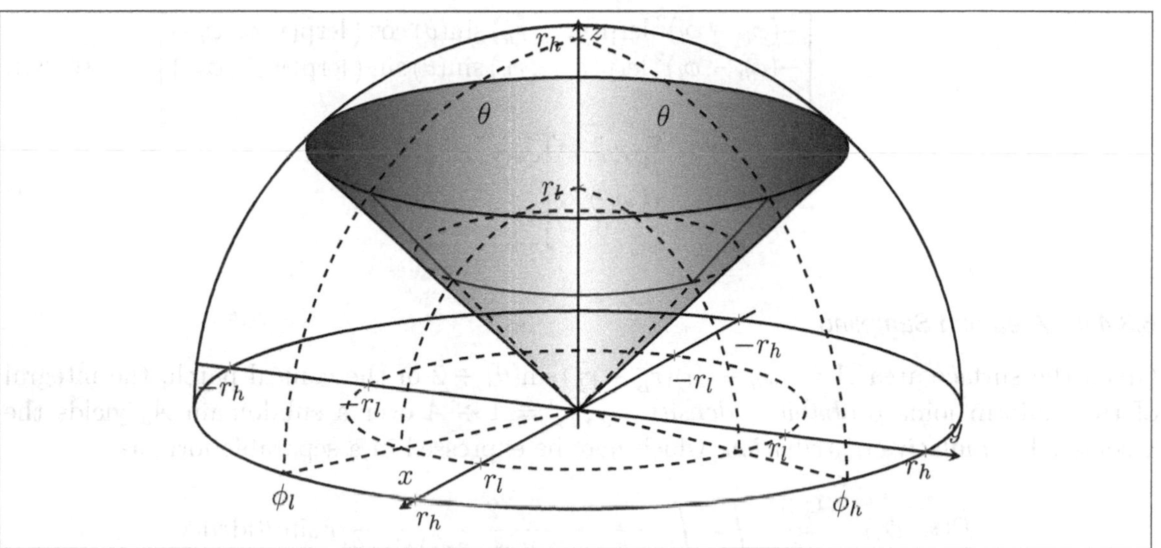

Figure 6.23: Cone Parameterization: Illustration of the parametric representation of the surface of a circular cone.

The first partial derivatives are then given by

$$\begin{aligned}
\frac{\partial \vec{p}(u, v)}{\partial u} &= \begin{bmatrix} (r_h - r_l) \sin(\theta) \cos\left(\operatorname{lerp}(v, \phi_l, \phi_h)\right) \\ (r_h - r_l) \sin(\theta) \sin\left(\operatorname{lerp}(v, \phi_l, \phi_h)\right) \\ (r_h - r_l) \cos(\theta) \end{bmatrix} && (6.286) \\
&= (r_h - r_l) \vec{p}(u, v) \div \operatorname{lerp}(u, r_l, r_h) && (6.287) \\
\frac{\partial \vec{p}(u, v)}{\partial v} &= \begin{bmatrix} -(\phi_h - \phi_l) \operatorname{lerp}(u, r_l, r_h) \sin(\theta) \sin\left(\operatorname{lerp}(v, \phi_l, \phi_h)\right) \\ (\phi_h - \phi_l) \operatorname{lerp}(u, r_l, r_h) \sin(\theta) \cos\left(\operatorname{lerp}(v, \phi_l, \phi_h)\right) \\ 0 \end{bmatrix} && (6.288) \\
&= (\phi_h - \phi_l) \begin{bmatrix} -p_y(u, v) \\ p_x(u, v) \\ 0 \end{bmatrix} && (6.289)
\end{aligned}$$

while the second partial derivatives read

$$\frac{\partial^2 \vec{p}(u,v)}{\partial u^2} = \vec{0} \tag{6.290}$$

$$\frac{\partial^2 \vec{p}(u,v)}{\partial u \partial v} = \begin{bmatrix} -(\phi_h - \phi_l)(r_h - r_l)\sin(\theta)\sin\left(\operatorname{lerp}(v, \phi_l, \phi_h)\right) \\ (\phi_h - \phi_l)(r_h - r_l)\sin(\theta)\cos\left(\operatorname{lerp}(v, \phi_l, \phi_h)\right) \\ 0 \end{bmatrix} \tag{6.291}$$

$$= (\phi_h - \phi_l)(r_h - r_l) \begin{bmatrix} -p_y(u,v) \\ p_x(u,v) \\ 0 \end{bmatrix} \div \operatorname{lerp}(u, r_l, r_h) \tag{6.292}$$

$$\frac{\partial^2 \vec{p}(u,v)}{\partial v^2} = \begin{bmatrix} -(\phi_h - \phi_l)^2 \operatorname{lerp}(u, r_l, r_h)\sin(\theta)\cos\left(\operatorname{lerp}(v, \phi_l, \phi_h)\right) \\ -(\phi_h - \phi_l)^2 \operatorname{lerp}(u, r_l, r_h)\sin(\theta)\sin\left(\operatorname{lerp}(v, \phi_l, \phi_h)\right) \\ 0 \end{bmatrix} \tag{6.293}$$

$$= -(\phi_h - \phi_l)^2 \begin{bmatrix} p_x(u,v) \\ p_y(u,v) \\ 0 \end{bmatrix} \tag{6.294}$$

6.3.4.4 Area and Sampling

Given the surface area $A \triangleq (\phi_h - \phi_l)(r_h^2 - r_l^2)\sin(\theta) \div 2$ of the conical patch, the integral
131 of the uniform joint *probability density* $p(r, \phi) \triangleq 1 \div A$ over a subdomain A_s yields the
132 associated *cumulative distribution*, which may be expressed in a separable form as

132

$$\begin{aligned} P(r_s, \phi_s) &\overset{(4.22)}{=} \int_{\phi_l}^{\phi_s} \int_{r_l}^{r_s} \frac{2}{(\phi_h - \phi_l)(r_h^2 - r_l^2)\sin(\theta)} r \sin(\theta) \mathrm{d}r \mathrm{d}\phi \\ &= \int_{\phi_l}^{\phi_s} \frac{1}{\phi_h - \phi_l} \mathrm{d}\phi \int_{r_l}^{r_s} \frac{2r}{r_h^2 - r_l^2} \mathrm{d}r \\ &= \left[\frac{\phi}{\phi_h - \phi_l}\right]_{\phi_l}^{\phi_s} \left[\frac{r^2}{r_h^2 - r_l^2}\right]_{r_l}^{r_s} \\ &= \frac{\phi_s - \phi_l}{\phi_h - \phi_l} \frac{r_s^2 - r_l^2}{r_h^2 - r_l^2} \end{aligned} \tag{6.295}$$

Integrating over the whole domain by substituting $\phi_s = \phi_h$ and $r_s = r_h$ then ensures
134 normalization, while applying *inverse-transform sampling* allows uniform sampling to be
readily carried as

$$\xi_\phi = \frac{\phi_s - \phi_l}{\phi_h - \phi_l} \implies \phi_s = \operatorname{lerp}(\xi_\phi, \phi_l, \phi_h) \tag{6.296}$$

$$\xi_r = \frac{r_s^2 - r_l^2}{r_h^2 - r_l^2} \implies r_s = \sqrt{\operatorname{lerp}(\xi_r, r_l^2, r_h^2)} \tag{6.297}$$

6.3.5 Quadric

6.3.5.1 Implicit Intersection

Let us consider the scalar field defined by the function

$$\begin{aligned} f(x,y,z) \triangleq\; & x_2(x - x_c)^2 + x_1(x - x_c) + x_0(y - y_c)(z - z_c) \\ +\; & y_2(y - y_c)^2 + y_1(y - y_c) + y_0(z - z_c)(x - x_c) \\ +\; & z_2(z - z_c)^2 + z_1(z - z_c) + z_0(x - x_c)(y - y_c) \end{aligned} \tag{6.298}$$

and its associated vector field

$$\nabla f(x,y,z) \overset{(6.20)}{=} \begin{bmatrix} x_2 2(x-x_c) + x_1 + y_0(z-z_c) + z_0(y-y_c) \\ y_2 2(y-y_c) + y_1 + z_0(x-x_c) + x_0(z-z_c) \\ z_2 2(z-z_c) + z_1 + x_0(y-y_c) + y_0(x-x_c) \end{bmatrix} \tag{6.299}$$ 239

Substituting the ray equation $\vec{r}(t) \triangleq \vec{o} + t\vec{d}$, the values of the scalar field along the ray are then defined as

$$\begin{aligned} f(t) &\overset{(6.21)}{=} x_2(x_o + tx_d - x_c)^2 + x_1(x_o + tx_d - x_c) + x_0(y_o + ty_d - y_c)(z_o + tz_d - z_c) \\ &+ y_2(y_o + ty_d - y_c)^2 + y_1(y_o + ty_d - y_c) + y_0(z_o + tz_d - z_c)(x_o + tx_d - x_c) \\ &+ z_2(z_o + tz_d - z_c)^2 + z_1(z_o + tz_d - z_c) + z_0(x_o + tx_d - x_c)(y_o + ty_d - y_c) \\ &= x_2(x_{co} + tx_d)^2 + x_1(x_{co} + tx_d) + x_0(y_{co} + ty_d)(z_{co} + tz_d) \\ &+ y_2(y_{co} + ty_d)^2 + y_1(y_{co} + ty_d) + y_0(z_{co} + tz_d)(x_{co} + tx_d) \\ &+ z_2(z_{co} + tz_d)^2 + z_1(z_{co} + tz_d) + z_0(x_{co} + tx_d)(y_{co} + ty_d) \\ &= (x_2 x_{co}^2 + y_2 y_{co}^2 + z_2 z_{co}^2 + x_1 x_{co} + y_1 y_{co} + z_1 z_{co} + x_0 y_{co} z_{co} + x_{co} y_0 z_{co} + x_{co} y_{co} z_0) \\ &+ (2x_2 x_{co} x_d + 2y_2 y_{co} y_d + 2z_2 z_{co} z_d + x_1 x_d + y_1 y_d + z_1 z_d + x_0 y_d z_{co} + x_0 y_{co} z_d \\ &\quad + x_{co} y_0 z_d + x_d y_0 z_{co} + x_d y_{co} z_0 + x_{co} y_d z_0)t \\ &+ (x_2 x_d^2 + y_2 y_d^2 + z_2 z_d^2 + x_0 y_d z_d + x_d y_0 z_d + x_d y_d z_0)t^2 \end{aligned} \tag{6.300}$$ 239

where $x_{co} \triangleq x_o - x_c$, $y_{co} \triangleq y_o - y_c$, $z_{co} \triangleq z_o - z_c$.

As illustrated in *Table 6.1*, a quadratic surface, also called *quadric* [Cychosz and Waggenspack, 1992], may then be defined as the set of points satisfying $f(x,y,z) = v$ for a given isovalue v, and whose points of intersection along the ray are determined by the solutions of the *quadratic equation* $f(t) = v$. 283 28

6.3.5.2 Hyperbolic Form

Let us now more specifically consider the special case of the above scalar field where $x_0 = y_0 = z_0 = x_1 = y_1 = z_1 = 0$ and

$$x_2 \triangleq \frac{1}{x_r|x_r|} \tag{6.301}$$

$$y_2 \triangleq \frac{1}{y_r|y_r|} \tag{6.302}$$

$$z_2 \triangleq \frac{1}{z_r|z_r|} \tag{6.303}$$

along with the isovalue

$$v \triangleq v_r|v_r| \tag{6.304}$$

yielding the following surface definition

$$f(x,y,z) \overset{(6.298)}{=} \frac{(x-x_c)^2}{x_r|x_r|} + \frac{(y-y_c)^2}{y_r|y_r|} + \frac{(z-z_c)^2}{z_r|z_r|} = v_r|v_r| \tag{6.305}$$ 278

This formulation allows several common quadrics to be represented. For instance, when $x_r > 0$, $y_r > 0$, $z_r > 0$ and $v_r > 0$, it defines an *ellipsoid* of radii $x_r v_r$, $y_r v_r$ and $z_r v_r$ in x, y and z, respectively. Furthermore, if all three radii are equal, $x_r v_r = y_r v_r = z_r v_r = r$, for instance by setting $x_r = y_r = z_r = 1$ and $v_r = r$, the ellipsoid degenerates into a *sphere* of 269 radius r

279

$$f(x,y,z) \stackrel{(6.305)}{=} (x-x_c)^2+(y-y_c)^2+(z-z_c)^2 = r^2 \tag{6.306}$$

which may be geometrically interpreted as the set of points satisfying $\|\vec{p}-\vec{c}\|^2 = r^2$. On the other hand, when $x_r > 0$, $y_r > 0$, $z_r < 0$ and $v_r = 0$, the above formulation instead
275 defines a *cone* oriented along the z axis and of half-opening angles $\arctan(-x_r \div z_r)$ and $\arctan(-y_r \div z_r)$ in x and y, respectively, that is, of radii x_r and y_r in the planes defined by $z - z_c = \pm z_r$.

In order to allow various other types of quadrics to be intuitively specified as well, let us define a reparameterization of the above formulation such that the surface observes some user-specified radii $x - x_c = x'_r$ and $y - y_c = y'_r$ at a given height $z - z_c = z'_r$. The relationship that x_r must satisfy can then be derived by considering the plane $y = y_c$, which yields

279

$$f(x'_r+x_c, y_c, z'_r+z_c) \stackrel{(6.305)}{=} \frac{x'^2_r}{x_r|x_r|}+\frac{z'^2_r}{z_r|z_r|} = v_r|v_r| \iff \frac{1}{x_r|x_r|} = \frac{z_r|z_r|v_r|v_r| - z'^2_r}{z_r|z_r|x'^2_r} \tag{6.307}$$

while the relationship that y_r must satisfy may be derived by considering the plane $x = x_c$, which yields

279

$$f(x_c, y'_r+y_c, z'_r+z_c) \stackrel{(6.305)}{=} \frac{y'^2_r}{y_r|y_r|}+\frac{z'^2_r}{z_r|z_r|} = v_r|v_r| \iff \frac{1}{y_r|y_r|} = \frac{z_r|z_r|v_r|v_r| - z'^2_r}{z_r|z_r|y'^2_r} \tag{6.308}$$

Substituting the above two results into the expression of $f(x,y,z)$ then yields

279

$$\begin{aligned} f(x,y,z) &\stackrel{(6.305)}{=} \frac{z_r|z_r|v_r|v_r| - z'^2_r}{z_r|z_r|x'^2_r}(x-x_c)^2 + \frac{z_r|z_r|v_r|v_r| - z'^2_r}{z_r|z_r|y'^2_r}(y-y_c)^2 + \frac{(z-z_c)^2}{z_r|z_r|} \\ &= v_r|v_r| \end{aligned} \tag{6.309}$$

which can be equivalently expressed by multiplying all sides by $z_r|z_r|$ and defining $v'_r = z_r v_r$

$$\begin{aligned} f'(x,y,z) &\triangleq \frac{v'_r|v'_r| - z'^2_r}{x'^2_r}(x-x_c)^2 + \frac{v'_r|v'_r| - z'^2_r}{y'^2_r}(y-y_c)^2 + (z-z_c)^2 \\ &= v'_r|v'_r| \end{aligned} \tag{6.310}$$

In order to handle the limiting case where $|v'_r| \to \infty$, an alternative expression may be obtained by dividing all terms by $|v'_r|v'_r| - z'^2_r|$, where the outer absolute value ensures consistency with the gradient orientation from the previous formulation

$$\begin{aligned} f''(x,y,z) &\triangleq \frac{\operatorname{sgn}(v'_r|v'_r| - z'^2_r)}{x'^2_r}(x-x_c)^2 + \frac{\operatorname{sgn}(v'_r|v'_r| - z'^2_r)}{y'^2_r}(y-y_c)^2 + \frac{(z-z_c)^2}{|v'_r|v'_r| - z'^2_r|} \\ &= \frac{v'_r|v'_r|}{|v'_r|v'_r| - z'^2_r|} \end{aligned} \tag{6.311}$$

which, whenever $|v'_r| = \infty$, simplifies to

$$f''(x,y,z) = \frac{\operatorname{sgn}(v'_r)}{x'^2_r}(x-x_c)^2 + \frac{\operatorname{sgn}(v'_r)}{y'^2_r}(y-y_c)^2 = \operatorname{sgn}(v'_r) \tag{6.312}$$

Overall, the reparameterization consequently reformulates the original equation of a quadratic surface in terms of the radii x'_r and y'_r at the given height z'_r as well as the isoradius v'_r, by setting $x_0 = y_0 = z_0 = x_1 = y_1 = z_1 = 0$ and then defining

$$x_2 = \frac{1}{x_r'^2} \times \begin{cases} v'_r|v'_r| - z_r'^2 & \text{if } |v'_r| \neq \infty \\ \text{sgn}(v'_r) & \text{if } |v'_r| = \infty \end{cases} \tag{6.313}$$

$$y_2 = \frac{1}{y_r'^2} \times \begin{cases} v'_r|v'_r| - z_r'^2 & \text{if } |v'_r| \neq \infty \\ \text{sgn}(v'_r) & \text{if } |v'_r| = \infty \end{cases} \tag{6.314}$$

$$z_2 = \begin{cases} 1 & \text{if } |v'_r| \neq \infty \\ 0 & \text{if } |v'_r| = \infty \end{cases} \tag{6.315}$$

$$v = \begin{cases} v'_r|v'_r| & \text{if } |v'_r| \neq \infty \\ \text{sgn}(v'_r) & \text{if } |v'_r| = \infty \end{cases} \tag{6.316}$$

which allows for both the definition of ellipsoids in terms of their radii by setting $z'_r = 0$, and
of *cones* in terms of their half-opening angles $\arctan(x'_r \div z'_r)$ and $\arctan(y'_r \div z'_r)$ by setting 275
$v'_r = 0$.

6.3.5.3 Parabolic Form

Another interesting special case of the general scalar field formulation is obtained for $x_0 = y_0 = z_0 = x_1 = y_1 = z_2 = 0$ and

$$x_2 \triangleq \frac{1}{x_r|x_r|} \tag{6.317}$$

$$y_2 \triangleq \frac{1}{y_r|y_r|} \tag{6.318}$$

$$z_1 \triangleq \frac{1}{z_r} \tag{6.319}$$

along with the isovalue

$$v \triangleq v_r|v_r| \tag{6.320}$$

The resulting formulation

$$f(x, y, z) \overset{(6.298)}{=} \frac{(x - x_c)^2}{x_r|x_r|} + \frac{(y - y_c)^2}{y_r|y_r|} + \frac{z - z_c}{z_r} = v_r|v_r| \tag{6.321}$$ 278

defines z-oriented *paraboloids* of radii $x_r v_r$ and $y_r v_r$ in x and y, respectively, at the height $z = z_c$, and with their extremity at $z - z_c = z_r v_r |v_r|$.

Let us define a reparameterization of the above formulation such that the surface observes some user-specified radii $x - x_c = x'_r$ and $y - y_c = y'_r$ at a given height $z - z_c = z'_r$. The relationship that x_r must satisfy may then be derived by considering the plane $y = y_c$, which yields

$$f(x'_r + x_c, y_c, z'_r + z_c) \overset{(6.321)}{=} \frac{x_r'^2}{x_r|x_r|} + \frac{z'_r}{z_r} = v_r|v_r| \iff \frac{1}{x_r|x_r|} = \frac{z_r v_r|v_r| - z'_r}{z_r x_r'^2} \tag{6.322}$$ 281

while the relationship that y_r must satisfy can be derived by considering the plane $x = x_c$, which yields

$$f(x_c, y'_r + y_c, z'_r + z_c) \overset{(6.321)}{=} \frac{y_r'^2}{y_r|y_r|} + \frac{z'_r}{z_r} = v_r|v_r| \iff \frac{1}{y_r|y_r|} = \frac{z_r v_r|v_r| - z'_r}{z_r y_r'^2} \tag{6.323}$$ 281

Substituting the above two results into the expression of $f(x, y, z)$ then yields

281 $$f(x, y, z) \overset{(6.321)}{=} \frac{z_r v_r |v_r| - z'_r}{z_r x'^2_r}(x - x_c)^2 + \frac{z_r v_r |v_r| - z'_r}{z_r y'^2_r}(y - y_c)^2 + \frac{z - z_c}{z_r} = v_r |v_r| \quad (6.324)$$

Multiplying all terms by z_r and defining $v'_r = z_r v_r |v_r|$, the above quadric formulation may then equivalently be expressed as

$$f'(x, y, z) \triangleq \frac{v'_r - z'_r}{x'^2_r}(x - x_c)^2 + \frac{v'_r - z'_r}{y'^2_r}(y - y_c)^2 + (z - z_c) = v'_r \quad (6.325)$$

In order to handle the limiting case where $|v'_r| \to \infty$ here as well, an alternative expression is similarly obtained by dividing all terms by $|v'_r - z'_r|$

$$\begin{aligned} f''(x, y, z) &\triangleq \frac{\operatorname{sgn}(v'_r - z'_r)}{x'^2_r}(x - x_c)^2 + \frac{\operatorname{sgn}(v'_r - z'_r)}{y'^2_r}(y - y_c)^2 + \frac{z - z_c}{|v'_r - z'_r|} \\ &= \frac{v'_r}{|v'_r - z'_r|} \end{aligned} \quad (6.326)$$

which, whenever $|v'_r| = \infty$, simplifies to

$$f''(x, y, z) = \frac{\operatorname{sgn}(v'_r)}{x'^2_r}(x - x_c)^2 + \frac{\operatorname{sgn}(v'_r)}{y'^2_r}(y - y_c)^2 = \operatorname{sgn}(v'_r) \quad (6.327)$$

Overall, the reparameterization reformulates the original equation of a quadratic surface in terms of the radii x'_r and y'_r at the given height z'_r as well as the iso-radius v'_r, by setting $x_0 = y_0 = z_0 = x_1 = y_1 = z_2 = 0$ and then defining

$$x_2 = \frac{1}{x'^2_r} \times \begin{cases} v'_r - z'_r & \text{if } |v'_r| \neq \infty \\ \operatorname{sgn}(v'_r) & \text{if } |v'_r| = \infty \end{cases} \quad (6.328)$$

$$y_2 = \frac{1}{y'^2_r} \times \begin{cases} v'_r - z'_r & \text{if } |v'_r| \neq \infty \\ \operatorname{sgn}(v'_r) & \text{if } |v'_r| = \infty \end{cases} \quad (6.329)$$

$$z_1 = \begin{cases} 1 & \text{if } |v'_r| \neq \infty \\ 0 & \text{if } |v'_r| = \infty \end{cases} \quad (6.330)$$

$$v = \begin{cases} v'_r & \text{if } |v'_r| \neq \infty \\ \operatorname{sgn}(v'_r) & \text{if } |v'_r| = \infty \end{cases} \quad (6.331)$$

Finally, it is worth noting that the two reparameterizations above can be generalized by replacing all squared x'_r, y'_r and z'_r terms by the product of the terms with their absolute value. This way, it is possible to transform an *elliptic paraboloid* into a *hyperbolic paraboloid* by simply setting the radius x'_r or y'_r to be negative.

6.3.5.4 Surface Parameterization

In the special case of a quadric exhibiting a rotational symmetry around the z axis (such as a *circular ellipsoid*, a *circular hyperboloid* or a *circular paraboloid*), a *circular patch* of extent $[\phi_l, \phi_h] \times [z_l, z_h]$ centered at the origin and oriented along the z axis of a given coordinate
69 system may alternatively be represented in *cylindrical coordinates* as a parametric surface

Table 6.1: Quadrics: The main types of quadrics defined using both the hyperbolic and parabolic forms. All surfaces use $x'_r = 0.4$, $y'_r = 0.2$ and $z'_r = 0.5$, and are clipped within the unit cube. Additional degenerate quadrics may be derived by instead letting either $x'_r = \infty$ or $y'_r = \infty$, such that a hyperboloid of one or two sheets becomes a hyperbolic cylinder, an elliptic cone becomes two intersecting planes and an elliptic paraboloid becomes a parabolic cylinder.

Parameter	Hyperbolic Form	Parabolic Form
$v'_r = +\infty$	Elliptic cylinder	Elliptic cylinder
$v'_r > z'_r$	Ellipsoid	Elliptic paraboloid
$v'_r = z'_r$	Parallel planes	Single plane
$0 < v'_r < z'_r$	Hyperboloid of two sheets	Elliptic paraboloid
$v'_r = 0$	Elliptic cone	Elliptic paraboloid
$v'_r < 0$	Hyperboloid of one sheet	Elliptic paraboloid
$v'_r = -\infty$	Elliptic cylinder	Elliptic cylinder

of the form

$$\vec{p}(u,v) \triangleq \begin{bmatrix} \rho(\operatorname{lerp}(u,z_l,z_h))\cos(\operatorname{lerp}(v,\phi_l,\phi_h)) \\ \rho(\operatorname{lerp}(u,z_l,z_h))\sin(\operatorname{lerp}(v,\phi_l,\phi_h)) \\ \operatorname{lerp}(u,z_l,z_h) \end{bmatrix} \tag{6.332}$$

whose normal is readily given as

240

$$\vec{n}(u,v) \overset{(6.27)}{=} \begin{bmatrix} -\cos(\operatorname{lerp}(v,\phi_l,\phi_h)) \\ -\sin(\operatorname{lerp}(v,\phi_l,\phi_h)) \\ \rho'(\operatorname{lerp}(u,z_l,z_h)) \end{bmatrix} \tag{6.333}$$

The first partial derivatives are then given by

$$\frac{\partial\vec{p}(u,v)}{\partial u} = \begin{bmatrix} (z_h - z_l)\rho'(\operatorname{lerp}(u,z_l,z_h))\cos(\operatorname{lerp}(v,\phi_l,\phi_h)) \\ (z_h - z_l)\rho'(\operatorname{lerp}(u,z_l,z_h))\sin(\operatorname{lerp}(v,\phi_l,\phi_h)) \\ (z_h - z_l) \end{bmatrix} \tag{6.334}$$

$$= (z_h - z_l)\begin{bmatrix} \rho'(\operatorname{lerp}(u,z_l,z_h))\cos(\operatorname{lerp}(v,\phi_l,\phi_h)) \\ \rho'(\operatorname{lerp}(u,z_l,z_h))\sin(\operatorname{lerp}(v,\phi_l,\phi_h)) \\ 1 \end{bmatrix} \tag{6.335}$$

$$\frac{\partial\vec{p}(u,v)}{\partial v} = \begin{bmatrix} -(\phi_h - \phi_l)\rho(\operatorname{lerp}(u,z_l,z_h))\sin(\operatorname{lerp}(v,\phi_l,\phi_h)) \\ (\phi_h - \phi_l)\rho(\operatorname{lerp}(u,z_l,z_h))\cos(\operatorname{lerp}(v,\phi_l,\phi_h)) \\ 0 \end{bmatrix} \tag{6.336}$$

$$= (\phi_h - \phi_l)\begin{bmatrix} -p_y(u,v) \\ p_x(u,v) \\ 0 \end{bmatrix} \tag{6.337}$$

while the second partial derivatives read

$$\frac{\partial^2\vec{p}(u,v)}{\partial u^2} = \begin{bmatrix} (z_h - z_l)^2\rho''(\operatorname{lerp}(u,z_l,z_h))\cos(\operatorname{lerp}(v,\phi_l,\phi_h)) \\ (z_h - z_l)^2\rho''(\operatorname{lerp}(u,z_l,z_h))\sin(\operatorname{lerp}(v,\phi_l,\phi_h)) \\ 0 \end{bmatrix} \tag{6.338}$$

$$= (z_h - z_l)^2\begin{bmatrix} \rho''(\operatorname{lerp}(u,z_l,z_h))\cos(\operatorname{lerp}(v,\phi_l,\phi_h)) \\ \rho''(\operatorname{lerp}(u,z_l,z_h))\sin(\operatorname{lerp}(v,\phi_l,\phi_h)) \\ 0 \end{bmatrix} \tag{6.339}$$

$$\frac{\partial^2\vec{p}(u,v)}{\partial u \partial v} = \begin{bmatrix} -(z_h - z_l)(\phi_h - \phi_l)\rho'(\operatorname{lerp}(u,z_l,z_h))\sin(\operatorname{lerp}(v,\phi_l,\phi_h)) \\ (z_h - z_l)(\phi_h - \phi_l)\rho'(\operatorname{lerp}(u,z_l,z_h))\cos(\operatorname{lerp}(v,\phi_l,\phi_h)) \\ 0 \end{bmatrix} \tag{6.340}$$

$$= (z_h - z_l)(\phi_h - \phi_l)\begin{bmatrix} -\rho'(\operatorname{lerp}(u,z_l,z_h))\sin(\operatorname{lerp}(v,\phi_l,\phi_h)) \\ \rho'(\operatorname{lerp}(u,z_l,z_h))\cos(\operatorname{lerp}(v,\phi_l,\phi_h)) \\ 0 \end{bmatrix} \tag{6.341}$$

$$\frac{\partial^2\vec{p}(u,v)}{\partial v^2} = \begin{bmatrix} -(\phi_h - \phi_l)^2\rho(\operatorname{lerp}(u,z_l,z_h))\cos(\operatorname{lerp}(v,\phi_l,\phi_h)) \\ -(\phi_h - \phi_l)^2\rho(\operatorname{lerp}(u,z_l,z_h))\sin(\operatorname{lerp}(v,\phi_l,\phi_h)) \\ 0 \end{bmatrix} \tag{6.342}$$

$$= -(\phi_h - \phi_l)^2\begin{bmatrix} p_x(u,v) \\ p_y(u,v) \\ 0 \end{bmatrix} \tag{6.343}$$

The corresponding expression of the radius $\rho(z) \triangleq \sqrt{(x - x_c)^2 + (y - y_c)^2}$ is then ob-
279 tained by substituting $x_r = y_r = \rho_r$ into the formulation of the *hyperbolic form* or *parabolic*

form, respectively 281

$$f(x,y,z) \overset{(6.305)}{=} \frac{\rho(z)^2}{\rho_r|\rho_r|} + \frac{(z-z_c)^2}{z_r|z_r|} = v_r|v_r| \implies \rho(z) = \sqrt{\rho_r|\rho_r|\left(v_r|v_r| - \frac{(z-z_c)^2}{z_r|z_r|}\right)}$$ 279

$$\implies \rho'(z) = -\frac{\rho_r|\rho_r|(z-z_c)}{z_r|z_r|\rho(z)} \quad (6.344)$$

$$f(x,y,z) \overset{(6.321)}{=} \frac{\rho(z)^2}{\rho_r|\rho_r|} + \frac{z-z_c}{z_r} = v_r|v_r| \implies \rho(z) = \sqrt{\rho_r|\rho_r|\left(v_r|v_r| - \frac{z-z_c}{z_r}\right)}$$ 281

$$\implies \rho'(z) = -\frac{\rho_r|\rho_r|}{2z_r\rho(z)} \quad (6.345)$$

6.3.5.5 *Area and Sampling*

The surface area of a quadric exhibiting a rotational symmetry around the z axis is then defined by that of a *surface of revolution*

$$A \triangleq \int_{\phi_l}^{\phi_h}\int_{s_l}^{s_h} \rho(s)\mathrm{d}s\mathrm{d}\phi = \int_{\phi_l}^{\phi_h}\mathrm{d}\phi\int_{s_l}^{s_h}\rho(s)\mathrm{d}s \overset{(6.37)}{=} (\phi_h - \phi_l)\int_{z_l}^{z_h}\rho(z)\sqrt{1+\left(\frac{\mathrm{d}\rho(z)}{\mathrm{d}z}\right)^2}\mathrm{d}z \quad (6.346)$$ 241

6.4 THIRD-ORDER SURFACES

6.4.1 Trilinear Patch

6.4.1.1 *Implicit Intersection*

Given sample values $s[i,j,k]$ at coordinates $[x_i, y_j, z_k]$ with sampling periods $T_x = x_1 - x_0$, $T_y = y_1 - y_0$ and $T_z = z_1 - z_0$, the *reconstruction* of a scalar field $f(x,y,z)$ within the cell 201
$[x_0, x_1] \times [y_0, y_1] \times [z_0, z_1]$ may be carried using a *separable filter* defined as the tensor product 203
of three *tent filters*. Substituting the semi-extent $t_m = 1$ of the filter and defining $[x_0, y_0, z_0]$ 206
as the origin of the coordinate system then yields

$$\begin{aligned}
f(x,y,z) &\overset{(5.183)}{=} \sum_{n_z=\left\lceil\frac{z-z_0}{T_z}-1\right\rceil}^{\left\lfloor\frac{z-z_0}{T_z}+1\right\rfloor}\ \sum_{n_y=\left\lceil\frac{y-y_0}{T_y}-1\right\rceil}^{\left\lfloor\frac{y-y_0}{T_y}+1\right\rfloor}\ \sum_{n_x=\left\lceil\frac{x-x_0}{T_x}-1\right\rceil}^{\left\lfloor\frac{x-x_0}{T_x}+1\right\rfloor} s[n_x,n_y,n_z]\left(1-\left|\frac{x-x_0}{T_x}-n_x\right|\right) \\
&\quad \times\left(1-\left|\frac{y-y_0}{T_y}-n_y\right|\right)\left(1-\left|\frac{z-z_0}{T_z}-n_z\right|\right) \\
&= \sum_{n_z=0}^{1}\sum_{n_y=0}^{1}\sum_{n_x=0}^{1} s[n_x,n_y,n_z](-1)^{1-n_x}\frac{x-x_{1-n_x}}{T_x} \\
&\quad \times(-1)^{1-n_y}\frac{y-y_{1-n_y}}{T_y}(-1)^{1-n_z}\frac{z-z_{1-n_z}}{T_z} \\
&= \frac{-1}{T_xT_yT_z}\sum_{n_x=0}^{1}(-1)^{n_x}(x-x_{1-n_x})\sum_{n_y=0}^{1}(-1)^{n_y}(y-y_{1-n_y}) \\
&\quad \times\sum_{n_z=0}^{1}(-1)^{n_z}(z-z_{1-n_z})s[n_x,n_y,n_z] \qquad (6.347) \\
&= \sum_{i=0}^{1}\sum_{j=0}^{1}\sum_{k=0}^{1} d_{ijk}x^iy^jz^k \qquad (6.348)
\end{aligned}$$ 203

where

$$d_{111} \triangleq \frac{-1}{T_xT_yT_z}\sum_{n_x=0}^{1}\sum_{n_y=0}^{1}\sum_{n_z=0}^{1}(-1)^{n_x+n_y+n_z}s[n_x,n_y,n_z] \tag{6.349}$$

$$d_{110} \triangleq \frac{1}{T_xT_yT_z}\sum_{n_x=0}^{1}\sum_{n_y=0}^{1}\sum_{n_z=0}^{1}(-1)^{n_x+n_y+n_z}z_{1-n_z}s[n_x,n_y,n_z] \tag{6.350}$$

$$d_{101} \triangleq \frac{1}{T_xT_yT_z}\sum_{n_x=0}^{1}\sum_{n_y=0}^{1}\sum_{n_z=0}^{1}(-1)^{n_x+n_y+n_z}y_{1-n_y}s[n_x,n_y,n_z] \tag{6.351}$$

$$d_{011} \triangleq \frac{1}{T_xT_yT_z}\sum_{n_x=0}^{1}\sum_{n_y=0}^{1}\sum_{n_z=0}^{1}(-1)^{n_x+n_y+n_z}x_{1-n_x}s[n_x,n_y,n_z] \tag{6.352}$$

$$d_{100} \triangleq \frac{-1}{T_xT_yT_z}\sum_{n_x=0}^{1}\sum_{n_y=0}^{1}\sum_{n_z=0}^{1}(-1)^{n_x+n_y+n_z}y_{1-n_y}z_{1-n_z}s[n_x,n_y,n_z] \tag{6.353}$$

$$d_{010} \triangleq \frac{-1}{T_xT_yT_z}\sum_{n_x=0}^{1}\sum_{n_y=0}^{1}\sum_{n_z=0}^{1}(-1)^{n_x+n_y+n_z}x_{1-n_x}z_{1-n_z}s[n_x,n_y,n_z] \tag{6.354}$$

$$d_{001} \triangleq \frac{-1}{T_xT_yT_z}\sum_{n_x=0}^{1}\sum_{n_y=0}^{1}\sum_{n_z=0}^{1}(-1)^{n_x+n_y+n_z}x_{1-n_x}y_{1-n_y}s[n_x,n_y,n_z] \tag{6.355}$$

$$d_{000} \triangleq \frac{1}{T_xT_yT_z}\sum_{n_x=0}^{1}\sum_{n_y=0}^{1}\sum_{n_z=0}^{1}(-1)^{n_x+n_y+n_z}x_{1-n_x}y_{1-n_y}z_{1-n_z}s[n_x,n_y,n_z] \tag{6.356}$$

yielding the associated vector field

239
$$\nabla f(x,y,z) \overset{(6.20)}{=} \begin{bmatrix}\sum_{j=0}^{1}\sum_{k=0}^{1}d_{1jk}y^jz^k\\ \sum_{i=0}^{1}\sum_{k=0}^{1}d_{i1k}x^iz^k\\ \sum_{i=0}^{1}\sum_{j=0}^{1}d_{ij1}x^iy^j\end{bmatrix} \tag{6.357}$$

Substituting the ray equation $\vec{r}(t) \triangleq \vec{o} + t\vec{d}$, the values of the scalar field along the ray are then defined as

239
$$\begin{aligned} f(t) &\overset{(6.21)}{=} \sum_{i=0}^{1}\sum_{j=0}^{1}\sum_{k=0}^{1}d_{ijk}(x_o+tx_d)^i(y_o+ty_d)^j(z_o+tz_d)^k\\ &= c_0 + c_1t + c_2t^2 + c_3t^3 \end{aligned} \tag{6.358}$$

where

$$c_0 \triangleq \sum_{i=0}^{1}\sum_{j=0}^{1}\sum_{k=0}^{1}d_{ijk}x_o^iy_o^jz_o^k \tag{6.359}$$

$$c_1 \triangleq x_d\sum_{j=0}^{1}\sum_{k=0}^{1}d_{1jk}y_o^jz_o^k + y_d\sum_{i=0}^{1}\sum_{k=0}^{1}d_{i1k}x_o^iz_o^k + z_d\sum_{i=0}^{1}\sum_{j=0}^{1}d_{ij1}x_o^iy_o^j \tag{6.360}$$

$$c_2 \triangleq y_dz_d\sum_{i=0}^{1}d_{i11}x_o^i + x_dz_d\sum_{j=0}^{1}d_{1j1}y_o^j + x_dy_d\sum_{k=0}^{1}d_{11k}z_o^k \tag{6.361}$$

$$c_3 \triangleq x_dy_dz_dd_{111} \tag{6.362}$$

287 As illustrated in *Figure 6.24*, a *trilinear patch* [Lin and Ching, 1996, Parker *et al.*, 1998, Parker *et al.*, 1999, Parker *et al.*, 2005] may then be defined as the set of points satisfying $f(x,y,z) = v$ for a given isovalue v, and whose points of intersection along the ray are
29 determined by the solutions of the *cubic equation* $f(t) = v$.

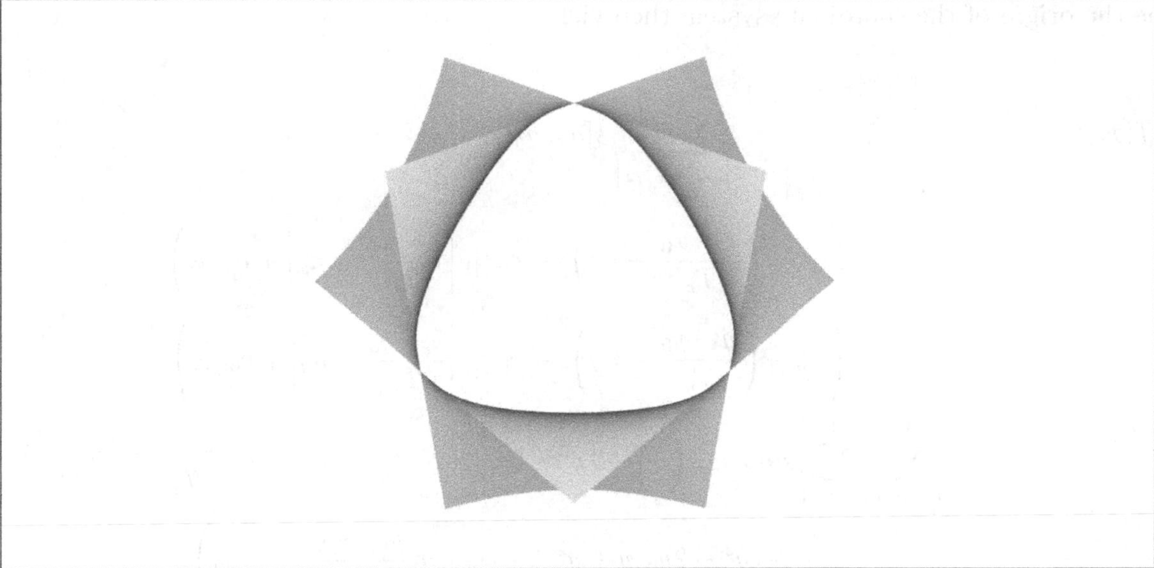

Figure 6.24: Trilinear Patch: Illustration of a trilinear patch.

6.4.2 Cubic Surfaces

Other notable cubic surfaces include:

- the Clebsch diagonal cubic surface
- the Cayley cubic surface
- the Ding-Dong surface
- the Möbius strip

6.5 FOURTH-ORDER SURFACES

6.5.1 Biquadratic Patch

6.5.1.1 Explicit Form

Given sample values $s[i, j]$ at coordinates $[x_i, y_j]$ with sampling periods $T_x = x_1 - x_0 = x_0 - x_{-1}$ and $T_y = y_1 - y_0 = y_0 - y_{-1}$, a *biquadratic patch* may be explicitly defined as the *reconstruction* of a height field $z = f(x, y)$ within the cell $\left[\frac{x_{-1}+x_0}{2}, \frac{x_0+x_1}{2}\right] \times \left[\frac{y_{-1}+y_0}{2}, \frac{y_0+y_1}{2}\right]$ 201
using a *separable filter* defined as the tensor product of two second-order *polynomial filters* 203
of the form 203

$$f_2(t) \triangleq \begin{cases} c_{02}|t|^2 + c_{01}|t| + c_{00} & \text{if } |t| \in [0, 1/2] \\ c_{12}|t|^2 + c_{11}|t| + c_{10} & \text{if } |t| \in [1/2, 3/2] \\ 0 & \text{otherwise} \end{cases} \quad (6.363)$$

such as the *quadratic filter*, the second-order *B-spline filter* or the *Dodgson filter*. As illustrated in *Figure 6.25*, substituting the semi-extent $t_m = 3/2$ of the filter and defining $[x_0, y_0]$ 208 220 226 289 as the origin of the coordinate system then yields

203

$$
\begin{aligned}
f(x,y) &\overset{(5.183)}{=} \sum_{n_y=\left\lceil \frac{y-y_0}{T_y}-3/2\right\rceil}^{\left\lfloor \frac{y-y_0}{T_y}+3/2\right\rfloor} \sum_{n_x=\left\lceil \frac{x-x_0}{T_x}-3/2\right\rceil}^{\left\lfloor \frac{x-x_0}{T_x}+3/2\right\rfloor} s[n_x,n_y] \\
&\quad \times \left(c_{|n_x|2}\left(\frac{x-x_0}{T_x}-n_x\right)^2 + c_{|n_x|1}\left|\frac{x-x_0}{T_x}-n_x\right| + c_{|n_x|0}\right) \\
&\quad \times \left(c_{|n_y|2}\left(\frac{y-y_0}{T_y}-n_y\right)^2 + c_{|n_y|1}\left|\frac{y-y_0}{T_y}-n_y\right| + c_{|n_y|0}\right) \\
&= \sum_{n_y=-1}^{1}\sum_{n_x=-1}^{1} s[n_x,n_y]\left(\frac{c_{|n_x|2}}{T_x^2}(x^2-2x_{n_x}x+x_{n_x}^2) + c_{|n_x|1}n_x\frac{x_{n_x}-x}{T_x} + c_{|n_x|0}\right) \\
&\quad \times \left(\frac{c_{|n_y|2}}{T_y^2}(y^2-2y_{n_y}y+y_{n_y}^2) + c_{|n_y|1}n_y\frac{y_{n_y}-y}{T_y} + c_{|n_y|0}\right) \\
&= \sum_{n_x=-1}^{1}\left(k_x[n_x,2]x^2 + k_x[n_x,1]x + k_x[n_x,0]\right) \\
&\quad \times \sum_{n_y=-1}^{1}\left(k_y[n_y,2]y^2 + k_y[n_y,1]y + k_y[n_y,0]\right)s[n_x,n_y] \qquad (6.364) \\
&= \sum_{i=0}^{2}\sum_{j=0}^{2} d_{ij}x^iy^j \qquad (6.365)
\end{aligned}
$$

where the expansion of the absolute values in the third equality assumes $c_{01}=0$ (as required for the filter to have a continuous first derivative at $t=0$) with $x_{n_x}=x_0+n_xT_x$ and $y_{n_y}=y_0+n_yT_y$, while the coefficients read

$$
\begin{aligned}
k_x[n_x,2] &\triangleq \frac{c_{|n_x|2}}{T_x^2} &(6.366)\\
k_x[n_x,1] &\triangleq -2\frac{c_{|n_x|2}}{T_x^2}x_{n_x} - n_x\frac{c_{|n_x|1}}{T_x} &(6.367)\\
k_x[n_x,0] &\triangleq \frac{c_{|n_x|2}}{T_x^2}x_{n_x}^2 + n_x\frac{c_{|n_x|1}}{T_x}x_{n_x} + c_{|n_x|0} &(6.368)\\
k_y[n_y,2] &\triangleq \frac{c_{|n_y|2}}{T_y^2} &(6.369)\\
k_y[n_y,1] &\triangleq -2\frac{c_{|n_y|2}}{T_y^2}y_{n_y} - n_y\frac{c_{|n_y|1}}{T_y} &(6.370)\\
k_y[n_y,0] &\triangleq \frac{c_{|n_y|2}}{T_y^2}y_{n_y}^2 + n_y\frac{c_{|n_y|1}}{T_y}y_{n_y} + c_{|n_y|0} &(6.371)
\end{aligned}
$$

such that $k_x[-1,2]=k_x[1,2]$ and $k_y[-1,2]=k_y[1,2]$, and where

$$
d_{ij} \triangleq \sum_{n_y=-1}^{1}\sum_{n_x=-1}^{1} s[n_x,n_y]k_x[n_x,i]k_y[n_y,j] \qquad (6.372)
$$

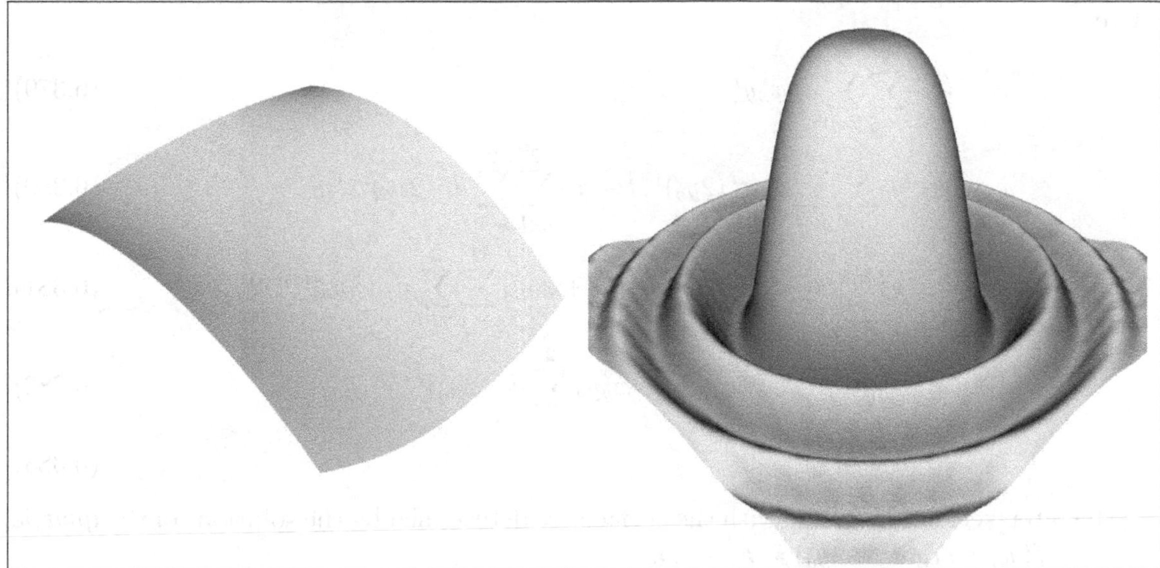

Figure 6.25: Biquadratic Patch: Illustration of a biquadratic patch (left), and of the biquadratic reconstruction of a height field (right).

The first partial derivatives are then given by

$$\frac{\partial f(x,y)}{\partial x} = \sum_{i=1}^{2}\sum_{j=0}^{2} d_{ij} i x^{i-1} y^j \tag{6.373}$$

$$\frac{\partial f(x,y)}{\partial y} = \sum_{i=0}^{2}\sum_{j=1}^{2} d_{ij} x^i j y^{j-1} \tag{6.374}$$

while the second partial derivatives read

$$\frac{\partial^2 f(x,y)}{\partial x^2} = 2\sum_{j=0}^{2} d_{2j} y^j \tag{6.375}$$

$$\frac{\partial^2 f(x,y)}{\partial x \partial y} = \sum_{i=1}^{2}\sum_{j=1}^{2} d_{ij} i x^{i-1} j y^{j-1} \tag{6.376}$$

$$\frac{\partial^2 f(x,y)}{\partial y^2} = 2\sum_{i=0}^{2} d_{i2} x^i \tag{6.377}$$

Substituting the ray equation $\vec{r}(t) \triangleq \vec{o} + t\vec{d}$, the values of the height field under the ray are then defined as

$$f(x_o + tx_d, y_o + ty_d) \overset{(6.364)}{=} \sum_{i=0}^{2}\sum_{j=0}^{2} d_{ij}(x_o + tx_d)^i (y_o + ty_d)^j$$ 288

$$= c_0 + c_1 t + c_2 t^2 + c_3 t^3 + c_4 t^4 \tag{6.378}$$

where

$$c_0 \triangleq \sum_{i=0}^{2}\sum_{j=0}^{2} d_{ij} x_o^i y_o^j \tag{6.379}$$

$$c_1 \triangleq y_d \sum_{i=0}^{2}\sum_{j=1}^{2} d_{ij} x_o^i (2y_o)^{j-1} + x_d \sum_{i=1}^{2}\sum_{j=0}^{2} d_{ij} (2x_o)^{i-1} y_o^j \tag{6.380}$$

$$c_2 \triangleq y_d^2 \sum_{i=0}^{2} d_{i2} x_o^i + x_d^2 \sum_{j=0}^{2} d_{2j} y_o^j + x_d y_d \sum_{i=1}^{2}\sum_{j=1}^{2} d_{ij} (2x_o)^{i-1} (2y_o)^{j-1} \tag{6.381}$$

$$c_3 \triangleq x_d y_d^2 \sum_{i=1}^{2} d_{i2} (2x_o)^{i-1} + x_d^2 y_d \sum_{j=1}^{2} d_{2j} (2y_o)^{j-1} \tag{6.382}$$

$$c_4 \triangleq x_d^2 y_d^2 d_{22} \tag{6.383}$$

and the intersections of the ray with the surface are determined by the solutions of the *quartic*
33 *equation* $f(x_o + tx_d, y_o + ty_d) = z_o + tz_d$.

Conversely, solving for the first two coordinates of the surface point at which the slopes are such that the normal is collinear with a given vector $\vec{n}$ yields

237

$$\sum_{i=1}^{2}\sum_{j=0}^{2} d_{ij} i x^{i-1} y^j \overset{(6.6)}{=} -\frac{n_x}{n_z} \tag{6.384}$$

237

$$\sum_{i=0}^{2}\sum_{j=1}^{2} d_{ij} x^i j y^{j-1} \overset{(6.7)}{=} -\frac{n_y}{n_z} \tag{6.385}$$

which can be expanded into

$$\sum_{j=0}^{2} d_{1j} y^j + 2x \sum_{j=0}^{2} d_{2j} y^j = -\frac{n_x}{n_z} \implies x = -\frac{\frac{n_x}{n_z} + \sum_{j=0}^{2} d_{1j} y^j}{2\sum_{j=0}^{2} d_{2j} y^j} \tag{6.386}$$

$$\sum_{i=0}^{2} d_{i1} x^i + 2y \sum_{i=0}^{2} d_{i2} x^i = -\frac{n_y}{n_z} \implies y = -\frac{\frac{n_y}{n_z} + \sum_{i=0}^{2} d_{i1} x^i}{2\sum_{i=0}^{2} d_{i2} x^i} \tag{6.387}$$

as well as into

$$\sum_{i=1}^{2} d_{i0} i x^{i-1} + y \sum_{i=1}^{2} d_{i1} i x^{i-1} + y^2 \sum_{i=1}^{2} d_{i2} i x^{i-1} = -\frac{n_x}{n_z} \tag{6.388}$$

$$\sum_{j=1}^{2} d_{0j} j y^{j-1} + x \sum_{j=1}^{2} d_{1j} j y^{j-1} + x^2 \sum_{j=1}^{2} d_{2j} j y^{j-1} = -\frac{n_y}{n_z} \tag{6.389}$$

Substituting the above expressions for x and y then yields

$$\begin{aligned} 0 = {} & 4\left(\sum_{i=0}^{2} d_{i2} x^i\right)^2 \left(\frac{n_x}{n_z} + \sum_{i=1}^{2} d_{i0} i x^{i-1}\right) + \left(\frac{n_y}{n_z} + \sum_{i=0}^{2} d_{i1} x^i\right)^2 \left(\sum_{i=1}^{2} d_{i2} i x^{i-1}\right) \\ & - 2\left(\sum_{i=0}^{2} d_{i2} x^i\right)\left(\frac{n_y}{n_z} + \sum_{i=0}^{2} d_{i1} x^i\right)\left(\sum_{i=1}^{2} d_{i1} i x^{i-1}\right) \end{aligned} \tag{6.390}$$

$$\begin{aligned} 0 = {} & 4\left(\sum_{j=0}^{2} d_{2j} y^j\right)^2 \left(\frac{n_y}{n_z} + \sum_{j=1}^{2} d_{0j} j y^{j-1}\right) + \left(\frac{n_x}{n_z} + \sum_{j=0}^{2} d_{1j} y^j\right)^2 \left(\sum_{j=1}^{2} d_{2j} j y^{j-1}\right) \\ & - 2\left(\sum_{j=0}^{2} d_{2j} y^j\right)\left(\frac{n_x}{n_z} + \sum_{j=0}^{2} d_{1j} y^j\right)\left(\sum_{j=1}^{2} d_{1j} j y^{j-1}\right) \end{aligned} \tag{6.391}$$

and expanding the previous-to-last equation gives

$$\sum_{i=0}^{5} k_i x^i = 0 \tag{6.392}$$

where

$$\begin{aligned}
k_0 &\triangleq 4d_x d_{02}^2 - 2d_{11}d_{02}d_y + d_{12}d_y^2 && (6.393)\\
k_1 &\triangleq 8d_x d_{02}d_{12} + 8d_{20}d_{02}^2 - 2d_{11}^2 d_{02} - 4d_{21}d_{02}d_y + 2d_{22}d_y^2 && (6.394)\\
k_2 &\triangleq 8d_x d_{02}d_{22} + 4d_x d_{12}^2 + 16d_{20}d_{02}d_{12} - 6d_{11}d_{02}d_{21}\\
&\qquad - d_{12}d_{11}^2 - 2d_{21}d_{12}d_y + 2d_{22}d_y d_{11} && (6.395)\\
k_3 &\triangleq 8d_x d_{12}d_{22} + 16d_{20}d_{02}d_{22} + 8d_{20}d_{12}^2 - 4d_{21}^2 d_{02} - 4d_{21}d_{12}d_{11} && (6.396)\\
k_4 &\triangleq 4d_x d_{22}^2 + 16d_{20}d_{12}d_{22} - 2d_{21}d_{11}d_{22} - 3d_{21}^2 d_{12} && (6.397)\\
k_5 &\triangleq 8d_{20}d_{22}^2 - 2d_{21}^2 d_{22} && (6.398)
\end{aligned}$$

with $d_x \triangleq \frac{n_x}{n_z} + d_{10}$ and $d_y \triangleq \frac{n_y}{n_z} + d_{01}$. The x coordinates are then given by the solutions of the *quintic equation*, from which the corresponding y coordinates may be readily computed, 36
such that the resulting points lie within the cell if both x and y are within range.

6.5.2 Torus

6.5.2.1 *Algebraic Intersection*

As illustrated in *Figure 6.26*, a *torus* [Cychosz, 1991] of center $\vec{c}$, axis $\hat{u}$, central radius R and 292
tubular radius r is defined as the set of points $\vec{p}$ such that

$$\begin{aligned}
r^2 &\overset{(3.96)}{=} \left(\|(\vec{p}-\vec{c})\times\hat{u}\| - R\right)^2 + \langle\vec{p}-\vec{c},\hat{u}\rangle^2 && (6.399)\\
&\overset{(3.78)}{=} \|(\vec{p}-\vec{c})\times\hat{u}\|^2 - 2R\|(\vec{p}-\vec{c})\times\hat{u}\| + R^2 + \langle\vec{p}-\vec{c},\hat{u}\rangle^2\\
&\overset{(3.98)}{=} \|\vec{p}-\vec{c}\|^2 - 2R\|(\vec{p}-\vec{c})\times\hat{u}\| + R^2 && (6.400)
\end{aligned}$$

80
77
80

Rearranging the terms, substituting $\vec{p}$ with the set of points defined by the ray equation $\vec{r}(t) \triangleq \vec{o} + t\vec{d}$ and squaring the result then yields

$$\begin{aligned}
& \left(2R\|(\vec{o}+t\vec{d}-\vec{c})\times\hat{u}\|\right)^2 = \left(\|\vec{o}+t\vec{d}-\vec{c}\|^2 + R^2 - r^2\right)^2\\
\Longleftrightarrow\ & \left(2R\|(t\vec{d}+\vec{co})\times\hat{u}\|\right)^2 = \left(\|t\vec{d}+\vec{co}\|^2 + R^2 - r^2\right)^2\\
\Longleftrightarrow\ & 4R^2\|t\vec{d}\times\hat{u} + \vec{co}\times\hat{u}\|^2 = \left(\langle t\vec{d}+\vec{co}, t\vec{d}+\vec{co}\rangle + R^2 - r^2\right)^2\\
\Longleftrightarrow\ & 4R^2\langle t\vec{d}\times\hat{u} + \vec{co}\times\hat{u}, t\vec{d}\times\hat{u} + \vec{co}\times\hat{u}\rangle \overset{(3.75)}{=} \left(t^2\|\vec{d}\|^2 + 2t\langle\vec{d},\vec{co}\rangle + \|\vec{co}\|^2 + R^2 - r^2\right)^2
\end{aligned} \tag{6.401}$$

76

where $\vec{co} = \vec{o} - \vec{c}$, whereas defining $k \triangleq \|\vec{co}\|^2 + R^2 - r^2$ leads to the *quartic equation* 33

$$\begin{aligned}
& 4R^2(t^2\|\vec{d}\times\hat{u}\|^2 + 2t\langle\vec{d}\times\hat{u},\vec{co}\times\hat{u}\rangle + \|\vec{co}\times\hat{u}\|^2)\\
&\quad = t^4\|\vec{d}\|^4 + 4t^2\langle\vec{d},\vec{co}\rangle^2 + k^2 + 2(2t^3\|\vec{d}\|^2\langle\vec{d},\vec{co}\rangle + t^2\|\vec{d}\|^2 k + 2t\langle\vec{d},\vec{co}\rangle k)\\
\Longleftrightarrow\ & t^2 4R^2\|\vec{d}\times\hat{u}\|^2 + t8R^2\langle\vec{d}\times\hat{u},\vec{co}\times\hat{u}\rangle + 4R^2\|\vec{co}\times\hat{u}\|^2\\
&\quad = t^4\|\vec{d}\|^4 + t^3 4\|\vec{d}\|^2\langle\vec{d},\vec{co}\rangle + t^2(4\langle\vec{d},\vec{co}\rangle^2 + 2\|\vec{d}\|^2 k) + t4\langle\vec{d},\vec{co}\rangle k + k^2
\end{aligned} \tag{6.402}$$

whose solutions determine the points of intersection along the ray, while a vector orthogonal to the surface at that point is readily given by $\vec{n} \triangleq \vec{p} - \vec{c} - R\hat{v}$, where $\hat{v} \triangleq \vec{v} \div \|\vec{v}\|$, with the
vector $\vec{v} \overset{(3.110)}{=} \vec{p} - \vec{c} - \langle\vec{p}-\vec{c},\hat{u}\rangle\hat{u}$ being orthogonal to $\hat{u}$ and in the same plane as $\vec{p}$. 82

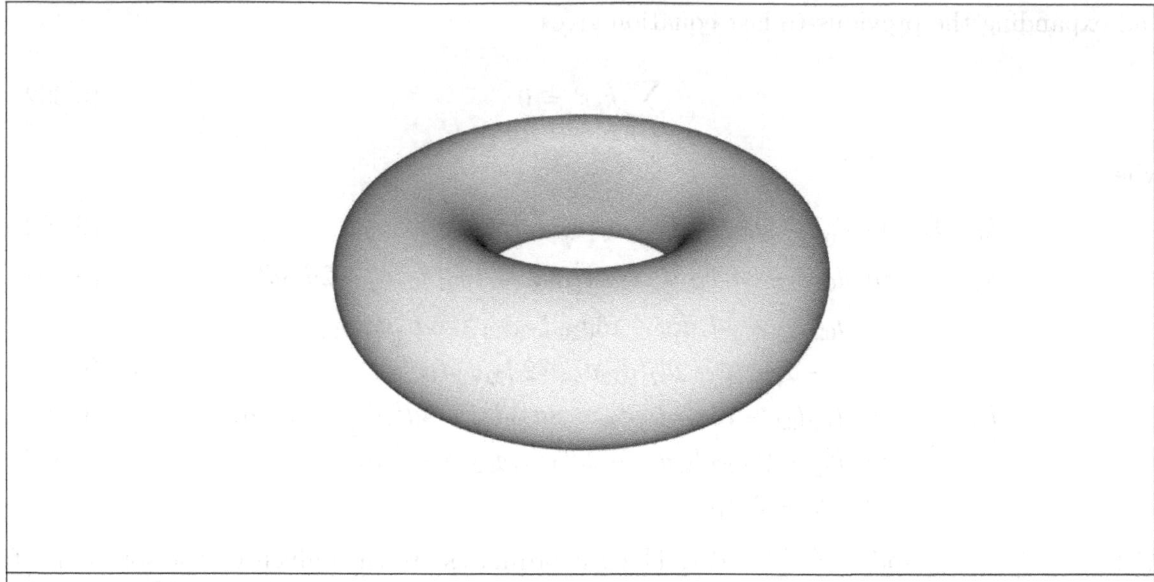

Figure 6.26: Torus: Illustration of a torus.

6.5.2.2 Distance Estimation

The distance from a point $\vec{p}$ to a torus of center $\vec{c}$, axis $\hat{u}$, central radius R and tubular radius r reads

80 77

$$f(\vec{p}) \overset{(3.96)}{\underset{(3.78)}{=}} \sqrt{\left(\|(\vec{p}-\vec{c})\times\hat{u}\| - R\right)^2 + \langle\vec{p}-\vec{c},\hat{u}\rangle^2} - r$$

$$= \sqrt{\|(\vec{p}-\vec{c})\times\hat{u}\|^2 - 2R\|(\vec{p}-\vec{c})\times\hat{u}\| + R^2 + \langle\vec{p}-\vec{c},\hat{u}\rangle^2} - r$$

80

$$\overset{(3.98)}{=} \sqrt{\|\vec{p}-\vec{c}\|^2 - 2R\|(\vec{p}-\vec{c})\times\hat{u}\| + R^2} - r$$

80 77

$$\overset{(3.96)}{\underset{(3.78)}{=}} \sqrt{\|\vec{p}-\vec{c}\|^2 + 2\langle\vec{p}-\vec{c}, -R\hat{v}\rangle + \|-R\hat{v}\|^2} - r$$

77

$$\overset{(3.79)}{=} \|\vec{p}-\vec{c}-R\hat{v}\| - r \tag{6.403}$$

82 where $\hat{v} \triangleq \vec{v} \div \|\vec{v}\|$, with the vector $\vec{v} \overset{(3.110)}{=} \vec{p}-\vec{c}-\langle\vec{p}-\vec{c},\hat{u}\rangle\hat{u}$ being orthogonal to $\hat{u}$ and in the same plane as $\vec{p}$.

6.5.2.3 Implicit Intersection

Let us consider the scalar field defined by the function

$$f(x,y,z) \triangleq \left(\sqrt{(x-x_c)^2+(y-y_c)^2} - r\right)^2 + (z-z_c)^2 \tag{6.404}$$

and its associated vector field

239

$$\nabla f(x,y,z) \overset{(6.20)}{=} \begin{bmatrix} 2(x-x_c)\frac{\sqrt{(x-x_c)^2+(y-y_c)^2}-r}{\sqrt{(x-x_c)^2+(y-y_c)^2}} \\ 2(y-y_c)\frac{\sqrt{(x-x_c)^2+(y-y_c)^2}-r}{\sqrt{(x-x_c)^2+(y-y_c)^2}} \\ 2(z-z_c) \end{bmatrix} \tag{6.405}$$

Substituting the ray equation $\vec{r}(t) \triangleq \vec{o} + t\vec{d}$, the values of the scalar field along the ray are then defined as

239

$$\begin{aligned}
f(t) &\overset{(6.21)}{=} \left(\sqrt{(x_o + tx_d - x_c)^2 + (y_o + ty_d - y_c)^2} - r\right)^2 + (z_o + tz_d - z_c)^2 \\
&= \left(\sqrt{(x_{co} + tx_d)^2 + (y_{co} + ty_d)^2} - r\right)^2 + (z_{co} + tz_d)^2 \\
&= (x_{co} + tx_d)^2 + (y_{co} + ty_d)^2 + (z_{co} + tz_d)^2 \\
&- 2r\sqrt{(x_{co} + tx_d)^2 + (y_{co} + ty_d)^2} + r^2 \\
&= x_{co}^2 + 2x_{co}tx_d + t^2x_d^2 + y_{co}^2 + 2y_{co}ty_d + t^2y_d^2 + z_{co}^2 + 2z_{co}tz_d + t^2z_d^2 \\
&- 2r\sqrt{x_{co}^2 + 2x_{co}tx_d + t^2x_d^2 + y_{co}^2 + 2y_{co}ty_d + t^2y_d^2} + r^2 \\
&= (x_{co}^2 + y_{co}^2 + z_{co}^2) + 2(x_{co}x_d + y_{co}y_d + z_{co}z_d)t + (x_d^2 + y_d^2 + z_d^2)t^2 \\
&- 2r\sqrt{(x_{co}^2 + y_{co}^2) + 2(x_{co}x_d + y_{co}y_d)t + (x_d^2 + y_d^2)t^2} + r^2 \qquad (6.406)
\end{aligned}$$

where $x_{co} \triangleq x_o - x_c$, $y_{co} \triangleq y_o - y_c$, $z_{co} \triangleq z_o - z_c$.

A torus may then be defined as the set of points satisfying $f(x, y, z) = v$ for a given isovalue v. By setting the isovalue $v = r'^2$, the formulation defines a torus of central radius r and tubular radius r'. Using a vector notation, the equation to be solved can be written as

$$2r\sqrt{(x_{co}^2 + y_{co}^2) + 2(x_{co}x_d + y_{co}y_d)t + (x_d^2 + y_d^2)t^2} = (\|\vec{co}\|^2 + r^2 - v) + 2\langle\vec{co}, \vec{d}\rangle t + \|\vec{d}\|^2t^2 \qquad (6.407)$$

which, when squaring both sides, yields

$$\begin{aligned}
&4r^2((x_{co}^2 + y_{co}^2) + 2(x_{co}x_d + y_{co}y_d)t + (x_d^2 + y_d^2)t^2) \\
&= (\|\vec{co}\|^2 + r^2 - v)^2 + 4(\|\vec{co}\|^2 + r^2 - v)\langle\vec{co}, \vec{d}\rangle t \qquad (6.408) \\
&+ (4\langle\vec{co}, \vec{d}\rangle^2 + 2(\|\vec{co}\|^2 + r^2 - v)\|\vec{d}\|^2)t^2 + 4\langle\vec{co}, \vec{d}\rangle\|\vec{d}\|^2t^3 + \|\vec{d}\|^4t^4
\end{aligned}$$

Rearranging the terms then leads to a *quartic equation* 33

$$0 = c_0 + c_1t + c_2t^2 + c_3t^3 + c_4t^4 \qquad (6.409)$$

whose coefficients read

$$\begin{aligned}
c_0 &\triangleq (\|\vec{co}\|^2 + r^2 - v)^2 - 4r^2(x_{co}^2 + y_{co}^2) \\
&= (\|\vec{co}\|^2 - r^2 - v)^2 + 4r^2(\|\vec{co}\|^2 - (x_{co}^2 + y_{co}^2) - v) \\
&= (\|\vec{co}\|^2 - r^2 - v)^2 + 4r^2(z_{co}^2 - v) \qquad (6.410) \\
c_1 &\triangleq 4(\|\vec{co}\|^2 + r^2 - v)\langle\vec{co}, \vec{d}\rangle - 8r^2(x_{co}x_d + y_{co}y_d) \\
&= 4(\|\vec{co}\|^2 - r^2 - v)\langle\vec{co}, \vec{d}\rangle + 8r^2(\langle\vec{co}, \vec{d}\rangle - (x_{co}x_d + y_{co}y_d)) \\
&= 4(\|\vec{co}\|^2 - r^2 - v)\langle\vec{co}, \vec{d}\rangle + 8r^2z_{co}z_d \qquad (6.411) \\
c_2 &\triangleq 4\langle\vec{co}, \vec{d}\rangle^2 + 2(\|\vec{co}\|^2 + r^2 - v)\|\vec{d}\|^2 - 4r^2(x_d^2 + y_d^2) \\
&= 4\langle\vec{co}, \vec{d}\rangle^2 + 2(\|\vec{co}\|^2 - r^2 - v)\|\vec{d}\|^2 + 4r^2(\|\vec{d}\|^2 - (x_d^2 + y_d^2)) \\
&= 4\langle\vec{co}, \vec{d}\rangle^2 + 2(\|\vec{co}\|^2 - r^2 - v)\|\vec{d}\|^2 + 4r^2z_d^2 \qquad (6.412) \\
c_3 &\triangleq 4\langle\vec{co}, \vec{d}\rangle\|\vec{d}\|^2 \qquad (6.413) \\
c_4 &\triangleq \|\vec{d}\|^4 \qquad (6.414)
\end{aligned}$$

6.5.2.4 Surface Parameterization

294 As illustrated in *Figure 6.27*, a *toroidal patch* of central radius R, tubular radius r and extent $[\theta_l, \theta_h] \times [\phi_l, \phi_h]$ centered at the origin and oriented along the z axis of a given coordinate system may alternatively be represented in toroidal coordinates as a parametric surface of the form

$$\vec{p}(u,v) \triangleq R\begin{bmatrix}\cos\left(\text{lerp}(v,\phi_l,\phi_h)\right)\\ \sin\left(\text{lerp}(v,\phi_l,\phi_h)\right)\\ 0\end{bmatrix} + r\hat{n}(u,v) \tag{6.415}$$

$$= \begin{bmatrix}\Big(R + r\sin\left(\text{lerp}(u,\theta_l,\theta_h)\right)\Big)\cos\left(\text{lerp}(v,\phi_l,\phi_h)\right)\\ \Big(R + r\sin\left(\text{lerp}(u,\theta_l,\theta_h)\right)\Big)\sin\left(\text{lerp}(v,\phi_l,\phi_h)\right)\\ r\cos\left(\text{lerp}(u,\theta_l,\theta_h)\right)\end{bmatrix} \tag{6.416}$$

whose unit normal is readily given as

240 $$\hat{n}(u,v) \overset{(6.27)}{=} \begin{bmatrix}\sin\left(\text{lerp}(u,\theta_l,\theta_h)\right)\cos\left(\text{lerp}(v,\phi_l,\phi_h)\right)\\ \sin\left(\text{lerp}(u,\theta_l,\theta_h)\right)\sin\left(\text{lerp}(v,\phi_l,\phi_h)\right)\\ \cos\left(\text{lerp}(u,\theta_l,\theta_h)\right)\end{bmatrix} \tag{6.417}$$

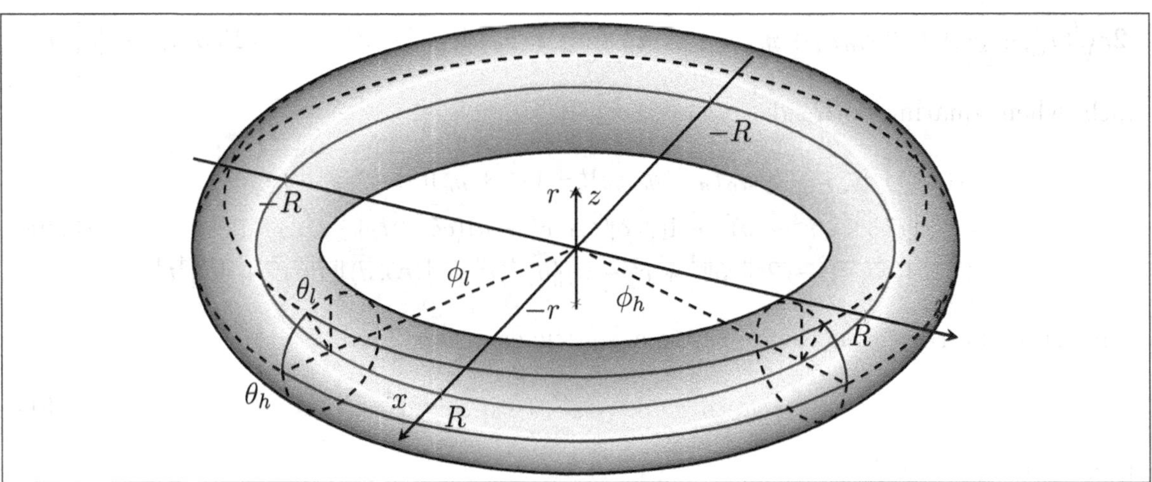

Figure 6.27: Torus Parameterization: Illustration of the parametric representation of the surface of a torus.

The first partial derivatives are then given by

$$\frac{\partial \vec{p}(u,v)}{\partial u} = \begin{bmatrix}(\theta_h - \theta_l)r\cos\left(\text{lerp}(u,\theta_l,\theta_h)\right)\cos\left(\text{lerp}(v,\phi_l,\phi_h)\right)\\ (\theta_h - \theta_l)r\cos\left(\text{lerp}(u,\theta_l,\theta_h)\right)\sin\left(\text{lerp}(v,\phi_l,\phi_h)\right)\\ -(\theta_h - \theta_l)r\sin\left(\text{lerp}(u,\theta_l,\theta_h)\right)\end{bmatrix} \tag{6.418}$$

$$= (\theta_h - \theta_l)\begin{bmatrix}p_z(u,v)\cos\left(\text{lerp}(v,\phi_l,\phi_h)\right)\\ p_z(u,v)\sin\left(\text{lerp}(v,\phi_l,\phi_h)\right)\\ -\sqrt{r^2 - p_z(u,v)^2}\end{bmatrix} \tag{6.419}$$

$$\frac{\partial \vec{p}(u,v)}{\partial v} = \begin{bmatrix} -(\phi_h - \phi_l)\Big(R + r\sin\big(\operatorname{lerp}(u,\theta_l,\theta_h)\big)\Big)\sin\big(\operatorname{lerp}(v,\phi_l,\phi_h)\big) \\ (\phi_h - \phi_l)\Big(R + r\sin\big(\operatorname{lerp}(u,\theta_l,\theta_h)\big)\Big)\cos\big(\operatorname{lerp}(v,\phi_l,\phi_h)\big) \\ 0 \end{bmatrix} \tag{6.420}$$

$$= (\phi_h - \phi_l)\begin{bmatrix} -p_y(u,v) \\ p_x(u,v) \\ 0 \end{bmatrix} \tag{6.421}$$

while the second partial derivatives read

$$\frac{\partial^2 \vec{p}(u,v)}{\partial u^2} = \begin{bmatrix} -(\theta_h - \theta_l)^2 r\sin\big(\operatorname{lerp}(u,\theta_l,\theta_h)\big)\cos\big(\operatorname{lerp}(v,\phi_l,\phi_h)\big) \\ -(\theta_h - \theta_l)^2 r\sin\big(\operatorname{lerp}(u,\theta_l,\theta_h)\big)\sin\big(\operatorname{lerp}(v,\phi_l,\phi_h)\big) \\ -(\theta_h - \theta_l)^2 r\cos\big(\operatorname{lerp}(u,\theta_l,\theta_h)\big) \end{bmatrix} \tag{6.422}$$

$$= -(\theta_h - \theta_l)^2 \begin{bmatrix} \sqrt{r^2 - p_z(u,v)^2}\cos\big(\operatorname{lerp}(v,\phi_l,\phi_h)\big) \\ \sqrt{r^2 - p_z(u,v)^2}\sin\big(\operatorname{lerp}(v,\phi_l,\phi_h)\big) \\ p_z(u,v) \end{bmatrix} \tag{6.423}$$

$$\frac{\partial^2 \vec{p}(u,v)}{\partial u \partial v} = \begin{bmatrix} -(\theta_h - \theta_l)(\phi_h - \phi_l) r\cos\big(\operatorname{lerp}(u,\theta_l,\theta_h)\big)\sin\big(\operatorname{lerp}(v,\phi_l,\phi_h)\big) \\ (\theta_h - \theta_l)(\phi_h - \phi_l) r\cos\big(\operatorname{lerp}(u,\theta_l,\theta_h)\big)\cos\big(\operatorname{lerp}(v,\phi_l,\phi_h)\big) \\ 0 \end{bmatrix} \tag{6.424}$$

$$= (\theta_h - \theta_l)(\phi_h - \phi_l)\begin{bmatrix} -p_z(u,v)\sin\big(\operatorname{lerp}(v,\phi_l,\phi_h)\big) \\ p_z(u,v)\cos\big(\operatorname{lerp}(v,\phi_l,\phi_h)\big) \\ 0 \end{bmatrix} \tag{6.425}$$

$$\frac{\partial^2 \vec{p}(u,v)}{\partial v^2} = \begin{bmatrix} -(\phi_h - \phi_l)^2\Big(R + r\sin\big(\operatorname{lerp}(u,\theta_l,\theta_h)\big)\Big)\cos\big(\operatorname{lerp}(v,\phi_l,\phi_h)\big) \\ -(\phi_h - \phi_l)^2\Big(R + r\sin\big(\operatorname{lerp}(u,\theta_l,\theta_h)\big)\Big)\sin\big(\operatorname{lerp}(v,\phi_l,\phi_h)\big) \\ 0 \end{bmatrix} \tag{6.426}$$

$$= -(\phi_h - \phi_l)^2 \begin{bmatrix} p_x(u,v) \\ p_y(u,v) \\ 0 \end{bmatrix} \tag{6.427}$$

The equation of the curve in a plane with constant azimuth ϕ is implicitly defined by $(\rho - R)^2 + z^2 = r^2$, whose corresponding explicit formulation over either the top or bottom half of the torus reads $z = \pm\sqrt{r^2 - (\rho - R)^2}$. It follows that the arc length of the upper/lower hemicircle is given as

$$s \overset{(6.37)}{=} \int_S \sqrt{1 + \left(\frac{\mathrm{d}z}{\mathrm{d}\rho}\right)^2}\,\mathrm{d}\rho$$ 241

$$= \int_S \sqrt{1 + \left(\mp\frac{\rho - R}{\sqrt{r^2 - (\rho - R)^2}}\right)^2}\,\mathrm{d}\rho$$

$$= \int_S \sqrt{1 + \frac{(\rho - R)^2}{r^2 - (\rho - R)^2}}\,\mathrm{d}\rho$$

$$= \int_S \frac{r}{\sqrt{r^2 - (\rho - R)^2}}\,\mathrm{d}\rho \tag{6.428}$$

6.5.2.5 *Area and Sampling*

Given the surface area $A \triangleq (\phi_h - \phi_l)2\pi r R$ of the toroidal patch, the integral of the uniform joint *probability density* $p(\rho, \phi) \triangleq 1 \div A$ over a subdomain A_s yields the associated *cumulative* 131

132 *distribution* over the half torus, which may be expressed in *cylindrical coordinates* in a
69 separable form as

132

$$\begin{aligned}
P(\rho_s, \phi_s) &\overset{(4.22)}{=} \int_{\phi_l}^{\phi_s} \int_{R-r}^{\rho_s} \frac{2}{(\phi_h - \phi_l)2\pi r R} \frac{r}{\sqrt{r^2 - (\rho - R)^2}} \rho \mathrm{d}\rho \mathrm{d}\phi \\
&= \int_{\phi_l}^{\phi_s} \frac{1}{\phi_h - \phi_l} \mathrm{d}\phi \int_{R-r}^{\rho_s} \frac{1}{\pi R} \frac{\rho}{\sqrt{r^2 - (\rho - R)^2}} \mathrm{d}\rho \\
&= \left[\frac{\phi}{\phi_h - \phi_l} \right]_{\phi_l}^{\phi_s} \frac{1}{\pi R} \left[R \arctan\left(\frac{\rho - R}{\sqrt{r^2 - (\rho - R)^2}} \right) - \sqrt{r^2 - (\rho - R)^2} \right]_{R-r}^{\rho_s} \\
&= \frac{\phi_s - \phi_l}{\phi_h - \phi_l} \left(\frac{\arctan\left(\frac{\rho_s - R}{\sqrt{r^2 - (\rho_s - R)^2}} \right) + \frac{\pi}{2}}{\pi} - \frac{\sqrt{r^2 - (\rho_s - R)^2}}{\pi R} \right) \\
&= \frac{\phi_s - \phi_l}{\phi_h - \phi_l} \left(\frac{\arctan\left(\frac{\frac{\rho_s - R}{r}}{\sqrt{1 - \left(\frac{\rho_s - R}{r}\right)^2}} \right) + \frac{\pi}{2}}{\pi} - \frac{r\sqrt{1 - \left(\frac{\rho_s - R}{r}\right)^2}}{\pi R} \right) \\
&= \frac{\phi_s - \phi_l}{\phi_h - \phi_l} \left(\frac{\theta_s + \frac{\pi}{2}}{\pi} - \frac{r \cos(\theta_s)}{\pi R} \right)
\end{aligned} \tag{6.429}$$

where $\theta_s \triangleq \arcsin\left(\frac{\rho_s - R}{r}\right) \in \left[-\frac{\pi}{2}, \frac{\pi}{2}\right]$.

Integrating over the whole domain by substituting $\phi_s = \phi_h$ and $\rho_s = R + r$ then ensures
134 normalization, while applying *inverse-transform sampling* allows uniform sampling to be readily carried as

$$\xi_\phi = \frac{\phi_s - \phi_l}{\phi_h - \phi_l} \quad \Longrightarrow \quad \phi_s = \mathrm{lerp}(\xi_\phi, \phi_l, \phi_h) \tag{6.430}$$

$$\xi_\rho = \frac{\theta_s + \frac{\pi}{2}}{\pi} - \frac{r\cos(\theta_s)}{\pi R} \quad \Longrightarrow \quad \frac{r}{R}\cos(\theta_s) = \theta_s - (2\xi_\rho - 1)\frac{\pi}{2} \tag{6.431}$$

where the latter equation, or equivalently $\frac{r}{R}\sin(\theta'_s) = \theta'_s - \pi\xi_h$ where $\theta'_s \triangleq \theta_s + \frac{\pi}{2} \in [0, \pi]$,
36 can be solved using a numerical *root finding* scheme as it has a unique solution given that the slope of the scaled cosine function is bounded by $\frac{r}{R} < 1$. The second half of the torus may then be similarly sampled by randomly distributing the sample coordinates in either the upper or lower half with equal probability.

6.5.3 Goursat Surface

6.5.3.1 Implicit Intersection

Let us consider the scalar field defined by the function

$$\begin{aligned} f(x,y,z) &\triangleq k_4\left((x-x_c)^4+(y-y_c)^4+(z-z_c)^4\right) \\ &+ k_3\left((x-x_c)^2+(y-y_c)^2+(z-z_c)^2\right)^2 \\ &+ k_2\left((x-x_c)^2+(y-y_c)^2+(z-z_c)^2\right) \qquad (6.432) \\ &= k_4\left((x-x_c)^4+(y-y_c)^4+(z-z_c)^4\right) \\ &+ k_3((x-x_c)^4+(y-y_c)^4+(z-z_c)^4+2(y-y_c)^2(z-z_c)^2 \\ &\quad + 2(z-z_c)^2(x-x_c)^2+2(x-x_c)^2(y-y_c)^2) \\ &+ k_2\left((x-x_c)^2+(y-y_c)^2+(z-z_c)^2\right) \\ &= (k_4+k_3)\left((x-x_c)^4+(y-y_c)^4+(z-z_c)^4\right) \\ &+ 2k_3\left((y-y_c)^2(z-z_c)^2+(z-z_c)^2(x-x_c)^2+(x-x_c)^2(y-y_c)^2\right) \\ &+ k_2\left((x-x_c)^2+(y-y_c)^2+(z-z_c)^2\right) \qquad (6.433) \end{aligned}$$

and its associated vector field

239

$$\nabla f(x,y,z) \overset{(6.20)}{=} \begin{bmatrix} 4(k_4+k_3)(x-x_c)^3+4k_3(x-x_c)\left((y-y_c)^2+(z-z_c)^2\right)+2k_2(x-x_c) \\ 4(k_4+k_3)(y-y_c)^3+4k_3(y-y_c)\left((z-z_c)^2+(x-x_c)^2\right)+2k_2(y-y_c) \\ 4(k_4+k_3)(z-z_c)^3+4k_3(z-z_c)\left((x-x_c)^2+(y-y_c)^2\right)+2k_2(z-z_c) \end{bmatrix} \qquad (6.434)$$

Substituting the ray equation $\vec{r}(t) \triangleq \vec{o} + t\vec{d}$, the values of the scalar field along the ray are then defined as

239

$$\begin{aligned} f(t) &\overset{(6.21)}{=} (k_4+k_3)\left((x_o+tx_d-x_c)^4+(y_o+ty_d-y_c)^4+(z_o+tz_d-z_c)^4\right) \\ &+ 2k_3((y_o+ty_d-y_c)^2(z_o+tz_d-z_c)^2 \\ &\quad + (z_o+tz_d-z_c)^2(x_o+tx_d-x_c)^2+(x_o+tx_d-x_c)^2(y_o+ty_d-y_c)^2) \\ &+ k_2\left((x_o+tx_d-x_c)^2+(y_o+ty_d-y_c)^2+(z_o+tz_d-z_c)^2\right) \\ &= (k_4+k_3)\left((x_{co}+tx_d)^4+(y_{co}+ty_d)^4+(z_{co}+tz_d)^4\right) \\ &+ 2k_3\left((y_{co}+ty_d)^2(z_{co}+tz_d)^2+(z_{co}+tz_d)^2(x_{co}+tx_d)^2+(x_{co}+tx_d)^2(y_{co}+ty_d)^2\right) \\ &+ k_2\left((x_{co}+tx_d)^2+(y_{co}+ty_d)^2+(z_{co}+tz_d)^2\right) \\ &= (k_4+k_3)\alpha(t)+2k_3\beta(t)+k_2\gamma(t) \\ &= c_0+c_1t+c_2t^2+c_3t^3+c_4t^4 \qquad (6.435) \end{aligned}$$

where $x_{co} \triangleq x_o - x_c$, $y_{co} \triangleq y_o - y_c$, $z_{co} \triangleq z_o - z_c$ and

$$
\begin{aligned}
\alpha(t) &\triangleq x_{co}^4 + 4x_{co}^3 x_d t + 6x_{co}^2 x_d^2 t^2 + 4x_{co} x_d^3 t^3 + x_d^4 t^4 \\
&+ y_{co}^4 + 4y_{co}^3 y_d t + 6y_{co}^2 y_d^2 t^2 + 4y_{co} y_d^3 t^3 + y_d^4 t^4 \\
&+ z_{co}^4 + 4z_{co}^3 z_d t + 6z_{co}^2 z_d^2 t^2 + 4z_{co} z_d^3 t^3 + z_d^4 t^4 \\
&= (x_{co}^4 + y_{co}^4 + z_{co}^4) + 4(x_{co}^3 x_d + y_{co}^3 y_d + z_{co}^3 z_d)t + 6(x_{co}^2 x_d^2 + y_{co}^2 y_d^2 + z_{co}^2 z_d^2)t^2 \\
&+ 4(x_{co} x_d^3 + y_{co} y_d^3 + z_{co} z_d^3)t^3 + (x_d^4 + y_d^4 + z_d^4)t^4 \qquad (6.436)\\
\beta(t) &\triangleq y_{co}^2 z_{co}^2 + 2(y_{co}^2 z_{co} z_d + z_{co}^2 y_{co} y_d)t + (y_{co}^2 z_d^2 + 4y_{co} y_d z_{co} z_d + z_{co}^2 y_d^2)t^2 \\
&+ 2(y_{co} y_d z_d^2 + z_{co} z_d y_d^2)t^3 + y_d^2 z_d^2 t^4 \\
&+ z_{co}^2 x_{co}^2 + 2(z_{co}^2 x_{co} x_d + x_{co}^2 z_{co} z_d)t + (z_{co}^2 x_d^2 + 4z_{co} z_d x_{co} x_d + x_{co}^2 z_d^2)t^2 \\
&+ 2(z_{co} z_d x_d^2 + x_{co} x_d z_d^2)t^3 + z_d^2 x_d^2 t^4 \\
&+ x_{co}^2 y_{co}^2 + 2(x_{co}^2 y_{co} y_d + y_{co}^2 x_{co} x_d)t + (x_{co}^2 y_d^2 + 4x_{co} x_d y_{co} y_d + y_{co}^2 x_d^2)t^2 \\
&+ 2(x_{co} x_d y_d^2 + y_{co} y_d x_d^2)t^3 + x_d^2 y_d^2 t^4 \\
&= (y_{co}^2 z_{co}^2 + z_{co}^2 x_{co}^2 + x_{co}^2 y_{co}^2) \\
&+ 2\left(x_{co}^2(y_{co} y_d + z_{co} z_d) + y_{co}^2(z_{co} z_d + x_{co} x_d) + z_{co}^2(x_{co} x_d + y_{co} y_d)\right)t \\
&+ (y_{co}^2 z_d^2 + z_{co}^2 y_d^2 + z_{co}^2 x_d^2 + x_{co}^2 z_d^2 + x_{co}^2 y_d^2 + y_{co}^2 x_d^2 \\
&\qquad + 4(y_{co} y_d z_{co} z_d + z_{co} z_d x_{co} x_d + x_{co} x_d y_{co} y_d))t^2 \\
&+ 2\left((y_{co} y_d + z_{co} z_d)x_d^2 + (z_{co} z_d + x_{co} x_d)y_d^2 + (x_{co} x_d + y_{co} y_d)z_d^2\right)t^3 \\
&+ (y_d^2 z_d^2 + z_d^2 x_d^2 + x_d^2 y_d^2)t^4 \qquad (6.437)\\
\gamma(t) &\triangleq (x_{co}^2 + 2x_{co} x_d t + x_d^2 t^2) + (y_{co}^2 + 2y_{co} y_d t + y_d^2 t^2) + (z_{co}^2 + 2z_{co} z_d t + z_d^2 t^2) \\
&= (x_{co}^2 + y_{co}^2 + z_{co}^2) + 2(x_{co} x_d + y_{co} y_d + z_{co} z_d)t + (x_d^2 + y_d^2 + z_d^2)t^2 \qquad (6.438)
\end{aligned}
$$

and with

$$
\begin{aligned}
c_0 &\triangleq (k_4 + k_3)(x_{co}^4 + y_{co}^4 + z_{co}^4) + 2k_3(y_{co}^2 z_{co}^2 + z_{co}^2 x_{co}^2 + x_{co}^2 y_{co}^2) + k_2(x_{co}^2 + y_{co}^2 + z_{co}^2) \qquad (6.439)\\
c_1 &\triangleq 4(k_4 + k_3)(x_{co}^3 x_d + y_{co}^3 y_d + z_{co}^3 z_d) + 2k_2(x_{co} x_d + y_{co} y_d + z_{co} z_d) \\
&+ 4k_3\left(x_{co}^2(y_{co} y_d + z_{co} z_d) + y_{co}^2(z_{co} z_d + x_{co} x_d) + z_{co}^2(x_{co} x_d + y_{co} y_d)\right) \qquad (6.440)\\
c_2 &\triangleq 6(k_4 + k_3)(x_{co}^2 x_d^2 + y_{co}^2 y_d^2 + z_{co}^2 z_d^2) + k_2(x_d^2 + y_d^2 + z_d^2) \\
&+ 2k_3\left(y_{co}^2 z_d^2 + z_{co}^2 y_d^2 + z_{co}^2 x_d^2 + x_{co}^2 z_d^2 + x_{co}^2 y_d^2 + y_{co}^2 x_d^2\right) \\
&+ 8k_3(y_{co} y_d z_{co} z_d + z_{co} z_d x_{co} x_d + x_{co} x_d y_{co} y_d) \qquad (6.441)\\
c_3 &\triangleq 4(k_4 + k_3)(x_{co} x_d^3 + y_{co} y_d^3 + z_{co} z_d^3) \\
&+ 4k_3\left((y_{co} y_d + z_{co} z_d)x_d^2 + (z_{co} z_d + x_{co} x_d)y_d^2 + (x_{co} x_d + y_{co} y_d)z_d^2\right) \qquad (6.442)\\
c_4 &\triangleq (k_4 + k_3)(x_d^4 + y_d^4 + z_d^4) + 2k_3(y_d^2 z_d^2 + z_d^2 x_d^2 + x_d^2 y_d^2) \qquad (6.443)
\end{aligned}
$$

299 As illustrated in *Figure 6.28*, a *Goursat surface* may then be defined as the set of points
satisfying $f(x, y, z) = v$ for a given isovalue v, and whose points of intersection along the ray
33 are determined by the solutions of the *quartic equation* $f(t) = v$.

6.5.4 Quartic Surfaces

Other notable quartic surfaces include:

- the Roman surface, also known as the Steiner surface

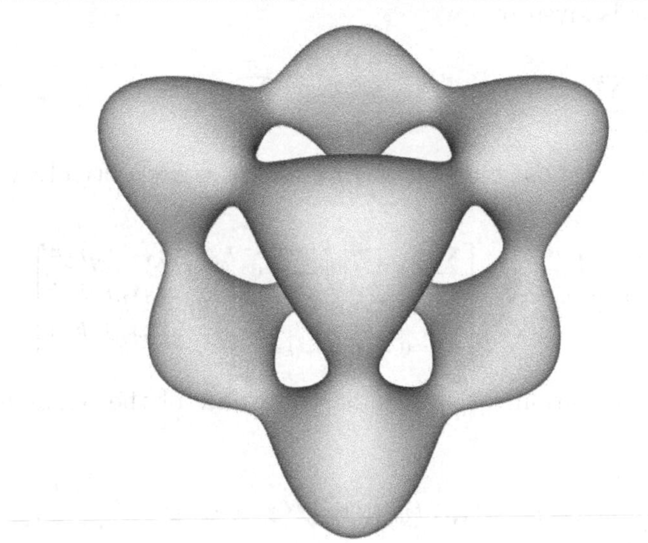

Figure 6.28: Goursat Surface: Illustration of a Goursat surface with parameters $k_4 = 1$, $k_3 = 0$, $k_2 = -5$ and $v = -11.8$, commonly known as the Tangle cube.

- the Apple and Lemon quartic surfaces
- the Eight and Octdong surfaces
- the Miter surface
- the Tooth surface
- ...

6.6 HIGHER-ORDER SURFACES

6.6.1 Polynomial Surfaces

6.6.1.1 Implicit Intersection

Let us consider the scalar field defined by the function

$$\begin{aligned} f(x,y,z) &\triangleq \sum_{i=0}^{n}\sum_{j=0}^{n-i}\sum_{k=0}^{n-i-j} c_{i,j,k}x^i y^j z^k && (6.444) \\ &= \sum_{i=0}^{n}\sum_{j=0}^{n-i}\sum_{k=j}^{n-i} c_{i,j,k-j}x^i y^j z^{k-j} \\ &= \sum_{i=0}^{n}\sum_{k=0}^{n-i}\sum_{j=0}^{k} c_{i,j,k-j}x^i y^j z^{k-j} \\ &= \sum_{i=0}^{n}\sum_{k=i}^{n}\sum_{j=0}^{k-i} c_{i,j,k-i-j}x^i y^j z^{k-i-j} \\ &= \sum_{k=0}^{n}\sum_{i=0}^{k}\sum_{j=0}^{k-i} c_{i,j,k-i-j}x^i y^j z^{k-i-j} && (6.445) \end{aligned}$$

whose numbers of terms is given by

15 15 $$\sum_{k=0}^{n}\sum_{i=0}^{k}\sum_{j=0}^{k-i} 1 = \sum_{k=0}^{n}\sum_{i=0}^{k} k-i+1 = \sum_{k=0}^{n}\sum_{j=1}^{k+1} j \overset{(2.1)}{=} \sum_{k=0}^{n} t_{k+1} = \sum_{k=1}^{n+1} t_k \overset{(2.7)}{=} T_{n+1} \tag{6.446}$$

15 where t_n and T_n are the *triangular and tetrahedral numbers*, respectively, while its associated vector field reads

239 $$\nabla f(x,y,z) \overset{(6.20)}{=} \begin{bmatrix} \sum_{i=1}^{n}\sum_{j=0}^{n-i}\sum_{k=0}^{n-i-j} c_{i,j,k} i x^{i-1} y^j z^k \\ \sum_{i=0}^{n}\sum_{j=1}^{n-i}\sum_{k=0}^{n-i-j} c_{i,j,k} j x^{i} y^{j-1} z^k \\ \sum_{i=0}^{n}\sum_{j=0}^{n-i}\sum_{k=1}^{n-i-j} c_{i,j,k} k x^{i} y^j z^{k-1} \end{bmatrix} \tag{6.447}$$

Substituting the ray equation $\vec{r}(t) \triangleq \vec{o} + t\vec{d}$, the values of the scalar field along the ray are then defined as

239 $$\begin{aligned}
f(t) &\overset{(6.21)}{=} \sum_{i=0}^{n}\sum_{j=0}^{n-i}\sum_{k=0}^{n-i-j} c_{i,j,k}(x_o + tx_d)^i (y_o + ty_d)^j (z_o + tz_d)^k \\
&= \sum_{i=0}^{n}\sum_{j=0}^{n-i}\sum_{k=0}^{n-i-j} c_{i,j,k} \left(\sum_{p=0}^{i}\binom{i}{p} x_o^{i-p} t^p x_d^p\right)\left(\sum_{q=0}^{j}\binom{j}{q} y_o^{j-q} t^q y_d^q\right)\left(\sum_{r=0}^{k}\binom{k}{r} z_o^{k-r} t^r z_d^r\right) \\
&= \sum_{i=0}^{n}\sum_{j=0}^{n-i}\sum_{k=0}^{n-i-j} c_{i,j,k} \sum_{p=0}^{i}\binom{i}{p} x_o^{i-p} x_d^p \sum_{q=0}^{j}\binom{j}{q} y_o^{j-q} y_d^q \sum_{r=0}^{k}\binom{k}{r} z_o^{k-r} z_d^r t^{p+q+r} \\
&= \sum_{i=0}^{n}\sum_{j=0}^{n-i}\sum_{k=0}^{n-i-j} c_{i,j,k} \sum_{p=0}^{i}\binom{i}{p} x_o^{i-p} x_d^p \sum_{q=0}^{j}\binom{j}{q} y_o^{j-q} y_d^q \\
&\quad \times \sum_{m=p+q}^{p+q+k} \binom{k}{m-p-q} z_o^{k-m+p+q} z_d^{m-p-q} t^m \\
&= \sum_{i=0}^{n}\sum_{j=0}^{n-i}\sum_{k=0}^{n-i-j} c_{i,j,k} \sum_{p=0}^{i}\binom{i}{p} x_o^{i-p} x_d^p \sum_{m=p}^{p+j+k} t^m \\
&\quad \times \sum_{q=\max\{0,m-p-k\}}^{\min\{j,m\}} \binom{j}{q} y_o^{j-q} y_d^q \binom{k}{m-p-q} z_o^{k-m+p+q} z_d^{m-p-q} \\
&= \sum_{i=0}^{n}\sum_{j=0}^{n-i}\sum_{k=0}^{n-i-j} c_{i,j,k} \sum_{m=0}^{i+j+k} t^m \sum_{p=\max\{0,m-j-k\}}^{\min\{i,m\}} \binom{i}{p} x_o^{i-p} x_d^p \\
&\quad \times \sum_{q=\max\{0,m-p-k\}}^{\min\{j,m\}} \binom{j}{q} y_o^{j-q} y_d^q \binom{k}{m-p-q} z_o^{k-m+p+q} z_d^{m-p-q} \\
&= \sum_{i=0}^{n}\sum_{j=0}^{n-i}\sum_{m=0}^{n} t^m \sum_{k=\max\{0,m-i-j\}}^{n-i-j} c_{i,j,k} \sum_{p=\max\{0,m-j-k\}}^{\min\{i,m\}} \binom{i}{p} x_o^{i-p} x_d^p \\
&\quad \times \sum_{q=\max\{0,m-p-k\}}^{\min\{j,m\}} \binom{j}{q} y_o^{j-q} y_d^q \binom{k}{m-p-q} z_o^{k-m+p+q} z_d^{m-p-q} \\
&= \sum_{m=0}^{n} t^m \sum_{i=0}^{n}\sum_{j=0}^{n-i} \sum_{k=\max\{0,m-i-j\}}^{n-i-j} c_{i,j,k} \sum_{p=\max\{0,m-j-k\}}^{\min\{i,m\}} \binom{i}{p} x_o^{i-p} x_d^p \\
&\quad \times \sum_{q=\max\{0,m-p-k\}}^{\min\{j,m\}} \binom{j}{q} y_o^{j-q} y_d^q \binom{k}{m-p-q} z_o^{k-m+p+q} z_d^{m-p-q}
\end{aligned} \tag{6.448}$$

A polynomial surface of order n may then be defined as the set of points satisfying $f(x, y, z) = v$ for a given isovalue v, and whose points of intersection along the ray are determined by the solutions of the *polynomial equation* $f(t) = v$. 26

6.7 COMPOSITE SURFACES

6.7.1 Clipped Geometry

Once the possibly many intersection points of a ray with a surface have been determined, an additional assertion on their coordinates may be carried, and an intersection point potentially discarded in order to clip parts of the geometry away. The simplest instance of this consists in discarding any intersection point whose parametric coordinates lie outside of a predefined range of parametric values. As illustrated in *Figure 6.29*, more general instances include the 301
clipping of geometry based on the value of an auxiliary scalar field evaluated at the point of intersection.

Figure 6.29: Clipped Geometry: Illustration of a sphere whose surface has been partially clipped by a scalar field.

6.7.2 Cuboid

6.7.2.1 *Algebraic Intersection*

A *cuboid* [Woo, 1990, Mahovsky and Wyvill, 2004, Mahovsky, 2005a, Williams *et al.*, 2005, Eisemann *et al.*, 2007], i.e., a rectangular parallelepiped, can be defined as the Boolean intersection of three sets of parallel *planes*, essentially discarding any point of a given set 247
that lies in the outer domain of the other two. The intersection of a ray $\vec{r}(t) \triangleq \vec{o} + t\vec{d}$ with an axis-aligned cuboid centered in $\vec{c} = [x_c, y_c, z_c]$ and of ∞-norm radii $\vec{r} = [x_r, y_r, z_r]$ may therefore be computed by first computing the individual ray intersections with the pairs of lower and upper planes defined by the three slabs spanning the x, y and z dimensions of the cuboid

$$[x_l, y_l, z_l] \triangleq \left[\frac{x_c - x_r - x_o}{x_d}, \frac{y_c - y_r - y_o}{y_d}, \frac{z_c - z_r - z_o}{z_d}\right] \tag{6.449}$$

$$[x_h, y_h, z_h] \triangleq \left[\frac{x_c + x_r - x_o}{x_d}, \frac{y_c + y_r - y_o}{y_d}, \frac{z_c + z_r - z_o}{z_d}\right] \tag{6.450}$$

and then sorting the near and far intersections along each axis according to the orientation of the ray

$$[x_n, y_n, z_n] \triangleq [\min\{x_l, x_h\}, \min\{y_l, y_h\}, \min\{z_l, z_h\}] \tag{6.451}$$
$$[x_f, y_f, z_f] \triangleq [\max\{x_l, x_h\}, \max\{y_l, y_h\}, \max\{z_l, z_h\}] \tag{6.452}$$

The t parameters at which the ray has entered and exited, respectively, the slabs in all three dimensions are then given by

$$t_n \triangleq \max\{x_n, y_n, z_n\} \tag{6.453}$$
$$t_f \triangleq \min\{x_f, y_f, z_f\} \tag{6.454}$$

from which follows that the box is intersected both at t_n and t_f only if $t_n < t_f$, that is, if
302 the ray has entered all three slabs before exiting any of them, as illustrated in *Figure 6.30*.

Figure 6.30: Cuboid: Illustration of a cuboid.

A vector field that, at points located on one of the faces of the cuboid, is orthogonal to
44 the associated face can then be defined in terms of the Kronecker *delta function* as

$$\nabla f(x, y, z) \triangleq \begin{bmatrix} (x - x_c)\delta(\lceil |x_u - m| \rceil) \\ (y - y_c)\delta(\lceil |y_u - m| \rceil) \\ (z - z_c)\delta(\lceil |z_u - m| \rceil) \end{bmatrix} \tag{6.455}$$

where $m \triangleq \max\{x_u, y_u, z_u\}$ and $[x_u, y_u, z_u] \triangleq \left[\left|\frac{x - x_c}{x_r}\right|, \left|\frac{y - y_c}{y_r}\right|, \left|\frac{z - z_c}{z_r}\right|\right]$.

6.7.2.2 Distance Estimation

The distance from a point $\vec{p}$ to an axis-aligned cuboid of center $\vec{c} = [x_c, y_c, z_c]$ and ∞-norm radii $\vec{r} = [x_r, y_r, z_r]$ reads

$$f(x, y, z) \triangleq \min\{\max\{x_l, y_l, z_l\}, \|[\max\{x_l, 0\}, \max\{y_l, 0\}, \max\{z_l, 0\}]\|\} \tag{6.456}$$

where $[x_l, y_l, z_l] \triangleq [|x - x_c| - |x_r|, |y - y_c| - |y_r|, |z - z_c| - |z_r|]$.

6.7.3 Constructive Solid Geometry

In *constructive solid geometry* (*CSG*), clipping the geometry is achieved by determining whether an intersection point lies inside or outside a secondary surface. Given an implicit representation of the latter, this simply entails comparing the value of its associated scalar field at the intersection point against its isovalue, while for arbitrary geometry, performing operations on the entry-exit intervals is generally required. Two surfaces clipping one another may therefore be combined in four different ways (depending on whether the geometry of one surface that is internal or external to the other surface is clipped away), which are classified according to three operators called *Boolean union*, *Boolean intersection* and *Boolean difference*, as illustrated in *Table 6.2*. 303

Table 6.2: Constructive Solid Geometry: Example of a cube and a sphere clipping parts of each other's internal or external geometry, as shown in the top row and left-hand column, resulting in four different geometric combinations classified according to three distinct Boolean operations.

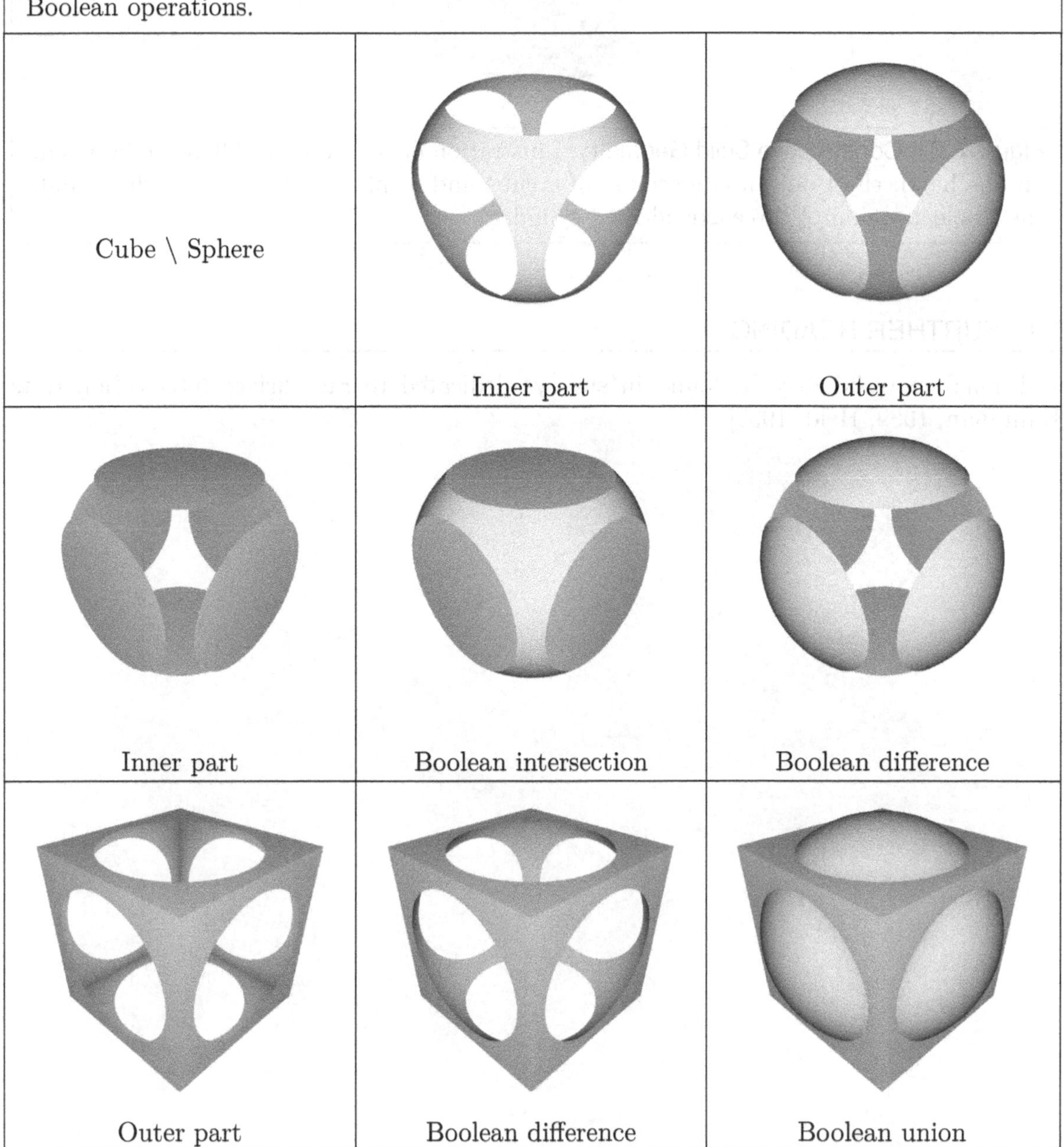

In turn, more elaborate shapes can be modeled by constructing a tree of such CSG
304 operations, as shown in *Figure 6.31*.

Figure 6.31: Constructive Solid Geometry: Illustration of the Boolean difference between, on one hand, the Boolean intersection of a cube and a sphere, and, on the other hand, the Boolean union of three axis-aligned cylinders.

6.8 FURTHER READING

Additional material may be found in surveys dedicated to ray–surface intersection tests [Hanrahan, 1989, Held, 1997].

CHAPTER 7

Implicit Surfaces

TABLE OF CONTENTS

7.1 DISTANCE ESTIMATION

7.1.1 Definition

A specific type of implicit surfaces are those for which the value of the scalar field, then
referred to as a *distance field*, at a given point in space corresponds to (a lower bound of)
the signed distance of that point to the surface, the latter being intrinsically defined by
36 the isovalue $v = 0$. Instead of resorting to a numerical *root finding* algorithm or iteratively
marching with a fixed step along the ray, the intersection of the latter with the surface can
instead be more efficiently computed by adaptively defining each ray-marching step based on
the absolute value of the distance field at the current location, the *distance-estimated surface*
being guaranteed not to be intersected within this radius in any direction around the point.
306 The resulting scheme, known as *sphere tracing* [Hart, 1996], is illustrated in *Figure 7.1*. The
iterative process may then be stopped whenever the magnitude of the distance falls below a
predefined threshold, indicating that the current position along the ray is sufficiently close
to the surface, while the surface normal at the intersection point is readily given by the field
gradient, which can be evaluated either analytically in simple cases, or numerically by using
a finite-differences scheme in the case of more complex functions.

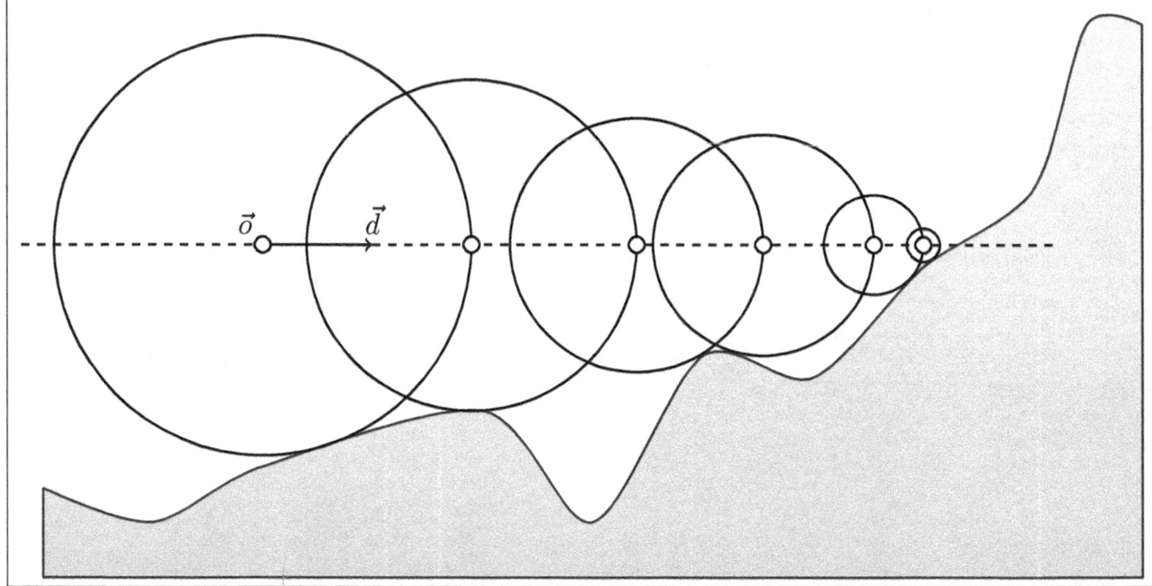

Figure 7.1: Distance Estimation: Diagram illustrating the iterative intersection evaluation by marching along the ray in steps whose length corresponds to the estimated distance to the surface (drawn after [Hart, 1996, Fig. 2 and 6]).

7.1.2 Algebraic Surfaces

236 Distance estimation techniques are readily applicable to various *analytic surfaces* of algebraic
form by means of their respective distance functions. Alternatively, various alterations of the
latter surfaces may also be obtained by substituting the aforementioned Euclidean distance
with a generalized p-norm metric.

7.1.3 CSG Operations

303 Boolean operations of the type defined in *constructive solid geometry* can be built in terms
of the minimum or maximum of the distance to two surfaces, or their opposite, as listed in

Table 7.1. A geometric surface may additionally be translated and/or rotated by applying the 307
inverse of the corresponding *transformation* matrix to the point $\vec{p}$, and an object scaled by a 102
factor f by dividing the coordinates of $\vec{p}$ by f while multiplying the corresponding distance by f.

Table 7.1: CSG Operations for Distance Estimated Surfaces: Definition of CSG Boolean operations in terms of the distance fields of two surfaces.

Boolean intersection: $\max\{f_a(x,y,z), f_b(x,y,z)\}$	Boolean difference: $\max\{f_a(x,y,z), -f_b(x,y,z)\}$
Boolean difference: $\max\{-f_a(x,y,z), f_b(x,y,z)\}$	Boolean union: $\min\{f_a(x,y,z), f_b(x,y,z)\}$

Finally, domain operations allow the generation of a finite number $2n+1$ of instances of an object by iteratively folding n times the coordinates along a given axis x, y and/or z as follows

$$x' = \begin{cases} -f_v - x & \text{if } x < -f_l \\ x & \text{if } x \in [-f_l, +f_l] \\ +f_v - x & \text{if } x > +f_l \end{cases} \tag{7.1}$$

where f_l and f_v are the so-called *folding limit* and *folding value*, respectively, where typically $f_v = 2f_l$. In the limit, infinite replication can be achieved by means of the (mirrored) modulus with periodicity f_v of the coordinates of $\vec{p}$ across the selected axes.

7.1.4 Iterated Function Systems

Based on the repeated replication of a geometric pattern transformed by an *iterated function* (i.e., a function recursively applied to itself a finite number of times), *iterated function systems* (*IFS*) are characterized by the exhibition of *self-similarity* at various feature scales. Three-dimensional instances of such fractals include the *Sierpinski pyramid* and *Menger sponge*,
illustrated in *Figure 7.2*. 308

Defining the distance field of the Menger sponge first entails formulating the distance to
a z-oriented pillar, i.e., to a *cuboid* centered at the origin $\vec{c} = [0,0,0]$ and with unit ∞-norm 301
radii in both x and y, and infinite size in z, such that $\vec{r} = [1,1,\infty]$, which yields

$$f_p(x,y,z) \triangleq \min\left\{\max\{x_l, y_l\}, \sqrt{\max\{x_l,0\}^2 + \max\{y_l,0\}^2}\right\} \tag{7.2}$$

where $x_l \triangleq |x| - 1$ and $y_l \triangleq |y| - 1$.

The distance of a cross with unit ∞-norm radii may then be defined as the union of three infinite pillars with swapped coordinates

$$f_c(x,y,z) \triangleq \min\{f_p(x,y,z), f_p(y,z,x), f_p(z,x,y)\} \tag{7.3}$$

while modulating the input coordinates to the latter as follows yields an infinite grid with a periodicity of six units

$$f_g(x,y,z) \triangleq f_c((x+3 \bmod 6) - 3, (y+3 \bmod 6) - 3, (z+3 \bmod 6) - 3) \tag{7.4}$$

The distance field f_n to the Menger sponge fractal of depth n is finally defined as the recursive Boolean difference of a box f_b centered in $\vec{c} = [0,0,0]$ and unit ∞-norm radii $\vec{r} = [1,1,1]$ with instances of the infinite grid scaled by a factor of $1/3^n$

$$f_n(x,y,z) \triangleq \begin{cases} f_b(x,y,z) & \text{if } n = 0 \\ \max\left\{f_{n-1}(x,y,z), -\frac{f_g(3^n x, 3^n y, 3^n z)}{3^n}\right\} & \text{if } n \geq 1 \end{cases} \tag{7.5}$$

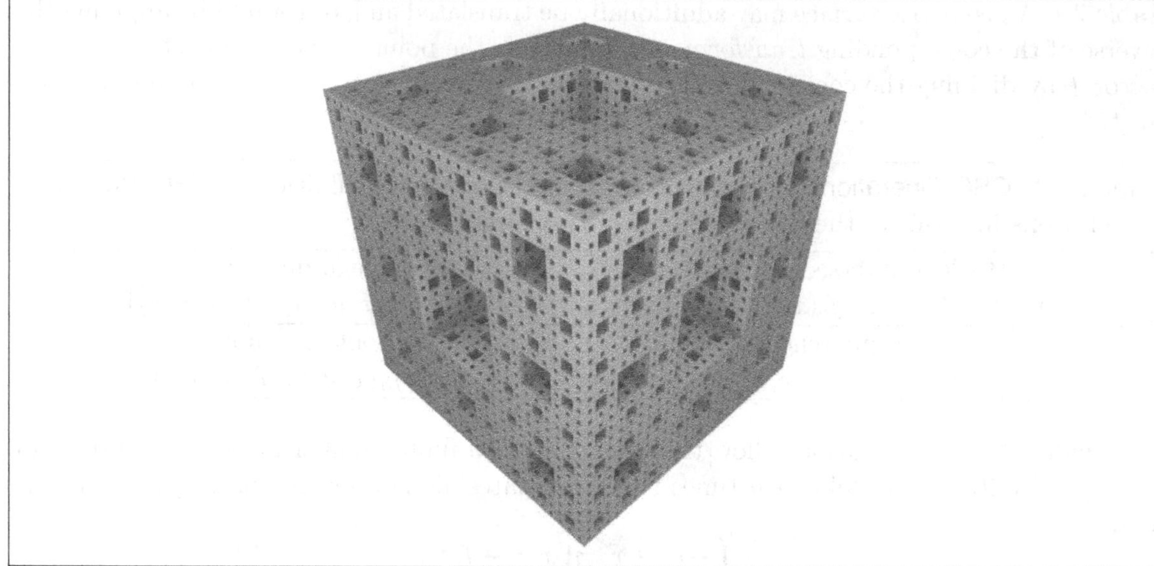

Figure 7.2: **Menger Sponge:** Illustration of a Menger sponge of depth 4.

7.1.5 Escape-Time Fractals

Based on mathematical recurrence, *escape-time fractals* are characterized by the exhibition
of *quasi-self-similarity* at various feature scales. Two-dimensional instances based on *complex*
85 *numbers* include the *Julia set* as well as the *multibrot set* (referred to as the *Mandelbrot set* in
309 the special case where $n = 2$) illustrated in *Figure 7.3*. Considering the *Cartesian coordinates*
67 88 of a point in space as the components of a *triplex number* p, three-dimensional extensions of
both sets of order n are analogously defined as the set of points for which the recursion

$$g_i(p) \triangleq \begin{cases} p & \text{if } i = 0 \\ g_{i-1}(p)^n + h(p) & \text{if } i \geq 1 \end{cases} \tag{7.6}$$

converges as $i \to \infty$ instead of escaping to infinity, with $h(p) = k$ for the Julia set given a hypercomplex constant k, and $h(p) = p$ for the multibrot set (then referred to as the *Mandelbulb* in the special case where $n = 8$ [Graf, 2010]).

85 Adapting the concepts initially introduced for *complex numbers* and *quaternions* [Hart *et*
90 *al.*, 1989], the *Green function* $G(p)$, also known as the *Hubbard–Douady electrostatic potential*,

$$G(p) \triangleq \lim_{i \to \infty} \frac{1}{n^i} \ln\left(|g_i(p)|\right) \tag{7.7}$$

defines an associated scalar field that is negative inside the set and positive outside of it, and whose gradient is readily given as

308

$$|G'(p)| \overset{(7.7)}{=} \lim_{i \to \infty} \frac{1}{n^i} \frac{|g'_i(p)|}{|g_i(p)|} \tag{7.8}$$

The derivative in the numerator is recursively defined as

308

$$g'_i(p) \overset{(7.6)}{=} \begin{cases} 1 & \text{if } i = 0 \\ n g_{i-1}(p)^{n-1} g'_{i-1}(p) + h'(p) & \text{if } i \geq 1 \end{cases} \tag{7.9}$$

where $h'(p) = 0$ for the Julia set and $h'(p) = 1$ for the multibrot set, while its magnitude is

Figure 7.3: Escape-Time Fractals: Illustration of the 2-D Julia set (top) and multibrot set of order 2 (known as the Mandelbrot set) (bottom left), and of the 3-D multibrot set of order 8 (known as the Mandelbulb) (bottom right).

instead typically estimated as

$$|g_i'(p)| \approx \tilde{g}_i(p) = \begin{cases} 1 & \text{if } i = 0 \\ n|g_{i-1}(p)^{n-1}|\tilde{g}_{i-1}(p) + |h'(p)| & \text{if } i \geq 1 \end{cases} \tag{7.10}$$

The distance field to the surface of the set is then bounded by

$$\frac{1}{2}\frac{\sinh(G(p))}{e^{G(p)}|G'(p)|} = \frac{1 - e^{-2G(p)}}{4|G'(p)|} < d(p) < 2\frac{\sinh(G(p))}{|G'(p)|} = \frac{e^{G(p)} - e^{-G(p)}}{|G'(p)|} \tag{7.11}$$

which, as an alternative to computing the gradient from the associated Jacobian matrix or numerically via finite differences, can be approximated by truncating the infinite loops given in *Equation 7.7* and *Equation 7.8* at a finite step i, such that 308
308

$$\frac{1 - e^{-2\frac{\ln(|g_i(p)|)}{n^i}}}{\frac{4}{n^i}\frac{|g_i'(p)|}{|g_i(p)|}} = \frac{1 - |g_i(p)|^{-\frac{2}{n^i}}}{\frac{4}{n^i}\frac{|g_i'(p)|}{|g_i(p)|}} < d(p) < \frac{e^{\frac{\ln(|g_i(p)|)}{n^i}} - e^{-\frac{\ln(|g_i(p)|)}{n^i}}}{\frac{1}{n^i}\frac{|g_i'(p)|}{|g_i(p)|}} = \frac{|g_i(p)|^{\frac{1}{n^i}} - |g_i(p)|^{-\frac{1}{n^i}}}{\frac{1}{n^i}\frac{|g_i'(p)|}{|g_i(p)|}} \tag{7.12}$$

For points not too distant from the surface of the set, where the magnitude of the potential
59 is small, the first-order *Taylor series* expansion $e^x \approx 1 + x, \forall x \approx 0$ might alternatively be
exploited, yielding

308
308
308
308

$$\frac{1}{2}\frac{G(p)}{|G'(p)|} \underset{(7.8)}{\overset{(7.7)}{=}} \lim_{i\to\infty} \frac{1}{2}\frac{|g_i(p)|}{|g_i'(p)|}\ln\left(|g_i(p)|\right) < d(p) < 2\frac{G(p)}{|G'(p)|} \underset{(7.8)}{\overset{(7.7)}{=}} \lim_{i\to\infty} 2\frac{|g_i(p)|}{|g_i'(p)|}\ln\left(|g_i(p)|\right) \tag{7.13}$$

or the more conservative approximation for the lower bound

$$\frac{1}{2|g_i(p)|^{\frac{1}{n^i}}}\frac{|g_i(p)|}{|g_i'(p)|}\ln\left(|g_i(p)|\right) < d(p) < 2\frac{|g_i(p)|}{|g_i'(p)|}\ln\left(|g_i(p)|\right) \tag{7.14}$$

which is consistent with the previous lower bound as $i \to \infty$, although in practice the distance is here again estimated within a finite number of iterations.

In practice, the iterative process may either be aborted when the magnitude of any term in the sequence $\|g_i(p)\|$ exceeds a predefined bailout radius b, in which case the point is assumed to have escaped to infinity and to therefore lie outside of the set, or when the number of iterations has exceeded the maximal number of allowed iterations, in which case the point is assumed to have converged and to therefore lie within the set. Because any point leading to $\|g_i(p)\| > 2$ is guaranteed to escape to infinity, the bailout radius is typically defined as $b = 2$. For much larger bailout values, though, the non-integer number of iterations $\nu(p)$ at which the bailout radius would have been precisely met can be determined by equating the potentials

$$\frac{\ln(\|g_i(p)\|)}{n^i} = \frac{\ln(b)}{n^{\nu(p)}} \tag{7.15}$$

and then solving the equation to yield

$$\nu(p) = \log_n\left(n^i\frac{\ln(b)}{\ln(\|g_i(p)\|)}\right) = i - \log_n\left(\frac{\ln(\|g_i(p)\|)}{\ln(b)}\right) \tag{7.16}$$

where the subtrahend on the right-hand side is guaranteed to lie in the interval $[0, 1)$ whenever
308 i is such that $\|g_{i-1}(p)\| \overset{(7.6)}{\approx} \|g_i(p)\|^{\frac{1}{n}} < b \leq \|g_i(p)\|$.

Alternative sequence definitions of g_i can finally be used in order to create a wide variety of fractal patterns. For instance, replacing the exponentiation of the previous term in the sequence by a box fold followed by a sphere fold and a scaling yields the so-called *Mandelbox*
311 fractal illustrated in *Figure 7.4*.

Figure 7.4: Mandelbox: Illustration of the classical Mandelbox (left), and of the internal structures exhibited by a variant of the latter (right).

7.2 FURTHER READING

Additional material may be found in books dedicated to hypercomplex iterations and distance estimation of fractals [Dang *et al.*, 2002].

CHAPTER 8

Parametric Curves & Surfaces

TABLE OF CONTENTS

8.1 SPLINE

Before the advent of computer-aided design (CAD), technical drafting in the shipbuilding and aircraft industries typically entailed hand-drawing smooth curves by means of thin flexible strips, so-called "flat splines," minimizing the bending energy when constrained at a set of predefined key points, so-called "knots," by duck-shaped lead weights referred to as "ducks." Named after its mechanical counterpart, spline interpolation provides a simple and efficient alternative avoiding the oscillation phenomena exhibited by high degree *polynomial*
17 *interpolation*.

Given a set of intervals $[t_0 < t_1 < \ldots < t_i < \ldots < t_{m-1} < t_m]$, a *spline* of degree n is mathematically defined as a piecewise-polynomial function of degree n

$$S(t) = \begin{cases} p_1(t) & \text{if } t \in [t_0, t_1] \\ \vdots & \vdots \\ p_i(t) & \text{if } t \in [t_{i-1}, t_i] \\ \vdots & \vdots \\ p_m(t) & \text{if } t \in [t_{m-1}, t_m] \end{cases} \tag{8.1}$$

whose free-form shape is determined by a set of so-called *control points*. The spline is then referred to as a *uniform spline* if the length of all intervals is equal, and as a *non-uniform spline* otherwise.

A one-dimensional spline function is said to be C_k-continuous if the junctions between successive intervals satisfy

$$p_i^{(j)}(t_i) = p_{i+1}^{(j)}(t_i), \quad \forall i \in [1, m-1], \forall j \in [0, k] \tag{8.2}$$

In the case of a multidimensional spline curve formed by the parametric combination of individual spline functions in each dimension, the spline similarly exhibits a parametric continuity of type C_k if

$$\vec{p}_i^{(j)}(t_i) = \vec{p}_{i+1}^{(j)}(t_i), \quad \forall i \in [1, m-1], \forall j \in [0, k] \tag{8.3}$$

whereas it is referred to as G_k-continuous under the milder geometric continuity condition

$$\vec{p}_i^{(j)}(t_i) \propto \vec{p}_{i+1}^{(j)}(t_i), \quad \forall i \in [1, m-1], \forall j \in [0, k] \tag{8.4}$$

315 As illustrated in *Figure 8.1*, a spline curve or surface consequently exhibits zeroth-order continuity if the position of the endpoints of adjacent segments coincide, possibly at an angle, thereby preventing geometric gaps but allowing sharp corners or edges between the segments. Likewise, first-order continuity additionally entails that the tangent lines or planes at the meeting points be parallel, and so do their normal vectors, thereby guaranteeing smooth corners or edges, and zeroth-order continuity of reflected highlights with it. In contrast, seamless highlights with first-order continuity require second-order curvature continuity at the curve or surface junctions.

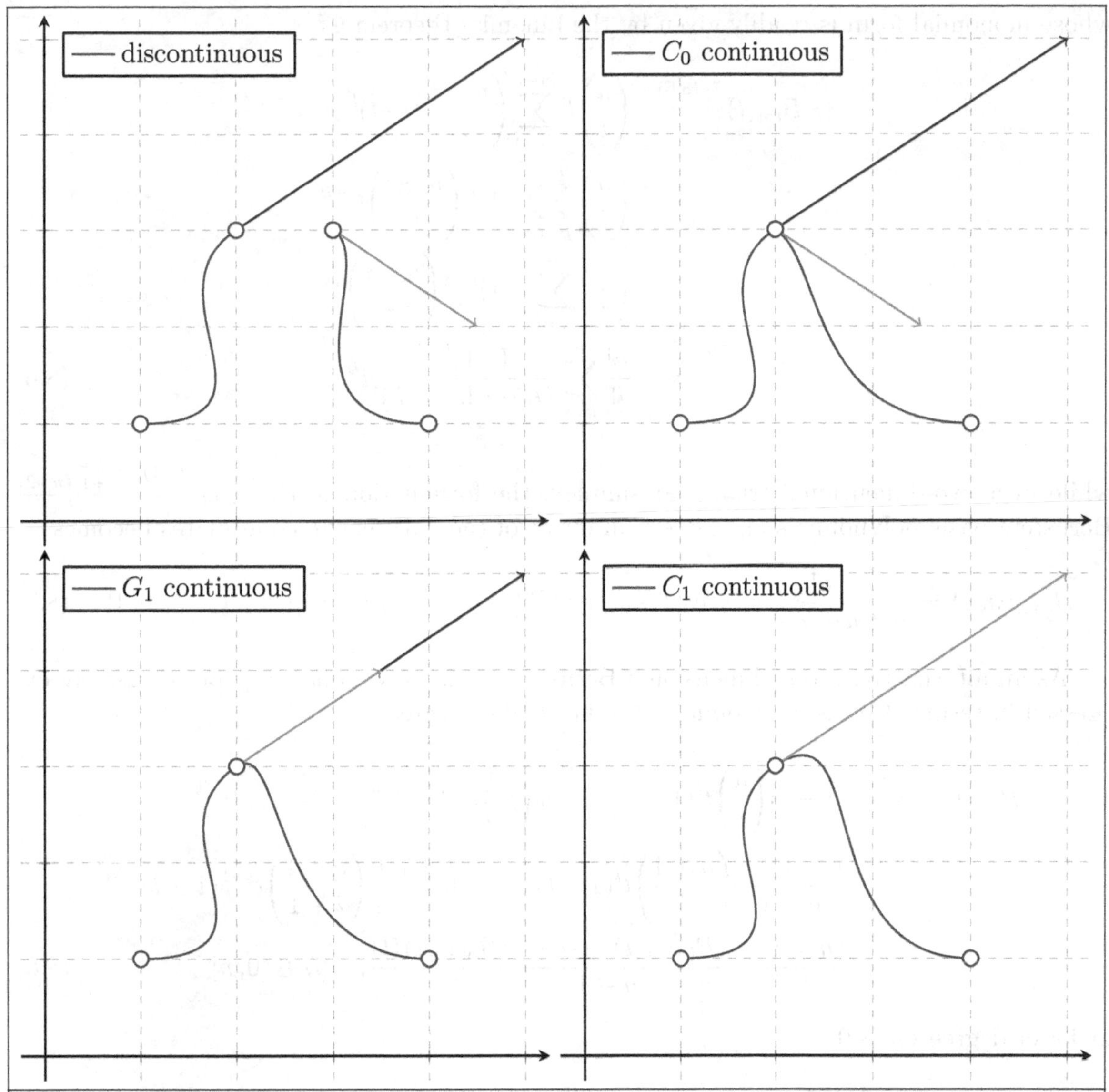

Figure 8.1: Spline Continuity: Illustration of the parametric and geometric continuity of different spline curves.

8.2 BÉZIER SPLINE

8.2.1 Bézier Function

8.2.1.1 Bernstein Basis Polynomial

As illustrated in *Figure 8.2*, the $n+1$ one-dimensional *Bernstein basis polynomials* of degree 317
$n \in \mathbb{N}$ are defined as

$$B_{i,n}(t) \triangleq \binom{n}{i} t^i (1-t)^{n-i}, \quad \forall i \in [0, n], \forall t \in [0, 1] \tag{8.5}$$

whose monomial form is readily given by the binomial theorem as

315

$$\begin{aligned} B_{i,n}(t) &\overset{(8.5)}{=} \binom{n}{i} t^i \sum_{k=0}^{n-i} \binom{n-i}{k} (-t)^k \\ &= \binom{n}{i} \sum_{k=0}^{n-i} (-1)^k \binom{n-i}{k} t^{i+k} \\ &= \binom{n}{i} \sum_{k=i}^{n} (-1)^{k-i} \binom{n-i}{k-i} t^k \\ &= \frac{n!}{i!} \sum_{k=i}^{n} \frac{(-1)^{k-i}}{(k-i)!(n-k)!} t^k \end{aligned} \tag{8.6}$$

15 while in a two-dimensional triangular simplex, the formulation of the $t_{n+1} \overset{(2.1)}{=} \frac{(n+1)(n+2)}{2}$ Bernstein basis polynomials of degree n in terms of the barycentric coordinates becomes

$$B_{i,j,n}(u,v) \triangleq \frac{n!}{i!j!(n-i-j)!} u^i v^j (1-u-v)^{n-i-j}, \quad \forall i+j \in [0,n], \forall u+v \in [0,1] \tag{8.7}$$

As an alternative, a one-dimensional Bernstein basis polynomial may be recursively expressed in terms of basis polynomials of either higher degree

315

$$\begin{aligned} B_{i,n}(t) &\overset{(8.5)}{=} (1-t)\binom{n}{i} t^i (1-t)^{n-i} + t\binom{n}{i} t^i (1-t)^{n-i} \\ &= \frac{n+1-i}{n+1} \binom{n+1}{i} t^i (1-t)^{n+1-i} + \frac{i+1}{n+1} \binom{n+1}{i+1} t^{i+1} (1-t)^{n-i} \\ &= \frac{(n+1-i) B_{i,n+1}(t) + (i+1) B_{i+1,n+1}(t)}{n+1}, \quad \forall i \in [0,n] \end{aligned} \tag{8.8}$$

or lower degree $\forall n > 0$

315

$$\begin{aligned} B_{i,n}(t) &\overset{(8.5)}{=} \begin{cases} \binom{n}{0}(1-t)^n & \text{if } i = 0 \\ \binom{n-1}{i-1} t^i (1-t)^{n-i} + \binom{n-1}{i} t^i (1-t)^{n-i} & \text{if } i \in [1, n-1] \\ \binom{n}{n} t^n & \text{if } i = n \end{cases} \\ &= \begin{cases} (1-t)\binom{n-1}{0}(1-t)^{n-1} & \text{if } i = 0 \\ t\binom{n-1}{i-1} t^{i-1} (1-t)^{n-i} + (1-t)\binom{n-1}{i} t^i (1-t)^{n-1-i} & \text{if } i \in [1, n-1] \\ t\binom{n-1}{n-1} t^{n-1} & \text{if } i = n \end{cases} \\ &= \begin{cases} (1-t) B_{0,n-1}(t) & \text{if } i = 0 \\ t B_{i-1,n-1}(t) + (1-t) B_{i,n-1}(t) & \text{if } i \in [1, n-1] \\ t B_{n-1,n-1}(t) & \text{if } i = n \end{cases} \end{aligned} \tag{8.9}$$

By means of the binomial theorem, the Bernstein basis polynomials form a partition of unity

315

$$\sum_{i=0}^{n} B_{i,n}(t) \overset{(8.5)}{=} \sum_{i=0}^{n} \binom{n}{i} t^i (1-t)^{n-i} = (t + (1-t))^n = 1 \tag{8.10}$$

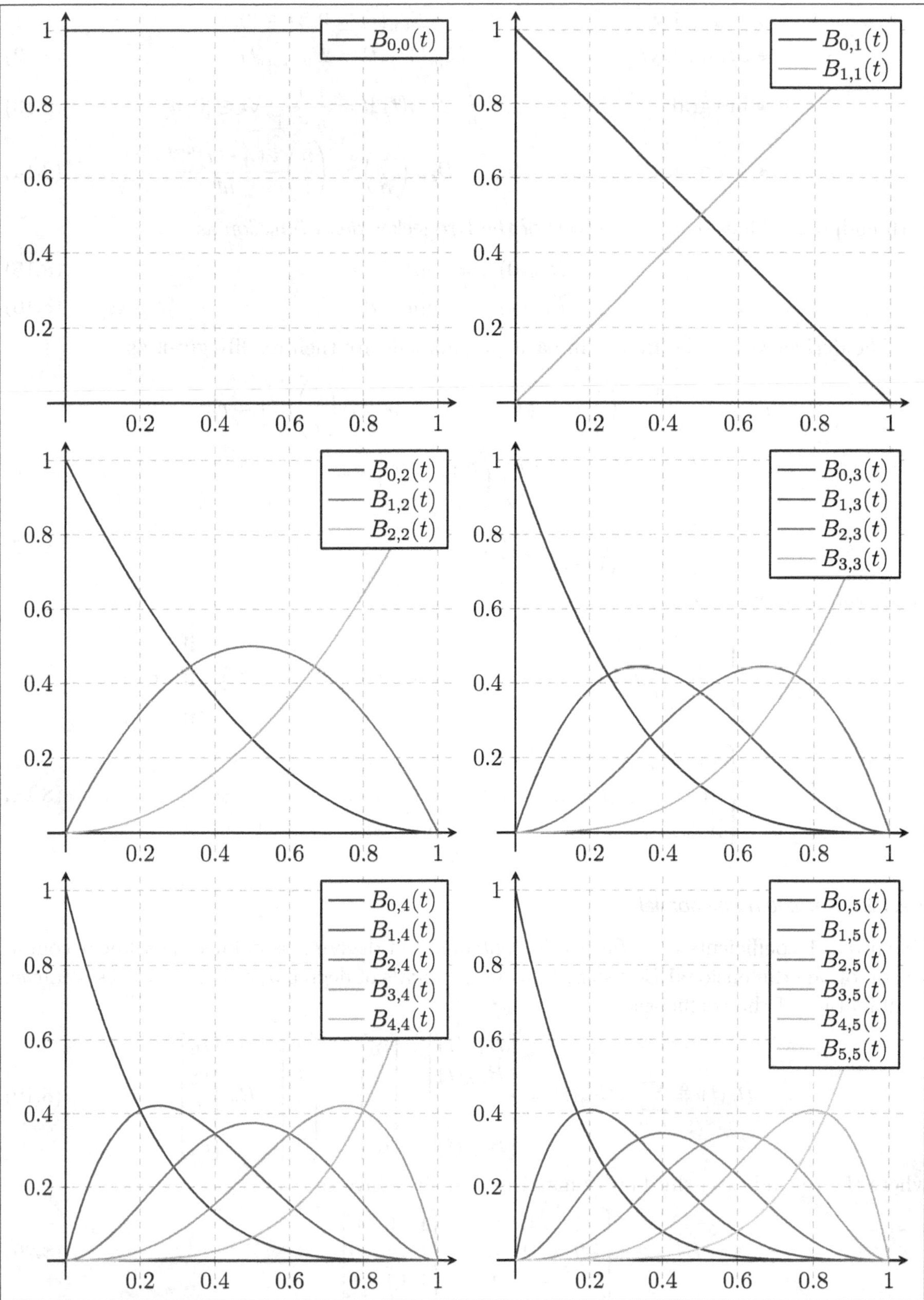

Figure 8.2: Bernstein Basis Polynomials: Plot of the Bernstein basis polynomials of various degrees.

while satisfying the following properties

- positivity: $$B_{i,n}(t) \geq 0, \forall t \in [0,1] \tag{8.11}$$
- symmetry: $$B_{i,n}(1-t) = B_{n-i,n}(t) \tag{8.12}$$
- integral: $$\int_0^1 B_{i,n}(t)dt = \frac{1}{n+1}, \forall i \in [0,n] \tag{8.13}$$
- maximum: $$B_{i,n}\left(\frac{i}{n}\right) = \binom{n}{i}\frac{i^i(n-i)^{n-i}}{n^n} \tag{8.14}$$

44 with endpoint values defined in terms of the Kronecker *delta function* as

$$\begin{aligned} B_{i,n}(0) &= \delta[i] & (8.15)\\ B_{i,n}(1) &= \delta[n-i] & (8.16) \end{aligned}$$

The derivatives of the Bernstein basis polynomials are then readily given as

315
$$\begin{aligned} B'_{i,n}(t) &\overset{(8.5)}{=} i\binom{n}{i}t^{i-1}(1-t)^{n-i} - (n-i)\binom{n}{i}t^i(1-t)^{n-i-1} \\ &= \left(\frac{i}{t} - \frac{n-i}{1-t}\right)\binom{n}{i}t^i(1-t)^{n-i} \\ &= \frac{i-tn}{t(1-t)}B_{i,n}(t) & (8.17) \end{aligned}$$

or alternatively $\forall n > 0$ as

315
$$\begin{aligned} B'_{i,n}(t) &\overset{(8.5)}{=} \begin{cases} -n(1-t)^{n-1} & \text{if } i = 0 \\ n\left(\binom{n-1}{i-1}t^{i-1}(1-t)^{n-1-(i-1)} - \binom{n-1}{i}t^i(1-t)^{n-1-i}\right) & \text{if } i \in [1, n-1] \\ nt^{n-1} & \text{if } i = n \end{cases} \\ &= \begin{cases} -nB_{0,n-1}(t) & \text{if } i = 0 \\ n(B_{i-1,n-1}(t) - B_{i,n-1}(t)) & \text{if } i \in [1, n-1] \\ nB_{n-1,n-1}(t) & \text{if } i = n \end{cases} & (8.18) \end{aligned}$$

8.2.1.2 Bernstein Polynomial

Given $n+1$ coefficients c_i, a *Bernstein polynomial* of degree n is defined as a linear combi-
315 nation of one-dimensional *Bernstein basis polynomials* of degree n, or conversely as a convex combination of the coefficients

$$B_n(t) \triangleq \sum_{i=0}^{n} c_i B_{i,n}(t) = \begin{bmatrix} B_{0,n}(t) \\ B_{1,n}(t) \\ \vdots \\ B_{n,n}(t) \end{bmatrix}^T \begin{bmatrix} c_0 \\ c_1 \\ \vdots \\ c_n \end{bmatrix} = \begin{bmatrix} 1 \\ t \\ \vdots \\ t^n \end{bmatrix}^T B_n \begin{bmatrix} c_0 \\ c_1 \\ \vdots \\ c_n \end{bmatrix} \tag{8.19}$$

where the second- and third-order matrices and their inverse read

$$B_2 = \begin{bmatrix} 1 & 0 & 0 \\ -2 & 2 & 0 \\ 1 & -2 & 1 \end{bmatrix} = \begin{bmatrix} 1 & 0 & 0 \\ 1 & \frac{1}{2} & 0 \\ 1 & 1 & 1 \end{bmatrix}^{-1} \tag{8.20}$$

$$B_3 = \begin{bmatrix} 1 & 0 & 0 & 0 \\ -3 & 3 & 0 & 0 \\ 3 & -6 & 3 & 0 \\ -1 & 3 & -3 & 1 \end{bmatrix} = \begin{bmatrix} 1 & 0 & 0 & 0 \\ 1 & \frac{1}{3} & 0 & 0 \\ 1 & \frac{2}{3} & \frac{1}{3} & 0 \\ 1 & 1 & 1 & 1 \end{bmatrix}^{-1} \tag{8.21}$$

while the monomial form is readily given as

$$B_n(t) \overset{(8.19)}{\underset{(8.6)}{=}} \sum_{i=0}^{n} c_i \frac{n!}{i!} \sum_{k=i}^{n} \frac{(-1)^{k-i}}{(k-i)!(n-k)!} t^k = \sum_{k=0}^{n} t^k \frac{n!}{(n-k)!} \sum_{i=0}^{k} c_i \frac{(-1)^{k-i}}{i!(k-i)!} \tag{8.22}$$

318
316

As an alternative, a Bernstein polynomial may be expressed in terms of basis polynomials of either higher degree by means of degree elevation

$$\begin{aligned}
B_n(t) &\overset{(8.19)}{\underset{(8.8)}{=}} \sum_{i=0}^{n} c_i \frac{(n+1-i)B_{i,n+1}(t) + (i+1)B_{i+1,n+1}(t)}{n+1} \\
&= \sum_{i=0}^{n} c_i \frac{n+1-i}{n+1} B_{i,n+1}(t) + \sum_{i=1}^{n+1} c_{i-1} \frac{i}{n+1} B_{i,n+1}(t) \\
&= \sum_{i=0}^{n+1} \left(c_i \left(1 - \frac{i}{n+1}\right) + c_{i-1} \frac{i}{n+1} \right) B_{i,n+1}(t) \qquad (8.23) \\
&= \vdots \\
&= \sum_{i=0}^{n+d} \left(\frac{n!}{(n+d)!} \sum_{j=0}^{d} c_{i-j} \binom{d}{j} \frac{(n+d-i)!}{(n+j-i)!} \frac{i!}{(i-j)!} \right) B_{i,n+d}(t) \\
&= \sum_{i=0}^{n+d} \left(\frac{1}{\binom{n+d}{n}} \sum_{j=0}^{d} c_{i-j} \binom{n+d-i}{n+j-i} \binom{i}{j} \right) B_{i,n+d}(t) \qquad (8.24)
\end{aligned}$$

318
316

where $c_i = 0, \forall i \notin [0, n]$, or lower degree $\forall n > 0$

$$\begin{aligned}
B_n(t) &\overset{(8.19)}{=} c_0 B_{0,n}(t) + c_n B_{n,n}(t) + \sum_{i=1}^{n-1} c_i B_{i,n}(t) \\
&\overset{(8.9)}{=} c_0(1-t)B_{0,n-1}(t) + c_n t B_{n-1,n-1}(t) + \sum_{i=1}^{n-1} c_i \left(t B_{i-1,n-1}(t) + (1-t)B_{i,n-1}(t)\right) \\
&= \sum_{i=1}^{n} c_i t B_{i-1,n-1}(t) + \sum_{i=0}^{n-1} c_i (1-t) B_{i,n-1}(t) \\
&= \sum_{i=0}^{n-1} (c_{i+1} t + c_i(1-t)) B_{i,n-1}(t) \qquad (8.25)
\end{aligned}$$

318
316

It follows that a Bernstein polynomial can be recursively evaluated in a more numerically stable fashion as

$$B_n(t) \overset{(8.25)}{=} t \sum_{i=0}^{n-1} c_{i+1} B_{i,n-1}(t) + (1-t) \sum_{i=0}^{n-1} c_i B_{i,n-1}(t) = B(t, [c_0, \ldots, c_n]) \tag{8.26}$$

319

with

$$B(t, [c_i, \ldots, c_j]) \triangleq \begin{cases} c_i & \text{if } j = i \\ tB(t, [c_{i+1}, \ldots, c_j]) + (1-t)B(t, [c_i, \ldots, c_{j-1}]) & \text{if } j > i \end{cases} \tag{8.27}$$

or equivalently by means of *de Casteljau's algorithm* (named after Citroën's physicist and mathematician Paul de Casteljau)

$$B_n(t) \overset{(8.19)}{=} \sum_{i=0}^{n} c_{i,n}(t) B_{i,n}(t) \overset{(8.25)}{=} \sum_{i=0}^{n-1} c_{i,n-1}(t) B_{i,n-1}(t) = \ldots = \sum_{i=0}^{0} c_{i,0}(t) B_{i,0}(t) = c_{0,0}(t) \tag{8.28}$$

318
319

whose coefficients

$$c_{i,j}(t) \triangleq \begin{cases} c_i & \text{if } j = n \\ c_{i+1,j+1}(t)t + c_{i,j+1}(t)(1-t) & \text{if } j < n \end{cases} \tag{8.29}$$

may be computed successively on each level of the tree from the leaves to the root

$$\begin{array}{ccccc} c_0 = c_{0,n}(t) & & & & \\ & c_{0,n-1}(t) & & & \\ c_1 = c_{1,n}(t) & & c_{0,n-2}(t) & & \\ \vdots & \vdots & \vdots & \ddots & \\ c_i = c_{i,n}(t) & & c_{i-1,n-2}(t) & & \\ & c_{i,n-1}(t) & & \cdots & c_{0,0}(t) \\ c_{i+1} = c_{i+1,n}(t) & & c_{i,n-2}(t) & & \\ \vdots & \vdots & \vdots & \iddots & \\ c_{n-1} = c_{n-1,n}(t) & & c_{n-2,n-2}(t) & & \\ & c_{n-1,n-1}(t) & & & \\ c_n = c_{n,n}(t) & & & & \end{array} \tag{8.30}$$

The first derivative of a Bernstein polynomial reads

318

318

$$\begin{aligned} B'_n(t) &\overset{(8.19)}{=} \sum_{i=0}^{n} c_i B'_{i,n}(t) \\ &= c_0 B'_{0,n}(t) + \sum_{i=1}^{n-1} c_i B'_{i,n}(t) + c_n B'_{n,n}(t) \\ &\overset{(8.18)}{=} -c_0 n B_{0,n-1}(t) + \sum_{i=1}^{n-1} c_i n (B_{i-1,n-1}(t) - B_{i,n-1}(t)) + c_n n B_{n-1,n-1}(t) \\ &= n \sum_{i=0}^{n-1} (c_{i+1} - c_i) B_{i,n-1}(t) \end{aligned} \tag{8.31}$$

while higher-order derivatives are readily given as

$$B''_n(t) = n(n-1) \sum_{i=0}^{n-2} (c_{i+2} - 2c_{i+1} + c_i) B_{i,n-2}(t) \tag{8.32}$$

$$B^{(d)}_n(t) = \frac{n!}{(n-d)!} \sum_{i=0}^{n-d} \left(\sum_{j=0}^{d} (-1)^{d-j} \binom{d}{j} c_{i+j} \right) B_{i,n-d}(t) \tag{8.33}$$

It follows that the values of a Bernstein polynomial at the endpoints are

318 318 46

$$B_n(0) \overset{(8.19)}{=} \sum_{i=0}^{n} c_i B_{i,n}(0) \overset{(8.15)}{=} \sum_{i=0}^{n} c_i \delta[i] \overset{(2.223)}{=} c_0 \tag{8.34}$$

318 318 46

$$B_n(1) \overset{(8.19)}{=} \sum_{i=0}^{n} c_i B_{i,n}(1) \overset{(8.16)}{=} \sum_{i=0}^{n} c_i \delta[n-i] \overset{(2.223)}{=} c_n \tag{8.35}$$

320 318 46

$$B'_n(0) \overset{(8.31)}{=} n \sum_{i=0}^{n-1} (c_{i+1} - c_i) B_{i,n-1}(0) \overset{(8.15)}{=} n \sum_{i=0}^{n-1} (c_{i+1} - c_i) \delta[i] \overset{(2.223)}{=} n(c_1 - c_0) \tag{8.36}$$

320 318 46

$$B'_n(1) \overset{(8.31)}{=} n \sum_{i=0}^{n-1} (c_{i+1} - c_i) B_{i,n-1}(1) \overset{(8.16)}{=} n \sum_{i=0}^{n-1} (c_{i+1} - c_i) \delta[n-1-i] \overset{(2.223)}{=} n(c_n - c_{n-1}) \tag{8.37}$$

Given a continuous function $f(x)$ defined on the interval $[0, 1]$, the sequence of Bernstein polynomials of degree n with coefficients $c_i = f(i/n)$ converges uniformly such that the *approximation error* obeys 21

$$\lim_{n\to\infty} \sup_{t\in[0,1]} \{|B_n(t) - f(t)|\} = 0 \tag{8.38}$$

thereby proving the Weierstrass approximation theorem. More generally, if $f(x)$ is a function with continuous k^{th} derivative, it holds that

$$\lim_{n\to\infty} \sup_{t\in[0,1]} \{|B_n^{(k)}(t) - f^{(k)}(t)|\} = 0 \tag{8.39}$$

8.2.1.3 Subdivision and Extrapolation

Based on de Casteljau's algorithm, a *Bernstein polynomial* may be subdivided at a given 318
parameter t_s into two *Bernstein polynomials* whose coefficients are readily given by the upper 318
and lower boundaries of the tree, respectively

$$B_n(t) = \begin{cases} \sum_{i=0}^{n} c_{0,n-i}(t) B_{i,n}\left(\frac{t}{t_s}\right) & \text{if } t \in [0, t_s] \\ \sum_{i=0}^{n} c_{i,i}(t) B_{i,n}\left(\frac{t-t_s}{1-t_s}\right) & \text{if } t \in [t_s, 1] \end{cases} \tag{8.40}$$

Similarly, a *Bernstein polynomial* may be extrapolated to the left/right by using its coeffi- 318
cients to form the lower/upper boundary of the tree, from which the remaining coefficients can then be progressively reconstructed, with the leaves corresponding to those of the extrapolating *Bernstein polynomial.* 318

As an alternative, both operations may be expressed in matrix form, such that, in the cubic case, the linear change of variable reads

318

$$\begin{aligned} B_3(o + dt) &\overset{(8.19)}{=} \begin{bmatrix} 1 \\ o + dt \\ (o + dt)^2 \\ (o + dt)^3 \end{bmatrix}^T B_3 \begin{bmatrix} c_0 \\ c_1 \\ c_2 \\ c_3 \end{bmatrix} \\ &= \begin{bmatrix} 1 \\ t \\ t^2 \\ t^3 \end{bmatrix}^T \begin{bmatrix} 1 & o & o^2 & o^3 \\ 0 & d & 2od & 3o^2d \\ 0 & 0 & d^2 & 3od^2 \\ 0 & 0 & 0 & d^3 \end{bmatrix} B_3 \begin{bmatrix} c_0 \\ c_1 \\ c_2 \\ c_3 \end{bmatrix} \\ &= \begin{bmatrix} 1 \\ t \\ t^2 \\ t^3 \end{bmatrix}^T B_3 S_{[o,o+d]} \begin{bmatrix} c_0 \\ c_1 \\ c_2 \\ c_3 \end{bmatrix} \end{aligned} \tag{8.41}$$

where

$$S_{[o,o+d]} \triangleq B_3^{-1} \begin{bmatrix} 1 & o & o^2 & o^3 \\ 0 & d & 2od & 3o^2d \\ 0 & 0 & d^2 & 3od^2 \\ 0 & 0 & 0 & d^3 \end{bmatrix} B_3 \tag{8.42}$$

The coefficients of the first half of the cubic *Bernstein polynomial* are then readily given as 318

321

$$B_3\left(\frac{t}{2}\right) \overset{(8.41)}{=} \begin{bmatrix} 1 \\ t \\ t^2 \\ t^3 \end{bmatrix}^T B_3 S_{[0,\frac{1}{2}]} \begin{bmatrix} c_0 \\ c_1 \\ c_2 \\ c_3 \end{bmatrix} = \begin{bmatrix} 1 \\ t \\ t^2 \\ t^3 \end{bmatrix}^T B_3 \begin{bmatrix} c_0 \\ \frac{c_0+c_1}{2} \\ \frac{c_0+2c_1+c_2}{4} \\ \frac{c_0+3c_1+3c_2+c_3}{8} \end{bmatrix} \tag{8.43}$$

where

321 318

$$S_{[0,\frac{1}{2}]} \overset{(8.42)}{=} B_3^{-1} \begin{bmatrix} 1 & 0 & 0 & 0 \\ 0 & \frac{1}{2} & 0 & 0 \\ 0 & 0 & \frac{1}{4} & 0 \\ 0 & 0 & 0 & \frac{1}{8} \end{bmatrix} B_3 \overset{(8.21)}{=} \begin{bmatrix} 1 & 0 & 0 & 0 \\ \frac{1}{2} & \frac{1}{2} & 0 & 0 \\ \frac{1}{4} & \frac{2}{4} & \frac{1}{4} & 0 \\ \frac{1}{8} & \frac{3}{8} & \frac{3}{8} & \frac{1}{8} \end{bmatrix} \tag{8.44}$$

while those of the second half read

321

$$B_3\left(\frac{1+t}{2}\right) \overset{(8.41)}{=} \begin{bmatrix} 1 \\ t \\ t^2 \\ t^3 \end{bmatrix}^T B_3 S_{[\frac{1}{2},1]} \begin{bmatrix} c_0 \\ c_1 \\ c_2 \\ c_3 \end{bmatrix} = \begin{bmatrix} 1 \\ t \\ t^2 \\ t^3 \end{bmatrix}^T B_3 \begin{bmatrix} \frac{c_0+3c_1+3c_2+c_3}{8} \\ \frac{c_1+2c_2+c_3}{4} \\ \frac{c_2+c_3}{2} \\ c_3 \end{bmatrix} \tag{8.45}$$

where

321 318

$$S_{[\frac{1}{2},1]} \overset{(8.42)}{=} B_3^{-1} \begin{bmatrix} 1 & \frac{1}{2} & \frac{1}{4} & \frac{1}{8} \\ 0 & \frac{1}{2} & \frac{2}{4} & \frac{3}{8} \\ 0 & 0 & \frac{1}{4} & \frac{3}{8} \\ 0 & 0 & 0 & \frac{1}{8} \end{bmatrix} B_3 \overset{(8.21)}{=} \begin{bmatrix} \frac{1}{8} & \frac{3}{8} & \frac{3}{8} & \frac{1}{8} \\ 0 & \frac{1}{4} & \frac{2}{4} & \frac{1}{4} \\ 0 & 0 & \frac{1}{2} & \frac{1}{2} \\ 0 & 0 & 0 & 1 \end{bmatrix} \tag{8.46}$$

318 Similarly, the coefficients of the doubled cubic *Bernstein polynomial* are given as

321

$$B_3(1+t) \overset{(8.41)}{=} \begin{bmatrix} 1 \\ t \\ t^2 \\ t^3 \end{bmatrix}^T B_3 S_{[1,2]} \begin{bmatrix} c_0 \\ c_1 \\ c_2 \\ c_3 \end{bmatrix} = \begin{bmatrix} 1 \\ t \\ t^2 \\ t^3 \end{bmatrix}^T B_3 \begin{bmatrix} c_3 \\ -c_2 + 2c_3 \\ c_1 - 4c_2 + 4c_3 \\ -c_0 + 6c_1 - 12c_2 + 8c_3 \end{bmatrix} \tag{8.47}$$

where

321 318

$$S_{[1,2]} \overset{(8.42)}{=} B_3^{-1} \begin{bmatrix} 1 & 1 & 1 & 1 \\ 0 & 1 & 2 & 3 \\ 0 & 0 & 1 & 3 \\ 0 & 0 & 0 & 1 \end{bmatrix} B_3 \overset{(8.21)}{=} \begin{bmatrix} 0 & 0 & 0 & 1 \\ 0 & 0 & -1 & 2 \\ 0 & 1 & -4 & 4 \\ -1 & 6 & -12 & 8 \end{bmatrix} \tag{8.48}$$

More generally, the polynomial segment $t \in \left[\frac{i}{2^j}, \frac{i+1}{2^j}\right]$ is readily given by the combination of j successive halving subdivisions followed by i doubling extrapolations

321

$$B_3\left(\frac{i+t}{2^j}\right) \overset{(8.41)}{=} \begin{bmatrix} 1 \\ t \\ t^2 \\ t^3 \end{bmatrix}^T B_3 S_{[1,2]}^i S_{[0,\frac{1}{2}]}^j \begin{bmatrix} c_0 \\ c_1 \\ c_2 \\ c_3 \end{bmatrix} \tag{8.49}$$

8.2.2 Bézier Curve

8.2.2.1 Non-Rational Bézier Curve

Given $n+1$ control points $\vec{p}_i \triangleq [x_i, y_i, z_i]^T$, a *non-rational Bézier curve* (named after Renault's engineer Pierre Bézier) of degree n is defined as a parametric combination of *Bernstein*
318 *polynomials* of degree n, or conversely as a convex combination of the control points

$$\vec{p}(t) \triangleq \begin{bmatrix} \sum_{i=0}^n x_i B_{i,n}(t) \\ \sum_{i=0}^n y_i B_{i,n}(t) \\ \sum_{i=0}^n z_i B_{i,n}(t) \end{bmatrix} = \sum_{i=0}^n \vec{p}_i B_{i,n}(t) = \begin{bmatrix} B_{0,n}(t) \\ B_{1,n}(t) \\ \vdots \\ B_{n,n}(t) \end{bmatrix}^T \begin{bmatrix} \vec{p}_0 \\ \vec{p}_1 \\ \vdots \\ \vec{p}_n \end{bmatrix} = \begin{bmatrix} 1 \\ t \\ \vdots \\ t^n \end{bmatrix}^T B_n \begin{bmatrix} \vec{p}_0 \\ \vec{p}_1 \\ \vdots \\ \vec{p}_n \end{bmatrix} \tag{8.50}$$

323 As illustrated in *Figure 8.3*, the geometric construction of a point on the curve, as well as

subdivision and extrapolation, readily follows from de Casteljau's algorithm by successive pairwise interpolation of points in the tree 321

$$
\begin{array}{rclllll}
\vec{p}_0 & = & \vec{p}_{0,n}(t) & & & & \\
 & & & \vec{p}_{0,n-1}(t) & & & \\
\vec{p}_1 & = & \vec{p}_{1,n}(t) & & \vec{p}_{0,n-2}(t) & & \\
 & \vdots & & \vdots & \vdots & \ddots & \\
\vec{p}_i & = & \vec{p}_{i,n}(t) & & \vec{p}_{i-1,n-2}(t) & & \\
 & & & \vec{p}_{i,n-1}(t) & & \dots & \vec{p}_{0,0}(t) \\
\vec{p}_{i+1} & = & \vec{p}_{i+1,n}(t) & & \vec{p}_{i,n-2}(t) & & \\
 & \vdots & & \vdots & \vdots & \cdot^{\cdot^{\cdot}} & \\
\vec{p}_{n-1} & = & \vec{p}_{n-1,n}(t) & & \vec{p}_{n-2,n-2}(t) & & \\
 & & & \vec{p}_{n-1,n-1}(t) & & & \\
\vec{p}_n & = & \vec{p}_{n,n}(t) & & & &
\end{array}
\tag{8.51}
$$

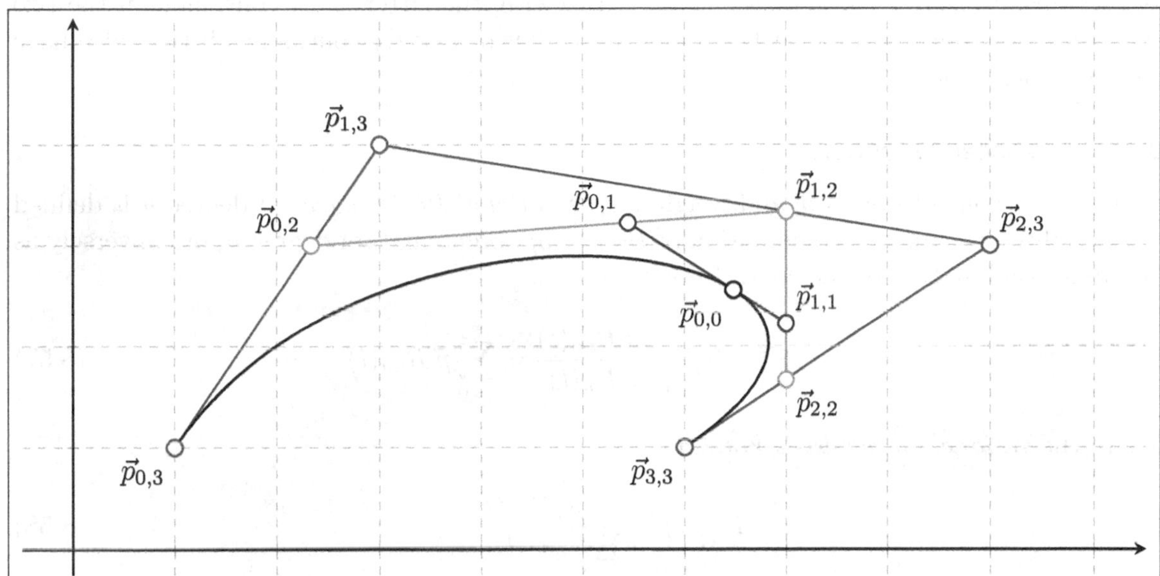

Figure 8.3: De Casteljau's Algorithm: Illustration of the geometric construction of a point on a cubic Bézier curve using de Casteljau's algorithm, and of the point sequence defining the control points of the subdivided curve.

Guaranties on the smoothness of a Bézier curve are provided by their *variation diminishing property*, which states that the number of intersections of a curve with a line (in 2-D) or a plane (in 3-D) is no greater than the number of intersections of the latter with the *polygonal chain* (i.e., the polygon in 2-D, or the *polyline* in arbitrary dimensions) defined by its control points (as can be shown by observing that degree elevation is a form of linear interpolation, which trivially satisfies the variation diminishing property, and that the limit of the control polyline for an infinite degree elevation is the curve itself). The curve is also guaranteed to lie within the convex hull of its control points, such that the curve forms a straight line if and only if all its control points are collinear. Finally, Bézier curves are affine invariant, and their *affine transformation* therefore corresponds to the curve defined by the transform of 115
their control points.

The tangent vector of a Bézier curve is readily given as 320

$$\vec{p}'(t) \overset{(8.31)}{=} n \sum_{i=0}^{n-1} (\vec{p}_{i+1} - \vec{p}_i) B_{i,n-1}(t) \tag{8.52}$$

yielding the endpoints

320 46

$$\vec{p}(0) \overset{(8.34)}{=} \sum_{i=0}^{n} \vec{p}_i \delta[i] \overset{(2.223)}{=} \vec{p}_0 \tag{8.53}$$

320 46

$$\vec{p}(1) \overset{(8.35)}{=} \sum_{i=0}^{n} \vec{p}_i \delta[n-i] \overset{(2.223)}{=} \vec{p}_n \tag{8.54}$$

320 46

$$\vec{p}'(0) \overset{(8.36)}{=} n \sum_{i=0}^{n-1} (\vec{p}_{i+1} - \vec{p}_i) \delta[i] \overset{(2.223)}{=} n(\vec{p}_1 - \vec{p}_0) \tag{8.55}$$

320 46

$$\vec{p}'(1) \overset{(8.37)}{=} n \sum_{i=0}^{n-1} (\vec{p}_{i+1} - \vec{p}_i) \delta[n-1-i] \overset{(2.223)}{=} n(\vec{p}_n - \vec{p}_{n-1}) \tag{8.56}$$

314 It follows that a piecewise-Bézier *spline* curve is C_0-continuous if the endpoints of the control polylines of adjacent Bézier curves coincide, in which case the spline is referred to as a *composite Bézier curve* or *poly-Bézier*. Likewise, the latter is G_1-continuous if the two end segments abutting a connection point are collinear, and C_1-continuous if they also have identical magnitudes.

8.2.2.2 Rational Bézier Curve

Given $n+1$ control points $\vec{p}_i$ and weights w_i, a *rational Bézier curve* of degree n is defined
318 as a weighted parametric combination of *Bernstein polynomials* of degree n, or conversely as an affine combination of the control points

$$\vec{p}(t) \triangleq \frac{\sum_{i=0}^{n} \vec{p}_i w_i B_{i,n}(t)}{\sum_{i=0}^{n} w_i B_{i,n}(t)} = \sum_{i=0}^{n} \vec{p}_i R_{i,n}(t) \tag{8.57}$$

where the *rational Bézier basis functions*

$$R_{i,n}(t) \triangleq \frac{w_i B_{i,n}(t)}{\sum_{j=0}^{n} w_j B_{j,n}(t)} \tag{8.58}$$

form a partition of unity

324

$$\sum_{i=0}^{n} R_{i,n}(t) \overset{(8.58)}{=} \sum_{i=0}^{n} \frac{w_i B_{i,n}(t)}{\sum_{j=0}^{n} w_j B_{j,n}(t)} = \frac{\sum_{i=0}^{n} w_i B_{i,n}(t)}{\sum_{j=0}^{n} w_j B_{j,n}(t)} = 1 \tag{8.59}$$

322 By generalizing *non-rational Bézier curves*, the rational form allows the exact representation of conic sections (i.e., curves resulting from the intersection of a plane with a cone,
325 such as parabolas, circular and ellipsoidal arcs and hyperbolas) as illustrated in *Figure 8.4*. Instead, if $w_i = 1, \forall i \in [0, n]$, the curve and its basis functions reduce to a *non-rational Bézier*
322 *curve* and to the *Bernstein basis polynomials*, respectively.

315 325 As illustrated in *Figure 8.5*, the geometric construction of a point on the rational curve first entails projecting the weighted control points $[w_i x_i, w_i y_i, w_i z_i, w_i]$ into a four-dimensional projective space, in which de Casteljau's algorithm may then be readily performed before
122 back-projecting the result into $\mathbb{R}^3$ by means of a *perspective projection*.

8.2.3 Bézier Surface

Given a net of control points, a *non-rational Bézier surface* is defined as a generalization
322 of *non-rational Bézier curves* to a two-dimensional parameter space, such that holding one

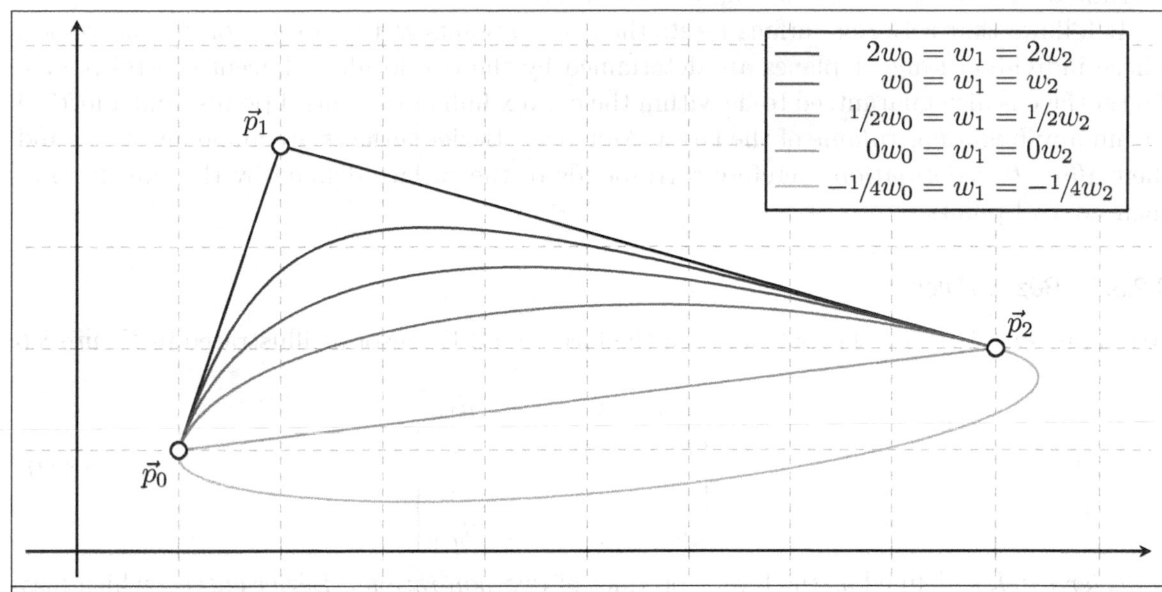

Figure 8.4: Rational Bézier Curve: Illustration of a rational Bézier curve with different weights.

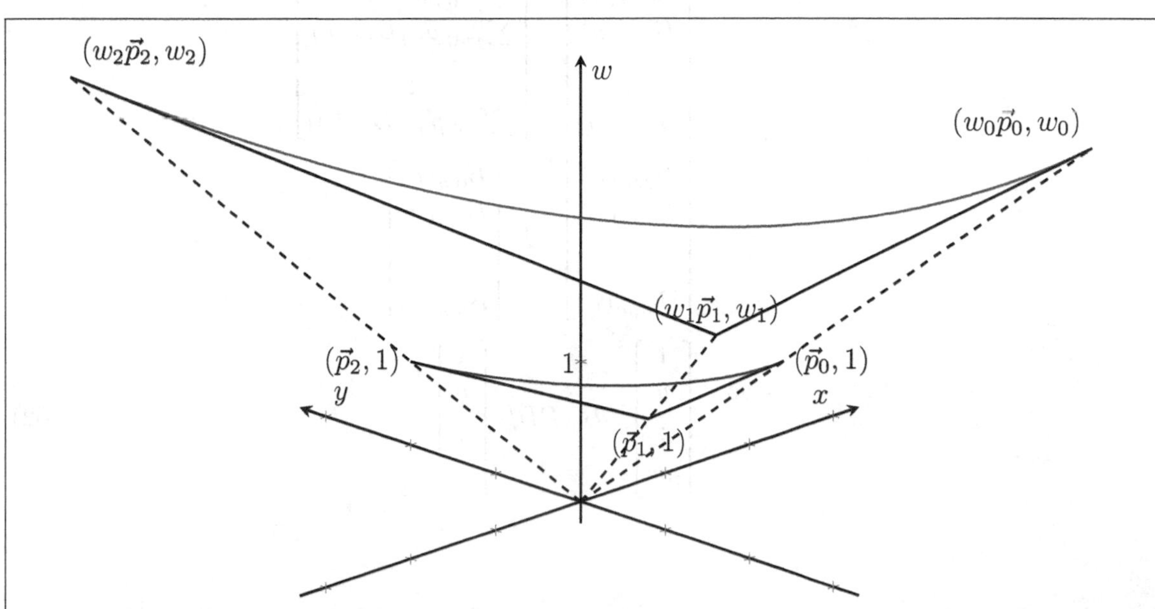

Figure 8.5: Homogeneous de Casteljau's Algorithm: Illustration of the geometric construction of a rational Bézier curve using de Casteljau's algorithm in homogeneous coordinates.

of the parameters constant yields a Bézier curve parameterized by the other parameter. In particular, the control points along the edges of the control net readily form the control polyline of the curves along the edges of the surface.

It follows that a Bézier surface meets the control points at the corners of its control net, whose individual tangent planes are determined by the two locally adjacent control points. The surface is also guaranteed to lie within the convex hull of its control points, and a fortiori
357 within any *bounding volume* of the latter. Moreover, Bézier surfaces are affine invariant, and
115 their *affine transformation* therefore corresponds to the surface defined by the transform of their control points.

8.2.3.1 Bézier Patch

327 Given an $(m+1) \times (n+1)$ control net in the form of a 3-D tensor as illustrated in *Figure 8.6*

$$P \triangleq \begin{bmatrix} \vec{p}_{0,0} & \vec{p}_{0,1} & \cdots & \vec{p}_{0,n} \\ \vec{p}_{1,0} & \vec{p}_{1,1} & \cdots & \vec{p}_{1,n} \\ \vdots & \vdots & \ddots & \vdots \\ \vec{p}_{m,0} & \vec{p}_{m,1} & \cdots & \vec{p}_{m,n} \end{bmatrix} \tag{8.60}$$

322 a *Bézier patch* is defined as the tensor product of two *non-rational Bézier curves*, which may be expressed in matrix form as

$$\vec{p}(u,v) \triangleq \sum_{i=0}^{m}\sum_{j=0}^{n} \vec{p}_{i,j} B_{i,m}(u) B_{j,n}(v) \tag{8.61}$$

$$= \sum_{i=0}^{m}\left(\sum_{j=0}^{n} \vec{p}_{i,j} B_{j,n}(v)\right) B_{i,m}(u)$$

$$= \begin{bmatrix} B_{0,m}(u) \\ B_{1,m}(u) \\ \vdots \\ B_{m,m}(u) \end{bmatrix}^T \begin{bmatrix} \sum_{j=0}^{n} \vec{p}_{0,j} B_{j,n}(v) \\ \sum_{j=0}^{n} \vec{p}_{1,j} B_{j,n}(v) \\ \vdots \\ \sum_{j=0}^{n} \vec{p}_{m,j} B_{j,n}(v) \end{bmatrix}$$

$$= \begin{bmatrix} B_{0,m}(u) \\ B_{1,m}(u) \\ \vdots \\ B_{m,m}(u) \end{bmatrix}^T P \begin{bmatrix} B_{0,n}(v) \\ B_{1,n}(v) \\ \vdots \\ B_{n,n}(v) \end{bmatrix}$$

322

$$\overset{(8.50)}{=} \begin{bmatrix} 1 \\ u \\ \vdots \\ u^m \end{bmatrix}^T B_m P B_n^T \begin{bmatrix} 1 \\ v \\ \vdots \\ v^n \end{bmatrix} \tag{8.62}$$

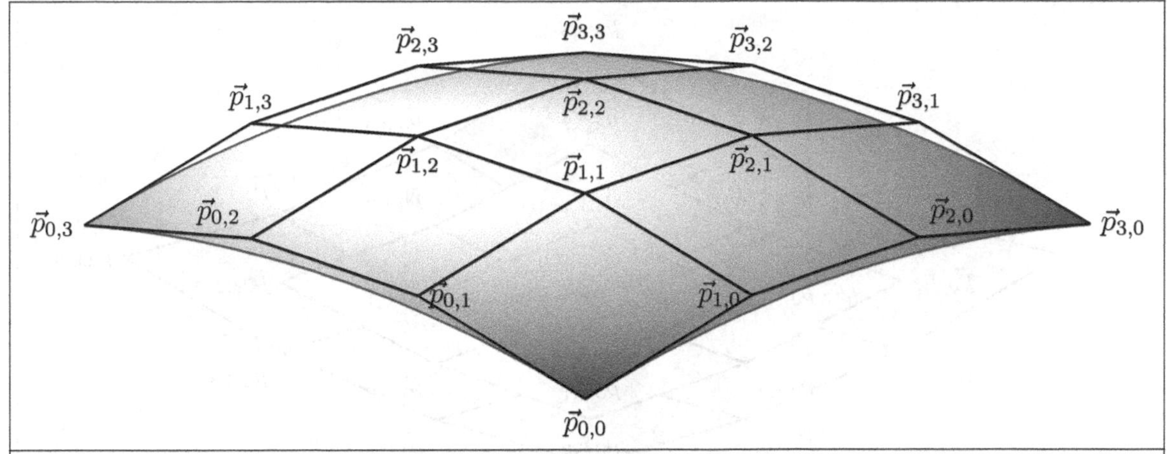

Figure 8.6: Bézier Patch: Illustration of the control net of a Bézier patch.

The first partial derivatives are then given by

$$\begin{aligned}\frac{\partial\vec{p}(u,v)}{\partial u} &= \sum_{j=0}^{n}\left(\sum_{i=0}^{m}\vec{p}_{i,j}B'_{i,m}(u)\right)B_{j,n}(v)\\ &\overset{(8.52)}{=} \sum_{j=0}^{n}\left(m\sum_{i=0}^{m-1}(\vec{p}_{i+1,j}-\vec{p}_{i,j})B_{i,m-1}(u)\right)B_{j,n}(v) \qquad (8.63)\end{aligned}$$ 323

$$\begin{aligned}\frac{\partial\vec{p}(u,v)}{\partial v} &= \sum_{i=0}^{m}\left(\sum_{j=0}^{n}\vec{p}_{i,j}B'_{j,n}(v)\right)B_{i,m}(u)\\ &\overset{(8.52)}{=} \sum_{i=0}^{m}\left(n\sum_{j=0}^{n-1}(\vec{p}_{i,j+1}-\vec{p}_{i,j})B_{j,n-1}(v)\right)B_{i,m}(u) \qquad (8.64)\end{aligned}$$ 323

As illustrated in *Figure 8.7*, the geometric construction of a point on the patch is readily 328
obtained by successive bilinear interpolation, as follows from de Casteljau's algorithm. Akin
to *non-rational Bézier curves*, *subdivision and extrapolation* of a cubic Bézier patch $\vec{p}(o_u +$ 322
$d_u u, o_v + d_v v)$ are then readily given by the control net $S_{[o_u,o_u+d_u]}PS^T_{[o_v,o_v+d_v]}$. 321

The intersections of a ray $\vec{r}(t) \triangleq \vec{o} + t\vec{d}$ with the patch may be determined by solving $\vec{p}(u,v) = \vec{r}(t)$ simultaneously in x, y and z, thereby yielding a non-linear system of 3 equations with the 3 unknowns t, u and v. As an alternative, the parametric coordinates of the intersection point can be estimated by procedurally subdividing the patch along both the u
and v axes, should the ray intersect the *bounding volume* of its control points, and then re- 357
cursively repeating the operation until a pre-determined subdivision level is reached, at which
point the geometry may either be approximated by proxy *triangles* or *bilinear patches*, or 250
the approximate intersection coordinates can be used as an initial guess for a numerical *root* 264
finding scheme such as *Householder's method*. 36 38

8.2.3.2 Bézier Triangle

Given a control net with $t_{n+1} \overset{(2.1)}{=} \frac{(n+1)(n+2)}{2}$ control points $\vec{p}_{i,j}$ as illustrated in *Figure 8.8*, a 15 328
Bézier triangle of degree n is defined as a parametric linear combination of two-dimensional
Bernstein basis polynomials of degree n, or conversely as a convex combination of the control 315

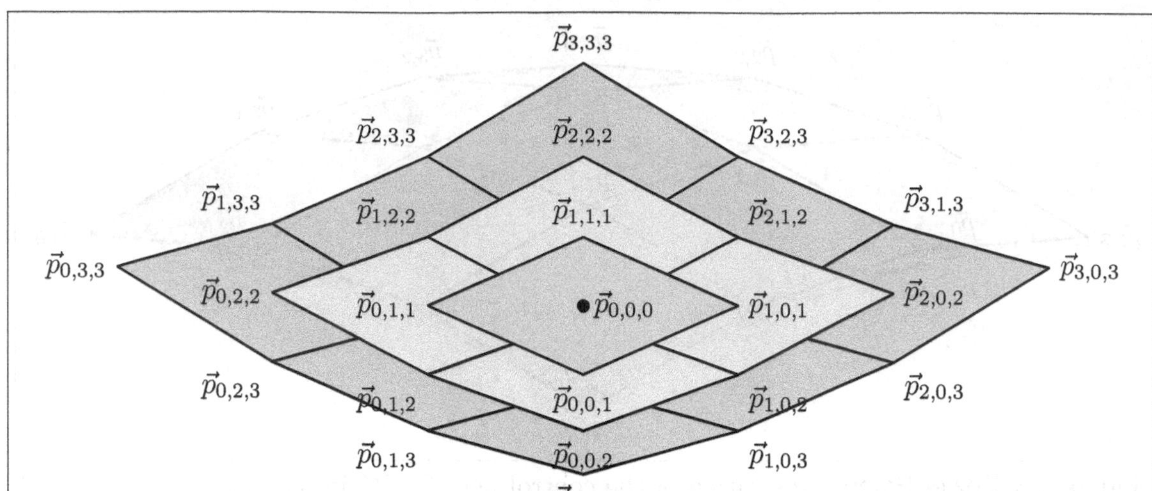

Figure 8.7: Quadrilateral de Casteljau's Algorithm: Illustration of the geometric construction of a point on a Bézier patch using de Casteljau's algorithm.

points

$$\vec{p}(u, v) \triangleq \sum_{i=0}^{n} \sum_{j=0}^{n-i} \vec{p}_{i,j} B_{i,j,n}(u, v) \tag{8.65}$$

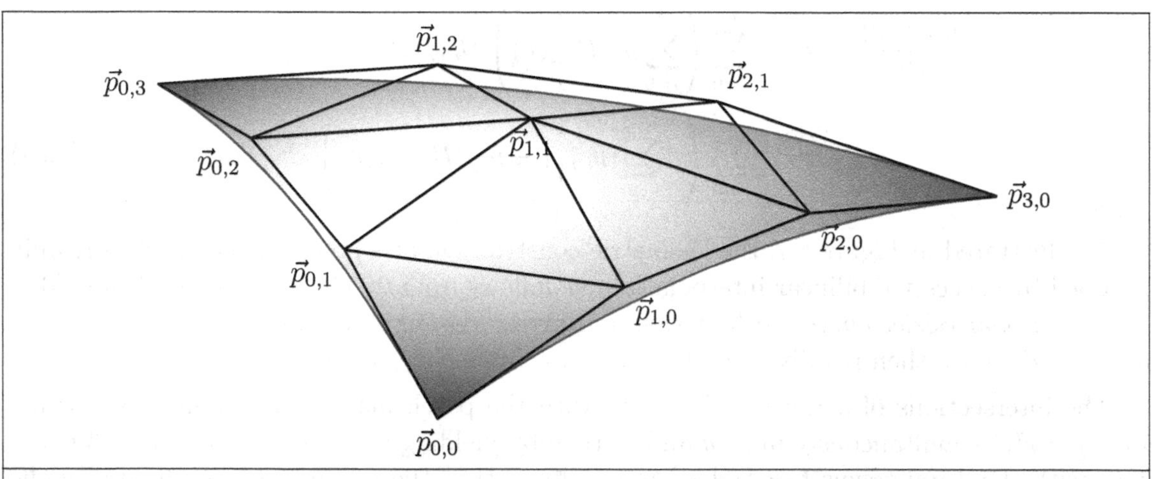

Figure 8.8: Bézier Triangle: Illustration of the control net of a Bézier triangle.

329 As illustrated in *Figure 8.9*, the geometric construction of a point on the curved triangle readily follows from an adaptation of de Casteljau's algorithm by successive barycentric interpolation

$$\vec{p}(u, v) = \vec{p}_{0,0,0}(u, v) \tag{8.66}$$

where

$$\vec{p}_{i,j,k}(u, v) \triangleq \begin{cases} \vec{p}_{i,j} & \text{if } k = n \\ \vec{p}_{i+1,j,k+1}(u, v)u + \vec{p}_{i,j+1,k+1}(u, v)v + \vec{p}_{i,j,k+1}(u, v)(1 - u - v) & \text{if } k < n \end{cases} \tag{8.67}$$

321 and so do *subdivision and extrapolation*, albeit in a form that does not refine the three boundary curves.

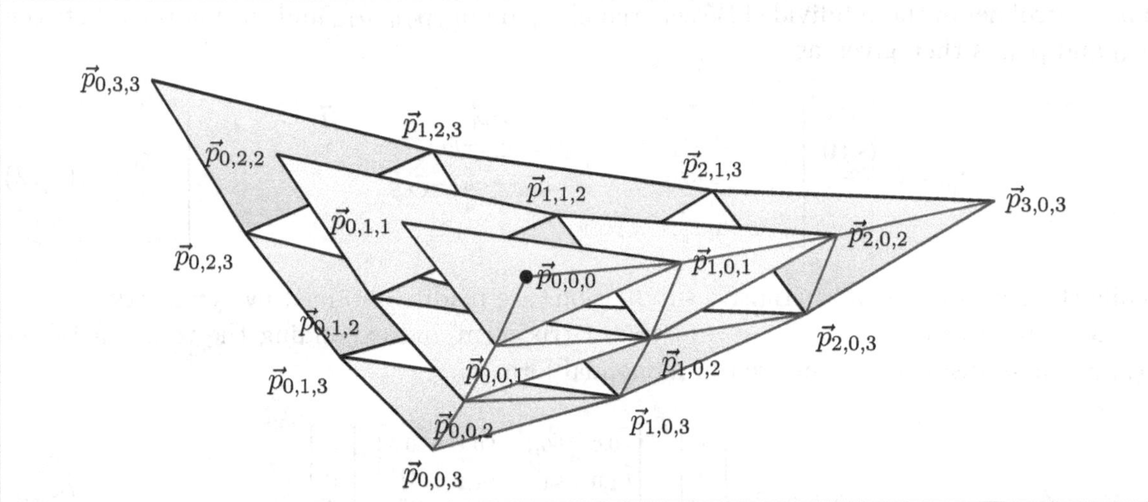

Figure 8.9: Triangular de Casteljau's Algorithm: Illustration of the geometric construction of a point on a Bézier triangle using de Casteljau's algorithm, and of the point sequence defining the control net of the subdivided curved triangle.

The first partial derivatives are then given by

$$\frac{\partial \vec{p}(u,v)}{\partial u} = \sum_{i=0}^{n-1} \sum_{j=0}^{n-1-i} \vec{p}_{i+1,j} B_{i,j,n-1}(u,v) \tag{8.68}$$

$$\frac{\partial \vec{p}(u,v)}{\partial v} = \sum_{i=0}^{n-1} \sum_{j=0}^{n-1-i} \vec{p}_{i,j+1} B_{i,j,n-1}(u,v) \tag{8.69}$$

As an alternative, a Bézier triangle may be expressed in matrix form, which, in the cubic case, reads

$$\begin{aligned}
\vec{p}(u,v) &= \vec{p}_{0,0}B_{0,0,3}(u,v) + \vec{p}_{0,1}B_{0,1,3}(u,v) + \vec{p}_{0,2}B_{0,2,3}(u,v) + \vec{p}_{0,3}B_{0,3,3}(u,v) \\
&+ \vec{p}_{1,0}B_{1,0,3}(u,v) + \vec{p}_{1,1}B_{1,1,3}(u,v) + \vec{p}_{1,2}B_{1,2,3}(u,v) \\
&+ \vec{p}_{2,0}B_{2,0,3}(u,v) + \vec{p}_{2,1}B_{2,1,3}(u,v) \\
&+ \vec{p}_{3,0}B_{3,0,3}(u,v) \\
&= \vec{p}_{0,0}w^3 + \vec{p}_{0,1}3vw^2 + \vec{p}_{0,2}3v^2w + \vec{p}_{0,3}v^3 \\
&+ \vec{p}_{1,0}3uw^2 + \vec{p}_{1,1}6uvw + \vec{p}_{1,2}3uv^2 \\
&+ \vec{p}_{2,0}3u^2w + \vec{p}_{2,1}3u^2v \\
&+ \vec{p}_{3,0}u^3 \\
&= \begin{bmatrix} 1 \\ u \\ u^2 \\ u^3 \end{bmatrix}^T \left(P \circ \begin{bmatrix} w^3 & w^2 & w & 1 \\ w^2 & w & 1 & 0 \\ w & 1 & 0 & 0 \\ 1 & 0 & 0 & 0 \end{bmatrix} \circ \begin{bmatrix} 1 & 3 & 3 & 1 \\ 3 & 6 & 3 & 0 \\ 3 & 3 & 0 & 0 \\ 1 & 0 & 0 & 0 \end{bmatrix} \right) \begin{bmatrix} 1 \\ v \\ v^2 \\ v^3 \end{bmatrix}
\end{aligned} \tag{8.70}$$

where $w \triangleq 1 - u - v$, and with control net

$$P \triangleq \begin{bmatrix} \vec{p}_{0,0} & \vec{p}_{0,1} & \vec{p}_{0,2} & \vec{p}_{0,3} \\ \vec{p}_{1,0} & \vec{p}_{1,1} & \vec{p}_{1,2} & \\ \vec{p}_{2,0} & \vec{p}_{2,1} & & \\ \vec{p}_{3,0} & & & \end{bmatrix} \tag{8.71}$$

The control net of the subdivided Bézier triangle spanning $\vec{p}_{0,0}$, $\vec{p}_{0,3}$ and the midpoint between $\vec{p}_{0,0}$ and $\vec{p}_{3,0}$ is then given as

322

$$S_{[0,\frac{1}{2}]}P \overset{(8.44)}{=} \begin{bmatrix} \vec{p}_{0,0} & \vec{p}_{0,1} & \vec{p}_{0,2} & \vec{p}_{0,3} \\ \frac{\vec{p}_{0,0}+\vec{p}_{1,0}}{2} & \frac{\vec{p}_{0,1}+\vec{p}_{1,1}}{2} & \frac{\vec{p}_{0,2}+\vec{p}_{1,2}}{2} & \\ \frac{\vec{p}_{0,0}+2\vec{p}_{1,0}+\vec{p}_{2,0}}{4} & \frac{\vec{p}_{0,1}+2\vec{p}_{1,1}+\vec{p}_{2,1}}{4} & & \\ \frac{\vec{p}_{0,0}+3\vec{p}_{1,0}+3\vec{p}_{2,0}+\vec{p}_{3,0}}{8} & & & \end{bmatrix} \tag{8.72}$$

while the control nets of alternative subdivisions are readily obtained by symmetry.

By substituting $w = 1 - u - v$ in the matrix form and expanding the terms, a Bézier triangle may instead be expressed in monomial form as

$$\vec{p}(u, v) = \begin{bmatrix} 1 \\ u \\ u^2 \\ u^3 \end{bmatrix}^T \begin{bmatrix} \vec{c}_{0,0} & \vec{c}_{0,1} & \vec{c}_{0,2} & \vec{c}_{0,3} \\ \vec{c}_{1,0} & \vec{c}_{1,1} & \vec{c}_{1,2} & \vec{0} \\ \vec{c}_{2,0} & \vec{c}_{2,1} & \vec{0} & \vec{0} \\ \vec{c}_{3,0} & \vec{0} & \vec{0} & \vec{0} \end{bmatrix} \begin{bmatrix} 1 \\ v \\ v^2 \\ v^3 \end{bmatrix} \tag{8.73}$$

where

$$\vec{c}_{0,0} \triangleq \vec{p}_{0,0} \tag{8.74}$$
$$\vec{c}_{0,1} \triangleq 3(-\vec{p}_{0,0} + \vec{p}_{0,1}) \tag{8.75}$$
$$\vec{c}_{0,2} \triangleq 3(\vec{p}_{0,0} - 2\vec{p}_{0,1} + \vec{p}_{0,2}) \tag{8.76}$$
$$\vec{c}_{0,3} \triangleq -\vec{p}_{0,0} + 3(\vec{p}_{0,1} - \vec{p}_{0,2}) + \vec{p}_{0,3} \tag{8.77}$$
$$\vec{c}_{1,0} \triangleq 3(-\vec{p}_{0,0} + \vec{p}_{1,0}) \tag{8.78}$$
$$\vec{c}_{1,1} \triangleq 6(\vec{p}_{0,0} - \vec{p}_{0,1} - \vec{p}_{1,0} + \vec{p}_{1,1}) \tag{8.79}$$
$$\vec{c}_{1,2} \triangleq -3(\vec{p}_{0,0} - 2\vec{p}_{0,1} + \vec{p}_{0,2}) + 3(\vec{p}_{1,0} - 2\vec{p}_{1,1} + \vec{p}_{1,2}) \tag{8.80}$$
$$\vec{c}_{2,0} \triangleq 3(\vec{p}_{0,0} - 2\vec{p}_{1,0} + \vec{p}_{2,0}) \tag{8.81}$$
$$\vec{c}_{2,1} \triangleq -3(\vec{p}_{0,0} - 2\vec{p}_{1,0} + \vec{p}_{2,0}) + 3(\vec{p}_{0,1} - 2\vec{p}_{1,1} + \vec{p}_{2,1}) \tag{8.82}$$
$$\vec{c}_{3,0} \triangleq -\vec{p}_{0,0} + 3(\vec{p}_{1,0} - \vec{p}_{2,0}) + \vec{p}_{3,0} \tag{8.83}$$

while the corresponding control net is conversely given by

$$\vec{p}_{0,0} \triangleq \vec{c}_{0,0} \tag{8.84}$$
$$\vec{p}_{0,1} \triangleq \vec{c}_{0,0} + {}^1\!/_3\vec{c}_{0,1} \tag{8.85}$$
$$\vec{p}_{0,2} \triangleq \vec{c}_{0,0} + {}^2\!/_3\vec{c}_{0,1} + {}^1\!/_3\vec{c}_{0,2} \tag{8.86}$$
$$\vec{p}_{0,3} \triangleq \vec{c}_{0,0} + \vec{c}_{0,1} + \vec{c}_{0,2} + \vec{c}_{0,3} \tag{8.87}$$
$$\vec{p}_{1,0} \triangleq \vec{c}_{0,0} + {}^1\!/_3\vec{c}_{1,0} \tag{8.88}$$
$$\vec{p}_{1,1} \triangleq \vec{c}_{0,0} + {}^1\!/_3\vec{c}_{0,1} + {}^1\!/_3\vec{c}_{1,0} + {}^1\!/_6\vec{c}_{1,1} \tag{8.89}$$
$$\vec{p}_{1,2} \triangleq (\vec{c}_{0,0} + {}^2\!/_3\vec{c}_{0,1} + {}^1\!/_3\vec{c}_{0,2}) + {}^1\!/_3(\vec{c}_{1,0} + \vec{c}_{1,1} + \vec{c}_{1,2}) \tag{8.90}$$
$$\vec{p}_{2,0} \triangleq \vec{c}_{0,0} + {}^2\!/_3\vec{c}_{1,0} + {}^1\!/_3\vec{c}_{2,0} \tag{8.91}$$
$$\vec{p}_{2,1} \triangleq (\vec{c}_{0,0} + {}^2\!/_3\vec{c}_{1,0} + {}^1\!/_3\vec{c}_{2,0}) + {}^1\!/_3(\vec{c}_{0,1} + \vec{c}_{1,1} + \vec{c}_{2,1}) \tag{8.92}$$
$$\vec{p}_{3,0} \triangleq \vec{c}_{0,0} + \vec{c}_{1,0} + \vec{c}_{2,0} + \vec{c}_{3,0} \tag{8.93}$$

332 As illustrated in *Figure 8.10*, the range of barycentric coordinates may then be subdivided

into four distinct subsets

$$\vec{p}\left(\frac{1+u}{2},\frac{v}{2},\frac{w}{2}\right)$$

$$\overset{(8.41)}{=} \begin{bmatrix}1\\u\\u^2\\u^3\end{bmatrix}^T \begin{bmatrix}1 & \frac{1}{2} & \frac{1}{4} & \frac{1}{8}\\ 0 & \frac{1}{2} & \frac{2}{4} & \frac{3}{8}\\ 0 & 0 & \frac{1}{4} & \frac{3}{8}\\ 0 & 0 & 0 & \frac{1}{8}\end{bmatrix} \begin{bmatrix}\vec{c}_{0,0} & \vec{c}_{0,1} & \vec{c}_{0,2} & \vec{c}_{0,3}\\ \vec{c}_{1,0} & \vec{c}_{1,1} & \vec{c}_{1,2} & \vec{0}\\ \vec{c}_{2,0} & \vec{c}_{2,1} & \vec{0} & \vec{0}\\ \vec{c}_{3,0} & \vec{0} & \vec{0} & \vec{0}\end{bmatrix} \begin{bmatrix}1 & 0 & 0 & 0\\ 0 & \frac{1}{2} & 0 & 0\\ 0 & 0 & \frac{1}{4} & 0\\ 0 & 0 & 0 & \frac{1}{8}\end{bmatrix}^T \begin{bmatrix}1\\v\\v^2\\v^3\end{bmatrix}$$ 321

$$= \begin{bmatrix}1\\u\\u^2\\u^3\end{bmatrix}^T \begin{bmatrix}\vec{c}_{0,0}+\frac{\vec{c}_{1,0}}{2}+\frac{\vec{c}_{2,0}}{4}+\frac{\vec{c}_{3,0}}{8} & \frac{\vec{c}_{0,1}}{2}+\frac{\vec{c}_{1,1}}{4}+\frac{\vec{c}_{2,1}}{8} & \frac{\vec{c}_{0,2}}{4}+\frac{\vec{c}_{1,2}}{8} & \frac{\vec{c}_{0,3}}{8}\\ \frac{\vec{c}_{1,0}}{2}+\frac{2\vec{c}_{2,0}}{4}+\frac{3\vec{c}_{3,0}}{8} & \frac{\vec{c}_{1,1}}{4}+\frac{2\vec{c}_{2,1}}{8} & \frac{\vec{c}_{1,2}}{8} & \vec{0}\\ \frac{\vec{c}_{2,0}}{4}+\frac{3\vec{c}_{3,0}}{8} & \frac{\vec{c}_{2,1}}{8} & \vec{0} & \vec{0}\\ \frac{\vec{c}_{3,0}}{8} & \vec{0} & \vec{0} & \vec{0}\end{bmatrix} \begin{bmatrix}1\\v\\v^2\\v^3\end{bmatrix} \quad (8.94)$$

$$\vec{p}\left(\frac{u}{2},\frac{1+v}{2},\frac{w}{2}\right)$$

$$\overset{(8.41)}{=} \begin{bmatrix}1\\u\\u^2\\u^3\end{bmatrix}^T \begin{bmatrix}1 & 0 & 0 & 0\\ 0 & \frac{1}{2} & 0 & 0\\ 0 & 0 & \frac{1}{4} & 0\\ 0 & 0 & 0 & \frac{1}{8}\end{bmatrix} \begin{bmatrix}\vec{c}_{0,0} & \vec{c}_{0,1} & \vec{c}_{0,2} & \vec{c}_{0,3}\\ \vec{c}_{1,0} & \vec{c}_{1,1} & \vec{c}_{1,2} & \vec{0}\\ \vec{c}_{2,0} & \vec{c}_{2,1} & \vec{0} & \vec{0}\\ \vec{c}_{3,0} & \vec{0} & \vec{0} & \vec{0}\end{bmatrix} \begin{bmatrix}1 & \frac{1}{2} & \frac{1}{4} & \frac{1}{8}\\ 0 & \frac{1}{2} & \frac{2}{4} & \frac{3}{8}\\ 0 & 0 & \frac{1}{4} & \frac{3}{8}\\ 0 & 0 & 0 & \frac{1}{8}\end{bmatrix}^T \begin{bmatrix}1\\v\\v^2\\v^3\end{bmatrix}$$ 321

$$= \begin{bmatrix}1\\u\\u^2\\u^3\end{bmatrix}^T \begin{bmatrix}\vec{c}_{0,0}+\frac{\vec{c}_{0,1}}{2}+\frac{\vec{c}_{0,2}}{4}+\frac{\vec{c}_{0,3}}{8} & \frac{\vec{c}_{0,1}}{2}+\frac{2\vec{c}_{0,2}}{4}+\frac{3\vec{c}_{0,3}}{8} & \frac{\vec{c}_{0,2}}{4}+\frac{3\vec{c}_{0,3}}{8} & \frac{\vec{c}_{0,3}}{8}\\ \frac{\vec{c}_{1,0}}{2}+\frac{\vec{c}_{1,1}}{4}+\frac{\vec{c}_{1,2}}{8} & \frac{\vec{c}_{1,1}}{4}+\frac{2\vec{c}_{1,2}}{8} & \frac{\vec{c}_{1,2}}{8} & \vec{0}\\ \frac{\vec{c}_{2,0}}{4}+\frac{\vec{c}_{2,1}}{8} & \frac{\vec{c}_{2,1}}{8} & \vec{0} & \vec{0}\\ \frac{\vec{c}_{3,0}}{8} & \vec{0} & \vec{0} & \vec{0}\end{bmatrix} \begin{bmatrix}1\\v\\v^2\\v^3\end{bmatrix} \quad (8.95)$$

$$\vec{p}\left(\frac{u}{2},\frac{v}{2},\frac{1+w}{2}\right)$$

$$\overset{(8.41)}{=} \begin{bmatrix}1\\u\\u^2\\u^3\end{bmatrix}^T \begin{bmatrix}1 & 0 & 0 & 0\\ 0 & \frac{1}{2} & 0 & 0\\ 0 & 0 & \frac{1}{4} & 0\\ 0 & 0 & 0 & \frac{1}{8}\end{bmatrix} \begin{bmatrix}\vec{c}_{0,0} & \vec{c}_{0,1} & \vec{c}_{0,2} & \vec{c}_{0,3}\\ \vec{c}_{1,0} & \vec{c}_{1,1} & \vec{c}_{1,2} & \vec{0}\\ \vec{c}_{2,0} & \vec{c}_{2,1} & \vec{0} & \vec{0}\\ \vec{c}_{3,0} & \vec{0} & \vec{0} & \vec{0}\end{bmatrix} \begin{bmatrix}1 & 0 & 0 & 0\\ 0 & \frac{1}{2} & 0 & 0\\ 0 & 0 & \frac{1}{4} & 0\\ 0 & 0 & 0 & \frac{1}{8}\end{bmatrix}^T \begin{bmatrix}1\\v\\v^2\\v^3\end{bmatrix}$$ 321

$$= \begin{bmatrix}1\\u\\u^2\\u^3\end{bmatrix}^T \begin{bmatrix}\vec{c}_{0,0} & \frac{\vec{c}_{0,1}}{2} & \frac{\vec{c}_{0,2}}{4} & \frac{\vec{c}_{0,3}}{8}\\ \frac{\vec{c}_{1,0}}{2} & \frac{\vec{c}_{1,1}}{4} & \frac{\vec{c}_{1,2}}{8} & \vec{0}\\ \frac{\vec{c}_{2,0}}{4} & \frac{\vec{c}_{2,1}}{8} & \vec{0} & \vec{0}\\ \frac{\vec{c}_{3,0}}{8} & \vec{0} & \vec{0} & \vec{0}\end{bmatrix} \begin{bmatrix}1\\v\\v^2\\v^3\end{bmatrix} \quad (8.96)$$

$$\vec{p}\left(\frac{1-u}{2},\frac{1-v}{2},\frac{1-w}{2}\right)$$

$$\overset{(8.41)}{=} \begin{bmatrix}1\\u\\u^2\\u^3\end{bmatrix}^T \begin{bmatrix}1 & \frac{1}{2} & \frac{1}{4} & \frac{1}{8}\\ 0 & -\frac{1}{2} & -\frac{2}{4} & -\frac{3}{8}\\ 0 & 0 & \frac{1}{4} & \frac{3}{8}\\ 0 & 0 & 0 & -\frac{1}{8}\end{bmatrix} \begin{bmatrix}\vec{c}_{0,0} & \vec{c}_{0,1} & \vec{c}_{0,2} & \vec{c}_{0,3}\\ \vec{c}_{1,0} & \vec{c}_{1,1} & \vec{c}_{1,2} & \vec{0}\\ \vec{c}_{2,0} & \vec{c}_{2,1} & \vec{0} & \vec{0}\\ \vec{c}_{3,0} & \vec{0} & \vec{0} & \vec{0}\end{bmatrix} \begin{bmatrix}1 & \frac{1}{2} & \frac{1}{4} & \frac{1}{8}\\ 0 & -\frac{1}{2} & -\frac{2}{4} & -\frac{3}{8}\\ 0 & 0 & \frac{1}{4} & \frac{3}{8}\\ 0 & 0 & 0 & -\frac{1}{8}\end{bmatrix}^T \begin{bmatrix}1\\v\\v^2\\v^3\end{bmatrix}$$ 321

$$= \begin{bmatrix}1\\u\\u^2\\u^3\end{bmatrix}^T \begin{bmatrix}\sum_{i=0}^{3}\sum_{j=0}^{3-i}\frac{\vec{c}_{i,j}}{2^{i+j}} & -\frac{\vec{c}_{0,1}+\vec{c}_{0,2}}{2}-\frac{\vec{c}_{1,1}+\vec{c}_{1,2}}{4}-\frac{3\vec{c}_{0,3}+\vec{c}_{2,1}}{8} & \frac{\vec{c}_{1,2}+2\vec{c}_{0,2}+3\vec{c}_{0,3}}{8} & -\frac{\vec{c}_{0,3}}{8}\\ -\frac{\vec{c}_{1,0}+\vec{c}_{2,0}}{2}-\frac{\vec{c}_{1,1}+\vec{c}_{2,1}}{4}-\frac{\vec{c}_{1,2}+3\vec{c}_{3,0}}{8} & \frac{\vec{c}_{1,1}+\vec{c}_{1,2}+\vec{c}_{2,1}}{4} & -\frac{\vec{c}_{1,2}}{8} & \vec{0}\\ \frac{\vec{c}_{2,1}+2\vec{c}_{2,0}+3\vec{c}_{3,0}}{8} & -\frac{\vec{c}_{2,1}}{8} & \vec{0} & \vec{0}\\ -\frac{\vec{c}_{3,0}}{8} & \vec{0} & \vec{0} & \vec{0}\end{bmatrix} \begin{bmatrix}1\\v\\v^2\\v^3\end{bmatrix} \quad (8.97)$$

Converting the monomial coefficients resulting from the previous to last sub-triangle into

Bézier coefficients yields the control net

322 $$S_{[0,\frac{1}{2}]}PS_{[0,\frac{1}{2}]}^T \overset{(8.44)}{=} \begin{bmatrix} \vec{p}_{0,0} & \frac{\vec{p}_{0,0}+\vec{p}_{0,1}}{2} & \frac{\vec{p}_{0,0}+2\vec{p}_{0,1}+\vec{p}_{0,2}}{4} & \sum_{j=0}^{3}\binom{3}{j}\frac{\vec{p}_{0,j}}{8} \\ \frac{\vec{p}_{0,0}+\vec{p}_{1,0}}{2} & \frac{\vec{p}_{0,0}+\vec{p}_{0,1}+\vec{p}_{1,0}+\vec{p}_{1,1}}{4} & \sum_{j=0}^{2}\binom{2}{j}\frac{\vec{p}_{0,j}+\vec{p}_{1,j}}{8} & \\ \frac{\vec{p}_{0,0}+2\vec{p}_{1,0}+\vec{p}_{2,0}}{4} & \sum_{i=0}^{2}\binom{2}{i}\frac{\vec{p}_{i,0}+\vec{p}_{i,1}}{8} & & \\ \sum_{i=0}^{3}\binom{3}{i}\frac{\vec{p}_{i,0}}{8} & & & \end{bmatrix} \tag{8.98}$$

whose entries can be generally expressed as

$$\left(S_{[0,\frac{1}{2}]}PS_{[0,\frac{1}{2}]}^T\right)_{mn} = \frac{1}{2^{m+n}}\sum_{i=0}^{m}\binom{m}{i}\sum_{j=0}^{n}\binom{n}{j}\vec{p}_{i,j} \tag{8.99}$$

while the control points of the remaining sub-triangles are readily obtained by symmetry, with the exception of the central control point of the last sub-triangle, which is given by

330
331
330
330

$$\begin{aligned} \vec{p}'_{1,1} &\underset{(8.97)}{\overset{(8.89)}{=}} \vec{c}_{0,0} + \frac{\vec{c}_{0,1}+\vec{c}_{1,0}}{2} + \frac{\vec{c}_{0,2}+\vec{c}_{1,1}+\vec{c}_{2,0}}{4} + \frac{\vec{c}_{0,3}+\vec{c}_{1,2}+\vec{c}_{2,1}+\vec{c}_{3,0}}{8} \\ &+ \frac{-\frac{\vec{c}_{0,1}+\vec{c}_{0,2}}{2} - \frac{\vec{c}_{1,1}+\vec{c}_{1,2}}{4} - \frac{3\vec{c}_{0,3}+\vec{c}_{2,1}}{8}}{3} + \frac{-\frac{\vec{c}_{1,0}+\vec{c}_{2,0}}{2} - \frac{\vec{c}_{1,1}+\vec{c}_{2,1}}{4} - \frac{\vec{c}_{1,2}+3\vec{c}_{3,0}}{8}}{3} + \frac{\frac{\vec{c}_{1,1}+\vec{c}_{1,2}+\vec{c}_{2,1}}{4}}{6} \\ &= \vec{c}_{0,0} + \frac{\vec{c}_{0,1}+\vec{c}_{1,0}}{3} + \frac{\vec{c}_{1,1}}{8} + \frac{\vec{c}_{0,2}+\vec{c}_{2,0}}{12} + \frac{\vec{c}_{1,2}+\vec{c}_{2,1}}{24} \\ &\underset{(8.83)}{\overset{(8.74)}{=}} \frac{2\vec{p}_{1,1}+\vec{p}_{0,1}+\vec{p}_{1,0}+\vec{p}_{0,2}+\vec{p}_{2,0}+\vec{p}_{1,2}+\vec{p}_{2,1}}{8} \end{aligned} \tag{8.100}$$

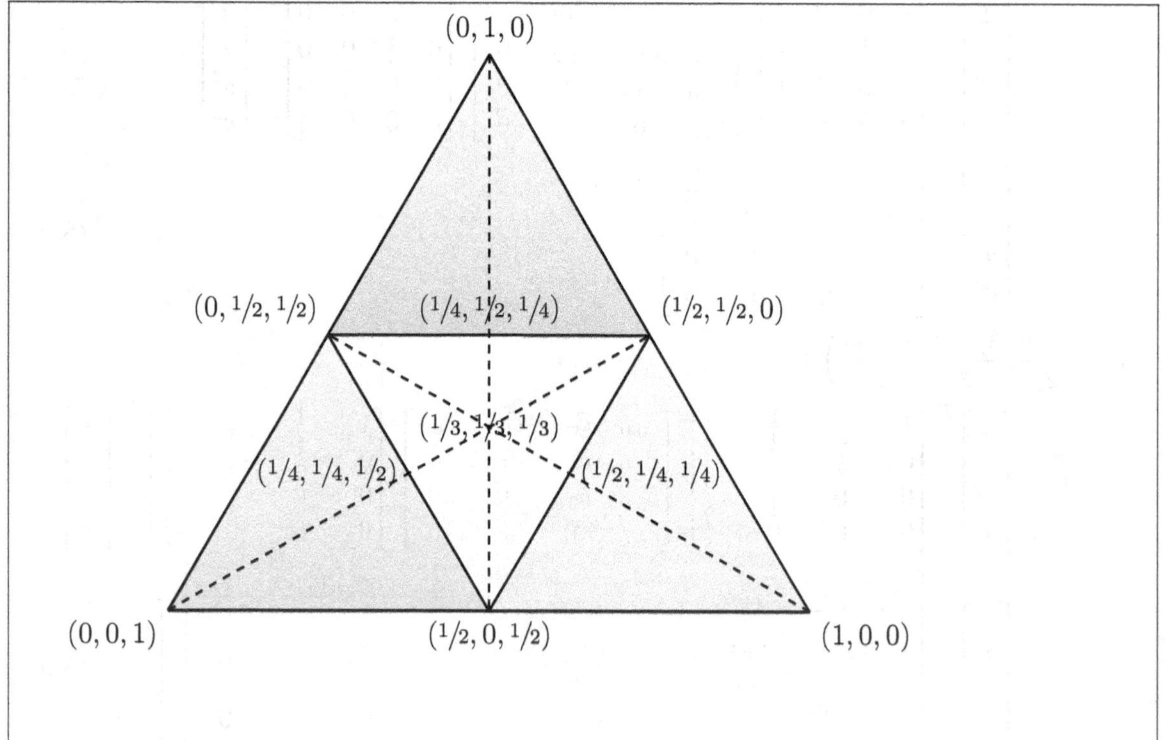

Figure 8.10: Bézier Triangle Subdivision: Illustration of the subdivision of the range of barycentric coordinates of a Bézier triangle into four distinct subsets.

As illustrated in *Figure 8.11*, the intersection of a ray with a Bézier triangle may then 333
be evaluated by recursively subdividing each sub-triangle for which the ray intersects the
bounding volume of its control points, until the extent of the latter falls below a given 357
threshold.

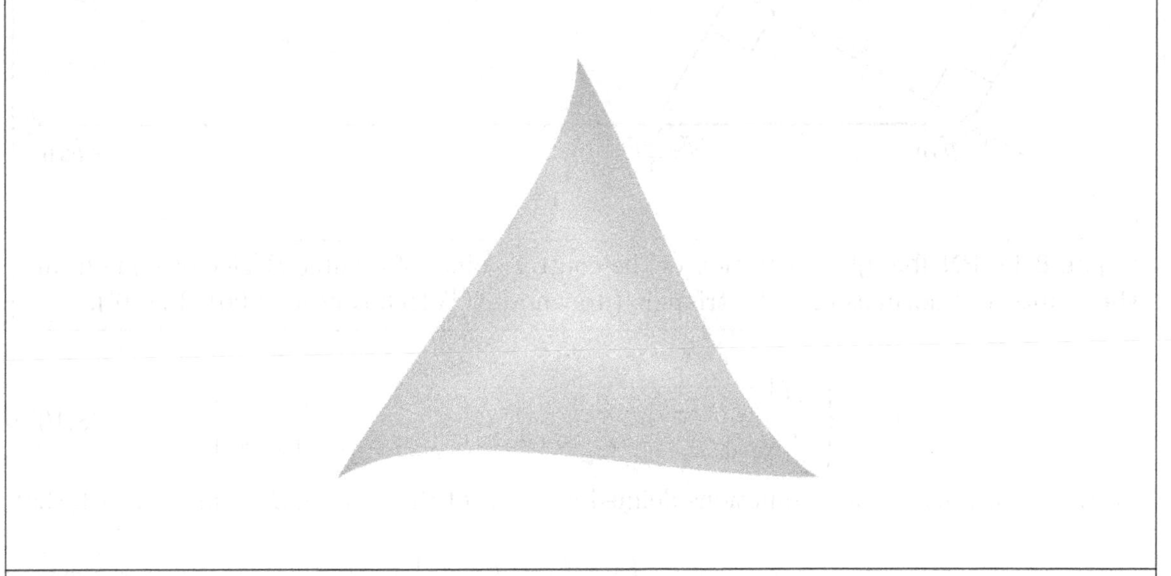

Figure 8.11: Bézier Triangle: Illustration of a Bézier triangle.

8.2.3.3 PN Triangle

Given three endpoints $\vec{p}_{i,j}$ and normal vectors $\vec{n}_{i,j}$, a *PN triangle* is defined as a cubic *Bézier*
triangle whose remaining points in the control net are implicitly inferred. As illustrated in 327
Figure 8.12, the six control points along the boundaries may then be computed by projecting 334
each third point of the edges onto the plane orthogonal to the normal of the nearest endpoint
[Vlachos *et al.*, 2001]

$$\begin{aligned}\vec{p}_{1,0} &\triangleq \frac{2\vec{p}_{0,0}+\vec{p}_{3,0}}{3} - \left\langle \frac{2\vec{p}_{0,0}+\vec{p}_{3,0}}{3} - \vec{p}_{0,0}, \frac{\vec{n}_{0,0}}{\|\vec{n}_{0,0}\|} \right\rangle \frac{\vec{n}_{0,0}}{\|\vec{n}_{0,0}\|} \\ &= \frac{2\vec{p}_{0,0}+\vec{p}_{3,0}+\langle \vec{p}_{0,0}-\vec{p}_{3,0}, \hat{n}_{0,0}\rangle \hat{n}_{0,0}}{3}\end{aligned} \tag{8.101}$$

while the inner control point can instead be computed as

$$\vec{p}_{1,1} \triangleq \frac{\vec{p}_{0,1}+\vec{p}_{0,2}+\vec{p}_{1,0}+\vec{p}_{1,2}+\vec{p}_{2,0}+\vec{p}_{2,1}}{4} - \frac{\vec{p}_{0,0}+\vec{p}_{0,3}+\vec{p}_{3,0}}{6} \tag{8.102}$$

8.3 B-SPLINE

8.3.1 B-Spline Function

8.3.1.1 B-Spline Basis Function

General Case Given knot values $[t_i \leq \ldots \leq t_{i+n+1}]$, a *B-spline basis function* of degree
$n \in \mathbb{N}$ (commonly said to be of order $n+1$) with support $[t_i, t_{i+n+1}]$ is a generalized *Bernstein*
basis polynomial recursively defined in terms of basis functions of lower degree 315

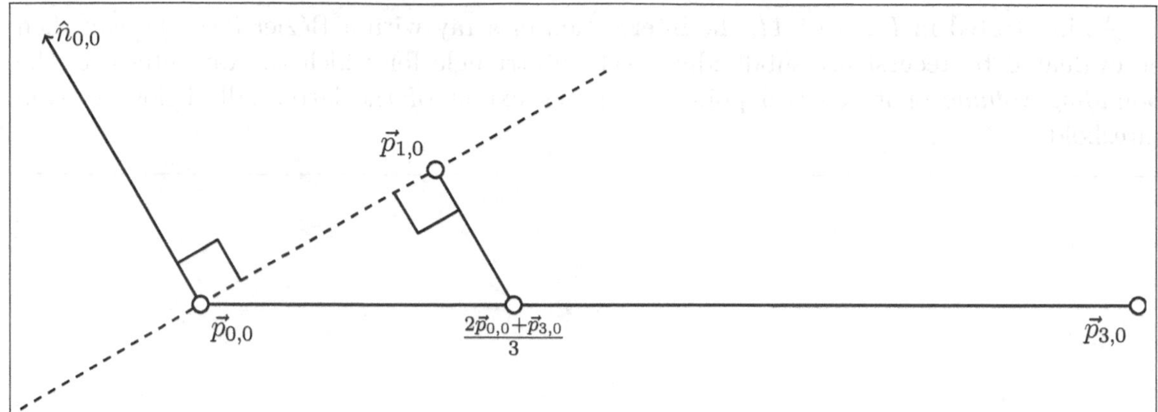

Figure 8.12: PN Triangle: Definition of the control points of a cubic Bézier triangle from the points and normals of a PN triangle (drawn after [Vlachos *et al.*, 2001, Fig. 6]).

$$S_{i,n}(t) \triangleq \begin{cases} \sqcap\left(\frac{(t-t_i)-(t_{i+1}-t)}{2(t_{i+1}-t_i)}\right) & \text{if } n = 0 \\ \frac{t-t_i}{t_{i+n}-t_i} S_{i,n-1}(t) + \frac{t_{i+n+1}-t}{t_{i+n+1}-t_{i+1}} S_{i+1,n-1}(t) & \text{if } n > 0 \end{cases} \tag{8.103}$$

46 with the zeroth-degree basis functions defined in terms of the *rectangular function* such that

$$S_{i,0}(t) = \begin{cases} 1 & \text{if } t \in [t_i, t_{i+1}] \\ 0 & \text{otherwise} \end{cases} \tag{8.104}$$

and which may be evaluated as

$$S_{i,n}(t) = S(t, [t_i, \ldots, t_{i+n+1}]) \tag{8.105}$$

with

$$S(t, [t_i, \ldots, t_j]) \triangleq \begin{cases} \sqcap\left(\frac{(t-t_i)-(t_j-t)}{2(t_j-t_i)}\right) & \text{if } j = i+1 \\ \frac{t-t_i}{t_{j-1}-t_i} S(t, [t_i, \ldots, t_{j-1}]) + \frac{t_j-t}{t_j-t_{i+1}} S(t, [t_{i+1}, \ldots, t_j]) & \text{if } j > i+1 \end{cases} \tag{8.106}$$

B-spline basis functions of degree n exhibit C_{n-1}-continuity at the knots if the latter are distinct, while their derivatives are readily given as

$$S'_{i,n}(t) = n\left(\frac{S_{i,n-1}(t)}{t_{i+n} - t_i} - \frac{S_{i+1,n-1}(t)}{t_{i+n+1} - t_{i+1}}\right), \quad \forall n > 0 \tag{8.107}$$

Given a so-called *knot vector* $[t_{k-n}, \ldots, t_{k+m}]$ of $n+m+1$ knots delimiting the piecewise-polynomial segments, the m B-spline basis functions of degree n form a partition of unity

$$\sum_{i=k-n}^{k-n+m-1} S_{i,n}(t) = 1, \quad \forall t \in [t_k, t_{k-n+m}] \tag{8.108}$$

335 over the natural interval overlapped by $n+1$ basis functions, as illustrated in *Figure 8.13*,
while satisfying positivity $S_{i,n}(t) \geq 0, \forall t \in [t_i, t_{i+n+1}]$. The knots $[t_k, t_{k-n+m}]$ defining the boundaries of the natural interval are then called *boundary knots*, while the knots $[t_{k+1}, \ldots, t_{k-n+m-1}]$ are referred to as *interior knots*, and the knots $[t_{k-n}, \ldots, t_{k-1}]$ and $[t_{k-n+m+1}, \ldots, t_{k+m}]$ as *exterior knots*.

It follows that when the exterior and boundary knots are merged into end knots $t_{k-n} =$
335 $\ldots = t_k$ and $t_{k-n+m} = \ldots = t_{k+m}$ with *multiplicity* $n+1$ as illustrated in *Figure 8.14*,
the natural interval extends to the whole domain. In the absence of internal knots, the
315 B-spline basis functions then reduce to the *Bernstein basis polynomials* over the domain
$[t_{k-n} = \ldots = t_k = 0, t_{k+1} = \ldots = t_{k+n+1} = 1]$.

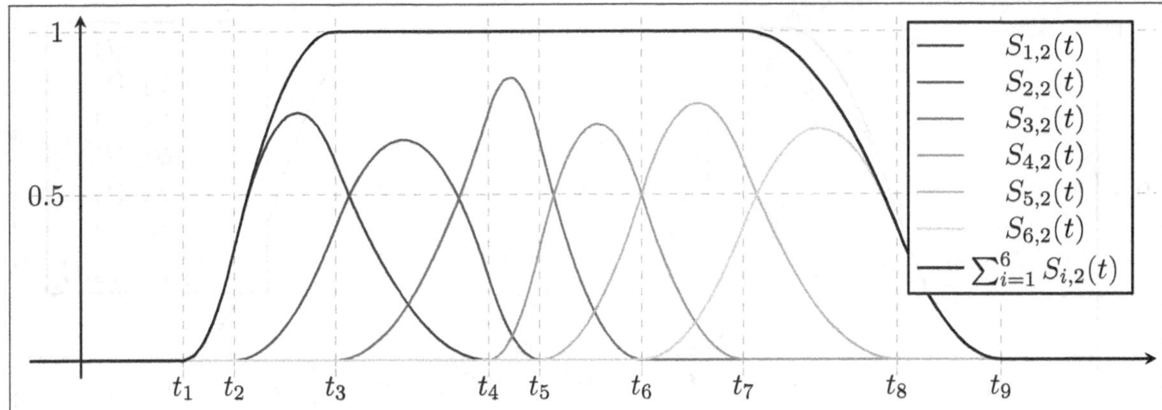

Figure 8.13: B-Spline Basis Functions: Illustration of the quadratic B-spline basis functions defined by a given knot vector.

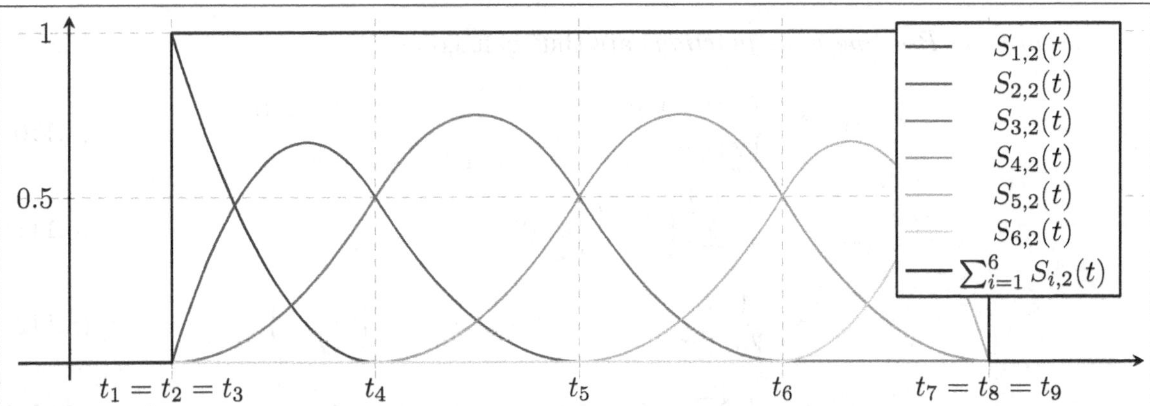

Figure 8.14: Clamped B-Spline Basis Functions: Illustration of the quadratic B-spline basis functions defined by a knot vector whose exterior knots are merged with the boundary knots.

Uniform Case In the special case of equally spaced knots $t_i = i$ as illustrated in *Figure 8.15*, 336
the *B-spline basis functions* become uniform and reduce to 333

$$S_{i,n}(t) = U_n(t - i) \tag{8.109}$$

where the *Irwin–Hall distributions* $U_n(t), \forall t \in [0, n+1]$ of degree n describe the *probability*
density of the sum $X = \sum_{k=0}^{n} U_k$ of $n+1$ independent and identically distributed uniform 131
random variables $U_k \in [0, 1]$, which, according to the central limit theorem, asymptotically 129
converge to a (shifted and scaled) normal *Gaussian* distribution as $n \to \infty$. Similarly, the 51
probability density of their mean $\frac{X}{n+1}$ is given by the *Bates distribution* $(n+1)U_n((n+1)t), \forall t \in [0, 1]$. 131

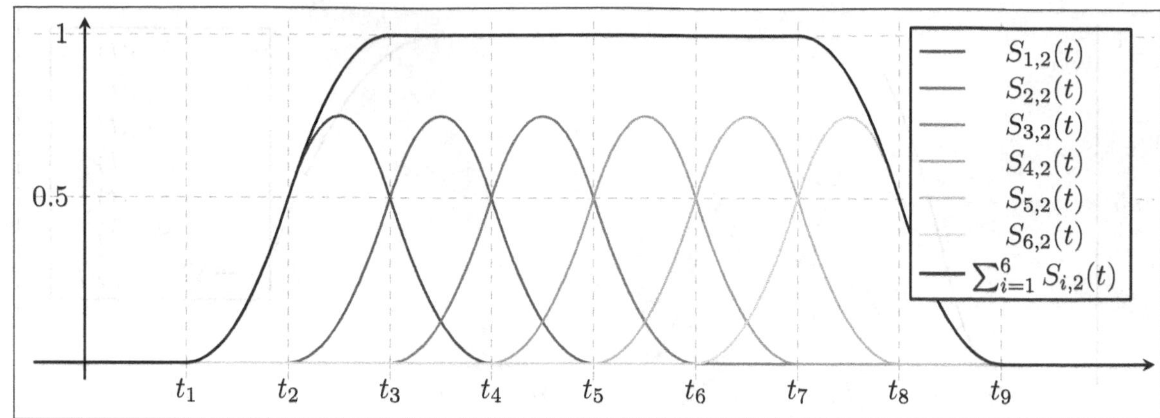

Figure 8.15: Uniform B-Spline Basis Functions: Illustration of uniform quadratic B-spline basis functions defined by an equally spaced knot vector.

The *uniform B-spline basis functions* are thus defined as

$$U_n(t) \triangleq \begin{cases} \sqcap(t - 1/2) & \text{if } n = 0 \\ \frac{t}{n} U_{n-1}(t) + \frac{n+1-t}{n} U_{n-1}(t-1) & \text{if } n > 0 \end{cases} \tag{8.110}$$

$$= \frac{1}{2^n} \sum_{k=0}^{n+1} \binom{n+1}{k} U_n(2t - k) \tag{8.111}$$

$$= \frac{1}{2n!} \sum_{k=0}^{n+1} (-1)^k \operatorname{sgn}(t-k)(t-k)^n \binom{n+1}{k} \tag{8.112}$$

$$= \frac{1}{n!} \sum_{k=0}^{n} a_i(k, n+1) t^k, \quad \forall t \in [i, i+1] \tag{8.113}$$

with

$$a_i(k, n+1) \triangleq \begin{cases} \delta[n-k] & \text{if } i = 0 \\ a_{i-1}(k, n+1) + (-1)^{n+i-k} \binom{n+1}{i} \binom{n}{k} i^{n-k} & \text{if } i > 0 \end{cases} \tag{8.114}$$

336 and exhibit a local maximum at $t = \frac{n+1}{2}$, as illustrated in *Figure 8.16*.

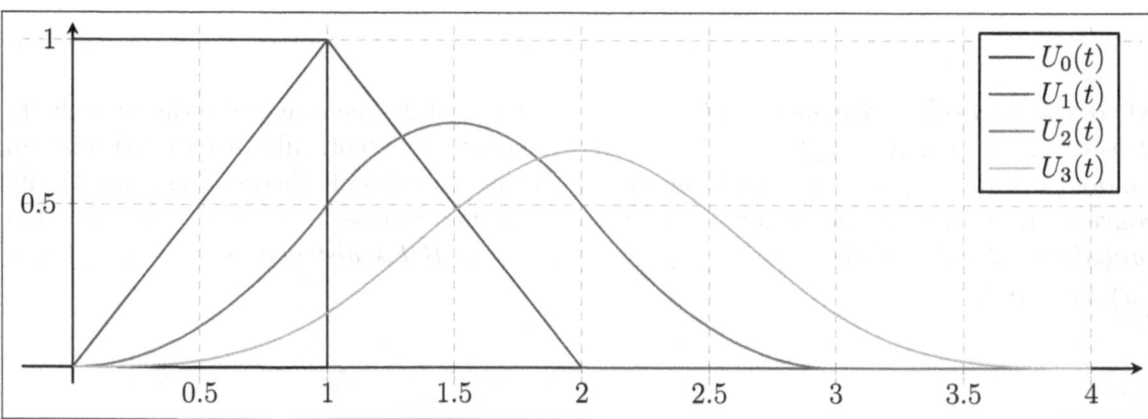

Figure 8.16: Irwin–Hall Distributions: Illustration of the uniform B-spline basis functions defined as Irwin–Hall distributions of various degrees.

The first few basis functions are then readily given as

$$U_0(t) = \frac{1}{0!}\begin{cases} 1 & \text{if } t \in [0,1] \\ 0 & \text{otherwise} \end{cases} \tag{8.115}$$

$$U_1(t) = \frac{1}{1!}\begin{cases} t & \text{if } t \in [0,1] \\ -t+2 & \text{if } t \in [1,2] \\ 0 & \text{otherwise} \end{cases} \tag{8.116}$$

$$U_2(t) = \frac{1}{2!}\begin{cases} t^2 & \text{if } t \in [0,1] \\ -2t^2+6t-3 & \text{if } t \in [1,2] \\ t^2-6t+9 & \text{if } t \in [2,3] \\ 0 & \text{otherwise} \end{cases} \tag{8.117}$$

$$U_3(t) = \frac{1}{3!}\begin{cases} t^3 & \text{if } t \in [0,1] \\ -3t^3+12t^2-12t+4 & \text{if } t \in [1,2] \\ 3t^3-24t^2+60t-44 & \text{if } t \in [2,3] \\ -t^3+12t^2-48t+64 & \text{if } t \in [3,4] \\ 0 & \text{otherwise} \end{cases} \tag{8.118}$$

$$U_4(t) = \frac{1}{4!}\begin{cases} t^4 & \text{if } t \in [0,1] \\ -4t^4+20t^3-30t^2+20t-5 & \text{if } t \in [1,2] \\ 6t^4-60t^3+210t^2-300t+155 & \text{if } t \in [2,3] \\ -4t^4+60t^3-330t^2+780t-655 & \text{if } t \in [3,4] \\ t^4-20t^3+150t^2-500t+625 & \text{if } t \in [4,5] \\ 0 & \text{otherwise} \end{cases} \tag{8.119}$$

while the shifted instances of the quadratic and cubic basis functions read

$$U_2(t-i) \overset{(8.117)}{=} \frac{1}{2}\begin{cases} t^2-2it+i^2 & \text{if } t \in [i+0,i+1] \\ -2t^2+(4i+6)t-(2i^2+6i+3) & \text{if } t \in [i+1,i+2] \\ t^2-(2i+6)t+(i^2+6i+9) & \text{if } t \in [i+2,i+3] \\ 0 & \text{otherwise} \end{cases} \tag{8.120}$$ 337

$$U_3(t-i) \overset{(8.118)}{=} \frac{1}{6}\begin{cases} t^3-3it^2+3i^2t-i^3 & \text{if } t \in [i+0,i+1] \\ \begin{aligned}-3t^3&+(9i+12)t^2-(9i^2+24i+12)t \\ &+(3i^3+12i^2+12i+4)\end{aligned} & \text{if } t \in [i+1,i+2] \\ \begin{aligned}3t^3&-(9i+24)t^2+(9i^2+48i+60)t \\ &-(3i^3+24i^2+60i+44)\end{aligned} & \text{if } t \in [i+2,i+3] \\ \begin{aligned}-t^3&+(3i+12)t^2-(3i^2+24i+48)t \\ &+(i^3+12i^2+48i+64)\end{aligned} & \text{if } t \in [i+3,i+4] \\ 0 & \text{otherwise} \end{cases} \tag{8.121}$$ 337

8.3.1.2 B-Spline Polynomial

General Case Given a knot vector $[t_{k-n}, \ldots, t_{k+m}]$ and m coefficients c_i, a basis spline polynomial, commonly referred to as *B-spline polynomial*, of degree n is defined as a linear combination of *B-spline basis functions* of degree n, or conversely as a convex combination 333 of the coefficients whenever $t \in [t_k, t_{k-n+m}]$

$$S_n(t) \triangleq \sum_{i=k-n}^{k-n+m-1} c_i S_{i,n}(t) = \sum_{i=k-n}^{k-n+m-1} \begin{cases} c_i S_{i,n}(t) & \text{if } t \in [t_i, t_{i+n+1}] \\ 0 & \text{otherwise} \end{cases} \tag{8.122}$$

Solely considering the basis functions spanning a given knot interval $\forall t \in [t_k, t_{k+1}]$ such that $m = n + 1$, a B-spline polynomial may alternatively be expressed in terms of basis functions of lower degree $\forall n > 0$

338

$$S_n(t) \overset{(8.122)}{=} \sum_{i=k-n}^{k} c_i S_{i,n}(t) \tag{8.123}$$

334

$$\begin{aligned} &\overset{(8.103)}{=} \sum_{i=k-n}^{k} c_i \left(\frac{t - t_i}{t_{i+n} - t_i} S_{i,n-1}(t) + \frac{t_{i+n+1} - t}{t_{i+n+1} - t_{i+1}} S_{i+1,n-1}(t) \right) \\ &= \sum_{i=k-n+1}^{k} c_i \frac{t - t_i}{t_{i+n} - t_i} S_{i,n-1}(t) + \sum_{i=k-n}^{k-1} c_i \frac{t_{i+n+1} - t}{t_{i+n+1} - t_{i+1}} S_{i+1,n-1}(t) \\ &= \sum_{i=k-n+1}^{k} \frac{c_i(t - t_i) + c_{i-1}(t_{i+n} - t)}{t_{i+n} - t_i} S_{i,n-1}(t) \end{aligned} \tag{8.124}$$

which can be recursively evaluated in a more numerically stable fashion by means of a generalization of de Casteljau's algorithm known as *de Boor's algorithm* (named after General Motors's mathematician Carl de Boor)

338

$$S_n(t) \overset{(8.122)}{=} \sum_{i=k-n}^{k} c_{i,n}(t) S_{i,n}(t)$$

338

$$\begin{aligned} &\overset{(8.124)}{=} \sum_{i=k-n+1}^{k} c_{i,n-1}(t) S_{i,n-1}(t) \\ &= \dots \\ &= \sum_{i=k-0}^{k} c_{i,0}(t) S_{i,0}(t) \\ &= c_{k,0}(t) \end{aligned} \tag{8.125}$$

whose coefficients

$$c_{i,j}(t) \triangleq \begin{cases} c_i & \text{if } j = n \\ \frac{c_{i,j+1}(t)(t - t_i) + c_{i-1,j+1}(t)(t_{i+j+1} - t)}{t_{i+j+1} - t_i} & \text{if } j < n \end{cases} \tag{8.126}$$

may be computed successively on each level of the tree from the leaves to the root

$$\begin{array}{ccccc} c_{k-n} = c_{k-n,n}(t) & & & & \\ & c_{k-n+1,n-1}(t) & & & \\ c_{k-n+1} = c_{k-n+1,n}(t) & & c_{k-n+2,n-2}(t) & & \\ \vdots & \vdots & \vdots & \ddots & \\ c_{k-n+i} = c_{k-n+i,n}(t) & & c_{k-n+i+1,n-2}(t) & & \\ & c_{k-n+i+1,n-1}(t) & & \dots & c_{k,0}(t) \\ c_{k-n+i+1} = c_{k-n+i+1,n}(t) & & c_{k-n+i+2,n-2}(t) & & \\ \vdots & \vdots & \vdots & \cdot^{\cdot^{\cdot}} & \\ c_{k-1} = c_{k-1,n}(t) & & c_{k,n-2}(t) & & \\ & c_{k,n-1}(t) & & & \\ c_k = c_{k,n}(t) & & & & \end{array} \tag{8.127}$$

The derivative of a B-spline polynomial is then readily given as

$$\begin{aligned} S_n'(t) &\overset{(8.123)}{=} \sum_{i=k-n}^{k} c_i S_{i,n}'(t) \\ &\overset{(8.107)}{=} n \sum_{i=k-n}^{k} c_i \left(\frac{S_{i,n-1}(t)}{t_{i+n} - t_i} - \frac{S_{i+1,n-1}(t)}{t_{i+n+1} - t_{i+1}} \right) \\ &= n \left(\sum_{i=k-n+1}^{k} c_i \frac{S_{i,n-1}(t)}{t_{i+n} - t_i} - \sum_{i=k-n}^{k-1} c_i \frac{S_{i+1,n-1}(t)}{t_{i+n+1} - t_{i+1}} \right) \\ &= n \sum_{i=k-n+1}^{k} \frac{c_i - c_{i-1}}{t_{i+n} - t_i} S_{i,n-1}(t) \end{aligned} \tag{8.128}$$ 338 334

Uniform Case Given a knot interval $\forall t \in [k, k+1]$ and $n+1$ coefficients c_i, a *uniform B-spline polynomial* of degree n is defined as a linear combination of uniform *B-spline basis functions* of degree n, or conversely as a convex combination of the coefficients whenever 333
$t \in [t_k, t_{k+1}]$, which may be expressed in matrix form as

$$S_n(t) \overset{(8.123)}{=} \sum_{i=k-n}^{k} c_i U_n(t-i) = \begin{bmatrix} U_n(t-k+n) \\ \vdots \\ U_n(t-k+1) \\ U_n(t-k) \end{bmatrix}^T \begin{bmatrix} c_{k-n} \\ \vdots \\ c_{k-1} \\ c_k \end{bmatrix} = \begin{bmatrix} 1 \\ t \\ \vdots \\ t^n \end{bmatrix}^T S_n \begin{bmatrix} c_{k-n} \\ \vdots \\ c_{k-1} \\ c_k \end{bmatrix} \tag{8.129}$$ 338

where the second- and third-order matrices read

$$S_2 \overset{(8.120)}{=} \frac{1}{2} \begin{bmatrix} k^2+4k+1 & -2k^2-2k+1 & k^2 \\ -2k-2 & 4k+2 & -2k \\ 1 & -2 & 1 \end{bmatrix} \tag{8.130}$$ 337

$$S_3 \overset{(8.121)}{=} \frac{1}{6} \begin{bmatrix} k^3+3k^2+3k+1 & -3k^3-6k^2+96k+4 & 3k^3+3k^2-3k+1 & -k^3 \\ -3k^2-6k-3 & 9k^2-24k & -9k^2-6k+3 & 3k^2 \\ 3k+3 & -9k-6 & 9k+3 & -3k \\ -1 & 3 & -3 & 1 \end{bmatrix} \tag{8.131}$$ 337

8.3.1.3 Subdivision

A *B-spline polynomial* may be subdivided into two *B-spline polynomials*, which, when the 337 337
knot vector is uniform, can be readily expressed in matrix form.

In the quadratic case, the linear change of variable reads

$$\begin{aligned} S_2(o+dt) &\overset{(8.129)}{=} \begin{bmatrix} 1 \\ o+dt \\ (o+dt)^2 \end{bmatrix}^T S_2 \begin{bmatrix} c_{k-2} \\ c_{k-1} \\ c_k \end{bmatrix} \\ &= \begin{bmatrix} 1 \\ t \\ t^2 \end{bmatrix}^T \begin{bmatrix} 1 & o & o^2 \\ 0 & d & 2od \\ 0 & 0 & d^2 \end{bmatrix} S_2 \begin{bmatrix} c_{k-2} \\ c_{k-1} \\ c_k \end{bmatrix} \\ &= \begin{bmatrix} 1 \\ t \\ t^2 \end{bmatrix}^T S_2 S_{[o,o+d]} \begin{bmatrix} c_{k-2} \\ c_{k-1} \\ c_k \end{bmatrix} \end{aligned} \tag{8.132}$$ 339

where

$$S_{[o,o+d]} \triangleq S_2^{-1} \begin{bmatrix} 1 & o & o^2 \\ 0 & d & 2od \\ 0 & 0 & d^2 \end{bmatrix} S_2 \tag{8.133}$$

337 For $k = 0$, the coefficients of the first half of the quadratic *B-spline polynomial* are then readily given as

339

$$S_2\left(\frac{t}{2}\right) \overset{(8.132)}{=} \begin{bmatrix} 1 \\ t \\ t^2 \end{bmatrix}^T S_2 S_{[0,\frac{1}{2}]} \begin{bmatrix} c_{-2} \\ c_{-1} \\ c_0 \end{bmatrix} = \begin{bmatrix} 1 \\ t \\ t^2 \end{bmatrix}^T S_2 \frac{1}{4} \begin{bmatrix} 3c_{-2} + c_{-1} \\ c_{-2} + 3c_{-1} \\ 3c_{-1} + c_0 \end{bmatrix} \tag{8.134}$$

where

340
339

$$S_{[0,\frac{1}{2}]} \overset{(8.133)}{=} S_2^{-1} \begin{bmatrix} 1 & 0 & 0 \\ 0 & \frac{1}{2} & 0 \\ 0 & 0 & \frac{1}{4} \end{bmatrix} S_2 \overset{(8.130)}{=} \frac{1}{4} \begin{bmatrix} 3 & 1 & 0 \\ 1 & 3 & 0 \\ 0 & 3 & 1 \end{bmatrix} \tag{8.135}$$

while those of the second half read

339

$$S_2\left(\frac{1+t}{2}\right) \overset{(8.132)}{=} \begin{bmatrix} 1 \\ t \\ t^2 \end{bmatrix}^T S_2 S_{[\frac{1}{2},1]} \begin{bmatrix} c_{-2} \\ c_{-1} \\ c_0 \end{bmatrix} = \begin{bmatrix} 1 \\ t \\ t^2 \end{bmatrix}^T S_2 \frac{1}{4} \begin{bmatrix} c_{-2} + 3c_{-1} \\ 3c_{-1} + c_0 \\ c_{-1} + 3c_0 \end{bmatrix} \tag{8.136}$$

where

340
339

$$S_{[\frac{1}{2},1]} \overset{(8.133)}{=} S_2^{-1} \begin{bmatrix} 1 & \frac{1}{2} & \frac{1}{4} \\ 0 & \frac{1}{2} & \frac{2}{4} \\ 0 & 0 & \frac{1}{4} \end{bmatrix} S_2 \overset{(8.130)}{=} \frac{1}{4} \begin{bmatrix} 1 & 3 & 0 \\ 0 & 3 & 1 \\ 0 & 1 & 3 \end{bmatrix} \tag{8.137}$$

which can be both combined into

$$S_{[0,\frac{1}{2},1]} \begin{bmatrix} c_{-2} \\ c_{-1} \\ c_0 \end{bmatrix} \triangleq \frac{1}{4} \begin{bmatrix} 3 & 1 & 0 \\ 1 & 3 & 0 \\ 0 & 3 & 1 \\ 0 & 1 & 3 \end{bmatrix} \begin{bmatrix} c_{-2} \\ c_{-1} \\ c_0 \end{bmatrix} = \frac{1}{4} \begin{bmatrix} 3c_{-2} + c_{-1} \\ c_{-2} + 3c_{-1} \\ 3c_{-1} + c_0 \\ c_{-1} + 3c_0 \end{bmatrix} \tag{8.138}$$

In the cubic case, the linear change of variable similarly reads

339

$$\begin{aligned} S_3(o + dt) &\overset{(8.129)}{=} \begin{bmatrix} 1 \\ o + dt \\ (o+dt)^2 \\ (o+dt)^3 \end{bmatrix}^T S_3 \begin{bmatrix} c_{k-3} \\ c_{k-2} \\ c_{k-1} \\ c_k \end{bmatrix} \\ &= \begin{bmatrix} 1 \\ t \\ t^2 \\ t^3 \end{bmatrix}^T \begin{bmatrix} 1 & o & o^2 & o^3 \\ 0 & d & 2od & 3o^2d \\ 0 & 0 & d^2 & 3od^2 \\ 0 & 0 & 0 & d^3 \end{bmatrix} S_3 \begin{bmatrix} c_{k-3} \\ c_{k-2} \\ c_{k-1} \\ c_k \end{bmatrix} \\ &= \begin{bmatrix} 1 \\ t \\ t^2 \\ t^3 \end{bmatrix}^T S_3 S_{[o,o+d]} \begin{bmatrix} c_{k-3} \\ c_{k-2} \\ c_{k-1} \\ c_k \end{bmatrix} \end{aligned} \tag{8.139}$$

where

$$S_{[o,o+d]} \triangleq S_3^{-1} \begin{bmatrix} 1 & o & o^2 & o^3 \\ 0 & d & 2od & 3o^2d \\ 0 & 0 & d^2 & 3od^2 \\ 0 & 0 & 0 & d^3 \end{bmatrix} S_3 \tag{8.140}$$

For $k = 0$, the coefficients of the first half of the cubic *B-spline polynomial* are then readily given as 337

$$S_3\left(\frac{t}{2}\right) \overset{(8.139)}{=} \begin{bmatrix}1\\t\\t^2\\t^3\end{bmatrix}^T S_3 S_{[0,\frac{1}{2}]} \begin{bmatrix}c_{-3}\\c_{-2}\\c_{-1}\\c_0\end{bmatrix} = \begin{bmatrix}1\\t\\t^2\\t^3\end{bmatrix}^T S_3 \frac{1}{8} \begin{bmatrix}4c_{-3}+4c_{-2}\\c_{-3}+6c_{-2}+c_{-1}\\4c_{-2}+4c_{-1}\\c_{-2}+6c_{-1}+c_0\end{bmatrix} \tag{8.141}$$ 340

where

$$S_{[0,\frac{1}{2}]} \overset{(8.140)}{=} S_3^{-1} \begin{bmatrix}1 & 0 & 0 & 0\\0 & \frac{1}{2} & 0 & 0\\0 & 0 & \frac{1}{4} & 0\\0 & 0 & 0 & \frac{1}{8}\end{bmatrix} S_3 \overset{(8.131)}{=} \frac{1}{8}\begin{bmatrix}4 & 4 & 0 & 0\\1 & 6 & 1 & 0\\0 & 4 & 4 & 0\\0 & 1 & 6 & 1\end{bmatrix} \tag{8.142}$$ 340 339

while those of the second half read

$$S_3\left(\frac{1+t}{2}\right) \overset{(8.139)}{=} \begin{bmatrix}1\\t\\t^2\\t^3\end{bmatrix}^T S_3 S_{[\frac{1}{2},1]} \begin{bmatrix}c_{-3}\\c_{-2}\\c_{-1}\\c_0\end{bmatrix} = \begin{bmatrix}1\\t\\t^2\\t^3\end{bmatrix}^T S_3 \frac{1}{8} \begin{bmatrix}c_{-3}+6c_{-2}+c_{-1}\\4c_{-2}+4c_{-1}\\c_{-2}+6c_{-1}+c_0\\4c_{-1}+4c_0\end{bmatrix} \tag{8.143}$$ 340

where

$$S_{[\frac{1}{2},1]} \overset{(8.140)}{=} S_3^{-1} \begin{bmatrix}1 & \frac{1}{2} & \frac{1}{4} & \frac{1}{8}\\0 & \frac{1}{2} & \frac{2}{4} & \frac{3}{8}\\0 & 0 & \frac{1}{4} & \frac{3}{8}\\0 & 0 & 0 & \frac{1}{8}\end{bmatrix} S_3 \overset{(8.131)}{=} \frac{1}{8}\begin{bmatrix}1 & 6 & 1 & 0\\0 & 4 & 4 & 0\\0 & 1 & 6 & 1\\0 & 0 & 4 & 4\end{bmatrix} \tag{8.144}$$ 340 339

which can be both combined into

$$S_{[0,\frac{1}{2},1]} \begin{bmatrix}c_{-3}\\c_{-2}\\c_{-1}\\c_0\end{bmatrix} \triangleq \frac{1}{8}\begin{bmatrix}4 & 4 & 0 & 0\\1 & 6 & 1 & 0\\0 & 4 & 4 & 0\\0 & 1 & 6 & 1\\0 & 0 & 4 & 4\end{bmatrix} \begin{bmatrix}c_{-3}\\c_{-2}\\c_{-1}\\c_0\end{bmatrix} = \frac{1}{8}\begin{bmatrix}4c_{-3}+4c_{-2}\\c_{-3}+6c_{-2}+c_{-1}\\4c_{-2}+4c_{-1}\\c_{-2}+6c_{-1}+c_0\\4c_{-1}+4c_0\end{bmatrix} \tag{8.145}$$

8.3.2 B-Spline Curve

B-spline curves are affine invariant, and their *affine transformation* therefore corresponds to the curve defined by the transform of their control points. 115

8.3.2.1 Non-Rational B-Spline Curve

Given a knot vector $[t_{k-n}, \ldots, t_{k+m}]$ and m control points $\vec{p}_i = [x_i, y_i, z_i]^T$, a *non-rational B-spline curve* of degree n is defined as a parametric combination of *B-spline polynomials* of degree n, or conversely as a convex combination of the control points whenever $t \in [t_k, t_{k-n+m}]$ 337

$$\vec{p}(t) \triangleq \begin{bmatrix}\sum_{i=k-n}^{k-n+m-1} x_i S_{i,n}(t)\\ \sum_{i=k-n}^{k-n+m-1} y_i S_{i,n}(t)\\ \sum_{i=k-n}^{k-n+m-1} z_i S_{i,n}(t)\end{bmatrix} = \sum_{i=k-n}^{k-n+m-1} \vec{p}_i S_{i,n}(t) = \sum_{i=k-n}^{k-n+m-1} \begin{cases}\vec{p}_i S_{i,n}(t) & \text{if } t \in [t_i, t_{i+n+1}]\\ 0 & \text{otherwise}\end{cases} \tag{8.146}$$

As illustrated in *Figure 8.17*, B-spline curves of degree n exhibit C_{n-1}-continuity at the 342
knots if the latter are distinct. In contrast, the continuity of a *spline* formed by juxtaposed 314
B-spline curves depends on whether the successive endpoints coincide and on the collinearity of the curves' tangents at those points.

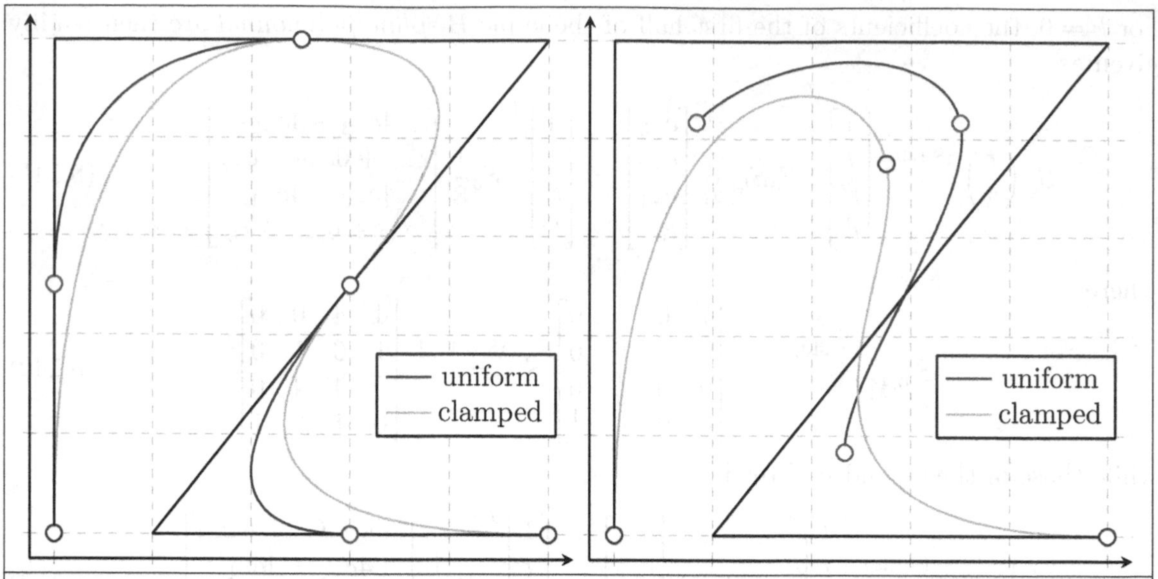

Figure 8.17: B-Spline Curve: Illustration of quadratic (left) and cubic (right) B-spline curves defined by a uniform and clamped uniform knot vector.

8.3.2.2 Rational B-Spline Curve

Given a knot vector $[t_{k-n}, \ldots, t_{k+m}]$ and m control points $\vec{p}_i$ and weights w_i, a *non-uniform rational B-spline curve*, commonly referred to as *NURBS curve*, of degree n is defined as a
337 weighted parametric combination of *B-spline polynomials* of degree n, or conversely as an
affine combination of the control points

$$\vec{p}(t) \triangleq \frac{\sum_{i=k-n}^{k-n+m-1} \vec{p}_i w_i S_{i,n}(t)}{\sum_{i=k-n}^{k-n+m-1} w_i S_{i,n}(t)} = \sum_{i=k-n}^{k-n+m-1} \vec{p}_i N_{i,n}(t) \tag{8.147}$$

where the *NURBS basis functions*

$$N_{i,n}(t) \triangleq \frac{w_i S_{i,n}(t)}{\sum_{j=k-n}^{k-n+m-1} w_j S_{j,n}(t)} \tag{8.148}$$

form a partition of unity

342 $$\sum_{i=k-n}^{k-n+m-1} N_{i,n}(t) \overset{(8.148)}{=} \sum_{i=k-n}^{k-n+m-1} \frac{w_i S_{i,n}(t)}{\sum_{j=k-n}^{k-n+m-1} w_j S_{j,n}(t)} = \frac{\sum_{i=k-n}^{k-n+m-1} w_i S_{i,n}(t)}{\sum_{j=k-n}^{k-n+m-1} w_j S_{j,n}(t)} = 1 \tag{8.149}$$

341 By generalizing *non-rational B-spline curves*, the rational form allows the exact representation of conic sections (i.e., curves resulting from the intersection of a plane with a cone,
such as parabolas, circular and ellipsoidal arcs and hyperbolas). Instead, if $w_i = 1, \forall i \in [0, n]$,
341 the curve and its basis functions reduce to a *non-rational B-spline curve* and to the *B-spline*
333 *basis functions*, respectively, $\forall t \in [t_k, t_{k-n+m}]$.
122 From a geometric standpoint, the rational curve corresponds to the *perspective projection*
into $\mathbb{R}^3$ of a non-rational curve embedded by means of homogeneous coordinates into a four-dimensional projective space.

8.3.3 B-Spline Surface

Given a net of control points, a *B-spline surface* is defined as a generalization of *B-spline*
341 *curves* to a two-dimensional parameter space. As such, B-spline surfaces are affine invariant,

and their *affine transformation* therefore corresponds to the surface defined by the transform 115
of their control points.

8.3.3.1 Non-Rational B-Spline Patch

Given two knot vectors and a control net P with control points $\vec{p}_{i,j}$, a *B-spline patch* is defined as the tensor product of two *non-rational B-spline curves* 341

$$\vec{p}(u,v) \triangleq \sum_i \sum_j \vec{p}_{i,j} S_{i,m}(u) S_{j,n}(v) \overset{(8.146)}{=} \sum_i \left(\sum_j \vec{p}_{i,j} S_{j,n}(v) \right) S_{i,m}(u) \tag{8.150}$$ 341

Akin to uniform *non-rational B-spline curves*, *subdivision* of a uniform biquadratic 341
or bicubic B-spline patch $\vec{p}(o_u + d_u u, o_v + d_v v)$ is readily given by the control net 339
$S_{[o_u,o_u+d_u]} P S^T_{[o_v,o_v+d_v]}$.

8.3.3.2 Rational B-Spline Patch

Given two knot vectors and a control net with control points $\vec{p}_{i,j}$ and weights $w_{i,j} = w_i w_j$, a *NURBS patch* (which can exactly represent spherical sections) is defined as the tensor product of two *rational B-spline curves*, or conversely as an affine combination of the control 342
points

$$\vec{p}(u,v) \triangleq \sum_i \sum_j \vec{p}_{i,j} N_{i,j}(u,v) \overset{(8.147)}{=} \sum_j \left(\sum_i \vec{p}_{i,j} N_{i,m}(u) \right) N_{j,n}(v) \tag{8.151}$$ 342

where the *NURBS basis functions*

$$N_{i,j}(u,v) \triangleq N_{i,m}(u) N_{j,n}(v) = \frac{w_{i,j} S_{i,m}(u) S_{j,n}(v)}{\sum_p \sum_q w_{p,q} S_{p,m}(u) S_{q,n}(v)} \tag{8.152}$$

form a partition of unity

$$\sum_i \sum_j N_{i,j}(u,v) \overset{(8.152)}{=} \sum_i \sum_j \frac{w_{i,j} S_{i,m}(u) S_{j,n}(v)}{\sum_p \sum_q w_{p,q} S_{p,m}(u) S_{q,n}(v)} = \frac{\sum_i \sum_j w_{i,j} S_{i,m}(u) S_{j,n}(v)}{\sum_p \sum_q w_{p,q} S_{p,m}(u) S_{q,n}(v)} = 1 \tag{8.153}$$ 343

8.4 HERMITE SPLINE

8.4.1 Hermite Function

8.4.1.1 Hermite Basis Function

Given a set of two distinct tuples of coordinates $[0, p_0, d_0]$ and $[1, p_1, d_1]$ containing the ordinates $p_{0|1}$ and the values of the first derivatives $d_{0|1}$ at abscissa 0 and 1, respectively, *Hermite interpolation* of degree 3 may be readily carried by considering a general cubic polynomial 20
and its derivative $\forall t \in [0,1]$

$$h(t) \triangleq c_3 t^3 + c_2 t^2 + c_1 t + c_0 \tag{8.154}$$

$$h'(t) = 3c_3 t^2 + 2c_2 t + c_1 \tag{8.155}$$

satisfying

$$\begin{aligned} h(0) &= c_0 &&= p_0 \\ h'(0) &= c_1 &&= d_0 \\ h(1) &= c_3 + c_2 + c_1 + c_0 &&= p_1 \\ h'(1) &= 3c_3 + 2c_2 + c_1 &&= d_1 \end{aligned} \tag{8.156}$$

such that the monomial coefficients of higher degree read

$$\begin{aligned} c_3 + c_2 + d_0 + p_0 = p_1 \quad &\Longrightarrow \quad c_2 = p_1 - c_3 - d_0 - p_0 \\ &\qquad\quad = 3(p_1 - p_0) - (2d_0 + d_1) \qquad (8.157) \\ 3c_3 + 2(p_1 - c_3 - d_0 - p_0) + d_0 = d_1 \quad &\Longrightarrow \quad c_3 = (d_0 + d_1) - 2(p_1 - p_0) \qquad (8.158) \end{aligned}$$

Instead, expressing the constraints in matrix form equivalently yields

$$\begin{bmatrix} h(0) \\ h'(0) \\ h(1) \\ h'(1) \end{bmatrix} = \begin{bmatrix} 1 & 0 & 0 & 0 \\ 0 & 1 & 0 & 0 \\ 1 & 1 & 1 & 1 \\ 0 & 1 & 2 & 3 \end{bmatrix} \begin{bmatrix} c_0 \\ c_1 \\ c_2 \\ c_3 \end{bmatrix} = \begin{bmatrix} 1 & 0 & 0 & 0 \\ 0 & 1 & 0 & 0 \\ 1 & 1 & 1 & 1 \\ 0 & 1 & 2 & 3 \end{bmatrix} H_3 \begin{bmatrix} p_0 \\ d_0 \\ p_1 \\ d_1 \end{bmatrix} = \begin{bmatrix} p_0 \\ d_0 \\ p_1 \\ d_1 \end{bmatrix} \qquad (8.159)$$

where

$$\begin{bmatrix} c_0 \\ c_1 \\ c_2 \\ c_3 \end{bmatrix} = H_3 \begin{bmatrix} p_0 \\ d_0 \\ p_1 \\ d_1 \end{bmatrix} = \begin{bmatrix} p_0 \\ d_0 \\ 3(p_1 - p_0) - (2d_0 + d_1) \\ (d_0 + d_1) - 2(p_1 - p_0) \end{bmatrix} \qquad (8.160)$$

with

$$H_3 \triangleq \begin{bmatrix} 1 & 0 & 0 & 0 \\ 0 & 1 & 0 & 0 \\ 1 & 1 & 1 & 1 \\ 0 & 1 & 2 & 3 \end{bmatrix}^{-1} = \begin{bmatrix} 1 & 0 & 0 & 0 \\ 0 & 1 & 0 & 0 \\ -3 & -2 & 3 & -1 \\ 2 & 1 & -2 & 1 \end{bmatrix} \qquad (8.161)$$

Substituting the expression of the coefficients into the cubic polynomial then yields

$$\begin{aligned} h(t) &= ((d_0 + d_1) - 2(p_1 - p_0))t^3 + (3(p_1 - p_0) - (2d_0 + d_1))t^2 + d_0 t + p_0 \qquad (8.162) \\ &= \begin{bmatrix} 1 \\ t \\ t^2 \\ t^3 \end{bmatrix}^T \begin{bmatrix} p_0 \\ d_0 \\ 3(p_1 - p_0) - (2d_0 + d_1) \\ (d_0 + d_1) - 2(p_1 - p_0) \end{bmatrix} \\ &= \begin{bmatrix} 1 \\ t \\ t^2 \\ t^3 \end{bmatrix}^T H_3 \begin{bmatrix} p_0 \\ d_0 \\ p_1 \\ d_1 \end{bmatrix} \qquad (8.163) \\ &= \begin{bmatrix} h_{p0}(t) \\ h_{d0}(t) \\ h_{p1}(t) \\ h_{d1}(t) \end{bmatrix}^T \begin{bmatrix} p_0 \\ d_0 \\ p_1 \\ d_1 \end{bmatrix} \\ &= p_0 h_{p0}(t) + d_0 h_{d0}(t) + p_1 h_{p1}(t) + d_1 h_{d1}(t) \qquad (8.164) \end{aligned}$$

where the *Hermite basis functions* read

$$\begin{aligned} h_{p0}(t) &\triangleq 2t^3 - 3t^2 + 1 &&= (2t + 1)(t - 1)^2 \\ h_{d0}(t) &\triangleq t^3 - 2t^2 + t &&= t(t - 1)^2 \\ h_{p1}(t) &\triangleq -2t^3 + 3t^2 &&= (3 - 2t)t^2 \\ h_{d1}(t) &\triangleq t^3 - t^2 &&= (t - 1)t^2 \end{aligned} \qquad (8.165)$$

As an alternative, a unit-interval cubic Hermite spline polynomial can be equivalently
318 formulated as a *Bernstein polynomial* in terms of *Bernstein basis polynomials* as
315

$$h(t) = \begin{bmatrix} 1 \\ t \\ t^2 \\ t^3 \end{bmatrix}^T B_3 \begin{bmatrix} 1 & 0 & 0 & 0 \\ 1 & \frac{1}{3} & 0 & 0 \\ 0 & 0 & 1 & -\frac{1}{3} \\ 0 & 0 & 1 & 0 \end{bmatrix} \begin{bmatrix} p_0 \\ d_0 \\ p_1 \\ d_1 \end{bmatrix} = \begin{bmatrix} B_{0,3}(t) \\ B_{1,3}(t) \\ B_{2,3}(t) \\ B_{3,3}(t) \end{bmatrix}^T \begin{bmatrix} p_0 \\ p_0 + \frac{d_0}{3} \\ p_1 - \frac{d_1}{3} \\ p_1 \end{bmatrix} \tag{8.166}$$

with the Hermite basis functions being related to *Bernstein basis polynomials* by 315

$$h_{p0}(t) = B_{0,3}(t) + B_{1,3}(t) \tag{8.167}$$
$$h_{d0}(t) = {}^1\!/_3 B_{1,3}(t) \tag{8.168}$$
$$h_{p1}(t) = B_{2,3}(t) + B_{3,3}(t) \tag{8.169}$$
$$h_{d1}(t) = -{}^1\!/_3 B_{2,3}(t) \tag{8.170}$$

Conversely, a cubic Bernstein polynomial may be equivalently formulated as a unit-interval cubic *Hermite spline polynomial* in terms of *Hermite basis functions* as 346 343

$$B_3(t) = \begin{bmatrix} 1 \\ t \\ t^2 \\ t^3 \end{bmatrix}^T H_3 \begin{bmatrix} 1 & 0 & 0 & 0 \\ -3 & 3 & 0 & 0 \\ 0 & 0 & 0 & 1 \\ 0 & 0 & -3 & 3 \end{bmatrix} \begin{bmatrix} c_0 \\ c_1 \\ c_2 \\ c_3 \end{bmatrix} = \begin{bmatrix} h_{p0}(t) \\ h_{d0}(t) \\ h_{p1}(t) \\ h_{d1}(t) \end{bmatrix}^T \begin{bmatrix} c_0 \\ 3(c_1 - c_0) \\ c_3 \\ 3(c_3 - c_2) \end{bmatrix} \tag{8.171}$$

with the Bernstein basis polynomials being related to *Hermite basis functions* by 343

$$B_{0,3}(t) = h_{p0}(t) - 3h_{d0}(t) \tag{8.172}$$
$$B_{1,3}(t) = 3h_{d0}(t) \tag{8.173}$$
$$B_{2,3}(t) = -3h_{d1}(t) \tag{8.174}$$
$$B_{3,3}(t) = h_{p1}(t) + 3h_{d1}(t) \tag{8.175}$$

As illustrated in *Figure 8.18*, the cubic Hermite basis functions satisfy 346

$$\begin{bmatrix} h_{p0}(0) & h_{d0}(0) & h_{p1}(0) & h_{d1}(0) \\ h'_{p0}(0) & h'_{d0}(0) & h'_{p1}(0) & h'_{d1}(0) \\ h_{p0}(1) & h_{d0}(1) & h_{p1}(1) & h_{d1}(1) \\ h'_{p0}(1) & h'_{d0}(1) & h'_{p1}(1) & h'_{d1}(1) \end{bmatrix} = \begin{bmatrix} 1 & 0 & 0 & 0 \\ 0 & 1 & 0 & 0 \\ 0 & 0 & 1 & 0 \\ 0 & 0 & 0 & 1 \end{bmatrix} \tag{8.176}$$

as well as

$$h_{p1}(t) = h_{p0}(1-t) \tag{8.177}$$
$$h_{d1}(t) = -h_{d0}(1-t) \tag{8.178}$$

such that

$$h_{p0}(t) + h_{p1}(t) = h_{p0}(t) + h_{p0}(1-t) = h_{p1}(t) + h_{p1}(1-t) = 1 \tag{8.179}$$

while their definite integrals over the interval $[0, 1]$ read

$$\int_0^1 h_{p0}(t)\mathrm{d}t = \left[\frac{1}{2}t^4 - t^3 + t\right]_0^1 = \frac{1}{2} - 1 + 1 = \frac{1}{2} \tag{8.180}$$
$$\int_0^1 h_{d0}(t)\mathrm{d}t = \left[\frac{1}{4}t^4 - \frac{2}{3}t^3 + \frac{1}{2}t^2\right]_0^1 = \frac{1}{4} - \frac{2}{3} + \frac{1}{2} = \frac{1}{12} \tag{8.181}$$
$$\int_0^1 h_{p1}(t)\mathrm{d}t = \left[-\frac{1}{2}t^4 + t^3\right]_0^1 = -\frac{1}{2} + 1 = \frac{1}{2} \tag{8.182}$$
$$\int_0^1 h_{d1}(t)\mathrm{d}t = \left[\frac{1}{4}t^4 - \frac{1}{3}t^3\right]_0^1 = \frac{1}{4} - \frac{1}{3} = -\frac{1}{12} \tag{8.183}$$

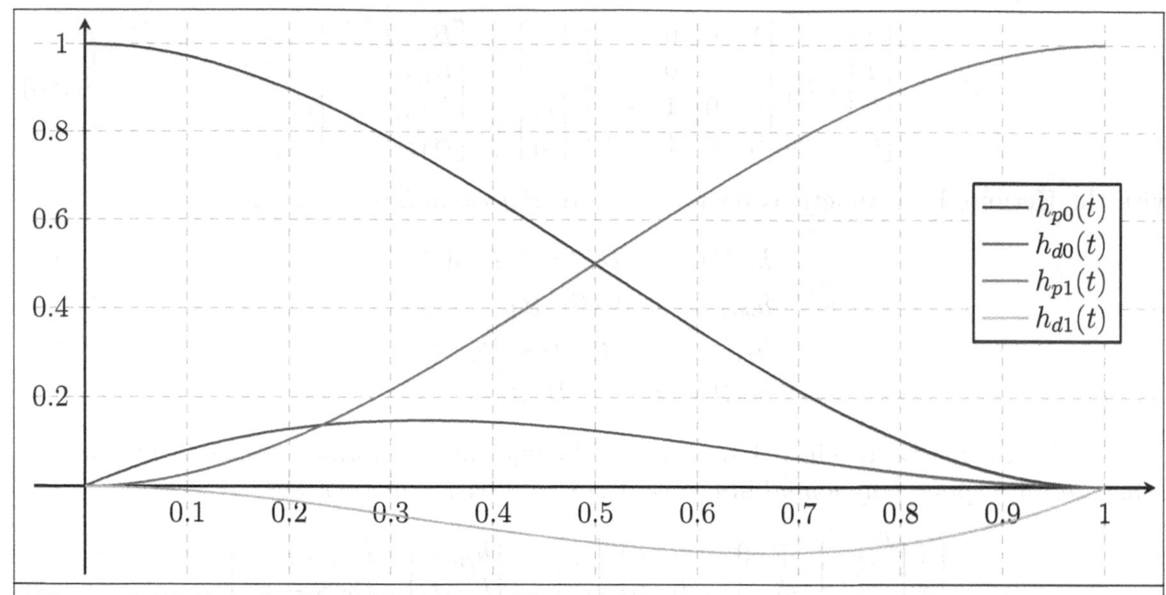

Figure 8.18: Hermite Basis Functions: Illustration of the cubic Hermite basis functions.

8.4.1.2 Hermite Spline Polynomial

Given a set of n distinct tuples of coordinates $[t_i, p_i, d_i], \forall i \in [1, n]$ containing the ordinates p_i and the values of the first derivatives d_i at abscissa t_i, a cubic *Hermite spline polynomial* is
343 defined as a juxtaposition of *Hermite basis functions* generalized to non-unit intervals $[t_i, t_{i+1}]$ by multiplying the derivative terms by the length of the intervals

$$\begin{aligned} h_i(t) &\triangleq ((t_{i+1} - t_i)(d_i + d_{i+1}) - 2(p_{i+1} - p_i))u^3 \\ &+ (3(p_{i+1} - p_i) - (t_{i+1} - t_i)(2d_i + d_{i+1}))u^2 \\ &+ (t_{i+1} - t_i)d_i u + p_i \\ &= p_i h_{p0}(u) + p_{i+1} h_{p1}(u) + (t_{i+1} - t_i)(d_i h_{d0}(u) + d_{i+1} h_{d1}(u)) \end{aligned} \tag{8.184}$$

where

$$u \triangleq \frac{t - t_i}{t_{i+1} - t_i} \tag{8.185}$$

The first and second derivatives are then given by

$$h_i'(t) = \left(3(d_i + d_{i+1}) - 6\frac{p_{i+1} - p_i}{t_{i+1} - t_i}\right)u^2 + \left(6\frac{p_{i+1} - p_i}{t_{i+1} - t_i} - (4d_i + 2d_{i+1})\right)u + d_i \tag{8.186}$$

$$h_i''(t) = \left(6\frac{d_i + d_{i+1}}{t_{i+1} - t_i} - 12\frac{p_{i+1} - p_i}{(t_{i+1} - t_i)^2}\right)u + \left(6\frac{p_{i+1} - p_i}{(t_{i+1} - t_i)^2} - \frac{4d_i + 2d_{i+1}}{t_{i+1} - t_i}\right) \tag{8.187}$$

such that $h_i'(t_i) = d_i$ and $h_i'(t_{i+1}) = d_{i+1}$, while

$$h_i''(t_i) = 6\frac{p_{i+1} - p_i}{(t_{i+1} - t_i)^2} - \frac{4d_i + 2d_{i+1}}{t_{i+1} - t_i} \tag{8.188}$$

$$h_i''(t_{i+1}) = \frac{2d_i + 4d_{i+1}}{t_{i+1} - t_i} - 6\frac{p_{i+1} - p_i}{(t_{i+1} - t_i)^2} \tag{8.189}$$

8.4.1.3 Natural Spline

347
346 As illustrated in *Figure 8.19*, a *natural spline* is defined as a *Hermite spline polynomial* that

minimizes bending akin to a mechanical *spline*. Given a set of n distinct pairs of coordinates 314
$[t_i, p_i], \forall i \in [1, n]$ containing the ordinates p_i at abscissa t_i, the first derivatives $h'_{i-1}(t_i) = h'_i(t_i) = d_i$ are intrinsically continuous and their values are thus determined so as to also ensure the continuity of the second derivatives at the junctions between successive spline segments by setting $h''_{i-1}(t_i) = h''_i(t_i), \forall i \in [2, n-1]$, which yields

$$2\frac{d_{i-1} + 2d_i}{t_i - t_{i-1}} - 6\frac{p_i - p_{i-1}}{(t_i - t_{i-1})^2} = 6\frac{p_{i+1} - p_i}{(t_{i+1} - t_i)^2} - 2\frac{2d_i + d_{i+1}}{t_{i+1} - t_i} \tag{8.190}$$

or equivalently

$$\frac{d_{i-1}}{t_i - t_{i-1}} + \left(\frac{2}{t_i - t_{i-1}} + \frac{2}{t_{i+1} - t_i}\right) d_i + \frac{d_{i+1}}{t_{i+1} - t_i} = 3\left(\frac{p_i - p_{i-1}}{(t_i - t_{i-1})^2} + \frac{p_{i+1} - p_i}{(t_{i+1} - t_i)^2}\right) \tag{8.191}$$

while causing the curvature to vanish at the endpoints by setting $h''_1(t_1) = 0$ and $h''_{n-1}(t_n) = 0$, which yields

$$\frac{2}{t_2 - t_1} d_1 + \frac{d_2}{t_2 - t_1} = 3\frac{p_2 - p_1}{(t_2 - t_1)^2} \tag{8.192}$$

$$\frac{d_{n-1}}{t_n - t_{n-1}} + \frac{2}{t_n - t_{n-1}} d_n = 3\frac{p_n - p_{n-1}}{(t_n - t_{n-1})^2} \tag{8.193}$$

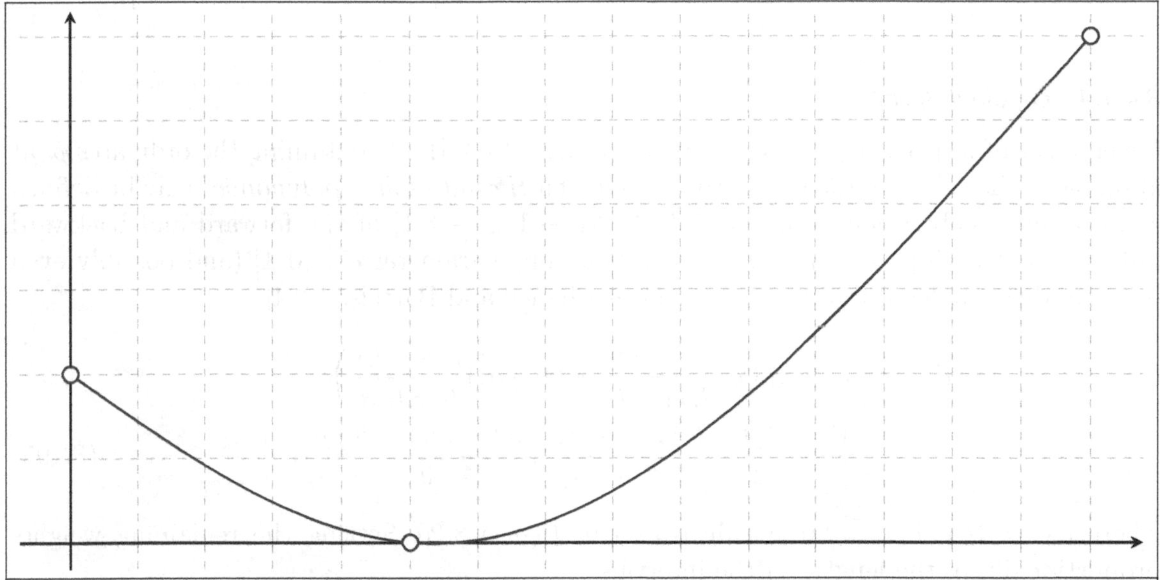

Figure 8.19: Natural Spline: Illustration of a natural spline interpolating pre-defined knots while minimizing the bending energy.

Expressing the constraints in matrix form, it then follows that the values of the first derivatives d_i are readily given as the solution of the tridiagonal system of linear equations

$$\begin{bmatrix} \frac{2}{t_2-t_1} & \frac{1}{t_2-t_1} & 0 & \cdots & \cdots & \cdots & \cdots & 0 \\ \frac{1}{t_2-t_1} & \frac{2}{t_2-t_1}+\frac{2}{t_3-t_2} & \ddots & 0 & \cdots & \cdots & \cdot^{\cdot^{\cdot}} & \vdots \\ 0 & \ddots & \ddots & \ddots & \ddots & \ddots & \vdots & \vdots \\ \vdots & 0 & \frac{1}{t_i-t_{i-1}} & \frac{2}{t_i-t_{i-1}}+\frac{2}{t_{i+1}-t_i} & \frac{1}{t_{i+1}-t_i} & & 0 & \vdots \\ \vdots & \vdots & \ddots & \ddots & \ddots & & \ddots & 0 \\ \vdots & \cdot^{\cdot^{\cdot}} & \cdots & 0 & \ddots & & \frac{2}{t_{n-1}-t_{n-2}}+\frac{2}{t_n-t_{n-1}} & \frac{1}{t_n-t_{n-1}} \\ 0 & \cdots & \cdots & \cdots & 0 & & \frac{1}{t_n-t_{n-1}} & \frac{2}{t_n-t_{n-1}} \end{bmatrix}$$

$$\times \begin{bmatrix} d_1 \\ d_2 \\ \vdots \\ d_i \\ \vdots \\ d_{n-1} \\ d_n \end{bmatrix} = 3 \begin{bmatrix} \frac{p_2-p_1}{(t_2-t_1)^2} \\ \frac{p_2-p_1}{(t_2-t_1)^2}+\frac{p_3-p_2}{(t_3-t_2)^2} \\ \vdots \\ \frac{p_i-p_{i-1}}{(t_i-t_{i-1})^2}+\frac{p_{i+1}-p_i}{(t_{i+1}-t_i)^2} \\ \vdots \\ \frac{p_{n-1}-p_{n-2}}{(t_{n-1}-t_{n-2})^2}+\frac{p_n-p_{n-1}}{(t_n-t_{n-1})^2} \\ \frac{p_n-p_{n-1}}{(t_n-t_{n-1})^2} \end{bmatrix} \tag{8.194}$$

8.4.1.4 Cardinal Spline

Given a set of n distinct pairs of coordinates $[t_i, p_i], \forall i \in [1, n]$ containing the ordinates p_i at
346 abscissa t_i, the values of the first derivatives d_i of a *Hermite spline polynomial* may be defined as an affine combination with "bias" $b_i \triangleq 2\alpha_i - 1 \in [-1, 1]$ of the forward and backward differences at each point, modulated by a "tension" parameter $c \in [0, 1]$ (and possibly even by an additional "continuity" parameter) [Kochanek and Bartels, 1984]

$$\begin{aligned} d_i &= (1-c)\left(\alpha_i \frac{p_{i+1}-p_i}{t_{i+1}-t_i} + (1-\alpha_i)\frac{p_i-p_{i-1}}{t_i-t_{i-1}}\right) \\ &= \frac{(1-c)(1+b_i)}{2}\frac{p_{i+1}-p_i}{t_{i+1}-t_i} + \frac{(1-c)(1-b_i)}{2}\frac{p_i-p_{i-1}}{t_i-t_{i-1}} \end{aligned} \tag{8.195}$$

350 where $\alpha_1 = 1$ and $\alpha_n = 0$, as illustrated in *Figure 8.20*. Setting the remaining weights proportionally to the lengths of the intervals

$$\alpha_i \triangleq \frac{t_{i+1}-t_i}{t_{i+1}-t_{i-1}}, \quad \forall i \in [2, n-1] \tag{8.196}$$

then results in the central difference scheme

$$\begin{aligned} d_i &= (1-c)\left(\frac{t_{i+1}-t_i}{t_{i+1}-t_{i-1}}\frac{p_{i+1}-p_i}{t_{i+1}-t_i} + \left(1 - \frac{t_{i+1}-t_i}{t_{i+1}-t_{i-1}}\right)\frac{p_i-p_{i-1}}{t_i-t_{i-1}}\right) \\ &= (1-c)\left(\frac{p_{i+1}-p_i}{t_{i+1}-t_{i-1}} + \frac{p_i-p_{i-1}}{t_{i+1}-t_{i-1}}\right) \\ &= (1-c)\frac{p_{i+1}-p_{i-1}}{t_{i+1}-t_{i-1}} \end{aligned} \tag{8.197}$$

yielding a so-called *cardinal spline*

346

$$\begin{aligned} h_i(t) &\overset{(8.184)}{=} p_i h_{p0}(u) + p_{i+1} h_{p1}(u) \\ &\quad + (t_{i+1} - t_i)(1-c)\left(\frac{p_{i+1} - p_{i-1}}{t_{i+1} - t_{i-1}} h_{d0}(u) + \frac{p_{i+2} - p_i}{t_{i+2} - t_i} h_{d1}(u)\right) \\ &= -p_{i-1} m_{0,i} h_{d0}(u) + p_i (h_{p0}(u) - m_{1,i} h_{d1}(u)) \\ &\quad + p_{i+1}(h_{p1}(u) + m_{0,i} h_{d0}(u)) + p_{i+2} m_{1,i} h_{d1}(u) \end{aligned} \tag{8.198}$$

where

$$m_{0,i} \triangleq (1-c)\frac{t_{i+1} - t_i}{t_{i+1} - t_{i-1}} \tag{8.199}$$

$$m_{1,i} \triangleq (1-c)\frac{t_{i+1} - t_i}{t_{i+2} - t_i} \tag{8.200}$$

and which, whenever $c = 0$, reduces to a *Catmull–Rom spline* [Catmull and Rom, 1974], while a different definition of the latter is given as

$$h_i(t) = \frac{(t_{i+1} - t)p_{i,1}(t) + (t - t_i)p_{i+1,1}(t)}{t_{i+1} - t_i} \tag{8.201}$$

whose coefficients

$$p_{i,1}(t) \triangleq \frac{(t_{i+1} - t)p_{i-1,2}(t) + (t - t_{i-1})p_{i,2}(t)}{t_{i+1} - t_{i-1}} \tag{8.202}$$

$$p_{i,2}(t) \triangleq \frac{(t_{i+1} - t)p_i + (t - t_i)p_{i+1}}{t_{i+1} - t_i} \tag{8.203}$$

may be computed successively on each level of the tree from the leaves to the root [Barry and Goldman, 1988]

$$\begin{array}{cccc} p_{i-1} & & & \\ & p_{i-1,2}(t) & & \\ p_i & & p_{i,1}(t) & \\ & p_{i,2}(t) & & h_i(t) \\ p_{i+1} & & p_{i+1,1}(t) & \\ & p_{i+1,2}(t) & & \\ p_{i+2} & & & \end{array} \tag{8.204}$$

In the case of uniformly spaced intervals, the latter coefficients become constant

$$m = -m_{0,i} = -m_{1,i} = -\frac{1-c}{2} \tag{8.205}$$

and defining the *cardinal basis functions* as

$$C_{-1}(u) \triangleq m h_{d0}(u) = mu^3 - 2mu^2 + mu \tag{8.206}$$

$$C_0(u) \triangleq h_{p0}(u) + m h_{d1}(u) = (2+m)u^3 - (3+m)u^2 + 1 \tag{8.207}$$

$$C_1(u) \triangleq h_{p1}(u) - m h_{d0}(u) = -(2+m)u^3 + (3+2m)u^2 - mu \tag{8.208}$$

$$C_2(u) \triangleq -m h_{d1}(u) = -mu^3 + mu^2 \tag{8.209}$$

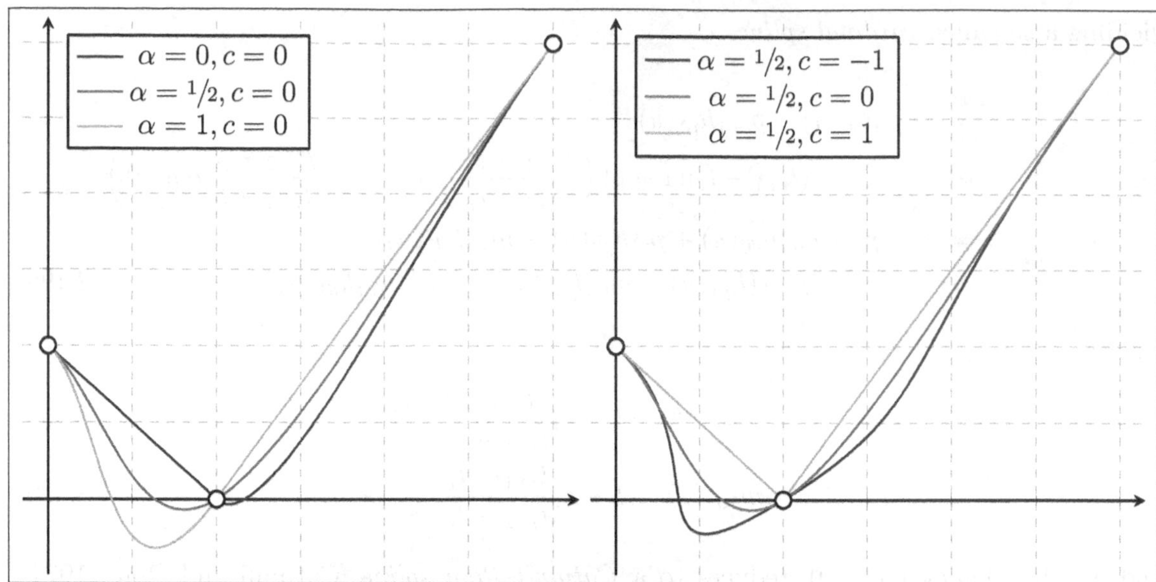

Figure 8.20: Kochanek–Bartels Spline Curve: Illustration of the impact of the bias and tension parameters on the shape of a Kochanek–Bartels spline curve.

reduces the formulation of the cardinal spline to the matrix form

$$h_i(t) = p_{i-1}C_{-1}(u) + p_iC_0(u) + p_{i+1}C_1(u) + p_{i+2}C_2(u) \tag{8.210}$$

$$= \begin{bmatrix} C_{-1}(u) \\ C_0(u) \\ C_1(u) \\ C_2(u) \end{bmatrix}^T \begin{bmatrix} p_{i-1} \\ p_i \\ p_{i+1} \\ p_{i+2} \end{bmatrix}$$

$$= \begin{bmatrix} 1 \\ u \\ u^2 \\ u^3 \end{bmatrix}^T C_3 \begin{bmatrix} p_{i-1} \\ p_i \\ p_{i+1} \\ p_{i+2} \end{bmatrix} \tag{8.211}$$

$$= \begin{bmatrix} 1 \\ u \\ u^2 \\ u^3 \end{bmatrix}^T \begin{bmatrix} p_i \\ m(p_{i-1} - p_{i+1}) \\ m(p_{i+2} - 2p_{i-1}) - (3+m)p_i + (3+2m)p_{i+1} \\ m(p_{i-1} - p_{i+2}) + (2+m)(p_i - p_{i+1}) \end{bmatrix} \tag{8.212}$$

with

$$C_3 \triangleq \begin{bmatrix} 0 & 1 & 0 & 0 \\ m & 0 & -m & 0 \\ -2m & -(3+m) & 3+2m & m \\ m & 2+m & -(2+m) & -m \end{bmatrix} \tag{8.213}$$

which, in the specific case of a Catmull–Rom spline where $c = 0$ or $m = -1/2$, becomes

$$C_3 = \frac{1}{2} \begin{bmatrix} 0 & 2 & 0 & 0 \\ -1 & 0 & 1 & 0 \\ 2 & -5 & 4 & -1 \\ -1 & 3 & -3 & 1 \end{bmatrix} \tag{8.214}$$

As an alternative, a uniform cardinal spline may be equivalently formulated as a *Hermite*
346 *spline polynomial* in terms of *Hermite basis functions* as
343

$$h_i(t) = \begin{bmatrix} 1 \\ u \\ u^2 \\ u^3 \end{bmatrix}^T H_3 \begin{bmatrix} 0 & 1 & 0 & 0 \\ m & 0 & -m & 0 \\ 0 & 0 & 1 & 0 \\ 0 & m & 0 & -m \end{bmatrix} \begin{bmatrix} p_{i-1} \\ p_i \\ p_{i+1} \\ p_{i+2} \end{bmatrix} = \begin{bmatrix} h_{p0}(u) \\ h_{d0}(u) \\ h_{p1}(u) \\ h_{d1}(u) \end{bmatrix}^T \begin{bmatrix} p_i \\ -m(p_{i+1} - p_{i-1}) \\ p_{i+1} \\ -m(p_{i+2} - p_i) \end{bmatrix} \tag{8.215}$$

or as a *Bernstein polynomial* in terms of *Bernstein basis polynomials* as 318 315

$$h_i(t) = \begin{bmatrix} 1 \\ u \\ u^2 \\ u^3 \end{bmatrix}^T B_3 \begin{bmatrix} 0 & 1 & 0 & 0 \\ \frac{m}{3} & 1 & -\frac{m}{3} & 0 \\ 0 & -\frac{m}{3} & 1 & \frac{m}{3} \\ 0 & 0 & 1 & 0 \end{bmatrix} \begin{bmatrix} p_{i-1} \\ p_i \\ p_{i+1} \\ p_{i+2} \end{bmatrix} = \begin{bmatrix} B_{0,3}(u) \\ B_{1,3}(u) \\ B_{2,3}(u) \\ B_{3,3}(u) \end{bmatrix}^T \begin{bmatrix} p_i \\ p_i - \frac{m}{3}(p_{i+1} - p_{i-1}) \\ p_{i+1} + \frac{m}{3}(p_{i+2} - p_i) \\ p_{i+1} \end{bmatrix} \tag{8.216}$$

8.4.2 Hermite Curve

8.4.2.1 Hermite Spline Curve

Given a set of n distinct tuples $[t_i, \vec{p}_i, \vec{d}_i], \forall i \in [1, n]$ containing the control points $\vec{p}_i$ and the tangents vectors $\vec{d}_i$ at parameters t_i as illustrated in *Figure 8.21*, a cubic *Hermite curve* is 351
defined $\forall t \in [t_i, t_{i+1}]$ as a parametric combination of cubic *Hermite spline polynomials* 346

$$\vec{p}_i(t) \triangleq \vec{p}_i h_{p0}(u) + \vec{p}_{i+1} h_{p1}(u) + (t_{i+1} - t_i)(\vec{d}_i h_{d0}(u) + \vec{d}_{i+1} h_{d1}(u)) \tag{8.217}$$

where

$$u \triangleq \frac{t - t_i}{t_{i+1} - t_i} \tag{8.218}$$

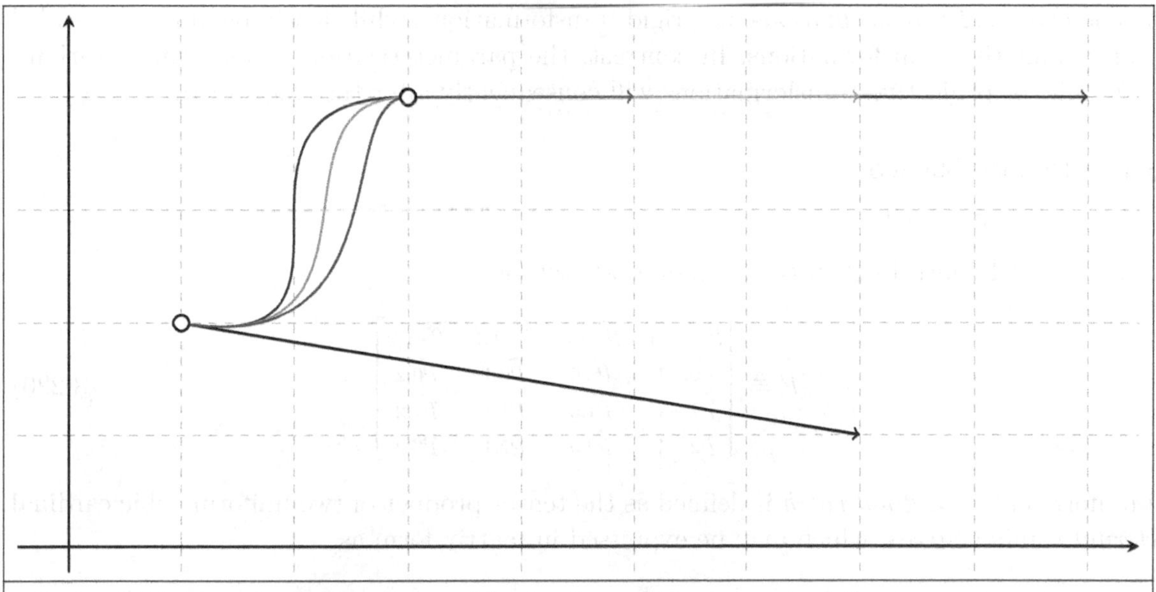

Figure 8.21: Hermite Spline Curve: Illustration of the impact of the tangent vectors on the shape of a Hermite spline curve.

Shall the parameter values t_i be unspecified, the latter may be computed from the control points as

$$t_i = \begin{cases} 0 & \text{if } i = 1 \\ t_{i-1} + \|\vec{p}_i - \vec{p}_{i-1}\|^\alpha = \sum_{j=2}^{i} \|\vec{p}_j - \vec{p}_{j-1}\|^\alpha & \text{if } i > 1 \end{cases} \tag{8.219}$$

where setting $\alpha = 0$ yields the *uniform parameterization*, while setting $\alpha = 1$ yields the

352 *chordal parameterization*, as illustrated in *Figure 8.22*. In contrast, setting $\alpha = {}^1\!/_2$ yields the so-called *centripetal parameterization*, which, in the case of a Catmull–Rom curve, is guaranteed not to exhibit cusps or loops (i.e., self-intersections in 2-D) within a parameter interval [Yuksel *et al.*, 2011].

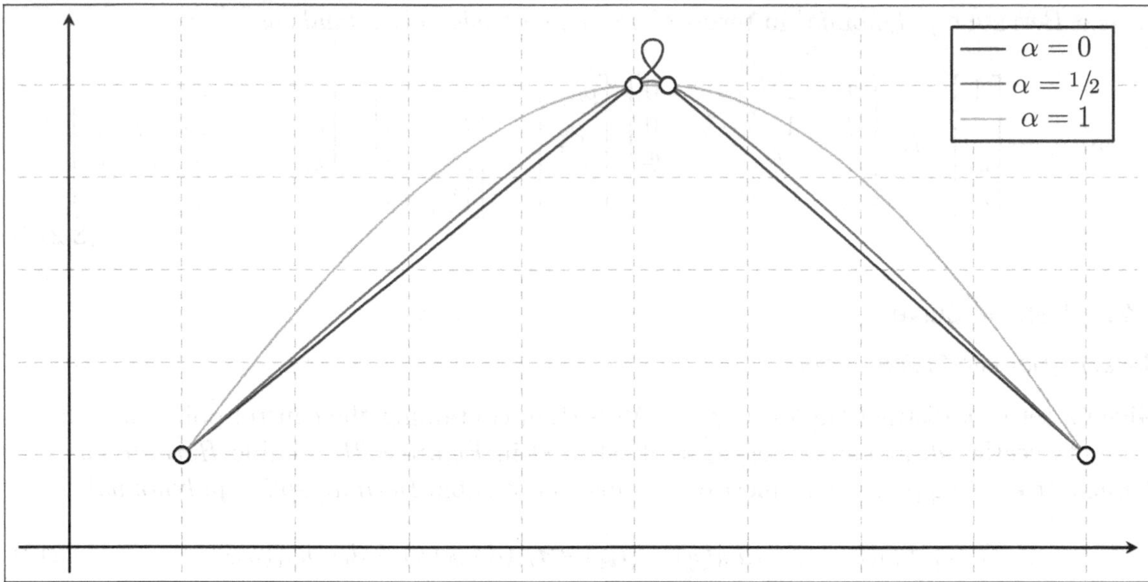

Figure 8.22: Catmull–Rom Curve Parameterization: Illustration of the uniform, chordal and centripetal parameterizations of a Catmull–Rom curve.

Due to its dependence on distance, the parameterization is strictly invariant under iso-
124 metric *classes of transformations*, i.e., rigid transformations, while it will be uniformly scaled under similarity transformations. In contrast, the parameterization is not affine invariant, and affine or projective transformations will consequently alter the shape of the curve.

8.4.3 Hermite Surface

8.4.3.1 *Cardinal Patch*

Given a 4×4 control net in the form of a 3-D tensor

$$P \triangleq \begin{bmatrix} \vec{p}_{-1,-1} & \vec{p}_{-1,0} & \vec{p}_{-1,1} & \vec{p}_{-1,2} \\ \vec{p}_{0,-1} & \vec{p}_{0,0} & \vec{p}_{0,1} & \vec{p}_{0,2} \\ \vec{p}_{1,-1} & \vec{p}_{1,0} & \vec{p}_{1,1} & \vec{p}_{1,2} \\ \vec{p}_{2,-1} & \vec{p}_{2,0} & \vec{p}_{2,1} & \vec{p}_{2,2} \end{bmatrix} \tag{8.220}$$

a uniform cubic *cardinal patch* is defined as the tensor product of two uniform cubic cardinal
351 *Hermite spline curves*, which may be expressed in matrix form as

$$\begin{aligned}
\vec{p}(u,v) &\triangleq \sum_{i=-1}^{2}\sum_{j=-1}^{2} \vec{p}_{i,j}C_i(u)C_j(v) && (8.221)\\
&= \sum_{i=-1}^{2}\left(\sum_{j=-1}^{2} \vec{p}_{i,j}C_j(v)\right)C_i(u)\\
&= \begin{bmatrix} C_{-1}(u)\\ C_0(u)\\ C_1(u)\\ C_2(u)\end{bmatrix}^T \begin{bmatrix} \sum_{j=-1}^{2}\vec{p}_{-1,j}C_j(v)\\ \sum_{j=-1}^{2}\vec{p}_{0,j}C_j(v)\\ \sum_{j=-1}^{2}\vec{p}_{1,j}C_j(v)\\ \sum_{j=-1}^{2}\vec{p}_{2,j}C_j(v)\end{bmatrix}\\
&= \begin{bmatrix} C_{-1}(u)\\ C_0(u)\\ C_1(u)\\ C_2(u)\end{bmatrix}^T P \begin{bmatrix} C_{-1}(v)\\ C_0(v)\\ C_1(v)\\ C_2(v)\end{bmatrix}\\
&\stackrel{(8.210)}{=} \begin{bmatrix} 1\\ u\\ u^2\\ u^3\end{bmatrix}^T C_3PC_3^T \begin{bmatrix} 1\\ v\\ v^2\\ v^3\end{bmatrix} && (8.222)
\end{aligned}$$

350

8.4.3.2 Bicubic Patch

A *bicubic patch* is a surface of order 6 defined as a height field $z = f(x,y)$ of the form

$$f(x,y) \triangleq \sum_{i=0}^{3}\sum_{j=0}^{3} m_{ij}x^iy^j, \quad \forall x,y \in [0,1]^2 \qquad (8.223)$$

whose partial derivatives read

$$\frac{\partial f(x,y)}{\partial x} = \sum_{i=1}^{3}\sum_{j=0}^{3} m_{ij}ix^{i-1}y^j \qquad (8.224)$$

$$\frac{\partial f(x,y)}{\partial y} = \sum_{i=0}^{3}\sum_{j=1}^{3} m_{ij}jx^iy^{j-1} \qquad (8.225)$$

$$\frac{\partial^2 f(x,y)}{\partial x\partial y} = \sum_{i=1}^{3}\sum_{j=1}^{3} m_{ij}ijx^{i-1}y^{j-1} \qquad (8.226)$$

Given the values of the height field and of its partial derivatives at the four corners of the unit square $[0,1]^2$, the coefficients may then be defined by means of the following system of linear equations

$$\begin{bmatrix}
1&0&0&0&0&0&0&0&0&0&0&0&0&0&0&0\\
1&1&1&1&0&0&0&0&0&0&0&0&0&0&0&0\\
1&0&0&0&1&0&0&0&1&0&0&0&1&0&0&0\\
1&1&1&1&1&1&1&1&1&1&1&1&1&1&1&1\\
0&1&0&0&0&0&0&0&0&0&0&0&0&0&0&0\\
0&1&2&3&0&0&0&0&0&0&0&0&0&0&0&0\\
0&1&0&0&0&1&0&0&0&1&0&0&0&1&0&0\\
0&1&2&3&0&1&2&3&0&1&2&3&0&1&2&3\\
0&0&0&0&1&0&0&0&0&0&0&0&0&0&0&0\\
0&0&0&0&1&1&1&1&0&0&0&0&0&0&0&0\\
0&0&0&0&1&0&0&0&2&0&0&0&3&0&0&0\\
0&0&0&0&1&1&1&1&2&2&2&2&3&3&3&3\\
0&0&0&0&0&1&0&0&0&0&0&0&0&0&0&0\\
0&0&0&0&0&1&2&3&0&0&0&0&0&0&0&0\\
0&0&0&0&0&1&0&0&0&2&0&0&0&3&0&0\\
0&0&0&0&0&1&2&3&0&2&4&6&0&3&6&9
\end{bmatrix}
\begin{bmatrix} m_{00}\\ m_{10}\\ m_{20}\\ m_{30}\\ m_{01}\\ m_{11}\\ m_{21}\\ m_{31}\\ m_{02}\\ m_{12}\\ m_{22}\\ m_{32}\\ m_{03}\\ m_{13}\\ m_{23}\\ m_{33} \end{bmatrix}
=
\begin{bmatrix} f(0,0)\\ f(1,0)\\ f(0,1)\\ f(1,1)\\ f_x(0,0)\\ f_x(1,0)\\ f_x(0,1)\\ f_x(1,1)\\ f_y(0,0)\\ f_y(1,0)\\ f_y(0,1)\\ f_y(1,1)\\ f_{xy}(0,0)\\ f_{xy}(1,0)\\ f_{xy}(0,1)\\ f_{xy}(1,1) \end{bmatrix}
\tag{8.227}$$

whose solution is readily given by the inverse matrix.

8.5 FURTHER READING

Additional material may be found in books dedicated to curves and surfaces for computer-aided geometric design [Farin, 1996, Farin, 2002], and spline-based geometric modeling [Cohen *et al.*, 2001].

CHAPTER 9

Indexing Structures

TABLE OF CONTENTS

9.1 OVERVIEW

Determining the closest intersection of a ray with a set of n objects is in essence a geometric range searching problem [Bentley and Friedman, 1979], just like collision detection, but more specifically concerned with determining the first, rather than all, objects from the set that intersect the given range query, i.e., the ray [Havran, 2007]. Without any a priori knowledge about the data, the search may be carried in a brute-force fashion by exhaustively evaluating the intersection (or the lack thereof) of the ray with every individual geometric entity in the set. However, the complexity of such a naive approach is $O(n)$ for n objects, therefore making the intersection test impractical for scenes comprised of a non-negligible amount of geometry.

As an alternative, the time complexity of the search can be reduced to a sub-linear cost by exploiting the spatial coherence that objects in a scene tend to exhibit [Gröller and Purgathofer, 1995], and preliminarily sorting the geometry by means of a data structure, commonly referred to as an *acceleration structure*, which may be classified based on the entity that its subdivision scheme operates on (e.g., the objects or space). Similarly to the way they allow the intersection of two objects to be quickly determined for collision detection purposes, such structures allow the ray-intersection routine to conservatively discard from the intersection test parts of the set that are a priori known not to intersect the ray (e.g., because they are far away from its trajectory), therefore providing the ray-tracing engine with some "intuition" as to which geometric entities the ray might or might not hit.

Exploiting the partial spatial sorting of the objects along the ray, the search process may be optimized further and preemptively aborted whenever an encountered intersection is guaranteed to have no other intersection point lying before it. Directing the search by testing the geometric entities in order of approximately increasing distance from the ray's origin therefore additionally allows the ray-intersection routine to conservatively discard from the intersection test parts of the set whose potential intersection point is a priori known to lie further away than other intersection points found earlier in the process.

9.2 OBJECT SUBDIVISION

An *object subdivision* scheme complementarily (i.e., in a mutually exclusive and exhaustive manner) partitions the geometric entities of a scene into a set of cells whose resulting spatial extents are mutually independent (i.e., potentially overlapping or disjoint), such that each object is referenced by exactly one cell, while a given point in space may be encompassed an arbitrary number of times. By considering all cells in turn, the ray-intersection routine can then be restricted to the entities contained within the cells whose spatial extent is found to overlap the trajectory of the ray.

Due to the fact that the spatial extent of the cells may overlap and that their sorting along the ray is therefore only partial, directing the traversal does not readily allow the search process to be anticipatively aborted upon intersection, as it is possible for an intersection point found in a cell to be farther from the ray's origin than an intersection point found in a subsequent cell. Given that an intersection is guaranteed to lie within the interval defined by the overlap between the ray and the *bounding volume*, any subsequent cell whose entry 357 point lies beyond the closest previously recorded intersection can nonetheless be readily discarded.

9.2.1 Bounding Volume

A *bounding volume* for a given (potentially compound) object is a volumetric subset of the 3-D space that contains all spatial points of the object. Any ray that does not overlap the bounding volume, which in the case of a closed volume reduces to asserting the absence of intersection between the ray and the volume's boundary, is therefore guaranteed not to intersect the object contained within, such that the latter test may be conservatively avoided. Although enclosing an object in a bounding volume might reduce the average computational cost of the ray-intersection test by a constant factor, doing so does not by itself impact the asymptotic behavior of the procedure, which remains linear in the number of objects.

Defining $\alpha \triangleq \frac{m}{n} \leq 1$ as the ratio of the number m of rays that overlap the bounding volume to the overall number n of rays to be tested for intersection, the average computational
27 cost of the intersection procedure for a single ray then becomes a generalized *linear equation* [Weghorst *et al.*, 1984]

$$C \triangleq \frac{nC_B + mC_O}{n} = C_B + \frac{m}{n}C_O = C_B + \alpha C_O \tag{9.1}$$

where C_B and C_O are the individual computational costs of the ray-intersection tests with the bounding volume and with its enclosed object, respectively. The conservative intersection procedure is therefore more efficient than a brute-force intersection with the object itself whenever the characteristics of its bounding volume are such that

$$C < C_O \iff \frac{C_B}{1-\alpha} < C_O \tag{9.2}$$

for which a necessary condition is $\alpha \neq 1$, and $C_B < C_O$ given that $C_B \leq \frac{C_B}{1-\alpha}$. For a fixed object-intersection cost C_O, minimizing C therefore requires both C_B and α to be made as small as possible.

Because simpler topologies generally entail cheaper overlap tests C_B, connexity of the bounding volume is typically made a prerequisite, and so is convexity. Together, those two requirements ensure that the potential overlap of a ray with the closed volume is restricted to a unique segment delimited on each end either by the origin of the ray or by its intersection with the volume's boundary.

On the other hand, minimizing α requires that the bounding volume tightly encompasses the contained object, which, under the assumption of convexity, is optimally achieved by its convex hull. Mathematically, given a ray whose origin is uniformly distributed in the plane
129 orthogonal to its direction, the *probability* of the bounding volume to be intersected by the ray is proportional to its projected area along the ray's direction $\hat{\omega}$, which for a convex solid reads

$$A(\hat{\omega}) \triangleq \int_S \max\{0, \langle \hat{n}_q, \hat{\omega} \rangle\} dA(\vec{q}) \tag{9.3}$$

where $\vec{q}$ is a point on the surface S of the bounding volume and $\hat{n}_q$ is the surface normal at that point. Assuming truly incoherent rays whose directions are uniformly distributed, the
129 overall *probability* of the bounding volume to be intersected by a ray is then proportional to the directional average of its projected area

$$\begin{aligned}
\frac{1}{4\pi}\int_{4\pi} A(\hat{\omega}) d\hat{\omega} &= \frac{1}{4\pi}\int_{4\pi}\int_S \max\{0, \langle \hat{n}_q, \hat{\omega} \rangle\} dA(\vec{q}) d\hat{\omega} \\
&= \frac{1}{4\pi}\int_S \int_{4\pi} \max\{0, \langle \hat{n}_q, \hat{\omega} \rangle\} d\hat{\omega} dA(\vec{q}) \\
&= \frac{1}{4\pi}\int_S \left(\int_{2\pi^-} 0 d\hat{\omega} + \int_{2\pi^+} \langle \hat{n}_q, \hat{\omega} \rangle d\hat{\omega} \right) dA(\vec{q}) \\
&= \frac{1}{4\pi}\int_S (0 + \pi) dA(\vec{q}) \\
&= \frac{S}{4}
\end{aligned} \tag{9.4}$$

which, according to *Cauchy's theorem*, states that the average projected area of a convex solid equals a fourth of its surface area.

Because complex volume boundaries parameterized by numerous degrees of freedom (including free orientation or any other *affine transformation*) generally allow for tighter object 115
bounds (although exploiting the parameterization in an optimal way might be rather non-
trivial) and vice versa, the two aforementioned requirements generally counterbalance each
other, and the optimal bounding volume is therefore the one providing the best compromise.
Nevertheless, the variety of bounding volumes conforming to the above restrictions still offers a broad range of cost/tightness trade-offs as illustrated in *Figure 9.1*. Instances include 359
various *quadrics*, ranging from cost-effective but potentially loose *spheres* [Ritter, 1990, Wu, 278
1992] to more versatile but computationally demanding ellipsoids [Bouville, 1985] and *cylin-* 269
ders (possibly capped with disks or hemispheres at each end, the latter case being commonly 272
referred to as a *capsule*). Other examples also include parallelepipeds such as axis-aligned or
oriented *cuboids* [Wu, 1992, Trumbore, 1992, Iones *et al.*, 1998] (commonly known as oriented 301
or *axis-aligned bounding boxes* (*AABB*)), and their generalization to the Boolean intersection
of oriented slabs (i.e., pairs of half-spaces) [Kay and Kajiya, 1986] to, for instance, form an
AABB (i.e., 3 slabs or 6 axis-aligned *planes*) beveled on all edges (i.e., 9 slabs or 18 planes 247
in total) as well as potentially on all corners (i.e., 13 slabs or 26 planes in total) (although
the resulting polyhedron may actually have fewer faces since some might degenerate to an
edge or a vertex), as well as arbitrary convex polyhedra (i.e., 3-D *discrete oriented polytopes*
(*DOP*)) defined by the intersection of *plane*-bounded half-spaces. Several bounding volumes 247
of the entire object may also be combined via their Boolean intersection, leading to an exit-upon-first-miss overlap test, whereas the Boolean union of bounding volumes for individual subsets of the object leads to an entry-upon-first-hit overlap test, although the latter case generally requires the aforementioned restriction on convexity to be alleviated.

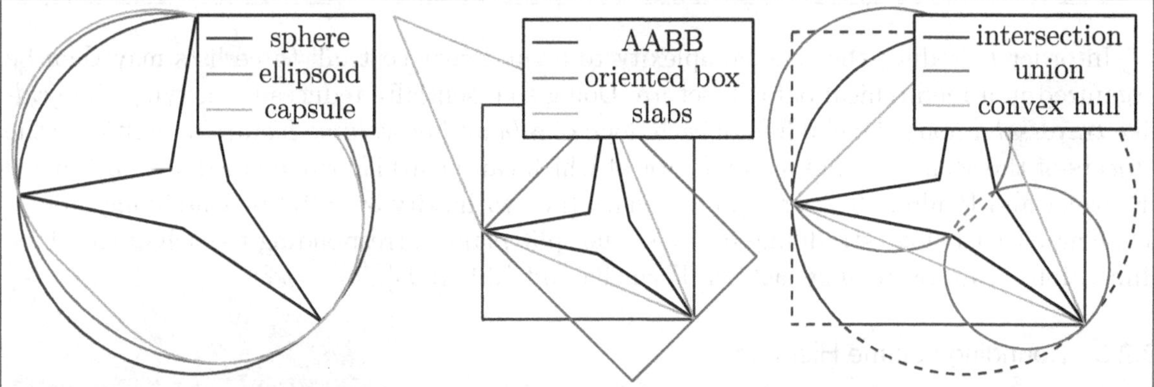

Figure 9.1: Bounding Volumes: Illustration of various bounding volumes for a given object, including a bounding sphere, a bounding ellipsoid, a bounding capsule, an axis-aligned bounding box, an oriented bounding box, the Boolean intersection of several bounding slabs, the Boolean intersection of several bounding volumes, the Boolean union of the bounding volumes for subsets of the object and the convex hull (drawn after [Arvo and Kirk, 1989, Fig. 5 and 6]).

9.2.2 Bounding Volume Grid

As illustrated in *Figure 9.2*, the order of potential intersection of a ray with a set of objects 360
may be accounted for by defining a set of 3 one-dimensional sorted lists of the minimum and maximum coordinates of their bounding boxes along each axis, thereby resulting in a

bounding volume grid (*BVG*). Traversing the structure then entails repeatedly considering the
closest parametric event simultaneously along all three dimensions (similarly to the 3-D DDA
369 373 *grid traversal*) while solely visiting an object whenever its bounds are entered in all three
dimensions before being exited in any dimension. Although the approach effectively discards
from the search procedure the bounding boxes located beyond any potential intersection
point, the asymptotic cost of the traversal remains linear since the total number of events to
consider along each axis is directly proportional to the number of objects in the scene.

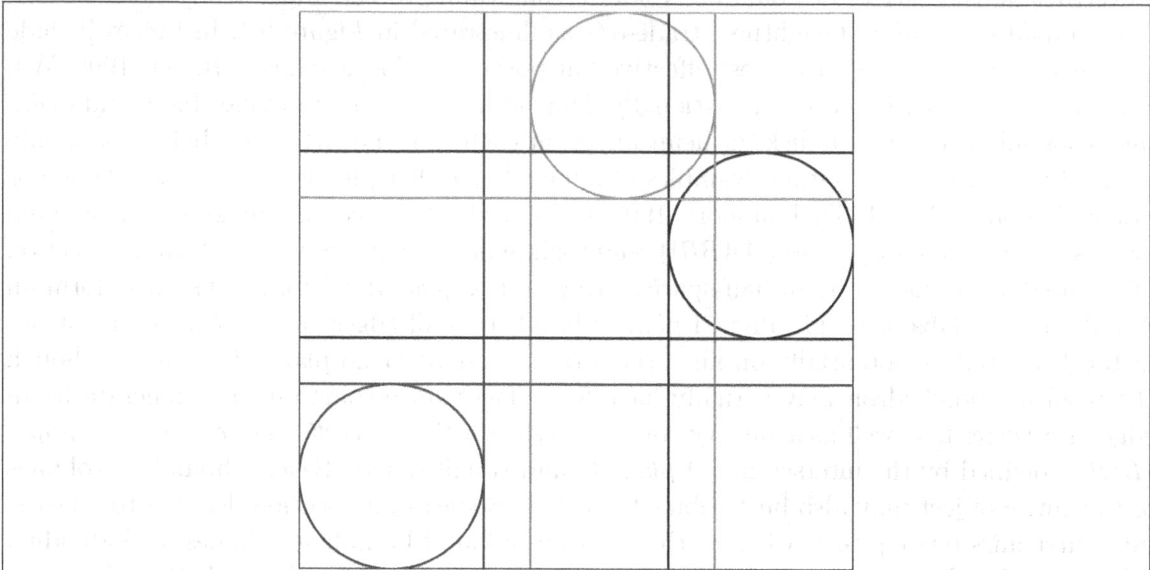

Figure 9.2: BVG Structure: Illustration of a grid of bounding volumes allowing a set of objects to be traversed in order of potential intersection along a given ray.

In order to reduce the time complexity to a sub-linear cost, all three lists may then be
369 organized in a hierarchical data structure. Doing so essentially reduces to carrying the *grid-*
373 360 *like traversal* among the children of each node of a *bounding volume hierarchy* built over the
objects of the scene, the branching factor of which can be arbitrarily defined, e.g., as binary
[Fournier and Poulin, 1993] or septenvicenary (i.e., with arity $3^3 = 27$) by classifying objects
247 as being either below, straddling or above the split *plane* corresponding to each of the three
378 dimensions in an *octree*-like fashion [Formella and Gill, 1995].

9.2.3 Bounding Volume Hierarchy

9.2.3.1 Definition

A *bounding volume hierarchy* (*BVH*, sometimes also called *hierarchy of extents*) defines a
tree structure whose leaf nodes correspond to the individual objects in the initial set (or
subsets of it if the tree is partially built), while each branch node represents a *bounding*
357 361 *volume* encompassing all of its children in a hierarchical fashion, as illustrated in *Figure 9.3*.

9.2.3.2 Construction

Whenever the relative arrangement of spatially adjacent objects (such as the joined limbs of
115 a human body for instance) is hierarchically determined via nested *affine transformations*,
the structure of the BVH tree may be readily defined as that of the corresponding scene
graph, as initially proposed in the context of rasterization [Clark, 1976a, Clark, 1976b], or
that of the CSG tree in the context of solid modeling [Roth, 1982]. Given that the previous

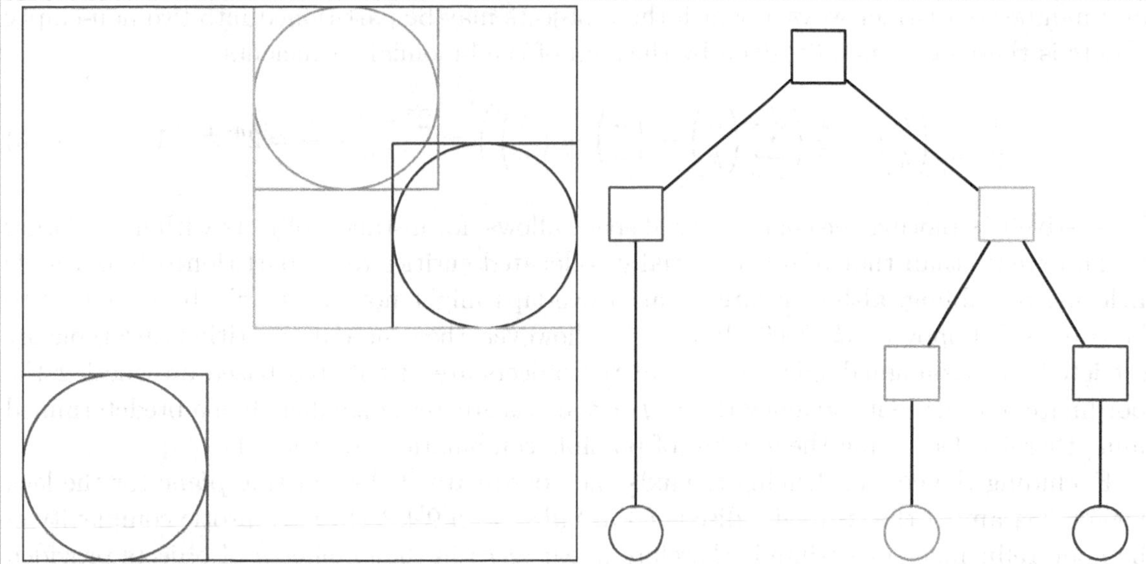

Figure 9.3: BVH Structure: Illustration of a BVH structure (formally described as a polytree, i.e., an oriented tree, as there exits exactly one path from the root to each object) recursively partitioning the set of objects referenced by each branch node into two subsets, where the nodes hold a bounding volume explicitly encompassing all respective children along all three dimensions.

structures are primarily designed for modeling purposes rather than for efficient traversal, though, early general approaches relied instead on the visual inspection of spatial proximity by the user who was then required to manually specify object clusters and to enclose them in a *bounding volume* via an interactive structure editor, successively building the individual 357 levels of the hierarchy from the leaves all the way up to the root of the tree [Rubin and Whitted, 1980].

In order to automate the construction process, each object can in turn be instead incrementally inserted in an insertion-sort fashion at the root of an initially empty structure, and trickle down the subtree that minimizes the increase in the tree's traversal cost as given in *Equation 9.29* until a leaf node is reached [Goldsmith and Salmon, 1987], although the 398 final structure of the tree is rather sensitive to the actual order of insertion of the individual objects since the higher levels of the hierarchy are solely determined by the first objects in the sequence. In an attempt to mitigate this issue, the object sequence may then be either randomly pre-shuffled (as opposed to pre-sorted along an axis) or repeatedly permuted by means of evolutionary genetic algorithms until a newly rebuilt structure with relatively low overall cost is obtained [Ng and Trifonov, 2003].

As an alternative, good quality trees are in general most effectively constructed by top-down build algorithms akin to quicksort, which recursively partition the objects into subsets progressing from the root towards the leaves, therefore putting greater emphasis on the higher levels of the tree such that entire subtrees can be pruned early during *traversal* [Wald, 2007]. 362 Competitive results may also be achieved via a bottom-up build algorithm akin to merge sort, which recursively agglomerates objects into clusters progressing from the leaves all the way up to the root, allowing the information readily available about the lower levels of the tree to more accurately guide the construction of higher levels [Walter, 2008].

As outlined in *Algorithm 9.1*, a binary BVH tree can be built via a top-down algorithm by 362 recursively partitioning the set of objects into its two children. Considering all individual set sizes k of the first partition, and then in each case all possible combinations of that size, the total number of distinct ways in which the n objects may be partitioned into two non-empty subsets is therefore generally given by the sum of the binomial coefficients

$$\frac{1}{2}\sum_{k=1}^{n-1}\binom{n}{k} = \frac{1}{2}\left(\sum_{k=0}^{n}\binom{n}{k} - \binom{n}{0} - \binom{n}{n}\right) = \frac{2^n - 1 - 1}{2} = 2^{n-1} - 1 \tag{9.5}$$

Exhaustively exploring the combinatorial space allows, for instance, objects with much larger spatial extents than that of other spatially collocated entities to be partitioned into a node enclosing its sibling, although large spatial overlaps might not necessarily be beneficial to
362 the *traversal* [Popov *et al.*, 2009]. In practice, however, the candidate partitions are typically restricted to axis-aligned splits, such that the objects are distributed based on whether the coordinate of their centroid along the x, y or z axis is greater or smaller than a predetermined value, thereby decreasing the number of possible combinations to $3(n-1)$.

247 Excluding the cost of defining the axis and coordinate of the splitting *plane* (or the lack
393 thereof) via any of the strategies discussed in *Subsection 9.4.2*, the asymptotic complexity of the node refinement procedure is therefore linear $O(n)$ in the number n of objects provided as input to the node. Starting with the original set of objects in the scene, the subsets associated with the child nodes can then be created upon branching by evaluating the side
247 of the splitting *plane* that the objects' centroid lies on, such that each object in the given set is assigned to one and only one child node. It is also common practice to approximate the centroid of the object under consideration by the center of its axis-aligned bounding box.

Algorithm 9.1: BVH Construction: Pseudocode for BVH construction.

```
Data: Set of objects S
Result: A BVH tree built over S
B ← BoundingBox(S);
[axis, coordinate] ← DefineSplit(S, B);
if axis ∈ {X, Y, Z} then
    S_l ← ∅;
    S_r ← ∅;
    foreach object o ∈ S do
        if coordinate of centroid of o along axis < coordinate then
            S_l ← S_l ∪ o;
        else
            S_r ← S_r ∪ o;
        end
    end
    Node n ← CreateInnerNode(B, BuildBVHTree(S_l), BuildBVHTree(S_r));
else
    Node n ← CreateLeafNode(B, S);
end
return n
```

9.2.3.3 Traversal

363 As illustrated in *Figure 9.4*, the tree hierarchy may be exploited during rendering in a fashion similar to its original use for visibility determination in rasterization [Clark, 1976a, Clark, 1976b], where all objects contained within a subtree are to be displayed if the associated

bounding volume is completely inside the view frustum. Conversely, all of its content is 357
anticipatively clipped if the *bounding volume* is entirely outside, while the child nodes must 357
be individually processed in case of a partial overlap.

Figure 9.4: BVH Traversal Cost: Color-coded illustration of the relative computational cost of BVH traversal for a Sierpinski tetrahedron.

Upon intersection of its *bounding volume* by a ray, which can be regarded as a degenerate 357
view frustum with a null horizontal and vertical angle of view, a BVH tree may be traversed
in a stack-less fashion by storing in each node a pointer to its left child and a pointer to
its right sibling or parent as defined by a fixed-order depth-first pattern, such that during
traversal the former is followed upon intersection with the node's *bounding volume* and the 357
latter followed otherwise [Smits, 1998, Smits, 2005]. Visiting sibling nodes in a front-to-back order can additionally be achieved by storing in each node a pointer to its parent, sibling and children, and selecting the node to follow based on the relationship of the previously processed node to the current one [Hapala *et al.*, 2011a].

In order to avoid accessing higher levels of the tree by restepping through all ancestors along the way, the BVH hierarchy may alternatively be traversed in a depth-first fashion by starting from the root of the tree and then recursively visiting the children of each branch
node shall the ray overlap the spatial extent of (none, any or all of) the latter, as outlined
in *Algorithm 9.2* for an arbitrary branching factor. The complete subtrees associated with 364
non-overlapping child nodes can then be entirely pruned, whereas in case of a leaf node the objects contained within are tested for intersection.

Exploiting the distance-based culling approach described for *object subdivision* schemes, 357
the base algorithm may be further optimized by initiating the traversal procedure with a
comparison of the *bounding volume*'s entry point against the closest intersection recorded 357
prior to visiting the given node. As illustrated in *Figure 9.5*, doing so then allows subtrees 364
entirely located beyond the latter to be anticipatively culled [Roth, 1982]. Rather than relying on a fixed predetermined ordering, this optimization can then be exploited to a greater extent by dynamically visiting the children of a given node in order of increasing distance of the entry point from the ray's origin (or approximated by the sign of the ray direction along the node's split axis [Mahovsky, 2005a]).

Algorithm 9.2: BVH Traversal: Pseudocode for BVH traversal.

```
Data: Ray r and node n
Result: Intersection found by traversing the BVH tree
Intersection i ← ∅;
if enter > prior intersections then
    Go to end;
end
if n is branch node then
    foreach node c ∈ children of n do
        if r overlaps bounding volume of c then
            i ← closest{i, TraverseBVHTree(r, c)};
        end
    end
else
    foreach object o ∈ set S_n of objects referenced by node n do
        i ← closest{i, Intersect(r, o)};
    end
end
return i
```

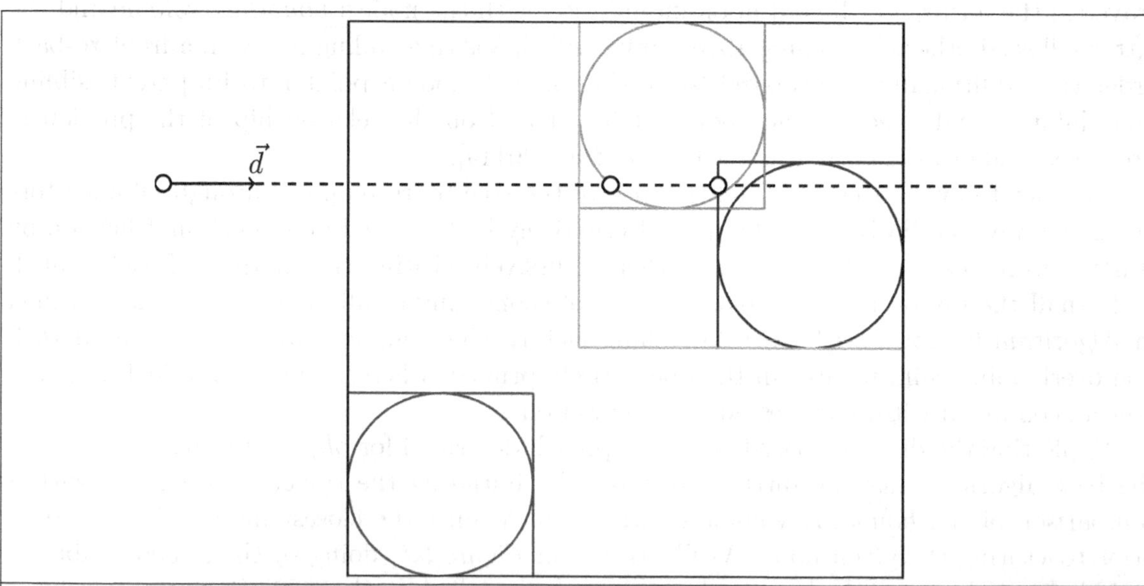

Figure 9.5: BVH Traversal: Illustration of the anticipated pruning of a BVH node and corresponding subtree whenever its associated bounding volume lies beyond an intersection point found earlier during the ray-traversal process, as is here the case if the two nodes are processed in order of increasing distance along the ray.

9.2.3.4 Storage

In addition to being flagged as a branch or as a leaf, each BVH node must also hold a
list of references to its associated objects in case of a leaf node, while a branch node ought
to store references to its children as well as the *bounding volume* of its associated subtree. 357
Recalling that a binary tree can contain up to about twice as many nodes as there are objects,
the memory requirements for a complete BVH structure, whose upper bound may then be
determined in advance, can therefore be quite substantial.

Observing that, in the case of axis-aligned bounding boxes, each of the six coordinates
of a node's bounding box is inherited by at least one of its children, the latter may together
introduce at most six new plane coordinates compared to their parent, leading not only to
redundant ray–*plane* intersection tests during *traversal* [Stürzlinger and Tobler, 1994], but 247
also to redundant data storage [Fabianowski and Dingliana, 2009]. By solely storing the 362
six new coordinates along with six binary flags indicating whether a node's coordinates are
inherited by its left or right child, both the memory footprint and the number of intersections
can be minimized, though at the cost of additional branching instructions to maintain the
active ray-interval via a BIH-like approach during *traversal* [Ernst and Woop, 2011]. 362

Aside from using larger branching factors, the memory footprint of the structure and
cache coherence may both be alternatively improved by quantizing the coordinates of the
bounding boxes, either relative to that of the root node [Cline *et al.*, 2006, Cline, 2007, Ch. 3],
or hierarchically relative to the parent of each node in order to minimize the loss of precision,
albeit at the cost of an additional dequantization overhead during *traversal* [Mahovsky, 2005b, 362
Mahovsky and Wyvill, 2006]. Compression via delta-encoding can similarly be extended to
exploit spatial coherence within clusters of nodes ordered according to a given layout (e.g.,
depth-first or cache-oblivious) as well as to the representation of the objects referenced by a
leaf node [Kim *et al.*, 2009a, Kim *et al.*, 2009b, Kim *et al.*, 2010], potentially encoding vertex
connectivity within a leaf node as *triangle* strips [Segovia and Ernst, 2010]. 250

In the case of a complete tree, which may either be built by completing an unbalanced
tree with empty nodes or by balancing the objects during *construction* via an *object-median* 360
split partitioning scheme, implicit indexing of a branch node's children can also be achieved 395
via a heap-like breadth-first layout [Cline *et al.*, 2006, Cline, 2007, Ch. 3]. As an alternative
to explicit storage via dynamically sized lists, the subset of objects associated with each leaf
node may likewise be implicitly represented by pairs of indices delineating segments in the
array of the initial set, each segment being then hierarchically reordered so as to group the
elements of a node's children into two contiguous sub-segments via a standard partitioning
procedure, such that the partitioning of the entire tree can be done in place [Wald, 2007].
Both approaches might finally be combined by allowing not only leaf nodes, but also branch
nodes to hold references to a fixed-size subset of the objects whose spatial extent defines
the node's bounding box, thereby allowing for an entirely implicit representation of the data
structure via a reordering of the objects in the set without requiring any additional storage
[Eisemann *et al.*, 2011, Eisemann *et al.*, 2012].

9.2.4 Bounding Interval Hierarchy

9.2.4.1 Definition

A *bounding interval hierarchy* (*BIH*) [Wächter and Keller, 2006] similarly defines a binary tree
structure whose branch nodes represent either an axis-aligned bounding *plane* (then referred 247
to as a *spatial k-D tree* (*S-KD tree*) [Ooi *et al.*, 1987] due to the conceptual resemblance with
a *k-D* tree), an axis-aligned bounding slab (then referred to as a *dual-extent tree* (*DE-tree*) 381
[Zuniga and Uhlmann, 2006] or as a *bounded k-D tree* (*B-KD tree*) [Woop *et al.*, 2006]) or

357 a mix of both with *bounding volumes* (then referred to as a *hybrid tree* (*H-tree*) [Havran *et al.*, 2006]).

366 As illustrated in *Figure 9.6*, the latter explicitly bound the extent of the associated subtrees along only one of the three major axes, whereas the remaining two dimensions of the volume are implicitly bounded by ancestor nodes higher up in the hierarchy. Each individual cell therefore has lower memory requirements than the nodes of a BVH, but at
367 the expense of the more frequent inspection of their content during *traversal* due to the looser
357 nature of the resulting *bounding volumes*. Rather than restricting sibling nodes to share an
247 identical bounding-*plane* axis, empty space may alternatively be more effectively cut out by allowing their orientation to be optimally determined individually for each node [Eisemann *et al.*, 2008].

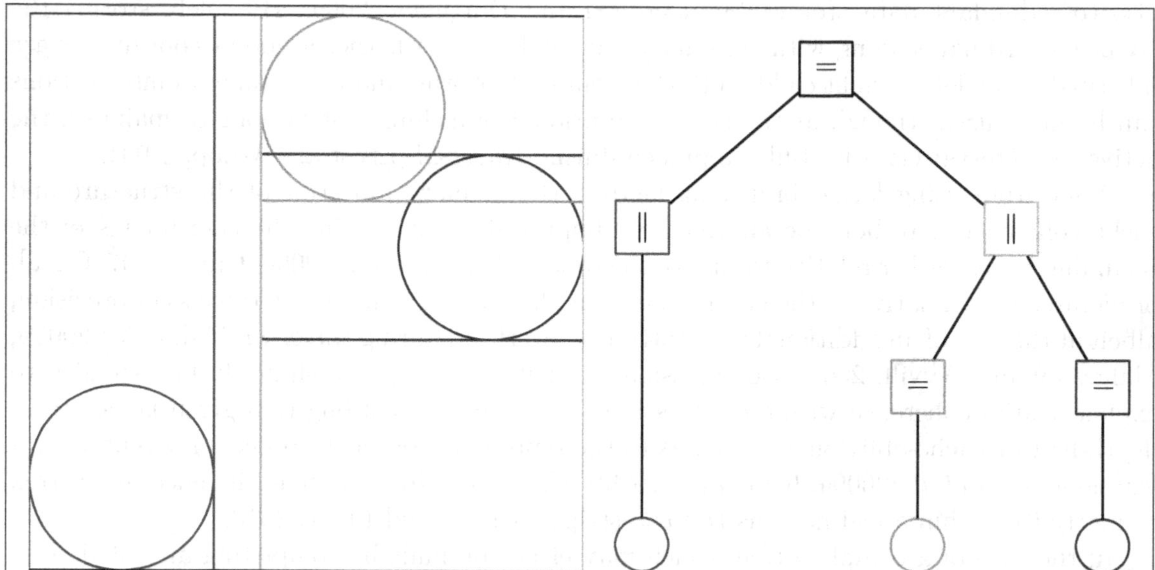

Figure 9.6: BIH Structure: Illustration of a BIH structure recursively partitioning the set of objects referenced by each branch node into two subsets, where the nodes hold a bounding interval explicitly encompassing all respective children along a single dimension while bounds on the remaining two dimensions are implicitly provided by ancestor nodes higher up in the hierarchy.

9.2.4.2 Construction

A BIH tree can be built via a top-down algorithm akin to the one introduced for BVH trees
360 in *Subsubsection 9.2.3.2*. Although exhaustively exploring the combinatorial space similarly allows objects with much larger spatial extents than that of other spatially collocated entities to be partitioned into a node enclosing its sibling and to be isolated at higher levels of the tree [Zuniga and Uhlmann, 2006] based on the concept of "oversized shelves" [Havran *et al.*, 2006], the candidate partitions are in practice also typically restricted to axis-aligned splits.

247 Excluding the cost of defining the axis and coordinate of the splitting *plane* (or the lack
393 thereof) via any of the strategies discussed in *Subsection 9.4.2*, the asymptotic complexity of the node refinement procedure is therefore also linear $O(n)$ in the number n of objects provided as input to the node. Starting with the original set of objects in the scene, the subsets associated with the child nodes may then be similarly created upon branching by
247 evaluating the side of the splitting *plane* that the objects' centroid lies on, such that each object in the given set is assigned to one and only one child node, which computes and stores

its bounding interval oriented along the previously chosen split axis. The process is then recursively repeated using new split axes, progressively proceeding from the root all the way down to the leaves.

9.2.4.3 Traversal

Upon intersection of its *bounding volume* by a ray, a BIH tree can be traversed in a depth- 357
first fashion similar to the *traversal* algorithm devised for BVHs, starting from the root of 362
the hierarchy and then recursively visiting the children of each branch node shall the ray
overlap the spatial extent of (none, any or all of) the latter, as illustrated in *Figure 9.7* for 367
an arbitrary branching factor.

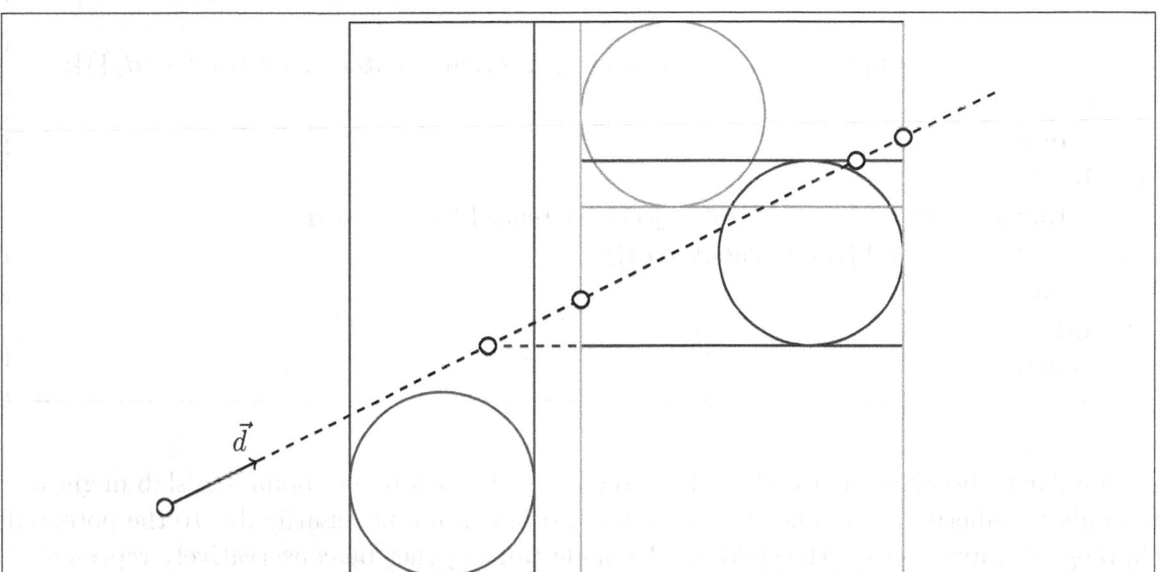

Figure 9.7: BIH Traversal: Illustration of the traversal of a BIH tree where the overlap interval resulting from higher levels in the hierarchy is recursively clipped against the bounding interval of the nodes.

Because the *bounding volume* associated with each node is implicitly defined by its 357
ancestors higher up in the tree, the procedure additionally requires the overlap interval
(initialized to that of the scene's bounding box at the root) to be explicitly maintained via a
k-D tree-like approach in order to clip the implicitly bounded dimensions of each subtree, as 381
outlined in *Algorithm 9.3*. Finally, the base algorithm may be further optimized by visiting 368
the child nodes in the order in which they are pierced by the ray based on the direction of the latter, and initiating the traversal procedure with a comparison of the current node's entry point against the closest intersection identified prior to visiting the given node, so as to anticipatively cull subtrees entirely located beyond the latter.

9.2.4.4 Storage

In addition to being flagged as a branch or as a leaf, each BIH node must also hold a list of references to its associated objects in case of a leaf node, while a branch node ought to store references to its children as well as the coordinates of its associated bounding interval and the axis along which it is oriented. However, because a bounding interval only contains a third or sixth of the data contained in a full bounding box, the memory footprint of a complete BIH structure can be substantially lower than that of a BVH tree, therefore improving both storage requirements and cache efficiency.

Algorithm 9.3: BIH Traversal: Pseudocode for BIH traversal.

Data: Ray r, node n and interval $[enter, exit]$
Result: Intersection found by traversing the BIH tree

```
Intersection i ← ∅;
if enter > prior intersections then
    Go to end;
end
if n is branch node then
    foreach node c ∈ children of n do
        if interval [enter, exit] along r overlaps bounding interval of c then
            i ← closest{i, TraverseBIHTree(r, c, max{enter, enter_c}, min{exit, exit_c})};
        end
    end
else
    foreach object o ∈ set S_n of objects referenced by node n do
        i ← closest{i, Intersect(r, o)};
    end
end
return i
```

Similarly observing that each of the two coordinates of a node's bounding slab might potentially be inherited from one of its ancestors (although not necessarily due to the potential clipping of empty space), the children of a node can together be conservatively represented
247 by two bounding *plane* coordinates instead. By additionally balancing the hierarchy via an
395 *object-median split* partitioning scheme, the nodes of the resulting complete tree may then
be implicitly indexed using a heap-like breadth-first layout, therefore minimizing the memory footprint of the whole structure [Bauszat *et al.*, 2010].

9.2.5 Performance

Because the spatial extent of the cells can be no smaller than that of the referenced objects, object-partitioning schemes typically yield rather shallow trees with relatively few but relatively loose cells, generally leading to moderate memory requirements and construction times, albeit at the cost of a relatively moderate traversal performance. Also, the systematic inspection of all children of a node is counterbalanced by the fact that each geometric entity is guaranteed to be visited no more than once, consequently making such subdivision schemes relatively suited for computationally costly objects.

Various caching schemes may be devised to improve the efficiency of the structure, such as caching in each node a per light reference to an object found to occlude a surface point within the node for prior testing against shadow rays cast from other surface points within the node, or even caching in each node the closest object intersected when casting a ray from a surface point within the node for prior testing against reflective rays cast from other surface points within the node. Nodes encompassing the common origin of a set of camera or shading rays, and therefore guaranteed to be intersected by them, can additionally be dispensed from further processing by building a list solely comprising their non-encompassing siblings that ought to be tested against the individual rays [Haines, 1991].

9.3 SPATIAL SUBDIVISION

A *spatial subdivision* scheme complementarily (i.e., in a mutually exclusive and exhaustive
manner) partitions the spatial extent of a scene (typically via *planes*) into a set of cells whose 247
resulting geometric entities are mutually independent (i.e., potentially overlapping), such that a given point in space is encompassed exactly once, while each object may be referenced by multiple cells. By exclusively considering the cells whose spatial extent is known to overlap the trajectory of the ray, the ray-intersection routine can then be restricted to the entities referenced by the visited cells.

Due to the fact that the geometry of the objects might extend beyond the spatial extent of the cells referencing them, the strict spatial sorting of the cells along the ray may only be exploited, by anticipatively aborting the search process upon intersection, if the latter lies inside the currently visited cell, such that its parametric coordinate is within the ray interval overlapped by the cell, therefore guaranteeing that the intersection point is closer to the ray's origin than any intersection point found in the subsequent cells. Rather than explicitly discarding intersections that fall beyond the extent of the currently visited cell though, a more robust alternative (e.g., for objects lying at the boundary between two adjacent cells) entails considering all intersections and aborting the traversal whenever the entry point of the subsequent cell lies beyond the closest previously recorded intersection [Lagae and Dutré, 2008c, Lagae and Dutré, 2008d].

9.3.1 Volume–Object Intersection

A volumetric subset of the 3-D space is said to intersect a given (potentially compound) object if the volume contains any of the spatial points of the object. Any object that is not intersected by any of the volumes pierced by a given ray and complementarily overlapping its trajectory is therefore guaranteed not to be intersected either by the ray, such that the latter test can be conservatively avoided. Because spatial subdivision schemes often partition the 3-D extent
of a scene into a set of cuboidal cells, assessing their overlap typically entails evaluating
the intersection of a box with a given object such as a *triangle* [Voorhies, 1992, Möller, 250
2001], a convex [Greene, 1994] or arbitrary [Green and Hatch, 1995] *polygon*, a *sphere* [Arvo, 262 269
1990a, Larsson *et al.*, 2007] or an ellipsoid [Larsson, 2008].

In order to reduce the computational cost, the object may alternatively be conservatively
substituted by its *bounding volume*, typically defined as a bounding box, although doing 357
so causes cells overlapping a given *bounding volume* to non-optimally reference the corre- 357
sponding object even if the latter doesn't itself overlap the cell. As illustrated in *Figure 9.8*, 370
addressing this issue then entails performing *split clipping* [Havran and Bittner, 2002] operations, in which the bounding box of objects straddling a given split *plane* is clipped against 247
the cells lying on each side of it. Minimal bounding boxes for a geometric subset of a *triangle* 250
can, for instance, be inexpensively determined by computing the intersection of its edges
with the given split *plane*, and then evaluating the bounding box of the latter points with 247
the *triangle* vertices lying on each side of it, intersected against the tight *bounding volume* 250 357
resulting from previous split-clipping operations [Soupikov *et al.*, 2008].

9.3.2 Grid

9.3.2.1 Definition

As illustrated in *Figure 9.9*, a *uniform grid* [Cosenza, 2008] regularly partitions the spatial 370
extent of a scene into a set of axis-aligned cuboidal volume elements referred to as *voxels*,
generally leading to low memory requirements and *construction* times, albeit at the cost of 371
a relatively low *traversal* performance. 373

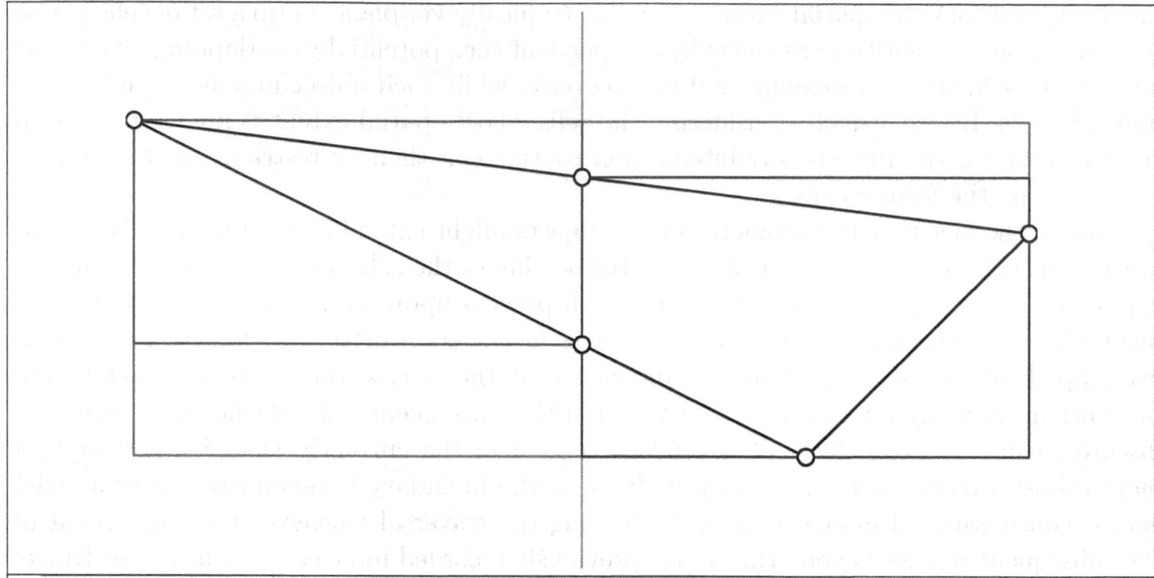

Figure 9.8: Split Clipping: Illustration of the clipping of a bounding box against a given split plane (drawn after [Havran and Bittner, 2002, Fig. 4] and [Soupikov *et al.*, 2008, Fig. 3]).

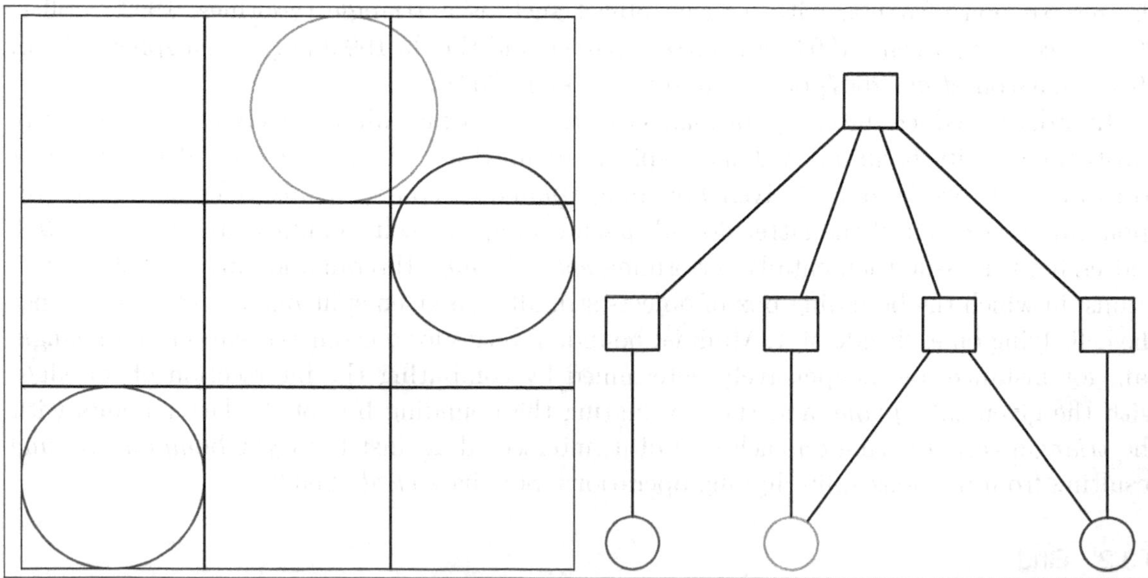

Figure 9.9: Grid Structure: Illustration of a grid structure (formally described as a bipartite graph) uniformly partitioning the spatial extent of a scene into a set of axis-aligned voxels.

In the special case of a height field in the form of a *triangle*-based *polyhedral terrain*, or 250
reconstructed using *bilinear patches* or *biquadratic patches*, or in the case of a volumetric 264
isosurface reconstructed using *trilinear patches*, as illustrated in *Figure 9.10*, the partition 287 285
may actually be intrinsically defined by the lattice layout of the regularly sampled data points. 371
Because each cell is known to contain exactly one (e.g., as in a height field) or at most one (e.g., as in an isosurface) geometric entity, the structure does not need to be explicitly built, thereby yielding a logical indexing scheme where the patch (if any) contained within a cell
is temporarily instantiated from the sampled data on the fly during the *traversal* of the cell. 373

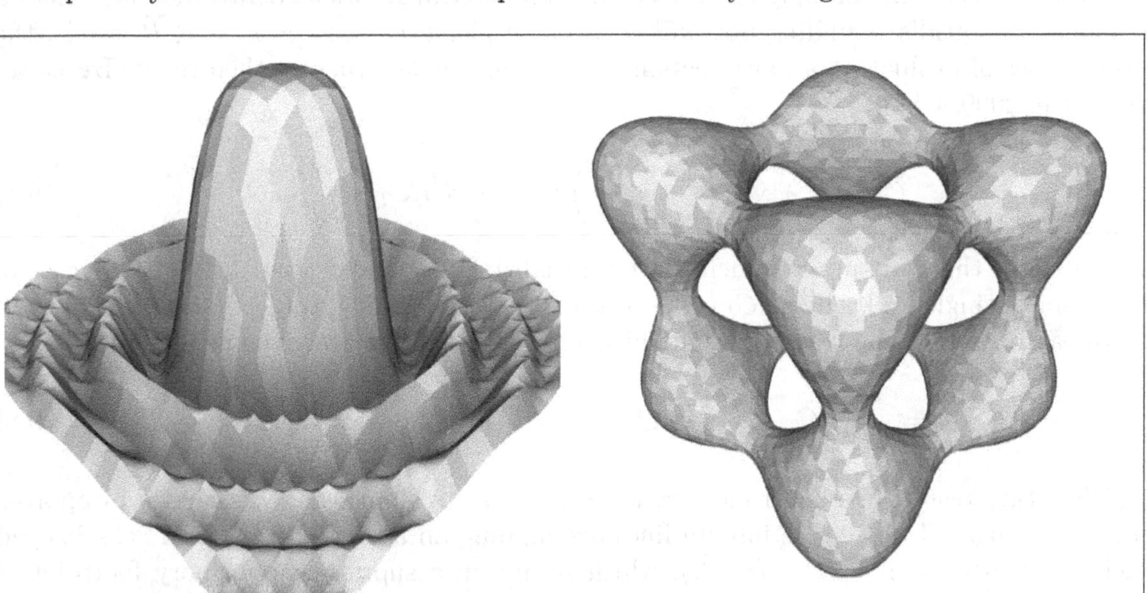

Figure 9.10: Height Field and Isosurface: Illustration of a height field (left) and of an isosurface (right), spatially indexed using a logical grid structure whose layout is implicitly defined by the lattice of the regularly sampled data points.

9.3.2.2 Construction

In contrast to the characteristics of hierarchical structures, which are typically determined as the tree is being populated, the properties of a grid structure need to be defined prior to its creation. While it might be implied by the scene itself in the case of a height field or a volumetric isosurface, setting the optimal resolution more generally involves a compromise between various competing factors. Whereas an insufficiently low resolution will cause the undervoxelized structure to require an excessive number of inspections of the heavily aggregated geometry due to the loose extent of the cells pierced by the ray, a disproportionately high resolution will conversely cause the overvoxelized structure to require an excessive
number of *traversal* steps in empty regions, increase memory consumption and potentially 373
degrade cache performance.

Rather than manually setting the grid resolution $r_{x|y|z}$, the latter may instead be defined in terms of the spatial extent of the scene $b_{x|y|z}$ in each dimension

$$r_{x|y|z} \triangleq \frac{b_{x|y|z}}{v_{x|y|z}} \tag{9.6}$$

where the voxel size $v_{x|y|z}$ is determined following the principles of any of the strategies
discussed in *Subsection 9.4.2*. For instance, considering the *probability* of intersection of the 393
individual cells, the size of the latter, which ought to be roughly cubical in shape, can be 129

defined from a given target surface area $s = 2(v_y v_z + v_z v_x + v_x v_y) = 6v_x^2$ to yield $v_x = v_y = v_z = \sqrt{\frac{s}{6}}$.

As an alternative, considering the workload associated with the individual cells, their total number $R \triangleq r_x r_y r_z = \alpha n$ may be defined proportionally to the number n of objects in the scene [Cleary and Wyvill, 1988], which are assumed to be uniformly distributed in space and to be punctual so as to overlap only a single grid cell, which on average holds ${}^{n}/_{R} = {}^{1}/_{\alpha}$
369 objects. Ignoring the distance-based culling optimization described for *spatial subdivision* schemes, for the sake of simplicity, such that an arbitrarily oriented ray that intersects a homogeneous grid's bounding box will on average pierce $r_x = r_y = r_z = \sqrt[3]{R}$ voxels, the overall cost of evaluating an intersection against the whole structure then reads [Ize *et al.*, 2007, Ize, 2009, Ch. 4]

$$C \triangleq C_S + \sqrt[3]{R}\left(C_T + \frac{C_I}{\alpha}\right) = C_S + \sqrt[3]{R}C_T + \frac{\sqrt[3]{R}}{R}nC_I \tag{9.7}$$

where C_S is the start-up cost incurred by initializing the grid traversal, C_T is the cost of traversing a single grid cell and C_I is the cost of intersecting a single object (assumed constant across all objects). The resolution minimizing the cost is therefore given as

$$\frac{\mathrm{d}C}{\mathrm{d}R} = \frac{1}{3R^{2/3}}C_T - \frac{2}{3R^{5/3}}nC_I = 0 \implies R = 2n\frac{C_I}{C_T} \implies \alpha = 2\frac{C_I}{C_T} \tag{9.8}$$

which in turn results in a linear memory footprint $O(n)$. A similar analysis carried by approximating elongated objects as infinite lines overlapping an average of $\sqrt[3]{R}$ grid cells instead yields a density of $\alpha = R \div (n\sqrt[3]{R})$, which results in a supra-linear memory footprint of $R = \left(n\frac{C_I}{C_T}\right)^{\frac{3}{2}}$ [Ize *et al.*, 2007, Ize, 2009, Ch. 4]. In practice, though, optimal grid resolutions for non-idealized geometry are expected to lie somewhere between these two theoretical extremes and can presumably be estimated by trial and error with several sample values.

In order to minimize the overlap of each object with multiple voxels, the voxel size might additionally be made proportional to the average spatial extent $o_{x|y|z}$ of the individual
129 objects in each dimension (albeit at the cost of increasing the intersection *probability* of each compared to a cubical shape)

$$v_{x|y|z} \triangleq \frac{\sqrt[3]{b_x b_y b_z}}{\sqrt[3]{\alpha n}} \frac{o_{x|y|z}}{\sqrt[3]{o_x o_y o_z}} \tag{9.9}$$

such that

371

$$r_{x|y|z} \overset{(9.6)}{=} \frac{b_{x|y|z}}{o_{x|y|z}} \frac{\sqrt[3]{o_x o_y o_z}}{\sqrt[3]{b_x b_y b_z}} \sqrt[3]{\alpha n} = \frac{f_{x|y|z}}{\sqrt[3]{f_x f_y f_z}} \sqrt[3]{\alpha n} = f_{x|y|z} \sqrt[3]{\frac{\alpha n}{f_x f_y f_z}} \tag{9.10}$$

with the scaling factors $f_{x|y|z} \triangleq \frac{b_{x|y|z}}{o_{x|y|z}}$. The surface area and the workload can then be both simultaneously taken into account by restoring the cubical shape of the voxels using $o_{x|y|z} = 1$, which yields

372

$$v_{x|y|z} \overset{(9.9)}{=} \sqrt[3]{\frac{b_x b_y b_z}{\alpha n}} \tag{9.11}$$

as well as $f_{x|y|z} = b_{x|y|z}$, such that [Klimaszewski, 1994, Klimaszewski and Sederberg, 1997]

372

$$r_{x|y|z} \overset{(9.10)}{=} b_{x|y|z} \sqrt[3]{\frac{\alpha n}{b_x b_y b_z}} \tag{9.12}$$

Once the resolution of the grid has been defined, the structure may be populated as outlined in *Algorithm 9.4*. In order to reference all objects that a given voxel intersects, 373
each object might be naively tested for intersection against the set of all voxels V in the grid, yielding an asymptotic complexity of $O(Rn) = O(\alpha n^2) \sim O(n^2)$. Because the average number of voxels intersecting a given object is determined by the ratio $\alpha = R \div n$, though, a more efficient approach entails restricting the range of voxels V to the lattice coordinates overlapping the extent of the object's bounding box in each dimension, thereby reducing the complexity to $O(\alpha n) \sim O(n)$. Conservatively referencing each object in all voxels overlapping its bounding box rather than the object itself then allows the intersection test to be skipped altogether, as illustrated in *Figure 9.11*. 373

Algorithm 9.4: Grid Construction: Pseudocode for grid construction.

Data: Set of objects S
Result: A grid built over S
$[n_x, n_y, n_z] \leftarrow$ `DefineResolution`(S);
foreach object $o \in S$ **do**
  foreach voxel $v \in$ set V **do**
    if voxel v intersects object o **then**
      Set $S_v \leftarrow S_v \cup o$;
    end
  end
end
return Grid g

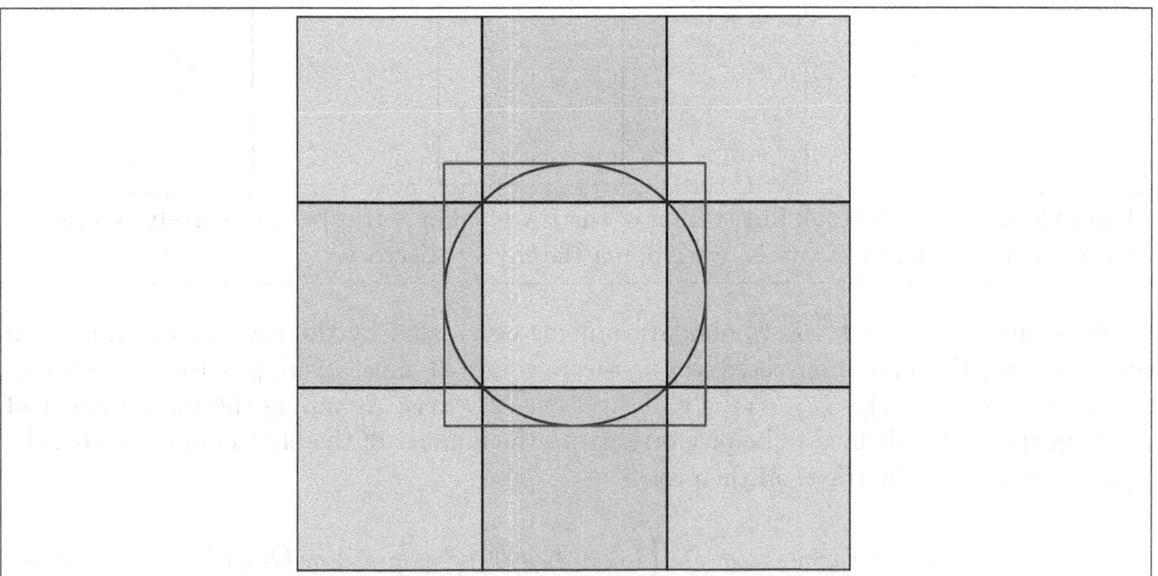

Figure 9.11: Grid Construction: Illustration of a grid structure conservatively built by referencing each object in all voxels overlapping its bounding box.

9.3.2.3 *Traversal*

Upon intersection of its *bounding volume* by a ray, a grid may be traversed by identifying the 357
voxels overlapping the trajectory of the ray in 3-D space. As illustrated in *Figure 9.12*, this 374

is in essence closely related to rasterizing a line via 2-D scan conversion, and both tasks can therefore be regarded as special cases of a general multidimensional discrete problem [Slater, 1992], in contrast to continuous ray generators stepping along the ray by an arbitrary amount regardless of the voxel boundaries [Endl and Sommer, 1994]. Rather than determining the unit-width subset of pixels that best approximate the trajectory of the line, the grid traversal ought to determine the set of all voxels pierced by the ray. In addition, because the ray may enter the grid at any location and with any direction, the endpoints of the line cannot be assumed to lie at voxel centers, therefore limiting the applicability of Bresenham-like [Bresenham, 1965] integer-based algorithms [Cohen, 1994, Liu *et al.*, 2004]. Instead, grid traversal is typically performed via a 3-D extension of the *digital differential analyzer* (*DDA*) algorithm, either unconditionally stepping along the main axis of the ray's direction and then determining whether a step along any of the two secondary axes should be taken as well [Fujimoto and Iwata, 1985, Fujimoto *et al.*, 1986], or by handling all three dimensions in a symmetrical manner [Snyder and Barr, 1987, Amanatides and Woo, 1987] so as to allow for various optimizations [Cleary and Wyvill, 1988].

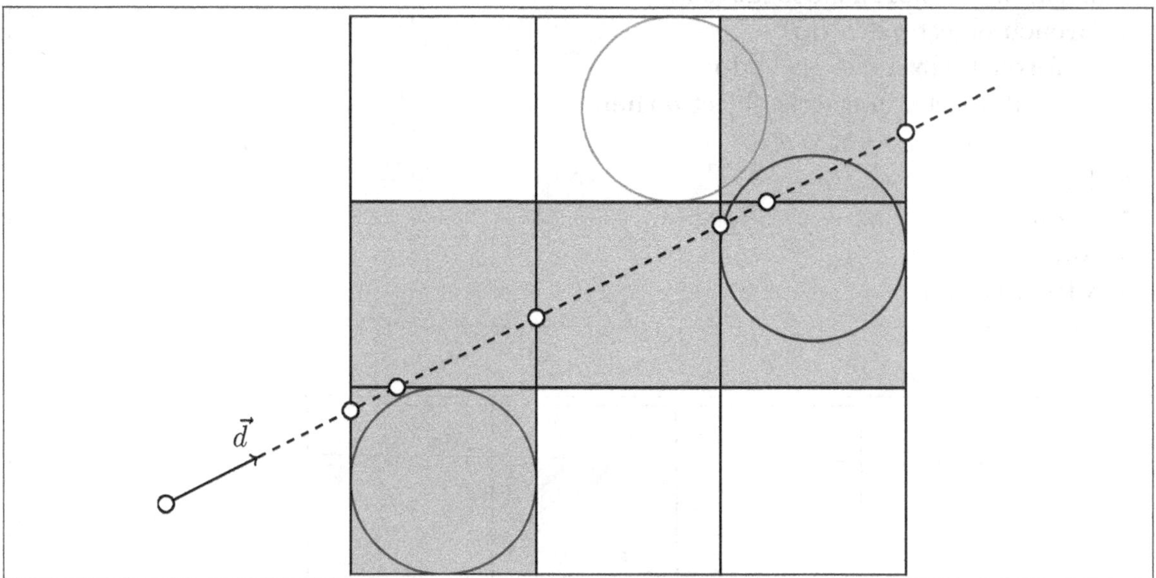

Figure 9.12: Grid Traversal: Illustration of the traversal of a grid by successively stepping through the sequence of voxels overlapping the ray's trajectory.

Since up to $r_{x|y|z} - 1$ voxel boundaries might be crossed by the ray in each dimension after entering the first intersected voxel, the ray may at most overlap a total number of $1 + (r_x - 1) + (r_y - 1) + (r_z - 1) = r_x + r_y + r_z - 2$ voxels. Assuming the total number of voxels in the grid is defined to be proportional to the number of the objects in the scene, the asymptotic cost of the traversal then reads

372

$$O(r_x + r_y + r_z) \overset{(9.10)}{=} O\left((f_x + f_y + f_z)\sqrt[3]{\frac{\alpha n}{f_x f_y f_z}}\right) \sim O(\sqrt[3]{n}) \tag{9.13}$$

In order to further optimize the search process, the distance-based culling approach described
369 for *spatial subdivision* schemes can additionally be exploited by visiting the voxels in the order
375 in which they are pierced by the ray, as illustrated in *Figure 9.13*.

376 As outlined in *Algorithm 9.5*, the integer-valued lattice indices $c_{x|y|z}$ of the first encountered voxel are initially determined by projecting the spatial coordinates of the entry point $e_{x|y|z}$ of the ray into the volume of the grid's bounding box, which may be either the closest intersection of the ray with the bounding box's surface, or the origin of the ray itself

Figure 9.13: Grid Traversal Cost: Color-coded illustration of the relative computational cost of grid traversal for a Sierpinski tetrahedron.

if the latter lies inside the bounding box. The values $s_{x|y|z}$ by which the lattice indices of the current voxel should be incremented in each dimension are also initialized based on the sign (i.e., $+1$ or -1) of the ray's direction $d_{x|y|z}$ along each axis. The parametric distances
$p_{x|y|z}$ at which the ray intersects each of the *planes* defined by the lower bounds $l_{x|y|z}$ of 247
the volume are then computed, and potentially pushed to the next *plane* boundary shall 247
the direction of the ray be positive along each axis. The parametric distances $\delta_{x|y|z}$ along the ray between two consecutive lattice boundaries in each dimension are finally initialized, and so are the parametric distances $t_{x|y|z}$ along the ray to the next lattice boundary to be crossed in each dimension. Each overlapping voxel can then be successively visited so as to evaluate its set of referenced objects for intersection against the ray. The next voxel in the sequence is incrementally determined by incrementing/decrementing the lattice index along the axis $a = x|y|z$ of the face through which the ray leaves the previous voxel, assuming a six-connected line such that an edge or corner intersection is implicitly treated as two or three successive face events, respectively. The parametric ray distance of the subsequent lattice boundary between two voxels along the latter dimension is subsequently updated as well, either by replicating the formulation with which it was initialized, or alternatively by using a slightly more efficient (albeit prone to the numerical accumulation of fixed-precision floating point rounding errors) incremental update based on the DDA-like formulation

$$t'_a \triangleq p_a + c'_a\delta_a = p_a + (c_a + s_a)\delta_a = p_a + c_a\delta_a + s_a\delta_a = t_a + s_a\delta_a = t_a + |\delta_a| \qquad (9.14)$$

where the last equality stems from the fact that the product $s_a\delta_a$ is always positive. Finally, the base algorithm may be further optimized by initiating the iterative loop with a comparison of the current voxel's entry point against the closest intersection identified so far, so as to anticipatively cull voxels entirely located beyond the latter.

Due to the regularity of their 3-D structure, uniform grids allow for the efficient *con-*
struction and traversal of each voxel despite the relatively costly initialization of the traver- 371
sal process. As such, they are particularly suited for roughly uniform object distributions, since the latter yield a relatively homogeneous repartition of the workload among voxels, in
turn increasing the *probability* of an intersection to be found within a few traversal steps. 129
However, their fixed resolution conversely precludes any form of local adaptation to the

Algorithm 9.5: Grid Traversal: Pseudocode for grid traversal.

Data: Ray r
Result: Intersection found by traversing the grid
Intersection $i \leftarrow \emptyset$;
$c_{x|y|z} \leftarrow \lfloor (e_{x|y|z} - l_{x|y|z}) \div v_{x|y|z} \rfloor$;
$s_{x|y|z} \leftarrow \text{sgn}(d_{x|y|z})$;
$p_{x|y|z} \leftarrow (l_{x|y|z} - o_{x|y|z}[+v_{x|y|z} \text{ if } s_{x|y|z} > 0]) \div d_{x|y|z}$;
$\delta_{x|y|z} \leftarrow v_{x|y|z} \div d_{x|y|z}$;
$t_{x|y|z} \leftarrow p_{x|y|z} + c_{x|y|z}\delta_{x|y|z}$;
while $[c_x, c_y, c_z]$ are within limits of grid resolution $[r_x, r_y, r_z]$ **do**
    if *enter* $> i$ **then**
        Go to end;
    end
    foreach object $o \in$ set S_v of voxel v **do**
        $i \leftarrow \texttt{closest}\{i, \texttt{Intersect}(r, o)\}$;
    end
    $a \leftarrow$ axis of $\min\{t_x, t_y, t_z\}$;
    $c_a \leftarrow c_a + s_a$;
    $t_a \leftarrow \texttt{Update}(t_a)$;
end
return i

input geometry, potentially impairing the performance of the overall ray-intersection test. This phenomenon, commonly known as the "teapot in a stadium" problem, illustrates the fact that the structure is in general unable to adequately accommodate both densely and sparsely populated regions simultaneously, as occurs when a small, finely tessellated teapot is placed inside a large, coarsely tessellated stadium. This typically leads to an increase of the average number of traversal steps due to the numerous underpopulated cells, whereas overpopulated cells conversely incur countless intersection tests. Although the latter prob-
247 lem can be partially mitigated by an irregular placement of the *plane* coordinates along each
377 axis as illustrated in *Figure 9.14*, the flexibility of *non-uniform grids* [Dippé and Swensen, 1984, Gigante, 1988] remains limited in practice by the separable nature of the partitioning scheme, causing the refinement of a given region of space to alter the density of the cells in other regions as a side effect.

9.3.2.4 Storage

Instead of resorting to the standard extension of the row-major or column-major order layout to represent multidimensional arrays in linear memory, cache efficiency may be substantially improved via a bricking approach in which the voxels of the grid are contiguously arranged as a set of volumetric blocks, although requiring a more complex indexing scheme. In order to reduce the overall memory footprint of the structure, and thus further improve cache efficiency with it, the grid can also be stored using a sparse multidimensional array representation, therefore avoiding the explicit storage of voxels whose list of object references is empty, albeit at the cost of additional indexing overheads incurred by the hashing function [Cleary and Wyvill, 1988, Wyvill, 1990].

Hashing may actually be combined with various representations of the reference lists associated with each grid cell [Lagae and Dutré, 2008c, Lagae and Dutré, 2008d], including

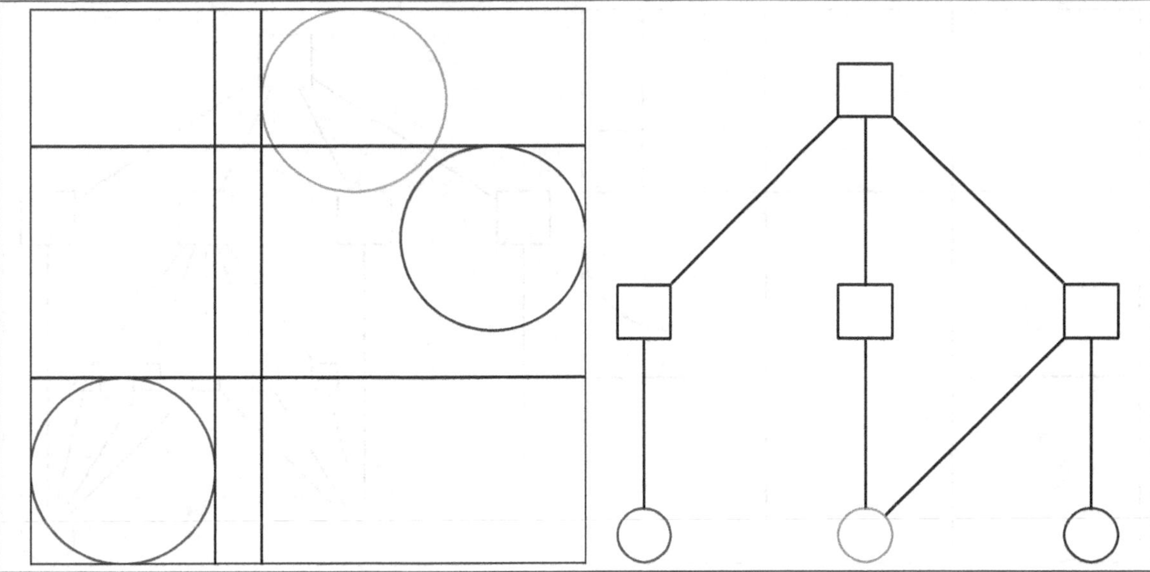

Figure 9.14: Non-Uniform Grid: Illustration of a non-uniform grid irregularly partitioning space (drawn after [Dippé and Swensen, 1984, Fig. 1a]).

dynamically resizable data structures such as linked lists or buffered dynamic arrays, which allow the build process to operate in a single pass. The storage requirements can instead be further minimized by resorting to fixed-size arrays, albeit requiring a two-stage construction process in order to determine their size in the first pass prior to allocating and populating them during the second pass. As an alternative to storing the size and address of the individual arrays in each grid cell, a more compact scheme may then be devised by contiguously storing all references in a single secondary array such that each grid cell solely needs to contain the index of its first reference while their number is readily obtained by subtracting it from the index contained in the following grid cell (e.g., based on a row-major ordering). Under this representation, a non-redundant construction scheme then entails iterating over the objects in a first pass and for each, populating the secondary array with object-cell index pairs, while sorting of the entries during the second pass allows the references to be grouped by their associated cell, the first index of which is then stored into the latter [Kalojanov and Slusallek, 2009].

9.3.3 Multilevel Grid

As illustrated in *Figure 9.15*, adaptation to non-uniformly distributed geometry may be 378
achieved by nesting *grids* of various spatial resolutions in a hierarchical fashion [Cosenza, 369
2008]. A *multilevel grid* built in a top-down fashion corresponds to a generalized multi-
branching tree structure recursively refining in densely populated regions, possibly stored
via a hash-based sparse representation, and which degenerates into a regular *grid* or an *oc-* 369
tree in the special cases of a single depth-level or a 2^3 branching factor, respectively [Jevans 378
and Wyvill, 1989]. As such, multilevel grids not only allow empty regions of space to be represented with a minimal memory footprint, but they also allow them to be readily skipped in an adaptive fashion during traversal [Hsiung and Thibadeau, 1992]. Optimal resolutions for the various levels of the hierarchy can then similarly be derived by generalizing the theoretical cost analysis devised for the *construction* of uniform *grids* [Ize *et al.*, 2007, Ize, 2009, 371
Ch. 4]. 369

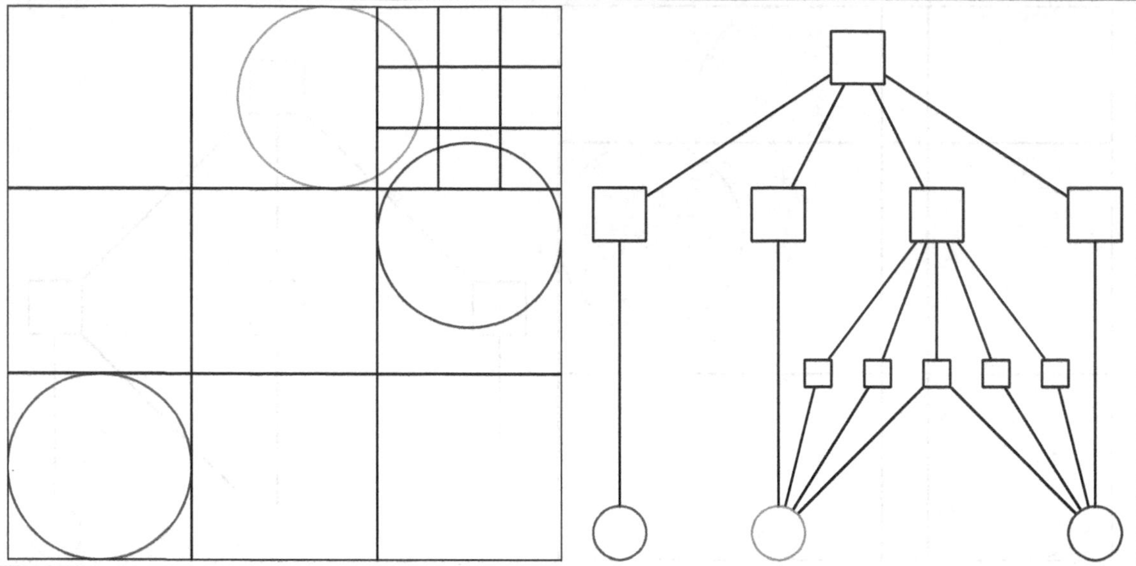

Figure 9.15: Multilevel Grid: Illustration of a hierarchical multilevel grid recursively partitioning densely populated regions of space.

9.3.4 Octree

9.3.4.1 Definition

Defined as the 3-D extension of a two-dimensional *quadtree*, an *octree* [Matsumoto and Murakami, 1983, Glassner, 1984], whose name stems from the contraction of oct-tree, is an octonary tree (i.e., with arity $2^3 = 8$) in which the spatial extent of each branch node is recursively partitioned into eight octants by a set of three orthogonal axis-aligned splitting
247 *planes*, while its leaf nodes hold references to the objects that their associated *bounding*
357 *volume* intersects. As illustrated in *Figure 9.16*, the hierarchical data structure may locally
379 adapt the size of the cells to the features of the input geometry, providing a fine subdivision
in densely populated regions while remaining relatively coarse in sparse regions. However, because the level of subdivision is uniform across all three dimensions, octrees are in general unable to adequately accommodate scenes with highly anisotropic geometric distributions, as would occur with degenerate height-field-like geometry, for instance.

9.3.4.2 Construction

An octree can be built via a top-down algorithm by recursively subdividing space into eight
379 octants, progressing from the root towards the leaves as outlined in *Algorithm 9.6*. Excluding
the cost of defining the coordinates of the center point of the split (or the lack thereof)
393 via any of the strategies discussed in *Subsection 9.4.2* (possibly independently along each
axis) [Whang *et al.*, 1995], the asymptotic complexity of the node refinement procedure is therefore linear $O(n)$ in the number n of objects provided as input to the node. Starting with the original set of objects in the scene and their bounding box, the subsets associated with the child nodes may then be created upon branching by evaluating whether the objects in the given set intersect the corresponding octants, such that each object is assigned to one or more child nodes.

9.3.4.3 Traversal

357 Upon intersection of its *bounding volume* by a ray, an octree structure might be sequentially

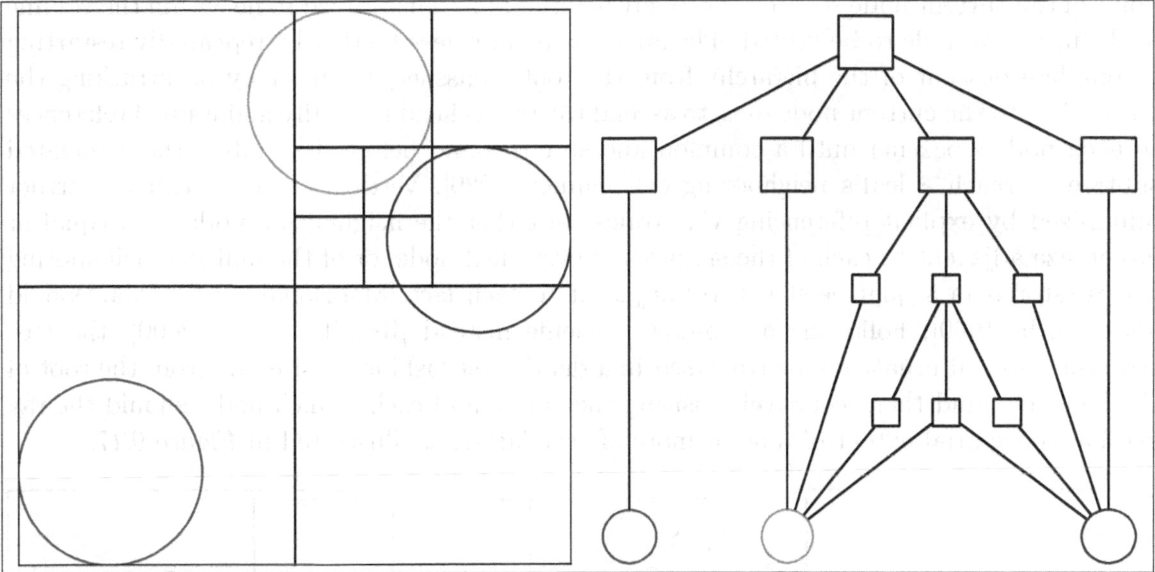

Figure 9.16: Octree Structure: Illustration of an octree structure recursively partitioning the spatial extent of each branch node into eight axis-aligned octants (here shown as a 2-D quadtree with arity 4 instead).

Algorithm 9.6: Octree Construction: Pseudocode for octree construction.

Data: Set of objects S and bounding box B
Result: An octree built over S

```
s_{x|y|z} ← DefineSplit(S, B);
if split s_{x|y|z} is valid then
    foreach child c ∈ 8 children do
        B_c ← SplitBoundingVolume(B, s_{x|y|z});
        S_c ← ∅;
    end
    foreach object o ∈ S do
        foreach child c ∈ 8 children do
            if bounding box of child B_c intersects object o then
                S_c ← S_c ∪ o;
            end
        end
    end
    Node
    n ← CreateInnerNode(s_{x|y|z}, BuildOctree(S_1, B_1), ..., BuildOctree(S_8, B_8));
else
    Node n ← CreateLeafNode(S);
end
return n
```

traversed in a stack-less fashion via point-location queries by infinitesimally offsetting the exit point of the current node so as to iteratively define a point guaranteed to lie within the volume of the next leaf node to be visited. The latter is then retrieved either by repeatedly restarting a complete descent of the hierarchy from the root [Glassner, 1984], or by backtracking the path taken to the current node so as to ascend the tree (via additionally maintained references to each node's parent) until a common ancestor is found before descending the associated subtree to reach a leaf's neighboring cell [Samet, 1989]. Vertical traversal can be further minimized by explicit referencing via "ropes" of either the neighboring node with equal or larger size adjacent to each of the six faces of every leaf node, or of the multiple neighboring leaves (stored in a quatree structure) adjacent to each face [MacDonald, 1988, MacDonald and Booth, 1990]. Following a top-down scheme instead [Revelles *et al.*, 2000], the tree structure may alternatively be traversed in a depth-first fashion by starting from the root of the hierarchy and then recursively visiting the children of each branch node, should the ray
380 overlap the spatial extent of (one or more of) the latter, as illustrated in *Figure 9.17.*

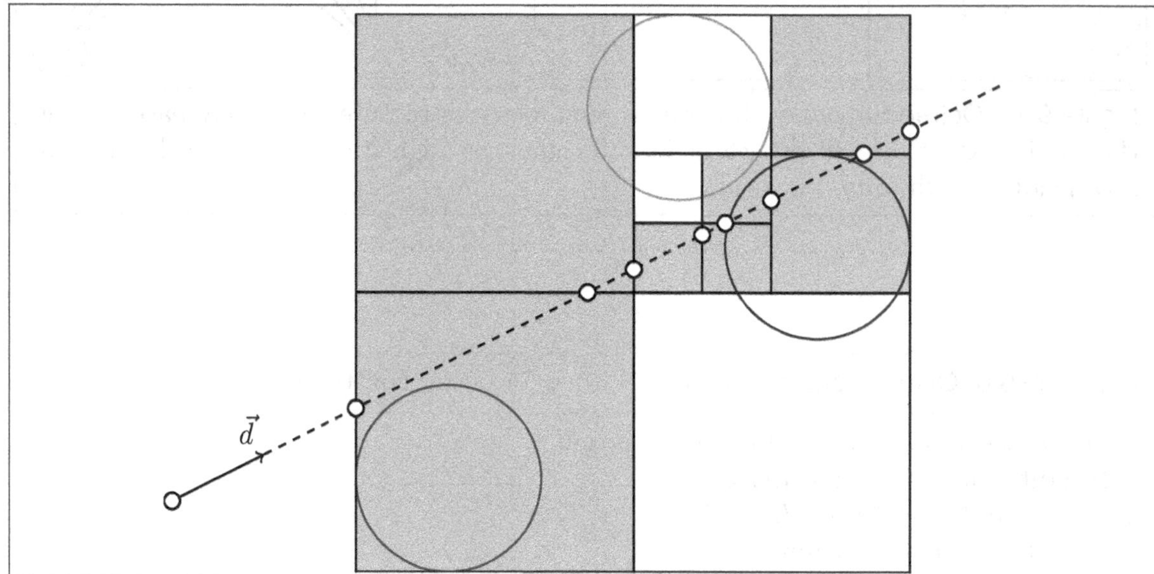

Figure 9.17: Octree Traversal: Illustration of the traversal of an octree by recursively visiting the children of a node.

369 Regarding the eight octants of a branch node as a *grid*-like structure of resolution $2 \times 2 \times 2$,
the overlapping children (whose number is at least 1, otherwise the current node wouldn't
have been visited in the first place, and at most $1 + (2 - 1) + (2 - 1) + (2 - 1) = 4$) can be
efficiently visited in order of increasing distance from the ray's origin using the aforementioned
373 grid *traversal* algorithm [Fujimoto and Iwata, 1985, Fujimoto *et al.*, 1986], or a dedicated
variant of it flipping the three axial bits encoding the octants' IDs along each dimension
247 according to the order in which the three split *planes* are intersected by the ray [Agate *et*
357 *al.*, 1991]. Because the *bounding volume* associated with each node is implicitly defined by
its ancestors higher up in the tree, the procedure additionally requires the overlap interval
(initialized to that of the scene's bounding box at the root) to be explicitly maintained, as
381 outlined in *Algorithm 9.7.* Finally, the base algorithm may be further optimized by initiating
the traversal procedure with a comparison of the current node's entry point against the
closest intersection identified prior to visiting the given node, so as to anticipatively cull
subtrees entirely located beyond the latter.

Algorithm 9.7: Octree Traversal: Pseudocode for octree traversal.

```
Data: Ray r, node n and interval [enter, exit]
Result: Intersection found by traversing the octree
Intersection i ← ∅;
if enter > prior intersections then
    Go to end;
end
if n is branch node then
    t_{x|y|z} ← (s_{x|y|z} − o_{x|y|z}) ÷ d_{x|y|z};
    foreach node c ∈ grid-like traversal of children of n do
        i ← closest{i, TraverseOctree(r, c, max{enter, enter_c}, min{exit, exit_c})};
    end
else
    foreach object o ∈ set S_n of objects referenced by node n do
        i ← closest{i, Intersect(r, o)};
    end
end
return i
```

9.3.4.4 Storage

In addition to being flagged as a branch or as a leaf, each octree node must also hold a list of references to its associated objects in case of a leaf node, while a branch node ought to store references to its children as well as the coordinates of its associated splitting *planes* along 247
each axis. In order to reduce the overall memory footprint of the structure, and thus further improve cache efficiency with it, the octree may be stored using a sparse representation, therefore avoiding the explicit storage of cells whose list of object references is empty, albeit at the cost of additional indexing overheads incurred by the hashing function [Glassner, 1984].

9.3.5 k-D Tree

9.3.5.1 Definition

A *k-D tree* [Bentley, 1975], whose name is the shorthand notation for a k-dimensional tree where $k = 3$ when applied to space partitioning [Sung and Shirley, 1992, Szécsi, 2003], is a binary tree in which the spatial extent of each branch node is recursively partitioned into two half-spaces by an axis-aligned splitting *plane* (thereby defining a special case of a restricted 247
BSP tree), while its leaf nodes hold references to the objects that their associated *bounding* 385
volume intersects. As illustrated in *Figure 9.18*, the hierarchical data structure may locally 357 382
adapt the level and axis of refinement to the distribution of the input geometry, providing a fine subdivision along the critical dimension of densely populated regions while remaining relatively coarse in sparse regions.

9.3.5.2 Construction

A k-D tree can be built via a top-down algorithm by recursively subdividing space into two half-spaces and assigning each object to one or both child nodes, progressing from the root towards the leaves. Excluding the cost of defining the axis and coordinate of the splitting *plane* (or the lack thereof) via any of the strategies discussed in *Subsection 9.4.2*, the asymp- 247 393

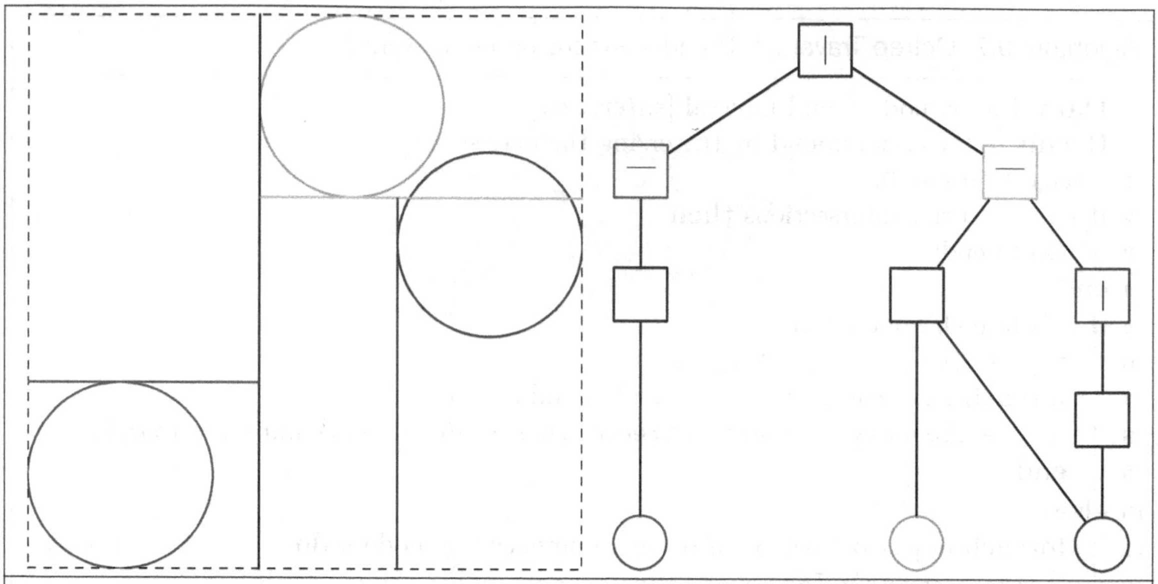

Figure 9.18: k-D Tree Structure: Illustration of a k-D tree structure (formally described as a directed acyclic graph (DAG) as each object may be connected to several leaf nodes of the polytree formed by the upper subgraph) recursively partitioning the spatial extent of each branch node into two axis-aligned half-spaces.

totic complexity of the node refinement procedure is therefore linear $O(n)$ in the number n of objects provided as input to the node. Starting with the original set of objects in the scene and their bounding box, the subsets associated with the child nodes may then be created upon branching by evaluating whether the objects in the given set intersect the corresponding bounding boxes, such that each object is assigned to one or both child nodes, while objects
247 embedded within the split *plane* may be assigned to either, as outlined in *Algorithm 9.8*.

383 Conservatively substituting the object by its bounding box, the object-child intersection test finally reduces to evaluating whether the object's bounding box overlaps each of the
247 semi-infinite half-spaces defined by the splitting *plane*, since clipping of the object via other faces of the node's bounding box then ought to have already occurred through higher levels of the hierarchy.

9.3.5.3 *Traversal*

357 Upon intersection of its *bounding volume* by a ray, a k-D tree might be sequentially traversed in a stack-less fashion via point-location queries by infinitesimally offsetting the exit point of the current node so as to iteratively define a point guaranteed to lie within the volume of the next leaf node to be visited. The latter is then retrieved either by repeatedly restarting a complete descent of the hierarchy from the root [Kaplan, 1985, Kaplan, 1987], or by backtracking the path taken to the current node so as to ascend the tree until a common ancestor is found before descending the associated subtree to reach a leaf's neighboring cell [Foley and Sugerman, 2005]. The latter approach then additionally requires maintaining either references to each node's parent, or references among ancestor nodes belonging to sparsely distributed levels of the tree so as to limit the number of nodes whose bounding box must be explicitly stored [Havran and Bittner, 2007a], in turn allowing a stackless variant of the scheme to solely restart the traversal from the highest node of a given subtree [Havran and Bittner, 2007b]. In addition to noting that the leaf node encompassing the intersection point of a ray may be readily used as the entry node of the subsequent ray along a path,

Algorithm 9.8: k-D Tree Construction: Pseudocode for k-D tree construction.

Data: Set of objects S and bounding box B
Result: A k-D tree built over S

$[axis, coordinate] \leftarrow$ `DefineSplit`(S, B);
if $axis \in \{X, Y, Z\}$ **then**
    $[B_l, B_r] \leftarrow$ `SplitBoundingVolume`$(B, axis, coordinate)$;
    $S_l \leftarrow \emptyset$;
    $S_r \leftarrow \emptyset$;
    foreach object $o \in S$ **do**
        if bounding box of left child B_l intersects object o **then**
            $S_l \leftarrow S_l \cup o$;
        end
        if bounding box of right child B_r intersects object $o \vee o \notin S_l$ **then**
            $S_r \leftarrow S_r \cup o$;
        end
    end
    Node $n \leftarrow$
    `CreateInnerNode`$(axis, coordinate,$ `BuildKDTree`$(S_l, B_l),$ `BuildKDTree`$(S_r, B_r))$;
else
    Node $n \leftarrow$ `CreateLeafNode`(S);
end
return n

vertical traversal can be further minimized by explicit referencing via "ropes" of either the neighboring node with equal or larger size adjacent to each of the six faces of every leaf node, or of the multiple neighboring leaves (stored in a two-dimensional k-D tree structure called *rope tree*) adjacent to each face [Havran *et al.*, 1998, Křivánek and Bubník, 2000].

Following a top-down scheme instead, the tree structure may alternatively be traversed
in a depth-first fashion [Jansen, 1986] by starting from the root of the hierarchy and then
recursively visiting the children of each branch node shall the ray overlap the spatial extent
of (one or both of) the latter. Because the *bounding volume* associated with each node is 357
implicitly defined by its ancestors higher up in the tree, the procedure additionally requires
the overlap interval (initialized to that of the scene's bounding box at the root) to be explicitly
maintained in order to clip the implicitly bounded dimensions of each subtree. The base
algorithm can be further optimized by visiting the child nodes in the order in which they
are pierced by the ray, and by initiating the traversal procedure with a comparison of the
current node's entry point against the closest intersection identified prior to visiting the given
node, so as to anticipatively cull subtrees entirely located beyond the latter, as illustrated in
Figure 9.19. 384

As illustrated in *Figure 9.20*, the order of the child nodes may be determined by defining 384
the near node as the one located on the same side of the split *plane* as the ray's origin 247
[Jansen, 1986], using its direction as a discriminant shall the origin lie within the *plane*, in 247
which case the ray pierces the near node only whenever $t_{split} \leq 0$ or $t_{max} \leq t_{split}$, the far node
only whenever $0 < t_{split} \leq t_{min}$ and both nodes whenever $t_{min} < t_{split} < t_{max}$. Although
this approach can be made overall more efficient and robust by evaluating the coordinates of
the points along the axis of the split *plane* rather than parametrically along the ray [Havran 247
et al., 1997, Havran, 2000, Ch. 5], a simpler alternative entails determining the order of the

Figure 9.19: ***k*-D Tree Traversal Cost:** Color-coded illustration of the relative computational cost of k-D tree traversal for a Sierpinski tetrahedron.

child nodes based on the ray's direction, using the location of its origin as a discriminant
247 shall the direction be parallel to the *plane*, in which case the ray pierces the near node only
whenever $t_{max} \leq t_{split}$, the far node only whenever $t_{split} \leq t_{min}$ and both nodes whenever
385 $t_{min} < t_{split} < t_{max}$, as outlined in *Algorithm 9.9*.

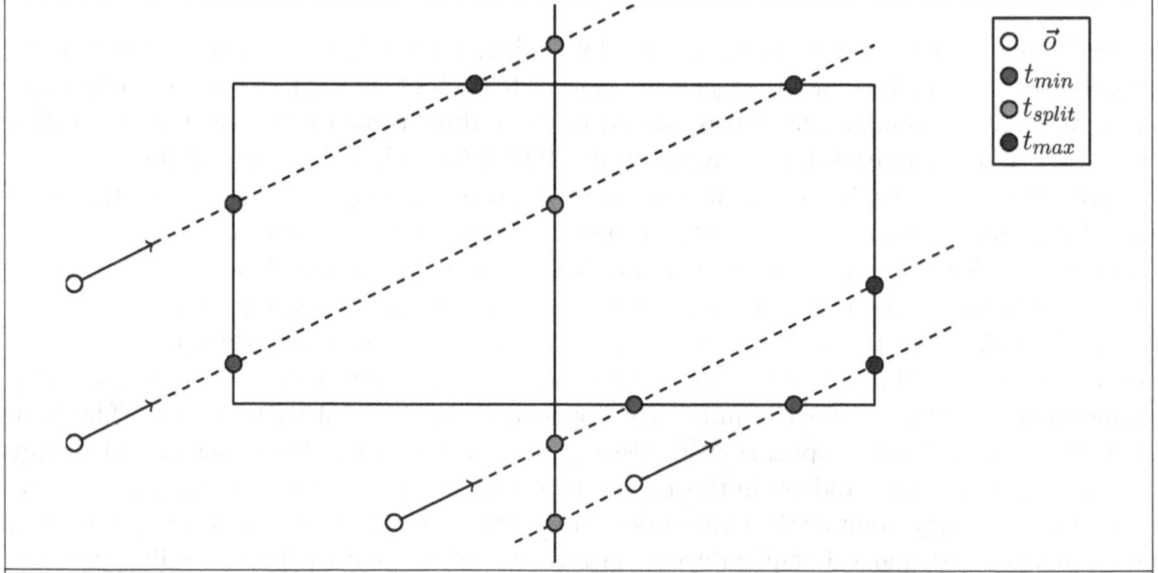

Figure 9.20: ***k*-D Tree Traversal:** Illustration of the ordering of the near and far child node based either on the ray's origin or on its direction (drawn after [Havran *et al.*, 1997, Fig. 1] and [Havran, 2000, Fig. 5.3]).

Further Reading Additional material may be found in surveys dedicated to k-D tree traversal algorithms for ray-tracing [Hapala and Havran, 2011].

Algorithm 9.9: k-D Tree Traversal: Pseudocode for k-D tree traversal.

```
Data: Ray r, node n and interval [enter, exit]
Result: Intersection found by traversing the k-D tree
Intersection i ← ∅;
if enter > prior intersections then
    Go to end;
end
if n is branch node then
    t ← (s − o_a) ÷ d_a;
    if t > enter then
        i ← closest{i, TraverseKDTree(r, c_near, enter, min{exit, t})};
    end
    if t < exit then
        i ← closest{i, TraverseKDTree(r, c_far, max{enter, t}, exit)};
    end
else
    foreach object o ∈ set S_n of objects referenced by node n do
        i ← closest{i, Intersect(r, o)};
    end
end
return i
```

9.3.5.4 Storage

In addition to being flagged as a branch or as a leaf, each k-D tree node must also hold a list and number of references to its associated objects in case of a leaf node, while a branch node ought to store references to its children as well as the coordinate of its associated splitting *plane* and the axis along which it is oriented. Because the four states of being either a leaf 247
node or a branch node with a splitting *plane* oriented in X, Y or Z are all mutually exclusive, 247
the type of a given node can be fully encoded in two bits of storage.

In order to improve cache efficiency, a node may be compactly represented by coalescing fields that are only relevant to either branch nodes or leaf nodes into a single variable. It is also common practice to store the two bits encoding the type of a node either in the lower bits of the reduced-precision split *plane* coordinate or object count, or in the unused last two 247
bits of the pointer to the memory-aligned location of the juxtaposed children or object list, yielding an 8-byte memory footprint under the assumption of a 32-bit addressing mode and floating-point representation.

Finally, the memory footprint of the structure might be reduced further by storing the references of sibling leaf nodes in a single contiguous array. The latter is then reordered into left-only, shared and right-only segment lists so as to avoid duplicating shared references [Soupikov *et al.*, 2008].

9.3.6 BSP Tree

9.3.6.1 Definition

First introduced to the field of computer graphics for visibility determination [Fuchs *et al.*, 1980], a ***binary space-partitioning tree***, commonly abbreviated *BSP tree*, is a binary tree in which the spatial extent of each branch node is recursively partitioned into two half-spaces

247 by an arbitrarily oriented splitting *plane* (thereby defining a generalized *k-D tree*), while its
381 357 leaf nodes hold references to the objects that their associated *bounding volume* intersects.
386 As illustrated in *Figure 9.21*, the hierarchical data structure may locally adapt, thanks to its relatively high degree of freedom, the level and orientation of refinement to the distribution of the input geometry, flexibly providing a fine subdivision along the critical angles of densely populated regions while remaining relatively coarse in sparse regions.

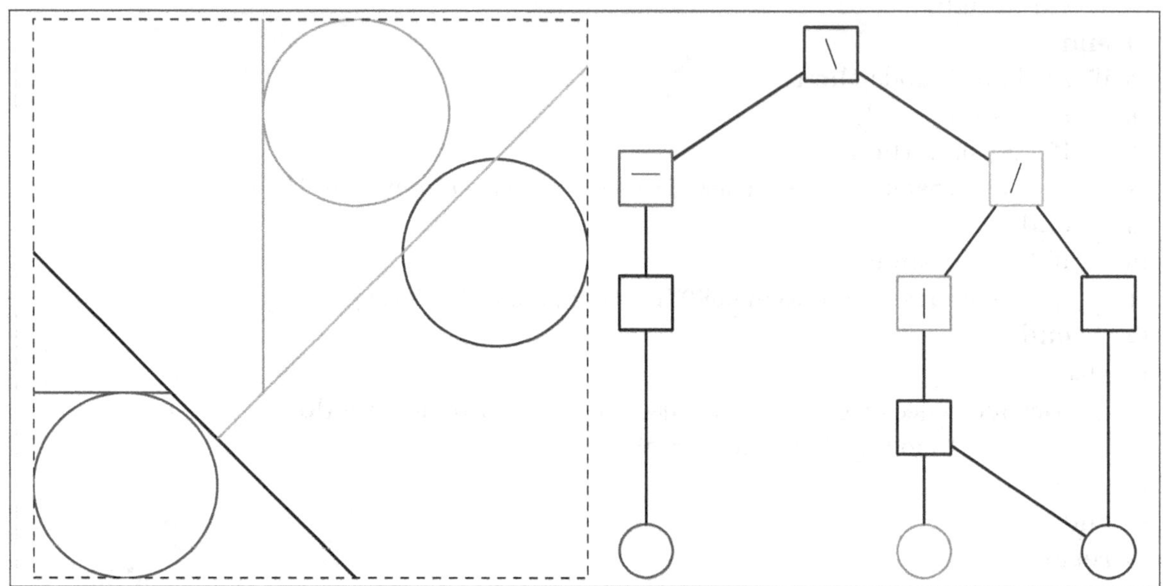

Figure 9.21: BSP Tree Structure: Illustration of a BSP tree structure recursively partitioning the spatial extent of each branch node into two arbitrarily oriented half-spaces.

9.3.6.2 Construction

A BSP tree can be built via a top-down algorithm similar to the one devised for the *con-*
381 *struction* of *k-D trees*. Excluding the cost of defining the axis and coordinate of the splitting
381 247 *plane* (or the lack thereof), the asymptotic complexity of the node refinement procedure is
therefore also linear $O(n)$ in the number n of objects provided as input to the node.

247 On the downside, the arbitrary orientation of each splitting *plane* significantly broadens
the dimensionality of the search space, and exploration schemes rely in practice either on evolutionary genetic algorithms applied to a population of split candidates tangent to the polygonal faces of the geometry [Cassen *et al.*, 1995], or on restricting the space of split
247 candidates to a predetermined set of *plane* orientations [Kammaje and Mora, 2007]. While
393 the latter approach allows some of the splitting strategies discussed in *Subsection 9.4.2* to
efficiently evaluate the surface area of the k-DOPs via linear programming techniques [Budge
247 *et al.*, 2008], the arbitrary orientation of the *planes* precludes the amortization of sort-based
approaches at the benefit of naive SAH computation, in addition to making the recursive classification sensitive to the numerical errors occurring in fixed-precision floating-point computation [Ize *et al.*, 2008, Ize, 2009, Ch. 3].

357 Finally, because the *bounding volume* associated with each child node is described by an
arbitrary convex polyhedron rather than by a simple axis-aligned bounding box, evaluating the overlap of the object (or its bounding box) with each of the semi-infinite half-spaces
247 defined by the splitting *plane* is generally a more practical conservative approximation than
an object-child intersection test.

9.3.6.3 *Traversal*

Upon intersection of its *bounding volume* by a ray, a BSP tree may be traversed in a depth- 357
first fashion similar to the *traversal* algorithm devised for *k-D trees*. However, the arbitrary 382
orientation of each splitting *plane* requires a general ray–*plane* intersection test as opposed 381 247
to a 1-D subset of it, similarly preventing the fixed-precision floating-point representation of 247
the normals to encode precise *plane* equations [Ize *et al.*, 2008, Ize, 2009, Ch. 3]. 247

9.3.6.4 *Storage*

In addition to being flagged as a branch or as a leaf, each BSP-tree node must also hold a
list of references to its associated objects in case of a leaf node, while a branch node ought to
store references to its children as well as the coordinate of its associated splitting *plane* and 247
the axis along which it is oriented. Also, although restricted splitting *planes* can be compactly 247
referenced by means of a *k-D tree*-like index [Kammaje and Mora, 2007], arbitrarily oriented 381
splitting *planes* more generally require an explicit encoding of their normal axis using a 247
floating-point representation.

9.3.7 Unstructured Mesh

As illustrated in *Figure 9.22*, a relatively versatile spatial-subdivision structure may be de- 387
vised as an unstructured mesh, such as a hexahedral mesh whose free-form cube-like cells provide a greater potential for adaptability [Dippé and Swensen, 1984]. In an attempt to approximately isolate a single object per cell, a Voronoi diagram can alternatively be built over the centroids of all objects in the scene, where each cell holds references to all objects ultimately overlapping its spatial extent [Márton, 1995a]. While an unstructured tetrahedral mesh might be readily provided as the output of a (e.g., heat/fluid flow) field solver based on finite element methods [Favre and Löhner, 1994], the connected triangles constituting a scene can be similarly embedded as faces of the mesh via constrained Delaunay tetrahedralization, thereby defining the data structure as a superset of the geometry rather than as a container of it [Lagae and Dutré, 2008a, Lagae and Dutré, 2008b].

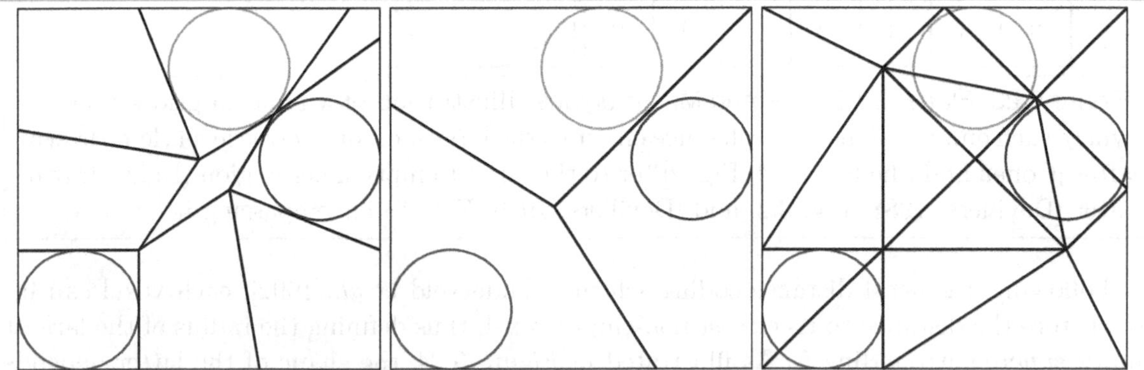

Figure 9.22: Unstructured Meshes: Illustration of various types of unstructured meshes, including a hexahedral mesh (drawn after [Dippé and Swensen, 1984, Fig. 1b]), a Voronoi diagram (drawn after [Márton, 1995a, Fig. 3]) and a tetrahedral mesh (drawn after [Dippé and Swensen, 1984, Fig. 1c] and [Lagae and Dutré, 2008a, Fig. 2]) (from left to right, respectively).

In contrast to hierarchical data structures where a local adaptation to the data globally impacts the higher levels of the tree, the non-hierarchical nature of locally adaptive unstructured meshes allows their computational cost to solely depend on the local complexity of the data in the vicinity of the ray. The latter may then traverse the structure by repeatedly following the reference to the neighboring cell adjacent to the wall through which it exits the cell being currently visited. In order to avoid repeatedly resorting to relatively expensive point location queries, though, the cell within which the intersection of a ray occurred might readily be used as the entry node of the subsequent ray along a path.

9.3.8 Distance Field

While spatial-subdivision schemes allow empty regions of space to be readily skipped during
traversal, empty-space leaping may alternatively be achieved by explicitly defining for each
individual position in space an empty region encompassing it. Rather than flattening an
378 *octree* hierarchy by storing in each empty voxel of a *grid* structure the level of its largest
369 empty ancestor node [Cohen and Sheffer, 1994], a more flexible approach entails storing in
each empty voxel a reference to an unconstrained cuboidal "macroregion" [Devillers, 1989,
388 Devillers, 1988, Ch. 3], as illustrated in *Figure 9.23*.

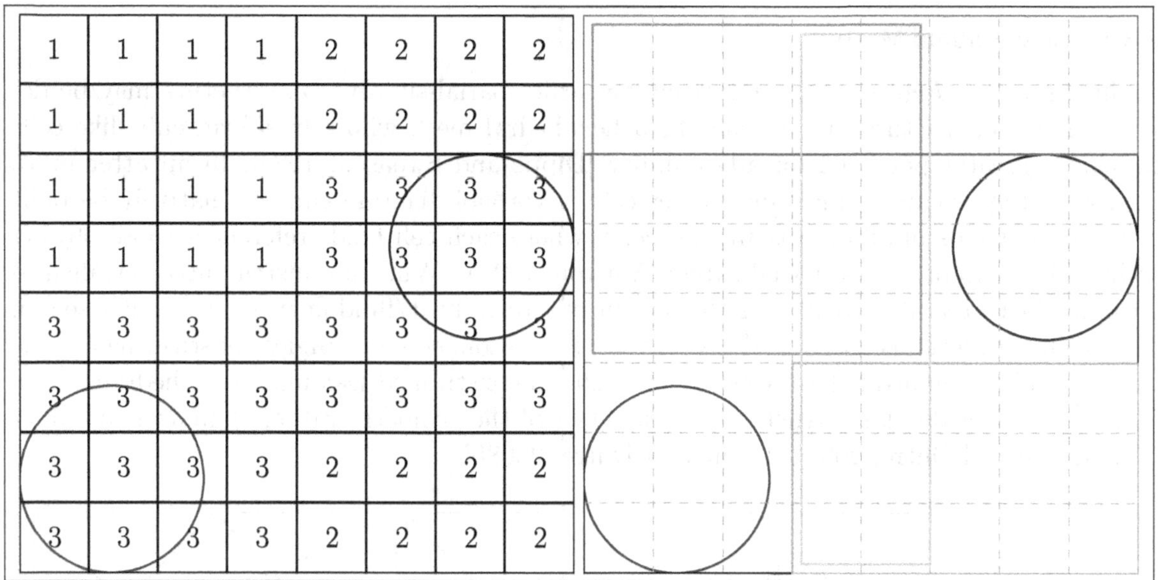

1	1	1	1	2	2	2	2
1	1	1	1	2	2	2	2
1	1	1	1	3	3	3	3
1	1	1	1	3	3	3	3
3	3	3	3	3	3	3	3
3	3	3	3	3	3	3	3
3	3	3	3	2	2	2	2
3	3	3	3	2	2	2	2

Figure 9.23: Flattened Octree and Macroregions: Illustration of a uniform grid structure where each empty cell holds a reference either to the largest empty octree level (left, drawn after [Cohen and Sheffer, 1994, Fig. 2]) or to the largest empty macroregion (right, drawn after [Devillers, 1988, Fig. 3.2] and [Devillers, 1989, Fig. 2]) encompassing it.

Following a general distance-coding scheme [Zuiderveld *et al.*, 1992], each voxel can instead store the distance to its closest non-empty voxel, thus defining the radius of the largest
269 empty *sphere* surrounding it. As illustrated in *Figure 9.24*, the shape of the latter depends
389 on the specific distance metric under consideration, and widely used instances include the
city-block metric (L^1 distance) [Cohen and Sheffer, 1994], approximations of the Euclidean
metric (L^2 distance) such as the Chamfer distance, as well as the chessboard metric (L^∞
distance) [Šrámek, 1994a, Šrámek, 1994b, Šrámek, 1995, Šrámek, 1996].

Considering a single orientation along a given axis, the distance of an empty voxel to the closest non-empty voxel before it (whose distance value is implicitly defined to be zero) may be incrementally computed as the sum of the empty voxel's distance to another visible preceding empty voxel and the distance value contained within the latter [Borgefors, 1986]. In the more general multidimensional case, the distance between the two voxels can be

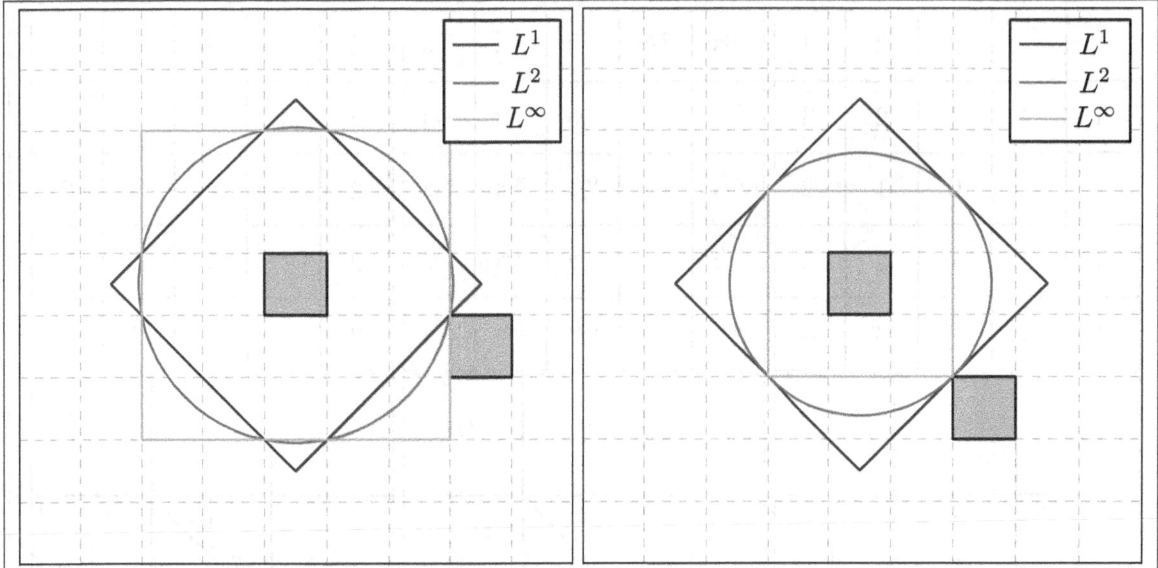

Figure 9.24: Distance Metrics: Illustration of the largest empty sphere around a given voxel for the city-block, quantized Euclidean and chessboard distance metrics (drawn after [Šrámek and Kaufman, 2000, Fig. 5]).

compactly represented as a mask whose values depend on the given distance metric, as illustrated in *Figure 9.25*. The incremental distance computation then entails carrying a 390
forward pass using the upper half of the mask, determining the distance of a voxel at the center of the mask to all objects to the top left of it as the smallest sum of the mask value and distance stored in the respective neighboring voxel (defined as infinity beyond the domain boundaries), followed by a backward pass using the lower half of the mask so as to determine the distance to all objects to the bottom right, while the distance transform finally attributes to each empty voxel the minimum of the two previously computed distances, thereby yielding an asymptotic cost $O(R)$ linear in the number of voxels R.

Rather than stepping through each voxel individually, the 3-D DDA grid algorithm may then readily exploit the distance information contained within each empty voxel encountered during the ray traversal to skip over empty regions of space. Because the step size is directly correlated to the proximity of geometric data, the distance field similarly allows the computational cost to locally adapt to the *probability* of intersection in the vicinity of the 129
ray.

In order to account not only for the spatial position along the ray but also for the direction of the latter, anisotropic distance fields encode within every empty voxel a distance for each of the eight octants corresponding to positive/negative ray directions along the $x/y/z$ axes, which can similarly be incrementally computed by considering the corresponding octant of the associated mask [Šrámek and Kaufman, 2000]. In the case of the chessboard distance metric, further extensions of the approach additionally entail expanding the empty region associated with a given octant along the axis yielding the maximum increase, thereby requiring each octant to store a distance per dimension rather than a single distance for all dimensions [Es *et al.*, 2006, Es and İşler, 2007].

9.3.9 Performance

Because the spatial extent of the cells may be smaller than that of the referenced objects (e.g., by means of split-clipping), hierarchical space-partitioning schemes typically yield rather

4	3	2	3	4
3	2	1	2	3
2	1	0	1	2
3	2	1	2	3
4	3	2	3	4

8/3	7/3	6/3	7/3	8/3
7/3	4/3	3/3	4/3	7/3
6/3	3/3	0/3	3/3	6/3
7/3	4/3	3/3	4/3	7/3
8/3	7/3	6/3	7/3	8/3

2	2	2	2	2
2	1	1	1	2
2	1	0	1	2
2	1	1	1	2
2	2	2	2	2

∞	1	∞
1	0	1
∞	1	∞

4/3	3/3	4/3
3/3	0/3	3/3
4/3	3/3	4/3

1	1	1
1	0	1
1	1	1

Figure 9.25: Distance Transforms: Illustration of the set of equidistant voxels (top, drawn after [Šrámek and Kaufman, 2000, Fig. 19]) and of the masks used to compute the discrete distance transform (bottom, drawn after [Cohen and Sheffer, 1994, Fig. 9 and 10]) based on the city-block, the 3-4 Chamfer and the chessboard distance (from left to right, respectively) decomposed into two halves for incremental evaluation of the distance values in row-major order.

deep trees with relatively many but tight cells, generally leading to a relatively high traversal performance, albeit at the cost of high memory requirements and construction times. Also, the seldom inspection of the children of a node is counterbalanced by the fact that each geometric entity might be visited more than once, consequently making such subdivision schemes relatively suited for computationally inexpensive objects.

In order to avoid the redundant computation of previously calculated intersections, each object in the scene may be assigned a container identifying whether the object has previously
391 been visited by a given ray, as illustrated in *Figure 9.26*. Upon inspection of an object by the ray, the content of the container is first evaluated such that the intersection test is readily skipped (and its result optionally retrieved from the container) shall the container report its previous occurrence. Otherwise, the intersection test proceeds and the container is marked accordingly (optionally storing the result of the intersection test), hence making the data readily available for subsequent inspections of the object by the ray, and thereby increasing performance proportionally to the ratio of the intersection's computational cost against the overhead incurred by the bookkeeping process.

The simplest instance of this approach relies on a single Boolean flag, which is set upon inspection of the object by a given ray, and reset for all objects prior to the traversal of the structure by a new ray [Subramanian, 1987, Fussell and Subramanian, 1988]. Instead, a more efficient alternative, commonly referred to as *mailboxing* [Arnaldi *et al.*, 1987], consists in assigning a unique identification number to each ray and in storing the ID of the last visiting ray in the containers, then referred to as mailboxes, such that an intersection test

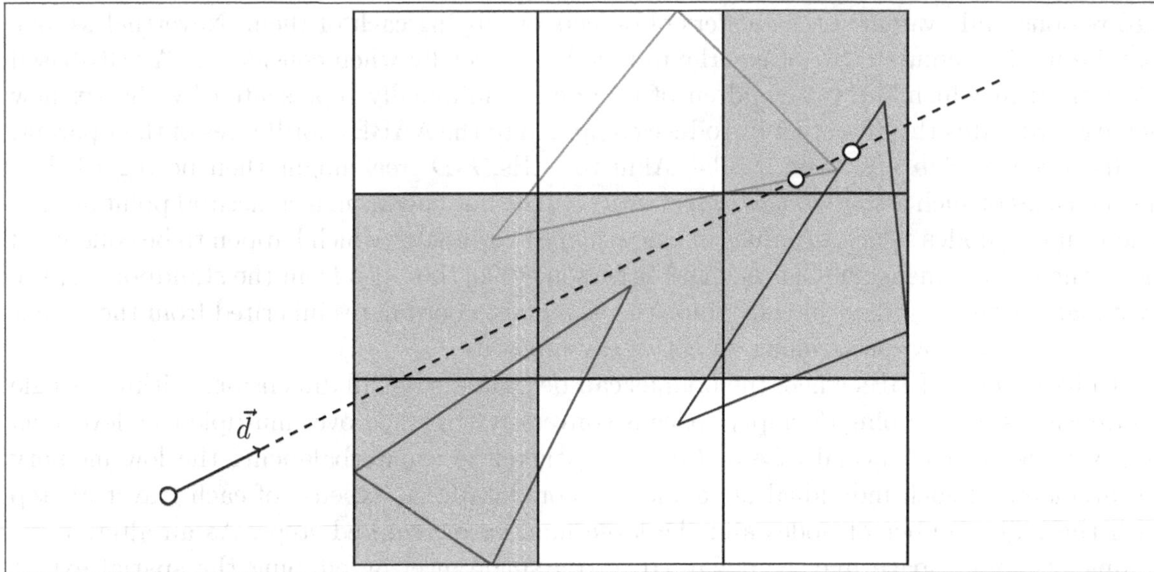

Figure 9.26: Mail Boxing: Illustration of an object straddling several cell boundaries, leading to the redundant computation of the intersection point in each referencing cell visited by the ray.

can be skipped if the ID of a ray matches the ID stored in the mailbox, while the ray ID is written into it otherwise, thereby implicitly resetting the ID of the previous ray [Amanatides and Woo, 1987]. In the case of instantiated geometry, though, for which the mailbox of a single physical object might be shared among different logical instances, the ID should instead uniquely identify the pairwise combination of a given ray traversing a given structure [Kirk and Arvo, 1991].

In order to avoid concurrency issues in parallel implementations, each object may either allocate a mailbox per thread, or hold instead a read-only residency mask whose bits indicate whether the object resides in each individual cell of the acceleration structure, while the bits of the mask associated with a ray are flipped in turn as the ray progresses through the cells of the acceleration structure, such that an object is known to have already been visited by the ray if a bit-wise logical AND of the object's mask and the ray's mask results in a non-zero value (i.e., at least one of the cells where the object resides has already been visited by the ray) [Cychosz, 1992]. As an inherently thread-safe alternative, *inverse mailboxing* [Shevtsov *et al.*, 2007] conversely stores in per ray caches the IDs of the n most recently visited objects, therefore eliminating most, but not all, redundant intersection tests.

9.4 SPACE–OBJECT SUBDIVISION

Even though the various aforementioned subdivision schemes might at first appear fundamentally different, their underlying data structures actually are conceptually closely related.
For instance, the distinction between the various *spatial subdivision* schemes such as uniform 369
grids, *multilevel grids*, *octrees*, *k-D trees* and *BSP trees* essentially lies in the height and 369
arity of their tree structures as well as in the (non-)uniform positioning and orientation of the 377 378
partitioning *planes*, such that any of the former may be emulated by imposing restrictions 381
on the degrees of freedom of the latter [Havran, 2007]. 385 247

A similar observation can be made regarding *object subdivision* versus *spatial subdivision* 357
schemes, which are dual of one another since the former partitions the set of objects into 369
clusters and evaluates the regions of spaces occupied by each, while the latter partitions space

into regions and evaluates the clusters of objects occupying each of them. Nevertheless, one
may be used to emulate the other [Havran, 2007], especially when considering AABB-based
BVH trees in which the two children of a node are minimally represented by the six new
247 *plane* coordinates they together introduce compared to the AABB coordinates of their parent,
365 381 as discussed in *Subsubsection 9.2.3.4.* Akin to BIHs, *k-D trees* might then be regarded as
special cases of such a *bounding box hierarchy* (*BBH*), not only from a structural point of view
247 where sibling nodes solely introduce two new *plane* coordinates which happen to be collocated
along the same dimension [Charney and Scherson, 1990], but also from the standpoint of the
247 traversal where redundant intersections with the *plane* coordinates inherited from the parent
node are avoided by maintaining an active ray interval.

Unlike general BBHs where the bounds can be tightened in all dimensions within a single
subdivision step, clipping of empty space is conversely stretched over multiple tree levels via
381 empty nodes in the special case of *k-D trees*, therefore counterbalancing the low memory
requirements of each individual node and low computational expense of each traversal step
with the high number of nodes and the large number of required steps. As an alternative,
culling of empty space may be collapsed into a single level by clipping the spatial extent
381 of the nodes of a *k-D tree* with explicitly stored bounding boxes tightly fitting the objects
within [Hook and Forward, 1995, Hook, 1995], thereby affecting the surface areas of the
child nodes [Subramanian and Fussell, 1990b, Subramanian, 1990, Ch. 6] and inducing a
piecewise quadratic (rather than piecewise linear) SAH cost function since both the length
and circumference of the bounding boxes vary linearly with the coordinate due to clipping, in
turn causing the exact minimum to no longer coincide with the face of an object's bounding
box [Stich *et al.*, 2009].

In order for the geometry to be exhaustively indexable by any such structure, the construction algorithm must then guarantee that any surface point is referenced by a node
357 encompassing it. Two incarnations of this requirement are *object subdivision* and *spatial*
369 *subdivision*, and either can be applied to build a valid BBH tree. Lifting the restriction of
single referencing in the latter structure, for instance, allows for a more efficient handling of
non-uniformly tessellated geometry via a tighter isolation of objects with large spatial extents,
either by split-clipping the latter such that the resulting localized bounding boxes referencing
it are treated as individual inputs by the construction algorithm [Ernst and Greiner, 2007], or
by solely subdividing objects whose bounding box contains large portions of empty space in
357 369 a pre-process [Dammertz and Keller, 2008]. Both *object subdivision* and *spatial subdivision*
may also be mixed within a single *spatial BVH* (*SBVH*) during the hierarchy construction
itself, either on a per node basis by selecting the scheme that will yield the overall optimal
SAH-based partition, or doing so on a per object basis by referencing each object that strad-
247 dles a given splitting *plane* either in the left/right child node (as in object partitioning) or
in both (as in spatial partitioning) [Stich *et al.*, 2009].

9.4.1 Definition

Most of the aforementioned subdivision schemes are based on a hierarchical representation of the data. Following the standard terminology, each branch node (also known as internal or inner node) of the underlying tree structure holds references to its children, starting from the root all the way down to the leaf nodes (also called external or outer nodes).

Considering a *perfect tree* (i.e., a tree in which every level is completely filled) with a branching factor b (so-called *arity* as it yields a b-ary tree) (such that every node has $b-1$ siblings, except for the root since it has no parent), the level of depth i (where the root has depth zero) contains exactly b^i cousin nodes. Conversely, a perfect tree whose last level contains $n \triangleq b^h$ leaf nodes therefore has a height of $h = \log_b(n)$, such that the total number of levels equals $1 + h$. It then follows that the total number of nodes in the tree is given by the *geometric series* 16

$$N \triangleq \sum_{i=0}^{h} b^i \overset{(2.10)}{=} \frac{b^{1+h} - 1}{b - 1} \tag{9.15}$$ 16

which, in the case where $h = \log_b(n)$, yields

$$N = \frac{b b^{\log_b(n)} - 1}{b - 1} = \frac{bn - 1}{b - 1} \tag{9.16}$$

thereby resulting in a linear memory footprint $O(n)$. In the typical case of a binary tree, where $b = 2$, the result simplifies to $N = 2n - 1$.

9.4.2 Construction

9.4.2.1 Overview

Thanks to the various degrees of freedom provided by each of their nodes, tree-based acceleration structures are generally able to locally adapt (to different extents) to the spatial distribution of the scene's geometry. However, exploiting the full potential of this versatility entails the exhaustive exploration of their associated search space [Popov *et al.*, 2009], whose cardinality is given by the ratio of all $n!$ possible combinations of the leaf nodes at the bottom level, to the number of topologically equivalent perfect tree configurations. Expressing the latter quantity as the accumulation for every level i but the last of the $b!$ arrangements of the child nodes of each of the b^i branch nodes, the total number of distinct possible trees then reads

$$\frac{n!}{\prod_{i=0}^{\log_b(n)-1} (b!)^{b^i}} = \frac{n!}{(b!)^{\sum_{i=0}^{\log_b(n)-1} b^i}} \overset{(2.10)}{=} \frac{n!}{(b!)^{\frac{b^{1+\log_b(n)-1}-1}{b-1}}} = \frac{n!}{(b!)^{\frac{n-1}{b-1}}} \tag{9.17}$$ 16

which reduces to $\frac{n!}{2^{n-1}}$ in the case of a binary structure where $b = 2$.

Under the simplifying assumption of a perfect tree built over n input objects, the asymptotic cost C of constructing the subtree associated with a node given a subset of n' objects may be expressed recursively as the sum of the cost C_P of processing the node and the cost of processing each of its children

$$C(n') \triangleq C_P(n') + \begin{cases} bC\left(\frac{n'}{b}\right) & \text{if } n' > \frac{n}{b^h} \\ 0 & \text{otherwise} \end{cases} \tag{9.18}$$

Rather than relying on the *master theorem* to derive bounds for restricted formulations of $C_P(n)$, the recurrence may instead be expanded into a sum over all levels of their corresponding time complexities. The latter are themselves defined as the product of the number of nodes at the given level with the complexity of refining a single node at that level, which is a function of the number of objects distributed among all nodes at that level, in turn yielding

$$C(n) = C_P(n) + bC\left(\frac{n}{b}\right) = C_P(n) + b\left(C_P\left(\frac{n}{b}\right) + bC\left(\frac{n}{b^2}\right)\right) = \ldots = \sum_{i=0}^{h} b^i C_P\left(\frac{n}{b^i}\right) \tag{9.19}$$

where the height h might be explicitly capped to a fixed maximum value in order to bound the level of recursion and the memory consumption of the tree structure with it. In practice, *object subdivision* schemes typically need to additionally abort the recursive refinement of 357
a subtree whenever the partitioning scheme fails to subdivide its input into distinct subsets (e.g., due to the spatial overlap of the objects in the set).

9.4.2.2 Spatial-Middle Split

357 Following Cauchy's theorem regarding the average projected area of convex *bounding volumes*
358 247 as introduced in *Equation 9.4*, the axis and coordinate of the splitting *plane* may be defined so
129 as to minimize the surface area, and therefore the *probability* of intersection, of the children
of the node being refined.

Considering a cuboid of dimensions x, y and z and constant inner volume $v \triangleq xyz$, the surface area

$$s \triangleq 2(yz + zx + xy) = 2\left(\frac{v}{x} + \frac{v}{y} + xy\right) \tag{9.20}$$

is minimum whenever the first-order partial derivatives of the multivariate function vanish, leading to

$$\frac{\partial s}{\partial x} = 2\left(-\frac{v}{x^2} + y\right) = 0 \iff v = yx^2 \tag{9.21}$$

$$\frac{\partial s}{\partial y} = 2\left(-\frac{v}{y^2} + x\right) = 0 \iff v = xy^2 \tag{9.22}$$

394 which yields $yx^2 = xy^2 \iff x = y$ as well as $z = \frac{v}{x^2} \overset{(9.21)}{=} \frac{yx^2}{x^2} = y$, and finally $x = y = z =$
$\sqrt[3]{v}$, which corresponds to a cube (while for the same volume but an arbitrary topology, the
269 absolute minimum surface area would be given by a *sphere*).

It then follows that in order to minimize their surface areas, the cuboidal volumes associated with the child nodes should be roughly cubical in shape. This can be achieved using the *spatial-middle split* strategy, which consists in splitting the parent's volume in half along the
378 axis of largest extent (rather than by cycling through the axes to emulate an *octree* [Kaplan,
129 1985, Kaplan, 1987]), thereby making the *probability* of intersection of the children equal
394 as illustrated in *Figure 9.27*. Similarly, the recursive refinement process might be terminated
whenever the surface area of the (non-empty) volume associated with the node under con-
129 sideration falls below a given threshold, in which case its absolute *probability* of intersection
is deemed to be negligible.

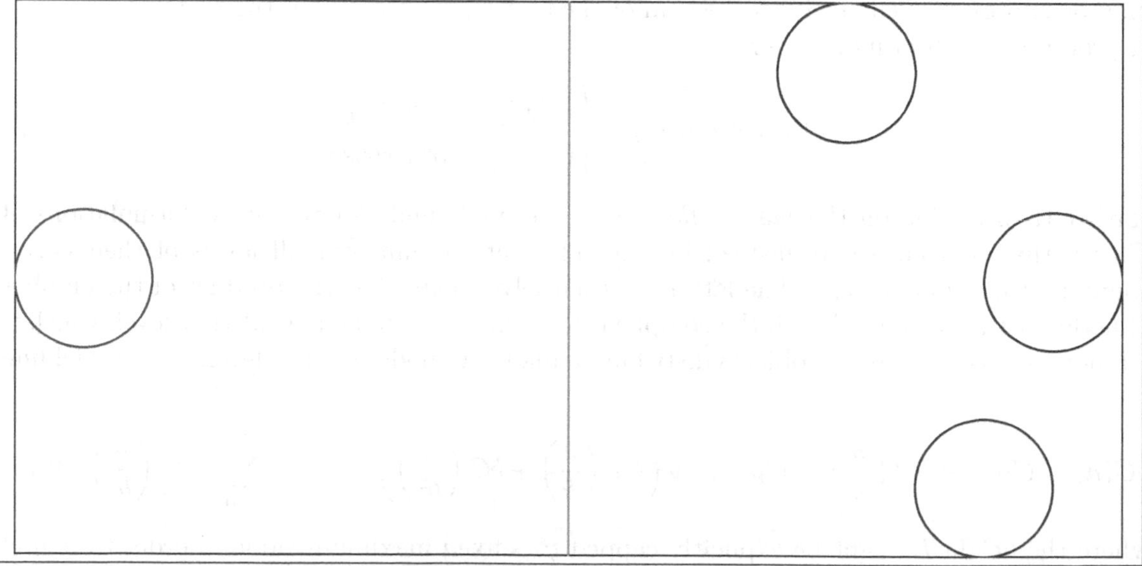

Figure 9.27: Spatial-Middle Split: Illustration of a node refinement step where the children are created by splitting the volume of the node under consideration in half along the axis of largest extent.

Because the axis and coordinate of the split can be determined in constant time as outlined in *Algorithm 9.10*, the cost of refining a single node remains linear, $C_P(n) = O(1) +$ 395
$O(n) \sim O(n)$, leading to an overall asymptotic complexity for the tree construction of

$$C(n) \overset{(9.19)}{=} \sum_{i=0}^{h} b^i O\left(\frac{n}{b^i}\right) = O\left(\sum_{i=0}^{h} n\right) = O(n(1+h)) \tag{9.23}$$ 393

which, in the case where $h = \log_b(n)$, yields

$$C(n) = O\Big(n(1 + \log_b(n))\Big) \sim O(n \log_b(n)) \tag{9.24}$$

Algorithm 9.10: Spatial-Middle Split: Pseudocode for the middle-based splitting strategy.

```
Data: Set of objects S and bounding box B
Result: A splitting plane in the spatial middle of S
if SurfaceArea(B) > threshold then
    axis ← LargestDimension(B);
    coordinate ← MiddlePoint(B, axis);
else
    axis ← ∅;
    coordinate ← ∅;
end
return Splitting plane [axis, coordinate]
```

9.4.2.3 Object-Median Split

As an alternative, the axis and coordinate of a splitting *plane* may instead be defined so as to 247
evenly distribute the number objects in the input set, and therefore the associated workload as would be optimal for proximity search tasks, among the children of the node being refined [Subramanian, 1987, Fussell and Subramanian, 1988]. This can be achieved using the *object-median split* strategy, which consists in splitting the parent's volume at the median along the chosen axis (e.g., selected in a round-robin fashion at each level of the tree), as illustrated in *Figure 9.28*. Similarly, the recursive refinement process might be terminated whenever the 396
number of objects in the input set falls below a given threshold, in which case its absolute workload is deemed to be negligible.

By selecting the $\frac{n}{2}^{\text{th}}$ smallest centroid coordinate along the chosen axis as outlined in
Algorithm 9.11, the median can be determined in linear time using an efficient selection 396
algorithm (such as quickselect), which only performs a partial sort rather than a complete sort of the elements in the list. The cost of refining a single node therefore remains linear, $C_P(n) = O(n) + O(n) \sim O(n)$, similarly leading to an overall asymptotic complexity for the
tree construction of $C(n) = O(n \log_b(n))$ whenever $h = \log_b(n)$, as shown in *Equation 9.24*. 395

9.4.2.4 SAH Split

Surface Area Heuristic Given a ray whose origin is uniformly distributed in the plane orthogonal to its direction $\hat{\omega}$, the conditional *probability* of a child node N_c to be intersected 129
by the ray given that the latter overlaps its parent N_p is defined as the ratio of the projected
areas of their *bounding volumes* onto the plane 357

Figure 9.28: Object-Median Split: Illustration of a node refinement step where the children are created by splitting the volume of the node under consideration at the median along the chosen axis.

Algorithm 9.11: Object-Median Split: Pseudocode for the median-based splitting strategy.

Data: Set of objects S and bounding box B
Result: A splitting plane in the object median of S

if $\|S\| > \textit{threshold}$ **then**
  $\textit{axis} \leftarrow$ `CyclingDimension()`;
  $\textit{coordinate} \leftarrow$ `SelectCandidate`$(S, \|S\| \div 2, \textit{axis})$;
else
  $\textit{axis} \leftarrow \emptyset$;
  $\textit{coordinate} \leftarrow \emptyset$;
end
return Splitting plane $[\textit{axis}, \textit{coordinate}]$

131

$$\Pr(N_c \mid N_p) \overset{(4.10)}{=} \frac{\Pr(N_c \cap N_p)}{\Pr(N_p)} = \frac{\Pr(N_c)}{\Pr(N_p)} = \frac{A_c(\hat{\omega})}{A_p(\hat{\omega})} \tag{9.25}$$

where the second equality follows from the fact a child node is guaranteed to be encapsulated
397 by its parent, as illustrated in *Figure 9.29*.

In the case of truly incoherent rays whose directions are uniformly distributed, as would
result from tracing a ray between two randomly selected points on the surface of the scene's
269 bounding *sphere* for instance, the *probability density* of rays actually intersecting the parent
131
357 node is similarly proportional to the projected area of its *bounding volume* onto the plane

$$p(\hat{\omega}) \triangleq \frac{A_p(\hat{\omega})}{\int_{4\pi} A_p(\hat{\omega}')\mathrm{d}\hat{\omega}'} \tag{9.26}$$

129 such that the expected conditional *probability* over all directions is readily given by the
357 surface areas S_c and S_p of the *bounding volumes* of the nodes

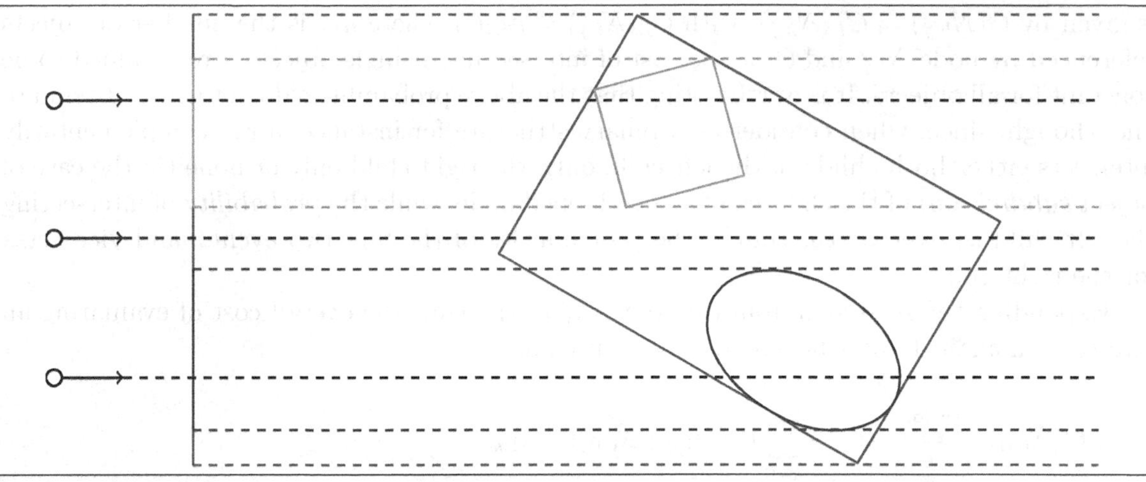

Figure 9.29: Projected Area of Bounding Volume: Illustration of the conditional probability of a child node to be intersected by a ray given that the latter overlaps its parent, which is defined by the ratio of the projected areas of their bounding volumes onto the plane orthogonal to the ray's direction.

$$\overline{\Pr}(N_c \mid N_p) \overset{(4.65)}{=} \int_{4\pi} \Pr(N_c \mid N_p) p(\hat{\omega}) d\hat{\omega}$$ 141

$$\overset{(9.25)}{\underset{(9.26)}{=}} \int_{4\pi} \frac{A_c(\hat{\omega})}{A_p(\hat{\omega})} \frac{A_p(\hat{\omega})}{\int_{4\pi} A_p(\hat{\omega}') d\hat{\omega}'} d\hat{\omega}$$ 396 396

$$= \frac{\int_{4\pi} A_c(\hat{\omega}) d\hat{\omega}}{\int_{4\pi} A_p(\hat{\omega}) d\hat{\omega}}$$

$$\overset{(9.4)}{=} \frac{4\pi \frac{S_c}{4}}{4\pi \frac{S_p}{4}}$$ 358

$$= \frac{S_c}{S_p} \tag{9.27}$$

Surface Area Cost Metric The *probability* of intersection of the individual cells and their 129
associated workload may be simultaneously taken into account by factoring both into a single
expression [Goldsmith and Salmon, 1987]. Adapting *Equation 9.1* to the case of hierarchical 358
object subdivision schemes and ignoring the distance-based culling optimization for the sake 357
of simplicity, the overall cost incurred by visiting the jth branch node $N_{i,j}$ at depth $i < h$ of a perfect tree with arity b is recursively defined as

$$\begin{aligned} C(N_{i,j}) &\triangleq \sum_{k=jb}^{(j+1)b-1} (C_B + \overline{\Pr}(N_{i+1,k} \mid N_{i,j}) C(N_{i+1,k})) \\ &= C_T + \sum_{k=jb}^{(j+1)b-1} \overline{\Pr}(N_{i+1,k} \mid N_{i,j}) C(N_{i+1,k}) \end{aligned} \tag{9.28}$$

where C_B is the cost of intersecting the *bounding volume* of each child node $N_{i+1,k}$, here 357
assumed to be constant for all *bounding volumes*. For *object subdivision* schemes, the cost 357
incurred by traversing the visited branch node itself therefore reads $C_T \triangleq \sum_{k=jb}^{(j+1)b-1} C_B =$ 357
bC_B, while for *spatial subdivision* schemes, it instead corresponds to the cost of identifying 369
the cells overlapping the ray. On the other hand, the cost incurred by visiting a leaf node

is given by $C(N_{h,j}) = C_L(N_{h,j})$, with $C_L(N_{i,j}) \triangleq n_{i,j}C_I$ where $n_{i,j}$ is the number of objects referenced by node $N_{i,j}$ and C_I is the cost of intersecting a single object, here assumed to be constant for all objects. It is worth noting that the above probabilities do not generally sum to one, though, since, when considering a binary structure for instance, a ray complementarily intersects either both children, the left child only, the right child only or none (in the case of
357 129 *object subdivision*) of the children of an overlapped node, while the *probability* of intersecting
129 the left child is given as the sum of the probabilities of the first two *events*, and vice versa
for the right child.

Expanding the recursion from the root $N_{0,0}$ of the tree, the overall cost of evaluating an intersection against the whole hierarchy then reads

397 $$C(N_{0,0}) \overset{(9.28)}{=} C_T + \sum_{k=0}^{b-1} \overline{\Pr}(N_{1,k} \mid N_{0,0})C(N_{1,k})$$

397 $$\overset{(9.28)}{=} C_T + \sum_{k=0}^{b-1} \overline{\Pr}(N_{1,k} \mid N_{0,0}) \left(C_T + \sum_{j=kb}^{(k+1)b-1} \overline{\Pr}(N_{2,j} \mid N_{1,k})C(N_{2,j}) \right)$$

397 $$\overset{(9.27)}{=} C_T + \sum_{k=0}^{b-1} \overline{\Pr}(N_{1,k} \mid N_{0,0})C_T + \sum_{k=0}^{b-1} \sum_{j=kb}^{(k+1)b-1} \overline{\Pr}(N_{2,j} \mid N_{0,0})C(N_{2,j})$$

$$= C_T + \sum_{j=0}^{b-1} \overline{\Pr}(N_{1,j} \mid N_{0,0})C_T + \sum_{j=0}^{b^2-1} \overline{\Pr}(N_{2,j} \mid N_{0,0})C(N_{2,j})$$

$$= \dots$$

$$= \sum_{i=0}^{h-1} \sum_{j=0}^{b^i-1} \overline{\Pr}(N_{i,j} \mid N_{0,0})C_T + \sum_{j=0}^{b^h-1} \overline{\Pr}(N_{h,j} \mid N_{0,0})C_L(N_{h,j}) \tag{9.29}$$

which, when assuming that all average conditional probabilities $\overline{\Pr}(N_{i+1,k} \mid N_{i,j}) = P_c$ and leaf costs $C_L(N_{h,j}) = C_L$ are constant, reduces to

398 16 $$C(N_{0,0}) \overset{(9.29)}{=} \sum_{i=0}^{h-1} b^i P_c^i C_T + b^h P_c^h C_L \overset{(2.10)}{=} \frac{1 - b^h P_c^h}{1 - bP_c} C_T + b^h P_c^h C_L \tag{9.30}$$

406 129 By considering the *traversal* cost $C_T \approx 0$ to be negligible, the average conditional *probability*
of the nodes can then be inversely expressed as a function of the branching factor, the number
406 of objects and the estimated tree *traversal* cost, so as to provide a rough load-independent
quality metric among various acceleration structures [Hunt *et al.*, 2007, Hunt, 2008b, Ch. 5].

Since, in practice, the actual properties of the subtrees are not known until the latter have been constructed, their costs may instead be conservatively estimated as those of leaf nodes $C(N_{i+1,k}) \approx C_L(N_{i+1,k})$, such that the cost formulation reduces to a typically parabola-shaped function of the axial coordinate known as the *surface area heuristic* (*SAH*) [MacDonald, 1988, MacDonald and Booth, 1990]

397 397 $$C(N_{i,j}) \underset{(9.27)}{\overset{(9.28)}{=}} C_T + \sum_{k=jb}^{(j+1)b-1} \frac{S_{i+1,k}}{S_{i,j}} C_L(N_{i+1,k}) = C_T + \frac{C_I}{S_{i,j}} \sum_{k=jb}^{(j+1)b-1} S_{i+1,k} n_{i+1,k} \tag{9.31}$$

247 The optimal split *plane* can then be greedily determined as the one for which the sum-
399 mation term is minimal, as illustrated in *Figure 9.30*, although it might be beneficial for
subdivision schemes providing loose spatial bounds to additionally favor nodes cutting out
regions of empty space by downscaling the cost estimation of the latter with a constant
369 sub-unit bias factor [Hurley *et al.*, 2002]. In the case of *spatial subdivision*, and under the

assumption of infinitely small objects such that none straddles the split *plane*, it may actually 247
be shown, via an analysis of the derivative of the SAH formulation, that the optimal split
coordinate ought to lie within the range defined by the spatial middle and the object median,
whose SAH costs turn out to be identical [MacDonald, 1988, MacDonald and Booth, 1990],
whereas the optimal partitioning might actually lie outside of this interval whenever objects
do straddle the split *plane*. 247

Terminating the construction of the hierarchy may similarly be driven by the SAH
cost model [Subramanian and Fussell, 1990a, Subramanian, 1990, Ch. 4] [Subramanian and
Fussell, 1991, Subramanian, 1990, Ch. 5]. To this end, the recursive refinement process might
stop whenever the cost incurred by visiting a leaf node would be smaller than that of visiting
the branch node with optimal split *plane* for that subtree 247

398

$$C_L(N_{i,j}) \leq C(N_{i,j}) \overset{(9.31)}{\iff} n_{i,j}C_I \leq C_T + \frac{C_I}{S_{i,j}} \sum_{k=jb}^{(j+1)b-1} S_{i+1,k}n_{i+1,k}$$

$$\iff S_{i,j}\left(n_{i,j} - \frac{C_T}{C_I}\right) \leq \sum_{k=jb}^{(j+1)b-1} S_{i+1,k}n_{i+1,k} \tag{9.32}$$

from which follows that the refinement criterion is solely impacted by the ratio of the *traversal* 406
and intersection costs rather than by their individual values. Due to the overestimation of
the subtree's costs via a linear rather than logarithmic term, though, it can be beneficial in
practice to encompass several levels in the subdivision criterion before terminating refinement
in order to better estimate the actual costs of the subtrees [Havran and Bittner, 2002].

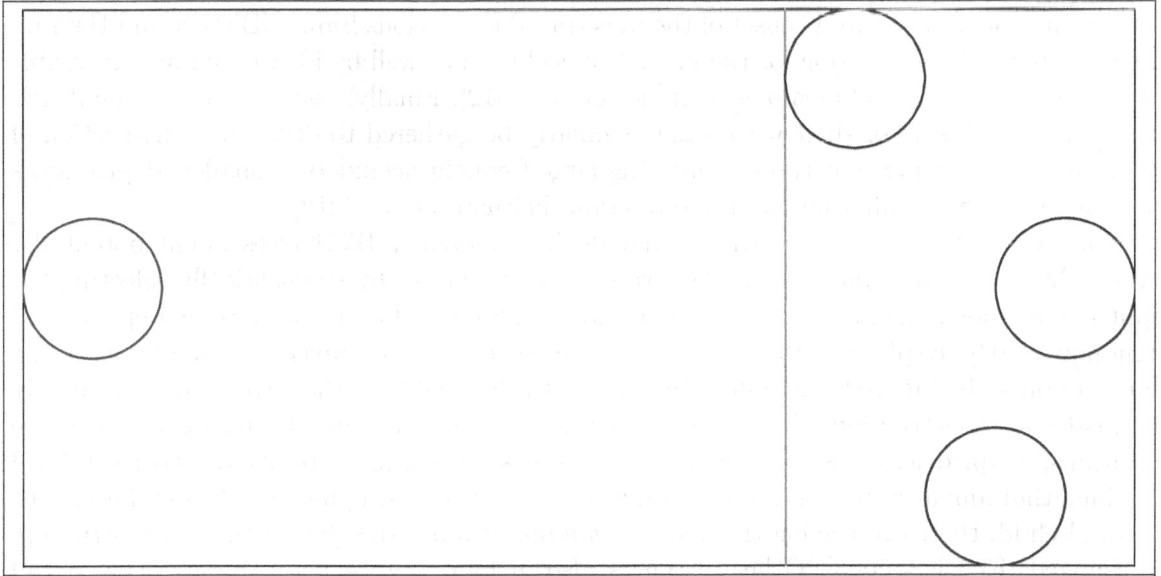

Figure 9.30: SAH-Based Split: Illustration of a node refinement step where the children are created by splitting the volume of the node under consideration so as to minimize the cost predicted by the surface area heuristic.

In order to minimize the *probability* of high-cost queries while maximizing the *proba-* 129
bility of low-cost ones, local heuristics inherently depend on the reliability of their expected 129
cost model for the specific task at hand, be it aimed at point, segment, ray, line or plane
classification [Naylor, 1996]. Because the assumptions on which the SAH builds do not necessarily hold in practice, though, more accurate cost prediction models may alternatively be
derived by generalization of the SAH, considering for instance the average *traversal* depth 406

406 of an actual tree or the impact of occlusion-based termination of the *traversal* upon intersection [Reinhard *et al.*, 1996]. Despite its practical relevance [Havran, 2000], the linear cost
estimate can, to this end, be substituted by a log-like function of the number of objects in
each local subtree [Szécsi and Benedek, 2002]. Besides its potential applicability to the tree
construction process [Havran, 2000], a generalized cost metric accounting for the impact of
406 partial occlusion between sibling nodes on *traversal* termination may also prove beneficial
406 when used during the tree *traversal* phase itself in order to prioritize the descent of the least
expensive of the ray-overlapping sibling subtrees in order-independent occlusion queries [Ize
and Hansen, 2011]. Aside from considering the impact of initializing the ray traversal (which
369 is, for instance, non-negligible in *grids*) as well as that of cache latencies [Havran, 2007], a
369 similar observation can be made regarding *spatial subdivision* structures augmented with
mailboxing, for which the SAH cost model ought to be adjusted by means of a correction
term subtracting the probabilistic cost of redundant intersections among sibling nodes [Hunt,
2008a, Hunt, 2008b, Ch. 4].

Provided with additional knowledge about the distribution of the rays in the scene, the
129 *probability* terms in the original SAH formulation may likewise be reformulated to better
model the expected workload. The probabilities for primary rays might, for instance, be evaluated as the ratio of the parallel/perspective projected area of a node's bounding box with
244 respect to the camera's viewport area, or as the ratio of their *solid angles* in the case of spherical projections [Havran and Bittner, 1999, Havran, 2000, Ch. 4], while reflection/refraction
rays may be better accounted for by assuming that the rays' origins are uniformly distributed
within the scene's bounding box [Fabianowski *et al.*, 2009]. In more general settings, though,
statistics about the actual distribution can alternatively be gathered from a sample set representative of the rays to be cast in the scene, defined either as a subset of the rays to be traced
for the current frame or as a subset of the rays traced in previous frames [Bittner and Havran,
2009], potentially accounting for the impact of occlusion as well by identifying mostly visible
objects from mostly occluded ones [Vinkler *et al.*, 2012]. Finally, statistics about the distribution and occlusion of shadow rays may similarly be gathered to drive the construction of
dedicated acceleration structures referencing large frequent occluders at shallow depths so as
to promote early termination upon intersection [Feltman *et al.*, 2012].

Due to the heuristic's limitations, though, better quality BVH trees might potentially
be sought via greedy randomized adaptive search procedures by stochastically selecting the
247 split *plane* among the most promising partition candidates of each subdivision step [Ng and
406 Trifonov, 2003]. Exploiting the ability to better estimate the *traversal* cost of the actual
subtrees once the hierarchy is built, adjustments to the quality of the latter can alternatively
be made postconstruction. For instance, this may be accomplished by means of local tree
rotations, coupled with a stochastic simulated annealing approach to avoid settling in local
406 minima, that aim at reducing the *traversal* cost of a node by swapping one of its children with
357 a grand-child, therefore leaving the node's *bounding volume* and that of the whole structure
unchanged [Kensler, 2008]. Other instances also include more general updates that entail
removing costly subtrees from the hierarchy and reinserting them at a more globally optimal
location [Bittner *et al.*, 2013].

247 **Data-Independent Candidates** Given a sample set of k candidate *planes*, the optimal split
may be determined by "scanning" through the individual candidates in turn. As outlined in
401 *Algorithm 9.12*, the SAH cost associated with each sample can then be estimated by iterating
over the set of objects in order to compute the parameters of the prospective child nodes
402 (i.e., their associated number of objects, and, as illustrated in *Figure 9.31*, the corresponding
357 surface area of their *bounding volume* in the case of *object subdivision* schemes) [Hunt *et*
357 *al.*, 2006, Hunt, 2008b, Ch. 5]. The cost of refining a single node therefore becomes $C_P(n) =$

$O(kn) + O(n) = O((k+1)n) \sim O(kn)$, leading to an overall asymptotic complexity for the tree construction of

$$C(n) \overset{(9.19)}{=} \sum_{i=0}^{h} b^i O\left(k\frac{n}{b^i}\right) = O\left(\sum_{i=0}^{h} kn\right) = O(kn(1+h)) \tag{9.33}$$ 393

which, in the case where $h = \log_b(n)$, yields

$$C(n) = O\Big(kn(1 + \log_b(n))\Big) \sim O(kn \log_b(n)) \tag{9.34}$$

Algorithm 9.12: Naive SAH Split: Pseudocode for the naive SAH splitting strategy.

Data: Set of objects S and bounding box B
Result: A splitting plane based on the naive SAH scheme

$axis \leftarrow \emptyset$;
$coordinate \leftarrow \emptyset$;
$cost \leftarrow \left(\|S\| - \frac{C_T}{C_I}\right) \times \texttt{SurfaceArea}(B)$;
foreach axis $a \in \{X, Y, Z\}$ **do**
  foreach candidate c along axis a **do**
    $S_l \leftarrow \emptyset$;
    $S_r \leftarrow \emptyset$;
    foreach object $o \in S$ **do**
      Add o to S_l and/or S_r based on subdivision scheme;
    end
    $[B_l, B_r] \leftarrow$ bounding volumes of child nodes based on subdivision scheme;
    $cost_c \leftarrow \|S_l\| \times \texttt{SurfaceArea}(B_l) + \|S_r\| \times \texttt{SurfaceArea}(B_r)$;
    if $cost_c < cost$ **then**
      $axis \leftarrow a$;
      $coordinate \leftarrow c$;
      $cost \leftarrow cost_c$;
    end
  end
end
return Splitting plane $[axis, coordinate]$

As an alternative, the cost function may be incrementally evaluated by "streaming" the
objects, and, for each, binning either its centroid and *bounding volume* in the case of *object* 357
subdivision, or the minimum or maximum coordinates of its *bounding volume* in the case of 357
spatial subdivision [Hurley *et al.*, 2002], into buckets associated with each interval between 357 369
consecutive split candidates (assumed to be uniformly distributed) [Popov *et al.*, 2006, Wald,
2007], as illustrated in *Figure 9.32*. The aggregated object count (and bounding volume in the 403
case of object subdivision) associated with each bin can then be incrementally cumulated via
a backward iteration through the bins so as to compute the partial sums corresponding to the
right side of each split *plane*. A forward iteration through the bins finally allows the partial 247
sums corresponding to the left side of each split *plane* to be similarly cumulated, and the SAH 247
cost associated with each candidate to be evaluated, as outlined in *Algorithm 9.13*. The cost 404
of refining a single node therefore becomes $C_P(n) = O(k+n) + O(n) = O(k+2n) \sim O(k+n)$,

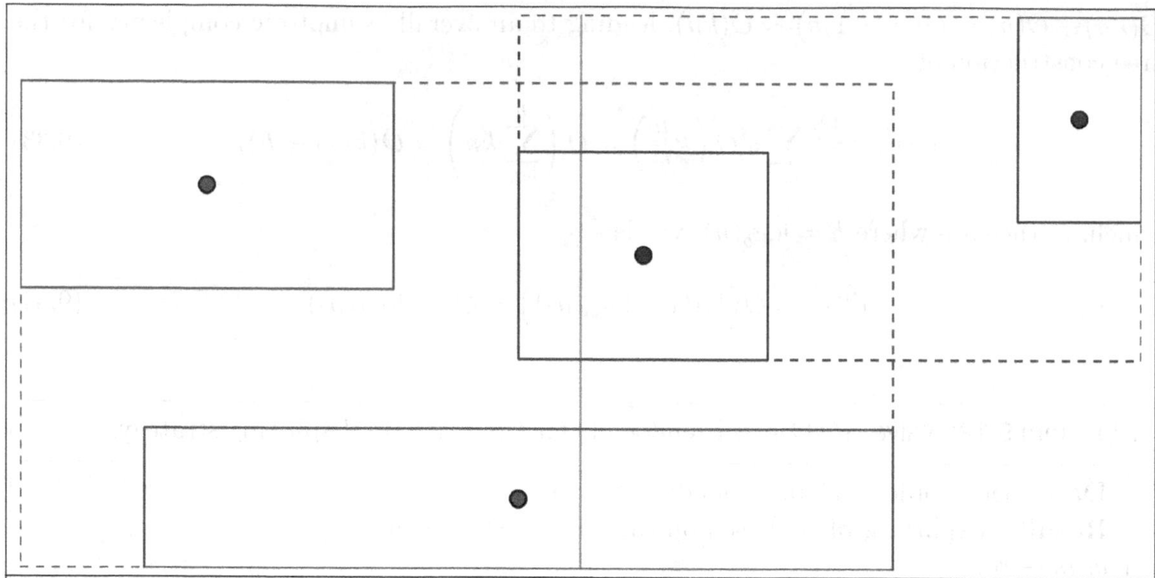

Figure 9.31: SAH-Based BVH: Illustration of the surface area heuristic used for optimal partitioning in an object-subdivision scheme.

leading to an overall asymptotic complexity for the tree construction of

393

$$C(n) \overset{(9.19)}{=} \sum_{i=0}^{h} b^i O\left(k + \frac{n}{b^i}\right)$$

$$= \sum_{i=0}^{h} O(b^i k + n)$$

$$= O\left(k\sum_{i=0}^{h} b^i + \sum_{i=0}^{h} n\right)$$

16

$$\overset{(2.10)}{=} O\left(k\frac{b^{1+h}-1}{b-1} + n(1+h)\right) \tag{9.35}$$

which, in the case where $h = \log_b(n)$, yields

$$\begin{aligned} C(n) &= O\left(k\frac{bb^{\log_b(n)}-1}{b-1} + n(1+\log_b(n))\right) \\ &= O\left(k\frac{bn-1}{b-1} + n(1+\log_b(n))\right) \\ &\sim O(kn + n\log_b(n)) \\ &= O\Big(n(k+\log_b(n))\Big) \end{aligned} \tag{9.36}$$

Finally, the latter binning approach might be adapted into an $O\Big(n\log\big(\log(n)\big)\Big)$ construction algorithm by relying on a radix-sort-like limited-precision 3-D discrete data representation.

In either case, the sampling process may be carried adaptively by noting that both the number of objects and the surface area associated with the left/right children of a node are monotonously increasing/decreasing functions of the split coordinate, and so are their associated cost functions. It then follows that the costs for the left/right children at two
247 candidate *planes* provide upper and lower bounds of the cost function over the interval

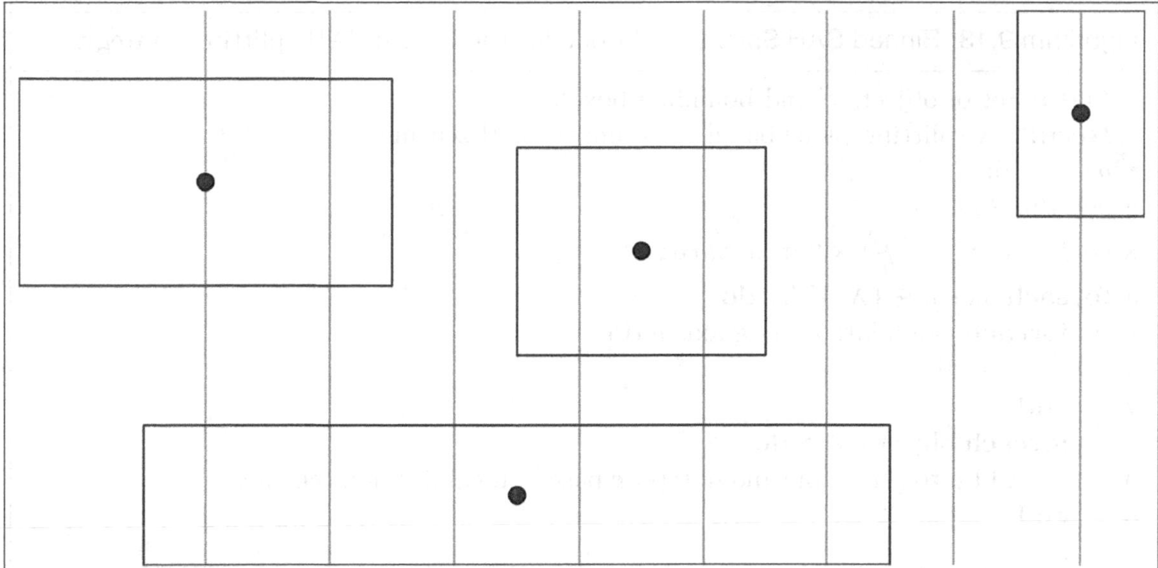

Figure 9.32: Binned SAH Split: Illustration of the computation of the SAH cost for several candidate planes by binning the objects into the resulting buckets.

between the *planes*. All intervals whose lower bound is greater than the smallest upper 247
bound are therefore guaranteed not to contain the absolute minimum and therefore do not
need to be sampled further [Popov *et al.*, 2006]. Furthermore, assuming a piecewise linear
representation of all four individual functions additionally allows for a more detailed error
analysis of the resulting piecewise quadratic approximation whose minimum can then be
analytically computed [Hunt *et al.*, 2006, Hunt, 2008b, Ch. 5].

Data-Specific Candidates In the case of *object subdivision*, data-specific candidates are gen- 357
erally defined as the *planes* between consecutive centroid coordinates along each dimension. 247
In the case of *spatial subdivision*, on the other hand, data-specific candidates are defined 369
as the *planes* located at the minimum and maximum coordinates (within the volume of the 247
node) of the *bounding volumes* (possibly having undergone split-clipping operations [Hurley 357
et al., 2002], in which case the candidates are then referred to as *perfect splits* [Soupikov *et al.*, 2008]) of the individual objects in all three dimensions. Given that the object counts are piecewise-constant functions with discontinuities at those points, the summation term behaves linearly between them, due to the linearity of the surface areas, while also presenting discontinuities at those points, where the absolute extremum therefore ought to occur.

In order to determine the optimal split, a naive algorithm entails independently considering each candidate *plane* in turn, as outlined in *Algorithm 9.12*. The cost of refining a single 247
node therefore becomes $C_P(n) = O(n^2) + O(n) \sim O(n^2)$, leading to an overall asymptotic 401
complexity for the tree construction of

$$C(n) \overset{(9.19)}{=} \sum_{i=0}^{h} b^i O\left(\left(\frac{n}{b^i}\right)^2\right) = O\left(\sum_{i=0}^{h} \frac{n^2}{b^i}\right) \overset{(2.10)}{=} O\left(n^2 \frac{1 - \frac{1}{b^{1+h}}}{1 - \frac{1}{b}}\right) \quad (9.37)$$ 393 16

which, in the case where $h = \log_b(n)$, yields

$$C(n) = O\left(n^2 \frac{1 - \frac{1}{bn}}{1 - \frac{1}{b}}\right) \sim O\left(n^2\right) \quad (9.38)$$

As an alternative, the list of split *plane* candidates may be preliminarily sorted and then 247

Algorithm 9.13: Binned SAH Split: Pseudocode for the binned SAH splitting strategy.

```
Data: Set of objects S and bounding box B
Result: A splitting plane based on a binned SAH scheme
axis ← ∅;
coordinate ← ∅;
cost ← (||S|| − C_T/C_I) × SurfaceArea(B);
foreach axis a ∈ {X, Y, Z} do
    foreach candidate c along axis a do
        S_c ← ∅;
    end
    foreach object o ∈ S do
        Add o to set S_c of candidate(s) c based on subdivision scheme;
    end
    S_r ← ∅;
    foreach candidate c along axis a in backward order do
        S_r ← S_r ∪ S_c;
        S_cr ← S_r;
        B_cr ← bounding volume of S_cr based on subdivision scheme;
    end
    S_l ← ∅;
    foreach candidate c along axis a in forward order do
        S_l ← S_l ∪ S_c;
        S_cl ← S_l;
        B_cl ← bounding volume of S_cl based on subdivision scheme;
        cost_c ← ||S_cl|| × SurfaceArea(B_cl) + ||S_cr|| × SurfaceArea(B_cr);
        if cost_c < cost then
            axis ← a;
            coordinate ← c;
            cost ← cost_c;
        end
    end
end
return Splitting plane [axis, coordinate]
```

processed in order [Szécsi, 2003], allowing both the number of objects associated with the
357 prospective child nodes and the surface area of their *bounding volumes* to be incrementally
405 updated, as outlined in *Algorithm 9.14.* Because *bounding volumes* can be incrementally
357 357 enlarged for each additional object but not shrunk upon their removal, *object subdivision*
schemes also generally need to preliminarily construct a list of the surface areas associated with the right child, incrementally built by considering the candidates in backward order, so that the data is readily available when "sweeping" forward through the candidates.

Considering the $n \log(n)$ average complexity of efficient comparison-based sorting algorithms (such as quicksort), the cost of refining a single node therefore becomes $C_P(n) = O(n \log_b(n)) + O(n) \sim O(n \log_b(n))$, leading to an overall asymptotic complexity for the tree construction of

$$
\begin{aligned}
C(n) &\overset{(9.19)}{=} \sum_{i=0}^{h} b^i O\left(\frac{n}{b^i}\log_b\left(\frac{n}{b^i}\right)\right) \\
&= O\left(\sum_{i=0}^{h} n(\log_b(n) - \log_b(b^i))\right) \\
&= O\left(n\left(\sum_{i=0}^{h}\log_b(n) - \sum_{i=0}^{h} i\right)\right) \\
&\overset{(2.1)}{=} O\left(n\left((1+h)\log_b(n) - \frac{(1+h)h}{2}\right)\right) \\
&= O\left(n(1+h)\left(\log_b(n) - \frac{h}{2}\right)\right)
\end{aligned}
\tag{9.39}
$$

393

15

which, in the case where $h = \log_b(n)$, yields

$$
C(n) = O\left(n(1+\log_b(n))\frac{\log_b(n)}{2}\right) \sim O(n\log_b(n)^2) \tag{9.40}
$$

Algorithm 9.14: Sort-Based SAH Split: Pseudocode for the sort-based SAH splitting strategy.

Data: Set of objects S and bounding box B

Result: A splitting plane based on the sort-based SAH scheme

```
axis ← ∅;
coordinate ← ∅;
cost ← (‖S‖ − C_T/C_I) × SurfaceArea(B);
foreach axis a ∈ {X, Y, Z} do
    Sort set of candidates C along axis a;
    S_l ← ∅;
    S_r ← S;
    [B_l, B_r] ← bounding volumes of child nodes based on subdivision scheme;
    foreach candidate c in sorted set C do
        Populate S_l and/or depopulate S_r based on subdivision scheme;
        Increase B_l and/or decrease B_r based on subdivision scheme;
        cost_c ← ‖S_l‖ × SurfaceArea(B_l) + ‖S_r‖ × SurfaceArea(B_r);
        if cost_c < cost then
            axis ← a;
            coordinate ← c;
            cost ← cost_c;
        end
    end
end
return Splitting plane [axis, coordinate]
```

Rather than repeatedly sorting the candidates for every partitioning step, the complete set of objects may alternatively be preliminarily sorted prior to the tree construction process [Müller and Fellner, 1999], albeit reducing the potential benefits of lazy construction

406 schemes where subtrees of the hierarchy are built on-demand during *traversal*. Each branch node therefore solely needs to maintain the ordering during the partitioning phase, although the presumably small number of perfect split candidates newly introduced by split-clipping
247 objects that straddle the split *plane* in *spatial subdivision* schemes still need to be sorted
369 on the fly before being merged with the pre-sorted list of candidates [Wald and Havran, 2006]. Because the axis and coordinate of the split can then be determined in linear time, the cost of refining a single node remains linear, $C_P(n) = O(n) + O(n) \sim O(n)$, leading to an overall asymptotic complexity for the tree construction of $C(n) = O(n \log_b(n))$ when-
395 ever $h = \log_b(n)$, as shown in *Equation 9.24*, which is the theoretical lower bound for any comparison-based spatial sorting algorithm. When dealing with a priori sorted data, though, such as given by a scene graph or the acceleration structure from the previous frame of an animation, both the sorting and sifting processes operated at each subdivision step may be restricted to a constant number of nodes from the preliminary structure, thereby yielding an asymptotic overall construction cost of $O(n)$ [Hunt *et al.*, 2007, Hunt, 2008b, Ch. 5].

9.4.3 Traversal

By exploiting a divide-and-conquer paradigm, tree-based hierarchical structures are able to loosely correlate the likelihood of subsets of objects to be anticipatively culled with their distance from the trajectory of a given ray, while recursively narrowing the focus of the search on objects that are more likely to be intersected. The search process entails evaluating an average of b^c immediate children of every branch node on the path from the root down
374 357 369 to a leaf, where $c = 1$ for *object subdivision* schemes and $c \overset{(9.13)}{=} 1/3$ for *spatial subdivision* schemes.

Assuming that the tree traversal terminates after descending a single path, the asymptotic complexity of the ray-intersection test using a perfect tree of height h with a branching factor b built over n leaf nodes is then given as $O\left(1 + \sum_{i=0}^{h-1} b^c\right) = O(1 + b^c h)$, which, in the case where $h = \log_b(n)$, yields $O(1 + b^c \log_b(n))$. The theoretically optimal branching factor then ought to satisfy

$$\frac{\mathrm{d}(1 + b^c \log_b(n))}{\mathrm{d}b} = b^{c-1} \log_b(n) \left(c - \frac{1}{\ln(b)}\right) = 0 \iff b = e^{\frac{1}{c}} \tag{9.41}$$

357 369 such that $b \approx 2.7$ for *object subdivision* schemes and $b \approx 20.1$ for *spatial subdivision* schemes, although better performance is typically observed for lower arity values in practice.
357 Upon intersection of its *bounding volume* by a ray, a general tree structure may be efficiently traversed in a depth-first fashion by starting from the root of the hierarchy and then recursively visiting the children of each branch node whose associated spatial extent
407 overlaps the ray's trajectory [Jansen, 1986], as outlined in *Algorithm 9.15* for an arbitrary branching factor.

Relegating the task of tracking the closest hit point as part of the intersection procedure, the recursive traversal of the child nodes actually reduces to a series of tail calls since no other action is performed afterwards besides potentially returning the computed intersection itself. In order to avoid the overhead of new stack frames being added to the call stack by the operating system, such a *tail recursion* can be eliminated and reformulated into an iterative loop by means of an explicitly managed stack of nodes to visit, the maximum size of the
407 latter being defined by the height of the tree, as outlined in *Algorithm 9.16*.
369 While *spatial subdivision* schemes allow such a stack-based traversal to defer the testing of siblings adjacent to the path upon an initial point-location of the leaf node enclosing
357 the entry point of the ray [Charney and Scherson, 1990], *object subdivision* schemes may

Algorithm 9.15: Recursive Tree Traversal: Pseudocode for recursive tree traversal.

```
Data: Ray r and node n [and interval [enter, exit]]
Result: Intersection found by recursively traversing the tree
Intersection i ← ∅;
if enter > prior intersections then
    Go to end;
end
if n is branch node then
    foreach node c ∈ front-to-back traversal of children of n overlapped by r do
        i ← closest{i, TraverseTree(r, c, [enter_c, exit_c])};
    end
else
    foreach object o ∈ set S_n of objects referenced by node n do
        i ← closest{i, Intersect(r, o)};
    end
end
return i
```

Algorithm 9.16: Iterative Tree Traversal: Pseudocode for iterative tree traversal.

```
Data: Ray r and node n [and interval [enter, exit]]
Result: Intersection found by iteratively traversing the tree
Stack S ← [n, enter, exit];
Intersection i ← ∅;
while S is not empty do
    [n, enter, exit] ← Pop(S);
    if enter > i then
        Go to end;
    end
    if n is branch node then
        foreach node c ∈ back-to-front traversal of children of n overlapped by r do
            S ← Push(S, [c, enter_c, exit_c]);
        end
    else
        foreach object o ∈ set S_n of objects referenced by node n do
            i ← closest{i, Intersect(r, o)};
        end
    end
end
return i
```

optionally substitute the LIFO stack of nodes to visit by a priority queue (e.g., efficiently
357 implemented as a heap data structure) sorted by the distance of the *bounding volumes*' entry
points, which allows the distance-culling optimization discussed therein to be fully exploited
[Kay and Kajiya, 1986], not only among sibling nodes, but more generally across all nodes
of arbitrary depth. By trading the depth-first traversal for an approximation of the order in
which the objects are actually pierced by the ray, the process can terminate as soon as the
first culled node is encountered.

In contrast, hardware architectures with limited memory resources such as graphics processing units (*GPUs*) may instead rely on a short stack of fixed maximum size, solely caching
the least recently inserted nodes and evicting older nodes upon overflow. Underflows occurring during unstacking operations can then be handled either by a full restart of the descent
369 from the root of the *spatial subdivision* structure to locate the origin of the ray newly offset
beyond the current cell [Horn *et al.*, 2007], or, due to the possible overlap of nodes in *object*
357 *subdivision* structures, by explicitly maintaining a trail where a single bit per level readily
indicates the per branch direction of the path to the next node in the sequence [Laine, 2010].

9.4.4 Storage

406 A first step towards improving cache efficiency during *traversal* consists in ensuring that
the nodes of the tree are contiguously allocated rather than being scattered in memory. In
order to reduce the overall memory footprint of the structure and therefore further improve
cache performance with it (as well as potentially allowing serialization for offline loading
from and storing to disk), the tree structure may additionally be flattened (either directly
393 during *construction* or as a postprocess) into a compact pointerless array representation
(potentially memory-aligned and whose elements might be padded to avoid straddling cache
lines) by recursively laying out the nodes with a contiguous depth-first ordering [Havran,
408 1997a, Havran, 1999, Havran, 2000, Ch. 7]. As illustrated in *Figure 9.33*, this induces the left
child of each branch node to immediately follow its parent in memory, such that the latter
only needs to explicitly store the index of its right child via a skip-pointer/index once the
latter has been processed, albeit yielding better cache coherence when accessing the left child
rather than the right one.

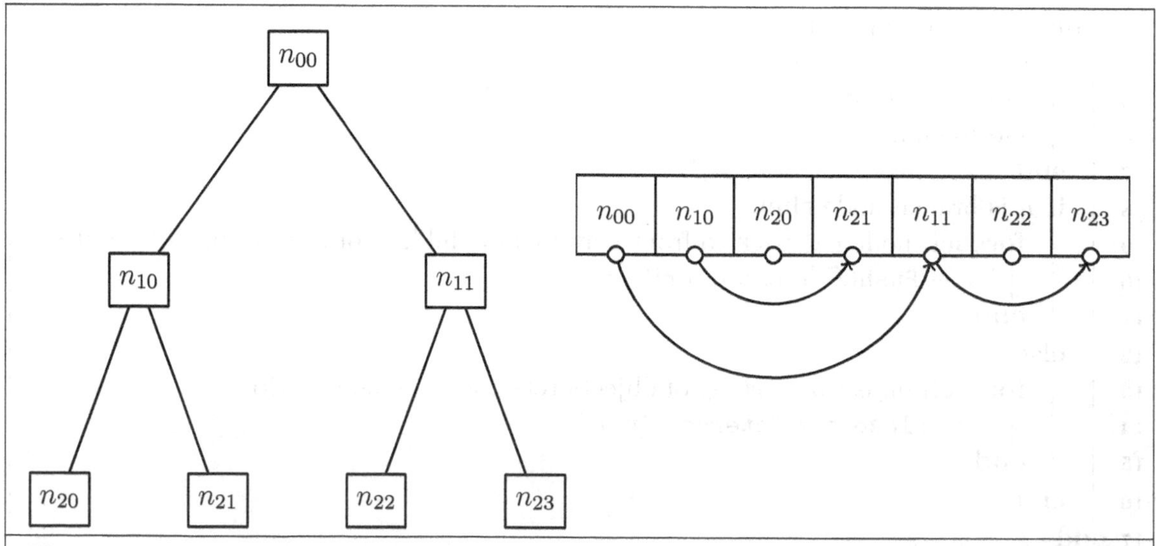

Figure 9.33: Tree Flattening: Illustration of the contiguous memory layout of a tree structure flattened into a pointerless array representation with depth-first ordering (drawn after [Pharr and Humphreys, 2010, Fig. 4.12]).

As an alternative, locality can be exploited to a greater extent by contiguously allocating entire subtrees of predetermined height, so called *treelets*, which additionally allows for a reduction of memory consumption via implicit indexing within a subtree [Havran, 1997a, Havran, 1999, Havran, 2000, Ch. 7], as well as by merging partially empty terminal subtrees with their parent shall the latter also be partially empty [Szécsi and Benedek, 2002]. Further gains in cache efficiency may also be achieved by means of more sophisticated layouts that account for both parent-child locality via clustering as well as spatial locality via a cache-oblivious layout of the clusters [Yoon and Manocha, 2006]. The overall footprint of the structure might additionally be a priori restricted to a given block of memory by partitioning the latter at each subdivision step of the in-place *construction* process among newly created 393
child nodes based on an estimate of their relative memory requirements, while terminating the recursion whenever a node cannot successfully subdivide within its attributed memory chunk [Wächter and Keller, 2007].

Based on the concept of *breadth-first ray tracing* [Nakamaru and Ohno, 1997], which consists in intersecting each object with all rays rather than each ray with all objects so as to better minimize thrashing of cached geometry, explicit storage can instead be avoided altogether by means of an on-the-fly divide-and-conquer strategy that recursively partitions the scene directly during *traversal* while amortizing the cost by simultaneously processing a 406
large number of rays. Starting with a list of all objects in the scene and a list of all rays to be traced, the implicitly defined *bounding volume hierarchy* [Keller and Wächter, 2011] or 360
k-D tree [Mora, 2011] structure is then created by recursively discarding the objects and the 381
unintersected rays not overlapping the node under consideration (both being achievable via in-place reordering of the sub-lists into contiguous sub-segments), thereby effectively subdividing solely those regions that are actually traversed by the given set of rays akin to a lazy *construction* algorithm. Aside from possible optimizations to better exploit hardware re- 393
sources and cache, should the set contain incoherent rays [Áfra, 2012], the overall complexity is theoretically bounded by the sum of the cost of partitioning objects as in the *construction* 393
of a traditional structure, and the cost of intersecting the rays against the cells as in the *traversal* of a traditional structure. However, as secondary rays can only be defined once the 406
intersection points of the primary rays have been computed, the different segments of the ray paths must be treated individually and the entire implicit construction/traversal process repeated separately for each of them.

9.5 OTHER SUBDIVISION

9.5.1 Metasubdivision

Akin to a simple list, an acceleration structure may be conceptually regarded as an aggregate object encompassing the set of geometric entities over which it is built. It can consequently be seamlessly treated as one of the constituents of a scene, providing the same intersection and *bounding volume* queries as an instanced object or any other geometric entity, and dealt 357
with as such in order to build meta-structures in a nested fashion [Kirk and Arvo, 1988, Arvo, 1990b], although at the risk of indiscriminately handling entities with dramatically different costs when constructing higher-level structures.

In order to better adapt to the geometric complexity of the scene, several *grid* structures 369
may, for instance, be loosely nested in a bottom-up fashion, either by merging nearby nodes from subtrees of the scene graph and recursively building individual *grids* over the resulting 369
geometric sets [Klimaszewski, 1994, Klimaszewski and Sederberg, 1997], or by filtering the objects into different levels based on their size and then clustering the objects of a level by spatial proximity, such that a uniform *grid* can be built for each cluster while recursively 369

369 nesting the *grids* from the lower levels to the higher levels of the meta-hierarchy [Cazals *et al.*, 1995, Cazals and Puech, 1997].
357 As *object subdivision* and *spatial subdivision* structures exhibit different characteris-
369 tics depending on the distribution and density of the objects in the scene, their respective
strengths may be similarly exploited by means of a hybrid hierarchy, nesting, for instance,
378 low-level BVHs within a high-level *octree* [Scherson and Caspary, 1987]. Because large lists of
369 uniformly distributed objects are generally more efficiently indexed by uniform *grids* whereas
small lists of sparsely distributed objects are better handled by BVHs, both structures can
369 likewise be either nested [Snyder and Barr, 1987], interleaved by substituting *grids* in place
of homogeneous sections of the BVH tree [Müller and Fellner, 1999] or combined with hier-
369 archical *grids* according to a generalized cost metric predicting which subtrees of the BVH
ought to be replaced [Massó and López, 2003].

9.5.2 Directional Subdivision

The coherence existing between rays emanating from or converging to localized regions of
space may be best exploited by a *directional subdivision* scheme [Simiakakis, 1995]. Such a
431 structure can, for instance, be built for a *point light* source by scan-converting the objects of
357 the scene (or their conservative *bounding volumes*) into a so-called *light buffer* [Haines and
410 Greenberg, 1986, Haines, 1986]. As illustrated in *Figure 9.34*, the latter consists of a cube
369 centered at the light position and whose individual faces are composed of uniform 2-D *grids*
122 corresponding to rectilinear *perspective projections* with a 90° *angle of view*, such that any
673 shadow ray cast to a given light may readily identify the cell corresponding to its direction
and solely traverse the distance-sorted list of objects recorded therein. Given that the objects
occluding nearby surface points are likely to reside in the vicinity of one another, shadow
queries might also be further accelerated by not only caching in the structure a reference to the
most recently intersected occluder, but also a reference (or tree of references) to the voxel of
the spatial acceleration structure containing it for prior testing of its elements [Pearce, 1991].

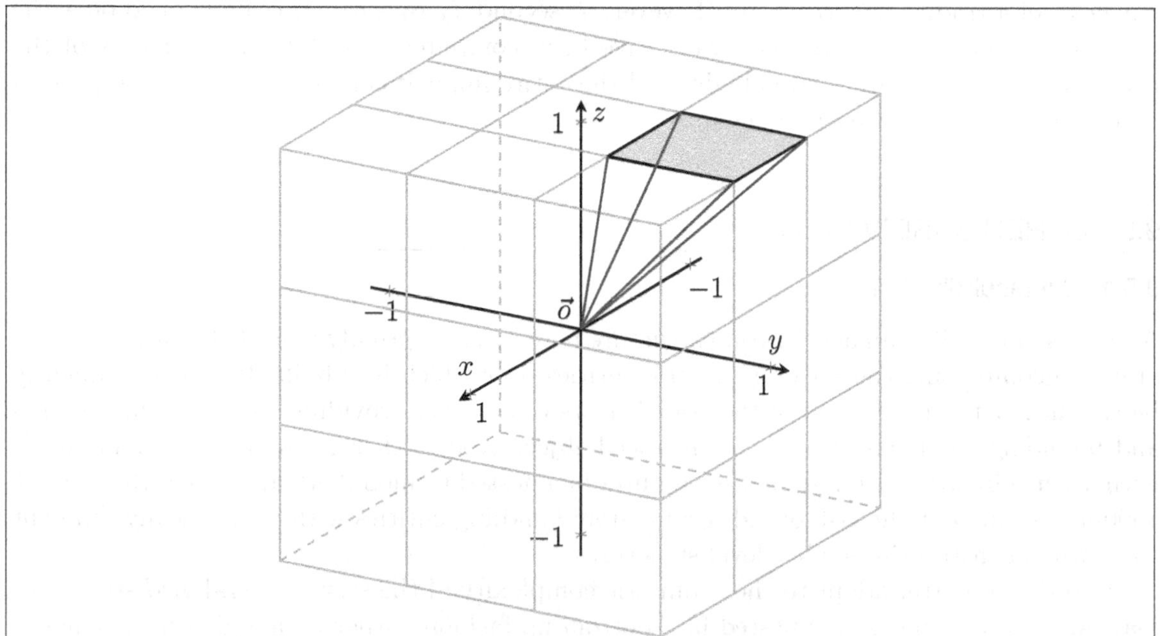

Figure 9.34: Light Buffer: Illustration of a directional subdivision structure consisting of a cube centered at the light and whose individual faces are composed of uniform 2-D grids (drawn after [Haines and Greenberg, 1986, Fig. 1]).

The approach may also be extended to *area lights* by sweeping the origin of each direc- 429
tional beam defined by a cell through the light's *bounding volume* while recording all objects 357
intersecting the swept beam. As illustrated in *Figure 9.35*, such a *ray coherence* structure 411
can be equivalently built in practice by recording each object in all directional cells whose
beam (originating from the light's center) overlaps the *cone* of apex angle $\pi/2 - \alpha$ between 275
the light and the object, where $\cos(\alpha) = \frac{r_1}{d - \frac{r_2}{\cos(\alpha)}} = \frac{r_1 + r_2}{d}$ is defined by the radii r_1 and r_2 and
the distance d between the centers of their respective bounding *spheres* [Ohta and Maekawa, 269
1987].

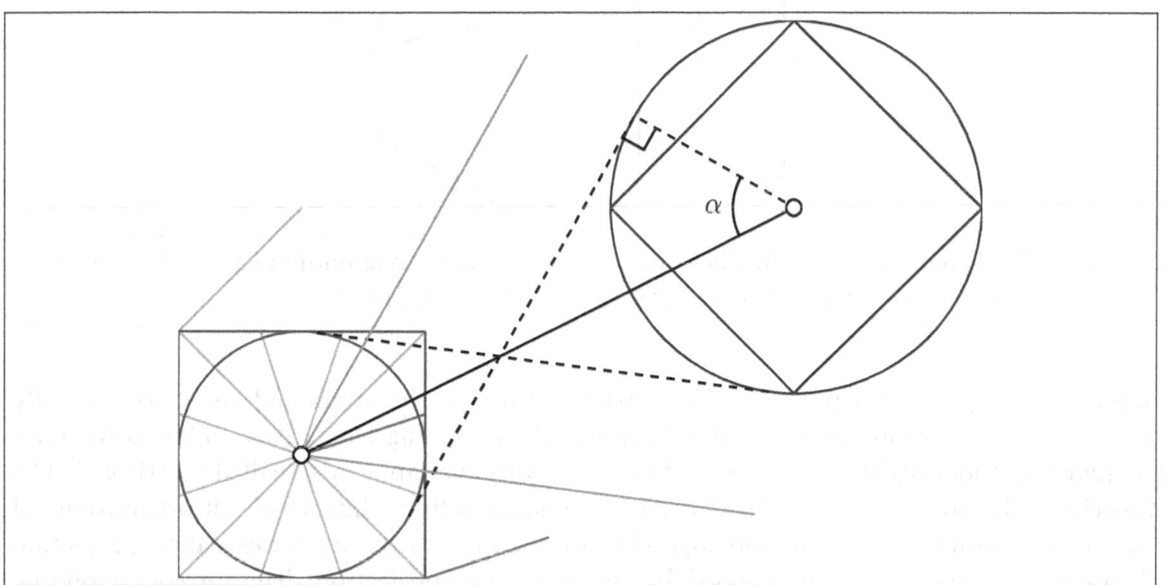

Figure 9.35: Ray Coherence: Illustration of the cone angle between the bounding spheres of an area light and a given object.

Directional subdivision may be more generally combined with *spatial subdivision* by 369
means of a five-dimensional duotricenary tree (i.e., with arity $2^5 = 32$). As illustrated in
Figure 9.36, such a *ray classification* structure partitions space into 3-D cells of 2-D direc- 412
tional cubes, each holding a list of references to all distance-sorted objects intersecting the
corresponding beam. Classifying a ray then entails traversing the hierarchical structure down
to the single 5-D hypercube leaf node corresponding to the ray's origin (or its entry point
into the scene's *bounding volume*) and direction. In order to reduce the amount of redundant 357
information due to the substantial overlap of neighboring beams, though, the distance-related
extent of the latter might alternatively be truncated and the traversal carried instead in the
spirit of a *spatial subdivision* structure by successively visiting the 3-D cells encompassing 369
the intersection point of the ray with the truncating *plane* of the previous hypercube [Arvo 247
and Kirk, 1987, Arvo and Kirk, 1988].

Observing that any ray defined by shifting another ray's origin along its axis forms a sub-/superset of the latter, redundancy may instead be reduced by folding the ray space onto a four-dimensional domain, for instance by apposing a directional cube onto the bounding box of the scene, whereby the objects intersecting the spatial beams defined by a pair of different-face cells are stored during construction. Despite the remaining redundancy due to the spatial overlap of the beams, the traversal of a ray then solely entails determining the cells through which it enters and exits the volume, thereby readily identifying the beam whose list of objects ought to be tested for intersection [Stürzlinger and Tobler, 1994]. As illustrated in
Figure 9.37, the *complementer plane* algorithm is another conceptually related ray-shooting 413
scheme from computational geometry, thereby exhibiting an $O(\log(n))$ worst case complexity.

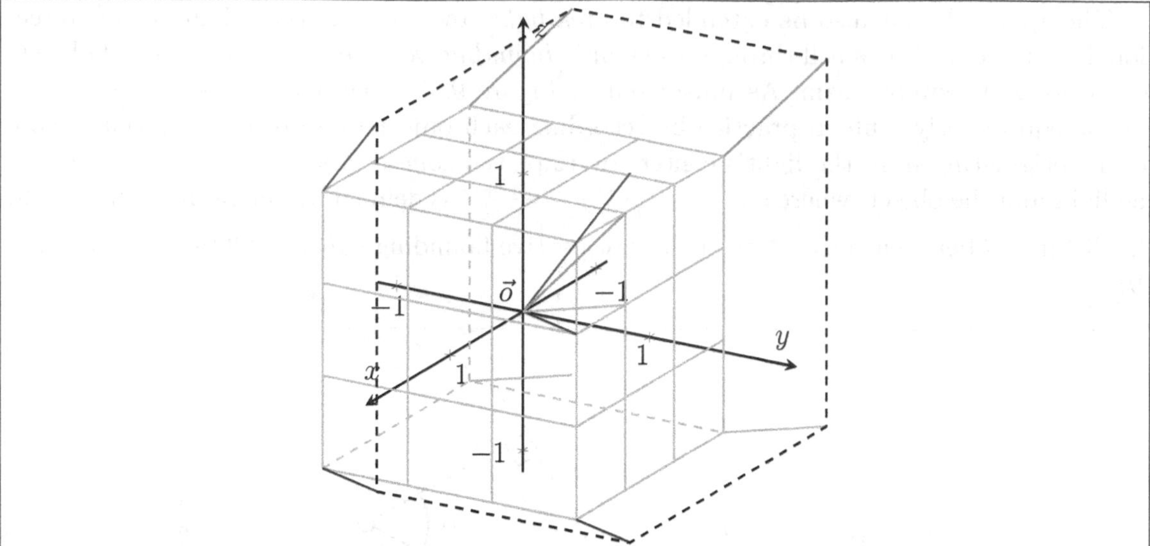

Figure 9.36: Ray Classification: Illustration of the beam corresponding to a node of a 5-D spatio-directional tree (drawn after [Arvo and Kirk, 1987, Fig. 1]).

Defining a complementer plane as a plane passing through the origin and being orthogonally oriented to a given direction, the algorithm entails projecting the objects of the scene onto the plane and identifying each region of homogeneous overlap as a so-called "territory." The directional domain is then subdivided into individual cells within which all orientations of the planes' normals result in topologically equivalent sets of territories called projection diagrams. Traversal is finally carried by retrieving the projection diagram corresponding to the ray's direction while the 2-D projection of its origin onto the complementer plane allows the associated territory to be readily identified by point location query, such that the ordered list of objects contained therein is finally traversed from the projection coordinate of the ray's origin onto the plane's normal axis [Fóris *et al.*, 1996, Szirmay-Kalos and Márton, 1997, Szirmay-Kalos and Márton, 1998].

In the case of rays emanating from a single point, efficient partitioning schemes can
alternatively be devised in perspective space whereby the center of projection is defined as
431 the camera's origin or the location of a given *point light* source (using one structure for each
369 of the six faces). A uniform *grid* then defines a Z-buffer-like structure built by transforming
250 the *triangles* into perspective space, while reducing the perspective-space traversal to a 1-D
process as the transformed rays become aligned with the z axis [Hunt and Mark, 2008b, Hunt,
662 2008b, Ch. 5]. On the other hand, off-axis *depth of field* camera rays and *area light* soft-
429 shadow rays originating in the vicinity of the center of projection require a more general
traversal along all three axes, and may be more effectively handled by an adaptive structure
381 such as a *k-D tree* whose per frame construction (as is often already required in dynamic
397 environments) is driven by a specialized *surface area cost metric* considering the origins of
the rays to be uniformly distributed over the area of the lens/light while their directions
follow a uniform distribution across the perspective plane [Hunt and Mark, 2008a, Hunt,
2008b, Ch. 4–6].

9.5.3 Metaocclusion

Rather than explicitly testing individual shadow rays directly against the actual geometry,
much of the information contained in an acceleration structure can actually be leveraged in
369 order to provide higher-level occlusion queries. To this end, every voxel of a uniform *grid*

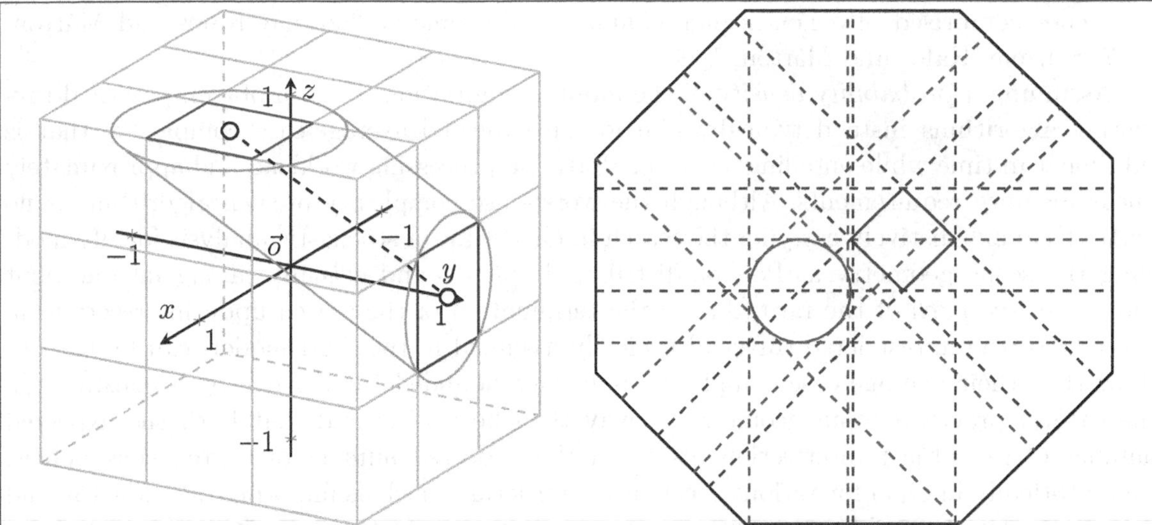

Figure 9.37: Directional Subdivision: Illustration of various directional subdivision schemes, including beams defined by the pairwise association of cells from different faces of a bounding cube (left, drawn after [Stürzlinger and Tobler, 1994, Fig. 4]) and the complementer plane algorithm (right, drawn after [Fóris *et al.*, 1996, Fig. 4] and [Szirmay-Kalos and Márton, 1998, Fig. 8]).

may, for instance, hold a flag for each *light source* indicating whether the light is fully visible, 429
fully occluded or partially visible/occluded from within the voxel. This can be determined by a preliminary scan conversion of the objects from the light's perspective, eventually allowing the traversal of shadow rays to be aborted as soon as a voxel whose visibility is fully resolved is encountered [Woo, 1989, Woo and Amanatides, 1990].

As an alternative, the voxels of an acceleration structure may themselves serve as proxies
for visibility testing. Non-empty *k-D tree* nodes can, for instance, readily provide approximate 381
information whose quality may be controlled by a threshold on the magnitude of the *inner*
product of the ray's direction and the average normal of the geometry within a node, thereby 76
allowing coarser nodes to be used as proxies in mainly front- or back-facing regions while requiring finer-level nodes to be used around the silhouettes [Djeu and Volchenok, 2008]. Exact information can also be obtained in the case of closed watertight meshes whose fully
enclosed *k-D tree* nodes may readily act as occluders and allow for an early termination of 381
the shadow ray traversal, the latter potentially being carried in an out-of-order fashion to prioritize nodes with a low processing cost and/or with a large spatial extent, in addition to caching most recently occluding nodes for prior processing [Djeu *et al.*, 2009].

9.6 PERFORMANCE ANALYSIS

9.6.1 Theoretical Analysis

Casting a ray against a set of objects is very closely related to the ray-shooting problem from the field of computational geometry [de Berg *et al.*, 1991, de Berg, 1992, de Berg *et al.*, 1994]. Being an inherent property of the problem itself, it may be proven by means of a simple algebraic decision tree model that the theoretical lower bound on the worst case complexity (as typically of concern in computational geometry) of ray shooting is $\Omega(\log(n))$, as is the case for the aforementioned complementer plane algorithm [Fóris *et al.*, 1996]. However, the theoretical lower bound on the memory and pre-processing requirements of any algorithm achieving this optimal limit is given by $\Omega(n^4)$, thereby making the approach impractical for scenes comprised of a non-negligible amount of geometry [Szirmay-Kalos and Márton, 1997, Szirmay-Kalos and Márton, 1998].

131 Assuming a *probability density* of the input configuration of the problem, practical ray-casting algorithms instead typically aim for an expected average-case complexity that is sub-linear in time while entailing a sub-quadratic preprocessing workload and approximately linear memory requirements. Although the worst-case complexity of such algorithms is no better than exhaustively carrying the search in $O(n)$ time, a stochastic analysis ideally mod-
269 eling the scene geometry as Poisson-distributed *spheres* and actually taking into account
464 the *mean free path* of the rays (due to the termination of the search upon intersection, in contrast to the unrestricted traversal typically assumed in the SAH model) can be used to show that their average-case complexity is in fact bounded from above by a constant. In the case of practical input geometry, it may then be conjectured that both the expected number of ray–object intersection tests and the expected number of visited cells behave
369 asymptotically in $O(1)$ for various acceleration structures such as uniform *grids* [Márton and
378 381 Szirmay-Kalos, 1995, Márton, 1995b] as well as *octrees* and *k-D trees* [Szirmay-Kalos and Márton, 1998, Szirmay-Kalos *et al.*, 2002].

9.6.2 Empirical Analysis

Although implicitly factored out of asymptotic analyses, the leading constants driving the actual computational costs can have in practice a non-negligible impact on the total time-to-image

$$t_i = t_b + rt_t \tag{9.42}$$

which is a linear function of the total number of rays r (expressed as the product of the number of rays per path, the number of paths per pixel, the number of pixels per frame and the total number of frames to be rendered) parameterized by the time t_b required to build a given acceleration structure and the time t_t required by each ray to traverse it. Minimizing the time-to-image therefore implies a trade-off between all three terms, and while for a sufficiently large number of rays it can pay off to devote a substantial amount of time constructing an
381 acceleration structure with minimal traversal time (such as a *k-D tree*), a compromise might, on the other hand, be more desirable for a moderate number of rays (by, for instance, resorting
360 to a *bounding volume hierarchy*), whereas for fewer rays an inexpensive construction cost
369 ought to be favored at the expense of an increase in traversal time (as exhibited by a *grid*), building no acceleration structure at all and resorting to an exhaustive search actually being the optimal alternative for a sufficiently small number of rays.

Additionally considering the fact that the performance characteristics of the various acceleration structures heavily depend on the distribution and density of the objects in the scene, it is consensually believed that there exists no single acceleration structure that performs best for all possible configurations of input geometry. A systematic assessment and comparison of the efficiency of a given acceleration scheme therefore prescribes the use of a standard set of geometric models [Haines, 1987] as well as the use of a standard benchmarking procedure by means of a common software framework [Raab *et al.*, 2007]. The empirical evaluation of the quality of a scheme also ought to be performed in the light of the various variables characterizing the properties of the data structure itself, such as the set of parameters influencing its construction algorithm, the miscellaneous implementation/compiler/hardware-specific time constants [Havran and Žára, 1997] and the statistical complexity of the scene, as well as the number of different nodes/references in the data structure, and the average number of nodes/references accessed per ray [Havran *et al.*, 2000, Havran, 2000, Ch. 3]. Given a model of the overall performance as a function of these parameters [Havran and Purgathofer, 2000, Havran, 2000, Ch. 2], the various statistics collected either during a preliminary

generic calibration phase, or for the given scene by means of an initial acceleration structure with a low construction cost (such as a uniform *grid*), may then be used to estimate which 369
of either, using the already-built initial structure for tracing a predefined number of rays, or building instead a higher-quality structure for the scene, will yield the smallest time-to-image [Hapala *et al.*, 2011b].

9.7 FURTHER READING

Additional material may be found in surveys and books dedicated to hierarchical data structures [Samet and Webber, 1988a, Samet and Webber, 1988b, Samet, 1990] and spatial data structures [Havran, 1997b, Havran and Bittner, 2006], as well as in surveys dedicated to acceleration [Arvo and Kirk, 1989] and geometric data structures [Chang, 2001] in general.

III

Physical Foundations

CHAPTER 10

Visible Light

TABLE OF CONTENTS

10.1 ELECTROMAGNETIC RADIATION

10.1.1 Electromagnetic Wave

In free space, an *electromagnetic wave* propagates at the constant *speed of light* c, which is related to the *vacuum permeability* μ_0 and the *vacuum permittivity*, also called *dielectric constant*, ϵ_0 (in F·m^{-1}) by

$$\epsilon_0 \triangleq \frac{1}{\mu_0 c^2} \tag{10.1}$$

whereas the *phase velocity* v (in m·s^{-1}) of the wave in a medium similarly obeys

$$\epsilon \triangleq \frac{1}{\mu v^2} \tag{10.2}$$

where the *medium permeability* μ and the *medium permittivity* ϵ are related to the *relative permeability* μ_r and the *relative permittivity* ϵ_r of the material by

$$\mu_r \triangleq \frac{\mu}{\mu_0} \tag{10.3}$$

$$\epsilon_r \triangleq \frac{\epsilon}{\epsilon_0} \tag{10.4}$$

421 As illustrated in *Figure 10.1*, a monochromatic wave is characterized by its *period* T (in s), or equivalently by its *frequency* of oscillation ν (in Hz)

$$\nu \triangleq \frac{1}{T} \tag{10.5}$$

or its *angular frequency* (in rd·s^{-1})

$$\omega \triangleq 2\pi\nu = \frac{2\pi}{T} \tag{10.6}$$

678 As it corresponds to the spectral sensitivity of the *human eye*, the subset of the electromagnetic spectrum ranging roughly between 383 THz and 783 THz in frequency, or between 783 nm and 383 nm in wavelength, is then referred to as *visible light*.

The *wavelengths* (in m) in free space and in a medium are then, respectively, defined as

$$\lambda_0 \triangleq cT = \frac{c}{\nu} \tag{10.7}$$

$$\lambda \triangleq vT = \frac{v}{\nu} \tag{10.8}$$

while the (angular) *wave number* (in rd·m^{-1}) is given as

420
420

$$k_0 \triangleq \frac{2\pi}{\lambda_0} \overset{(10.7)}{=} \frac{2\pi}{c}\nu \overset{(10.6)}{=} \frac{\omega}{c} \tag{10.9}$$

420
420

$$k \triangleq \frac{2\pi}{\lambda} \overset{(10.8)}{=} \frac{2\pi}{v}\nu \overset{(10.6)}{=} \frac{\omega}{v} \tag{10.10}$$

which, together with the direction of propagation $\hat{k}$ of the wave, defines the *wave vector* $\vec{k} \triangleq k\hat{k}$, such that $k = \|\vec{k}\|$.

From a physical standpoint, the properties of the wave in a medium relative to its prop-
420 erties in a vacuum are determined by the spectrally dependent *index of refraction*

420
420
420
420
420

$$n \triangleq \sqrt{\mu_r \epsilon_r} \underset{(10.4)}{\overset{(10.3)}{=}} \sqrt{\frac{\mu\epsilon}{\mu_0\epsilon_0}} \underset{(10.2)}{\overset{(10.1)}{=}} \frac{c}{v} \underset{(10.8)}{\overset{(10.7)}{=}} \frac{\lambda_0}{\lambda} \underset{(10.10)}{\overset{(10.9)}{=}} \frac{k}{k_0} \tag{10.11}$$

420
420 where $n = 1$ in a vacuum whereas $n > 1$ typically holds in most media. The *refractivity* of a medium is then defined as $N \triangleq n - 1$.

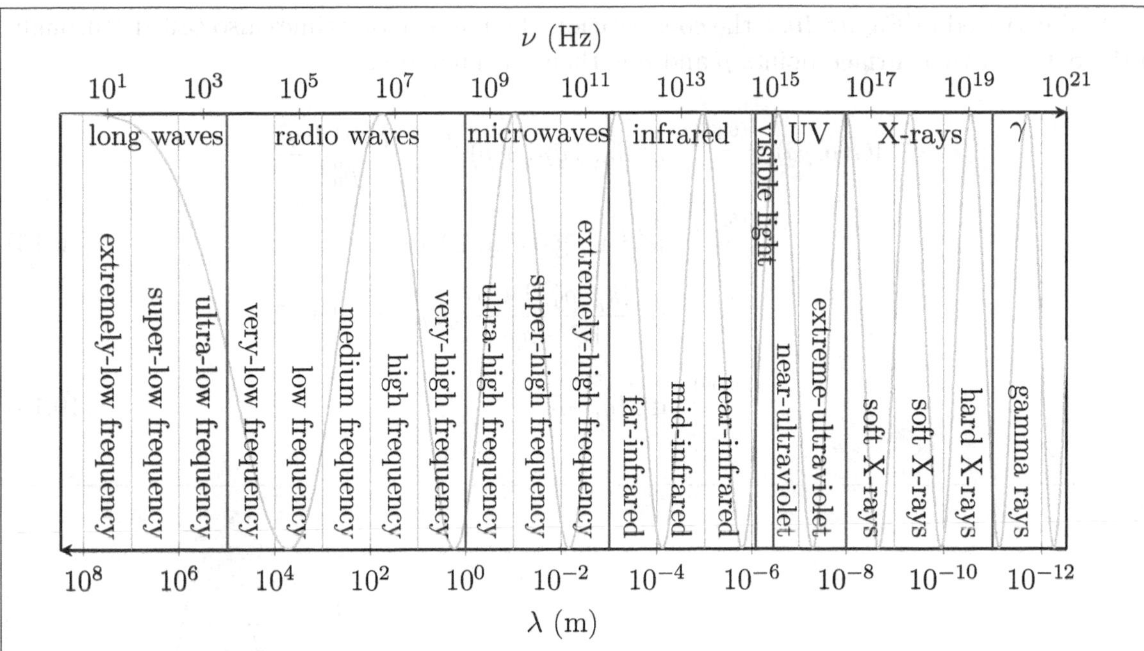

Figure 10.1: Electromagnetic Spectrum: Illustration of the different frequency bands in the electromagnetic spectrum.

10.1.2 Étendue

As illustrated in *Figure 10.2*, the projected differential area of a surface at point $\vec{p}$ with 421
normal $\hat{n}$ and the projected differential *solid angle* are, respectively, defined as 244

$$\mathrm{d}A_\perp(\vec{p}) \triangleq \langle \hat{n}, \hat{\omega} \rangle \mathrm{d}A(\vec{p}) \tag{10.12}$$

$$\mathrm{d}\vec{\omega}_\perp \triangleq \langle \hat{n}, \hat{\omega} \rangle \mathrm{d}\hat{\omega} \tag{10.13}$$

while the differential *étendue* of an object subtending a differential *solid angle* $\mathrm{d}\hat{\omega}$ at $\vec{p}$ on 244
a surface of differential area $\mathrm{d}A(\vec{p})$ is defined in terms of the index of refraction n of the medium as

$$\mathrm{d}G(\vec{p}, \hat{\omega}) \triangleq n^2 \langle \hat{n}, \hat{\omega} \rangle \mathrm{d}A(\vec{p}) \mathrm{d}\hat{\omega} = n^2 \mathrm{d}A_\perp(\vec{p}) \mathrm{d}\hat{\omega} = n^2 \mathrm{d}A(\vec{p}) \mathrm{d}\vec{\omega}_\perp \tag{10.14}$$

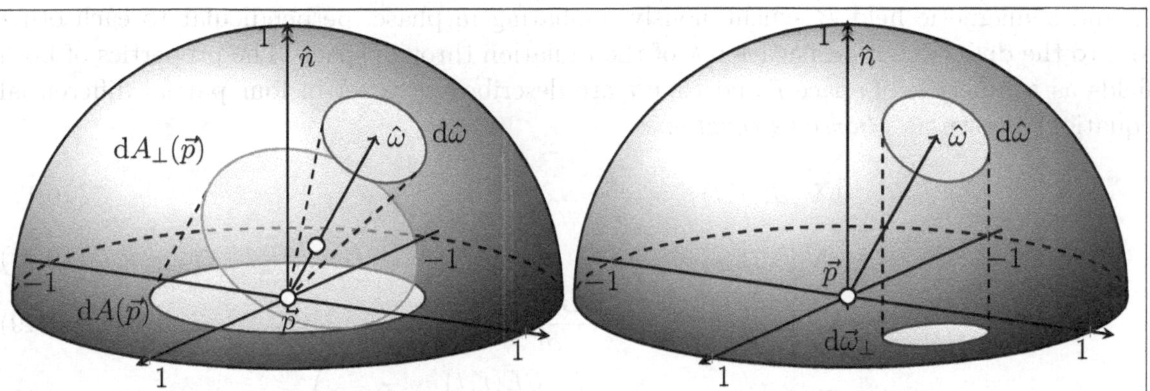

Figure 10.2: Étendue: Illustration of the étendue at a surface point in terms of projected differential area (left) and projected differential solid angle (right).

422 As illustrated in *Figure 10.3*, the conservation of étendue (sometimes also called "throughput") between two surface points $\vec{p}$ and $\vec{q}$ is then formulated as

245 $$\mathrm{d}G(\vec{p},\widehat{pq}) \overset{(6.66)}{=} n^2\langle\hat{n}_p,\widehat{pq}\rangle\mathrm{d}A(\vec{p})\frac{\langle\hat{n}_q,-\widehat{pq}\rangle\mathrm{d}A(\vec{q})}{\|\vec{q}-\vec{p}\|^2}$$

246 $$\overset{(6.71)}{=} n^2\mathrm{d}A(\vec{p})G(\vec{p},\vec{q})\mathrm{d}A(\vec{q}) \tag{10.15}$$

246 $$\overset{(6.71)}{=} n^2\frac{\langle\hat{n}_p,\widehat{pq}\rangle\mathrm{d}A(\vec{p})}{\|\vec{q}-\vec{p}\|^2}\langle\hat{n}_q,-\widehat{pq}\rangle\mathrm{d}A(\vec{q})$$

245 $$\overset{(6.66)}{=} \mathrm{d}G(\vec{q},-\widehat{pq}) \tag{10.16}$$

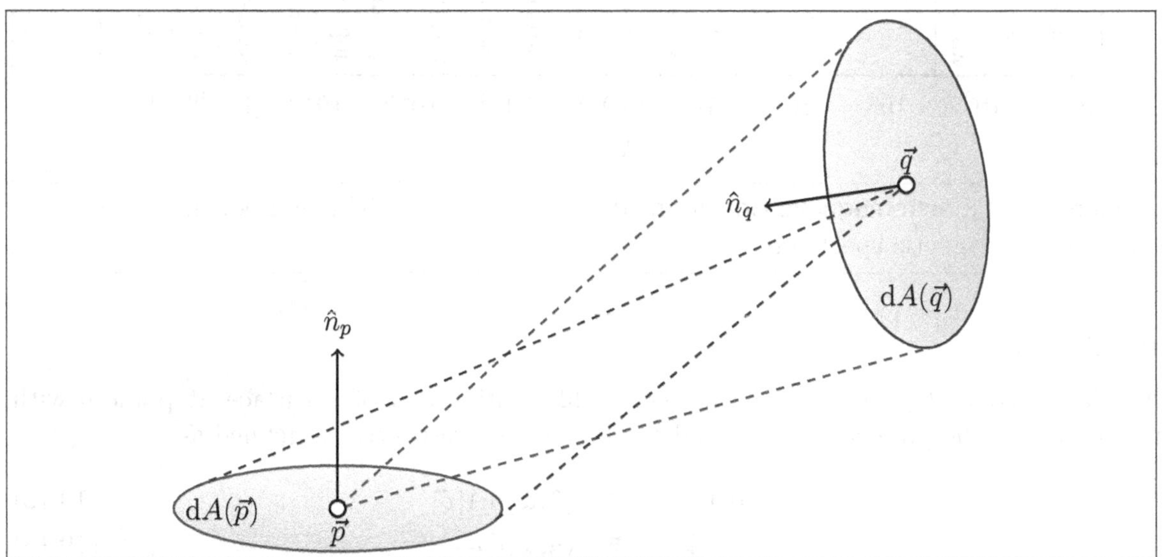

Figure 10.3: Étendue Conservation: Illustration of the conservation of étendue between two surface points.

10.1.3 Maxwell's Equations

423 As illustrated in *Figure 10.4*, an *electromagnetic radiation* is composed of an electric field $\vec{E}$ and a magnetic field $\vec{B}$ synchronously oscillating in phase, perpendicular to each other and to the direction of propagation $\hat{k}$ of the radiation through space. The properties of both fields as a function of space $\vec{r}$ and time t are described by a set of four partial differential equations known as *Maxwell's equations*

$$\nabla\cdot\vec{E}(\vec{r},t) = \frac{\rho}{\epsilon_0} \tag{10.17}$$

$$\nabla\cdot\vec{B}(\vec{r},t) = 0 \tag{10.18}$$

$$\nabla\times\vec{E}(\vec{r},t) = -\frac{\partial\vec{B}(\vec{r},t)}{\partial t} \tag{10.19}$$

$$\nabla\times\vec{B}(\vec{r},t) = \mu_0\left(\epsilon_0\frac{\partial\vec{E}(\vec{r},t)}{\partial t}+\vec{J}(\vec{r},t)\right) \tag{10.20}$$

where ρ is the total charge density and $\vec{J}$ is the current density.

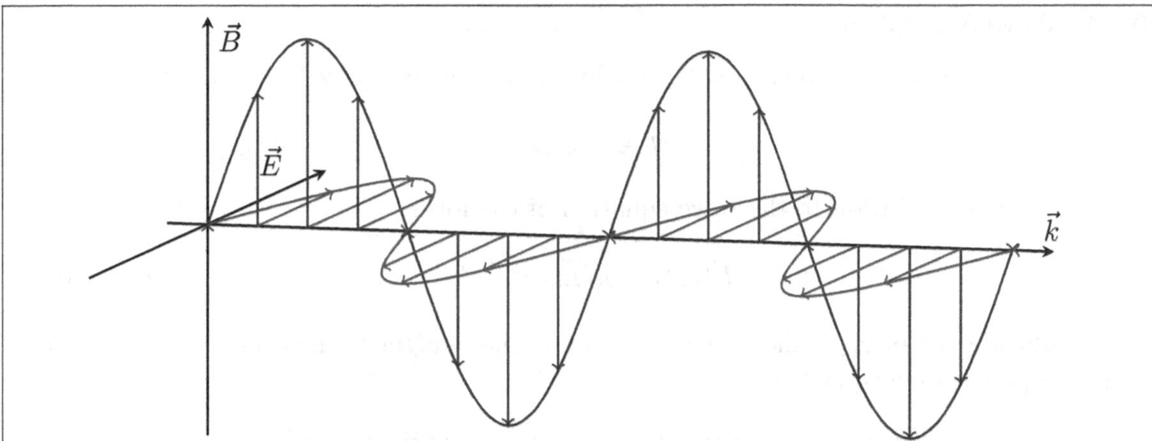

Figure 10.4: Electromagnetic Wave: Illustration of the electric and magnetic fields of an electromagnetic wave.

In free space, where there are no charges $\rho = 0$ and no currents $\vec{J}(\vec{r}, t) = \vec{0}$, Maxwell's equations reduce to

$$\begin{aligned} \nabla \cdot \vec{E}(\vec{r}, t) &= 0 && (10.21) \\ \nabla \cdot \vec{B}(\vec{r}, t) &= 0 && (10.22) \\ \nabla \times \vec{E}(\vec{r}, t) &= -\frac{\partial \vec{B}(\vec{r}, t)}{\partial t} && (10.23) \\ \nabla \times \vec{B}(\vec{r}, t) &\overset{(10.1)}{=} \frac{1}{c^2}\frac{\partial \vec{E}(\vec{r}, t)}{\partial t} && (10.24) \end{aligned}$$ 420

such that

$$\begin{aligned} \nabla^2 \vec{E} &\overset{(10.21)}{=} \nabla^2 \vec{E} - \nabla(\nabla \cdot \vec{E}) \overset{(3.133)}{=} -\nabla \times (\nabla \times \vec{E}) \\ &\overset{(10.23)}{=} -\nabla \times \left(-\frac{\partial \vec{B}}{\partial t}\right) = \frac{\partial(\nabla \times \vec{B})}{\partial t} \overset{(10.24)}{=} \frac{1}{c^2}\frac{\partial^2 \vec{E}}{\partial t^2} && (10.25) \end{aligned}$$ 423 84 423 423

$$\begin{aligned} \nabla^2 \vec{B} &\overset{(10.22)}{=} \nabla^2 \vec{B} - \nabla(\nabla \cdot \vec{B}) \overset{(3.133)}{=} -\nabla \times (\nabla \times \vec{B}) \\ &\overset{(10.24)}{=} -\nabla \times \left(\frac{1}{c^2}\frac{\partial \vec{E}}{\partial t}\right) = -\frac{1}{c^2}\frac{\partial(\nabla \times \vec{E})}{\partial t} \overset{(10.23)}{=} \frac{1}{c^2}\frac{\partial^2 \vec{B}}{\partial t^2} && (10.26) \end{aligned}$$ 423 84 423 423

It then follows that both the electric and magnetic fields obey the differential *wave equation*

$$\frac{1}{c^2}\frac{\partial^2 \vec{v}}{\partial t^2} - \nabla^2 \vec{v} = \left(\frac{1}{c^2}\frac{\partial^2}{\partial t^2} - \nabla^2\right)\vec{v} = \Box \vec{v} = 0 \qquad (10.27)$$

where the *d'Alembertian operator* reads

$$\Box = \frac{1}{c^2}\frac{\partial^2}{\partial t^2} - \nabla^2 \qquad (10.28)$$

and whose general solution is given by any second differentiable function f of the form

$$\vec{E}(\vec{r}, t) = f(\hat{k} \cdot \vec{r} - ct) \overset{(10.10)}{=} f\left(\frac{\vec{k} \cdot \vec{r} - \omega t}{k}\right) \qquad (10.29)$$ 420

10.1.4 Wave Absorption

Given the *absorption coefficient* κ_a of the medium, the *complex-valued wave number* is defined as

$$\underline{k} \triangleq k + \imath\frac{\kappa_a}{2} \tag{10.30}$$

Considering a solution to the wave equation of the form

$$\vec{E}(\vec{r}, t) = \Re(\vec{E}_0 e^{\imath(\vec{\underline{k}}\cdot\vec{r} - \omega t)}) \tag{10.31}$$

with amplitude vector $\vec{E}_0$ while propagating along the z-aligned direction $\hat{k} = [0, 0, 1]^T$ then yields the plane wave equation

$$\vec{E}(z, t) = \Re\left(\vec{E}_0 e^{\imath(\underline{k}z - \omega t)}\right) = \Re\left(e^{-\frac{\kappa_a}{2}z}\vec{E}_0 e^{\imath(kz - \omega t)}\right) \tag{10.32}$$

such that the intensity of the wave becomes

$$I(z) = \int |\vec{E}_0 e^{\imath(\underline{k}z - \omega t)}|^2 \mathrm{d}t = \int |e^{-\frac{\kappa_a}{2}z}\vec{E}_0 e^{\imath(kz - \omega t)}|^2 \mathrm{d}t = |e^{-\frac{\kappa_a}{2}z}|^2 \int |\vec{E}_0 e^{\imath(kz - \omega t)}|^2 \mathrm{d}t = e^{-\kappa_a z} I_0 \tag{10.33}$$

where I_0 is the absorption-free intensity. It follows that the distance at which the amplitude is divided by e, known as the *skin depth*, reads $z = \frac{2}{\kappa_a}$, whereas the distance at which the
464 intensity of the wave is divided by e, known as the *penetration depth* or *mean free path*, is given as $z = \frac{1}{\kappa_a}$.

Similarly, the wavelength-dependent *complex-valued index of refraction* reads

424
420

$$\underline{n} \triangleq \sqrt{\mu_r \underline{\epsilon}_r} = \frac{\underline{k}}{k_0} \overset{(10.30)}{=} \frac{k}{k_0} + \imath\frac{\kappa_a}{2k_0} \overset{(10.11)}{=} n + \imath\kappa \tag{10.34}$$

where $\kappa \triangleq \frac{\kappa_a}{2k_0}$ is the *absorption index* of the surface, while the *complex-valued relative permittivity* $\underline{\epsilon}_r$ is defined in terms of the *complex-valued permittivity* $\underline{\epsilon}$ as

$$\underline{\epsilon}_r \triangleq \frac{\underline{\epsilon}}{\epsilon_0} = \epsilon_1 + \imath\epsilon_2 \tag{10.35}$$

Because most natural materials are non-magnetic within the visible spectrum, it generally holds that $\mu_r \approx 1$, such that the complex-valued index of refraction reduces to $\underline{n} = \sqrt{\underline{\epsilon}_r}$, whose real and imaginary parts, respectively, read

88

$$n = \Re(\sqrt{\underline{\epsilon}_r}) \overset{(3.173)}{=} \sqrt{\frac{\sqrt{\epsilon_1^2 + \epsilon_2^2} + \epsilon_1}{2}} \tag{10.36}$$

88

$$\kappa = \Im(\sqrt{\underline{\epsilon}_r}) \overset{(3.173)}{=} \sqrt{\frac{\sqrt{\epsilon_1^2 + \epsilon_2^2} - \epsilon_1}{2}} \tag{10.37}$$

while the complex-valued relative permittivity is conversely given by $\underline{\epsilon}_r = \underline{n}^2$, such that

$$\epsilon_1 = \Re(\underline{n}^2) = n^2 - \kappa^2 \tag{10.38}$$

$$\epsilon_2 = \Im(\underline{n}^2) = 2n\kappa \tag{10.39}$$

10.1.5 Wave–Particle Duality

An electromagnetic radiation exhibits both wave-like and particle-like properties, a phenomenon known as the *wave–particle duality*. The quantum of the electromagnetic field is an elementary particle called a *photon*, whose energy is defined by the *Planck–Einstein equation* as

$$E = h\nu \overset{(10.6)}{=} \frac{h\omega}{2\pi} = \hbar\omega \tag{10.40}$$ 420

where h is the *Planck constant* and $\hbar \triangleq \frac{h}{2\pi}$ is the *reduced Planck constant*.

The *momentum* of the photon is then given as

$$p \triangleq \frac{E}{v} = \frac{h\nu}{v} \overset{(10.8)}{=} \frac{h}{\lambda} = \frac{h}{2\pi}\frac{2\pi}{\lambda} \overset{(10.10)}{=} \hbar k \tag{10.41}$$ 420 420

from which the *momentum vector* of the photon is defined as $\vec{p} \triangleq p\hat{k} = \hbar k\hat{k} = \hbar\vec{k}$, such that $p = \|\vec{p}\|$. *Heisenberg's uncertainty principle* then states that the *standard deviations* of 146
position σ_x and momentum σ_p obey the inequality

$$\sigma_x\sigma_p \geq \frac{\hbar}{2} \tag{10.42}$$

At frequencies lower than the visible range, electromagnetic radiation mainly alters cells and other materials due to bulk heating effects from multiple photons, which is determined by the radiation power, the frequency of the radiation affecting mainly the depth of penetration into the material. On the other hand, the energy of a single photon in the visible range is sufficiently high to change the bond structure of some individual molecules, such as that of the
retinal *photoreceptors* in the *human eye* or that of the molecule of chlorophyll responsible for 681
photosynthesis. At frequencies greater than the visible range, though, photons carry enough 678
energy to break chemical bonds and to cause a permanent rearrangement of certain molecules, while at the higher end of the ultraviolet range, the energy of photons is sufficiently large to free individual electrons from their atoms in a process called *photo-ionisation*.

10.1.6 Radiometry

As illustrated in *Table 10.1*, *radiometry* is the science of measuring electromagnetic radiation, 426
whose *radiant energy* is determined by the aggregate energy of its individual photons

$$Q_e \overset{(10.46)}{=} \int_0^T \Phi_e(t)\mathrm{d}t \tag{10.43}$$ 426

The *radiant exposure* of a surface is then defined as the incident radiant energy received per unit area $\mathrm{d}A$

$$H_e(\vec{p}) \triangleq \frac{\mathrm{d}Q_e}{\mathrm{d}A(\vec{p})} \overset{(10.53)}{=} \int_0^T E_e(t,\vec{p})\mathrm{d}t \tag{10.44}$$ 426

whereas *radiant energy density* corresponds to the density of radiant energy per unit volume $\mathrm{d}V$

$$w_e(\vec{p}) \triangleq \frac{\mathrm{d}Q_e}{\mathrm{d}V(\vec{p})} \tag{10.45}$$

Table 10.1: Radiometric Quantities: Nomenclature of radiometric quantities.

Quantity	Symbol	SI Unit
Radiant energy	Q_e	J
Radiant exposure/fluence	H_e	$\text{J}\cdot\text{m}^{-2}$
Radiant energy density	w_e	$\text{J}\cdot\text{m}^{-3}$
Radiant flux/power	Φ_e	$\text{W} \equiv \text{J}\cdot\text{s}^{-1}$
Radiant intensity	I_e	$\text{W}\cdot\text{sr}^{-1}$
Radiant exitance/emittance (emitted)	M_e	$\text{W}\cdot\text{m}^{-2}$
Radiosity (emitted and reflected)	J_e / B_e	$\text{W}\cdot\text{m}^{-2}$
Irradiance (incident)	E_e	$\text{W}\cdot\text{m}^{-2}$
Radiance	L_e	$\text{W}\cdot\text{m}^{-2}\cdot\text{sr}^{-1}$

Instead, *radiant flux* is defined as the radiant energy per unit of time $\text{d}t$

427

$$\Phi_e(t) \triangleq \frac{\text{d}Q_e}{\text{d}t} \overset{(10.57)}{=} \int_\Omega \int_S L_e(t,\vec{p},\hat{\omega})\langle\hat{n},\hat{\omega}\rangle \text{d}A(\vec{p})\text{d}\hat{\omega} \quad (10.46)$$

426
421

$$\overset{(10.49)}{=} \int_\Omega I_e(t,\hat{\omega})\text{d}\hat{\omega} \overset{(10.12)}{=} \int_\Omega \int_{S_\perp} L_e(t,\vec{p},\hat{\omega})\text{d}A_\perp(\vec{p})\text{d}\hat{\omega} \quad (10.47)$$

426
421

$$\overset{(10.50)}{=} \int_S M|J|E_e(t,\vec{p})\text{d}A(\vec{p}) \overset{(10.13)}{=} \int_{\Omega_\perp} \int_S L_e(t,\vec{p},\hat{\omega})\text{d}A(\vec{p})\text{d}\hat{\omega}_\perp \quad (10.48)$$

244 and *radiant intensity* as the radiant flux per unit *solid angle* $\text{d}\hat{\omega}$

427
421

$$I_e(t,\hat{\omega}) \triangleq \frac{\text{d}\Phi_e(t)}{\text{d}\hat{\omega}} \overset{(10.55)}{=} \int_S L_e(t,\vec{p},\hat{\omega})\langle\hat{n},\hat{\omega}\rangle\text{d}A(\vec{p}) \overset{(10.12)}{=} \int_{S_\perp} L_e(t,\vec{p},\hat{\omega})\text{d}A_\perp(\vec{p}) \quad (10.49)$$

Similarly, *radiant exitance*, *radiosity* and *irradiance* are defined as the flux density of emitted, emitted-and-reflected, and incident, respectively, radiation per unit surface area $\text{d}A$

427
421

$$M|J|E_e(t,\vec{p}) \triangleq \frac{\text{d}\Phi_e(t)}{\text{d}A(\vec{p})} \overset{(10.56)}{=} \int_\Omega L_e(t,\vec{p},\hat{\omega})\langle\hat{n},\hat{\omega}\rangle\text{d}\hat{\omega} \overset{(10.13)}{=} \int_{\Omega_\perp} L_e(t,\vec{p},\hat{\omega})\text{d}\hat{\omega}_\perp \quad (10.50)$$

whereas *scalar irradiance* is defined as

$$e(t,\vec{p}) \triangleq \int_\Omega L_e(t,\vec{p},\hat{\omega})\text{d}\hat{\omega} \quad (10.51)$$

and *vector irradiance* as

$$\vec{E}(t,\vec{p}) \triangleq \int_\Omega L_e(t,\vec{p},\hat{\omega})\hat{\omega}\text{d}\hat{\omega} \quad (10.52)$$

such that, whenever Ω belongs to the positive hemisphere around $\hat{n}$, irradiance may be formulated as

$$E_e(t,\vec{p}) \triangleq \frac{\text{d}H_e(\vec{p})}{\text{d}t} \quad (10.53)$$

426

$$\begin{aligned} &\overset{(10.50)}{=} \int_\Omega L_e(t,\vec{p},\hat{\omega})\left(\sum_{i\in\{x,y,z\}} n_i\omega_i\right)\text{d}\hat{\omega} \\ &= \sum_{i\in\{x,y,z\}} n_i \int_\Omega L_e(t,\vec{p},\hat{\omega})\omega_i\text{d}\hat{\omega} \\ &= \left\langle \hat{n}, \int_\Omega L_e(t,\vec{p},\hat{\omega})\hat{\omega}\text{d}\hat{\omega} \right\rangle \end{aligned}$$

426

$$\overset{(10.52)}{=} \langle\hat{n},\vec{E}(t,\vec{p})\rangle \quad (10.54)$$

Finally, *radiance* is defined as the radiant flux per unit *solid angle* $\mathrm{d}\hat{\omega}$ per unit surface area $\mathrm{d}A(\vec{p})$ projected orthogonally to the direction of propagation $\hat{\omega}$ 244

$$L_e(t,\vec{p},\hat{\omega}) \triangleq \frac{\mathrm{d}I_e(t,\hat{\omega})}{\langle\hat{n},\hat{\omega}\rangle \mathrm{d}A(\vec{p})} \overset{(10.12)}{=} \frac{\mathrm{d}I_e(t,\hat{\omega})}{\mathrm{d}A_\perp(\vec{p})} \tag{10.55}$$ 421

$$= \frac{\mathrm{d}M|J|E_e(t,\vec{p})}{\langle\hat{n},\hat{\omega}\rangle \mathrm{d}\hat{\omega}} \overset{(10.13)}{=} \frac{\mathrm{d}M|J|E_e(t,\vec{p})}{\mathrm{d}\hat{\omega}_\perp} \tag{10.56}$$ 421

$$= \frac{\mathrm{d}^2\Phi_e(t)}{\langle\hat{n},\hat{\omega}\rangle \mathrm{d}A(\vec{p})\mathrm{d}\hat{\omega}} \overset{(10.14)}{=} n^2\frac{\mathrm{d}^2\Phi_e(t)}{\mathrm{d}G(\vec{p},\hat{\omega})} \tag{10.57}$$ 421

from which, together with the conservation of *étendue*, follows the conservation of *basic radiance* in a non-attenuating medium of refractive index n 421

$$\frac{L_e(t,\vec{p},\hat{\omega})}{n^2} \overset{(10.57)}{=} \frac{\mathrm{d}^2\Phi_e(t)}{\mathrm{d}G(\vec{p},\hat{\omega})} \overset{(10.16)}{=} \frac{\mathrm{d}^2\Phi_e(t)}{\mathrm{d}G(\vec{q},-\hat{\omega})} \overset{(10.57)}{=} \frac{L_e(t,\vec{q},-\hat{\omega})}{n^2} \tag{10.58}$$ 427 422 427

as well as the conservation of *basic spectral radiance* $\frac{L_{e\nu}}{n^2}$ or $\frac{L_{e\lambda}}{n^3}$.

Formally, *spectral power distribution* (*SPD*) is defined as the distribution of radiant flux per spectral unit (i.e., either per unit frequency $\mathrm{d}\nu$ or per unit wavelength $\mathrm{d}\lambda$), although the term is more generally used to refer to the spectral distribution of any radiometric quantity

$$X_{e\nu}(\nu) \triangleq \frac{\mathrm{d}X_e}{\mathrm{d}\nu} \tag{10.59}$$

$$X_{e\lambda}(\lambda) \triangleq \frac{\mathrm{d}X_e}{\mathrm{d}\lambda} \tag{10.60}$$

A radiometric quantity is then related to its spectral distribution by

$$X_e = \int_0^\infty X_{e\nu}(\nu)\mathrm{d}\nu \overset{(10.8)}{=} \int_0^\infty X_{e\nu}\left(\frac{v}{\lambda}\right)\frac{v}{\lambda^2}\mathrm{d}\lambda \tag{10.61}$$ 420

$$= \int_0^\infty X_{e\lambda}(\lambda)\mathrm{d}\lambda \overset{(10.8)}{=} \int_0^\infty X_{e\lambda}\left(\frac{v}{\nu}\right)\frac{v}{\nu^2}\mathrm{d}\nu \tag{10.62}$$ 420

Because most radiometric quantities generally vary with wavelength, the dependence is commonly implied and omitted from the notation in order to simplify the latter. Likewise, radiometric quantities typically refer to light in a steady rather than a transient state, and the time dependence is also commonly omitted.

10.1.7 Blackbody Radiation

Whereas a *white body* is an idealized diffuse reflector that uniformly reflects all incident electromagnetic radiation in all directions, a *blackbody* is a similarly idealized body that perfectly absorbs all incident radiation. A blackbody also is an ideal diffuse emitter that radiates uniformly in all directions. Its spectral energy density, which solely depends on the temperature T (in K), is then given by *Planck's law* according to Bose–Einstein statistics as

$$w_\nu(T,\nu) = \frac{8\pi h\nu^3}{c^3}\frac{1}{e^{\frac{h\nu}{kT}}-1} \tag{10.63}$$

$$w_\lambda(T,\lambda) = \frac{8\pi hc}{\lambda^5}\frac{1}{e^{\frac{hc}{\lambda kT}}-1} \tag{10.64}$$

where k is the *Boltzmann constant*, such that $w_s(T_1,s) < w_s(T_2,s), \forall s \in \mathbb{R}^+$ for any two temperatures $T_1 < T_2$. As illustrated in *Figure 10.5*, multiplying the spectral energy density 428 by $\frac{c}{4\pi}$ (in m·s^{-1}·sr^{-1}) then yields the corresponding spectral radiance

$$L_\nu(T,\nu) = \frac{2h\nu^3}{c^2}\frac{1}{e^{\frac{h\nu}{kT}}-1} \quad (10.65)$$

$$L_\lambda(T,\lambda) = \frac{2hc^2}{\lambda^5}\frac{1}{e^{\frac{hc}{\lambda kT}}-1} \quad (10.66)$$

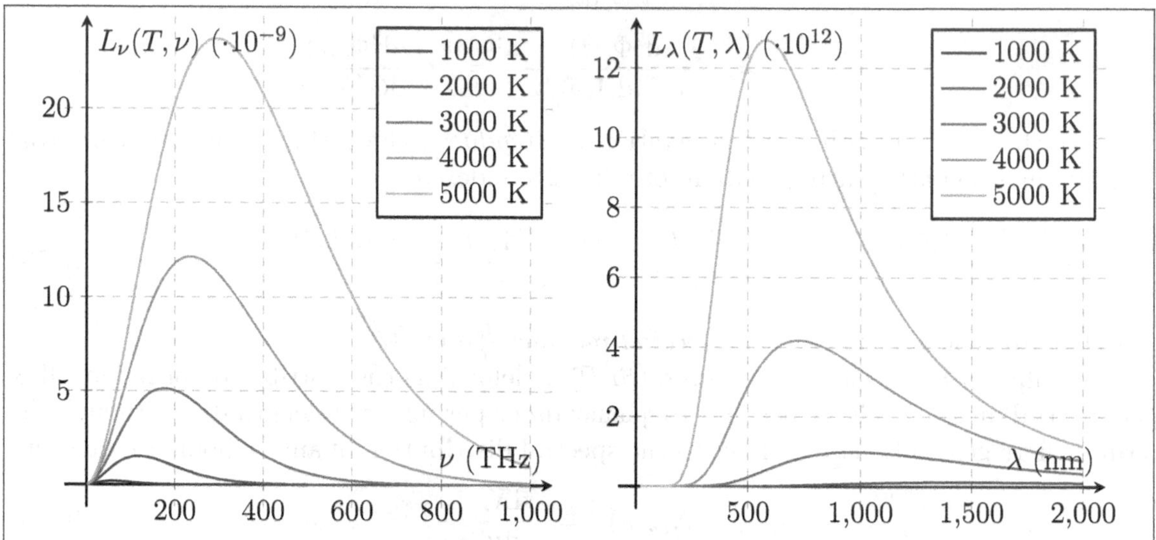

Figure 10.5: **Blackbody Radiation:** Spectral radiance emitted by a blackbody at various temperatures as a function of frequency (left) and wavelength (right).

The derivatives of the spectral radiance are then readily given as

$$\begin{aligned}\frac{\partial L_\nu(T,\nu)}{\partial \nu} &= \frac{2h}{c^2}\left(3\nu^2\frac{1}{e^{\frac{h\nu}{kT}}-1} - \nu^3\frac{\frac{h}{kT}e^{\frac{h\nu}{kT}}}{\left(e^{\frac{h\nu}{kT}}-1\right)^2}\right)\\ &= \frac{2h\nu^2}{c^2}\frac{1}{e^{\frac{h\nu}{kT}}-1}\left(3-\frac{h\nu}{kT}\frac{e^{\frac{h\nu}{kT}}}{e^{\frac{h\nu}{kT}}-1}\right) \quad (10.67)\end{aligned}$$

$$\begin{aligned}\frac{\partial L_\lambda(T,\nu)}{\partial \lambda} &= 2hc^2\left(\frac{1}{\lambda^5}\frac{hc}{\lambda^2 kT}\frac{e^{\frac{hc}{\lambda kT}}}{\left(e^{\frac{hc}{\lambda kT}}-1\right)^2} - \frac{5}{\lambda^6}\frac{1}{e^{\frac{hc}{\lambda kT}}-1}\right)\\ &= \frac{2hc^2}{\lambda^6}\frac{1}{e^{\frac{hc}{\lambda kT}}-1}\left(\frac{hc}{\lambda kT}\frac{e^{\frac{hc}{\lambda kT}}}{e^{\frac{hc}{\lambda kT}}-1}-5\right) \quad (10.68)\end{aligned}$$

from which follows *Wien's displacement law*, which states that as the temperature increases, the peak of the spectrum at which the emission is maximal shifts from the infrared range towards the ultraviolet

$$\frac{\partial L_\nu(T,\nu)}{\partial \nu} = 0 \implies \frac{h\nu}{kT} \approx 2.821439372 \quad (10.69)$$

$$\frac{\partial L_\lambda(T,\nu)}{\partial \lambda} = 0 \implies \frac{hc}{\lambda kT} \approx 4.965114231 \quad (10.70)$$

Conversely, integrating the spectral radiance over the entire spectrum yields the total emitted radiance

427

$$L_e(T) \overset{(10.61)}{=} \frac{2h}{c^2}\int_0^\infty \frac{\nu^3}{e^{\frac{h\nu}{kT}}-1}\mathrm{d}\nu = \frac{2h}{c^2}\left(\frac{kT}{h}\right)^4\frac{\pi^4}{15} = \frac{2k^4\pi^4}{15c^2h^3}T^4 \quad (10.71)$$

from which the radiant exitance is given by the *Stefan–Boltzmann law* as

$$M_e(T) \overset{(10.50)}{=} \int_{2\pi^+} \frac{2k^4\pi^4}{15c^2h^3} T^4 \langle \hat{n}, \hat{\omega} \rangle \mathrm{d}\hat{\omega} = \frac{2k^4\pi^4}{15c^2h^3} T^4 \int_{2\pi^+} \langle \hat{n}, \hat{\omega} \rangle \mathrm{d}\hat{\omega} = \sigma T^4 \tag{10.72}$$ 426

where $\sigma \triangleq \frac{2k^4\pi^5}{15c^2h^3}$ is the *Stefan–Boltzmann constant.*

The *directional emissivity* and *hemispherical emissivity* $\epsilon \in [0, 1]$ of a point $\vec{p}$ on a surface at a temperature T_p are then, respectively, defined as

$$\epsilon(t, \vec{p}, \hat{\omega}) \triangleq \frac{L_e(t, \vec{p}, \hat{\omega})}{L_e(T_p)} \tag{10.73}$$

$$\epsilon(t, \vec{p}) \triangleq \frac{M_e(t, \vec{p})}{M_e(T_p)} \tag{10.74}$$

In thermal equilibrium (i.e., at constant temperature), *Kirchoff's law* states that the (spectral) emissivity of an object equals its (spectral) absorptance/absorptivity

$$\epsilon(t, \vec{p}, \hat{\omega}) = \alpha(t, \vec{p}, \hat{\omega}) \tag{10.75}$$

Because it is an ideal absorber with $\alpha(t, \vec{p}, \hat{\omega}) = 1, \forall \hat{\omega} \in 2\pi^+$, a blackbody consequently is an ideal emitter with maximal emissivity, such that no other body at the same temperature can radiate more energy than it.

10.2 LIGHT SOURCE

10.2.1 Volumetric Light

Given a medium with volumetric flux density $\rho_e(t, \vec{p}) = \frac{\mathrm{d}\Phi_e(t)}{\mathrm{d}V(\vec{p})}$ at each point $\vec{p}$, an upper bound on the total power received by an illuminated scene is readily given by the total emitted flux of the *volumetric light* source [Zhang *et al.*, 2011]

$$\Phi_e = \int_V \rho_e(\vec{p}) \mathrm{d}V(\vec{p}) \tag{10.76}$$

while a sample position may be drawn according to the distribution of $\rho_e(\vec{p})$.

10.2.2 Area Light

Given a directional distribution $f(\hat{\omega})$ normalized such that

$$\int_{2\pi^+} f(\hat{\omega}) \langle \hat{n}, \hat{\omega} \rangle \mathrm{d}\hat{\omega} = 1 \tag{10.77}$$

the emitted radiance of a surface can be expressed in a separable form as

$$L_e(\vec{p}, \hat{\omega}) = M_e(\vec{p}) f(\hat{\omega}) \tag{10.78}$$

such that the radiant emittance at a point $\vec{p}$ reads

$$M_e(\vec{p}) \overset{(10.50)}{=} \int_{2\pi^+} M_e(\vec{p}) f(\hat{\omega}) \langle \hat{n}, \hat{\omega} \rangle \mathrm{d}\hat{\omega} = M_e(\vec{p}) \int_{2\pi^+} f(\hat{\omega}) \langle \hat{n}, \hat{\omega} \rangle \mathrm{d}\hat{\omega} \tag{10.79}$$ 426

An upper bound on the total power received by an illuminated scene is then readily given
by the total emitted flux of the *area light* source illustrated in *Figure 10.6* and *Figure 10.7*, 430 431
while a sample position on the surface of the latter may be drawn either uniformly, as in the
case of *analytic surfaces*, or according to the distribution of $M_e(\vec{p})$, and a sample direction 236
drawn from $f(\hat{\omega}) \langle \hat{n}, \hat{\omega} \rangle$.

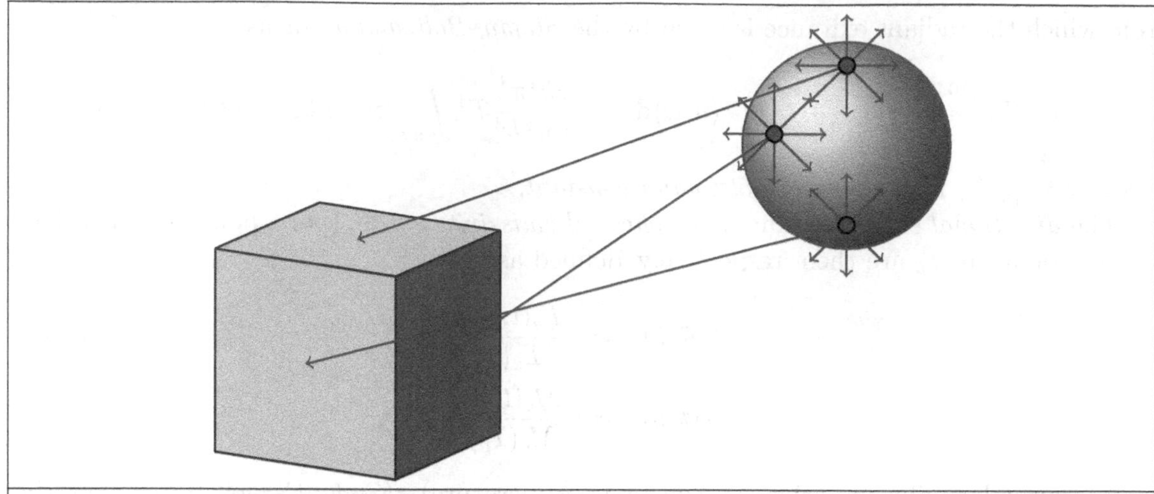

Figure 10.6: Area Light: Illustration of an area light source.

10.2.3 Linear Light

429 Given a cylindrical *area light* of radius r whose emitted radiance is inversely proportional to its circumference $C = 2\pi r$ and independent of the azimuthal coordinate c of the position $\vec{p}$

$$L_e(\vec{p}, \hat{\omega}) = \frac{\pi}{C} l_e(s, \hat{\omega}) \tag{10.80}$$

244 the emitted radiant flux per unit length per unit *solid angle* at arc-length s reads

$$l_e(s, \hat{\omega}) = \int_C L_e(\vec{p}, \hat{\omega}) \langle \hat{n}, \hat{n}_\omega \rangle \mathrm{d}c = \frac{\pi}{C} l_e(s, \hat{\omega}) \int_C \langle \hat{n}, \hat{n}_\omega \rangle \mathrm{d}c = \frac{\pi}{2\pi r} l_e(s, \hat{\omega}) 2r \tag{10.81}$$

where $\hat{n}_\omega$ is the orthogonalization of $\hat{\omega}$ with respect to the tangent $\hat{t}$ at point $\vec{p}$, as given by
81 the *vector triple product*.

432 As illustrated in *Figure 10.8*, in the limit of an infinitely small radius $r \to 0$, the *cylinder*
272 reduces to a *linear light* source of infinite emitted radiance, but finite l_e. Defining the separable directional distribution $f(\hat{\omega}) = g(\phi)h(\theta)$ normalized such that

$$\int_{4\pi} f(\hat{\omega}) \langle \hat{n}, \hat{\omega} \rangle \mathrm{d}\hat{\omega} = \int_{2\pi} g(\phi) \mathrm{d}\phi \int_{\pi} h(\theta) \cos(\theta) \mathrm{d}\theta = 1 \tag{10.82}$$

244 the emitted radiant flux per unit length per unit *solid angle* can then be formulated in a separable form as

$$l_e(s, \hat{\omega}) = \rho_e(s) f(\hat{\omega}) \tag{10.83}$$

Given a segment with linear flux density $\rho_e(t, s) = \frac{\mathrm{d}\Phi_e(t)}{\mathrm{d}s}$ emitted at a given arc-length s

$$\rho_e(s) = \int_{4\pi} l_e(s, \hat{\omega}) \langle \hat{n}, \hat{\omega} \rangle \mathrm{d}\hat{\omega} = \rho_e(s) \int_{4\pi} f(\hat{\omega}) \langle \hat{n}, \hat{\omega} \rangle \mathrm{d}\hat{\omega} \tag{10.84}$$

an upper bound on the total power received by an illuminated scene is readily given by the total emitted flux

$$\Phi_e = \int_L \rho_e(s) \mathrm{d}s \tag{10.85}$$

while a sample position may be drawn according to the distribution of $\rho_e(s)$, and a sample direction drawn from $f(\hat{\omega}) \langle \hat{n}, \hat{\omega} \rangle$.

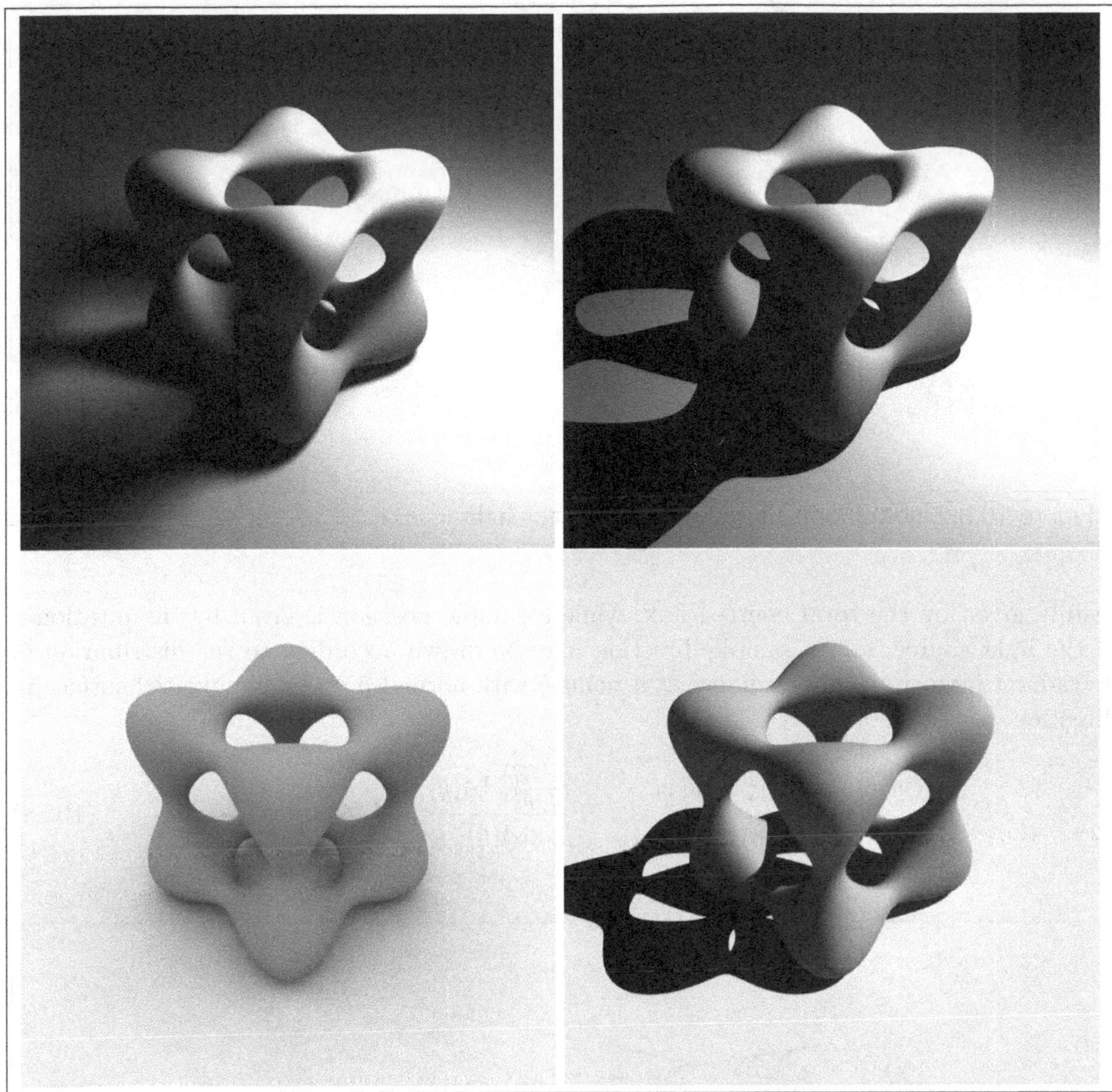

Figure 10.7: Light Source: Qualitative appearance of the illumination of a scene by an area light (top left), an isotropic point light (top right), an environmental light (bottom left) and a directional light (bottom right).

10.2.4 Point Light

Given a spherical *area light* of radius r whose emitted radiance is inversely proportional to 429
its surface area $A = 4\pi r^2$ and independent of position $\vec{p}$

$$L_e(\vec{p}, \hat{\omega}) = \frac{4}{A} I_e(\hat{\omega}) \tag{10.86}$$

the radiant intensity emitted along a given direction $\hat{\omega}$ reads

426

$$I_e(\hat{\omega}) \overset{(10.49)}{=} \int_S \frac{4}{A} I_e(\hat{\omega}) \langle \hat{n}, \hat{\omega} \rangle \mathrm{d}A(\vec{p}) = \frac{4}{A} I_e(\hat{\omega}) \int_S \langle \hat{n}, \hat{\omega} \rangle \mathrm{d}A(\vec{p}) = \frac{4}{4\pi r^2} I_e(\hat{\omega}) \pi r^2 \tag{10.87}$$

In the limit of an infinitely small radius $r \to 0$, the sphere reduces to a *point light* source of infinite emitted radiance, but finite radiant intensity, as illustrated in *Figure 10.9* and 432
Figure 10.7. An upper bound on the total power received by an illuminated scene is then 431

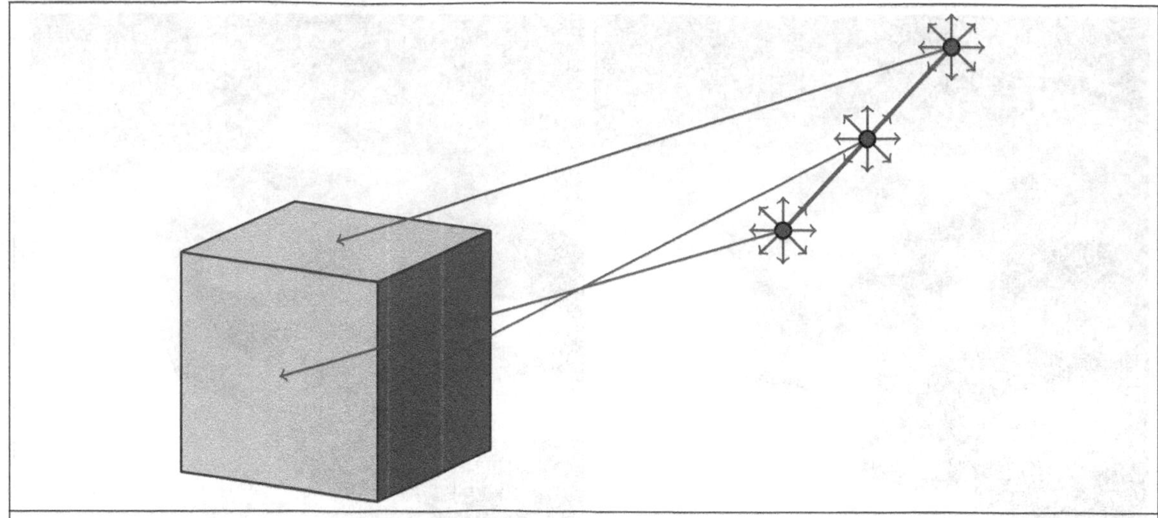

Figure 10.8: Linear Light: Illustration of a linear light source.

readily given by the total emitted flux, while a sample position is given by the position $\vec{p}$ of the light source, and a sample direction may be drawn according to the distribution of its radiant intensity. The irradiance at a point $\vec{q}$ with normal $\hat{n}$ on an illuminated surface in direction $\hat{\omega} = \widehat{pq}$ then reads

426
426
245

$$E_e(\vec{q}) \overset{(10.50)}{=} \frac{\mathrm{d}\Phi_e}{\mathrm{d}\hat{\omega}} \frac{\mathrm{d}\hat{\omega}}{\mathrm{d}A(\vec{q})} \underset{(6.66)}{\overset{(10.49)}{=}} I_e(\hat{\omega}) \frac{\frac{\langle \hat{n}, -\widehat{pq} \rangle}{\|\vec{q}-\vec{p}\|^2} \mathrm{d}A(\vec{q})}{\mathrm{d}A(\vec{q})} = I_e(\hat{\omega}) \frac{\langle \hat{n}, -\hat{\omega} \rangle}{\|\vec{q}-\vec{p}\|^2} \tag{10.88}$$

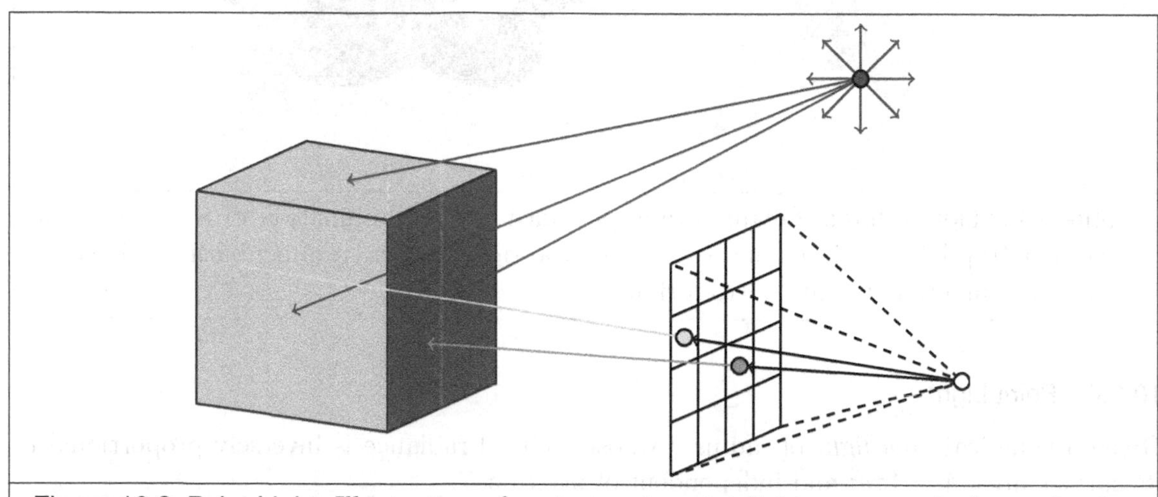

Figure 10.9: Point Light: Illustration of an isotropic point light source and of a projective light.

The distribution of the radiant intensity might be specified analytically by substituting
the fixed light orientation $\hat{\omega}_l$ and the illumination direction $\hat{\omega}$ in place of the incident and
444 exitant directions of a normalized *phase function*, such as an *isotropic* or the cosine-lobe
446 *Warn* spotlight [Warn, 1983] distribution (possibly restricting illumination within a *cone*)
447
275

$$I_e(\hat{\omega}) = \Phi_e f_p(\hat{\omega}_l, \hat{\omega}) \tag{10.89}$$

such that the total emitted flux reads

$$\Phi_e \overset{(10.46)}{=} \int_{4\pi} \Phi_e f_p(\hat{\omega}_l, \hat{\omega}) \mathrm{d}\hat{\omega} = \Phi_e \int_{4\pi} f_p(\hat{\omega}_l, \hat{\omega}) \mathrm{d}\hat{\omega} \tag{10.90}$$ 426

while a sample direction may be drawn from $f_p(\hat{\omega}_l, \hat{\omega})$.

Instead, the directional distribution might be tabulated by means of a spherical or cubical
goniometric diagram akin to the sphere map or cube map representing an *environmental light*, 433
and then sampled accordingly.

Moreover, the directional distribution may be restricted to a *spherical rectangle* akin to 260
the perspective projection of a video projector. Assuming a piecewise-constant representation
divided into cells of *solid angle* Ω_c and value k_c, the associated *probability density* reads 244 131

$$\int_{\Omega} p(\hat{\omega}) \mathrm{d}\hat{\omega} = \sum_{\Omega_c \in \Omega} \int_{\Omega_c} \frac{k_c}{C} \mathrm{d}\hat{\omega} = \frac{1}{C} \sum_{\Omega_c \in \Omega} k_c \Omega_c = 1 \tag{10.91}$$

where the normalization constant is defined as $C = \sum_{\Omega_c \in \Omega} k_c \Omega_c$. It follows that *importance*
sampling of the illumination can be carried by first randomly selecting a cell from a PMF 155
with weights proportional to the product of the value and *solid angle* of each cell. A sample 244
direction may then be drawn within the cell by uniformly sampling either its surface area
relative to the virtual geometry of the projection screen, or its subtended *spherical rectangle*. 260

10.2.5 Environmental Light

Given a convex spherical or cuboidal *area light* enclosing a scene centered around a point $\vec{c}$, 429
the radiant emittance within the *solid angle* Ω_S subtended by the scene at a point $\vec{p}$ on the 244
light source in the limit of an infinite radius $\|\vec{c} - \vec{p}\| \to \infty, \forall \vec{p} \in S$ such that $\hat{\omega} \to \frac{\vec{c}-\vec{p}}{\|\vec{c}-\vec{p}\|}$ reads

$$M_e(\vec{p}) \overset{(10.50)}{=} \int_{\Omega_S} L_e(\vec{p}, \hat{\omega}) \langle \hat{n}, \hat{\omega} \rangle \mathrm{d}\hat{\omega} = L_e(\vec{p}, \hat{\omega}) \langle \hat{n}, \hat{\omega} \rangle \Omega_S \tag{10.92}$$ 426

While the surface area of the *environmental light* source is infinite, and so is its total
emitted flux, the total power received by the illuminated scene is finite, as illustrated in
Figure 10.7, and bounded by 431

$$\Phi_e \overset{(10.46)}{=} \int_S L_e(\vec{p}, \hat{\omega}) \langle \hat{n}, \hat{\omega} \rangle \Omega_S \mathrm{d}\vec{p} \overset{(6.66)}{=} \int_{4\pi} L_e(\vec{p}, \hat{\omega}) \langle \hat{n}, \hat{\omega} \rangle \Omega_S \frac{\|\vec{c} - \vec{p}\|^2}{\langle \hat{n}, \hat{\omega} \rangle} \mathrm{d}\hat{\omega} = \int_{4\pi} L_e(\vec{p}, \hat{\omega}) A_\perp(\hat{\omega}) \mathrm{d}\hat{\omega} \tag{10.93}$$ 426 245

where the *solid angle* $\Omega_S = \frac{A_\perp(\hat{\omega})}{\|\vec{c}-\vec{p}\|^2}$ is expressed in terms of the projected area of the scene 244
$A_\perp(\hat{\omega})$ along $\hat{\omega}$, whose upper bound is readily given by the direction-independent projected
area of its bounding sphere.

In practice, the radiance values are typically stored in a (possibly HDR) image, called
environment map, in which case the illumination of a virtual scene by the latter is commonly
referred to as *image-based lighting* [Debevec, 1998, Debevec, 2002, Debevec *et al.*, 2003, Debevec, 2005]. Based on *panoramic photography*, equi-solid-angle or equi-angular *light probes* 674
can be acquired from a real environment by means of an orthographic camera imaging a
convex spherical or parabolic mirror [Heidrich and Seidel, 1998]. However, both azimuthal
projections are prone to distortion and undersampling of the incident radiation near the
peripheral area, as illustrated in *Figure 10.10*. 434

Instead, environmental illumination may be represented as an equi-rectangular map,
typically relying on an equi-angular projection linearly mapping the *spherical coordinates* 70

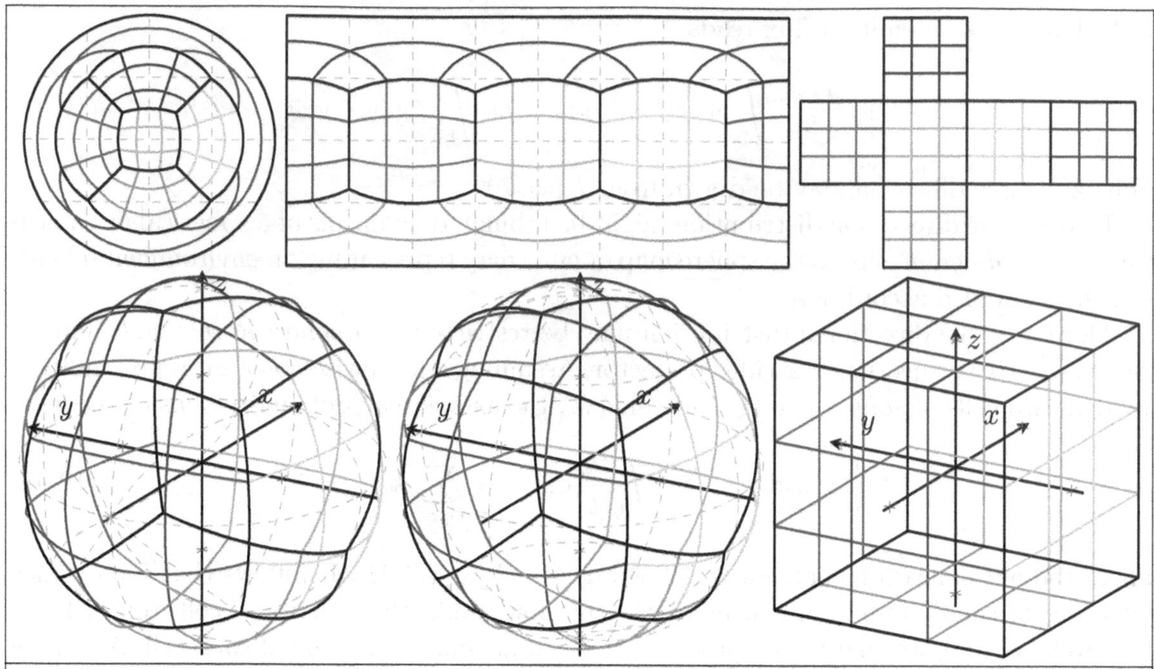

Figure 10.10: Environment Map: Environmental illumination represented as an equi-angular map, as an equi-rectangular map and as a cube map (from left to right, respectively).

$\phi \in (-\pi, \pi]$ and $\theta \in [0, \pi]$ to normalized image space $s \in [0, 1]$ and $t \in [0, 1]$ by a transformation of the form

$$s = \frac{1}{2}\left(1 - \frac{\phi}{\pi}\right) \tag{10.94}$$

$$t = 1 - \frac{\theta}{\pi} \tag{10.95}$$

244 Assuming a piecewise-constant PDF representation divided into cells of *solid angle* Ω_c (whose
values may either be defined as the cell luminances of a cell-centered piecewise-constant map,
or by averaging the corner values of a piecewise-linear node-centered map), normalization of
131 the *probability density* yields

$$\begin{aligned}
\int_{4\pi} p(\hat{\omega}) \mathrm{d}\hat{\omega} &= \int_{4\pi} \frac{L_e(\vec{p}(\hat{\omega}), \hat{\omega})}{C} \mathrm{d}\hat{\omega} \\
&= \frac{1}{C} \sum_{\Omega_c \in 4\pi} \int_{\Omega_c} L_e(\vec{p}(\hat{\omega}), \hat{\omega}) \mathrm{d}\hat{\omega} \\
&= \frac{1}{C} \sum_{\Omega_c \in 4\pi} L_e(\vec{p}(\hat{\omega}_c), \hat{\omega}_c) \Omega_c \\
&= 1
\end{aligned} \tag{10.96}$$

where $\vec{p}(\hat{\omega})$ is the point of the sphere whose normal is collinear with $\hat{\omega}$, and $\hat{\omega}_c \in \Omega_c$, while the
normalization constant is defined as $C = \sum_{\Omega_c \in 4\pi} L_e(\vec{p}(\hat{\omega}_c), \hat{\omega}_c)$. It follows that *importance*
155 *sampling* of the illumination can be carried by first randomly selecting a cell from a PMF
244 with weights proportional to the product of the emitted radiance and *solid angle* of each cell,
and then uniformly drawing a sample direction within the spherical patch defined by the cell
131 with a constant *probability density* $1 \div \Omega_c$.

As an alternative, environmental illumination may be represented as a cube map composed of six rectilinear projections with a 90° *angle of view* each, such that the axis a and 673
normalized image-space coordinates s and t corresponding to a given direction $\hat{\omega}$ read

$$[a, s, t] = \begin{cases} \left[\operatorname{sgn}(\omega_x)1, \frac{\omega_y}{|\omega_x|}, \frac{\omega_z}{|\omega_x|}\right] & \text{if } |\omega_x| > |\omega_y| \wedge |\omega_x| > |\omega_z| \\ \left[\operatorname{sgn}(\omega_y)2, \frac{\omega_z}{|\omega_y|}, \frac{\omega_x}{|\omega_y|}\right] & \text{if } |\omega_y| > |\omega_z| \wedge |\omega_y| > |\omega_x| \\ \left[\operatorname{sgn}(\omega_z)3, \frac{\omega_x}{|\omega_z|}, \frac{\omega_y}{|\omega_z|}\right] & \text{if } |\omega_z| > |\omega_x| \wedge |\omega_z| > |\omega_y| \end{cases} \tag{10.97}$$

Assuming a piecewise-constant map representation divided into cells of *solid angle* Ω_c, nor- 244
malization of the associated *probability density* yields 131

$$\begin{aligned} \int_{4\pi} p(\hat{\omega})\mathrm{d}\hat{\omega} &= \sum_{\Omega_a \in 4\pi} \int_{\Omega_a} \frac{L_e(\vec{p}(\hat{\omega}), \hat{\omega})}{C} \mathrm{d}\hat{\omega} \\ &= \frac{1}{C} \sum_{\Omega_a \in 4\pi} \sum_{\Omega_c \in \Omega_a} \int_{\Omega_c} L_e(\vec{p}(\hat{\omega}), \hat{\omega}) \mathrm{d}\hat{\omega} \\ &= \frac{1}{C} \sum_{\Omega_a \in 4\pi} \sum_{\Omega_c \in \Omega_a} L_e(\vec{p}(\hat{\omega}_c), \hat{\omega}_c)\Omega_c \\ &= 1 \end{aligned} \tag{10.98}$$

where $\Omega_a = \frac{2}{3}\pi$ represents the *solid angle* of the 90° angles of view oriented along each of 244
the six major axes. It follows that *importance sampling* of the illumination can be similarly 155
carried by first randomly selecting a main axis Ω_a from a PMF with weights proportional
to the cumulated products of the emitted radiance and *solid angle* of the cells within each 244
cube face, and then stochastically choosing a cell Ω_c within that face. A sample direction
may finally be drawn within the cell by uniformly sampling either its surface area relative to
the virtual geometry of the face or its subtended *spherical rectangle*. 260

A sample position can then be uniformly sampled within the disk given by the projected disk of the bounding sphere along the sample direction $\hat{\omega}$.

10.2.6 Directional Light

Given an isotropic *point light* at position $\vec{p}$ whose radiant intensity is proportional to the 431
square of the distance to a scene centered around a point $\vec{c}$

$$I_e(\hat{\omega}) = M_e\|\vec{c} - \vec{p}\|^2 \tag{10.99}$$

the total emitted flux reads

426

$$\Phi_e \overset{(10.46)}{=} \int_{4\pi} M_e\|\vec{c} - \vec{p}\|^2 \mathrm{d}\hat{\omega} = M_e\|\vec{c} - \vec{p}\|^2 4\pi \tag{10.100}$$

In the limit of an infinitely distant scene $\|\vec{c}-\vec{p}\| \to \infty$, all light rays reaching it are parallel
and oriented along $\hat{\omega} = \frac{\vec{c}-\vec{p}}{\|\vec{c}-\vec{p}\|}$ as illustrated in *Figure 10.11* and *Figure 10.7* (similarly to the 436 431
light rays from the sun reaching the earth). While the total flux emitted by a *directional light*
is infinite, the total power received by the illuminated scene is finite and reads

426

$$\Phi_e \overset{(10.46)}{=} \int_{\Omega_S} M_e\|\vec{c} - \vec{p}\|^2 \mathrm{d}\hat{\omega} = M_e\|\vec{c} - \vec{p}\|^2 \Omega_S = M_e A_\perp(\hat{\omega}) \tag{10.101}$$

where $\Omega_S = \frac{A_\perp(\hat{\omega})}{\|\vec{c}-\vec{p}\|^2}$ is the *solid angle* subtended by the scene at $\vec{p}$, and $A_\perp(\hat{\omega})$ is its projected 244

area along $\hat{\omega}$. The latter may then be bounded by the projected area of the scene's *bounding*
357 *volume*. In the case of a bounding box, the projected area can itself be bounded by the area of the disk whose diameter is given by the maximal projected length of each of the four diagonal vectors of the box. A sample position may then be uniformly drawn within the projected disk, while a sample direction is readily given by the orientation of the light source $\hat{\omega}$.

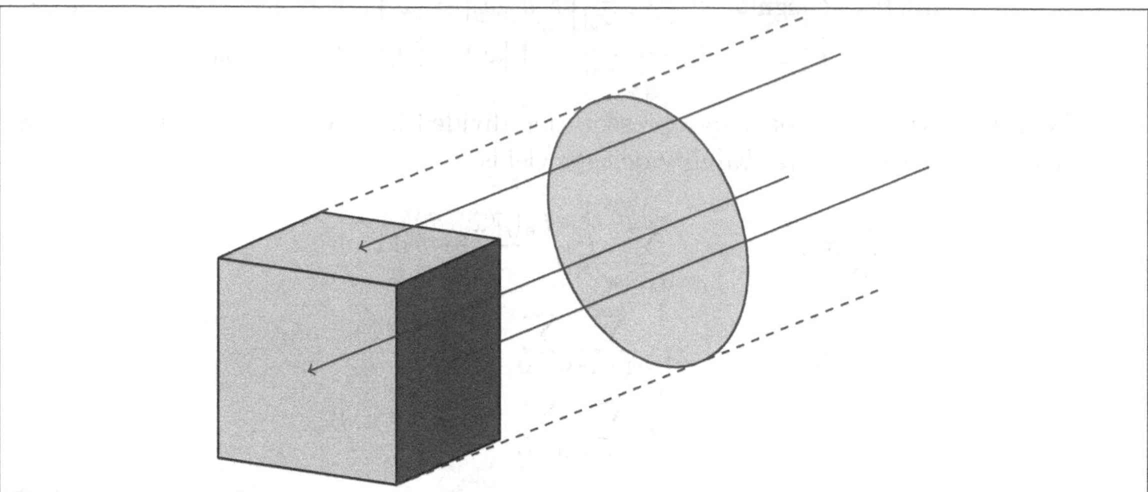

Figure 10.11: Directional Light: Illustration of a directional light source.

10.2.7 Collimated Beam Light

429 Given a planar *area light* whose emitted radiance is expressed in a separable form $L_e(\vec{p}, \hat{\omega}) =$ $M_e(\vec{p})f(\hat{\omega})$, where the directional distribution $f(\hat{\omega}) = \delta(\hat{\omega} - \hat{n})$ is described by a Dirac *delta*
44 *function*, the radiant emittance at a point $\vec{p}$ reads

426
45

$$M_e(\vec{p}) \overset{(10.50)}{=} \int_{2\pi^+} M_e(\vec{p})\delta(\hat{\omega} - \hat{n})\langle \hat{n}, \hat{\omega} \rangle \mathrm{d}\hat{\omega} \overset{(2.218)}{=} M_e(\vec{p})\langle \hat{n}, \hat{n} \rangle \tag{10.102}$$

An upper bound on the total power received by an illuminated scene is then readily
437 given by the total emitted flux of the *collimated beam light* source illustrated in *Figure 10.12*
431 (as obtained when placing a *point light* at the focus $(0, 1/4a)$ of a convex parabolic mirror $y = ax^2$). The surface of the latter may be sampled either uniformly, as in the case of *analytic*
236 *surfaces*, or according to the distribution of $M_e(\vec{p})$, as in the case of an orthographic video projector, while a sample direction is readily given by the orientation of the light source $\hat{n}$.

10.2.8 Ray Light

431 Given a *point light* source whose emitted radiant intensity is independent of direction within
244 a directional cone of *solid angle* Ω and inversely proportional to the latter

$$I_e(\hat{\omega}) = \frac{\Phi_e}{\Omega} \tag{10.103}$$

the total emitted flux reads

426

$$\Phi_e \overset{(10.46)}{=} \int_{\Omega} \frac{\Phi_e}{\Omega} \mathrm{d}\hat{\omega} = \frac{\Phi_e}{\Omega}\Omega \tag{10.104}$$

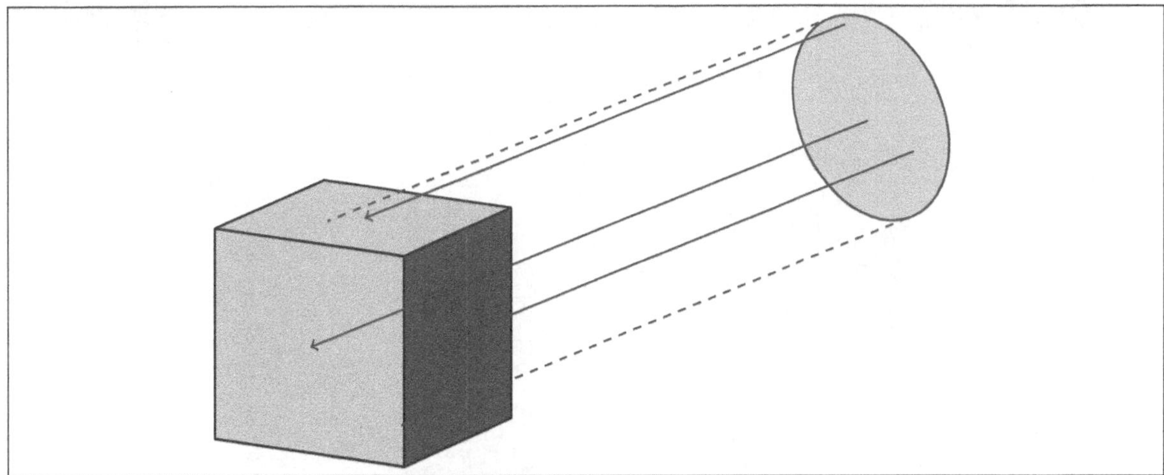

Figure 10.12: Collimated Beam Light: Illustration of a collimated beam light source.

Alternatively, given a *collimated beam light* source whose radiant emittance is indepen- 436
dent of position and inversely proportional to its area A

$$M_e(\vec{p}) = \frac{\Phi_e}{A} \tag{10.105}$$

the total emitted flux reads

426

$$\Phi_e \overset{(10.46)}{=} \int_A \frac{\Phi_e}{A} \mathrm{d}A(\vec{p}) = \frac{\Phi_e}{A} A \tag{10.106}$$

In the limit of an infinitely small *solid angle* $\Omega \to 0$ or infinitely small area $A \to 0$, the 244
emitted radiant intensity and radiant emittance are infinite, but the total emitted flux of the
ray light source (i.e., an ideal laser pointer) illustrated in *Figure 10.13* is finite, and gives an 437
upper bound on the total power received by an illuminated scene. A sample position is then
readily given by the position of the light source $\vec{p}$, while a sample direction is similarly given
by its orientation $\hat{\omega}$.

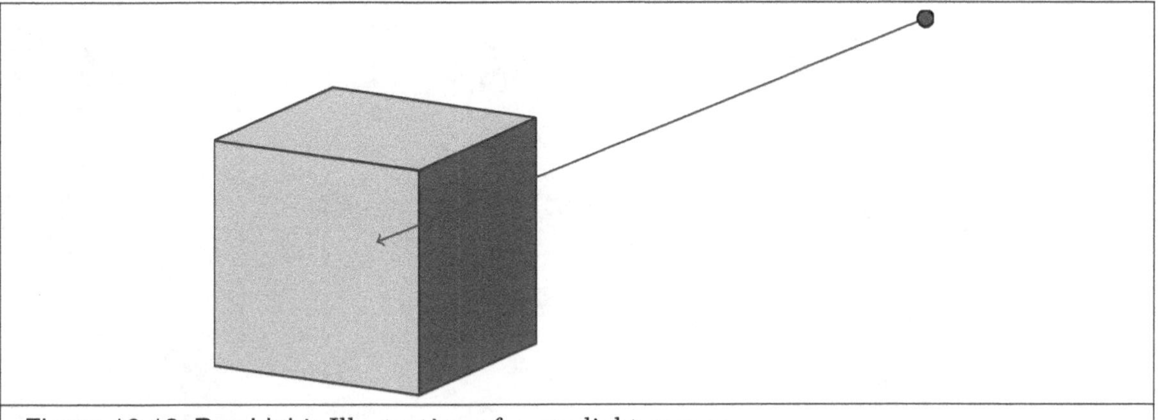

Figure 10.13: Ray Light: Illustration of a ray light source.

10.3 FURTHER READING

Additional material may be found in books dedicated to optics [Bass, 1995a, Bass, 1995b, Bass, 1995c, Bass, 1995d].

CHAPTER 11

Participating Media

TABLE OF CONTENTS

11.1 APPLICATIONS

Participating media model the interaction of light as photons penetrate through a given material, and are used to simulate a wide variety of elements in the natural world. Examples include many organic and inorganic translucent solids, whose visual appearance is mostly affected by subsurface scattering, such as marble, wax, leaves, fruits and skin. Similar phenomena are observed in various liquids, including milk and water in its various phases (e.g., flowing fluid as in oceans, ice crystals responsible for halos, snow flakes, droplets forming clouds and fog or producing rainbows), while the non-linear propagation of light through refractive media is responsible for mirages due to temperature gradients in air layers. Their scope also encompasses light absorption in fumes as well as scattering in many gases and aerosols, such as smoke, dust particles, haze and the earth's atmosphere causing the common variations in sky color and the blue coating of our planet when seen from space. Finally, participating media are used to model several emissive volumes, either due to thermal radiation or luminescence, including fire, fluorescent gases and plasmas such as lightning, auroras, stars and nebulae.

Within the realm of the entertainment industry, their applications encompass realistic visual effects [Wrenninge *et al.*, 2010, Wrenninge and Bin Zafar, 2011, Wrenninge *et al.*, 2011, Wrenninge, 2012] such as virtual characters, underwater scenes, explosions, god rays and other atmospheric phenomena. The trade-offs between visual accuracy and interactive feedback are typically of greater concern in flight simulators [Nielsen, 2003] and other training scenarios too dangerous or too costly to be deployed experimentally (such as virtual-environment firefighting), as well as in safety-oriented research where typical tasks entail predicting the visibility of traffic signs in foggy weather or emergency exit signs in a smoke-filled room. In addition, applications have also emerged in the study of cultural heritage [Sundstedt *et al.*, 2005, Gutierrez *et al.*, 2007, Gutierrez *et al.*, 2008b], in medicine [Sakas and Pommert, 1997, Sakas *et al.*, 2009] and, more broadly, among the scientific visualization community, where photo-realistic volume rendering techniques provide scientists with valuable insights facilitating the exploration and analysis of both simulated and acquired (e.g., CT or MRI) volumetric data sets [Kroes *et al.*, 2012].

11.2 OPTICAL PROPERTIES

11.2.1 Interaction Events

The optical properties of a medium at a given position in space and along a given direction depend on bulk material characteristics such as the temperature, density and spectral properties of the various chemical species. As illustrated in *Figure 11.1*, the mesoscopic in- 442
teractions that may occur between a photon traveling through a participating medium and the particles in suspension within it can be classified as follows:

- *absorption*: a photon traveling through the medium may be destroyed upon collision with a particle (as a net result of the effects of pure photo-absorption and stimulated emission) and its energy converted to some other form such as kinetic or thermal energy.
- *emission*: a new photon may be generated by the medium, for instance as a result of atomic or molecular collisions due to thermal agitation, extracting kinetic energy from the medium.
- *out-scattering*: a photon may change trajectory upon collision with a particle and be effectively removed from the flux in the considered direction of propagation.

- *in-scattering*: a photon may change trajectory upon collision with a particle and be effectively added to the flux in the considered direction of propagation.

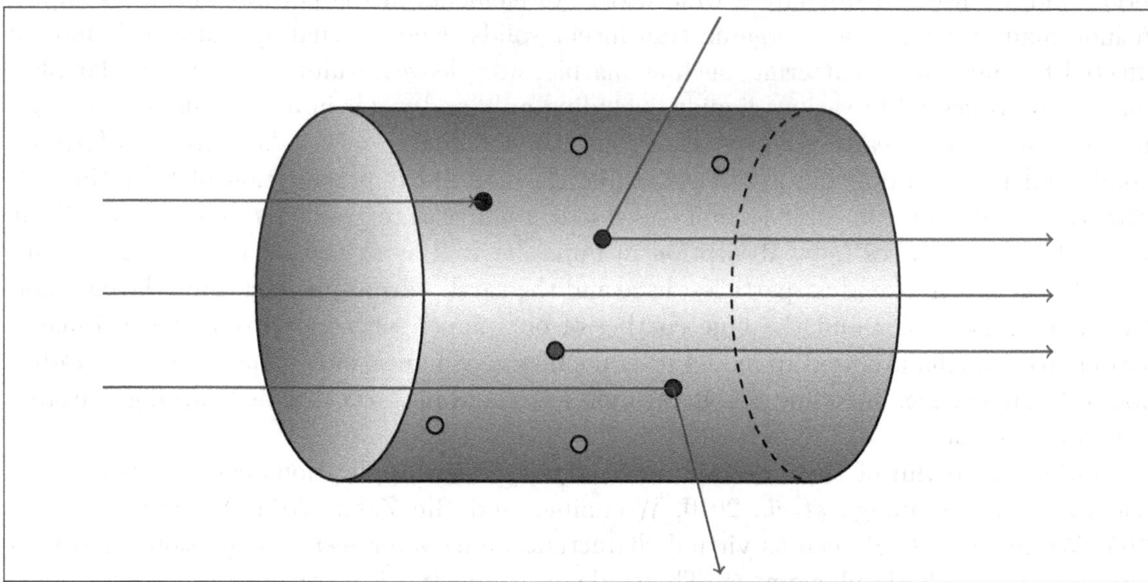

Figure 11.1: Photon–Particle Interactions: Illustration of the absorption, emission, out-scattering and in-scattering interactions that may occur between a photon and the particles in suspension within a participating medium.

11.2.2 Optical Coefficients

Under the assumption of a given type of idealized spherical particles of radius r, their *geo-*
443 *metric cross section* reads $\sigma \triangleq \pi r^2$. As illustrated in *Figure 11.2*, the latter may, however, be smaller or larger than the size of the *effective cross section* (in m^2) effectively altering any radiation incident upon the particles. The effective *absorption cross section* σ_a, *scattering cross section* σ_s and *attenuation cross section* $\sigma_t \triangleq \sigma_a + \sigma_s$, also called *extinction cross section*, are related to the geometric cross-section as follows

$$\sigma_{a|s|t} \triangleq Q_{a|s|t}\sigma \tag{11.1}$$

where the dimensionless constants of proportionality Q_a, Q_s and $Q_t \triangleq Q_a + Q_s$ are, respectively, called absorption, scattering and extinction *efficiency factors*.

Defining the *number density* $n(\vec{p}) \triangleq \frac{\mathrm{d}N}{\mathrm{d}V}$ (in m^{-3}) as the number N of particles per unit volume V, the optical properties of the medium may then be physically characterized by a set of three coefficients

$$\kappa_{a|s|t}(\vec{p}) \triangleq n(\vec{p})\sigma_{a|s|t} \tag{11.2}$$

The *absorption coefficient* κ_a describes the absorption properties of a medium at position $\vec{p}$, while the *scattering coefficient* κ_s similarly provides a quantitative measure of its local scattering properties (such as out-scattering). A cumulative measure of both properties is then given by the *attenuation coefficient*, also called *extinction coefficient*

$$\kappa_t \triangleq \kappa_a + \kappa_s \tag{11.3}$$

All three entities are measured in inverse units of length (in m^{-1}) and must obey $\kappa_{a|s|t} \geq 0$ to be physically valid. A medium in which all three coefficients are independent of position

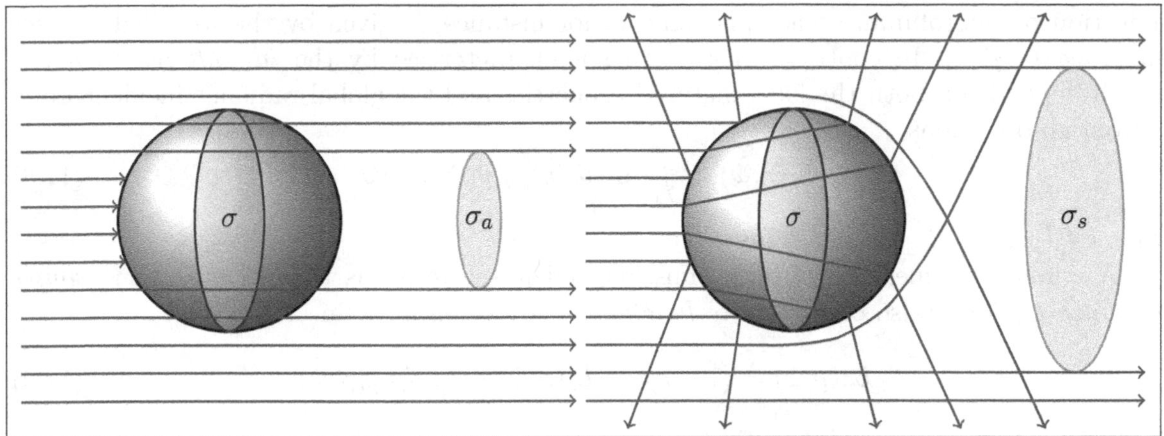

Figure 11.2: Effective Cross Sections: Illustration of the effective absorption and scattering cross sections (drawn after [Premože, 2003, Fig. 2.12]).

is then referred to as a *homogeneous medium*, and as a *heterogeneous medium* otherwise. Similarly, in the typical case of coefficients exhibiting no directional dependence, the latter are said to be isotropic, while those of non-spherically symmetric particles (e.g., ice crystals) are conversely said to be anisotropic.

In the more general case of a medium consisting of a discrete mixture of m different types of particles, the optical properties of the external mixture are given by the sums of the properties of each individual compound i

$$\kappa_{a|s|t}(\vec{p}) = \sum_{i=1}^{m} n_i(\vec{p})\sigma_{a|s|t}[i] \tag{11.4}$$

while in the case of a continuous mixture of particles with radius density distribution $N(\vec{p}, r)$ for radii r in the range $[r_{min}, r_{max}]$, the effective coefficients become

$$\kappa_{a|s|t}(\vec{p}) = \int_{r_{min}}^{r_{max}} N(\vec{p}, r)\sigma_{a|s|t}(r)\mathrm{d}r \tag{11.5}$$

11.2.3 Radiative Terms

Upon a single collision of a photon with a particle, the *probability* of the event being a 129
scattering event rather than an absorption event is given by the so-called single-scattering *albedo*, which is the dimensionless ratio of the likelihood of scattering to the sum of the likelihoods of both absorption and scattering

$$\rho_p(\vec{p}) \triangleq \frac{\kappa_s(\vec{p})}{\kappa_t(\vec{p})} \in [0, 1] \tag{11.6}$$

while the probability of the event being an absorption event is complementarily defined as

$$1 - \rho_p(\vec{p}) = \frac{\kappa_t(\vec{p})}{\kappa_t(\vec{p})} - \frac{\kappa_s(\vec{p})}{\kappa_t(\vec{p})} \overset{(11.3)}{=} \frac{\kappa_a(\vec{p})}{\kappa_t(\vec{p})} \in [0, 1] \tag{11.7}$$ 442

It follows that if $\rho_p = 1$, all collisions are scattering events and there is no absorption at position $\vec{p}$, whereas all collisions are absorption events and no scattering events occur if $\rho_p = 0$.

A quantitative measure of the local emission properties of the medium, due to thermal agitation or photoluminescence phenomena, for instance, is given by the so-called *emitted radiance* $L_e(\vec{p}, \hat{\omega})$. In contrast, in-scattering is characterized by the *in-scattered radiance*, which depends on both the local material properties and the global radiance incident upon $\vec{p}$ from all directions

$$L_p(\vec{p}, \hat{\omega}) \triangleq \int_{4\pi} L_i(\vec{p}, \hat{\omega}_i) f_p(\vec{p}, \hat{\omega}, \hat{\omega}_i) \mathrm{d}\hat{\omega}_i \tag{11.8}$$

444 where $f_p(\vec{p}, \hat{\omega}, \hat{\omega}_i)$ is the *phase function*.

A cumulative measure of both emission and in-scattering is then given by the *source radiance* $L_u(\vec{p}, \hat{\omega})$ (also called *source function* or *source term*) defined as

$$L_u(\vec{p}, \hat{\omega}) \triangleq (1 - \rho_p(\vec{p})) L_e(\vec{p}, \hat{\omega}) + \rho_p(\vec{p}) L_p(\vec{p}, \hat{\omega}) \tag{11.9}$$

such that

443 $$\kappa_t(\vec{p}) L_u(\vec{p}, \hat{\omega}) \overset{(11.6)}{=} \kappa_a(\vec{p}) L_e(\vec{p}, \hat{\omega}) + \kappa_s(\vec{p}) L_p(\vec{p}, \hat{\omega}) \tag{11.10}$$

11.3 PHASE FUNCTION

11.3.1 Definition

At a microscopic level, scattering events may be caused by the reflection of the *electromag-*
420 *netic waves* off the surface of the particle, their refraction through the particle, their diffraction when passing nearby the particle even though they are not in direct contact with it, as well as their temporary absorption immediately followed by their re-emission in a different direction of propagation but without change in the energy of the radiation. At a mesoscopic level, the spherical density distribution of scattered radiance upon a single scattering event at point $\vec{p}$ is described by the so-called (single-scattering) *phase function*, which is expressed
244 in inverse units of *solid angle* (sr^{-1}), and which will thereafter be referred to as *bidirectional phase distribution function* (*BPDF*) for the sake of brevity.

In order to be physically valid, a phase function must be non-negative (such that the medium doesn't scatter negative radiation)

$$f_p(\vec{p}, \hat{\omega}_o, \hat{\omega}_i) \geq 0, \quad \forall \hat{\omega}_o, \hat{\omega}_i \in 4\pi \tag{11.11}$$

fulfill the *Helmholtz reciprocity rule* [von Helmholtz, 1867] (such that reverting the direction of propagation by exchanging the locations of a source and a sensor leaves the ratio of scattered radiation unaffected)

$$f_p(\vec{p}, \hat{\omega}_o, \hat{\omega}_i) = f_p(\vec{p}, \hat{\omega}_i, \hat{\omega}_o), \quad \forall \hat{\omega}_o, \hat{\omega}_i \in 4\pi \tag{11.12}$$

and obey *energy conservation* (such that the radiant flux scattered by the medium equals that incident upon it, therefore ensuring that no energy is gained or lost upon scattering)

$$1 = \int_{4\pi} f_p(\vec{p}, \hat{\omega}_o, \hat{\omega}_i) \mathrm{d}\hat{\omega}_i \tag{11.13}$$

244 $$\overset{(6.63)}{=} \int_0^{2\pi} \int_0^{\pi} f_p(\vec{p}, \hat{\omega}_o, \theta, \phi) \sin(\theta) \mathrm{d}\theta \mathrm{d}\phi$$

244 $$\overset{(6.64)}{=} \int_0^{2\pi} \int_{-1}^{+1} f_p(\vec{p}, \hat{\omega}_o, \arccos(\mu), \phi) \mathrm{d}\mu \mathrm{d}\phi, \quad \forall \hat{\omega}_o \in 4\pi \tag{11.14}$$

where $\mu \triangleq \cos(\theta) = \langle \hat{\omega}_o, \hat{\omega}_i \rangle$. Without any a priori knowledge about the distribution of the incident radiation, importance sampling of the in-scattered radiance integrand over the spherical domain may therefore be optimally carried using the phase function as a normalized *probability density* 131

$$p(\vec{p}, \hat{\omega}_o, \hat{\omega}_i) \triangleq f_p(\vec{p}, \hat{\omega}_o, \hat{\omega}_i) \tag{11.15}$$

The extent of asymmetry of a phase function is characterized by its *asymmetry coefficient* g, also called *average cosine* or *mean cosine* of the scattering angle, defined as

$$g \triangleq \int_{4\pi} f_p(\vec{p}, \hat{\omega}_o, \hat{\omega}_i)\langle\hat{\omega}_o, \hat{\omega}_i\rangle \mathrm{d}\hat{\omega}_i \tag{11.16}$$

$$\overset{(6.63)}{=} \int_0^{2\pi}\int_0^{\pi} f_p(\vec{p}, \hat{\omega}_o, \theta, \phi)\cos(\theta)\sin(\theta)\mathrm{d}\theta\mathrm{d}\phi$$ 244

$$\overset{(6.64)}{=} \int_0^{2\pi}\int_{-1}^{+1} f_p(\vec{p}, \hat{\omega}_o, \arccos(\mu), \phi)\mu\mathrm{d}\mu\mathrm{d}\phi, \quad \forall\hat{\omega}_o \in 4\pi \tag{11.17}$$ 244

such that

$$-1 \overset{(11.13)}{=} \int_{4\pi} f_p(\vec{p}, \hat{\omega}_o, \hat{\omega}_i)(-1)\mathrm{d}\hat{\omega}_i \leq g \leq \int_{4\pi} f_p(\vec{p}, \hat{\omega}_o, \hat{\omega}_i)(+1)\mathrm{d}\hat{\omega}_i \overset{(11.13)}{=} +1 \tag{11.18}$$ 444 444

and which is positive (respectively negative) if the phase function predominantly scatters light forward (respectively backward), while energy is equally distributed forward and backward if the asymmetry coefficient equals zero.

In practice, most phase functions are actually symmetrical around $\hat{\omega}_o$ and therefore only depend on the *phase angle* θ, also called *scattering angle*, or its cosine $\mu = \cos(\theta) = \langle\hat{\omega}_o, \hat{\omega}_i\rangle$. It follows that the 2-D *probability density* is separable and can be expressed as the product 131
of two 1-D PDFs to independently importance sample the polar coordinate $\theta \in [0, \pi]$ and azimuthal coordinate $\phi \in [0, 2\pi)$. The integral of the phase function over a spherical domain Ω_i then reads

$$\int_{\Omega_i} f_p(\vec{p}, \langle\hat{\omega}_o, \hat{\omega}_i\rangle)\mathrm{d}\hat{\omega}_i \overset{(6.63)}{=} \int_0^{\phi_i}\int_0^{\theta_i} f_p(\vec{p}, \cos(\theta))\sin(\theta)\mathrm{d}\theta\mathrm{d}\phi$$ 244

$$= \int_0^{\phi_i}\frac{1}{2\pi}\mathrm{d}\phi\int_0^{\theta_i} 2\pi f_p(\vec{p}, \cos(\theta))\sin(\theta)\mathrm{d}\theta$$

$$\overset{(6.64)}{=} \int_0^{\phi_i}\frac{1}{2\pi}\mathrm{d}\phi\int_{\cos(\theta_i)}^{1} 2\pi f_p(\vec{p}, \mu)\mathrm{d}\mu \tag{11.19}$$ 244

such that the normalization condition reduces to

$$1 \overset{(11.13)}{=} \int_{4\pi} f_p(\vec{p}, \langle\hat{\omega}_o, \hat{\omega}_i\rangle)\mathrm{d}\hat{\omega}_i \tag{11.20}$$ 444

$$\overset{(6.63)}{=} \int_0^{2\pi}\int_0^{\pi} f_p(\vec{p}, \cos(\theta))\sin(\theta)\mathrm{d}\theta\mathrm{d}\phi$$ 244

$$= 2\pi\int_0^{\pi} f_p(\vec{p}, \cos(\theta))\sin(\theta)\mathrm{d}\theta$$

$$\overset{(6.64)}{=} 2\pi\int_{-1}^{+1} f_p(\vec{p}, \mu)\mathrm{d}\mu \tag{11.21}$$ 244

and the expression of the asymmetry coefficient becomes

445 $$g \overset{(11.16)}{=} \int_{4\pi} f_p(\vec{p}, \langle \hat{\omega}_o, \hat{\omega}_i \rangle) \langle \hat{\omega}_o, \hat{\omega}_i \rangle \mathrm{d}\hat{\omega}_i \tag{11.22}$$

244 $$\overset{(6.63)}{=} \int_0^{2\pi} \int_0^{\pi} f_p(\vec{p}, \cos(\theta)) \cos(\theta) \sin(\theta) \mathrm{d}\theta \mathrm{d}\phi$$

$$= 2\pi \int_0^{\pi} f_p(\vec{p}, \cos(\theta)) \cos(\theta) \sin(\theta) \mathrm{d}\theta$$

244 $$\overset{(6.64)}{=} 2\pi \int_{-1}^{+1} f_p(\vec{p}, \mu) \mu \mathrm{d}\mu \tag{11.23}$$

Several regimes exist in order to model light scattering by different types of particles. While *geometric optics* describe interactions with scatterers much bigger than the wavelength of the incident radiation, for which $2\pi r \gg \lambda$, *Mie theory* models scattering by spherical particles of roughly the same size as the wavelength. These include liquid water droplets in clouds, fog and vapor, whereas solid particles such as complex ice crystals have various irregular and non-spherical shapes. Scattering by particles of this size is rather non-selective as visible wavelengths are mostly scattered uniformly, hence the white appearance of the medium. In contrast, *Rayleigh theory* describes scattering by spherical particles much smaller in size than the wavelength of the incident light, for which $2\pi r \ll \lambda$, such as air molecules in the Earth's atmosphere with diameters less than 10% of the wavelength. The small size of the gas particles also induces the occurrence of *selective scattering* due to the strong wavelength dependence of the scattering coefficient. The latter is roughly proportional to λ^{-4}, causing shorter wavelengths of the visible sunlight to be scattered about 10 times more than longer wavelength. Due to the dual source-extinction nature of scattering, this induces both the blue appearance of the sky dome during daytime when in-scattering prevails and the red sunsets caused by predominant out-scattering phenomena.

11.3.2 Isotropic

11.3.2.1 Formulation

The phase function of a particle that scatters light equally in all directions is characterized by the *isotropic phase function*

$$f_p(\vec{p}, \hat{\omega}_o, \hat{\omega}_i) \triangleq \frac{1}{4\pi} \tag{11.24}$$

which is a constant independent of the incident and exitant directions, as illustrated in
447 *Figure 11.3*.

11.3.2.2 Normalization and Sampling

132 Its *cumulative distribution* over the domain Ω_i may be expressed in a separable form as

445 $$\int_{\Omega_i} f_p(\vec{p}, \hat{\omega}_o, \hat{\omega}_i) \mathrm{d}\hat{\omega}_i \overset{(11.19)}{=} \int_0^{\phi_i} \frac{1}{2\pi} \mathrm{d}\phi \int_{\cos(\theta_i)}^{1} \frac{1}{2} \mathrm{d}\mu = \left[\frac{\phi}{2\pi}\right]_0^{\phi_i} \left[\frac{\mu}{2}\right]_{\cos(\theta_i)}^{1} = \frac{\phi_i}{2\pi} \frac{1 - \cos(\theta_i)}{2} \tag{11.25}$$

Integrating over the whole spherical domain by substituting $\phi_i = 2\pi$ and $\theta_i = \pi$ then en-
134 sures normalization, while applying *inverse-transform sampling* allows *importance sampling*
155

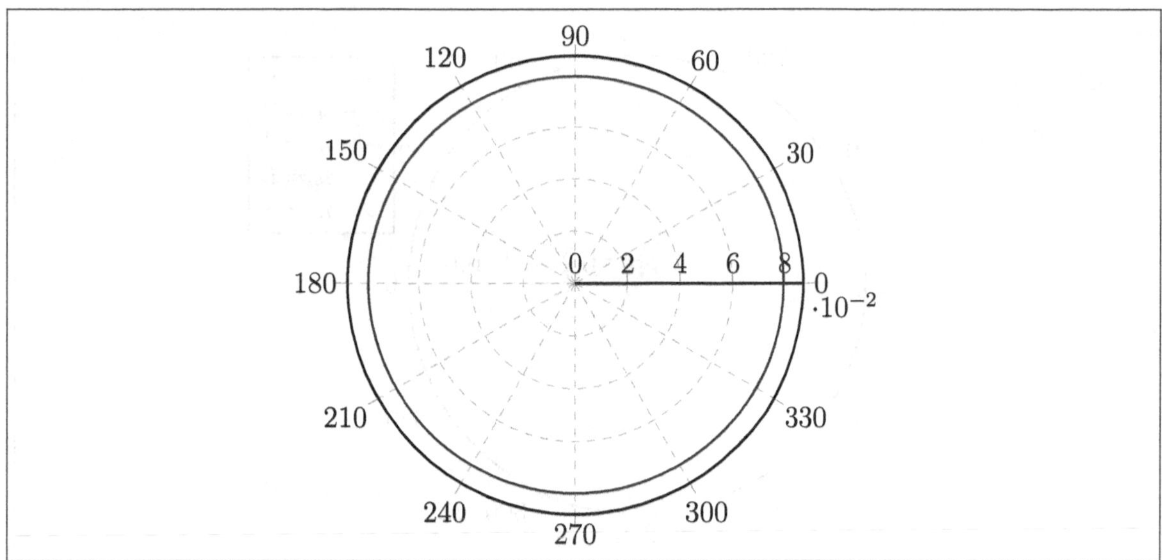

Figure 11.3: Isotropic BPDF: Illustration of the angular distribution of the isotropic phase function.

to be readily carried as

$$\xi_\phi = \frac{\phi_i}{2\pi} \quad \Longrightarrow \quad \phi_i = 2\pi\xi_\phi \tag{11.26}$$

$$\xi_\theta = \frac{1-\cos(\theta_i)}{2} \quad \Longrightarrow \quad \theta_i = \arccos(1-2\xi_\theta) \tag{11.27}$$

11.3.3 Warn

11.3.3.1 Formulation

Inspired by the cosine-lobe formulation for spot-like *point light* sources, the *Warn phase* 431
function is here defined as a simple anisotropic phase function with symmetric forward and backward scattering distributions of the form

$$f_p(\vec{p}, \hat{\omega}_o, \hat{\omega}_i) \triangleq \frac{n+1}{4\pi} \langle \hat{\omega}_o, \hat{\omega}_i \rangle^n \tag{11.28}$$

where the exponent n determines the sharpness of the lobes, such that $n = 0$ yields an *isotropic* distribution, as illustrated in *Figure 11.4*. It is also worth noting that, as written 446 448
above, this formulation requires n to be even in order to guarantee positivity. Otherwise, the formulation should either be adjusted so as to replace the cosine term with its absolute value, or the backward lobe should be clamped to zero and the magnitude of the forward lobe doubled in order to maintain energy conservation.

11.3.3.2 Normalization and Sampling

Its *cumulative distribution* over the domain Ω_i may be expressed in a separable form as 132

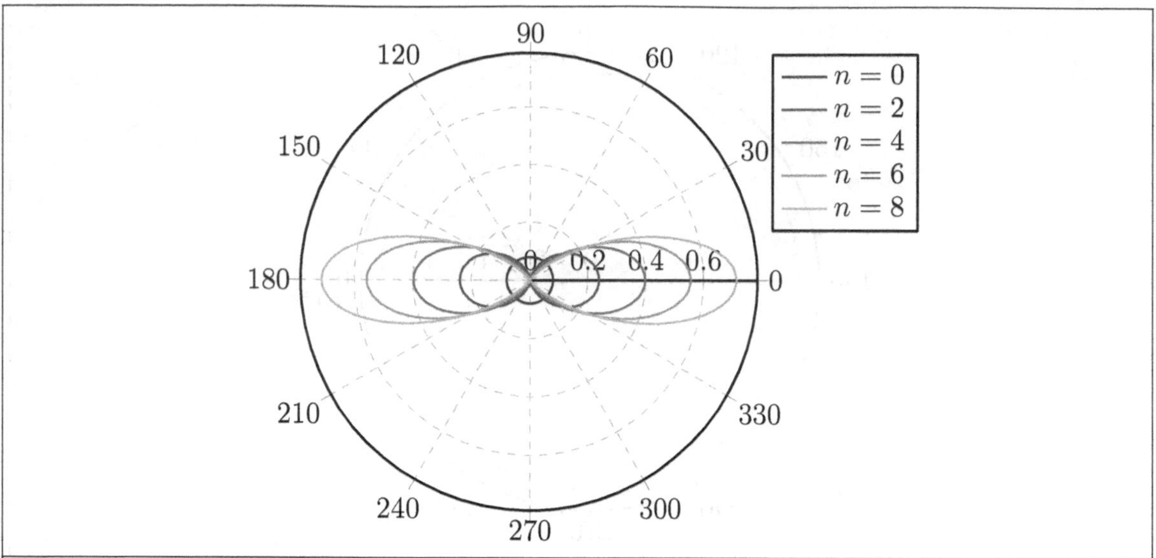

Figure 11.4: Warn BPDF: Illustration of the angular distribution of the Warn phase function.

445

$$\begin{aligned}\int_{\Omega_i} f_p(\vec{p}, \hat{\omega}_o, \hat{\omega}_i)\mathrm{d}\hat{\omega}_i &\overset{(11.19)}{=} \int_0^{\phi_i} \frac{1}{2\pi}\mathrm{d}\phi \int_{\cos(\theta_i)}^{1} \frac{n+1}{2}\mu^n \mathrm{d}\mu \\ &= \left[\frac{\phi}{2\pi}\right]_0^{\phi_i} \frac{n+1}{2}\left[\frac{\mu^{n+1}}{n+1}\right]_{\cos(\theta_i)}^{1} \\ &= \frac{\phi_i}{2\pi}\frac{1-\cos(\theta_i)^{n+1}}{2}\end{aligned} \quad (11.29)$$

Integrating over the whole spherical domain by substituting $\phi_i = 2\pi$ and $\theta_i = \pi$ then en-
134 sures normalization, while applying *inverse-transform sampling* allows *importance sampling*
155 to be readily carried as

$$\xi_\phi = \frac{\phi_i}{2\pi} \implies \phi_i = 2\pi\xi_\phi \quad (11.30)$$

$$\xi_\theta = \frac{1-\cos(\theta_i)^{n+1}}{2} \implies \theta_i = \arccos\left(\sqrt[n+1]{1-2\xi_\theta}\right) \quad (11.31)$$

11.3.4 Rayleigh

11.3.4.1 Formulation

The distribution of scattering events occurring in the Earth's atmosphere may be modeled
446 as a convex combination of the *isotropic* BPDF and the *Warn* BPDF with a fixed exponent
447 $n = 2$ [Sloup, 2002]

$$f_p(\vec{p}, \hat{\omega}_o, \hat{\omega}_i) \triangleq \alpha\frac{1}{4\pi} + (1-\alpha)\frac{3\langle\hat{\omega}_o, \hat{\omega}_i\rangle^2}{4\pi} = \frac{1}{4\pi}\frac{3}{2}\frac{1+k+(1-k)\langle\hat{\omega}_o, \hat{\omega}_i\rangle^2}{2+k} \quad (11.32)$$

where the parameters $\alpha \triangleq \frac{3+3k}{4+2k} \in [0,1]$ and $k = -\frac{4\alpha-3}{2\alpha-3} \in [-1,+1]$ control the distribution
446 of the scattered light, such that setting $\alpha = 1$ or $k = +1$ yields the *isotropic* BPDF, while
447 setting $\alpha = 0$ or $k = -1$ yields the *Warn* BPDF.

In the special case where $\alpha = 3/4$ or $k = 0$, the formulation yields the *Rayleigh phase function* [Strutt, 1871a, Strutt, 1871b]

$$f_p(\vec{p}, \hat{\omega}_o, \hat{\omega}_i) = \frac{3}{4}\frac{1}{4\pi} + \frac{1}{4}\frac{3\langle\hat{\omega}_o, \hat{\omega}_i\rangle^2}{4\pi} = \frac{3}{4}\frac{1 + \langle\hat{\omega}_o, \hat{\omega}_i\rangle^2}{4\pi} \tag{11.33}$$

which exhibits symmetric forward and backward scattering lobes, as illustrated in *Figure 11.5*. 449

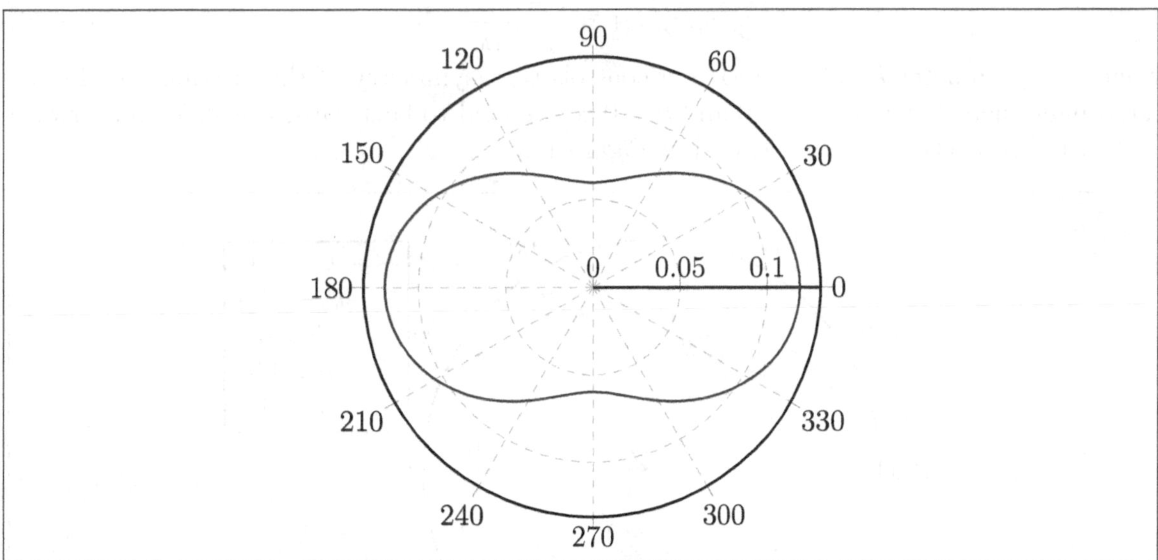

Figure 11.5: Rayleigh BPDF: Illustration of the angular distribution of the Rayleigh phase function.

11.3.4.2 Normalization and Sampling

Its *cumulative distribution* over the domain Ω_i may be expressed in a separable form as 132

445

$$\begin{aligned}\int_{\Omega_i} f_p(\vec{p}, \hat{\omega}_o, \hat{\omega}_i)\mathrm{d}\hat{\omega}_i &\overset{(11.19)}{=} \int_0^{\phi_i} \frac{1}{2\pi}\mathrm{d}\phi \int_{\cos(\theta_i)}^{1} \frac{3}{4}\frac{1 + k + (1-k)\mu^2}{2+k}\mathrm{d}\mu \\ &= \left[\frac{\phi}{2\pi}\right]_0^{\phi_i} \left[\frac{3(1+k)\mu + (1-k)\mu^3}{4(2+k)}\right]_{\cos(\theta_i)}^{1} \\ &= \frac{\phi_i}{2\pi}\frac{2(2+k) - 3(1+k)\cos(\theta_i) - (1-k)\cos(\theta_i)^3}{4(2+k)}\end{aligned} \tag{11.34}$$

Integrating over the whole spherical domain by substituting $\phi_i = 2\pi$ and $\theta_i = \pi$ then ensures normalization, while applying *inverse-transform sampling* allows *importance sampling* to be readily carried as 134 155

$$\xi_\phi = \frac{\phi_i}{2\pi} \implies \phi_i = 2\pi\xi_\phi \tag{11.35}$$

$$\begin{aligned}\xi_\theta = \frac{2(2+k) - 3(1+k)\cos(\theta_i) - (1-k)\cos(\theta_i)^3}{4(2+k)} &\implies \\ (1-k)\cos(\theta_i)^3 + 3(1+k)\cos(\theta_i) &= 2(2+k)(1-2\xi_\theta)\end{aligned} \tag{11.36}$$

where the cosine angle is the first solution of the depressed *cubic equation* with discriminant 29

31

$$\Delta \overset{(2.119)}{=} 4\left((2+k)^2(1-2\xi_\theta)^2 + \frac{(1+k)^3}{1-k}\right) \geq 0, \quad \forall \xi_\theta \in [0,1] \tag{11.37}$$

11.3.5 Eddington

11.3.5.1 Formulation

The simplest phase function that allows for some degree of asymmetry is known as the *Eddington phase function*, also referred to as the *linear anisotropic phase function*, which reads

$$f_p(\vec{p}, \hat{\omega}_o, \hat{\omega}_i) \triangleq \frac{1 + k\langle \hat{\omega}_o, \hat{\omega}_i \rangle}{4\pi} \tag{11.38}$$

where the parameter $k = 3g \in [-1, +1]$ controls the asymmetry of the distribution of scat-
446 tered light such that $k < 0$, $k = 0$ and $k > 0$ correspond to backward, *isotropic* and forward
450 scattering, respectively, as illustrated in *Figure 11.6*.

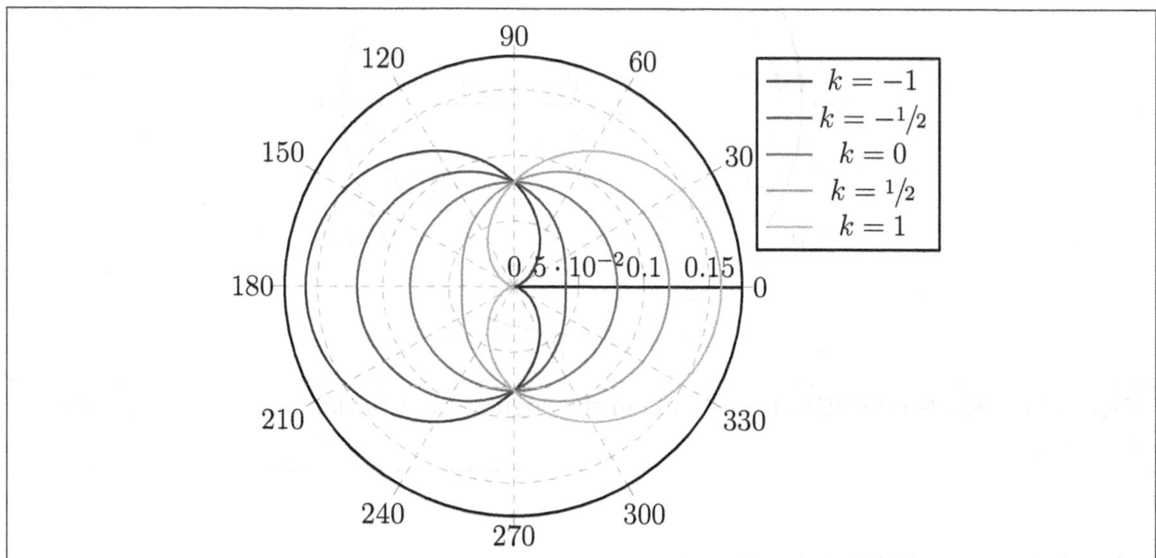

Figure 11.6: Eddington BPDF: Illustration of the angular distribution of the Eddington phase function.

11.3.5.2 Normalization and Sampling

132 Its *cumulative distribution* over the domain Ω_i may be expressed in a separable form as

445

$$\begin{aligned}\int_{\Omega_i} f_p(\vec{p}, \hat{\omega}_o, \hat{\omega}_i)\mathrm{d}\hat{\omega}_i &\overset{(11.19)}{=} \int_0^{\phi_i} \frac{1}{2\pi}\mathrm{d}\phi \int_{\cos(\theta_i)}^1 \frac{1 + k\mu}{2}\mathrm{d}\mu \\ &= \left[\frac{\phi}{2\pi}\right]_0^{\phi_i} \frac{1}{2}\left[\mu + k\frac{\mu^2}{2}\right]_{\cos(\theta_i)}^1 \\ &= \frac{\phi_i}{2\pi} \frac{1 + \frac{k}{2} - \cos(\theta_i) - \frac{k}{2}\cos(\theta_i)^2}{2}\end{aligned} \tag{11.39}$$

Integrating over the whole spherical domain by substituting $\phi_i = 2\pi$ and $\theta_i = \pi$ then en-
134 sures normalization, while applying *inverse-transform sampling* allows *importance sampling*
155 to be readily carried as

$$\xi_\phi = \frac{\phi_i}{2\pi} \implies \phi_i = 2\pi\xi_\phi \tag{11.40}$$

$$\xi_\theta = \frac{1 + \frac{k}{2} - \cos(\theta_i) - \frac{k}{2}\cos(\theta_i)^2}{2} \implies \theta_i = \arccos\left(\frac{\sqrt{1 + 2k(1 - 2\xi_\theta) + k^2} - 1}{k}\right) \tag{11.41}$$

whenever $k \neq 0$ while resorting to isotropic sampling otherwise.

11.3.6 Liu

11.3.6.1 Formulation

Generalizing the *Eddington* BPDF by exponentiation yields the *Liu phase function* [Liu, 450
1994]

$$f_p(\vec{p}, \hat{\omega}_o, \hat{\omega}_i) \triangleq \frac{1}{4\pi} \frac{2k(n+1)}{(1+k)^{n+1} - (1-k)^{n+1}} (1 + k\langle\hat{\omega}_o, \hat{\omega}_i\rangle)^n \tag{11.42}$$

where the parameter $k \in [-1, +1]$ controls the asymmetry of the distribution of scattered
light such that $k < 0$ and $k > 0$ correspond to backward and forward scattering, respectively.
The parameter must also satisfy $k \neq 0$ to avoid a singularity of the normalization factor
in the phase function, which tends towards the *isotropic* BPDF as $k \to 0$, and which may 446
consequently be replaced by it whenever $k = 0$. On the other hand, the exponent n determines
the sharpness of the lobes, such that $n = 0$ yields an *isotropic* distribution, as illustrated in 446
Figure 11.7. 451

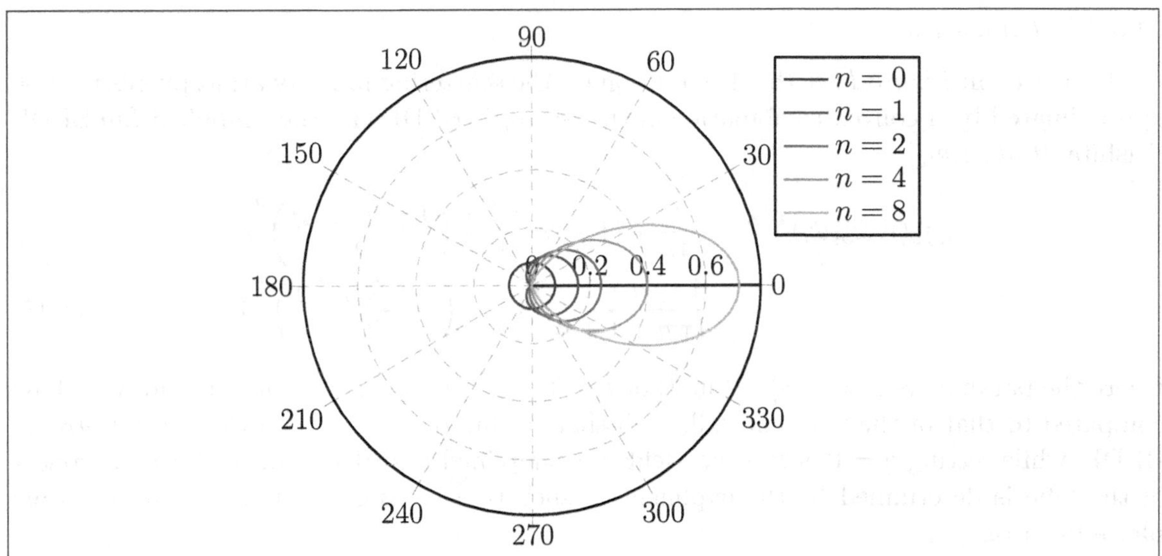

Figure 11.7: Liu BPDF: Illustration of the angular distribution of the simplified Liu phase function.

In the special case where $k = 1$, the formulation simplifies into

$$f_p(\vec{p}, \hat{\omega}_o, \hat{\omega}_i) = \frac{n+1}{4\pi} \left(\frac{1 + \langle\hat{\omega}_o, \hat{\omega}_i\rangle}{2} \right)^n \tag{11.43}$$

11.3.6.2 Normalization and Sampling

Its *cumulative distribution* over the domain Ω_i may be expressed in a separable form as 132

445

$$\begin{aligned}
\int_{\Omega_i} f_p(\vec{p}, \hat{\omega}_o, \hat{\omega}_i) \mathrm{d}\hat{\omega}_i &\overset{(11.19)}{=} \int_0^{\phi_i} \frac{1}{2\pi} \mathrm{d}\phi \int_{\cos(\theta_i)}^1 \frac{k(n+1)}{(1+k)^{n+1} - (1-k)^{n+1}} (1 + k\mu)^n \mathrm{d}\mu \\
&= \left[\frac{\phi}{2\pi} \right]_0^{\phi_i} \frac{k(n+1)}{(1+k)^{n+1} - (1-k)^{n+1}} \left[\frac{(1 + k\mu)^{n+1}}{k(n+1)} \right]_{\cos(\theta_i)}^1 \\
&= \frac{\phi_i}{2\pi} \frac{(1+k)^{n+1} - (1 + k\cos(\theta_i))^{n+1}}{(1+k)^{n+1} - (1-k)^{n+1}} \qquad (11.44)
\end{aligned}$$

Integrating over the whole spherical domain by substituting $\phi_i = 2\pi$ and $\theta_i = \pi$ then en-
134 sures normalization, while applying *inverse-transform sampling* allows *importance sampling*
155 to be readily carried as

$$\xi_\phi = \frac{\phi_i}{2\pi} \implies \phi_i = 2\pi\xi_\phi \tag{11.45}$$

$$\begin{aligned} \xi_\theta &= \frac{(1+k)^{n+1} - (1+k\cos(\theta_i))^{n+1}}{(1+k)^{n+1} - (1-k)^{n+1}} \\ \implies \theta_i &= \arccos\left(\frac{\sqrt[n+1]{(1+k)^{n+1} - ((1+k)^{n+1} - (1-k)^{n+1})\xi_\theta} - 1}{k}\right) \end{aligned} \tag{11.46}$$

whenever $k \neq 0$ while resorting to isotropic sampling otherwise.

11.3.7 Hazy–Murky

11.3.7.1 Formulation

452 As illustrated in *Figure 11.8*, the distribution of *Mie* scattering in foggy atmospheres may be
457
446 approximated by a convex combination of the *isotropic* BPDF and the simplified *Liu* BPDF
451 [Nishita *et al.*, 1987]

$$\begin{aligned} f_p(\vec{p}, \hat{\omega}_o, \hat{\omega}_i) &\triangleq \alpha\frac{1}{4\pi} + (1-\alpha)\frac{n+1}{4\pi}\left(\frac{1+\langle\hat{\omega}_o,\hat{\omega}_i\rangle}{2}\right)^n \\ &= \frac{1}{4\pi}\frac{n+1}{n+1+k}\left(1+k\left(\frac{1+\langle\hat{\omega}_o,\hat{\omega}_i\rangle}{2}\right)^n\right) \end{aligned} \tag{11.47}$$

where the parameters $\alpha \triangleq \frac{n+1}{n+1+k} \in [0,1]$ or $k \in [0,\infty)$ control the weight of the forward lobe
446 compared to that of the isotropic tail, such that setting $\alpha = 1$ or $k = 0$ yields the *isotropic*
451 BPDF, while setting $\alpha = 0$ or $k \to \infty$ yields the simplified *Liu* BPDF. Instead, the sharpness
446 of the lobe is determined by the exponent n, such that setting $n = 0$ yields the *isotropic*
phase function.

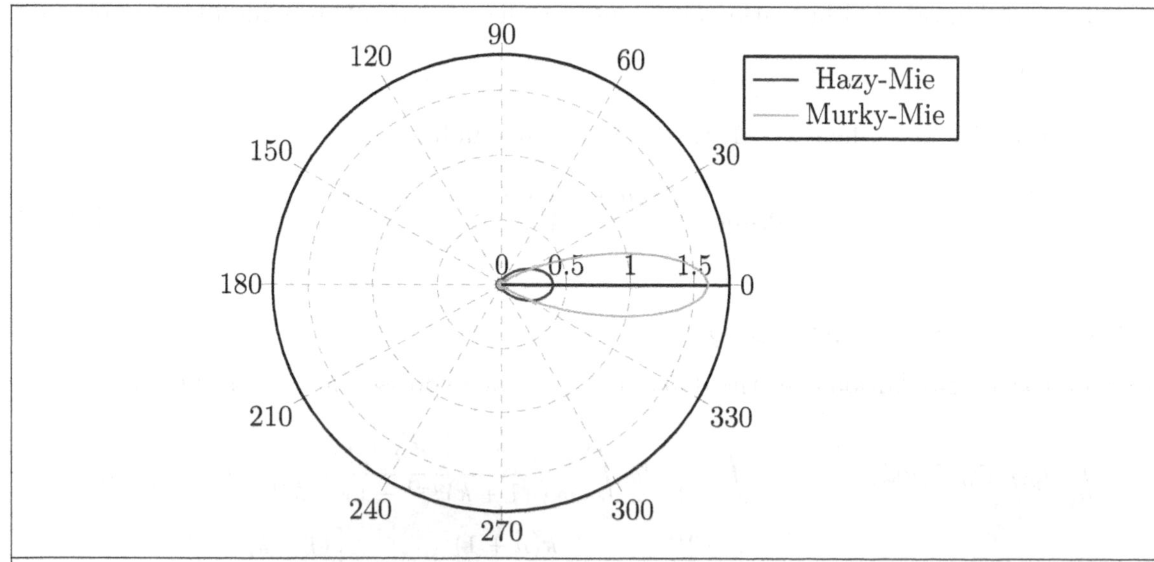

Figure 11.8: **Hazy–Murky BPDF:** Illustration of the angular distribution of the hazy–murky phase function.

457 *Mie* scattering in low-density atmospheres may then be approximated by the set of pa-

rameters $k = 9$ and $n = 8$, coined as the *hazy–Mie phase function*

$$f_p(\vec{p}, \hat{\omega}_o, \hat{\omega}_i) = \frac{1}{4\pi}\frac{1}{2}\left(1 + 9\left(\frac{1 + \langle\hat{\omega}_o, \hat{\omega}_i\rangle}{2}\right)^8\right) = \frac{1}{4\pi}\frac{1}{2}\left(1 + 9\cos\left(\frac{\theta}{2}\right)^{16}\right) \tag{11.48}$$

while *Mie* scattering in high-density atmospheres may instead be approximated by the set 457
of parameters $k = 50$ and $n = 32$, coined as the *murky–Mie phase function*

$$f_p(\vec{p}, \hat{\omega}_o, \hat{\omega}_i) = \frac{1}{4\pi}\frac{33}{83}\left(1 + 50\left(\frac{1 + \langle\hat{\omega}_o, \hat{\omega}_i\rangle}{2}\right)^{32}\right) = \frac{1}{4\pi}\frac{33}{83}\left(1 + 50\cos\left(\frac{\theta}{2}\right)^{64}\right) \tag{11.49}$$

11.3.7.2 Normalization and Sampling

Its *cumulative distribution* over the domain Ω_i may be expressed in a separable form as 132

445

$$\begin{aligned}
&\int_{\Omega_i} f_p(\vec{p}, \hat{\omega}_o, \hat{\omega}_i)\mathrm{d}\hat{\omega}_i \\
\overset{(11.19)}{=}\ & \int_0^{\phi_i} \frac{1}{2\pi}\mathrm{d}\phi \int_{\cos(\theta_i)}^{1} \frac{1}{2}\frac{n+1}{n+1+k}\left(1 + k\left(\frac{1+\mu}{2}\right)^n\right)\mathrm{d}\mu \\
=\ & \left[\frac{\phi}{2\pi}\right]_0^{\phi_i} \frac{1}{2}\frac{n+1}{n+1+k}\left[\mu + \frac{k}{2^n}\frac{(1+\mu)^{n+1}}{n+1}\right]_{\cos(\theta_i)}^{1} \\
=\ & \frac{\phi_i}{2\pi}\frac{1}{2}\frac{n+1}{n+1+k}\left(1 + \frac{2k}{n+1} - \cos(\theta_i) - \frac{k}{2^n}\frac{(1+\cos(\theta_i))^{n+1}}{n+1}\right)
\end{aligned} \tag{11.50}$$

and carrying the integral over the whole spherical domain by substituting $\phi_i = 2\pi$ and $\theta_i = \pi$ then ensures normalization.

11.3.8 Schlick

11.3.8.1 Formulation

Introduced as an alternative relying on a relatively cheaper exponentiation than the *Henyey–Greenstein* phase function, the *Schlick phase function* [Blasi *et al.*, 1993] reads 454

$$f_p(\vec{p}, \hat{\omega}_o, \hat{\omega}_i) \triangleq \frac{1}{4\pi}\frac{1 - k^2}{(1 - k\langle\hat{\omega}_o, \hat{\omega}_i\rangle)^2} \tag{11.51}$$

where the parameter $k \in (-1, +1)$ controls the asymmetry of the distribution of scattered
light such that $k < 0$, $k = 0$ and $k > 0$ correspond to backward, *isotropic* and forward 446
scattering, respectively, as illustrated in *Figure 11.9.* 454

11.3.8.2 Normalization and Sampling

Its *cumulative distribution* over the domain Ω_i may be expressed in a separable form as 132

445

$$\begin{aligned}
\int_{\Omega_i} f_p(\vec{p}, \hat{\omega}_o, \hat{\omega}_i)\mathrm{d}\hat{\omega}_i \overset{(11.19)}{=}\ & \int_0^{\phi_i} \frac{1}{2\pi}\mathrm{d}\phi \int_{\cos(\theta_i)}^{1} \frac{1}{2}\frac{1-k^2}{(1-k\mu)^2}\mathrm{d}\mu \\
=\ & \int_0^{\phi_i} \frac{1}{2\pi}\mathrm{d}\phi \int_{1-k\cos(\theta_i)}^{1-k} \frac{1-k^2}{2}\frac{1}{v^2}\frac{\mathrm{d}v}{-k} \\
=\ & \left[\frac{\phi}{2\pi}\right]_0^{\phi_i} \frac{1-k^2}{2k}\left[\frac{1}{v}\right]_{1-k\cos(\theta_i)}^{1-k} \\
=\ & \frac{\phi_i}{2\pi}\frac{1-k^2}{2k}\left(\frac{1}{1-k} - \frac{1}{1-k\cos(\theta_i)}\right)
\end{aligned} \tag{11.52}$$

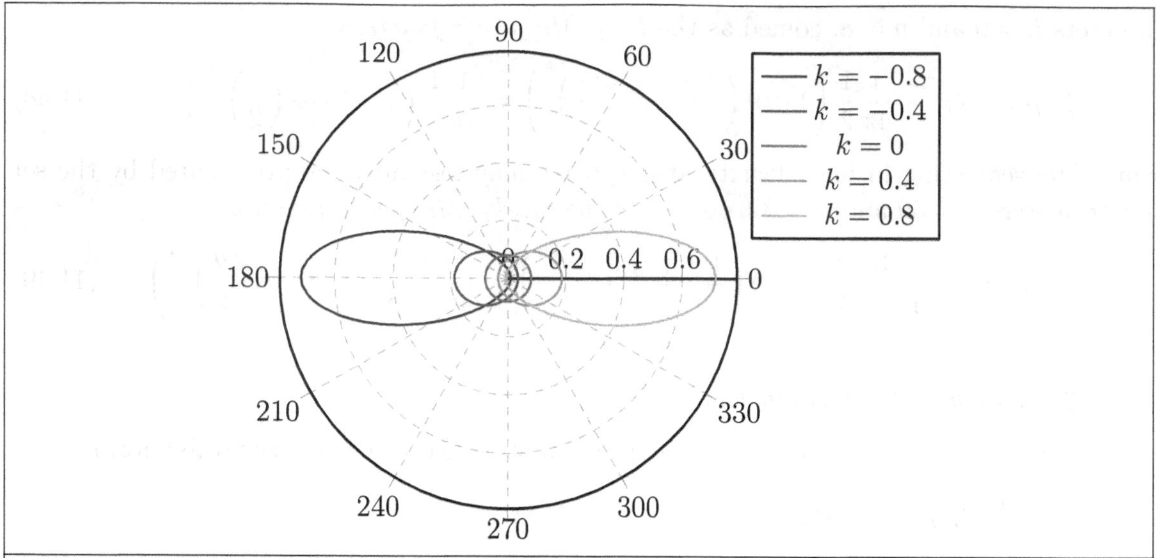

Figure 11.9: Schlick BPDF: Illustration of the angular distribution of the Schlick phase function.

where $\upsilon = 1 - k\mu$.

Integrating over the whole spherical domain by substituting $\phi_i = 2\pi$ and $\theta_i = \pi$ then en-
134 155 sures normalization, while applying *inverse-transform sampling* allows *importance sampling*
to be readily carried as

$$\xi_\phi = \frac{\phi_i}{2\pi} \implies \phi_i = 2\pi\xi_\phi \tag{11.53}$$

$$\xi_\theta = \frac{1-k^2}{2k}\left(\frac{1}{1-k} - \frac{1}{1-k\cos(\theta_i)}\right) \implies \theta_i = \arccos\left(\frac{k+1-2\xi_\theta}{1+k(1-2\xi_\theta)}\right) \tag{11.54}$$

11.3.9 Henyey–Greenstein

11.3.9.1 Formulation

Initially introduced to model scattering of radiation in the galaxy, the *Henyey–Greenstein*
phase function [Henyey and Greenstein, 1941] is an elliptical approximation to the more
457 complex *Mie* scattering phase function, and reads

$$f_p(\vec{p}, \hat{\omega}_o, \hat{\omega}_i) \triangleq \frac{1}{4\pi}\frac{1-g^2}{(1+g^2-2g\langle\hat{\omega}_o,\hat{\omega}_i\rangle)^{\frac{3}{2}}} \tag{11.55}$$

where the mean cosine $g \in (-1, +1)$ controls the asymmetry of the distribution of scattered
446 light such that $g < 0$, $g = 0$ and $g > 0$ correspond to backward, *isotropic* and forward
455 scattering, respectively, as illustrated in *Figure 11.10.*

11.3.9.2 Normalization and Sampling

132 Its *cumulative distribution* over the domain Ω_i may be expressed in a separable form as

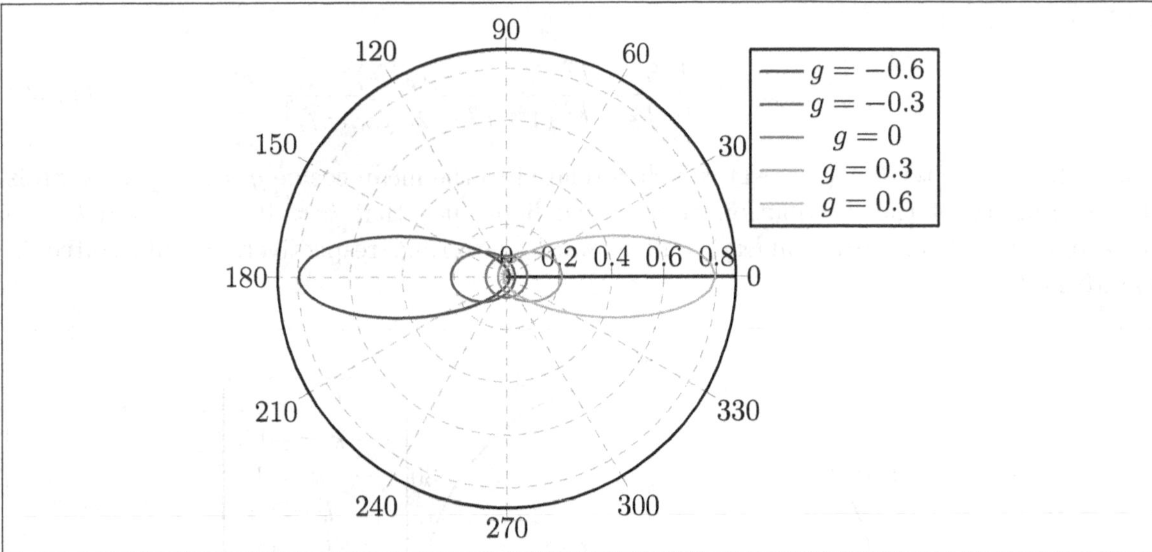

Figure 11.10: Henyey–Greenstein BPDF: Illustration of the angular distribution of the Henyey–Greenstein phase function.

$$\begin{aligned}\int_{\Omega_i} f_P(\vec{p},\hat{\omega}_o,\hat{\omega}_i)\mathrm{d}\hat{\omega}_i &\overset{(11.19)}{=} \int_0^{\phi_i}\frac{1}{2\pi}\mathrm{d}\phi\int_{\cos(\theta_i)}^{1}\frac{1}{2}\frac{1-g^2}{(1+g^2-2g\mu)^{\frac{3}{2}}}\mathrm{d}\mu \\ &= \int_0^{\phi_i}\frac{1}{2\pi}\mathrm{d}\phi\int_{1+g^2-2g\cos(\theta_i)}^{1+g^2-2g}\frac{1-g^2}{2}\frac{1}{\upsilon^{\frac{3}{2}}}\frac{\mathrm{d}\upsilon}{-2g} \\ &= \left[\frac{\phi}{2\pi}\right]_0^{\phi_i}\frac{1-g^2}{4g}\left[\frac{2}{\sqrt{\upsilon}}\right]_{1+g^2-2g\cos(\theta_i)}^{(1-g)^2} \\ &= \frac{\phi_i}{2\pi}\frac{1-g^2}{2g}\left(\frac{1}{1-g}-\frac{1}{\sqrt{1+g^2-2g\cos(\theta_i)}}\right) \qquad (11.56)\end{aligned}$$ 445

where $\upsilon \triangleq 1+g^2-2g\mu$.

Integrating over the whole spherical domain by substituting $\phi_i = 2\pi$ and $\theta_i = \pi$ then ensures normalization, while applying *inverse-transform sampling* allows *importance sampling* 134
to be readily carried as 155

$$\xi_\phi = \frac{\phi_i}{2\pi} \implies \phi_i = 2\pi\xi_\phi \qquad (11.57)$$

$$\xi_\theta = \frac{1-g^2}{2g}\left(\frac{1}{1-g}-\frac{1}{\sqrt{1+g^2-2g\cos(\theta_i)}}\right) \implies \theta_i = \arccos\left(\frac{1+g^2-\left(\frac{1-g^2}{1+g(1-2\xi_\theta)}\right)^2}{2g}\right) \qquad (11.58)$$

whenever $g \neq 0$ while resorting to *isotropic* sampling otherwise. 446

11.3.10 Cornette–Shanks

11.3.10.1 Formulation

A more physically reasonable elaboration of the *Henyey–Greenstein* phase function is given 454
by the *Cornette–Shanks phase function* [Cornette and Shanks, 1992, Cornette and Shanks,

1995], which reads

$$f_p(\vec{p}, \hat{\omega}_o, \hat{\omega}_i) \triangleq \frac{1}{4\pi} \frac{3}{2} \frac{1-k^2}{2+k^2} \frac{1 + \langle \hat{\omega}_o, \hat{\omega}_i \rangle^2}{(1 + k^2 - 2k\langle \hat{\omega}_o, \hat{\omega}_i \rangle)^{\frac{3}{2}}} \tag{11.59}$$

where the parameter $k \in (-1, +1)$, which is related to the mean cosine $g = k\frac{3}{5}\frac{4+k^2}{2+k^2}$, controls the asymmetry of the distribution of scattered light such that $k < 0$, $k = 0$ and $k > 0$
448 corresponds to backward, *Rayleigh* and forward scattering, respectively, as illustrated in
456 *Figure 11.11*.

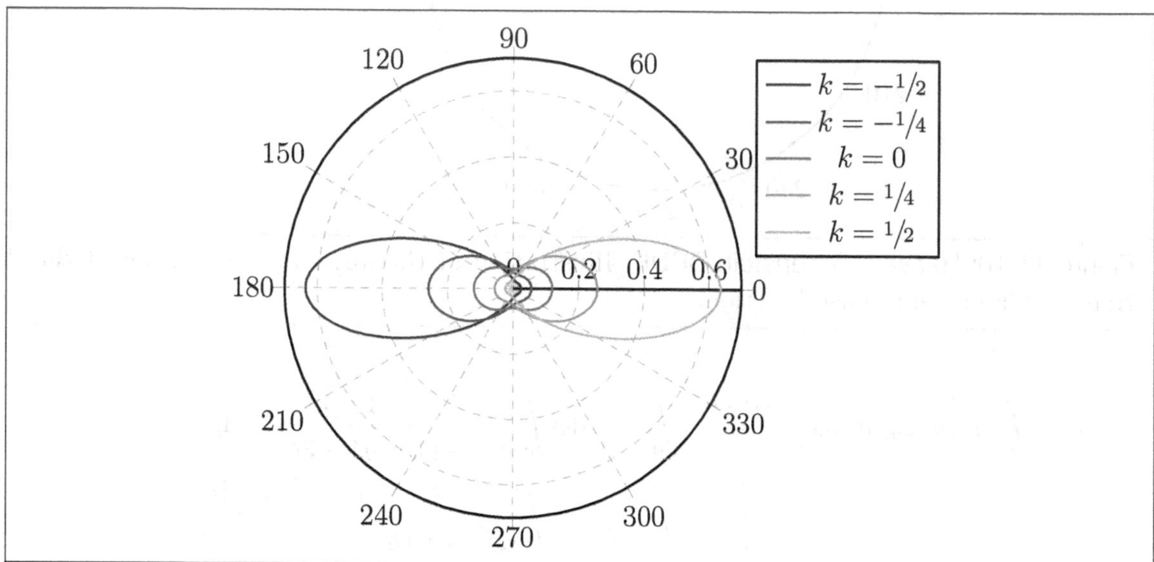

Figure 11.11: Cornette–Shanks BPDF: Illustration of the angular distribution of the Cornette–Shanks phase function.

11.3.10.2 Normalization and Sampling

132 Its *cumulative distribution* over the domain Ω_i may be expressed in a separable form as

445

$$\begin{aligned}
\int_{\Omega_i} f_p(\vec{p}, \hat{\omega}_o, \hat{\omega}_i) \mathrm{d}\hat{\omega}_i &\overset{(11.19)}{=} \int_0^{\phi_i} \frac{1}{2\pi} \mathrm{d}\phi \int_{\cos(\theta_i)}^{1} \frac{3}{4} \frac{1-k^2}{2+k^2} \frac{1+\mu^2}{(1+k^2-2k\mu)^{\frac{3}{2}}} \mathrm{d}\mu \\
&= \left[\frac{\phi}{2\pi}\right]_0^{\phi_i} \frac{3}{4} \frac{1-k^2}{2+k^2} \left[\frac{2(1+k^4) - 2k(1+k^2)\mu + k^2(7-\mu^2)}{3k^3\sqrt{1+k^2-2k\mu}}\right]_{\cos(\theta_i)}^{1} \\
&= \frac{\phi_i}{2\pi} a \left(b - \frac{c - d\cos(\theta_i) - k^2\cos(\theta_i)^2}{\sqrt{1+k^2-2k\cos(\theta_i)}}\right)
\end{aligned} \tag{11.60}$$

where

$$a \triangleq \frac{1}{4k^3} \frac{1-k^2}{2+k^2} \tag{11.61}$$

$$b \triangleq \frac{2(1+k^4) - 2k(1+k^2) + 6k^2}{1-k} \tag{11.62}$$

$$c \triangleq 2(1+k^4) + 7k^2 \tag{11.63}$$

$$d \triangleq 2k(1+k^2) \tag{11.64}$$

Integrating over the whole spherical domain by substituting $\phi_i = 2\pi$ and $\theta_i = \pi$ then en-
134 sures normalization, while applying *inverse-transform sampling* allows *importance sampling*
155

to be readily carried as

$$\xi_\phi = \frac{\phi_i}{2\pi} \quad \Longrightarrow \quad \phi_i = 2\pi\xi_\phi \tag{11.65}$$

$$\xi_\theta = a\left(b - \frac{c - d\mu - k^2\mu^2}{\sqrt{1 + k^2 - 2k\mu}}\right) \quad \Longrightarrow \quad c_4\mu^4 + c_3\mu^3 + c_2\mu^2 + c_1\mu + c_0 = 0 \tag{11.66}$$

where the cosine angle $\mu \triangleq \cos(\theta_i)$ is the solution of the *quartic equation* with coefficients 33

$$c_4 = k^4 \tag{11.67}$$

$$c_3 = 2dk^2 \tag{11.68}$$

$$c_2 = d^2 - 2ck^2 \tag{11.69}$$

$$c_1 = 2k\left(b - \frac{\xi_\theta}{a}\right)^2 - 2cd \tag{11.70}$$

$$c_0 = c^2 - (1 + k^2)\left(b - \frac{\xi_\theta}{a}\right)^2 \tag{11.71}$$

11.3.11 Mie

Mie theory [Mie, 1908], also called Lorenz–Mie theory or Lorenz–Mie–Debye theory, is an
analytical solution to Maxwell's equations for the scattering of *electromagnetic waves* by 420
spherical particles. As illustrated in *Figure 11.12*, the *Mie phase function* exhibits distinctive 457
features such as a backward-scattering peak responsible for the *glory* effect in clouds, two wavelength-dependent off-backward peaks responsible for *rainbows* and *fogbows* in rain and cloud droplets, respectively, as well as a strong forward-scattering peak responsible for the *corona* effect.

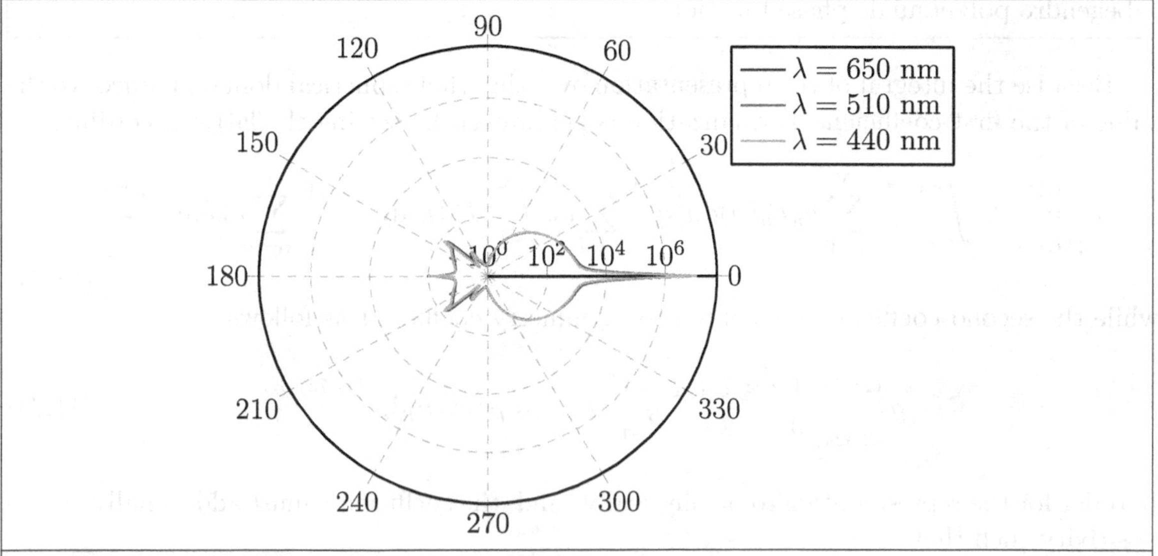

Figure 11.12: Mie BPDF: Illustration of the angular distribution of the Mie phase function for an average of a given range of particle sizes.

11.3.12 Legendre Polynomials

Legendre polynomials form a widely used basis to represent general symmetric phase func- 62
tions [Chandrasekhar, 1960], which, as illustrated in *Figure 11.13*, may be expressed as a

458 series of the form

$$f_p(\vec{p}, \hat{\omega}_o, \hat{\omega}_i) \triangleq \frac{1}{4\pi} \sum_{n=0}^{N} a_n P_n(\langle \hat{\omega}_o, \hat{\omega}_i \rangle) \tag{11.72}$$

where, noting $\mu \triangleq \langle \hat{\omega}_o, \hat{\omega}_i \rangle$, the coefficients are defined as

64

$$a_n \overset{(2.347)}{=} \frac{2n+1}{2} \int_{-1}^{+1} 4\pi f_p(\vec{p}, \mu) P_n(\mu) \mathrm{d}\mu \tag{11.73}$$

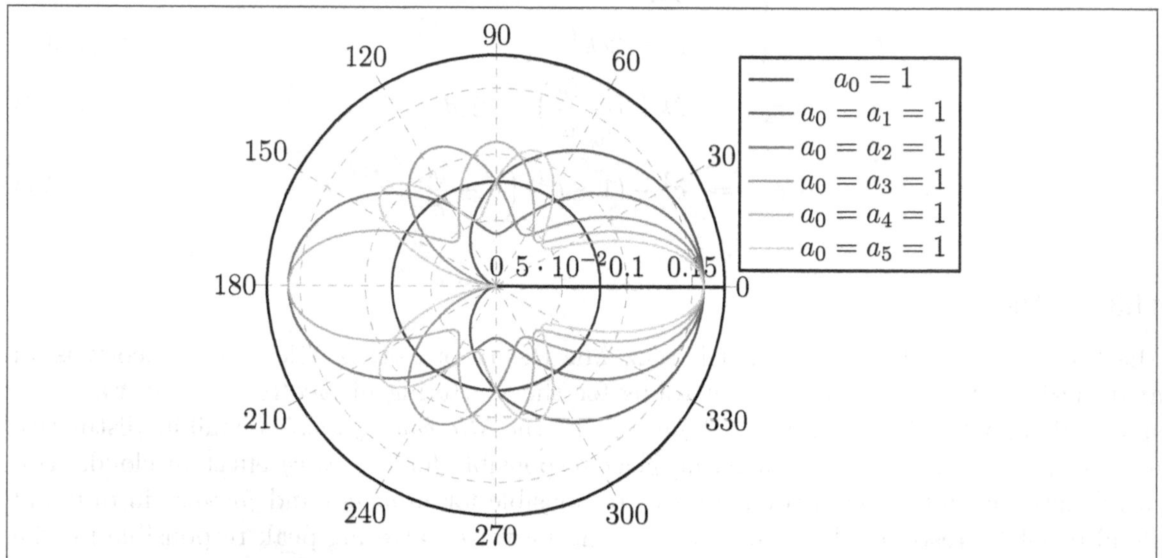

Figure 11.13: Legendre Polynomials BPDF: Illustration of the angular distribution of the Legendre polynomials phase function.

Because the integral of the representation over the whole spherical domain reduces to the value of the first coefficient, normalization is guaranteed by setting the latter accordingly

445
64
46
458

$$1 \underset{(11.72)}{\overset{(11.21)}{=}} 2\pi \int_{-1}^{+1} \frac{1}{4\pi} \sum_{n=0}^{N} a_n P_n(\mu) \mathrm{d}\mu = \frac{1}{2} \sum_{n=0}^{N} a_n \int_{-1}^{+1} P_n(\mu) \mathrm{d}\mu \overset{(2.344)}{=} \sum_{n=0}^{N} a_n \delta[n] \overset{(2.223)}{=} a_0 \tag{11.74}$$

while the second coefficient relates to the asymmetry coefficient as follows

446
458
62

$$g \underset{(2.324)}{\overset{(11.23)}{=}} \frac{1}{3} \frac{2 \times 1 + 1}{2} \int_{-1}^{+1} 4\pi f_p(\vec{p}, \mu) P_1(\mu) \mathrm{d}\mu \overset{(11.73)}{=} \frac{a_1}{3} \tag{11.75}$$

In order for the representation to be physically valid, the coefficients must additionally ensure positivity such that

$$0 \leq \sum_{n=0}^{N} a_n P_n(\mu), \quad \forall \mu \in [-1, +1] \tag{11.76}$$

Several phase functions may be represented in this polynomial basis, either exactly with a finite number of terms or approximately via truncation of the expansion into an infinite
459 series. Coefficients for common scattering modes are reported in *Table 11.1* while expansions for more complex distributions such as the Mie phase function may be found elsewhere [Chu and Churchill, 1955, Fowler, 1983].

Table 11.1: Legendre Polynomials Coefficients: Coefficients of Legendre polynomials for several common phase functions.

Phase Function	Order	Coefficients
Isotropic	0	$a_0 = 1$
Eddington	1	$a_0 = 1,\ a_1 = k$
Rayleigh	2	$a_0 = 1,\ a_1 = 0,\ a_2 = 1/2$
Henyey–Greenstein	∞	$a_n = (2n+1)g^n$
Cornette–Shanks	∞	$a_n = \frac{3}{2}\frac{1}{2+k^2}\left(\frac{n(n-1)}{2n-1}k^{n-2} + \left(\frac{5n^2-1}{2n-1} + \frac{(n+1)^2}{2n+3}\right)k^n + \frac{(n+1)(n+2)}{2n+3}k^{n+2}\right)$

11.3.13 Monomial Basis

Symmetric phase functions can more generally be expressed as a polynomial of the cosine angle

$$f_p(\vec{p}, \hat{\omega}_o, \hat{\omega}_i) \triangleq \sum_{n=0}^{N} c_n \langle \hat{\omega}_o, \hat{\omega}_i \rangle^n \tag{11.77}$$

This basis provides an exact representation for most distributions, including the *isotropic*, 446
Warn, *Rayleigh*, *Eddington*, *Liu* and *hazy–murky* phase functions. Distributions formulated 447
in terms of *Legendre polynomials* may also be precisely projected into this representation by 448 450
converting their coefficients as per *Equation 2.349.* 451

In contrast, a few rational formulations, such as the *Schlick*, *Henyey–Greenstein* and 452 457
Cornette–Shanks phase functions, are not exactly representable in this basis and must be 64
approximated via an expansion, either into a series of *Legendre polynomials*, or into a *Taylor* 453 454
series, which tends to rapidly converge with only a few terms in practice due to the zero- 455
valued limit of the repeated exponentiations of the cosine angle $\mu \in [-1, +1]$. To this end, 457 59
a formulation of the successive derivatives of the *Henyey–Greenstein* BPDF with respect to 454
the cosine angle reads [Pegoraro *et al.*, 2010]

$$f_p^{(n)}(\vec{p}, \hat{\omega}_o, \hat{\omega}_i) \overset{(11.55)}{=} \frac{1}{4\pi} \frac{1-g^2}{(1+g^2-2g\langle \hat{\omega}_o, \hat{\omega}_i \rangle)^{\frac{3}{2}+n}} \left(\frac{g}{2}\right)^n \frac{(2n+1)!}{n!} \tag{11.78}$$ 454

from which the monomial coefficients may be readily computed.

11.3.14 Composite Distributions

11.3.14.1 Formulation

More complex phase functions may be modeled as a convex combination of simpler BPDFs

$$f_p(\vec{p}, \hat{\omega}_o, \hat{\omega}_i) \triangleq \sum_{j=1}^{n} w_j f_j(\vec{p}, \hat{\omega}_o, \hat{\omega}_i) \tag{11.79}$$

where the weights $w_j \geq 0$ obey $\sum_{j=1}^{n} w_j = 1$.

As illustrated in *Figure 11.14*, two-lobed scattering events that cannot be described with 460
a single lobe may then be modeled as a convex combination of a forward and a backward
Henyey–Greenstein BPDF with weight $\alpha \in [0, 1]$, yielding the so-called *double Henyey–* 454
Greenstein phase function

$$f_p(\vec{p}, \hat{\omega}_o, \hat{\omega}_i) = \alpha f_p^{g_1>0}(\vec{p}, \hat{\omega}_o, \hat{\omega}_i) + (1-\alpha) f_p^{g_2<0}(\vec{p}, \hat{\omega}_o, \hat{\omega}_i) \tag{11.80}$$

Several phase functions such as the *Rayleigh* and *hazy–murky* BPDFs may also be approxi- 448
mated by linearly combining two *Schlick* phase functions with different parameters [Blasi *et* 452 453

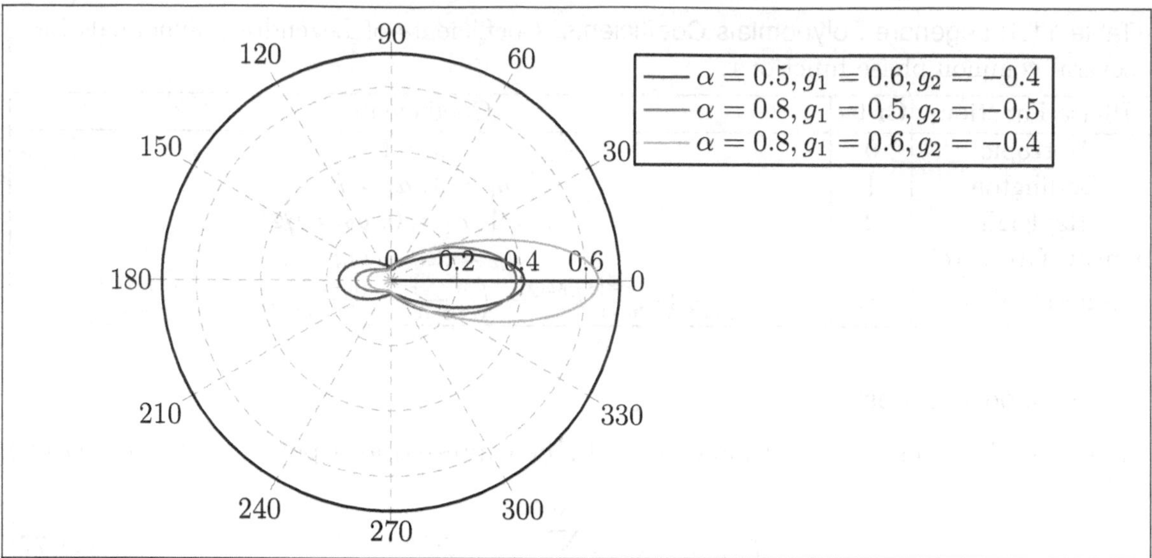

Figure 11.14: Double Henyey–Greenstein BPDF: Illustration of the angular distribution of the double Henyey–Greenstein phase function.

al., 1993].

Similarly, if the medium consists of a discrete mixture of n different types of particles with number density $n_j(\vec{p})$, the phase function of the external mixture is given by the average of the BPDFs of each individual compound j weighted by the scattering coefficients

442 $$f_p(\vec{p}, \hat{\omega}_o, \hat{\omega}_i) = \frac{\sum_{j=1}^{n} \kappa_s^j(\vec{p}) f_p^j(\vec{p}, \hat{\omega}_o, \hat{\omega}_i)}{\sum_{j=1}^{n} \kappa_s^j(\vec{p})} \overset{(11.2)}{=} \frac{\sum_{j=1}^{n} n_j(\vec{p}) \sigma_s[j] f_p^j(\vec{p}, \hat{\omega}_o, \hat{\omega}_i)}{\sum_{j=1}^{n} n_j(\vec{p}) \sigma_s[j]} \tag{11.81}$$

while in the case of a continuous mixture of particles with radius density distribution $N(\vec{p}, r)$ for radii r in the range $[r_{min}, r_{max}]$, the effective phase function becomes

$$f_p(\vec{p}, \hat{\omega}_o, \hat{\omega}_i) = \frac{\int_{r_{min}}^{r_{max}} N(\vec{p}, r) \sigma_s(r) f_p^r(\vec{p}, \hat{\omega}_o, \hat{\omega}_i) \mathrm{d}r}{\int_{r_{min}}^{r_{max}} N(\vec{p}, r) \sigma_s(r) \mathrm{d}r} \tag{11.82}$$

11.3.14.2 Normalization and Sampling

132 Its *cumulative distribution* over the domain Ω_i may be expressed as

$$\int_{\Omega_i} f_p(\vec{p}, \hat{\omega}_o, \hat{\omega}_i) \mathrm{d}\hat{\omega}_i = \int_{\Omega_i} \sum_{j=1}^{n} w_j f_j(\vec{p}, \hat{\omega}_o, \hat{\omega}_i) \mathrm{d}\hat{\omega}_i = \sum_{j=1}^{n} w_j \int_{\Omega_i} f_j(\vec{p}, \hat{\omega}_o, \hat{\omega}_i) \mathrm{d}\hat{\omega}_i \tag{11.83}$$

Integrating over the whole spherical domain by substituting $\Omega_i = 4\pi$ then ensures normalization

$$\int_{4\pi} f_p(\vec{p}, \hat{\omega}_o, \hat{\omega}_i) \mathrm{d}\hat{\omega}_i = \sum_{j=1}^{n} w_j \int_{4\pi} f_j(\vec{p}, \hat{\omega}_o, \hat{\omega}_i) \mathrm{d}\hat{\omega}_i = \sum_{j=1}^{n} w_j = 1 \tag{11.84}$$

while drawing random samples from the mixture of distributions may be readily carried by
155 means of mixture *importance sampling*.

11.3.15 Multiple Scattering

The previously introduced single-scattering phase functions describe the distribution of energy for processes in which light undergoes a single scattering event. In contrast, a *multiple-scattering phase function* describes the angular distribution resulting from processes in which light undergoes n interactions with particles. Such a BPDF may be computed by convolving n times the single-scattering phase function with itself, which tends to smooth the original distribution and, in the limit as $n \to \infty$, yields an *isotropic* BPDF. 446

In the case of a *Henyey–Greenstein* phase function, the resulting distribution can actually 454
be expressed in closed form as another *Henyey–Greenstein* BPDF with asymmetry coefficient 454
g^n, such that $\lim_{n\to\infty} g^n = 0$, which is in agreement with the isotropization phenomenon. This property is often exploited in highly scattering media where diffusion is assumed to dominate.

11.4 RADIATIVE TRANSFER

11.4.1 Radiative Transport Equation

Radiative transfer refers to the physical transfer of energy in the form of *electromagnetic radiation*, so-called light transport in the visible range, whose propagation through the medium 420
is affected by the various absorption, emission and scattering phenomena. Considering the geometrical model illustrated in *Figure 11.1*, the total number of particles N contained within 442
the infinitely small cylinder is proportional to the number density $n(\vec{p})$ of the particles, which is assumed to be constant within the infinitely small volume, and to the volume of the cylinder oriented along the direction $\hat{\omega}$, itself being proportional to its cross-sectional area a and its length ds, leading to

$$N = n(\vec{p})a\mathrm{d}s \tag{11.85}$$

Assuming the particles are distributed sparsely enough so that the *mean free path* is much 464
larger than their size, any overlap of their projection onto the base of the cylinder may be considered negligible and collision events are therefore independent [Ishimaru, 1978]. The product of the total number of particles N and their effective cross section $\sigma_{a|s|t}$ is then directly proportional to their aggregate projected area, whose ratio to the total cross-sectional area of the cylinder defines the ratio of differential radiation to incident radiation

$$-\frac{\mathrm{d}L(\vec{p}+s\hat{\omega},\hat{\omega})}{L(\vec{p}+s\hat{\omega},\hat{\omega})} = \frac{\sigma_{a|s|t}N}{a} = \frac{\sigma_{a|s|t}n(\vec{p}+s\hat{\omega})a\mathrm{d}s}{a} \overset{(11.2)}{=} \kappa_{a|s|t}(\vec{p}+s\hat{\omega})\mathrm{d}s \tag{11.86}$$ 442

Proceeding similarly for all four types of light-matter interaction and aggregating the contributions then yields the equation of radiative transfer, formally known as the *radiative transport equation* (*RTE*), which mathematically describes light transport through the medium, as illustrated in *Figure 11.15*. The RTE is a steady-state balance equation equating 462
variations in radiance at position $\vec{p}$ over an infinitesimal distance along a ray of direction $\hat{\omega}$ with gains from emission and in-scattering as well as losses from absorption and out-scattering, leading to the following integro-differential (due to the integral nature of the in-scattered radiance) equation

$$\begin{aligned}\langle\hat{\omega}, \nabla L(\vec{s},\hat{\omega})\rangle \overset{(3.116)}{=} \frac{\mathrm{d}L(\vec{s},\hat{\omega})}{\mathrm{d}s} &= -\underbrace{\kappa_a(\vec{s})L(\vec{s},\hat{\omega})}_{absorption} + \underbrace{\kappa_a(\vec{s})L_e(\vec{s},\hat{\omega})}_{emission} \\ &\quad -\underbrace{\kappa_s(\vec{s})L(\vec{s},\hat{\omega})}_{out\text{-}scattering} + \underbrace{\kappa_s(\vec{s})L_p(\vec{s},\hat{\omega})}_{in\text{-}scattering} \\ &= -\underbrace{\kappa_t(\vec{s})L(\vec{s},\hat{\omega})}_{losses} + \underbrace{\kappa_t(\vec{s})L_u(\vec{s},\hat{\omega})}_{gains}\end{aligned} \tag{11.87}$$ 83

with the shorthand notation $\vec{s} = \vec{p} + s\hat{\omega}$.

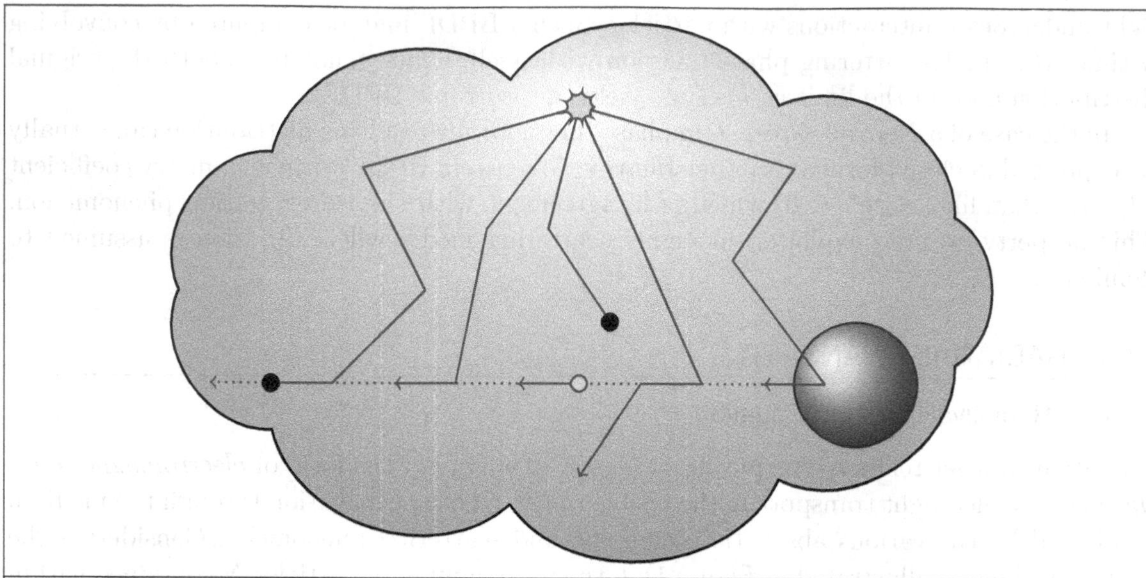

Figure 11.15: Radiative Transport: Illustration of absorption, emission and scattering events that light may undergo on its way between the light source and the sensor (drawn after [Pegoraro, 2009, Fig. 4.8]).

11.4.2 Beer's Law

The RTE is a first-order differential equation, and the definition of a *boundary condition* is therefore necessary to determine the constant of integration and give the equation a fully physical meaning. The boundary condition is typically defined as the radiance leaving the surface bounding the medium, which is referred to as *background radiance*. The latter may either be explicitly described by the local properties of the background such as its emitted radiance, or implicitly formulated as a function of the radiance incident on the background, itself being dependent on the light transport phenomena occurring in the medium.

Assuming that extinction phenomena dominate and that the source radiance $L_u(\vec{p},\hat{\omega})$ is negligible along the path, the RTE simplifies into

461

$$\frac{\mathrm{d}L(\vec{p}+s\hat{\omega},\hat{\omega})}{\mathrm{d}s} \overset{(11.87)}{=} -\kappa_t(\vec{p}+s\hat{\omega})L(\vec{p}+s\hat{\omega},\hat{\omega}) \tag{11.88}$$

which can be solved by first rearranging the terms as follows

$$\frac{\frac{\mathrm{d}L(\vec{p}+s\hat{\omega},\hat{\omega})}{\mathrm{d}s}}{L(\vec{p}+s\hat{\omega},\hat{\omega})} = \frac{\mathrm{d}\ln\left(L(\vec{p}+s\hat{\omega},\hat{\omega})\right)}{\mathrm{d}s} = -\kappa_t(\vec{p}+s\hat{\omega}) \tag{11.89}$$

Integrating both sides from s_b to s_c then gives

$$\begin{aligned}\int_{s_b}^{s_c}\frac{\mathrm{d}\ln\left(L(\vec{p}+s\hat{\omega},\hat{\omega})\right)}{\mathrm{d}s}\mathrm{d}s &= \left[\ln\left(L(\vec{p}+s\hat{\omega},\hat{\omega})\right)\right]_{s_b}^{s_c}\\ &= \ln\left(\frac{L(\vec{p}+s_c\hat{\omega},\hat{\omega})}{L(\vec{p}+s_b\hat{\omega},\hat{\omega})}\right)\\ &= -\int_{s_b}^{s_c}\kappa_t(\vec{p}+s\hat{\omega})\mathrm{d}s\end{aligned} \tag{11.90}$$

and rearranging the terms finally yields the so-called *Beer–Lambert–Bouguer law* [Bouguer,

1729, Lambert, 1760], commonly referred to as *Beer's law*, with the boundary condition defined by the background radiance $L(\vec{p} + s_b\hat{\omega}, \hat{\omega})$

$$L(\vec{p} + s_c\hat{\omega}, \hat{\omega}) = e^{-\int_{s_b}^{s_c} \kappa_t(\vec{p}+s\hat{\omega})\mathrm{d}s} L(\vec{p} + s_b\hat{\omega}, \hat{\omega}) \tag{11.91}$$

11.4.3 Optical Measures

The impact of absorption and scattering phenomena over distance are, respectively, characterized by the *absorbance*

$$A(\vec{p} + s_a\hat{\omega}, \vec{p} + s_b\hat{\omega}) \triangleq \int_{s_a}^{s_b} \kappa_a(\vec{p} + s\hat{\omega})\mathrm{d}s \tag{11.92}$$

and the *scatterance*

$$B(\vec{p} + s_a\hat{\omega}, \vec{p} + s_b\hat{\omega}) \triangleq \int_{s_a}^{s_b} \kappa_s(\vec{p} + s\hat{\omega})\mathrm{d}s \tag{11.93}$$

Similarly, *attenuance*, also called *optical thickness* or *optical depth*, is a dimensionless cumulative measure of extinction over distance in the medium. It relates the physical distance between two points to optical distance as

$$\tau(\vec{p}+s_a\hat{\omega}, \vec{p}+s_b\hat{\omega}) \triangleq A(\vec{p}+s_a\hat{\omega}, \vec{p}+s_b\hat{\omega}) + B(\vec{p}+s_a\hat{\omega}, \vec{p}+s_b\hat{\omega}) \overset{(11.92)}{\underset{(11.93)}{=}} \int_{s_a}^{s_b} \kappa_t(\vec{p}+s\hat{\omega})\mathrm{d}s \tag{11.94}$$

463
463

Given a layer of medium delimited by two given points, the latter is said to be optically thick if $\tau \gg 1$, while it is said to be optically thin if $\tau \ll 1$.

Considering n non-overlapping intervals along a ray such that $s_0 < s_1 < \ldots < s_{n-1} < s_n$, it follows that

$$\begin{aligned} \tau(\vec{p} + s_0\hat{\omega}, \vec{p} + s_n\hat{\omega}) &\overset{(11.94)}{=} \int_{s_0}^{s_n} \kappa_t(\vec{p} + s\hat{\omega})\mathrm{d}s \\ &= \sum_{i=1}^{n} \int_{s_{i-1}}^{s_i} \kappa_t(\vec{p} + s\hat{\omega})\mathrm{d}s \\ &\overset{(11.94)}{=} \sum_{i=1}^{n} \tau(\vec{p} + s_{i-1}\hat{\omega}, \vec{p} + s_i\hat{\omega}) \end{aligned} \tag{11.95}$$

463
463

The complement of the ratio of unabsorbed incident radiation is then defined as

$$\alpha(\vec{p} + s_a\hat{\omega}, \vec{p} + s_b\hat{\omega}) \triangleq 1 - e^{-A(\vec{p}+s_a\hat{\omega}, \vec{p}+s_b\hat{\omega})} \tag{11.96}$$

while the complement of the ratio of unscattered incident radiation reads

$$\beta(\vec{p} + s_a\hat{\omega}, \vec{p} + s_b\hat{\omega}) \triangleq 1 - e^{-B(\vec{p}+s_a\hat{\omega}, \vec{p}+s_b\hat{\omega})} \tag{11.97}$$

Similarly, a dimensionless measure of the amount of light that has not undergone any extinction event when traveling between two points in the medium is then given by the *transmittance*

$$T(\vec{p} + s_a\hat{\omega}, \vec{p} + s_b\hat{\omega}) \triangleq e^{-\tau(\vec{p}+s_a\hat{\omega}, \vec{p}+s_b\hat{\omega})} \tag{11.98}$$

while the attenuation of light through the medium is conversely quantified by the *opacity*

$$O(\vec{p} + s_a\hat{\omega}, \vec{p} + s_b\hat{\omega}) \triangleq 1 - T(\vec{p} + s_a\hat{\omega}, \vec{p} + s_b\hat{\omega}) \tag{11.99}$$

where $T \in (0, 1]$ and $O \in [0, 1)$. It follows that if the medium is fully transparent, then $T = 1$ and $O = 0$ and no intensity is lost, while if the medium is fully opaque then, in the limit, $T \to 0$ and $O \to 1$ and no light is transmitted.

Considering n non-overlapping intervals along a ray such that $s_0 < s_1 < \ldots < s_{n-1} < s_n$, it follows that

463 463 463

$$\begin{aligned} T(\vec{p} + s_0\hat{\omega}, \vec{p} + s_n\hat{\omega}) &\overset{(11.98)}{=} e^{-\tau(\vec{p}+s_0\hat{\omega},\vec{p}+s_n\hat{\omega})} \\ &\overset{(11.95)}{=} e^{-\sum_{i=1}^{n} \tau(\vec{p}+s_{i-1}\hat{\omega},\vec{p}+s_i\hat{\omega})} \\ &= \prod_{i=1}^{n} e^{-\tau(\vec{p}+s_{i-1}\hat{\omega},\vec{p}+s_i\hat{\omega})} \\ &\overset{(11.98)}{=} \prod_{i=1}^{n} T(\vec{p} + s_{i-1}\hat{\omega}, \vec{p} + s_i\hat{\omega}) \end{aligned} \quad (11.100)$$

as well as

463 463

$$\begin{aligned} O(\vec{s}_0, \vec{s}_n) &\overset{(11.99)}{=} 1 - T(\vec{s}_0, \vec{s}_n) \\ &= 1 - T(\vec{s}_0, \vec{s}_{n-1})T(\vec{s}_{n-1}, \vec{s}_n) \\ &\overset{(11.99)}{=} 1 - (1 - O(\vec{s}_0, \vec{s}_{n-1}))(1 - O(\vec{s}_{n-1}, \vec{s}_n)) \\ &= O(\vec{s}_0, \vec{s}_{n-1}) + (1 - O(\vec{s}_0, \vec{s}_{n-1}))O(\vec{s}_{n-1}, \vec{s}_n) \\ &= \ldots \\ &= \sum_{i=1}^{n} (1 - O(\vec{s}_0, \vec{s}_{i-1}))O(\vec{s}_{i-1}, \vec{s}_i) \end{aligned} \quad (11.101)$$

with the shorthand notation $\vec{s}_\square = \vec{p} + s_\square\hat{\omega}$.

11.4.4 Mean Free Path

129 From a probabilistic standpoint, transmittance expresses the *probability* of the radiation to not undergo any extinction event when traveling a given distance between two points in
129 the medium, while opacity conversely expresses the *probability* of such an event to occur.
129 Defining the *random variable* $S \in [s_a, \infty)$ as the coordinate along the ray where an extinction
132 event occurs, its *cumulative distribution* is then readily given by the opacity as

132 463 463

$$P(s) \overset{(4.21)}{=} \Pr(S \leq s) = O(\vec{p} + s_a\hat{\omega}, \vec{p} + s\hat{\omega}) \underset{(11.98)}{\overset{(11.99)}{=}} 1 - e^{-\tau(\vec{p}+s_a\hat{\omega},\vec{p}+s\hat{\omega})} \quad (11.102)$$

such that $P(s_a) = 0$ while carrying the integral over the whole domain by substituting $s \to \infty$ ensures normalization $\lim_{s\to\infty} P(s) = 1$, assuming a virtual blackbody at infinity such that $\lim_{s\to\infty} \tau(\vec{p} + s_a\hat{\omega}, \vec{p} + s\hat{\omega}) = \infty$.

131 Deriving the previous expression consequently yields the *probability density* of the dis-
131 tribution, which defines the *probability density* of collision per unit distance

133 463

$$p(s) \overset{(4.23)}{=} \frac{\mathrm{d}P(s)}{\mathrm{d}s} \overset{(11.94)}{=} \frac{\mathrm{d}(1 - e^{-\int_{s_a}^{s} \kappa_t(\vec{p}+s'\hat{\omega})\mathrm{d}s'})}{\mathrm{d}s} = e^{-\int_{s_a}^{s} \kappa_t(\vec{p}+s'\hat{\omega})\mathrm{d}s'} \kappa_t(\vec{p} + s\hat{\omega}) \quad (11.103)$$

such that the average distance the radiation travels before being either absorbed or scattered is given by the *mean free path* (in m) as the integral to infinity of the transmittance along the ray

$$
\begin{aligned}
\ell &\triangleq \mathrm{E}[S] - s_a \\
&\overset{(4.64)}{=} \int_{s_a}^{\infty} s p(s) \mathrm{d}s - s_a \\
&= \int_{s_a}^{\infty} s e^{-\int_{s_a}^{s} \kappa_t(\vec{p}+s'\hat{\omega})\mathrm{d}s'} \kappa_t(\vec{p}+s\hat{\omega}) \mathrm{d}s - s_a \\
&= \left[-s e^{-\int_{s_a}^{s} \kappa_t(\vec{p}+s'\hat{\omega})\mathrm{d}s'} \right]_{s_a}^{\infty} - \int_{s_a}^{\infty} -e^{-\int_{s_a}^{s} \kappa_t(\vec{p}+s'\hat{\omega})\mathrm{d}s'} \mathrm{d}s - s_a \\
&= (-0 + s_a) + \int_{s_a}^{\infty} e^{-\tau(\vec{p}+s_a\hat{\omega}, \vec{p}+s\hat{\omega})} \mathrm{d}s - s_a \\
&\overset{(11.98)}{=} \int_{s_a}^{\infty} T(\vec{p}+s_a\hat{\omega}, \vec{p}+s\hat{\omega}) \mathrm{d}s
\end{aligned}
\qquad (11.104)
$$

141

463

In the special case of a homogeneous medium, the mean free path simplifies into the reciprocal of the extinction coefficient

$$
\ell \overset{(11.98)}{=} \int_{s_a}^{\infty} e^{-(s-s_a)\kappa_t} \mathrm{d}s = \left[-\frac{e^{-(s-s_a)\kappa_t}}{\kappa_t} \right]_{s_a}^{\infty} = -\frac{0}{\kappa_t} + \frac{1}{\kappa_t} = \frac{1}{\kappa_t} \qquad (11.105)
$$

463

and the optical depth therefore represents the number of mean free paths between two points in the medium

$$
\tau(\vec{p}+s_a\hat{\omega}, \vec{p}+(s_a+\alpha\ell)\hat{\omega}) \overset{(11.94)}{=} \int_{s_a}^{s_a+\alpha\ell} \kappa_t \mathrm{d}s = \kappa_t(s_a+\alpha\ell-s_a) = \kappa_t \alpha \frac{1}{\kappa_t} = \alpha \qquad (11.106)
$$

463

such that the attenuation of a radiation traveling a distance equal to the mean free path through the volume reads

$$
O(\vec{p}+s_a\hat{\omega}, \vec{p}+(s_a+\ell)\hat{\omega}) \underset{(11.98)}{\overset{(11.99)}{=}} 1 - e^{-\tau(\vec{p}+s_a\hat{\omega}, \vec{p}+(s_a+\ell)\hat{\omega})} = 1 - e^{-1} \approx 0.63212\ldots \qquad (11.107)
$$

463

463

Similarly, the absorptance defines the *probability* of occurrence of an absorption event, 129
and the inverse of the absorption coefficient $\frac{1}{\kappa_a}$ then gives the average distance a radiation will travel in a homogeneous medium before being absorbed. Conversely, the scatterance defines the *probability* of occurrence of a scattering event, and the reciprocal of the scattering 129
coefficient $\frac{1}{\kappa_s}$ defines the average distance a radiation will travel in a homogeneous medium before being scattered, i.e., the average distance between two consecutive scattering events.

11.4.5 Integral Form of the RTE

Rearranging the terms in the *radiative transport equation* and dividing both sides by the 461
integrating factor $T(\vec{p}+s_b\hat{\omega}, \vec{p}+s\hat{\omega})$ [Williams and Max, 1992] yields

$$
\begin{aligned}
e^{\int_{s_b}^{s} \kappa_t(\vec{s}')\mathrm{d}s'} \kappa_t(\vec{s}) L_u(\vec{s}, \hat{\omega}) &\overset{(11.87)}{=} e^{\int_{s_b}^{s} \kappa_t(\vec{s}')\mathrm{d}s'} \left(\frac{\mathrm{d}L(\vec{s}, \hat{\omega})}{\mathrm{d}s} + \kappa_t(\vec{s}) L(\vec{s}, \hat{\omega}) \right) \\
&= \frac{\mathrm{d}}{\mathrm{d}s} \left[e^{\int_{s_b}^{s} \kappa_t(\vec{s}')\mathrm{d}s'} L(\vec{s}, \hat{\omega}) \right]
\end{aligned}
\qquad (11.108)
$$

461

such that integrating both sides from s_b to s_c gives

$$\begin{aligned}\int_{s_b}^{s_c} e^{\int_{s_b}^{s}\kappa_t(\vec{s}')\mathrm{d}s'}\kappa_t(\vec{s})L_u(\vec{s},\hat{\omega})\mathrm{d}s &= \int_{s_b}^{s_c}\frac{\mathrm{d}}{\mathrm{d}s}\left[e^{\int_{s_b}^{s}\kappa_t(\vec{s}')\mathrm{d}s'}L(\vec{s},\hat{\omega})\right]\mathrm{d}s \\ &= \left[e^{\int_{s_b}^{s}\kappa_t(\vec{s}')\mathrm{d}s'}L(\vec{s},\hat{\omega})\right]_{s_b}^{s_c} \\ &= e^{\int_{s_b}^{s_c}\kappa_t(\vec{s}')\mathrm{d}s'}L(\vec{s}_c,\hat{\omega})-L(\vec{s}_b,\hat{\omega}) \qquad (11.109)\end{aligned}$$

461 Rearranging the terms finally yields an integral form of the *radiative transport equation* that integrates contributions from the background boundary condition to the sensor, following the direction of propagation of physical light

$$\begin{aligned}L(\vec{s}_c,\hat{\omega}) &= e^{-\int_{s_b}^{s_c}\kappa_t(\vec{s}')\mathrm{d}s'}L(\vec{s}_b,\hat{\omega})+\int_{s_b}^{s_c}e^{-\int_{s}^{s_c}\kappa_t(\vec{s}')\mathrm{d}s'}\kappa_t(\vec{s})L_u(\vec{s},\hat{\omega})\mathrm{d}s \\ &= \underbrace{T(\vec{s}_b,\vec{s}_c)L(\vec{s}_b,\hat{\omega})}_{L_r(\vec{s}_b,\vec{s}_c,\hat{\omega})}+\underbrace{\int_{s_b}^{s_c}T(\vec{s},\vec{s}_c)\kappa_t(\vec{s})L_u(\vec{s},\hat{\omega})\mathrm{d}s}_{L_m(\vec{s}_b,\vec{s}_c,\hat{\omega})} \qquad (11.110)\end{aligned}$$

Alternatively, inverting the orientation of the axis so as to change the sign of ds in the differential form of the RTE, and then rearranging the terms and multiplying both sides by $T(\vec{p}+s_a\hat{\omega},\vec{p}+s\hat{\omega})$, yields

461

$$\begin{aligned}e^{-\int_{s_a}^{s}\kappa_t(\vec{s}')\mathrm{d}s'}\kappa_t(\vec{s})L_u(\vec{s},\hat{\omega}) &\overset{(11.87)}{=} e^{-\int_{s_a}^{s}\kappa_t(\vec{s}')\mathrm{d}s'}\left(-\frac{\mathrm{d}L(\vec{s},\hat{\omega})}{\mathrm{d}s}+\kappa_t(\vec{s})L(\vec{s},\hat{\omega})\right) \\ &= \frac{\mathrm{d}}{\mathrm{d}s}\left[-e^{-\int_{s_a}^{s}\kappa_t(\vec{s}')\mathrm{d}s'}L(\vec{s},\hat{\omega})\right] \qquad (11.111)\end{aligned}$$

such that integrating both sides from s_a to s_b gives

$$\begin{aligned}\int_{s_a}^{s_b}e^{-\int_{s_a}^{s}\kappa_t(\vec{s}')\mathrm{d}s'}\kappa_t(\vec{s})L_u(\vec{s},\hat{\omega})\mathrm{d}s &= \int_{s_a}^{s_b}\frac{\mathrm{d}}{\mathrm{d}s}\left[-e^{-\int_{s_a}^{s}\kappa_t(\vec{s}')\mathrm{d}s'}L(\vec{s},\hat{\omega})\right]\mathrm{d}s \\ &= \left[-e^{-\int_{s_a}^{s}\kappa_t(\vec{s}')\mathrm{d}s'}L(\vec{s},\hat{\omega})\right]_{s_a}^{s_b} \\ &= -e^{-\int_{s_a}^{s_b}\kappa_t(\vec{s}')\mathrm{d}\vec{s}'}L(\vec{s}_b,\hat{\omega})+L(\vec{s}_a,\hat{\omega}) \qquad (11.112)\end{aligned}$$

461 Rearranging the terms finally yields an integral form of the *radiative transport equation* that integrates contributions from the sensor to the background boundary condition, in order of decreasing potential

$$\begin{aligned}L(\vec{s}_a,\hat{\omega}) &= \int_{s_a}^{s_b}e^{-\int_{s_a}^{s}\kappa_t(\vec{s}')\mathrm{d}s'}\kappa_t(\vec{s})L_u(\vec{s},\hat{\omega})\mathrm{d}s+e^{-\int_{s_a}^{s_b}\kappa_t(\vec{s}')\mathrm{d}s'}L(\vec{s}_b,\hat{\omega}) \\ &= \underbrace{\int_{s_a}^{s_b}T(\vec{s}_a,\vec{s})\kappa_t(\vec{s})L_u(\vec{s},\hat{\omega})\mathrm{d}s}_{L_m(\vec{s}_a,\vec{s}_b,\hat{\omega})}+\underbrace{T(\vec{s}_a,\vec{s}_b)L(\vec{s}_b,\hat{\omega})}_{L_r(\vec{s}_a,\vec{s}_b,\hat{\omega})} \qquad (11.113)\end{aligned}$$

Both integral forms express the radiance reaching the sensor in terms of the background
462 radiance attenuated by *Beer's law*, which is referred to as the *reduced radiance* $L_r(\vec{s}_0,\vec{s}_1,\hat{\omega})$, and the contributions of the source term within the medium itself, which is referred to as the *medium radiance* $L_m(\vec{s}_0,\vec{s}_1,\hat{\omega})$. Using the chain rule [Max *et al.*, 1990] and applying

integration by parts, the latter may alternatively be formulated as

$$
\begin{aligned}
L_m(\vec{s}_a, \vec{s}_b, \hat{\omega}) &= \int_{s_a}^{s_b} T(\vec{s}_a, \vec{s})\kappa_t(\vec{s})L_u(\vec{s}, \hat{\omega})\mathrm{d}s && (11.114)\\
&\overset{(11.98)}{=} \int_{s_a}^{s_b} e^{-\int_{s_a}^{s} \kappa_t(\vec{s}')\mathrm{d}s'}\kappa_t(\vec{s})L_u(\vec{s}, \hat{\omega})\mathrm{d}s\\
&= \int_{s_a}^{s_b} -\frac{\mathrm{d}e^{-\int_{s_a}^{s} \kappa_t(\vec{s}')\mathrm{d}s'}}{\mathrm{d}s}L_u(\vec{s}, \hat{\omega})\mathrm{d}s\\
&= -\left[e^{-\int_{s_a}^{s} \kappa_t(\vec{s}')\mathrm{d}s'}L_u(\vec{s}, \hat{\omega})\right]_{s_a}^{s_b} + \int_{s_a}^{s_b} e^{-\int_{s_a}^{s} \kappa_t(\vec{s}')\mathrm{d}s'}\frac{\mathrm{d}L_u(\vec{s}, \hat{\omega})}{\mathrm{d}s}\mathrm{d}s\\
&= L_u(\vec{s}_a, \hat{\omega}) - e^{-\int_{s_a}^{s_b} \kappa_t(\vec{s}')\mathrm{d}s'}L_u(\vec{s}_b, \hat{\omega}) + \int_{s_a}^{s_b} e^{-\int_{s_a}^{s} \kappa_t(\vec{s}')\mathrm{d}s'}\mathrm{d}L_u(\vec{s}, \hat{\omega})\\
&\overset{(11.98)}{=} L_u(\vec{s}_a, \hat{\omega}) - T(\vec{s}_a, \vec{s}_b)L_u(\vec{s}_b, \hat{\omega}) + \int_{s_a}^{s_b} T(\vec{s}_a, \vec{s})\mathrm{d}L_u(\vec{s}, \hat{\omega}) && (11.115)
\end{aligned}
$$

463 463

11.5 TRANSPORT REGIMES

11.5.1 Absorption

Assuming that emission and scattering are negligible, the differential form of the RTE becomes

$$\frac{\mathrm{d}L(\vec{s}, \hat{\omega})}{\mathrm{d}s} \overset{(11.87)}{=} -\kappa_a(\vec{s})L(\vec{s}, \hat{\omega}) \tag{11.116}$$ 461

and substituting $L_e(\vec{s}, \hat{\omega}) = 0$ and $\kappa_s(\vec{s}) = 0$ into its integral form then yields

$$L(\vec{s}_a, \hat{\omega}) \overset{(11.113)}{=} T(\vec{s}_a, \vec{s}_b)L(\vec{s}_b, \hat{\omega}) \tag{11.117}$$ 466

As illustrated in *Figure 11.16*, the radiance emanating from a purely absorptive medium consequently consists solely of the attenuated background radiation, which must therefore be luminous in order for the radiance reaching the sensor to be non-zero. Because all values along the ray equally contribute to the final attenuation, no self-occlusion occurs, hence allowing a see-through visualization of a volume as in fluoroscopic medical images, whose negative yields the more familiar X-ray images. 469

11.5.2 Emission

Assuming that scattering is negligible, and considering the limit where absorption is infinitely low and emission infinitely high in a compensating manner such that the *emission coefficient* $j(\vec{s}, \hat{\omega}) = \kappa_a(\vec{s})L_e(\vec{s}, \hat{\omega})$ (in J·s^{-1}·m^{-3}·sr^{-1}) tends towards a finite value, the differential form of the RTE becomes

$$\frac{\mathrm{d}L(\vec{s}, \hat{\omega})}{\mathrm{d}s} \overset{(11.87)}{=} j(\vec{s}, \hat{\omega}) \tag{11.118}$$ 461

and substituting $\kappa_s(\vec{s}) = 0$ and $\kappa_a(\vec{s}) \to 0$, such that the transmittance equals one, and $\kappa_a(\vec{s})L_e(\vec{s}, \hat{\omega}) = j(\vec{s}, \hat{\omega})$ into its integral form then yields

$$L(\vec{s}_a, \hat{\omega}) \overset{(11.113)}{=} \int_{s_a}^{s_b} j(\vec{s}, \hat{\omega})\mathrm{d}s + L(\vec{s}_b, \hat{\omega}) \tag{11.119}$$ 466

As illustrated in *Figure 11.16*, the radiance emanating from a purely emissive medium 469 consequently consists of the background radiance to which the integrated contributions from the medium are added in a purely cumulative manner. Because all values along the ray equally contribute to the final exitant radiance, no self-occlusion occurs, hence allowing a see-through visualization of a volume as observed in highly transparent emitting media such as auroras.

11.5.3 Absorption and Emission

Assuming that scattering is negligible, the differential form of the RTE becomes

461 $$\frac{\mathrm{d}L(\vec{s},\hat{\omega})}{\mathrm{d}s} \overset{(11.87)}{=} \kappa_a(\vec{s})\big(L_e(\vec{s},\hat{\omega}) - L(\vec{s},\hat{\omega})\big) \tag{11.120}$$

and substituting $\kappa_s(\vec{s}) = 0$ into its integral form then yields

466 $$L(\vec{s}_a,\hat{\omega}) \overset{(11.113)}{=} \int_{s_a}^{s_b} T(\vec{s}_a,\vec{s})\kappa_a(\vec{s})L_e(\vec{s},\hat{\omega})\mathrm{d}s + T(\vec{s}_a,\vec{s}_b)L(\vec{s}_b,\hat{\omega}) \tag{11.121}$$

469 As illustrated in *Figure 11.16*, the radiance emanating from a purely absorptive-emissive medium consequently consists of a weighted mixture of the contributions along the ray, whose weight decreases as the distance from the sensor increases. Because all values along the ray do not equally contribute to the final exitant radiance, partial occlusion phenomena occur, hence providing information about the spatial ordering of the volumetric data.

11.5.4 Scattering

Assuming that absorption is negligible, the differential form of the RTE becomes

461 $$\frac{\mathrm{d}L(\vec{s},\hat{\omega})}{\mathrm{d}s} \overset{(11.87)}{=} \kappa_s(\vec{s})\big(L_p(\vec{s},\hat{\omega}) - L(\vec{s},\hat{\omega})\big) \tag{11.122}$$

and substituting $\kappa_a(\vec{s}) = 0$ into its integral form then yields

466 $$L(\vec{s}_a,\hat{\omega}) \overset{(11.113)}{=} \int_{s_a}^{s_b} T(\vec{s}_a,\vec{s})\kappa_s(\vec{s})L_p(\vec{s},\hat{\omega})\mathrm{d}s + T(\vec{s}_a,\vec{s}_b)L(\vec{s}_b,\hat{\omega}) \tag{11.123}$$

469 As illustrated in *Figure 11.16*, the radiance emanating from a purely scattering medium consequently consists of a weighted mixture of the contributions along the ray, whose weight decreases as the distance from the sensor increases, due to the dual source-extinction nature of scattering. Because all values along the ray do not equally contribute to the final exitant radiance, partial occlusion phenomena occur, hence providing information about the spatial ordering of the volumetric data, as well as additional perceptual cues due to non-local shading which helps better conveying depth information and spatial relationships.

Scattering phenomena may actually be further categorized by splitting the incident radiance within the in-scattered radiance formulation into its reduced and medium contributions such that

444
466 $$L_p(\vec{s},\hat{\omega}) \underset{(11.113)}{\overset{(11.8)}{=}} \int_{4\pi} L_m(\vec{s},\hat{\omega}_i)f_p(\vec{s},\hat{\omega},\hat{\omega}_i)\mathrm{d}\hat{\omega}_i + \int_{4\pi} L_r(\vec{s},\hat{\omega}_i)f_p(\vec{s},\hat{\omega},\hat{\omega}_i)\mathrm{d}\hat{\omega}_i \tag{11.124}$$

In optically thin low-albedo media such as low-density smoke, photons typically undergo very few scattering events and the contributions of the medium radiance in the above equation can consequently be considered negligible, an assumption commonly referred to as *single*

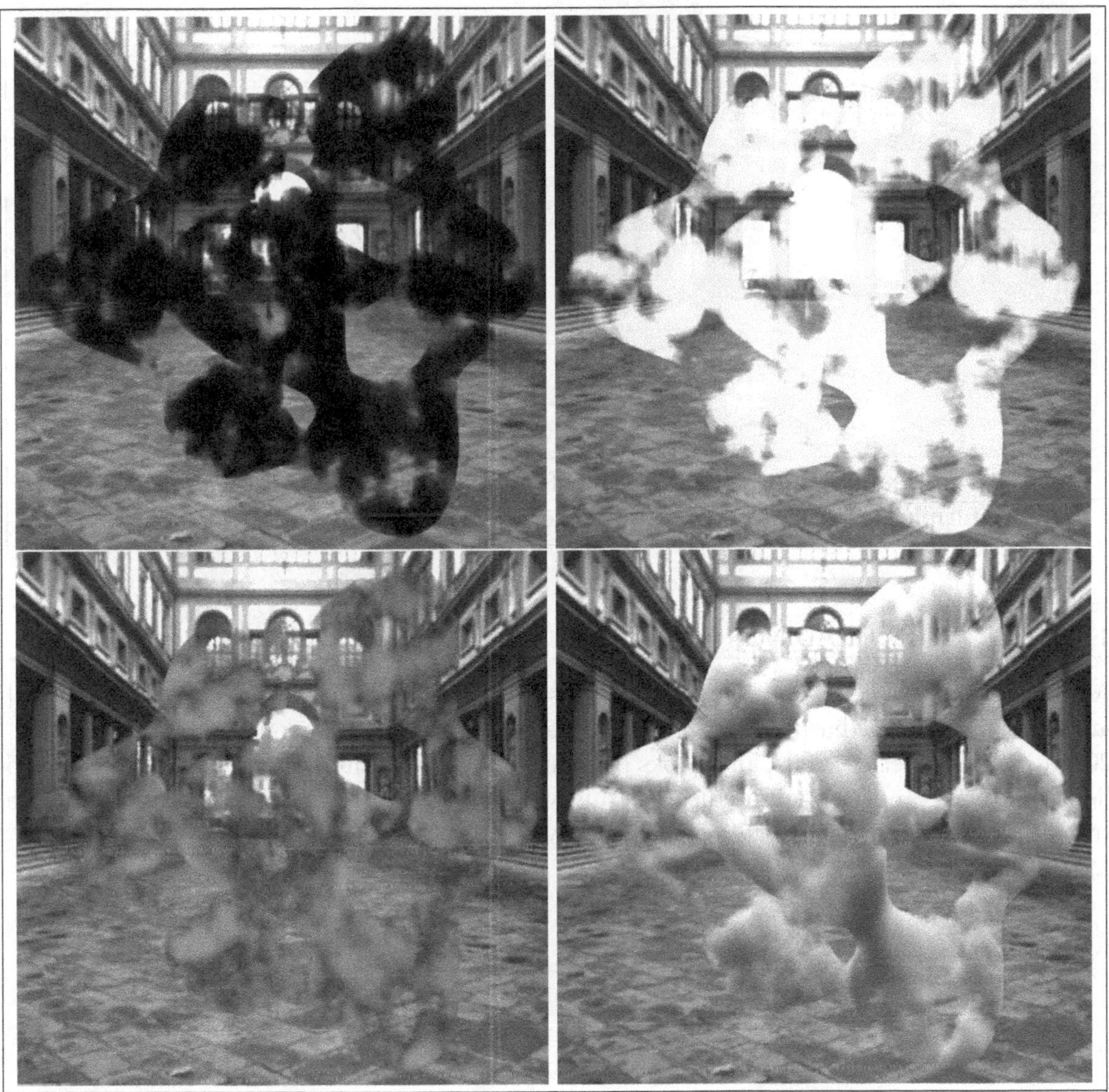

Figure 11.16: Optical Properties: Qualitative appearance of a participating medium whose optical properties are dominated by absorption (top left), emission (top right), absorption and emission (bottom left) and scattering (bottom right) (light probe courtesy of Paul Debevec).

scattering. As the optical thickness and the albedo increase, though, *multiple scattering* becomes increasingly important and higher-order events may be considered by progressively accounting for the medium radiance up to an arbitrary degree of recursion in the integral
equation. As illustrated in *Figure 11.17*, *diffusion* in highly scattering media such as clouds 470
results in a spatial and angular spreading of the incident radiation.

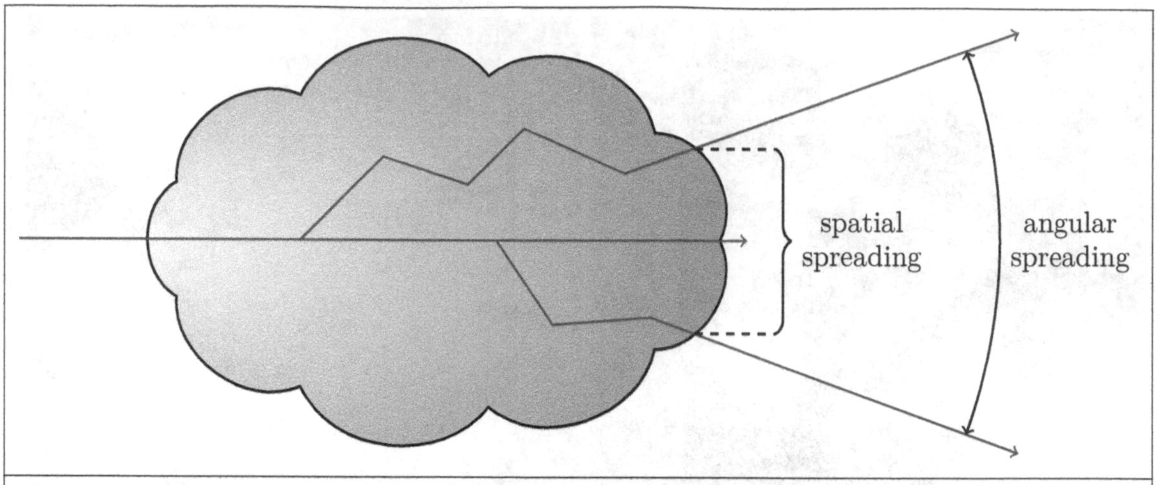

Figure 11.17: **Beam Spreading:** Illustration of the spatial and angular spreading of a beam due to multiple scattering events (drawn after [Premože, 2003, Fig. 8.1]).

11.6 FURTHER READING

Additional material may be found in surveys dedicated to volume rendering [Max, 1995] and participating media [Pérez *et al.*, 1997, Cerezo *et al.*, 2005], in courses [Gutierrez *et al.*, 2008a, Gutierrez *et al.*, 2009] and books [van de Hulst, 1957, van de Hulst, 1980] dedicated to light scattering and in books dedicated to wave propagation [Ishimaru, 1978] and radiative transfer [Chandrasekhar, 1960, Siegel and Howell, 1981, Modest, 2003].

CHAPTER 12

Surface Reflectance

TABLE OF CONTENTS

12.1 APPLICATIONS

As the composition of materials may be inferred from their visual appearance, surface reflectance modeling has come to span a broad range of applications. Within the realm of the entertainment industry [Hoffman *et al.*, 2010, McAuley *et al.*, 2012, McAuley *et al.*, 2013, Hill *et al.*, 2014], those encompass realistic material representations in both film [Borshukov, 2003] and game production, whereas the trade-offs between visual quality and interactive feedback are typically of greater concern for virtual try-on [Wacker *et al.*, 2005] consumer services, digital product design and marketing, as well as in driving simulators [Nakamae *et al.*, 1990].

Physical accuracy is also important in the context of virtual reality [Meseth, 2006] and virtual prototyping [Klein *et al.*, 2003] of automotive paint [Meyer *et al.*, 2005, Meyer and Shimizu, 2005, Meyer, 2009] and car interiors [Schregle *et al.*, 2013], as well as for military camouflage of stealth aircraft from infrared-sensing radars. Broader applications also exist in remote sensing (e.g., of vegetation canopies), and in the field of computer vision where reflectance properties represent a building block of shape-from-shading algorithms, object recognition and surface classification.

12.2 BIDIRECTIONAL DISTRIBUTION FUNCTION

12.2.1 Definition

As the extinction coefficient of a participating medium increases, light penetrates less deeply underneath the surface of the material, progressively exhibiting more localized subsurface scattering as illustrated in *Figure 12.1*. The reflectance properties of a heterogeneous material 473
may then be macroscopically described using an 8-D function known as the *bidirectional scattering-surface reflectance distribution function* (*BSSRDF*) [Nicodemus *et al.*, 1977, ANSI, 2010], which defines the amount of light propagating between a pair of incident position and direction and a pair of exitant position and direction. In the case of a homogeneous material, the effect of subsurface scattering solely depends on the difference between the incident and exitant positions, resulting in a 6-D function known as the *bidirectional subsurface-scattering distribution function* (*BSSDF*).

Figure 12.1: Subsurface Scattering: An isotropic participating medium whose extinction coefficient progressively increases, leading in the limit to a diffuse reflectance distribution due to purely local interaction phenomena (light probe courtesy of Paul Debevec).

As illustrated in *Figure 12.2*, the dependence of mesoscopic subsurface scattering effects 474
on the incident position might alternatively be locally aggregated to yield a 6-D function known as the *bidirectional texture function* (*BTF*) [Müller *et al.*, 2004, Filip and Haindl, 2009], and whose individual texels therefore do not generally represent physically plausible

BRDFs per se. In the limit of a medium with an infinite extinction coefficient, all types of light-matter interaction essentially become purely local phenomena. The reflectance properties of a heterogeneous material may then be described using a 6-D function known as the *spatially varying bidirectional reflectance distribution function* (*SVBRDF*), essentially corresponding to a BRDF with spatially dependent properties.

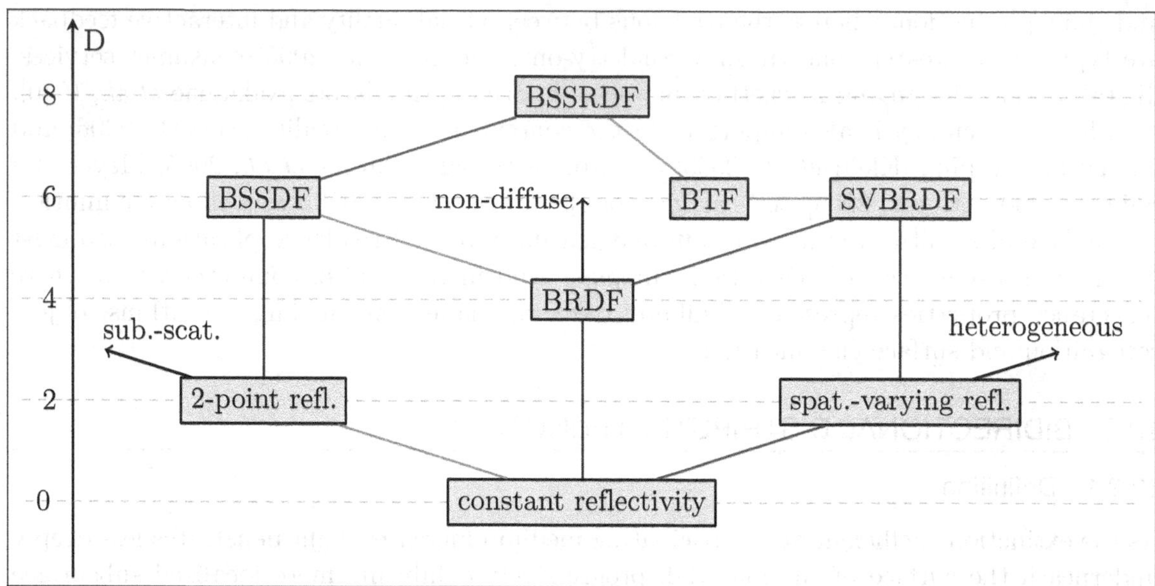

Figure 12.2: Reflectance Nomenclature: Nomenclature of the various reflectance functions (drawn after [Lensch, 2003, Fig. 2.3] and [Lensch *et al.*, 2005, Fig. 3.3]).

Given a dense and homogeneous material, the reflectance properties of the surface in the upper hemisphere $2\pi^+$ can then be macroscopically described using a 4-D function called the *directional–directional reflectance*, also known as the *bidirectional reflectance distribution function* (*BRDF*) [Nicodemus *et al.*, 1977, ANSI, 2010]. In the general case where the reflectance properties vary as the material is rotated around the normal axis, as occurs with velvet, satin and brushed aluminum, for instance, the BRDF is said to be an *anisotropic BRDF* and does depend on all four directional input parameters. In contrast, reflectance properties that are invariant under rotation around the normal are described by a so-called *isotropic BRDF*, which reduces to a 3-D function parameterized by θ_o, θ_i and $|\phi_o - \phi_i|$, while a diffuse BRDF is a 0-D constant reflectivity independent of direction.

Conversely, the distribution of light that is transmitted through a thin slab of material into the lower hemisphere $2\pi^-$ is macroscopically described using a 4-D function known as the *bidirectional transmittance distribution function* (*BTDF*). Combining the BRDF and BTDF of a material then yields a so-called *bidirectional scattering distribution function* (*BSDF*), which describes the aggregate distribution of reflected and transmitted radiation.

It should be noted that the actual dimensionality of the above bidirectional distribution functions is furthermore subject to their dependence on additional parameters. For instance, wavelength dependence and time-varying reflectance characteristics each require an additional parameterization in terms of either the frequency or time, respectively, of
the radiation. Photoluminescence phenomena such as *fluorescence*, causing an incident *elec-*
420 *tromagnetic wave* to be inelastically re-radiated at a longer less energetic wavelength, and
420 *phosphorescence*, causing an incident *electromagnetic wave* to be non-instantly re-radiated,
similarly require a parameterization in terms of either the frequency or time, respectively, of both the incident and exitant radiations.

The reflectance properties of a given material may then be represented either with a
numerical model, by reconstructing previously measured reflectance data samples, or an
analytical model via a mathematical function characterizing the reflectance distribution.
Analytical models are further categorized into *phenomenological models*, which aim at em- 498
pirically capturing via an ad hoc set of intuitive parameters the salient features of a given
observable phenomenon, and physically based models, which are derived by analyzing the
underlying physical mechanisms based on potentially measurable, physically meaningful parameters. Among physically based models can finally be distinguished *turbid models*, which 478
are derived from the equations of radiative transfer in *participating media*, geometric mod- 440
els, which are based on geometrical optics and ray theory, and theoretical models, which are
based on physical optics and wave theory.

12.2.2 Physical Properties

A BRDF describes the hemispherical density distribution of incident radiance upon a surface
scattering event, and it is therefore expressed in inverse units of *solid angle* (sr^{-1}). Mathe- 244
matically, the BRDF is defined as the ratio of the differential reflected radiance in a given
direction to the differential incident irradiance

427

$$f_r(\vec{p}, \hat{\omega}_o, \hat{\omega}_i) \triangleq \frac{\mathrm{d}L_r(\vec{p}, \hat{\omega}_o)}{\mathrm{d}E_i(\vec{p}, \hat{\omega}_i)} \overset{(10.56)}{=} \frac{\mathrm{d}L_r(\vec{p}, \hat{\omega}_o)}{L_i(\vec{p}, \hat{\omega}_i)\langle \hat{n}, \hat{\omega}_i \rangle \mathrm{d}\hat{\omega}_i} \tag{12.1}$$

such that the *reflectance integral* over the upper hemisphere centered around the surface normal $\hat{n}$ reads

$$L_r(\vec{p}, \hat{\omega}_o) = \int_{2\pi^+} L_i(\vec{p}, \hat{\omega}_i) f_r(\vec{p}, \hat{\omega}_o, \hat{\omega}_i) \langle \hat{n}, \hat{\omega}_i \rangle \mathrm{d}\hat{\omega}_i = \rho(\vec{p}, \hat{\omega}_o) L_k(\vec{p}, \hat{\omega}_o) \tag{12.2}$$

with the kernel radiance

$$L_k(\vec{p}, \hat{\omega}_o) \triangleq \int_{2\pi^+} L_i(\vec{p}, \hat{\omega}_i) f_k(\vec{p}, \hat{\omega}_o, \hat{\omega}_i) \mathrm{d}\hat{\omega}_i \tag{12.3}$$

and the scattering kernel

$$f_k(\vec{p}, \hat{\omega}_o, \hat{\omega}_i) \triangleq \frac{f_r(\vec{p}, \hat{\omega}_o, \hat{\omega}_i) \langle \hat{n}, \hat{\omega}_i \rangle}{\rho(\vec{p}, \hat{\omega}_o)} \tag{12.4}$$

normalized such that

$$\int_{2\pi^+} f_k(\vec{p}, \hat{\omega}_o, \hat{\omega}_i) \mathrm{d}\hat{\omega}_i \overset{(12.4)}{=} \frac{1}{\rho(\vec{p}, \hat{\omega}_o)} \int_{2\pi^+} f_r(\vec{p}, \hat{\omega}_o, \hat{\omega}_i) \langle \hat{n}, \hat{\omega}_i \rangle \mathrm{d}\hat{\omega}_i \overset{(12.9)}{=} 1 \tag{12.5}$$

475
476

Based on Kirchoff's law of thermal radiation, the radiance emitted by the surface may instead be formulated as [Wilkie and Weidlich, 2011]

$$L_e(\vec{p}, \hat{\omega}_o) \overset{(10.73)}{=} \epsilon(\vec{p}, \hat{\omega}_o) L_e(T_p) \overset{(10.75)}{=} \alpha(\vec{p}, \hat{\omega}_o) L_e(T_p) \overset{(12.13)}{=} (1 - \rho(\vec{p}, \hat{\omega}_o)) L_e(T_p) \tag{12.6}$$

429
429
476

The total exitant radiance is then defined by the *rendering equation* [Kajiya, 1986] as

$$\begin{aligned} L_o(\vec{p}, \hat{\omega}_o) &\triangleq L_e(\vec{p}, \hat{\omega}_o) + L_r(\vec{p}, \hat{\omega}_o) && (12.7) \\ &\underset{(12.2)}{\overset{(12.6)}{=}} (1 - \rho(\vec{p}, \hat{\omega}_o)) L_e(T_p) + \rho(\vec{p}, \hat{\omega}_o) L_k(\vec{p}, \hat{\omega}_o) && (12.8) \end{aligned}$$

475
475

Integrating the BRDF and the cosine angle over the whole hemispherical domain $[0, 2\pi] \times [0, \pi/2]$ yields the so-called *directional–hemispherical reflectance*, more commonly referred to as the *albedo* or *reflectivity*, defined as

$$\rho(\vec{p}, \hat{\omega}) \triangleq \int_{2\pi^+} f_r(\vec{p}, \hat{\omega}, \hat{\omega}') \langle \hat{n}, \hat{\omega}' \rangle \mathrm{d}\hat{\omega}' \tag{12.9}$$

244

$$\overset{(6.63)}{=} \int_0^{2\pi} \int_0^{\frac{\pi}{2}} f_r(\vec{p}, \hat{\omega}, \theta, \phi) \cos(\theta) \sin(\theta) \mathrm{d}\theta \mathrm{d}\phi \tag{12.10}$$

244

$$\overset{(6.64)}{=} \int_0^{2\pi} \int_0^1 f_r(\vec{p}, \hat{\omega}, \arccos(\mu), \phi) \mu \mathrm{d}\mu \mathrm{d}\phi \tag{12.11}$$

244

$$\overset{(6.65)}{=} \int_0^{2\pi} \int_0^1 f_r(\vec{p}, \hat{\omega}, \arcsin(\rho), \phi) \rho \mathrm{d}\rho \mathrm{d}\phi \tag{12.12}$$

77
70 where $\mu \triangleq \langle \hat{n}, \hat{\omega}' \rangle \overset{(3.77)}{=} \cos(\theta) = \sqrt{1 - \sin(\theta)^2} \overset{(3.25)}{=} \sqrt{1 - \rho^2}$, thereby implicitly encompassing the cosine term within the projection of the hemispherical domain onto the underlying unit disc. The resulting aggregate reflectance actually corresponds to the radiance reflected off a surface placed in a furnace, where the incident radiance is a unit constant. Because closed-form expressions for the albedo of different types of BRDFs are not always readily available, the analytic evaluation is generally limited to that of an upper bound, while the 2-D tabulation of sample values of the albedo typically requires the use of numerical integration schemes. Conversely, the ratio of absorbed to incident radiance is given by the *directional absorptance*, also called *directional absorptivity*,

$$\alpha(\vec{p}, \hat{\omega}) \triangleq 1 - \rho(\vec{p}, \hat{\omega}) \tag{12.13}$$

The *hemispherical–hemispherical reflectance*, or *mean albedo*, is then defined as

$$\rho(\vec{p}) \triangleq \frac{\int_{2\pi^+} \rho(\vec{p}, \hat{\omega}) \langle \hat{n}, \hat{\omega} \rangle \mathrm{d}\hat{\omega}}{\int_{2\pi^+} \langle \hat{n}, \hat{\omega} \rangle \mathrm{d}\hat{\omega}} = \frac{1}{\pi} \int_{2\pi^+} \rho(\vec{p}, \hat{\omega}) \langle \hat{n}, \hat{\omega} \rangle \mathrm{d}\hat{\omega} \tag{12.14}$$

and the *hemispherical absorptance*, also called *hemispherical absorptivity*, as

$$\begin{aligned} \alpha(\vec{p}) &\triangleq \frac{1}{\pi} \int_{2\pi^+} \alpha(\vec{p}, \hat{\omega}) \langle \hat{n}, \hat{\omega} \rangle \mathrm{d}\hat{\omega} && (12.15) \\ &= \frac{1}{\pi} \int_{2\pi^+} (1 - \rho(\vec{p}, \hat{\omega})) \langle \hat{n}, \hat{\omega} \rangle \mathrm{d}\hat{\omega} \\ &= \frac{1}{\pi} \int_{2\pi^+} \langle \hat{n}, \hat{\omega} \rangle \mathrm{d}\hat{\omega} - \frac{1}{\pi} \int_{2\pi^+} \rho(\vec{p}, \hat{\omega}) \langle \hat{n}, \hat{\omega} \rangle \mathrm{d}\hat{\omega} \\ &= 1 - \rho(\vec{p}) && (12.16) \end{aligned}$$

such that, in the case of an isotropic albedo, the following equalities hold

$$\begin{aligned} \rho(\vec{p}) &= \rho(\vec{p}, \hat{\omega}) && (12.17) \\ \alpha(\vec{p}) &= \alpha(\vec{p}, \hat{\omega}) && (12.18) \end{aligned}$$

In order to be physically plausible [Lewis, 1994], a BRDF must be non-negative (such that the surface does not reflect anti-radiation)

$$f_r(\vec{p}, \hat{\omega}_o, \hat{\omega}_i) \geq 0, \quad \forall \hat{\omega}_o, \hat{\omega}_i \in 2\pi^+ \tag{12.19}$$

fulfill the *Helmholtz reciprocity rule* [von Helmholtz, 1867] (such that reverting the direction of propagation by exchanging the locations of a source and a sensor leaves the ratio of reflected radiation unaffected)

$$f_r(\vec{p}, \hat{\omega}_o, \hat{\omega}_i) = f_r(\vec{p}, \hat{\omega}_i, \hat{\omega}_o), \quad \forall \hat{\omega}_o, \hat{\omega}_i \in 2\pi^+ \tag{12.20}$$

and obey *energy conservation* [Neumann *et al.*, 1998a, Neumann *et al.*, 1999b] (such that the radiant flux density reflected by the surface isn't greater than the irradiance incident upon it)

$$\frac{B_r(\vec{p})}{E(\vec{p})} \overset{(10.50)}{=} \frac{\int_{2\pi^+} L_r(\vec{p}, \hat{\omega}_o)\langle \hat{n}, \hat{\omega}_o\rangle \mathrm{d}\hat{\omega}_o}{\int_{2\pi^+} L_i(\vec{p}, \hat{\omega}_i)\langle \hat{n}, \hat{\omega}_i\rangle \mathrm{d}\hat{\omega}_i}$$ 426

$$\overset{(12.2)}{=} \frac{\int_{2\pi^+}\int_{2\pi^+} L_i(\vec{p}, \hat{\omega}_i) f_r(\vec{p}, \hat{\omega}_o, \hat{\omega}_i)\langle \hat{n}, \hat{\omega}_i\rangle \mathrm{d}\hat{\omega}_i \langle \hat{n}, \hat{\omega}_o\rangle \mathrm{d}\hat{\omega}_o}{\int_{2\pi^+} L_i(\vec{p}, \hat{\omega}_i)\langle \hat{n}, \hat{\omega}_i\rangle \mathrm{d}\hat{\omega}_i}$$ 475

$$= \frac{\int_{2\pi^+} L_i(\vec{p}, \hat{\omega}_i) \int_{2\pi^+} f_r(\vec{p}, \hat{\omega}_o, \hat{\omega}_i)\langle \hat{n}, \hat{\omega}_o\rangle \mathrm{d}\hat{\omega}_o \langle \hat{n}, \hat{\omega}_i\rangle \mathrm{d}\hat{\omega}_i}{\int_{2\pi^+} L_i(\vec{p}, \hat{\omega}_i)\langle \hat{n}, \hat{\omega}_i\rangle \mathrm{d}\hat{\omega}_i}$$

$$\overset{(12.9)}{=} \frac{\int_{2\pi^+} L_i(\vec{p}, \hat{\omega}_i)\rho(\vec{p}, \hat{\omega}_i)\langle \hat{n}, \hat{\omega}_i\rangle \mathrm{d}\hat{\omega}_i}{\int_{2\pi^+} L_i(\vec{p}, \hat{\omega}_i)\langle \hat{n}, \hat{\omega}_i\rangle \mathrm{d}\hat{\omega}_i}$$ 476

$$\leq 1 \tag{12.21}$$

for an arbitrary incident radiance, therefore leading to $\rho(\vec{p}, \hat{\omega}) \in [0, 1], \forall \hat{\omega} \in 2\pi^+$ and $\alpha(\vec{p}, \hat{\omega}) \in [0, 1], \forall \hat{\omega} \in 2\pi^+$, while in a furnace, where $L_i(\vec{p}, \hat{\omega}_i) = 1$, it holds that $\rho(\vec{p}) \overset{(12.14)}{=} \frac{B_r(\vec{p})}{E(\vec{p})}$ and 476
$\alpha(\vec{p}) \overset{(12.15)}{=} \frac{E(\vec{p})-B_r(\vec{p})}{E(\vec{p})}$. 476

In the more general case of a non-opaque surface, the above properties similarly apply to the BSDF

$$f_s(\vec{p}, \hat{\omega}_o, \hat{\omega}_i) \triangleq \begin{cases} f_r(\vec{p}, \hat{\omega}_o, \hat{\omega}_i) & \text{if } \langle \hat{n}, \hat{\omega}_o\rangle\langle \hat{n}, \hat{\omega}_i\rangle \geq 0 \\ f_t(\vec{p}, \hat{\omega}_o, \hat{\omega}_i) & \text{otherwise} \end{cases} \tag{12.22}$$

$$= \frac{f_r(\vec{p}, \hat{\omega}_o, \hat{\omega}_i)\max\{\langle \hat{n}, \hat{\omega}_i\rangle, 0\} + f_t(\vec{p}, \hat{\omega}_o, \hat{\omega}_i)\max\{\langle \hat{n}, -\hat{\omega}_i\rangle, 0\}}{|\langle \hat{n}, \hat{\omega}_i\rangle|} \tag{12.23}$$

or alternatively $f_s(\vec{p}, \hat{\omega}_o, \hat{\omega}_i) = f_r(\vec{p}, \hat{\omega}_o, \hat{\omega}_i) + f_t(\vec{p}, \hat{\omega}_o, \hat{\omega}_i)$ where

$$f_r(\vec{p}, \hat{\omega}_o, \hat{\omega}_i) = 0, \quad \text{if } \langle \hat{n}, \hat{\omega}_o\rangle\langle \hat{n}, \hat{\omega}_i\rangle \leq 0 \tag{12.24}$$

$$f_t(\vec{p}, \hat{\omega}_o, \hat{\omega}_i) = 0, \quad \text{if } \langle \hat{n}, \hat{\omega}_o\rangle\langle \hat{n}, \hat{\omega}_i\rangle \geq 0 \tag{12.25}$$

for which the reciprocity rule generalizes to

$$\frac{f_s(\vec{p}, \hat{\omega}_o, \hat{\omega}_i)}{n_o^2} = \frac{f_s(\vec{p}, \hat{\omega}_i, \hat{\omega}_o)}{n_i^2}, \quad \forall \hat{\omega}_o, \hat{\omega}_i \in 4\pi^+ \tag{12.26}$$

with n_o and n_i being the refractive indices of the exitant and incident media, respectively.

The scattered radiance then reads

$$L_s(\vec{p}, \hat{\omega}_o) \triangleq \int_{4\pi} L_i(\vec{p}, \hat{\omega}_i) f_s(\vec{p}, \hat{\omega}_o, \hat{\omega}_i)|\langle \hat{n}, \hat{\omega}_i\rangle| \mathrm{d}\hat{\omega}_i \tag{12.27}$$

$$\begin{aligned} &= \int_{4\pi} L_i(\vec{p}, \hat{\omega}_i) f_r(\vec{p}, \hat{\omega}_o, \hat{\omega}_i)\max\{\langle \hat{n}, \hat{\omega}_i\rangle, 0\} \mathrm{d}\hat{\omega}_i \\ &+ \int_{4\pi} L_i(\vec{p}, \hat{\omega}_i) f_t(\vec{p}, \hat{\omega}_o, \hat{\omega}_i)\max\{\langle \hat{n}, -\hat{\omega}_i\rangle, 0\} \mathrm{d}\hat{\omega}_i \\ &= L_r(\vec{p}, \hat{\omega}_o) + L_t(\vec{p}, \hat{\omega}_o) \end{aligned} \tag{12.28}$$

with the reflected and transmitted radiances defined as

475
$$L_r(\vec{p},\hat{\omega}_o) \overset{(12.2)}{=} \int_{2\pi^+} L_i(\vec{p},\hat{\omega}_i) f_r(\vec{p},\hat{\omega}_o,\hat{\omega}_i)\langle\hat{n},\hat{\omega}_i\rangle \mathrm{d}\hat{\omega}_i \tag{12.29}$$
$$L_t(\vec{p},\hat{\omega}_o) \triangleq \int_{2\pi^-} L_i(\vec{p},\hat{\omega}_i) f_t(\vec{p},\hat{\omega}_o,\hat{\omega}_i)\langle\hat{n},-\hat{\omega}_i\rangle \mathrm{d}\hat{\omega}_i \tag{12.30}$$

155 131 Ideal *importance sampling* of a BSDF is given by the sub-critical *probability density*

$$p(\vec{p},\hat{\omega}_o,\hat{\omega}_i) \propto f_s(\vec{p},\hat{\omega}_o,\hat{\omega}_i)|\langle\hat{n},\hat{\omega}_i\rangle| \tag{12.31}$$

which, after normalization, reads

$$p(\vec{p},\hat{\omega}_o,\hat{\omega}_i) = \frac{f_s(\vec{p},\hat{\omega}_o,\hat{\omega}_i)|\langle\hat{n},\hat{\omega}_i\rangle|}{\rho(\vec{p},\hat{\omega}_o)} \tag{12.32}$$

12.3 TURBID MODELS

A partially translucent material is referred to as a *turbid material* whenever all subsurface light transport phenomena occur locally at a microscopic scale. Under various assumptions and/or approximations, the reflectance and transmittance properties of the material may
440 then be analytically derived from the equation of radiative transfer in *participating media* [Premože, 2002].

12.3.1 Kubelka–Munk

Given a non-emissive diffuse participating medium such as pigmented paint, the *Kubelka–Munk theory* [Kubelka and Munk, 1931] models light transport within a uniformly illuminated plane-parallel coating layer as a 1-D two-stream process assuming that light (whether incident from the source, transmitted through the medium, scattered by the pigment particles or reflected off the substrate) can only propagate downward or upward, and where the in-scattered radiance of one stream is defined by the radiance of the other stream (presumably
444 due to a forward Dirac *phase function*), yielding the following differential equations

461
$$-\frac{\mathrm{d}L(\vec{s},\hat{\omega})}{\mathrm{d}s} \overset{(11.87)}{=} -\kappa_t(\vec{s})L(\vec{s},\hat{\omega}) + \kappa_s(\vec{s})L(\vec{s},-\hat{\omega}) \tag{12.33}$$
461
$$\frac{\mathrm{d}L(\vec{s},-\hat{\omega})}{\mathrm{d}s} \overset{(11.87)}{=} -\kappa_t(\vec{s})L(\vec{s},-\hat{\omega}) + \kappa_s(\vec{s})L(\vec{s},\hat{\omega}) \tag{12.34}$$

479 where the distance s is measured from the substrate, as illustrated in *Figure 12.3*.

Dividing by the radiance terms and adding the two equations then yields

$$\begin{aligned}
\frac{\frac{\mathrm{d}L(\vec{s},-\hat{\omega})}{\mathrm{d}s}}{L(\vec{s},-\hat{\omega})} - \frac{\frac{\mathrm{d}L(\vec{s},\hat{\omega})}{\mathrm{d}s}}{L(\vec{s},\hat{\omega})} &= \frac{\mathrm{d}\ln(L(\vec{s},-\hat{\omega}))}{\mathrm{d}s} - \frac{\mathrm{d}\ln(L(\vec{s},\hat{\omega}))}{\mathrm{d}s} \\
&= \frac{\mathrm{d}\Big(\ln(L(\vec{s},-\hat{\omega})) - \ln(L(\vec{s},\hat{\omega}))\Big)}{\mathrm{d}s} \\
&= -2\kappa_t(\vec{s}) + \kappa_s(\vec{s})\left(\frac{L(\vec{s},-\hat{\omega})}{L(\vec{s},\hat{\omega})} + \frac{L(\vec{s},\hat{\omega})}{L(\vec{s},-\hat{\omega})}\right)
\end{aligned} \tag{12.35}$$

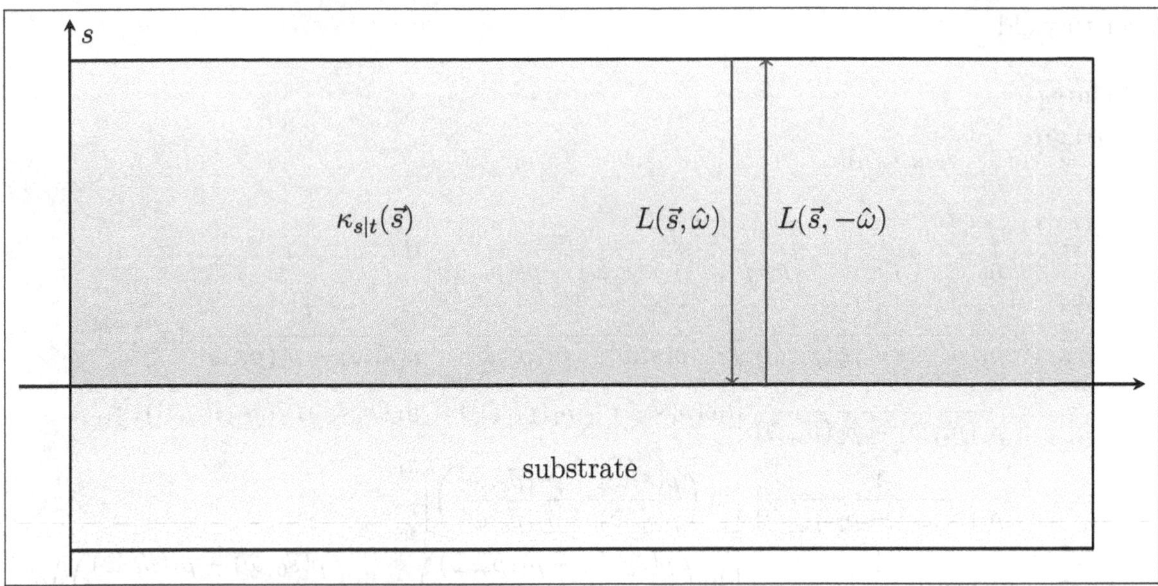

Figure 12.3: Kubelka–Munk Theory: Illustration of the geometric terms involved in computing the albedo of a thin layer of non-emissive participating medium as defined by the Kubelka–Munk theory (drawn after [Haase and Meyer, 1992, Fig. 20]).

while defining the surface albedo as $\rho(\vec{s},\hat{\omega}) = \frac{L(\vec{s},-\hat{\omega})}{L(\vec{s},\hat{\omega})}$ gives

$$\frac{\mathrm{d}\ln\left(\rho(\vec{s},\hat{\omega})\right)}{\mathrm{d}s} = \frac{\frac{\mathrm{d}\rho(\vec{s},\hat{\omega})}{\mathrm{d}s}}{\rho(\vec{s},\hat{\omega})} = -2\kappa_t(\vec{s}) + \kappa_s(\vec{s})\left(\rho(\vec{s},\hat{\omega}) + \frac{1}{\rho(\vec{s},\hat{\omega})}\right) \tag{12.36}$$

Multiplying both sides by $\frac{\rho(\vec{s},\hat{\omega})}{\kappa_t(\vec{s})}$ and defining the volumetric albedo as $\rho_p(\vec{s}) \overset{(11.6)}{=} \frac{\kappa_s(\vec{s})}{\kappa_t(\vec{s})}$ 443
then yields

$$\begin{aligned}\frac{1}{\kappa_t(\vec{s})}\frac{\mathrm{d}\rho(\vec{s},\hat{\omega})}{\mathrm{d}s} &= \rho_p(\vec{s})\rho(\vec{s},\hat{\omega})^2 - 2\rho(\vec{s},\hat{\omega}) + \rho_p(\vec{s}) \\ &= \left(\rho(\vec{s},\hat{\omega}) - \rho_1(\vec{s},\hat{\omega})\right)\left(\rho(\vec{s},\hat{\omega}) - \rho_2(\vec{s},\hat{\omega})\right)\end{aligned} \tag{12.37}$$

where the reduced discriminant of the quadratic polynomial is $\Delta'(\vec{s}) \overset{(2.103)}{=} 1 - \rho_p(\vec{s})^2 \geq 0$ 29
while its roots read

$$\rho_1(\vec{s},\hat{\omega}) \overset{(2.104)}{=} \frac{1-\sqrt{\Delta'(\vec{s})}}{\rho_p(\vec{s})} \tag{12.38}$$ 29

$$\rho_2(\vec{s},\hat{\omega}) \overset{(2.104)}{=} \frac{1+\sqrt{\Delta'(\vec{s})}}{\rho_p(\vec{s})} \tag{12.39}$$ 29

Assuming that the material is homogeneous in the vicinity of a point $\vec{p}_s$ along the ray such that the volumetric albedo is locally constant [Kubelka, 1954], both sides of the previous equation may then be integrated by partial fraction decomposition over the thickness of the layer to yield

$$\tau(\vec{s}_0, \vec{s}_d)$$

463 $$\stackrel{(11.94)}{=} \int_0^{d(\vec{p}_s)} \kappa_t(\vec{s})\mathrm{d}s$$

479 $$\stackrel{(12.37)}{=} \int_0^{d(\vec{p}_s)} \frac{\frac{\mathrm{d}\rho(\vec{s},\hat{\omega})}{\mathrm{d}s}}{(\rho(\vec{s},\hat{\omega}) - \rho_1(\vec{p}_s,\hat{\omega}))(\rho(\vec{s},\hat{\omega}) - \rho_2(\vec{p}_s,\hat{\omega}))}\mathrm{d}s$$

$$\begin{aligned}
&= \frac{1}{\rho_1(\vec{p}_s,\hat{\omega}) - \rho_2(\vec{p}_s,\hat{\omega})} \int_{\vec{s}_0}^{\vec{s}_d} \frac{1}{\rho(\vec{s},\hat{\omega}) - \rho_1(\vec{p}_s,\hat{\omega})} - \frac{1}{\rho(\vec{s},\hat{\omega}) - \rho_2(\vec{p}_s,\hat{\omega})}\mathrm{d}\rho(\vec{s},\hat{\omega}) \\
&= \frac{1}{\rho_1(\vec{p}_s,\hat{\omega}) - \rho_2(\vec{p}_s,\hat{\omega})} \left[\ln\left(\rho(\vec{s},\hat{\omega}) - \rho_1(\vec{p}_s,\hat{\omega})\right) - \ln\left(\rho(\vec{s},\hat{\omega}) - \rho_2(\vec{p}_s,\hat{\omega})\right)\right]_{\vec{s}_0}^{\vec{s}_d} \\
&= \frac{1}{\rho_1(\vec{p}_s,\hat{\omega}) - \rho_2(\vec{p}_s,\hat{\omega})} \left[\ln\left(\frac{\rho(\vec{s},\hat{\omega}) - \rho_1(\vec{p}_s,\hat{\omega})}{\rho(\vec{s},\hat{\omega}) - \rho_2(\vec{p}_s,\hat{\omega})}\right)\right]_{\vec{s}_0}^{\vec{s}_d} \\
&= \frac{1}{\rho_1(\vec{p}_s,\hat{\omega}) - \rho_2(\vec{p}_s,\hat{\omega})} \left(\ln\left(\frac{\rho(\vec{s}_d,\hat{\omega}) - \rho_1(\vec{p}_s,\hat{\omega})}{\rho(\vec{s}_d,\hat{\omega}) - \rho_2(\vec{p}_s,\hat{\omega})}\right) - \ln\left(\frac{\rho(\vec{s}_0,\hat{\omega}) - \rho_1(\vec{p}_s,\hat{\omega})}{\rho(\vec{s}_0,\hat{\omega}) - \rho_2(\vec{p}_s,\hat{\omega})}\right)\right) \\
&= \frac{1}{\rho_1(\vec{p}_s,\hat{\omega}) - \rho_2(\vec{p}_s,\hat{\omega})} \ln\left(\frac{\rho(\vec{s}_d,\hat{\omega}) - \rho_1(\vec{p}_s,\hat{\omega})}{\rho(\vec{s}_d,\hat{\omega}) - \rho_2(\vec{p}_s,\hat{\omega})}\frac{\rho(\vec{s}_0,\hat{\omega}) - \rho_2(\vec{p}_s,\hat{\omega})}{\rho(\vec{s}_0,\hat{\omega}) - \rho_1(\vec{p}_s,\hat{\omega})}\right) \qquad (12.40)
\end{aligned}$$

where $\rho(\vec{s}_d,\hat{\omega})$ refers to the surface albedo atop the layer and $\rho(\vec{s}_0,\hat{\omega})$ to that of the substrate.

Rearranging the terms then gives

$$\frac{\rho(\vec{s}_d,\hat{\omega}) - \rho_1(\vec{p}_s,\hat{\omega})}{\rho(\vec{s}_d,\hat{\omega}) - \rho_2(\vec{p}_s,\hat{\omega})} = \frac{\rho(\vec{s}_0,\hat{\omega}) - \rho_1(\vec{p}_s,\hat{\omega})}{\rho(\vec{s}_0,\hat{\omega}) - \rho_2(\vec{p}_s,\hat{\omega})} e^{\left(\rho_1(\vec{p}_s,\hat{\omega}) - \rho_2(\vec{p}_s,\hat{\omega})\right)\tau(\vec{s}_0,\vec{s}_d)} \qquad (12.41)$$

and solving for the albedo finally yields

$$\rho(\vec{s}_d,\hat{\omega}) = \frac{\rho_1(\vec{p}_s,\hat{\omega}) - \rho_2(\vec{p}_s,\hat{\omega})\frac{\rho(\vec{s}_0,\hat{\omega}) - \rho_1(\vec{p}_s,\hat{\omega})}{\rho(\vec{s}_0,\hat{\omega}) - \rho_2(\vec{p}_s,\hat{\omega})} e^{\left(\rho_1(\vec{p}_s,\hat{\omega}) - \rho_2(\vec{p}_s,\hat{\omega})\right)\tau(\vec{s}_0,\vec{s}_d)}}{1 - \frac{\rho(\vec{s}_0,\hat{\omega}) - \rho_1(\vec{p}_s,\hat{\omega})}{\rho(\vec{s}_0,\hat{\omega}) - \rho_2(\vec{p}_s,\hat{\omega})} e^{\left(\rho_1(\vec{p}_s,\hat{\omega}) - \rho_2(\vec{p}_s,\hat{\omega})\right)\tau(\vec{s}_0,\vec{s}_d)}} \qquad (12.42)$$

where, in the special case of an infinitely optically thick layer, the exponential terms vanish since $\rho_1(\vec{p}_s,\hat{\omega}) - \rho_2(\vec{p}_s,\hat{\omega}) \le 0$, resulting in $\rho(\vec{s}_\infty,\hat{\omega}) = \rho_1(\vec{p}_s,\hat{\omega}) = \frac{1}{\rho_p(\vec{p}_s)} - \sqrt{\frac{1}{\rho_p(\vec{p}_s)^2} - 1} \in [0,1]$ with $\frac{1}{\rho_p(\vec{p}_s)} = 1 + \frac{\kappa_a(\vec{p}_s)}{\kappa_s(\vec{p}_s)}$.

By considering the actual distribution of the incident light, whose reciprocal cosine angle determines the length of traversal through the layer, the model may also be generalized to yield [Kubelka, 1948b, Kubelka, 1948a]

$$\rho_r(\vec{p}_s,\hat{\omega}_o) = \frac{\rho_p(\vec{p}_s) - \rho(\vec{s}_0,\hat{\omega}) + \rho(\vec{s}_0,\hat{\omega})\sqrt{\Delta'(\vec{p}_s)}\coth\left(\sqrt{\Delta'(\vec{p}_s)}\tau(\vec{s}_0,\vec{s}_d)\right)}{1 - \rho_p(\vec{p}_s)\rho(\vec{s}_0,\hat{\omega}) + \sqrt{\Delta'(\vec{p}_s)}\coth\left(\sqrt{\Delta'(\vec{p}_s)}\tau(\vec{s}_0,\vec{s}_d)\right)} \qquad (12.43)$$

whereas in the case of no substrate such that $\rho(\vec{s}_0,\hat{\omega}) = 0$, the reflective and transmissive albedos, respectively, read

$$\rho_r(\vec{p}_s,\hat{\omega}_o) = \frac{\rho_p(\vec{p}_s)\sinh\left(\sqrt{\Delta'(\vec{p}_s)}\tau(\vec{s}_0,\vec{s}_d)\right)}{\sinh\left(\sqrt{\Delta'(\vec{p}_s)}\tau(\vec{s}_0,\vec{s}_d)\right) + \sqrt{\Delta'(\vec{p}_s)}\cosh\left(\sqrt{\Delta'(\vec{p}_s)}\tau(\vec{s}_0,\vec{s}_d)\right)} \qquad (12.44)$$

$$\rho_t(\vec{p}_s,\hat{\omega}_o) = \frac{\sqrt{\Delta'(\vec{p}_s)}}{\sinh\left(\sqrt{\Delta'(\vec{p}_s)}\tau(\vec{s}_0,\vec{s}_d)\right) + \sqrt{\Delta'(\vec{p}_s)}\cosh\left(\sqrt{\Delta'(\vec{p}_s)}\tau(\vec{s}_0,\vec{s}_d)\right)} \qquad (12.45)$$

which, in the special case of an infinitely optically thick layer, yields the previous formulation of the reflective albedo as the hyperbolic cotangent converges to one, while the transmissive albedo vanishes to zero as both the hyperbolic sine and cosine grow to infinity.

By accounting for the successive interactions of light between layers [Kubelka, 1954], the approach can additionally be extended to multilayer stacks as illustrated in *Figure 12.4.* Using 481
the shorthand notations $R^{\downarrow|\uparrow}$ and $T^{\downarrow|\uparrow}$ to refer to the reflective and transmissive albedos of two individual layers in the downward and upward directions, respectively, their combined albedos are then given by the infinite geometric series

$$\begin{aligned}
\rho_r(\vec{p}_s, \hat{\omega}_o) &= R_1^{\downarrow} + T_1^{\downarrow} R_2^{\downarrow}\Big(T_1^{\uparrow} + R_1^{\uparrow} R_2^{\downarrow}(T_1^{\uparrow} + R_1^{\uparrow} R_2^{\downarrow}(T_1^{\uparrow} + \ldots))\Big) \\
&= R_1^{\downarrow} + T_1^{\downarrow} R_2^{\downarrow} T_1^{\uparrow}(1 + (R_1^{\uparrow} R_2^{\downarrow}) + (R_1^{\uparrow} R_2^{\downarrow})^2 + \ldots) \\
&= R_1^{\downarrow} + T_1^{\downarrow} R_2^{\downarrow} T_1^{\uparrow} \sum_{i=0}^{\infty} (R_1^{\uparrow} R_2^{\downarrow})^i \\
&\overset{(2.11)}{=} R_1^{\downarrow} + T_1^{\downarrow} R_2^{\downarrow} T_1^{\uparrow} \frac{1}{1 - R_1^{\uparrow} R_2^{\downarrow}} \qquad (12.46)
\end{aligned}$$

16

$$\begin{aligned}
\rho_t(\vec{p}_s, \hat{\omega}_o) &= T_1^{\downarrow}\Big(T_2^{\downarrow} + R_2^{\downarrow} R_1^{\uparrow}(T_2^{\downarrow} + R_2^{\downarrow} R_1^{\uparrow}(T_2^{\downarrow} + \ldots))\Big) \\
&= T_1^{\downarrow} T_2^{\downarrow}(1 + (R_2^{\downarrow} R_1^{\uparrow}) + (R_2^{\downarrow} R_1^{\uparrow})^2 + \ldots) \\
&= T_1^{\downarrow} T_2^{\downarrow} \sum_{i=0}^{\infty} (R_2^{\downarrow} R_1^{\uparrow})^i \\
&\overset{(2.11)}{=} T_1^{\downarrow} T_2^{\downarrow} \frac{1}{1 - R_2^{\downarrow} R_1^{\uparrow}} \qquad (12.47)
\end{aligned}$$

16

where the last identities stem from the inequality $|R_1^{\uparrow} R_2^{\downarrow}| < 1$. Regarding the stack of layers as a single meta-layer, the impact of additional layers on the combined albedos may then similarly be evaluated in a recursive fashion.

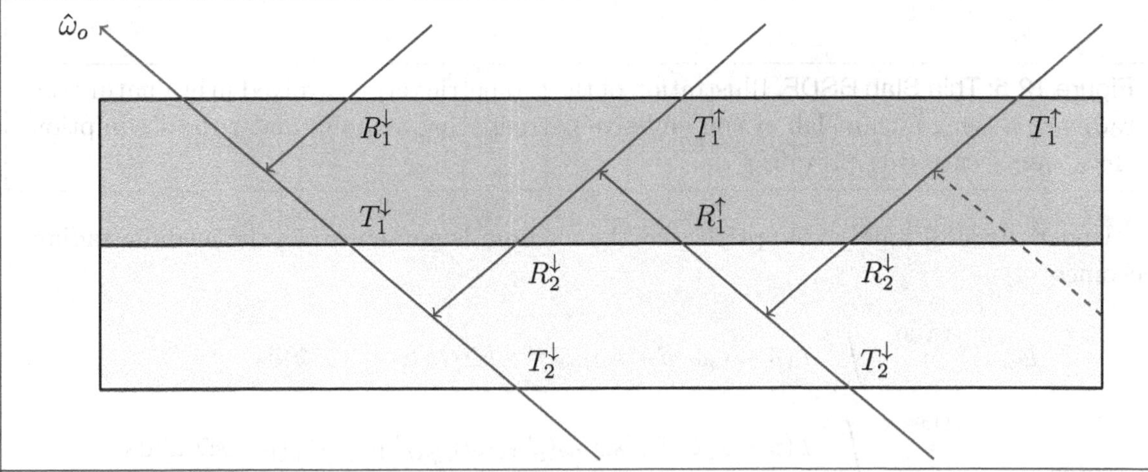

Figure 12.4: Multilayer Kubelka–Munk Theory: Illustration of the geometric terms involved in evaluating the reflective and transmissive albedos of a stack of turbid layers (drawn after [Kubelka, 1954, Fig. 1]).

12.3.2 Thin Slab

12.3.2.1 Formulation

Considering a thin slab of locally homogeneous participating medium as illustrated in *Figure 12.5* and defining $\vec{p}_s$ as a neighboring point lying on the macroscopic surface of the slab
482 such that any radiance term depending on it suffers no further interaction with the slab, the reduced radiance reads [Blinn, 1982]

466
463
463

$$\begin{aligned} L_r &\overset{(11.113)}{=} T(\vec{p}+s_a\hat{\omega},\vec{p}+s_b\hat{\omega})L(\vec{p}+s_b\hat{\omega},\hat{\omega}) \\ &\overset{(11.98)}{=} e^{-(s_b-s_a)\kappa_t(\vec{p}_s)}L(\vec{p}_s,\hat{\omega}) \\ &\overset{(11.94)}{=} e^{-\frac{d(\vec{p}_s)}{\langle\hat{n},\hat{\omega}_o\rangle}\kappa_t(\vec{p}_s)}L(\vec{p}_s,\hat{\omega}) \end{aligned} \tag{12.48}$$

where $d(\vec{p}_s)$ is the local thickness of the slab, such that $\frac{d(\vec{p}_s)}{s_b-s_a} = \langle\hat{n},\hat{\omega}_o\rangle$.

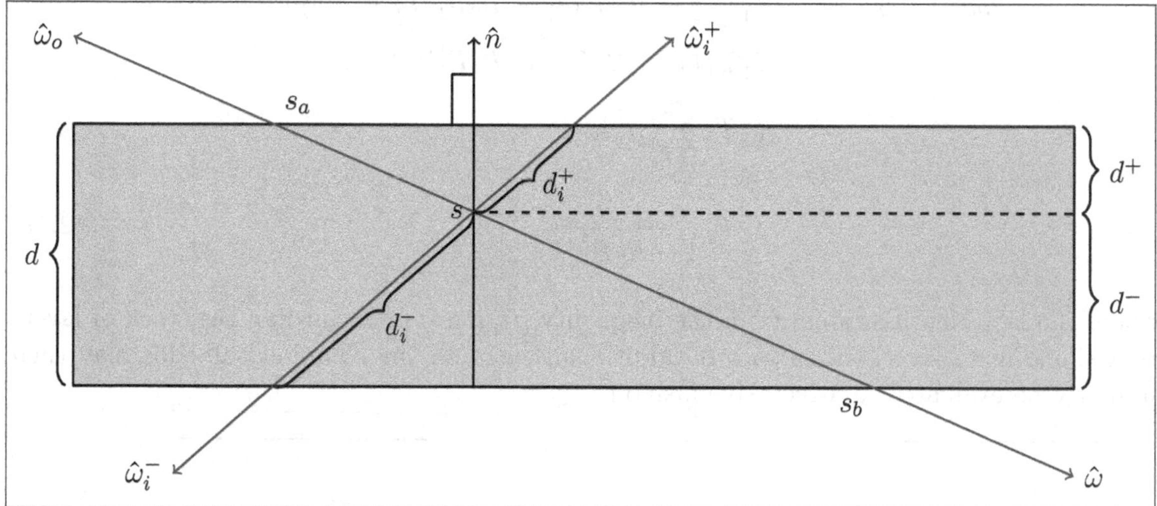

Figure 12.5: Thin Slab BSDF: Illustration of the geometric terms involved in evaluating the radiance leaving a thin slab of non-emissive participating medium under the assumption that single-scattering prevails.

Under the additional assumption that the medium is non-emissive, the medium radiance becomes

466
444
463
463

$$\begin{aligned} L_m &\overset{(11.113)}{=} \int_{s_a}^{s_b} T(\vec{p}+s_a\hat{\omega},\vec{p}+s\hat{\omega})\kappa_t(\vec{p}+s\hat{\omega})L_u(\vec{p}+s\hat{\omega},\hat{\omega})\mathrm{d}s \\ &\overset{(11.9)}{=} \int_{s_a}^{s_b} T(\vec{p}+s_a\hat{\omega},\vec{p}+s\hat{\omega})\kappa_t(\vec{p}+s\hat{\omega})\rho_p(\vec{p}+s\hat{\omega})L_p(\vec{p}+s\hat{\omega},\hat{\omega})\mathrm{d}s \\ &\underset{(11.94)}{\overset{(11.98)}{=}} \int_{s_a}^{s_b} e^{-(s-s_a)\kappa_t(\vec{p}_s)}\kappa_t(\vec{p}_s)\rho_p(\vec{p}_s)L_p(\vec{p}+s\hat{\omega},\hat{\omega})\mathrm{d}s \end{aligned} \tag{12.49}$$

Additionally assuming that single-scattering prevails, the in-scattered radiance reads

$$
\begin{aligned}
L_p(\vec{p}',\hat{\omega}) &\overset{(11.8)}{=} \int_{4\pi} f_p(\vec{p}',\hat{\omega},\hat{\omega}_i)L(\vec{p}',\hat{\omega}_i)\mathrm{d}\hat{\omega}_i && 444\\
&= \int_{4\pi} f_p(\vec{p}',\hat{\omega},\hat{\omega}_i)T(\vec{p}',\vec{p}'+d_i\hat{\omega}_i)L(\vec{p}'+d_i\hat{\omega}_i,\hat{\omega}_i)\mathrm{d}\hat{\omega}_i\\
&\underset{(11.94)}{\overset{(11.98)}{=}} \int_{4\pi} f_p(\vec{p}_s,\hat{\omega},\hat{\omega}_i)e^{-d_i\kappa_t(\vec{p}_s)}L(\vec{p}_s,\hat{\omega}_i)\mathrm{d}\hat{\omega}_i \qquad (12.50) && 463\ \ 463
\end{aligned}
$$

Substituting the formulation of the in-scattered radiance, and observing that whenever $\hat{\omega}_i$ points towards the upper hemisphere, the identities $\frac{d^+}{s-s_a} = \langle\hat{n},\hat{\omega}_o\rangle$ and $\frac{d^+}{d_i} = \langle\hat{n},\hat{\omega}_i\rangle$ hold, with $\hat{\omega}_o = -\hat{\omega}$, while whenever $\hat{\omega}_i$ points towards the lower hemisphere, the identities $\frac{d^-}{s_b-s} = \langle\hat{n},\hat{\omega}_o\rangle$ and $\frac{d^-}{d_i} = -\langle\hat{n},\hat{\omega}_i\rangle$ hold instead, the medium radiance then reads

$$
\begin{aligned}
L_m &= \int_{s_a}^{s_b} e^{-(s-s_a)\kappa_t(\vec{p}_s)}\kappa_t(\vec{p}_s)\rho_p(\vec{p}_s)\int_{4\pi} f_p(\vec{p}_s,\hat{\omega},\hat{\omega}_i)e^{-d_i\kappa_t(\vec{p}_s)}L(\vec{p}_s,\hat{\omega}_i)\mathrm{d}\hat{\omega}_i\mathrm{d}s\\
&= \int_{4\pi}\rho_p(\vec{p}_s)f_p(\vec{p}_s,\hat{\omega},\hat{\omega}_i)\int_{s_a}^{s_b} e^{-(s-s_a+d_i)\kappa_t(\vec{p}_s)}\kappa_t(\vec{p}_s)\mathrm{d}sL(\vec{p}_s,\hat{\omega}_i)\mathrm{d}\hat{\omega}_i\\
&= \int_{2\pi^+}\rho_p(\vec{p}_s)f_p(\vec{p}_s,\hat{\omega},\hat{\omega}_i)i_s(s_a)L(\vec{p}_s,\hat{\omega}_i)\mathrm{d}\hat{\omega}_i\\
&+ \int_{2\pi^-}\rho_p(\vec{p}_s)f_p(\vec{p}_s,\hat{\omega},\hat{\omega}_i)e^{-(s_b-s_a)\kappa_t(\vec{p}_s)}i_s(s_b)L(\vec{p}_s,\hat{\omega}_i)\mathrm{d}\hat{\omega}_i \qquad (12.51)
\end{aligned}
$$

where, assuming $\langle\hat{n},\hat{\omega}_i\rangle \neq -\langle\hat{n},\hat{\omega}_o\rangle$,

$$
\begin{aligned}
i_s(s_x) &\triangleq \int_{s_a}^{s_b} e^{-(s-s_x)\left(1+\frac{\langle\hat{n},\hat{\omega}_o\rangle}{\langle\hat{n},\hat{\omega}_i\rangle}\right)\kappa_t(\vec{p}_s)}\kappa_t(\vec{p}_s)\mathrm{d}s = \left[\frac{e^{-(s-s_x)\left(1+\frac{\langle\hat{n},\hat{\omega}_o\rangle}{\langle\hat{n},\hat{\omega}_i\rangle}\right)\kappa_t(\vec{p}_s)}}{-\left(1+\frac{\langle\hat{n},\hat{\omega}_o\rangle}{\langle\hat{n},\hat{\omega}_i\rangle}\right)}\right]_{s_a}^{s_b}\\
&= \frac{e^{-(s_a-s_x)\left(1+\frac{\langle\hat{n},\hat{\omega}_o\rangle}{\langle\hat{n},\hat{\omega}_i\rangle}\right)\kappa_t(\vec{p}_s)} - e^{-(s_b-s_x)\left(1+\frac{\langle\hat{n},\hat{\omega}_o\rangle}{\langle\hat{n},\hat{\omega}_i\rangle}\right)\kappa_t(\vec{p}_s)}}{\langle\hat{n},\hat{\omega}_i\rangle + \langle\hat{n},\hat{\omega}_o\rangle}\langle\hat{n},\hat{\omega}_i\rangle \qquad (12.52)
\end{aligned}
$$

such that

$$
\begin{aligned}
i_s(s_a) &= \frac{e^0 - e^{-(s_b-s_a)\left(1+\frac{\langle\hat{n},\hat{\omega}_o\rangle}{\langle\hat{n},\hat{\omega}_i\rangle}\right)\kappa_t(\vec{p}_s)}}{\langle\hat{n},\hat{\omega}_i\rangle + \langle\hat{n},\hat{\omega}_o\rangle}\langle\hat{n},\hat{\omega}_i\rangle\\
&= \frac{1 - e^{-d(\vec{p}_s)\left(\frac{1}{\langle\hat{n},\hat{\omega}_o\rangle}+\frac{1}{\langle\hat{n},\hat{\omega}_i\rangle}\right)\kappa_t(\vec{p}_s)}}{\langle\hat{n},\hat{\omega}_i\rangle + \langle\hat{n},\hat{\omega}_o\rangle}\langle\hat{n},\hat{\omega}_i\rangle \qquad (12.53)\\
i_s(s_b) &= \frac{e^{-(s_a-s_b)\left(1+\frac{\langle\hat{n},\hat{\omega}_o\rangle}{\langle\hat{n},\hat{\omega}_i\rangle}\right)\kappa_t(\vec{p}_s)} - e^0}{\langle\hat{n},\hat{\omega}_i\rangle + \langle\hat{n},\hat{\omega}_o\rangle}\langle\hat{n},\hat{\omega}_i\rangle\\
&= -\frac{1 - e^{d(\vec{p}_s)\left(\frac{1}{\langle\hat{n},\hat{\omega}_o\rangle}+\frac{1}{\langle\hat{n},\hat{\omega}_i\rangle}\right)\kappa_t(\vec{p}_s)}}{\langle\hat{n},\hat{\omega}_i\rangle + \langle\hat{n},\hat{\omega}_o\rangle}\langle\hat{n},\hat{\omega}_i\rangle \qquad (12.54)
\end{aligned}
$$

where the latter fraction is always positive $\forall\hat{\omega}_o,\hat{\omega}_i$, while in the limit where $\langle\hat{n},\hat{\omega}_i\rangle = -\langle\hat{n},\hat{\omega}_o\rangle$, which may only occur when $\hat{\omega}_i$ points towards the lower hemisphere, then

$$
\lim_{\langle\hat{n},\hat{\omega}_i\rangle\to-\langle\hat{n},\hat{\omega}_o\rangle} i_s(s_b) = \int_{s_a}^{s_b} e^0\kappa_t(\vec{p}_s)\mathrm{d}s = (s_b-s_a)\kappa_t(\vec{p}_s) = \frac{d(\vec{p}_s)}{\langle\hat{n},\hat{\omega}_o\rangle}\kappa_t(\vec{p}_s) \qquad (12.55)
$$

The expression of the observed radiance finally reads

466

$$
\begin{aligned}
L(\vec{p}, \hat{\omega}) &\overset{(11.113)}{=} \int_{2\pi^+} L(\vec{p}_s, \hat{\omega}_i) f_r(\vec{p}_s, \hat{\omega}_o, \hat{\omega}_i) \langle \hat{n}, \hat{\omega}_i \rangle \mathrm{d}\hat{\omega}_i \\
&+ \int_{2\pi^-} L(\vec{p}_s, \hat{\omega}_i) f_t(\vec{p}_s, \hat{\omega}_o, \hat{\omega}_i) \langle \hat{n}, \hat{\omega}_i \rangle \mathrm{d}\hat{\omega}_i \\
&+ e^{-\frac{d(\vec{p}_s)}{\langle \hat{n}, \hat{\omega}_o \rangle} \kappa_t(\vec{p}_s)} L(\vec{p}_s, \hat{\omega})
\end{aligned}
\tag{12.56}
$$

where the reflectance and transmittance distributions read

$$
f_r(\vec{p}_s, \hat{\omega}_o, \hat{\omega}_i) \triangleq \rho_p(\vec{p}_s) f_p(\vec{p}_s, -\hat{\omega}_o, \hat{\omega}_i) \frac{i_s(s_a)}{\langle \hat{n}, \hat{\omega}_i \rangle} \tag{12.57}
$$

$$
f_t(\vec{p}_s, \hat{\omega}_o, \hat{\omega}_i) \triangleq \rho_p(\vec{p}_s) f_p(\vec{p}_s, -\hat{\omega}_o, \hat{\omega}_i) \frac{i_s(s_b)}{-\langle \hat{n}, \hat{\omega}_i \rangle} e^{-\frac{d(\vec{p}_s)}{\langle \hat{n}, \hat{\omega}_o \rangle} \kappa_t(\vec{p}_s)} \tag{12.58}
$$

resulting in a surface appearance that depends both on the optical thickness of the slab and
444 on the *phase function* of the medium, as illustrated in *Figure 12.6* and *Figure 12.7*.
487
488

12.3.2.2 Albedo and Sampling

155 In turn, *importance sampling* may be carried by drawing random directions from the *proba-*
131 *bility density* associated with the *phase function*. Moreover, in the special case of an *isotropic*
444
446 BPDF, as might, for instance, be used to simulate diffusely scattering semi-transparent materials like cloth [Frisvad *et al.*, 2005], the albedo can be expressed in terms of the *exponential*
56 *integral* function as

476

$$
\rho_r(\vec{p}_s, \hat{\omega}_o) \overset{(12.11)}{=} \frac{\rho_p(\vec{p}_s)}{4\pi} \int_0^{2\pi} \mathrm{d}\phi \int_0^1 \frac{1 - e^{-d(\vec{p}_s)\left(\frac{1}{\langle \hat{n}, \hat{\omega}_o \rangle} + \frac{1}{\mu}\right)\kappa_t(\vec{p}_s)}}{\mu + \langle \hat{n}, \hat{\omega}_o \rangle} \mu \mathrm{d}\mu
$$

56

$$
\begin{aligned}
&\overset{(2.281)}{=} \frac{\rho_p(\vec{p}_s)}{4\pi} [\phi]_0^{2\pi} \Bigg[\mu - \langle \hat{n}, \hat{\omega}_o \rangle \ln(\mu + \langle \hat{n}, \hat{\omega}_o \rangle) - \mu e^{-d(\vec{p}_s)\left(\frac{1}{\langle \hat{n}, \hat{\omega}_o \rangle} + \frac{1}{\mu}\right)\kappa_t(\vec{p}_s)} \\
&+ \langle \hat{n}, \hat{\omega}_o \rangle \operatorname{Ei}\left(-d(\vec{p}_s) \left(\frac{1}{\langle \hat{n}, \hat{\omega}_o \rangle} + \frac{1}{\mu} \right) \kappa_t(\vec{p}_s) \right) \\
&- (\langle \hat{n}, \hat{\omega}_o \rangle + d(\vec{p}_s)\kappa_t(\vec{p}_s)) e^{-\frac{d(\vec{p}_s)}{\langle \hat{n}, \hat{\omega}_o \rangle} \kappa_t(\vec{p}_s)} \operatorname{Ei}\left(-\frac{d(\vec{p}_s)}{\mu} \kappa_t(\vec{p}_s) \right) \Bigg]_0^1
\end{aligned}
$$

56

$$
\begin{aligned}
&\overset{(2.282)}{=} \frac{\rho_p(\vec{p}_s)}{2} \Bigg(1 - \langle \hat{n}, \hat{\omega}_o \rangle \ln\left(\frac{1 + \langle \hat{n}, \hat{\omega}_o \rangle}{\langle \hat{n}, \hat{\omega}_o \rangle} \right) - e^{-d(\vec{p}_s)\left(\frac{1}{\langle \hat{n}, \hat{\omega}_o \rangle} + 1\right)\kappa_t(\vec{p}_s)} \\
&+ \langle \hat{n}, \hat{\omega}_o \rangle \operatorname{Ei}\left(-d(\vec{p}_s) \left(\frac{1}{\langle \hat{n}, \hat{\omega}_o \rangle} + 1 \right) \kappa_t(\vec{p}_s) \right) \\
&- (\langle \hat{n}, \hat{\omega}_o \rangle + d(\vec{p}_s)\kappa_t(\vec{p}_s)) e^{-\frac{d(\vec{p}_s)}{\langle \hat{n}, \hat{\omega}_o \rangle} \kappa_t(\vec{p}_s)} \operatorname{Ei}\left(-d(\vec{p}_s)\kappa_t(\vec{p}_s) \right) \Bigg)
\end{aligned}
\tag{12.59}
$$

$$
\begin{aligned}
\rho_t(\vec{p}_s, \hat{\omega}_o) &\overset{(12.11)}{=} \frac{\rho_p(\vec{p}_s)}{4\pi} e^{-\frac{d(\vec{p}_s)}{\langle \hat{n}, \hat{\omega}_o \rangle}\kappa_t(\vec{p}_s)} \int_0^{2\pi} \mathrm{d}\phi \int_{-0}^{-1} \frac{1 - e^{d(\vec{p}_s)\left(\frac{1}{\langle \hat{n}, \hat{\omega}_o \rangle} + \frac{1}{\mu}\right)\kappa_t(\vec{p}_s)}}{\mu + \langle \hat{n}, \hat{\omega}_o \rangle} \mu \mathrm{d}\mu \\
&\overset{(2.281)}{=} \frac{\rho_p(\vec{p}_s)}{4\pi} e^{-\frac{d(\vec{p}_s)}{\langle \hat{n}, \hat{\omega}_o \rangle}\kappa_t(\vec{p}_s)} [\phi]_0^{2\pi} \Bigg[\mu - \langle \hat{n}, \hat{\omega}_o \rangle \ln(|\mu + \langle \hat{n}, \hat{\omega}_o \rangle|) \\
&- \mu e^{d(\vec{p}_s)\left(\frac{1}{\langle \hat{n}, \hat{\omega}_o \rangle} + \frac{1}{\mu}\right)\kappa_t(\vec{p}_s)} + \langle \hat{n}, \hat{\omega}_o \rangle \operatorname{Ei}\left(d(\vec{p}_s) \left(\frac{1}{\langle \hat{n}, \hat{\omega}_o \rangle} + \frac{1}{\mu} \right) \kappa_t(\vec{p}_s) \right) \\
&- \left(\langle \hat{n}, \hat{\omega}_o \rangle - d(\vec{p}_s)\kappa_t(\vec{p}_s)\right) e^{\frac{d(\vec{p}_s)}{\langle \hat{n}, \hat{\omega}_o \rangle}\kappa_t(\vec{p}_s)} \operatorname{Ei}\left(\frac{d(\vec{p}_s)}{\mu} \kappa_t(\vec{p}_s) \right) \Bigg]_{-0}^{-1} \\
&\overset{(2.282)}{=} \frac{\rho_p(\vec{p}_s)}{2} e^{-\frac{d(\vec{p}_s)}{\langle \hat{n}, \hat{\omega}_o \rangle}\kappa_t(\vec{p}_s)} \Bigg(-1 - \langle \hat{n}, \hat{\omega}_o \rangle \ln\left(\frac{1 - \langle \hat{n}, \hat{\omega}_o \rangle}{\langle \hat{n}, \hat{\omega}_o \rangle} \right) \\
&+ e^{d(\vec{p}_s)\left(\frac{1}{\langle \hat{n}, \hat{\omega}_o \rangle} - 1\right)\kappa_t(\vec{p}_s)} + \langle \hat{n}, \hat{\omega}_o \rangle \operatorname{Ei}\left(d(\vec{p}_s) \left(\frac{1}{\langle \hat{n}, \hat{\omega}_o \rangle} - 1 \right) \kappa_t(\vec{p}_s) \right) \\
&- \left(\langle \hat{n}, \hat{\omega}_o \rangle - d(\vec{p}_s)\kappa_t(\vec{p}_s)\right) e^{\frac{d(\vec{p}_s)}{\langle \hat{n}, \hat{\omega}_o \rangle}\kappa_t(\vec{p}_s)} \operatorname{Ei}\left(- d(\vec{p}_s)\kappa_t(\vec{p}_s) \right) \Bigg) \qquad (12.60)
\end{aligned}
$$

476 56 56

such that, for a given exitant direction $\hat{\omega}_o$, the transmittance term, upper hemisphere and lower hemisphere may be importance sampled with probabilities proportional to $e^{-\frac{d(\vec{p}_s)}{\langle \hat{n}, \hat{\omega}_o \rangle}\kappa_t(\vec{p}_s)}$, $\rho_r(\vec{p}_s, \hat{\omega}_o)$ and $\rho_t(\vec{p}_s, \hat{\omega}_o)$, respectively.

12.3.3 Hapke–Irvine

12.3.3.1 Formulation

Considering the case of an infinite optical thickness in the *thin slab* model, the transmitted 482
terms vanish as illustrated in *Figure 12.6* and *Figure 12.7*, and the reflectance distribution 487 488
simplifies into the *Hapke–Irvine BRDF* [Hapke, 1963, Irvine, 1966]

$$
f_r(\vec{p}, \hat{\omega}_o, \hat{\omega}_i) \overset{(12.57)}{=} \rho_p(\vec{p}) \frac{f_p(\vec{p}, -\hat{\omega}_o, \hat{\omega}_i)}{\langle \hat{n}, \hat{\omega}_i \rangle + \langle \hat{n}, \hat{\omega}_o \rangle} \qquad (12.61)
$$

484

Whenever the viewer and the light source are aligned, then $\langle \hat{n}, \hat{\omega}_i \rangle = \langle \hat{n}, \hat{\omega}_o \rangle$ holds and the expression reduces to

$$
\lim_{\hat{\omega}_i \to \hat{\omega}_o} f_r(\vec{p}, \hat{\omega}_o, \hat{\omega}_i) = \rho_p(\vec{p}) \frac{f_p(\vec{p}, -\hat{\omega}_o, \hat{\omega}_i)}{2\langle \hat{n}, \hat{\omega}_i \rangle} \qquad (12.62)
$$

such that the cosine term in the denominator cancels out with the cosine term in the rendering equation. This results in a constant exitant radiance regardless of the orientation of the surface normal, therefore reproducing the rather uniform brightness of the full moon.

Considering the limit of an *isotropic multiple scattering phase function* and similarly 446
assuming that contributions due to multiple scattering are independent of the azimuthal 460 444
angle [Ambarzumian, 1942], the model can then be extended to account for higher-order scattering events by adding the term $\frac{H(\vec{p}, \langle \hat{n}, \hat{\omega}_o \rangle) H(\vec{p}, \langle \hat{n}, \hat{\omega}_i \rangle) - 1}{4\pi}$ to the BPDF in the numerator, where the solution to the integral equation [Hapke, 1993]

$$
H(\vec{p}, \mu) = 1 + \frac{\rho_p(\vec{p})}{2} \mu H(\vec{p}, \mu) \int_0^1 \frac{H(\vec{p}, \mu')}{\mu + \mu'} \mathrm{d}\mu' \qquad (12.63)
$$

might be approximated as

$$
H(\vec{p}, \mu) \approx \frac{1 + 2\mu}{1 + 2\mu\sqrt{1 - \rho_p(\vec{p})}} \qquad (12.64)
$$

Further extensions may additionally account for the *opposition effect*, which corresponds to a sudden surge in brightness near the retroreflection direction, by multiplying the expression
444 of the *phase function* in the numerator with an angle-dependent scaling factor [Premože, 2002].

12.3.3.2 Albedo and Sampling

The albedo is then bounded by

476

$$\rho(\vec{p},\hat{\omega}_o) \overset{(12.9)}{=} \int_{2\pi^+} \rho_p(\vec{p}) \frac{f_p(\vec{p},-\hat{\omega}_o,\hat{\omega}_i)}{\langle \hat{n},\hat{\omega}_i\rangle + \langle \hat{n},\hat{\omega}_o\rangle} \langle \hat{n},\hat{\omega}_i\rangle \mathrm{d}\hat{\omega}_i$$

$$\leq \rho_p(\vec{p}) \int_{2\pi^+} f_p(\vec{p},-\hat{\omega}_o,\hat{\omega}_i)\mathrm{d}\hat{\omega}_i$$

444

$$\overset{(11.13)}{\leq} \rho_p(\vec{p}) \tag{12.65}$$

12.3.4 Lommel–Seeliger

12.3.4.1 Formulation

444 Considering the special case where the *phase function* is *isotropic* in the *Hapke–Irvine* model
446
485 yields the *Lommel–Seeliger BRDF* [Lommel, 1889, von Seeliger, 1888]

485
446

$$f_r(\vec{p},\hat{\omega}_o,\hat{\omega}_i) \underset{(11.24)}{\overset{(12.61)}{=}} \frac{\rho_p(\vec{p})}{4\pi} \frac{1}{\langle \hat{n},\hat{\omega}_i\rangle + \langle \hat{n},\hat{\omega}_o\rangle} \tag{12.66}$$

487 illustrated in *Figure 12.6* and *Figure 12.7*.
488

12.3.4.2 Albedo and Sampling

The albedo then reads

476

$$\rho(\vec{p},\hat{\omega}_o) \overset{(12.11)}{=} \frac{\rho_p(\vec{p})}{4\pi} \int_0^{2\pi} \mathrm{d}\phi \int_0^1 \frac{\mu}{\mu + \langle \hat{n},\hat{\omega}_o\rangle} \mathrm{d}\mu$$

$$= \frac{\rho_p(\vec{p})}{4\pi} [\phi]_0^{2\pi} [\mu - \langle \hat{n},\hat{\omega}_o\rangle \ln(\mu + \langle \hat{n},\hat{\omega}_o\rangle)]_0^1$$

$$= \frac{\rho_p(\vec{p})}{2} \left(1 - \langle \hat{n},\hat{\omega}_o\rangle \ln\left(\frac{1+\langle \hat{n},\hat{\omega}_o\rangle}{\langle \hat{n},\hat{\omega}_o\rangle}\right)\right) \tag{12.67}$$

whose maximum $\frac{\rho_p(\vec{p})}{2}$ occurs at grazing angles where $\langle \hat{n},\hat{\omega}_o\rangle = 0$.

12.4 SPECULAR SURFACES

12.4.1 Directions of Propagation

489 In the case of an ideally smooth surface as illustrated in *Figure 12.8*, a portion of the incident light beam can solely be reflected in a perfectly specular fashion along the direction defined by $\theta_o = \theta_i$ and $\phi_o = \phi_i \pm \pi$, such that

$$\hat{\omega}_o = \tau_r(\hat{n},\hat{\omega}_i) \tag{12.68}$$

$$\hat{\omega}_i = \tau_r(\hat{n},\hat{\omega}_o) \tag{12.69}$$

106 where the reflection direction function is defined as the opposite of the Householder *reflection*

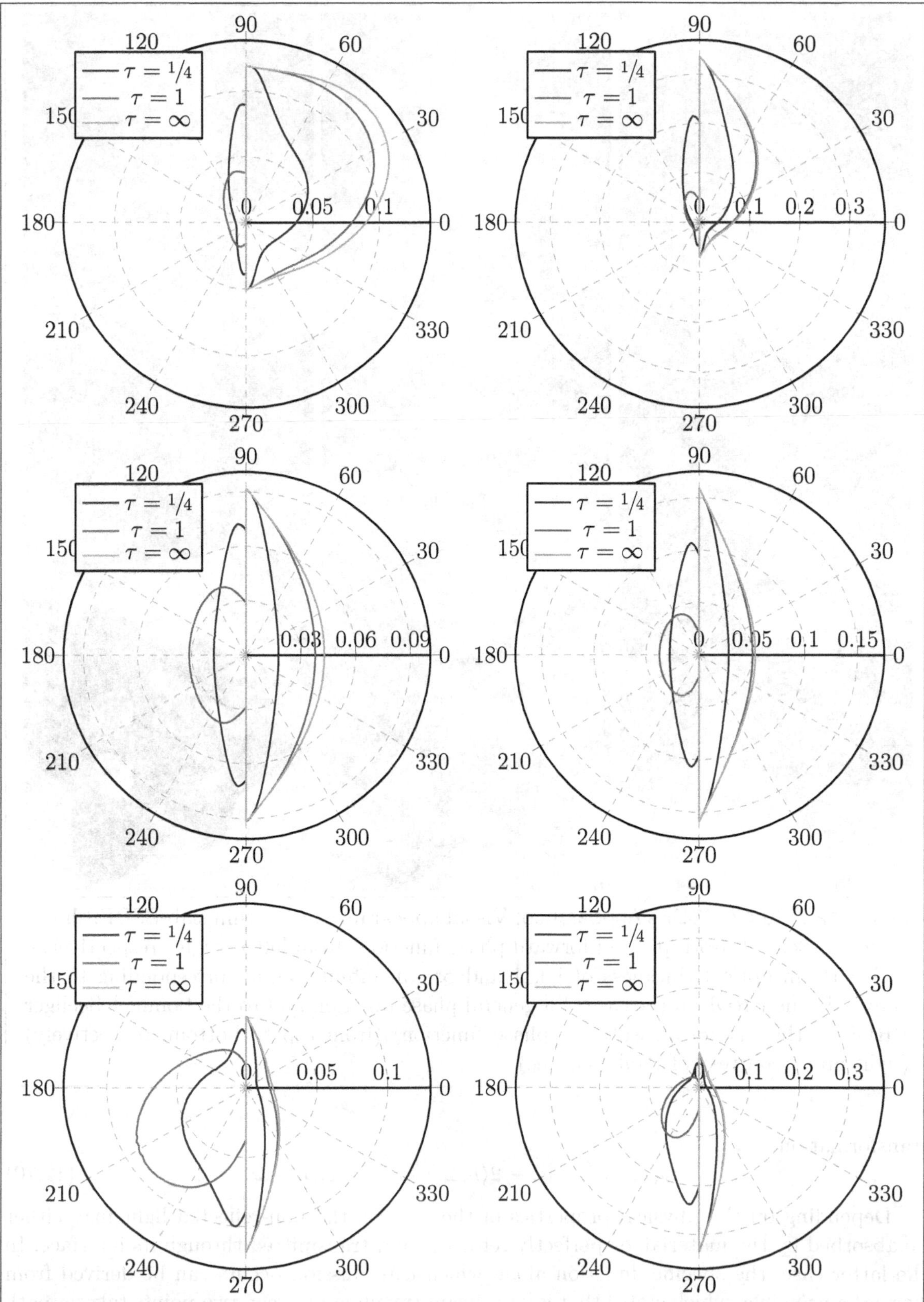

Figure 12.6: Turbid BSDFs Plots: Angular distribution of the thin slab BSDF, shown with a backward, isotropic and forward phase function (from top to bottom, respectively) for various optical thicknesses (an infinite value corresponding to the Hapke–Irvine BRDF in the case of a general phase function and to the Lommel–Seeliger BRDF in the case of an isotropic phase function), and with an incidence angle of 30° (left) and 60° (right).

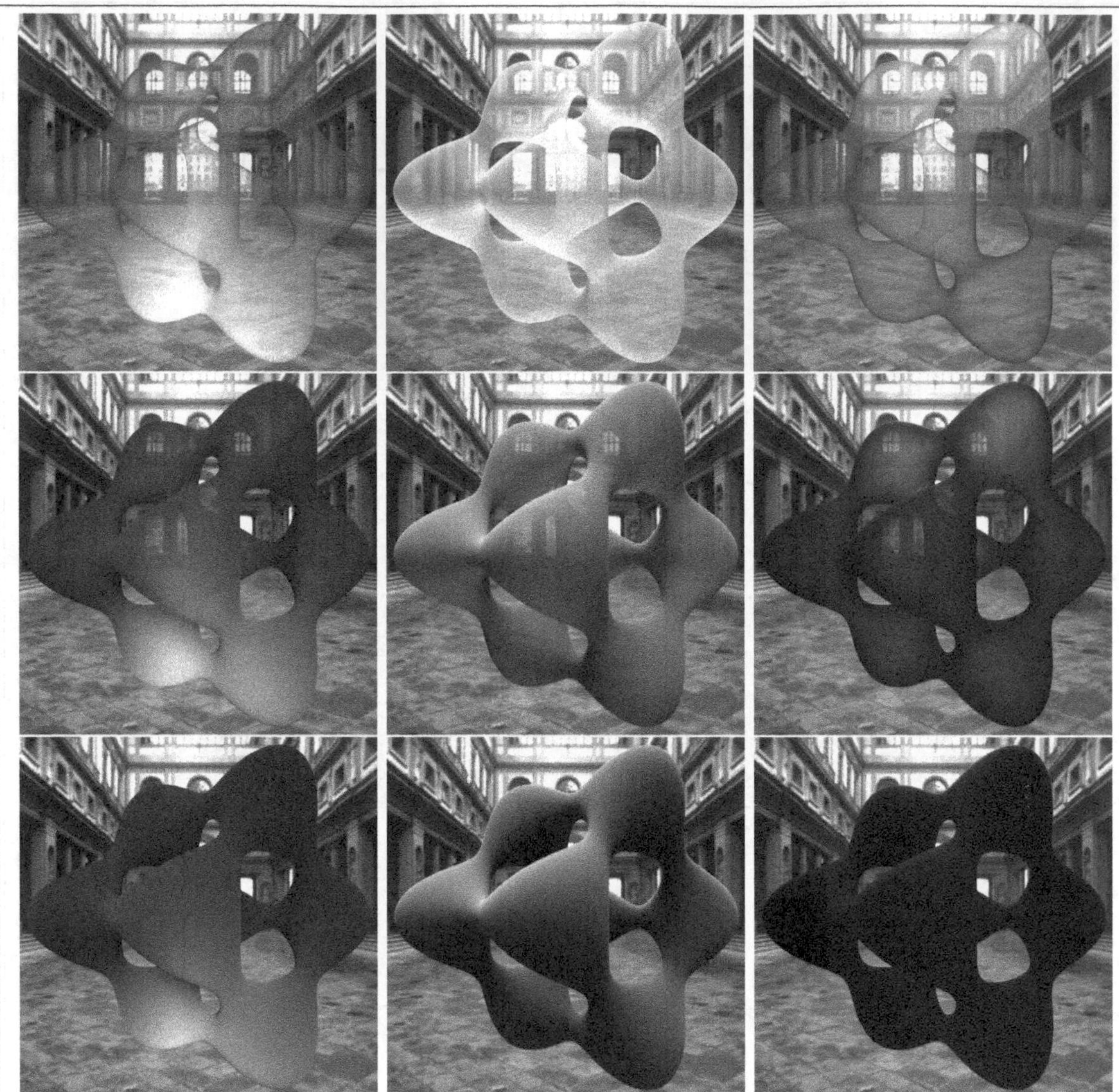

Figure 12.7: Turbid BSDFs Appearance: Visual appearance of the thin slab BSDF, shown with a backward, isotropic and forward phase function (from left to right, respectively), and with an optical thickness of 1/4, 1 and ∞ (an infinite value corresponding to the Hapke–Irvine BRDF in the case of a general phase function and to the Lommel–Seeliger BRDF in the case of an isotropic phase function) (from top to bottom, respectively) (light probe courtesy of Paul Debevec).

transformation

$$\tau_r(\hat{n}, \hat{\omega}) \triangleq -(\hat{\omega} - 2\langle \hat{n}, \hat{\omega} \rangle \hat{n}) = 2\langle \hat{n}, \hat{\omega} \rangle \hat{n} - \hat{\omega} \tag{12.70}$$

Depending on the physical properties of the surface, the non-reflected light may either be absorbed by the material, or perfectly refracted and transmitted through its interface. In the latter case, the specific direction along which transmission occurs can be derived from *Fermat's principle*, which states that a light beam traveling between two points takes a path of stationary (i.e., minimal or maximal) optical length. Without loss of generality, let us consider a planar surface orthogonal to the y axis. The travel time between a point $\vec{p}_i$ in the incident material and a point $\vec{p}_t$ in the transmission material may then be expressed in terms

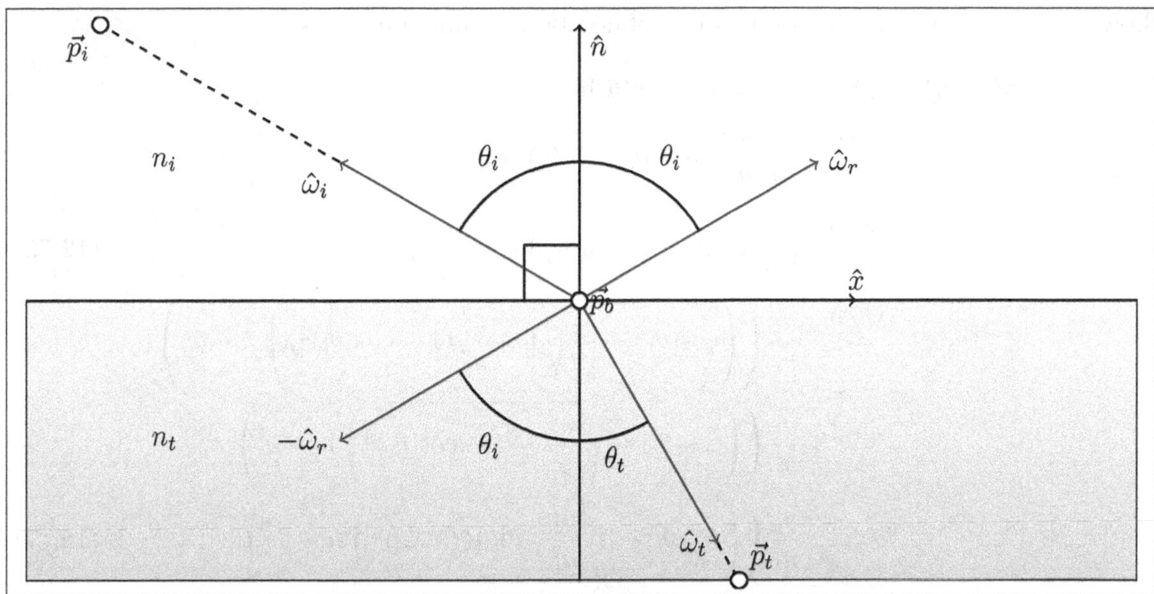

Figure 12.8: Specular Reflection and Refraction: Illustration of the geometric terms involved in reflection and refraction phenomena.

of the coordinates of the point $\vec{p}_b$ at the interface boundary as

$$\begin{aligned} t_{it}(x_b) &= t_{ib}(x_b) + t_{bt}(x_b) \\ &= \frac{\|\vec{p}_b - \vec{p}_i\|}{v_i} + \frac{\|\vec{p}_b - \vec{p}_t\|}{v_t} \\ &= \frac{\sqrt{(x_b - x_i)^2 + (y_b - y_i)^2}}{v_i} + \frac{\sqrt{(x_b - x_t)^2 + (y_b - y_t)^2}}{v_t} \end{aligned} \tag{12.71}$$

where v_i and v_t are the speed of light in the incident and transmission media, respectively. The derivative of the optical path length with respect to x_b then reads

$$\begin{aligned} \frac{\mathrm{d}t_{it}(x_b)}{\mathrm{d}x_b} &= \frac{x_b - x_i}{v_i\sqrt{(x_b - x_i)^2 + (y_b - y_i)^2}} + \frac{x_b - x_t}{v_t\sqrt{(x_b - x_t)^2 + (y_b - y_t)^2}} \\ &= \frac{x_b - x_i}{v_i\|\vec{p}_b - \vec{p}_i\|} + \frac{x_b - x_t}{v_t\|\vec{p}_b - \vec{p}_t\|} \\ &= \frac{\sin(\theta_i)}{v_i} - \frac{\sin(\theta_t)}{v_t} \end{aligned} \tag{12.72}$$

Solving for the extremum (i.e., minimum or maximum) finally leads to *Snell's law*, which formulates the following relationship between the polar angles

$$\frac{\mathrm{d}t_{it}(x_b)}{\mathrm{d}x_b} \overset{(10.11)}{=} \frac{n_i \sin(\theta_i)}{c} - \frac{n_t \sin(\theta_t)}{c} = 0 \iff n_i \sin(\theta_i) = n_t \sin(\theta_t) \tag{12.73}$$ 420

while the azimuthal angle is defined as $\phi_t = \phi_i \pm \pi$.

Using a similar geometrical construction as for reflection then yields

$$\sin(\theta_i)\hat{x} = \cos(\theta_i)\hat{n} - \hat{\omega}_i \tag{12.74}$$

and formulating the cosine of the angle of refraction as

$$\cos(\theta_t) = \sqrt{1 - \sin(\theta_t)^2} = \sqrt{1 - \frac{n_i^2}{n_t^2}\sin(\theta_i)^2} = \sqrt{1 - \frac{n_i^2}{n_t^2}(1 - \cos(\theta_i)^2)} \tag{12.75}$$

allows the transmission direction to be defined by the function

$$\tau_t(\hat{n}, \hat{\omega}_i) \triangleq \sin(\theta_t)\hat{x} - \cos(\theta_t)\hat{n}$$

489
$$\overset{(12.74)}{=} \frac{\sin(\theta_t)}{\sin(\theta_i)}\big(\cos(\theta_i)\hat{n} - \hat{\omega}_i\big) - \cos(\theta_t)\hat{n}$$

489
$$\overset{(12.73)}{=} \left(\frac{n_i}{n_t}\cos(\theta_i) - \cos(\theta_t)\right)\hat{n} - \frac{n_i}{n_t}\hat{\omega}_i \tag{12.76}$$

489
$$\overset{(12.75)}{=} \frac{n_i}{n_t}\left(\left(\cos(\theta_i) - \frac{n_t}{n_i}\sqrt{1 - \frac{n_i^2}{n_t^2}(1 - \cos(\theta_i)^2)}\right)\hat{n} - \hat{\omega}_i\right)$$

$$= \frac{n_i}{n_t}\left(\left(\cos(\theta_i) - \sqrt{\frac{n_t^2}{n_i^2} - 1 + \cos(\theta_i)^2}\right)\hat{n} - \hat{\omega}_i\right)$$

$$= \frac{n_i}{n_t}\left(\left(\langle\hat{n}, \hat{\omega}_i\rangle - \sqrt{\frac{n_t^2}{n_i^2} - 1 + \langle\hat{n}, \hat{\omega}_i\rangle^2}\right)\hat{n} - \hat{\omega}_i\right) \tag{12.77}$$

It follows that when $n_i < n_t$, the orientation of the refracted ray is closer to the axis of the normal than the incident ray. Conversely, if $n_i > n_t$, as occurs when a beam of light
494 exits a *dielectric* material, the orientation of the refracted ray is farther away from the axis of the normal than the incident ray, allowing the entire hemisphere above the surface to be observed from a fish's eye under water (and after which was coined the lens of the same
491 name) within a smaller angle of view known as *Snell's window*, as illustrated in *Figure 12.9*. In this case, it is possible for the angle of refraction to increase up until $\theta_t = \frac{\pi}{2}$ as the angle of incidence θ_i reaches the so-called *critical angle*

$$\theta_c \triangleq \arcsin\left(\frac{n_t}{n_i}\right) \tag{12.78}$$

Therefore, whenever $\theta_i \geq \theta_c$, no transmission occurs and radiation is completely reflected back into the medium, a phenomenon known as *total internal reflection*, which is the principle at the heart of optical fibers.

12.4.2 Fresnel Equations

For a given incident cosine angle $\mu \triangleq \cos(\theta_i) = \langle\hat{n}, \hat{\omega}_i\rangle$, the fraction of reflected and potentially transmitted radiation actually depends on the polarization of the incident light with respect to the plane encompassing $\hat{n}$, $\hat{\omega}_i$, $\hat{\omega}_r$ and $\hat{\omega}_t$. The reflection coefficient $R_\perp$ for light whose electric field is perpendicular to the plane, so called *s*-polarized from the German translation "senkrecht," and the reflection coefficient $R_\parallel$ for light whose electric field is parallel to that plane, so called *p*-polarized, are both given by the *Fresnel equations*

$$R_\perp(\mu) \triangleq \frac{\|\sqrt{\varepsilon} - \mu\|^2}{\|\sqrt{\varepsilon} + \mu\|^2} = \frac{(a - \mu)^2 + b^2}{(a + \mu)^2 + b^2} \in [0, 1] \tag{12.79}$$

$$R_{\parallel/\perp}(\mu) \triangleq \frac{\left\|\sqrt{\varepsilon} - \frac{1-\mu^2}{\mu}\right\|^2}{\left\|\sqrt{\varepsilon} + \frac{1-\mu^2}{\mu}\right\|^2} = \frac{\left(a - \frac{1-\mu^2}{\mu}\right)^2 + b^2}{\left(a + \frac{1-\mu^2}{\mu}\right)^2 + b^2} \in [0, 1] \tag{12.80}$$

$$R_\parallel(\mu) \triangleq R_\perp(\mu)R_{\parallel/\perp}(\mu) = \frac{\left\|\sqrt{\varepsilon} + \frac{1-\mu^2}{\sqrt{\varepsilon}} - \frac{1}{\mu}\right\|^2}{\left\|\sqrt{\varepsilon} + \frac{1-\mu^2}{\sqrt{\varepsilon}} + \frac{1}{\mu}\right\|^2} \in [0, 1] \tag{12.81}$$

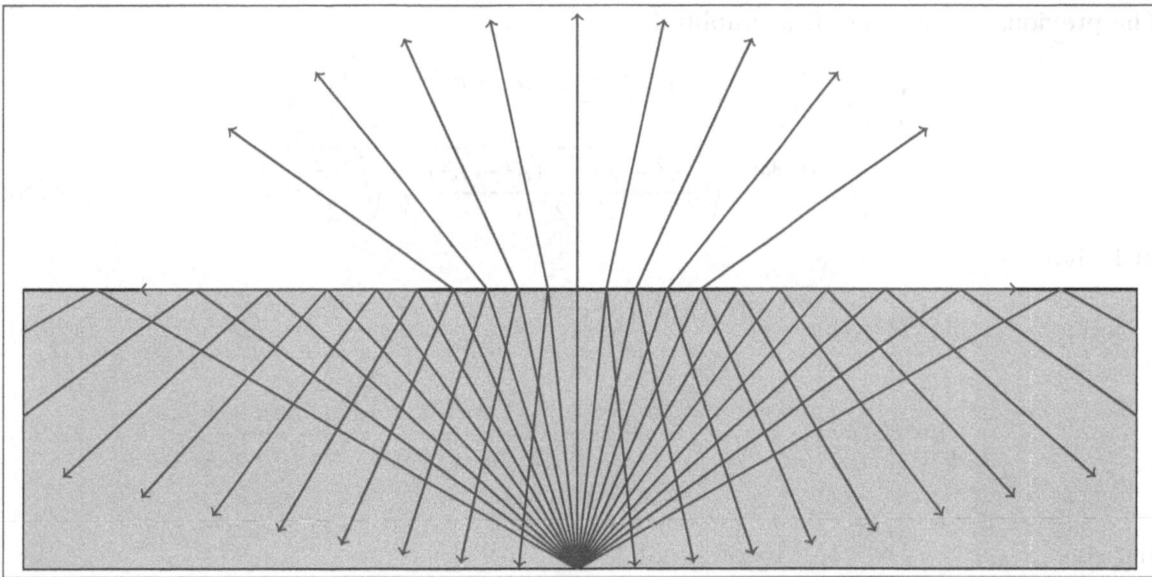

Figure 12.9: Total Internal Reflection: Illustration of Snell's window, allowing a wide angle of view of the environment above the water surface to be seen from a fish's eye, while light rays whose direction is outside the window span are subject to total internal reflection.

with $\varepsilon \triangleq (n + \imath\kappa)^2 - (1 - \mu^2) = c + \imath 2n\kappa$ such that

$$a \triangleq \Re(\sqrt{\varepsilon}) \overset{(3.173)}{\underset{(3.147)}{=}} \sqrt{\frac{\sqrt{c^2 + 4n^2\kappa^2} + c}{2}} \tag{12.82}$$

88 86

$$b \triangleq \Im(\sqrt{\varepsilon}) \overset{(3.173)}{\underset{(3.147)}{=}} \sqrt{\frac{\sqrt{c^2 + 4n^2\kappa^2} - c}{2}} \tag{12.83}$$

88 86

$$c \triangleq \Re(\varepsilon) = n^2 - \kappa^2 - \left(1 - \mu^2\right) \tag{12.84}$$

where the relative index of refraction $n \triangleq \frac{n_t n_i + \kappa_t \kappa_i}{n_i^2 + \kappa_i^2}$ (such that $n = \frac{n_t}{n_i}$ whenever $\kappa_i = 0$, as presumed for light to propagate through the medium of incidence) and the relative absorption index $\kappa \triangleq \frac{\kappa_t n_i - n_t \kappa_i}{n_i^2 + \kappa_i^2}$ (such that $\kappa = \frac{\kappa_t}{n_i}$ whenever $\kappa_i = 0$) are the real and imaginary parts, respectively, of the complex-valued relative index of refraction $\underline{n} \triangleq \frac{n_t + \imath\kappa_t}{n_i + \imath\kappa_i} = n + \imath\kappa$. The reflection coefficient for unpolarized light is then simply given as the average of the reflection coefficients for s-polarized and p-polarized radiation

$$F(\mu) \triangleq \frac{R_\perp(\mu) + R_\parallel(\mu)}{2} \overset{(12.81)}{=} R_\perp(\mu) \frac{1 + R_{\parallel/\perp}(\mu)}{2} \in [0, 1] \tag{12.85}$$

490

At grazing angles, $\theta_i = \frac{\pi}{2}$ and $\mu = 0$ hold, such that $F(0) = R_\perp(0) = R_\parallel(0) = R_{\parallel/\perp}(0) = 1$ and all light is reflected. Conversely, under normal incidence, $\theta_i = 0$ holds such that $\mu = 1$ and $c = n^2 - \kappa^2$, yielding

$$\lim_{\mu \to 1} \sqrt{c^2 + 4n^2\kappa^2} = \sqrt{(n^2 - \kappa^2)^2 + 4n^2\kappa^2} = \sqrt{n^4 + 2n^2\kappa^2 + \kappa^4} = n^2 + \kappa^2 \tag{12.86}$$

The previous expressions then simplify into

491 $$\lim_{\mu\to 1} a \overset{(12.82)}{=} \sqrt{\frac{(n^2+\kappa^2)+(n^2-\kappa^2)}{2}} = \sqrt{\frac{2n^2}{2}} = n \tag{12.87}$$

491 $$\lim_{\mu\to 1} b \overset{(12.83)}{=} \sqrt{\frac{(n^2+\kappa^2)-(n^2-\kappa^2)}{2}} = \sqrt{\frac{2\kappa^2}{2}} = \kappa \tag{12.88}$$

such that

490 $$\lim_{\mu\to 1} R_{\perp}(\mu) \overset{(12.79)}{=} \frac{(n-\mu)^2+\kappa^2}{(n+\mu)^2+\kappa^2} = \frac{(n^2+\kappa^2)-2n\mu+\mu^2}{(n^2+\kappa^2)+2n\mu+\mu^2} \tag{12.89}$$

490 $$\lim_{\mu\to 1} R_{\parallel}(\mu) \overset{(12.81)}{=} \frac{\left(n-\frac{1}{\mu}\right)^2+\kappa^2}{\left(n+\frac{1}{\mu}\right)^2+\kappa^2} = \frac{(n^2+\kappa^2)\mu^2-2n\mu+1}{(n^2+\kappa^2)\mu^2+2n\mu+1} \tag{12.90}$$

490 and since $R_{\parallel/\perp}(1) \overset{(12.80)}{=} 1$, it follows that

491 $$F(1) \overset{(12.85)}{=} R_{\perp}(1) = R_{\parallel}(1) = \frac{(n-1)^2+\kappa^2}{(n+1)^2+\kappa^2} \tag{12.91}$$

from which the physical parameters n and κ may be determined (within one degree of freedom) by measuring the reflectance of a given material under normal incidence

492 $$\kappa \overset{(12.91)}{=} \sqrt{\frac{(n+1)^2F(1)-(n-1)^2}{1-F(1)}} \tag{12.92}$$

492
29 $$n \underset{(2.104)}{\overset{(12.91)}{=}} \frac{1+F(1)+\sqrt{(1+F(1))^2-(1-F(1))^2(\kappa^2+1)}}{1-F(1)} \tag{12.93}$$

28 where the latter result, which is the solution to the reduced *quadratic equation*

$$(1-F(1))n^2 - 2(1+F(1))n + (1-F(1))(\kappa^2+1) = 0 \tag{12.94}$$

reduces whenever $\kappa = 0$ to [Cook, 1981, Cook and Torrance, 1981, Cook and Torrance, 1982]

$$\begin{aligned} n &= \frac{1+F(1)+\sqrt{(1+F(1))^2-(1-F(1))^2}}{1-F(1)} \\ &= \frac{1+F(1)+2\sqrt{F(1)}}{1-F(1)} \\ &= \frac{(1+\sqrt{F(1)})^2}{1-F(1)} \\ &= \frac{1+\sqrt{F(1)}}{1-\sqrt{F(1)}} \end{aligned} \tag{12.95}$$

As an alternative, computationally inexpensive approximations of the overall Fresnel reflectance include [Lazányi and Szirmay-Kalos, 2005]

$$F(\mu) \approx \frac{(n-1)^2+\kappa^2+4n(1-\mu)^5}{(n+1)^2+\kappa^2} \tag{12.96}$$

as well as Schlick's approximation [Schlick, 1993, Schlick, 1994b], which is readily expressed in terms of the material's reflectance at normal incidence $F_0 \triangleq F(1)$

$$F(\mu) \approx F_0 + (1-F_0)(1-\mu)^5 \tag{12.97}$$

12.4.3 Conductors and Dielectrics

As illustrated in *Figure 12.10*, two idealized classes of specular materials may be distinguished 493
based on the value of the extinction index, namely *conductors* and *dielectrics*. Representative 494
values of the complex-valued refractive index at a fixed wavelength are provided in *Table 12.1* 494 493
for various types of *conductors* and *dielectrics*, while wavelength-dependent formulas for 494 494
common types of *dielectrics* are readily reported in *Section B.2.* 494 748

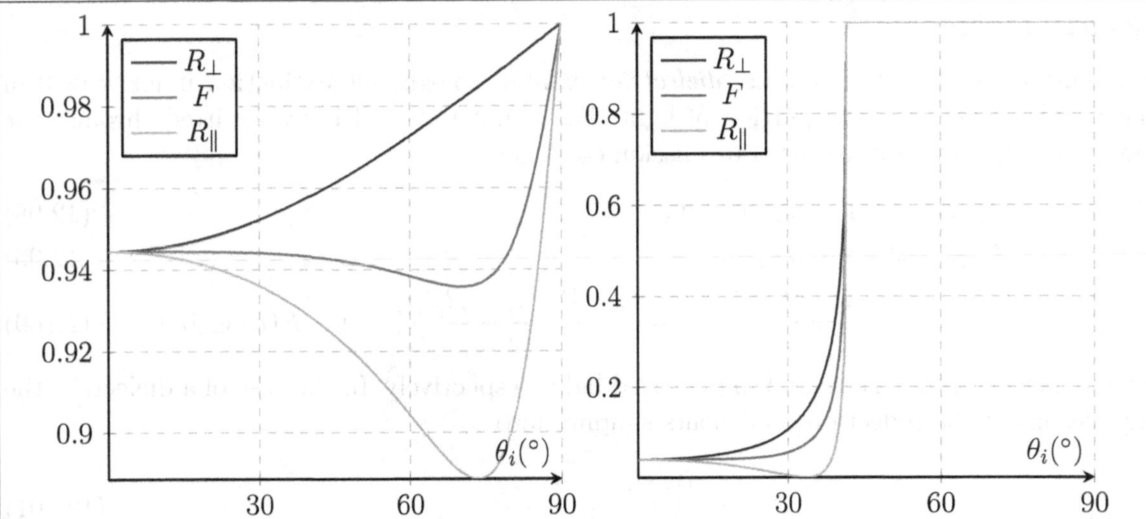

Figure 12.10: Fresnel Coefficients: Angular distribution of the Fresnel reflection coefficients for a sample conductor material (left), and for a sample dielectric (right), the latter illustrating Brewster's angle at which no *p*-polarized light is reflected, and the critical angle beyond which total internal reflection occurs.

Table 12.1: Refractive Indices: Representative complex-valued indices of refraction for sample dielectrics and metals at a wavelength of 589.29 nm (yellow doublet sodium D line).

Material	n	κ
Vacuum	1	0
Air (15°C)	1.0002772	0
Ice (−7°C)	1.3097	4.8204×10^{-9}
Water (25°C)	1.3324	7.7727×10^{-9}
Fused silica	1.4584	0
Crown glass	1.50–1.54	0
Flint glass	1.60–1.62	0
Diamond	2.39–2.42	0
Silver	0.1210	3.6513
Gold	0.2656	2.9579
Copper	0.4828	2.8013
Aluminum	1.2066	7.0674
Chromium	3.2112	3.3008

12.4.3.1 Conductor

Electrical *conductors* are characterized by a non-negligible extinction index $\kappa \gg 0$, and the portion of light that is not reflected is consequently absorbed by the medium, thereby yielding negligible penetration depths. The refractive and extinction indices of several metals such as copper and gold are strongly wavelength-dependent, therefore determining the dominant tint of the material.

12.4.3.2 Dielectric

Behaving as electrical insulators, *dielectrics* exhibit a negligible extinction index $\kappa \approx 0$ in the visible range, and the portion of light that is not reflected is transmitted through the medium proportionally to the transmission coefficients

$$T_\perp(\mu) \triangleq 1 - R_\perp(\mu) \in [0,1] \tag{12.98}$$

$$T_\parallel(\mu) \triangleq 1 - R_\parallel(\mu) \in [0,1] \tag{12.99}$$

$$T(\mu) \triangleq \frac{T_\perp(\mu) + T_\parallel(\mu)}{2} = \frac{2 - R_\perp(\mu) - R_\parallel(\mu)}{2} = 1 - F(\mu) \in [0,1] \tag{12.100}$$

for *s*-polarized, *p*-polarized and unpolarized light, respectively. In the case of a dielectric, the expressions of the reflection coefficients simplify into

491
$$a \overset{(12.82)}{=} \sqrt{\frac{|c| + c}{2}} \tag{12.101}$$

491
$$b \overset{(12.83)}{=} \sqrt{\frac{|c| - c}{2}} \tag{12.102}$$

491
$$c \overset{(12.84)}{=} n^2 - \left(1 - \mu^2\right) \tag{12.103}$$

Whenever $\theta_i \geq \theta_c$, then $\sin(\theta_i)^2 \geq \frac{n_t^2}{n_i^2}$ and $c \leq 0$ such that $a = 0$ and $b = \sqrt{-c}$, from which
491 490 490 490 follows that $F(\mu) \overset{(12.85)}{=} R_\perp(\mu) \overset{(12.79)}{=} R_\parallel(\mu) \overset{(12.81)}{=} R_{\parallel/\perp}(\mu) \overset{(12.80)}{=} 1$, which is in agreement with the law of total internal reflection. Conversely, whenever $\theta_i \leq \theta_c$, then $\sin(\theta_i)^2 \leq \frac{n_t^2}{n_i^2}$ and $c \geq 0$ such that $b = 0$ and

489
489
$$\begin{aligned} a &= \sqrt{c} = \sqrt{n^2 - (1 - \cos(\theta_i)^2)} = n\sqrt{1 - \frac{\sin(\theta_i)^2}{n^2}} \overset{(12.73)}{=} n\sqrt{1 - \sin(\theta_t)^2} \\ &= n\cos(\theta_t) = \frac{n_t}{n_i}\cos(\theta_t) \overset{(12.73)}{=} \frac{\sin(\theta_i)\cos(\theta_t)}{\sin(\theta_t)} = \frac{\sin(\theta_i)}{\tan(\theta_t)} \end{aligned} \tag{12.104}$$

from which follows that

490
$$\begin{aligned} R_\perp(\mu) &\overset{(12.79)}{=} \left(\frac{a - \mu}{a + \mu}\right)^2 = \left(\frac{n\cos(\theta_t) - \cos(\theta_i)}{n\cos(\theta_t) + \cos(\theta_i)}\right)^2 \\ &= \left(\frac{n_t\cos(\theta_t) - n_i\cos(\theta_i)}{n_t\cos(\theta_t) + n_i\cos(\theta_i)}\right)^2 = \left(\frac{\sin(\theta_i - \theta_t)}{\sin(\theta_i + \theta_t)}\right)^2 \end{aligned} \tag{12.105}$$

490
$$R_{\parallel/\perp}(\mu) \overset{(12.80)}{=} \left(\frac{a - \frac{1-\mu^2}{\mu}}{a + \frac{1-\mu^2}{\mu}}\right)^2 = \left(\frac{\frac{\sin(\theta_i)\cos(\theta_t)}{\sin(\theta_t)} - \frac{\sin(\theta_i)^2}{\cos(\theta_i)}}{\frac{\sin(\theta_i)\cos(\theta_t)}{\sin(\theta_t)} + \frac{\sin(\theta_i)^2}{\cos(\theta_i)}}\right)^2 = \left(\frac{\cos(\theta_i + \theta_t)}{\cos(\theta_i - \theta_t)}\right)^2 \tag{12.106}$$

490
$$R_\parallel(\mu) \overset{(12.81)}{=} \left(\frac{n_i\cos(\theta_t) - n_t\cos(\theta_i)}{n_i\cos(\theta_t) + n_t\cos(\theta_i)}\right)^2 = \left(\frac{\tan(\theta_i - \theta_t)}{\tan(\theta_i + \theta_t)}\right)^2 \tag{12.107}$$

where $R_\perp(\mu)$ and $R_\parallel(\mu)$ are both symmetric with respect to incidence and transmittance, such that $T_\perp(\cos(\theta_i))$, $T_\parallel(\cos(\theta_i))$ and $T(\cos(\theta_i))$ evaluated with a relative index of refraction n equal $T_\perp(\cos(\theta_t))$, $T_\parallel(\cos(\theta_t))$ and $T(\cos(\theta_t))$ evaluated with the reciprocal relative refraction index $1/n$, respectively.

A notable property of dielectrics is that when the direction of refraction is perpendicular
to the direction of reflection, $R_{\parallel/\perp}(\cos(\theta_b)) = R_\parallel(\cos(\theta_b)) = 0$, such that p-polarized radiation is entirely transmitted through the material, and all radiation reflected by the surface
is therefore s-polarized, as illustrated in *Figure 12.11*. The corresponding angle of incidence 495
θ_i, known as *Brewster's angle* θ_b, may be derived by substituting the condition $\theta_b + \theta_t = \frac{\pi}{2}$
into Snell's law 489

$$n_i \sin(\theta_b) \overset{(12.73)}{=} n_t \sin\left(\frac{\pi}{2} - \theta_b\right) = n_t \cos(\theta_b) \tag{12.108}$$

which finally leads to

$$\theta_b \triangleq \arctan\left(\frac{n_t}{n_i}\right) \tag{12.109}$$

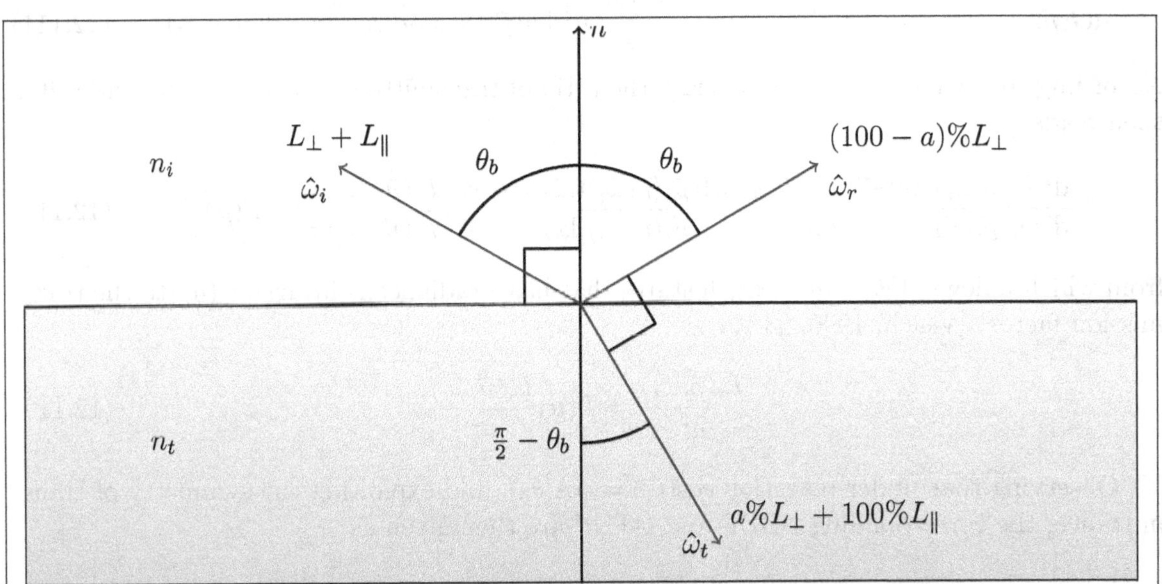

Figure 12.11: Brewster's Angle: Illustration of Brewster's angle of incidence, at which p-polarized light is entirely transmitted as opposed to being partially reflected.

12.4.4 Bidirectional Distributions

Although the flux of photons is only affected by the transmission coefficient upon refraction
at the interface, the *solid angle* subtended by a collection of rays does decrease as light 244
penetrates into a medium with greater index of refraction, gathering less energy per initial
solid angle, which effectively reduces radiance, thereby forming an exception to the radiance- 244
based reciprocity rule. Conversely, the *solid angle* subtended by the set of rays increases as 244
the latter enter a medium with lower index of refraction, effectively increasing radiance.

Exploiting the identity between polar angles established by Snell's law, the Jacobian
relating the differential *solid angles* is then given by 244

244 489 489

$$
\begin{aligned}
\frac{d\hat{\omega}_t}{d\hat{\omega}_i} &\overset{(6.62)}{=} \frac{\sin(\theta_t)d\theta_t d\phi_t}{\sin(\theta_i)d\theta_i d\phi_i} \\
&\overset{(12.73)}{=} \frac{\sin(\theta_t)}{\sin(\theta_i)} \frac{d \arcsin\left(\frac{n_i}{n_t}\sin(\theta_i)\right)}{d\theta_i} \\
&= \frac{n_i}{n_t} \frac{\frac{n_i}{n_t}\cos(\theta_i)}{\sqrt{1-\frac{n_i^2}{n_t^2}\sin(\theta_i)^2}} \\
&\overset{(12.73)}{=} \frac{n_i^2}{n_t^2} \frac{\cos(\theta_i)}{\sqrt{1-\sin(\theta_t)^2}} \\
&= \frac{n_i^2 \cos(\theta_i)}{n_t^2 \cos(\theta_t)} \qquad (12.110)
\end{aligned}
$$

421 such that the *étendue* is preserved

421 496 421

$$
dG(\vec{p},\hat{\omega}_i) \overset{(10.14)}{=} n_i^2 dA(\vec{p})\langle\hat{n},\hat{\omega}_i\rangle d\hat{\omega}_i \overset{(12.110)}{=} n_t^2 dA(\vec{p})\langle\hat{n},\hat{\omega}_t\rangle d\hat{\omega}_t \overset{(10.14)}{=} dG(\vec{p},\hat{\omega}_t) \qquad (12.111)
$$

According to the conservation of energy, the ratio of transmitted to incident differential flux then reads

427 496

$$
\frac{d^2\Phi_t(\vec{p},\hat{\omega}_t)}{d^2\Phi_i(\vec{p},\hat{\omega}_i)} \overset{(10.57)}{=} \frac{L_t(\vec{p},\hat{\omega}_t)dA(\vec{p})\langle\hat{n},\hat{\omega}_t\rangle d\hat{\omega}_t}{L_i(\vec{p},\hat{\omega}_i)dA(\vec{p})\langle\hat{n},\hat{\omega}_i\rangle d\hat{\omega}_i} \overset{(12.110)}{=} \frac{L_t(\vec{p},\hat{\omega}_t)n_i^2}{L_i(\vec{p},\hat{\omega}_i)n_t^2} = T(\mu) \qquad (12.112)
$$

from which follows *Abbe's law*, which states that basic radiance is invariant (up to the transmission factor) [Veach, 1996, §3.1]

$$
\frac{L_t(\vec{p},\hat{\omega}_t)}{n_t^2} = T(\mu)\frac{L_i(\vec{p},\hat{\omega}_i)}{n_i^2} \qquad (12.113)
$$

Observing that under reflection $\cos(\theta_i) = \cos(\theta_o)$, and exploiting the symmetry of transmittance, the corresponding BRDF and BTDF are then given as

$$
\begin{aligned}
f_r(\vec{p},\hat{\omega}_o,\hat{\omega}_i) &\triangleq \frac{\delta(\hat{\omega}_i - \tau_r(\hat{n},\hat{\omega}_o))}{\langle\hat{n},\hat{\omega}_i\rangle} F(\langle\hat{n},\hat{\omega}_i\rangle) && (12.114) \\
&= \frac{\delta(\hat{\omega}_i - \tau_r(\hat{n},\hat{\omega}_o))}{\langle\hat{n},\hat{\omega}_i\rangle} F(\langle\hat{n},\hat{\omega}_o\rangle) && (12.115) \\
f_t(\vec{p},\hat{\omega}_o,\hat{\omega}_i) &\triangleq \frac{\delta(\hat{\omega}_i - \tau_t(\hat{n},\hat{\omega}_o))}{-\langle\hat{n},\hat{\omega}_i\rangle} T_{\frac{n_o}{n_i}}(\langle\hat{n},\hat{\omega}_i\rangle)\frac{n_o^2}{n_i^2} && (12.116) \\
&= \frac{\delta(\hat{\omega}_i - \tau_t(\hat{n},\hat{\omega}_o))}{-\langle\hat{n},\hat{\omega}_i\rangle} T_{\frac{n_i}{n_o}}(\langle\hat{n},\hat{\omega}_o\rangle)\frac{n_o^2}{n_i^2} && (12.117)
\end{aligned}
$$

497 497 resulting in the visual appearance illustrated in *Figure 12.12* and *Figure 12.13*.

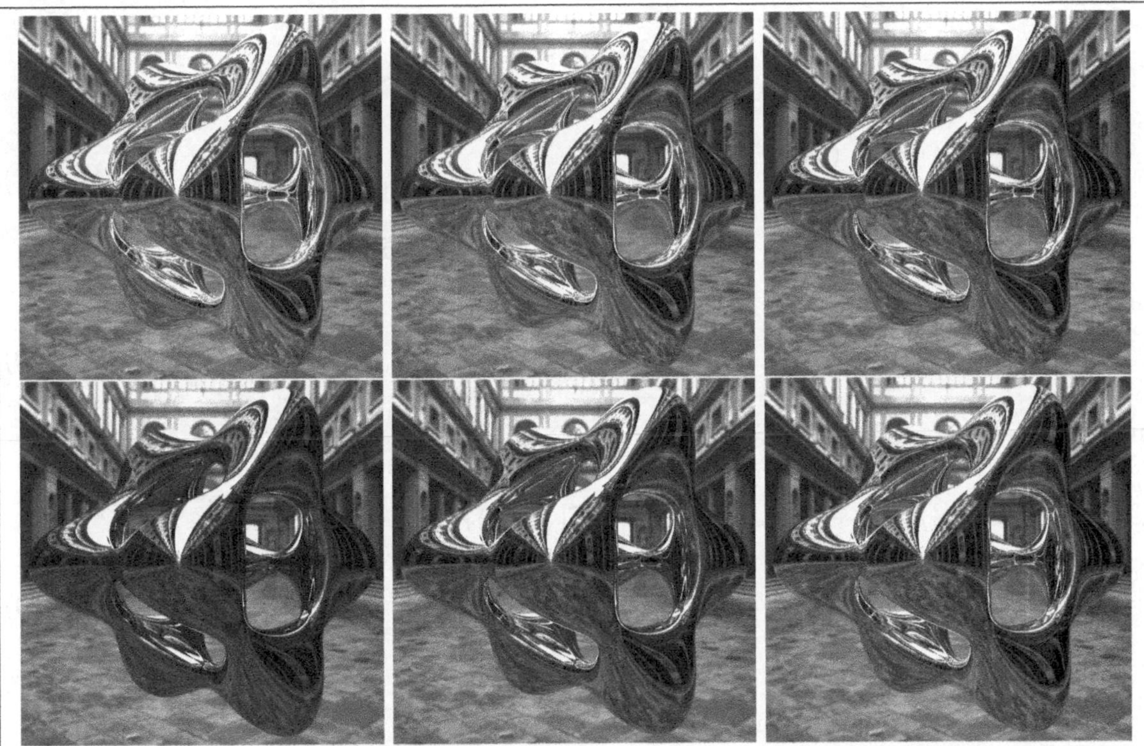

Figure 12.12: Specular Conductors: Visual appearance of specular conductors rendered with 8 spectral samples using the measured refractive and extinction indices of a perfect reflector (top left), silver (top center), aluminum (top right), chromium (bottom left), copper (bottom center) and gold (bottom right) (light probe courtesy of Paul Debevec).

Figure 12.13: Specular Dielectrics: Visual appearance of specular dielectrics rendered using the refractive indices of ice, glass and diamond (from left to right, respectively) (light probe courtesy of Paul Debevec).

12.4.5 Albedo and Sampling

The respective albedos then read

476 496 45

$$\rho_r(\vec{p}, \hat{\omega}_o) \overset{(12.9)}{\underset{(12.114)}{=}} \int_{2\pi^+} \frac{\delta(\hat{\omega}_i - \tau_r(\hat{n}, \hat{\omega}_o))}{\langle \hat{n}, \hat{\omega}_i \rangle} F(\langle \hat{n}, \hat{\omega}_o \rangle) \langle \hat{n}, \hat{\omega}_i \rangle \mathrm{d}\hat{\omega}_i \overset{(2.218)}{=} F(\langle \hat{n}, \hat{\omega}_o \rangle) \tag{12.118}$$

476 496 45

$$\rho_t(\vec{p}, \hat{\omega}_o) \overset{(12.9)}{\underset{(12.116)}{=}} \int_{2\pi^-} \frac{\delta(\hat{\omega}_i - \tau_t(\hat{n}, \hat{\omega}_o))}{-\langle \hat{n}, \hat{\omega}_i \rangle} T(\langle \hat{n}, \hat{\omega}_o \rangle) \frac{n_o^2}{n_i^2} |\langle \hat{n}, \hat{\omega}_i \rangle| \mathrm{d}\hat{\omega}_i \overset{(2.218)}{=} T(\langle \hat{n}, \hat{\omega}_o \rangle) \frac{n_o^2}{n_i^2} \tag{12.119}$$

such that

494

$$\begin{aligned} \rho_r(\vec{p}, \hat{\omega}_o) + \rho_t(\vec{p}, \hat{\omega}_o) &\overset{(12.100)}{=} F(\langle \hat{n}, \hat{\omega}_o \rangle) + (1 - F(\langle \hat{n}, \hat{\omega}_o \rangle)) \frac{n_o^2}{n_i^2} \\ &= (1 - F(\langle \hat{n}, \hat{\omega}_o \rangle)) \left(\frac{n_o^2}{n_i^2} - 1 \right) + 1 \end{aligned} \tag{12.120}$$

12.5 PHENOMENOLOGICAL MODELS

12.5.1 Cosine-Lobe Distribution

131 The cosine-lobe distribution is a *probability density* centered around a zenith direction $\hat{\omega}_z$ and defined as

$$c_n(\hat{\omega}_z, \hat{\omega}_i) \triangleq \frac{n+1}{2\pi} \langle \hat{\omega}_z, \hat{\omega}_i \rangle^n \tag{12.121}$$

whose integral over the domain Ω_i may be expressed in a separable form as

244

$$\begin{aligned} \int_{\Omega_i} c_n(\hat{\omega}_z, \hat{\omega}_i) \mathrm{d}\hat{\omega}_i &\overset{(6.64)}{=} \int_0^{\phi_i} \frac{1}{2\pi} \mathrm{d}\phi \int_{\cos(\theta_i)}^1 (n+1) \mu^n \mathrm{d}\mu \\ &= \left[\frac{\phi}{2\pi} \right]_0^{\phi_i} \left[\mu^{n+1} \right]_{\cos(\theta_i)}^1 \\ &= \frac{\phi_i}{2\pi} \left(1 - \cos(\theta_i)^{n+1} \right) \end{aligned} \tag{12.122}$$

where $\mu \triangleq \cos(\theta) = \langle \hat{\omega}_z, \hat{\omega}_i \rangle$.

Integrating over the whole hemispherical domain by substituting $\phi_i = 2\pi$ and $\theta_i = \frac{\pi}{2}$ then ensures normalization

$$\int_{2\pi^+} c_n(\hat{\omega}_z, \hat{\omega}_i) \mathrm{d}\hat{\omega}_i = 1 \tag{12.123}$$

134 155 while applying *inverse-transform sampling* allows *importance sampling* to be readily carried as

$$\xi_\phi = \frac{\phi_i}{2\pi} \implies \phi_i = 2\pi \xi_\phi \tag{12.124}$$

$$\xi_\theta = 1 - \cos(\theta_i)^{n+1} \implies \theta_i = \arccos\left(\sqrt[n+1]{1 - \xi_\theta} \right) \tag{12.125}$$

Uniform sampling can then be achieved by letting $n = 0$, which is equivalent to sampling a unit-radius spherical cap of apex angle $\theta_a = \frac{\pi}{2}$, while in the special case where $n = 1$, the expression of the polar angle simplifies into $\theta_i = \arccos\left(\sqrt{1-\xi_\theta}\right) = \arcsin\left(\sqrt{\xi_\theta}\right)$ from which follow the *Cartesian coordinates* of the sample incident direction 67

$$\hat{\omega}_i \triangleq \begin{bmatrix} x_i \\ y_i \\ z_i \end{bmatrix} \overset{(3.6)}{\underset{(3.8)}{\overset{(3.7)}{=}}} \begin{bmatrix} \sin(\theta_i)\cos(\phi_i) \\ \sin(\theta_i)\sin(\phi_i) \\ \cos(\theta_i) \end{bmatrix} = \begin{bmatrix} \sqrt{\xi_\theta}\cos(2\pi\xi_\phi) \\ \sqrt{\xi_\theta}\sin(2\pi\xi_\phi) \\ \sqrt{1-\xi_\theta} \end{bmatrix} \tag{12.126}$$

67 67 67

By exploiting the fact that carrying the integral of the cosine term over the hemisphere is equivalent to integrating over the area of the subtended disk, the above sampling distribution may alternatively be achieved by drawing a random sample uniformly distributed over the unit disk $(r_i, \phi_i) = (\sqrt{\xi_r}, 2\pi\xi_\phi)$, and projecting it straight up onto the hemisphere such that $\theta_i = \arcsin(r_i)$.

12.5.2 Lambertian

12.5.2.1 Formulation

The reflectance distribution of a perfectly diffusive material is characterized by Lambert's law of diffuse reflection and modeled by the *Lambertian BRDF* [Lambert, 1760]

$$f_r(\vec{p}, \hat{\omega}_o, \hat{\omega}_i) \triangleq \frac{1}{\pi} \tag{12.127}$$

which is a constant independent of the incident and exitant directions, as illustrated in *Figure 12.14.* 499

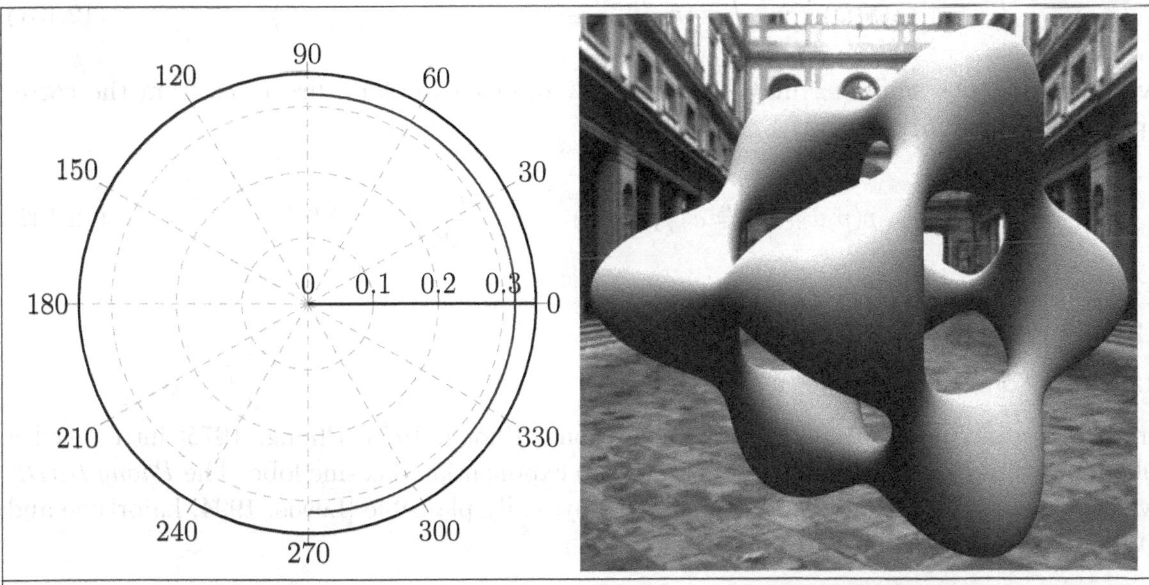

Figure 12.14: Lambertian BRDF: Angular distribution (left) and visual appearance (right, light probe courtesy of Paul Debevec) of the Lambertian BRDF.

12.5.2.2 Albedo and Sampling

Expressing the product of the BRDF and cosine factor in terms of the *cosine-lobe distribution*, the albedo is readily given as 498

$$\rho(\vec{p}, \hat{\omega}) \overset{(12.9)}{=} \int_{2\pi^+} c_1(\hat{n}, \hat{\omega}')\mathrm{d}\hat{\omega}' \overset{(12.123)}{=} 1 \tag{12.128}$$

476 498

155 while *importance sampling* may be carried by drawing random directions from the corre-
131 sponding *probability density*

498
$$p(\vec{p}, \hat{\omega}_o, \hat{\omega}_i) \triangleq c_1(\hat{n}, \hat{\omega}_i) \overset{(12.121)}{=} \frac{1}{\pi}\langle \hat{n}, \hat{\omega}_i \rangle \tag{12.129}$$

12.5.3 Minnaert

12.5.3.1 Formulation

Originally introduced as an empirical characterization of the reflectance off of lunar dust, the *Minnaert BRDF* [Minnaert, 1941] reads

$$f_r(\vec{p}, \hat{\omega}_o, \hat{\omega}_i) \triangleq \frac{n+2}{2\pi}\langle \hat{n}, \hat{\omega}_o \rangle^n \langle \hat{n}, \hat{\omega}_i \rangle^n \tag{12.130}$$

503 as illustrated in *Figure 12.16* and *Figure 12.17*, and where the range $n \in [-1/2, 0)$ is most
504 adequate to model the reflectance properties of the moon's surface, while the model reduces
499 to a *Lambertian* BRDF whenever $n = 0$.

12.5.3.2 Albedo and Sampling

498 Expressing the product of the BRDF and cosine factor in terms of the *cosine-lobe distribution*,
the albedo is readily given as

476
498
$$\rho(\vec{p}, \hat{\omega}) \overset{(12.9)}{=} \int_{2\pi^+} \langle \hat{n}, \hat{\omega} \rangle^n c_{n+1}(\hat{n}, \hat{\omega}')\mathrm{d}\hat{\omega}' \overset{(12.123)}{=} \langle \hat{n}, \hat{\omega} \rangle^n \tag{12.131}$$

155 while *importance sampling* may be carried by drawing random directions from the corre-
131 sponding *probability density*

498
$$p(\vec{p}, \hat{\omega}_o, \hat{\omega}_i) \triangleq c_{n+1}(\hat{n}, \hat{\omega}_i) \overset{(12.121)}{=} \frac{n+2}{2\pi}\langle \hat{n}, \hat{\omega}_i \rangle^{n+1} \tag{12.132}$$

12.5.4 Phong

12.5.4.1 Formulation

In order to simulate specular highlights, Phong [Phong, 1973, Phong, 1975] introduced a phenomenological reflection model based on an exponentiated cosine lobe. The *Phong BRDF* was subsequently modified so as to make it physically plausible [Lewis, 1994, Lafortune and Willems, 1994b], yielding

$$f_r(\vec{p}, \hat{\omega}_o, \hat{\omega}_i) \triangleq \frac{n+2}{2\pi}\max\{0, c(\hat{\omega}_o, \hat{\omega}_i)\}^n \tag{12.133}$$

503 as illustrated in *Figure 12.16* and *Figure 12.17*, which reduces to a *Lambertian* BRDF
504
499 whenever $n = 0$ (exploiting the identity $0^0 = 1$ for the portion of the hemisphere where
$c(\hat{\omega}_o, \hat{\omega}_i) \leq 0$), and where

488
$$c(\hat{\omega}_o, \hat{\omega}_i) \triangleq \langle \hat{\omega}_o, \tau_r(\hat{n}, \hat{\omega}_i) \rangle = \langle \tau_r(\hat{n}, \hat{\omega}_o), \hat{\omega}_i \rangle \overset{(12.70)}{=} 2\langle \hat{n}, \hat{\omega}_o \rangle \langle \hat{n}, \hat{\omega}_i \rangle - \langle \hat{\omega}_o, \hat{\omega}_i \rangle \tag{12.134}$$

12.5.4.2 Albedo and Sampling

Whenever the exitant direction is normal to the surface, then

$$\lim_{\hat{\omega}_o \to \hat{n}} c(\hat{\omega}_o, \hat{\omega}_i) \overset{(12.134)}{=} \langle \hat{n}, \hat{\omega}_i \rangle \tag{12.135}$$ 500

and the product of the BRDF and cosine factor can be expressed in terms of the *cosine-lobe*
distribution. Given that the albedo is maximal in such a setting, its upper bound is then 498
readily given as

$$\rho(\vec{p}, \hat{\omega}) \le \rho(\vec{p}, \hat{n}) \overset{(12.9)}{=} \int_{2\pi^+} c_{n+1}(\hat{n}, \hat{\omega}')\mathrm{d}\hat{\omega}' \overset{(12.123)}{=} 1 \tag{12.136}$$ 476 498

In turn, *importance sampling* may be carried by drawing random directions from the 155
following *probability density* 131

$$\begin{aligned} p(\vec{p}, \hat{\omega}_o, \hat{\omega}_i) &\triangleq \max\{0, c_n(\tau_r(\hat{n}, \hat{\omega}_o), \hat{\omega}_i)\} \\ &\overset{(12.121)}{=} \frac{n+1}{2\pi} \max\{0, \langle \tau_r(\hat{n}, \hat{\omega}_o), \hat{\omega}_i \rangle\}^n \\ &\overset{(12.134)}{=} \frac{n+1}{2\pi} \max\{0, c(\hat{\omega}_o, \hat{\omega}_i)\}^n \end{aligned} \tag{12.137}$$ 498 500

which might generate sample directions that point underneath the surface, where the BRDF
is implicitly assumed to be zero. A more efficient *acceptance–rejection sampling* strategy can 135
alternatively be devised by considering the *probability density* to be solely positive over the 131
upper hemisphere, for which, in the case of an integer exponent, the normalization factor may
be obtained by applying the concepts of *axial moments* to integrate the distribution over the 246
positive spherical digon illustrated in *Figure 12.15*, a special case for which the evaluation 501
procedure can be substantially optimized [Arvo, 1995b].

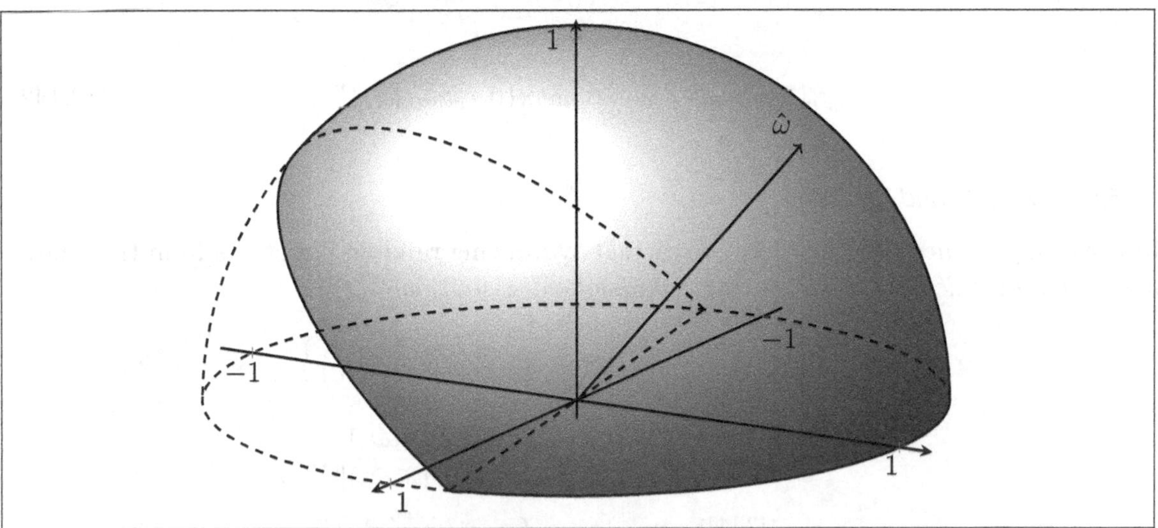

Figure 12.15: Spherical Digon: Illustration of the spherical lune, also called spherical digon, over which the Phong BRDF is positive.

12.5.5 Lafortune

12.5.5.1 Formulation

The aforementioned cosine lobe models may be generalized by first expressing a direction $\hat{\omega}$ in terms of its coordinates within a frame defined by the surface tangent, bi-tangent and normal

$$\hat{\omega} = \langle \vec{u}, \hat{\omega} \rangle \vec{u} + \langle \vec{v}, \hat{\omega} \rangle \vec{v} + \langle \hat{n}, \hat{\omega} \rangle \hat{n} \tag{12.138}$$

500 and then substituting the reflection function $\tau_r(\hat{n}, \hat{\omega})$ used in the *Phong* BRDF with the
more general transformation

$$t_c(\hat{n}, \hat{\omega}) \triangleq x_c \langle \vec{u}, \hat{\omega} \rangle \vec{u} + y_c \langle \vec{v}, \hat{\omega} \rangle \vec{v} + z_c \langle \hat{n}, \hat{\omega} \rangle \hat{n} \tag{12.139}$$

503 As illustrated in *Figure 12.16* and *Figure 12.17*, various reflection behaviors can then
504 be modeled by adjusting the coefficient vector $\vec{c} = [x_c, y_c, z_c]$. For instance, defining $\vec{c} =$
488
500 $[-1, -1, +1]$ yields $t_c(\hat{n}, \hat{\omega}) \overset{(12.70)}{=} \tau_r(\hat{n}, \hat{\omega})$, resulting in the *Phong* BRDF, while defining
500 $\vec{c} = [0, 0, 1]$ instead yields $t_c(\hat{n}, \hat{\omega}) = \langle \hat{n}, \hat{\omega} \rangle \hat{n}$, resulting in the *Minnaert* BRDF. Retroreflection
phenomena, as observed on safety vests and road signs, may also be modeled by defining $\vec{c} = [1, 1, 1]$ such that $t_c(\hat{n}, \hat{\omega}) = \hat{\omega}$, and off-specular peaks captured with $-x_c = -y_c > z_c > 0$. Additionally, the extension allows anisotropic reflectance properties to be accounted for by letting $x_c \neq y_c$ and aligning either the tangent or bi-tangent vector along the major axis of anisotropy. Finally, the overall flexibility of the model actually makes it a suitable basis for fitting of experimentally measured data.

The corresponding *Lafortune BRDF* [Lafortune *et al.*, 1997] is then obtained by substituting the $c(\hat{\omega}_o, \hat{\omega}_i)$ function from Phong's model with

$$c_c(\hat{\omega}_o, \hat{\omega}_i) \triangleq \langle \hat{\omega}_o, t_c(\hat{n}, \hat{\omega}_i) \rangle = \langle t_c(\hat{n}, \hat{\omega}_o), \hat{\omega}_i \rangle \tag{12.140}$$

502

$$\overset{(12.139)}{=} x_c \langle \vec{u}, \hat{\omega}_o \rangle \langle \vec{u}, \hat{\omega}_i \rangle + y_c \langle \vec{v}, \hat{\omega}_o \rangle \langle \vec{v}, \hat{\omega}_i \rangle + z_c \langle \hat{n}, \hat{\omega}_o \rangle \langle \hat{n}, \hat{\omega}_i \rangle \tag{12.141}$$

to yield

$$f_r(\vec{p}, \hat{\omega}_o, \hat{\omega}_i) \triangleq \frac{n+2}{2\pi} \max\{0, c_c(\hat{\omega}_o, \hat{\omega}_i)\}^n \tag{12.142}$$

12.5.5.2 Albedo and Sampling

155 In turn, *importance sampling* may be carried by drawing random directions from the follow-
131 ing *probability density* based on the *cosine-lobe distribution*
498

$$p(\vec{p}, \hat{\omega}_o, \hat{\omega}_i) \triangleq \max\left\{0, c_n\left(\frac{t_c(\hat{n}, \hat{\omega}_o)}{\|t_c(\hat{n}, \hat{\omega}_o)\|}, \hat{\omega}_i\right)\right\}$$

498

$$\overset{(12.121)}{=} \frac{n+1}{2\pi} \max\left\{0, \left\langle \frac{t_c(\hat{n}, \hat{\omega}_o)}{\|t_c(\hat{n}, \hat{\omega}_o)\|}, \hat{\omega}_i \right\rangle\right\}^n$$

502

$$\overset{(12.140)}{=} \frac{n+1}{2\pi} \max\left\{0, \frac{c_c(\hat{\omega}_o, \hat{\omega}_i)}{\|t_c(\hat{n}, \hat{\omega}_o)\|}\right\}^n \tag{12.143}$$

which might similarly generate sample directions that point underneath the surface, unless such samples are appropriately rejected using a scheme such as the one described for the
500 *Phong* BRDF.

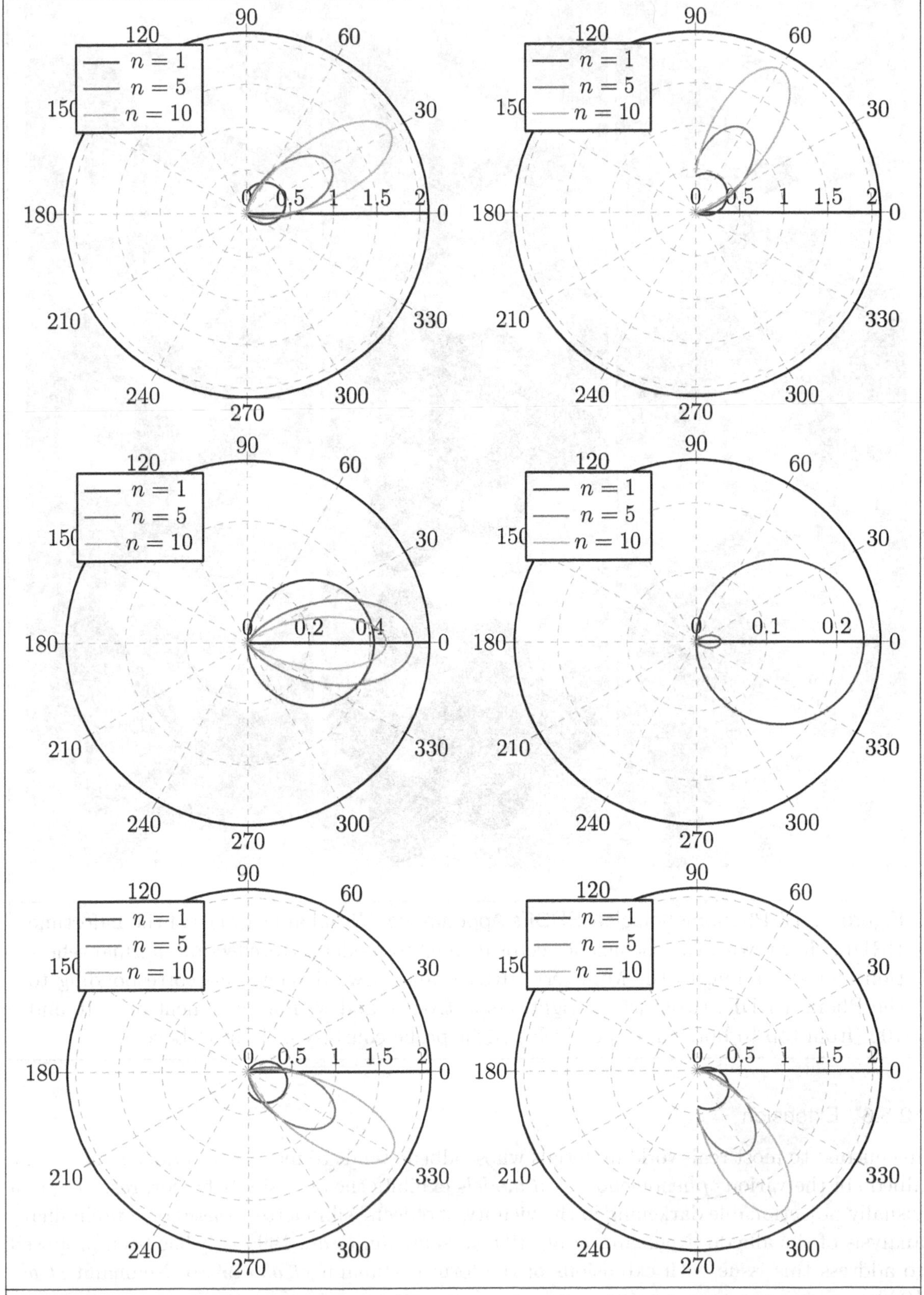

Figure 12.16: Phenomenological BRDFs Plots: Angular distribution of the Lafortune BRDF, shown for various exponents with the coefficient vector defined to model retroreflection, normal-reflection (corresponding to the Minnaert BRDF), and forward-reflection (corresponding to the Phong BRDF) (from top to bottom, respectively), and with an incidence angle of 30° (left) and 60° (right).

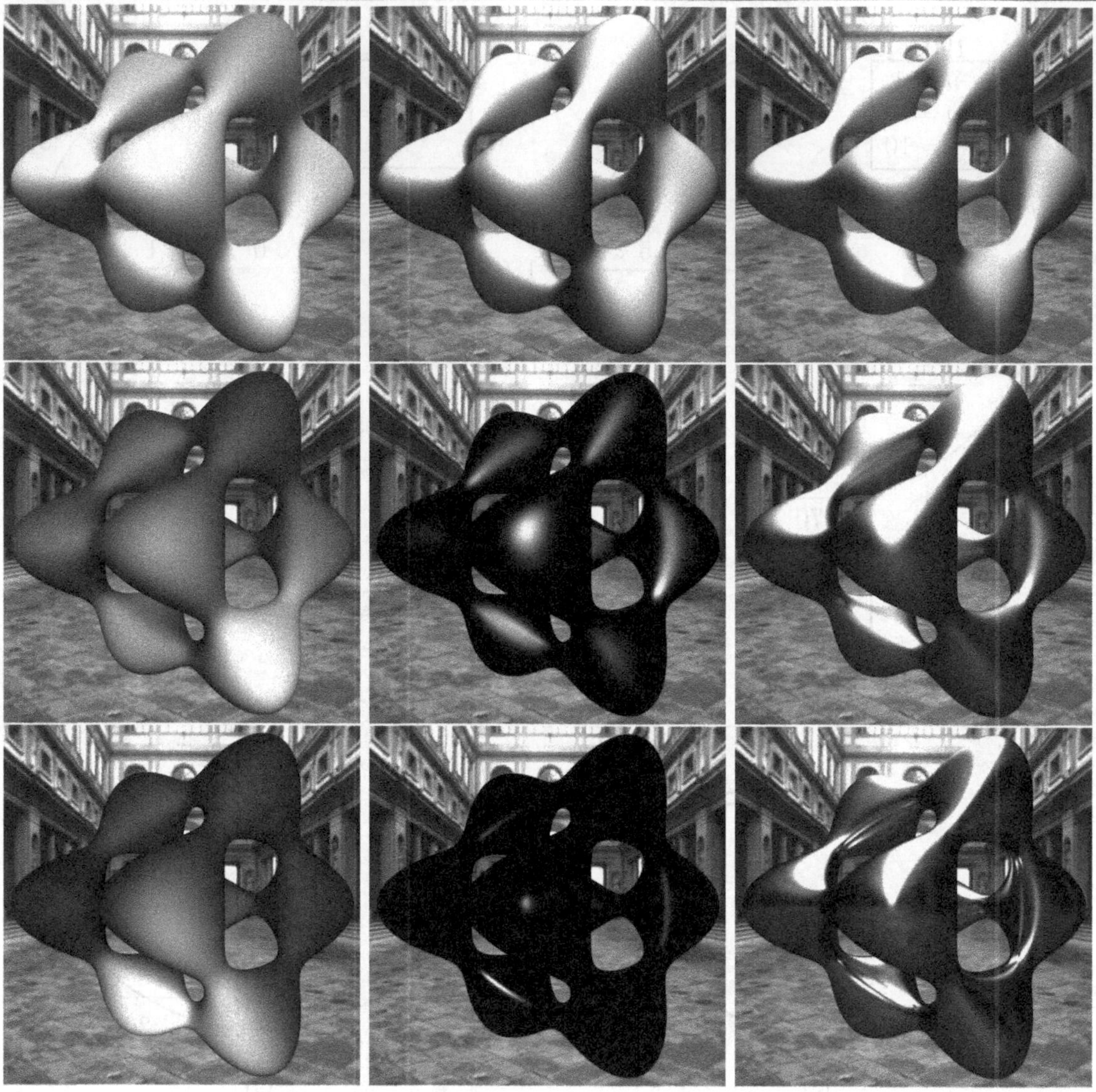

Figure 12.17: Phenomenological BRDFs Appearance: Visual appearance of the Lafortune BRDF, shown with the coefficient vector defined to model retroreflection, normal reflection (corresponding to the Minnaert BRDF), and forward reflection (corresponding to the Phong BRDF) (from left to right, respectively), and with an exponent of 1, 10 and 100 (from top to bottom, respectively) (light probe courtesy of Paul Debevec).

12.5.6 Extension

In contrast to most real-world materials whose albedo tends to increase at grazing angles, the
498 albedo of the various *phenomenological models* exhibits the opposite behavior, resulting in a visually objectionable darkening in the vicinity of objects' silhouettes. Based on a preliminary analysis of the albedo [Neumann *et al.*, 1998a, Neumann *et al.*, 1999b], it has been proposed to address this issue with extensions of the form [Neumann *et al.*, 1998b, Neumann *et al.*, 1999a]

$$f_r(\vec{p}, \hat{\omega}_o, \hat{\omega}_i) \triangleq \frac{f'_r(\vec{p}, \hat{\omega}_o, \hat{\omega}_i)}{\max\{\langle \hat{n}, \hat{\omega}_o \rangle, \langle \hat{n}, \hat{\omega}_i \rangle\}^p} \tag{12.144}$$

where $f'_r(\vec{p}, \hat{\omega}_o, \hat{\omega}_i)$ represents any of the aforementioned phenomenological BRDF models, and where $p \in [0, 1]$ is such that $p = 0$ corresponds to the original models and $p = 1$ to the associated extended model. In turn, *importance sampling* may be carried by drawing 155 random directions from the *probability density* associated with the original BRDF. 131

12.5.7 Transmission

Observing that a forward (respectively backward) *phase function* in the *thin slab* model 444 482 yields a distribution of transmission via scattering that is predominantly centered around the opposite (respectively symmetric) of the incident direction in the lower hemisphere, a generalized model for glossy transmission through *thin slabs* can be empirically derived by 482 reflecting the exitant direction provided to an arbitrary BRDF model as follows

$$f_t(\vec{p}, \hat{\omega}_o, \hat{\omega}_i) \triangleq f_r(\vec{p}, \tau_r(\hat{n}, -\hat{\omega}_o), \hat{\omega}_i) \tag{12.145}$$

such that a forward-reflective or retroreflective BRDF yields a distribution phenomenologically in agreement with a forward or backward scattering *phase function*, respectively. 444

Noting that glossy reflections typically describe distributions that are predominantly centered around the mirror direction, a phenomenological model for transmission through a glossy *dielectric* interface may similarly be defined as a distribution centered around the 494 direction of ideal refraction by refracting and then mirroring the exitant direction provided to an arbitrary BRDF model as follows

$$f_t(\vec{p}, \hat{\omega}_o, \hat{\omega}_i) \triangleq f_r\Big(\vec{p}, r(\hat{n}, \tau_t(\hat{n}, \hat{\omega}_o)), \hat{\omega}_i\Big) \tag{12.146}$$

12.6 MICRO-GEOMETRY MODELS

First introduced by Bouguer in 1760 [Bouguer, 1760], micro-geometry models assume that a given surface may be represented as a collection of microscopic asperities, such as micro-hemispheres or micro-facets, whose scale is presumed to be negligible compared to the total size of the microscopic surface sample, itself being of size negligible compared to the size of the macroscopic surface so that the latter can be considered locally flat.

Given a macroscopic surface point $\vec{p}$ with macro-normal $\hat{n} = \hat{\nabla}(\vec{p})$ as illustrated in *Figure 12.18*, let us define the integral transform $\mathcal{T}$, which measures a given function f over the 506 differential area $\mathrm{d}A(\vec{p}_m)$ in the vicinity A_m of the microscopic geometry where the micro-normal $\hat{\nabla}(\vec{p}_m)$ corresponds to a given direction $\hat{m}$

$$\begin{aligned}
\mathcal{T}\{f(\vec{p}_m)\}(\vec{p}, \hat{m}) &\triangleq \int_{A_m} \delta(\hat{\nabla}(\vec{p}_m) - \hat{m}) f(\vec{p}_m) \mathrm{d}A(\vec{p}_m) && (12.147)\\
&= \lim_{\Omega_m \to \hat{m}} \frac{\int_{A_m} \delta[\hat{\nabla}(\vec{p}_m) \in \Omega_m] f(\vec{p}_m) \mathrm{d}A(\vec{p}_m)}{\int_{\Omega_m} \mathrm{d}\hat{m}}\\
&= \sum_{\vec{p}_m | \hat{\nabla}(\vec{p}_m) = \hat{m}} f(\vec{p}_m) \frac{\mathrm{d}A(\vec{p}_m)}{\mathrm{d}\hat{m}}\\
&= \sum_{\vec{p}_m | \hat{\nabla}(\vec{p}_m) = \hat{m}} \frac{f(\vec{p}_m)}{|K(\vec{p}_m)|} && (12.148)
\end{aligned}$$

where the change from a Dirac to a Kronecker *delta function* is given by the limit $\delta(\hat{\nabla}(\vec{p}_m) - \hat{m}) = \lim_{\Omega_m \to \hat{m}} \frac{\delta[\hat{\nabla}(\vec{p}_m) \in \Omega_m]}{\int_{\Omega_m} \mathrm{d}\hat{m}}$, while $K(\vec{p}_m)$ denotes the Gaussian curvature [Levi, 2009, p. 140] 44 at the microscopic surface point $\vec{p}_m$.

From the definition then follows that the integral of the weighted transform over *solid angles* can be equivalently expressed as an integral over the microscopic surface as 244

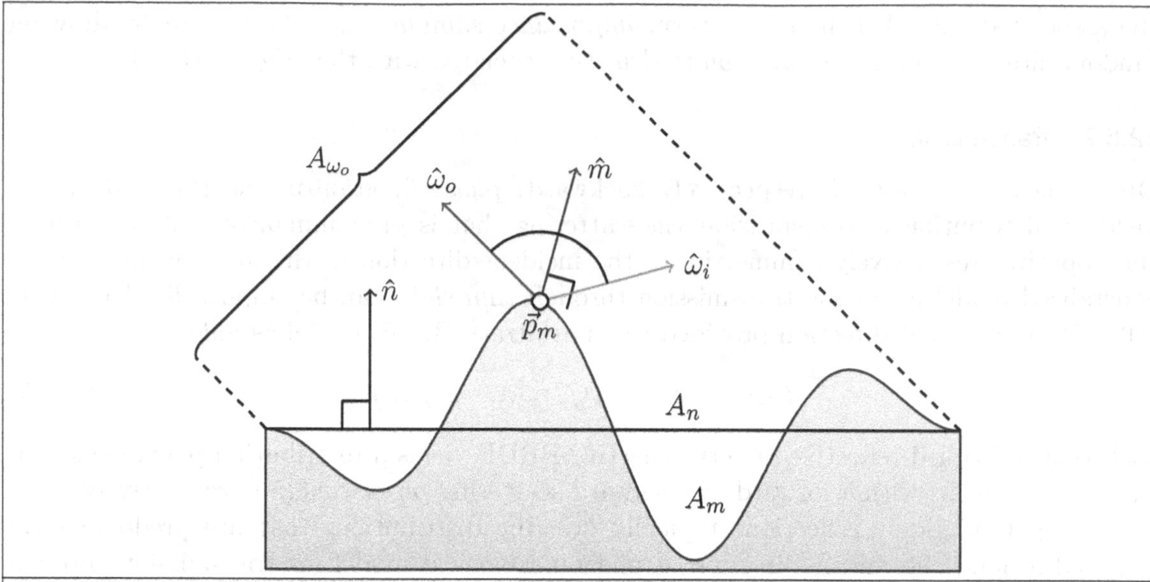

Figure 12.18: Micro-Geometry Models: Illustration of the geometric properties of the macroscopic surface and its microscopic height field.

$$\begin{aligned}
\int_{2\pi^+} \mathcal{T}\{f(\vec{p}_m)\}(\vec{p},\hat{m})g(\hat{m})\mathrm{d}\hat{m} &= \int_{2\pi^+}\int_{A_m} \delta(\hat{\nabla}(\vec{p}_m)-\hat{m})f(\vec{p}_m)\mathrm{d}A(\vec{p}_m)g(\hat{m})\mathrm{d}\hat{m} \\
&= \int_{A_m} f(\vec{p}_m)\int_{2\pi^+} \delta(\hat{\nabla}(\vec{p}_m)-\hat{m})g(\hat{m})\mathrm{d}\hat{m}\mathrm{d}A(\vec{p}_m)
\end{aligned}$$

45 $$\overset{(2.218)}{=} \int_{A_m} f(\vec{p}_m)g(\hat{\nabla}(\vec{p}_m))\mathrm{d}A(\vec{p}_m) \quad (12.149)$$

12.6.1 Normal Distribution Function

12.6.1.1 Normal Distribution

Definition The *normal distribution function* (*NDF*) measures the statistical orientation of the micro-structures as the ratio of the area of the microscopic surface orthogonal to $\hat{m}$

$$D(\vec{p},\hat{m}) \triangleq \frac{\mathcal{T}\{1\}(\vec{p},\hat{m})}{A_n} \quad (12.150)$$

relative to the total area of the macroscopic surface

$$A_n = \int_{A_n} \mathrm{d}A(\vec{p}_n) = \int_{A_m} \langle\hat{n},\hat{\nabla}(\vec{p}_m)\rangle \mathrm{d}A(\vec{p}_m) \quad (12.151)$$

In order to be physically plausible, an NDF must be non-negative

$$D(\vec{p},\hat{m}) \geq 0 \quad (12.152)$$

and, in the typical case where the underlying microscopic surface is a height field, ensure that all micro-structures face towards the upper hemisphere

$$D(\vec{p},\hat{m}) = 0, \quad \forall\hat{m} \mid \langle\hat{n},\hat{m}\rangle \leq 0 \quad (12.153)$$

244 The integral of the NDF over *solid angles* yields the ratio of the area A_m of the micro-

surface to the area A_n of the macroscopic surface

$$\begin{aligned}
\int_{2\pi^+} D(\vec{p},\hat{m})\mathrm{d}\hat{m} &\overset{(12.150)}{=} \int_{2\pi^+} \frac{\mathcal{T}\{1\}(\vec{p},\hat{m})}{A_n}\mathrm{d}\hat{m} \\
&\overset{(12.149)}{=} \frac{1}{A_n}\int_{A_m} \mathrm{d}A(\vec{p}_m) \\
&= \frac{A_m}{A_n} \\
&\geq 1 \qquad (12.154)
\end{aligned}$$

506
506

Conversely, given a direction $\hat{\omega}$, the strong normalization constraint, which is a distinctive property of an actual manifold micro-surface, states that the integral of the cosine-weighted NDF over *solid angles* yields the ratio of the signed area A_ω of the micro-surface projected along $\hat{\omega}$, which is the same as the projected area of the macroscopic surface itself, to the total area A_n of the latter 244

$$\begin{aligned}
g(\vec{p},\hat{\omega}) &\triangleq \int_{2\pi^+} D(\vec{p},\hat{m})\langle\hat{\omega},\hat{m}\rangle\mathrm{d}\hat{m} \qquad (12.155) \\
&\overset{(12.150)}{=} \int_{2\pi^+} \frac{\mathcal{T}\{1\}(\vec{p},\hat{m})}{A_n}\langle\hat{\omega},\hat{m}\rangle\mathrm{d}\hat{m} \\
&\overset{(12.149)}{=} \frac{1}{A_n}\int_{A_m} \langle\hat{\omega},\hat{\nabla}(\vec{p}_m)\rangle\mathrm{d}A(\vec{p}_m) \\
&= \frac{1}{A_n}\int_{A_\omega} \mathrm{d}A(\vec{p}_\omega) \\
&= \frac{A_\omega}{A_n} \\
&= \langle\hat{n},\hat{\omega}\rangle \qquad (12.156) \\
&\leq 1 \qquad (12.157)
\end{aligned}$$

506
506

which may alternatively be expressed as the sum $g(\vec{p},\hat{\omega}) = g^+(\vec{p},\hat{\omega}) + g^-(\vec{p},\hat{\omega})$ of its positive and negative components

$$\begin{aligned}
g^+(\vec{p},\hat{\omega}) &\triangleq \int_{\Omega_m|\langle\hat{n},\hat{\omega}\rangle\langle\hat{m},\hat{\omega}\rangle>0} D(\vec{p},\hat{m})\langle\hat{\omega},\hat{m}\rangle\mathrm{d}\hat{m} \qquad (12.158) \\
g^-(\vec{p},\hat{\omega}) &\triangleq \int_{\Omega_m|\langle\hat{n},\hat{\omega}\rangle\langle\hat{m},\hat{\omega}\rangle\leq 0} D(\vec{p},\hat{m})\langle\hat{\omega},\hat{m}\rangle\mathrm{d}\hat{m} \qquad (12.159)
\end{aligned}$$

Considering the special case where $\hat{\omega} = \hat{n}$ then yields the weak normalization constraint

$$g(\vec{p},\hat{n}) \overset{(12.155)}{=} \int_{2\pi^+} D(\vec{p},\hat{m})\langle\hat{n},\hat{m}\rangle\mathrm{d}\hat{m} \overset{(12.156)}{=} \langle\hat{n},\hat{n}\rangle = 1 \qquad (12.160)$$

507
507

The normalization constraints given above are necessary conditions for an NDF to correspond to a physical surface profile. However, it is important to observe that these constraints are not, by themselves, sufficient to characterize a given surface as there may exist many different profiles (e.g., their central symmetry about a given point) having identical normal distributions.

Micro-Facets In the case of a non-manifold surface made of a finite collection F of planar micro-facets f, each with normal $\hat{\nabla}(f)$ as illustrated in *Figure 12.19*, the integral can be 508

independently carried over each individual micro-facet and the NDF reduces to a discrete set
44 of Dirac *delta functions* weighted by the area A_f of the facets

$$\begin{aligned} D(\vec{p}, \hat{m}) &= \frac{1}{A_n} \sum_{f \in F} \int_{A_f} \delta(\hat{\nabla}(\vec{p}_m) - \hat{m}) \mathrm{d}A(\vec{p}_m) \\ &= \frac{1}{A_n} \sum_{f \in F} \delta(\hat{\nabla}(f) - \hat{m}) \int_{A_f} \mathrm{d}A(\vec{p}_m) \\ &= \frac{1}{A_n} \sum_{f \in F} \delta(\hat{\nabla}(f) - \hat{m}) A_f \end{aligned} \tag{12.161}$$

which generally does not obey the strong, and possibly not the weak either, normalization constraint

45

$$\begin{aligned} g(\vec{p}, \hat{\omega}) &= \int_{2\pi^+} \frac{1}{A_n} \sum_{f \in F} \delta(\hat{\nabla}(f) - \hat{m}) A_f \langle \hat{\omega}, \hat{m} \rangle \mathrm{d}\hat{m} \\ &= \frac{1}{A_n} \sum_{f \in F} A_f \int_{2\pi^+} \delta(\hat{\nabla}(f) - \hat{m}) \langle \hat{\omega}, \hat{m} \rangle \mathrm{d}\hat{m} \\ &\overset{(2.218)}{=} \frac{1}{A_n} \sum_{f \in F} A_f \langle \hat{\omega}, \hat{\nabla}(f) \rangle \\ &\neq \frac{A_\omega}{A_n} \end{aligned} \tag{12.162}$$

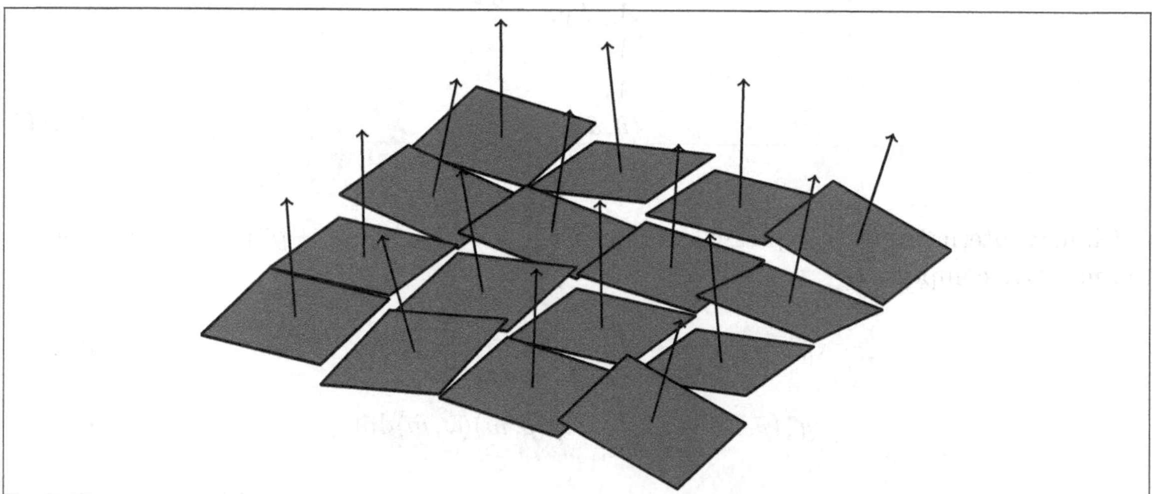

Figure 12.19: Micro-Facets Surface: Illustration of a non-manifold surface made of a finite collection of planar micro-facets.

Sampling Whenever the weak normalization constraint holds, the cosine-weighted NDF forms a normalized distribution over the hemisphere, and it may therefore be used as a
131 155 *probability density* for *importance sampling* of a random micro-normal. Substituting the
formulation of the NDF and reformulating the PDF in the space of the micro-geometry then

yields

$$\begin{aligned}\int_{2\pi^+} D(\vec{p}, \hat{m})\langle \hat{n}, \hat{m}\rangle \mathrm{d}\hat{m} &= \int_{2\pi^+} \frac{\mathcal{T}\{1\}(\vec{p}, \hat{m})}{A_n}\langle \hat{n}, \hat{m}\rangle \mathrm{d}\hat{m} \\ &\overset{(12.149)}{=} \int_{A_m} \frac{1}{A_n}\langle \hat{n}, \hat{\nabla}(\vec{p}_m)\rangle \mathrm{d}A(\vec{p}_m) \\ &= \int_{A_n} \frac{1}{A_n}\mathrm{d}A(\vec{p}_n) \qquad (12.163)\end{aligned}$$ 506

while the resulting PDF is shown to be constant in the space of the underlying macroscopic surface.

This sampling strategy is therefore equivalent to uniformly drawing a point in the underlying area of the macroscopic surface, and then projecting it along the macro-normal onto the micro-geometry of the height field, from which the sample micro-normal is obtained. Shall the albedo of the micro-structures be taken into account, the sampling scheme may then be extended by instead drawing points according to the projection of the albedo onto the underlying area of the macroscopic surface, such that, under projective mapping, the PDF is readily defined by the texture itself.

In case the microscopic height field of infinite extent is created by procedural periodic instantiation of a base rectangular tile, *importance sampling* of the micro-normals can be 155
readily carried from the base tile only, as it is an entirely local operation just like point location, curvature calculation and micro-normal computation.

12.6.1.2 Slope Distribution

As an alternative, an NDF may also be expressed as a two-dimensional slope distribution $D(\vec{p}, u, v)$ in terms of the derivatives of the *Cartesian coordinates* of the points on the surface 67

$$u \triangleq \frac{\mathrm{d}z}{\mathrm{d}x} \qquad (12.164)$$

$$v \triangleq \frac{\mathrm{d}z}{\mathrm{d}y} \qquad (12.165)$$

which are related to the micro-structures' inclination angle $\theta_m = \angle(\hat{n}, \hat{m}) \overset{(3.77)}{=} \arccos(\langle \vec{n}, \vec{m}\rangle)$ 77
and azimuthal angle ϕ_m by

$$\theta_m \triangleq \arctan\left(\sqrt{u^2 + v^2}\right) \qquad (12.166)$$

$$\phi_m \triangleq \operatorname{arctan2}(-v, -u) \qquad (12.167)$$

and reciprocally by

$$u = -\tan(\theta_m)\cos(\phi_m) \qquad (12.168)$$

$$v = -\tan(\theta_m)\sin(\phi_m) \qquad (12.169)$$

with $\tan(\theta_m)$ being the absolute slope.

Alternatively, expressing the *spherical coordinates* of the micro-normal in terms of its 70
Cartesian coordinates yields 67

$$u \underset{(3.8)}{\overset{(3.6)}{=}} -\frac{x_m}{z_m} \overset{(3.61)}{=} -\frac{x_m}{\sqrt{1 - x_m^2 - y_m^2}} \qquad (12.170)$$ 67 74 67

$$v \underset{(3.8)}{\overset{(3.7)}{=}} -\frac{y_m}{z_m} \overset{(3.61)}{=} -\frac{y_m}{\sqrt{1 - x_m^2 - y_m^2}} \qquad (12.171)$$ 67 74 67

and conversely

$$\begin{aligned} x_m &= \frac{-u}{\sqrt{u^2+v^2+1}} && (12.172) \\ y_m &= \frac{-v}{\sqrt{u^2+v^2+1}} && (12.173) \\ z_m &= \frac{1}{\sqrt{u^2+v^2+1}} && (12.174) \end{aligned}$$

such that the cosine and sine inclination angles read

$$\begin{aligned} \cos(\theta_m) &= z_m = \frac{1}{\sqrt{u^2+v^2+1}} && (12.175) \\ \sin(\theta_m) &= \sqrt{x_m^2+y_m^2} = \sqrt{\frac{u^2+v^2}{u^2+v^2+1}} && (12.176) \end{aligned}$$

The Jacobian matrix of the transformation then reads

$$J_T \triangleq \begin{bmatrix} \frac{\partial \theta_m}{\partial u} & \frac{\partial \theta_m}{\partial v} \\ \frac{\partial \phi_m}{\partial u} & \frac{\partial \phi_m}{\partial v} \end{bmatrix} = \begin{bmatrix} \frac{u}{\sqrt{u^2+v^2}(u^2+v^2+1)} & \frac{v}{\sqrt{u^2+v^2}(u^2+v^2+1)} \\ -\frac{v}{u^2+v^2} & \frac{u}{u^2+v^2} \end{bmatrix} \qquad (12.177)$$

98 with Jacobian *determinant*

100

$$\begin{aligned} \det(J_T) &\overset{(3.306)}{=} \frac{u}{\sqrt{u^2+v^2}(u^2+v^2+1)} \frac{u}{u^2+v^2} + \frac{v}{\sqrt{u^2+v^2}(u^2+v^2+1)} \frac{v}{u^2+v^2} \\ &= \frac{u^2+v^2}{\sqrt{u^2+v^2}(u^2+v^2+1)(u^2+v^2)} \\ &= \frac{1}{\sqrt{u^2+v^2}(u^2+v^2+1)} && (12.178) \end{aligned}$$

while the Jacobian matrix of the inverse transformation reads

$$J_T^{-1} \triangleq \begin{bmatrix} \frac{\partial u}{\partial \theta_m} & \frac{\partial u}{\partial \phi_m} \\ \frac{\partial v}{\partial \theta_m} & \frac{\partial v}{\partial \phi_m} \end{bmatrix} = \begin{bmatrix} -\frac{\cos(\phi_m)}{\cos(\theta_m)^2} & \tan(\theta_m)\sin(\phi_m) \\ -\frac{\sin(\phi_m)}{\cos(\theta_m)^2} & -\tan(\theta_m)\cos(\phi_m) \end{bmatrix} \qquad (12.179)$$

98 with Jacobian *determinant*

100

$$\begin{aligned} \det(J_T^{-1}) &\overset{(3.306)}{=} \frac{\cos(\phi_m)}{\cos(\theta_m)^2}\tan(\theta_m)\cos(\phi_m) + \frac{\sin(\phi_m)}{\cos(\theta_m)^2}\tan(\theta_m)\sin(\phi_m) \\ &= \frac{\tan(\theta_m)}{\cos(\theta_m)^2}\big(\cos(\phi_m)^2+\sin(\phi_m)^2\big) \\ &= \tan(\theta_m)\big(\tan(\theta_m)^2+1\big) && (12.180) \end{aligned}$$

The weak NDF normalization constraint then reads

507

510

510

510

$$\begin{aligned} g(\vec{p},\hat{n}) &\overset{(12.160)}{=} \int_0^{2\pi}\int_0^{\frac{\pi}{2}} D(\vec{p},\hat{m})\cos(\theta_m)\sin(\theta_m)\mathrm{d}\theta_m\mathrm{d}\phi_m \\ &\overset{(12.175)(12.176)(12.178)}{=} \int_{-\infty}^{+\infty}\int_{-\infty}^{+\infty} D(\vec{p},\hat{m})\frac{\sqrt{u^2+v^2}}{u^2+v^2+1}\frac{\mathrm{d}u\mathrm{d}v}{\sqrt{u^2+v^2}(u^2+v^2+1)} \\ &= \int_{-\infty}^{+\infty}\int_{-\infty}^{+\infty} \frac{D(\vec{p},\hat{m})}{(u^2+v^2+1)^2}\mathrm{d}u\mathrm{d}v \\ &= \int_{-\infty}^{+\infty}\int_{-\infty}^{+\infty} D(\vec{p},u,v)\mathrm{d}u\mathrm{d}v && (12.181) \end{aligned}$$

from which follows that the joint *probability density* of the slopes $D(\vec{p}, u, v)\mathrm{d}u\mathrm{d}v =$ 131
$D(\vec{p}, \hat{m})\langle\hat{n}, \hat{m}\rangle\mathrm{d}\hat{m}$ is related to that of the NDF by

$$D(\vec{p}, u, v) = \frac{D(\vec{p}, \hat{m})}{(u^2 + v^2 + 1)^2} \overset{(12.168)}{\underset{(12.169)}{=}} \frac{D(\vec{p}, \hat{m})}{\left(\tan(\theta_m)^2 + 1\right)^2} = D(\vec{p}, \hat{m})\cos(\theta_m)^4 = D(\vec{p}, \hat{m})\langle\hat{n}, \hat{m}\rangle^4 \tag{12.182}$$
509
509

while the measures are related by

$$\mathrm{d}u\mathrm{d}v = \frac{\mathrm{d}\hat{m}}{\langle\hat{n}, \hat{m}\rangle^3} \tag{12.183}$$

Similarly, the strong NDF normalization constraint may then be readily obtained by expressing the macro-normal $\hat{n} = [0, 0, 1]$, micro-normal $\hat{m} = [x_m, y_m, z_m]$ and projection direction $\hat{\omega} = [x_\omega, y_\omega, z_\omega]$ in *Cartesian coordinates* to yield 67

$$\begin{aligned} g(\vec{p}, \hat{\omega}) &\overset{(12.155)}{=} \int_{2\pi^+} D(\vec{p}, \hat{m}) \frac{\langle\hat{\omega}, \hat{m}\rangle}{\langle\hat{n}, \hat{m}\rangle} \langle\hat{n}, \hat{m}\rangle\mathrm{d}\hat{m} \\ &\overset{(12.181)}{=} \int_{-\infty}^{+\infty}\int_{-\infty}^{+\infty} D(\vec{p}, u, v)\frac{x_\omega x_m + y_\omega y_m + z_\omega z_m}{z_m}\mathrm{d}u\mathrm{d}v \\ &\overset{(12.170)}{\underset{(12.171)}{=}} \int_{-\infty}^{+\infty}\int_{-\infty}^{+\infty} D(\vec{p}, u, v)(-x_\omega u - y_\omega v + z_\omega)\mathrm{d}u\mathrm{d}v \end{aligned} \tag{12.184}$$
507
510
509
509

NDFs are generally formulated so as to provide control over the degree of roughness of the surface, typically in terms of the root-mean-square (RMS) slope of the micro-geometry $m \in [0, \infty)$ (although most often in practice $m \in [0, 1/2)$), impacting the standard deviation of the distribution. Lower roughness values consequently yield gentle micro-slopes and typically more specular reflectance properties (assuming the micro-structures are themselves specular), while larger roughness values lead to steeper slopes and rather diffuse reflectance distributions (although there exists no NDF that can result in an ideal *Lambertian* BRDF). In order to 499
compare the degree of roughness of various NDFs in a uniform manner, it is convenient to express their roughness parameter in terms of the slope angle β at which the distribution drops to half its peak value at $\theta_m = 0$ [Blinn, 1977].

12.6.1.3 Beckmann

Formulation The *Beckmann NDF* [Beckmann and Spizzichino, 1963, Beckmann, 1965] is defined as an isotropic 2-D *Gaussian* distribution of slopes 51

$$D(\vec{p}, u, v) \triangleq \frac{e^{-\frac{u^2+v^2}{m^2}}}{\pi m^2} \tag{12.185}$$

which, as illustrated in *Figure 12.20* and *Figure 12.21*, corresponds to the normal distribution 512 512
function

$$D(\vec{p}, \hat{m}) \overset{(12.166)}{\underset{(12.182)}{=}} \frac{e^{-\frac{\tan(\theta_m)^2}{m^2}}}{\pi m^2 \cos(\theta_m)^4} = \frac{e^{-\frac{1-\langle\hat{n},\hat{m}\rangle^2}{m^2\langle\hat{n},\hat{m}\rangle^2}}}{\pi m^2 \langle\hat{n}, \hat{m}\rangle^4} \tag{12.186}$$
509
511

and solving for the roughness parameter in terms of the median slope angle yields

$$\frac{e^{-\frac{\tan(\beta)^2}{m^2}}}{\pi m^2 \cos(\beta)^4} = \frac{1}{2}\frac{1}{\pi m^2} \implies m = \frac{\tan(\beta)}{\sqrt{\ln(2) - 4\ln(\cos(\beta))}} = \frac{1}{\cos(\beta)}\sqrt{\frac{\cos(\beta)^2 - 1}{\ln\left(\frac{\cos(\beta)^4}{2}\right)}} \tag{12.187}$$

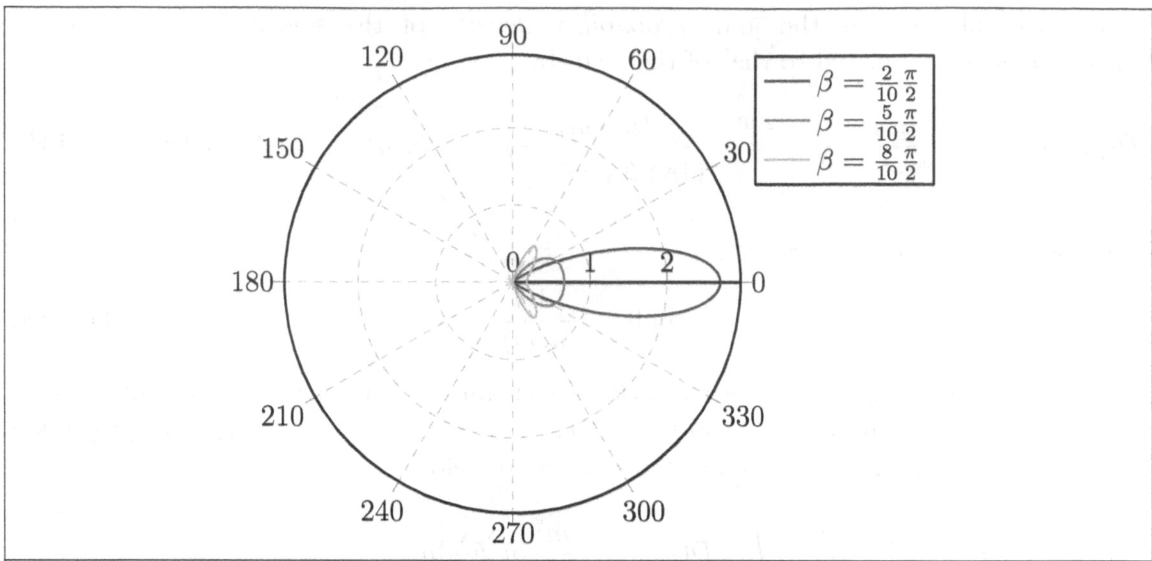

Figure 12.20: Beckmann NDF Plots: Angular distribution of the Beckmann normal distribution function, shown for various median slope angles.

Figure 12.21: Beckmann NDF Appearance: Visual appearance of the Beckmann NDF with a median slope angle of $\frac{1}{10}\frac{\pi}{2}$, $\frac{5}{10}\frac{\pi}{2}$ and $\frac{9}{10}\frac{\pi}{2}$ (from left to right, respectively) (light probe courtesy of Paul Debevec).

131 **Normalization and Sampling** Defining the joint *probability density* as the product of the NDF and the cosine factor

$$p_m(\vec{p}, \hat{m}) \triangleq D(\vec{p}, \hat{m})\langle \hat{n}, \hat{m}\rangle = \frac{e^{-\frac{1-\langle \hat{n}, \hat{m}\rangle^2}{m^2\langle \hat{n}, \hat{m}\rangle^2}}}{\pi m^2 \langle \hat{n}, \hat{m}\rangle^3} \tag{12.188}$$

132 the joint *cumulative distribution* over the domain Ω_m may be expressed in a separable form as

244

$$\begin{aligned}\int_{\Omega_m} D(\vec{p}, \hat{m})\langle \hat{n}, \hat{m}\rangle \mathrm{d}\hat{m} &\overset{(6.64)}{=} \int_0^{\phi_m} \frac{1}{2\pi}\mathrm{d}\phi \int_{\cos(\theta_m)}^1 2\frac{e^{-\frac{1-\mu^2}{m^2\mu^2}}}{m^2\mu^3}\mathrm{d}\mu \\ &= \left[\frac{\phi}{2\pi}\right]_0^{\phi_m} \left[e^{-\frac{1-\mu^2}{m^2\mu^2}}\right]_{\cos(\theta_m)}^1 \\ &= \frac{\phi_m}{2\pi}\left(1 - e^{-\frac{1-\cos(\theta_m)^2}{m^2\cos(\theta_m)^2}}\right)\end{aligned} \tag{12.189}$$

where $\mu = \cos(\theta) = \langle \hat{n}, \hat{m} \rangle$.

Integrating over the whole hemispherical domain by substituting $\phi_m = 2\pi$ and $\theta_m = \frac{\pi}{2}$ then ensures normalization, while applying *inverse-transform sampling* allows *importance* 134
sampling to be readily carried as 155

$$\xi_\phi = \frac{\phi_m}{2\pi} \implies \phi_m = 2\pi\xi_\phi \tag{12.190}$$

$$\xi_\theta = 1 - e^{-\frac{1-\cos(\theta_m)^2}{m^2\cos(\theta_m)^2}} \implies \theta_m = \arccos\left(\frac{1}{\sqrt{1 - m^2\ln(1-\xi_\theta)}}\right) \tag{12.191}$$

$$\implies \theta_m = \arctan\left(\sqrt{-m^2\ln(1-\xi_\theta)}\right) \tag{12.192}$$

12.6.1.4 Trowbridge–Reitz

Formulation The *Trowbridge–Reitz NDF* [Trowbridge and Reitz, 1975], also referred to as the *GGX NDF* [Walter *et al.*, 2007], is an isotropic distribution of slopes of the form

$$D(\vec{p}, u, v) \triangleq \frac{1}{\pi k^2\left(1 + \frac{u^2}{k^2} + \frac{v^2}{k^2}\right)^2} = \frac{k^2}{\pi(k^2 + u^2 + v^2)^2} \tag{12.193}$$

which, as illustrated in *Figure 12.22* and *Figure 12.23*, corresponds to the normal distribution 514 514
function

$$D(\vec{p}, \hat{m}) \overset{(12.166)}{\underset{(12.182)}{=}} \frac{k^2}{\pi\left(k^2 + \tan(\theta_m)^2\right)^2\cos(\theta_m)^4} = \frac{k^2}{\pi\left(1 + (k^2-1)\langle \hat{n}, \hat{m} \rangle^2\right)^2} \tag{12.194}$$

509 511

and solving for the roughness parameter in terms of the median slope angle yields

$$\frac{k^2}{\pi\left(1 + (k^2-1)\cos(\beta)^2\right)^2} = \frac{1}{2}\frac{1}{\pi k^2} \implies k = \sqrt{\frac{1 - \cos(\beta)^2}{\sqrt{2} - \cos(\beta)^2}} \tag{12.195}$$

Normalization and Sampling Defining the joint *probability density* as the product of the 131
NDF and the cosine factor

$$p_m(\vec{p}, \hat{m}) \triangleq D(\vec{p}, \hat{m})\langle \hat{n}, \hat{m} \rangle = \frac{k^2\langle \hat{n}, \hat{m} \rangle}{\pi\left(1 + (k^2-1)\langle \hat{n}, \hat{m} \rangle^2\right)^2} \tag{12.196}$$

the joint *cumulative distribution* over the domain Ω_m may be expressed in a separable form 132
as

244

$$\begin{aligned}
\int_{\Omega_m} D(\vec{p}, \hat{m})\langle \hat{n}, \hat{m} \rangle \mathrm{d}\hat{m} &\overset{(6.64)}{=} \int_0^{\phi_m} \frac{1}{2\pi}\mathrm{d}\phi \int_{\cos(\theta_m)}^1 \frac{2k^2}{\left(1 + (k^2-1)\mu^2\right)^2}\mu\mathrm{d}\mu \\
&= \left[\frac{\phi}{2\pi}\right]_0^{\phi_m}\left[\frac{k^2}{k^2-1}\frac{-1}{1 + (k^2-1)\mu^2}\right]_{\cos(\theta_m)}^1 \\
&= \frac{\phi_m}{2\pi}\frac{1}{k^2-1}\left(\frac{k^2}{1 + (k^2-1)\cos(\theta_m)^2} - 1\right) \\
&= \frac{\phi_m}{2\pi}\frac{1}{k^2-1}\frac{k^2 - 1 - (k^2-1)\cos(\theta_m)^2}{1 + (k^2-1)\cos(\theta_m)^2} \\
&= \frac{\phi_m}{2\pi}\frac{1 - \cos(\theta_m)^2}{1 + (k^2-1)\cos(\theta_m)^2}
\end{aligned} \tag{12.197}$$

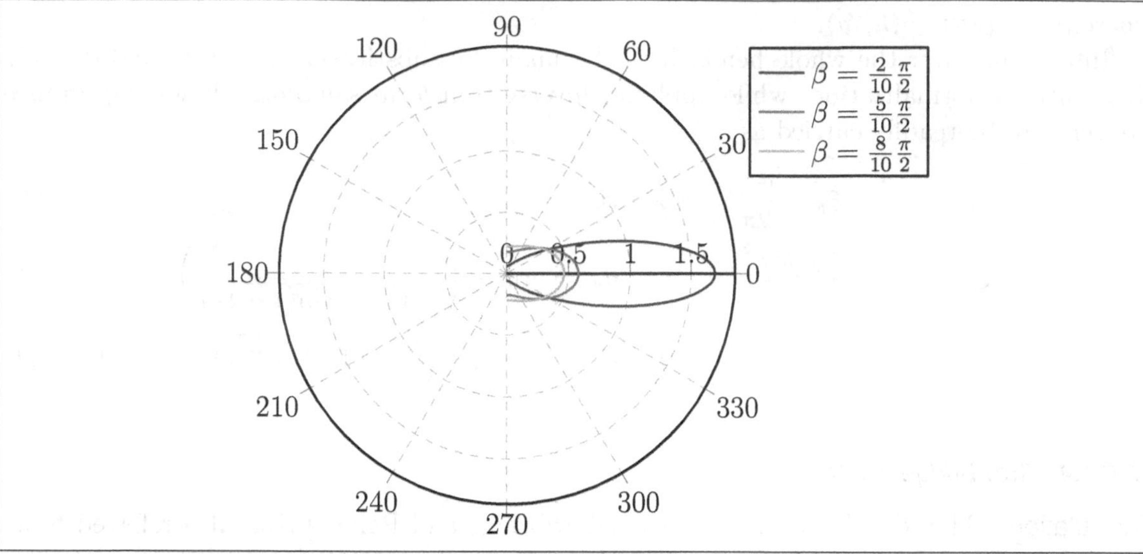

Figure 12.22: Trowbridge–Reitz NDF Plots: Angular distribution of the Trowbridge–Reitz normal distribution function, shown for various median slope angles.

Figure 12.23: Trowbridge–Reitz NDF Appearance: Visual appearance of the Trowbridge–Reitz NDF with a median slope angle of $\frac{1}{10}\frac{\pi}{2}$, $\frac{5}{10}\frac{\pi}{2}$ and $\frac{9}{10}\frac{\pi}{2}$ (from left to right, respectively) (light probe courtesy of Paul Debevec).

where $\mu \triangleq \cos(\theta) = \langle \hat{n}, \hat{m} \rangle$.

Integrating over the whole hemispherical domain by substituting $\phi_m = 2\pi$ and $\theta_m = \frac{\pi}{2}$
134 then ensures normalization, while applying *inverse-transform sampling* allows *importance*
155 *sampling* to be readily carried as

$$\xi_\phi = \frac{\phi_m}{2\pi} \quad \Longrightarrow \quad \phi_m = 2\pi\xi_\phi \tag{12.198}$$

$$\xi_\theta = \frac{1 - \cos(\theta_m)^2}{1 + (k^2 - 1)\cos(\theta_m)^2} \quad \Longrightarrow \quad \theta_m = \arccos\left(\sqrt{\frac{1 - \xi_\theta}{1 - \xi_\theta + \xi_\theta k^2}}\right) \tag{12.199}$$

$$\Longrightarrow \quad \theta_m = \arccos\left(\frac{1}{\sqrt{1 + \frac{\xi_\theta}{1-\xi_\theta} k^2}}\right)$$

$$\Longrightarrow \quad \theta_m = \arctan\left(k\sqrt{\frac{\xi_\theta}{1 - \xi_\theta}}\right) \tag{12.200}$$

12.6.1.5 Blinn

Formulation The *Blinn NDF* [Blinn, 1977] is an isotropic distribution of slopes of the form

$$D(\vec{p}, u, v) \triangleq \frac{n+2}{2\pi} \frac{1}{\left(\sqrt{u^2+v^2+1}\right)^{n+4}} \tag{12.201}$$

which, as illustrated in *Figure 12.24* and *Figure 12.25*, corresponds to the *Phong*-like [Fisher 515
and Woo, 1994] normal distribution function 516 500

$$D(\vec{p}, \hat{m}) \overset{(12.175)}{\underset{(12.182)}{=}} \frac{n+2}{2\pi} \cos(\theta_m)^n = \frac{n+2}{2\pi} \langle \hat{n}, \hat{m} \rangle^n \tag{12.202}$$

510 511

and solving for the roughness parameter in terms of the median slope angle yields

$$\frac{n+2}{2\pi} \cos(\beta)^n = \frac{1}{2} \frac{n+2}{2\pi} \implies n = -\frac{\ln(2)}{\ln\left(\cos(\beta)\right)} \tag{12.203}$$

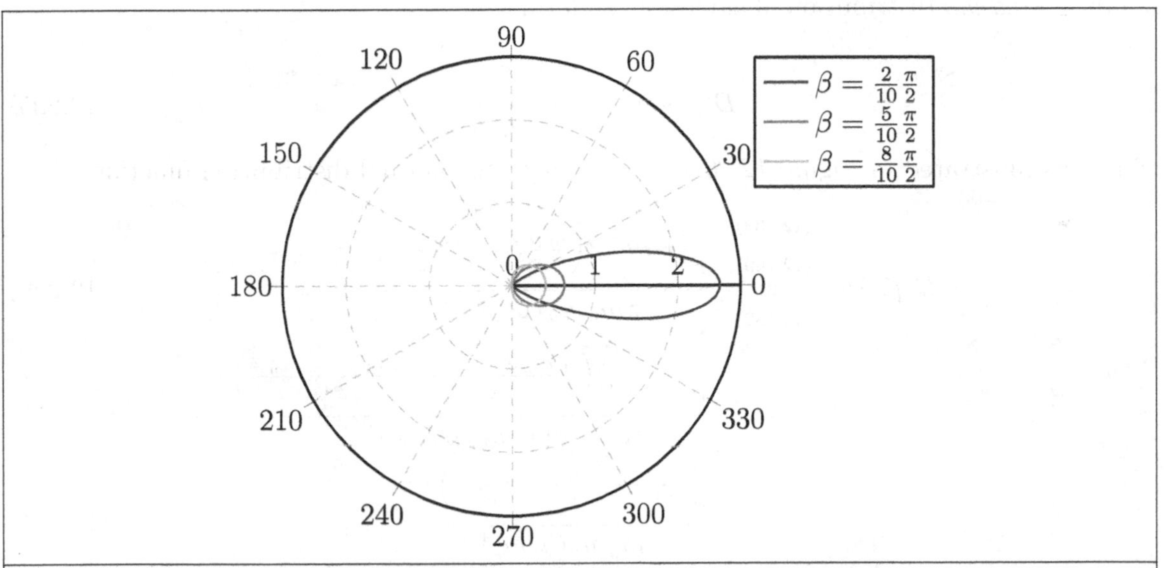

Figure 12.24: Blinn NDF Plots: Angular distribution of the Blinn normal distribution function, shown for various median slope angles.

Normalization and Sampling Defining the joint *probability density* as the product of the 131
NDF and the cosine factor

$$p_m(\vec{p}, \hat{m}) \triangleq D(\vec{p}, \hat{m}) \langle \hat{n}, \hat{m} \rangle = c_{n+1} \langle \hat{n}, \hat{m} \rangle \overset{(12.121)}{=} \frac{n+2}{2\pi} \langle \hat{n}, \hat{m} \rangle^{n+1} \tag{12.204}$$

498

the joint *cumulative distribution* over the domain Ω_m may be expressed in a separable form 132
in terms of the *cosine-lobe distribution*. 498

Integrating over the whole hemispherical domain by substituting $\phi_m = 2\pi$ and $\theta_m = \frac{\pi}{2}$
then ensures normalization, while applying *inverse-transform sampling* allows *importance* 134
sampling to be readily carried. 155

Figure 12.25: Blinn NDF Appearance: Visual appearance of the Blinn NDF with a median slope angle of $\frac{1}{10}\frac{\pi}{2}$, $\frac{5}{10}\frac{\pi}{2}$ and $\frac{9}{10}\frac{\pi}{2}$ (from left to right, respectively) (light probe courtesy of Paul Debevec).

12.6.1.6 Ward

Formulation The *Ward NDF* [Ward Larson, 1992] is an anisotropic generalization of *Beck-*
511 *mann*'s *Gaussian* distribution of slopes of the form
51

$$D(\vec{p}, u, v) \triangleq \frac{e^{-\left(\frac{u^2}{m_u^2}+\frac{v^2}{m_v^2}\right)}}{\pi m_u m_v} \tag{12.205}$$

517 which, as illustrated in *Figure 12.26*, corresponds to the normal distribution function

509
509
511

$$D(\vec{p}, \hat{m}) \overset{(12.168)}{\underset{(12.182)}{\overset{(12.169)}{=}}} \frac{e^{-\tan(\theta_m)^2\left(\frac{\cos(\phi_m)^2}{m_u^2}+\frac{\sin(\phi_m)^2}{m_v^2}\right)}}{\pi m_u m_v \cos(\theta_m)^4} \tag{12.206}$$

$$= \frac{e^{-\frac{1}{\cos(\theta_m)^2}\left(\frac{\sin(\theta_m)^2\cos(\phi_m)^2}{m_u^2}+\frac{\sin(\theta_m)^2\sin(\phi_m)^2}{m_v^2}\right)}}{\pi m_u m_v \cos(\theta_m)^4}$$

$$= \frac{e^{-\frac{1}{\langle\hat{n},\hat{m}\rangle^2}\left(\frac{\langle\vec{u},\hat{m}\rangle^2}{m_u^2}+\frac{\langle\vec{v},\hat{m}\rangle^2}{m_v^2}\right)}}{\pi m_u m_v \langle\hat{n},\hat{m}\rangle^4} \tag{12.207}$$

511 therefore reducing to the isotropic *Beckmann* NDF whenever $m_u = m_v = m$.

131 **Normalization and Sampling** Defining the joint *probability density* as the product of the
NDF and the cosine factor [Walter, 2005]

$$p_m(\vec{p}, \hat{m}) \triangleq D(\vec{p}, \hat{m})\langle\hat{n}, \hat{m}\rangle = \frac{e^{-\frac{1}{\langle\hat{n},\hat{m}\rangle^2}\left(\frac{\langle\vec{u},\hat{m}\rangle^2}{m_u^2}+\frac{\langle\vec{v},\hat{m}\rangle^2}{m_v^2}\right)}}{\pi m_u m_v \langle\hat{n},\hat{m}\rangle^3} \tag{12.208}$$

132 the joint *cumulative distribution* over the domain Ω_m may be expressed as

244

$$\int_{\Omega_m} D(\vec{p}, \hat{m})\langle\hat{n}, \hat{m}\rangle \mathrm{d}\hat{m} \overset{(6.64)}{=} \int_0^{\phi_m} p(\phi, \theta_m)\mathrm{d}\phi \tag{12.209}$$

where

$$p(\phi, \theta_m) \triangleq \int_{\cos(\theta_m)}^1 \frac{e^{-\frac{1-\mu^2}{\mu^2}\alpha}}{\pi m_u m_v \mu^3}\mathrm{d}\mu = \frac{1}{\pi m_u m_v}\left[\frac{e^{-\frac{1-\mu^2}{\mu^2}\alpha}}{2\alpha}\right]_{\cos(\theta_m)}^1 = \frac{1 - e^{-\frac{1-\cos(\theta_m)^2}{\cos(\theta_m)^2}\alpha}}{2\pi m_u m_v \alpha} \tag{12.210}$$

Figure 12.26: Ward NDF: Visual appearance of the Ward NDF with median slope angles of $\frac{1}{10}\frac{\pi}{2}$ and $\frac{9}{10}\frac{\pi}{2}$ (left) and $\frac{9}{10}\frac{\pi}{2}$ and $\frac{1}{10}\frac{\pi}{2}$ (right) (light probe courtesy of Paul Debevec).

with $\mu \triangleq \cos(\theta) = \langle \hat{n}, \hat{m} \rangle$ and $\alpha \triangleq \frac{\cos(\phi)^2}{m_u^2} + \frac{\sin(\phi)^2}{m_v^2}$. The marginal *probability density* is then 131
given as

$$p(\phi, {}^{\pi}\!/_{2}) = \frac{1}{2\pi m_u m_v \alpha} \tag{12.211}$$

from which follows the marginal *cumulative distribution* 132

$$\begin{aligned} \int_0^{\phi_m} p(\phi, {}^{\pi}\!/_{2}) \mathrm{d}\phi &= \int_0^{\phi_m} \frac{1}{2\pi m_u m_v} \frac{1}{\frac{\cos(\phi)^2}{m_u^2} + \frac{\sin(\phi)^2}{m_v^2}} \mathrm{d}\phi \\ &= \frac{1}{2\pi m_u m_v} \left[m_u m_v \arctan\left(\frac{m_u}{m_v} \tan(\phi) \right) \right]_0^{\phi_m} \\ &= \frac{1}{2\pi} \arctan\left(\frac{m_u}{m_v} \tan(\phi_m) \right) \end{aligned} \tag{12.212}$$

as well as the conditional *cumulative distribution* 132

$$\frac{p(\phi, \theta_m)}{p(\phi, {}^{\pi}\!/_{2})} = 1 - e^{-\frac{1-\cos(\theta_m)^2}{\cos(\theta_m)^2} \left(\frac{\cos(\phi)^2}{m_u^2} + \frac{\sin(\phi)^2}{m_v^2} \right)} \tag{12.213}$$

Integrating over the whole hemispherical domain by substituting $\phi_m = 2\pi$ and $\theta_m = \frac{\pi}{2}$ then ensures normalization, while applying *inverse-transform sampling* allows *importance* 134
sampling to be readily carried as 155

$$\xi_\phi = \frac{1}{2\pi} \arctan\left(\frac{m_u}{m_v}\tan(\phi_m)\right) \implies \phi_m = \operatorname{arctan2}\left(m_v \sin(2\pi\xi_\phi), m_u \cos(2\pi\xi_\phi)\right) \tag{12.214}$$

$$\xi_\theta = 1 - e^{-\frac{1-\cos(\theta_m)^2}{\cos(\theta_m)^2}\left(\frac{\cos(\phi_m)^2}{m_u^2}+\frac{\sin(\phi_m)^2}{m_v^2}\right)} \implies \theta_m = \arccos\left(\frac{1}{\sqrt{1 - \frac{\ln(1-\xi_\theta)}{\frac{\cos(\phi_m)^2}{m_u^2}+\frac{\sin(\phi_m)^2}{m_v^2}}}}\right) \tag{12.215}$$

$$\implies \theta_m = \arctan\left(\sqrt{\frac{-\ln(1-\xi_\theta)}{\frac{\cos(\phi_m)^2}{m_u^2}+\frac{\sin(\phi_m)^2}{m_v^2}}}\right) \tag{12.216}$$

12.6.1.7 Schlick

Formulation The *Schlick NDF* [Schlick, 1993, Schlick, 1994b] is an anisotropic generalization
513 of the *Trowbridge–Reitz* NDF given as a separable distribution of the form

$$D(\vec{p}, \hat{m}) \triangleq D_z(\vec{p}, \hat{m}) D_a(\vec{p}, \hat{m}) \tag{12.217}$$

where the zenithal dependency, parameterized by the roughness factor $r \in [0, 1]$ modeling from purely specular to purely diffuse distributions, reads

$$D_z(\vec{p}, \hat{m}) \triangleq \frac{2r}{\left(1 + (r-1)\cos(\theta_m)^2\right)^2} = \frac{2r}{\left(1 + (r-1)\langle\hat{n}, \hat{m}\rangle^2\right)^2} \tag{12.218}$$

while the azimuthal dependency, parameterized by the isotropy factor $p \in [0, 1]$ modeling from purely anisotropic to purely isotropic distributions, is given by the polar equation of an ellipse centered at the origin

$$D_a(\vec{p}, \hat{m}) \triangleq \frac{1}{2\pi}\sqrt{\frac{p}{p^2 - p^2\cos(\phi_m)^2 + \cos(\phi_m)^2}} \tag{12.219}$$

12.6.1.8 ATR

Formulation The *ATR NDF* [Heitz, 2014] is an anisotropic generalization of *Trowbridge–*
513 *Reitz*'s distribution of slopes of the form

$$D(\vec{p}, u, v) \triangleq \frac{1}{\pi k_u k_v \left(1 + \frac{u^2}{k_u^2} + \frac{v^2}{k_v^2}\right)^2} \tag{12.220}$$

519 which, as illustrated in *Figure 12.27*, corresponds to the normal distribution function

509

509

511

$$D(\vec{p}, \hat{m}) \overset{(12.168)}{\underset{(12.182)}{\overset{(12.169)}{=}}} \frac{1}{\pi k_u k_v \left(1 + \tan(\theta_m)^2\left(\frac{\cos(\phi_m)^2}{k_u^2} + \frac{\sin(\phi_m)^2}{k_v^2}\right)\right)^2 \cos(\theta_m)^4} \tag{12.221}$$

$$= \frac{1}{\pi k_u k_v \left(\cos(\theta_m)^2 + \frac{\sin(\theta_m)^2\cos(\phi_m)^2}{k_u^2} + \frac{\sin(\theta_m)^2\sin(\phi_m)^2}{k_v^2}\right)^2}$$

$$= \frac{1}{\pi k_u k_v \left(\langle\hat{n}, \hat{m}\rangle^2 + \frac{\langle\vec{u}, \hat{m}\rangle^2}{k_u^2} + \frac{\langle\vec{v}, \hat{m}\rangle^2}{k_v^2}\right)^2} \tag{12.222}$$

513 therefore reducing to the isotropic *Trowbridge–Reitz* NDF whenever $k_u = k_v = k$.

Figure 12.27: ATR NDF: Visual appearance of the ATR NDF with median slope angles of $\frac{1}{10}\frac{\pi}{2}$ and $\frac{9}{10}\frac{\pi}{2}$ (left) and $\frac{9}{10}\frac{\pi}{2}$ and $\frac{1}{10}\frac{\pi}{2}$ (right) (light probe courtesy of Paul Debevec).

Normalization and Sampling Defining the joint *probability density* as the product of the 131
NDF and the cosine factor

$$p_m(\vec{p}, \hat{m}) \triangleq D(\vec{p}, \hat{m})\langle \hat{n}, \hat{m}\rangle = \frac{\langle \hat{n}, \hat{m}\rangle}{\pi k_u k_v \left(\langle \hat{n}, \hat{m}\rangle^2 + \frac{\langle \vec{u}, \hat{m}\rangle^2}{k_u^2} + \frac{\langle \vec{v}, \hat{m}\rangle^2}{k_v^2}\right)^2} \tag{12.223}$$

the joint *cumulative distribution* over the domain Ω_m may be expressed as 132

244

$$\int_{\Omega_m} D(\vec{p}, \hat{m})\langle \hat{n}, \hat{m}\rangle \mathrm{d}\hat{m} \overset{(6.64)}{=} \int_0^{\phi_m} p(\phi, \theta_m)\mathrm{d}\phi \tag{12.224}$$

where

$$\begin{aligned} p(\phi, \theta_m) &\triangleq \int_{\cos(\theta_m)}^{1} \frac{\mu}{\pi k_u k_v (\mu^2 + (1-\mu^2)\alpha)^2} \mathrm{d}\mu \\ &= \frac{1}{\pi k_u k_v} \left[\frac{1}{2(\alpha - 1)(\alpha - \mu^2\alpha + \mu^2)}\right]_{\cos(\theta_m)}^{1} \\ &= \frac{1}{2\pi k_u k_v (\alpha - 1)} \left(1 - \frac{1}{\alpha - \cos(\theta_m)^2\alpha + \cos(\theta_m)^2}\right) \\ &= \frac{1}{2\pi k_u k_v (\alpha - 1)} \left(\frac{\alpha - \cos(\theta_m)^2\alpha + \cos(\theta_m)^2 - 1}{\alpha - \cos(\theta_m)^2\alpha + \cos(\theta_m)^2}\right) \\ &= \frac{1}{2\pi k_u k_v} \left(\frac{1 - \cos(\theta_m)^2}{\alpha - \cos(\theta_m)^2\alpha + \cos(\theta_m)^2}\right) \end{aligned} \tag{12.225}$$

with $\mu \triangleq \cos(\theta) = \langle \hat{n}, \hat{m}\rangle$ and $\alpha \triangleq \frac{\cos(\phi)^2}{k_u^2} + \frac{\sin(\phi)^2}{k_v^2}$. The marginal *probability density* is then 131
given as

$$p(\phi, {}^{\pi}\!/_{2}) = \frac{1}{2\pi k_u k_v \alpha} \tag{12.226}$$

from which follows the marginal *cumulative distribution* 132

$$\begin{aligned}\int_0^{\phi_m} p(\phi, \pi/2)\mathrm{d}\phi &= \int_0^{\phi_m} \frac{1}{2\pi k_u k_v} \frac{1}{\frac{\cos(\phi)^2}{k_u^2} + \frac{\sin(\phi)^2}{k_v^2}} \mathrm{d}\phi \\ &= \frac{1}{2\pi k_u k_v} \left[k_u k_v \arctan\left(\frac{k_u}{k_v}\tan(\phi)\right)\right]_0^{\phi_m} \\ &= \frac{1}{2\pi} \arctan\left(\frac{k_u}{k_v}\tan(\phi_m)\right) \end{aligned} \tag{12.227}$$

132 as well as the conditional *cumulative distribution*

$$\begin{aligned}\frac{p(\phi, \theta_m)}{p(\phi, \pi/2)} &= \frac{(1-\cos(\theta_m)^2)\left(\frac{\cos(\phi)^2}{k_u^2} + \frac{\sin(\phi)^2}{k_v^2}\right)}{(1-\cos(\theta_m)^2)\left(\frac{\cos(\phi)^2}{k_u^2} + \frac{\sin(\phi)^2}{k_v^2}\right) + \cos(\theta_m)^2} \\ &= \frac{1}{1 + \frac{\cos(\theta_m)^2}{(1-\cos(\theta_m)^2)\left(\frac{\cos(\phi)^2}{k_u^2} + \frac{\sin(\phi)^2}{k_v^2}\right)}} \end{aligned} \tag{12.228}$$

Integrating over the whole hemispherical domain by substituting $\phi_m = 2\pi$ and $\theta_m = \frac{\pi}{2}$
134 then ensures normalization, while applying *inverse-transform sampling* allows *importance*
155 *sampling* to be readily carried as

$$\begin{aligned} \xi_\phi &= \frac{1}{2\pi}\arctan\left(\frac{k_u}{k_v}\tan(\phi_m)\right) \\ &\implies \phi_m = \operatorname{arctan2}\left(k_v \sin(2\pi\xi_\phi), k_u \cos(2\pi\xi_\phi)\right) \end{aligned} \tag{12.229}$$

$$\begin{aligned} \xi_\theta &= \frac{1}{1 + \frac{\cos(\theta_m)^2}{(1-\cos(\theta_m)^2)\left(\frac{\cos(\phi_m)^2}{k_u^2} + \frac{\sin(\phi_m)^2}{k_v^2}\right)}} \\ &\implies \theta_m = \arccos\left(\sqrt{\frac{1-\xi_\theta}{1-\xi_\theta + \frac{\xi_\theta}{\frac{\cos(\phi_m)^2}{k_u^2} + \frac{\sin(\phi_m)^2}{k_v^2}}}}\right) \end{aligned} \tag{12.230}$$

$$\begin{aligned} &\implies \theta_m = \arccos\left(\frac{1}{\sqrt{1 + \frac{\xi_\theta}{(1-\xi_\theta)\left(\frac{\cos(\phi_m)^2}{k_u^2} + \frac{\sin(\phi_m)^2}{k_v^2}\right)}}}\right) \\ &\implies \theta_m = \arctan\left(\sqrt{\frac{\xi_\theta}{(1-\xi_\theta)\left(\frac{\cos(\phi_m)^2}{k_u^2} + \frac{\sin(\phi_m)^2}{k_v^2}\right)}}\right) \end{aligned} \tag{12.231}$$

12.6.1.9 Ashikhmin–Shirley

521 **Formulation** As illustrated in *Figure 12.28*, the *Ashikhmin–Shirley NDF* [Ashikhmin and
515 Shirley, 2000b, Ashikhmin and Shirley, 2000a] is an anisotropic generalization of *Blinn's* NDF of the form

$$D(\vec{p}, \hat{m}) \triangleq \frac{\sqrt{(n_u+2)(n_v+2)}}{2\pi} \cos(\theta_m)^{n_u \cos(\phi_m)^2 + n_v \sin(\phi_m)^2} \tag{12.232}$$

$$\begin{aligned} &= \frac{\sqrt{(n_u+2)(n_v+2)}}{2\pi} \cos(\theta_m)^{\frac{n_u \sin(\theta_m)^2 \cos(\phi_m)^2 + n_v \sin(\theta_m)^2 \sin(\phi_m)^2}{1-\cos(\theta_m)^2}} \\ &= \frac{\sqrt{(n_u+2)(n_v+2)}}{2\pi} \langle \hat{n}, \hat{m}\rangle^{\frac{n_u \langle \vec{u}, \hat{m}\rangle^2 + n_v \langle \vec{v}, \hat{m}\rangle^2}{1-\langle \hat{n}, \hat{m}\rangle^2}} \end{aligned} \tag{12.233}$$

515 therefore reducing to the isotropic *Blinn* NDF whenever $n_u = n_v = n$.

Figure 12.28: Ashikhmin–Shirley NDF: Visual appearance of the Ashikhmin–Shirley NDF with median slope angles of $\frac{1}{10}\frac{\pi}{2}$ and $\frac{9}{10}\frac{\pi}{2}$ (left) and $\frac{9}{10}\frac{\pi}{2}$ and $\frac{1}{10}\frac{\pi}{2}$ (right) (light probe courtesy of Paul Debevec).

Normalization and Sampling Defining the joint *probability density* as the product of the NDF and the cosine factor 131

$$p_m(\vec{p}, \hat{m}) \triangleq D(\vec{p}, \hat{m})\langle \hat{n}, \hat{m} \rangle = \frac{\sqrt{(n_u + 2)(n_v + 2)}}{2\pi} \langle \hat{n}, \hat{m} \rangle^{\frac{n_u \langle \vec{u}, \hat{m} \rangle^2 + n_v \langle \vec{v}, \hat{m} \rangle^2}{1 - \langle \hat{n}, \hat{m} \rangle^2} + 1} \tag{12.234}$$

the joint *cumulative distribution* over the domain Ω_m may be expressed as 132

$$\int_{\Omega_m} D(\vec{p}, \hat{m})\langle \hat{n}, \hat{m} \rangle \mathrm{d}\hat{m} \overset{(6.64)}{=} \int_0^{\phi_m} p(\phi, \theta_m)\mathrm{d}\phi \tag{12.235}$$ 244

where

$$\begin{aligned} p(\phi, \theta_m) &\triangleq \int_{\cos(\theta_m)}^1 \frac{\sqrt{(n_u + 2)(n_v + 2)}}{2\pi} \mu^{\alpha+1} \mathrm{d}\mu \\ &= \frac{\sqrt{(n_u + 2)(n_v + 2)}}{2\pi} \left[\frac{\mu^{\alpha+2}}{\alpha + 2} \right]_{\cos(\theta_m)}^1 \\ &= \frac{\sqrt{(n_u + 2)(n_v + 2)}}{2\pi} \frac{1 - \cos(\theta_m)^{\alpha+2}}{\alpha + 2} \end{aligned} \tag{12.236}$$

with $\mu \triangleq \cos(\theta) = \langle \hat{n}, \hat{m} \rangle$ and $\alpha \triangleq n_u \cos(\phi)^2 + n_v \sin(\phi)^2$. The marginal *probability density* is then given as 131

$$p(\phi, {}^{\pi}\!/_{2}) = \frac{\sqrt{(n_u + 2)(n_v + 2)}}{2\pi} \frac{1}{\alpha + 2} \tag{12.237}$$

from which follows the marginal *cumulative distribution* 132

$$\int_0^{\phi_m} p(\phi, \pi/2)\mathrm{d}\phi = \int_0^{\phi_m} \frac{\sqrt{(n_u+2)(n_v+2)}}{2\pi} \frac{1}{n_u \cos(\phi)^2 + n_v \sin(\phi)^2 + 2}\mathrm{d}\phi$$
$$= \frac{\sqrt{(n_u+2)(n_v+2)}}{2\pi} \left[\frac{\arctan\left(\frac{\sqrt{n_v+2}}{\sqrt{n_u+2}} \tan(\phi)\right)}{\sqrt{n_u+2}\sqrt{n_v+2}} \right]_0^{\phi_m}$$
$$= \frac{1}{2\pi} \arctan\left(\frac{\sqrt{n_v+2}}{\sqrt{n_u+2}} \tan(\phi_m)\right) \tag{12.238}$$

132 as well as the conditional *cumulative distribution*

$$\frac{p(\phi, \theta_m)}{p(\phi, \pi/2)} = 1 - \cos(\theta_m)^{n_u \cos(\phi)^2 + n_v \sin(\phi)^2 + 2} \tag{12.239}$$

Integrating over the whole hemispherical domain by substituting $\phi_m = 2\pi$ and $\theta_m = \frac{\pi}{2}$
134 then ensures normalization, while applying *inverse-transform sampling* allows *importance*
155 *sampling* to be readily carried as

$$\xi_\phi = \frac{1}{2\pi} \arctan\left(\frac{\sqrt{n_v+2}}{\sqrt{n_u+2}} \tan(\phi_m)\right)$$
$$\implies \phi_m = \operatorname{arctan2}\left(\frac{\sin(2\pi\xi_\phi)}{\sqrt{n_v+2}}, \frac{\cos(2\pi\xi_\phi)}{\sqrt{n_u+2}}\right) \tag{12.240}$$
$$\implies \phi_m = \operatorname{arctan2}\left(\sqrt{n_u+2}\sin(2\pi\xi_\phi), \sqrt{n_v+2}\cos(2\pi\xi_\phi)\right) \tag{12.241}$$
$$\xi_\theta = 1 - \cos(\theta_m)^{n_u \cos(\phi_m)^2 + n_v \sin(\phi_m)^2 + 2}$$
$$\implies \theta_m = \arccos\left(\sqrt[n_u \cos(\phi_m)^2 + n_v \sin(\phi_m)^2 + 2]{1 - \xi_\theta}\right) \tag{12.242}$$

12.6.1.10 Composite NDF

Formulation More complex normal distributions (such as those with multiple directions of anisotropy for instance) may be modeled as a linear combination of simpler NDFs

$$D(\vec{p}, \hat{m}) \triangleq \sum_{j=1}^{n} w_j D_j(\vec{p}, \hat{m}) \tag{12.243}$$

where the weights $w_j \geq 0$ obey $\sum_{j=1}^{n} w_j = 1$.

131 **Normalization and Sampling** Defining the joint *probability density* as the product of the NDF and the cosine factor

$$p_m(\vec{p}, \hat{m}) \triangleq D(\vec{p}, \hat{m})\langle \hat{n}, \hat{m} \rangle = \sum_{j=1}^{n} w_j D_j(\vec{p}, \hat{m})\langle \hat{n}, \hat{m} \rangle \tag{12.244}$$

132 the joint *cumulative distribution* over the domain Ω_m may be expressed as

$$\int_{\Omega_m} D(\vec{p}, \hat{m})\langle \hat{n}, \hat{m} \rangle \mathrm{d}\hat{m} = \int_{\Omega_m} \sum_{j=1}^{n} w_j D_j(\vec{p}, \hat{m})\langle \hat{n}, \hat{m} \rangle \mathrm{d}\hat{m} = \sum_{j=1}^{n} w_j \int_{\Omega_m} D_j(\vec{p}, \hat{m})\langle \hat{n}, \hat{m} \rangle \mathrm{d}\hat{m} \tag{12.245}$$

Integrating over the whole hemispherical domain by substituting $\Omega_m = 2\pi^+$ then ensures normalization

507

$$\int_{2\pi^+} D(\vec{p}, \hat{m})\langle \hat{n}, \hat{m} \rangle \mathrm{d}\hat{m} = \sum_{j=1}^{n} w_j \int_{2\pi^+} D_j(\vec{p}, \hat{m})\langle \hat{n}, \hat{m} \rangle \mathrm{d}\hat{m} \overset{(12.160)}{=} \sum_{j=1}^{n} w_j = 1 \tag{12.246}$$

while drawing random samples from the mixture of distributions may be readily carried by
155 means of mixture *importance sampling*.

12.6.2 Bidirectional Distribution Function

12.6.2.1 Halfway Vector

Reflection Assuming the surface of the micro-structures is ideally smooth, light may only be reflected in agreement with the reflection direction established for *specular surfaces*, and 486
therefore by those points of the micro-geometry whose normal is defined by the vector halfway between the incident and exitant directions

$$\hat{h}_r \triangleq \frac{\hat{\omega}_o + \hat{\omega}_i}{\|\hat{\omega}_o + \hat{\omega}_i\|} \tag{12.247}$$

such that

$$\begin{aligned} \hat{\omega}_o &= \tau_r(\hat{h}_r, \hat{\omega}_i) && (12.248) \\ \hat{\omega}_i &= \tau_r(\hat{h}_r, \hat{\omega}_o) && (12.249) \end{aligned}$$

The normalization factor evaluates to

$$\frac{\|\hat{\omega}_o + \hat{\omega}_i\|}{2} = \langle \hat{h}_r, \hat{\omega}_o \rangle = \langle \hat{h}_r, \hat{\omega}_i \rangle = \frac{\langle \hat{\omega}_o, \hat{\omega}_i \rangle + 1}{\|\hat{\omega}_o + \hat{\omega}_i\|} = \sqrt{\frac{\langle \hat{\omega}_o, \hat{\omega}_i \rangle + 1}{2}} \tag{12.250}$$

from which follows that

$$\langle \hat{n}, \hat{h}_r \rangle \overset{(12.247)}{=} \left\langle \hat{n}, \frac{\hat{\omega}_o + \hat{\omega}_i}{\|\hat{\omega}_o + \hat{\omega}_i\|} \right\rangle \overset{(12.250)}{=} \frac{\langle \hat{n}, \hat{\omega}_o \rangle + \langle \hat{n}, \hat{\omega}_i \rangle}{\sqrt{2}\sqrt{\langle \hat{\omega}_o, \hat{\omega}_i \rangle + 1}} \tag{12.251}$$

523
523

where

$$\begin{aligned} \langle \hat{\omega}_o, \hat{\omega}_i \rangle &\overset{(3.70)}{\underset{(3.7)}{\overset{(3.6)}{=}}} \sin(\theta_o)\cos(\phi_o)\sin(\theta_i)\cos(\phi_i) + \sin(\theta_o)\sin(\phi_o)\sin(\theta_i)\sin(\phi_i) + \cos(\theta_o)\cos(\theta_i) \\ &\overset{(3.8)}{=} \sin(\theta_o)\sin(\theta_i)\cos(\phi_o - \phi_i) + \cos(\theta_o)\cos(\theta_i) \end{aligned} \tag{12.252}$$

76
67
67
67

The halfway vector can then be expressed in *spherical coordinates* as 70

$$\begin{aligned} \theta_h &\triangleq \arccos(\langle \hat{n}, \hat{h}_r \rangle) \\ &\overset{(12.251)}{\underset{(12.252)}{=}} \arccos\left(\frac{\cos(\theta_o) + \cos(\theta_i)}{\sqrt{2}\sqrt{\sin(\theta_o)\sin(\theta_i)\cos(\phi_o - \phi_i) + \cos(\theta_o)\cos(\theta_i) + 1}} \right) && (12.253) \\ \phi_h &\triangleq \operatorname{arctan2}(\langle \hat{v}, \hat{h}_r \rangle, \langle \hat{u}, \hat{h}_r \rangle) \\ &= \operatorname{arctan2}\left(\sin(\theta_o)\sin(\phi_o) + \sin(\theta_i)\sin(\phi_i), \sin(\theta_o)\cos(\phi_o) + \sin(\theta_i)\cos(\phi_i) \right) && (12.254) \end{aligned}$$

523
523

Rather than expressing the incident direction relative to the standard frame defined by the surface normal, it may alternatively be defined within the frame whose zenith direction is aligned with the halfway vector [Rusinkiewicz, 1998] as illustrated in *Figure 12.29*, yielding 524
the difference coordinates

$$\begin{aligned} \theta_d &\triangleq \arccos(\langle \hat{h}_r, \hat{\omega}_o \rangle) \overset{(12.250)}{=} \arccos(\langle \hat{h}_r, \hat{\omega}_i \rangle) \overset{(12.250)}{=} \arccos\left(\frac{\|\hat{\omega}_o + \hat{\omega}_i\|}{2} \right) \\ &\overset{(12.250)}{\underset{(12.252)}{=}} \arccos\left(\sqrt{\frac{\sin(\theta_o)\sin(\theta_i)\cos(\phi_o - \phi_i) + \cos(\theta_o)\cos(\theta_i) + 1}{2}} \right) && (12.255) \\ \phi_d &\triangleq \operatorname{arctan2}(\langle \hat{v}', \hat{\omega}_i \rangle, \langle \hat{u}', \hat{\omega}_i \rangle) && (12.256) \end{aligned}$$

523
523
523
523

70 where the vectors of the local frame are given in *spherical coordinates* as $\hat{v}' \triangleq [1, \pi/2, \phi_h + \pi/2]$ and $\hat{u}' \triangleq [1, \theta_h + \pi/2, \phi_h]$. A notable property of the resulting coordinate system is that Helmholtz's reciprocity reduces to a symmetry between ϕ_d and $\phi_d \pm \pi$, and that isotropic BRDFs are independent of ϕ_h. Also, the parameterization tends to align the main BRDF
444 features, such that the influence of the underlying normal distribution or *phase function* become majoritarily stationary, and vary only predominantly with respect to either θ_h or θ_d, respectively.

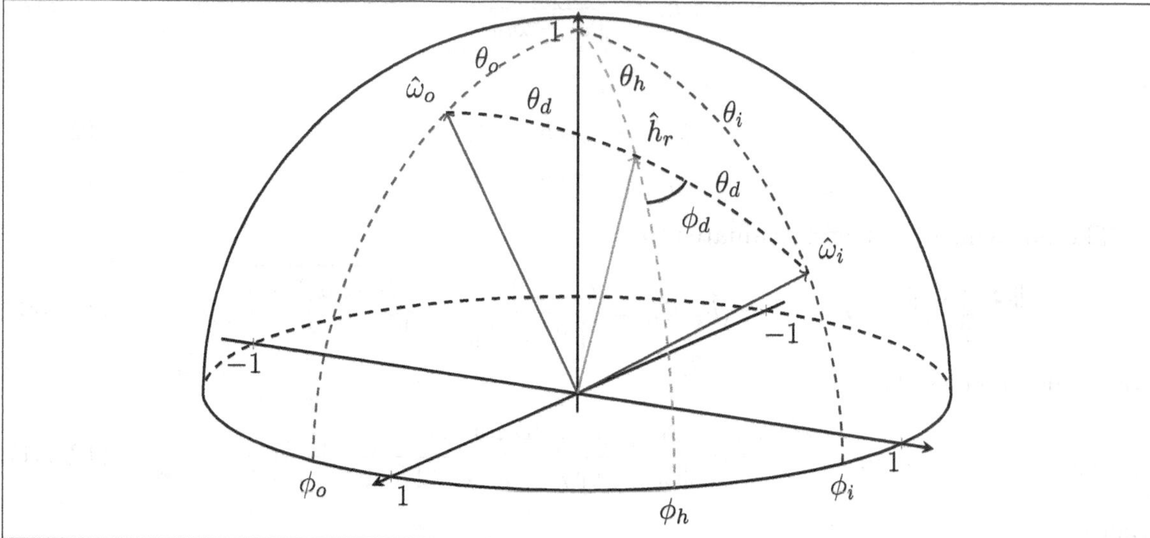

Figure 12.29: BRDF Parameterizations: Illustration of BRDF parameterization in terms of incident and exitant angles, and in terms of halfway and difference angles (drawn after [Rusinkiewicz, 1998, Fig. 2]).

133 Recalling the dependence between *transformed probability density* functions on different spaces, the sampling distribution of the halfway vector and incident direction are accordingly related by the absolute value of the Jacobian determinant of the transformation. Without loss of generality, let us consider a coordinate system where the exitant vector is aligned with the zenith direction such that $\theta_o = 0$, allowing the previous expressions for the reflective case to simplify into

523
$$\begin{aligned}\lim_{\theta_o \to 0} \theta_h &\overset{(12.253)}{=} \arccos\left(\frac{1+\cos(\theta_i)}{\sqrt{2}\sqrt{\cos(\theta_i)+1}}\right) = \arccos\left(\sqrt{\frac{\cos(\theta_i)+1}{2}}\right) \\ &= \arccos\left(\sqrt{\cos\left(\frac{\theta_i}{2}\right)^2}\right) = \frac{\theta_i}{2}\end{aligned} \tag{12.257}$$

523
$$\lim_{\theta_o \to 0} \phi_h \overset{(12.254)}{=} \operatorname{arctan2}\left(\sin(\phi_i), \cos(\phi_i)\right) = \phi_i \tag{12.258}$$

from which follows the relationship between the respective PDFs [Torrance and Sparrow,

1966, Torrance and Sparrow, 1967]

$$\frac{p_i(\vec{p},\hat{\omega}_o,\hat{\omega}_i)}{p_m(\vec{p},\hat{h}_r)} \overset{(4.31)}{=} \frac{\mathrm{d}\hat{h}_r}{\mathrm{d}\hat{\omega}_i} \overset{(6.62)}{=} \frac{\sin(\theta_h)}{\sin(\theta_i)}\frac{\mathrm{d}\theta_h}{\mathrm{d}\theta_i}\frac{\mathrm{d}\phi_h}{\mathrm{d}\phi_i} \underset{(12.258)}{\overset{(12.257)}{=}} \frac{\sin(\theta_h)}{\sin(2\theta_h)}\frac{1}{2} = \frac{\sin(\theta_h)}{2\cos(\theta_h)\sin(\theta_h)}\frac{1}{2}$$

133 244 524 524

$$= \frac{1}{4\cos(\theta_h)} = \frac{1}{4\langle\hat{h}_r,\hat{\omega}_o\rangle} \overset{(12.250)}{=} \frac{1}{4\langle\hat{h}_r,\hat{\omega}_i\rangle} \qquad (12.259)$$

523

$$\overset{(12.250)}{=} \frac{\langle\hat{h}_r,\hat{\omega}_i\rangle}{\|\hat{\omega}_o+\hat{\omega}_i\|^2} \overset{(12.250)}{=} \frac{\langle\hat{h}_r,\hat{\omega}_i\rangle}{(\langle\hat{h}_r,\hat{\omega}_o\rangle+\langle\hat{h}_r,\hat{\omega}_i\rangle)^2} \qquad (12.260)$$

523 523

Refraction Similarly, light may only be refracted by ideally smooth micro-structures in agreement with the transmission direction established for *specular surfaces*, and therefore by 486
those points of the micro-geometry whose normal satisfies Snell's law

$$\begin{aligned}
& n_o\sqrt{1-\langle\hat{m},\hat{\omega}_o\rangle^2} \overset{(12.73)}{=} n_i\sqrt{1-\langle\hat{m},\hat{\omega}_i\rangle^2} \\
\Longrightarrow\ & n_o^2(1-\langle\hat{m},\hat{\omega}_o\rangle^2) = n_i^2(1-\langle\hat{m},\hat{\omega}_i\rangle^2) \\
\Longrightarrow\ & n_o^2-\langle\hat{m},n_o\hat{\omega}_o\rangle^2 = n_i^2-\langle\hat{m},n_i\hat{\omega}_i\rangle^2 \\
\Longrightarrow\ & n_o^2-n_i^2 = \langle\hat{m},n_o\hat{\omega}_o\rangle^2-\langle\hat{m},n_i\hat{\omega}_i\rangle^2 \\
\Longrightarrow\ & (n_o+n_i)(n_o-n_i) = (\langle\hat{m},n_o\hat{\omega}_o\rangle+\langle\hat{m},n_i\hat{\omega}_i\rangle)(\langle\hat{m},n_o\hat{\omega}_o\rangle-\langle\hat{m},n_i\hat{\omega}_i\rangle) \\
& = \langle\hat{m},n_o\hat{\omega}_o+n_i\hat{\omega}_i\rangle\langle\hat{m},n_o\hat{\omega}_o-n_i\hat{\omega}_i\rangle \\
\Longrightarrow\ & 1 = \left\langle\hat{m},\tfrac{n_o\hat{\omega}_o+n_i\hat{\omega}_i}{n_o+n_i}\right\rangle\left\langle\hat{m},\tfrac{n_o\hat{\omega}_o-n_i\hat{\omega}_i}{n_o-n_i}\right\rangle
\end{aligned} \qquad (12.261)$$

489

from which follows that

$$\hat{h}_t = \operatorname{sgn}(n_o-n_i)\frac{n_o\hat{\omega}_o+n_i\hat{\omega}_i}{\|n_o\hat{\omega}_o+n_i\hat{\omega}_i\|} = \operatorname{sgn}\left(1-\frac{n_i}{n_o}\right)\frac{n_o\hat{\omega}_o+n_i\hat{\omega}_i}{\|n_o\hat{\omega}_o+n_i\hat{\omega}_i\|} \qquad (12.262)$$

where the normalization factor evaluates to

$$\begin{aligned}
\|n_o\hat{\omega}_o+n_i\hat{\omega}_i\| &= \sqrt{\langle n_o\hat{\omega}_o+n_i\hat{\omega}_i,n_o\hat{\omega}_o+n_i\hat{\omega}_i\rangle} \\
&= \sqrt{\langle n_o\hat{\omega}_o,n_o\hat{\omega}_o\rangle+2\langle n_o\hat{\omega}_o,n_i\hat{\omega}_i\rangle+\langle n_i\hat{\omega}_i,n_i\hat{\omega}_i\rangle} \\
&= \sqrt{n_o^2+2n_on_i\langle\hat{\omega}_o,\hat{\omega}_i\rangle+n_i^2}
\end{aligned} \qquad (12.263)$$

While the Jacobian of the reflective and refractive transformations can be computed
by expressing the differential *solid angles* in terms of intermediate differential *Cartesian* 244
coordinates [Stam, 2001], both may alternatively be obtained by geometric construction 67
[Walter *et al.*, 2007] as illustrated in *Figure 12.30*. The relationship between the respective 526

measure densities for the refractive case is then similarly given by

133 $$\frac{p_i(\vec{p},\hat{\omega}_o,\hat{\omega}_i)}{p_m(\vec{p},\hat{h}_t)} \overset{(4.31)}{=} \frac{\mathrm{d}\hat{h}_t}{\mathrm{d}\hat{\omega}_i} = \frac{n_i^2\langle\hat{h}_t,\hat{\omega}_i\rangle}{\|n_o\hat{\omega}_o+n_i\hat{\omega}_i\|^2} \quad (12.264)$$

525 $$\overset{(12.262)}{=} \frac{n_i^2\langle\hat{h}_t,\hat{\omega}_i\rangle}{(\langle\hat{h}_t,n_o\hat{\omega}_o+n_i\hat{\omega}_i\rangle)^2} \quad (12.265)$$

$$= \frac{1}{\frac{(n_o\langle\hat{h}_t,\hat{\omega}_o\rangle+n_i\langle\hat{h}_t,\hat{\omega}_i\rangle)^2}{n_i^2\langle\hat{h}_t,\hat{\omega}_i\rangle^2}\langle\hat{h}_t,\hat{\omega}_i\rangle}$$

$$= \frac{1}{\left(\frac{n_o\langle\hat{h}_t,\hat{\omega}_o\rangle}{n_i\langle\hat{h}_t,\hat{\omega}_i\rangle}+1\right)^2\langle\hat{h}_t,\hat{\omega}_i\rangle} \quad (12.266)$$

525 $$\overset{(12.262)}{=} \frac{1}{\left(\frac{\langle n_o\hat{\omega}_o+n_i\hat{\omega}_i,n_o\hat{\omega}_o\rangle}{\langle n_o\hat{\omega}_o+n_i\hat{\omega}_i,n_i\hat{\omega}_i\rangle}+1\right)^2\langle\hat{h}_t,\hat{\omega}_i\rangle}$$

$$= \frac{1}{\left(\frac{n_o^2+\langle n_o\hat{\omega}_o,n_i\hat{\omega}_i\rangle}{n_i^2+\langle n_o\hat{\omega}_o,n_i\hat{\omega}_i\rangle}+1\right)^2\langle\hat{h}_t,\hat{\omega}_i\rangle} \quad (12.267)$$

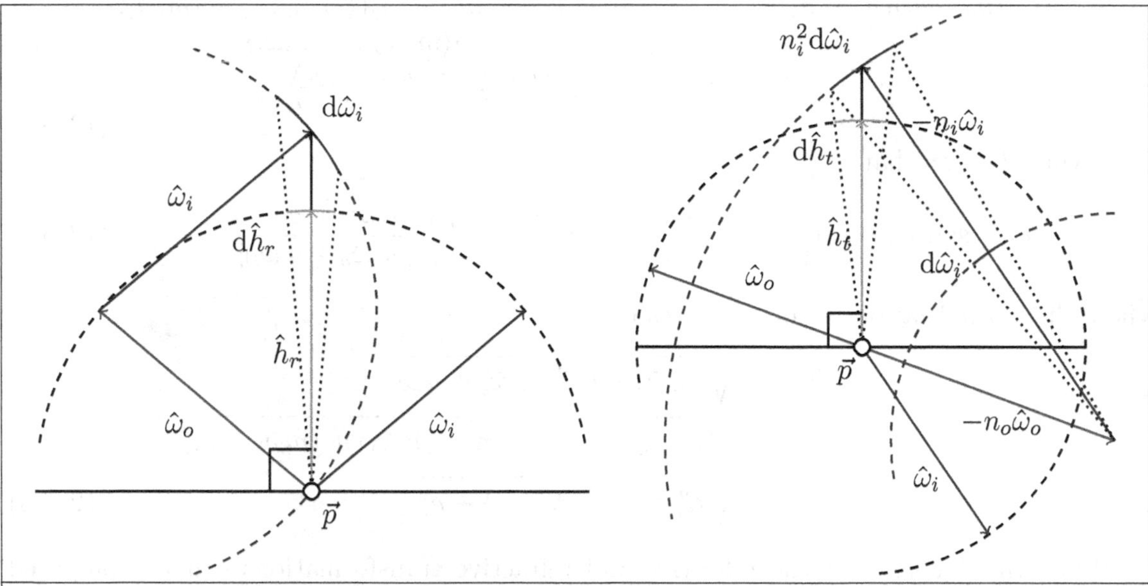

Figure 12.30: Jacobian of Reflection and Refraction: Illustration of the geometric construction of the Jacobian for the reflective and refractive transformations (drawn after [Walter *et al.*, 2007, Fig. 6 and 7]).

12.6.2.2 Bidirectional Distributions

Definition Under the assumption of single light scattering, the radiance reflected/transmitted in direction $\hat{\omega}_o$ by a point $\vec{p}_m$ on the microscopic surface is defined in terms of the BSDF f_m of the micro-structures as

475 $$L_{r|t}(\vec{p}_m,\hat{\omega}_o) \overset{(12.2)}{=} \int_\Omega L_i(\vec{p}_m,\hat{\omega}_i)f_m(\vec{p}_m,\hat{\omega}_o,\hat{\omega}_i)|\langle\hat{\nabla}(\vec{p}_m),\hat{\omega}_i\rangle|\mathrm{d}\hat{\omega}_i$$

$$= \int_\Omega L_i(\vec{p},\hat{\omega}_i)T(\vec{p}_m,\hat{\omega}_i)f_m(\vec{p}_m,\hat{\omega}_o,\hat{\omega}_i)|\langle\hat{\nabla}(\vec{p}_m),\hat{\omega}_i\rangle|\mathrm{d}\hat{\omega}_i \quad (12.268)$$

The radiance scattered by the macroscopic surface at point $\vec{p}$ then reads

$$\begin{aligned} L_{r|t}(\vec{p}, \hat{\omega}_o) &\triangleq \frac{1}{A_{\omega_o}} \int_{A_{\omega_o}} L_{r|t}(\vec{p}_{\omega_o}, \hat{\omega}_o) \mathrm{d}A(\vec{p}_{\omega_o}) \\ &= \frac{1}{A_{\omega_o}} \int_{A_m} L_{r|t}(\vec{p}_m, \hat{\omega}_o) T(\vec{p}_m, \hat{\omega}_o) |\langle \hat{\omega}_o, \hat{\nabla}(\vec{p}_m) \rangle| \mathrm{d}A(\vec{p}_m) \\ &\overset{(12.149)}{=} \frac{1}{A_{\omega_o}} \int_{2\pi^+} \mathcal{T}\{L_{r|t}(\vec{p}_m, \hat{\omega}_o) T(\vec{p}_m, \hat{\omega}_o)\}(\vec{p}, \hat{m}) |\langle \hat{\omega}_o, \hat{m} \rangle| \mathrm{d}\hat{m} \quad (12.269) \end{aligned}$$ 506

which, when substituting the formulation of $L_{r|t}(\vec{p}_m, \hat{\omega}_o)$, becomes

$$\begin{aligned} L_{r|t}(\vec{p}, \hat{\omega}_o) &= \frac{1}{A_{\omega_o}} \int_{A_m} \int_{\Omega} L_i(\vec{p}, \hat{\omega}_i) T(\vec{p}_m, \hat{\omega}_i) f_m(\vec{p}_m, \hat{\omega}_o, \hat{\omega}_i) |\langle \hat{\nabla}(\vec{p}_m), \hat{\omega}_i \rangle| \mathrm{d}\hat{\omega}_i \\ &\quad \times T(\vec{p}_m, \hat{\omega}_o) |\langle \hat{\omega}_o, \hat{\nabla}(\vec{p}_m) \rangle| \mathrm{d}A(\vec{p}_m) \\ &= \frac{1}{A_n |\langle \hat{n}, \hat{\omega}_o \rangle|} \int_{\Omega} L_i(\vec{p}, \hat{\omega}_i) \int_{A_m} T(\vec{p}_m, \hat{\omega}_o) T(\vec{p}_m, \hat{\omega}_i) f_m(\vec{p}_m, \hat{\omega}_o, \hat{\omega}_i) \\ &\quad \times |\langle \hat{\nabla}(\vec{p}_m), \hat{\omega}_o \rangle \langle \hat{\nabla}(\vec{p}_m), \hat{\omega}_i \rangle| \mathrm{d}A(\vec{p}_m) \mathrm{d}\hat{\omega}_i \quad (12.270) \end{aligned}$$

It then follows that the macroscopic BRDF/BTDF corresponding to first-order scattering events is given by

$$\begin{aligned} f_{r|t}(\vec{p}, \hat{\omega}_o, \hat{\omega}_i) &\overset{(12.1)}{=} \frac{\mathrm{d}L_{r|t}(\vec{p}, \hat{\omega}_o)}{L_i(\vec{p}, \hat{\omega}_i) |\langle \hat{n}, \hat{\omega}_i \rangle| \mathrm{d}\hat{\omega}_i} \\ &= \frac{1}{A_n |\langle \hat{n}, \hat{\omega}_o \rangle \langle \hat{n}, \hat{\omega}_i \rangle|} \int_{A_m} T(\vec{p}_m, \hat{\omega}_o) T(\vec{p}_m, \hat{\omega}_i) f_m(\vec{p}_m, \hat{\omega}_o, \hat{\omega}_i) \\ &\quad \times |\langle \hat{\nabla}(\vec{p}_m), \hat{\omega}_o \rangle \langle \hat{\nabla}(\vec{p}_m), \hat{\omega}_i \rangle| \mathrm{d}A(\vec{p}_m) \\ &\overset{(12.149)}{=} \frac{1}{A_n |\langle \hat{n}, \hat{\omega}_o \rangle \langle \hat{n}, \hat{\omega}_i \rangle|} \int_{2\pi^+} \mathcal{T}\{T(\vec{p}_m, \hat{\omega}_o) T(\vec{p}_m, \hat{\omega}_i) f_m(\vec{p}_m, \hat{\omega}_o, \hat{\omega}_i)\}(\vec{p}, \hat{m}) \\ &\quad \times |\langle \hat{m}, \hat{\omega}_o \rangle \langle \hat{m}, \hat{\omega}_i \rangle| \mathrm{d}\hat{m} \quad (12.271) \end{aligned}$$ 475 506

which, in the special case where all points of the micro-surface with a given micro-normal have an identical micro-BRDF/BTDF, are expressible as a product of the *normal distribution* 506
and the *bi-static visibility G* 533

$$\begin{aligned} f_{r|t}(\vec{p}, \hat{\omega}_o, \hat{\omega}_i) &= \frac{1}{A_n |\langle \hat{n}, \hat{\omega}_o \rangle \langle \hat{n}, \hat{\omega}_i \rangle|} \int_{2\pi^+} \mathcal{T}\{T(\vec{p}_m, \hat{\omega}_o) T(\vec{p}_m, \hat{\omega}_i)\}(\vec{p}, \hat{m}) \\ &\quad \times f_m(\vec{p}_m \mid \hat{\nabla}(\vec{p}_m) = \hat{m}, \hat{\omega}_o, \hat{\omega}_i) |\langle \hat{m}, \hat{\omega}_o \rangle \langle \hat{m}, \hat{\omega}_i \rangle| \mathrm{d}\hat{m} \\ &\underset{(12.305)}{\overset{(12.150)}{=}} \frac{1}{|\langle \hat{n}, \hat{\omega}_o \rangle \langle \hat{n}, \hat{\omega}_i \rangle|} \int_{2\pi^+} D(\vec{p}, \hat{m}) G(\vec{p}, \hat{m}, \hat{\omega}_o, \hat{\omega}_i) f_m(\vec{p}_m \mid \hat{\nabla}(\vec{p}_m) = \hat{m}, \hat{\omega}_o, \hat{\omega}_i) \\ &\quad \times |\langle \hat{m}, \hat{\omega}_o \rangle \langle \hat{m}, \hat{\omega}_i \rangle| \mathrm{d}\hat{m} \quad (12.272) \end{aligned}$$ 506 533

Specular Micro-Structures Under the assumption of micro-structures modeled as perfect *specular surfaces*, the microscopic BRDF is defined as 486

$$\begin{aligned} f_m(\vec{p}_m, \hat{\omega}_o, \hat{\omega}_i) &\overset{(12.114)}{=} \frac{\delta(\hat{\omega}_i - \mathcal{T}_r(\hat{m}, \hat{\omega}_o))}{\langle \hat{m}, \hat{\omega}_i \rangle} F(\langle \hat{m}, \hat{\omega}_o \rangle) \\ &= \frac{\delta(\hat{h}_r - \hat{m})}{\langle \hat{m}, \hat{\omega}_i \rangle} \left| \frac{\mathrm{d}\hat{h}_r}{\mathrm{d}\hat{\omega}_i} \right| F(\langle \hat{m}, \hat{\omega}_o \rangle) \\ &= \frac{\delta(\hat{h}_r - \hat{m})}{\langle \hat{m}, \hat{\omega}_i \rangle} \frac{F(\langle \hat{m}, \hat{\omega}_o \rangle)}{4 |\langle \hat{h}_r, \hat{\omega}_o \rangle|} \quad (12.273) \end{aligned}$$ 496

and the expression of the macroscopic BRDF simplifies into [Cook, 1981, Cook and Torrance, 1981, Cook and Torrance, 1982]

527

$$f_r(\vec{p},\hat{\omega}_o,\hat{\omega}_i) \overset{(12.272)}{=} \frac{1}{|\langle\hat{n},\hat{\omega}_o\rangle\langle\hat{n},\hat{\omega}_i\rangle|}\int_{2\pi^+} D(\vec{p},\hat{m})G(\vec{p},\hat{m},\hat{\omega}_o,\hat{\omega}_i) \times \frac{\delta(\hat{h}_r-\hat{m})}{\langle\hat{m},\hat{\omega}_i\rangle}\frac{F(\langle\hat{m},\hat{\omega}_o\rangle)}{4|\langle\hat{h}_r,\hat{\omega}_o\rangle|}|\langle\hat{m},\hat{\omega}_o\rangle\langle\hat{m},\hat{\omega}_i\rangle|\mathrm{d}\hat{m}$$

45

$$\overset{(2.218)}{=} \frac{D(\vec{p},\hat{h}_r)G(\vec{p},\hat{h}_r,\hat{\omega}_o,\hat{\omega}_i)}{|\langle\hat{n},\hat{\omega}_o\rangle\langle\hat{n},\hat{\omega}_i\rangle|}\frac{F(\langle\hat{h}_r,\hat{\omega}_o\rangle)}{4} \tag{12.274}$$

Similarly, the microscopic BTDF is defined as

496

$$f_m(\vec{p}_m,\hat{\omega}_o,\hat{\omega}_i) \overset{(12.116)}{=} \frac{\delta(\hat{\omega}_i-\tau_t(\hat{m},\hat{\omega}_o))}{-\langle\hat{m},\hat{\omega}_i\rangle}T(\langle\hat{m},\hat{\omega}_o\rangle)\frac{n_o^2}{n_i^2}$$
$$= \frac{\delta(\hat{h}_t-\hat{m})}{-\langle\hat{m},\hat{\omega}_i\rangle}\left|\frac{\mathrm{d}\hat{h}_t}{\mathrm{d}\hat{\omega}_i}\right|T(\langle\hat{m},\hat{\omega}_o\rangle)\frac{n_o^2}{n_i^2}$$
$$= \frac{\delta(\hat{h}_t-\hat{m})}{-\langle\hat{m},\hat{\omega}_i\rangle}\frac{-n_o^2\langle\hat{h}_t,\hat{\omega}_i\rangle T(\langle\hat{m},\hat{\omega}_o\rangle)}{(n_o\langle\hat{h}_t,\hat{\omega}_o\rangle+n_i\langle\hat{h}_t,\hat{\omega}_i\rangle)^2} \tag{12.275}$$

and the expression of the macroscopic BTDF becomes [Walter *et al.*, 2007]

527

$$f_t(\vec{p},\hat{\omega}_o,\hat{\omega}_i) \overset{(12.272)}{=} \frac{1}{|\langle\hat{n},\hat{\omega}_o\rangle\langle\hat{n},\hat{\omega}_i\rangle|}\int_{2\pi^+} D(\vec{p},\hat{m})G(\vec{p},\hat{m},\hat{\omega}_o,\hat{\omega}_i)\frac{\delta(\hat{h}_t-\hat{m})}{-\langle\hat{m},\hat{\omega}_i\rangle} \times \frac{-n_o^2\langle\hat{h}_t,\hat{\omega}_i\rangle T(\langle\hat{m},\hat{\omega}_o\rangle)}{(n_o\langle\hat{h}_t,\hat{\omega}_o\rangle+n_i\langle\hat{h}_t,\hat{\omega}_i\rangle)^2}|\langle\hat{m},\hat{\omega}_o\rangle\langle\hat{m},\hat{\omega}_i\rangle|\mathrm{d}\hat{m}$$

45

$$\overset{(2.218)}{=} \frac{D(\vec{p},\hat{h}_t)G(\vec{p},\hat{h}_t,\hat{\omega}_o,\hat{\omega}_i)}{|\langle\hat{n},\hat{\omega}_o\rangle\langle\hat{n},\hat{\omega}_i\rangle|}\frac{n_o^2T(\langle\hat{h}_t,\hat{\omega}_o\rangle)|\langle\hat{h}_t,\hat{\omega}_o\rangle\langle\hat{h}_t,\hat{\omega}_i\rangle|}{(n_o\langle\hat{h}_t,\hat{\omega}_o\rangle+n_i\langle\hat{h}_t,\hat{\omega}_i\rangle)^2} \tag{12.276}$$

which is not reciprocal but instead obeys

$$\frac{f_t(\vec{p},\hat{\omega}_o,\hat{\omega}_i)}{n_o^2} = \frac{f_t(\vec{p},\hat{\omega}_i,\hat{\omega}_o)}{n_i^2} \tag{12.277}$$

529 while modeling refraction through rough surfaces as illustrated in *Figure 12.31*.

Alternatively, these results can also be derived by considering the numerical simulation performed by virtual gonio-reflectometers, which evaluate the cosine-weighted single-scattering BRDF/BTDF of the macroscopic surface as a limit integral of the geometric and optical properties of the micro-structures over the projection space orthogonal to the direction of exitance. Rewriting the numerator as an integral over the microscopic surface and the denominator as an integral over micro-normals then yields

$$f_{r|t}(\vec{p},\hat{\omega}_o,\hat{\omega}_i)|\langle\hat{n},\hat{\omega}_i\rangle|$$
$$\triangleq \lim_{\Omega_i\to\hat{\omega}_i}\frac{\int_{A_{\omega_o}}\delta[\tau_{r|t}(\hat{\nabla}(\vec{p}_{\omega_o}),\hat{\omega}_o)\in\Omega_i]T(\vec{p}_{\omega_o},\hat{\omega}_o)T(\vec{p}_{\omega_o},\hat{\omega}_i)\rho_{r|t}(\vec{p}_{\omega_o},\hat{\omega}_o)\mathrm{d}A(\vec{p}_{\omega_o})}{A_{\omega_o}\int_{\Omega_i}\mathrm{d}\hat{\omega}_i}$$
$$= \lim_{\Omega_m\to\hat{h}_{r|t}}\frac{\int_{A_m}\delta[\hat{\nabla}(\vec{p}_m)\in\Omega_m]T(\vec{p}_m,\hat{\omega}_o)T(\vec{p}_m,\hat{\omega}_i)\rho_{r|t}(\vec{p}_m,\hat{\omega}_o)\langle\hat{h}_{r|t},\hat{\omega}_o\rangle\mathrm{d}A(\vec{p}_m)}{A_n\langle\hat{n},\hat{\omega}_o\rangle\int_{\Omega_m}\frac{\mathrm{d}\hat{\omega}_i}{\mathrm{d}\hat{h}_{r|t}}\mathrm{d}\hat{m}}$$
$$= \frac{\langle\hat{h}_{r|t},\hat{\omega}_o\rangle}{\langle\hat{n},\hat{\omega}_o\rangle\frac{\mathrm{d}\hat{\omega}_i}{\mathrm{d}\hat{h}_{r|t}}}\lim_{\Omega_m\to\hat{h}_{r|t}}\frac{\int_{A_m}\delta[\hat{\nabla}(\vec{p}_m)\in\Omega_m]T(\vec{p}_m,\hat{\omega}_o)T(\vec{p}_m,\hat{\omega}_i)\rho_{r|t}(\vec{p}_m,\hat{\omega}_o)\mathrm{d}A(\vec{p}_m)}{A_n\int_{\Omega_m}\mathrm{d}\hat{m}} \tag{12.278}$$

Figure 12.31: Micro-Geometry BSDF: Visual appearance of a micro-geometry BSDF simulating rough glass (light probe courtesy of Paul Debevec).

where the spatially varying reflection/transmission microscopic albedos are defined in terms
of the *Fresnel equations* as 490

$$\rho_r(\vec{p}_m, \hat{\omega}_o) \overset{(12.118)}{=} F(\vec{p}_m, \langle \hat{\nabla}(\vec{p}_m), \hat{\omega}_o \rangle) \qquad (12.279)$$ 498

$$\rho_t(\vec{p}_m, \hat{\omega}_o) \overset{(12.119)}{=} T(\vec{p}_m, \langle \hat{\nabla}(\vec{p}_m), \hat{\omega}_o \rangle) \frac{n_o^2}{n_i^2} \qquad (12.280)$$ 498

Dividing both sides by the cosine term then yields the following formulations of the BRDF and BTDF

$$f_{r|t}(\vec{p}, \hat{\omega}_o, \hat{\omega}_i) \overset{(12.147)}{=} A_{r|t}(\hat{\omega}_o, \hat{\omega}_i) \frac{\mathcal{T}\{T(\vec{p}_m, \hat{\omega}_o) T(\vec{p}_m, \hat{\omega}_i) \rho_{r|t}(\vec{p}_m, \hat{\omega}_o)\}(\vec{p}, \hat{h}_{r|t})}{A_n} \qquad (12.281)$$ 505

where the auxiliary functions read

$$A_{r|t}(\hat{\omega}_o, \hat{\omega}_i) \triangleq \frac{\langle \hat{h}_{r|t}, \hat{\omega}_o \rangle}{\langle \hat{n}, \hat{\omega}_o \rangle |\langle \hat{n}, \hat{\omega}_i \rangle|} \frac{\mathrm{d}\hat{h}_{r|t}}{\mathrm{d}\hat{\omega}_i} \qquad (12.282)$$

such that

$$A_r(\hat{\omega}_o, \hat{\omega}_i) \overset{(12.259)}{=} \frac{1}{4 \langle \hat{n}, \hat{\omega}_o \rangle \langle \hat{n}, \hat{\omega}_i \rangle} \qquad (12.283)$$ 525

$$A_t(\hat{\omega}_o, \hat{\omega}_i) \overset{(12.264)}{=} \frac{n_i^2}{(n_o \langle \hat{h}_t, \hat{\omega}_o \rangle + n_i \langle \hat{h}_t, \hat{\omega}_i \rangle)^2} \left| \frac{\langle \hat{h}_t, \hat{\omega}_o \rangle \langle \hat{h}_t, \hat{\omega}_i \rangle}{\langle \hat{n}, \hat{\omega}_o \rangle \langle \hat{n}, \hat{\omega}_i \rangle} \right| \qquad (12.284)$$ 526

where the n_i^2 term cancels out with the denominator of $\frac{n_o^2}{n_i^2}$ in $\rho_t(\vec{p}_m, \hat{\omega}_o)$.

In the special case where all points of the micro-surface with a given micro-normal have an identical micro-BRDF/BTDF, and therefore an identical micro-albedo for a given exitant direction

$$\rho_r(\vec{p}_m, \hat{\omega}_o) \overset{(12.279)}{=} F(\langle \hat{\nabla}(\vec{p}_m), \hat{\omega}_o \rangle) \qquad (12.285)$$ 529

$$\rho_t(\vec{p}_m, \hat{\omega}_o) \overset{(12.280)}{=} T(\langle \hat{\nabla}(\vec{p}_m), \hat{\omega}_o \rangle) \frac{n_o^2}{n_i^2} \qquad (12.286)$$ 529

the formulations of the BRDF and BTDF are readily expressible as a product of the *normal*
506 *distribution* and the *bi-static visibility* G
533

529

$$f_{r|t}(\vec{p},\hat{\omega}_o,\hat{\omega}_i) \overset{(12.281)}{=} A_{r|t}(\hat{\omega}_o,\hat{\omega}_i)\frac{\mathcal{T}\{T(\vec{p}_m,\hat{\omega}_o)T(\vec{p}_m,\hat{\omega}_i)\}(\vec{p},\hat{h}_{r|t})}{A_n}\rho_{r|t}(\vec{p}_m \mid \hat{\nabla}(\vec{p}_m)=\hat{h}_{r|t},\hat{\omega}_o)$$

506
533

$$\overset{(12.150)}{\underset{(12.305)}{=}} A_{r|t}(\hat{\omega}_o,\hat{\omega}_i)D(\vec{p},\hat{h}_{r|t})G(\vec{p},\hat{h}_{r|t},\hat{\omega}_o,\hat{\omega}_i)\rho_{r|t}(\vec{p}_m \mid \hat{\nabla}(\vec{p}_m)=\hat{h}_{r|t},\hat{\omega}_o) \quad (12.287)$$

12.6.2.3 Albedo

In order to prove the energy-conservation property of the BRDF/BTDF, a bound on the albedo may be derived by formulating the latter as an integral over micro-normals. For a given exitant direction, the set of incident directions $\hat{\omega}_i \in 2\pi$ describes a subset of the space of micro-normals $\hat{m}$ in the corresponding hemisphere, whose complementary subset corresponds to incident directions pointing in the opposite hemisphere, where the BRDF/BTDF is implicitly assumed to be zero. The expression of the albedo then becomes

476

$$\begin{aligned}\rho_{r|t}(\vec{p},\hat{\omega}_o) &\overset{(12.9)}{=} \int_{\Omega_i} f_{r|t}(\vec{p},\hat{\omega}_o,\hat{\omega}_i)|\langle\hat{n},\hat{\omega}_i\rangle|\mathrm{d}\hat{\omega}_i \\ &= \int_{\Omega_m|\hat{\omega}_i\in\Omega_i} f_{r|t}(\vec{p},\hat{\omega}_o,\tau_{r|t}(\hat{m},\hat{\omega}_o))|\langle\hat{n},\tau_{r|t}(\hat{m},\hat{\omega}_o)\rangle|\frac{\mathrm{d}\hat{\omega}_i}{\mathrm{d}\hat{h}_{r|t}}\mathrm{d}\hat{m} \\ &= \int_{2\pi^+} f_{r|t}(\vec{p},\hat{\omega}_o,\tau_{r|t}(\hat{m},\hat{\omega}_o))|\langle\hat{n},\tau_{r|t}(\hat{m},\hat{\omega}_o)\rangle|\frac{\mathrm{d}\hat{\omega}_i}{\mathrm{d}\hat{h}_{r|t}}\mathrm{d}\hat{m}\end{aligned} \quad (12.288)$$

526 Substituting the formulation of the *bidirectional distributions*, and exploiting the physical range of the micro-albedos $\rho_{r|t}(\vec{p}_m) \in [0,1]$ and of the visibility function $T \in [0,1]$, an upper bound on the macroscopic albedo is then readily obtained as

529
529
532

$$\begin{aligned}\rho_{r|t}(\vec{p},\hat{\omega}_o) &\overset{(12.281)}{=} \int_{2\pi^+} A_{r|t}(\hat{\omega}_o,\tau_{r|t}(\hat{m},\hat{\omega}_o))\frac{\mathcal{T}\{T(\vec{p}_m,\hat{\omega}_o)T(\vec{p}_m,\tau_{r|t}(\hat{m},\hat{\omega}_o))\rho_{r|t}(\vec{p}_m,\hat{\omega}_o)\}(\vec{p},\hat{m})}{A_n} \\ &\quad\times|\langle\hat{n},\tau_{r|t}(\hat{m},\hat{\omega}_o)\rangle|\frac{\mathrm{d}\hat{\omega}_i}{\mathrm{d}\hat{h}_{r|t}}\mathrm{d}\hat{m} \\ &\overset{(12.282)}{=} \frac{1}{\langle\hat{n},\hat{\omega}_o\rangle}\int_{2\pi^+}\frac{\mathcal{T}\{T(\vec{p}_m,\hat{\omega}_o)T(\vec{p}_m,\tau_{r|t}(\hat{m},\hat{\omega}_o))\rho_{r|t}(\vec{p}_m,\hat{\omega}_o)\}(\vec{p},\hat{m})}{A_n}\langle\hat{\omega}_o,\hat{m}\rangle\mathrm{d}\hat{m} \\ &\leq \frac{1}{\langle\hat{n},\hat{\omega}_o\rangle}\int_{2\pi^+}\frac{\mathcal{T}\{T(\vec{p}_m,\hat{\omega}_o)\}(\vec{p},\hat{m})}{A_n}\langle\hat{\omega}_o,\hat{m}\rangle\mathrm{d}\hat{m} \\ &\overset{(12.299)}{=} \frac{g(\vec{p},\hat{\omega}_o)}{\langle\hat{n},\hat{\omega}_o\rangle} \\ &= 1\end{aligned} \quad (12.289)$$

or equivalently in the special case of homogeneous micro-structures as

$$\begin{aligned}
\rho_{r|t}(\vec{p}, \hat{\omega}_o) &\overset{(12.287)}{=} \int_{2\pi^+} A_{r|t}(\hat{\omega}_o, \tau_{r|t}(\hat{m}, \hat{\omega}_o)) D(\vec{p}, \hat{m}) G(\vec{p}, \hat{m}, \hat{\omega}_o, \tau_{r|t}(\hat{m}, \hat{\omega}_o)) \\
&\quad \times \rho_{r|t}(\vec{p}_m, \hat{\omega}_o) |\langle \hat{n}, \tau_{r|t}(\hat{m}, \hat{\omega}_o)\rangle| \frac{d\hat{\omega}_i}{d\hat{h}_{r|t}} d\hat{m} \\
&\overset{(12.282)}{=} \frac{1}{\langle \hat{n}, \hat{\omega}_o\rangle} \int_{2\pi^+} D(\vec{p}, \hat{m}) G(\vec{p}, \hat{m}, \hat{\omega}_o, \tau_{r|t}(\hat{m}, \hat{\omega}_o)) \rho_{r|t}(\vec{p}_m, \hat{\omega}_o) \langle \hat{\omega}_o, \hat{m}\rangle d\hat{m} \\
&\leq \frac{1}{\langle \hat{n}, \hat{\omega}_o\rangle} \int_{2\pi^+} D(\vec{p}, \hat{m}) V(\vec{p}, \hat{m}, \hat{\omega}_o) \langle \hat{\omega}_o, \hat{m}\rangle d\hat{m} \\
&\overset{(12.299)}{=} \frac{g(\vec{p}, \hat{\omega}_o)}{\langle \hat{n}, \hat{\omega}_o\rangle} \\
&= 1
\end{aligned} \tag{12.290}$$

530 529 532

Under the assumption of the weak normalization constraint, energy conservation of the BRDF may alternatively be guaranteed by letting [Edwards *et al.*, 2006]

$$\begin{aligned}
\rho_r(\vec{p}, \hat{\omega}_o) &\overset{(12.259)}{=} \int_{2\pi^+} f_r(\vec{p}, \hat{\omega}_o, \tau_r(\hat{m}, \hat{\omega}_o)) |\langle \hat{n}, \tau_r(\hat{m}, \hat{\omega}_o)\rangle| 4\langle \hat{h}_r, \hat{\omega}_o\rangle d\hat{m} \\
&\leq \int_{2\pi^+} D(\vec{p}, \hat{h}_r) \langle \hat{n}, \hat{h}_r\rangle d\hat{h}_r \\
&\overset{(12.160)}{=} g(\vec{p}, \hat{n}) \\
&\overset{(12.160)}{=} 1
\end{aligned} \tag{12.291}$$

525 507 507

for which a sufficient condition, on the space of micro-normals corresponding to incident directions pointing in the upper hemisphere, is given by the conservative bound

$$f_r(\vec{p}, \hat{\omega}_o, \hat{\omega}_i) \leq D(\vec{p}, \hat{h}_r) \frac{\langle \hat{n}, \hat{h}_r\rangle}{4\langle \hat{h}_r, \hat{\omega}_o\rangle \langle \hat{n}, \hat{\omega}_i\rangle} \tag{12.292}$$

$$\overset{(12.247)}{=} D\left(\vec{p}, \frac{\hat{\omega}_o + \hat{\omega}_i}{\|\hat{\omega}_o + \hat{\omega}_i\|}\right) \frac{\langle \hat{n}, \hat{\omega}_o\rangle + \langle \hat{n}, \hat{\omega}_i\rangle}{4(\langle \hat{\omega}_o, \hat{\omega}_i\rangle + 1)\langle \hat{n}, \hat{\omega}_i\rangle} \tag{12.293}$$ 523

12.6.3 Visibility Function

12.6.3.1 Mono-Static Visibility

Definition Given a microscopic normal $\hat{m}$ and a direction $\hat{\omega}$, the *mono-static visibility function* (*MVF*) defines the aggregate fraction of the microscopic surface orthogonal to $\hat{m}$ that is visible from $\hat{\omega}$, relative to the total area of the microscopic surface that is orthogonal to $\hat{m}$

$$V(\vec{p}, \hat{m}, \hat{\omega}) \triangleq \frac{\mathcal{T}\{T(\vec{p}_m, \hat{\omega})\}(\vec{p}, \hat{m})}{\mathcal{T}\{1\}(\vec{p}, \hat{m})} \tag{12.294}$$

which statistically characterizes the non-local probability of a point of the micro-surface with normal-orientation $\hat{m}$ to be unoccluded from direction $\hat{\omega}$

$$V(\vec{p}, \hat{m}, \hat{\omega}) = \Pr(\hat{\omega}) \tag{12.295}$$

In order to be physically plausible, the MVF must be bounded

$$V(\vec{p},\hat{m},\hat{\omega}) \in [0,1] \tag{12.296}$$

and explicitly guarantee that the front/back face of the micro-structures is only visible from the front/back face of the macroscopic surface

$$V(\vec{p},\hat{m},\hat{\omega}) = 0, \quad \text{if } \langle\hat{n},\hat{\omega}\rangle\langle\hat{m},\hat{\omega}\rangle \leq 0 \tag{12.297}$$

while satisfying an alternative form of the strong normalization constraint for *normal distri-*
506 *butions* expressed in terms of unsigned projected areas by clamping occluded portions (both front-facing and back-facing) of the micro-geometry [Ashikhmin *et al.*, 2000]

507 506 531 506

$$\begin{aligned}
g(\vec{p},\hat{\omega}) &\overset{(12.155)}{=} \int_{2\pi^+} D(\vec{p},\hat{m})V(\vec{p},\hat{m},\hat{\omega})\langle\hat{\omega},\hat{m}\rangle \mathrm{d}\hat{m} && (12.298)\\
&\underset{(12.294)}{\overset{(12.150)}{=}} \int_{2\pi^+} \frac{\mathcal{T}\{T(\vec{p}_m,\hat{\omega})\}(\vec{p},\hat{m})}{A_n}\langle\hat{\omega},\hat{m}\rangle \mathrm{d}\hat{m}\\
&\overset{(12.149)}{=} \frac{1}{A_n}\int_{A_m} T(\vec{p}_m,\hat{\omega})\langle\hat{\omega},\hat{\nabla}(\vec{p}_m)\rangle \mathrm{d}A(\vec{p}_m)\\
&= \frac{1}{A_n}\int_{A_\omega} \mathrm{d}A(\vec{p}_\omega)\\
&= \frac{A_\omega}{A_n}\\
&= \langle\hat{n},\hat{\omega}\rangle && (12.299)\\
&\leq 1 && (12.300)
\end{aligned}$$

from which follows that

$$\begin{aligned}
g(\vec{p},\hat{\omega}) &= \int_{\Omega_m|\langle\hat{n},\hat{\omega}\rangle\langle\hat{m},\hat{\omega}\rangle>0} D(\vec{p},\hat{m})\langle\hat{\omega},\hat{m}\rangle \mathrm{d}\hat{m} + \int_{\Omega_m|\langle\hat{n},\hat{\omega}\rangle\langle\hat{m},\hat{\omega}\rangle\leq 0} D(\vec{p},\hat{m})\langle\hat{\omega},\hat{m}\rangle \mathrm{d}\hat{m} && (12.301)\\
&= \int_{\Omega_m|\langle\hat{n},\hat{\omega}\rangle\langle\hat{m},\hat{\omega}\rangle>0} D(\vec{p},\hat{m})V(\vec{p},\hat{m},\hat{\omega})\langle\hat{\omega},\hat{m}\rangle \mathrm{d}\hat{m} + \cancel{\int_{\Omega_m|\langle\hat{n},\hat{\omega}\rangle\langle\hat{m},\hat{\omega}\rangle\leq 0} D(\vec{p},\hat{m})V(\vec{p},\hat{m},\hat{\omega})\langle\hat{\omega},\hat{m}\rangle \mathrm{d}\hat{m}} && (12.302)
\end{aligned}$$

and therefore

$$\int_{\Omega_m|\langle\hat{n},\hat{\omega}\rangle\langle\hat{m},\hat{\omega}\rangle>0} D(\vec{p},\hat{m})(1-V(\vec{p},\hat{m},\hat{\omega}))\langle\hat{\omega},\hat{m}\rangle \mathrm{d}\hat{m} = -\int_{\Omega_m|\langle\hat{n},\hat{\omega}\rangle\langle\hat{m},\hat{\omega}\rangle\leq 0} D(\vec{p},\hat{m})\langle\hat{\omega},\hat{m}\rangle \mathrm{d}\hat{m} \tag{12.303}$$

The normalization constraints given above are necessary conditions for an MVF to correspond to a physical surface profile. However, it is important to observe that, for a given
506 *normal distribution*, these constraints are not, by themselves, sufficient to characterize a given surface as there may exist many different profiles, each having a unique normalized visibility function, thereby resulting in different reflectance properties.

155 **Sampling** Whenever the strong MVF normalization constraint holds, *importance sampling* of a random micro-normal can be restricted only to those that are actually visible from a given exitant direction $\hat{\omega}$ [Heitz and d'Eon, 2014]. Substituting the formulations of the *normal*
506 *distribution* and MVF and reformulating the *probability density* function in the space of the
131

micro-geometry then yields

$$\begin{aligned}\int_{2\pi^+} \frac{D(\vec{p},\hat{m})V(\vec{p},\hat{m},\hat{\omega})\langle\hat{\omega},\hat{m}\rangle}{\langle\hat{n},\hat{\omega}\rangle}\mathrm{d}\hat{m} &\overset{(12.150)}{\underset{(12.294)}{=}} \int_{2\pi^+} \frac{1}{A_n\langle\hat{n},\hat{\omega}\rangle}\mathcal{T}\{T(\vec{p}_m,\hat{\omega})\}(\vec{p},\hat{m})\langle\hat{\omega},\hat{m}\rangle\mathrm{d}\hat{m} \\ &\overset{(12.149)}{=} \int_{A_m} \frac{1}{A_n\langle\hat{n},\hat{\omega}\rangle}T(\vec{p}_m,\hat{\omega})\langle\hat{\omega},\hat{\nabla}(\vec{p}_m)\rangle\mathrm{d}A(\vec{p}_m) \\ &= \int_{A_\omega} \frac{1}{A_\omega}\mathrm{d}A(\vec{p}_\omega) \end{aligned} \quad (12.304)$$

506 531 506

while the resulting PDF is shown to be constant in the space of the projection along $\hat{\omega}$.

This sampling strategy is therefore equivalent to uniformly drawing a point in the plane orthogonal to $\hat{\omega}$, and then projecting it along $\hat{\omega}$ onto the micro-geometry of the height field, from which the sample micro-normal is obtained. It is also worth noting that this sampling strategy is, in essence, similar to the one devised by a virtual gonio-reflectometer. Shall the albedo of the micro-structures be taken into account, the sampling scheme may then be extended by subjecting the points drawn in the first phase to *acceptance–rejection sampling*, 135
preserving a point if a realization of the uniform random variable in the range [0, 1] is smaller than the albedo at the point, and rejecting it otherwise, such that the resulting distribution corresponds to the projection of the albedo onto the plane orthogonal to $\hat{\omega}$.

In case the microscopic height field of infinite extent is created by procedural periodic instantiation of a base rectangular tile, the sampling of visible normals can be achieved by generating rays whose origins are uniformly distributed in the projection *polygon* of the 262
tile's bounding box onto the infinitely distant *plane* orthogonal to $\hat{\omega}$. As visibility is a global 247
property that depends on partial occlusion phenomena between neighboring tiles, a sample micro-normal is readily obtained from the first intersection point of the ray with the infinite height field only if the point lies within the base tile, whereas *acceptance–rejection sampling* 135
is carried and the process reiterated otherwise.

12.6.3.2 Bi-Static Visibility

The *bi-static visibility function* (*BVF*), also known as the "geometric term," defines the aggregate fraction of the microscopic surface orthogonal to $\hat{m}$ that is simultaneously visible from two given directions $\hat{\omega}_o$ and $\hat{\omega}_i$ relative to the total area of the microscopic surface that is orthogonal to $\hat{m}$

$$G(\vec{p},\hat{m},\hat{\omega}_o,\hat{\omega}_i) \triangleq \frac{\mathcal{T}\{T(\vec{p}_m,\hat{\omega}_o)T(\vec{p}_m,\hat{\omega}_i)\}(\vec{p},\hat{m})}{\mathcal{T}\{1\}(\vec{p},\hat{m})} \quad (12.305)$$

which statistically characterizes partial visibility due to both shadowing (along direction $\hat{\omega}_i$ towards the light source) and masking (along direction $\hat{\omega}_o$ towards the sensor) of the micro-structures by one another

$$G(\vec{p},\hat{m},\hat{\omega}_o,\hat{\omega}_i) = \Pr(\hat{\omega}_o \cap \hat{\omega}_i) = \Pr(\hat{\omega}_o \mid \hat{\omega}_i)\Pr(\hat{\omega}_i) = \Pr(\hat{\omega}_i \mid \hat{\omega}_o)\Pr(\hat{\omega}_o) \quad (12.306)$$

thereby, in the limit where shadowing and masking are uncorrelated as may occur for azimuthally distant incident and exitant directions, reducing to

$$G(\vec{p},\hat{m},\hat{\omega}_o,\hat{\omega}_i) = \Pr(\hat{\omega}_o)\Pr(\hat{\omega}_i) \quad (12.307)$$

In order to be physically plausible, the geometric term must be bounded by the *mono-static visibility* 531

$$G(\vec{p}, \hat{m}, \hat{\omega}_o, \hat{\omega}_i) \in [0, \min\{V(\vec{p}, \hat{m}, \hat{\omega}_o), V(\vec{p}, \hat{m}, \hat{\omega}_i)\}] \tag{12.308}$$

and therefore guarantee that the front/back face of the micro-structures is only visible from the macroscopic upper/lower hemisphere

$$G(\vec{p}, \hat{m}, \hat{\omega}_o, \hat{\omega}_i) = 0, \quad \text{if } \langle \hat{n}, \hat{\omega}_o \rangle \langle \hat{m}, \hat{\omega}_o \rangle \leq 0 \vee \langle \hat{n}, \hat{\omega}_i \rangle \langle \hat{m}, \hat{\omega}_i \rangle \leq 0 \tag{12.309}$$

while satisfying reciprocity such that

$$G(\vec{p}, \hat{m}, \hat{\omega}_o, \hat{\omega}_i) = G(\vec{p}, \hat{m}, \hat{\omega}_i, \hat{\omega}_o) \tag{12.310}$$

12.6.3.3 *Torrance et al.*

51 Originally formulated in terms of a *Gaussian* distribution of slopes, the *Torrance BRDF*
[Torrance and Sparrow, 1966, Torrance and Sparrow, 1967] was derived in order to model
off-specular peaks experimentally observed in the reflectance distribution of rough metallic
and non-metallic (such as ceramic and plastic) surfaces whose root-mean-square roughness
is comparable to or greater than the wavelength of the incident radiation, i.e., $m \gtrsim \lambda$. The
model was later introduced to the field of computer graphics [Blinn, 1977] using a *Trowbridge–*
513 *Reitz* NDF and subsequently re-adapted [Cook, 1981, Cook and Torrance, 1981, Cook and
511 Torrance, 1982] using a *Beckmann* NDF, while further revisions [Mikkelsen, 2009] additionally
considered the applicability of the von Mises–Fisher distribution.

Assuming the micro-structures form elongated symmetric V-shaped groove cavities as il-
535 lustrated in *Figure 12.32*, determining their visibility essentially reduces to a two-dimensional
problem in the plane defined by $\hat{n}$ and $\hat{m}$. In the case of partial occlusion, the *mono-static*
531 *visibility* is then expressible in terms of the ratio of occluded length by means of the law of
sines

80

$$\begin{aligned} v(\vec{p}, \hat{m}, \hat{\omega}) &\triangleq \frac{v}{l} \\ &\overset{(3.97)}{=} \frac{d}{l} \frac{\sin(\theta')}{\sin(\pi - \theta_m - \theta')} \\ &= \frac{2l\cos(\theta_m)}{l} \frac{\sin(\pi/2 - \theta)}{\sin(\pi/2 - \theta_m + \theta)} \\ &= \frac{2\cos(\theta_m)\cos(\theta)}{\cos(\theta - \theta_m)} \\ &= \frac{2\langle \hat{n}, \hat{m} \rangle \langle \hat{n}, \hat{\omega} \rangle}{\langle \hat{m}, \hat{\omega} \rangle} \end{aligned} \tag{12.311}$$

This result can alternatively be obtained by considering the NDF of a single V-shaped cavity with micro-normals at a fixed angle from the macroscopic normal [Heitz, 2014]

$$D(\vec{p}, \hat{m}) \triangleq \frac{\delta(\hat{m} - \hat{m}_\backslash)}{2\langle \hat{n}, \hat{m}_\backslash \rangle} + \frac{\delta(\hat{m} - \hat{m}_/)}{2\langle \hat{n}, \hat{m}_/ \rangle} \tag{12.312}$$

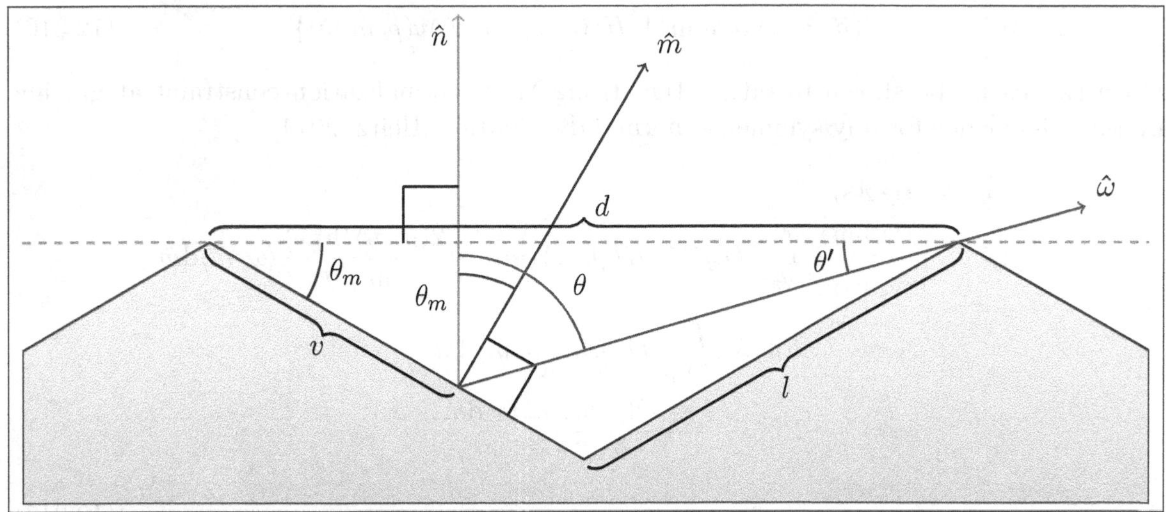

Figure 12.32: Torrance Visibility Function: Illustration of the geometric terms involved in computing the visibility ratio of V-shaped cavities (drawn after [Torrance and Sparrow, 1967, Fig. 4 and 5] and [Kelemen and Szirmay-Kalos, 2001, Fig. 10]).

which satisfies the weak NDF normalization constraint

$$\begin{aligned} g(\vec{p},\hat{n}) &\overset{(12.160)}{=} \int_{2\pi^+} \left(\frac{\delta(\hat{m}-\hat{m}_{\backslash})}{2\langle \hat{n},\hat{m}_{\backslash}\rangle} + \frac{\delta(\hat{m}-\hat{m}_{/})}{2\langle \hat{n},\hat{m}_{/}\rangle} \right) \langle \hat{n},\hat{m}\rangle \mathrm{d}\hat{m} \\ &= \int_{2\pi^+} \frac{\delta(\hat{m}-\hat{m}_{\backslash})}{2\langle \hat{n},\hat{m}_{\backslash}\rangle} \langle \hat{n},\hat{m}\rangle \mathrm{d}\hat{m} + \int_{2\pi^+} \frac{\delta(\hat{m}-\hat{m}_{/})}{2\langle \hat{n},\hat{m}_{/}\rangle} \langle \hat{n},\hat{m}\rangle \mathrm{d}\hat{m} \\ &\overset{(2.218)}{=} \frac{1}{2\langle \hat{n},\hat{m}_{\backslash}\rangle}\langle \hat{n},\hat{m}_{\backslash}\rangle + \frac{1}{2\langle \hat{n},\hat{m}_{/}\rangle}\langle \hat{n},\hat{m}_{/}\rangle \\ &= \frac{1}{2} + \frac{1}{2} \\ &= 1 \end{aligned} \tag{12.313}$$

507

45

Substituting the formulation into the strong MVF normalization constraint then yields

$$\begin{aligned} g(\vec{p},\hat{\omega}) &\overset{(12.298)}{=} \int_{2\pi^+} \left(\frac{\delta(\hat{m}-\hat{m}_{\backslash})}{2\langle \hat{n},\hat{m}_{\backslash}\rangle} + \frac{\delta(\hat{m}-\hat{m}_{/})}{2\langle \hat{n},\hat{m}_{/}\rangle} \right) V(\vec{p},\hat{m},\hat{\omega})\langle \hat{\omega},\hat{m}\rangle \mathrm{d}\hat{m} \\ &= \int_{2\pi^+} \frac{\delta(\hat{m}-\hat{m}_{\backslash})}{2\langle \hat{n},\hat{m}_{\backslash}\rangle} V(\vec{p},\hat{m},\hat{\omega})\langle \hat{\omega},\hat{m}\rangle \mathrm{d}\hat{m} + \int_{2\pi^+} \frac{\delta(\hat{m}-\hat{m}_{/})}{2\langle \hat{n},\hat{m}_{/}\rangle} V(\vec{p},\hat{m},\hat{\omega})\langle \hat{\omega},\hat{m}\rangle \mathrm{d}\hat{m} \\ &\overset{(2.218)}{=} \frac{V(\vec{p},\hat{m}_{\backslash},\hat{\omega})\langle \hat{\omega},\hat{m}_{\backslash}\rangle}{2\langle \hat{n},\hat{m}_{\backslash}\rangle} + \frac{V(\vec{p},\hat{m}_{/},\hat{\omega})\langle \hat{\omega},\hat{m}_{/}\rangle}{2\langle \hat{n},\hat{m}_{/}\rangle} \qquad (12.314) \\ &\overset{(12.299)}{=} \langle \hat{n},\hat{\omega}\rangle \end{aligned}$$

532

45

532

which, whenever the face with micro-normal $\hat{m}_{/}$ is occluded such that $V(\vec{p},\hat{m}_{\backslash},\hat{\omega}) = v(\vec{p},\hat{m}_{\backslash},\hat{\omega})$ and $V(\vec{p},\hat{m}_{/},\hat{\omega}) = 0$, yields

$$v(\vec{p},\hat{m}_{\backslash},\hat{\omega}) = \frac{2\langle \hat{n},\hat{m}_{\backslash}\rangle\langle \hat{n},\hat{\omega}\rangle}{\langle \hat{\omega},\hat{m}_{\backslash}\rangle} \tag{12.315}$$

Conversely, when both faces are unoccluded, $v = l$ and $V(\vec{p},\hat{m},\hat{\omega}) = 1$. The minimum value of the two configurations then yields the complete *mono-static visibility* 531

$$V(\vec{p}, \hat{m}, \hat{\omega}) = \min\{1, H(\langle \hat{n}, \hat{\omega}\rangle\langle \hat{m}, \hat{\omega}\rangle)v(\vec{p}, \hat{m}, \hat{\omega})\} \tag{12.316}$$

which can easily be shown to satisfy the strong MVF normalization constraint at grazing
506 angles of incidence for any symmetric *normal distribution* [Heitz, 2014]

532 536 534

$$\begin{aligned} g(\vec{p}, \hat{\omega}) &\overset{(12.298)}{\underset{(12.311)}{\overset{(12.316)}{=}}} \int_{2\pi^+} D(\vec{p}, \hat{m}) H(\langle \hat{n}, \hat{\omega}\rangle\langle \hat{m}, \hat{\omega}\rangle) \frac{2\langle \hat{n}, \hat{m}\rangle\langle \hat{n}, \hat{\omega}\rangle}{\langle \hat{m}, \hat{\omega}\rangle} \langle \hat{\omega}, \hat{m}\rangle \mathrm{d}\hat{m} \\ &= 2\langle \hat{n}, \hat{\omega}\rangle \int_{\Omega_m | \langle \hat{n}, \hat{\omega}\rangle\langle \hat{m}, \hat{\omega}\rangle > 0} D(\vec{p}, \hat{m}) \langle \hat{n}, \hat{m}\rangle \mathrm{d}\hat{m} \\ &= 2\langle \hat{n}, \hat{\omega}\rangle \frac{\int_{2\pi^+} D(\vec{p}, \hat{m}) \langle \hat{n}, \hat{m}\rangle \mathrm{d}\hat{m}}{2} \\ &\overset{(12.160)}{=} \langle \hat{n}, \hat{\omega}\rangle \end{aligned} \tag{12.317}$$

507

while a more involved demonstration would show that this property generally holds for arbitrary angles of incidence, thereby guaranteeing the energy conservation of the BRDF.

Assuming that shadowing and masking are correlated, as is the case when the incident
533 and exitant directions are azimuthally close, the *bi-static visibility* is defined as the minimum
of the three ratios corresponding to full visibility, partial masking and partial shadowing

536

$$\begin{aligned} &G(\vec{p}, \hat{m}, \hat{\omega}_o, \hat{\omega}_i) \\ &\quad \triangleq \min\{V(\vec{p}, \hat{m}, \hat{\omega}_o), V(\vec{p}, \hat{m}, \hat{\omega}_i)\} \\ &\quad \overset{(12.316)}{=} \min\{1, H(\langle \hat{n}, \hat{\omega}_o\rangle\langle \hat{m}, \hat{\omega}_o\rangle)v(\hat{m}, \hat{\omega}_o), H(\langle \hat{n}, \hat{\omega}_i\rangle\langle \hat{m}, \hat{\omega}_i\rangle)v(\hat{m}, \hat{\omega}_i)\} \end{aligned} \tag{12.318}$$

and reformulating the ratio of the geometric term and the denominator leads to

$$\begin{aligned} &\frac{G(\vec{p}, \hat{m}, \hat{\omega}_o, \hat{\omega}_i)}{4\langle \hat{n}, \hat{\omega}_o\rangle\langle \hat{n}, \hat{\omega}_i\rangle} \\ &= \min\left\{\frac{1}{4\langle \hat{n}, \hat{\omega}_o\rangle\langle \hat{n}, \hat{\omega}_i\rangle}, \frac{H(\langle \hat{n}, \hat{\omega}_o\rangle\langle \hat{m}, \hat{\omega}_o\rangle)v(\hat{m}, \hat{\omega}_o)}{4\langle \hat{n}, \hat{\omega}_o\rangle\langle \hat{n}, \hat{\omega}_i\rangle}, \frac{H(\langle \hat{n}, \hat{\omega}_i\rangle\langle \hat{m}, \hat{\omega}_i\rangle)v(\hat{m}, \hat{\omega}_i)}{4\langle \hat{n}, \hat{\omega}_o\rangle\langle \hat{n}, \hat{\omega}_i\rangle}\right\} \\ &= \min\left\{\frac{1}{4\langle \hat{n}, \hat{\omega}_o\rangle\langle \hat{n}, \hat{\omega}_i\rangle}, \frac{H(\langle \hat{n}, \hat{\omega}_o\rangle\langle \hat{m}, \hat{\omega}_o\rangle)2\langle \hat{n}, \hat{m}\rangle}{4\langle \hat{m}, \hat{\omega}_o\rangle\langle \hat{n}, \hat{\omega}_i\rangle}, \frac{H(\langle \hat{n}, \hat{\omega}_i\rangle\langle \hat{m}, \hat{\omega}_i\rangle)2\langle \hat{n}, \hat{m}\rangle}{4\langle \hat{m}, \hat{\omega}_i\rangle\langle \hat{n}, \hat{\omega}_o\rangle}\right\} \end{aligned} \tag{12.319}$$

In the case where $\hat{m} = \hat{h}_r$, the MVF may alternatively be expressed as

534 523

$$v(\vec{p}, \hat{h}_r, \hat{\omega}) \overset{(12.311)}{\underset{(12.247)}{=}} 2\frac{\langle \hat{n}, \hat{\omega}_o\rangle + \langle \hat{n}, \hat{\omega}_i\rangle}{\langle \hat{\omega}_o, \hat{\omega}\rangle + \langle \hat{\omega}_i, \hat{\omega}\rangle}\langle \hat{n}, \hat{\omega}\rangle \tag{12.320}$$

and the BVF as

$$\frac{G(\vec{p}, \hat{h}_r, \hat{\omega}_o, \hat{\omega}_i)}{4\langle \hat{n}, \hat{\omega}_o\rangle\langle \hat{n}, \hat{\omega}_i\rangle} = \min\left\{\frac{1}{4\cos(\theta_o)\cos(\theta_i)}, \frac{2\cos(\theta_h)}{4\cos(\theta_d)\cos(\theta_i)}, \frac{2\cos(\theta_h)}{4\cos(\theta_d)\cos(\theta_o)}\right\} \tag{12.321}$$

from which follows that the conservative energy-conservation requirement introduced in
531 *Equation 12.293* is met within a constant factor of 2 for an arbitrary NDF, as illustrated in
540 537 *Figure 12.36* and *Figure 12.33*, thereby yielding a loose upper bound of 2 on the albedo.

Even though the V-cavity visibility function itself does not explicitly depend on the
506 *normal distribution*, it does depend on the orientation of the micro-normal, whose distribution
is defined by the NDF, thereby implicitly making the aggregate amount of masking in the

Figure 12.33: Torrance BVF: Visual appearance of the Torrance bi-static visibility function for a Beckmann NDF with a median slope angle of $\frac{1}{10}\frac{\pi}{2}$, $\frac{5}{10}\frac{\pi}{2}$ and $\frac{9}{10}\frac{\pi}{2}$ (from left to right, respectively) (light probe courtesy of Paul Debevec).

BRDF NDF-dependent. However, near grazing angles of incidence, the resulting distribution of visible normals reduces to the uniform projection of all micro-structures onto the macro-surface

$$\frac{D(\vec{p},\hat{m})V(\vec{p},\hat{m},\hat{\omega})\langle\hat{\omega},\hat{m}\rangle}{\langle\hat{n},\hat{\omega}\rangle} \overset{(12.316)}{\underset{(12.311)}{=}} \frac{D(\vec{p},\hat{m})H(\langle\hat{n},\hat{\omega}\rangle\langle\hat{m},\hat{\omega}\rangle)\frac{2\langle\hat{n},\hat{m}\rangle\langle\hat{n},\hat{\omega}\rangle}{\langle\hat{m},\hat{\omega}\rangle}\langle\hat{\omega},\hat{m}\rangle}{\langle\hat{n},\hat{\omega}\rangle}$$
536
534
$$= 2H(\langle\hat{n},\hat{\omega}\rangle\langle\hat{m},\hat{\omega}\rangle)D(\vec{p},\hat{m})\langle\hat{n},\hat{m}\rangle \qquad (12.322)$$

without accounting for their direction-dependent projected area (aside from back-face culling), thereby simulating an unrealistic geometrically flat micro-surface with perturbed normals that does not reproduce the shift of the reflectance lobe towards the back-scattering direction exhibited by physical surfaces at increasing roughness [Heitz, 2014, Heitz and d'Eon, 2014].

12.6.3.4 Ward

Originally formulated in terms of a *Ward* NDF, the *Ward BRDF* [Ward Larson, 1992] stems 516
from a simplification of the *Torrance et al.* model, substituting the geometric term with 534

$$G(\vec{p},\hat{m},\hat{\omega}_o,\hat{\omega}_i) \triangleq \cos(\theta_m)^4\sqrt{\cos(\theta_o)\cos(\theta_i)} = \langle\hat{n},\hat{m}\rangle^4\sqrt{\langle\hat{n},\hat{\omega}_o\rangle\langle\hat{n},\hat{\omega}_i\rangle} \qquad (12.323)$$

and whose albedo was subsequently improved by removing the square root term [Dür, 2005, Dür, 2006].

As an alternative, a lower bound on the *Torrance et al.* geometric factor may be derived 534
by first considering the identity

$$\begin{aligned} 1 &\geq \cos(\theta_o-\theta_i) = \cos(\theta_o)\cos(\theta_i)+\sin(\theta_o)\sin(\theta_i) \\ &\geq \cos(\theta_o)\cos(\theta_i)-\sin(\theta_o)\sin(\theta_i)\cos(\phi_o-\phi_i) \end{aligned} \qquad (12.324)$$

given θ_o and $\theta_i \in [0, \pi/2]$, from which follows that

$$\sin(\theta_o)\sin(\theta_i)\cos(\phi_o-\phi_i)+\cos(\theta_o)\cos(\theta_i)+1 \geq 2\cos(\theta_o)\cos(\theta_i) \qquad (12.325)$$

and therefore

$$\frac{\langle\hat{\omega}_o,\hat{\omega}_i\rangle+1}{2} = \langle\hat{h}_r,\hat{\omega}_o\rangle\langle\hat{h}_r,\hat{\omega}_i\rangle \geq \langle\hat{n},\hat{\omega}_o\rangle\langle\hat{n},\hat{\omega}_i\rangle \qquad (12.326)$$

Additionally observing that whenever $\hat{m} = \hat{h}_r$ the following inequalities hold

534 523

$$\frac{v(\hat{h}_r, \hat{\omega}_o)}{2\langle\hat{n}, \hat{\omega}_o\rangle\langle\hat{n}, \hat{\omega}_i\rangle} \overset{(12.311)}{=} \frac{\langle\hat{n}, \hat{h}_r\rangle}{\langle\hat{h}_r, \hat{\omega}_o\rangle\langle\hat{n}, \hat{\omega}_i\rangle} \overset{(12.247)}{=} \frac{\langle\hat{n}, \hat{\omega}_o\rangle + \langle\hat{n}, \hat{\omega}_i\rangle}{(\langle\hat{\omega}_o, \hat{\omega}_i\rangle + 1)\langle\hat{n}, \hat{\omega}_i\rangle} \geq \frac{1}{\langle\hat{\omega}_o, \hat{\omega}_i\rangle + 1} \quad (12.327)$$

534 523

$$\frac{v(\hat{h}_r, \hat{\omega}_i)}{2\langle\hat{n}, \hat{\omega}_o\rangle\langle\hat{n}, \hat{\omega}_i\rangle} \overset{(12.311)}{=} \frac{\langle\hat{n}, \hat{h}_r\rangle}{\langle\hat{h}_r, \hat{\omega}_i\rangle\langle\hat{n}, \hat{\omega}_o\rangle} \overset{(12.247)}{=} \frac{\langle\hat{n}, \hat{\omega}_o\rangle + \langle\hat{n}, \hat{\omega}_i\rangle}{(\langle\hat{\omega}_o, \hat{\omega}_i\rangle + 1)\langle\hat{n}, \hat{\omega}_o\rangle} \geq \frac{1}{\langle\hat{\omega}_o, \hat{\omega}_i\rangle + 1} \quad (12.328)$$

a lower bound on the geometric factor is readily given as

536 523

$$\frac{G(\vec{p}, \hat{h}_r, \hat{\omega}_o, \hat{\omega}_i)}{4\langle\hat{n}, \hat{\omega}_o\rangle\langle\hat{n}, \hat{\omega}_i\rangle} \overset{(12.319)}{\geq} \frac{1}{4\langle\hat{h}_r, \hat{\omega}_o\rangle\langle\hat{h}_r, \hat{\omega}_i\rangle} \overset{(12.250)}{=} \frac{1}{2(\langle\hat{\omega}_o, \hat{\omega}_i\rangle + 1)} \quad (12.329)$$

534 Substituting the lower bound in place of the *Torrance et al.* geometric factor then results in the following geometric formulation [Kelemen and Szirmay-Kalos, 2001]

$$\frac{G(\vec{p}, \hat{m}, \hat{\omega}_o, \hat{\omega}_i)}{4\langle\hat{n}, \hat{\omega}_o\rangle\langle\hat{n}, \hat{\omega}_i\rangle} \triangleq \frac{1}{4\langle\hat{m}, \hat{\omega}_o\rangle\langle\hat{m}, \hat{\omega}_i\rangle} = \frac{V(\vec{p}, \hat{m}, \hat{\omega}_o)V(\vec{p}, \hat{m}, \hat{\omega}_i)}{4\langle\hat{n}, \hat{\omega}_o\rangle\langle\hat{n}, \hat{\omega}_i\rangle} \quad (12.330)$$

where, under the assumption that shadowing and masking are uncorrelated, the MVF reads

$$V(\vec{p}, \hat{m}, \hat{\omega}) \triangleq \frac{\langle\hat{n}, \hat{\omega}\rangle}{\langle\hat{m}, \hat{\omega}\rangle} \quad (12.331)$$

Whenever $\hat{m} = \hat{h}_r$, the expression reduces to

523

$$\frac{G(\vec{p}, \hat{h}_r, \hat{\omega}_o, \hat{\omega}_i)}{4\langle\hat{n}, \hat{\omega}_o\rangle\langle\hat{n}, \hat{\omega}_i\rangle} = \frac{1}{4\cos(\theta_d)^2} \overset{(12.250)}{=} \frac{1}{2(\langle\hat{\omega}_o, \hat{\omega}_i\rangle + 1)} \quad (12.332)$$

and therefore also satisfies the conservative energy-conservation requirement introduced in
531 *Equation 12.293* within a constant factor for an arbitrary NDF, as illustrated in *Figure 12.36*
540 538 and *Figure 12.34*, since $\frac{\langle\hat{n}, \hat{\omega}_i\rangle}{\langle\hat{n}, \hat{\omega}_o\rangle + \langle\hat{n}, \hat{\omega}_i\rangle} \leq 1$, such that the albedo is bounded by 2. In the
516 special case where the normal distribution is described by the *Ward* NDF, numerical evidence additionally showed that the model actually is energy conserving [Geisler-Moroder and Dür, 2010b, Geisler-Moroder and Dür, 2010a].

Figure 12.34: Ward BVF: Visual appearance of the Ward bi-static visibility function for a Beckmann NDF with a median slope angle of $\frac{1}{10}\frac{\pi}{2}$, $\frac{5}{10}\frac{\pi}{2}$ and $\frac{9}{10}\frac{\pi}{2}$ (from left to right, respectively) (light probe courtesy of Paul Debevec).

12.6.3.5 Ashikhmin et al.

Originally formulated in terms of an *Ashikhmin–Shirley* NDF, the *Ashikhmin BRDF* 520
[Ashikhmin and Shirley, 2000b, Ashikhmin and Shirley, 2000a] was initially defined as

$$\frac{G(\vec{p},\hat{m},\hat{\omega}_o,\hat{\omega}_i)}{4\langle\hat{n},\hat{\omega}_o\rangle\langle\hat{n},\hat{\omega}_i\rangle} \triangleq \frac{\langle\hat{n},\hat{m}\rangle}{4\sqrt{\langle\hat{m},\hat{\omega}_o\rangle\langle\hat{m},\hat{\omega}_i\rangle}\max\{\langle\hat{n},\hat{\omega}_o\rangle,\langle\hat{n},\hat{\omega}_i\rangle\}} \tag{12.333}$$

which whenever $\hat{m}=\hat{h}_r$ reduces to

$$\frac{G(\vec{p},\hat{h}_r,\hat{\omega}_o,\hat{\omega}_i)}{4\langle\hat{n},\hat{\omega}_o\rangle\langle\hat{n},\hat{\omega}_i\rangle} \overset{(12.255)}{=} \frac{\cos(\theta_h)}{4\cos(\theta_d)\max\{\cos(\theta_o),\cos(\theta_i)\}} \tag{12.334}$$ 523

and satisfies the conservative energy-conservation requirement introduced in *Equation 12.293* 531
for an arbitrary NDF since $\langle\hat{n},\hat{\omega}_i\rangle \leq \max\{\langle\hat{n},\hat{\omega}_o\rangle,\langle\hat{n},\hat{\omega}_i\rangle\}$.

In order to remove potentially visible banding artifacts due to the discontinuity in the denominator, the latter was subsequently substituted by the complement of a bilinear term, and the leading cosine angle optionally omitted to better match experimental measurements, yielding [Ashikhmin and Premože, 2007]

$$\begin{aligned}\frac{G(\vec{p},\hat{m},\hat{\omega}_o,\hat{\omega}_i)}{4\langle\hat{n},\hat{\omega}_o\rangle\langle\hat{n},\hat{\omega}_i\rangle} &\triangleq \frac{\langle\hat{n},\hat{m}\rangle}{4[\sqrt{\langle\hat{m},\hat{\omega}_o\rangle\langle\hat{m},\hat{\omega}_i\rangle}](1-(1-\langle\hat{n},\hat{\omega}_o\rangle)(1-\langle\hat{n},\hat{\omega}_i\rangle))} &(12.335)\\ &= \frac{\langle\hat{n},\hat{m}\rangle}{4[\sqrt{\langle\hat{m},\hat{\omega}_o\rangle\langle\hat{m},\hat{\omega}_i\rangle}](\langle\hat{n},\hat{\omega}_o\rangle+\langle\hat{n},\hat{\omega}_i\rangle-\langle\hat{n},\hat{\omega}_o\rangle\langle\hat{n},\hat{\omega}_i\rangle)} &(12.336)\end{aligned}$$

which whenever $\hat{m}=\hat{h}_r$ reduces to

$$\begin{aligned}\frac{G(\vec{p},\hat{h}_r,\hat{\omega}_o,\hat{\omega}_i)}{4\langle\hat{n},\hat{\omega}_o\rangle\langle\hat{n},\hat{\omega}_i\rangle} &\overset{(12.255)}{=} \frac{\cos(\theta_h)}{4[\cos(\theta_d)]\Big(1-(1-\cos(\theta_o))(1-\cos(\theta_i))\Big)} &(12.337)\\ &= \frac{\cos(\theta_h)}{4[\cos(\theta_d)](\cos(\theta_o)+\cos(\theta_i)-\cos(\theta_o)\cos(\theta_i))} &(12.338)\end{aligned}$$ 523

coined the d-BRDF, which actually imposes an even more conservative bound on the albedo given that $\max\{\langle\hat{n},\hat{\omega}_o\rangle,\langle\hat{n},\hat{\omega}_i\rangle\} \leq \langle\hat{n},\hat{\omega}_o\rangle+\langle\hat{n},\hat{\omega}_i\rangle-\langle\hat{n},\hat{\omega}_o\rangle\langle\hat{n},\hat{\omega}_i\rangle$, and $\langle\hat{h}_r,\hat{\omega}_i\rangle \leq 1$, as
illustrated in *Figure 12.36* and *Figure 12.35*. 540 540

12.6.3.6 Extension

Inspired by the *Ashikhmin et al.* BRDF, the previous geometric terms may also be generalized 539
by adding a variable exponent to the denominator in order to provide more flexibility when fitting measured data [Kurt *et al.*, 2010]

$$\frac{G(\vec{p},\hat{m},\hat{\omega}_o,\hat{\omega}_i)}{4\langle\hat{n},\hat{\omega}_o\rangle\langle\hat{n},\hat{\omega}_i\rangle} \triangleq \frac{\langle\hat{n},\hat{m}\rangle}{4\sqrt{\langle\hat{m},\hat{\omega}_o\rangle\langle\hat{m},\hat{\omega}_i\rangle}(\langle\hat{n},\hat{\omega}_o\rangle\langle\hat{n},\hat{\omega}_i\rangle)^\alpha} \tag{12.339}$$

which whenever $\hat{m}=\hat{h}_r$ reduces to

$$\frac{G(\vec{p},\hat{h}_r,\hat{\omega}_o,\hat{\omega}_i)}{4\langle\hat{n},\hat{\omega}_o\rangle\langle\hat{n},\hat{\omega}_i\rangle} \overset{(12.255)}{=} \frac{\cos(\theta_h)}{4\cos(\theta_d)\big(\cos(\theta_o)\cos(\theta_i)\big)^\alpha} \tag{12.340}$$ 523

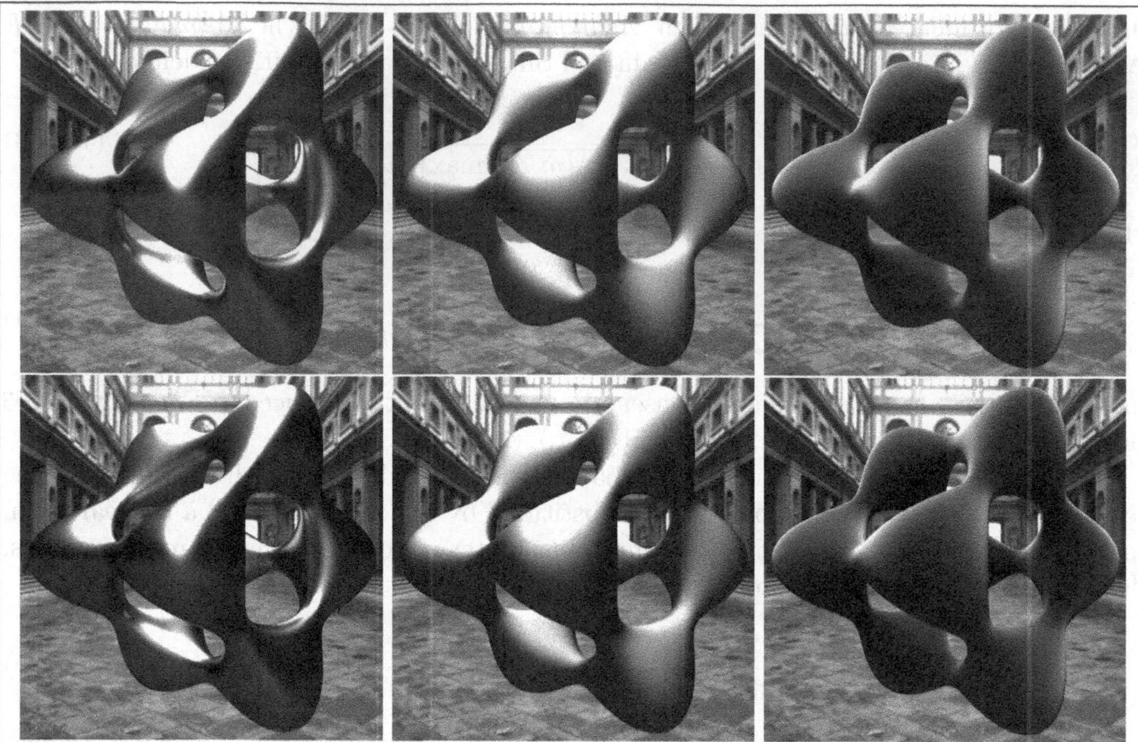

Figure 12.35: Ashikhmin BVF: Visual appearance of the Ashikhmin bi-static visibility function with a maximum term (top) and a bilinear term (bottom), for a Beckmann NDF with a median slope angle of $\frac{1}{10}\frac{\pi}{2}$, $\frac{5}{10}\frac{\pi}{2}$ and $\frac{9}{10}\frac{\pi}{2}$ (from left to right, respectively) (light probe courtesy of Paul Debevec).

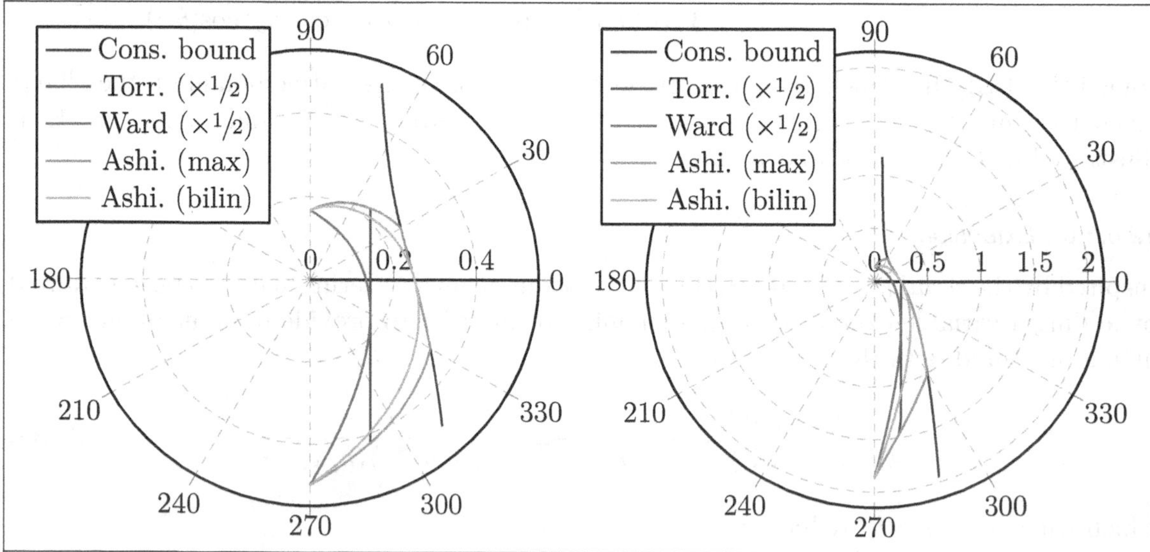

Figure 12.36: Geometric Terms: Angular distribution of the geometric factor, shown for various micro-geometry BRDF models, and with an incidence angle of 30° (left) and 60° (right).

12.6.3.7 Beard–Maxwell

The *Beard–Maxwell BRDF* [Maxwell *et al.*, 1973], subsequently introduced in the field of computer graphics [Westlund and Meyer, 2002], empirically formulates the geometric term as

$$G(\vec{p}, \hat{m}, \hat{\omega}_o, \hat{\omega}_i) \triangleq \frac{1 + \frac{\arccos(\langle \hat{n}, \hat{m} \rangle)}{\Omega} e^{-2\frac{\arccos(\sqrt{\langle \hat{m}, \hat{\omega}_o \rangle \langle \hat{m}, \hat{\omega}_i \rangle})}{\tau}}}{1 + \frac{\arccos(\langle \hat{n}, \hat{m} \rangle)}{\Omega}} \left[\frac{1}{1 + \frac{\phi_n}{\Omega} \frac{\arccos(\langle \hat{n}, \hat{\omega}_i \rangle)}{\Omega}} \right] \tag{12.341}$$

which whenever $\hat{m} = \hat{h}_r$ reduces to

$$G(\vec{p}, \hat{h}_r, \hat{\omega}_o, \hat{\omega}_i) \overset{(12.253)}{\underset{(12.255)}{=}} \frac{1 + \frac{\theta_h}{\Omega} e^{-2\frac{\theta_d}{\tau}}}{1 + \frac{\theta_h}{\Omega}} \left[\frac{1}{1 + \frac{\phi_n}{\Omega} \frac{\theta_i}{\Omega}} \right] \tag{12.342}$$

523
523

where the parameters Ω and τ, respectively, control the falloff in the forward and backward-scattered directions of the geometric term, while ϕ_n is a geometry-dependent parameter affecting its rate of change. In order to maintain reciprocity, the model was then modified by setting $\phi_n = 0$ for use with the Nonconventional Exploitation Factors Data System (NEFDS), which provides a large database from the field of remote sensing.

12.6.3.8 NDF-Generated

Given an arbitrary *normal distribution*, the *NDF-generated BRDF* [Ashikhmin *et al.*, 2000] 506
guarantees energy conservation by enforcing the strong normalization constraint for *mono-*
static visibility. Assuming that the orientation of the micro-normal at a point isn't corre- 531
lated with its height, and therefore with its likelihood of being occluded as illustrated in
Figure 12.37, the MVF can be expressed as the product of a term accounting for the local 542
sidedness of the microscopic and macroscopic front/back faces by means of the *Heaviside*
step function, and a term accounting for global masking/shadowing that is independent of 42
the micro-normal

$$V(\vec{p}, \hat{m}, \hat{\omega}) \triangleq H(\langle \hat{n}, \hat{\omega} \rangle \langle \hat{m}, \hat{\omega} \rangle) V(\vec{p}, \hat{\omega}) \tag{12.343}$$

whose substitution into the strong MVF normalization constraint yields

$$\begin{aligned} g(\vec{p}, \hat{\omega}) &\overset{(12.298)}{=} \int_{2\pi^+} D(\vec{p}, \hat{m}) H(\langle \hat{n}, \hat{\omega} \rangle \langle \hat{m}, \hat{\omega} \rangle) V(\vec{p}, \hat{\omega}) \langle \hat{\omega}, \hat{m} \rangle d\hat{m} \\ &= V(\vec{p}, \hat{\omega}) \int_{\Omega_m | \langle \hat{n}, \hat{\omega} \rangle \langle \hat{m}, \hat{\omega} \rangle > 0} D(\vec{p}, \hat{m}) \langle \hat{\omega}, \hat{m} \rangle d\hat{m} \\ &\overset{(12.158)}{=} V(\vec{p}, \hat{\omega}) g^+(\vec{p}, \hat{\omega}) \\ &\overset{(12.299)}{=} \langle \hat{n}, \hat{\omega} \rangle \end{aligned} \tag{12.344}$$

532
507
532

from which follows that

$$V(\vec{p}, \hat{\omega}) = \frac{\langle \hat{n}, \hat{\omega} \rangle}{g^+(\vec{p}, \hat{\omega})} \tag{12.345}$$

with the 2-D function $g^+(\vec{p}, \hat{\omega})$ being generally tabulated by means of a numerical integration scheme.

Defining the correlation factor $C(\hat{\omega}_o, \hat{\omega}_i) \in [0, 1]$ as a reciprocal and supposedly monotonic
function of the azimuthal distance between the incident and exitant directions, the *bi-static*
visibility may then be formulated as an interpolation between correlated and uncorrelated 533

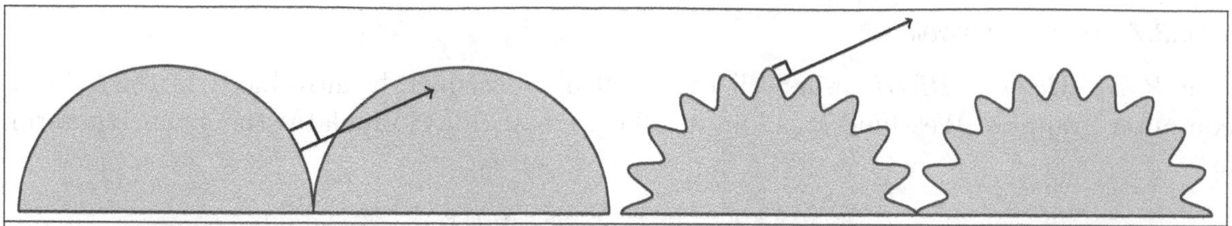

Figure 12.37: Height–Normal Correlation: Illustration of a microscopic surface where points with quasi-horizontal micro-normals predominantly occur at lower heights, thereby inducing a higher probability of occlusion (left), compared against a surface where the orientation of the micro-normal at a point and its height are mostly uncorrelated (right) (drawn after [Ashikhmin *et al.*, 2000, Fig. 3]).

shadowing and masking of the form

$$\begin{aligned} G(\vec{p}, \hat{m}, \hat{\omega}_o, \hat{\omega}_i) &\triangleq (1 - C(\hat{\omega}_o, \hat{\omega}_i))V(\vec{p}, \hat{m}, \hat{\omega}_o)V(\vec{p}, \hat{m}, \hat{\omega}_i) \\ &+ C(\hat{\omega}_o, \hat{\omega}_i) \min\{V(\vec{p}, \hat{m}, \hat{\omega}_o), V(\vec{p}, \hat{m}, \hat{\omega}_i)\} \end{aligned} \quad (12.346)$$

which, whenever shadowing and masking are uncorrelated so that $C(\hat{\omega}_o, \hat{\omega}_i) = 0$, reduces to

$$\frac{G(\vec{p}, \hat{m}, \hat{\omega}_o, \hat{\omega}_i)}{4\langle \hat{n}, \hat{\omega}_o \rangle \langle \hat{n}, \hat{\omega}_i \rangle} = \frac{V(\vec{p}, \hat{m}, \hat{\omega}_o)V(\vec{p}, \hat{m}, \hat{\omega}_i)}{4\langle \hat{n}, \hat{\omega}_o \rangle \langle \hat{n}, \hat{\omega}_i \rangle}$$

541

$$\overset{(12.343)}{=} \frac{H(\langle \hat{n}, \hat{\omega}_o \rangle \langle \hat{m}, \hat{\omega}_o \rangle)V(\vec{p}, \hat{\omega}_o)H(\langle \hat{n}, \hat{\omega}_i \rangle \langle \hat{m}, \hat{\omega}_i \rangle)V(\vec{p}, \hat{\omega}_i)}{4\langle \hat{n}, \hat{\omega}_o \rangle \langle \hat{n}, \hat{\omega}_i \rangle}$$

541

$$\overset{(12.345)}{=} \frac{H(\langle \hat{n}, \hat{\omega}_o \rangle \langle \hat{m}, \hat{\omega}_o \rangle)H(\langle \hat{n}, \hat{\omega}_i \rangle \langle \hat{m}, \hat{\omega}_i \rangle)}{4g^+(\vec{p}, \hat{\omega}_o)g^+(\vec{p}, \hat{\omega}_i)} \quad (12.347)$$

In the case of NDFs not satisfying the weak normalization constraint, such as 2-D tabulated NDF data extracted from a 4-D gonio-reflectometric measurement by inversion of the micro-geometry BRDF formulation (e.g., by solely considering the 2-D subset corresponding to the retroreflective direction $\hat{\omega}_o = \hat{\omega}_i = \hat{h}_r$ [Ashikhmin and Premože, 2007]), renormalization entails a division of the NDF by $g(\vec{p}, \hat{n})$, which is equivalent to introducing the latter term as a multiplicative factor in the visibility function [Ashikhmin *et al.*, 2000]

$$V(\vec{p}, \hat{\omega}) = \frac{\langle \hat{n}, \hat{\omega} \rangle}{g^+(\vec{p}, \hat{\omega})} g(\vec{p}, \hat{n}) \quad (12.348)$$

while simplification with the denominator of the renormalized NDF yields

$$\frac{D(\vec{p}, \hat{m})}{g(\vec{p}, \hat{n})} \frac{G(\vec{p}, \hat{m}, \hat{\omega}_o, \hat{\omega}_i)}{4\langle \hat{n}, \hat{\omega}_o \rangle \langle \hat{n}, \hat{\omega}_i \rangle} = D(\vec{p}, \hat{m}) \frac{H(\langle \hat{n}, \hat{\omega}_o \rangle \langle \hat{m}, \hat{\omega}_o \rangle)H(\langle \hat{n}, \hat{\omega}_i \rangle \langle \hat{m}, \hat{\omega}_i \rangle)}{4g^+(\vec{p}, \hat{\omega}_o)g^+(\vec{p}, \hat{\omega}_i)} g(\vec{p}, \hat{n}) \quad (12.349)$$

12.6.3.9 Smith

51 **Mono-Static Visibility** Originally introduced for a *Gaussian* distribution of slopes, the *Smith*
509 *BRDF* [Smith, 1967] and its generalization to other *slope distributions* [Brown, 1980] assume
that the orientation of the micro-normal at a point isn't correlated with its height, and
542 therefore with its likelihood of being occluded as illustrated in *Figure 12.37*. The *mono-static*
531 *visibility* can then be expressed as the product of a term accounting for the local sidedness of
42 the microscopic and macroscopic front/back faces by means of the *Heaviside step function*,

and a term accounting for global masking/shadowing that is independent of the micro-normal but that explicitly accounts for the NDF of the micro-geometry

$$V(\vec{p},\hat{m},\hat{\omega}) \triangleq H(\langle\hat{n},\hat{\omega}\rangle\langle\hat{m},\hat{\omega}\rangle)V(\vec{p},\hat{\omega}) \tag{12.350}$$

For a given *normal distribution*, the expression of the NDF-dependent global term may 506
be derived by representing the microscopic surface as a random height field whose height z
relative to the macroscopic surface is distributed according to the *probability density* $p_z(z)$, 131
such that the marginal *probability density* along the axis parallel to the plane of incidence 131
of the ray is obtained by integrating the distribution of slopes along the axis perpendicular to it

$$p_s(u) \triangleq \int_{-\infty}^{+\infty} D(\vec{p},u,v)\mathrm{d}v \tag{12.351}$$

which, due to the weak NDF normalization constraint, is also normalized, and, in the case of a symmetric distribution, is an even function such that

510

$$\int_{-\infty}^{+\infty} p_s(u)\mathrm{d}u \overset{(12.181)}{=} 1 \tag{12.352}$$

$$\int_{-\infty}^{+\infty} u p_s(u)\mathrm{d}u = 0 \tag{12.353}$$

Considering a ray with origin at a surface point of height z_0 and oriented in direction $\hat{\omega}$, the height of any point along the ray is then given by the line equation $z = sx + z_0$ where x is the projected distance of the point to the ray's origin, while the ray's slope reads

$$s(\hat{\omega}) \triangleq \left|\frac{1}{\tan(\theta)}\right| = \left|\frac{\cos(\theta)}{\sin(\theta)}\right| = \frac{|\langle\hat{n},\hat{\omega}\rangle|}{\sqrt{1-\langle\hat{n},\hat{\omega}\rangle^2}} \tag{12.354}$$

As illustrated in *Figure 12.38*, a point with abscissa x is therefore above the surface with 544
height z and slope u if $sx + z_0 > z$, and below it at abscissa $x + \delta x$ if $s(x + \delta x) + z_0 < z + u\delta x \iff sx + z_0 < z + (u - s)\delta x$, such that the fraction of rays that intersect the surface within the interval $[x, x + \delta x]$ is given by

$$\kappa(x) \triangleq \frac{p_z(sx+z_0)}{\int_{-\infty}^{sx+z_0} p_z(z)\mathrm{d}z} P_s(s) \tag{12.355}$$

whose denominator expresses the probability of height $sx + z_0$ to be above the surface, and where

$$P_s(s) \triangleq \int_s^{\infty} (u-s)p_s(u)\mathrm{d}u \tag{12.356}$$

Expressing the fraction of rays whose first surface intersection lies in the interval $[x, x+\delta x]$ as $\kappa(x)\delta x$, the statistical optical thickness of the surface points along the ray then reads

543

$$\tau(z_0,s) \triangleq \int_0^{\infty} \kappa(x)\mathrm{d}x \overset{(12.355)}{=} \left[\frac{\ln\left(\int_{-\infty}^{sx+z_0} p_z(z)\mathrm{d}z\right)}{s}\right]_0^{\infty} P_s(s) = -\ln\left(\int_{-\infty}^{z_0} p_z(z)\mathrm{d}z\right)\Lambda(s) \tag{12.357}$$

where the auxiliary function Λ is defined as

$$\Lambda(s) \triangleq \frac{P_s(s)}{s} \tag{12.358}$$

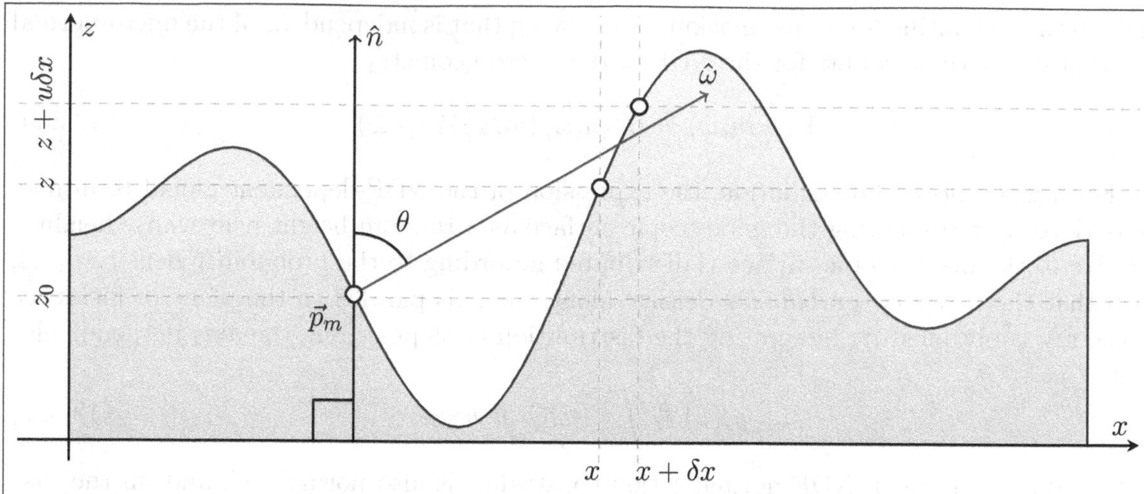

Figure 12.38: Smith Visibility Function: Illustration of the geometric terms involved in the derivation of Smith's NDF-dependent visibility term (drawn after [Walter *et al.*, 2007, Fig. 16]).

The probability of a surface point of height z to be visible along the ray is thus given by the transmittance-like term

543 $$T(z_0, s) \triangleq e^{-\tau(z_0,s)} \overset{(12.357)}{=} e^{\ln\left(\int_{-\infty}^{z_0} p_z(z)\mathrm{d}z\right)\Lambda(s)} = \left(\int_{-\infty}^{z_0} p_z(z)\mathrm{d}z\right)^{\Lambda(s)} \quad (12.359)$$

such that the expected visibility over all surface heights reads

$$T(s) \triangleq \int_{-\infty}^{+\infty} T(z_0, s) p_z(z_0)\mathrm{d}z_0 = \left[\frac{\left(\int_{-\infty}^{z_0} p_z(z)\mathrm{d}z\right)^{\Lambda(s)+1}}{\Lambda(s)+1}\right]_{-\infty}^{+\infty} = \frac{1}{\Lambda(s)+1} \quad (12.360)$$

Similarly, under the assumption that shadowing and masking are directionally uncorrelated, the probability of a surface point of height z to be simultaneously visible from both directions is given by the product of their individual probabilities

$$T(z_0, s_o, s_i) \triangleq T(z_0, s_o)T(z_0, s_i) = \left(\int_{-\infty}^{z_0} p_z(z)\mathrm{d}z\right)^{\Lambda(s_o)+\Lambda(s_i)} \quad (12.361)$$

such that the expected joint visibility over all surface heights reads

$$\begin{aligned} T(s_o, s_i) &\triangleq \int_{-\infty}^{+\infty} T(z_0, s_o, s_i) p_z(z_0)\mathrm{d}z_0 \\ &= \left[\frac{\left(\int_{-\infty}^{z_0} p_z(z)\mathrm{d}z\right)^{\Lambda(s_o)+\Lambda(s_i)+1}}{\Lambda(s_o)+\Lambda(s_i)+1}\right]_{-\infty}^{+\infty} \\ &= \frac{1}{\Lambda(s_o)+\Lambda(s_i)+1} \end{aligned} \quad (12.362)$$

Assuming, without loss of generality, that the x axis of the Cartesian coordinate system is aligned with the projection direction $\hat{\omega} = [x_\omega, y_\omega, z_\omega]$ such that $y_\omega = 0$ and its slope is $\frac{z_\omega}{x_\omega}$, this result can alternatively be derived by solving the positive component of the strong NDF
509 normalization constraint for a given *slope distribution*

$$
\begin{aligned}
g^+(\vec{p},\hat{\omega}) &\overset{(12.158)}{\underset{(12.184)}{=}} \int_{-\infty}^{+\infty}\int_{-\infty}^{\frac{z_\omega}{x_\omega}} D(\vec{p},u,v)(-x_\omega u - y_\omega v + z_\omega)\mathrm{d}u\mathrm{d}v \\
&\overset{(12.351)}{=} \int_{-\infty}^{\frac{z_\omega}{x_\omega}} (z_\omega - x_\omega u)p_s(u)\mathrm{d}u \\
&= \int_{-\infty}^{+\infty} (z_\omega - x_\omega u)p_s(u)\mathrm{d}u - \int_{\frac{z_\omega}{x_\omega}}^{+\infty} (z_\omega - x_\omega u)\, p_s(u)\mathrm{d}u \\
&= z_\omega \int_{-\infty}^{+\infty} p_s(u)\mathrm{d}u - \cancel{x_\omega \int_{-\infty}^{+\infty} u p_s(u)\mathrm{d}u} + x_\omega \int_{\frac{z_\omega}{x_\omega}}^{+\infty} \left(u - \frac{z_\omega}{x_\omega}\right) p_s(u)\mathrm{d}u \\
&\overset{(12.352)\,(12.353)}{\underset{(12.356)}{=}} z_\omega + x_\omega P_s\left(\frac{z_\omega}{x_\omega}\right) \qquad (12.363)
\end{aligned}
$$

507 511 543 543 543 543

Recalling the *Cartesian coordinates* of the macro-normal $\hat{n} = [0,0,1]$, the closed-form solution 67
to the *NDF-generated* global visibility function expressed in slope space is then readily given 541
as [Heitz, 2014]

$$
V(\vec{p},\hat{\omega}) \overset{(12.345)}{\underset{(12.363)}{=}} \frac{z_\omega}{z_\omega + x_\omega P_s\left(\frac{z_\omega}{x_\omega}\right)} = \frac{1}{1 + \frac{x_\omega}{z_\omega} P_s\left(\frac{z_\omega}{x_\omega}\right)} \overset{(12.358)}{=} \frac{1}{1 + \Lambda\left(\frac{z_\omega}{x_\omega}\right)} \qquad (12.364)
$$

541 543 545

The visibility function is finally obtained by substituting the formulation of the ray's slope to yield

$$
V(\vec{p},\hat{\omega}) = T(s(\hat{\omega})) \overset{(12.360)}{=} \frac{1}{\Lambda(s(\hat{\omega})) + 1} \qquad (12.365)
$$

544

Shall it be needed for other physics problems beyond BRDF evaluation, an average visibility term over the whole micro-surface may also be calculated by integrating the formulation of $V(\vec{p},\hat{\omega})$ over all directions.

Bi-Static Visibility Assuming shadowing and masking are uncorrelated, the *bi-static visibility* 533
can be formulated as the separable product

$$
\begin{aligned}
G(\vec{p},\hat{m},\hat{\omega}_o,\hat{\omega}_i) &\triangleq V(\vec{p},\hat{m},\hat{\omega}_o)V(\vec{p},\hat{m},\hat{\omega}_i) \\
&\overset{(12.350)}{\underset{(12.365)}{=}} \frac{H(\langle\hat{n},\hat{\omega}_o\rangle\langle\hat{m},\hat{\omega}_o\rangle)}{\Lambda(s(\hat{\omega}_o)) + 1}\frac{H(\langle\hat{n},\hat{\omega}_i\rangle\langle\hat{m},\hat{\omega}_i\rangle)}{\Lambda(s(\hat{\omega}_i)) + 1} \\
&= \frac{H(\langle\hat{n},\hat{\omega}_o\rangle\langle\hat{m},\hat{\omega}_o\rangle)H(\langle\hat{n},\hat{\omega}_i\rangle\langle\hat{m},\hat{\omega}_i\rangle)}{\Lambda(s(\hat{\omega}_o))\Lambda(s(\hat{\omega}_i)) + \Lambda(s(\hat{\omega}_o)) + \Lambda(s(\hat{\omega}_i)) + 1} \qquad (12.366)
\end{aligned}
$$

543 545

However, because some degree of correlation always exists between shadowing and masking, this formulation systematically overestimates occlusion effects. Instead, assuming that shadowing and masking are fully correlated yields

$$
\begin{aligned}
G(\vec{p},\hat{m},\hat{\omega}_o,\hat{\omega}_i) &\triangleq \min\{V(\vec{p},\hat{m},\hat{\omega}_o), V(\vec{p},\hat{m},\hat{\omega}_i)\} \\
&\overset{(12.350)}{\underset{(12.365)}{=}} \min\left\{\frac{H(\langle\hat{n},\hat{\omega}_o\rangle\langle\hat{m},\hat{\omega}_o\rangle)}{\Lambda(s(\hat{\omega}_o)) + 1}, \frac{H(\langle\hat{n},\hat{\omega}_i\rangle\langle\hat{m},\hat{\omega}_i\rangle)}{\Lambda(s(\hat{\omega}_i)) + 1}\right\} \\
&= \frac{H(\langle\hat{n},\hat{\omega}_o\rangle\langle\hat{m},\hat{\omega}_o\rangle)H(\langle\hat{n},\hat{\omega}_i\rangle\langle\hat{m},\hat{\omega}_i\rangle)}{\max\{\Lambda(s(\hat{\omega}_o)), \Lambda(s(\hat{\omega}_i))\} + 1} \qquad (12.367)
\end{aligned}
$$

543 545

As an alternative, accounting for partial height correlation, due to the fact that the probabilities of masking and shadowing both depend on the elevation of the micro-surface, yields the joint visibility function

$$G(\vec{p}, \hat{m}, \hat{\omega}_o, \hat{\omega}_i) \triangleq H(\langle \hat{n}, \hat{\omega}_o\rangle\langle \hat{m}, \hat{\omega}_o\rangle)H(\langle \hat{n}, \hat{\omega}_i\rangle\langle \hat{m}, \hat{\omega}_i\rangle)T(s(\hat{\omega}_o), s(\hat{\omega}_i))$$

544

$$\stackrel{(12.362)}{=} \frac{H(\langle \hat{n}, \hat{\omega}_o\rangle\langle \hat{m}, \hat{\omega}_o\rangle)H(\langle \hat{n}, \hat{\omega}_i\rangle\langle \hat{m}, \hat{\omega}_i\rangle)}{\Lambda(s(\hat{\omega}_o)) + \Lambda(s(\hat{\omega}_i)) + 1} \quad (12.368)$$

Generalizing the above formula to account for both height and directional dependence may then be achieved by means of a correlation factor $C(\hat{\omega}_o, \hat{\omega}_i) \in [0, 1]$ defined as a reciprocal and supposedly monotonic function of the azimuthal distance between the incident and exitant directions [Heitz *et al.*, 2013]

$$G(\vec{p}, \hat{m}, \hat{\omega}_o, \hat{\omega}_i) \triangleq \frac{H(\langle \hat{n}, \hat{\omega}_o\rangle\langle \hat{m}, \hat{\omega}_o\rangle)H(\langle \hat{n}, \hat{\omega}_i\rangle\langle \hat{m}, \hat{\omega}_i\rangle)}{\max\{\Lambda(s(\hat{\omega}_o)), \Lambda(s(\hat{\omega}_i))\} + (1 - C(\hat{\omega}_o, \hat{\omega}_i)) \min\{\Lambda(s(\hat{\omega}_o)), \Lambda(s(\hat{\omega}_i))\} + 1} \quad (12.369)$$

which reduces to the fully correlated form whenever $C(\hat{\omega}_o, \hat{\omega}_i) = 1$, and to the height-correlated form whenever $C(\hat{\omega}_o, \hat{\omega}_i) = 0$.

511 **Applications** In the case of the *Beckmann* NDF, the marginal slope distribution reads

543

511

$$p_s(u) \underset{(12.185)}{\stackrel{(12.351)}{=}} \int_{-\infty}^{+\infty} \frac{e^{-\frac{u^2+v^2}{m^2}}}{\pi m^2} dv$$

55

$$\stackrel{(2.270)}{=} \frac{1}{\pi m^2} \left[\frac{m\sqrt{\pi}}{2} e^{-\frac{u^2}{m^2}} \operatorname{erf}\left(\frac{v}{m}\right)\right]_{-\infty}^{+\infty}$$

55

$$\stackrel{(2.272)}{=} \frac{1}{2\sqrt{\pi}m} e^{-\frac{u^2}{m^2}} (1 + 1)$$

$$= \frac{e^{-\frac{u^2}{m^2}}}{\sqrt{\pi}m} \quad (12.370)$$

55 which is expressed in terms of the *error function*, such that

543

$$P_s(s) \stackrel{(12.356)}{=} \int_s^{\infty} (u - s) \frac{e^{-\frac{u^2}{m^2}}}{\sqrt{\pi}m} du$$

$$= \frac{1}{\sqrt{\pi}m} \left[-\frac{1}{2}\left(\sqrt{\pi}ms \operatorname{erf}\left(\frac{u}{m}\right) + m^2 e^{-\frac{u^2}{m^2}}\right)\right]_s^{\infty}$$

$$= -\frac{1}{2\sqrt{\pi}m}\left(\sqrt{\pi}ms + 0 - \sqrt{\pi}ms \operatorname{erf}\left(\frac{s}{m}\right) - m^2 e^{-\frac{s^2}{m^2}}\right)$$

$$= \frac{1}{2}\left(s \operatorname{erf}\left(\frac{s}{m}\right) + \frac{m}{\sqrt{\pi}} e^{-\frac{s^2}{m^2}} - s\right) \quad (12.371)$$

yielding the expected visibility [Walter *et al.*, 2007]

544

$$T(s) \stackrel{(12.360)}{=} \frac{1}{\frac{s \operatorname{erf}\left(\frac{s}{m}\right) + \frac{m}{\sqrt{\pi}} e^{-\frac{s^2}{m^2}} - s}{2s} + 1} = \frac{2}{\operatorname{erf}\left(\frac{s}{m}\right) + \frac{m}{s\sqrt{\pi}} e^{-\frac{s^2}{m^2}} + 1} \quad (12.372)$$

513 In the case of the *Trowbridge–Reitz* NDF, the marginal slope distribution instead reads

$$p_s(u) \overset{(12.351)}{\underset{(12.193)}{=}} \int_{-\infty}^{+\infty} \frac{k^2}{\pi(k^2+u^2+v^2)^2} \mathrm{d}v$$ 543 513

$$= \frac{k^2}{\pi} \left[\frac{v}{2(k^2+u^2)(k^2+u^2+v^2)} + \frac{\arctan\left(\frac{v}{\sqrt{k^2+u^2}}\right)}{2(k^2+u^2)^{\frac{3}{2}}} \right]_{-\infty}^{+\infty}$$

$$= \frac{k^2}{\pi} \left(0 + \frac{\frac{\pi}{2}}{2(k^2+u^2)^{\frac{3}{2}}} - 0 - \frac{-\frac{\pi}{2}}{2(k^2+u^2)^{\frac{3}{2}}} \right)$$

$$= \frac{k^2}{2(k^2+u^2)^{\frac{3}{2}}} \tag{12.373}$$

such that

$$P_s(s) \overset{(12.356)}{=} \int_s^{\infty} (u-s) \frac{k^2}{2(k^2+u^2)^{\frac{3}{2}}} \mathrm{d}u$$ 543

$$= \frac{k^2}{2} \left[\frac{-k^2 - su}{k^2\sqrt{k^2+u^2}} \right]_s^{\infty}$$

$$= \frac{k^2}{2} \left(-\frac{s}{k^2} - \frac{-k^2-s^2}{k^2\sqrt{k^2+s^2}} \right)$$

$$= \frac{\sqrt{k^2+s^2} - s}{2} \tag{12.374}$$

yielding the expected visibility [Walter *et al.*, 2007]

$$T(s) \overset{(12.360)}{=} \frac{1}{\frac{\sqrt{k^2+s^2}-s}{2s} + 1} = \frac{2}{\sqrt{\frac{k^2}{s^2}+1}+1} \tag{12.375}$$ 544

An approximation for the *Schlick* NDF is alternatively given by [Schlick, 1993, Schlick, 1994b] 518

$$T(s) = \frac{\langle \hat{n}, \hat{\omega} \rangle}{r - r\langle \hat{n}, \hat{\omega} \rangle + \langle \hat{n}, \hat{\omega} \rangle} \tag{12.376}$$

while no closed-form solution exists for the *Blinn* NDF. 515

12.6.4 He et al.

Rather than relying on geometric optics, the *He BRDF* [He *et al.*, 1991, He, 1993] is a comprehensive model based on physical optics and Kirchhoff's electromagnetic theory. While the full model accounts for wave effects such as diffraction and interference as well as for polarization, the formulation for unpolarized light simplifies substantially.

The average depth of the asperities is specified by means of a height-correlation function, defined as a *Gaussian* distribution parameterized by the RMS roughness σ_0 51

$$p(z) \triangleq \frac{e^{-\frac{z^2}{2\sigma_0^2}}}{\sigma_0\sqrt{2\pi}} \tag{12.377}$$

while the average distance between the asperities is characterized by the autocorrelation length τ of the surface, whose ratio is proportional to the RMS of the *slope distribution* 509
$m \propto \frac{\sigma_0}{\tau}$. The corresponding NDF is then given as

$$D(\vec{p}, \hat{\omega}_o, \hat{\omega}_i) \triangleq G\frac{\pi\tau^2}{\lambda^2} \sum_{i=1}^{\infty} \frac{g^i e^{-g}}{i!\, i} e^{-\frac{\|\hat{n}\times(\hat{\omega}_o+\hat{\omega}_i)\|^2\tau^2}{4i}} \tag{12.378}$$

where the apparent roughness

$$g \triangleq \left(\frac{2\pi\sigma}{\lambda}(\cos(\theta_o) + \cos(\theta_i))\right)^2 \tag{12.379}$$

is a function of the effective surface roughness

$$\sigma \triangleq \frac{\sigma_0}{\sqrt{1 + \frac{z_0^2}{\sigma_0^2}}} \tag{12.380}$$

introduced as an extension of earlier work [Stogryn, 1967] in order to model the fact that surfaces appear less rough at grazing angles. The z_0 term in the above equation is given as the solution of the following equation

$$\sqrt{\frac{\pi}{2}} z_0 = \frac{\sigma_0}{4}(K(\hat{\omega}_o) + K(\hat{\omega}_i))e^{-\frac{z_0^2}{2\sigma_0^2}} \tag{12.381}$$

with

$$K(\hat{\omega}) \triangleq \tan(\theta)\left(1 - \operatorname{erf}\left(\frac{\tau}{2\sigma_0 \tan(\theta)}\right)\right) \tag{12.382}$$

55 which is expressed in terms of the *error function.*

The leading geometric factor is readily given as

$$G \triangleq \frac{\|\hat{\omega}_o + \hat{\omega}_i\|^4}{\langle\hat{n}, \hat{\omega}_o + \hat{\omega}_i\rangle^2} \frac{(\langle\vec{s}_o, \hat{\omega}_i\rangle^2 + \langle\vec{p}_o, \hat{\omega}_i\rangle^2)(\langle\vec{s}_i, \hat{\omega}_o\rangle^2 + \langle\vec{p}_i, \hat{\omega}_o\rangle^2)}{(1 - \langle\hat{\omega}_o, \hat{\omega}_i\rangle^2)^2} \tag{12.383}$$

where

$$\hat{s}_i \triangleq \frac{\hat{n} \times \hat{\omega}_i}{\|\hat{n} \times \hat{\omega}_i\|} \tag{12.384}$$

$$\vec{p}_i \triangleq \hat{s}_i \times \hat{\omega}_i \tag{12.385}$$

$$\hat{s}_o \triangleq \frac{\hat{n} \times \hat{\omega}_o}{\|\hat{n} \times \hat{\omega}_o\|} \tag{12.386}$$

$$\vec{p}_o \triangleq \hat{s}_o \times \hat{\omega}_o \tag{12.387}$$

Assuming that shadowing and masking are uncorrelated, the BVF is then formulated as

$$G(\vec{p}, \hat{m}, \hat{\omega}_o, \hat{\omega}_i) \triangleq V(\vec{p}, \hat{\omega}_o)V(\vec{p}, \hat{\omega}_i) \tag{12.388}$$

542 where the *Smith* visibility function averaged over all micro-normals reads

$$V(\vec{p}, \hat{\omega}) \triangleq \frac{1 - \frac{1 - \operatorname{erf}\left(\frac{\tau}{2\sigma_0 \tan(\theta)}\right)}{2}}{\frac{1}{2\sqrt{\pi}} \frac{2\sigma_0 \tan(\theta)}{\tau} + 1 - \frac{1 - \operatorname{erf}\left(\frac{\tau}{2\sigma_0 \tan(\theta)}\right)}{2}} \tag{12.389}$$

such that the reflectance of a perfectly specular surface is defined by the product of the Fresnel coefficient with $e^{-g}G(\vec{p}, \hat{m}, \hat{\omega}_o, \hat{\omega}_i)$ [Davies, 1954a, Davies, 1954b].

In order to reduce the computational cost of the evaluation process, the infinite sum of the NDF may be tabulated as a pre-process and cheaply evaluated by spline interpolation during rendering [He *et al.*, 1992]. Following an empirical validation of the model [Li and Torrance, 2005b], the normal distribution may alternatively be reduced to the Beckmann NDF (then generalizable to the anisotropic Ward NDF) formulated in terms of the wave vector change
490 $\vec{v} = \frac{2\pi}{\lambda}(\hat{\omega}_o + \hat{\omega}_i)$, possibly in correlation with other approximations of the *Fresnel equations* using Schlick's formulation, of Smith's visibility term as

$$V(\vec{p}, \hat{\omega}) = 1 - (1 - \langle\hat{n}, \hat{\omega}\rangle)^{\frac{\tau}{\sigma}} \tag{12.390}$$

and of the effective roughness formulation [Li and Torrance, 2005a, Li, 2005].

12.6.5 Oren–Nayar

Rather than considering perfectly specular microscopic reflectance properties, the *Oren–*
Nayar BRDF [Oren and Nayar, 1994, Nayar and Oren, 1995] assumes *Lambertian* micro- 499
structures instead in order to model diffusely back-scattering surfaces such as plaster, sand, paper, clay, concrete and cloth. The microscopic BRDF is therefore defined as

499

$$f_m(\vec{p}_m, \hat{\omega}_o, \hat{\omega}_i) \overset{(12.127)}{=} \frac{1}{\pi} \tag{12.391}$$

while the slope distribution of the micro-structures is modeled as a *Gaussian*. Based on the 51
Torrance et al. visibility function introduced for V-groove cavities, the geometric term is 534
additionally adjusted to

$$G(\vec{p}, \hat{m}, \hat{\omega}_o, \hat{\omega}_i) \triangleq \min\{1, \max\{0, V(\vec{p}, \hat{m}, \hat{\omega}_o), V(\vec{p}, \hat{m}, \hat{\omega}_i)\}\} \tag{12.392}$$

Due to the non-analyticity of the resulting integral, functional approximations to the BRDFs describing first-order and second-order scattering events, respectively, are then given as

$$f_r^1(\vec{p}, \hat{\omega}_o, \hat{\omega}_i) \triangleq \frac{1}{\pi}\left(1 - c_1 + c_2 c_2' \tan(\beta) + c_3 c_3' \tan\left(\frac{\alpha+\beta}{2}\right)\right) \tag{12.393}$$

$$f_r^2(\vec{p}, \hat{\omega}_o, \hat{\omega}_i) \triangleq \frac{1}{\pi} c_4 \left(1 - \gamma\left(\frac{2\beta}{\pi}\right)^2\right) \tag{12.394}$$

both depending on the following variables

$$\alpha \triangleq \max\{\theta_o, \theta_i\} = \max\{\arccos(\langle\hat{n}, \hat{\omega}_o\rangle), \arccos(\langle\hat{n}, \hat{\omega}_i\rangle)\} \tag{12.395}$$

$$\beta \triangleq \min\{\theta_o, \theta_i\} = \min\{\arccos(\langle\hat{n}, \hat{\omega}_o\rangle), \arccos(\langle\hat{n}, \hat{\omega}_i\rangle)\} \tag{12.396}$$

$$\gamma \triangleq \cos(\phi_o - \phi_i) = \frac{\langle\hat{\omega}_o, \hat{\omega}_i\rangle - \cos(\theta_o)\cos(\theta_i)}{\sin(\theta_o)\sin(\theta_i)} = \frac{\langle\hat{\omega}_o, \hat{\omega}_i\rangle - \langle\hat{n}, \hat{\omega}_o\rangle\langle\hat{n}, \hat{\omega}_i\rangle}{\sqrt{1 - \langle\hat{n}, \hat{\omega}_o\rangle^2}\sqrt{1 - \langle\hat{n}, \hat{\omega}_i\rangle^2}} \tag{12.397}$$

The various coefficients are expressed in terms of the roughness parameter σ as follows

$$c_1 \triangleq \frac{0.5\sigma^2}{\sigma^2 + 0.33} \tag{12.398}$$

$$c_2 \triangleq \frac{0.45\sigma^2}{\sigma^2 + 0.09} \tag{12.399}$$

$$c_3 \triangleq \frac{0.125\sigma^2}{\sigma^2 + 0.09} \tag{12.400}$$

$$c_4 \triangleq \frac{0.17\sigma^2}{\sigma^2 + 0.13} \tag{12.401}$$

such that the distribution reduces to a *Lambertian* BRDF whenever $\sigma = 0$. 499

The remaining terms are given as

$$c_2' \triangleq \gamma \times \begin{cases} \sin(\alpha) & \text{if } \gamma \geq 0 \\ c_2'' & \text{otherwise} \end{cases} \tag{12.402}$$

$$c_3' \triangleq (1 - |\gamma|)\left(\frac{4\alpha\beta}{\pi^2}\right)^2 \tag{12.403}$$

with

$$c_2'' \triangleq \sin(\alpha) - \left(\frac{2\beta}{\pi}\right)^3 \tag{12.404}$$

550 As illustrated in *Figure 12.39* and *Figure 12.40*, the first-order BRDF is discontinuous at
550 $\theta_i = \theta_o$ and exhibits a relatively flat appearance. The full BRDF model is then defined as a linear combination of the first- and second-order distributions, parameterized by the surface albedo ρ as follows

$$f_r(\vec{p}, \hat{\omega}_o, \hat{\omega}_i) \triangleq \rho f_r^1(\vec{p}, \hat{\omega}_o, \hat{\omega}_i) + \rho^2 f_r^2(\vec{p}, \hat{\omega}_o, \hat{\omega}_i) \tag{12.405}$$

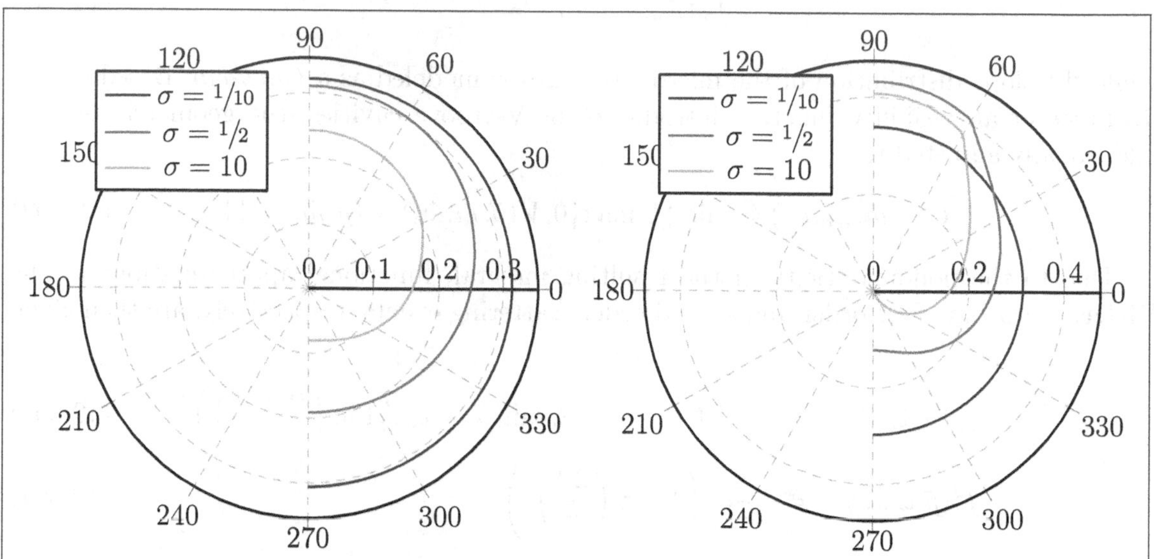

Figure 12.39: Oren–Nayar BRDF Plots: Angular distribution of the Oren–Nayar BRDF, shown for various roughness parameters with an incidence angle of 30° (left) and 60° (right).

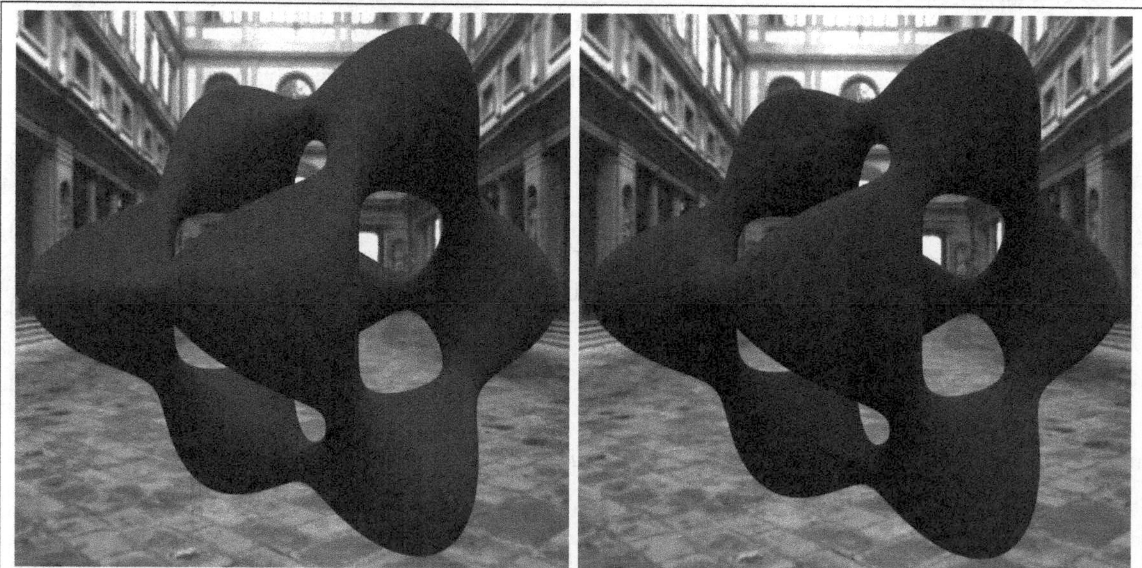

Figure 12.40: Oren–Nayar BRDF Appearance: Visual appearance of the Oren–Nayar BRDF, shown for a roughness parameter of 1/2 (left) and 10 (right) (light probe courtesy of Paul Debevec).

As a qualitative alternative, a simplified model may also be obtained by ignoring interreflections such that $f_r^2(\vec{p}, \hat{\omega}_o, \hat{\omega}_i) = 0$, while redefining $c_3' = 0$ as well as $c_2'' = 0$ such that

$c_2' = \max\{0, \gamma\} \sin(\alpha)$, overall resulting into

$$f_r(\vec{p}, \hat{\omega}_o, \hat{\omega}_i) \triangleq \frac{1}{\pi}(1 - c_1 + c_2 \max\{0, \gamma\} \sin(\alpha) \tan(\beta)) \tag{12.406}$$

essentially replacing the quadrant opposite to the incident direction in the first-order term
with a constant *Lambertian* term, therefore introducing an additional discontinuity at $\theta_i = 0$. 499

12.7 MICRO-CYLINDERS MODEL

Following early work on simulating anisotropic reflectance [Miller, 1988], the micro-*cylinders* 272
model [Poulin and Fournier, 1990] assumes that a given surface may be represented as a
collection of microscopic cylindrical bulges or cavities, as illustrated in *Figure 12.41*. 551

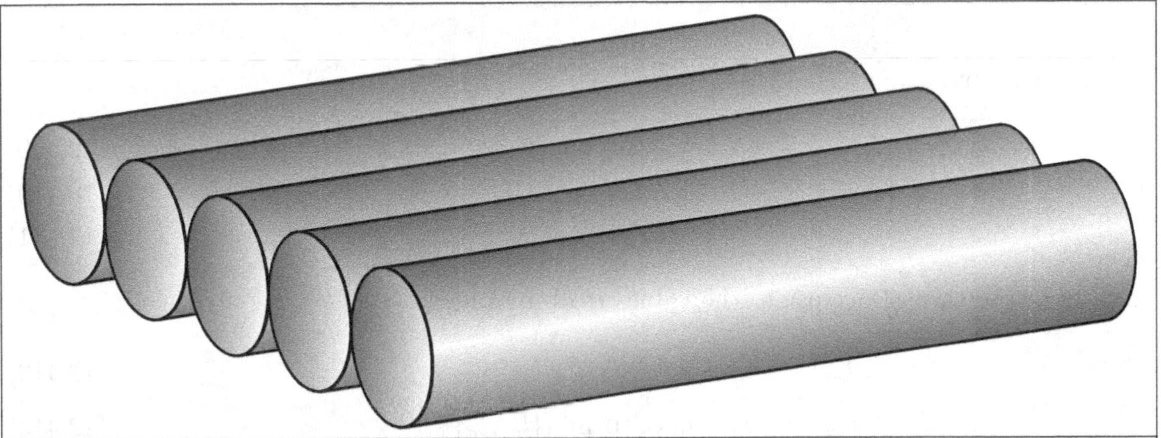

Figure 12.41: Micro-Cylinders Surface: Illustration of the microscopic cylindrical structures composing a surface whose reflectance is described by the micro-cylinders model.

Assuming, without loss of generality, that all distances are expressed proportionally to
the radius of the *cylinders*, whose relative value is then one, the degree of anisotropy of the 272
surface is controlled by the distance $d \in [0, \infty)$ between the centers of two adjacent cylinders
and by the height $h \in [0, 1]$ of the substrate between them. Considering the case of positive
cylinders bulging out of the surface as illustrated in *Figure 12.42*, the polar angle at which 272
two adjacent cylinders intersect each other, as they do if $d < 2$, then reads 552

$$\theta_d \triangleq \begin{cases} \arcsin\left(\frac{d}{2}\right) & \text{if } d < 2 \\ \frac{\pi}{2} & \text{otherwise} \end{cases} \tag{12.407}$$

whereas the polar angle at which a *cylinder* intersects the substrate is defined as $\theta_h \triangleq$ 272
$\arccos(h)$, such that the angular extent of uncovered cylindrical surface and the length of
uncovered substrate are readily given as

$$[\theta_g, l_g] \triangleq \begin{cases} [\theta_h, d - 2\sin(\theta_h)] & \text{if } \theta_h < \theta_d \\ [\theta_d, 0] & \text{otherwise} \end{cases} \tag{12.408}$$

with $\sin(\theta_h) = \sqrt{1 - h^2}$.

Considering a ray that strikes the surface at an angle θ_r as illustrated in *Figure 12.43*, the 553
entire surface will be fully unoccluded whenever $\frac{\pi}{2} - \theta_r > \theta_g$, such that the angular extent
of cylindrical surface that isn't self-occluded θ_{so}, the length of unoccluded substrate l_{uo} and
the angular extent of cylindrical surface that isn't mutually occluded by an adjacent *cylinder* 272

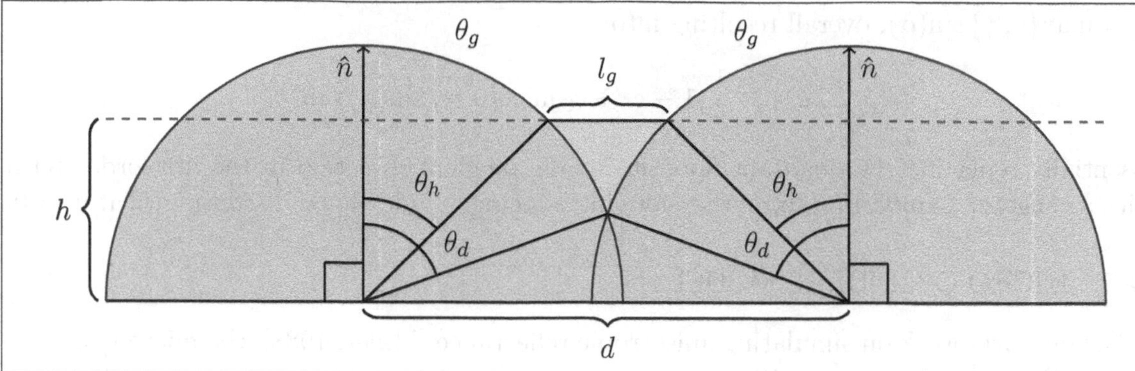

Figure 12.42: Micro-Cylinders Geometry: Illustration of the geometric terms involved in computing the uncovered portion of the micro-structures.

θ_{mo} are given by

$$\begin{aligned} \theta_{so} &= \theta_g && (12.409) \\ l_{uo} &= l_g && (12.410) \\ \theta_{mo} &= \theta_g && (12.411) \end{aligned}$$

whereas in the case of occlusion, the values read instead

$$\begin{aligned} \theta_{so} &= \frac{\pi}{2} - \theta_r && (12.412) \\ l_{uo} &= l_g - \max\{0, \min\{l_{oo}, l_g\}\} && (12.413) \\ \theta_{mo} &= \begin{cases} \min\{\theta_r + \theta_t, \theta_g\} & \text{if } \frac{1}{\cos(\theta_r)} > d - 1 \\ \theta_g & \text{otherwise} \end{cases} && (12.414) \end{aligned}$$

where the last conditional statement evaluates whether the tangential ray intersects the
272 adjacent positive hemi-*cylinder*, while the additional terms verify

$$l_{oo} = \frac{1}{\cos(\theta_r)} - \sin(\theta_h) - h\tan(\theta_r) \tag{12.415}$$

as well as

$$\cos(\theta_r) = \frac{1 + \sin(\theta_t)}{d} \tag{12.416}$$

such that

$$\theta_t = \arcsin\left(d\cos(\theta_r) - 1\right) \tag{12.417}$$

Masking and shadowing can then both be determined by letting the occlusion ray point
429 either to the sensor or to the *light source*, respectively. In case both the view and light vectors
lie on the same side (i.e., to the left or to the right) of the surface normal, the portions of
272 the *cylinders* and of the substrate that are simultaneously visible and illuminated are then
readily given as

$$\begin{aligned} \theta_s &= \min\{\theta_{sm}, \theta_{ss}\} && (12.418) \\ l_u &= \min\{l_{um}, l_{us}\} && (12.419) \\ \theta_m &= \min\{\theta_{mm}, \theta_{ms}\} && (12.420) \end{aligned}$$

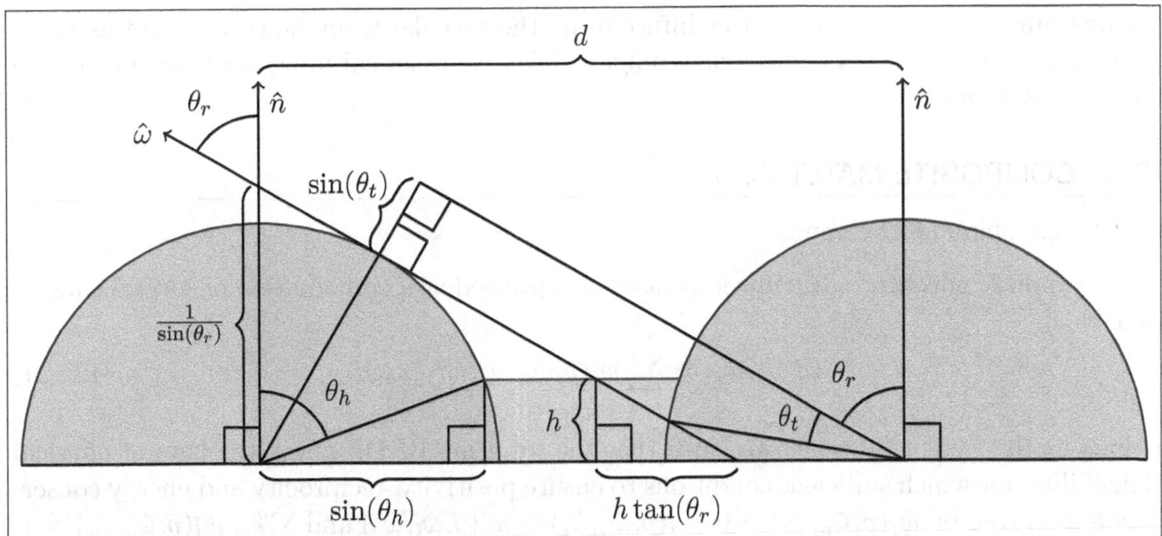

Figure 12.43: Micro-Cylinders Occlusion: Illustration of the geometric terms involved in computing the occluded portion of the micro-structures (drawn after [Poulin and Fournier, 1990, Fig. 3]).

whereas they otherwise read

$$\theta_s = \min\{\theta_{sm}, \theta_{ms}\} \quad (12.421)$$

$$l_u = \max\{0, l_{um} + l_{us} - l_g\} \quad (12.422)$$

$$\theta_m = \min\{\theta_{mm}, \theta_{ss}\} \quad (12.423)$$

A similar geometric construction may alternatively be carried for cylindrical cavities, in which case the height of the substrate lies below the macroscopic surface, as illustrated in *Figure 12.44*. Because the *cylinders* cannot occlude one another, though, nor can they occlude 553
the substrate, self-occlusion solely needs to be considered. 272

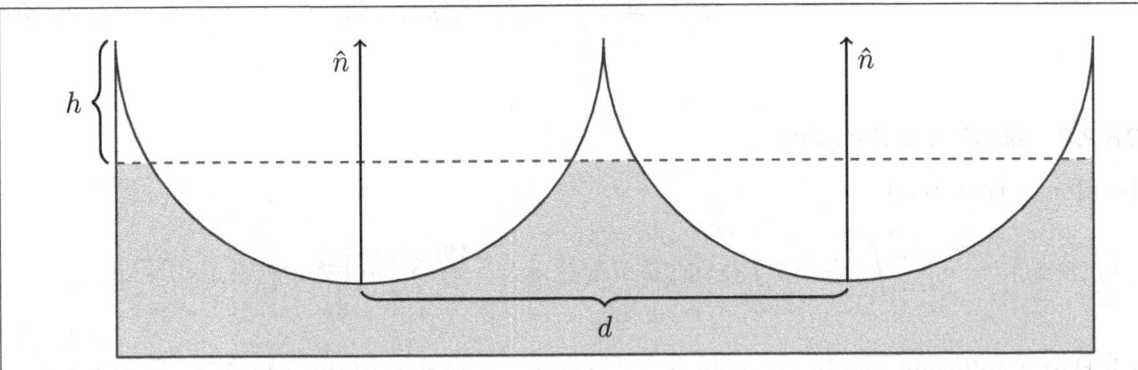

Figure 12.44: Cylindrical Micro-Cavities: Illustration of the geometric configuration corresponding to cylindrical micro-cavities (drawn after [Poulin and Fournier, 1990, Fig. 7])

Given the microscopic reflectance properties of the *cylinders*, the macroscopic reflectance 272
distribution of the surface may then be computed by integrating the visible and illuminated contributions over the projected macroscopic surface area. Doing so entails considering the tilt angle of the corresponding micro-normal lying on the *cylinder's* surface while expressing 272
all vectors in the surface's normal–tangent–bitangent coordinate frame. Whereas the integral

can be evaluated analytically for the diffuse term, the specular term, however, requires either approximations in terms of Chebyshev polynomials, or numerical integration by means of a sampling scheme.

12.8 COMPOSITE MATERIALS

12.8.1 Combined Reflectance

More complex reflectance distributions may be expressed as a combination of several simpler BRDFs

$$f_r(\vec{p}, \hat{\omega}_o, \hat{\omega}_i) \triangleq \sum_{j=1}^{n} w_j(\vec{p}, \hat{\omega}_o, \hat{\omega}_i) f_j(\vec{p}, \hat{\omega}_o, \hat{\omega}_i) \tag{12.424}$$

as long as the weight functions are such that the resulting BRDF obeys the laws of physical plausibility, for which sufficient conditions to ensure positivity, reciprocity and energy conservation are given by $w_j(\vec{p}, \hat{\omega}_o, \hat{\omega}_i) \geq 0$, $w_j(\vec{p}, \hat{\omega}_o, \hat{\omega}_i) = w_j(\vec{p}, \hat{\omega}_i, \hat{\omega}_o)$ and $\sum_{j=1}^{n} w_j(\vec{p}, \hat{\omega}_o, \hat{\omega}_i) \leq 1$, respectively.

Each of the BRDFs on the right-hand side can actually be itself a composite reflectance distribution, thereby resulting in a hierarchical reflectance model akin to a shade tree [Cook,
155 1984]. In turn, *importance sampling* may be carried by drawing random directions from a mixture of the PDFs associated with each distribution, proportionally to the respective albedos of the weighted BRDFs, or, less optimally, to the product of the albedo of the respective BRDFs and the hemispherical average of their weighting functions.

12.8.2 Constant Weight

12.8.2.1 Formulation

The simplest form of such a composite reflectance model relies on constant weights, oftentimes
556 to combine a diffuse and a glossy/specular term, as illustrated in *Figure 12.45*. The combined BRDF then becomes

554
$$f_r(\vec{p}, \hat{\omega}_o, \hat{\omega}_i) \overset{(12.424)}{=} \sum_{j=1}^{n} w_j(\vec{p}) f_j(\vec{p}, \hat{\omega}_o, \hat{\omega}_i) \tag{12.425}$$

12.8.2.2 Albedo and Sampling

The albedo then reads

476
476
$$\rho(\vec{p}, \hat{\omega}_o) \overset{(12.9)}{=} \sum_{j=1}^{n} \int_{2\pi^+} w_j(\vec{p}) f_j(\vec{p}, \hat{\omega}_o, \hat{\omega}_i) \langle \hat{n}, \hat{\omega}_i \rangle \mathrm{d}\hat{\omega}_i \overset{(12.9)}{=} \sum_{j=1}^{n} w_j(\vec{p}) \rho_j(\vec{p}, \hat{\omega}_o) \leq \sum_{j=1}^{n} w_j(\vec{p}) \tag{12.426}$$

such that a sufficient condition to ensure energy conservation is given by $\sum_{j=1}^{n} w_j(\vec{p}) \leq 1$.
155 In turn, *importance sampling* may be carried by drawing random directions from a mixture of the PDFs associated with each distribution as follows

$$p(\vec{p}, \hat{\omega}_o, \hat{\omega}_i) \triangleq \frac{\sum_{j=1}^{n} w_j(\vec{p}) \rho_j(\vec{p}, \hat{\omega}_o) p_j(\vec{p}, \hat{\omega}_o, \hat{\omega}_i)}{\sum_{j=1}^{n} w_j(\vec{p}) \rho_j(\vec{p}, \hat{\omega}_o)} \tag{12.427}$$

$$= \frac{\sum_{j=1}^{n} w_j(\vec{p}) f_j(\vec{p}, \hat{\omega}_o, \hat{\omega}_i) \langle \hat{n}, \hat{\omega}_i \rangle}{\sum_{j=1}^{n} w_j(\vec{p}) \rho_j(\vec{p}, \hat{\omega}_o)}$$

554
$$\overset{(12.425)}{=} \frac{f_r(\vec{p}, \hat{\omega}_o, \hat{\omega}_i) \langle \hat{n}, \hat{\omega}_i \rangle}{\rho(\vec{p}, \hat{\omega}_o)} \tag{12.428}$$

where the second equality holds for individually optimal PDFs, in which case the combined *probability density* is also optimal as shown by the last equality. 131

12.8.3 Albedo Coupling

12.8.3.1 Formulation

The weight functions may alternatively be defined so as to couple different BRDFs based on their individual albedos. Attributing a unit weight $w_1(\vec{p}, \hat{\omega}_o, \hat{\omega}_i) = 1$ to a primary term of albedo $\rho_1(\vec{p}, \hat{\omega})$, energy conservation can then be ensured by bounding the weight function of the secondary term by $w_2(\vec{p}, \hat{\omega}_o, \hat{\omega}_i) \leq 1 - \rho_1(\vec{p}, \hat{\omega}_o)$, while reciprocity may be maintained by defining [Shirley *et al.*, 1997]

$$w_2(\vec{p}, \hat{\omega}_o, \hat{\omega}_i) \triangleq (1 - \rho_1(\vec{p}, \hat{\omega}_o))(1 - \rho_1(\vec{p}, \hat{\omega}_i)) \tag{12.429}$$

The composite BRDF then becomes

$$f_r(\vec{p}, \hat{\omega}_o, \hat{\omega}_i) \overset{(12.424)}{=} f_1(\vec{p}, \hat{\omega}_o, \hat{\omega}_i) + (1 - \rho_1(\vec{p}, \hat{\omega}_o))(1 - \rho_1(\vec{p}, \hat{\omega}_i)) f_2(\vec{p}, \hat{\omega}_o, \hat{\omega}_i) \tag{12.430}$$ 554

12.8.3.2 Albedo and Sampling

The albedo is bounded by

$$\begin{aligned} \rho(\vec{p}, \hat{\omega}_o) &\overset{(12.9)}{=} \int_{2\pi^+} f_1(\vec{p}, \hat{\omega}_o, \hat{\omega}_i) \langle \hat{n}, \hat{\omega}_i \rangle \mathrm{d}\hat{\omega}_i \\ &+ (1 - \rho_1(\vec{p}, \hat{\omega}_o)) \int_{2\pi^+} (1 - \rho_1(\vec{p}, \hat{\omega}_i)) f_2(\vec{p}, \hat{\omega}_o, \hat{\omega}_i) \langle \hat{n}, \hat{\omega}_i \rangle \mathrm{d}\hat{\omega}_i \\ &\overset{(12.9)}{\leq} \rho_1(\vec{p}, \hat{\omega}_o) + (1 - \rho_1(\vec{p}, \hat{\omega}_o)) \rho_2(\vec{p}, \hat{\omega}_o) \end{aligned} \tag{12.431}$$ 476 476

In turn, *importance sampling* may be carried by drawing random directions from a mixture of the PDFs associated with each distribution as follows 155

$$p(\vec{p}, \hat{\omega}_o, \hat{\omega}_i) \triangleq \frac{\rho_1(\vec{p}, \hat{\omega}_o) p_1(\vec{p}, \hat{\omega}_o, \hat{\omega}_i) + (1 - \rho_1(\vec{p}, \hat{\omega}_o)) \rho_2(\vec{p}, \hat{\omega}_o) p_2(\vec{p}, \hat{\omega}_o, \hat{\omega}_i)}{\rho_1(\vec{p}, \hat{\omega}_o) + (1 - \rho_1(\vec{p}, \hat{\omega}_o)) \rho_2(\vec{p}, \hat{\omega}_o)} \tag{12.432}$$

12.8.4 Fresnel Layer

12.8.4.1 Formulation

The *albedo coupling* approach is especially appropriate to model the fact that the ratio of light that is not directly reflected in a specular/glossy fashion by the surface will typically undergo higher-order scattering events onto the micro-geometry so as to be ultimately re-radiated in a diffuse fashion. Such behavior is often observed in layered materials with a clear coating, including ceramics, plastics, rubbers and varnished wood, where a portion of the incident light is partially reflected by the (typically gray specular/glossy) upper layer (therefore producing generally colorless highlights, in contrast to metals) while the remaining portion is transmitted toward the (typically diffuse) lower substrate of the material, possibly interacting with the deeper layers in a recursive fashion, as illustrated in *Figure 12.45*. 555 556

Modeling the interface of the upper specular/glossy layer (presumed not to already contain a Fresnel term) as perfectly specular micro-structures [Schlick, 1993, Schlick, 1994b],

Figure 12.45: Fresnel Layer: Visual appearance of a two-layer BRDF composed of a partially reflective specular interface beneath which lies a diffuse substrate, modeled using manually tuned constant weights (left) and Fresnel-based weights (right) (light probe courtesy of Paul Debevec).

the weight functions can then be defined by bounding its albedo as follows [Ashikhmin and Shirley, 2000b, Ashikhmin and Shirley, 2000a]

476

476

$$\begin{aligned}
\rho_s(\vec{p},\hat{\omega}_o) &\overset{(12.9)}{=} \int_{2\pi^+} F(\langle\hat{h}_r,\hat{\omega}_o\rangle) f_1(\vec{p},\hat{\omega}_o,\hat{\omega}_i)\langle\hat{n},\hat{\omega}_i\rangle \mathrm{d}\hat{\omega}_i \\
&\leq F_m(\vec{p},\hat{\omega}_o)\int_{2\pi^+} f_1(\vec{p},\hat{\omega}_o,\hat{\omega}_i)\langle\hat{n},\hat{\omega}_i\rangle \mathrm{d}\hat{\omega}_i \\
&\overset{(12.9)}{=} F_m(\vec{p},\hat{\omega}_o)\rho_1(\vec{p},\hat{\omega}_o) \\
&\leq F_m(\vec{p},\hat{\omega}_o)
\end{aligned} \tag{12.433}$$

where $F_m(\vec{p},\hat{\omega}_o)$ is the maximal value that the Fresnel term may take for a given exitant direction and an arbitrary incident direction, such that

555

$$\begin{aligned}
f_r(\vec{p},\hat{\omega}_o,\hat{\omega}_i) &\overset{(12.430)}{=} F(\langle\hat{h}_r,\hat{\omega}_o\rangle) f_1(\vec{p},\hat{\omega}_o,\hat{\omega}_i) \\
&+ (1-F_m(\vec{p},\hat{\omega}_o))(1-F_m(\vec{p},\hat{\omega}_i)) f_2(\vec{p},\hat{\omega}_o,\hat{\omega}_i)
\end{aligned} \tag{12.434}$$

12.8.4.2 Albedo and Sampling

The albedo is bounded by

476

476

$$\begin{aligned}
\rho(\vec{p},\hat{\omega}_o) &\overset{(12.9)}{=} \int_{2\pi^+} F(\langle\hat{h}_r,\hat{\omega}_o\rangle) f_1(\vec{p},\hat{\omega}_o,\hat{\omega}_i)\langle\hat{n},\hat{\omega}_i\rangle \mathrm{d}\hat{\omega}_i \\
&+ \int_{2\pi^+} (1-F_m(\vec{p},\hat{\omega}_o))(1-F_m(\vec{p},\hat{\omega}_i)) f_2(\vec{p},\hat{\omega}_o,\hat{\omega}_i)\langle\hat{n},\hat{\omega}_i\rangle \mathrm{d}\hat{\omega}_i \\
&\overset{(12.9)}{\leq} F_m(\vec{p},\hat{\omega}_o)\rho_1(\vec{p},\hat{\omega}_o) + (1-F_m(\vec{p},\hat{\omega}_o))\rho_2(\vec{p},\hat{\omega}_o)
\end{aligned} \tag{12.435}$$

From the behavior of the *Fresnel equations*, it can be observed that this maximum occurs 490
either when $\theta_d = 0$ or when θ_d has maximal value for the given exitant direction, that is, when $\langle \hat{n}, \hat{\omega}_i \rangle = 0$ and $\phi_o - \phi_i = \pi$, such that its cosine reads

$$
\begin{aligned}
c_m(\hat{\omega}_o) &\triangleq \cos\left(\frac{\theta_o + \frac{\pi}{2}}{2}\right) = \sqrt{\frac{1 + \cos\left(\theta_o + \frac{\pi}{2}\right)}{2}} \\
&= \sqrt{\frac{1 - \sin(\theta_o)}{2}} = \sqrt{\frac{1 - \sqrt{1 - \langle \hat{n}, \hat{\omega}_o \rangle^2}}{2}}
\end{aligned}
\tag{12.436}
$$

therefore leading to

$$
F_m(\vec{p}, \hat{\omega}_o) = \max\{F(1), F(c_m(\hat{\omega}_o))\}
\tag{12.437}
$$

When using Schlick's monotonous approximation to the *Fresnel equations*, the maximum 490
actually always occurs at the latter value of the cosine angle, and the weight function of the lower layer simplifies to

$$
\begin{aligned}
w_2(\vec{p}, \hat{\omega}_o, \hat{\omega}_i) &\overset{(12.429)}{=} \Big(1 - F(c_m(\hat{\omega}_o))\Big)\Big(1 - F(c_m(\hat{\omega}_i))\Big) \\
&\overset{(12.97)}{=} \Big(1 - F_0 - (1 - F_0)(1 - c_m(\hat{\omega}_o))^5\Big)\Big(1 - F_0 - (1 - F_0)(1 - c_m(\hat{\omega}_i))^5\Big) \\
&= (1 - F_0)^2\Big(1 - (1 - c_m(\hat{\omega}_o))^5\Big)\Big(1 - (1 - c_m(\hat{\omega}_i))^5\Big)
\end{aligned}
\tag{12.438}
$$

555 492

where the $(1 - F_0)^2$ factor is actually overly conservative and can instead be replaced with $(1 - F_0)$ while still ensuring energy conservation. Specific knowledge about the BRDF of the layers might additionally be used in order to relax the conservative nature of the normalization [Kelemen and Szirmay-Kalos, 2001].

In turn, *importance sampling* may be carried by drawing random directions from a mix- 155
ture of the PDFs associated with each distribution as follows

$$
p(\vec{p}, \hat{\omega}_o, \hat{\omega}_i) \triangleq \frac{F_m(\vec{p}, \hat{\omega}_o)\rho_1(\vec{p}, \hat{\omega}_o)p_1(\vec{p}, \hat{\omega}_o, \hat{\omega}_i) + (1 - F_m(\vec{p}, \hat{\omega}_o))\rho_2(\vec{p}, \hat{\omega}_o)p_2(\vec{p}, \hat{\omega}_o, \hat{\omega}_i)}{F_m(\vec{p}, \hat{\omega}_o)\rho_1(\vec{p}, \hat{\omega}_o) + (1 - F_m(\vec{p}, \hat{\omega}_o))\rho_2(\vec{p}, \hat{\omega}_o)}
\tag{12.439}
$$

12.8.5 Thin Layer

12.8.5.1 Formulation

In the case of a material covered with a thin layer of participating medium, the *thin slab* 482
model can be extended by noting that the light transmitted through the slab will be similarly attenuated on its way back to the surface, while ignoring the contributions of light transmitted via scattering, overall resulting in the following combined BRDF

$$
\begin{aligned}
f_r(\vec{p}, \hat{\omega}_o, \hat{\omega}_i) &\underset{(12.56)}{\overset{(12.57)}{=}} \left(1 - e^{-d(\vec{p})\left(\frac{1}{\langle \hat{n}, \hat{\omega}_o \rangle} + \frac{1}{\langle \hat{n}, \hat{\omega}_i \rangle}\right)\kappa_t(\vec{p})}\right) f_1(\vec{p}, \hat{\omega}_o, \hat{\omega}_i) \\
&+ e^{-d(\vec{p})\left(\frac{1}{\langle \hat{n}, \hat{\omega}_o \rangle} + \frac{1}{\langle \hat{n}, \hat{\omega}_i \rangle}\right)\kappa_t(\vec{p})} f_2(\vec{p}, \hat{\omega}_o, \hat{\omega}_i)
\end{aligned}
\tag{12.440}
$$

484 484

where the reflectance properties $f_1(\vec{p}, \hat{\omega}_o, \hat{\omega}_i)$ of the upper layer are described by the *Hapke–Irvine* BRDF, and that of the lower layer by an arbitrary BRDF $f_2(\vec{p}, \hat{\omega}_o, \hat{\omega}_i)$. 485

12.8.5.2 Albedo and Sampling

The albedo of the resulting BRDF is bounded by

476

$$\begin{aligned}\rho(\vec{p},\hat{\omega}_o) &\overset{(12.9)}{=} \int_{2\pi^+}\left(1-e^{-d(\vec{p})\left(\frac{1}{\langle\hat{n},\hat{\omega}_o\rangle}+\frac{1}{\langle\hat{n},\hat{\omega}_i\rangle}\right)\kappa_t(\vec{p})}\right) f_1(\vec{p},\hat{\omega}_o,\hat{\omega}_i)\langle\hat{n},\hat{\omega}_i\rangle \mathrm{d}\hat{\omega}_i \\ &+ \int_{2\pi^+} e^{-d(\vec{p})\left(\frac{1}{\langle\hat{n},\hat{\omega}_o\rangle}+\frac{1}{\langle\hat{n},\hat{\omega}_i\rangle}\right)\kappa_t(\vec{p})} f_2(\vec{p},\hat{\omega}_o,\hat{\omega}_i)\langle\hat{n},\hat{\omega}_i\rangle \mathrm{d}\hat{\omega}_i \\ &\leq \left(1-e^{-d(\vec{p})\left(\frac{1}{\langle\hat{n},\hat{\omega}_o\rangle}+\frac{1}{0}\right)\kappa_t(\vec{p})}\right)\int_{2\pi^+} f_1(\vec{p},\hat{\omega}_o,\hat{\omega}_i)\langle\hat{n},\hat{\omega}_i\rangle \mathrm{d}\hat{\omega}_i \\ &+ e^{-d(\vec{p})\left(\frac{1}{\langle\hat{n},\hat{\omega}_o\rangle}+\frac{1}{1}\right)\kappa_t(\vec{p})}\int_{2\pi^+} f_2(\vec{p},\hat{\omega}_o,\hat{\omega}_i)\langle\hat{n},\hat{\omega}_i\rangle \mathrm{d}\hat{\omega}_i\end{aligned}$$

476

$$\overset{(12.9)}{=} \rho_1(\vec{p},\hat{\omega}_o) + e^{-d(\vec{p})\left(\frac{1}{\langle\hat{n},\hat{\omega}_o\rangle}+1\right)\kappa_t(\vec{p})}\rho_2(\vec{p},\hat{\omega}_o) \tag{12.441}$$

155 In turn, *importance sampling* may be carried by drawing random directions from a mixture of the PDFs associated with each distribution, weighted by the hemispherical average of the weighting function

$$w(\vec{p},\hat{\omega}_o) \triangleq \int_{2\pi^+} e^{-d(\vec{p})\left(\frac{1}{\langle\hat{n},\hat{\omega}_o\rangle}+\frac{1}{\langle\hat{n},\hat{\omega}_i\rangle}\right)\kappa_t(\vec{p})}\mathrm{d}\hat{\omega}_i$$

244

$$\begin{aligned}&\overset{(6.64)}{=} \int_0^{2\pi}\mathrm{d}\phi\int_0^1 e^{-\frac{d(\vec{p})\kappa_t(\vec{p})}{\langle\hat{n},\hat{\omega}_o\rangle}} e^{-\frac{d(\vec{p})\kappa_t(\vec{p})}{\mu}}\mathrm{d}\mu \\ &= [\phi]_0^{2\pi} e^{-\frac{d(\vec{p})\kappa_t(\vec{p})}{\langle\hat{n},\hat{\omega}_o\rangle}}\left[\mu e^{-\frac{d(\vec{p})\kappa_t(\vec{p})}{\mu}} + d(\vec{p})\kappa_t(\vec{p})\,\mathrm{Ei}\left(-\frac{d(\vec{p})\kappa_t(\vec{p})}{\mu}\right)\right]_0^1 \\ &= 2\pi e^{-\frac{d(\vec{p})\kappa_t(\vec{p})}{\langle\hat{n},\hat{\omega}_o\rangle}}\left(e^{-d(\vec{p})\kappa_t(\vec{p})} + d(\vec{p})\kappa_t(\vec{p})\,\mathrm{Ei}\left(-d(\vec{p})\kappa_t(\vec{p})\right)\right)\end{aligned} \tag{12.442}$$

where $\mu \triangleq \langle\hat{n},\hat{\omega}_i\rangle$, such that

$$p(\vec{p},\hat{\omega}_o,\hat{\omega}_i) \triangleq \frac{\left(1-\frac{w(\vec{p},\hat{\omega}_o)}{2\pi}\right)\rho_1(\vec{p},\hat{\omega}_o)p_1(\vec{p},\hat{\omega}_o,\hat{\omega}_i) + \frac{w(\vec{p},\hat{\omega}_o)}{2\pi}\rho_2(\vec{p},\hat{\omega}_o)p_2(\vec{p},\hat{\omega}_o,\hat{\omega}_i)}{\left(1-\frac{w(\vec{p},\hat{\omega}_o)}{2\pi}\right)\rho_1(\vec{p},\hat{\omega}_o) + \frac{w(\vec{p},\hat{\omega}_o)}{2\pi}\rho_2(\vec{p},\hat{\omega}_o)} \tag{12.443}$$

12.8.6 Multilayer Materials

559 As illustrated in *Figure 12.46*, the *thin layer* composite BRDF can itself be used to char-
557 acterize the lower layer of the *Fresnel layer* composite model, approximately describing a
555 material with a non-clear coating, composed of a partially reflective interface beneath which
482 lies a *thin slab* of scattering medium, itself covering a substrate material. Besides the impact of volumetric extinction [Neumann and Neumann, 1989] and possibly single in-scattering within each layer, perfectly specular refraction of the rays at the interface between the layers and (energy loss due to) total internal reflection may also be recursively accounted for by procedurally simulating the path of the ray as light propagates from one layer to the next [Weidlich and Wilkie, 2007, Weidlich and Wilkie, 2009, Weidlich and Wilkie, 2011] as
559 illustrated in *Figure 12.47*, thereby yielding a computationally inexpensive reflectance model [Elek, 2010] that avoids the explicit numerical simulation of more general mesoscopic light scattering among the layers.

Figure 12.46: **Multilayer BRDF Appearance:** Visual appearance of a three-layer BRDF composed of a partially reflective specular interface, beneath which lies a thin layer of scattering medium, itself covering a diffusive substrate material, shown with an optical thickness that varies from zero (corresponding to a clear coating such that the medium layer is ineffective), to a medium range value (such that all three layers are effective) and to infinity (such that the bottom layer is ineffective) (from left to right, respectively) (light probe courtesy of Paul Debevec).

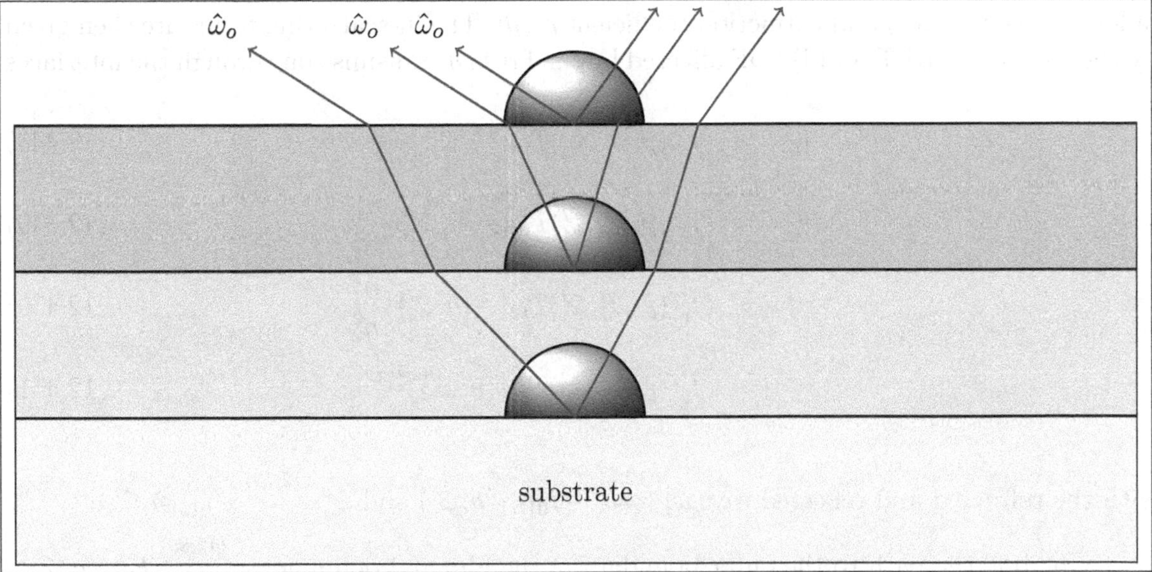

Figure 12.47: **Multilayer BRDF Geometry:** Illustration of the refracted light paths in a multilayer material (drawn after [Weidlich and Wilkie, 2007, Fig. 4]).

12.8.7 Thin Film

By embedding the medium in a *dielectric* material with perfectly smooth interfaces on both 494
sides as illustrated in *Figure 12.48*, the *thin slab* model may be extended by considering 561
the refraction of the transmitted and reflectively/transmissively scattered rays, besides ac- 482
counting for an additional specular reflection term [Hanrahan and Krueger, 1993]. While still neglecting multiple volumetric scattering, secondary specular reflection and reflective scattering can also be simulated by considering the specular transmission and upward scattering of rays reflected off the lower interface [Gu *et al.*, 2007]. More generally, higher-order terms
may be accounted for by adapting the *Kubelka–Munk* layered-stack model where each *di-* 478
electric interface is regarded as an individual layer with its own reflective and transmissive 494
albedos. Assuming the incidence angle is beyond the critical angle so as to prevent total

internal reflection (as is the case if $n_0 \leq n_1$ and $n_2 \leq n_1$), the contributions reaching the
490 interior of the upper interface of the thin film along the direction $\hat{\omega}'_o \overset{(12.77)}{=} -t_{01}(\hat{n}, \hat{\omega}_o)$ from the upper and lower hemispheres can then be recursively formulated as

$$\begin{aligned} \rho^+ &= v_0^+ + t_m r_{12}(v_2^- + t_m(t_{10} + r_{10}\rho^+)) & (12.444) \\ &= v_0^+ + t_m r_{12}(v_2^- + t_m t_{10}) + t_m r_{12} t_m r_{10}\rho^+ \\ &= \frac{v_0^+ + t_m r_{12}(v_2^- + t_m t_{10})}{1 - t_m^2 r_{12} r_{10}} & (12.445) \\ \rho^- &= v_0^- + t_m(t_{12} + r_{12}(v_2^+ + t_m r_{10}\rho^-)) & (12.446) \\ &= v_0^- + t_m(t_{12} + r_{12}v_2^+) + t_m r_{12} t_m r_{10}\rho^- \\ &= \frac{v_0^- + t_m(t_{12} + r_{12}v_2^+)}{1 - t_m^2 r_{12} r_{10}} & (12.447) \end{aligned}$$

491
494 where $r_{10|12} \overset{(12.85)}{=} F_{10|12}(\langle \hat{n}, \hat{\omega}'_o \rangle)$ and $t_{10|12} = t'_{10|12}\frac{n_1^2}{n_{0|2}^2}$ with $t'_{10|12} \overset{(12.100)}{=} T_{10|12}(\langle \hat{n}, \hat{\omega}'_o \rangle)$ are the Fresnel reflection and transmission coefficients of the interfaces, respectively, and $t_m = e^{-\frac{d(\vec{p})}{\langle \hat{n}, \hat{\omega}'_o \rangle}\kappa_t(\vec{p})}$ is the volumetric transmittance between two successive bounces within the film of local thickness $d(\vec{p})$ and extinction coefficient $\kappa_t(\vec{p})$. The in-scattering terms are then given
482 by the *thin slab* BRDF and BTDF affected by the Fresnel transmission through the interfaces

$$\begin{aligned} v_0^+ &= f_r^{ts}(\vec{p}, \hat{\omega}'_o, \hat{\omega}'_i) T_{10}(\langle \hat{n}, \hat{\omega}'_i \rangle)\frac{n_1^2}{n_0^2} & (12.448) \\ v_0^- &= f_t^{ts}(\vec{p}, \hat{\omega}'_o, \hat{\omega}'_i) T_{12}(-\langle \hat{n}, \hat{\omega}'_i \rangle)\frac{n_1^2}{n_2^2} & (12.449) \\ v_2^+ &= f_r^{ts}(\vec{p}, \hat{\omega}''_o, \hat{\omega}'_i) T_{12}(-\langle \hat{n}, \hat{\omega}'_i \rangle)\frac{n_1^2}{n_2^2} & (12.450) \\ v_2^- &= f_t^{ts}(\vec{p}, \hat{\omega}''_o, \hat{\omega}'_i) T_{10}(\langle \hat{n}, \hat{\omega}'_i \rangle)\frac{n_1^2}{n_0^2} & (12.451) \end{aligned}$$

490
488 with the refracted and reflected rays $\hat{\omega}'_i \overset{(12.77)}{=} -t_{01|21}(\hat{n}, \hat{\omega}_i)$ and $\hat{\omega}''_o \overset{(12.70)}{=} -r_{12}(\hat{n}, \hat{\omega}'_o)$.

491
Extending the path to the outer boundary of the film and defining $r_{01} \overset{(12.85)}{=} F_{01}(\langle \hat{n}, \hat{\omega}_o \rangle)$
494 and $t_{01} = t'_{01}\frac{n_0^2}{n_1^2}$ with $t'_{01} \overset{(12.100)}{=} T_{01}(\langle \hat{n}, \hat{\omega}_o \rangle)$, the corresponding BRDF and BTDF are then given by

$$\begin{aligned} f_r(\vec{p}, \hat{\omega}_o, \hat{\omega}_i) &\triangleq \frac{\delta(\hat{\omega}_i - r_{01}(\hat{n}, \hat{\omega}_o))}{\langle \hat{n}, \hat{\omega}_i \rangle}\rho_r^s(\vec{p}, \hat{\omega}_o) + f_r^t(\vec{p}, \hat{\omega}_o, \hat{\omega}_i) & (12.452) \\ f_t(\vec{p}, \hat{\omega}_o, \hat{\omega}_i) &\triangleq \frac{\delta(\hat{\omega}_i - t_{02}(\hat{n}, \hat{\omega}_o))}{-\langle \hat{n}, \hat{\omega}_i \rangle}\rho_t^s(\vec{p}, \hat{\omega}_o) + f_t^t(\vec{p}, \hat{\omega}_o, \hat{\omega}_i) & (12.453) \end{aligned}$$

where the albedos of the specular terms, respectively, read

$$\begin{aligned} \rho_r^s(\vec{p}, \hat{\omega}_o) &\triangleq r_{01} + t'_{01}\frac{n_0^2}{n_1^2}\frac{t_m r_{12} t_m t'_{10}\frac{n_1^2}{n_0^2}}{1 - t_m^2 r_{12} r_{10}} = r_{01} + t_m r_{12} t'_{10}\frac{t'_{01} t_m}{1 - t_m^2 r_{12} r_{10}} & (12.454) \\ \rho_t^s(\vec{p}, \hat{\omega}_o) &\triangleq t'_{01}\frac{n_0^2}{n_1^2}\frac{t_m t'_{12}\frac{n_1^2}{n_2^2}}{1 - t_m^2 r_{12} r_{10}} = t'_{12}\frac{t'_{01} t_m}{1 - t_m^2 r_{12} r_{10}}\frac{n_0^2}{n_2^2} & (12.455) \end{aligned}$$

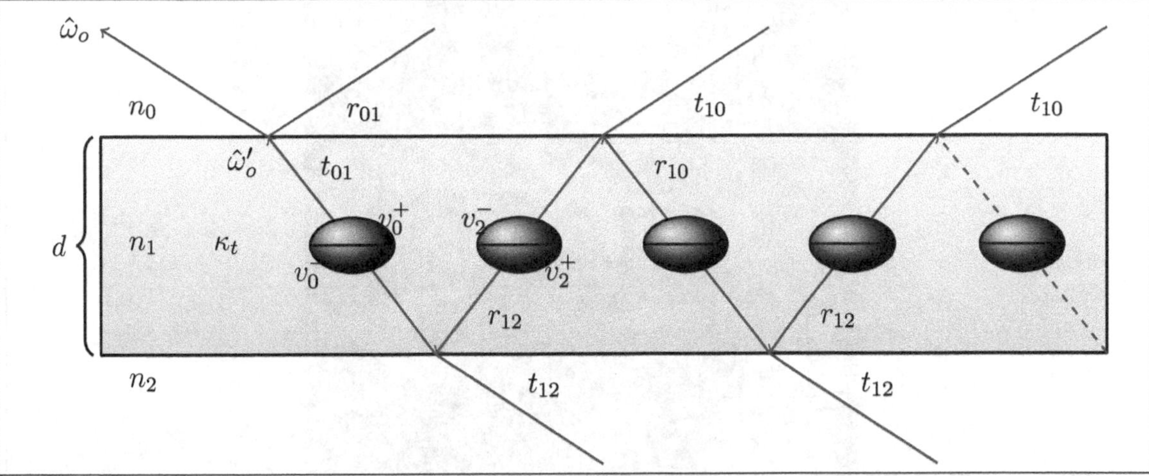

Figure 12.48: Thin Film Geometry: Illustration of the geometric terms defining reflection, transmission and scattering phenomena in a thin dielectric film (drawn after [Glassner, 2000, Fig. 6 and 7]).

while the turbid terms are given by

$$\begin{aligned} f_r^t(\vec{p},\hat{\omega}_o,\hat{\omega}_i) &\triangleq t'_{01}\frac{n_0^2}{n_1^2}\frac{f_r^{ts}(\vec{p},\hat{\omega}'_o,\hat{\omega}'_i)+t_m r_{12} f_t^{ts}(\vec{p},\hat{\omega}''_o,\hat{\omega}'_i)}{1-t_m^2 r_{12} r_{10}} T_{10}(\langle\hat{n},\hat{\omega}'_i\rangle)\frac{n_1^2}{n_0^2} \\ &= t'_{01}\frac{f_r^{ts}(\vec{p},\hat{\omega}'_o,\hat{\omega}'_i)+t_m r_{12} f_t^{ts}(\vec{p},\hat{\omega}''_o,\hat{\omega}'_i)}{1-t_m^2 r_{12} r_{10}} T_{10}(\langle\hat{n},\hat{\omega}'_i\rangle) \quad (12.456) \\ f_t^t(\vec{p},\hat{\omega}_o,\hat{\omega}_i) &\triangleq t'_{01}\frac{n_0^2}{n_1^2}\frac{f_t^{ts}(\vec{p},\hat{\omega}'_o,\hat{\omega}'_i)+t_m r_{12} f_r^{ts}(\vec{p},\hat{\omega}''_o,\hat{\omega}'_i)}{1-t_m^2 r_{12} r_{10}} T_{12}(-\langle\hat{n},\hat{\omega}'_i\rangle)\frac{n_1^2}{n_2^2} \\ &= t'_{01}\frac{f_t^{ts}(\vec{p},\hat{\omega}'_o,\hat{\omega}'_i)+t_m r_{12} f_r^{ts}(\vec{p},\hat{\omega}''_o,\hat{\omega}'_i)}{1-t_m^2 r_{12} r_{10}} T_{12}(-\langle\hat{n},\hat{\omega}'_i\rangle)\frac{n_0^2}{n_2^2} \quad (12.457) \end{aligned}$$

In the special case of a non-scattering medium, both of the above terms actually vanish to zero, thereby yielding a closed-form solution for multiple interreflections within a thin *dielectric* sheet, as illustrated in *Figure 12.49.* 494

By exploiting the assumption of single volumetric scattering, the properties of a stack of 562
layers may then be evaluated as the sum of the first-order scattering contributions of the individual turbid slabs attenuated by the transmittance along the refracted path to the surface
on either side [Hanrahan and Krueger, 1993], as illustrated in *Figure 12.50.* Given a two-layer 562
stack, secondary specular reflection and reflective scattering can also be simulated by considering the specular transmission and upward scattering of rays reflected off the lower interface
of the bottom layer [Gu *et al.*, 2007]. Alternatively regarding a composite *dielectric*-turbid 494
layer as a single meta-layer in which the identity $t'_{ij} = 1 - r_{ij}$ no longer necessarily holds, the impact of multiple interreflections caused by additional layers on the overall reflectance and transmittance may more generally be evaluated by recursively combining the specular terms via the given closed-form expression.

12.9 FURTHER READING

Additional material may be found in surveys and books dedicated to surface physics [Glassner, 1989b], to illumination/reflectance models and shading [Hall, 1986, Hall, 1989] [Schlick, 1994a] or to reflectance modeling [Claustres, 2000a, Claustres, 2000b] [Paulin, 2006, Kurt and Edwards, 2009] [Dorsey and Rushmeier, 2005, Dorsey *et al.*, 2006, Dorsey *et al.*, 2008]. Additional material can also be found in surveys dedicated to reflectance measurement [Lensch

Figure 12.49: Thin Film Appearance: Visual appearance of a thin dielectric film with the refractive index of glass (light probe courtesy of Paul Debevec).

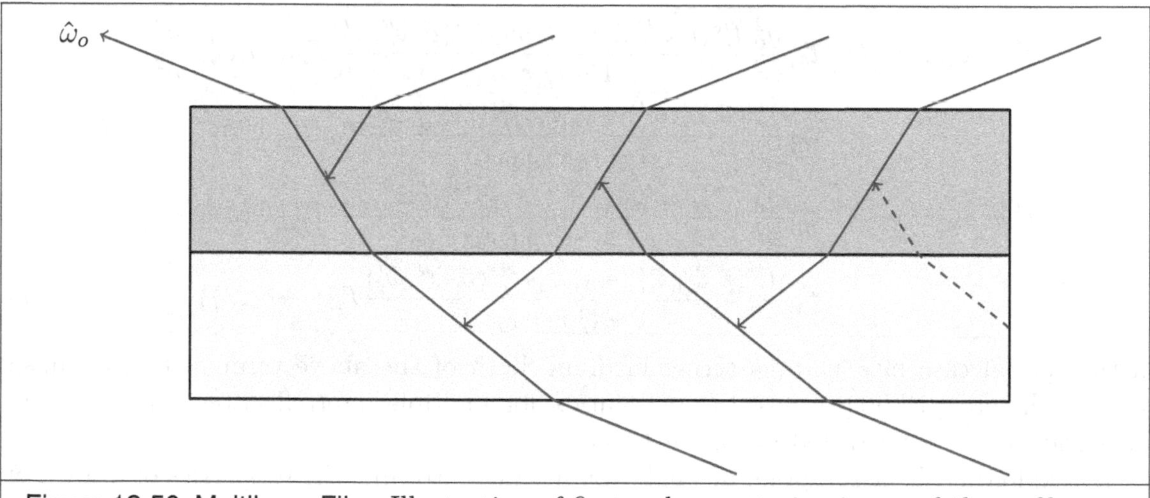

Figure 12.50: Multilayer Film: Illustration of first-order scattering in a multilayer film.

et al., 2005, Lensch *et al.*, 2007], to reflectance representation [Rusinkiewicz, 1997] or to both [Ashikhmin *et al.*, 2001a] [Weyrich *et al.*, 2008a, Weyrich *et al.*, 2008b].

CHAPTER 13

Light Transport

TABLE OF CONTENTS

13.1 APPLICATIONS

As the relative arrangement of objects may be inferred from the interplay of light between them, light transport simulation has come to span a broad range of applications. Within the realm of the entertainment industry [Křivánek *et al.*, 2010], those not only encompass animated films and visual effects [Christensen, 1997] in movie production [Keller *et al.*, 2015], but video games as well.

In addition, applications have also emerged among the scientific visualization community, where natural lighting models provide enhanced perceptual cues better conveying depth information and spatial relationships, both in the context of surface data [Gribble and Parker, 2005, Gribble and Parker, 2006] and volume rendering [Lindemann and Ropinski, 2011].

13.2 RADIOSITY EQUATION

554 Given a *constant weight Lambertian* BRDF
499

554
554
476
499

$$f_r(\vec{p}, \hat{\omega}_o, \hat{\omega}_i) \underset{(12.127)}{\overset{(12.425)}{=}} \frac{w(\vec{p})}{\pi} \underset{(12.128)}{\overset{(12.426)}{=}} \frac{\rho(\vec{p}, \hat{\omega}_o)}{\pi} \overset{(12.17)}{=} \frac{\rho(\vec{p})}{\pi} \tag{13.1}$$

499 the reflected radiance readily reads

475
426

$$L_r(\vec{p}, \hat{\omega}_o) \overset{(12.2)}{=} \int_{2\pi^+} L_i(\vec{p}, \hat{\omega}_i) \frac{\rho(\vec{p})}{\pi} \langle \hat{n}, \hat{\omega}_i \rangle \mathrm{d}\hat{\omega}_i = \frac{\rho(\vec{p})}{\pi} \int_{2\pi^+} L_i(\vec{p}, \hat{\omega}_i) \langle \hat{n}, \hat{\omega}_i \rangle \mathrm{d}\hat{\omega}_i \overset{(10.50)}{=} \frac{\rho(\vec{p})}{\pi} E_e(\vec{p}) \tag{13.2}$$

which is independent of direction, and so is the emitted radiance

475
476

$$L_e(\vec{p}, \hat{\omega}_o) \underset{(12.17)}{\overset{(12.6)}{=}} (1 - \rho(\vec{p})) L_e(T_p) \tag{13.3}$$

as well as the exitant radiance

475

$$L_o(\vec{p}, \hat{\omega}_o) \overset{(12.7)}{=} (1 - \rho(\vec{p})) L_e(T_p) + \frac{\rho(\vec{p})}{\pi} E_e(\vec{p}) \tag{13.4}$$

The radiant emittance, radiant reflectance and radiosity then become

426

$$M|B|J_e(\vec{p}) \overset{(10.50)}{=} \int_{2\pi^+} L_{e|r|o}(\vec{p}, \hat{\omega}_o) \langle \hat{n}, \hat{\omega}_o \rangle \mathrm{d}\hat{\omega}_o = L_{e|r|o}(\vec{p}, \hat{\omega}_o) \int_{2\pi^+} \langle \hat{n}, \hat{\omega}_o \rangle \mathrm{d}\hat{\omega}_o = L_{e|r|o}(\vec{p}, \hat{\omega}_o) \pi \tag{13.5}$$

from which follows the *radiosity equation*

564
564
564
475

$$J_e(\vec{p}) \underset{(12.7)}{\overset{(13.5)}{=}} (L_e(\vec{p}, \hat{\omega}_o) + L_r(\vec{p}, \hat{\omega}_o)) \pi \overset{(13.5)}{=} M_e(\vec{p}) + B_e(\vec{p}) \overset{(13.2)}{=} M_e(\vec{p}) + \rho(\vec{p}) E_e(\vec{p}) \tag{13.6}$$

13.3 SURFACE TRANSPORT

13.3.1 Radiance Transport

Reformulating the reflectance integral over surface area yields

475
427
246

$$L_r(\vec{p}, \hat{\omega}_o) \underset{(6.70)}{\overset{(12.2)\,(10.58)}{=}} \int_S f_r(\vec{p}, \hat{\omega}_o, \widehat{pq}) G(\vec{p}, \vec{q}) L_o(\vec{q}, -\widehat{pq}) \mathrm{d}A(\vec{q}) \tag{13.7}$$

whose dependence on the squared distance in the denominator of the geometric term is commonly referred to as the *inverse-square law*.

Defining a surface point $\vec{o}$ such that $\widehat{po} = \hat{\omega}_o$ as well as the shorthand notations $L_{o|e}(\vec{p} \to \vec{o}) \triangleq L_{o|e}(\vec{p}, \widehat{po})$ and $f_r(\vec{o}, \vec{p}, \vec{q}) \triangleq f_r(\vec{p}, \widehat{po}, \widehat{pq})$, the rendering equation may then be expressed
as a Fredholm *integral equation* of the second kind known as the three-point form [Kajiya, 150
1986]

$$L_o(\vec{p} \to \vec{o}) \overset{(12.7)}{\underset{(13.7)}{=}} L_e(\vec{p} \to \vec{o}) + \int_S f_r(\vec{o}, \vec{p}, \vec{q}) G(\vec{p}, \vec{q}) L_o(\vec{q} \to \vec{p}) \mathrm{d}A(\vec{q}) \tag{13.8}$$

475
564

$$= L_e(\vec{p} \to \vec{o}) + (\mathcal{T}_L L_o)(\vec{p} \to \vec{o})$$

$$= (\mathcal{S}_L L_e)(\vec{p} \to \vec{o}) \tag{13.9}$$

where the *radiance transport operator* reads

$$(\mathcal{T}_L L_o)(\vec{p} \to \vec{o}) \triangleq \int_S f_r(\vec{o}, \vec{p}, \vec{q}) G(\vec{p}, \vec{q}) L_o(\vec{q} \to \vec{p}) \mathrm{d}A(\vec{q}) \tag{13.10}$$

while the solution operator $\mathcal{S}_L \overset{(4.128)}{=} 1 + \mathcal{T}_L \mathcal{S}_L = (1 - \mathcal{T}_L)^{-1}$ is defined in terms of the *global* 150
reflectance distribution function (*GRDF*) f_g [Dutré *et al.*, 1994, Lafortune and Willems, 1994a, Lafortune, 1996] as

$$(\mathcal{S}_L L_e)(\vec{p} \to \vec{o}) \triangleq \int_S \int_S f_g(\vec{o}, \vec{p}, \vec{q}, \vec{r}) G(\vec{q}, \vec{r}) L_e(\vec{r} \to \vec{q}) \mathrm{d}A(\vec{q}) \mathrm{d}A(\vec{r}) \tag{13.11}$$

13.3.2 Importance Transport

Considering adjoint photons, called *importons*, conceptually emanating from the sensor and
propagating into the scene towards the light sources, *radiance transport* may alternatively 564
be mathematically described in terms of an adjoint quantity known as *importance*. Given the emitted importance $W_e(\vec{p}, \hat{\omega}_i)$ of the sensor's surface at point $\vec{p}$ (such as the local response
defining the *exposure* of a film or the radiosity of a surface patch in the *radiosity method*), 657
the exitant importance is given by the *importance equation* [Pattanaik and Mudur, 1993c, 593
Pattanaik, 1993a, Ch. 6] as

$$W_o(\vec{p}, \hat{\omega}_i) \triangleq W_e(\vec{p}, \hat{\omega}_i) + W_r(\vec{p}, \hat{\omega}_i) \tag{13.12}$$

where, by exploiting the adjoint conservation of importance in free space to reformulate the incident importance $W_i(\vec{p}, \hat{\omega}_o) \triangleq W_o(v(\vec{p}, \hat{\omega}_o), -\hat{\omega}_o)$, the reflected importance reads

$$W_r(\vec{p}, \hat{\omega}_i) \triangleq \int_\Omega W_i(\vec{p}, \hat{\omega}_o) f_r(\vec{p}, \hat{\omega}_o, \hat{\omega}_i) \langle \hat{n}_p, \hat{\omega}_o \rangle \mathrm{d}\hat{\omega}_o \tag{13.13}$$

$$\overset{(6.70)}{=} \int_S W_o(\vec{o}, -\widehat{po}) f_r(\vec{p}, \widehat{po}, \hat{\omega}_i) G(\vec{o}, \vec{p}) \mathrm{d}A(\vec{o}) \tag{13.14}$$

246

Defining a surface point $\vec{q}$ such that $\widehat{pq} = \hat{\omega}_i$ as well as the shorthand notations $W_{o|e}(\vec{p} \to \vec{q}) \triangleq W_{o|e}(\vec{p}, \widehat{pq})$, the importance equation may then be expressed as a Fredholm *integral*
equation of the second kind known as the three-point form 150

$$W_o(\vec{p} \to \vec{q}) \overset{(13.12)}{\underset{(13.14)}{=}} W_e(\vec{p} \to \vec{q}) + \int_S W_o(\vec{o} \to \vec{p}) G(\vec{o}, \vec{p}) f_r(\vec{o}, \vec{p}, \vec{q}) \mathrm{d}A(\vec{o}) \tag{13.15}$$

565
565

$$= W_e(\vec{p} \to \vec{q}) + (\mathcal{T}_W W_o)(\vec{p} \to \vec{q})$$

$$= (\mathcal{S}_W W_e)(\vec{p} \to \vec{q}) \tag{13.16}$$

where the *importance transport operator* reads

$$(\mathcal{T}_W W_o)(\vec{p} \to \vec{q}) \triangleq \int_S W_o(\vec{o} \to \vec{p}) G(\vec{o}, \vec{p}) f_r(\vec{o}, \vec{p}, \vec{q}) \mathrm{d}A(\vec{o}) \tag{13.17}$$

150 while the solution operator $\mathcal{S}_W \overset{(4.128)}{=} 1 + \mathcal{T}_W \mathcal{S}_W = (1 - \mathcal{T}_W)^{-1}$ is defined in terms of the GRDF as

$$(\mathcal{S}_W W_e)(\vec{q} \to \vec{r}) \triangleq \int_S \int_S W_e(\vec{o} \to \vec{p}) G(\vec{o}, \vec{p}) f_g(\vec{o}, \vec{p}, \vec{q}, \vec{r}) \mathrm{d}A(\vec{p}) \mathrm{d}A(\vec{o}) \tag{13.18}$$

13.3.3 Measurement Equation

657 Similarly to incident power or the *exposure* of an optical system, a *measurement* is defined by the so-called *measurement equation* as the integral of incident radiance modulated by the sensor's importance function

$$M \triangleq \int_S \int_\Omega L_i(\vec{p}, \hat{\omega}_i) W_e(\vec{p}, \hat{\omega}_i) \langle \hat{n}_p, \hat{\omega}_i \rangle \mathrm{d}\hat{\omega}_i \mathrm{d}A(\vec{p}) \tag{13.19}$$

427
246

$$\overset{(10.58)}{\underset{(6.70)}{=}} \int_S \int_S W_e(\vec{p}, \widehat{pq}) G(\vec{p}, \vec{q}) L_o(\vec{q}, -\widehat{pq}) \mathrm{d}A(\vec{q}) \mathrm{d}A(\vec{p}) \tag{13.20}$$

$$= \int_S \int_S W_e(\vec{p} \to \vec{q}) G(\vec{p}, \vec{q}) L_o(\vec{q} \to \vec{p}) \mathrm{d}A(\vec{q}) \mathrm{d}A(\vec{p}) \tag{13.21}$$

Recursively substituting the three-point form of the rendering equation into the measurement equation then yields

566

$$M \overset{(13.21)}{=} \int_S \int_S W_e(\vec{p}_0 \to \vec{p}_1) G(\vec{p}_0, \vec{p}_1) L_o(\vec{p}_1 \to \vec{p}_0) \mathrm{d}A(\vec{p}_1) \mathrm{d}A(\vec{p}_0)$$

565

$$\overset{(13.8)}{=} \int_S \int_S W_e(\vec{p}_0 \to \vec{p}_1) G(\vec{p}_0, \vec{p}_1) \times \left(L_e(\vec{p}_1 \to \vec{p}_0) + \int_S f_r(\vec{p}_0, \vec{p}_1, \vec{p}_2) G(\vec{p}_1, \vec{p}_2) L_o(\vec{p}_2 \to \vec{p}_1) \mathrm{d}A(\vec{p}_2) \right) \mathrm{d}A(\vec{p}_1) \mathrm{d}A(\vec{p}_0)$$

567

$$\overset{(13.24)}{=} \int_S \int_S W_e(\vec{p}_0 \to \vec{p}_1) G(\vec{p}_0, \vec{p}_1) L_e(\vec{p}_1 \to \vec{p}_0) \mathrm{d}A(\vec{p}_1) \mathrm{d}A(\vec{p}_0) + \int_S \int_S \int_S W_e(\vec{p}_0 \to \vec{p}_1) F(\vec{p}_0, \ldots, \vec{p}_2) L_o(\vec{p}_2 \to \vec{p}_1) \mathrm{d}A(\vec{p}_2) \mathrm{d}A(\vec{p}_1) \mathrm{d}A(\vec{p}_0)$$

$$= \vdots$$

566

$$\overset{(13.23)}{=} \sum_{n=1}^{\infty} M_n \tag{13.22}$$

567
568 where, as illustrated in *Figure 13.1* and *Figure 13.2*, the contribution of path length n is given by the *path integral*

$$M_n \triangleq \int_S \cdots \int_S W_e(\vec{p}_0 \to \vec{p}_1) F(\vec{p}_0, \ldots, \vec{p}_n) L_e(\vec{p}_n \to \vec{p}_{n-1}) \mathrm{d}A(\vec{p}_n) \ldots \mathrm{d}A(\vec{p}_0) \tag{13.23}$$

while the *path throughput* is defined as

$$
\begin{aligned}
F(\vec{p}_m, \ldots, \vec{p}_n) &\triangleq G(\vec{p}_m, \vec{p}_{m+1}) \prod_{i=m+2}^{n} f_r(\vec{p}_{i-2}, \vec{p}_{i-1}, \vec{p}_i) G(\vec{p}_{i-1}, \vec{p}_i) && (13.24)\\
&= G(\vec{p}_n, \vec{p}_{n-1}) \prod_{i=m+2}^{n} f_r(\vec{p}_{i-2}, \vec{p}_{i-1}, \vec{p}_i) G(\vec{p}_{i-2}, \vec{p}_{i-1})\\
&= G(\vec{p}_n, \vec{p}_{n-1}) \prod_{i=m}^{n-2} f_r(\vec{p}_i, \vec{p}_{i+1}, \vec{p}_{i+2}) G(\vec{p}_{i+1}, \vec{p}_i) && (13.25)
\end{aligned}
$$

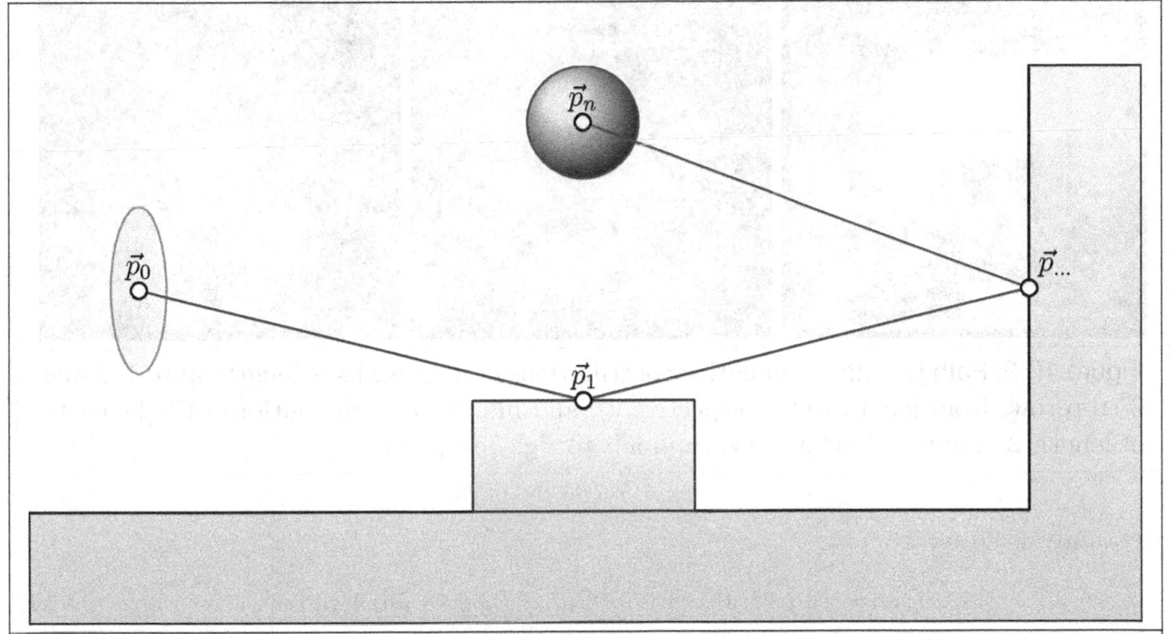

Figure 13.1: Path Integral: Illustration of the contribution of paths between the light source and the sensor as a multidimensional integral over surface points.

Due to the symmetry between radiance and importance [Pattanaik, 1993b, Pattanaik, 1993a, Ch. 6], the measurement may conversely be formulated as

$$M \overset{(13.22)}{=} \sum_{n=1}^{\infty} M_n$$ 566

$$= \vdots$$

$$\overset{(13.23)}{=} \int_S \int_S W_e(\vec{p}_{n-1} \to \vec{p}_n) G(\vec{p}_{n-1}, \vec{p}_n) L_e(\vec{p}_n \to \vec{p}_{n-1}) \mathrm{d}A(\vec{p}_{n-1}) \mathrm{d}A(\vec{p}_n)$$ 566

$$+ \int_S \int_S \int_S W_o(\vec{p}_{n-2} \to \vec{p}_{n-1}) F(\vec{p}_{n-2}, \ldots, \vec{p}_n) L_e(\vec{p}_n \to \vec{p}_{n-1}) \mathrm{d}A(\vec{p}_{n-2}) \mathrm{d}A(\vec{p}_{n-1}) \mathrm{d}A(\vec{p}_n)$$

$$\overset{(13.25)}{=} \int_S \int_S \Big(W_e(\vec{p}_{n-1} \to \vec{p}_n) + \int_S W_o(\vec{p}_{n-2} \to \vec{p}_{n-1}) G(\vec{p}_{n-2}, \vec{p}_{n-1}) \times f_r(\vec{p}_{n-2}, \vec{p}_{n-1}, \vec{p}_n) \mathrm{d}A(\vec{p}_{n-2}) \Big) G(\vec{p}_{n-1}, \vec{p}_n) L_e(\vec{p}_n \to \vec{p}_{n-1}) \mathrm{d}A(\vec{p}_{n-1}) \mathrm{d}A(\vec{p}_n)$$ 567

$$\overset{(13.15)}{=} \int_S \int_S W_o(\vec{p}_{n-1} \to \vec{p}_n) G(\vec{p}_{n-1}, \vec{p}_n) L_e(\vec{p}_n \to \vec{p}_{n-1}) \mathrm{d}A(\vec{p}_{n-1}) \mathrm{d}A(\vec{p}_n) \qquad (13.26)$$ 565

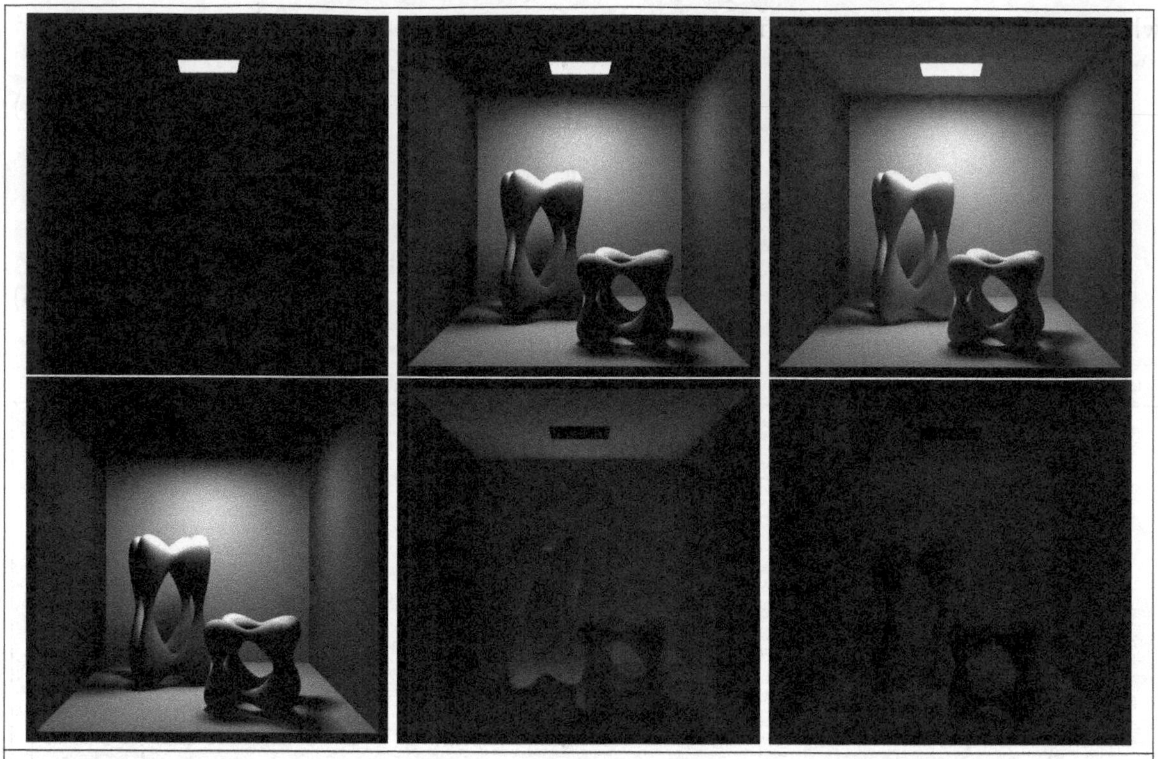

Figure 13.2: Path Length: Cumulative contributions of light paths of length up to 1, 2 and 3 (top row, from left to right, respectively), and individual contributions of light paths of length 2, 3 and 4 (bottom row, from left to right, respectively).

eventually yielding

$$\begin{aligned} M &= \int_S \int_S W_o(\vec{p} \to \vec{q}) G(\vec{p}, \vec{q}) L_e(\vec{q} \to \vec{p}) \mathrm{d}A(\vec{p}) \mathrm{d}A(\vec{q}) && (13.27) \\ &= \int_S \int_S W_o(\vec{p}, \widehat{pq}) G(\vec{p}, \vec{q}) L_e(\vec{q}, -\widehat{pq}) \mathrm{d}A(\vec{p}) \mathrm{d}A(\vec{q}) && (13.28) \\ &\overset{(6.71)}{\underset{(6.66)}{=}} \int_S \int_\Omega L_e(\vec{q}, \hat{\omega}_o) W_i(\vec{q}, \hat{\omega}_o) \langle \hat{n}_q, \hat{\omega}_o \rangle \mathrm{d}\hat{\omega}_o \mathrm{d}A(\vec{q}) && (13.29) \end{aligned}$$

246
245

which can be equivalently formulated in terms of the GRDF as

566
565
568
566

$$M \overset{(13.21)}{\underset{(13.18)}{\overset{(13.11)}{\underset{(13.27)}{=}}}} \int_S \int_S \int_S \int_S W_e(\vec{o} \to \vec{p}) G(\vec{o}, \vec{p}) f_g(\vec{o}, \vec{p}, \vec{q}, \vec{r}) G(\vec{q}, \vec{r}) L_e(\vec{r} \to \vec{q}) \mathrm{d}A(\vec{q}) \mathrm{d}A(\vec{r}) \mathrm{d}A(\vec{p}) \mathrm{d}A(\vec{o}) \quad (13.30)$$

421 422 In essence, the measurement evaluates to an inner product with respect to the *étendue* measure $\mathrm{d}G(\vec{p}, \widehat{pq}) \overset{(10.15)}{=} G(\vec{p}, \vec{q}) \mathrm{d}A(\vec{p}) \mathrm{d}A(\vec{q})$ [Dutré *et al.*, 1994, Dutré, 1996, Ch. 2]

566
565
568
565

$$\begin{aligned} M &\overset{(13.21)}{=} \langle W_e(\vec{p} \to \vec{q}), L_o(\vec{q} \to \vec{p}) \rangle \overset{(13.9)}{=} \langle W_e(\vec{p} \to \vec{q}), (\mathcal{S}_L L_e)(\vec{q} \to \vec{p}) \rangle && (13.31) \\ &\overset{(13.27)}{=} \langle W_o(\vec{p} \to \vec{q}), L_e(\vec{q} \to \vec{p}) \rangle \overset{(13.16)}{=} \langle (\mathcal{S}_W W_e)(\vec{p} \to \vec{q}), L_e(\vec{q} \to \vec{p}) \rangle && (13.32) \end{aligned}$$

from which follows that the radiance and importance solution operators $\mathcal{S}_L = \mathcal{S}_W^*$ are adjoint of one another, and so are the respective transport operators $\mathcal{T}_L = \mathcal{T}_W^*$ [Christensen *et al.*, 1993, Christensen, 2003]. The latter are then said to be self-adjoint if $\mathcal{S}_L = \mathcal{S}_W$, or equivalently if $\mathcal{T}_L \overset{(13.10)}{\underset{(13.17)}{=}} \mathcal{T}_W$. Given that $G(\vec{p}, \vec{q}) \overset{(6.71)}{=} G(\vec{q}, \vec{p})$, self-adjointness therefore holds 565 246 566

in the case of surface reflection since $f_r(\vec{o}, \vec{p}, \vec{q}) \overset{(12.20)}{=} f_r(\vec{q}, \vec{p}, \vec{o})$. In the case of transmissive scattering events between two media with different indices of refraction, though (such as the interface of *dielectric* materials), self-adjointness may be established by instead propagating basic radiance via BSDFs satisfying the generalized reciprocity rule while explicitly accounting for the index of refraction in the *étendue* measure [Veach, 1996, Veach, 1997, Ch. 7]. 477 494 421

13.4 VOLUME TRANSPORT

13.4.1 Scattering Integral

Observing that both the *phase function* f_p (with flipped exitant direction) of a participating 444
medium and the kernel function f_k associated with the *bidirectional distribution function* of 473
a surface are normalized scattering functions obeying

$$\int_\Omega f_{p|k}(\vec{p}, \hat{\omega}_o, \hat{\omega}_i) \mathrm{d}\hat{\omega}_i \overset{(11.13)}{\underset{(12.5)}{=}} 1 \tag{13.33}$$

444 475

the in-scattered radiance integral and the reflectance integral can be seamlessly formulated as a scattering integral of the form

$$L_{p|k}(\vec{p}, \hat{\omega}_o) \overset{(11.8)}{\underset{(12.3)}{=}} \int_\Omega L_i(\vec{p}, \hat{\omega}_i) f_{p|k}(\vec{p}, \hat{\omega}_o, \hat{\omega}_i) \mathrm{d}\hat{\omega}_i \tag{13.34}$$

444 475

$$\overset{(10.58)}{\underset{(6.66)}{=}} \int_S L_o(\vec{q}, -\widehat{pq}) f_{p|k}(\vec{p}, \hat{\omega}_o, \widehat{pq}) \frac{T(\vec{p}, \vec{q}) \langle \hat{n}_q, -\widehat{pq} \rangle}{\|\vec{q} - \vec{p}\|^2} \mathrm{d}A(\vec{q}) \tag{13.35}$$

427 245

such that the volumetric source radiance and the surface rendering equation may both be expressed in terms of the volumetric albedo ρ_p or surface albedo ρ_r of the material as

$$L_{u|o}(\vec{p}, \hat{\omega}_o) \overset{(11.9)}{\underset{(12.8)}{=}} (1 - \rho_{p|r}(\vec{p}, \hat{\omega}_o)) L_e(T_p) + \rho_{p|r}(\vec{p}, \hat{\omega}_o) L_{p|k}(\vec{p}, \hat{\omega}_o) \tag{13.36}$$

444 475

$$= L_e(\vec{p}, \hat{\omega}_o) + \rho_{p|r}(\vec{p}, \hat{\omega}_o) L_{p|k}(\vec{p}, \hat{\omega}_o) \tag{13.37}$$

13.4.2 Path Integral

In environments containing *participating media*, the *generalized path integral* [Pauly *et al.*, 440
2000, §3] is readily given as

$$M_n \triangleq \int_{\mathcal{D}_0} \cdots \int_{\mathcal{D}_n} W_e(\vec{p}_0 \to \vec{p}_1) F(\vec{p}_0, \ldots, \vec{p}_n) L_e(\vec{p}_n \to \vec{p}_{n-1}) \mathrm{d}\mu(\vec{p}_n) \ldots \mathrm{d}\mu(\vec{p}_0) \tag{13.38}$$

where the domain of integration $\mathcal{D}_i = S \cup V$ over a point $\vec{p}_i$ is the union of all surfaces and volumes, and the corresponding measure reads

$$\mathrm{d}\mu(\vec{p}_i) = \begin{cases} \mathrm{d}A(\vec{p}_i) & \text{if } \vec{p}_i \in S \\ \mathrm{d}V(\vec{p}_i) & \text{if } \vec{p}_i \in V \end{cases} \tag{13.39}$$

while the *generalized path throughput* is defined as

$$\begin{aligned} F(\vec{p}_m, \ldots, \vec{p}_n) &\triangleq G(\vec{p}_m, \vec{p}_{m+1}) \prod_{i=m+2}^{n} f(\vec{p}_{i-2}, \vec{p}_{i-1}, \vec{p}_i) G(\vec{p}_{i-1}, \vec{p}_i) && (13.40) \\ &= G(\vec{p}_n, \vec{p}_{n-1}) \prod_{i=m+2}^{n} f(\vec{p}_{i-2}, \vec{p}_{i-1}, \vec{p}_i) G(\vec{p}_{i-2}, \vec{p}_{i-1}) \\ &= G(\vec{p}_n, \vec{p}_{n-1}) \prod_{i=m}^{n-2} f(\vec{p}_i, \vec{p}_{i+1}, \vec{p}_{i+2}) G(\vec{p}_{i+1}, \vec{p}_i) && (13.41) \end{aligned}$$

where

443

$$f(\vec{o}, \vec{p}, \vec{q}) \triangleq \begin{cases} f_r(\vec{o}, \vec{p}, \vec{q}) & \text{if } \vec{p} \in S \\ \kappa_t(\vec{p}) \rho_p(\vec{p}) f_p(\vec{o}, \vec{p}, \vec{q}) \overset{(11.6)}{=} \kappa_s(\vec{p}) f_p(\vec{o}, \vec{p}, \vec{q}) & \text{if } \vec{p} \in V \end{cases} \quad (13.42)$$

and the *generalized geometric term* reads

$$G(\vec{p}, \vec{q}) \triangleq \begin{cases} \langle \hat{n}_p, \widehat{pq} \rangle \frac{T(\vec{p},\vec{q})}{\|\vec{q}-\vec{p}\|^2} \langle \hat{n}_q, -\widehat{pq} \rangle & \text{if } \vec{p} \in S \wedge \vec{q} \in S \\ \langle \hat{n}_p, \widehat{pq} \rangle \frac{T(\vec{p},\vec{q})}{\|\vec{q}-\vec{p}\|^2} & \text{if } \vec{p} \in S \wedge \vec{q} \in V \\ \frac{T(\vec{p},\vec{q})}{\|\vec{q}-\vec{p}\|^2} \langle \hat{n}_q, -\widehat{pq} \rangle & \text{if } \vec{p} \in V \wedge \vec{q} \in S \\ \frac{T(\vec{p},\vec{q})}{\|\vec{q}-\vec{p}\|^2} & \text{if } \vec{p} \in V \wedge \vec{q} \in V \end{cases} \quad (13.43)$$

As an alternative, the generalized path integral can be formulated as

$$\begin{aligned} M_n = \int_{\mathcal{D}_0} \cdots \int_{\mathcal{D}_n} & W_e(\vec{p}_0 \to \vec{p}_1) \langle \hat{n}_{p_0}, \widehat{p_0 p_1} \rangle F_r(\vec{p}_0, \ldots, \vec{p}_n) \\ & \langle \hat{n}_{p_n}, \widehat{p_n p_{n-1}} \rangle L_e(\vec{p}_n \to \vec{p}_{n-1}) \mathrm{d}\mu(\vec{p}_n) \ldots \mathrm{d}\mu(\vec{p}_0) \quad (13.44) \end{aligned}$$

with the *reduced path throughput* being defined as

$$\begin{aligned} F_r(\vec{p}_m, \ldots, \vec{p}_n) &\triangleq g(\vec{p}_m, \vec{p}_{m+1}) \prod_{i=m+2}^{n} f(\vec{p}_{i-2}, \vec{p}_{i-1}, \vec{p}_i) g(\vec{p}_{i-1}, \vec{p}_i) && (13.45) \\ &= g(\vec{p}_n, \vec{p}_{n-1}) \prod_{i=m+2}^{n} f(\vec{p}_{i-2}, \vec{p}_{i-1}, \vec{p}_i) g(\vec{p}_{i-2}, \vec{p}_{i-1}) \\ &= g(\vec{p}_n, \vec{p}_{n-1}) \prod_{i=m}^{n-2} f(\vec{p}_i, \vec{p}_{i+1}, \vec{p}_{i+2}) g(\vec{p}_{i+1}, \vec{p}_i) && (13.46) \end{aligned}$$

where

443

$$f(\vec{o}, \vec{p}, \vec{q}) \triangleq \begin{cases} \langle \hat{n}_p, \widehat{po} \rangle f_r(\vec{o}, \vec{p}, \vec{q}) \langle \hat{n}_p, \widehat{pq} \rangle & \text{if } \vec{p} \in S \\ \kappa_t(\vec{p}) \rho_p(\vec{p}) f_p(\vec{o}, \vec{p}, \vec{q}) \overset{(11.6)}{=} \kappa_s(\vec{p}) f_p(\vec{o}, \vec{p}, \vec{q}) & \text{if } \vec{p} \in V \end{cases} \quad (13.47)$$

while the *reduced geometric term* reads

$$g(\vec{p}, \vec{q}) \triangleq \frac{T(\vec{p}, \vec{q})}{\|\vec{q} - \vec{p}\|^2} \quad (13.48)$$

13.5 PATH NOTATION

The *bidirectional distribution function* (or *phase function*) associated with each scattering 473
event along a transport path may be categorized as one or a combination of components 444
identified by the following alphabet:

- D: ideal diffuse
- G: glossy
- S: ideal specular

while additionally introducing symbols for source and sink events:

- L: emission of light from a source
- E: absorption of light by the sensor or the eye

Using the above notation, the nature of a transport path can then be characterized by a regular expression [Heckbert, 1990, §3.1 ¶3] using standard operators denoting:

- (): a group of symbols
- []: an optional group of symbols
- |: either instance of the left or right symbol
- *: zero or more instances of the superscripted symbol
- $^+$: one or more instances of the superscripted symbol

such that the set of all possible paths is denoted by an expression of the form $E(D|G|S)^*L$.

13.6 FURTHER READING

Additional material may be found in courses dedicated to global illumination [Heckbert, 1992, Arvo, 1993].

IV

Computational Foundations

CHAPTER 14

Analytic Methods

TABLE OF CONTENTS

14.1 OVERVIEW

563 Due to the intricacy of radiative *light transport*, analytic solutions to the equation of transfer
can only be derived for special cases. Such solutions therefore inherently rely on a number of
429 simplifying assumptions with respect to the characteristics of the *light source*, the geometric
configuration of the scene and/or the properties of the surface materials or *participating*
440 *media*.

Nevertheless, those theoretical results are of fundamental importance as they allow the generation of reference solutions against which both the accuracy of approximate approaches and the convergence of numerical methods can be evaluated. Moreover, the derivation of those solutions provides valuable insights on the complexity of the mathematical mechanisms underlying the physical problems of concern.

14.2 DIRECT ILLUMINATION

14.2.1 Collimated Light

435 Given a *directional light* or *collimated beam light* of emitted radiance $L_e(\vec{q}, \hat{\omega}_o) = M_e(\vec{q})\delta(\hat{v}_l-$
436
569 $\hat{\omega}_o)$ oriented along the direction $\hat{v}_l$, the *scattering integral* reduces to

569
$$L_{p|k}(\vec{p}, \hat{\omega}_o) \overset{(13.34)}{=} \int_{\Omega} M_e(\vec{p} + \infty\hat{\omega}_i)\delta(\hat{v}_l + \hat{\omega}_i)T(\vec{p}, \vec{p} + \infty\hat{\omega}_i) f_{p|k}(\vec{p}, \hat{\omega}_o, \hat{\omega}_i) d\hat{\omega}_i$$

45
$$\overset{(2.218)}{=} M_e(\vec{p} - \infty\hat{v}_l)T(\vec{p}, \vec{p} - \infty\hat{v}_l) f_{p|k}(\vec{p}, \hat{\omega}_o, -\hat{v}_l) \quad (14.1)$$

444 In the case of a spatially homogeneous *phase function* $f_p(\vec{p}, \hat{\omega}_o, \hat{\omega}_i) = f_p(\hat{\omega}_o, \hat{\omega}_i)$ and
435 *directional light* $M_e(\vec{p}) = M_e$, and under the simplifying assumption that the transmittance
429 term $T(\vec{p}, \vec{p} - \infty\hat{v}_l) = T_0$ to the *light source* is invariant along a segment $[\vec{s}_a, \vec{s}_b]$ of the ray
of origin $\vec{p}$ and direction $\hat{\omega}$, the in-scattered radiance reduces to a constant for that segment, and in a non-emissive participating medium with a homogeneous albedo, so does the source radiance

444
$$L_u(\vec{p}, \hat{\omega}) \overset{(11.9)}{=} \rho_p M_e T_0 f_p(\hat{\omega}, -\hat{v}_l) \quad (14.2)$$

such that the medium radiance becomes

467
$$L_m(\vec{s}_a, \vec{s}_b, \hat{\omega}) \overset{(11.115)}{=} (1 - T(\vec{s}_a, \vec{s}_b))\rho_p M_e T_0 f_p(\hat{\omega}, -\hat{v}_l) \quad (14.3)$$

where the transmittance between $\vec{s}_a$ and $\vec{s}_b$ can be determined in closed form for analytically integrable expressions of the extinction coefficient, such as a constant [Hoffman and Preetham, 2002, Hoffman and Preetham, 2003] or an exponential function of elevation from a flat ground [Riley *et al.*, 2004] as often used to model single scattering of directional sun light in the earth's atmosphere.

14.2.2 Gaussian RBF

14.2.2.1 Gaussian Extinction

51 Considering a *Gaussian* radial basis function (*RBF*) with amplitude $a > 0$ and scale $b > 0$
centered at a given point $\vec{q}$, the extinction coefficient at a point $\vec{p}$ in a participating medium may be defined as

$$\kappa_t(\vec{p}) = ae^{-b\|\vec{p}-\vec{q}\|^2} \quad (14.4)$$

for instance, as a substitute to the more physically plausible exponential decay of particle density in the earth's atmosphere as a linear function of elevation [Max *et al.*, 1992], or for the scientific visualization of volumetric data mapped by means of a transfer function [Kniss *et al.*, 2003a, Kniss *et al.*, 2003b].

Defining the distance $h > 0$ from $\vec{q}$ to a given ray, the coordinate s_h of its projection onto it and the shorthand notation $\vec{s} = \vec{p} + s\hat{\omega}$, the optical thickness then reads

$$\tau(\vec{s}_a, \vec{s}_b) \overset{(11.94)}{=} \int_{s_a}^{s_b} \kappa_t(\vec{s})\mathrm{d}s = \int_{s_a}^{s_b} ae^{-b\left(h^2+(s-s_h)^2\right)}\mathrm{d}s = ae^{-b\left(h^2+s_h^2\right)} \int_{s_a}^{s_b} e^{-bs^2+2bs_h s}\mathrm{d}s \quad (14.5)$$ 463

whose closed-form solution is given by *Equation 2.279* in terms of the *error function.* 56
The additional assumption that the source radiance L_u is constant along the ray then 55
readily yields an analytical solution to the medium radiance integral

$$L_m(\vec{s}_a, \vec{s}_b, \hat{\omega}) \overset{(11.115)}{=} (1 - T(\vec{s}_a, \vec{s}_b))L_u(\vec{s}, \hat{\omega}) \overset{(11.98)}{=} (1 - e^{-\tau(\vec{s}_a, \vec{s}_b)})L_u(\vec{s}, \hat{\omega}) \quad (14.6)$$ 467 463

14.2.2.2 Gaussian Source

Considering a *Gaussian* radial basis function with amplitude $a > 0$ and scale $b > 0$ centered 51
at a given point $\vec{q}$, the source radiance at a point $\vec{p}$ in a participating medium may be defined as

$$L_u(\vec{p}, \hat{\omega}) = ae^{-b\|\vec{p}-\vec{q}\|^2} \quad (14.7)$$

Defining the distance $h > 0$ from $\vec{q}$ to a given ray, the coordinate s_h of its projection onto it and the short-hand notation $\vec{s} = \vec{p} + s\hat{\omega}$, the medium radiance then reads

$$\begin{aligned} L_m(\vec{s}_a, \vec{s}_b, \hat{\omega}) &\overset{(11.114)}{=} \int_{s_a}^{s_b} e^{-\kappa_t(s-s_a)}\kappa_t L_u(\vec{s}, \hat{\omega})\mathrm{d}s \\ &= \kappa_t \int_{s_a}^{s_b} e^{-\kappa_t(s-s_a)} ae^{-b\left(h^2+(s-s_h)^2\right)}\mathrm{d}s \\ &= \kappa_t ae^{\kappa_t s_a - b(h^2+s_h^2)} \int_{s_a}^{s_b} e^{-bs^2+(2bs_h-\kappa_t)s}\mathrm{d}s \end{aligned} \quad (14.8)$$ 467

whose closed-form solution is given by *Equation 2.279* in terms of the *error function.* 56 55

14.2.3 Point Light

14.2.3.1 Overview

Considering the limit of an infinitely small source resulting in a *point light* of radiant intensity 431
$I_e(\hat{\omega})$ located at position $\vec{q} = \vec{p_l}$, the *scattering integral* reduces to 569

$$\begin{aligned} L_{p|k}(\vec{p}, \hat{\omega}_o) &\overset{(13.35)}{=} f_{p|k}(\vec{p}, \hat{\omega}_o, \widehat{pp_l})\frac{T(\vec{p}, \vec{p_l})}{\|\vec{p_l} - \vec{p}\|^2} \int_S L_e(\vec{p_l}, -\widehat{pp_l})\langle \hat{n}_{p_l}, -\widehat{pp_l}\rangle \mathrm{d}A(\vec{p_l}) \\ &\overset{(10.49)}{=} f_{p|k}(\vec{p}, \hat{\omega}_o, \widehat{pp_l})\frac{T(\vec{p}, \vec{p_l})}{\|\vec{p_l} - \vec{p}\|^2} I_e(-\widehat{pp_l}) \end{aligned} \quad (14.9)$$ 569 426

where $\widehat{pp_l}$ is a unit vector oriented from the surface point $\vec{p}$ toward the *light source.* 429
Parameterizing the azimuthally symmetric *phase function* $f_p(\vec{p}, \hat{\omega}, \hat{\omega}_i) = f_c(\langle \hat{\omega}_i, \hat{v}_e\rangle)$ in 444
terms of the cosine angle with the view-dependent normalized direction $\hat{\omega} = \hat{v}_e$, and the radiant intensity $I_e(\hat{\omega}) = I_c(\langle \hat{\omega}, \hat{v}_l\rangle)$ in terms of the cosine angle with the predefined normalized direction $\hat{v}_l$, the in-scattered radiance of a non-emissive homogeneous participating medium may alternatively be formulated as

$$L_p(\vec{p}, \hat{\omega}) \overset{(11.98)}{=} f_c\left(\left\langle \frac{\vec{p_l} - \vec{p}}{\|\vec{p_l} - \vec{p}\|}, \hat{v}_e \right\rangle\right) \frac{e^{-\kappa_t\|\vec{p_l}-\vec{p}\|}}{\|\vec{p_l} - \vec{p}\|^2} I_c\left(\left\langle -\frac{\vec{p_l} - \vec{p}}{\|\vec{p_l} - \vec{p}\|}, \hat{v}_l \right\rangle\right)$$ 463

578 As illustrated in *Figure 14.1*, parameterizing the position $\vec{p} = \vec{s} = \vec{p}_e + s\hat{v}_e$ along the view ray of origin $\vec{p}_e$ and direction $\hat{v}_e$ then yields [Pegoraro and Parker, 2009, Pegoraro, 2009, Ch. 7]

$$\begin{aligned} L_p(\vec{s}, \hat{\omega}) &= f_c\left(\frac{\langle \vec{p}_l - \vec{p}_e - s\hat{v}_e, \hat{v}_e\rangle}{\|\vec{p}_l - \vec{p}_e - s\hat{v}_e\|}\right) \frac{e^{-\kappa_t\|\vec{p}_l - \vec{p}_e - s\hat{v}_e\|}}{\|\vec{p}_l - \vec{p}_e - s\hat{v}_e\|^2} I_c\left(-\frac{\langle \vec{p}_l - \vec{p}_e - s\hat{v}_e, \hat{v}_l\rangle}{\|\vec{p}_l - \vec{p}_e - s\hat{v}_e\|}\right) \\ &= f_c\left(\frac{\langle \vec{v}_{el}, \hat{v}_e\rangle - s\langle \hat{v}_e, \hat{v}_e\rangle}{\|\vec{v}_{el} - s\hat{v}_e\|}\right) \frac{e^{-\kappa_t\|\vec{v}_{el} - s\hat{v}_e\|}}{\|\vec{v}_{el} - s\hat{v}_e\|^2} I_c\left(-\frac{\langle \vec{v}_{el}, \hat{v}_l\rangle - s\langle \hat{v}_e, \hat{v}_l\rangle}{\|\vec{v}_{el} - s\hat{v}_e\|}\right) \\ &= f_c\left(\frac{s_h - s}{\sqrt{h^2 + (s - s_h)^2}}\right) \frac{e^{-\kappa_t\sqrt{h^2 + (s - s_h)^2}}}{h^2 + (s - s_h)^2} I_c\left(\frac{d_{lel} + sd_{el}}{\sqrt{h^2 + (s - s_h)^2}}\right) \end{aligned} \tag{14.10}$$

where $h > 0$ is the distance from the light to the given ray and $s_h \triangleq \langle \vec{v}_{el}, \hat{v}_e\rangle$ the coordinate of its projection onto it, and where $d_{el} \triangleq \langle \hat{v}_e, \hat{v}_l\rangle$ and $d_{lel} \triangleq -\langle \vec{v}_{el}, \hat{v}_l\rangle$ with $\vec{v}_{el} \triangleq \vec{p}_l - \vec{p}_e$.

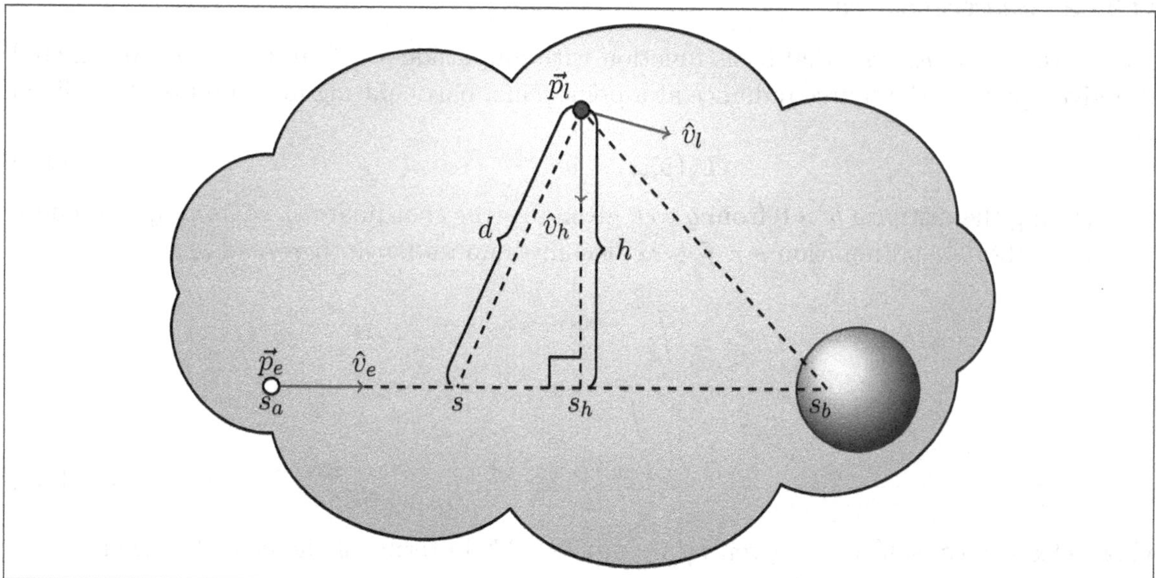

Figure 14.1: Air-Light Integral: Illustration of the terms involved in the computation of the closed-form solution to the single-scattering air-light integral in homogeneous participating media (drawn after [Pegoraro and Parker, 2009, Pegoraro *et al.*, 2010, Pegoraro *et al.*, 2011, Fig. 1] and [Pegoraro, 2009, Fig. 7.1]).

The formulation of the medium radiance then becomes

467
444

$$\begin{aligned} L_m(\vec{s}_a, \vec{s}_b, \hat{\omega}) &\overset{(11.114)}{\underset{(11.10)}{=}} \int_{s_a}^{s_b} e^{-\kappa_t\|\vec{s} - \vec{s}_a\|} \kappa_s L_p(\vec{s}, \hat{\omega}) \mathrm{d}s \\ &= \kappa_s e^{\kappa_t s_a} \int_{s_a}^{s_b} \frac{e^{-\kappa_t\left(s + \sqrt{h^2 + (s - s_h)^2}\right)}}{h^2 + (s - s_h)^2} f_c\left(\frac{s_h - s}{\sqrt{h^2 + (s - s_h)^2}}\right) \\ &\quad \times I_c\left(\frac{d_{lel} + sd_{el}}{\sqrt{h^2 + (s - s_h)^2}}\right) \mathrm{d}s \end{aligned} \tag{14.11}$$

where $s \in (-\infty, s_h, +\infty)$ with the three-variate interval notation specifying the lower endpoint, light projection coordinate and upper endpoint, respectively, of the space of integration.

Using the change of variable $u \triangleq \frac{s - s_h}{h} \in (-\infty, 0, +\infty)$, which maps coordinates before s_h to negative values and those beyond s_h to positive ones, the integrand may then be reduced to a function of 4 parameters instead of 6 (or only 2 instead of 4 when considering isotropic *light sources*), yielding the following simplified formulation of the medium radiance 429

$$\begin{aligned}
L_m(\vec{s}_a, \vec{s}_b, \hat{\omega}) \\
&= \kappa_s e^{\kappa_t s_a} \int_{u_a}^{u_b} \frac{e^{-\kappa_t\left(s_h+hu+\sqrt{h^2+h^2u^2}\right)}}{h^2+h^2u^2} f_c\left(-\frac{hu}{\sqrt{h^2+h^2u^2}}\right) I_c\left(\frac{d_{lel}+(s_h+hu)d_{el}}{\sqrt{h^2+h^2u^2}}\right) hdu \\
&= \kappa_s e^{\kappa_t (s_a-s_h)} \int_{u_a}^{u_b} \frac{e^{-\kappa_t\left(hu+h\sqrt{1+u^2}\right)}}{h^2(1+u^2)} f_c\left(-\frac{hu}{h\sqrt{1+u^2}}\right) I_c\left(\frac{d_{lel}+s_h d_{el}+hud_{el}}{h\sqrt{1+u^2}}\right) hdu \\
&= \frac{\kappa_s}{h} e^{\kappa_t (s_a-s_h)} \int_{u_a}^{u_b} \frac{e^{-H\left(u+\sqrt{1+u^2}\right)}}{1+u^2} f_c\left(-\frac{u}{\sqrt{1+u^2}}\right) I_c\left(\frac{d_c+ud_{el}}{\sqrt{1+u^2}}\right) du \qquad (14.12)
\end{aligned}$$

where the bounds of integration become $u_a \triangleq \frac{s_a-s_h}{h}$ and $u_b \triangleq \frac{s_b-s_h}{h}$, while defining the optical distance from the *light source* to the ray as $H \triangleq \kappa_t h$ and the constant $d_c \triangleq \frac{d_{el}s_h+d_{lel}}{h} = \langle \hat{v}_h, \hat{v}_l \rangle$ 429
with $\hat{v}_h \triangleq \frac{s_h\hat{v}_e-\vec{v}_{el}}{h}$ being the unit-length projection vector of the *light source* onto the ray 429
given s_a at the origin.

Substituting $v \triangleq u+\sqrt{1+u^2} \in (0,1,\infty)$, which uniquely defines $u = \frac{v^2-1}{2v}$ such that

$$\sqrt{1+u^2} = v - \frac{v^2-1}{2v} = \frac{2v^2-v^2+1}{2v} = \frac{v^2+1}{2v} \qquad (14.13)$$

finally yields

$$\begin{aligned}
L_m(\vec{s}_a, \vec{s}_b, \hat{\omega}) &= \frac{\kappa_s}{h} e^{\kappa_t (s_a-s_h)} \int_{v_a}^{v_b} \frac{e^{-Hv}}{\left(\frac{v^2+1}{2v}\right)^2} f_c\left(-\frac{\frac{v^2-1}{2v}}{\frac{v^2+1}{2v}}\right) I_c\left(\frac{d_c+\frac{v^2-1}{2v}d_{el}}{\frac{v^2+1}{2v}}\right) \frac{v^2+1}{2v^2} dv \\
&= \frac{\kappa_s}{h} e^{\kappa_t (s_a-s_h)} 2 \int_{v_a}^{v_b} \frac{e^{-Hv}}{v^2+1} f_c\left(-\frac{v^2-1}{v^2+1}\right) I_c\left(\frac{2vd_c+(v^2-1)d_{el}}{v^2+1}\right) dv \qquad (14.14)
\end{aligned}$$

where the bounds of integration are defined as $v_a \triangleq u_a+\sqrt{1+u_a^2}$ and $v_b \triangleq u_b+\sqrt{1+u_b^2}$.

14.2.3.2 Angular Distributions

Assuming the *phase function* is generically expressed as a polynomial of the cosine angle 444

$$f_c(\mu) \triangleq \sum_{n=0}^{N_f} c_f(n)\mu^n \qquad (14.15)$$

then yields [Pegoraro *et al.*, 2010, Pegoraro, 2009, Ch. 7]

$$\begin{aligned}
f_c\left(-\frac{v^2-1}{v^2+1}\right) &= \sum_{n=0}^{N_f} c_f(n)\left(-\frac{v^2-1}{v^2+1}\right)^n \\
&= \sum_{n=0}^{N_f} \frac{c_f(n)}{(v^2+1)^n} \sum_{k=0}^{n} \binom{n}{k} 1^{n-k}(-v^2)^k \\
&= \sum_{n=0}^{N_f} \frac{c_f(n)}{(v^2+1)^n} \sum_{k=0}^{n} \binom{n}{k} (-1)^k v^{2k} \\
&= \sum_{n=0}^{N_f} \frac{c_f(n)}{(v^2+1)^n} \sum_{\substack{k=0\\k+=2}}^{2n} \binom{n}{\frac{k}{2}} (-1)^{\frac{k}{2}} v^k \\
&= \sum_{n=0}^{N_f} c_f(n) \sum_{\substack{k=0\\k+=2}}^{2n} d_f(n,k)\frac{v^k}{(v^2+1)^n} \qquad (14.16)
\end{aligned}$$

where the coefficients read

$$d_f(n,k) \triangleq (-1)^{\frac{k}{2}} \binom{n}{\frac{k}{2}} = (-1)^{\frac{k}{2}} \frac{n!}{\left(\frac{k}{2}\right)!\left(n-\frac{k}{2}\right)!} \tag{14.17}$$

Making the same assumption for the angular distribution of the light intensity

$$I_c(\mu) \triangleq \sum_{n=0}^{N_I} c_I(n)\mu^n \tag{14.18}$$

similarly yields

$$\begin{aligned}
I_c\left(\frac{d_{el}(v^2-1)+2d_c v}{v^2+1}\right) &= \sum_{n=0}^{N_I} c_I(n)\left(\frac{d_{el}(v^2-1)+2d_c v}{v^2+1}\right)^n \\
&= \sum_{n=0}^{N_I} \frac{c_I(n)}{(v^2+1)^n} \sum_{i=0}^{n} \binom{n}{i} (2d_c)^{n-i} v^{n-i} d_{el}^i (v^2-1)^i \\
&= \sum_{n=0}^{N_I} \frac{c_I(n)}{(v^2+1)^n} \sum_{i=0}^{n} \binom{n}{i} (2d_c)^{n-i} v^{n-i} d_{el}^i \sum_{j=0}^{i} \binom{i}{j} (-1)^{i-j} v^{2j} \\
&= \sum_{n=0}^{N_I} \frac{c_I(n)}{(v^2+1)^n} \sum_{i=0}^{n} \binom{n}{i} (2d_c)^{n-i} d_{el}^i \sum_{j=0}^{i} \binom{i}{j} (-1)^{i-j} v^{n-i+2j} \\
&= \sum_{n=0}^{N_I} \frac{c_I(n)}{(v^2+1)^n} \sum_{i=0}^{n} \binom{n}{i} (2d_c)^{n-i} d_{el}^i \sum_{\substack{k=n-i\\k+=2}}^{n+i} \binom{i}{\frac{i+k-n}{2}} (-1)^{\frac{i-k+n}{2}} v^k \\
&= \sum_{n=0}^{N_I} \frac{c_I(n)}{(v^2+1)^n} \sum_{k=0}^{2n} \sum_{\substack{i=|n-k|\\i+=2}}^{\leq n} (2d_c)^{n-i} d_{el}^i \binom{n}{i} \binom{i}{\frac{i+k-n}{2}} (-1)^{\frac{i-k+n}{2}} v^k \\
&= \sum_{n=0}^{N_I} c_I(n) \sum_{k=0}^{2n} d_I(n,k) \frac{v^k}{(v^2+1)^n}
\end{aligned} \tag{14.19}$$

where the coefficients read

$$\begin{aligned}
d_I(n,k) &\triangleq \sum_{\substack{i=|n-k|\\i+=2}}^{\leq n} (-1)^{\frac{i-k+n}{2}} (2d_c)^{n-i} d_{el}^i \binom{n}{i} \binom{i}{\frac{i+k-n}{2}} \\
&= \sum_{\substack{i=|n-k|\\i+=2}}^{\leq n} (-1)^{\frac{i-k+n}{2}} (2d_c)^{n-i} d_{el}^i \frac{n!}{(n-i)!(\frac{i+k-n}{2})!(\frac{i-k+n}{2})!}
\end{aligned} \tag{14.20}$$

$$\begin{aligned}
&= \sum_{\substack{l=(n-|n-k|) \bmod 2\\l+=2}}^{n-|n-k|} (-1)^{n-\frac{k+l}{2}} (2d_c)^l d_{el}^{n-l} \binom{n}{l} \binom{n-l}{\frac{k-l}{2}} \\
&= \sum_{\substack{l=k \bmod 2\\l+=2}}^{n-|n-k|} (-1)^{n-\frac{k+l}{2}} (2d_c)^l d_{el}^{n-l} \frac{n!}{l!\left(\frac{k-l}{2}\right)!\left(n-\frac{k+l}{2}\right)!}
\end{aligned} \tag{14.21}$$

444 The product of the *phase function* and light distribution then becomes

$$
\begin{aligned}
&f_c\left(-\frac{v^2-1}{v^2+1}\right) I_c\left(\frac{d_{el}(v^2-1)+2d_c v}{v^2+1}\right)\\
&\overset{(14.16)}{\underset{(14.19)}{=}} \left(\sum_{n_f=0}^{N_f} c_f(n_f) \sum_{\substack{k_f=0\\k_f+=2}}^{2n_f} d_f(n_f,k_f)\frac{v^{k_f}}{(v^2+1)^{n_f}}\right)\left(\sum_{n_I=0}^{N_I} c_I(n_I)\sum_{k_I=0}^{2n_I} d_I(n_I,k_I)\frac{v^{k_I}}{(v^2+1)^{n_I}}\right)
\end{aligned}
$$

579
580

$$
\begin{aligned}
&= \sum_{n_f=0}^{N_f} c_f(n_f) \sum_{\substack{k_f=0\\k_f+=2}}^{2n_f} d_f(n_f,k_f) \sum_{n_I=0}^{N_I} c_I(n_I) \sum_{k_I=0}^{2n_I} d_I(n_I,k_I)\frac{v^{k_f+k_I}}{(v^2+1)^{n_f+n_I}}\\
&= \sum_{n_f=0}^{N_f} c_f(n_f) \sum_{\substack{k_f=0\\k_f+=2}}^{2n_f} d_f(n_f,k_f) \sum_{n=n_f}^{n_f+N_I} c_I(n-n_f) \sum_{k=k_f}^{k_f+2(n-n_f)} d_I(n-n_f,k-k_f)\frac{v^k}{(v^2+1)^n}\\
&= \sum_{n_f=0}^{N_f} c_f(n_f) \sum_{n=n_f}^{n_f+N_I} c_I(n-n_f) \sum_{\substack{k_f=0\\k_f+=2}}^{2n_f} d_f(n_f,k_f) \sum_{k=k_f}^{k_f+2(n-n_f)} d_I(n-n_f,k-k_f)\frac{v^k}{(v^2+1)^n}\\
&= \sum_{n=0}^{N_f+N_I} \sum_{n_f=\max\{0,n-N_I\}}^{\min\{N_f,n\}} c_f(n_f)c_I(n-n_f)\\
&\qquad \times \sum_{k=0}^{2n} \sum_{\substack{k_f=\max\{0,2\lceil\frac{k}{2}\rceil-2(n-n_f)\}\\k_f+=2}}^{\min\{2n_f,2\lfloor\frac{k}{2}\rfloor\}} d_f(n_f,k_f)d_I(n-n_f,k-k_f)\frac{v^k}{(v^2+1)^n}\\
&= \sum_{n=0}^{N_f+N_I}\sum_{k=0}^{2n} d_{fI}(n,k)\frac{v^k}{(v^2+1)^n} \qquad (14.22)
\end{aligned}
$$

where $k \triangleq k_f + k_I$ and $n \triangleq n_f + n_I$ and where the coefficients read

$$
d_{fI}(n,k) \triangleq \sum_{n_f=\max\{0,n-N_I\}}^{\min\{N_f,n\}} c_f(n_f)c_I(n-n_f) \sum_{\substack{k_f=\max\{0,2\lceil\frac{k}{2}\rceil-2(n-n_f)\}\\k_f+=2}}^{\min\{2n_f,2\lfloor\frac{k}{2}\rfloor\}} d_f(n_f,k_f)d_I(n-n_f,k-k_f) \qquad (14.23)
$$

More generally, the product of the *phase function* and light distribution may therefore be represented as an expression of the form 444

$$
f_c\left(-\frac{v^2-1}{v^2+1}\right) I_c\left(\frac{d_{el}(v^2-1)+2d_c v}{v^2+1}\right) = b\sum_{n=0}^{N} c(n)\sum_{k=0}^{2n} d(n,k)\frac{v^k}{(v^2+1)^n} \qquad (14.24)
$$

where whenever both the *phase function* and *light source* are anisotropic, the coefficients 444
are defined as $b = 1$, $N = N_f + N_I$, $c(n) = 1$ and $d(n,k) = d_{fI}(n,k)$. However, if the 429
light source is isotropic, the coefficients simplify into $b = c_I(0)$, $N = N_f$, $c(n) = c_f(n)$ and 429
$d(n,k) = (1-(k \bmod 2))d_f(n,k)$, while, on the other hand, if the *phase function* is *isotropic*, 444
the coefficients read instead $b = c_f(0)$, $N = N_I$, $c(n) = c_I(n)$ and $d(n,k) = d_I(n,k)$. Finally, 446
whenever both are *isotropic*, the coefficients reduce to $b = c_f(0)c_I(0)$, $N = 0$, $c(n) = 1$ and 446
$d(n,k) = 1$.

14.2.3.3 Closed-Form Solution

Substituting the expression of the product of the *phase function* and light distribution into 444 the formulation of the medium radiance finally yields

579 581

$$L_m(\vec{s}_a, \vec{s}_b, \hat{\omega}) \overset{(14.14)}{\underset{(14.24)}{=}} \frac{\kappa_s}{h} e^{\kappa_t(s_a - s_h)} 2 \int_{v_a}^{v_b} \frac{e^{-Hv}}{v^2+1} b \sum_{n=0}^{N} c(n) \sum_{k=0}^{2n} d(n,k) \frac{v^k}{(v^2+1)^n} \mathrm{d}v$$

$$= \frac{\kappa_s}{h} e^{\kappa_t(s_a - s_h)} 2b \sum_{n=0}^{N} c(n) \sum_{k=0}^{2n} d(n,k) \int_{v_a}^{v_b} \frac{e^{-Hv}}{(v^2+1)^{n+1}} v^k \mathrm{d}v \quad (14.25)$$

583 As illustrated in *Figure 14.2*, the above integral can then be solved in closed form using the following antiderivative (i.e., indefinite integral) [Pegoraro *et al.*, 2011]

$$\int \frac{e^{av}}{(v^2+1)^m} v^n \mathrm{d}v = \frac{1}{2^{m-1}} \left(F_1(a,v,m,n) + e^{av} F_2(a,v,m,n) + e^{av} F_3(a,v,m,n)\right) \quad (14.26)$$

where $n \in \mathbb{N}$ and $m \in \mathbb{N}^*$ and the functions read

$$F_1(a,v,m,n) \triangleq \sum_{l=0}^{m-1} \frac{a^l}{l!} C(m-1, n, m-1-l) E(a, v, 2m-n-1-l) \quad (14.27)$$

$$F_2(a,v,m,n) \triangleq \sum_{l=0}^{m-2} a^l \sum_{k=0}^{m-2-l} \frac{1}{(v^2+1)^{k+1}} \frac{k!}{(l+1+k)!} C(m-1, n, m-2-l-k)$$
$$\times \sum_{\substack{j=n+1+l \bmod 2 \\ j+=2}}^{k+1} v^j \binom{k+1}{j} (-1)^{\frac{2m-n-1-l-2k+j}{2}} \quad (14.28)$$

$$F_3(a,v,m,n) \triangleq \sum_{l=0}^{n-2m} \frac{1}{a^{l+1}} \sum_{\substack{k=(n+l) \bmod 2 \\ k+=2}}^{n-2m-l} v^k (-1)^{\frac{n-2m+l-k}{2}} \frac{(l+k)!}{k!} C(m-1, n-1-l-k, m-1)$$
$$(14.29)$$

with the coefficients defined as

$$C(m', n', l') \triangleq \sum_{i=\max\{0, l'-n'\}}^{l'} \left(-\frac{1}{2}\right)^i \binom{m'+i}{m'} \binom{n'}{l'-i} \quad (14.30)$$

$$= \sum_{j=0}^{\min\{l', n'\}} \left(-\frac{1}{2}\right)^{l'-j} \binom{m'+l'-j}{m'} \binom{n'}{j} \quad (14.31)$$

56 The auxiliary function is then defined in terms of the complex-valued *exponential integral* as

$$E(a,v,j) \triangleq \frac{1}{2}\left(\frac{\imath^j}{e^{\imath a}} \operatorname{Ei}(av + \imath a) + \frac{e^{\imath a}}{\imath^j} \operatorname{Ei}(av - \imath a)\right)$$
$$= (-1)^{\lfloor \frac{j}{2} \rfloor} i_{(1-(j \bmod 2))}(a, v) \quad (14.32)$$

where

$$i_0(a,v) \triangleq \int \frac{e^{av}}{v^2+1} \mathrm{d}v$$
$$= \frac{\imath}{2}\left(e^{-\imath a} \operatorname{Ei}(av + \imath a) - e^{\imath a} \operatorname{Ei}(av - \imath a)\right)$$
$$= \Im(e^{\imath a} \operatorname{Ei}(av - \imath a)) \quad (14.33)$$

$$i_1(a,v) \triangleq \int \frac{e^{av}}{v^2+1} v \mathrm{d}v$$
$$= \frac{1}{2}\left(e^{-\imath a} \operatorname{Ei}(av + \imath a) + e^{\imath a} \operatorname{Ei}(av - \imath a)\right)$$
$$= \Re(e^{\imath a} \operatorname{Ei}(av - \imath a)) \quad (14.34)$$

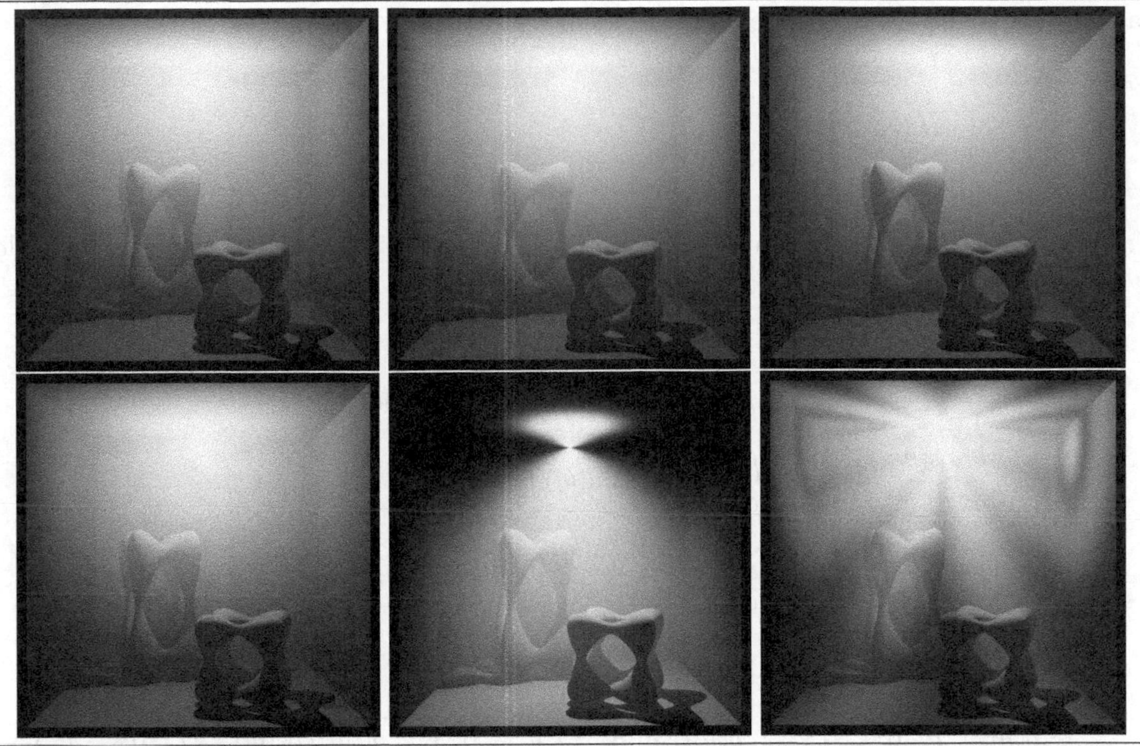

Figure 14.2: Closed-Form Single Scattering: Closed-form evaluation of the single-scattering air-light integral in a homogeneous participating medium illuminated by a point light source, shown for an isotropic angular distribution (top left), for a forward and backward Eddington phase function (top middle and top right), for a Rayleigh phase function (bottom left), for a Warn spotlight (bottom middle) and for a light distribution expressed in terms of Legendre polynomials (bottom right).

from which only $i_0(a, v)$ is involved shall both the *phase function* and the light distribution 444
be *isotropic*. 446

14.2.4 Environmental Light

Assuming that the illumination in a scene is solely due to an infinitely distant *environmental light* whose exitant radiance therefore only depends on direction, the radiance incident upon 433
a surface in the scene becomes

427

$$L_i(\vec{p}, \hat{\omega}_i) \overset{(10.58)}{=} L_e(\vec{p} + \infty\hat{\omega}_i, -\hat{\omega}_i)T(\vec{p}, \vec{p} + \infty\hat{\omega}_i) \tag{14.35}$$

which, in the absence of occlusion, and in the case of an *Eddington* distribution oriented 450
along the direction $\hat{v}_l$, becomes

450

$$L_i(\vec{p}, \hat{\omega}_i) \overset{(11.38)}{=} \frac{1 + k\langle\hat{v}_l, \hat{\omega}_i\rangle}{4\pi}, \quad \forall k \in [-1, +1] \tag{14.36}$$

The radiance reflected off a convex surface with a *constant weight Lambertian* BRDF 554
499

can then be determined in closed form as follows

475 564

$$
\begin{aligned}
&L_r(\vec{p}, \hat{\omega}_o)\\
&\overset{(12.2)}{\underset{(13.1)}{=}} \int_{2\pi^+} \frac{1 + k\langle \hat{\upsilon}_l, \hat{\omega}_i\rangle}{4\pi} \frac{\rho(\vec{p})}{\pi} \langle \hat{n}, \hat{\omega}_i\rangle \mathrm{d}\hat{\omega}_i\\
&= \frac{\rho(\vec{p})}{4\pi^2} \int_0^{2\pi} \int_0^{\frac{\pi}{2}} (1 + k\sin(\theta_l)\sin(\theta_i)\cos(\phi_l - \phi_i) + k\cos(\theta_l)\cos(\theta_i))\cos(\theta_i)\sin(\theta_i)\mathrm{d}\theta_i\mathrm{d}\phi_i\\
&= \frac{\rho(\vec{p})}{4\pi^2} \int_0^{2\pi} \mathrm{d}\phi_i \int_0^{\frac{\pi}{2}} \cos(\theta_i)\sin(\theta_i)\mathrm{d}\theta_i\\
&+ \frac{\rho(\vec{p})k\sin(\theta_l)}{4\pi^2} \int_0^{2\pi} \cos(\phi_l - \phi_i)\mathrm{d}\phi_i \int_0^{\frac{\pi}{2}} \cos(\theta_i)\sin(\theta_i)^2\mathrm{d}\theta_i\\
&+ \frac{\rho(\vec{p})k\cos(\theta_l)}{4\pi^2} \int_0^{2\pi} \mathrm{d}\phi_i \int_0^{\frac{\pi}{2}} \cos(\theta_i)^2\sin(\theta_i)\mathrm{d}\theta_i\\
&= \frac{\rho(\vec{p})}{4\pi^2}[\phi_i]_0^{2\pi}\left[-\frac{\cos(\theta_i)^2}{2}\right]_0^{\frac{\pi}{2}} + \frac{\rho(\vec{p})k\sin(\theta_l)}{4\pi^2}[-\sin(\phi_l - \phi_i)]_0^{2\pi}\left[\frac{\sin(\theta_i)^3}{3}\right]_0^{\frac{\pi}{2}}\\
&\quad + \frac{\rho(\vec{p})k\cos(\theta_l)}{4\pi^2}[\phi_i]_0^{2\pi}\left[-\frac{\cos(\theta_i)^3}{3}\right]_0^{\frac{\pi}{2}}\\
&= \frac{\rho(\vec{p})}{4\pi^2}2\pi\left(-\frac{0^2}{2} + \frac{1^2}{2}\right) + \frac{\rho(\vec{p})k\sin(\theta_l)}{4\pi^2}0\left(\frac{1^3}{3} - \frac{0^3}{3}\right) + \frac{\rho(\vec{p})k\cos(\theta_l)}{4\pi^2}2\pi\left(-\frac{0^3}{3} + \frac{1^3}{3}\right)\\
&= \frac{\rho(\vec{p})}{4\pi}\left(1 + \frac{2k}{3}\cos(\theta_l)\right)\\
&= \frac{\rho(\vec{p})}{4\pi}\left(1 + \frac{2k}{3}\langle \hat{\upsilon}_l, \hat{n}\rangle\right)
\end{aligned}
\tag{14.37}
$$

14.2.5 Polygonal Light

More general distributions raised to an integer exponent may also be evaluated analytically based on the concept of irradiance tensors [Arvo, 1995b, Arvo, 1995a, Ch. 4], whose elements, called angular moments, are weighted integrals of the radiation field with respect to a given direction. Example applications not only include diffuse reflections of directional luminaires, but also glossy reflections and transmissions of diffuse luminaires reflected by a cosine-lobe
500 500 BRDF or BTDF such as the *Minnaert*, *Phong* or *Lafortune* distributions, all leading to
502 integrals of the form

$$\int_{\Omega} \langle \hat{\omega}, \hat{\omega}_i\rangle^n \langle \hat{n}, \hat{\omega}_i\rangle \mathrm{d}\hat{\omega}_i \tag{14.38}$$

while the combination of a directional luminaire and glossy BRDF/BTDF would require the evaluation of triple-axis moments.

246 Based on the concepts of *axial moments* with respect to projected polygonal geometry,
such integrals can be readily evaluated as a double-axis moment about both the surface
normal $\hat{n}$ and a vector $\hat{\omega}$ defining either the orientation of the light distribution or that of
585 the cosine lobe, as illustrated in *Figure 14.3* and *Figure 14.4*. However, it should be noted
585 262 that the *spherical polygon* defining the corresponding domain of integration ought to be
clipped against the upper/lower hemisphere boundary, as well as potentially against the boundary of the hemisphere in which the cosine-lobe of the glossy BRDF/BTDF is positive. Extending the latter clipping procedure to polygonal occluders [Nishita and Nakamae, 1985] similarly allows the approach to be generalized to the analytical evaluation of soft shadows in penumbra regions.

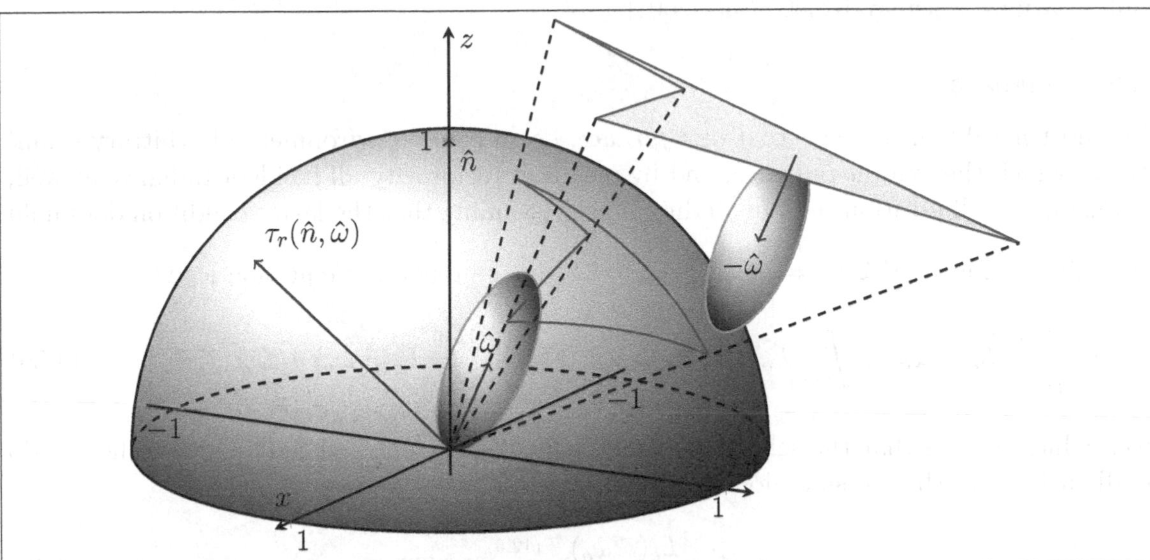

Figure 14.3: Polygonal Luminaire: Illustration of the axial moment defined by a polygonal luminaire, shown either for a directional light distribution or for a cosine-lobed glossy BRDF (drawn after [Arvo, 1995b, Fig. 4] and [Arvo, 1995a, Fig. 4.14]).

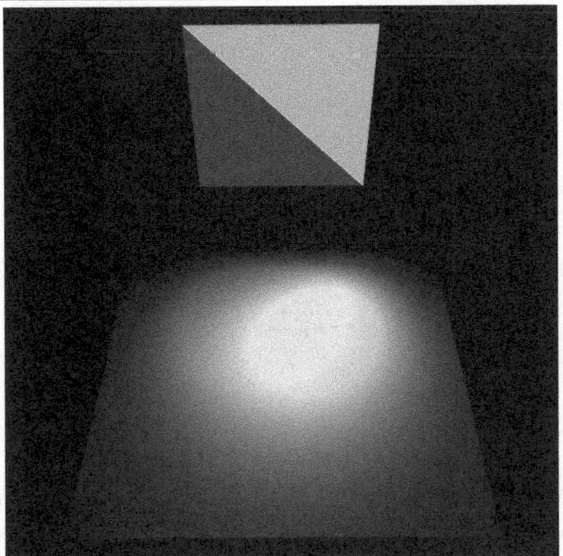

Figure 14.4: Polygonal Light: Analytic evaluation of the radiance reflecting off a surface illuminated by a polygonal light.

14.3 GLOBAL ILLUMINATION

The impact of indirect illumination may also be evaluated in closed form for specific geometric configurations [Szirmay-Kalos *et al.*, 2001].

14.3.1 Furnace

The most notable instance is that of a *furnace*, i.e., a closed environment of arbitrary geometry in which the exitant radiance, and by means of reciprocity all incident radiance as well, is constant at all positions and in all directions. Assuming that the latter condition does hold
427 and substituting $L_i(\vec{p}, \hat{\omega}_i) \overset{(10.58)}{=} L_o(\vec{q}, -\hat{\omega}_i) = L_o$ in the rendering equation leads to

475
476
475

$$L_o \underset{(12.2)}{\overset{(12.7)}{=}} L_e(\vec{p}, \hat{\omega}_o) + \int_{2\pi^+} L_o f_r(\vec{p}, \hat{\omega}_o, \hat{\omega}_i) \langle \hat{n}, \hat{\omega}_i \rangle \mathrm{d}\hat{\omega}_i \overset{(12.9)}{=} L_e(\vec{p}, \hat{\omega}_o) + L_o \rho(\vec{p}, \hat{\omega}_o) \tag{14.39}$$

from which follows that the solution is valid as long as the emitted radiance and the albedo of all surfaces in the scene are locally related by

475

$$L_o = \frac{L_e(\vec{p}, \hat{\omega}_o)}{1 - \rho(\vec{p}, \hat{\omega}_o)} \overset{(12.6)}{=} L_e(T_p) \tag{14.40}$$

14.3.2 Closed Sphere

Another instance is that of the inner surface S of an empty sphere of radius r, where every
586 point of the surface is visible to every other point, and where, as illustrated in *Figure 14.5*, the identity $\cos(\theta_p) = \cos(\theta_q) = \frac{\|\vec{q}-\vec{p}\|}{2r}$ holds due to symmetry.

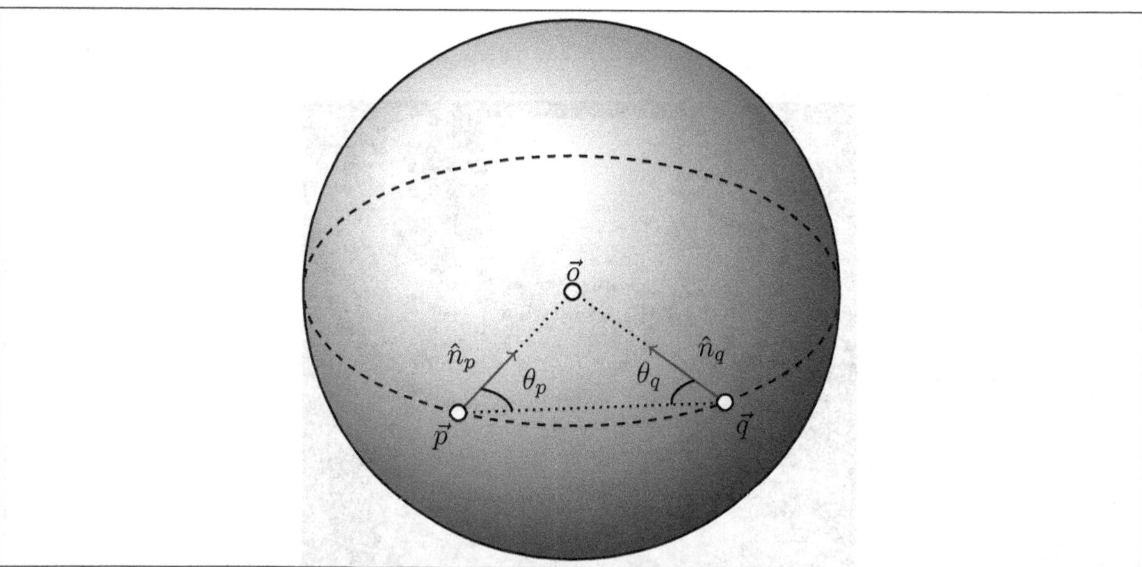

Figure 14.5: Closed Sphere: Illustration of the geometrical terms involved in analytically solving global illumination in the interior of a sphere (drawn after [Szirmay-Kalos *et al.*, 2001, Fig. 3]).

14.3.2.1 *Diffuse Surface*

564
554
499 Given a homogeneous *constant weight Lambertian* BRDF $f_r(\vec{p}, \hat{\omega}_o, \hat{\omega}_i) \overset{(13.1)}{=} \frac{\rho}{\pi}$ independent

of position and substituting $L_i(\vec{p},\hat{\omega}_i) \overset{(10.58)}{=} L_o(\vec{q},-\hat{\omega}_i)$, the expression of the direction- 427
independent reflected radiance becomes

$$L_r(\vec{p}) \overset{(12.2)}{\underset{(6.66)}{=}} \int_S L_o(\vec{q},-\widehat{pq}) \frac{\rho}{\pi} \frac{\frac{\|\vec{q}-\vec{p}\|}{2r}\frac{\|\vec{q}-\vec{p}\|}{2r}}{\|\vec{q}-\vec{p}\|^2} 1 \mathrm{d}A(\vec{q}) = \frac{\rho}{\pi}\frac{1}{4r^2}\int_S L_o(\vec{q},-\widehat{pq}) \mathrm{d}A(\vec{q}) \quad (14.41)$$

475
245

564
Given that the emitted radiance $L_e(\vec{p},\hat{\omega}_o) \overset{(13.3)}{=} L_e(\vec{p})$ is also diffuse, repeatedly substituting the expression of the exitant radiance $L_o(\vec{p},\hat{\omega}_o) = L_o(\vec{p})$ given by the rendering equation then yields

475

$$\begin{aligned}
L_o(\vec{p}) &\overset{(12.7)}{=} L_e(\vec{p}) + \frac{\rho}{\pi}\frac{1}{4r^2}\int_S L_o(\vec{q}) \, \mathrm{d}A(\vec{q}) \\
&= L_e(\vec{p}) + \frac{\rho}{\pi}\frac{1}{4r^2}\int_S L_e(\vec{q}) + \frac{\rho}{\pi}\frac{1}{4r^2}\int_S L_o(\vec{q}') \, \mathrm{d}A(\vec{q}')\mathrm{d}A(\vec{q}) \\
&= L_e(\vec{p}) + \frac{\rho}{\pi}\frac{1}{4r^2}\int_S L_e(\vec{q})\mathrm{d}A(\vec{q}) + \left(\frac{\rho}{\pi}\frac{1}{4r^2}\right)^2 \int_S \mathrm{d}A(\vec{q}) \int_S L_o(\vec{q}') \, \mathrm{d}A(\vec{q}') \\
&= L_e(\vec{p}) + \frac{\rho}{\pi}\frac{1}{4r^2}\int_S L_e(\vec{q})\mathrm{d}A(\vec{q}) + \left(\frac{\rho}{\pi}\frac{1}{4r^2}\right)^2 4\pi r^2 \int_S L_o(\vec{q}') \, \mathrm{d}A(\vec{q}') \\
&= L_e(\vec{p}) + \frac{\rho}{\pi}\frac{1}{4r^2}\int_S L_e(\vec{q})\mathrm{d}A(\vec{q}) + \frac{\rho^2}{\pi}\frac{1}{4r^2}\int_S L_o(\vec{q}') \, \mathrm{d}A(\vec{q}') \\
&= \ldots \\
&= L_e(\vec{p}) + \frac{1}{\pi}\frac{1}{4r^2}\left(\sum_{i=1}^{\infty}\rho^i\right)\int_S L_e(\vec{q})\mathrm{d}A(\vec{q}) \\
&\overset{(2.11)}{=} L_e(\vec{p}) + \frac{1}{\pi}\frac{1}{4r^2}\frac{\rho}{1-\rho}\int_S L_e(\vec{q})\mathrm{d}A(\vec{q}), \quad \forall\rho < 1 \qquad (14.42)
\end{aligned}$$

16

14.3.2.2 Mirror Surface

Instead, if the surface is an ideal mirror, then the angle of incidence at each successive bounce remains unchanged due to the symmetry of both the BRDF and the spherical geometry. Assuming the emitted radiance $L_e(\vec{p},\hat{\omega}_o) = L_e(\langle\hat{n}_p,\hat{\omega}_o\rangle)$ is solely parameterized by the cosine angle with the surface normal, and repeatedly substituting the expression of the exitant radiance $L_o(\vec{p},\hat{\omega}_o) = L_o(\langle\hat{n}_p,\hat{\omega}_o\rangle)$ given by the rendering equation then yields

$$\begin{aligned}
L_o(\langle\hat{n}_p,\hat{\omega}_o\rangle) &= L_e(\langle\hat{n}_p,\hat{\omega}_o\rangle) + \rho(\langle\hat{n}_p,\hat{\omega}_o\rangle)L_o(\langle\hat{n}_p,\hat{\omega}_o\rangle) \\
&= L_e(\langle\hat{n}_p,\hat{\omega}_o\rangle) + \rho(\langle\hat{n}_p,\hat{\omega}_o\rangle)L_e(\langle\hat{n}_p,\hat{\omega}_o\rangle) + \rho(\langle\hat{n}_p,\hat{\omega}_o\rangle)^2 L_o(\langle\hat{n}_p,\hat{\omega}_o\rangle) \\
&= \ldots \\
&= L_e(\langle\hat{n}_p,\hat{\omega}_o\rangle)\sum_{i=0}^{\infty}\rho(\langle\hat{n}_p,\hat{\omega}_o\rangle)^i \\
&\overset{(2.11)}{=} \frac{L_e(\langle\hat{n}_p,\hat{\omega}_o\rangle)}{1-\rho(\langle\hat{n}_p,\hat{\omega}_o\rangle)}, \quad \forall\rho(\langle\hat{n}_p,\hat{\omega}_o\rangle) < 1 \qquad (14.43) \\
&\overset{(12.6)}{=} L_e(T_p) \qquad (14.44)
\end{aligned}$$

16
475

CHAPTER 15

Deterministic Methods

TABLE OF CONTENTS

15.1 DIRECT ILLUMINATION

15.1.1 Volumetric Scattering

Splitting the domain of integration $[s_a, s_b]$ into n non-overlapping intervals along the ray such
465 that $s_a = s_0 < s_1 < \ldots < s_{n-1} < s_n = s_b$, the *integral form of the RTE in participating
440 *media* may be reformulated as

466
$$
\begin{aligned}
L(\vec{s}_a, \hat{\omega}) &\overset{(11.113)}{=} \sum_{j=1}^{n} \int_{s_{j-1}}^{s_j} T(\vec{s}_a, \vec{s})\kappa_t(\vec{s})L_u(\vec{s}, \hat{\omega})\mathrm{d}s + T(\vec{s}_a, \vec{s}_b)L(\vec{s}_b, \hat{\omega}) \\
&= \sum_{j=1}^{n} T(\vec{s}_0, \vec{s}_{j-1}) \int_{s_{j-1}}^{s_j} T(\vec{s}_{j-1}, \vec{s})\kappa_t(\vec{s})L_u(\vec{s}, \hat{\omega})\mathrm{d}s + T(\vec{s}_0, \vec{s}_n)L(\vec{s}_b, \hat{\omega}) \\
&= \sum_{j=1}^{n} \left(\prod_{i=1}^{j-1} T(\vec{s}_{i-1}, \vec{s}_i) \right) L_m(\vec{s}_{j-1}, \vec{s}_j, \hat{\omega}) + \left(\prod_{i=1}^{n} T(\vec{s}_{i-1}, \vec{s}_i) \right) L(\vec{s}_b, \hat{\omega}) \quad (15.1)
\end{aligned}
$$

Although the most obvious approach consists in using a fixed step size, the sampling process can be made more effective by coarsely evaluating the portions of the integration domain that are likely to have a smaller impact on the final estimate. Without any a priori knowledge about the radiance term, the size of the intervals may be optimally defined such that the cumulated opacity increases in constant steps. Doing so uniformly distributes the
132 samples in the domain of the associated *cumulative distribution*, effectively leading to coarser steps as the cumulated transmittance factor of the intervals decreases.

15.1.1.1 Constant Terms

Assuming that the source radiance is constant within the jth interval such that $L_u(\vec{s}, \hat{\omega}) = L_u[j], \forall s \in [s_{j-1}, s_j]$, as in the limit when $n \to \infty$, the medium radiance of the given segment simplifies into

467
$$
L_m(\vec{s}_{j-1}, \vec{s}_j, \hat{\omega}) \overset{(11.115)}{=} (1 - T(\vec{s}_{j-1}, \vec{s}_j))L_u[j] = O(\vec{s}_{j-1}, \vec{s}_j)L_u[j] \quad (15.2)
$$

Defining the opacity of the jth segment as $\alpha[j] \triangleq O(\vec{s}_{j-1}, \vec{s}_j)$, the individual contributions
of the various intervals can then be cumulated from the background to the sensor, yielding
590 the *back-to-front compositing* algorithm [Max, 1995] illustrated in *Algorithm 15.1*, which is
465 conceptually close to the first *integral form of the RTE*. This algorithm is most adequate to
raster-based volume rendering by alpha-blending textured slices to preserve the coherence in
execution across fragments of the screen.

Algorithm 15.1: Back-to-Front Compositing: Pseudocode for back-to-front compositing.

Data: Source radiance $L_u[]$ and discrete opacities $\alpha[]$
Result: Radiance integrated through the volume

```
Radiance L ← L_u(s_b);
for j ← n to 1 do
    L ← α[j] × L_u[j] + (1 − α[j]) × L;
end
return L
```

As an alternative, the contributions may instead be cumulated from the sensor to the
background, yielding the *front-to-back compositing* algorithm illustrated in *Algorithm 15.2*, 591
which is conceptually close to the second *integral form of the RTE*. This algorithm is most 465
adequate to ray-tracing volume densities, where, by letting $\epsilon \in (0, 1]$, the *ray marching* procedure might be allowed to prematurely abort whenever the cumulated opacity is sufficiently close to one [Levoy, 1990].

Algorithm 15.2: Front-to-Back Compositing: Pseudocode for front-to-back compositing.

Data: Source radiance $L_u[]$ and discrete opacities $\alpha[]$
Result: Radiance integrated through the volume

```
Radiance L ← 0;
Opacity O ← 0;
for j ← 1 to n do
    L ← L + (1 − O) × α[j] × L_u[j];
    O ← O + (1 − O) × α[j];
    if O > (1 − ε) then
        Go to end;
    end
end
L ← L + (1 − O) × L_u(s_b);
return L
```

As illustrated in *Figure 15.1*, the evaluation of the opacity of each interval can similarly 592
be simplified by assuming that the extinction coefficient is also piecewise constant such that
$\kappa_t(\vec{s}) = \kappa_t[j], \forall s \in [s_{j-1}, s_j]$, potentially even expanding the exponential term into a first-
order *Taylor series* to finally yield 59

463

$$\alpha[j] \overset{(11.99)}{\underset{(11.98)}{=}} 1 - e^{-(s_j - s_{j-1})\kappa_t[j]} = 1 - (1 - (s_j - s_{j-1})\kappa_t[j] + \ldots) \approx (s_j - s_{j-1})\kappa_t[j] \quad (15.3)$$

463

15.1.1.2 Linear Terms

Assuming that the extinction coefficient varies linearly within the jth interval such that

$$\kappa_t(\vec{s}) = \frac{s_j - s}{s_j - s_{j-1}}\kappa_t(\vec{s}_{j-1}) + \frac{s - s_{j-1}}{s_j - s_{j-1}}\kappa_t(\vec{s}_j) = k_1 s + k_0, \quad \forall s \in [s_{j-1}, s_j] \quad (15.4)$$

with

$$k_0 \triangleq \frac{s_j \kappa_t(\vec{s}_{j-1}) - s_{j-1}\kappa_t(\vec{s}_j)}{s_j - s_{j-1}} \quad (15.5)$$

$$k_1 \triangleq \frac{\kappa_t(\vec{s}_j) - \kappa_t(\vec{s}_{j-1})}{s_j - s_{j-1}} \quad (15.6)$$

the optical thickness along the given segment reads

463

$$\tau(\vec{s}_{j-1}, \vec{s}) \overset{(11.94)}{=} \int_{s_{j-1}}^{s} k_1 s' + k_0 \mathrm{d}s' = \left[\frac{k_1}{2}s'^2 + k_0 s'\right]_{s_{j-1}}^{s} = \frac{k_1}{2}\left(s^2 - s_{j-1}^2\right) + k_0\left(s - s_{j-1}\right) \quad (15.7)$$

Figure 15.1: Ray Marching: Illustration of direct volume rendering using ray-marching, shown at a low sampling rate based on a coarse step size (left), and at a high sampling rate based on a fine step size (right).

Additionally assuming that the source radiance is also piecewise linear such that

$$L_u(\vec{s},\hat{\omega}) = \frac{s_j - s}{s_j - s_{j-1}} L_u(\vec{s}_{j-1},\hat{\omega}) + \frac{s - s_{j-1}}{s_j - s_{j-1}} L_u(\vec{s}_j,\hat{\omega}) = l_1 s + l_0, \quad \forall s \in [s_{j-1}, s_j] \tag{15.8}$$

with

$$l_0 \triangleq \frac{s_j L_u(\vec{s}_{j-1},\hat{\omega}) - s_{j-1} L_u(\vec{s}_j,\hat{\omega})}{s_j - s_{j-1}} \tag{15.9}$$

$$l_1 \triangleq \frac{L_u(\vec{s}_j,\hat{\omega}) - L_u(\vec{s}_{j-1},\hat{\omega})}{s_j - s_{j-1}} \tag{15.10}$$

the medium radiance of the given segment then simplifies into [Williams and Max, 1992]

467

$$\begin{aligned} L_m(\vec{s}_{j-1},\vec{s}_j,\hat{\omega}) &\overset{(11.115)}{=} (l_1 s_{j-1} + l_0) - e^{-\frac{k_1}{2}(s_j^2 - s_{j-1}^2) - k_0(s_j - s_{j-1})}(l_1 s_j + l_0) \\ &+ \int_{s_{j-1}}^{s_j} e^{-\frac{k_1}{2}(s^2 - s_{j-1}^2) - k_0(s - s_{j-1})} l_1 \mathrm{d}s \\ &= (l_1 s_{j-1} + l_0) - e^{\frac{k_1}{2}s_{j-1}^2 + k_0 s_{j-1}} \left(e^{-\frac{k_1}{2}s_j^2 - k_0 s_j}(l_1 s_j + l_0) - l_1 \int_{s_{j-1}}^{s_j} e^{-\frac{k_1}{2}s^2 - k_0 s} \mathrm{d}s \right) \end{aligned} \tag{15.11}$$

56 whose closed-form solution is given by *Equation 2.279* in terms of the *error function.*

55 Such a solution is directly applicable to non-scattering media represented by an unstructured mesh of tetrahedra, within each of which both the absorption coefficient and emitted radiance vary linearly along a ray (assuming a pre-classification of the vertices shall a transfer function be used to define their optical properties), although its actual implementation requires great care in practice to avoid numerical overflow of the various exponential terms [Williams *et al.*, 1998].

15.2 GLOBAL ILLUMINATION

15.2.1 Radiosity Method

15.2.1.1 Principles

Given a scene whose surface S is composed of n patches S_i with *constant weight Lambertian* 554
BRDFs, the irradiance at a point $\vec{p}$ may be formulated as 499

$$E_e(\vec{p}) \underset{(6.70)}{\overset{(10.50)}{\overset{(10.58)}{=}}} \int_S L_o(\vec{q}, -\widehat{\vec{p}\vec{q}})G(\vec{p},\vec{q})\mathrm{d}A(\vec{q}) \overset{(13.5)}{=} \frac{1}{\pi}\sum_{j=1}^{n}\int_{S_j} J_e(\vec{q})G(\vec{p},\vec{q})\mathrm{d}A(\vec{q}) \tag{15.12}$$

426
427
564
246

Assuming that each patch has a constant radiosity $J_e(\vec{q}) = J_e[j], \forall \vec{q} \in S_j$, the expression of the average irradiance over the area A_i of patch i reads

$$\begin{aligned} E_e[i] &\triangleq \frac{1}{A_i}\int_{S_i} E_e(\vec{p})\mathrm{d}A(\vec{p}) \\ &= \frac{1}{\pi A_i}\sum_{j=1}^{n}\int_{S_i}\int_{S_j} J_e(\vec{q})G(\vec{p},\vec{q})\mathrm{d}A(\vec{q})\mathrm{d}A(\vec{p}) \qquad (15.13) \\ &= \frac{1}{\pi A_i}\sum_{j=1}^{n} J_e[j]\int_{S_i}\int_{S_j} G(\vec{p},\vec{q})\mathrm{d}A(\vec{q})\mathrm{d}A(\vec{p}) \\ &= \frac{1}{\pi A_i}\sum_{j=1}^{n} J_e[j]F_{ij} \qquad (15.14) \end{aligned}$$

where the *étendue* between patches i and j is defined by the *form factor* 421

$$F_{ij} \triangleq \int_{S_i}\int_{S_j} G(\vec{p},\vec{q})\mathrm{d}A(\vec{q})\mathrm{d}A(\vec{p}) \tag{15.15}$$

such that $F_{ij} = F_{ji}$ and

$$\begin{aligned} \sum_{j=1}^{n} F_{ij} &= \sum_{j=1}^{n}\int_{S_i}\int_{S_j} G(\vec{p},\vec{q})\mathrm{d}A(\vec{q})\mathrm{d}A(\vec{p}) \\ &= \int_{S_i}\sum_{j=1}^{n}\int_{S_j} G(\vec{p},\vec{q})\mathrm{d}A(\vec{q})\mathrm{d}A(\vec{p}) \\ &= \int_{S_i}\int_{S} G(\vec{p},\vec{q})\mathrm{d}A(\vec{q})\mathrm{d}A(\vec{p}) \\ &\overset{(6.70)}{\leq} \int_{S_i}\int_{2\pi^+} \langle \hat{n}_p, \hat{\omega}\rangle \mathrm{d}\hat{\omega}\mathrm{d}A(\vec{p}) \\ &= \pi\int_{S_i}\mathrm{d}A(\vec{p}) \\ &= \pi A_i \qquad (15.16) \end{aligned}$$

246

Similarly assuming that each patch has a constant radiant emittance $M_e(\vec{q}) = M_e[j], \forall \vec{q} \in$
S_j and a constant albedo $\rho(\vec{q}) = \rho[j], \forall \vec{q} \in S_j$, the *radiosity equation* can then be written in 564
discrete form as

$$J_e[i] \overset{(13.6)}{=} M_e[i] + \rho[i]E_e[i] \overset{(15.14)}{=} M_e[i] + \frac{\rho[i]}{\pi A_i}\sum_{j=1}^{n} F_{ij}J_e[j] \tag{15.17}$$

564
593

yielding the linear system of equations

$$
\begin{aligned}
\begin{bmatrix} J_e[1] \\ J_e[2] \\ \vdots \\ J_e[n] \end{bmatrix}
&= \begin{bmatrix} M_e[1] \\ M_e[2] \\ \vdots \\ M_e[n] \end{bmatrix}
+ \frac{1}{\pi}
\begin{bmatrix} \frac{\rho[1]}{A_1} & 0 & \dots & 0 \\ 0 & \frac{\rho[2]}{A_2} & \dots & 0 \\ \vdots & \vdots & \ddots & \vdots \\ 0 & \dots & 0 & \frac{\rho[n]}{A_n} \end{bmatrix}
\begin{bmatrix} F_{11} & F_{12} & \dots & F_{1n} \\ F_{21} & F_{22} & \dots & F_{2n} \\ \vdots & \vdots & \ddots & \vdots \\ F_{n1} & F_{n2} & \dots & F_{nn} \end{bmatrix}
\begin{bmatrix} J_e[1] \\ J_e[2] \\ \vdots \\ J_e[n] \end{bmatrix} \\
&= \begin{bmatrix} M_e[1] \\ M_e[2] \\ \vdots \\ M_e[n] \end{bmatrix}
+ \frac{1}{\pi}
\begin{bmatrix} \frac{\rho[1]}{A_1}F_{11} & \frac{\rho[1]}{A_1}F_{12} & \dots & \frac{\rho[1]}{A_1}F_{1n} \\ \frac{\rho[2]}{A_2}F_{21} & \frac{\rho[2]}{A_2}F_{22} & \dots & \frac{\rho[2]}{A_2}F_{2n} \\ \vdots & \vdots & \ddots & \vdots \\ \frac{\rho[n]}{A_n}F_{n1} & \frac{\rho[n]}{A_n}F_{n2} & \dots & \frac{\rho[n]}{A_n}F_{nn} \end{bmatrix}
\begin{bmatrix} J_e[1] \\ J_e[2] \\ \vdots \\ J_e[n] \end{bmatrix} \\
&= \begin{bmatrix} 1-\frac{\rho[1]}{\pi A_1}F_{11} & -\frac{\rho[1]}{\pi A_1}F_{12} & \dots & -\frac{\rho[1]}{\pi A_1}F_{1n} \\ -\frac{\rho[2]}{\pi A_2}F_{21} & 1-\frac{\rho[2]}{\pi A_2}F_{22} & \dots & -\frac{\rho[2]}{\pi A_2}F_{2n} \\ \vdots & \vdots & \ddots & \vdots \\ -\frac{\rho[n]}{\pi A_n}F_{n1} & -\frac{\rho[n]}{\pi A_n}F_{n2} & \dots & 1-\frac{\rho[n]}{\pi A_n}F_{nn} \end{bmatrix}^{-1}
\begin{bmatrix} M_e[1] \\ M_e[2] \\ \vdots \\ M_e[n] \end{bmatrix}
\end{aligned}
\qquad (15.18)
$$

While the system can theoretically be solved directly via matrix inversion, the associated computational cost is generally prohibitive in practice. Instead, the solution may be computed using one of various iterative schemes, whose convergence to a fixed point is favored by the diagonally dominant nature of the matrix, while its sub-unit norm (or spectral radius as per Gelfand's formula) guarantees the convergence of its expansion into a Neumann series. The system might then be solved by means of the *Jacobi iterative method*, a technique known as *classic radiosity* [Goral *et al.*, 1984], successively resolving the contributions of increasing
595 path length, as illustrated in *Algorithm 15.3.* As an alternative, the convergence rate can be increased by evaluating the radiosity values using the results computed during the previous steps of each iteration, a scheme known as the *Gauss–Seidel iterative method*, which is a
609 *gathering scheme* as each patch collects the contributions it receives from all other patches, also called *full matrix radiosity* as it involves a full matrix multiplication at each iteration, as
595 illustrated in *Algorithm 15.4.* Conversely, the radiosity of each patch may be propagated to
611 all others by means of a *shooting scheme* such as the *Southwell iterative method* illustrated in
596 *Algorithm 15.5*, a technique known as *progressive radiosity* as a single column of the matrix of form factors is involved in each iteration.

In order for the solution to be resolved more finely in regions of rapidly changing illumination, the patches representing the surfaces in the scene might be progressively refined between the iterations of the iterative solver, a technique known as *adaptive mesh refinement*, or along the edges of predicted discontinuities in the radiosity solution (e.g., shadow edges), which is then referred to as *discontinuity meshing.* Conversely, the computational cost of the evaluation scheme can be reduced by hierarchically clustering neighboring patches, a technique known as *hierarchical radiosity*, so that distant energy exchanges can be limited to the higher levels while pushing/pulling the corresponding values to/from the lower levels of the tree. As an alternative, smoother solutions may also be obtained by generalizing the piecewise-constant patch representation to higher-order basis functions.

Based on the underlying assumptions, the radiosity method is solely able to resolve ED^*L
486 paths. In order to support *specular surfaces*, the technique can be adapted by means of *extended form factors*, accounting for the indirect contributions due to one or more specular reflections, while the handling of more general reflectance properties typically necessitates some form of spatio-directional discretization. As an alternative, the transport paths unaccounted for by the radiosity method may instead be resolved during a subsequent pass using

Algorithm 15.3: Jacobi Iteration: Pseudocode for the Jacobi iterative scheme.

Data: Radiant exitance $M[]$, albedos $\rho[]$ and form factors $F[]$

Result: Radiosity of the patches

```
for i ← 1 to n do
    J[i] ← M[i];
end
for n ← 1 to pathLength do
    for i ← 1 to n do
        S ← 0;
        for j ← 1 to n do
            S ← S + F[i,j]J[j];
        end
        T[i] ← M[i] + ρ[i]S ÷ (πA_i);
    end
    for i ← 1 to n do
        J[i] ← T[i];
    end
end
return J[]
```

Algorithm 15.4: Gauss–Seidel Iteration: Pseudocode for the Gauss–Seidel iterative scheme.

Data: Radiant exitance $M[]$, albedos $\rho[]$ and form factors $F[]$

Result: Radiosity of the patches

```
for i ← 1 to n do
    J[i] ← M[i];
end
while not converged do
    for i ← 1 to n do
        S ← 0;
        for j ← 1 to n do
            S ← S + F[i,j]J[j];
        end
        J[i] ← M[i] + ρ[i]S ÷ (πA_i);
    end
end
return J[]
```

Algorithm 15.5: Southwell Iteration: Pseudocode for the Southwell iterative scheme.

```
Data: Radiant exitance M[], albedos ρ[] and form factors F[]
Result: Radiosity of the patches
for i ← 1 to n do
    J[i] ← M[i];
    ΔJ[i] ← M[i];
end
while not converged do
    j ← index of max{A_1 ΔJ[1], ..., A_n ΔJ[n]};
    for i ← 1 to n do
        S ← F[i, j] ΔJ[j];
        S ← ρ[i] S ÷ (π A_i);
        J[i] ← J[i] + S;
        ΔJ[i] ← ΔJ[i] + S;
    end
    ΔJ[j] ← 0;
end
return J[]
```

598 a *ray tracing* or *path tracing* scheme. Rather than directly visualizing the radiosity solution,
613 whose mesh resolution is typically coarser than that of the pixels on the sensor, the final
609 measurements might instead be computed by means of a *gathering scheme* based on length-
two eye paths integrating the contributions of all patches visible to the hit point along each
primary view ray, a technique known as *final gathering*. By extending the length of the eye
598 path as in recursive *ray tracing*, the approach may then be adapted to additionally capture
ES^*D^*L paths.

15.2.1.2 Further Reading

Additional material may be found in books dedicated to the radiosity method [Cohen and Wallace, 1993, Ashdown, 1994, Sillion and Puech, 1994].

CHAPTER 16

Stochastic Methods

TABLE OF CONTENTS

16.1 DIRECT ILLUMINATION

16.1.1 Ray Tracing

Based on the geometric principles of Leonardo da Vinci's perspectograph, and, even more so, on those of subsequent instruments for perspective drawing introduced during the European Renaissance [Dürer, 1525, Dürer, 1538] [Hofmann, 1990], *ray casting* generates a 2-D projection of a three-dimensional virtual scene by casting an individual ray for each pixel in the image plane. Such a primary ray, whose origin and orientation are defined by the camera model, traverses the scene in a front-to-back order. The illumination for the given pixel is then determined based on the purely local interaction of the light sources with either the material properties of the first intersected surface, or the volumetric properties of visible
440 *participating media* integrated along the overlapping ray interval.

166 In order to account for non-local shadowing effects, *ray tracing* resorts to *splitting* and
additionally traces secondary rays that evaluate the transmittance between each primary in-
431 tersection point and all *point light* sources [Appel, 1968], thereby resolving $E(D|G)L$ paths,
486 while *specular surfaces* may similarly be deterministically simulated by recursively tracing
a reflection ray and a refraction ray, effectively generating a binary ray tree additionally
598 capturing $ES^*(D|G)L$ paths [Whitted, 1979, Whitted, 1980]. As illustrated in *Figure 16.1*,
distribution ray tracing [Cook *et al.*, 1984, Cook, 1989] further extends the approach to
$E(D|G|S)^*L$ paths (including direct illumination paths of the form $E[D|G|S]L$) by stochas-
429 tically distributing the sampling rays over time, lens area, *area light* and about the specular
surface reflection and refraction directions in order to also simulate motion blur, *depth of*
662 *field*, penumbrae, gloss and translucency, respectively, in addition to resorting to jittered
sampling over pixel area for anti-aliasing [Cook, 1986, Cook, 1988, Cook, 1989].

Figure 16.1: Ray Tracing: Visual comparison of ray casting solely considering local illumination (left), against ray tracing additionally accounting for non-local shadowing effects (middle), and against distribution ray tracing also resolving partial occlusion in penumbra regions (right).

16.1.2 Material Sampling

16.1.2.1 BDF Sampling

Without any a priori knowledge about the distribution of the incident radiation, direct il-
155 lumination may be evaluated by *importance sampling* the *scattering integral* according to
569
131 a *probability density* p resembling the material's scattering function $f_{p|k}$. The integral is

therefore rewritten as

$$L_{p|k}(\vec{p}, \hat{\omega}_o) \overset{(13.34)}{=} \mathrm{E}\left[\frac{L_e(v(\vec{p}, \hat{\omega}_i), -\hat{\omega}_i) f_{p|k}(\vec{p}, \hat{\omega}_o, \hat{\omega}_i)}{p(\vec{p}, \hat{\omega}_o, \hat{\omega}_i)}\right] \tag{16.1}$$ 569

yielding the following *estimator* 139

$$\tilde{L}_{p|k}(\vec{p}, \hat{\omega}_o) = \frac{1}{n}\sum_{i=1}^{n} \frac{L_e(v(\vec{p}, \hat{\omega}_i), -\hat{\omega}_i) f_{p|k}(\vec{p}, \hat{\omega}_o, \hat{\omega}_i)}{p(\vec{p}, \hat{\omega}_o, \hat{\omega}_i)} \tag{16.2}$$

In case of an optimal *probability density* that is proportional to the scattering function, 131
the *estimator* reduces to 139

$$\tilde{L}_{p|k}(\vec{p}, \hat{\omega}_o) = \frac{1}{n}\sum_{i=1}^{n} \frac{L_e(v(\vec{p}, \hat{\omega}_i), -\hat{\omega}_i) f_{p|k}(\vec{p}, \hat{\omega}_o, \hat{\omega}_i)}{f_{p|k}(\vec{p}, \hat{\omega}_o, \hat{\omega}_i)} = \frac{1}{n}\sum_{i=1}^{n} L_e(v(\vec{p}, \hat{\omega}_i), -\hat{\omega}_i) \tag{16.3}$$

whose *variance* then reads 143

144

$$\mathrm{V}[\tilde{L}_{p|k}(\vec{p}, \hat{\omega}_o)] \overset{(4.92)}{=} \frac{1}{n}\mathrm{V}\left[L_e(v(\vec{p}, \hat{\omega}_i), -\hat{\omega}_i)\right] \tag{16.4}$$

The quality of the above *estimator* is therefore directly determined by the *variance* of the 139 143
emission term over the hemispherical domain with respect to the chosen distribution function.
It follows that this sampling strategy yields low *variance* when dealing with glossy/specular 143
surfaces illuminated by homogeneously spread visible luminaires, while *variance* will increase 143
for diffuse surfaces illuminated by heterogeneously focused partially occluded *light sources*, 429
as illustrated in *Figure 16.2*. 599

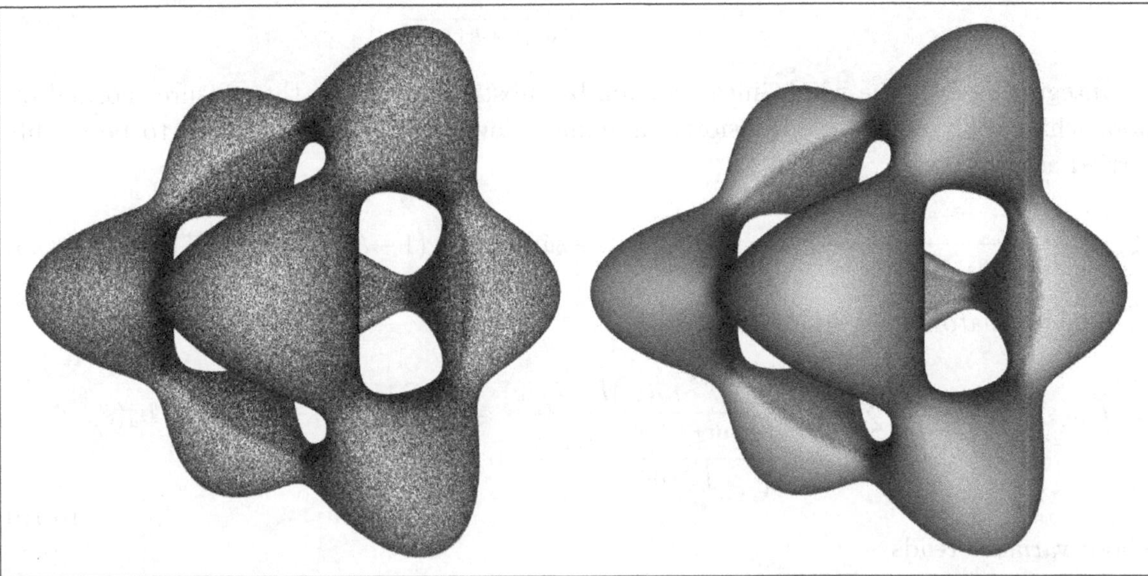

Figure 16.2: Material Sampling: Illustration of the variance resulting from direct illumination estimators based on uniform sampling (left) and importance sampling (right) of a Phong BRDF with an exponent of 10 illuminated by a uniform environmental light, both using 16 samples per pixel.

16.1.2.2 Free-Path Sampling

Medium Sampling Without any a priori knowledge about the distribution of the incident
155 radiance, direct illumination may be evaluated by *importance sampling* the medium radiance
131 integral according to a *probability density* resembling the medium's extinction distribution.
The integral is therefore rewritten as

467

$$L_m(\vec{s}_a, \vec{s}_b, \hat{\omega}) \overset{(11.114)}{=} \mathrm{E}\left[\frac{e^{-\int_{s_a}^{s} \kappa_t(\vec{s}')\mathrm{d}s'}\kappa_t(\vec{s})L_u(\vec{s}, \hat{\omega})}{p(s)}\right] \tag{16.5}$$

139 yielding the following *estimator*

$$\tilde{L}_m(\vec{s}_a, \vec{s}_b, \hat{\omega}) = \frac{1}{n}\sum_{i=1}^{n}\frac{e^{-\int_{s_a}^{s_i} \kappa_t(\vec{s}')\mathrm{d}s'}\kappa_t(\vec{s}_i)L_u(\vec{s}_i, \hat{\omega})}{p(s_i)} \tag{16.6}$$

132 Recalling that opacity relates to the *cumulative distribution* of occurrence of an extinction
131 event as radiation travels in a medium, the associated *probability density* of collision per
unit distance may be normalized over the integration domain so as to yield a so-called *forced*
interaction [Pattanaik and Mudur, 1993a, §7.1] by means of the denominator $O(\vec{p}+s_a\hat{\omega}, \vec{p}+$
131 $s_b\hat{\omega})$, such that the *probability density* becomes

$$p(s) = \frac{e^{-\int_{s_a}^{s} \kappa_t(\vec{p}+s'\hat{\omega})\mathrm{d}s'}\kappa_t(\vec{p}+s\hat{\omega})}{1-e^{-\int_{s_a}^{s_b} \kappa_t(\vec{p}+s'\hat{\omega})\mathrm{d}s'}} \tag{16.7}$$

132 whose *cumulative distribution* over the domain $[s_a, s_b]$ reads

$$P(s) = \frac{1-e^{-\tau(\vec{p}+s_a\hat{\omega}, \vec{p}+s\hat{\omega})}}{1-e^{-\tau(\vec{p}+s_a\hat{\omega}, \vec{p}+s_b\hat{\omega})}} \tag{16.8}$$

Integrating over the whole linear domain by substituting $s = s_b$ then ensures normaliza-
134 tion, while applying *inverse-transform sampling* allows *importance sampling* to be readily
155 carried as

$$\xi_s = \frac{1-e^{-\tau(\vec{p}+s_a\hat{\omega}, \vec{p}+s\hat{\omega})}}{O(\vec{p}+s_a\hat{\omega}, \vec{p}+s_b\hat{\omega})} \implies \tau(\vec{p}+s_a\hat{\omega}, \vec{p}+s\hat{\omega}) = -\ln\left(1-\xi_s O(\vec{p}+s_a\hat{\omega}, \vec{p}+s_b\hat{\omega})\right) \tag{16.9}$$

139 The *estimator* then reduces to

$$\tilde{L}_m(\vec{s}_a, \vec{s}_b, \hat{\omega}) = \frac{1}{n}\sum_{i=1}^{n}\frac{e^{-\int_{s_a}^{s_i} \kappa_t(\vec{s}')\mathrm{d}s'}\kappa_t(\vec{s}_i)L_u(\vec{s}_i, \hat{\omega})}{\frac{e^{-\int_{s_a}^{s_i} \kappa_t(\vec{p}+s'\hat{\omega})\mathrm{d}s'}\kappa_t(\vec{p}+s_i\hat{\omega})}{1-e^{-\int_{s_a}^{s_b} \kappa_t(\vec{p}+s'\hat{\omega})\mathrm{d}s'}}} = \frac{O(\vec{p}+s_a\hat{\omega}, \vec{p}+s_b\hat{\omega})}{n}\sum_{i=1}^{n}L_u(\vec{s}_i, \hat{\omega}) \tag{16.10}$$

143 whose *variance* reads

144

$$\mathrm{V}[\tilde{L}_m(\vec{s}_a, \vec{s}_b, \hat{\omega})] \overset{(4.92)}{=} \frac{O(\vec{p}+s_a\hat{\omega}, \vec{p}+s_b\hat{\omega})^2}{n}\mathrm{V}\left[L_u(\vec{s}, \hat{\omega})\right] \tag{16.11}$$

139 The quality of the above *estimator* is therefore directly determined by the *variance* of the
143 source term over the ray-segment domain with respect to the chosen distribution function.
143 It follows that this sampling strategy yields low *variance* when dealing with homogeneously
143 illuminated media, while *variance* will increase for media that are heterogeneously lit.

Medium–Background Sampling Both the medium radiance and the reduced radiance may
be evaluated via the subcritical *probability density* 131

$$p(s) = e^{-\int_{s_a}^{s} \kappa_t(\vec{p}+s'\hat{\omega})\mathrm{d}s'} \kappa_t(\vec{p}+s\hat{\omega}) \tag{16.12}$$

whose *cumulative distribution* over the domain $[s_a, \infty]$ reads 132

$$P(s) = 1 - e^{-\tau(\vec{p}+s_a\hat{\omega},\vec{p}+s\hat{\omega})} \overset{(11.98)}{=} 1 - T(\vec{s}_a, \vec{s}) \overset{(11.99)}{=} O(\vec{s}_a, \vec{s}) \tag{16.13}$$ 463 463

Integrating over the whole virtual domain by substituting $s = \infty$ then ensures normalization by assuming a virtual blackbody at infinity such that

$$T(\vec{s}_a, \vec{s}_b) \overset{(11.99)}{=} 1 - O(\vec{s}_a, \vec{s}_b) = O(\vec{s}_a, \vec{s}_\infty) - O(\vec{s}_a, \vec{s}_b) = P(\infty) - P(s_b) = \int_{s_b}^{\infty} p(s)\mathrm{d}s \tag{16.14}$$ 463

while applying *inverse-transform sampling* allows *importance sampling* to be readily carried 134
as 155

$$\xi_s = 1 - e^{-\tau(\vec{p}+s_a\hat{\omega},\vec{p}+s\hat{\omega})} \implies \tau(\vec{p}+s_a\hat{\omega}, \vec{p}+s\hat{\omega}) = -\ln(1-\xi_s) \tag{16.15}$$

The *integral form of the RTE* can then be reformulated as a single integral by rewriting 465
the transmittance term that appears in the expression of the reduced radiance as [Lafortune and Willems, 1996]

$$\begin{aligned} L(\vec{s}_a, \hat{\omega}) &\overset{(11.113)}{=} O(\vec{s}_a, \vec{s}_b) \int_{s_a}^{s_b} \frac{T(\vec{s}_a, \vec{s})\kappa_t(\vec{s})}{O(\vec{s}_a, \vec{s}_b)} L_u(\vec{s}, \hat{\omega})\mathrm{d}s + T(\vec{s}_a, \vec{s}_b)L(\vec{s}_b, \hat{\omega}) \\ &= \int_{s_a}^{s_b} p(s)L_u(\vec{s}, \hat{\omega})\mathrm{d}s + \int_{s_b}^{\infty} p(s)\mathrm{d}s L(\vec{s}_b, \hat{\omega}) \\ &= \int_{s_a}^{\infty} p(s)L_g(\vec{s}, \hat{\omega})\mathrm{d}s \end{aligned} \tag{16.16}$$ 466

where

$$L_g(\vec{s}, \hat{\omega}) = \begin{cases} L_u(\vec{s}, \hat{\omega}) & \text{if } s < s_b \\ L(\vec{s}_b, \hat{\omega}) & \text{otherwise} \end{cases} \tag{16.17}$$

It follows that the medium source radiance is sampled with *probability* $O(\vec{s}_a, \vec{s}_b)$ and 129
the background radiance with *probability* $T(\vec{s}_a, \vec{s}_b)$. Rather than repeatedly using individual 129
samples, the convergence rate of the estimation process may additionally be increased by resorting to stratified importance sampling.

Similarly, an expression for the transmittance through the medium can be formulated as

$$T(\vec{s}_a, \vec{s}_b) = \int_{s_a}^{s_b} p(s)0\mathrm{d}s + \int_{s_b}^{\infty} p(s)\mathrm{d}s1 = \int_{s_a}^{\infty} p(s)t_g(\vec{s})\mathrm{d}s \tag{16.18}$$

where

$$t_g(\vec{s}) = \begin{cases} 0 & \text{if } s < s_b \\ 1 & \text{otherwise} \end{cases} \tag{16.19}$$

It is also worth observing that because of its simultaneous appearance in both the numerator and the denominator of the estimates, the *probability density* term cancels out 131
and therefore intervenes only implicitly in the case of a gray extinction coefficient, or that of calculations carried out independently for each wavelength. However, when dealing with multiple wavelengths in parallel using a single sample distribution, the terms in the numerator and denominator generally no longer cancel out, and the distributions must be explicitly evaluated as their ratio becomes an integral part of the estimates. Although this can be done analytically in the case of a homogeneous medium, evaluating the distributions in an unbiased manner typically requires masking a subset of the wavelengths when dealing with heterogeneous media so as to solve for each wavelength separately [Raab *et al.*, 2006].

Homogeneous Media In case of a constant extinction coefficient $\kappa_t(\vec{p}) = \kappa_t$, the optical
134 depth can be evaluated in closed form and *inverse-transform sampling* may be carried out
analytically to yield

$$(s - s_a)\kappa_t = -\ln(1 - \xi_s) \quad \Longrightarrow \quad s = s_a - \frac{\ln(1 - \xi_s)}{\kappa_t} \tag{16.20}$$

464 such that the mean sample distance equals the *mean free path*

$$\mathrm{E}[S - s_a] = \mathrm{E}\left[-\frac{\ln(1 - \xi_s)}{\kappa_t}\right]$$

141
$$\overset{(4.67)}{=} -\frac{\mathrm{E}[\ln(1 - \xi_s)]}{\kappa_t}$$

141
$$\overset{(4.65)}{=} -\frac{\int_0^1 \ln(1 - \xi)\mathrm{d}\xi}{\kappa_t}$$

$$= -\frac{\lim_{\xi_s \to 1} \left[(1 - \xi)(1 - \ln(1 - \xi))\right]_0^{\xi_s}}{\kappa_t}$$

$$= -\frac{\lim_{\xi_s \to 1}(1 - \xi_s)(1 - \ln(1 - \xi_s)) - 1}{\kappa_t}$$

$$= -\frac{0 - 1}{\kappa_t}$$

$$= \frac{1}{\kappa_t}$$

465
$$\overset{(11.105)}{=} \ell \tag{16.21}$$

Heterogeneous Media Whenever the optical depth can not be evaluated or inverted analytically, it is possible to resort to a deterministic approach instead by assuming that the medium is piecewise-constant along the ray, and progressively carrying ray-marching until the cumulated optical depths of two consecutive steps in the iteration bracket the sample optical depth [Pattanaik and Mudur, 1993a, §3][Pauly *et al.*, 2000]. The associated distances may then be used to bracket the sample extinction distance itself, although the systematic error introduced by the Riemann summation process yields biased estimates.

As an alternative, *Woodcock tracking* [Woodcock *et al.*, 1965], also called fictitious interaction tracking, pseudoscattering, hole-tracking, self-scattering or delta-tracking, provides an unbiased means of stochastically simulating extinction events as can be proven by showing that $\Pr(S \leq s) = O(\vec{p} + s_a\hat{\omega}, \vec{p} + s\hat{\omega}) = P(s)$ [Coleman, 1968]. As illustrated in *Fig-*
603 *ure 16.3*, the technique is based on a conceptual abstraction that consists in introducing
444 in the medium virtual particles with unit albedo and whose *phase function* is described by
44 a Dirac *delta function* [Raab *et al.*, 2006]. Rather than being explicitly specified, the density $\kappa_t^v(\vec{s})$ of those particles is instead implicitly defined by a majoring extinction coefficient $\kappa_t^m(\vec{s}) = \kappa_t^v(\vec{s}) + \kappa_t(\vec{s}) \geq \kappa_t(\vec{s}), \forall s > s_a$ such that the corresponding majoring optical depth is analytically integrable and invertible.

135 In the spirit of *acceptance–rejection sampling*, the free path may be sampled from the
majorant distribution $p^m(s)$ defined in terms of $\kappa_t^m(\vec{s})$, and each extinction event is then
129 stochastically attributed to a real, rather than virtual, particle with *probability* $0 \leq \frac{\kappa_t(\vec{s})}{\kappa_t^m(\vec{s})} \leq$
1. More precisely, the algorithm first draws a tentative sample distance s from the envelope distribution $p^m(s)$, and then a uniformly distributed random value $\xi \in [0, 1)$. If $\xi\kappa_t^m(\vec{s}) \leq \kappa_t(\vec{s})$, the sample distance s is accepted as a realization of the real particle distribution $p(s)$,

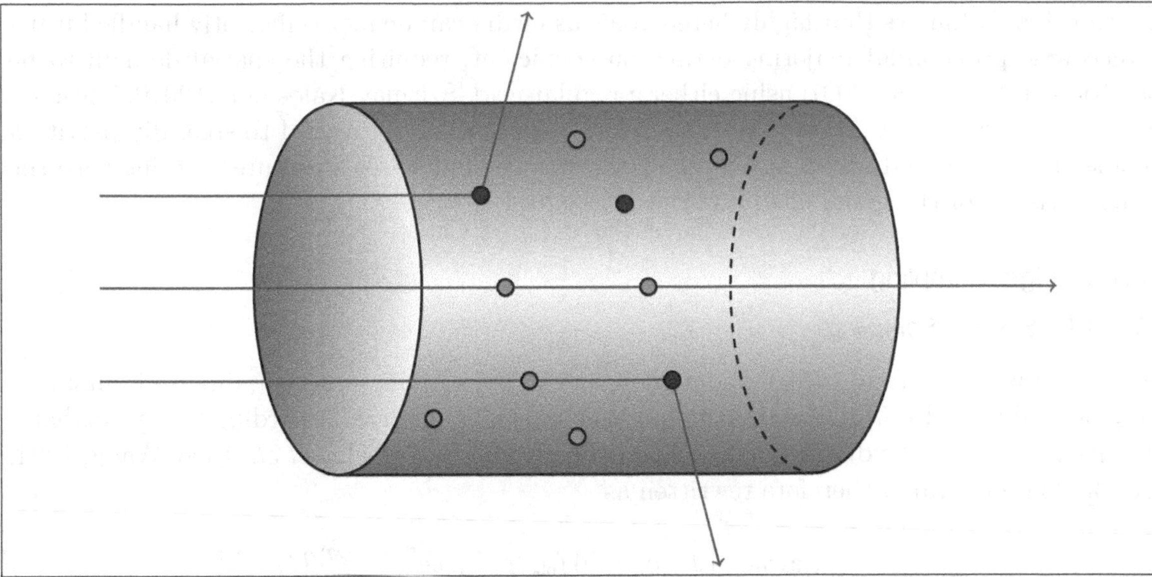

Figure 16.3: Virtual Particles: Illustration of the conceptual abstraction that Woodcock tracking is based on, i.e., the introduction in the medium of virtual particles with unit albedo and whose phase function is described by a Dirac delta distribution (drawn after [Szirmay-Kalos *et al.*, 2011, Fig. 2]).

and it is rejected otherwise, effectively attributing the collision to the virtual particles, which leaves the properties of the beam unaffected such that the process repeats from the current sample location until either a real collision event occurs or until the ray leaves the medium, as illustrated in *Figure 16.4*. 603

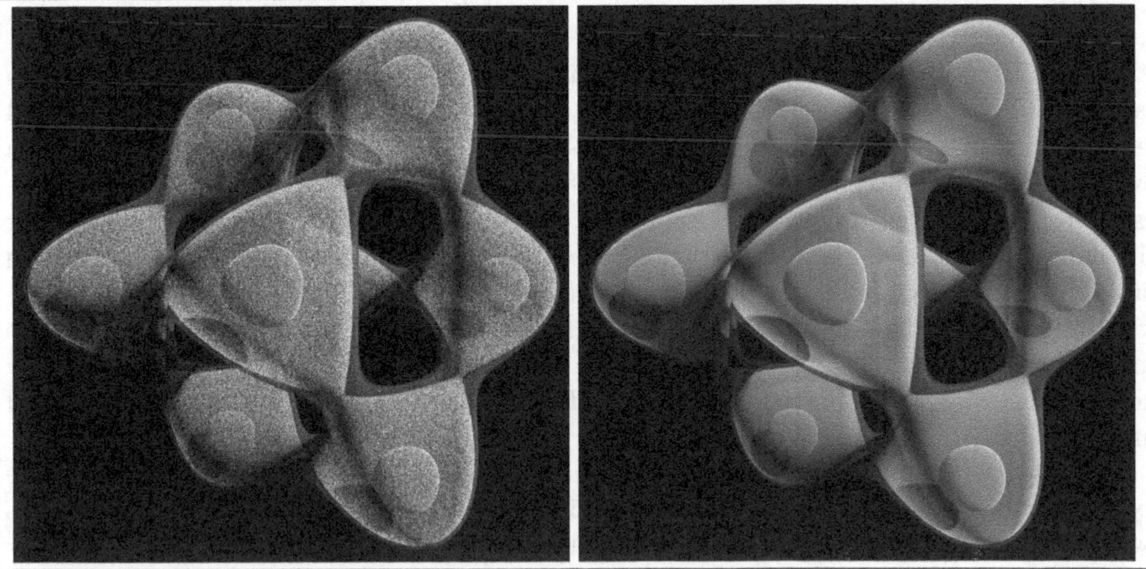

Figure 16.4: Woodcock Tracking: Illustration of direct volume rendering using Woodcock tracking, shown both at a low (left) and at a high (right) sampling rate.

Rather than resorting to high-order density representations, the majorant distribution is often described by a constant or trilinear extinction coefficient. As in *acceptance–rejection sampling*, though, the efficiency of the algorithm directly depends on the acceptance *prob-* 135
ability of the collision events, and therefore on the proximity of the majorant to the target 129

distribution. It follows that highly heterogeneous media can be more efficiently handled using
a piecewise polynomial majoring extinction coefficient, requiring the spatial domain to be
369 partitioned [Leppänen, 2007] using either a regular *grid* [Szirmay-Kalos *et al.*, 2010, Szirmay-
381 Kalos *et al.*, 2011], a *k-D tree* [Yue *et al.*, 2010] (potentially also used to spatially partition
378 geometric data as well) or an *octree*, the performance of all three structures varying with the
characteristics of the given medium [Yue *et al.*, 2011].

16.1.3 Light Sampling

16.1.3.1 Surface Sampling

Without any a priori knowledge about the material's scattering function, direct illumination
155 569 may be evaluated by *importance sampling* the *scattering integral* according to a *probability*
131 *density* resembling the distribution of the incident radiation [Shirley *et al.*, 1996, Wang, 1994,
Ch. 3]. The integral is therefore rewritten as

569
$$L_{p|k}(\vec{p},\hat{\omega}_o) \overset{(13.35)}{=} \mathrm{E}\left[\frac{L_e(\vec{q},-\widehat{pq})f_{p|k}(\vec{p},\hat{\omega}_o,\widehat{pq})\frac{\langle\hat{n}_q,-\widehat{pq}\rangle}{\|\vec{q}-\vec{p}\|^2}T(\vec{p},\vec{q})}{p(\vec{q})}\right] \tag{16.22}$$

139 with $\vec{q}\in S_e$, yielding the following *estimator*

$$\tilde{L}_{p|k}(\vec{p},\hat{\omega}_o) = \frac{1}{n}\sum_{i=1}^{n}\frac{L_e(\vec{q}_i,-\widehat{pq_i})f_{p|k}(\vec{p},\hat{\omega}_o,\widehat{pq_i})\frac{\langle\hat{n}_q,-\widehat{pq_i}\rangle}{\|\vec{q}_i-\vec{p}\|^2}T(\vec{p},\vec{q}_i)}{p(\vec{q}_i)} \tag{16.23}$$

143 whose *variance* then reads

144
$$\mathrm{V}[\tilde{L}_{p|k}(\vec{p},\hat{\omega}_o)] \overset{(4.92)}{=} \frac{1}{n}\mathrm{V}\left[\frac{L_e(\vec{q},-\widehat{pq})f_{p|k}(\vec{p},\hat{\omega}_o,\widehat{pq})\frac{\langle\hat{n}_q,-\widehat{pq}\rangle}{\|\vec{q}-\vec{p}\|^2}T(\vec{p},\vec{q})}{p(\vec{q})}\right] \tag{16.24}$$

236 Resorting to the area sampling procedures introduced for *analytic surfaces*, the estimation
can be readily carried by uniformly drawing a sample point on the light's surface of area A
131 with a constant *probability density* $p(\vec{q}) = 1 \div A$. Aside from the variations of the emission
over the light's surface and that of the transmittance/visibility, the quality of the above
139 143 *estimator* is therefore directly determined by the *variance* of the scattering function over
244 the subtended *solid angle* as well that of the geometric term with respect to the chosen
distribution function. It follows that this sampling strategy yields low variance when dealing
with diffuse surfaces illuminated by distant homogeneously focused visible luminaires that are
roughly planar, while variance will increase for glossy/specular surfaces illuminated by nearby
429 heterogeneously spread, partially occluded *light sources* with high curvature, as illustrated
605 in *Figure 16.5*.

143 In order to reduce *variance*, the local characteristics of the light's surface may first be
exploited to remove from the transmittance/visibility term the variations due to the light's
own geometry. Mathematically, this entails restricting the domain of integration to $S_{ev}(\vec{p}) =$
$S_e \backslash S_{env}(\vec{p})$, where $S_{env}(\vec{p}) \mid T(\vec{p},\vec{q}) = 0, \forall\vec{q}\in S_{env}(\vec{p})$ is the set of emissive surfaces that are
429 a priori occluded from $\vec{p}$. Considering, for instance, the case of a spherical *light source* of
radius r and center $\vec{c}$ illuminating a point $\vec{p}$ not contained within it such that $r < \|\vec{c}-\vec{p}\|$,
272 $\vec{q}_i$ can be uniformly drawn from the *spherical cap* of radius r centered in $\vec{c}$ of apex angle
269 $\theta_a = \arccos(r \div \|\vec{c}-\vec{p}\|)$ visible to $\vec{p}$ rather than from the remaining portion of the *sphere*
605 that is a priori known to be occluded from $\vec{p}$, as illustrated in *Figure 16.5*. Assuming a non-
emissive interior to avoid the special handling of regions to which the extremities are visible,
a similar strategy may also be devised for cylindrical luminaires of radius r [Zimmerman,

1995] by restricting the uniform sampling domain to the partial *cylinder* of apex angle $\theta_a =$ 272
$\arccos(r \div d)$ visible to $\vec{p}$, where d is the distance from $\vec{p}$ to the *cylinder*'s axis, as illustrated 272
in *Figure 16.6*. 606

The *probability density* can additionally be made proportional to the geometric term by 131
instead implicitly drawing $\vec{q} = v(\vec{p}, \hat{\omega}_i)$ as the first intersection of the light's surface with a
ray of origin $\vec{p}$ and oriented in a direction $\hat{\omega}_i \in \Omega$ that is sampled with PDF $p(\vec{p}, \hat{\omega}_o, \hat{\omega}_i)$ in the
solid angle Ω subtended at point $\vec{p}$ by the *light source*. Defining $p(\vec{q}) \overset{(6.69)}{=} p(\vec{p}, \hat{\omega}_o, \widehat{pq}) \frac{\langle \hat{n}_q, -\widehat{pq} \rangle}{\|\vec{q}-\vec{p}\|^2}$, 245 244 429
the *estimator* reduces to 139

$$
\begin{aligned}
\tilde{L}_{p|k}(\vec{p}, \hat{\omega}_o) &= \frac{1}{n} \sum_{i=1}^{n} \frac{L_e(\vec{q}_i, -\widehat{pq_i}) f_{p|k}(\vec{p}, \hat{\omega}_o, \widehat{pq_i}) \frac{\langle \hat{n}_q, -\widehat{pq_i} \rangle}{\|\vec{q}_i - \vec{p}\|^2} T(\vec{p}, \vec{q}_i)}{p(\vec{p}, \hat{\omega}_o, \hat{\omega}_i) \frac{\langle \hat{n}_q, -\widehat{pq_i} \rangle}{\|\vec{q}_i - \vec{p}\|^2}} \\
&= \frac{1}{n} \sum_{i=1}^{n} \frac{L_e(\vec{q}_i, -\widehat{pq_i}) f_{p|k}(\vec{p}, \hat{\omega}_o, \widehat{pq_i}) T(\vec{p}, \vec{q}_i)}{p(\vec{p}, \hat{\omega}_o, \hat{\omega}_i)} \qquad (16.25)
\end{aligned}
$$

whose *variance* then reads 143

144

$$
\mathrm{V}[\tilde{L}_{p|k}(\vec{p}, \hat{\omega}_o)] \overset{(4.92)}{=} \frac{1}{n} \mathrm{V}\left[\frac{L_e(\vec{q}, -\widehat{pq}) f_{p|k}(\vec{p}, \hat{\omega}_o, \widehat{pq}) T(\vec{p}, \vec{q})}{p(\vec{p}, \hat{\omega}_o, \hat{\omega}_i)} \right] \qquad (16.26)
$$

Aside from the variations of the emission over the light's surface and that of the trans-
mittance/visibility, the quality of the above *estimator* is therefore directly determined by 139
the *variance* of the scattering function over the subtended *solid angle* with respect to the 143
chosen distribution function. It follows that this sampling strategy yields low *variance* when 244 143
dealing with diffuse surfaces illuminated by homogeneously focused visible luminaires, while
variance will increase for glossy/specular surfaces illuminated by heterogeneously spread, 143
partially occluded *light sources*, as illustrated in *Figure 16.5*. 429 605

Figure 16.5: Light Sampling: Illustration of the variance resulting from direct illumination estimators that draw a point on the light's surface based on uniform area sampling (left), uniform sampling of the area visible to the point being illuminated (middle), and uniform sampling of the solid angle subtended at the point being illuminated (right), all using 16 samples per pixel.

Considering again the case of a spherical *light source* of radius r and center $\vec{c}$ illuminating 429
a point $\vec{p}$ not contained within it such that $r < \|\vec{c} - \vec{p}\|$, $\vec{q}_i$ may instead be uniformly drawn
with PDF $p(\vec{p}, \hat{\omega}_o, \hat{\omega}_i) = 1 \div \Omega$ by first sampling a direction from the *spherical cap* of unit 272
radius centered in $\vec{p}$ with apex angle $\theta_a = \arcsin(r \div \|\vec{c} - \vec{p}\|)$ [Shirley and Wang, 1991, Wang,
1992] as illustrated in *Figure 16.6*, and then determining the coordinates of $\vec{q}_i$ by clamping the 606

269 term under the square root to zero in the *geometric intersection* test shall it be negative due
to numerical precision errors. A similar strategy can also be devised for triangular luminaires
255 by uniformly sampling the subtended *spherical triangle* and then computing the intersection
247 250 of the corresponding ray with the *plane* defined by the *triangle*.

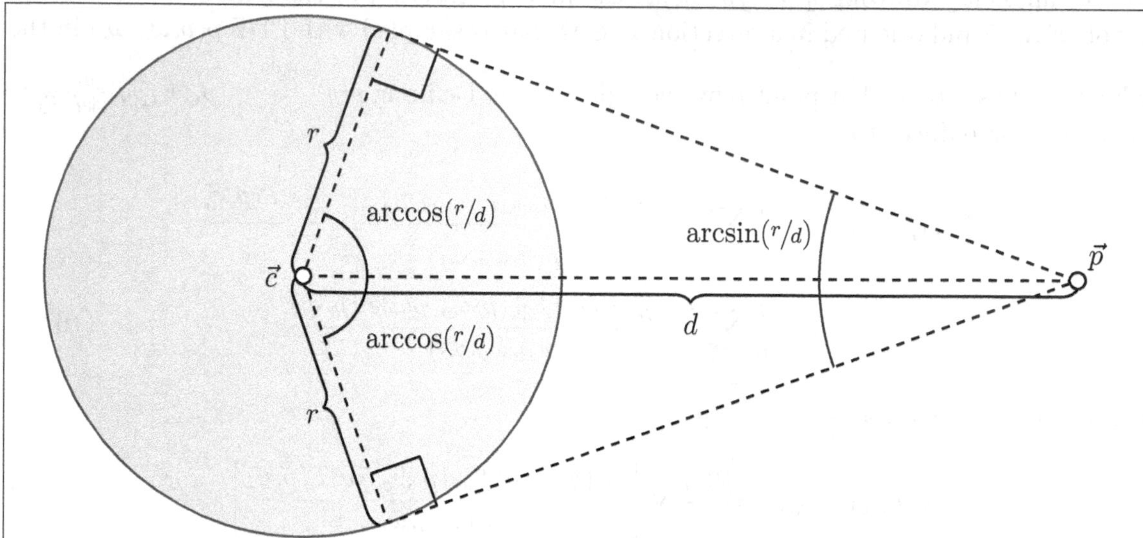

Figure 16.6: Visible Circular Sampling: Geometric terms involved in sampling the subset of the surface of a sphere or cylinder that is visible from a point (drawn after [Shirley and Wang, 1991, Fig. 3], [Wang, 1992, Fig. 2] and [Zimmerman, 1995, Fig. 2]).

16.1.3.2 Emission Sampling

143 In the case of a heterogeneous luminaire, *variance* may be reduced by defining the *probability*
131 *density* to be proportional to the emission term over the light's surface

$$p(\vec{p},\hat{\omega}_o,\hat{\omega}_i) \triangleq \frac{L_e(v(\vec{p},\hat{\omega}_i),-\hat{\omega}_i)}{\int_\Omega L_e(v(\vec{p},\hat{\omega}_i),-\hat{\omega}_i)\mathrm{d}\hat{\omega}_i} \tag{16.27}$$

244 where Ω is the *solid angle* subtended by the *light source* at point $\vec{p}$.
429 139 The *estimator* then reduces to

605

$$\begin{aligned}\tilde{L}_{p|k}(\vec{p},\hat{\omega}_o) &\overset{(16.25)}{=} \frac{1}{n}\sum_{i=1}^{n}\frac{L_e(\vec{q}_i,-\widehat{pq_i})f_{p|k}(\vec{p},\hat{\omega}_o,\widehat{pq_i})T(\vec{p},\vec{q}_i)}{\frac{L_e\left(v(\vec{p},\hat{\omega}_i),-\hat{\omega}_i\right)}{\int_\Omega L_e\left(v(\vec{p},\hat{\omega}_i),-\hat{\omega}_i\right)\mathrm{d}\hat{\omega}_i}} \\ &= \frac{\int_\Omega L_e(v(\vec{p},\hat{\omega}_i),-\hat{\omega}_i)\mathrm{d}\hat{\omega}_i}{n}\sum_{i=1}^{n} f_{p|k}(\vec{p},\hat{\omega}_o,\widehat{pq_i})T(\vec{p},\vec{q}_i)\end{aligned} \tag{16.28}$$

143 whose *variance* reads

144

$$\mathrm{V}[\tilde{L}_{p|k}(\vec{p},\hat{\omega}_o)] \overset{(4.92)}{=} \frac{\left(\int_\Omega L_e(v(\vec{p},\hat{\omega}_i),-\hat{\omega}_i)\mathrm{d}\hat{\omega}_i\right)^2}{n}\mathrm{V}\left[f_{p|k}(\vec{p},\hat{\omega}_o,\widehat{pq})T(\vec{p},\vec{q})\right] \tag{16.29}$$

Aside from the variations of the transmittance/visibility, the quality of the above *esti-*
139 *mator* is therefore directly determined by the *variance* of the scattering function over the
143 subtended *solid angle* with respect to the chosen distribution function. It follows that this
244 143 sampling strategy yields low *variance* when dealing with diffuse surfaces illuminated by visible

luminaires, while *variance* will increase for glossy/specular surfaces illuminated by partially occluded light sources. 143

As illustrated in *Figure 16.7*, the reduction in *variance* achieved by this sampling strategy 607 143
is most substantial when dealing with highly heterogeneous luminaires. This is especially relevant in the context of illumination by an HDR *environmental light.* 433

Figure 16.7: Emission Sampling: Illustration of the variance resulting from direct illumination estimators based on uniform sampling (left) and importance sampling (right) of an environmental light illuminating a Lambertian BRDF, both using 16 samples per pixel (light probe courtesy of Paul Debevec).

16.1.3.3 Lit-Path Sampling

Without any a priori knowledge about the medium's extinction distribution, direct illumination may be evaluated by *importance sampling* the medium radiance integral according 155
to a *probability density* resembling the distribution of the incident radiation [Kulla and Fa- 131
jardo, 2011, Kulla and Fajardo, 2012]. Considering, for instance, the case of a non-emissive participating medium illuminated by a *point light* source of radiant intensity $I_o(\hat{\omega})$ located 431
at position $\vec{p}_l$, the source radiance reduces to

$$L_u(\vec{p},\hat{\omega}) \overset{(11.9)}{\underset{(14.10)}{=}} \rho_p(\vec{p}) f_p(\vec{p},\hat{\omega},\widehat{pp_l}) \frac{T(\vec{p},\vec{p}_l)}{\|\vec{p}_l-\vec{p}\|^2} I_o(-\widehat{pp_l}) \tag{16.30}$$

444 577

and the integral is therefore rewritten as

$$L_m(\vec{s}_a,\vec{s}_b,\hat{\omega}) \overset{(11.114)}{=} \mathrm{E}\left[\frac{e^{-\int_{s_a}^{s}\kappa_t(\vec{s}')\mathrm{d}s'}\kappa_t(\vec{s})\rho_p(\vec{s}) f_p(\vec{s},\hat{\omega},\widehat{sp_l}) \frac{T(\vec{s},\vec{p}_l)}{\|\vec{p}_l-\vec{s}\|^2} I_o(-\widehat{sp_l})}{p(s)}\right] \tag{16.31}$$

467

yielding the following *estimator* 139

$$\tilde{L}_m(\vec{s}_a,\vec{s}_b,\hat{\omega}) = \frac{1}{n}\sum_{i=1}^{n}\frac{e^{-\int_{s_a}^{s_i}\kappa_t(\vec{s}')\mathrm{d}s'}\kappa_t(\vec{s}_i)\rho_p(\vec{s}_i) f_p(\vec{s}_i,\hat{\omega},\widehat{s_ip_l}) \frac{T(\vec{s}_i,\vec{p}_l)}{\|\vec{p}_l-\vec{s}_i\|^2} I_o(-\widehat{s_ip_l})}{p(s_i)} \tag{16.32}$$

131 Defining the *probability density* to be proportional to the reciprocal squared distance yields

$$p(s) \triangleq \frac{h}{\arctan\left(\frac{s_b - s_h}{h}\right) - \arctan\left(\frac{s_a - s_h}{h}\right)} \frac{1}{h^2 + (s - s_h)^2} \tag{16.33}$$

where $h > 0$ is the distance from the light to the given ray and s_h the coordinate of its
132 projection onto it. Its *cumulative distribution* over the domain $[s_a, s_b]$ therefore reads

132

$$\begin{aligned} P(s) &\overset{(4.21)}{=} \int_{s_a}^{s} \frac{h}{\arctan\left(\frac{s_b - s_h}{h}\right) - \arctan\left(\frac{s_a - s_h}{h}\right)} \frac{1}{h^2 + (s' - s_h)^2} \mathrm{d}s' \\ &= \left[\frac{\arctan\left(\frac{s' - s_h}{h}\right)}{\arctan\left(\frac{s_b - s_h}{h}\right) - \arctan\left(\frac{s_a - s_h}{h}\right)} \right]_{s_a}^{s} \\ &= \frac{\arctan\left(\frac{s - s_h}{h}\right) - \arctan\left(\frac{s_a - s_h}{h}\right)}{\arctan\left(\frac{s_b - s_h}{h}\right) - \arctan\left(\frac{s_a - s_h}{h}\right)} \end{aligned} \tag{16.34}$$

Integrating over the whole linear domain by substituting $s = s_b$ then ensures normaliza-
134 tion, while applying *inverse-transform sampling* allows *importance sampling* to be readily
155 carried as

$$\xi_s = \frac{\theta(s) - \theta(s_a)}{\theta(s_b) - \theta(s_a)} \implies s = s_h + h \tan\Big(\theta(s_a) + \xi_s(\theta(s_b) - \theta(s_a))\Big) \tag{16.35}$$

where $\theta(s) = \arctan\left(\frac{s - s_h}{h}\right)$, thereby resulting in a uniform sampling of the angular extent subtended by the ray segment $[\vec{s}_a, \vec{s}_b]$ at point $\vec{p}_l$.
139 The *estimator* then reduces to

$$\begin{aligned} \tilde{L}_m(\vec{s}_a, \vec{s}_b, \hat{\omega}) &= \frac{1}{n} \sum_{i=1}^{n} \frac{e^{-\int_{s_a}^{s_i} \kappa_t(\vec{s}')\mathrm{d}s'} \kappa_t(\vec{s}_i) L_u(\vec{s}_i, \hat{\omega})}{\frac{h}{\theta(s_b) - \theta(s_a)} \frac{1}{h^2 + (s_i - s_h)^2}} \\ &= \frac{\theta(s_b) - \theta(s_a)}{hn} \sum_{i=1}^{n} e^{-\int_{s_a}^{s_i} \kappa_t(\vec{s}')\mathrm{d}s'} \kappa_t(\vec{s}_i) \|\vec{p}_l - \vec{s}_i\|^2 L_u(\vec{s}_i, \hat{\omega}) \end{aligned} \tag{16.36}$$

143 whose *variance* reads

144

$$\mathrm{V}[\tilde{L}_m(\vec{s}_a, \vec{s}_b, \hat{\omega})] \overset{(4.92)}{=} \frac{\big(\theta(s_b) - \theta(s_a)\big)^2}{h^2 n} \mathrm{V}\left[e^{-\int_{s_a}^{s} \kappa_t(\vec{s}')\mathrm{d}s'} \kappa_t(\vec{s}) \|\vec{p}_l - \vec{s}\|^2 L_u(\vec{s}, \hat{\omega})\right] \tag{16.37}$$

139 Aside from the variations of $\|\vec{p}_l - \vec{p}\|^2 L_u(\vec{p}, \hat{\omega})$, the quality of the above *estimator* is
143 therefore directly determined by the *variance* of the transmittance and extinction term over the ray-segment domain with respect to the chosen distribution function. It follows that this
143 sampling strategy yields low *variance* when dealing with smoothly varying thin media that
143 are homogeneously illuminated, while *variance* will increase for fluctuating thick media that are heterogeneously lit.
429 Finally, the approach can also be extended to *area light* sources by first drawing a sample position on the light's surface, either by sampling its geometry or its emission, and then performing equi-angular sampling along the ray with respect to the chosen surface position.

16.1.4 Combined Sampling

598 In order to exploit the complementary strengths and weaknesses of implicit *material sampling*
604 and explicit *light sampling* of direct illumination [Shirley and Wang, 1992], the two strategies
158 may be combined via *multiple importance sampling* [Veach and Guibas, 1995, Veach, 1997,
609 Ch. 9] as illustrated in *Figure 16.8*. Because the first *probability density* is generally expressed
131
244 over *solid angles* while the second might be expressed over surface area, *combined sampling*
157 typically requires their conversion into an identical space measure by means of *Equation 6.69*.
245

Figure 16.8: Combined Sampling: Illustration of the variance resulting from direct illumination estimators based on material importance sampling, light importance sampling and multiple importance sampling (from left to right, respectively), using a Phong BRDF with an exponent of 10 illuminated by an environmental light (top, light probe courtesy of Paul Debevec) and using a Lambertian BRDF and an area light source (bottom), all using 16 samples per pixel.

16.2 GLOBAL ILLUMINATION

16.2.1 Overview

The *measurement equation* may be evaluated by formulating each term in the series as the 566
expected value $M_n = \mathrm{E}[\tilde{M}_n]$ of an *estimator* of the form 141 139

$$\tilde{M}_n \underset{(4.158)}{\overset{(13.23)}{=}} \frac{W_e(\vec{p}_0 \to \vec{p}_1)F(\vec{p}_0, \ldots, \vec{p}_n)L_e(\vec{p}_n \to \vec{p}_{n-1})}{p(\vec{p}_0, \ldots, \vec{p}_n)} \tag{16.38}$$

566 156

with a given joint *probability density* p. Rather than drawing each sample point independently via a separable PDF 131

$$p(\vec{p}_0, \ldots, \vec{p}_n) \overset{(4.19)}{=} \prod_{i=0}^{n} p(\vec{p}_i) \tag{16.39}$$

132

reductions in *variance* can be achieved by resorting to *importance sampling*. Akin to the use 143
of Markov chains to solve *integral equations* in the fields of neutron transport and radiative 155 150
heat transfer, the PDF is then constructed by means of a random walk through the scene.

16.2.1.1 Gathering Scheme

Defining a state as a surface position and incident direction, a *gathering scheme* gathers radiance by shooting importance particles "backward" from the sensor towards the luminaires based on directional PDFs of the form

$$p(\widehat{\vec{p}_{i-1}\vec{p}_i} \mid \vec{p}_m, \ldots, \vec{p}_{i-1}) \triangleq f(\vec{p}_{i-1} \to \vec{p}_i)\langle \hat{n}_{\vec{p}_{i-1}}, \widehat{\vec{p}_{i-1}\vec{p}_i}\rangle, \quad \forall i \in [m+1, n] \tag{16.40}$$

such that the transition PDF over surfaces from one state of the Markov chain to the next reads

245

$$p(\vec{p}_i \mid \vec{p}_m, \ldots, \vec{p}_{i-1}) \overset{(6.69)}{=} p(\widehat{\vec{p}_{i-1}\vec{p}_i} \mid \vec{p}_0, \ldots, \vec{p}_{i-1}) \frac{\langle \hat{n}_{\vec{p}_i}, -\widehat{\vec{p}_{i-1}\vec{p}_i}\rangle}{\|\vec{p}_i - \vec{p}_{i-1}\|^2} T(\vec{p}_{i-1}, \vec{p}_i)$$

610

$$\overset{(16.40)}{=} f(\vec{p}_{i-1} \to \vec{p}_i)\langle \hat{n}_{\vec{p}_{i-1}}, \widehat{\vec{p}_{i-1}\vec{p}_i}\rangle \frac{\langle \hat{n}_{\vec{p}_i}, -\widehat{\vec{p}_{i-1}\vec{p}_i}\rangle}{\|\vec{p}_i - \vec{p}_{i-1}\|^2} T(\vec{p}_{i-1}, \vec{p}_i)$$

246

$$\overset{(6.71)}{=} f(\vec{p}_{i-1} \to \vec{p}_i) G(\vec{p}_{i-1}, \vec{p}_i), \quad \forall i \in [m+1, n] \tag{16.41}$$

131 Given the PDF of the initial state $p(\vec{p}_m)$, the overall *probability density* of the chain in path space then reads

132

$$\begin{aligned} p(\vec{p}_m, \ldots, \vec{p}_n) &\overset{(4.18)}{=} p(\vec{p}_m, \ldots, \vec{p}_{n-1}) p(\vec{p}_n \mid \vec{p}_m, \ldots, \vec{p}_{n-1}) \\ &= \vdots \\ &= p(\vec{p}_m) \prod_{i=m+1}^{n} p(\vec{p}_i \mid \vec{p}_m, \ldots, \vec{p}_{i-1}) \end{aligned}$$

610

$$\overset{(16.41)}{=} p(\vec{p}_m) \prod_{i=m+1}^{n} f(\vec{p}_{i-1} \to \vec{p}_i) G(\vec{p}_{i-1}, \vec{p}_i) \tag{16.42}$$

and the score associated with the random walk is thus defined as

$$W_j \triangleq \frac{W_e(\vec{p}_0 \to \vec{p}_1) F(\vec{p}_0, \ldots, \vec{p}_j)}{p(\vec{p}_0, \ldots, \vec{p}_j)}$$

567
610

$$\underset{(16.42)}{\overset{(13.24)}{=}} \frac{W_e(\vec{p}_0 \to \vec{p}_1) G(\vec{p}_0, \vec{p}_1) \prod_{i=2}^{j} f_r(\vec{p}_{i-2}, \vec{p}_{i-1}, \vec{p}_i) G(\vec{p}_{i-1}, \vec{p}_i)}{p(\vec{p}_0) f(\vec{p}_0 \to \vec{p}_1) G(\vec{p}_0, \vec{p}_1) \prod_{i=2}^{j} f(\vec{p}_{i-1} \to \vec{p}_i) G(\vec{p}_{i-1}, \vec{p}_i)}$$

$$= \frac{W_e(\vec{p}_0 \to \vec{p}_1)}{p(\vec{p}_0) f(\vec{p}_0 \to \vec{p}_1)} \prod_{i=2}^{j} \frac{f_r(\vec{p}_{i-2}, \vec{p}_{i-1}, \vec{p}_i)}{f(\vec{p}_{i-1} \to \vec{p}_i)}, \quad \forall j \in [1, n] \tag{16.43}$$

Given the potential density and aggregate potential of the sensor

$$W_e(\vec{p}_0) \triangleq \int_{\Omega} W_e(\vec{p}_0, \hat{\omega}) \langle \hat{n}_{\vec{p}_0}, \hat{\omega}\rangle \mathrm{d}\hat{\omega} \tag{16.44}$$

$$W_e \triangleq \int_{S} W_e(\vec{p}) \mathrm{d}A(\vec{p}) \tag{16.45}$$

155 ideal *importance sampling* of the initial and secondary states is defined by the spatial and directional distributions

$$p(\vec{p}_0) \triangleq \frac{W_e(\vec{p}_0)}{W_e} \tag{16.46}$$

$$f(\vec{p}_0 \to \vec{p}_1) \triangleq \frac{W_e(\vec{p}_0 \to \vec{p}_1)}{W_e(\vec{p}_0)} \tag{16.47}$$

while that of the subsequent states is given by the directional transition distributions

475

$$f(\vec{p}_{i-1} \to \vec{p}_i) \overset{(12.4)}{=} \frac{f_r(\vec{p}_{i-2}, \vec{p}_{i-1}, \vec{p}_i)}{\rho(\vec{p}_{i-1}, \widehat{\vec{p}_{i-1}\vec{p}_{i-2}})}, \quad \forall i \in [2, n] \tag{16.48}$$

in which case the expression of the score reduces to

$$W_j \overset{(16.43)}{=} W_e \prod_{i=2}^{j} \rho(\vec{p}_{i-1}, \widehat{p_{i-1}p_{i-2}}), \quad \forall j \in [1, n] \tag{16.49}$$ 610

16.2.1.2 Shooting Scheme

Defining a state as a surface position and incident direction, a *shooting scheme* gathers importance by shooting light particles "forward" from the luminaires towards the sensor based on directional PDFs of the form

$$p(\widehat{p_{i+1}p_i} \mid \vec{p}_{i+1}, \ldots, \vec{p}_n) \triangleq f(\vec{p}_{i+1} \to \vec{p}_i)\langle \hat{n}_{p_{i+1}}, \widehat{p_{i+1}p_i} \rangle, \quad \forall i \in [0, n-1] \tag{16.50}$$

such that the transition PDF over surfaces from one state of the Markov chain to the next reads

$$p(\vec{p}_i \mid \vec{p}_{i+1}, \ldots, \vec{p}_n) \overset{(6.69)}{=} p(\widehat{p_{i+1}p_i} \mid \vec{p}_{i+1}, \ldots, \vec{p}_n) \frac{\langle \hat{n}_{p_i}, -\widehat{p_{i+1}p_i} \rangle}{\|\vec{p}_i - \vec{p}_{i+1}\|^2} T(\vec{p}_{i+1}, \vec{p}_i)$$ 245

$$\overset{(16.50)}{=} f(\vec{p}_{i+1} \to \vec{p}_i)\langle \hat{n}_{p_{i+1}}, \widehat{p_{i+1}p_i} \rangle \frac{\langle \hat{n}_{p_i}, -\widehat{p_{i+1}p_i} \rangle}{\|\vec{p}_i - \vec{p}_{i+1}\|^2} T(\vec{p}_{i+1}, \vec{p}_i)$$ 611

$$\overset{(6.71)}{=} f(\vec{p}_{i+1} \to \vec{p}_i) G(\vec{p}_{i+1}, \vec{p}_i), \quad \forall i \in [0, n-1] \tag{16.51}$$ 246

Given the PDF of the initial state $p(\vec{p}_n)$, the overall *probability density* of the chain in 131
path space then reads

$$p(\vec{p}_m, \ldots, \vec{p}_n) \overset{(4.18)}{=} p(\vec{p}_{m+1}, \ldots, \vec{p}_n) p(\vec{p}_m \mid \vec{p}_{m+1}, \ldots, \vec{p}_n)$$ 132

$$= \vdots$$

$$= p(\vec{p}_n) \prod_{i=m}^{n-1} p(\vec{p}_i \mid \vec{p}_{i+1}, \ldots, \vec{p}_n)$$

$$\overset{(16.51)}{=} p(\vec{p}_n) \prod_{i=m}^{n-1} f(\vec{p}_{i+1} \to \vec{p}_i) G(\vec{p}_{i+1}, \vec{p}_i) \tag{16.52}$$ 611

and the score associated with the random walk is thus defined as

$$L_j \triangleq \frac{F(\vec{p}_j, \ldots, \vec{p}_n) L_e(\vec{p}_n \to \vec{p}_{n-1})}{p(\vec{p}_j, \ldots, \vec{p}_n)}$$

$$\overset{(13.25)}{\underset{(16.52)}{=}} \frac{L_e(\vec{p}_n \to \vec{p}_{n-1}) G(\vec{p}_n, \vec{p}_{n-1}) \prod_{i=j}^{n-2} f_r(\vec{p}_i, \vec{p}_{i+1}, \vec{p}_{i+2}) G(\vec{p}_{i+1}, \vec{p}_i)}{p(\vec{p}_n) f(\vec{p}_n \to \vec{p}_{n-1}) G(\vec{p}_n, \vec{p}_{n-1}) \prod_{i=j}^{n-2} f(\vec{p}_{i+1} \to \vec{p}_i) G(\vec{p}_{i+1}, \vec{p}_i)}$$ 567 611

$$= \frac{L_e(\vec{p}_n \to \vec{p}_{n-1})}{p(\vec{p}_n) f(\vec{p}_n \to \vec{p}_{n-1})} \prod_{i=j}^{n-2} \frac{f_r(\vec{p}_i, \vec{p}_{i+1}, \vec{p}_{i+2})}{f(\vec{p}_{i+1} \to \vec{p}_i)}, \quad \forall j \in [0, n-1] \tag{16.53}$$

Given the radiant flux and radiant exitance of the luminaire

$$\Phi_e \overset{(10.46)}{=} \int_S M_e(\vec{p}) \mathrm{d}A(\vec{p}) \tag{16.54}$$ 426

$$M_e(\vec{p}_n) \overset{(10.50)}{=} \int_\Omega L_e(\vec{p}_n, \hat{\omega}) \langle \hat{n}_{p_n}, \hat{\omega} \rangle \mathrm{d}\hat{\omega} \tag{16.55}$$ 426

155 ideal *importance sampling* of the initial and secondary states is defined by the spatial and directional distributions

$$p(\vec{p}_n) \triangleq \frac{M_e(\vec{p}_n)}{\Phi_e} \tag{16.56}$$

$$f(\vec{p}_n \to \vec{p}_{n-1}) \triangleq \frac{L_e(\vec{p}_n \to \vec{p}_{n-1})}{M_e(\vec{p}_n)} \tag{16.57}$$

while that of the subsequent states is given by the directional transition distributions

475

$$f(\vec{p}_{i+1} \to \vec{p}_i) \overset{(12.4)}{=} \frac{f_r(\vec{p}_i, \vec{p}_{i+1}, \vec{p}_{i+2})}{\rho(\vec{p}_{i+1}, \widehat{p_{i+1}p_{i+2}})}, \quad \forall i \in [0, n-2] \tag{16.58}$$

in which case the expression of the score reduces to

611

$$L_j \overset{(16.53)}{=} \Phi_e \prod_{i=j}^{n-2} \rho(\vec{p}_{i+1}, \widehat{p_{i+1}p_{i+2}}), \quad \forall j \in [0, n-1] \tag{16.59}$$

16.2.1.3 Path Termination

566 Based on the formulation of the *measurement equation* as an infinite sum over paths of all lengths, a random walk may only be terminated upon leakage, i.e., upon escape (if ever) of the environment, a technique known as *implicit capture*. In closed environments, though, limiting the path length to a finite number of steps requires an explicit termination of the random walk. To this end, deterministic approaches entail truncating the path either once a predetermined maximal length is reached, or whenever the throughput of the walk or its score falls below a predetermined threshold, both approaches introducing bias in the result due to systematic underestimation of longer path lengths.

613 As illustrated in *Figure 16.9*, unbiased estimates of the infinite sum can alternatively
163 be obtained by means of *Russian roulette*, probabilistically deciding on whether to evaluate
129 each summand, in which case the latter ought to be divided by the *probability* of sampling
paths of the corresponding length. When constructing paths by appending vertices to paths
of shorter length, this process may be carried progressively by stochastically continuing the
129 walk at each scattering step i with a *probability* p_i by which the score is then divided, or
terminating the walk otherwise [Arvo and Kirk, 1990]. Instead of resorting to an arbitrary
129 constant *probability*, the walks might be sampled proportionally to their expected contribu-
609 tions, thereby, respectively, yielding for the *gathering scheme* and *shooting scheme*
611

611

$$p_i(\vec{p}_{i-1} \to \vec{p}_i) \overset{(16.49)}{=} \rho(\vec{p}_{i-1}, \widehat{p_{i-1}p_{i-2}}) \tag{16.60}$$

612

$$p_i(\vec{p}_{i+1} \to \vec{p}_i) \overset{(16.59)}{=} \rho(\vec{p}_{i+1}, \widehat{p_{i+1}p_{i+2}}) \tag{16.61}$$

or more generally

610

$$p_i(\vec{p}_{i-1} \to \vec{p}_i) \overset{(16.43)}{=} \min\left\{\frac{f_r(\vec{p}_{i-2}, \vec{p}_{i-1}, \vec{p}_i)}{f(\vec{p}_{i-1} \to \vec{p}_i)}, 1\right\} \tag{16.62}$$

611

$$p_i(\vec{p}_{i+1} \to \vec{p}_i) \overset{(16.53)}{=} \min\left\{\frac{f_r(\vec{p}_i, \vec{p}_{i+1}, \vec{p}_{i+2})}{f(\vec{p}_{i+1} \to \vec{p}_i)}, 1\right\} \tag{16.63}$$

Because the efficiency of continuing a path is determined by the trade-off between the

Figure 16.9: Russian Roulette: Equal time comparison of path tracing without Russian roulette (left) and with a continuation probability set to 20% of the path throughput (right).

associated computational cost and the resulting reduction in *variance*, the termination *prob-* 143
ability may be adjusted (typically so as to increase the average path length in order to 129
amortize the cost of generating the path) by means of an additional factor dividing the first
argument of the min function in the above expressions, and the argument potentially be substituted with the product term from the score of the current subpath in order to cumulatively
account for previous scattering events whose *probability* may have been clamped by the min 129
function. As an alternative to resorting to a user-defined factor, the value maximizing the
trade-off between computational cost and *variance* might then be estimated by maintain- 143
ing estimates of both quantities, a technique known as efficiency-optimized *Russian roulette* 163
[Veach, 1997, §10.4].

16.2.2 Path Tracing

Generalizing distribution *ray tracing* to resolve reflections and refractions of arbitrary surface 598
materials while avoiding the exponential growth of the ray tree incurred by *splitting* the 166
rays at each scattering event, *path tracing* [Kajiya, 1986] is a *gathering scheme*, recursively 609
evaluating the rendering equation by drawing a single sample direction at each scattering
event, thereby constructing unary ray trees, or "paths."

16.2.2.1 Unidirectional

Defined as a pure *gathering scheme*, the *unidirectional path tracing estimator* reads 609 139

$$\tilde{M}_n \overset{(16.38)}{=} \frac{W_e(\vec{p}_0 \to \vec{p}_1)F(\vec{p}_0, \ldots, \vec{p}_n)}{p(\vec{p}_0, \ldots, \vec{p}_n)} L_e(\vec{p}_n \to \vec{p}_{n-1}) \overset{(16.43)}{=} W_n L_e(\vec{p}_n \to \vec{p}_{n-1}) \tag{16.64}$$ 609 610

whose *variance* is mostly sensitive to the spatio-directional variations of the luminaires. As 143
such, the technique is highly suited to resolve ES^*L paths in the presence of a *pinhole*
camera and *area light* source, but its efficiency decreases in the presence of small but bright 648
luminaires, whose high contribution is sampled with a relatively low *probability*, thereby 429 129
failing to evaluate illumination in the limit of a *point light* source. 431

16.2.2.2 Next-Event Estimation

609 Defined as a hybrid *gathering scheme*, *next-event estimation path tracing* explicitly draws
the last vertex along the path from the spatial distribution of the luminaire, such that the
131 *probability density* of the path is expressed in a separable form as

132
$$p(\vec{p}_0, \ldots, \vec{p}_n) \overset{(4.19)}{=} p(\vec{p}_0, \ldots, \vec{p}_{n-1})p(\vec{p}_n) \tag{16.65}$$

while reformulating the path throughput as

567
$$F(\vec{p}_0, \ldots, \vec{p}_n) \overset{(13.24)}{=} F(\vec{p}_0, \ldots, \vec{p}_{n-1})f_r(\vec{p}_{n-2}, \vec{p}_{n-1}, \vec{p}_n)G(\vec{p}_{n-1}, \vec{p}_n) \tag{16.66}$$

139 The *estimator* then reads

609 610
$$\begin{aligned} \tilde{M}_n &\overset{(16.38)}{=} \frac{W_e(\vec{p}_0 \to \vec{p}_1)F(\vec{p}_0, \ldots, \vec{p}_{n-1})f_r(\vec{p}_{n-2}, \vec{p}_{n-1}, \vec{p}_n)G(\vec{p}_{n-1}, \vec{p}_n)L_e(\vec{p}_n \to \vec{p}_{n-1})}{p(\vec{p}_0, \ldots, \vec{p}_{n-1})p(\vec{p}_n)} \\ &\overset{(16.43)}{=} W_{n-1}f_r(\vec{p}_{n-2}, \vec{p}_{n-1}, \vec{p}_n)G(\vec{p}_{n-1}, \vec{p}_n)L_n \end{aligned} \tag{16.67}$$

where

$$L_n \triangleq \frac{L_e(\vec{p}_n \to \vec{p}_{n-1})}{p(\vec{p}_n)} \tag{16.68}$$

which, in case of locally ideal PDFs, reduces to

612 612
$$L_n \underset{(16.57)}{\overset{(16.56)}{=}} \Phi_e f(\vec{p}_n \to \vec{p}_{n-1}) \tag{16.69}$$

143 such that the *variance* of the *estimator* is mostly sensitive to the directional and geometric
139 variations between the previous-to-last point and the one on the luminaire. As such, the
technique is highly suited to resolve ES^*DL paths, but its efficiency decreases in the presence
of small but brightly lit parts of the scene being directly illuminated, whose high contribution
129 is sampled with a relatively low *probability*, while failing to evaluate illumination in the limit
429 486 of $E(D|G|S)^*SL$ paths, including reflections of *light sources* off *specular surfaces* via paths
431 of the type ESL, as well as caustics due to the reflections or refractions of *point lights* off
486 *specular surfaces* via paths of the type $E(D|G|S)^+SL$.

16.2.2.3 Combination

139 Rather than evaluating each *estimator* independently, *next-event estimation* can be readily
614 613 carried by reusing the subpath $[\vec{p}_0, \ldots, \vec{p}_{n-1}]$ generated by the *unidirectional* estimator while
166 *splitting* the path at the previous-to-last point $\vec{p}_{n-1}$ [Arvo and Kirk, 1990], and combining
158 both estimators by means of *multiple importance sampling*, as illustrated in *Figure 16.10*.
615 139 For a given path length n, the combined *estimator* then reads

159 613 614 610
$$\begin{aligned} \tilde{M}_n &\overset{(4.176)}{\underset{(16.67)}{\overset{(16.64)}{=}}} w_n(\vec{p}_0, \ldots, \vec{p}_n)W_n L_e(\vec{p}_n \to \vec{p}_{n-1}) \\ &+ w_{n-1}(\vec{p}_0, \ldots, \vec{p}_n)W_{n-1}f_r(\vec{p}_{n-2}, \vec{p}_{n-1}, \vec{p}_n)G(\vec{p}_{n-1}, \vec{p}_n)L_n \\ &\overset{(16.43)}{=} W_{n-1}f_r(\vec{p}_{n-2}, \vec{p}_{n-1}, \vec{p}_n) \\ &\left(w_n(\vec{p}_0, \ldots, \vec{p}_n)\frac{L_e(\vec{p}_n \to \vec{p}_{n-1})}{f(\vec{p}_{n-1} \to \vec{p}_n)} + w_{n-1}(\vec{p}_0, \ldots, \vec{p}_n)G(\vec{p}_{n-1}, \vec{p}_n)L_n\right) \end{aligned} \tag{16.70}$$

Figure 16.10: Path Tracing: Rendering of a scene with an area light source and a pinhole camera, using unidirectional path tracing, path tracing with next event estimation and both combined with multiple importance sampling (from left to right, respectively), all with 16 paths per pixels.

with the weight functions

$$\frac{1}{w_n(\vec{p}_0,\ldots,\vec{p}_n)} \overset{(4.180)}{\underset{(16.65)}{=}} 1+\left(\frac{p(\vec{p}_0,\ldots,\vec{p}_{n-1})p(\vec{p}_n)}{p(\vec{p}_0,\ldots,\vec{p}_n)}\right)^{\beta}$$ 159 614

$$\overset{(16.42)}{=} 1+\left(\frac{p(\vec{p}_0)\prod_{i=1}^{n-1} f(\vec{p}_{i-1}\to\vec{p}_i)G(\vec{p}_{i-1},\vec{p}_i)}{p(\vec{p}_0)\prod_{i=1}^{n} f(\vec{p}_{i-1}\to\vec{p}_i)G(\vec{p}_{i-1},\vec{p}_i)}p(\vec{p}_n)\right)^{\beta}$$ 610

$$= 1+\left(\frac{p(\vec{p}_n)}{f(\vec{p}_{n-1}\to\vec{p}_n)G(\vec{p}_{n-1},\vec{p}_n)}\right)^{\beta} \quad (16.71)$$

$$\frac{1}{w_{n-1}(\vec{p}_0,\ldots,\vec{p}_n)} \overset{(4.180)}{\underset{(16.65)}{=}} 1+\left(\frac{p(\vec{p}_0,\ldots,\vec{p}_n)}{p(\vec{p}_0,\ldots,\vec{p}_{n-1})p(\vec{p}_n)}\right)^{\beta}$$ 159 614

$$\overset{(16.42)}{=} 1+\left(\frac{p(\vec{p}_0)\prod_{i=1}^{n} f(\vec{p}_{i-1}\to\vec{p}_i)G(\vec{p}_{i-1},\vec{p}_i)}{p(\vec{p}_0)\prod_{i=1}^{n-1} f(\vec{p}_{i-1}\to\vec{p}_i)G(\vec{p}_{i-1},\vec{p}_i)p(\vec{p}_n)}\right)^{\beta}$$ 610

$$= 1+\left(\frac{f(\vec{p}_{n-1}\to\vec{p}_n)G(\vec{p}_{n-1},\vec{p}_n)}{p(\vec{p}_n)}\right)^{\beta} \quad (16.72)$$

It follows that the subsequent extension of the random walk by the *unidirectional estimator* essentially results in the implicit *stratified sampling* of the rendering equation at $\vec{p}_{n-1}$ into indirect and *direct illumination*, while allowing the iterative summation of the terms of increasing length without requiring the explicit storage of the complete path. 613 139 153 598

16.2.3 Light Tracing

Simulating the physical propagation of light, *light tracing* [Dutré *et al.*, 1993, Dutré, 1996, Ch. 5] is a *shooting scheme*, recursively evaluating the importance equation by drawing a sample direction at each scattering event, thereby constructing unary ray trees. 611

16.2.3.1 Unidirectional

Defined as a pure *shooting scheme*, the *unidirectional path tracing estimator* reads 611 139

$$\tilde{M}_n \overset{(16.38)}{=} W_e(\vec{p}_0\to\vec{p}_1)\frac{F(\vec{p}_0,\ldots,\vec{p}_n)L_e(\vec{p}_n\to\vec{p}_{n-1})}{p(\vec{p}_0,\ldots,\vec{p}_n)} \overset{(16.53)}{=} W_e(\vec{p}_0\to\vec{p}_1)L_0 \quad (16.73)$$ 609 611

143 whose *variance* is mostly sensitive to the spatio-directional variations of the sensor. As such,
the technique is highly suited to resolve ES^*L paths in the presence of a *finite aperture*
648 *camera* and *point light* source, but its efficiency decreases in the presence of a small but
431 129 highly sensitive sensor, whose high contribution is sampled with a relatively low *probability*,
648 thereby failing to evaluate illumination in the limit of a *pinhole camera*.

16.2.3.2 Next-Event Estimation

611 Defined as a hybrid *shooting scheme*, *next-event estimation light tracing* explicitly draws the
last vertex along the path from the spatial distribution of the sensor, such that the *probability*
131 *density* of the path is expressed in a separable form as

132

$$p(\vec{p}_0, \ldots, \vec{p}_n) \overset{(4.19)}{=} p(\vec{p}_0)p(\vec{p}_1, \ldots, \vec{p}_n) \tag{16.74}$$

while reformulating the path throughput as

567

$$F(\vec{p}_0, \ldots, \vec{p}_n) \overset{(13.25)}{=} G(\vec{p}_0, \vec{p}_1) f_r(\vec{p}_0, \vec{p}_1, \vec{p}_2) F(\vec{p}_1, \ldots, \vec{p}_n) \tag{16.75}$$

139 The *estimator* then reads

609

611

$$\begin{aligned} \tilde{M}_n &\overset{(16.38)}{=} \frac{W_e(\vec{p}_0 \to \vec{p}_1) G(\vec{p}_0, \vec{p}_1) f_r(\vec{p}_0, \vec{p}_1, \vec{p}_2) F(\vec{p}_1, \ldots, \vec{p}_n) L_e(\vec{p}_n \to \vec{p}_{n-1})}{p(\vec{p}_0) p(\vec{p}_1, \ldots, \vec{p}_n)} \\ &\overset{(16.53)}{=} W_0 G(\vec{p}_0, \vec{p}_1) f_r(\vec{p}_0, \vec{p}_1, \vec{p}_2) L_1 \end{aligned} \tag{16.76}$$

where

$$W_0 \triangleq \frac{W_e(\vec{p}_0 \to \vec{p}_1)}{p(\vec{p}_0)} \tag{16.77}$$

which, in case of locally ideal PDFs, reduces to

610

610

$$W_0 \underset{(16.47)}{\overset{(16.46)}{=}} W_e f(\vec{p}_0 \to \vec{p}_1) \tag{16.78}$$

143 such that the *variance* of the *estimator* is mostly sensitive to the directional and geometric
139 variations between the first visible point and the one on the sensor. As such, the technique
is highly suited to resolve EDS^*L paths (including caustic paths of the form EDS^+L), but
its efficiency decreases in the presence of small but measurably important parts of the scene
129 being directly visible, whose high contribution is sampled with a relatively low *probability*,
while failing to evaluate illumination in the limit of $ES(D|G|S)^*L$ paths, i.e., reflections off
486 *specular surfaces*.

16.2.3.3 Combination

139 Rather than evaluating each *estimator* independently, *next-event estimation* can be readily
616 615 carried by reusing the subpath $[\vec{p}_1, \ldots, \vec{p}_n]$ generated by the *unidirectional* estimator while
166 *splitting* the path at the previous-to-last point $\vec{p}_1$ [Arvo and Kirk, 1990], and combining both
158 estimators by means of *multiple importance sampling*, as illustrated in *Figure 16.11*.
617

Figure 16.11: Light Tracing: Rendering of a scene with a point light source and a thin lens camera, using unidirectional light tracing, light tracing with next event estimation and both combined with multiple importance sampling (from left to right, respectively), all with 16 times as many paths as the number of pixels.

For a given path length n, the combined *estimator* then reads 139

159 615 616 611

$$\begin{aligned}\tilde{M}_n &\overset{(4.176)}{\underset{(16.76)}{\overset{(16.73)}{=}}} w_{-1}(\vec{p}_0,\ldots,\vec{p}_n)W_e(\vec{p}_0\to\vec{p}_1)L_0 + w_0(\vec{p}_0,\ldots,\vec{p}_n)W_0G(\vec{p}_0,\vec{p}_1)f_r(\vec{p}_0,\vec{p}_1,\vec{p}_2)L_1\\ &\overset{(16.53)}{=} L_1 f_r(\vec{p}_0,\vec{p}_1,\vec{p}_2)\left(w_{-1}(\vec{p}_0,\ldots,\vec{p}_n)\frac{W_e(\vec{p}_0\to\vec{p}_1)}{f(\vec{p}_1\to\vec{p}_0)} + w_0(\vec{p}_0,\ldots,\vec{p}_n)W_0G(\vec{p}_0,\vec{p}_1)\right)\end{aligned} \tag{16.79}$$

with the weight functions

159 616 611

$$\begin{aligned}\frac{1}{w_{-1}(\vec{p}_0,\ldots,\vec{p}_n)} &\overset{(4.180)}{\underset{(16.74)}{=}} 1+\left(\frac{p(\vec{p}_0)p(\vec{p}_1,\ldots,\vec{p}_n)}{p(\vec{p}_0,\ldots,\vec{p}_n)}\right)^{\beta}\\ &\overset{(16.52)}{=} 1+\left(p(\vec{p}_0)\frac{p(\vec{p}_n)\prod_{i=1}^{n-1} f(\vec{p}_{i+1}\to\vec{p}_i)G(\vec{p}_{i+1},\vec{p}_i)}{p(\vec{p}_n)\prod_{i=0}^{n-1} f(\vec{p}_{i+1}\to\vec{p}_i)G(\vec{p}_{i+1},\vec{p}_i)}\right)^{\beta}\\ &= 1+\left(\frac{p(\vec{p}_0)}{f(\vec{p}_1\to\vec{p}_0)G(\vec{p}_1,\vec{p}_0)}\right)^{\beta}\end{aligned} \tag{16.80}$$

159 616 611

$$\begin{aligned}\frac{1}{w_0(\vec{p}_0,\ldots,\vec{p}_n)} &\overset{(4.180)}{\underset{(16.74)}{=}} 1+\left(\frac{p(\vec{p}_0,\ldots,\vec{p}_n)}{p(\vec{p}_0)p(\vec{p}_1,\ldots,\vec{p}_n)}\right)^{\beta}\\ &\overset{(16.52)}{=} 1+\left(p(\vec{p}_0)\frac{p(\vec{p}_n)\prod_{i=0}^{n-1} f(\vec{p}_{i+1}\to\vec{p}_i)G(\vec{p}_{i+1},\vec{p}_i)}{p(\vec{p}_n)\prod_{i=1}^{n-1} f(\vec{p}_{i+1}\to\vec{p}_i)G(\vec{p}_{i+1},\vec{p}_i)}\right)^{\beta}\\ &= 1+\left(\frac{f(\vec{p}_1\to\vec{p}_0)G(\vec{p}_1,\vec{p}_0)}{p(\vec{p}_0)}\right)^{\beta}\end{aligned} \tag{16.81}$$

It follows that the subsequent extension of the random walk by the *unidirectional esti-* 613
mator essentially results in the implicit *stratified sampling* of the importance equation at 139 153
$\vec{p}_1$ into indirect and direct visibility, while allowing the iterative summation of the terms of increasing length without requiring the explicit storage of the complete path.

16.2.4 Bidirectional Path Tracing

16.2.4.1 Definition

609 Defined as a composite *gathering scheme* and *shooting scheme*, *bidirectional path tracing*
611 (*BDPT*) [Lafortune and Willems, 1993, Lafortune and Willems, 1994a, Lafortune, 1996, §4.3][Veach and Guibas, 1994, Veach, 1997, Ch. 10] constructs a subset of the paths starting from the sensor towards the luminaires, and the other subset from the luminaires towards
131 the sensor, such that the *probability density* of the path is expressed in a separable form as

132

$$p(\vec{p}_0, \ldots, \vec{p}_n) \overset{(4.19)}{=} p(\vec{p}_0, \ldots, \vec{p}_j) p(\vec{p}_{j+1}, \ldots, \vec{p}_n) \tag{16.82}$$

while reformulating the path throughput as

567

$$F(\vec{p}_0, \ldots, \vec{p}_n) \overset{(13.24)}{=} F(\vec{p}_0, \ldots, \vec{p}_j) f_r(\vec{p}_{j-1}, \vec{p}_j, \vec{p}_{j+1}) G(\vec{p}_j, \vec{p}_{j+1}) f_r(\vec{p}_j, \vec{p}_{j+1}, \vec{p}_{j+2}) F(\vec{p}_{j+1}, \ldots, \vec{p}_n) \tag{16.83}$$

139 The *estimator* then reads

609 610 611

$$\begin{aligned} \tilde{M}_n &\overset{(16.38)}{=} \frac{W_e(\vec{p}_0 \to \vec{p}_1) F(\vec{p}_0, \ldots, \vec{p}_j) f_r(\vec{p}_{j-1}, \vec{p}_j, \vec{p}_{j+1}) G(\vec{p}_j, \vec{p}_{j+1}) \times f_r(\vec{p}_j, \vec{p}_{j+1}, \vec{p}_{j+2}) F(\vec{p}_{j+1}, \ldots, \vec{p}_n) L_e(\vec{p}_n \to \vec{p}_{n-1})}{p(\vec{p}_0, \ldots, \vec{p}_j) p(\vec{p}_{j+1}, \ldots, \vec{p}_n)} \\ &\underset{(16.53)}{\overset{(16.43)}{=}} W_j f_r(\vec{p}_{j-1}, \vec{p}_j, \vec{p}_{j+1}) G(\vec{p}_j, \vec{p}_{j+1}) f_r(\vec{p}_j, \vec{p}_{j+1}, \vec{p}_{j+2}) L_{j+1}, \quad \forall j \in [1, n-2] \end{aligned} \tag{16.84}$$

143 whose *variance* is mostly sensitive to the directional and geometric variations between the endpoints of the eye and light paths. As such, the technique is highly suited to resolve ES^*DDS^*L paths, but its efficiency decreases in the presence of small but measurably important or brightly lit parts of the scene being indirectly visible or illuminated, whose
129 high contribution is sampled with a relatively low *probability*, while failing to evaluate
486 $E(D|G|S)^*SDS(D|G|S)^*L$ paths, i.e., reflections of caustics off *specular surfaces*, in the
648 431 limit of a *pinhole camera* and *point light* source.

16.2.4.2 Combination

139 Rather than evaluating each *estimator* independently, the latter can be readily constructed by joining every point of the eye path to every point of the light path [Lafortune and Willems, 1993, Lafortune, 1996], therefore requiring the explicit storage of one of the two paths. While
139 the convex combination of the *estimators* of a given path length may resort to arbitrarily defined weights (e.g., based on the specularity of the materials at each point of the path
143 [Lafortune and Willems, 1993, Lafortune, 1996]), *variance* can be reduced more effectively
158 by means of *multiple importance sampling* [Veach and Guibas, 1994, Veach and Guibas,
619 1995, Veach, 1997, Ch. 10], as illustrated in *Figure 16.12*.
139 For a given path length n, the combined *estimator* then reads

159 618

$$\tilde{M}_n \underset{(16.84)}{\overset{(4.176)}{=}} \sum_{j=1}^{n-2} w_j(\vec{p}_0, \ldots, \vec{p}_n) W_j f_r(\vec{p}_{j-1}, \vec{p}_j, \vec{p}_{j+1}) G(\vec{p}_j, \vec{p}_{j+1}) f_r(\vec{p}_j, \vec{p}_{j+1}, \vec{p}_{j+2}) L_{j+1} \tag{16.85}$$

613 614 615 616 with the weight functions (here also including *path tracing* with *next-event estimation* and *light tracing* with *next-event estimation*)

159 618

$$\frac{1}{w_j(\vec{p}_0, \ldots, \vec{p}_n)} \underset{(16.82)}{\overset{(4.180)}{=}} 1 + \sum_{\substack{k=0 \\ k \neq j}}^{n-1} \left(\frac{p(\vec{p}_0, \ldots, \vec{p}_k) p(\vec{p}_{k+1}, \ldots, \vec{p}_n)}{p(\vec{p}_0, \ldots, \vec{p}_j) p(\vec{p}_{j+1}, \ldots, \vec{p}_n)} \right)^{\beta} = w_j + 1 + l_j \tag{16.86}$$

Figure 16.12: BDPT Estimators: Comparison of various bidirectional path tracing estimators with light paths of length 0 to 3 (from left to right, respectively) and eye paths of length 0 to 3 (from top to bottom, brightened by a factor of 1, 2, 4 and 8, respectively), all with 16 times as many paths as the number of pixels.

where

$$\begin{aligned} w_j &\triangleq \sum_{k=0}^{j-1} \left(\frac{p(\vec{p}_0, \ldots, \vec{p}_k) p(\vec{p}_{k+1}, \ldots, \vec{p}_n)}{p(\vec{p}_0, \ldots, \vec{p}_j) p(\vec{p}_{j+1}, \ldots, \vec{p}_n)} \right)^{\beta} \\ &\overset{(16.42)}{\underset{(16.52)}{=}} \sum_{k=0}^{j-1} \left(\frac{p(\vec{p}_0) \prod_{i=1}^{k} f(\vec{p}_{i-1} \rightarrow \vec{p}_i) G(\vec{p}_{i-1}, \vec{p}_i)}{p(\vec{p}_0) \prod_{i=1}^{j} f(\vec{p}_{i-1} \rightarrow \vec{p}_i) G(\vec{p}_{i-1}, \vec{p}_i)} \frac{p(\vec{p}_n) \prod_{i=k+1}^{n-1} f(\vec{p}_{i+1} \rightarrow \vec{p}_i) G(\vec{p}_{i+1}, \vec{p}_i)}{p(\vec{p}_n) \prod_{i=j+1}^{n-1} f(\vec{p}_{i+1} \rightarrow \vec{p}_i) G(\vec{p}_{i+1}, \vec{p}_i)} \right)^{\beta} \\ &= \sum_{k=0}^{j-1} \left(\prod_{i=k+1}^{j} \frac{f(\vec{p}_{i+1} \rightarrow \vec{p}_i) G(\vec{p}_{i+1}, \vec{p}_i)}{f(\vec{p}_{i-1} \rightarrow \vec{p}_i) G(\vec{p}_{i-1}, \vec{p}_i)} \right)^{\beta} \end{aligned} \tag{16.87}$$

610 611

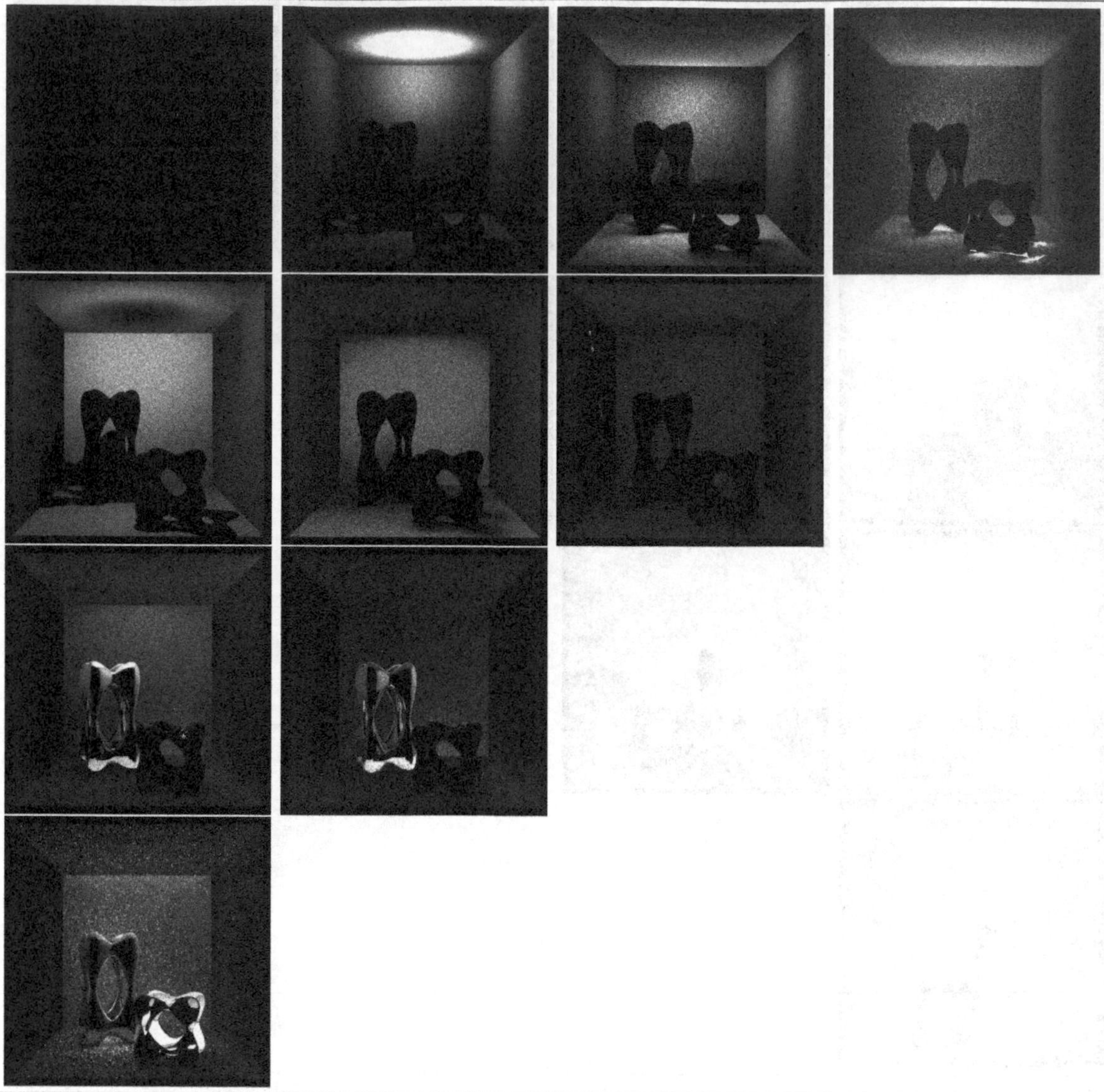

Figure 16.13: MIS-Weighted BDPT Contributions: Comparison of the MIS-weighted contributions of various bidirectional path tracing estimators with light paths of length 0 to 3 (from left to right, respectively) and eye paths of length 0 to 3 (from top to bottom, brightened by a factor of 1, 2, 4 and 8, respectively), all with 16 times as many paths as the number of pixels.

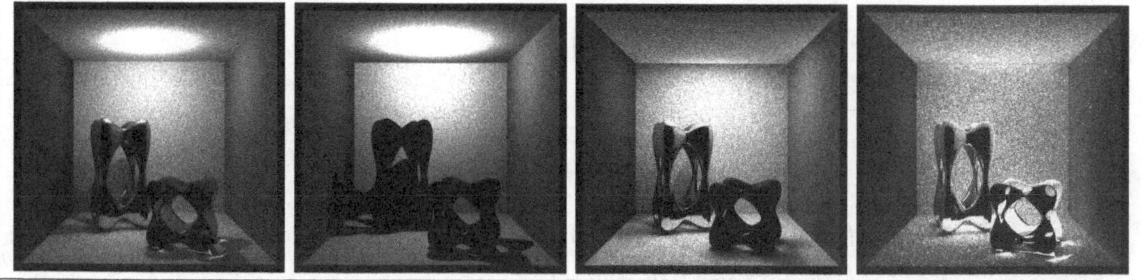

Figure 16.14: Bidirectional Path Tracing: Multiple importance sampling of paths of lengths 0-3 and 1 to 3 (from left to right, brightened by a factor of 1, 2, 4 and 8, respectively), all with 16 times as many paths as the number of pixels.

$$
\begin{aligned}
&= \left(\frac{f(\vec{p}_{j+1} \to \vec{p}_j)G(\vec{p}_{j+1}, \vec{p}_j)}{f(\vec{p}_{j-1} \to \vec{p}_j)G(\vec{p}_{j-1}, \vec{p}_j)}\right)^\beta + \sum_{k=0}^{j-2} \left(\prod_{i=k+1}^{j} \frac{f(\vec{p}_{i+1} \to \vec{p}_i)G(\vec{p}_{i+1}, \vec{p}_i)}{f(\vec{p}_{i-1} \to \vec{p}_i)G(\vec{p}_{i-1}, \vec{p}_i)}\right)^\beta \\
&= \left(\frac{f(\vec{p}_{j+1} \to \vec{p}_j)G(\vec{p}_{j+1}, \vec{p}_j)}{f(\vec{p}_{j-1} \to \vec{p}_j)G(\vec{p}_{j-1}, \vec{p}_j)}\right)^\beta \left(1 + \sum_{k=0}^{j-2} \left(\prod_{i=k+1}^{j-1} \frac{f(\vec{p}_{i+1} \to \vec{p}_i)G(\vec{p}_{i+1}, \vec{p}_i)}{f(\vec{p}_{i-1} \to \vec{p}_i)G(\vec{p}_{i-1}, \vec{p}_i)}\right)^\beta\right) \\
&= \left(\frac{f(\vec{p}_{j+1} \to \vec{p}_j)G(\vec{p}_{j+1}, \vec{p}_j)}{f(\vec{p}_{j-1} \to \vec{p}_j)G(\vec{p}_{j-1}, \vec{p}_j)}\right)^\beta (1 + w_{j-1}) \qquad (16.88)
\end{aligned}
$$

and

$$
\begin{aligned}
l_j &\triangleq \sum_{k=j+1}^{n-1} \left(\frac{p(\vec{p}_0, \ldots, \vec{p}_k)p(\vec{p}_{k+1}, \ldots, \vec{p}_n)}{p(\vec{p}_0, \ldots, \vec{p}_j)p(\vec{p}_{j+1}, \ldots, \vec{p}_n)}\right)^\beta \\
&\overset{(16.42)}{\underset{(16.52)}{=}} \sum_{k=j+1}^{n-1} \left(\frac{p(\vec{p}_0)\prod_{i=1}^{k} f(\vec{p}_{i-1} \to \vec{p}_i)G(\vec{p}_{i-1}, \vec{p}_i)\, p(\vec{p}_n)\prod_{i=k+1}^{n-1} f(\vec{p}_{i+1} \to \vec{p}_i)G(\vec{p}_{i+1}, \vec{p}_i)}{p(\vec{p}_0)\prod_{i=1}^{j} f(\vec{p}_{i-1} \to \vec{p}_i)G(\vec{p}_{i-1}, \vec{p}_i)\, p(\vec{p}_n)\prod_{i=j+1}^{n-1} f(\vec{p}_{i+1} \to \vec{p}_i)G(\vec{p}_{i+1}, \vec{p}_i)}\right)^\beta \\
&= \sum_{k=j+1}^{n-1} \left(\prod_{i=j+1}^{k} \frac{f(\vec{p}_{i-1} \to \vec{p}_i)G(\vec{p}_{i-1}, \vec{p}_i)}{f(\vec{p}_{i+1} \to \vec{p}_i)G(\vec{p}_{i+1}, \vec{p}_i)}\right)^\beta \qquad (16.89) \\
&= \left(\frac{f(\vec{p}_j \to \vec{p}_{j+1})G(\vec{p}_j, \vec{p}_{j+1})}{f(\vec{p}_{j+2} \to \vec{p}_{j+1})G(\vec{p}_{j+2}, \vec{p}_{j+1})}\right)^\beta + \sum_{k=j+2}^{n-1} \left(\prod_{i=j+1}^{k} \frac{f(\vec{p}_{i-1} \to \vec{p}_i)G(\vec{p}_{i-1}, \vec{p}_i)}{f(\vec{p}_{i+1} \to \vec{p}_i)G(\vec{p}_{i+1}, \vec{p}_i)}\right)^\beta \\
&= \left(\frac{f(\vec{p}_j \to \vec{p}_{j+1})G(\vec{p}_j, \vec{p}_{j+1})}{f(\vec{p}_{j+2} \to \vec{p}_{j+1})G(\vec{p}_{j+2}, \vec{p}_{j+1})}\right)^\beta \left(1 + \sum_{k=j+2}^{n-1} \left(\prod_{i=j+2}^{k} \frac{f(\vec{p}_{i-1} \to \vec{p}_i)G(\vec{p}_{i-1}, \vec{p}_i)}{f(\vec{p}_{i+1} \to \vec{p}_i)G(\vec{p}_{i+1}, \vec{p}_i)}\right)^\beta\right) \\
&= \left(\frac{f(\vec{p}_j \to \vec{p}_{j+1})G(\vec{p}_j, \vec{p}_{j+1})}{f(\vec{p}_{j+2} \to \vec{p}_{j+1})G(\vec{p}_{j+2}, \vec{p}_{j+1})}\right)^\beta (1 + l_{j+1}) \qquad (16.90)
\end{aligned}
$$

610
611

which may both be incrementally computed during the generation of an eye or light path,
respectively. A notable special case occurs in the presence of *specular surfaces*, as both the 486
numerator and denominator of w_j and l_j may contain a Dirac *delta function*, hence requiring 44
special treatment [Veach, 1997, §10.3.5].

Bidirectional path tracing can similarly be extended to *participating media* by sam- 440
pling the volumetric interactions of the eye and light paths by means of *free-path sampling*, 600
and combining the different *estimators* using *multiple importance sampling* [Lafortune and 139 158
Willems, 1996]. In the case of inhomogeneous media, though, the transmittance terms involved in each *probability density* defining the MIS weights cannot be analytically evaluated, 131
and typically need to be either stochastically estimated via *free-path sampling* or determin- 600
istically approximated via ray marching [Raab *et al.*, 2006].

16.2.5 Metropolis Light Transport

Rather than evaluating the path integral by *importance sampling* a subset of its integrand, 155
Metropolis light transport (*MLT*) [Veach and Guibas, 1997, Veach, 1997, Ch. 11] resorts to a
probability density proportional to the overall contribution of each path to the measurement 131
by means of *Metropolis–Hastings sampling*. By defining the state space $\Omega = \bigcup_{n=1}^{\infty} S^n$ as the 136
union of all paths of all lengths, the sum of path integrals defining the *measurement equation* 566

can be interpreted as a single multidimensional integral over paths $\vec{P} = \vec{p}_0 \dots \vec{p}_n$ of all lengths

566
566

$$M \overset{(13.22)}{\underset{(13.23)}{=}} \sum_{n=1}^{\infty} \int_S \cdots \int_S W_e(\vec{p}_0 \to \vec{p}_1) F(\vec{p}_0, \dots, \vec{p}_n) L_e(\vec{p}_n \to \vec{p}_{n-1}) \mathrm{d}A(\vec{p}_n) \dots \mathrm{d}A(\vec{p}_0)$$
$$= \int_\Omega f(\vec{P}) \mathrm{d}\mu(\vec{P}) \tag{16.91}$$

with cumulative product measure $\mathrm{d}\mu(\vec{P}) = \sum_{n=1}^{\infty} \mathrm{d}\mu_n(\vec{P} \cap S^n)$ where $\mathrm{d}\mu_n(\vec{P}_n) = \mathrm{d}A(\vec{p}_n) \dots \mathrm{d}A(\vec{p}_0)$.

While the method may be prone to the introduction of start-up bias [Szirmay-Kalos *et al.*, 1999], the correlation between samples does not impact the asymptotic behavior of its
143 *variance*, which, akin to that of methods relying on independent samples, decreases linearly with the number of path samples [Ashikhmin *et al.*, 2001b].

618 Mutations based on *bidirectional path tracing* might discard a subpath $\vec{p}_l \dots \vec{p}_m$ (i.e., all edges and vertices between $\vec{p}_l$ and $\vec{p}_m$, but preserving those endpoints) from the current
129 path with *probability* $p_d(l, m)$, normalized over all $l < m$ and with a non-zero probability of discarding the complete path so as to guarantee ergodicity. A new subpath is then generated, containing K new vertices with a given probability, and a number of eye/light vertices with
129 another probability, the product of which defines the overall *probability* $p_a(k, K-k)$ of generating a new subpath with k additional eye vertices and $K-k$ additional light vertices. In order to maximize the acceptance probability and minimize the regeneration cost, the deletion probabilities favor short path lengths while the regeneration process favors paths of
429 similar length. Abusing the notation $\vec{p}_n$ to represent a point on the *light source* rather than a
129 point at fixed path length n from $\vec{p}_0$, the terms of the acceptance *probability* are then readily given by

138
609
618

$$\frac{f(\vec{P}_i)}{p_p(\vec{P}_i \mid \vec{P}_{i-1})} \overset{(4.51)}{\underset{(16.38)}{=}} \frac{W_e(\vec{p}_0 \to \vec{p}_1) F(\vec{p}_0, \dots, \vec{p}_n) L_e(\vec{p}_n \to \vec{p}_{n-1})}{p_d(l, m) \sum_{k=0}^{K} p_a(k, K-k) p(\vec{p}_0, \dots, \vec{p}_{l+k}) p(\vec{p}_{m-K+k}, \dots, \vec{p}_n)}$$
$$= \left(p_d(l, m) \sum_{k=0}^{K} p_a(k, K-k) \frac{p(\vec{p}_0, \dots, \vec{p}_{l+k}) p(\vec{p}_{m-K+k}, \dots, \vec{p}_n)}{W_e(\vec{p}_0 \to \vec{p}_1) F(\vec{p}_0, \dots, \vec{p}_n) L_e(\vec{p}_n \to \vec{p}_{n-1})} \right)^{-1}$$
$$\overset{(16.84)}{=} \left(p_d(l, m) \sum_{k=0}^{K} \frac{p_a(k, K-k)}{\begin{array}{c} W_{l+k} f_r(\vec{p}_{l+k-1}, \vec{p}_{l+k}, \vec{p}_{m-K+k}) G(\vec{p}_{l+k}, \vec{p}_{m-K+k}) \\ \times f_r(\vec{p}_{l+k}, \vec{p}_{m-K+k}, \vec{p}_{m-K+k+1}) L_{m-K+k} \end{array}} \right)^{-1} \tag{16.92}$$

while systematically rejecting mutations for which the path fails to be constructed with successive surface intersections.

One of the main strengths of the technique lies in its ability to incorporate dedicated mutations specifically designed for certain special cases, while rejecting those mutations with a marginal computational overhead in cases where they are not effective. As such, hard-to-find bright paths may be better explored by slightly perturbing the vertices of a given subpath (especially those at the beginning of the eye path), either via positional (for $\vec{p}_0$) or
131 directional (for inner vertices) perturbations by means of a radial *probability density* of the
132 form $p(\rho) \propto \rho^{-2}, \forall \rho \in [\rho_0, \rho_1]$ with *cumulative distribution*

$$1 - \xi = \int_{\rho_0}^{\rho_s} \frac{1}{\rho^2 \ln\left(\frac{\rho_1}{\rho_0}\right)} \rho \mathrm{d}\rho = \frac{[\ln(\rho)]_{\rho_0}^{\rho_s}}{\ln\left(\frac{\rho_1}{\rho_0}\right)} = \frac{\ln\left(\frac{\rho_s}{\rho_0}\right)}{\ln\left(\frac{\rho_1}{\rho_0}\right)} \implies \rho_s = \rho_1 \exp\left(-\xi \ln\left(\frac{\rho_1}{\rho_0}\right)\right) \tag{16.93}$$

Strategies following a gathering approach include lens perturbations, shifting $ES^*D(D|L)$

subpaths by perturbing the direction $\widehat{\vec{p}_0\vec{p}_1}$ (or equivalently by perturbing the corresponding projection onto the film plane), and multichain perturbations, shifting $ES^*DS^*(D|L)$ subpaths by additionally perturbing the direction at each subsequent diffuse vertex so as to target reflections of caustics off *specular surfaces*. Conversely, strategies following a shoot- 486
ing approach include caustic perturbations, shifting $EDS^*(D|L)$ subpaths by perturbing the direction at the second diffuse vertex, and propagation perturbations, shifting the volume point $\vec{p}_1$ by perturbing the scattering distance along $\widehat{\vec{p}_2\vec{p}_1}$ in *participating media* [Pauly, 440
1999, Pauly *et al.*, 2000, Raab *et al.*, 2006]. In order for all pixels to be sampled at a similar rate, better stratification over the image plane may likewise be achieved by means of lens subpath mutations, discarding the beginning of the eye path and replacing it with newly generated vertices. Given a sampled path seed containing a chain of successive (nearly) *specular surfaces* with known differential geometry, neighboring subpaths can similarly be explored 486
upon mutation of one of the two non-specular ends of the chain by means of an extended geometric term. The latter relates the differential projected *solid angle* at one end to the 244
differential area at the other, thereby providing a first-order approximation from which a Newton-like scheme may reconstruct the mutated specular subpath by iteratively predicting the mutated direction at one end and correcting it by tracing the resulting subpath until convergence of the other end to the target point [Jakob and Marschner, 2012a, Jakob and Marschner, 2012b, Jakob, 2013]. Instead, MLT might rely on *path tracing* [Cline and Eg- 613
bert, 2005], similarly redistributing the energy of the paths over the image plane by means of mutations, while ergodicity can be guaranteed by a series of periodically reseeded short Markov chains so as to provide better stratification over the image plane than a uniquely seeded longer chain with an ergodic transition kernel [Cline *et al.*, 2005, Cline, 2007, Ch. 8].

As an alternative, mutations may be readily carried in the primary unit sample space of the inverse CDFs at each scattering event along both the eye and light subpaths, thereby adaptively yielding small path mutations where the proposal density is large, and large path mutations where it is small, in turn reducing correlation by increasing the acceptance *probability* (e.g., based on the maximum contribution of the estimators formed by all eye 129
subpaths and light subpaths combinations) [Kelemen *et al.*, 2002, Szirmay-Kalos and Antal, 2003]. The approach similarly extends to *participating media*, although extra care is required 440
in the case of Woodcock tracking as the number of *random variables* associated with a 129
scattering event is a priori unknown [Raab *et al.*, 2006]. Instead, the estimator corresponding to a specific length of the eye and light paths can itself be defined as being part of the state to be mutated, thereby allowing the associated MIS weight to be incorporated within the target function so as to favor the most effective estimators [Hachisuka *et al.*, 2014]. In order to reduce the start-up bias and guarantee ergodicity, the local mutations of the current state may be probabilistically replaced by large uncorrelated steps independent of it, from which the normalization factor of the target PDF can be progressively evaluated [Kelemen *et al.*, 2002, Szirmay-Kalos and Antal, 2003]. Based on statistics such as the average acceptance *probability* of the small and large steps, and the average probability of large steps to propose 129
paths with a non-zero contribution, the probability of generating large steps may then be defined so as to maximize the speed of exploration of the sample space if the integrand is relatively flattened in primary sample space, while favoring local exploration by small steps if it still contains high variations [Zsolnai and Szirmay-Kalos, 2013].

16.3 FURTHER READING

Additional material may be found in surveys dedicated to Monte Carlo methods for global illumination [Szirmay-Kalos, 1999, Szirmay-Kalos, 2000] and in books dedicated to global illumination in general [Dutré *et al.*, 2002, Dutré *et al.*, 2006], in courses dedicated to Monte

Carlo ray tracing for realistic image synthesis [Jensen *et al.*, 2001a] and in surveys dedicated to unbiased physically based rendering [van Antwerpen, 2010, van Antwerpen, 2011].

CHAPTER 17

Statistic Methods

TABLE OF CONTENTS

17.1 GLOBAL ILLUMINATION

17.1.1 (Ir)radiance Caching

17.1.1.1 Irradiance Caching

Based on the observation that indirect lighting generally is a low-frequency signal compared to direct illumination, *irradiance caching* [Ward Larson *et al.*, 1988] consists in pre-computing the former at a sparse set of sample points in the scene and then approximating irradiance at an arbitrary location by interpolating the nearby samples.

Given a position $\vec{p}$ with surface normal $\hat{n}$, the positional and directional errors with respect to a cache sample s at position $\vec{p}_s$ with surface normal $\hat{n}_s$ may be, respectively, defined as

$$r_s(\vec{p}) \triangleq \frac{\|\vec{p}-\vec{p}_s\|}{r_t} \tag{17.1}$$

$$a_s(\vec{p}) \triangleq \left(1 - \frac{\langle \hat{n}, \hat{n}_s\rangle - c_t}{1-c_t}\right)^{\alpha} = \left(\frac{1-\langle \hat{n}, \hat{n}_s\rangle}{1-c_t}\right)^{\alpha} \tag{17.2}$$

with the tolerance on distance r_t and on cosine angle c_t, and where typically $\alpha \in [1/2, 1]$.

The weight of each sample can then be evaluated as

$$w_s(\vec{p}) \triangleq \frac{1}{r_s(\vec{p}) + a_s(\vec{p})} \tag{17.3}$$

such that $w_s(\vec{p}_s) = \infty$, while typically clamping the weight to zero if it falls below a given threshold w_t. Alternatively, the weight may be defined in terms of any non-negative mono-
44 tonically decreasing *kernel function* K (such as the *triangular function*) as [Tabellion and
47 Lamorlette, 2004, Tabellion and Lamorlette, 2008]

$$w_s(\vec{p}) \triangleq K(\max\{r_s(\vec{p}), a_s(\vec{p})\}) = \min\{K(r_s(\vec{p})), K(a_s(\vec{p}))\} \tag{17.4}$$

or as [Schwarzhaupt *et al.*, 2012]

$$w_s(\vec{p}) \triangleq K(r_s(\vec{p}))K(a_s(\vec{p})) \tag{17.5}$$

Shall the errors be too high, such that the number of samples whose weight is greater than the threshold w_t is too small, or alternatively such that the sum of the weights $\sum_s w_s$ is smaller than a threshold w_t, a new irradiance sample is computed and added to the cache, possibly during an overture pass preliminarily populating the cache prior to the rendering pass. Otherwise, the irradiance at point $\vec{p}$ is estimated as the weighted average

$$E_e(\vec{p}) \approx \frac{\sum_s w_s(\vec{p})(E_s + \langle \hat{n}_s \times \hat{n}, \nabla_r E_s\rangle + \langle \vec{p}-\vec{p}_s, \nabla_t E_s\rangle)}{\sum_s w_s(\vec{p})} \tag{17.6}$$

of the cached sample irradiance values E_s, potentially extrapolated via a first-order Taylor expansion by means of the rotational gradient $\nabla_r E_s$ and translational gradient $\nabla_t E_s$ [Ward Larson and Heckbert, 1992, Ward Larson and Heckbert, 2008]. When estimating the
153 sample irradiance values by *stratified sampling* of the hemisphere, the gradients may be evaluated by interpreting the incident radiance and geometric distance in the strata as a piecewise constant (or piecewise linear via tesselation into triangular patches [Schwarzhaupt *et al.*, 2012]) representation of the environment surrounding each sample point, potentially
440 also taking the influence of *participating media* on surface irradiance into account [Jarosz *et al.*, 2008c, Jarosz, 2008].

Rather than using a fixed tolerance radius r_t, the latter is typically set individually for each irradiance sample in the cache, either as the harmonic mean [Ward Larson *et al.*, 1988]

or as the minimal distance [Tabellion and Lamorlette, 2004, Tabellion and Lamorlette, 2008] of the neighboring surfaces. The consistency in the detection of geometric features might then be improved by clamping the radius to the sum of the distance to and radius of each neighboring sample, which, according to the triangle inequality, is the maximum possible distance to a potentially missed geometric feature that has been detected by a neighboring cache sample [Křivánek *et al.*, 2006, Křivánek *et al.*, 2008a, Křivánek *et al.*, 2008d, Křivánek and Gautron, 2009]. Such a geometric definition allows samples in occluded regions where, akin to regions with changing surface orientation, indirect illumination is more likely to rapidly vary, to have a smaller radius of influence, in turn leading to a higher density of cache samples. The radius of each sample may additionally be perceptually adjusted so as to limit
the variation of extrapolated irradiance after being processed with a *tone mapping* operator 732
[Smyk and Myszkowski, 2002], or by clamping it between a minimum and a maximum rate based on the projected area of the pixels onto the geometry so as to control the density of the samples in screen space [Tabellion and Lamorlette, 2004, Tabellion and Lamorlette, 2008]. As an alternative, elliptical radii of influence can be defined anisotropically within the tangent plane of each irradiance sample by means of a radiometric bound on the integral of the (absolute or relative) error due to first-order extrapolation, estimated with respect to a second-order Taylor extrapolation based on the translational irradiance Hessian [Jarosz *et al.*, 2012], which, akin to the gradient, can be evaluated from a piecewise-constant or piecewise-linear [Schwarzhaupt *et al.*, 2012] hemispherical representation of the surrounding environment.

In order to accelerate the search of samples for which the point $\vec{p}$ is within radial range,
the cached data may be stored in one of a variety of *indexing structures*. In the case of an 356
octree, each sample can be stored in the single node containing $\vec{p}_s$ at the lowest level of 378
the tree whose size encompasses the sample's diameter, such that traversal explores the at-most 8 nodes whose doubled size encompasses the query point $\vec{p}$. Alternatively, each sample might be stored in all of the at-most 8 same-level nodes whose spatial extent overlaps its sphere of influence, such that traversal readily proceeds down the branch containing $\vec{p}$ while considering all stored samples whose radial extent overlaps $\vec{p}$.

In the case of a *constant weight Lambertian* BRDF independent of direction, the reflected 554
radiance readily evaluates to 499

564

$$L_r(\vec{p}, \hat{\omega}_o) \overset{(13.2)}{\underset{(13.1)}{=}} f_r(\vec{p}, \hat{\omega}_o, \hat{\omega}_i) E_e(\vec{p}) \tag{17.7}$$

564

In the case of more general BRDFs instead, the average direction $\hat{\omega}_s$ of the incident illumination at each sample in the cache can be computed as a linear combination of the incident directions with weights given by the luminance of the incident radiance along that direction. Assuming that the illumination at a given point $\vec{p}$ is solely due to the radiance $L_i(\vec{p}, \hat{\omega}_i) = L_a(\vec{p})\delta(\hat{\omega}_i - \hat{\omega}_p)$ coming from a single average direction [Tabellion and Lamorlette, 2004, Tabellion and Lamorlette, 2008]

$$\hat{\omega}_p \triangleq \frac{\sum_s w_s(\vec{p})\hat{\omega}_s}{\|\sum_s w_s(\vec{p})\hat{\omega}_s\|} \tag{17.8}$$

the irradiance at the point reduces to

426

$$E_e(\vec{p}) \overset{(10.50)}{=} \int_{2\pi^+} L_a(\vec{p})\delta(\hat{\omega}_i - \hat{\omega}_p)\langle \hat{n}, \hat{\omega}_i \rangle \mathrm{d}\hat{\omega}_i \overset{(2.218)}{=} L_a(\vec{p})\langle \hat{n}, \hat{\omega}_p \rangle \tag{17.9}$$

45

such that $L_a(\vec{p}) = \frac{E_e(\vec{p})}{\langle \hat{n}, \hat{\omega}_p \rangle}$. It then follows that $L_i(\vec{p}, \hat{\omega}_i) = \frac{E_e(\vec{p})}{\langle \hat{n}, \hat{\omega}_p \rangle}\delta(\hat{\omega}_i - \hat{\omega}_p)$, and the reflected radiance therefore becomes

475 45
$$L_r(\vec{p},\hat{\omega}_o) \overset{(12.2)}{=} \int_{2\pi^+} \frac{E_e(\vec{p})}{\langle \hat{n},\hat{\omega}_p\rangle}\delta(\hat{\omega}_i-\hat{\omega}_p)f_r(\vec{p},\hat{\omega}_o,\hat{\omega}_i)\langle \hat{n},\hat{\omega}_i\rangle \mathrm{d}\hat{\omega}_i \overset{(2.218)}{=} E_e(\vec{p})f_r(\vec{p},\hat{\omega}_o,\hat{\omega}_p) \quad (17.10)$$

566 In both cases, the *measurement equation* is then evaluated via length-1 eye paths as

566 475
$$\begin{aligned} M &\underset{(12.7)}{\overset{(13.20)}{=}} \int_S\int_S (L_e(\vec{q},-\widehat{pq})+L_r(\vec{q},-\widehat{pq}))W_e(\vec{p},\widehat{pq})G(\vec{p},\vec{q})\mathrm{d}A(\vec{q})\mathrm{d}A(\vec{p}) \\ &= \int_S\int_S (L_e(\vec{q},-\widehat{pq})+f_r(\vec{q},-\widehat{pq},\hat{\omega}_q)E_e(\vec{q}))W_e(\vec{p},\widehat{pq})G(\vec{p},\vec{q})\mathrm{d}A(\vec{q})\mathrm{d}A(\vec{p}) \quad (17.11) \end{aligned}$$

17.1.1.2 Radiance Caching

626 499 The proper generalization of *irradiance caching* to non-*Lambertian* BRDFs consists in storing the radiance incident at each cache point, a technique known as *radiance caching* [Křivánek and Žára, 2004, Křivánek *et al.*, 2005b, Křivánek, 2005, Křivánek *et al.*, 2008c]. By projecting both incident radiance and low-frequency glossy BRDFs onto a (hemi-)spherical harmonic basis, the reflectance integral can then be evaluated as the dot product of their respective coefficients. While doing so requires the explicit directional realignment of the basis functions via harmonic rotations, thereby bypassing the need for rotational extrapolation, a first-order Taylor extrapolation in the spatial domain may be readily carried by means of the translational gradients [Křivánek *et al.*, 2005a, Křivánek, 2005, Křivánek *et al.*, 2008b].

626 Akin to *irradiance caching*, the consistency in the detection of geometric features might be improved by clamping the radius of influence of each cache sample to the sum of the distance and radius of each neighboring sample. Moreover, the threshold w_t below which the weight $w_s(\vec{p})$ at a given interpolation point $\vec{p}$ is clamped to zero can be individually adapted at each cache sample and reduced such that its contribution to the reflected radiance at $\vec{p}$ (which accounts for the BRDF properties) relative to that of neighboring cache samples falls below a perceptible threshold, in turn leading to an increased density of cache samples [Křivánek, 2005, Křivánek *et al.*, 2006, Křivánek *et al.*, 2008a].

440 The radiance caching scheme may be similarly extended to *participating media* by resorting to spherical harmonics and by generalizing the translational gradient to account for volumetric scattering [Jarosz *et al.*, 2007, Jarosz *et al.*, 2008a, Jarosz, 2008]. On the other hand, handling high-frequency glossy BRDFs requires the explicit storage of each individual directional radiance sample, progressively evaluated and cached akin to the spatial samples,
155 in which case the reflectance integral is evaluated by *importance sampling* the BRDF and interpolating the incident radiance from the directional samples cached in the neighboring spatial samples [Gassenbauer *et al.*, 2009].

17.1.2 Instant Radiosity

17.1.2.1 Overview

554 Initially introduced for diffuse surfaces with *constant weight Lambertian* BRDFs whose ra-
499 564 diosity and exitant radiance are related by $J_e(\vec{p}) \overset{(13.5)}{=} L_o(\vec{p},\hat{\omega}_o)\pi$, *instant radiosity* [Keller,
618 139 1997] is a form of *bidirectional path tracing* solely relying on *estimators* with length-1 eye paths

618
$$\tilde{M}_n \overset{(16.84)}{=} W_1 f_r(\vec{p}_0,\vec{p}_1,\vec{p}_2)G(\vec{p}_1,\vec{p}_2)f_r(\vec{p}_1,\vec{p}_2,\vec{p}_3)L_2 \quad (17.12)$$

It follows that the *variance* of the *estimator* is mainly affected by the reflectance and 143 139
geometric variations between the primary surface point visible from the sensor and the points
of the light paths. As such, the technique is highly suited to resolve $EDDS^*L$ paths, but
its efficiency decreases whenever $\vec{p}_1$ or $\vec{p}_2$ lie on highly glossy or *specular surfaces*, as well 486
as in the proximity of visible geometry where the distance term in the denominator of the
geometric term might become arbitrarily small, the high contribution of both being sampled
with a relatively low probability.

Rather than generating a new light path for each eye path, though, the light subpaths
are typically precomputed and stored so as to amortize their computational cost over all eye
subpaths. Incrementally constructing each *estimator* $\tilde{M}_n$ of path length n by extending an 139
estimator $\tilde{M}_{n-1}$ of path length $n-1$ with an additional vertex then entails storing all vertices 139
of the light paths rather than just their endpoints.

Each vertex of a light path therefore acts as a virtual *point light* (*VPL*) "instantly" 431
illuminating the scene with the properties of the material that it is incident upon, thereby
correlating the estimation error across pixels. Instead of random noise, the correlation most
notably manifests itself by hard shadows cast by the VPLs, as well as by bright spots in
the vicinity of concave geometric corners, a phenomenon know as the *weak singularity*, as
illustrated in *Figure 17.1*. From a statistical standpoint, the result is still unbiased, and the 629
bright spots merely correspond to correlated estimates with an arbitrarily large *variance*, 143
hence requiring an arbitrarily large number of samples to compensate the result so as to
converge to an accurate estimate.

Figure 17.1: Instant Radiosity: Visual comparison of instant radiosity with 16 paths per pixel, without (left) and with (right) clamping.

17.1.2.2 Clamping and Bias Compensation

In order to reduce the impact of the weak singularities, the geometric term may be clamped
to a fixed predetermined bound G_b, thereby introducing bias in the *estimator* 139

628
$$\tilde{M}_n \overset{(17.12)}{=} W_1 f_r(\vec{p}_0, \vec{p}_1, \vec{p}_2) \min\{G(\vec{p}_1, \vec{p}_2), G_b\} f_r(\vec{p}_1, \vec{p}_2, \vec{p}_3) L_2 \quad (17.13)$$

which leads to a darkening of the estimated illumination near geometric corners.

To in turn address this issue, *bias compensation* [Kollig and Keller, 2004] evaluates the
139 missing contributions by means of a secondary *estimator* based on length-2 eye paths. From
the identity

$$\begin{aligned} G(\vec{p}_1,\vec{p}_2) &= \min\{G(\vec{p}_1,\vec{p}_2),G_b\}+G(\vec{p}_1,\vec{p}_2)-\min\{G(\vec{p}_1,\vec{p}_2),G_b\} \\ &= \min\{G(\vec{p}_1,\vec{p}_2),G_b\}+\max\{0,G(\vec{p}_1,\vec{p}_2)-G_b\} \end{aligned} \tag{17.14}$$

can then be defined the complementary weights

$$w_1(\vec{p}_0,\ldots,\vec{p}_n) \triangleq \frac{\min\{G(\vec{p}_1,\vec{p}_2),G_b\}}{G(\vec{p}_1,\vec{p}_2)} = \min\left\{1,\frac{G_b}{G(\vec{p}_1,\vec{p}_2)}\right\} \tag{17.15}$$

$$w_2(\vec{p}_0,\ldots,\vec{p}_n) \triangleq \frac{\max\{0,G(\vec{p}_1,\vec{p}_2)-G_b\}}{G(\vec{p}_1,\vec{p}_2)} = \max\left\{0,1-\frac{G_b}{G(\vec{p}_1,\vec{p}_2)}\right\} \tag{17.16}$$

139 forming a particular heuristic with which to combine the two bidirectional *estimators* via
158 *multiple importance sampling*

618

$$\begin{aligned} \tilde{M}_n &\overset{(16.85)}{=} \sum_{j=1}^{2} w_j(\vec{p}_0,\ldots,\vec{p}_n)W_j f_r(\vec{p}_{j-1},\vec{p}_j,\vec{p}_{j+1})G(\vec{p}_j,\vec{p}_{j+1})f_r(\vec{p}_j,\vec{p}_{j+1},\vec{p}_{j+2})L_{j+1} \\ &= \frac{\min\{G(\vec{p}_1,\vec{p}_2),G_b\}}{G(\vec{p}_1,\vec{p}_2)}W_1 f_r(\vec{p}_0,\vec{p}_1,\vec{p}_2)G(\vec{p}_1,\vec{p}_2)f_r(\vec{p}_1,\vec{p}_2,\vec{p}_3)L_2 \\ &+ \frac{\max\{0,G(\vec{p}_1,\vec{p}_2)-G_b\}}{G(\vec{p}_1,\vec{p}_2)}W_2 f_r(\vec{p}_1,\vec{p}_2,\vec{p}_3)G(\vec{p}_2,\vec{p}_3)f_r(\vec{p}_2,\vec{p}_3,\vec{p}_4)L_3 \\ &= W_1 f_r(\vec{p}_0,\vec{p}_1,\vec{p}_2)\min\{G(\vec{p}_1,\vec{p}_2),G_b\}f_r(\vec{p}_1,\vec{p}_2,\vec{p}_3)L_2 \\ &+ W_2 f_r(\vec{p}_1,\vec{p}_2,\vec{p}_3)\max\left\{0,1-\frac{G_b}{G(\vec{p}_1,\vec{p}_2)}\right\}G(\vec{p}_2,\vec{p}_3)f_r(\vec{p}_2,\vec{p}_3,\vec{p}_4)L_3 \end{aligned} \tag{17.17}$$

139 As the weight of the second *estimator* is zero for all surface points $\vec{p}_2$ at which

246

$$G(\vec{p}_1,\vec{p}_2) \overset{(6.71)}{=} \langle \hat{n}_{p_1},\widehat{p_1p_2}\rangle \frac{T(\vec{p}_1,\vec{p}_2)}{\|\vec{p}_2-\vec{p}_1\|^2}\langle \hat{n}_{p_2},-\widehat{p_1p_2}\rangle \leq \frac{\langle \hat{n}_{p_1},\widehat{p_1p_2}\rangle}{\|\vec{p}_2-\vec{p}_1\|^2} \leq G_b \tag{17.18}$$

the hemispherical sampling of $\vec{p}_2$ can be restricted to surface points satisfying

$$\|\vec{p}_2-\vec{p}_1\| \leq \sqrt{\frac{\langle \hat{n}_{p_1},\widehat{p_1p_2}\rangle}{G_b}} \tag{17.19}$$

139 Recursively clamping and compensating the bias of each subsequent *estimator* then yields
the weights

$$w_j(\vec{p}_0,\ldots,\vec{p}_n) = \begin{cases} 0 & \text{if } j=0 \\ \min\left\{1,\frac{G_b}{G(\vec{p}_j,\vec{p}_{j+1})}\right\}p_j & \text{if } j\in[1,n-1] \\ p_j & \text{if } j=n \end{cases} \tag{17.20}$$

139 where $p_j = \prod_{i=1}^{j-1} 1-w_i(\vec{p}_0,\ldots,\vec{p}_n)$, such that the combination of bidirectional *estimators*
reads

618

$$\begin{aligned} \tilde{M}_n &\overset{(16.85)}{=} \sum_{j=1}^{n-2}\min\left\{1,\frac{G_b}{G(\vec{p}_j,\vec{p}_{j+1})}\right\}p_j W_j f_r(\vec{p}_{j-1},\vec{p}_j,\vec{p}_{j+1})G(\vec{p}_j,\vec{p}_{j+1})f_r(\vec{p}_j,\vec{p}_{j+1},\vec{p}_{j+2})L_{j+1} \\ &= \sum_{j=1}^{n-2} p_j W_j f_r(\vec{p}_{j-1},\vec{p}_j,\vec{p}_{j+1})\min\{G(\vec{p}_j,\vec{p}_{j+1}),G_b\}f_r(\vec{p}_j,\vec{p}_{j+1},\vec{p}_{j+2})L_{j+1} \end{aligned} \tag{17.21}$$

139 to which is similarly added the contributions of the *estimators* based on *path tracing* with
613 *next-event estimation* and *unidirectional path tracing*, with weights $w_{n-1}(\vec{p}_0,\ldots,\vec{p}_n)$ and
614 $w_n(\vec{p}_0,\ldots,\vec{p}_n)$, respectively.
613
613

17.1.2.3 VPL Sampling

In order to decrease the *variance* remaining from the geometric term, each VPL may be 143
probabilistically discarded during a preliminary phase based on its average contribution to
the sensor relative to that of the other VPLs (estimated by connecting the VPL to a small
set of sample points on primary surfaces visible from the camera), while dividing by their
acceptance probability (and thereby uniformizing) the global contribution of the remaining
VPLs [Georgiev and Slusallek, 2010, Georgiev, 2015, Ch. 5]. The relative contributions of the
latter to each individual primary sample point can additionally be cached and interpolated
at neighboring shading points so as to yield probability mass functions proportional to the
local contributions of the VPLs in different parts of the scene, although the robustness
of the resulting *estimator* might require a combination with more conservative PMFs that 139
ignore translational occlusion and bound the effect of rotational variations [Georgiev *et al.*,
2012b, Georgiev, 2015, Ch. 6].

As an alternative, the set of VPLs generated along the light paths may be complemented
by tracing length-2 eye paths and instantiating "reverse" VPLs at their endpoints (whose
illumination can be determined by standard instant radiosity via connections to light-path
VPLs, while their PDF is given as the marginal density of the eye paths integrated over the
first two path vertices), each VPL of either type being then probabilistically discarded or
reweighted based on its average contribution to the sensor, similarly estimated at a small set
of sample points on primary surfaces visible from the camera [Segovia *et al.*, 2006, Segovia,
2007, Ch. 7]. Instead, a distribution with uniform average contribution to the sensor might
be directly obtained by instantiating a diffuse VPL (with associated multiplicity) at the
(potentially collocated) third eye vertex along bidirectional paths generated by multiple-try
Metropolis light transport [Segovia *et al.*, 2007, Segovia, 2007, Ch. 8]. 621

17.1.2.4 Glossy Surfaces

In the case of glossy surfaces, the weak singularities may additionally be caused by peaks in the BRDFs at the two ends of the segment connecting the eye and light paths. In order to address this issue, clamping can be extended to account for the BRDF of the primary surface by means of a variable bound defined as [Kollig and Keller, 2004]

$$G_b \triangleq \frac{G_f}{f_r(\vec{p}_0, \vec{p}_1, \vec{p}_2)} \tag{17.22}$$

in terms of a fixed threshold G_f, such that hemispherical sampling of $\vec{p}_2$ becomes restricted to surface points satisfying

$$\|\vec{p}_2 - \vec{p}_1\| \overset{(17.19)}{\leq} \sqrt{\frac{f_r(\vec{p}_0, \vec{p}_1, \vec{p}_2)\langle \hat{n}_{p_1}, \widehat{\vec{p}_1\vec{p}_2}\rangle}{G_f}} \tag{17.23}$$ 630

although recursive bias compensation typically tends to degenerate into *path tracing* in the 613
case of highly peaked BRDFs.

Clamping can be similarly extended to also account for the BRDF of the secondary
surface, while bias compensation may be locally evaluated from a set of reverse VPLs (potentially tailored to the image tile from which the eye path originated) [Davidovič *et al.*,
2010]. Instead, the effect of the weak singularities can be preemptively reduced by blurring
each VPL (i.e., splatting its power onto its vicinity) into a virtual spherical light (*VSL*) whose
radius is determined by the distance to the k nearest virtual lights, while its contribution
at a point in the scene might be evaluated by *multiple importance sampling* of the uniform 158
cone subtended by the VSL and of the BRDFs at the shading point and at the virtual light
[Hašan *et al.*, 2009].

17.1.2.5 *Participating Media*

440 Clamping and bias compensation can similarly be extended to *participating media*, in which case the compensation step ought to integrate the contributions from the entire volume surrounding a given shading point [Raab *et al.*, 2006]. Due to the exponential decay of transmittance, though, bias compensation is typically restricted to a single recursion step, while explicitly sampling the volume within a given distance of each ray-marching step along the primary ray by means of a locally homogeneous extinction coefficient, and connecting the resulting sample point to a random subset of the VPLs [Engelhardt *et al.*, 2010, Engelhardt *et al.*, 2012].

As an alternative, the effect of the weak singularities may be preemptively reduced by
436 instantiating virtual *ray lights* (*VRL*) at the segments of the light paths in place of VPLs at their vertices, and estimating their contributions at a primary surface point or along primary
155 volumetric rays by *importance sampling* the corresponding 1-D or 2-D integral, respectively [Novák *et al.*, 2012b]. In the spirit of VSLs, the effect of the weak singularities might be further reduced by blurring each VRL into a cylindrical virtual beam light, whose radius can then be progressively reduced during rendering in order to yield biased but consistent estimates [Novák *et al.*, 2012a].

17.1.2.6 *Further Reading*

Additional material may be found in courses and surveys dedicated to many-light methods [Křivánek *et al.*, 2012, Dachsbacher *et al.*, 2014].

17.1.3 Particle Tracing

17.1.3.1 *Overview*

44 By expanding the dimensionality of integration by means of a Dirac *delta function* and
44 substituting the latter with an arbitrary *kernel function* K (typically in the form of a *radial*
204 *filter*), the reflectance integral may be approximated as

475
45

$$\begin{aligned} L_r(\vec{p}, \hat{\omega}_o) &\overset{(12.2)}{\underset{(2.218)}{=}} \int_{2\pi^+} f_r(\vec{p}, \hat{\omega}_o, \hat{\omega}_i) \int_S \delta(\|\vec{q} - \vec{p}\|) L_i(\vec{q}, \hat{\omega}_i) \langle \hat{n}_q, \hat{\omega}_i \rangle \mathrm{d}A(\vec{q}) \mathrm{d}\hat{\omega}_i \\ &\approx \int_{2\pi^+} f_r(\vec{p}, \hat{\omega}_o, \hat{\omega}_i) \int_S K(\|\vec{q} - \vec{p}\|) L_i(\vec{q}, \hat{\omega}_i) \langle \hat{n}_q, \hat{\omega}_i \rangle \mathrm{d}A(\vec{q}) \mathrm{d}\hat{\omega}_i \\ &= \int_S \int_{2\pi^+} L_i(\vec{q}, \hat{\omega}_i) f_r(\vec{p}, \hat{\omega}_o, \vec{q}, \hat{\omega}_i) \langle \hat{n}_q, \hat{\omega}_i \rangle \mathrm{d}\hat{\omega}_i \mathrm{d}A(\vec{q}) \end{aligned} \tag{17.24}$$

essentially substituting the BRDF $f_r(\vec{p}, \hat{\omega}_o, \hat{\omega}_i)$ with a higher-dimensional BSSRDF
554
499 $f_r(\vec{p}, \hat{\omega}_o, \vec{q}, \hat{\omega}_i) \triangleq f_r(\vec{p}, \hat{\omega}_o, \hat{\omega}_i) K(\|\vec{q} - \vec{p}\|)$. Considering a *constant weight Lambertian* BRDF, the formulation of the reflectance integral becomes

564
426

$$\begin{aligned} L_r(\vec{p}, \hat{\omega}_o) &\overset{(13.1)}{\approx} \int_S \int_{2\pi^+} L_i(\vec{q}, \hat{\omega}_i) \frac{\rho(\vec{p})}{\pi} K(\|\vec{q} - \vec{p}\|) \langle \hat{n}_q, \hat{\omega}_i \rangle \mathrm{d}\hat{\omega}_i \mathrm{d}A(\vec{q}) \\ &= \frac{\rho(\vec{p})}{\pi} \int_S K(\|\vec{q} - \vec{p}\|) \int_{2\pi^+} L_i(\vec{q}, \hat{\omega}_i) \langle \hat{n}_q, \hat{\omega}_i \rangle \mathrm{d}\hat{\omega}_i \mathrm{d}A(\vec{q}) \\ &\overset{(10.50)}{=} \frac{\rho(\vec{p})}{\pi} \int_S K(\|\vec{q} - \vec{p}\|) E_e(\vec{q}) \mathrm{d}A(\vec{q}) \end{aligned} \tag{17.25}$$

which, in the case of a cylindrical kernel $K(\|\vec{q} - \vec{p}\|) = \frac{\chi_{[0,r]}(\|\vec{q} - \vec{p}\|)}{\Delta A(\vec{p})}$ of support $\Delta A(\vec{p}) = \pi r^2$ with radius r expressed in terms of the indicator function, might be evaluated by *density*
167 *estimation* of the incident flux as

$$L_r(\vec{p}, \hat{\omega}_o) \approx \frac{\rho(\vec{p})}{\pi} \int_S \frac{\chi_{[0,r]}(\|\vec{q}-\vec{p}\|)}{\Delta A(\vec{p})} E_e(\vec{q}) \mathrm{d}A(\vec{q}) = \frac{\rho(\vec{p})}{\pi} \frac{\int_{\Delta A(\vec{p})} E_e(\vec{q}) \mathrm{d}A(\vec{q})}{\Delta A(\vec{p})} \overset{(10.48)}{=} \frac{\rho(\vec{p})}{\pi} \frac{\Delta \Phi_e(\vec{p})}{\Delta A(\vec{p})} \tag{17.26}$$ 426

When introducing the above approximation at a given depth in the path integral, the
latter then formulates contributions M_n of path length n in terms of $n+2$, rather than
$n+1$, nested surface integrals. Crude *particle tracing* is then defined as an extended form of
bidirectional path tracing solely relying on *estimators* with length-1 eye paths 618 139

$$\tilde{M}_n \overset{(17.39)}{\approx} W_1 f_r(\vec{p}_0, \vec{p}_1, \vec{p}_2) K(\|\vec{p}_1^W - \vec{p}_1^L\|) L_1 \tag{17.27}$$ 642

where the depth-1 vertex $\vec{p}_1^L$ generated by the light path acts as a light particle illuminating the depth-1 vertex $\vec{p}_1^W$ generated by the eye path.

It follows that the *variance* of the *estimator* is mainly affected by the reflectance variations 143
between the primary surface point visible from the sensor and the light particles. As such, 139
the technique is highly suited to resolve EDS^*L paths (including caustic paths of the form
EDS^+L), but its efficiency decreases whenever $\vec{p}_1$ lies on a highly glossy surface whose
high contribution is sampled with a relatively low probability, thereby failing to evaluate
illumination in the limit of $ES(D|G|S)^*L$ paths, i.e., reflections off *specular surfaces*. 486

Rather than generating a new light path for each eye path, though, the light subpaths are
typically precomputed and stored in one of various forms so as to amortize the computational
cost of their generation over all eye subpaths. Incrementally constructing each *estimator* $\tilde{M}_n$ 139
of path length n by extending an *estimator* $\tilde{M}_{n-1}$ of path length $n-1$ with an additional 139
vertex then entails accounting for all vertices of the light paths rather than just their endpoints.

Irradiance Mapping In the case of diffuse surfaces, the contributions of incident particles may
be bilinearly accumulated in the texels of fixed-resolution textures [Arvo, 1986], referred to as
irradiance maps, whose irradiance values are readily given by the density of aggregated flux
per world-space area of the respective texels. Instead, adapting the resolution of the irradiance
maps to the density of the particle entails resorting to hierarchical structures such as quadtree
textures, subdividing each node whenever the number of photons contained within exceeds
a given threshold [Heckbert, 1990]. On the other hand, smoother reconstructions of the
irradiance signal can be obtained by projecting the flux of the incident particles onto higher-
order *B-spline basis functions*, the coefficients of which are similarly stored in the texels of 333
the irradiance maps [Redner *et al.*, 1995].

The approach may also be applied to *composite surfaces* such as *constructive solid ge-* 301
ometry by assigning a separate irradiance map to each individual CSG primitive, although 303
estimating the surface area associated with texels that overlap partially clipped geometry
might require their subdivision into sub-texels using an adaptive structure such as a quadtree [Wilkie *et al.*, 1998, Wilkie, 2001, Ch. 5]. More complex geometry for which no intrinsic
texture parameterization exists might instead be handled via a directional mapping parameterized by the normal of the surface at the particles (the surface area associated with each
texel being given by the cumulative area of all surfaces whose normal maps to the texel),
and by hierarchically allocating one such map at each node of the scene graph in order to
mitigate the assumption that similarly oriented surfaces have similar irradiance values, with
the *variance* reduction provided by aggregating a greater number of particle contributions 143
towards the higher levels of the tree [Wilkie *et al.*, 2000, Wilkie *et al.*, 2001, Wilkie, 2001,
Ch. 6].

Stochastic Radiosity Whereas soft indirect illumination due to multiple diffuse reflections
593 is adequately handled by the progressive refinement *radiosity method*, the latter can be
633 combined with *irradiance mapping* in order to capture sharp indirect illumination such as
155 caustics due to specular light paths reaching a diffuse surface (possibly *importance sampling*
429 directions towards specular objects by means of a spherical grid per *light source*), while
598 handling direct illumination and primary specular reflections using recursive *ray tracing*
[Shirley, 1990]. An interruptible adaptation of such a scheme then allows the results to be
progressively computed and displayed, while ultimately substituting the radiosity solution
613 with one computed using *path tracing* [Chen *et al.*, 1991].

By exploiting the relationship between radiosity and irradiance given by the *radiosity*
564 *equation*, the radiosity solution may alternatively be directly computed via particle tracing
by estimating the flux density of each patch of a tesselated representation of the scene
geometry [Shirley *et al.*, 1995], a technique commonly referred to as *stochastic radiosity*.
593 Akin to the *radiosity method*, structuring the mesh according to the density of the particles
is then readily achievable via adaptive refinement [Pattanaik and Mudur, 1992, Pattanaik,
1993a, Ch. 4].

634 **Photon Mapping** As illustrated in *Figure 17.2*, the particles reaching surfaces for which
a texture parameterization or meshing is problematic can be represented with an infinite
resolution as individual photon particles, either solely defined by their position and light
contribution onto diffuse surfaces [Jensen and Christensen, 1995b], or by additionally storing
499 their direction of incidence in order to resolve illumination on non-*Lambertian* materials
[Jensen, 1996b, Jensen, 1997], a technique known as *photon mapping*.

Figure 17.2: Photon Mapping: Rendering of a scene with a point light source and a pinhole camera using photon mapping, with as many paths as the number of rows/columns in the image (left) and with 16 times as many paths as the number of pixels (right).

In order to be queried with a sub-linear complexity during the subsequent rendering pass,
356 the photons are typically stored in one of a variety of *indexing structures*, then commonly
369 referred to as the *photon map*, such as a *grid* or a *k-D tree*. Rather than building the latter on
381 381 the fly during the light tracing pass [Jensen and Christensen, 1995b], the *k-D tree* may be a
posteriori constructed in a balanced manner so as to yield faster tree traversals, and possibly
represented in a compact manner as a heap so as to reduce its memory requirements [Jensen,

1996b, Jensen, 1997]. In order to further reduce the tree depth and increase performance, a
separate photon map might instead be associated with each group of geometrically connected
polygons whose pairwise angle with adjacent *polygons* falls below a given threshold, thereby 262
explicitly separating photons whose surface orientation would significantly differ from the 262
normal at the query point [Larsen and Christensen, 2003]. As an alternative, efficient trees
can be constructed by adapting the *surface area heuristic*, modified by substituting the 395
surface area of the nodes by the surface area of the geometry within their bounding volume
extended by the kernel radius, which is readily approximated by the volume of the latter
[Wald *et al.*, 2004].

17.1.3.2 Bias Reduction

By filtering the particles with a *kernel function*, *density estimation* introduces bias in the 44
reconstructed signal. As illustrated in *Figure 17.3*, the bias manifests itself in different forms 167
depending on the geometric configuration of the surfaces in the vicinity of the query point, 635
and is typically categorized as:

- *proximity bias*: blurring of the incident illumination on planar surfaces
- *topological bias*: brightening due to the underestimation of the underlying area on curved surfaces
- *boundary bias*: darkening due to the overestimation of the underlying area in the vicinity of geometric edges
- *occlusion bias*: light leaks and shadow leaks in the vicinity of geometric occluders

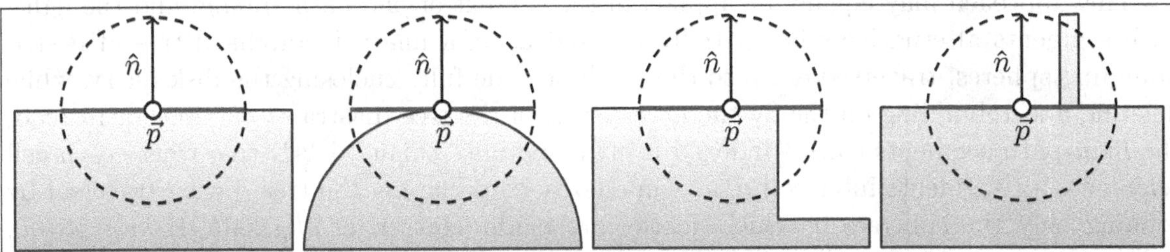

Figure 17.3: Bias Types: Illustration of the various types of bias that particle tracing is prone to, known as proximity, topological, boundary and occlusion bias (from left to right, respectively).

When setting the radius of a cylindrical kernel to the distance to the kth nearest neighbor,
including the latter within the support of the kernel results in a systematic density overestimation [Jarosz *et al.*, 2012, §4.4] while excluding it yields a systematic underestimation.
To address this issue, the kth nearest neighbor ought to be weighted by the transitional value
of the *rectangular function* at its boundary, or the radius of the cylindrical kernel should 46
instead be set to the average distance between the kth and $k+1^{\text{th}}$ nearest neighbors [García
et al., 2012].

Support Correction In order to mitigate the impact of topological bias, the contribution of
a particle to the density estimate at a point is typically weighted by the cosine angle between
their respective normals, effectively projecting the surface onto the tangent plane at the query
point, in turn resulting in a darkening due to the overestimation of the underlying projected
area akin to boundary bias. On the other hand, in the context of *stochastic radiosity*, it has 633

167 been proposed to address boundary bias by first performing a preliminary *density estimation* followed by a least-squares regression to fit a linear polynomial to the estimated density at kernel-weighted nearby observations, thereby maintaining the density estimates unchanged in non-boundary regions [Walter *et al.*, 1997, Walter, 1998, Ch. 4].

634 In the context of *photon mapping*, it has alternatively been proposed to address both boundary and topological bias by querying both the neighboring photons and the polygonal
378 geometry (spatially indexed using an *octree*) lying within and clipped to an axis-aligned cubical search region centered around the query point, and evaluating the flux density of each photon projected onto the actual geometry [Hey and Purgathofer, 2002]. On the other hand, occlusion bias may be addressed by estimating the surface area of the convex hull of the neighboring photons with that of their bounding octagon in the tangent plane (possibly using one individual octagon for each octant around the query point to handle concave corners) in order to avoid shadow leaks, while avoiding light leaks by tracing feeler rays along the tangent plane to detect nearby occluding geometry [Tobler and Maierhofer, 2006].

633 **Light Rays** In the context of *stochastic radiosity*, it has been proposed to address boundary bias by extruding the edges of the triangles at geometric boundaries by the radius of the kernel, and to additionally account for the contributions of particles whose ray trajectory intersects the extension during the light tracing pass [Lavignotte and Paulin, 2002]. Boundary bias may be similarly eliminated and topological bias reduced by performing *density estima-*
167 *tion* based on the light-path segments that strike the tangent disk at the query point, while
369 indexing the segments into a set of directional cells, each holding a 2-D *grid* structure oriented orthogonally to the cell's main direction, such that the path segments potentially intersecting
369 a given disk can be queried in sub-linear time by traversing the *grid* cells overlapping the projected disk in each of the directional cells [Lastra *et al.*, 2002a].

634 This approach may equally be applied in the context of *photon mapping*, and the light-path segments alternatively be spatially indexed using a unary hierarchical tree of nested bounding spheres, traversed down to the smallest node fully enclosing the disk query, while deleting and rebuilding on the fly the lower levels of the tree [Lastra *et al.*, 2002b]. Instead,
381 the light-path segments can be indexed using a spatially balanced *k-D tree* where each cell references all segments intersecting it, while lazily constructing the tree during traversal by refining only the subtrees in which queries are made [Havran *et al.*, 2004, Havran *et al.*, 2005a, Herzog, 2005, Ch. 7].

As an alternative, each photon ray may be approximately represented by a set of particles referencing it, regularly spaced (by a factor of the kernel radius) along the ray, and indexed
381 in a *k-D tree* akin to photon particles, so as to (possibly redundantly) retrieve the photon rays intersecting a query disk/sphere by gathering the neighboring reference particles (whose
369 instances can be limited to the cells of the scene's 3-D *grid* and their neighboring cells
381 that do contain geometry) [Zinke and Weber, 2006]. Instead, the *k-D tree* can be built over the intersection points of the primary view rays, and the contributions of the light-path segments (extruded into hemispherically end-capped conical frustums by the orthogonally oriented kernel) splatted onto the viewpoints directly during the photon-tracing pass by means of a conical frustum traversal of the tree [Herzog *et al.*, 2007]. In order to better preserve high-frequency illumination features such as shadow edges, visibility changes along
381 cylindrical photon beams may additionally be accounted for using a *k-D tree*-based voxelized representation of the scene [Herzog and Seidel, 2007].

633 **Bandwidth Selection** In the context of *irradiance mapping*, it has been proposed to address proximity bias by distributing the contributions of the incident particles among texels us-

ing a kernel, whose size is determined by the spatial spread between the intersection points
of the light paths originating from the adjacent cells of a directional grid structure encap-
sulating the *light source*, thereby allowing sharp gradients to be resolved in regions where 429
the wavefront converges while yielding smooth gradients where it diverges [Collins, 1995].
In the context of *stochastic radiosity*, it has also been suggested to mitigate the trade-off 633
between proximity bias and *variance* by preliminarily estimating the bandwidth minimizing 143
the combined *error* (expressed in terms of the kernel function and its second derivative as 148
per a method known as least-squares cross validation in the *density estimation* literature) 167
at each triangular patch, allowing the mesh to be adaptively subdivided to match the local
bandwidth, while distributing the contributions of the particles among the mesh vertices
using a kernel with locally optimal bandwidth during the particle-tracing pass [Lavignotte
and Paulin, 2002].

In the context of *photon mapping*, it has similarly been proposed to iteratively increase 634
the number of nearest neighbors until the density estimate monotonically increases or decreases (as in the vicinity of sharp illumination features) instead of exhibiting a differential
whose sign oscillates (as in regions of constant illumination) [Jensen and Christensen, 1995b,
§3.3 ¶5]. The kernel bandwidth locally minimizing the combined *error* may also be estimated 148
via a binary search between a user-defined minimum (assumed to yield no bias) and maximum number of nearest neighbors, recursing in the lower or upper half of the search domain
if the *error* resulting from the median number of nearest neighbors is probabilistically esti- 148
mated to be dominated by proximity bias or by *variance*, respectively, thereby allowing a 143
larger number of photons to be used in homogeneous regions while restricting the number
of nearest neighbors in regions of highly varying illumination [Schregle, 2003, Schregle, 2004,
Ch. 5].

Observing that some light paths reaching a surface might contain high-frequency illumination while others might instead contain low-frequency illumination, the kernel bandwidth
may be alternatively defined for each photon in terms of the *probability density* of the com- 131
plete light path [Bekaert *et al.*, 2003], or solely in terms of the conditional PDF of its last
segment [Herzog *et al.*, 2007], so as to account for the angular spread of the scattering events.

Instead, *variance* can be reduced along edge-like illumination features without increasing 143
proximity bias across them by means of an anisotropic kernel. The bandwidths of the latter
might then be locally determined by estimating the illumination gradient at each particle in
the photon map, allowing a structure tensor, and in turn a diffusion tensor, to be computed
at a given query point [Schjøth, 2005, Schjøth *et al.*, 2007a, Schjøth *et al.*, 2008, Schjøth,
2009, Ch. 4]. As an alternative, the bandwidths of the anisotropic kernel can be evaluated
from the positional (rather than directional) ray differentials along the light paths [Schjøth
et al., 2007b, Schjøth, 2009, Ch. 5].

Progressive Photon Mapping In the case of a k-NN bandwidth, increasing the number of
particles induces a reduction of the kernel radius, thereby allowing all types of bias to vanish
in the limit, and making *photon mapping* a theoretically consistent *estimator*, although 634 139
actual limitations on the memory requirements of the photon map invalidate this property in
practice. By instead resorting to multiple particle-tracing passes, and progressively reducing
the radius of the cylindrical kernel independently at each query point based on the local
number of photons cumulated after each pass, the *estimator* can then be made consistent 139
in the limit of infinitely many passes, a technique known as *progressive photon mapping*
(*PPM*) [Hachisuka *et al.*, 2008, Hachisuka, 2011, Ch. 5]. The approach may also be extended
to handle distribution *ray tracing* effects such as pixel anti-aliasing and *depth of field* by 598 662
additionally tracing new length-1 eye paths at each pass so as to redefine the query points,
the local statistics of which being then shared with the previous query points that originated

from the same pixel on the sensor [Hachisuka and Jensen, 2009, Hachisuka, 2011, Ch. 7]. Besides generalizing the technique to arbitrary kernels, evaluating the bias of the estimates
143 (in terms of the Laplacian of the kernel) as well as the *variance* of the bias-corrected estimates
148 then allows a probabilistic *error* bound to be derived, thereby providing an automated means of terminating the rendering process as a function of a given target error threshold [Hachisuka *et al.*, 2010b, Hachisuka *et al.*, 2010a, Hachisuka, 2011, Ch. 6].

As an alternative, the reduction factor of the kernel radius can be probabilistically derived and defined globally so as to solely depend on the pass number rather than on sequentially updated local statistics [Knaus and Zwicker, 2011]. Given a d-dimensional kernel of radius
143 139 r, the *variance* of the primary *estimator* and its bias, as given in *Equation 4.232* and *Equa-*
171 171 *tion 4.231*, respectively, can more generally be shown to obey

$$\mathrm{V}[\tilde{f}] \overset{\sim}{\propto} r^{-d} \tag{17.28}$$
$$\mathrm{B}[\tilde{f}] \propto r^{2} \tag{17.29}$$

143 139 which are invariant per pass. For a static kernel radius, the *variance* of a secondary *estimator* $F \triangleq \frac{1}{n}\sum_{j=1}^{n} \tilde{f}_j$ then obeys $\mathrm{V}[F] \propto n^{-1}$ and its bias $\mathrm{B}[F] \propto n^{-0}$. Instead, progressively reducing the kernel radius after each pass according to the sequence

$$\frac{r_j^d}{r_i^d} \triangleq \prod_{k=i}^{j-1} \frac{k+\alpha}{k+1} = \frac{\prod_{k=i}^{j-1} k+\alpha}{\prod_{k=i+1}^{j} k} = \frac{i}{j} \prod_{k=i}^{j-1} \frac{k+\alpha}{k} \overset{i \ll j}{\to} \Theta\left(\frac{i^{1-\alpha}}{j^{1-\alpha}}\right), \quad \forall i \leq j, \forall \alpha \in [0,1] \tag{17.30}$$

where $j = m + i$ after a pass with m new observations, induces a progressive increase in the
143 139 *variance* of the primary *estimator* while decreasing its bias. In contrast, the *variance* of the
143 139 secondary *estimator* still vanishes asymptotically as

144 638
$$\mathrm{V}[F] = \mathrm{V}\left[\frac{1}{n}\sum_{j=1}^{n} \tilde{f}_j\right] \overset{(4.92)}{=} \frac{1}{n^2}\sum_{j=1}^{n} \mathrm{V}[\tilde{f}_j] \overset{(17.28)}{\approx} \frac{\mathrm{V}[\tilde{f}_1]}{n^2}\sum_{j=1}^{n} \frac{r_1^d}{r_j^d} \overset{n\to\infty}{\propto} \frac{1}{n^2} n n^{1-\alpha} = n^{-\alpha} \tag{17.31}$$

and its bias as

638
$$\mathrm{B}[F] = \mathrm{B}\left[\frac{1}{n}\sum_{j=1}^{n} \tilde{f}_j\right] = \frac{1}{n}\sum_{j=1}^{n} \mathrm{B}[\tilde{f}_j] \overset{(17.29)}{\approx} \frac{\mathrm{B}[\tilde{f}_1]}{n}\sum_{j=1}^{n} \left(\frac{r_j^d}{r_1^d}\right)^{\frac{2}{d}} \overset{n\to\infty}{\propto} \frac{1}{n} n n^{\frac{2}{d}(\alpha-1)} = n^{-\frac{2}{d}(1-\alpha)} \tag{17.32}$$

148 139 The mean squared *error* of the *estimator* then reads

148
$$\mathrm{MSE}[F] \overset{(4.115)}{=} \mathrm{V}[F] + \mathrm{B}[F]^2 = O(n^{-\alpha}) + O(n^{-\frac{4}{d}(1-\alpha)}) \tag{17.33}$$

whose asymptotically optimal rate is given by

$$\alpha = \frac{4}{d}(1-\alpha) \iff \alpha = \frac{4}{d+4} \tag{17.34}$$

with a radius sequence

638
$$r_j^d \overset{(17.30)}{=} r_1^d \Theta(j^{\alpha-1}) \iff r_j = r_1 \Theta(j^{-\frac{1-\alpha}{d}}) = r_1 \Theta(j^{-\frac{1}{d+4}}) \tag{17.35}$$

167 In the case of *density estimation* on surfaces using a 2-D kernel, the above equations then
638 638 yield $\alpha \overset{(17.34)}{=} {}^2\!/_3$ and $r_j \overset{(17.35)}{=} r_1 \Theta(j^{-1/6})$ [Kaplanyan and Dachsbacher, 2013, §4.2]. While the asymptotic analysis defines the global relative rate of reduction of the kernel radius, its initial

value r_1, or more generally its local absolute scale factor given a finite number of observations,
still ought to be locally determined in order to minimize the *error*, to which end the bias 148
may be similarly estimated via progressive *density estimation* with an asymptotically optimal 167
radius reduction parameter of $\alpha = {}^3\!/\!_4$ for a 2-D Laplacian kernel whose corresponding radius
reduction rate is then given as $r_j \overset{(17.35)}{=} r_1\Theta(j^{-1/8})$ [Kaplanyan and Dachsbacher, 2013]. 638

17.1.3.3 Variance Reduction

Final Gathering In order to address proximity and occlusion bias, the *density estimation* 167
kernel may be corrected by the inverse ratio of the BRDFs and geometric term of the segment between a photon and its predecessor along the light path, and substituting them with the BRDFs and geometric term (including visibility) of the segment joining the photon's predecessor to the query point instead, although the approach prevents caustics due to specular BRDFs to be resolved [Bekaert *et al.*, 2003].

As an alternative, all types of bias can be reduced by classifying the photons based on the characteristics of the light path from which they emanate. As they result in high-density caustics where a k-NN search yields small kernel radii, photons emanating from DS^*L subpaths (potentially generated with an even greater probability by means of a directional map labeling the specular objects surrounding each *light source*) are then stored in a high-resolution 429
caustic photon map, and their contributions evaluated via direct *density estimation*. On the 167
other hand, photons emanating from light paths containing diffuse reflections, which result in lower densities and therefore larger kernel radii, are stored in a lower-resolution *global*
photon map, and their contributions instead evaluated by means of an alternative *estimator* 139
based on length-2 eye paths

$$\tilde{M}_n \overset{(17.39)}{\approx} W_2 f_r(\vec{p}_1, \vec{p}_2, \vec{p}_3) K(\|\vec{p}_2^{\,W} - \vec{p}_2^{\,L}\|) L_2 \qquad (17.36)$$ 642

a technique known as *final gathering* [Jensen and Christensen, 1995b].

While the latter might be accelerated whenever $\vec{p}_1$ lies on a diffuse surface by storing and
interpolating the results via *irradiance caching*, the second *estimator* additionally provides a 626
means of reducing the *variance* due to the variations in reflectance at $\vec{p}_1$ whenever the latter 139 143
lies on a highly glossy or specular surface. However, in the case of close spatial proximity such as in corners, the spread of the gather rays emanating from $\vec{p}_1$ towards $\vec{p}_2$ is spatially confined, thereby limiting the averaging capability of the final gathering scheme. Extending
the length of the eye path as in *path tracing* then addresses this issue while allowing higher- 613
order glossy/specular scattering events to be similarly handled, at each of which the incident illumination can be importance sampled from the k nearest photons, either by projecting their cumulated contributions into the directional cells of a hemispherical grid-based piecewise-constant PDF (potentially multiplied by the BRDF value corresponding to the photon's incident direction) [Jensen, 1995], or by probabilistically selecting one of the k nearest photons based on their kernel weights and drawing a random direction within a cone centered around
its direction of incidence, both approaches being potentially combined with *BDF sampling* 598
via *multiple importance sampling*. 158

Because *density estimation* is unable to resolve sharp shadow boundaries, the latter are 167
instead evaluated by means of a *direct illumination estimator*. Rather than discarding the 598 139
corresponding photons, though, the particles may be augmented with the ID of the *light*
source from which they emanate and stored in a *direct-illumination photon map* along with 429
"negative" photons created at all subsequent intersections along the ray from that *light*
source, which is then assumed to be fully visible/occluded from a query point during the 429
rendering pass if all neighboring photons with the corresponding ID are positive/negative,

while resolving the penumbra by tracing shadow rays to it if the photons are of mixed sign
[Jensen and Christensen, 1995a]. Alternatively, the ratio of photons with each ID might be
429 directly used to importance sample the corresponding *light source* based on its estimated
contribution to the given measurement [Keller and Wald, 2000, §3]. By combining together
634 the different techniques, *photon mapping* therefore provides a means of efficiently simulating
caustics on both diffuse and non-diffuse surfaces, as well as soft indirect illumination and
598 *direct illumination* [Jensen, 1996a].

554 499 In the case of *constant weight Lambertian* BRDFs, final gathering can be accelerated by
167 precomputing the irradiance at each photon via *density estimation*, the irradiance value being
then readily retrieved from the single photon nearest and with similar normal orientation to
the query point of each gather ray [Christensen, 1999] (which may be efficiently queried by
reducing the initial search radius at each necessarily closer newly visited photon). Rather
than storing the individual photons and their irradiance values, the latter may instead be
369 378 averaged into the voxels of 3-D *grid* bricks hierarchically organized into the nodes of an *octree*,
such that the irradiance value at each gather ray query point can be linearly interpolated
378 from the corresponding voxels in the brick at the *octree* level corresponding to the kernel
radius [Christensen and Batali, 2004].

Assuming that the number of gather ray query points is greater than the number of
photons, final gathering may alternatively be accelerated by preliminarily storing and build-
381 ing a *k-D tree* over the query points, thereby allowing the contributions of the photons to
be splatted onto the neighboring query points during the light-tracing pass [Havran *et al.*,
2005b, Herzog, 2005, Ch. 6]. Instead, the contributions of the photons at each level of the
381 *k-D tree* might be hierarchically redistributed to the spatially neighboring photons stored
in higher levels, such that each query can limit the tree traversal to fewer macrophotons
(aggregating the contributions of the photons at finer tree levels) based on the kernel radius
as well as on the geometric and radiometric coherence of the photons in the traversed nodes
[Spencer and Jones, 2009a].

633 **Particle Distribution** In the context of *stochastic radiosity*, instrumental particles may be
preliminarily traced from each patch into the tesselated scene until they reach the sensor
in order to evaluate their respective surface-averaged cosine-weighted hemispherical importance, which can then be importance sampled (dismissing mutually invisible patches) at each
scattering event during the light-tracing pass [Pattanaik and Mudur, 1993b]. By exploiting
564 565 the adjointness of *radiance transport* and *importance transport*, the technique thereby provides a means of steering the light particles towards visually important regions of the scene
[Pattanaik and Mudur, 1995]. By also preliminarily tracing instrumental particles from each
429 *light source* and aggregating their interactions with the cells of a voxelized representation of
the scene, the visual importance of each individual light can similarly be determined from
the voxels lying within the view frustum so as to form a probability mass function used to
429 importance sample the number of paths emanating from each *light source* during the actual
particle-tracing pass [Pattanaik and Bouatouch, 1995].

634 In the context of *photon mapping*, importons may instead be preliminarily traced from
381 the sensor into the scene and a *k-D tree* built over them (potentially also gathering im-
429 portons along paths traced from small *light sources* in order to refine the importance estimates of the latter), similarly allowing the visual importance at each scattering event of
the particle-tracing pass to be importance sampled from the k nearest importons by projecting their cumulated contributions into the directional cells of a hemispherical grid-based
piecewise-constant PDF (multiplied by the BRDF value corresponding to the importon's
incident direction) [Peter and Pietrek, 1998]. As an alternative, importons can be used to
probabilistically control the deposition of photons in the photon map proportionally to the

estimated local importance [Keller and Wald, 2000, §2], or to locally bound their density by redistributing the contribution of new photons to existing neighboring photons if the local density exceeds a given importance-aware error threshold [Suykens and Willems, 2000].

Instead, the contributions of the photons resulting from the particle-tracing pass may be
homogenized via a series of relaxation steps using a repulsion vector at each photon based
on the offset to its neighbors, while restricting its amplitude along the gradient direction
so as to preserve edges, thereby progressively migrating the photons into a hexagonal-like
distribution with a blue-noise spectrum, yielding a Voronoi-like diagram where the area
of each cell is inversely proportional to the contribution of its photon, which reduces the
variance of the density estimates and allows for a decrease of the kernel radius, in turn 143
reducing bias [Spencer and Jones, 2009b]. The relaxation can also be carried progressively
by redistributing the contribution of new photons to existing neighboring photons so as to
improve their estimates and further refine their distribution [Spencer and Jones, 2013]. As an
alternative, an importance-aware *error* might be evaluated in each cell of a progressively built 148
k-D tree based on the bias-corrected *variance* of the photons contained therein, allowing new 381 143
photon scattering events to be importance sampled by projecting the error of the neighboring
k-D tree nodes into the directional cells of a hemispherical grid-based PDF (multiplied by 381
the BRDF value corresponding to the cell's direction) [Liu and Zheng, 2014].

When dealing with complex *light sources* or BSDFs for which no suitable *importance* 429
sampling scheme exists, the light paths may instead be generated so as to yield photons with 155
more homogeneous contributions by resorting to *Metropolis light transport* as a sampling 621
mechanism for particle tracing [Leeson, 2003]. More generally, a distribution with greater
relative density in regions of the scene that are visually important for *final gathering* can 639
alternatively be obtained by instantiating photons at the first diffuse eye vertices along
bidirectional paths generated by *Metropolis light transport* (optionally seeded with user- 621
defined paths), thereby allowing for a reduction of the kernel radius and of the resulting bias
[Fan *et al.*, 2005]. In order to solely distribute the photons in visually important regions,
the particle tracing might also be carried using Metropolis sampling in the primary unit
sample space of the inverse CDFs with the importance function being defined as the path
visibility, such that a mutation has an acceptance probability of one if the resulting path is
visible to eye gather points, and zero otherwise, while adaptively adjusting the parameters
of the mutation strategies based on the outcome of the previous mutations, and resorting
to replica exchange by simultaneously drawing new paths in the uniform CDF space and
probabilistically exchanging them with the mutated paths in order to provide an automatic
mixture of uniform random samples and mutations that effectively explores the sampling
space and avoids getting stuck in the local maxima of the importance function [Hachisuka
and Jensen, 2011, Hachisuka, 2011, Ch. 8].

Bidirectional Photon Mapping The *estimator* based on direct *density estimation* and the one 139
based on *final gathering* may be combined using *multiple importance sampling* in a way that 167 639
effectively reduces *variance* so long as not both $\vec{p}_1$ and $\vec{p}_2$ lie on highly glossy or *specular* 158
surfaces [Bekaert *et al.*, 2003]. In order to handle a wider range of material configurations, 143 486
bidirectional photon mapping (*BDPM*) [Vorba, 2011] constructs a subset of the paths starting
from the sensor towards the luminaires, and the other subset from the luminaires towards
the sensor, such that the *probability density* of the path is expressed in a separable form as 131
132

$$p(\vec{p}_0, \ldots, \vec{p}_n) \overset{(4.19)}{=} p(\vec{p}_0, \ldots, \vec{p}_j^{W}) p(\vec{p}_j^{L}, \ldots, \vec{p}_n) \tag{17.37}$$

while reformulating the path throughput as

567

$$F(\vec{p}_0,\ldots,\vec{p}_n) \overset{(13.24)}{\approx} F(\vec{p}_0,\ldots,\vec{p}_j^W) f_r(\vec{p}_{j-1},\vec{p}_j,\vec{p}_{j+1}) K(\|\vec{p}_j^W - \vec{p}_j^L\|) F(\vec{p}_j^L,\ldots,\vec{p}_n) \quad (17.38)$$

139 The *estimator* then reads

609 610 611

$$\begin{aligned}\tilde{M}_n &\overset{(16.38)}{\approx} \frac{\begin{aligned}W_e(\vec{p}_0 \to \vec{p}_1) F(\vec{p}_0,\ldots,\vec{p}_j^W) f_r(\vec{p}_{j-1},\vec{p}_j,\vec{p}_{j+1})\\ \times K(\|\vec{p}_j^W - \vec{p}_j^L\|) F(\vec{p}_j^L,\ldots,\vec{p}_n) L_e(\vec{p}_n \to \vec{p}_{n-1})\end{aligned}}{p(\vec{p}_0,\ldots,\vec{p}_j^W) p(\vec{p}_j^L,\ldots,\vec{p}_n)}\\ &\underset{(16.53)}{\overset{(16.43)}{=}} W_j f_r(\vec{p}_{j-1},\vec{p}_j,\vec{p}_{j+1}) K(\|\vec{p}_j^W - \vec{p}_j^L\|) L_j, \quad \forall j \in [1, n-1]\end{aligned} \quad (17.39)$$

143 whose *variance* is mostly sensitive to the reflectance variations between the endpoints of
the eye and light paths. As such, the technique is highly suited to resolve ES^*DS^*L paths
486 (including reflections of caustics off *specular surfaces* via paths of the form ES^+DS^+L), but
its efficiency decreases whenever $\vec{p}_j$ lies on a highly glossy or specular surface, whose high
contribution is sampled with a relatively low probability.

143 139 In order to effectively reduce *variance*, the *estimators* may be combined using *multiple*
158 139 *importance sampling*. For a given path length n, the combined *estimator* then reads

159 642

$$\tilde{M}_n \underset{(17.39)}{\overset{(4.176)}{\approx}} \sum_{j=1}^{n-1} w_j(\vec{p}_0,\ldots,\vec{p}_n) W_j f_r(\vec{p}_{j-1},\vec{p}_j,\vec{p}_{j+1}) K(\|\vec{p}_j^W - \vec{p}_j^L\|) L_j \quad (17.40)$$

with the weight functions

159 641

$$\frac{1}{w_j(\vec{p}_0,\ldots,\vec{p}_n)} \underset{(17.37)}{\overset{(4.180)}{=}} 1 + \sum_{\substack{k=1\\k\neq j}}^{n-1} \left(\frac{p(\vec{p}_0,\ldots,\vec{p}_k^W) p(\vec{p}_k^L,\ldots,\vec{p}_n)}{p(\vec{p}_0,\ldots,\vec{p}_j^W) p(\vec{p}_j^L,\ldots,\vec{p}_n)}\right)^\beta \quad (17.41)$$

139 The above *estimators* can similarly be combined with those based on *bidirectional path*
618 *tracing* using the extended form of *multiple importance sampling*. In the case of a cylindrical
158 kernel $K(\|\vec{q} - \vec{p}\|) = \frac{\chi_{[0,r]}(\|\vec{q}-\vec{p}\|)}{\Delta A(\vec{p})}$ of support $\Delta A(\vec{p}) = \pi r^2$ with radius r expressed in terms
of the indicator function, the weights of the extended balance heuristic are obtained by
139 dividing the joint PDF of the BDPM *estimators* by [Georgiev *et al.*, 2011, Georgiev *et al.*,
2012a, Georgiev, 2012, Georgiev, 2015, Ch. 7–8]

$$\int_S K(\|\vec{q} - \vec{p}\|)^2 \mathrm{d}A(\vec{q}) = \int_S \left(\frac{\chi_{[0,r]}(\|\vec{q} - \vec{p}\|)}{\Delta A(\vec{p})}\right)^2 \mathrm{d}A(\vec{q}) = \int_{\Delta A(\vec{p})} \frac{1}{(\Delta A(\vec{p}))^2} \mathrm{d}A(\vec{q}) = \frac{1}{\Delta A(\vec{p})} \quad (17.42)$$

139 or equivalently by multiplying the joint PDF of the BDPT *estimators* by it instead [Hachisuka
139 *et al.*, 2012b, Hachisuka, 2011, Ch. 9]. Rather than evaluating each *estimator* independently,
the latter can be readily constructed by preliminarily generating and storing the light paths,
and joining every point of an eye path to all photons within the kernel radius, but connecting
it via shadow rays to a single light path in order to limit both correlation and computational
637 cost. Embedding BDPM in the framework of *progressive photon mapping* then results in a
139 consistent combined *estimator* whose weights initially favor BDPM due to the large kernel
radii, thereby yielding a comparable convergence rate, while progressively favoring BDPT
as the kernel radii decrease, ultimately exhibiting the same asymptotic convergence rate for
transport paths that can be resolved by it.

17.1.3.4 Participating Media

In order to handle *participating media*, *stochastic radiosity* can be extended by simulating 440
scattering events via *free-path sampling* while cumulating the volumetric contributions of the 633 600
particles in the voxels of a 3-D regular *grid*, whose values are subsequently integrated along 369
the discretized primary view rays using ray marching [Pattanaik and Mudur, 1993a, Pattanaik, 1993a, Ch. 5]. Similarly, extending *photon mapping* entails storing individual scat- 634
tered particles in a *volume photon map*, which are then queried to perform volumetric *density*
estimation at each ray-marching step by means of a three-dimensional kernel [Jensen and 167
Christensen, 1998], possibly in the fashion of *progressive photon mapping* via an asymptoti- 637
cally optimal radius reduction parameter of $\alpha \overset{(17.34)}{=} 4/7$ whose corresponding radius reduction 638
rate reads $r_j \overset{(17.35)}{=} r_1 \Theta(j^{-1/7})$ [Kaplanyan and Dachsbacher, 2013, §9 ¶3]. 638

As an alternative, the contributions of the photons may be continuously integrated along
the primary view rays, either by splatting each photon as a 2-D sprite onto the screen
[Boudet *et al.*, 2005], or by holistically querying the photons overlapping a given view ray
by means of a *bounding volume hierarchy* built over their k-NN-based kernel radii [Jarosz 360
et al., 2008d, Jarosz *et al.*, 2008e, Jarosz, 2008]. In the case of an *isotropic phase function*, 446
density estimation might instead be carried in a *parametric* fashion by progressively fitting 444 167
a *bounding volume hierarchy* of truncated anisotropic *Gaussian sources* to the photon den- 168
sity using an accelerated form of expectation maximization, the nodes of which being then 360 577
queried based on their projected footprint and transmittance to the sensor, while analytically
integrating their contributions along the ray in homogeneous media [Jakob *et al.*, 2011].

By similarly considering continuous segments of the light paths as well as kernels of different dimensionalities, the approach then gives rise to a complete set of *estimators*, including 139
the pointwise gathering of photon particles (using a 3-D kernel), the beam gathering of photon particles (using a 2-D or 3-D kernel), the pointwise gathering of photon beams (using
a 2-D or 3-D kernel) and the beam gathering of photon beams (using a 3-D kernel, a 2-D
kernel orthogonal to either the view beam or the photon beam or a 1-D kernel parameterized
by the shortest distance between the view ray and the photon ray) [Jarosz *et al.*, 2011a]. In
the case of a photon beam using a 2-D kernel, its contribution to a view ray whose origin lies
within the beam might alternatively be integrated using Gaussian quadrature [Johnson *et al.*,
2011]. Instead, the beam gathering of photon beams using a 1-D kernel can be extended in
the spirit of *progressive photon mapping* [Jarosz *et al.*, 2011b] by means of an asymptotically 637
optimal radius reduction parameter of $\alpha \overset{(17.34)}{=} 4/5$ whose corresponding radius reduction rate 638
reads $r_j \overset{(17.35)}{=} r_1 \Theta(j^{-1/5})$ [Kaplanyan and Dachsbacher, 2013, §9 ¶3]. By defining the beams 638
either as finite ray segments with a binary transmittance delimited by the scattering event,
or as semi-infinite rays with an exponentially decreasing transmittance, the set may then
be extended further, and the *estimators* therein combined with those based on *bidirectional* 139
path tracing using the extended form of *multiple importance sampling* so as to minimize 618
variance (rather than bias) [Křivánek *et al.*, 2014]. 158 143

17.1.3.5 Further Reading

Additional material may be found in books [Jensen, 2001, Marlon, 2003] and courses [Jensen *et al.*, 2001b, Jensen *et al.*, 2002, Jensen, 2004] [Jensen and Christensen, 2007, Jarosz *et al.*, 2008b] dedicated to photon mapping, as well as in courses dedicated to photon-density estimation [Hachisuka *et al.*, 2012a, Hachisuka *et al.*, 2013].

17.2 FURTHER READING

Additional material may be found in books dedicated to global illumination [Dutré *et al.*, 2002, Dutré *et al.*, 2006], in surveys dedicated to interactive global illumination [Heidrich, 2000, Ritschel *et al.*, 2012], as well as in surveys and courses dedicated to global illumination for interactive applications and animations [Damez *et al.*, 2002, Damez *et al.*, 2003a, Damez *et al.*, 2003b].

V

Perceptual Foundations

CHAPTER 18

Image-Forming Optical Systems

TABLE OF CONTENTS

18.1 PINHOLE CAMERA

648 As illustrated in *Figure 18.1*, a scene can be imaged either directly onto a screen for real-time viewing or painting as in a *camera obscura* (Latin for dark chamber), or onto the film or sensor of a *photographic camera*, by placing the target surface behind an opaque panel through which a small hole has been poked. The discovery of this phenomenon was first documented in ancient China by Mohist philosopher Mozi (ca. 470–391 BC), and in the west by the Greek philosopher Aristotle (384–322 BC) who reported observing the crescent-shaped projection of a solar eclipse on the ground through the gaps between the leaves of a plane tree in his collection of problems *Problemata*. Experimentations with dark chambers were later described in the east by Chinese scientist Shen Kuo (1031–1095 AD) in his *Dream Pool Essays* (1088 AD), in the middle-east by Iraqi scientist Abu Ali Ibn al-Haytham (latinized as Alhazen or Alhacen) in his *Kitab al-Manazir* (Arabic for *Book of Optics*, 1021 AD) and in the west by Leonardo da Vinci in his *Codex Atlanticus* (1502 AD).

In the limit of an infinitely small hole, the theoretical abstraction, known as the *pinhole camera* model, ought to generate a sharp image with perfect focus at all distances since photons emanating from any given location in the scene would strike the film or sensor at a unique position. However, in practice, the small aperture induces diffraction patterns
657 to appear, and its infinitesimal area requires an infinitely long *exposure* time in order to compensate for the low flux of photons passing through it.

Although diffraction may be reduced and a greater flux admitted by increasing the size of the hole, doing so also allows photons emanating from any given location in the scene to strike the film or sensor at various positions over a finite area, hence producing a blurred image at all distances. In order to obtain a sharper result, the light rays of common origin may be refocused onto a single image point by placing a lens within the aperture.

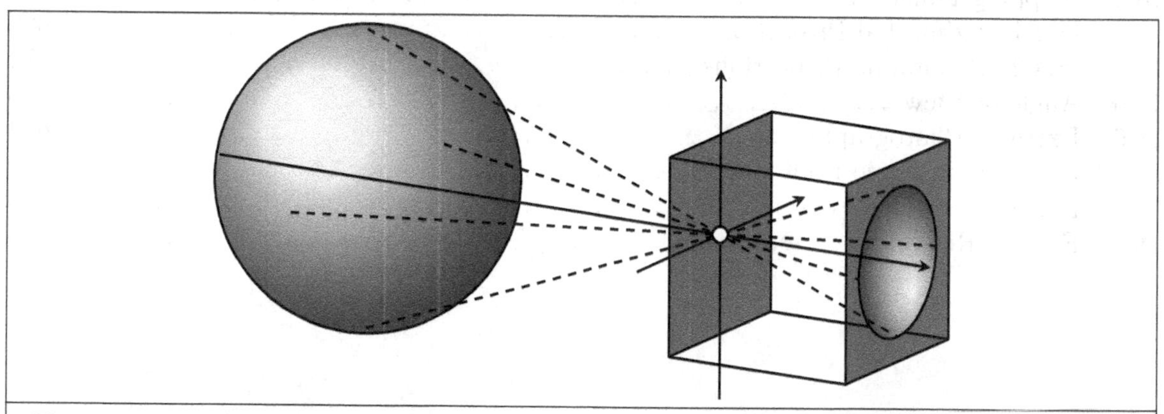

Figure 18.1: Pinhole Camera: Illustration of the pinhole camera model.

18.2 FINITE APERTURE CAMERA

18.2.1 Simple Lens

A *simple lens* consists of a single optical element, most often made of glass or transparent plastic. A mass-produced lens typically is a *spherical lens*, whose front and back surfaces are spherical patches as this is the easiest shape to grind and polish. The *optical axis* of the lens is then defined as the line joining the centers of the two spheres forming its surfaces. By convention, the orientation of the axis is such that the position of the light source is negative, defining the front side of the lens. The signs of the radii (or equivalently the signs of the position of the spheres' origins offset by half the thickness of the lens) then define the curvature of each of the two surfaces, such that a positive (respectively negative) radius defines a convex (respectively concave) front surface, whereas a positive (respectively negative) radius defines a concave (respectively convex) back surface, while a radius of infinite magnitude defines a planar surface, as illustrated in *Figure 18.2*. 649

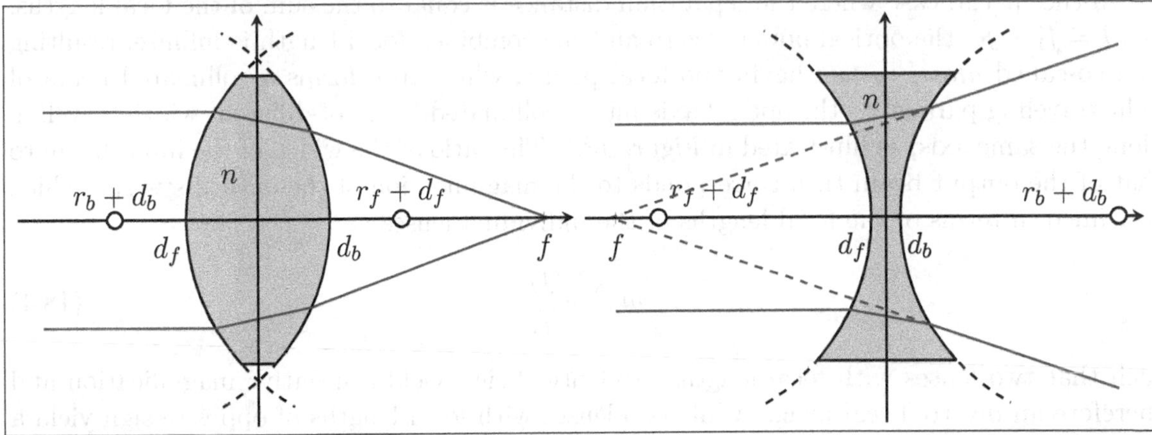

Figure 18.2: Simple Lens: Illustration of the convergence and divergence of parallel light rays as they interact with a positive (left) and a negative (right) simple lens.

The various types of lenses may then be classified according to the curvature of their optical surfaces, which in turn define their *vergence*. For instance, corrective lenses are typically convex-concave, also called meniscus, and consist of one convex and one concave surface. On the other hand, a biconvex lens (with two convex surfaces) or plano-convex lens (with one flat and one convex surface) forms a converging (or positive) optical system, focusing a collimated beam of light traveling parallel to the lens axis into a single focal point on the axis at a positive distance from the center of the lens. Finally, a biconcave lens (with two concave surfaces) or plano-concave lens (with one flat and one concave surface) forms a diverging (or negative) optical system, spreading a collimated beam of light traveling parallel to the lens axis as if it was emanating from a single focal point on the axis at a negative distance from the center of the lens.

The distance between the focal point and the center of the lens is referred to as the *focal length* (in m), which measures the potential of the optical system to focus light. Given a lens in air with medium of refractive index n, thickness $d \triangleq d_b - d_f$ measured along the optical axis, and signed front and back radii of curvature r_f and r_b, respectively, the reciprocal of the focal length f, also known as the *optical power* of the lens (in dpt), is given by the *lensmaker's equation*

$$\frac{1}{f} \triangleq (n-1)\left(\frac{1}{r_f} - \frac{1}{r_b} + \frac{(n-1)d}{n r_f r_b}\right) \tag{18.1}$$

which, for a *thin lens* (with negligible thickness $d \approx 0$), becomes 652

$$\lim_{d \to 0} \frac{1}{f} = (n-1)\left(\frac{1}{r_f} - \frac{1}{r_b}\right) \tag{18.2}$$

18.2.2 Compound Lens

A *compound lens* consists of a collection of multiple *simple lenses* arranged along a common 648
optical axis. Given two *thin lenses* in air of focal lengths f_1 and f_2 separated by some distance 652

l, the reciprocal of the effective focal length f of the combined system reads

$$\frac{1}{f} \triangleq \frac{1}{f_1} + \frac{1}{f_2} - \frac{l}{f_1 f_2} = \frac{f_1 + f_2 - l}{f_1 f_2} \tag{18.3}$$

In the special case where the separation distance is equal to the sum of the focal lengths, i.e., $l = f_1 + f_2$, the optical power is zero and the combined focal length is infinite, resulting in a so-called *afocal system* having no focal points, which transforms a collimated beam of light traveling parallel to the optical axis into a collimated beam of different width traveling
650 along the same axis, as illustrated in *Figure 18.3*. The ratio of the width of the input beam to that of the output beam then corresponds to the magnification of the optical system, which is defined in terms of the focal lengths of the individual lenses as

$$m \triangleq -\frac{f_2}{f_1} \tag{18.4}$$

such that two lenses with focal lengths of identical sign yield a negative magnification and therefore an inverted real image, while two lenses with focal lengths of opposite sign yield a positive magnification and therefore an upright virtual image, as detailed in the context of
652 the *thin lens* model.

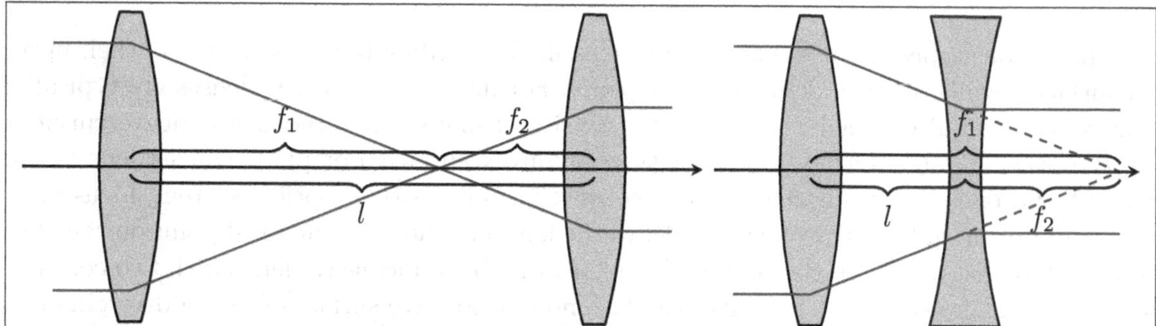

Figure 18.3: Afocal System: Example of an afocal system with two positive lenses (left), and one with a positive and a negative lens (right).

An example of such an optical system is a *zoom lens* (also referred to as *superzoom lens* or *hyperzoom lens* in the case of a very large range of focal lengths), which allows the focal length, and therefore the field of view, to be mechanically modified by sliding individual lenses along the optical axis. This is in contrast to a *unifocal lens*, also called *prime lens*, which has a fixed focal length, but usually offers a larger maximum aperture than zoom lenses due to the simpler design, making it more suitable for low-light/fast-shutter conditions and for
662 shallow *depth of field*. Zoom lenses are typically characterized by the ratio z of the longest to shortest focal lengths, so-called *optical zoom*, often denoted as $z:1$ or $z\times$. A zoom lens that loses focus as its focal length changes is called a *varifocal lens*, while one that maintains focus, either by mechanically displacing the complete lens assembly or by optically maintaining the position of the focal plane, is called a *parfocal lens*. Such an optically compensated zoom lens may, for instance, be built by combining an afocal system, consisting of a diverging lens placed between two converging lenses of equal focal length, with a standard unifocal focusing
651 lens, as illustrated in *Figure 18.4*. A *primary lens* may also be used in conjunction with a (typically simpler) *secondary lens*, designed to be mounted either between the subject and the primary lens, or between the latter and the film or sensor.

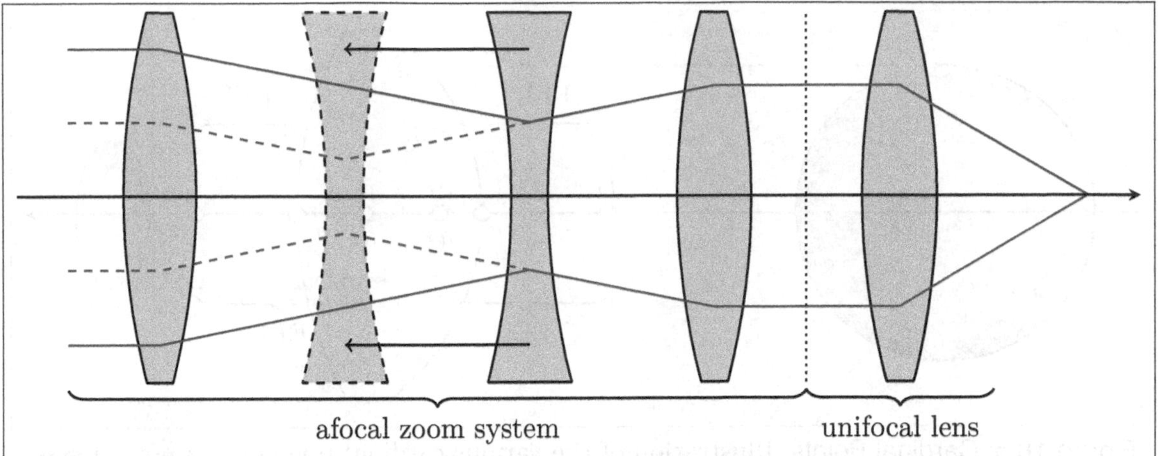

Figure 18.4: Zoom Lens: A simple optically compensated parfocal zoom lens consisting of an afocal system, which does not alter the position of the focal plane of the lens, combined with a unifocal lens.

18.2.3 Cardinal Points

The back *focal point* of an optical system (either a thin, thick or compound lens) is defined as the locus at which incident rays parallel to the optical axis are focused. Conversely, the front focal point is defined as the locus from which emanating rays will emerge from the system parallel to the optical axis. In both cases, the plane that passes through the front (respectively back) focal point orthogonally to the optical axis is called the front (respectively back) *focal plane*. The set of points at which the incident and exitant rays appear to cross then forms the so-called front (respectively back) *principal plane*, which might potentially lie outside of the lens, and whose intersection with the optical axis is referred to as the front (respectively back) *principal point*.

Additionally, the front *nodal point* and its rear counterpart are defined such that a light ray that appears to pass through one is refracted by the lens into a parallel ray that appears to pass through the other. For an optical system placed within the same medium on both sides, the front and back nodal points coincide with the front and back principal points, respectively. In order to determine the location at which the image of a given object position is formed, the locations of the afore-defined cardinal points are typically described with respect to the physically measurable points where the front (respectively back) surface of the system crosses the optical axis, known as the front (respectively back) *surface vertex*, as
illustrated in *Figure 18.5*. 652

The distance from the front and rear principal planes to their respective focal points then corresponds to the *effective focal length* (*EFL*) of the optical system multiplied by the index of refraction of the medium surrounding it, a product which in air may be approximated by the EFL itself. Similarly, the *front focal length* (*FFL*) is defined as the distance from the front focal point of the system to the front surface vertex, while the *back focal length* (*BFL*) is the distance from the back focal point to the back surface vertex, which, respectively, read

$$f_f \triangleq f\left(1+\frac{(n-1)d}{nr_b}\right) \tag{18.5}$$

$$f_b \triangleq f\left(1-\frac{(n-1)d}{nr_f}\right) \tag{18.6}$$

For a *compound lens*, the latter become 649

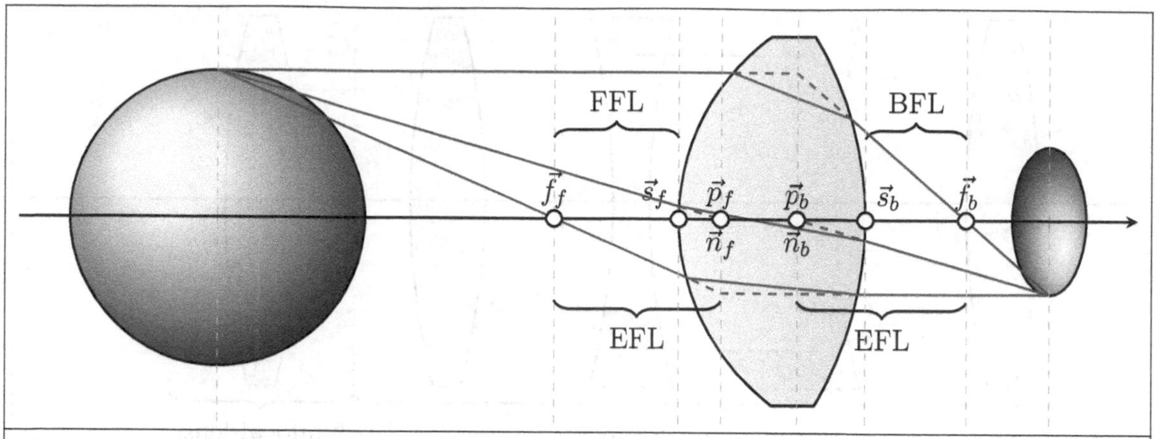

Figure 18.5: Cardinal Points: Illustration of the various cardinal points of an optical system, including its focal, principal and nodal points, as well as its surface vertices defining the corresponding front, back and effective focal lengths.

$$f_f = \frac{f_1(l - f_2)}{l - (f_1 + f_2)} \tag{18.7}$$

$$f_b = \frac{f_2(l - f_1)}{l - (f_1 + f_2)} \tag{18.8}$$

652 which, as $l \to 0$, converge to the value of the effective focal length of two *thin lenses* in
650 contact provided in *Equation 18.3*.

18.2.4 Thin Lens

653 Applying Thales's intercept theorem to Gauss's ray construction shown in *Figure 18.6*, the focal length f of a *thin lens*, i.e., a lens whose thickness is considered to be negligible, may be related with its distance s_o to an object of height h_o and the distance s_i to its converged image of height h_i, such that

$$\frac{h_o}{s_o} = \frac{h_i}{s_i} \tag{18.9}$$

$$\frac{h_o}{f} = \frac{h_i}{s_i - f} \tag{18.10}$$

$$\frac{h_o}{s_o - f} = \frac{h_i}{f} \tag{18.11}$$

Optical *magnification* is then defined as the ratio of the image size of an object to its actual size. Following the previous sign convention from optics, a negative magnification corresponds to a *real image*, which appears on the back side of the lens and is inverted (upside down) with respect to the object, while a positive magnification corresponds to a *virtual image*, which appears on the front side of the lens and is upright. However, in photography, heights and distances are usually defined to be positive, and so is magnification despite the typically inverted real image, resulting in the following expression of the dimensionless magnification factor

652
652
652

$$m \triangleq \frac{h_i}{h_o} \overset{(18.9)}{=} \frac{s_i}{s_o} \overset{(18.10)}{=} \frac{s_i - f}{f} \overset{(18.11)}{=} \frac{f}{s_o - f} \tag{18.12}$$

An image larger than the object therefore corresponds to $|m| > 1$, while $|m| < 1$ results in a minification, and $|m| = 1$ is obtained for $s_i = s_o = 2f$. It also follows that if s_o is fixed (as in

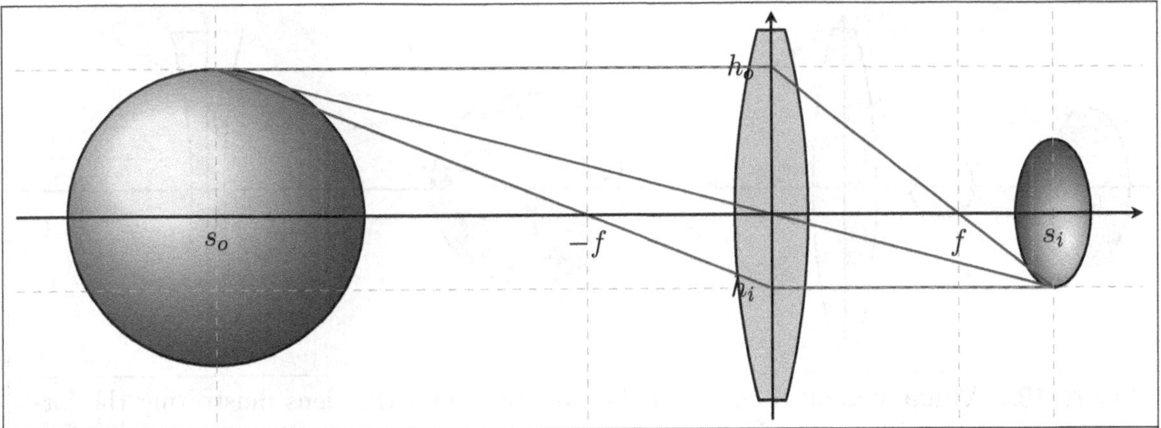

Figure 18.6: Gauss Construction: Illustration of Gauss's ray construction where light rays emanating from points in the object plane are focused on the image plane by a converging lens to form a real image.

photography or telescopy), magnification increases with focal length, whereas when s_o can vary while maintaining s_i fixed (as in microscopy), magnification decreases as focal length increases. In *macro photography*, magnification is alternatively given by the *reproduction ratio* 675
$m:1$ (or $1:\frac{1}{m}$ in case of minification), such that a $1:1$ ratio corresponds to a life-size image.

The distance s_o of an object in front of a positive lens and the distance s_i behind the lens at which its image is sharply focused onto the image plane are then related to the focal length f and magnification m by

$$\frac{s_o}{f} \overset{(18.12)}{=} \frac{s_i}{s_i - f} \overset{(18.12)}{=} \frac{m+1}{m} \quad (18.13)$$ 652 652

$$\frac{s_i}{f} \overset{(18.12)}{=} \frac{s_o}{s_o - f} \overset{(18.12)}{=} m+1 \quad (18.14)$$ 652 652

while the previous equations may also be rearranged to yield the so-called *thin lens equation* (sometimes also referred to as the *Gaussian lens formula*)

$$\frac{1}{f} \overset{(18.12)}{=} \frac{1}{s_i} + \frac{1}{s_o} \quad (18.15)$$ 652

It follows that an object infinitely far from a converging optical system is sharply imaged at the rear focal plane, while conversely, objects closer than the focal length cannot be sharply imaged as the resulting light rays diverge. Indeed, if $s_o > f$, a (typically smaller) real image of the object is projected onto the film plane, whereas if $s_o < f$, then s_i is negative and a (typically larger) virtual image of the apparent object from which light seems to be emanating
may be observed, as illustrated in *Figure 18.7*. Therefore, for magnifying glasses and optical 654
microscopes where $s_o < f$, angular magnification is used instead of magnification, which is expressed in terms of the apparent angle subtended by the object at the virtual focal point.

As illustrated in *Figure 18.8*, the Jacobian of the transformation relating differential area 654
to differential solid angle in image and object space are, respectively, given by

$$\frac{dA(\vec{q}_i)}{d\hat{\omega}_i} \overset{(6.66)}{=} \frac{\left(\frac{s_i}{\cos(\theta_i)}\right)^2}{\cos(\theta_i)} = \frac{s_i^2}{\cos(\theta_i)^3} \quad (18.16)$$ 245

$$\frac{dA(\vec{q}_o)}{d\hat{\omega}_o} \overset{(6.66)}{=} \frac{\left(\frac{s_o}{\cos(\theta_o)}\right)^2}{\cos(\theta_o)} = \frac{s_o^2}{\cos(\theta_o)^3} \quad (18.17)$$ 245

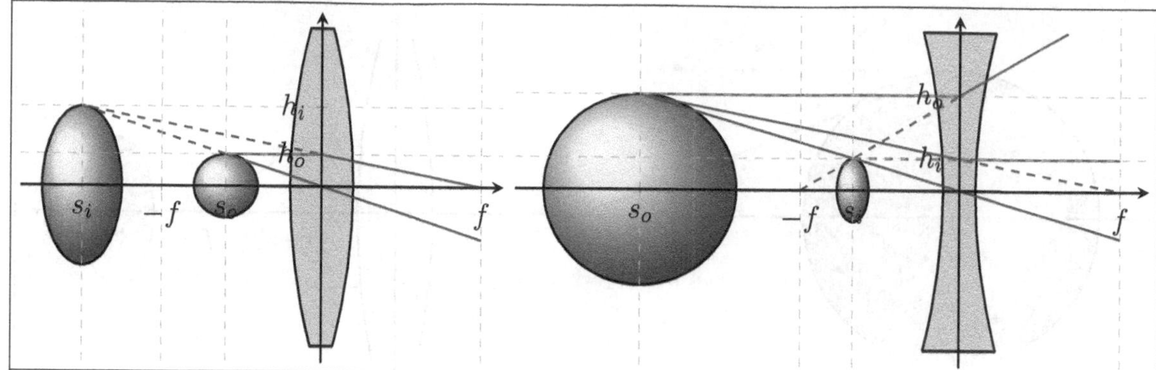

Figure 18.7: Virtual Image: Diagram of the ray optics of a thin lens illustrating the formation of a virtual image with a converging lens (left) and with a diverging lens (right).

while the differential area in image and object space are related by

$$\frac{\mathrm{d}A(\vec{q}_i)}{\mathrm{d}A(\vec{q}_o)} = \frac{s_i^2}{s_o^2} \tag{18.18}$$

It then follows that the Jacobian of the transformation relating differential area in image space to differential solid angle in object space is given by

$$\frac{\mathrm{d}A(\vec{q}_i)}{\mathrm{d}\hat{\omega}_o} = \frac{\mathrm{d}A(\vec{q}_i)}{\mathrm{d}A(\vec{q}_o)}\frac{\mathrm{d}A(\vec{q}_o)}{\mathrm{d}\hat{\omega}_o} = \frac{s_i^2}{s_o^2}\frac{s_o^2}{\cos(\theta_o)^3} = \frac{s_i^2}{\cos(\theta_o)^3} \tag{18.19}$$

and that relating the differential image-space and object-space solid angles as

$$\frac{\mathrm{d}\hat{\omega}_i}{\mathrm{d}\hat{\omega}_o} = \frac{\mathrm{d}\hat{\omega}_i}{\mathrm{d}A(\vec{q}_i)}\frac{\mathrm{d}A(\vec{q}_i)}{\mathrm{d}\hat{\omega}_o} = \frac{\cos(\theta_i)^3}{s_i^2}\frac{s_i^2}{\cos(\theta_o)^3} = \frac{\cos(\theta_i)^3}{\cos(\theta_o)^3} \tag{18.20}$$

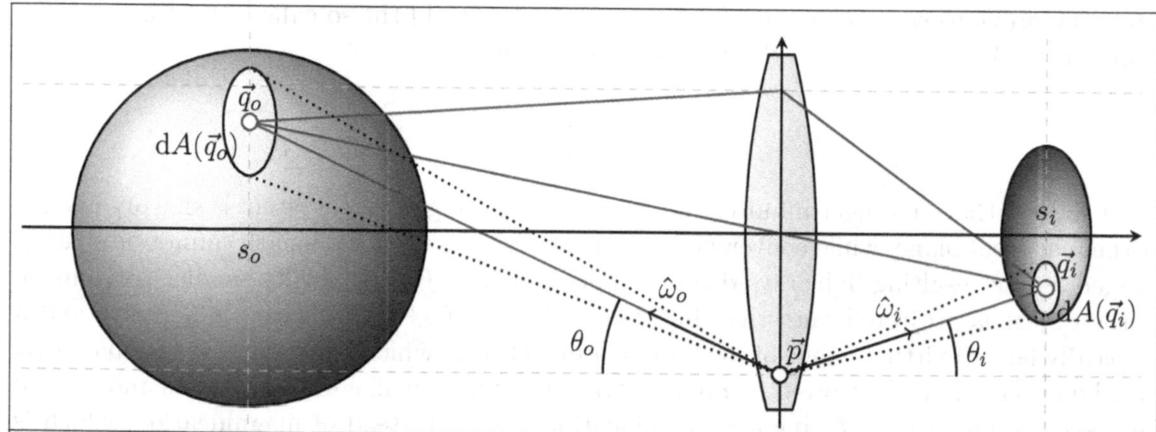

Figure 18.8: Thin Lens: Illustration of the geometric terms involved in computing the Jacobian of the transformation relating differential areas and solid angles in the image and object spaces of a thin lens.

Assuming that the lens is a perfect transmitter, the ratio of image-space to object-space differential flux then reads

427

$$\frac{\mathrm{d}^2\Phi_i(\vec{p},\hat{\omega}_i)}{\mathrm{d}^2\Phi_o(\vec{p},\hat{\omega}_o)} \overset{(10.57)}{=} \frac{L_i(\vec{p},\hat{\omega}_i)\mathrm{d}A(\vec{p})\langle\hat{n},\hat{\omega}_i\rangle\mathrm{d}\hat{\omega}_i}{L_o(\vec{p},\hat{\omega}_o)\mathrm{d}A(\vec{p})\langle\hat{n},\hat{\omega}_o\rangle\mathrm{d}\hat{\omega}_o} = \frac{L_i(\vec{p},\hat{\omega}_i)\cos(\theta_i)}{L_o(\vec{p},\hat{\omega}_o)\cos(\theta_o)}\frac{\mathrm{d}\hat{\omega}_i}{\mathrm{d}\hat{\omega}_o} = 1 \tag{18.21}$$

from which follows that the ratio of incident to exitant radiance is equal to

$$\frac{L_o(\vec{p}, \hat{\omega}_o)}{L_i(\vec{p}, \hat{\omega}_i)} = \frac{\cos(\theta_i)\, \mathrm{d}\hat{\omega}_i}{\cos(\theta_o)\, \mathrm{d}\hat{\omega}_o} \tag{18.22}$$

More generally, the above formulas similarly hold for thick and compound lenses, provided that s_o and s_i are measured from the front and rear principal planes of the optical system, respectively. It therefore follows that, for the sake of analysis, a complex optical system may be regarded as a thin lens with equivalent optical parameters.

Finally, while both the image plane and the plane of focus are here assumed to be orthogonal to the optical axis, the orientation of the plane of focus may actually be modified by using a *tilt–shift lens*. Based on the *Scheimpflug principle*, tilting the lens orientation relative to the image plane and shifting it parallel to the latter then allows the object plane to be similarly tilted such that all three planes intersect along a single line as illustrated in *Figure 18.9*. 655

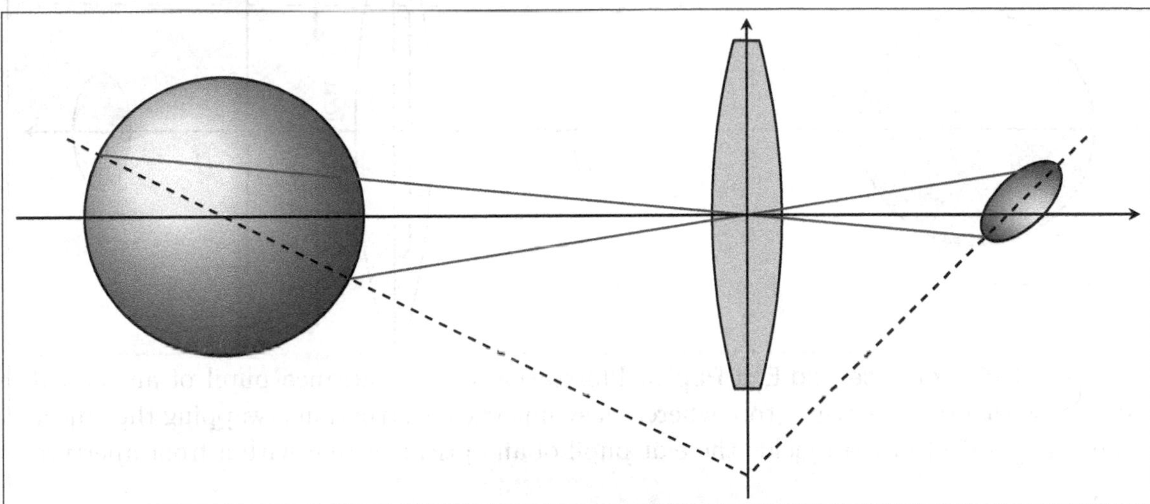

Figure 18.9: Scheimpflug Principle: Illustration of the Scheimpflug principle, which states that the lens plane intersects the object and image planes along a single line.

18.2.5 Aperture

The size of the lens opening is referred to as the *aperture*, and is typically controlled by a *diaphragm* such as a biological or mechanical iris centered around and orthogonal to the optical axis. The aperture is characterized by the *f-number* N (sometimes also called focal ratio, f-ratio, f-stop or relative aperture), which is the dimensionless ratio of the focal length f and the effective aperture diameter A of the entrance pupil

$$N \triangleq \frac{f}{A} \tag{18.23}$$

from which stems the notation $A = f/N$ commonly used to report the f-number. Modern lenses typically use a standard f-stop scale in which the f-numbers are the terms of a geometric sequence with common ratio $\sqrt{2}$, e.g., $f/\sqrt{2}^0 = f/1$, $f/\sqrt{2}^1 \approx f/1.4$, $f/\sqrt{2}^2 = f/2$, $f/\sqrt{2}^3 \approx f/2.8$, …, $f/\sqrt{2}^9 \approx f/22$, such that every stop increment/decrement on the scale corresponds to a halving/doubling of the aperture area

$$a \triangleq \pi \left(\frac{A}{2}\right)^2 \overset{(18.23)}{=} \pi \left(\frac{f}{2N}\right)^2 \tag{18.24}$$ 655

656 As illustrated in *Figure 18.10*, the *entrance pupil* (whose center is the center of perspective) of an optical system with a rear aperture stop (such as a camera) is the virtual image of the physical aperture stop through which light rays from an infinitely distant object can enter the system and reach the sensor. However, when focusing on a closer subject (especially
675 in *macro photography* where the distance is comparable to that between the lens and the film), the effective aperture A_w decreases and the light-gathering ability of the optical system is better characterized by the so-called *effective f-number* or *working f-number*. Similarly, the *exit pupil* of an optical system with a front aperture stop (such as a telescope or a microscope) is the virtual image of the physical aperture stop through which light rays can exit the system and reach the entrance pupil of an observer's eye (whose distance from the last surface of the eyepiece at which a full viewing angle can be obtained is called the *eye relief*).

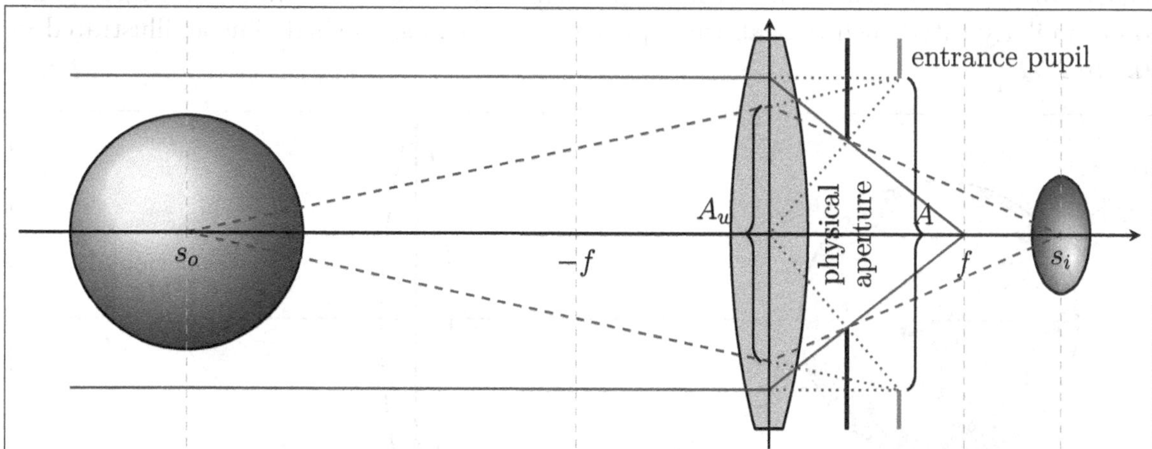

Figure 18.10: Entrance and Exit Pupils: Illustration of the entrance pupil of an optical system with a rear aperture stop, whereas a symmetric construction (swapping the object and image sides) instead yields the exit pupil of an optical system with a front aperture stop.

657 As illustrated in *Figure 18.11*, the ray joining a given off-axis object point to the center of the pupil is called the *principal ray* or *chief ray*. The plane that contains both the chief ray and the optical axis is then known as the *tangential plane* or *meridional plane*, and the rays lying within as *tangential rays* or *meridional rays*. Conversely, any plane that contains the chief ray but not the optical axis is referred to as a *skew plane*, and the rays lying within as *skew rays*. In particular, the skew plane that is orthogonal to the tangential plane is called the *sagittal plane*, and the rays lying within are called *sagittal rays* or *transverse rays*. Instead, the meridional ray joining the intersection of the object plane with the optical axis to the edge of the pupil is known as the *marginal ray*, whose distance to the optical axis at the loci of the entrance and exit pupils define their respective radii, while a ray that is almost parallel to the optical axis and lies close to it is referred to as a *paraxial ray*, which can be modeled by means of the paraxial approximation.

Decreasing the f-number increases the blur in out-of-focus portions of a scene, whose aesthetic quality for small features is determined by the shape of the aperture and referred to as the *bokeh*. Conversely, as increasing the f-number decreases the aperture area, it allows a larger range of distances to be sharply focused by only admitting relatively collimated rays
662 of light to reach the image plane, therefore increasing the *depth of field*, and resulting, in the
648 limit, in a *pinhole camera*. In practice, however, decreasing the aperture also exacerbates the
176 diffraction of light passing through it and results in the *convolution* of incident light with the point spread function of a punctual source located on the optical axis. In the specific case of

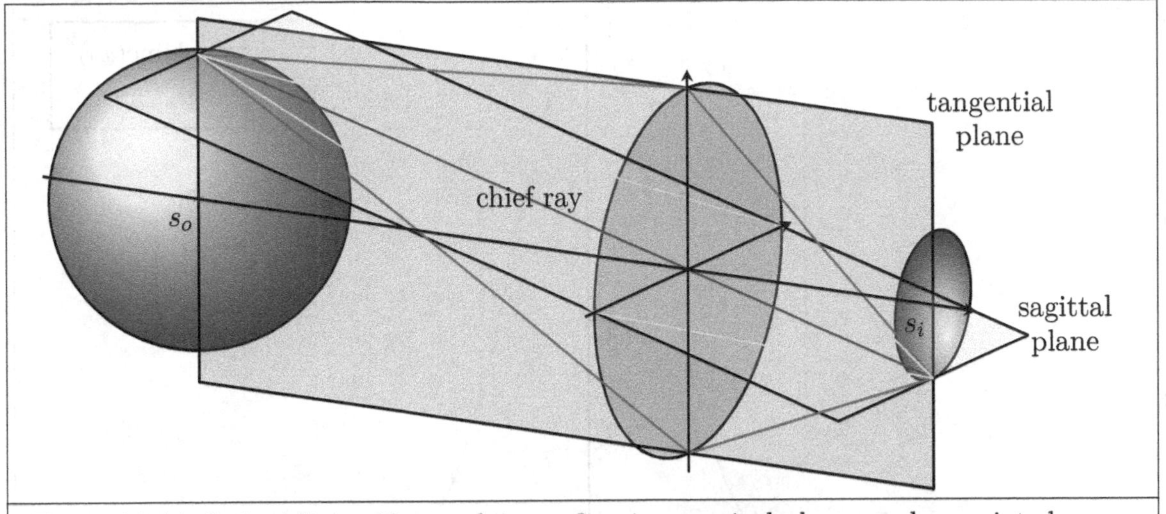

Figure 18.11: **Optical Rays:** Nomenclature of various optical planes and associated rays.

a circular aperture, the diffraction pattern is composed of a central lobe known as the *Airy disk*, which together with the surrounding concentric rings form the so-called *Airy pattern*
illustrated in *Figure 18.12*, and whose intensity at an angle θ from the optical axis is given 658
by the squared modulus of the *Fourier transform* of the aperture, akin to that of a radially 178
symmetric *box filter*, expressed in terms of the *jinc function* as 204 52

$$I(\theta) = I_0(2\,\mathrm{jinc}(\alpha))^2 \approx I_0 e^{-\frac{\alpha^2}{2\pi^2 c^2}} \tag{18.25}$$

where I_0 is the maximum intensity of the pattern at the center of the disc, and $\alpha \triangleq \frac{kA}{2}\sin(\theta)$ with k being the wave number, such that the spread of the function is proportional to N and predominant for longer wavelengths. Due to the rapid fall-off but infinite tails of the function, its most noticeable impact is the bleeding of bright features into darker adjacent
regions, known as the *bloom* effect, which may in practice be approximated as a *Gaussian* 51
blur by means of the constant $c \approx 0.42$ (for minimal error) or $c \approx 0.45$ (for identical volume). The counterbehavior of defocus blur and diffraction blur therefore leads to a trade-off in the choice of the f-number minimizing the size of the combined blur spot in order to achieve optimal image sharpness.

18.2.6 Exposure

The amount of time elapsed between the opening and closing of the *shutter* when capturing a photograph corresponds to the *exposure time* (in seconds), whose reciprocal is defined as the *shutter speed*. In an animated set-up, *high-speed photography* makes use of very fast shutter speeds in order to freeze the apparent motion of rapidly occurring phenomena. In contrast, decreasing the shutter speed, and therefore increasing the exposure time, accentuates the effect of *motion blur*. The latter may be reduced by an *image stabilization* system to compensate for camera shake, which is especially impactful at a narrow angle of view, or may be used for artistic purposes in the context of *light-painting*, in which the trajectory of an animated light source is recorded on the film or sensor, or of a *zoom burst* effect, which entails modifying the focal length during the time of exposure.

While the *photoreceptors* in the *human eye* are actually sensitive to the incident light 681 678
flux, a digital camera's CCD or CMOS sensor instead converts the energy of photons incident over time upon the surface of a single photoreceptor into a representative sample electrical measurement for that pixel. The luminous (respectively radiant) exposure of a film or sensor

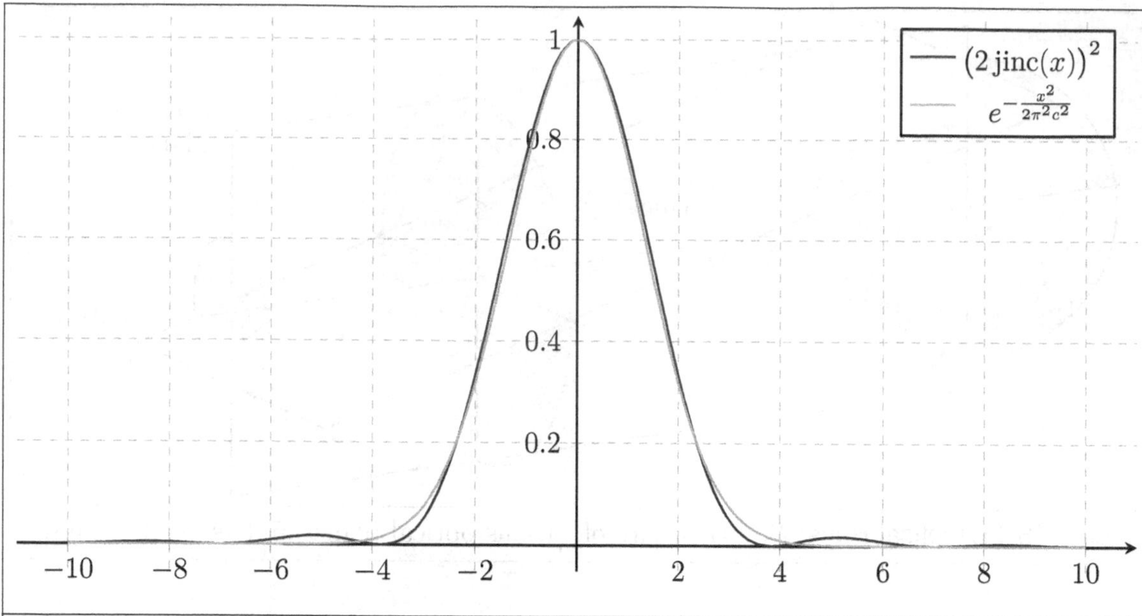

Figure 18.12: Airy Pattern: Plot of the Airy pattern and its Gaussian approximation.

is then independent of the specifications of the sensor and of its surface area, and, in the
658 limit of an infinitely small photoreceptor p as illustrated in *Figure 18.13*, may be formulated in terms of the flux leaving the perceived surface patch P as

425 426 426 426

$$H \overset{(10.44)}{=} E\,t \overset{(10.50)}{=} \Phi\frac{t}{p} \overset{(10.48)}{=} J\frac{P}{\cos(\theta)}\frac{t}{p} \overset{(10.50)}{=} L\cos(\theta)\Omega\frac{P}{\cos(\theta)}\frac{t}{p} = L\Omega P\frac{t}{p}$$

245 655

$$\overset{(6.66)}{=} L\frac{a}{s_o^2}P\frac{t}{p} = L\frac{a}{s_i^2}t \overset{(18.24)}{=} L\frac{\pi\left(\frac{f}{2N}\right)^2}{s_i^2}t \approx L\frac{\pi}{4}\frac{t}{N^2} \tag{18.26}$$

where t is the exposure time, a is the aperture area, E is the image-plane illuminance (respectively irradiance), J is the luminosity (respectively radiosity) of the scene and L is the scene luminance (respectively radiance).

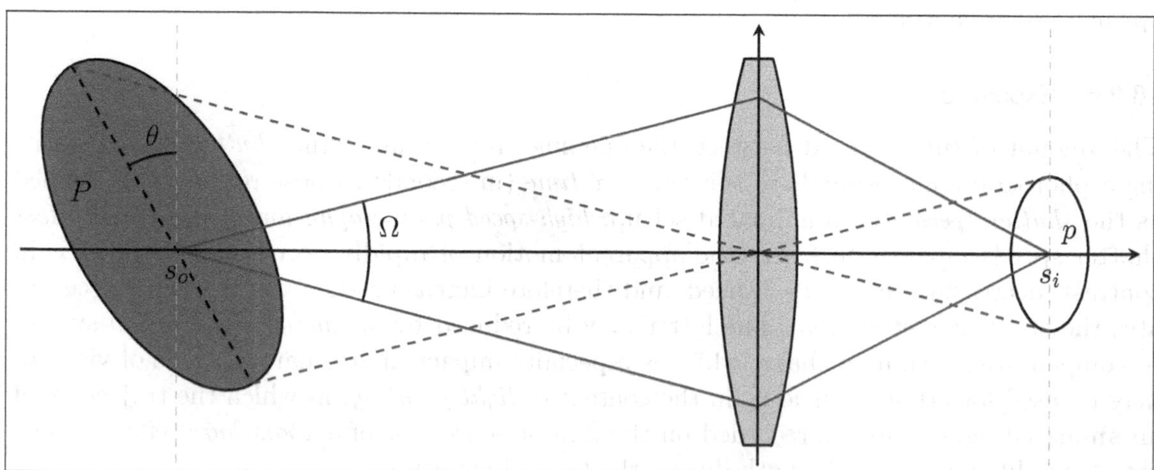

Figure 18.13: Exposure Geometry: Illustration of the terms involved in the computation of the exposure.

Due to physical limitations, a given photographic film or sensor setting can typically only adequately image a limited *dynamic range* of exposure. Underexposure causes the resulting 732 value to be noisy, while overexposure can lead to saturation and, for a sensor, to charge spilling to nearby pixels. The *dynamic range* of the device depends on its sensitivity, which is 732 measured in terms of the *film speed*. The latter is most commonly expressed in the arithmetic ISO scale (corresponding to the arithmetic ASA system), stating that a relatively fast film that is twice as sensitive as a slower film with half the speed index will require a smaller exposure to produce an image of similar brightness.

For a given average scene luminance L and illuminance E, the nominal exposure is determined by the *exposure equation* as

$$\frac{N^2}{t} = S\frac{L}{K} = S\frac{E}{C} \tag{18.27}$$

where S is the ISO arithmetic speed, and $K \approx 12.5$–14 and $C \approx 250$–340 are the reflected-light and incident-light meter calibration constants, respectively. The *exposure value* is then defined such that halving/doubling the exposure corresponds to an increment/decrement of one EV unit, commonly referred to as a *stop*, and it is given as

$$E_v \triangleq \log_2\left(\frac{N^2}{t}\right) \overset{(18.27)}{=} \log_2\left(S\frac{L}{K}\right) \overset{(18.27)}{=} \log_2\left(S\frac{E}{C}\right) \tag{18.28}$$ 659 659

or, according to the APEX system, as

$$E_v = A_v + T_v = S_v + B_v = S_v + I_v \tag{18.29}$$

where the aperture value and time value read $A_v \triangleq \log_2(N^2)$ and $T_v \triangleq \log_2(t^{-1})$, respectively (which some camera models allow control over), while the speed (or sensitivity) value, luminance (or brightness) value and incident-light value are defined as $S_v \triangleq \log_2(nS)$, $B_v \triangleq \log_2\left(\frac{L}{nK}\right)$ and $I_v \triangleq \log_2\left(\frac{E}{nC}\right)$, respectively, with the constant $n = 2^{-\frac{7}{4}}$.

For predetermined lighting conditions, a given exposure value denotes all combinations of lens aperture and shutter speed resulting in the same exposure. The reduction (respectively increase) in the amount of light reaching the sensor due to an increase (respectively a decrease) of the f-number should therefore be compensated by a longer (respectively shorter) exposure time, leading to a trade-off between defocus blur and motion blur. Conversely, an increase of the exposure value due to a decrease of the film exposure by a given factor, either by increasing the f-number and/or decreasing the exposure time, should similarly be compensated by an increase of the film speed by the same factor in order to produce an image of identical brightness. Increasing the ISO speed, however, generally leads to a reduced image quality due to the coarser grain of the film or to a lower signal-to-noise ratio (SNR) resulting from the correspondingly lower photon density. As illustrated in *Figure 18.14*, the 660 loci of identical image brightness consequently describe a manifold embedded in the three-dimensional space formed by the above parameters, thereby providing a trade-off between their associated side effects.

The exposure value computed by the *exposure metering* system of modern cameras can generally be manually adjusted by a given number of EV units, a technique known as *exposure compensation*. However, the offset is applied opposite to the sense of the EV scale, such that a positive exposure compensation results in a smaller exposure value, in turn yielding an increased exposure. The degree by which the exposure can be varied without causing the resulting image to be objectionably over- or underexposed is then referred to as the *exposure latitude*, which in turn directly depends on the *dynamic range* of the sensor. 732

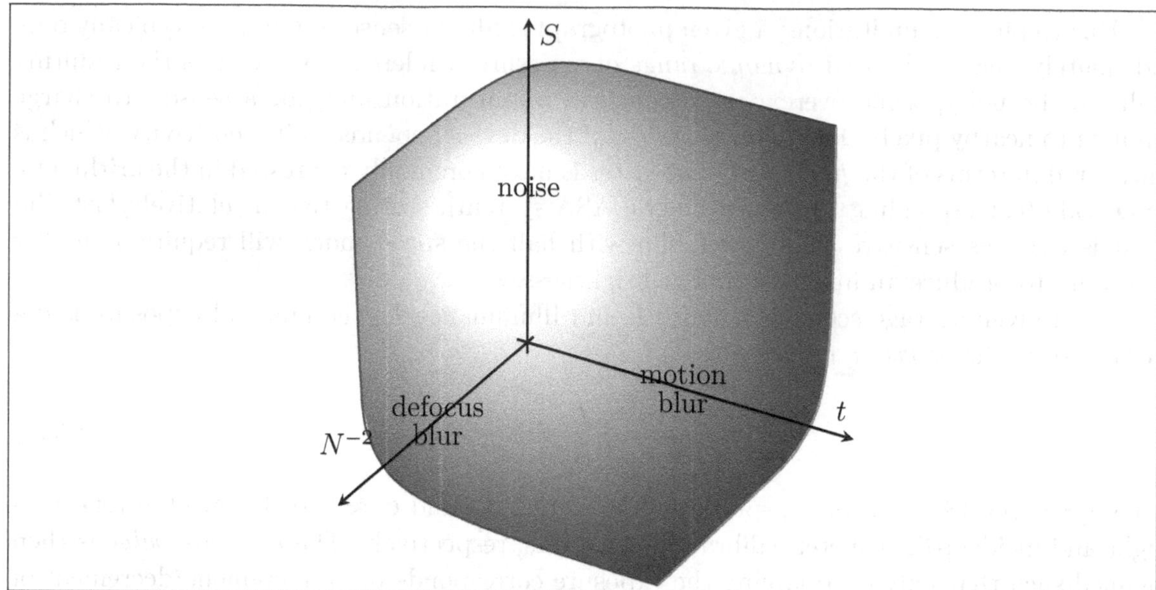

Figure 18.14: Image Brightness: Illustration of the three-dimensional space in which the loci of identical image brightness are parameterized by the shutter speed, f-number and film speed, each entailing a different type of side effect.

The exposure value corresponding to a given ISO speed S_2 may be derived from the one corresponding to a different ISO speed S_1 as

659
659

$$E_V^{S_2} \overset{(18.28)}{=} \log_2\left(S_2 \frac{L}{K}\right) \overset{(18.28)}{=} \log_2\left(S_2 \frac{2^{E_V^{S_1}}}{S_1}\right) = E_V^{S_1} + \log_2\left(\frac{S_2}{S_1}\right) \tag{18.30}$$

Given the sensitivity function $W(\vec{q}_i, \hat{\omega}) = f(\vec{q}_i)$ of the film plane at position $\vec{q}_i$ in direction
201 $\hat{\omega}$ expressed in terms of the response of the anti-aliasing *filter*, a measurement at a given pixel or sensor cell more specifically evaluates to

566

$$M \overset{(13.19)}{=} \int_S \int_\Omega L(\vec{q}_i, \hat{\omega}) W(\vec{q}_i, \hat{\omega}) \cos(\theta_i) \mathrm{d}\hat{\omega} \mathrm{d}A(\vec{q}_i) \tag{18.31}$$

245

$$\overset{(6.66)}{=} \int_S \int_a L(\vec{q}_i, \widehat{q_i p}) W(\vec{q}_i, \widehat{q_i p}) \frac{\cos(\theta_i)^2}{\|\vec{p} - \vec{q}_i\|^2} \mathrm{d}A(\vec{p}) \mathrm{d}A(\vec{q}_i)$$

427

$$\overset{(10.58)}{=} \int_S \int_a L_i(\vec{p}, -\widehat{q_i p}) W(\vec{q}_i, \widehat{q_i p}) \frac{\cos(\theta_i)^4}{s_i^2} \mathrm{d}A(\vec{p}) \mathrm{d}A(\vec{q}_i) \tag{18.32}$$

653

$$\overset{(18.16)}{=} \int_a \int_\Omega L_i(\vec{p}, \hat{\omega}_i) W(\vec{q}_i, -\hat{\omega}_i) \cos(\theta_i) \mathrm{d}\hat{\omega}_i \mathrm{d}A(\vec{p})$$

655

$$\overset{(18.22)}{=} \int_a \int_S L_o(\vec{p}, \hat{\omega}_o) W(\vec{q}_i, \widehat{q_i p}) \cos(\theta_o) \frac{\mathrm{d}\hat{\omega}_o}{\mathrm{d}A(\vec{q}_i)} \mathrm{d}A(\vec{q}_i) \mathrm{d}A(\vec{p}) \tag{18.33}$$

$$= \int_a \int_\Omega L_o(\vec{p}, \hat{\omega}_o) W(\vec{q}_i, -\hat{\omega}_i) \cos(\theta_o) \mathrm{d}\hat{\omega}_o \mathrm{d}A(\vec{p}) \tag{18.34}$$

where S is the surface of the sensor or film, $\vec{p}$ is a point on the surface of the lens and a is the aperture area.

18.2.7 Circle of Confusion

For a given magnification and focal length, an optical system can only establish a precise focus for object points located at a well-defined *focus distance*. The light rays emanating from a point located at another object distance do not perfectly converge onto the image plane, and such a defocused object point is consequently imaged as a blur spot shaped like the lens aperture (usually assumed to be circular), and whose diameter increases with the distance of the point to the plane of focus, as illustrated in *Figure 18.15*. 661

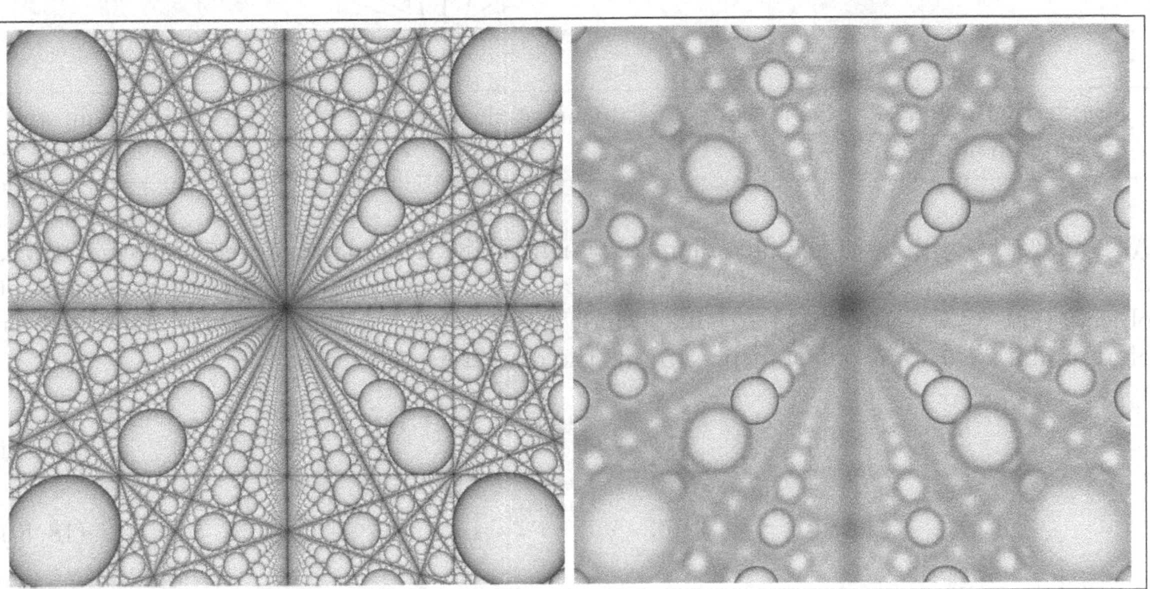

Figure 18.15: Depth of Field: A spatial field comprising infinitely many spheres, imaged with a pinhole camera model producing sharp focus at all objects points (left), and with a thin-lens camera model such that only the spheres lying in the plane of focus appear sharp (right).

Applying Thales's intercept theorem to the geometric setting shown in *Figure 18.16*, the 662
diameter B of the blur circle in the focused object plane at distance s_o, corresponding to the unfocused virtual image of an object at distance s'_o, may be defined in terms of the entrance aperture diameter A as

$$B \triangleq A\frac{|s'_o - s_o|}{s'_o} = A\frac{|s'_o - s_o|}{s_o \pm |s'_o - s_o|} \tag{18.35}$$

where the latter formulation uses a minus sign for foreground objects, for which $s'_o < s_o$, and the plus sign for background objects, for which $s'_o > s_o$.

The diameter b of the blur spot of the out-of-focus subject in the image plane can be similarly calculated, or may alternatively be obtained by multiplying B by the magnification, which yields

$$b \triangleq A\frac{|s'_i - s_i|}{s'_i} \overset{(18.12)}{=} Bm \underset{(18.12)}{\overset{(18.35)}{=}} A\frac{|s'_o - s_o|}{s'_o}\frac{f}{s_o - f} \tag{18.36}$$

652
661
652

In the limit of an infinitely close, out-of-focus subject with a finite focus distance, the diameters of the blur disks become

$$\lim_{s'_o \to 0} B \overset{(18.35)}{=} \infty \tag{18.37}$$

661

$$\lim_{s'_o \to 0} b \overset{(18.36)}{=} \infty \tag{18.38}$$

661

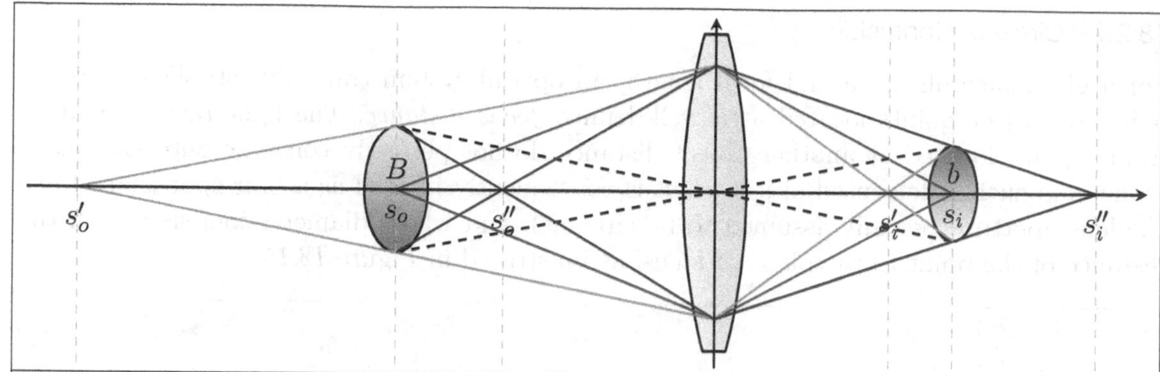

Figure 18.16: Circle of Confusion: Illustration of the image blur spot resulting from an out-of-focus object point.

Although large values of the blur diameter might make foreground objects unrecognizable, it makes close proximity with the lens especially useful to smear out the contributions of objects that would otherwise partially occlude the targeted subject. Conversely, in the limit of an infinitely distant out-of-focus subject, the diameters become

661

$$\lim_{s'_o \to \infty} B \overset{(18.35)}{=} A \tag{18.39}$$

661

$$\lim_{s'_o \to \infty} b \overset{(18.36)}{=} Am \tag{18.40}$$

Finally, in the limit of an infinite focus distance, the diameters of the blur spots become

661

$$\lim_{s_o \to \infty} B \overset{(18.35)}{=} \infty \tag{18.41}$$

661

$$\lim_{s_o \to \infty} b \overset{(18.36)}{=} A\frac{f}{s'_o} \tag{18.42}$$

The limit diameter of the largest blur spot that is sufficiently small to be indistinguishable from a point, and to therefore appear to be in focus, is then referred to as the (maximum permissible) *circle of confusion* (*CoC*). The acceptable sharpness is itself a function of visual acuity, viewing conditions (e.g., viewing distance) and image enlargement.

18.2.8 Depth of Field

As the diameter of the blur spot increases with the distance of an object to the plane of focus, the sharpness of the image gradually decreases. Applying Thales's intercept theorem
663 to the symmetrical lens setting illustrated in *Figure 18.17*, the near and far image space
661 limit distances s_{in} and s_{if} at which the blur spot diameter is equal to the *circle of confusion* criterion c may be related to the hyperfocal magnification m_h as follows

665
661
661
662

$$m_h \overset{(18.62)}{=} \frac{c}{A} \overset{(18.36)}{=} \frac{s_{in} - s_i}{s_{in}} \overset{(18.36)}{=} \frac{s_i - s_{if}}{s_{if}} \overset{(18.44)}{=} \frac{s_{in} - s_{if}}{s_{in} + s_{if}} \tag{18.43}$$

where the last equality stems from the fact that the corresponding focus distance in image space can be expressed as the harmonic mean of the limits by rearranging the third equality

662

$$s_i \overset{(18.43)}{=} 2\frac{s_{in}s_{if}}{s_{in} + s_{if}} = \frac{2}{\frac{1}{s_{if}} + \frac{1}{s_{in}}} \tag{18.44}$$

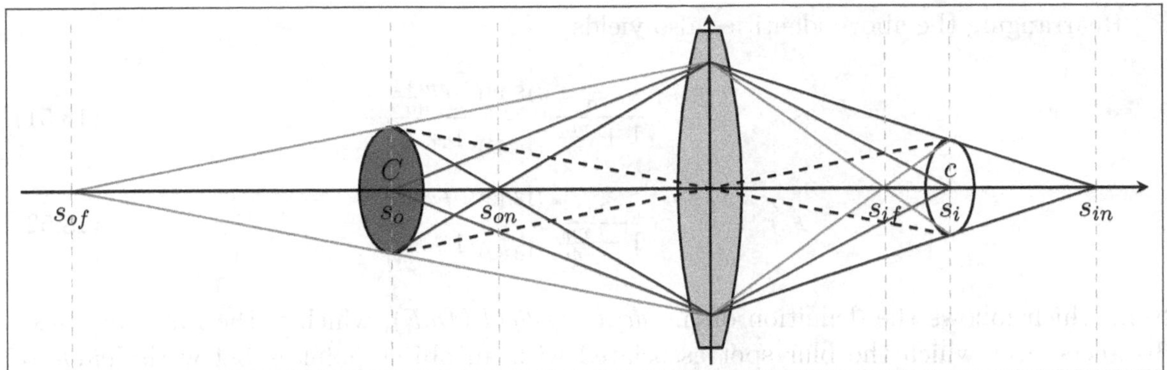

Figure 18.17: Depth of Field Geometry: Illustration of the parameters involved in computing the depth of focus and depth of field.

Rearranging the above identities also yields

$$s_{in} \overset{(18.43)}{=} \frac{s_i}{1 - m_h} \underset{(18.62)}{\overset{(18.14)}{=}} \frac{f(m+1)}{1 - \frac{cN}{f}} \tag{18.45}$$ 662 653 665

$$s_{if} \overset{(18.43)}{=} \frac{s_i}{1 + m_h} \underset{(18.62)}{\overset{(18.14)}{=}} \frac{f(m+1)}{1 + \frac{cN}{f}} \tag{18.46}$$ 662 653 665

from which the *depth of focus*, which is the image-space conjugate of the depth of field (DoF), is then defined as the extent

$$d_i \triangleq s_{in} - s_{if} \underset{(18.46)}{\overset{(18.45)}{=}} \frac{2s_i}{\frac{1}{m_h} - m_h} \underset{(18.62)}{\overset{(18.14)}{=}} \frac{2f(m+1)}{\frac{f}{cN} - \frac{cN}{f}} \tag{18.47}$$ 663 653 663 665

being asymmetrical about the image plane. The term "depth of focus" is also sometimes used to instead refer to the range over which the image plane may be displaced while maintaining a single object plane in acceptably sharp focus, in which case it actually is symmetrical about the image plane and reads

$$d_i' \triangleq 2s_i m_h \underset{(18.62)}{\overset{(18.14)}{=}} 2(m+1)cN \tag{18.48}$$ 653 665

The corresponding foreground and background object distances s_{on} and s_{of}, which are, respectively, called the near and far *DoF limits*, similarly verify

$$\frac{m_h}{m} = \frac{C}{A} \overset{(18.35)}{=} \frac{s_o - s_{on}}{s_{on}} \overset{(18.35)}{=} \frac{s_{of} - s_o}{s_{of}} \overset{(18.50)}{=} \frac{s_{of} - s_{on}}{s_{of} + s_{on}} \tag{18.49}$$ 661 661 663

where the last equality analogously stems from the fact that the corresponding focus distance in object space may be expressed as the harmonic mean of the limits by rearranging the third equality

$$s_o \overset{(18.49)}{=} 2\frac{s_{on}s_{of}}{s_{on} + s_{of}} = \frac{2}{\frac{1}{s_{of}} + \frac{1}{s_{on}}} \tag{18.50}$$ 663

Rearranging the above identities also yields

663
653
665

$$s_{on} \overset{(18.49)}{=} \frac{s_o}{1+\frac{m_h}{m}} \underset{(18.62)}{\overset{(18.13)}{=}} \frac{f\frac{m+1}{m}}{1+\frac{cN}{mf}} \tag{18.51}$$

663
653
665

$$s_{of} \overset{(18.49)}{=} \frac{s_o}{1-\frac{m_h}{m}} \underset{(18.62)}{\overset{(18.13)}{=}} \frac{f\frac{m+1}{m}}{1-\frac{cN}{mf}} \tag{18.52}$$

from which follows the definition of the *depth of field* (*DoF*), which is the range of object distances over which the blur spot associated with an object point is below the *circle of*
661 *confusion* criterion

664
653
664
665

$$d_o \triangleq s_{of} - s_{on} \underset{(18.52)}{\overset{(18.51)}{=}} \frac{2s_o}{\frac{m}{m_h} - \frac{m_h}{m}} \underset{(18.62)}{\overset{(18.13)}{=}} \frac{2f\frac{m+1}{m}}{\frac{mf}{cN} - \frac{cN}{mf}} \tag{18.53}$$

The near and far extents of the DoF read

664
653
665

$$s_o - s_{on} \overset{(18.51)}{=} \frac{s_o}{\frac{m}{m_h}+1} \underset{(18.62)}{\overset{(18.13)}{=}} \frac{f\frac{m+1}{m}}{\frac{mf}{cN}+1} \tag{18.54}$$

664
653
665

$$s_{of} - s_o \overset{(18.52)}{=} \frac{s_o}{\frac{m}{m_h}-1} \underset{(18.62)}{\overset{(18.13)}{=}} \frac{f\frac{m+1}{m}}{\frac{mf}{cN}-1} \tag{18.55}$$

whose ratio, called the near:far *DoF ratio*, characterizes the asymmetry of the depth of field about the plane of focus

664
665
664

$$\frac{s_o - s_{on}}{s_{of} - s_o} \underset{(18.55)}{\overset{(18.54)}{=}} \frac{m - m_h}{m + m_h} \overset{(18.62)}{=} \frac{m - \frac{cN}{f}}{m + \frac{cN}{f}} \tag{18.56}$$

As the in-focus subject distance decreases given a fixed focal length, the magnification increases and so does the near:far DoF ratio, approaching one in the limit. Conversely, increasing the in-focus subject distance decreases the near:far DoF ratio. From the magnitude range of the near:far DoF ratio then follows that the DoF extent beyond the plane of focus is always greater than that in front of it.

Although a defocused object of size h'_o is not imaged with a distinct boundary, the concept of magnification introduced earlier may be extended by referring to its "average" image size h_i, such that

652

$$m' \triangleq \frac{h_i}{h'_o} \overset{(18.12)}{=} \frac{s_i}{s'_o} \tag{18.57}$$

Because distant objects appear smaller in the image plane than those that are close to the optical system, it may be argued that the diameter of their associated blur spot should be proportionally smaller in order for background and foreground objects to be equally distinguishable. Rather than relying on a uniform absolute blur size as in the traditional DoF approach, this technique, often referred to as the *object field method*, therefore relies on a relative CoC criterion for the near and far DoF limits, characterized by the ratio

664
664

$$\frac{b}{h_i} \overset{(18.57)}{=} \frac{b}{m'h'_o} \overset{(18.57)}{=} \frac{s'_o b}{s_i h'_o} \tag{18.58}$$

18.2.9 Hyperfocal Distance

Rearranging the formulation of the far DoF limit to solve for the in-focus subject distance yields

$$s_o \overset{(18.52)}{=} s_{of}\left(1 - \frac{m_h}{m}\right) \overset{(18.12)}{=} s_{of}\left(1 - m_h\frac{s_o - f}{f}\right) = \frac{m_h + 1}{\frac{1}{s_{of}} + \frac{m_h}{f}} \tag{18.59}$$

664 652

The smallest in-focus subject distance for which the far DoF limit is infinite is then called the *hyperfocal distance*, which reads

$$H \triangleq \lim_{s_{of}\to\infty} s_o \overset{(18.59)}{=} f\frac{m_h + 1}{m_h} \overset{(18.62)}{=} f\frac{cN + f}{cN} \tag{18.60}$$

665 665

from which follows that the f-number corresponding to a given hyperfocal distance is defined as

$$N \overset{(18.60)}{=} \frac{f^2}{c(H - f)} \tag{18.61}$$

665

The greatest foreground extent of the *depth of field* for which the background extent is 662
infinite is obtained when $s_o = H$, therefore providing the largest total DoF extent. Although the far DoF limit remains infinite whenever $s_o \geq H$ and so does the *depth of field*, yielding 662
a zero-valued near:far DoF ratio, focusing beyond the hyperfocal distance does decrease the foreground DoF extent and the total DoF extent with it, which might seem wasteful in terms of conventional DoF calculations. However, when adapting the size of the blur spot to the object distance as in the object field method, focusing beyond the hyperfocal distance, sometimes close to infinity, becomes necessary.

The *hyperfocal magnification* may then be obtained by substituting $s_o = H$ in the expression of the magnification, which yields

$$m_h \triangleq \lim_{s_{of}\to\infty} m \overset{(18.12)}{=} \frac{f}{H - f} \overset{(18.60)}{=} \frac{cN}{f} \overset{(18.23)}{=} \frac{c}{A} \tag{18.62}$$

652 665 655

such that the near DoF limit becomes

$$\lim_{s_{of}\to\infty} s_{on} \overset{(18.51)}{=} \frac{H}{2} \tag{18.63}$$

664

18.2.10 Aberrations

Although it is most often adequate to characterize the properties of an optical system, the mathematical model previously described does rely on a number of assumptions that cannot necessarily be made by lens designers. The model builds on *Gaussian optics*, assuming idealized spherical surfaces, and relies on the *paraxial approximation*, under the assumption that the angle between the direction of travel of the light rays and the optical axis is small, which allows for a first-order approximation of the trigonometric functions involved in describing the path of a light beam through an optical system, overall yielding simplified formulations for the various optical parameters. By building on geometrical optics rather than wave optics, the impact of diffraction is ignored, and the light rays focused by the presumed stigmatic lens are assumed to perfectly converge into an infinitely small point.

In practice, however, real lenses do not exhibit perfect convergence even at best focus. A point source is rather imaged as a blur spot whose minimal achievable size is called the *circle of least confusion*, and the actual response of an optical system to an impulse may be more

667 generally described by a point spread function. As illustrated in *Figure 18.18*, the limitations of the model and other imperfections therefore cause the actual performance of the system to depart from the theoretical predictions, such a deviation being referred to as an *optical aberration*, categorized as follows

- *spherical aberration*: although spherical lenses are much cheaper to design and manufacture than aspherical profiles, they exhibit a focal length that increases from the periphery towards the center of the lens, thereby resulting in a *soft focus* by which paraxial rays focus farther away behind the lens than marginal rays instead of coming into perfect focus at a single location as they would with a lens that is hyperbolic in shape

- *comatic aberration* (or coma): light rays traveling at an angle from the optical axis actually come into focus either farther from or closer to the axis (respectively being called positive and negative coma) as the distance at which they hit the lens from its center increases, such that the superposition of the *comatic circles* (i.e., the image of rings of rays passing through the lens at a given distance from its center) forms a V-shaped comet-like pattern

- *field curvature*: parallel beams of rays at a given angle from the optical axis do not focus on a flat image plane but on a curved surface in image space, as is the case in the human eye

- *astigmatism*: biological lenses (such as that of the human eye) may also exhibit a non-symmetry about the optical axis, causing tangential and sagittal light rays to converge at different foci

- *chromatic aberration*: the refractive index of the lens material is wavelength-dependent, typically increasing at shorter wavelengths, causing the spectral light rays to come to a focus at different locations via dispersion, called longitudinal or axial chromatic aberration, and to form images of different sizes, called lateral or transverse chromatic aberration, although the resulting colored fringes appearing along boundaries in the image may be reduced by use of an *achromatic doublet* (i.e., the combination of a convex lens made of crown glass with a plano-concave lens made of flint glass)

667 As illustrated in *Figure 18.19*, undesirable spatial distortions might additionally be incurred by the lens, and are commonly approximated by the radial mapping $r \mapsto r + c_3 r^3 + c_5 r^5$. For instance, *barrel distortion* ($c_3 < 0$, $c_5 = 0$) causes image magnification to decrease as the distance from the optical axis increases, thereby making straight lines appear as if they had been mapped around a barrel, and is often associated with wide-angle lenses. Conversely, *pincushion distortion* ($c_3 > 0$, $c_5 = 0$) causes image magnification to increase with the distance from the optical axis, thereby making straight lines appear as if they had been mapped onto a pincushion, and is often associated with long-focus lenses. Finally, *mustache distortion* ($c_3 < 0$, $c_5 > 0$) progressively transitions from barrel distortion to pincushion distortion as the distance from the optical axis increases, thereby making straight lines appear as mustache-shaped curves, and is often associated with large-range zoom lenses.

Finally, stray interreflection between lens elements can produce an overall *glare* and reduce contrast, or cause bright light sources to create a *flare*. Their effect may, however, be reduced by anti-reflection coatings and lens hoods, respectively.

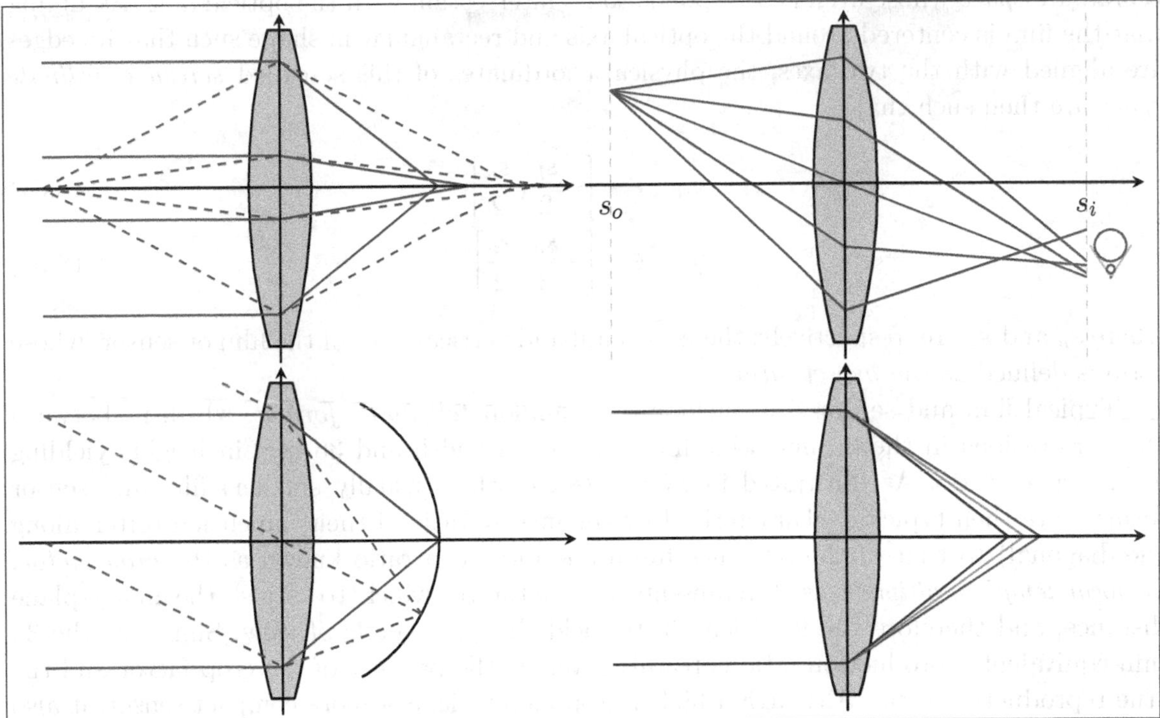

Figure 18.18: Lens Aberrations: Illustration of various types of lens aberrations, including spherical aberration (top left), comatic aberration (top right), field curvature (bottom left) and chromatic aberration (bottom right).

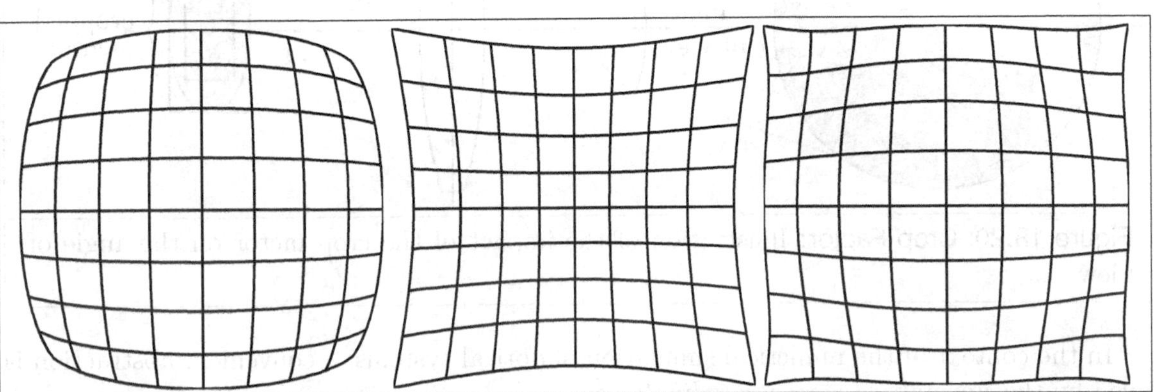

Figure 18.19: Lens Distortion: Illustration of various types of lens distortion, including barrel, pincushion and mustache distortion (from left to right, respectively).

18.3 IMAGE-PLANE COORDINATE SPACES

A point location on the image plane may be formally described by defining an embedded 2-D *coordinate space* whose origin corresponds to its intersection with the optical axis. Assuming that the film is centered around the optical axis and rectangular in shape such that its edges are aligned with the two axes, the physical coordinates of this so-called *screen coordinate space* are then such that

$$x_{sc} \in \left[-\frac{s_h}{2}, \frac{s_h}{2}\right] \tag{18.64}$$

$$y_{sc} \in \left[-\frac{s_v}{2}, \frac{s_v}{2}\right] \tag{18.65}$$

where s_h and s_v are, respectively, the horizontal and vertical sizes of the film or sensor, whose ratio is defined as the *aspect ratio.*

Typical film and sensor sizes include the common *full-frame format*, which is, between the perforations in the 35 mm wide film, 24 mm in width and 36 mm in height, yielding
668 a 3:2 aspect ratio. As illustrated in *Figure 18.20*, other (usually smaller) film and sensor formats are then typically characterized by the inverse ratio of their dimension (often along the diagonal) to that of the reference full-frame format, a ratio known as the *crop factor*, or *focal length multiplier* as it represents the factor by which to adjust the image-plane
673 distance, and therefore the focal length, to yield the same *angle of view*. Similarly, the 35 mm-equivalent reproduction ratio is readily given as the product of the crop factor and the true reproduction ratio. Although a higher crop factor yields a more compact sensor, it also reduces the integration area of each pixel element (assuming their number is constant) and the received photon flux density with it, potentially increasing noise in the resulting images. Additionally, a smaller sensor requires a smaller focal length for a similar angle of view, and
655 657 therefore a smaller effective *aperture* for a similar f-number/*exposure*, in turn increasing the
662 *depth of field*.

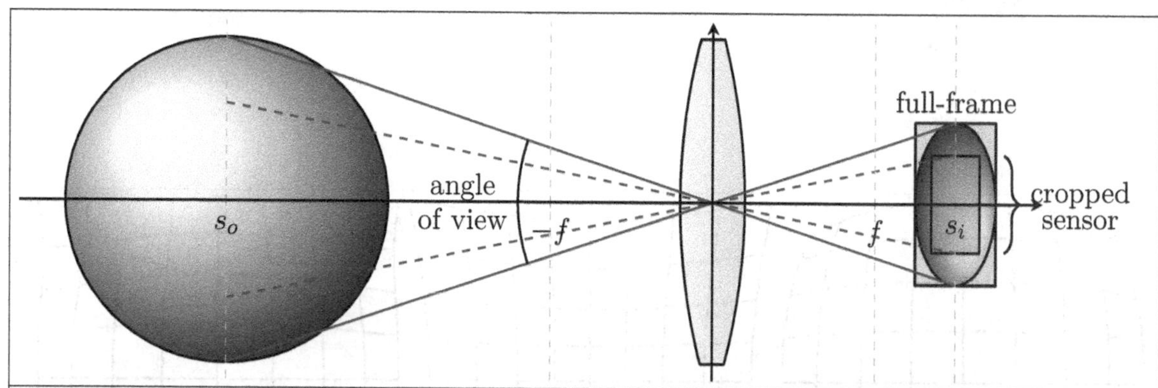

Figure 18.20: Crop Factor: Illustration of the impact of the crop factor on the angle of view.

In the context of the numerical simulation of optical systems, a convenient abstraction is given by the *normalized screen coordinate space*

$$x_{nsc} \triangleq 2\frac{x_{sc}}{s_h} \in [-1, 1] \quad \Longrightarrow \quad \frac{\mathrm{d}x_{nsc}}{\mathrm{d}x_{sc}} = \frac{2}{s_h} \tag{18.66}$$

$$y_{nsc} \triangleq 2\frac{y_{sc}}{s_v} \in [-1, 1] \quad \Longrightarrow \quad \frac{\mathrm{d}y_{nsc}}{\mathrm{d}y_{sc}} = \frac{2}{s_v} \tag{18.67}$$

which then leads to the *normalized device coordinate space* (*NDC space*)

$$x_{ndc} \triangleq \frac{x_{nsc}+1}{2} \in [0,1] \quad \Longrightarrow \quad \frac{\mathrm{d}x_{ndc}}{\mathrm{d}x_{nsc}} = \frac{1}{2} \tag{18.68}$$

$$y_{ndc} \triangleq \frac{y_{nsc}+1}{2} \in [0,1] \quad \Longrightarrow \quad \frac{\mathrm{d}y_{ndc}}{\mathrm{d}y_{nsc}} = \frac{1}{2} \tag{18.69}$$

Finally, the coordinates of the *raster coordinate space* may be computed as

$$x_r \triangleq x_{ndc} r_h \in [0, r_h] \quad \Longrightarrow \quad \frac{\mathrm{d}x_r}{\mathrm{d}x_{ndc}} = r_h \tag{18.70}$$

$$y_r \triangleq y_{ndc} r_v \in [0, r_v] \quad \Longrightarrow \quad \frac{\mathrm{d}y_r}{\mathrm{d}y_{ndc}} = r_v \tag{18.71}$$

either in a cell-centered fashion by defining r_h and r_v as the horizontal and vertical resolutions (or number of pixels) of the sensor such that integer raster coordinates indicate pixel edges while pixel centers correspond to raster coordinates that are integers offset by a half, or in a node-centered fashion by instead defining r_h and r_v as the horizontal and vertical resolutions minus one such that pixel centers readily correspond to integer raster coordinates.

It follows that any double integral over the screen coordinates (such as the measurement equation) expressed in terms of a function of raster coordinates (such as an anti-aliasing *filter*) may be reformulated as 201

$$\int_{-\frac{s_v}{2}}^{+\frac{s_v}{2}} \int_{-\frac{s_h}{2}}^{+\frac{s_h}{2}} f\left(\left(\frac{x_{sc}}{s_h}+\frac{1}{2}\right) r_h, \left(\frac{y_{sc}}{s_v}+\frac{1}{2}\right) r_v\right) \mathrm{d}x_{sc}\mathrm{d}y_{sc} = \int_0^{r_v} \int_0^{r_h} f(x_r, y_r) \frac{s_h}{r_h}\frac{s_v}{r_v} \mathrm{d}x_r \mathrm{d}y_r \tag{18.72}$$

18.4 MAPPING FUNCTIONS

18.4.1 Azimuthal Projections

Under rotational symmetry around the optical axis, the mapping function $f_m(\theta_o)$ of an optical system determines the extent to which the angle that a light ray makes with the optical axis will vary as the ray crosses the lens through its center. It therefore relates the object-space angle θ_o from the optical axis with the distance s_i between the lens and the image plane together with the distance $r = \sqrt{x_s^2 + y_s^2}$ of a point on the image plane from the image center as follows

$$\tan(\theta_i) = \frac{r}{s_i} = f_m(\theta_o) \tag{18.73}$$

The case where the direction of travel of the rays remains unchanged is described by the so-called *gnomonic mapping* function. The latter results in a *perspective projection*, which is characteristic of a *rectilinear lens* with which straight features in object space appear as straight lines on the image plane, as occurs with a pinhole camera or in the human eye. Such a projection causes the apparent convergence of each set of parallel lines that are not parallel to the image plane into a *vanishing point*, whose number typically varies between 1 and 3, and associated to either end of each of the 3-D axes.

In order to maintain the image size of an object, the variation of the distance between the lens and the image plane may be compensated by adapting the distance to the object such that magnification is constant, resulting in a *dolly zoom* effect. In the theoretical limit of an infinitely distant image plane and entrance pupil, as may be achieved in practice with an object-space *telecentric lens* design, the system only images light rays traveling parallel to the optical axis, resulting in a so-called *orthographic projection* having no vanishing points.

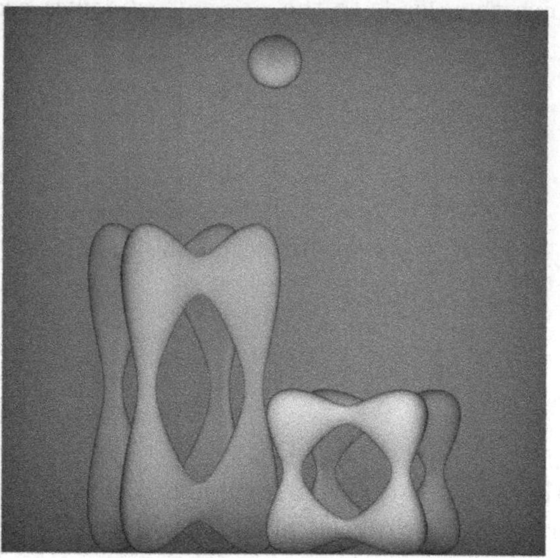

Figure 18.21: Perspective and Orthographic Projections: Comparison of the images produced by two different rectilinear optical systems, including a perspective projection (left) and an orthographic projection (right), set up so that the image sizes of the front of the box are identical.

Although the latter provides a lower sense of depth, it allows the alignment of geometric
670 features to be more easily established, as illustrated in *Figure 18.21*.

In contrast, a *fish-eye projection* does alter the direction in which light rays travel, whose behavior may be characterized by various mapping functions, including the least-distortive conformal *stereographic mapping*, the common *equi-angular mapping*, the common *equi-solid-angle mapping*, which corresponds to the distribution of initially parallel rays reflected off of a convex spherical mirror and the most-distortive *orthographic mapping*. As illustrated in
671 *Figure 18.22*, such a *curvilinear lens* displaces from the image center the position of sideways objects, typically resulting in up to 5 vanishing points corresponding to both ends of each of the 3-D axes except for the one end located behind the image plane.

70 Defining the inclination angle θ_o and the azimuthal angle ϕ_o as the *spherical coordinates* whose zenith axis is aligned with the optical axis and whose azimuthal axis is arbitrarily
671 oriented within the image plane as illustrated in *Figure 18.23*, the Jacobian of the transformation relating the differential image-space and object-space solid angles is given by

244
669

$$\frac{\mathrm{d}\hat{\omega}_i}{\mathrm{d}\hat{\omega}_o} \overset{(6.62)}{=} \frac{\sin(\theta_i)\mathrm{d}\theta_i\mathrm{d}\phi_i}{\sin(\theta_o)\mathrm{d}\theta_o\mathrm{d}\phi_o} \overset{(18.73)}{=} \frac{\sin(\theta_i)}{\sin(\theta_o)}\frac{\mathrm{d}\arctan\left(f_m(\theta_o)\right)}{\mathrm{d}\theta_o} \tag{18.74}$$

671 and, as detailed in *Table 18.1*, that relating differential area in image space to differential solid angle in object space as

653

$$\frac{\mathrm{d}A(\vec{q}_i)}{\mathrm{d}\hat{\omega}_o} = \frac{\mathrm{d}A(\vec{q}_i)}{\mathrm{d}\hat{\omega}_i}\frac{\mathrm{d}\hat{\omega}_i}{\mathrm{d}\hat{\omega}_o} \overset{(18.16)}{=} \frac{s_i^2}{\cos(\theta_i)^3}\frac{\sin(\theta_i)}{\sin(\theta_o)}\frac{\mathrm{d}\arctan\left(f_m(\theta_o)\right)}{\mathrm{d}\theta_o} \tag{18.75}$$

where

669

$$s_i^2\frac{\sin(\theta_i)}{\cos(\theta_i)^3} = s_i^2\frac{\tan(\theta_i)}{\cos(\theta_i)^2} \overset{(18.73)}{=} s_i^2\frac{r}{s_i}\frac{s_i^2+r^2}{s_i^2} = r\left(s_i + \frac{r^2}{s_i}\right) \tag{18.76}$$

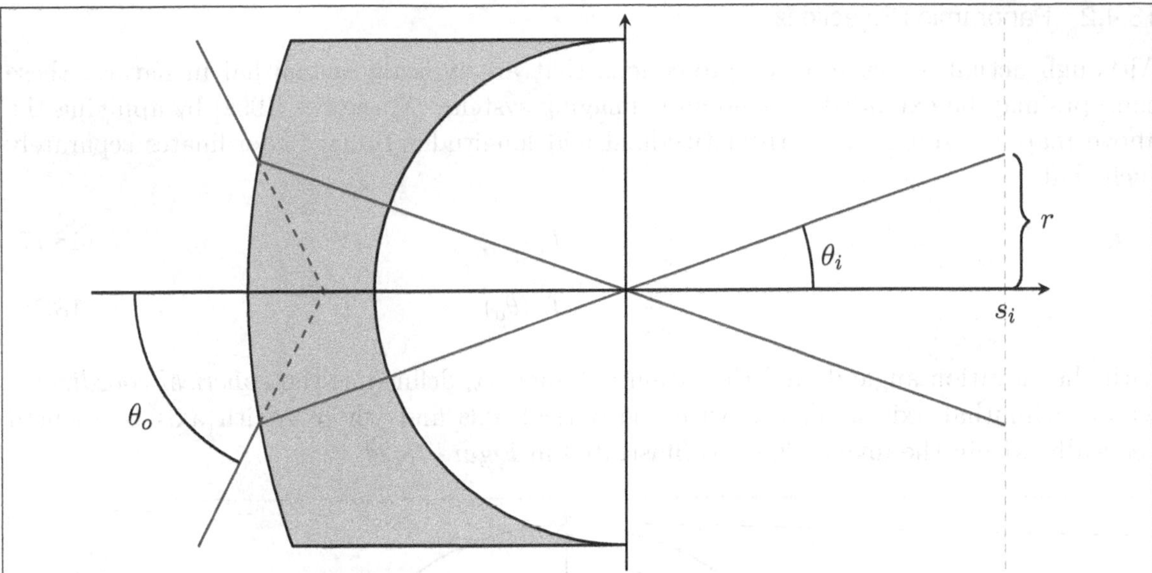

Figure 18.22: Fish-Eye Lens: Simplified illustration of the trajectory of a light ray being altered upon interaction with a fish-eye lens.

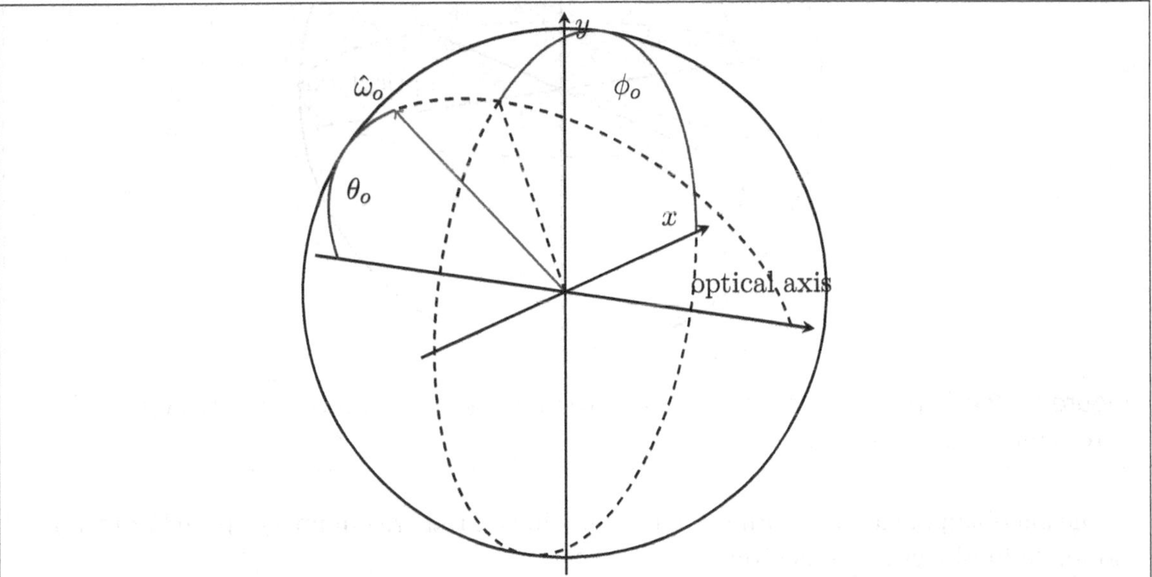

Figure 18.23: Azimuthal Projection: Illustration of the spherical coordinate system characterizing an azimuthal projection.

Table 18.1: Mapping Functions: Formulation of various mapping functions and their respective derivatives, given in order of increasing distortion.

Mapping	$f_m(\theta_o)$	$\frac{\mathrm{d}f_m(\theta_o)}{\mathrm{d}\theta_o}$	$\frac{\mathrm{d}\arctan\left(f_m(\theta_o)\right)}{\mathrm{d}\theta_o}$
Gnomonic	$\tan(\theta_o) = \frac{\sqrt{1-\cos(\theta_o)^2}}{\cos(\theta_o)}$	$\frac{1}{\cos(\theta_o)^2}$	1
Stereographic	$2\tan\left(\frac{\theta_o}{2}\right) = 2\sqrt{\frac{1-\cos(\theta_o)}{1+\cos(\theta_o)}}$	$\frac{1}{\cos\left(\frac{\theta_o}{2}\right)^2} = \frac{2}{1+\cos(\theta_o)}$	$\frac{2}{5-3\cos(\theta_o)}$
Equi-angular	θ_o	1	$\frac{1}{1+\theta_o^2}$
Equi-solid-angle	$2\sin\left(\frac{\theta_o}{2}\right) = 2\sqrt{\frac{1-\cos(\theta_o)}{2}}$	$\cos\left(\frac{\theta_o}{2}\right) = \sqrt{\frac{1+\cos(\theta_o)}{2}}$	$\frac{\cos\left(\frac{\theta_o}{2}\right)}{3-2\cos(\theta_o)} = \frac{\sqrt{\frac{1+\cos(\theta_o)}{2}}}{3-2\cos(\theta_o)}$
Orthographic	$\sin(\theta_o) = \sqrt{1-\cos(\theta_o)^2}$	$\cos(\theta_o)$	$\frac{\cos(\theta_o)}{1+\sin(\theta_o)^2} = \frac{\cos(\theta_o)}{2-\cos(\theta_o)^2}$

18.4.2 Panoramic Projections

Although actual lenses produce projections that are typically azimuthal in nature, these concepts may be extended to panoramic imaging systems [Musgrave, 1992] by applying the above mapping functions to the latitudinal and longitudinal image coordinates separately such that

$$\frac{x_{sc}}{s_i} = f_m(\phi_o) \tag{18.77}$$

$$\frac{y_{sc}}{s_i} = f_m(\theta_o) \tag{18.78}$$

70 with the elevation angle θ_o and the azimuthal angle ϕ_o defined as the *spherical coordinates* whose azimuthal axis is aligned with the optical axis and whose zenith axis is oriented
672 vertically within the image plane, as illustrated in *Figure 18.24*.

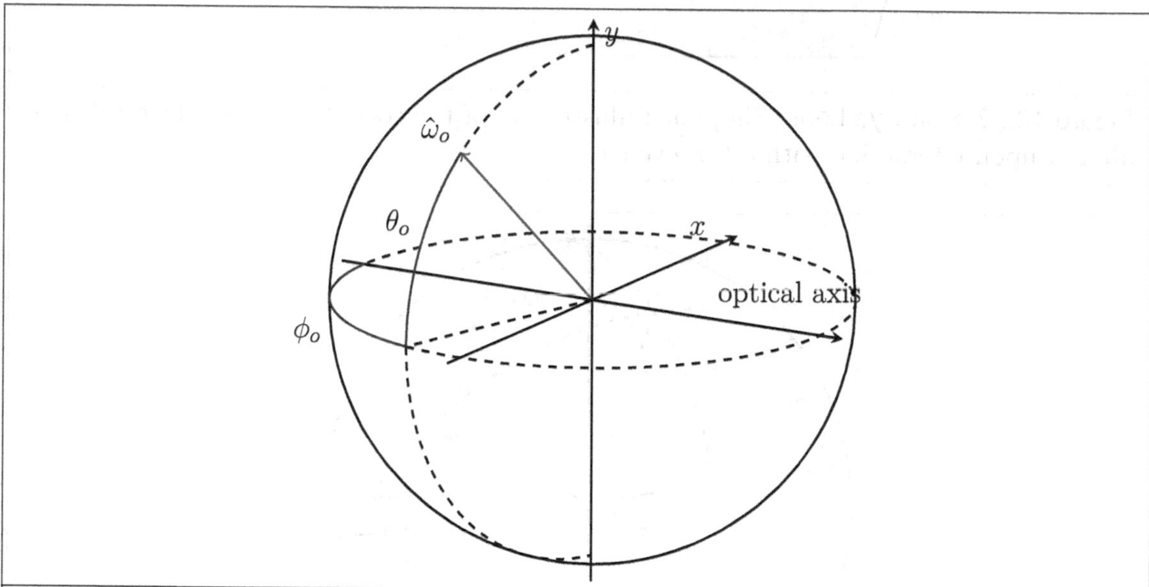

Figure 18.24: Panoramic Projection: Illustration of the spherical coordinate system characterizing a panoramic projection.

The Jacobian of the transformation relating differential area in image space to differential solid angle in object space is given by

$$\frac{\mathrm{d}A(\vec{q}_i)}{\mathrm{d}\hat{\omega}_o} = \frac{\mathrm{d}x_{sc}\mathrm{d}y_{sc}}{\cos(\theta_o)\mathrm{d}\theta_o\mathrm{d}\phi_o} = \frac{s_i^2}{\cos(\theta_o)}\frac{\mathrm{d}f_m(\phi_o)}{\mathrm{d}\phi_o}\frac{\mathrm{d}f_m(\theta_o)}{\mathrm{d}\theta_o} \tag{18.79}$$

where the cosine rather than sine term in the denominator is due to the use of the elevation (as opposed to inclination) angle, and that relating the differential image-space and object-space solid angles as

653
$$\frac{\mathrm{d}\hat{\omega}_i}{\mathrm{d}\hat{\omega}_o} = \frac{\mathrm{d}\hat{\omega}_i}{\mathrm{d}A(\vec{q}_i)}\frac{\mathrm{d}A(\vec{q}_i)}{\mathrm{d}\hat{\omega}_o} \overset{(18.16)}{=} \frac{\cos(\theta_i)^3}{s_i^2}\frac{s_i^2}{\cos(\theta_o)}\frac{\mathrm{d}f_m(\phi_o)}{\mathrm{d}\phi_o}\frac{\mathrm{d}f_m(\theta_o)}{\mathrm{d}\theta_o} = \frac{\cos(\theta_i)^3}{\cos(\theta_o)}\frac{\mathrm{d}f_m(\phi_o)}{\mathrm{d}\phi_o}\frac{\mathrm{d}f_m(\theta_o)}{\mathrm{d}\theta_o} \tag{18.80}$$

The resulting *equirectangular projection*, sometimes also referred to as latitude/longitude projection, is distinctively rectilinear in one axis while being curvilinear in the other, typically resulting in only up to 3 vanishing points corresponding to the two ends of one of the 3-D axes and the one end of a second axis located in front of the image plane, as illustrated in
673 *Figure 18.25*.

Figure 18.25: Mapping Functions: A scene imaged with an azimuthal projection (top) and a panoramic projection (bottom), both with an angle of view of 170°, using a gnomonic, conform (stereographic), equi-angular, equi-solid-angle and orthographic mapping (from left to right, respectively) (light probe courtesy of Paul Debevec).

18.5 ANGLE OF VIEW

The maximum angular extent that can be imaged with an optical system is defined as its *angle of view* (in radians), while the corresponding portion of the scene that is captured is referred to as the *field of view*. The horizontal, vertical or diagonal angle of view is formally expressed in terms of the inverse of the mapping function as well as the width, height or diagonal size s of the film, respectively, as follows

$$\alpha \triangleq 2f_m^{-1}\left(\frac{s}{2s_i}\right) \tag{18.81}$$

In the specific case of an optical system with a symmetric lens perspectively projecting a rectilinear image of distant objects as illustrated in *Figure 18.26*, the expression becomes 674

$$\alpha = 2\arctan\left(\frac{s}{2s_i}\right) \stackrel{(18.14)}{=} 2\arctan\left(\frac{s}{2f(m+1)}\right) \tag{18.82}$$ 653

which, whenever $s \ll 2s_i$, may be approximated by

$$\alpha \approx \frac{s}{s_i} \tag{18.83}$$

Assuming that $s_i \approx f$, the angle of view may be widened by reducing the focal length (possibly by means of a secondary optical lens called a *telecompressor*), which below 35 mm (on a 35 mm film format) is referred to as a *wide-angle lens* (potentially having a *retrofocus lens* design, i.e., an inverted telephoto configuration combining negative lens groups at the front with positive lens groups, so as to increase the back focal distance beyond the focal length in order to leave room for additional optical or mechanical parts such as the mirror in a single-lens reflex camera). An intermediate focal length of about 50 mm (on a 35 mm film format) is instead referred to as a *normal lens* as the angle of view closely matches the central angle of view that mostly impacts perception in the human eye. Conversely, the angle of view may be narrowed by increasing the focal length (possibly by means of a secondary optical lens called a *teleconverter*), which above 80 mm (on a 35 mm film format) is referred to as a *long-focus lens* (potentially having a *telephoto lens* design, which combines positive lens

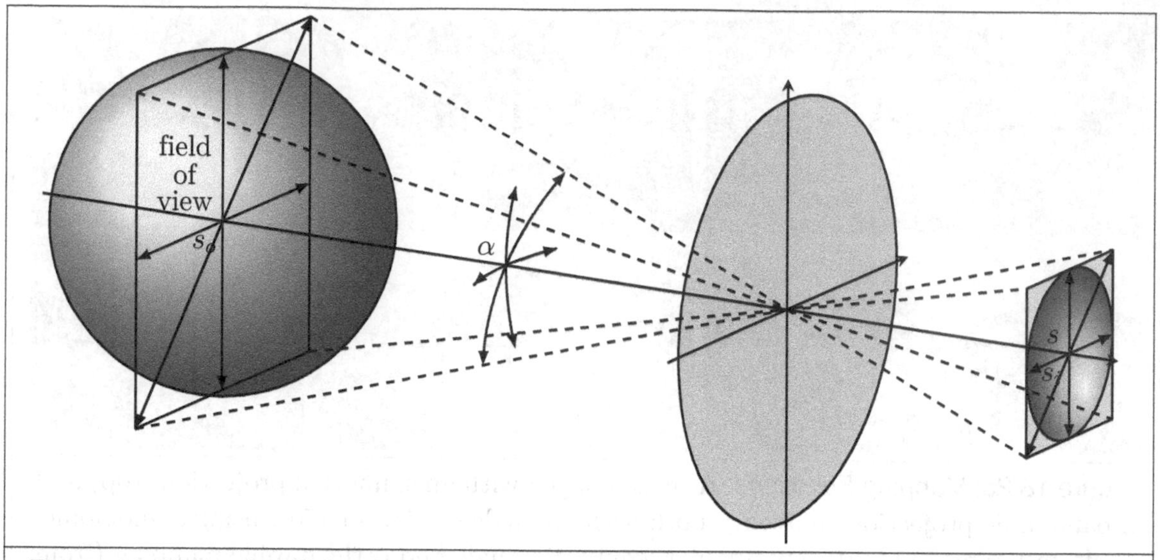

Figure 18.26: Angle of View: Illustration of the terms involved in the computation of the angle of view in the case of a perspective projection.

groups at the front with negative lens groups, so as to decrease the back focal distance below the focal length in order to make the physical dimensions shorter and less cumbersome), resulting in an orthographic projection in the conceptual limit of a focal length at infinity.

In practice, it is possible for the effective field of view to be limited by the angular field that can actually be imaged by the lens, so-called *angle of coverage*. Darkening artifacts might appear near the periphery of the picture either due to the decrease of the irradiance reaching a pixel on the sensor as a function of the cosines and distance to the aperture, so-called *natural vignetting* characterized by an illumination falloff proportional to the fourth power of
660 the cosine of the angle at which the light impinges on the film or sensor as per *Equation 18.32*,
or due to shadowing of oblique incident rays inside each pixel, so-called *pixel vignetting*, both of which may be reduced in the theoretical limit of an infinitely distant exit pupil to yield a zero angle of incidence as may be achieved in practice with an image-space *telecentric lens* design. Vignetting may also be due to the image circle produced by the lens not being large enough compared to the size of the film or sensor, then called *optical vignetting* if caused by multiple lens elements as occurs at wide apertures, or *mechanical vignetting* if caused by add-on filters or lens hoods, such that the image circle itself might even become visible in the limit as often occurs when using a wide-angle fish-eye lens.

18.6 EXTREME PHOTOGRAPHY

18.6.1 Panoramic Photography

In *panoramic photography*, a fully omniscient angle of view may be achieved using a *catadioptric system*, where a convex curved (spherical or parabolic) mirror is used to reflect the
675 incident light into the lens, as illustrated in *Figure 18.27*. In contrast, a *rotation camera* scans
a sequence of 1-D signals as the lens/camera pivots around its rear nodal point, either by exposing only a linear strip at a time of the 2-D film or sensor through a slit, or by means of a digital line sensor. Alternatively, segmented panoramic images may be obtained by stitching several partially overlapping photographs of a scene taken while rotating a standard camera (preferably mounted on a tripod equipped with a panoramic head) about the center of the entrance pupil of the (preferably wide-angle or fish-eye) lens in order to avoid parallax errors,
657 in which case both the *exposure* and the white balance should be kept constant across the

different shots in order to make the stitching post-process more consistent.

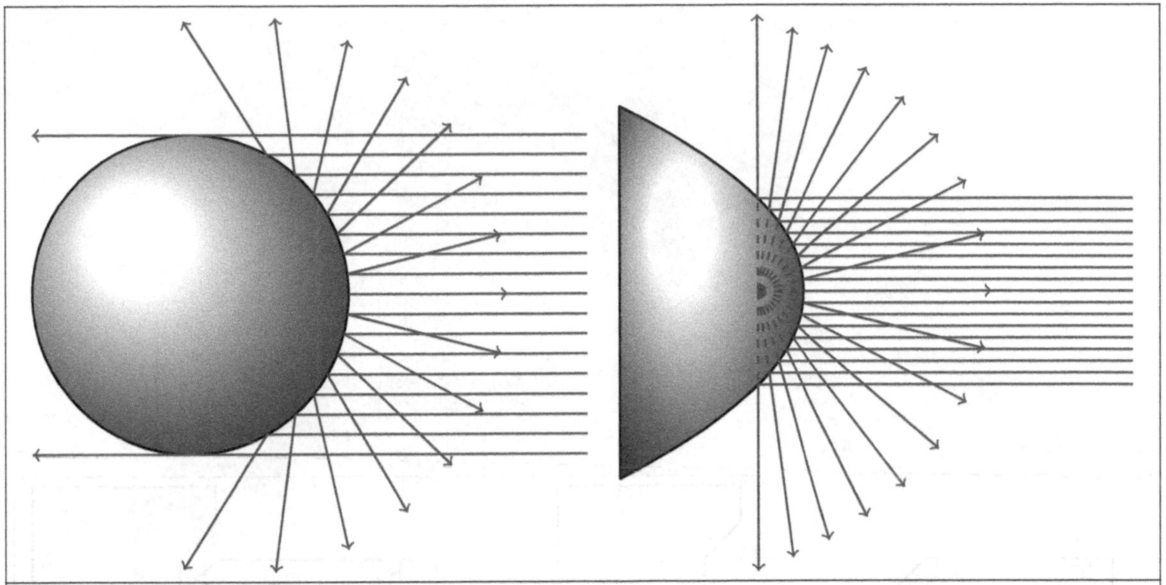

Figure 18.27: Panoramic Photography: Illustration of panoramic photography using either a reflective sphere or a parabolic mirror (drawn after [Heidrich and Seidel, 1998, Fig. 2]).

18.6.2 Macro Photography

In *macro photography*, a greater-than-life-size 35 mm-equivalent reproduction ratio (such that a 24 × 36 mm subject fills the frame) is achieved by reducing the minimal lens-to-subject focusing distance. As an alternative to a specialized *macro lens*, an ordinary primary lens may be mounted onto a non-optical element, such as a fixed-length *extension tube* or a continuously adjustable *bellows*, so as to extend the distance between the lens and the film or sensor. Instead, the primary lens can be equipped with a secondary lens called *close-up filter*, with a wide-angle lens that is mounted in reverse so as to invert its reproduction ratio,
or with a *microscope objective*, as illustrated in *Figure 18.28*. Although small sensor formats 676
offer a greater *depth of field*, the latter is in the general case rather limited for close focus 662
distances. Sharply imaging the entire subject thus typically requires taking a series of multiple photographies with a different focus distance each, a technique known as *focus bracketing*, and combining the individual in-focus regions into a single image via *focus stacking*.

18.7 FURTHER READING

Additional material may be found in books dedicated to pinhole photography [Renner, 2009], to photographic processes [Salvaggio, 2009] or to the science of photography [Johnson, 2010].

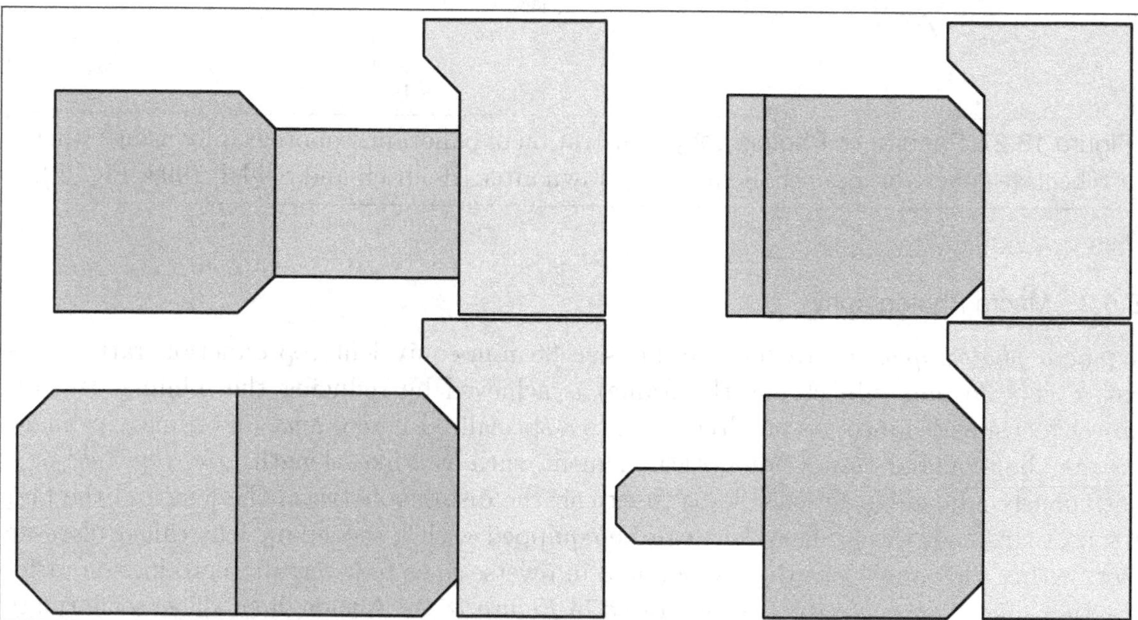

Figure 18.28: Macro Photography: Close focusing in macro photography, using either an extension tube (top left), a close-up filter (top right), a reverse-mounted lens (bottom left) or a microscope objective (bottom right).

CHAPTER 19

Visual Perception

TABLE OF CONTENTS

19.1 HISTORY

During the classical Greek antiquity, Sicilian philosopher Empedocles (ca. 490–430 BC) postulated that everything was composed of four classical elements (air, earth, fire and water), and that human vision was possible due to the goddess Aphrodite lighting the fire within the eyes, thereby emitting rays of light. This school of thought, known as the *emission theory* or *extramission theory*, was supported by subsequent thinkers such as Plato (ca. 427–347 BC), Euclid (ca. 300 BC) and Ptolemy (ca. 100–170 AD).

In contrast, Aristotle (384–322 BC) advocated the *intromission theory*, which states that vision is possible due to rays of light entering the eye. This theory was later developed by Abu Ali Ibn al-Haytham (latinized as Alhazen or Alhacen) in his *Kitab al-Manazir* (Arabic for *Book of Optics*, 1021 AD), as well as by Leonardo da Vinci in his *Codex Atlanticus* (1519 AD).

19.2 HUMAN EYE

19.2.1 Anatomy

678 As illustrated in *Figure 19.1*, the earliest form of light-sensitive organ was an unstructured
spot of photoreceptor protein, called *eyespot* or *pigment spot ocellus*, able to sense ambient
light levels but not to image the environment, as still found in some flatworms, jellyfishes and
sea stars. Throughout evolution, some of these organs depressed into a cavity to form a *pit*
eye or *stemma*, allowing rough directional sensitivity, as in the case of the infrared-sensing pit
organs of pit vipers, while others evolved further into the biological equivalent of a *pinhole*
648 *camera*, such as that of the nautilus, potentially followed by the development of one or more
focusing lenses, as in vertebrates.

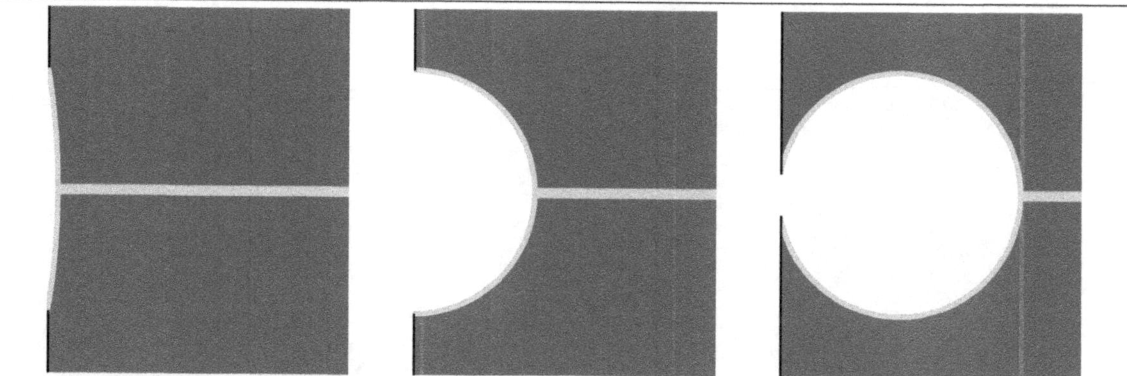

Figure 19.1: Eye Evolution: Illustration of the layout of the photosensitive cells in the eye organ, evolving from an eyespot, to a pit eye, and then to a pinhole eye (from left to right).

679 647 As illustrated in *Figure 19.2*, human eyes are spheroidal *image-forming optical systems*
composed of a white elastic chamber of about 12 mm in radius called *sclera*, often referred
679 to as the "white of the eye," at the opening of which lies the *crystalline lens* and a biological
681 diaphragm called *iris*. The interior wall of the eye is lined with a curved sensor called *retina*,
692 681 which contains *photoreceptors*, and whose outer and middle layers are irrigated by a vascular
layer called *choroid*, lying between the retina and the sclera, while its inner layers are supplied
by a tree of blood vessels branching off from the central retinal artery.

Random scattering of light within the eyeball is reduced by absorption from a dark pigment, called melanin, contained within the opaque choroid of non-albino humans. Bright

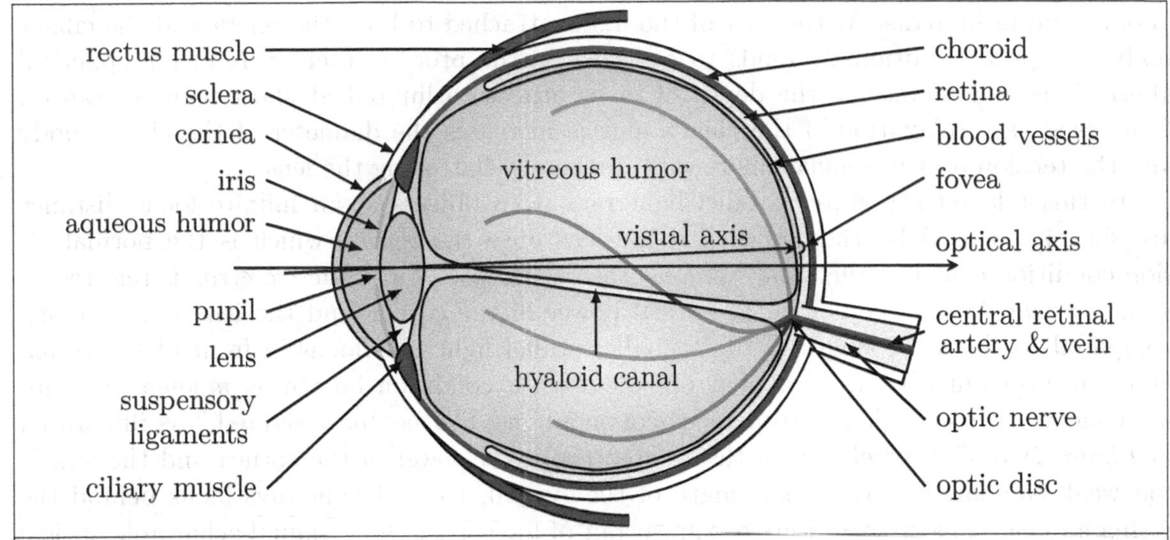

Figure 19.2: Human Eye: Illustration of the anatomy of the human eye, here showing a top view of the right eye.

light sources such as flashes may still cause a non-negligible amount of the incident light to scatter and exit the eyeball through the pupil, a phenomenon commonly observed as the *red-eye effect* in photography. Instead of melanin, areas of the choroid of various animals contain a reflective layer, known as the *tapetum lucidum*, which redirects stray light so as to augment night vision (potentially at the cost of a lower acuity), thereby causing the *eyeshine* commonly observed under illumination from automotive headlights.

The horizontal *angle of view* of the human eye gazing forwards is 95–110° temporal 673
(towards the temple) and about 60° nasal (towards the nose), whereas the vertical *angle of*
view is 70–80° inferior (downwards) and about 60° superior (upwards). The ranges of angles 673
less than 30°, between 30° and 60° and beyond 60° are then typically referred to as *near-*
peripheral vision, *mid-peripheral vision* and *far-peripheral vision*, respectively. It follows that
the total static *angle of view* of the two eyes of an average human being extends to about 673
190–220° horizontally and 130–140° vertically, and up to 270° horizontally when accounting
for the rotation of the eye ball.

19.2.2 Crystalline Lens

For aquatic vertebrates, the focusing power of the *cornea* is generally negligible as its refractive index of about 1.38 (being similar to that of the *aqueous humor* and *vitreous humor*, which are about 1.34) is comparable to that of water. In air, however, the focusing power of the cornea is substantial, representing about 43 diopters in humans, and generally accounts for about 2/3 of the eye's total optical power, albeit with a fixed focus.

In order to maintain a sharp focus onto the *retina* for various object distances (especially 692
in dimmer lighting conditions where the pupil aperture is larger), the vertebrate eye is able to
adapt by a process known as *accommodation*. Among most fishes, cephalopods, amphibians
and snakes, the latter occurs by means of muscles controlling the distance between the rigid
lens and the *retina*. In contrast, mammals, birds and reptiles have a flexible *crystalline lens* 692
whose curvature is controlled by the surrounding *ciliary muscle*. As the latter contracts, it
reduces the diameter of the *ciliary body*, which loosens the *zonule of Zinn* in the suspensory
ligaments, and allows the *lens capsule* to relax into a more biconvex shape, thereby increasing
its optical power up to 14 diopters and reducing the focus distance from infinity down to

681 about 7 cm in humans. As the root of the *iris* is attached to both the sclera and the ciliary
body, the pupil additionally tends to constrict in the process, thereby reducing spherical
aberrations and increasing the depth of focus otherwise limited at short focus distances.
Conversely, the relaxation of the ciliary muscle increases the diameter of the ciliary body
and the tension on the zonular fibers with it, thereby flattening the lens.

In this relaxed eye state, parallel light rays from objects at an infinite focus distance
692 are sharply focused by the cornea and the lens onto the *retina*, which is the normal vision condition called *emmetropia*, whereas the occurrence of a *refractive error* is referred to
as *ametropia*. When the combined optical power of the cornea and the lens is too strong
692 compared to the axial length of the eyeball, parallel light rays focus in front of the *retina*
and cause distant objects to appear out of focus, a condition known as *myopia* prescribing concave corrective lenses to persons commonly said to be "near-sighted," as illustrated
680 in *Figure 19.3*. Conversely, when the combined optical power of the cornea and the lens is
too weak compared to the axial length of the eyeball, parallel light rays focus behind the
692 *retina* and cause close-by objects to appear out of focus past the maximal achievable optical
power, a condition known as *hyperopia* or *hypermetropia* prescribing convex corrective lenses
to persons commonly said to be "far-sighted."

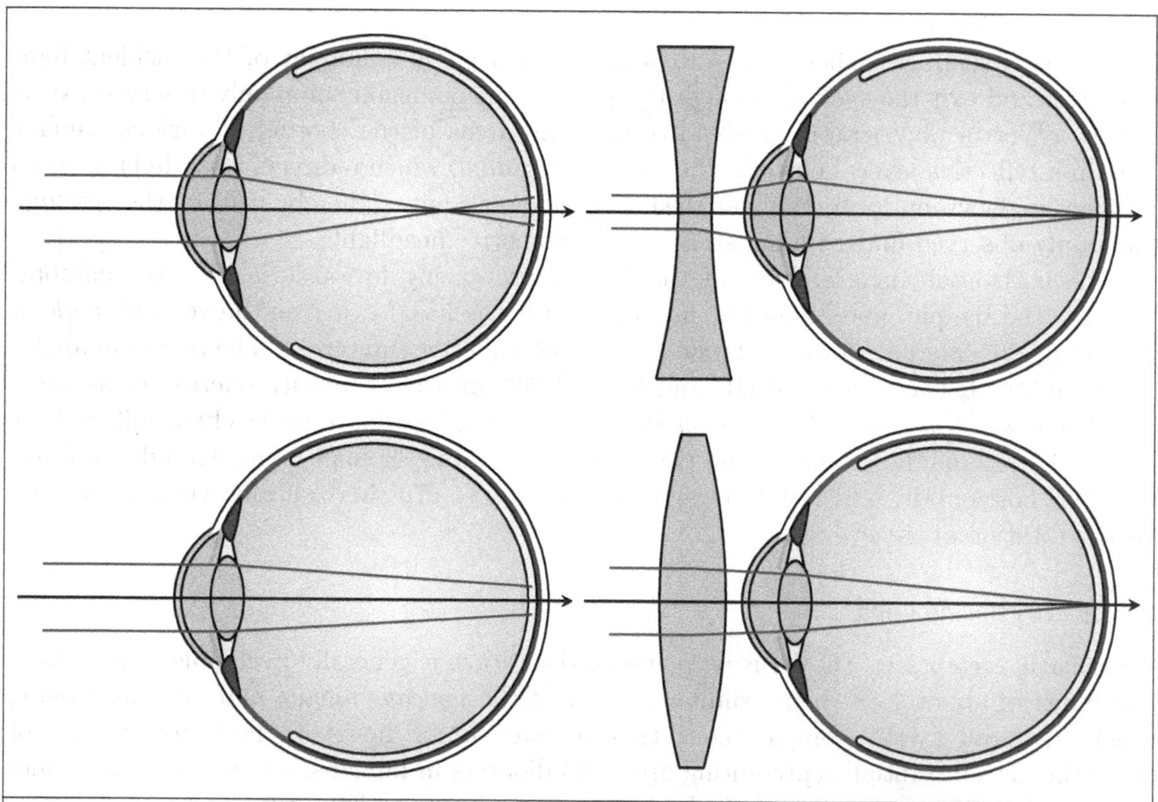

Figure 19.3: Crystalline Lens: Illustration of the focusing of light rays in a human eye affected by myopia (top) and hyperopia (bottom), both before (left) and after (right) optical correction.

When the cornea or the lens exhibit an axial asymmetry (either regular, or irregular such
as a scar) causing varying degrees of curvature along different meridians, light rays belonging
to different meridional planes focus at different points, hence prescribing cylindrical corrective
lenses. This condition is known as simple/double myopic or hyperopic *astigmatism* when
692 one/both focal points lie either in front of or behind the *retina*, respectively, and as mixed
astigmatism when the two focal points lie on each side of it.

Due to the loss of elasticity of the lens and/or the loss of power of the ciliary muscles, the maximal optical power achievable by the human eye tends to decrease with age, progressively bringing the closest focus distance beyond the reading distance, a condition known as *presbyopia*. In order to correct the latter, emmetropic persons generally require convex lenses for near vision, while myopic persons might potentially do without concave corrective lenses for near vision, whereas hyperopic persons typically require convex lenses with an increased optical power for near vision.

19.2.3 Iris

The pigments of the *iris* determine what is colloquially referred to as the "eye color," while its physical aperture is called the *pupil*. The size of the latter is controlled by the *pupillary light reflex* (*PLR*), by which a (potentially unilateral) bright stimulus causes both pupils (under normal conditions, due to the consensual response of the unstimulated eye) to constrict, or conversely to dilate in dimmer lighting conditions.

While the slit-shaped pupil of cats roughly provides a 135-fold change in aperture area, the circular pupil of the human eye only allows for a 10-fold adaptation to external illumination levels. Due to refraction in the cornea, though, the actual aperture of the physical pupil slightly differs from the effective aperture of the entrance pupil, whose diameter typically varies between 1–2 and 7–8 mm.

19.2.4 Photoreceptors

A *photoreceptor cell* is a light-sensitive nerve cell that biologically converts incident light
radiation into an electrical signal, a process known as *phototransduction*. The latter is due to
opsin photopigment proteins, whose *spectral sensitivity* determines the relative *probability* of 129
absorption of photons at a given wavelength. The human *retina* contains two main categories 692
of visual photoreceptors, namely rods and cones, and is therefore said to be a *duplex retina*.

The human *retina* counts an average of about 120 ± 30 million *rod cells*, which are highly 692
sensitive to incident light as their response can be stimulated by only a few photons while
bleaching under bright illumination. Their light detection ability is increased by *temporal*
summation of the incident photons over a period of about 100–200 milliseconds depending
on the intensity of the light stimulus, thereby making their response relatively slow while
yielding a *flicker fusion threshold* of about 15 Hz above which an intermittent light appears
steady. Rods contain a single type of *rhodopsin photopigment*, whose spectral sensitivity peaks
at about 498 nm as illustrated in *Figure 19.4*, thereby providing an intrinsically achromatic 682
vision.

The human *retina* additionally counts an average of about 6 ± 1 million *cone cells*, which 692
exhibit a much lower sensitivity as stimulating their response requires tens to hundreds of photons while vanishing under low illumination. Because their response time is relatively fast, cones have a much greater temporal resolution, even more so at higher light intensities (up to a plateau), and are able to detect more rapid changes in the light stimulus, thereby yielding a maximum flicker fusion rate of about 60 Hz, whereas the *persistence of vision* on the retina is considered to correspond to an animated motion at a frame rate of about 16 Hz (i.e., with up to 4 flickers per frame). As first postulated by Thomas Young and further developed by Hermann von Helmholtz in the nineteenth century, about 60–65%, 30–35% and 5% of the human cones are most sensitive to either long (L), medium (M) or short (S) wavelengths, depending on whether the *iodopsin photopigment* contained within is the *photopsin photopigment* of type I, II or III, whose spectral sensitivities normally peak at about 564 nm, 534 nm and 420 nm, respectively, thereby enabling chromatic vision.

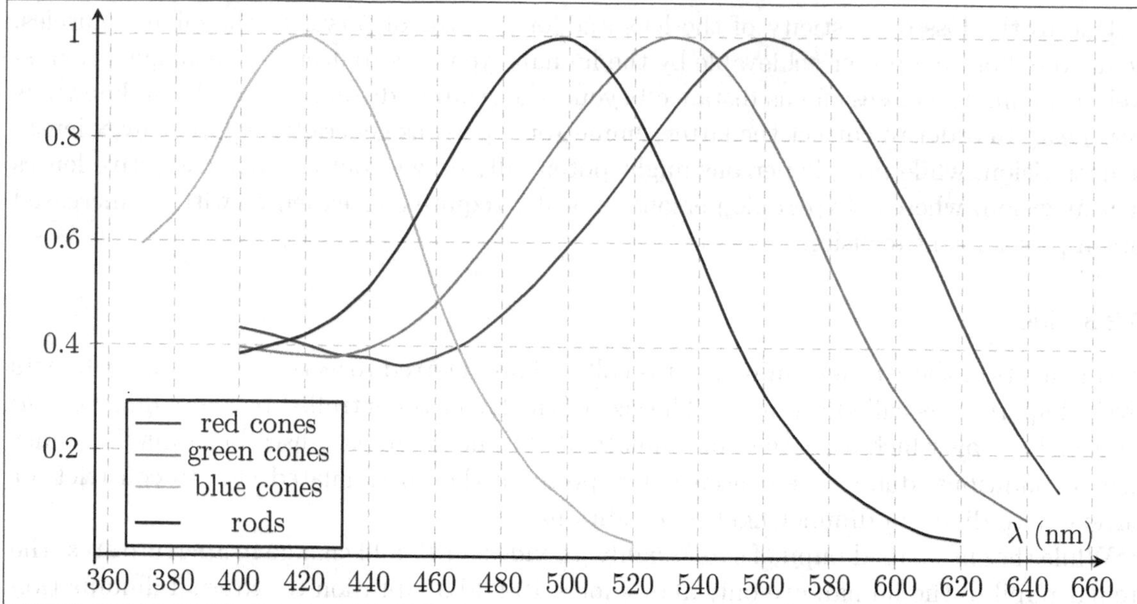

Figure 19.4: Opsin Spectral Sensitivity: Plot of the normalized absorption spectra of the rhodopsin and three types of photopsins in the human eye (plotted after data from [Bowmaker and Dartnall, 1980, Dartnall *et al.*, 1983, Table 2]).

Initially, primitive vertebrates were tetrachromats, and possessed cones sensitive to the long, medium, short and ultraviolet wavelengths. Various species of animals have preserved all four types of cones from their ancestors throughout evolution. In contrast, most placental mammals lost both long and ultra-short cone types and became dichromats, unable to perceive red or ultraviolet light. Trichromacy subsequently reappeared among primates by means of a genetic duplication of the medium cone type towards longer wavelengths. Instances among current living species include:

1. *monochromacy*: marine mammals (including cetaceans and pinnipeds), some New World monkeys (e.g., the night monkey)

2. *dichromacy*: most terrestrial non-primate placental mammals, males of most species of New World monkeys

3. *trichromacy*: most primates (including apes, Old World monkeys and about 60% of females of most species of New World monkeys), marsupial mammals, some insects (e.g., honeybees, sensitive to ultraviolet but not to red light)

4. *tetrachromacy*: most fishes, most reptiles, most birds, most amphibians, most insects

5. *pentachromacy*: some birds (e.g., pigeons), some insects (e.g., some species of butterflies)

whereas mantis shrimps, whose eyes contain 12 different types of photopigments, are dodecachromats.

19.2.5 Color Blindness

While humans are normally trichromats, various types of cone deficiencies may limit their ability to discriminate colors under normal lighting conditions. This condition, known as *color blindness*, is often diagnosed by means of the *Ishihara color test*, which consists of a series of circular images containing a random arrangement of spots whose colors depict Arabic numerals discriminable under normal color vision, but not under a certain type of color deficiency, or inversely. While color blindness is usually regarded as a disability, dichromats tend to better make use of geometric and textural cues, thereby increasing their ability to penetrate color camouflages and to distinguish objects under dim lighting conditions.

The most severe form, called *total color blindness* or *rod monochromacy*, is very rare especially among females, and corresponds to the deficiency or lack of all three types of cones, thereby resulting in a visual impairment at daylight illumination levels. Instead, *cone monochromacy* refers to the deficiency or lack of two types of cones, thereby providing an achromatic vision at both dim and bright light intensities.

A less severe form corresponds to the deficiency or lack of a single type of cones, thereby resulting in a pathological form of *dichromacy*. The deficiency or lack of the first cone type L, so-called *protanopia*, affects about 1% of males and 0.02% of females, and induces a shortening of the visible spectrum at longer wavelengths, such that wavelengths shorter or longer than the neutral point at about 492 nm are perceived as blue or yellow opponent colors, respectively, causing red to appear as black, orange/yellow/green as different shades of yellow, cyan as white and blue/violet/purple as different shades of blue. The deficiency or lack of the second cone type M, so-called *deuteranopia* or *Daltonism* (although the latter term is sometimes more broadly used to refer to color blindness in general) after the deuteranopic English chemist John Dalton who first studied the subject, affects about 1% of males and 0.01% of females, and induces wavelengths shorter or longer than the neutral point at about 498 nm to be perceived as blue or yellow opponent colors, respectively, causing red/orange/yellow/green to appear as different shades of yellow, green-cyan as white, blue/violet as different shades of blue and purples as a spectral color of a given wavelength. The deficiency of the third cone type S, so-called *tritanopia*, affects less than 0.02% of both males and females, and induces a shortening of the visible spectrum at shorter wavelengths, such that wavelengths shorter or longer than the neutral point at about 570 nm are perceived as green or red opponent colors, respectively, causing purple/red/orange/yellow to appear as different shades of red, and cyan/blue/violet as different shades of green.

The least severe form corresponds to the alteration of the spectral sensitivity of a single type of cones due to the mutation of its pigment, so-called *anomalous trichromacy*. The alteration of the first cone type L, so-called *protanomaly*, affects about 1% of males and less than 0.02% of females, and induces a shift of the spectral sensitivity towards shorter wavelengths and a greater overlap with that of M cones, thereby resulting in reduced sensitivity to red, which appears darker, and in poor red/orange/yellow/green hue discrimination. The alteration of the second cone type M, so-called *deuteranomaly*, affects about 5% of males and 0.35% of females, and induces a shift of the spectral sensitivity towards longer wavelengths and a greater overlap with that of L cones, thereby resulting in reduced sensitivity to green, but without loss of intensity, and in poor red/orange/yellow/green hue discrimination. The alteration of the third cone type S, so-called *tritanomaly*, affects less than 0.01% of both males and females, and induces a shift of the spectral sensitivity towards longer wavelength and a greater overlap with that of M cones, thereby resulting in poor red/orange/yellow and green/blue hue discrimination.

While all types of color blindness are hereditary, the genes defining the traits of the pigment of the S cone type are encoded on chromosome 7, such that *blue-yellow color blindness* (i.e., tritanopia and tritanomaly) is not sex-linked and equally unprevalent among both males and females, as most color-blind people retain blue-yellow discrimination.

In contrast, the genes defining the traits of the pigments of the L and M cone types are encoded on the X chromosome, such that *red-green color blindness* (i.e., protanopia/protanomaly and deuteranopia/deuteranomaly) is sex-linked and affects about

8% of men (for whom the gene of their XY pair is always expressed) versus 0.4% of women
(for whom each chromosome of their XX pair needs to carry the same deficiency in order
129 for the recessive gene to be expressed, thereby squaring the mathematical *probability*). It
follows that an affected male cannot transmit the gene to his sons as they receive his Y
chromosome, but will transmit it to all of his daughters through the X chromosome, whereas
a female carrier has a 50% chance of transmitting the gene to her children, and to affect her
sons, while her daughters will only be affected if receiving the gene from both parents. Due
to the random inactivation of one of each pair of heterozygotic alleles in each cell, daughters
receiving X chromosomes that each carry either the protanomalic or deuteranomalic gene
may possess a fourth type of cones whose spectral sensitivity lies between that of L and M
cone types, as is the case for 2–3% of women, similarly to how the majority of females of
most species of New World monkeys possess trichromatic vision. Although the scope of colors
measurable by the vertebrate retina is determined by the number of different cone types, the
ability of the visual system as a whole to perceive and discriminate colors also depends on the
overall aptitude to transmit and process the color information through independent channels
681 from the *photoreceptors* to the brain, and women with four cone types rarely happen to be
"functional" tetrachromats in practice.

19.2.6 LMS

The functional chromacy of a visual system intrinsically determines the effective dimensionality of the sensory color space, which, in the case of humans with normal trichromatic vision, is three-dimensional, such that the set of all perceivable colors can be characterized by a linear combination of three primary colors. As each of the three cone types is able to discriminate over 100 different gradations, assuming that their combinations can be transmitted and processed by the brain, an average human being can distinguish about 1–10 million different colors, although the just-noticeable difference in wavelength can vary from about 1 nm in the green-yellow range to more than 10 nm in the red or blue ends of the visible spectrum.

681 While the spectral sensitivity of the *photoreceptors* spans the near-ultraviolet range,
679 most electromagnetic radiation within 300–400 nm is absorbed by the *crystalline lens* of the
human eye, while the cornea is increasingly absorptive to shorter wavelengths, such that the
range of radiation visible to humans generally vanishes below approximately 380 nm. People
whose eyes are lacking a lens, a condition known as *aphakia*, perceive ultraviolet light down
to about 300 nm as whitish-violet/blue, due to the similar, though decreasing, sensitivity of
the S, L and M cone types in that order.

685 As illustrated in *Figure 19.5*, the resulting *tristimulus functions* $\bar{l}$, $\overline{m}$ and $\bar{s}$ of the three
cone types peak at about 570 nm, 540 nm and 440 nm, corresponding to yellowish, greenish
and blueish, respectively, although variations may be observed even among individuals considered to have normal color vision. Physiological measurements of the cone responses of an
individual are rather impractical, though, and the tristimulus functions are instead evaluated
704 by means of color-matching experiments using adjustable *RGB* primaries. The tristimulus
values of a spectral distribution I in the physiological *LMS color space* are then defined by
the projection coordinates

$$L \triangleq \int_0^\infty I(\lambda)\bar{l}(\lambda)\mathrm{d}\lambda \tag{19.1}$$

$$M \triangleq \int_0^\infty I(\lambda)\overline{m}(\lambda)\mathrm{d}\lambda \tag{19.2}$$

$$S \triangleq \int_0^\infty I(\lambda)\bar{s}(\lambda)\mathrm{d}\lambda \tag{19.3}$$

whose relative ratios determine the *color* sensation perceived in response to the spectral stimulus I.

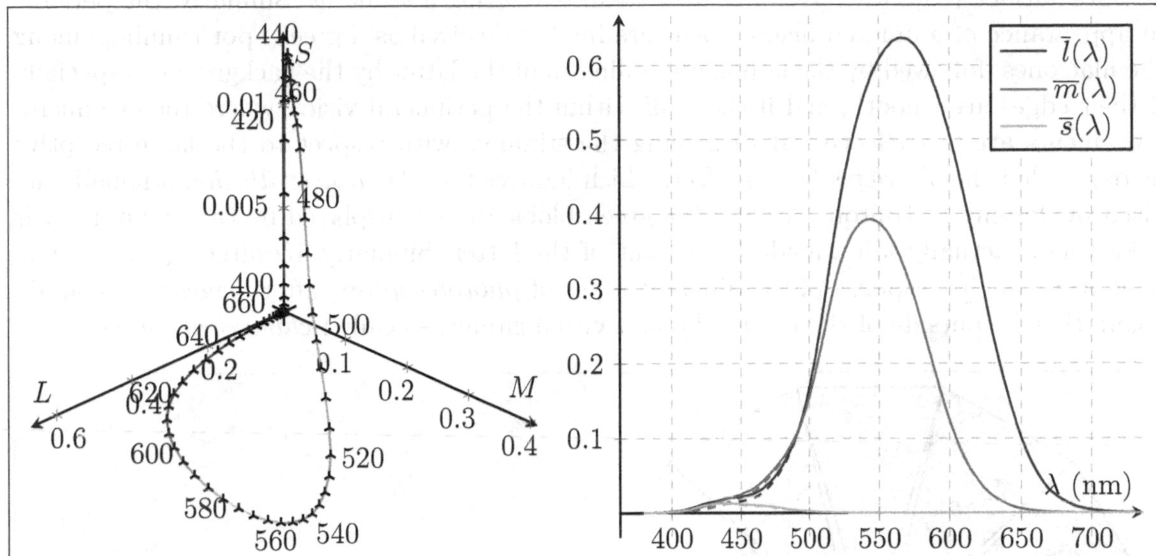

Figure 19.5: LMS Color Space: Illustration of the LMS virtual primaries (left), and plot of the corresponding tristimulus functions (dashed [Vos and Walraven, 1971] and solid [Smith and Pokorny, 1975]) (right).

The set of all spectral distributions projects into a subset of the LMS color space called the *human visual gamut*, and can be characterized by a conic combination of its primaries. The latter are said to be "virtual" as there exists no physical spectrum whose LMS coordinates are $[1, 0, 0]$, $[0, 1, 0]$ or $[0, 0, 1]$ due to their overlapping spectral sensitivities. Because of the loss of dimensionality entailed by the projection of a continuous spectrum into a finite basis, different stimuli may project to the same triplet of LMS coordinates, and therefore appear as identical colors to a human observer, a phenomenon known as *metamerism*. Whereas colors on the spectral locus correspond to a single specific wavelength, non-spectral colors may result from infinitely many different spectra such as the linear combinations of different monochromatic primaries, and the range of metameric spectra is therefore increasingly large as saturation decreases.

Metameric matching is especially relevant in the automotive industry, where the multiple parts of a car interior, although made of various materials exhibiting different spectral distributions, are intended to appear uniform in color. Conversely, the loss of color matching under varying conditions is referred to as *metameric failure*, including *illuminant metameric failure* due to variations in the illumination spectra (e.g., discrete fluorescent versus continuous incandescent distributions), as well as *geometric metameric failure* due to variations in viewing angles (e.g., pearlescent automotive paint). Similarly, *observer metameric failure* refers to variations in the spectral sensitivities among humans (e.g., colorblindness or biological heterogeneity), while *field-size metameric failure* is linked with variations in the distribution of the different cone types in the *retina* (e.g., fovea versus periphery). 692

From a physiological standpoint, the continuous exposition of sensory neurons to a constant stimulus causes the progressive decay of their response, a phenomenon generally known as *neural adaptation*. While usually unnoticed due to the fast and frequent jittering movements of the eyes, the overstimulation of certain cone types, by prolonged fixation of a color they are sensitive to, causes the progressive exhaustion of their photopigments and a temporary reduction in the strength of the output signal. As illustrated in *Figure 19.6*, this 686

mechanism is responsible for various *optical illusions*, such as the appearance of an image in complementary/opponent colors, called *negative afterimage*, when looking away towards a white surface (e.g., a white wall) after steadily fixating a stimulus. Similarly, the periodic disappearance of animated lilac blobs is gradually perceived as a green spot running among the lilac ones, followed by the fading and filling-in of the latter by the background (especially if their edges are smooth, and if they fall within the peripheral vision where the eye micro-movements are less effective at displacing the stimulus with respect to the large receptive fields), called the *Troxler's fading effect*, which induces the *lilac chaser illusion* originally devised by Jeremy L. Hinton. Because the green blobs are not displayed by the monitor, their color might actually fall outside the gamut of the latter. Similarly, by altering the relative
681 magnitude of the response of the different types of *photoreceptors*, afterimages may contain colors that lie outside of the normal human visual gamut, so-called *chimerical colors*.

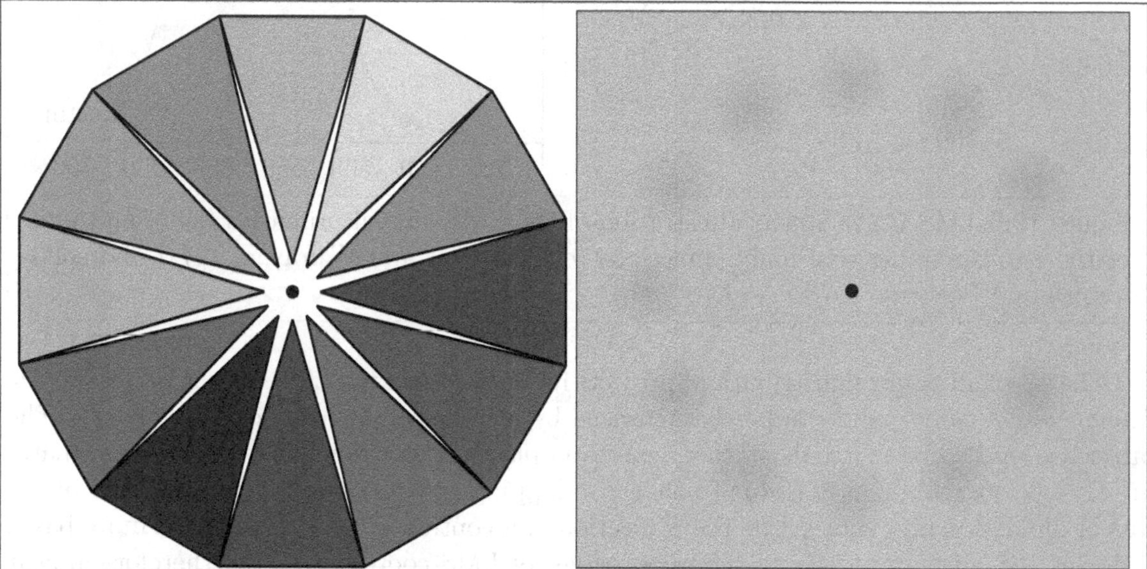

Figure 19.6: Afterimage: Illustration of an afterimage appearing when looking at a white surface after fixation of the central dot for about 30 seconds (left) and of Hinton's lilac chaser illusion (right).

19.2.7 Photometry

The average spectral brightness sensitivity of human vision is characterized by the dimensionless *luminous efficiency function*, also called standard *luminosity function*, $V(\lambda)$. As the cones are not sensitive enough to contribute to vision under low-light conditions, so-called *scotopic vision*, the *scotopic luminosity function* $V_s(\lambda)$ [CIE, 1951] corresponds to the spec-
681 tral sensitivity of the rod *photoreceptors* filtered by the spectral absorption of the cornea-lens
687 system, normalized to have a unit peak value at about 507 nm, as illustrated in *Figure 19.7*. Conversely, because the rods are saturated at high illumination levels and cones solely contribute to the so-called *photopic vision*, the *photopic luminosity function* $V_p(\lambda)$ [CIE, 1931]
684 corresponds to the aggregate of the three *LMS* tristimulus functions, normalized to have a unit peak value at 555 nm (or 540 nm and 560 nm in the case of protanopia and deuteranopia, respectively). However, the function standardized by the *Commission Internationale de l'Éclairage* (*CIE*) (i.e., French for International Commission on Illumination) is known to underestimate the perception of shorter wavelengths and various corrections have subsequently been proposed [Judd, 1951, Vos, 1978].

Since both rods and cones partially contribute to vision under intermediate lighting conditions, so-called *mesopic vision*, the *mesopic luminosity function* $V_m(\lambda)$ corresponds to a convex combination of the scotopic and photopic luminosity functions

$$V_m(\lambda) = (1 - \alpha)V_s(\lambda) + \alpha V_p(\lambda) \tag{19.4}$$

whose weighting factor α behaves similarly to a *smooth step function* or a scaled/offset 42
sigmoid function parameterized by the ambient light intensity. It follows that when the illu- 41
mination level decreases from the photopic toward the scotopic range, the mesopic transition from color to gray vision is accompanied by a progressive shift of the peak of spectral sensitivity away from yellow-green towards the green-blue range of the spectrum, a phenomenon known as the *Purkinje effect*.

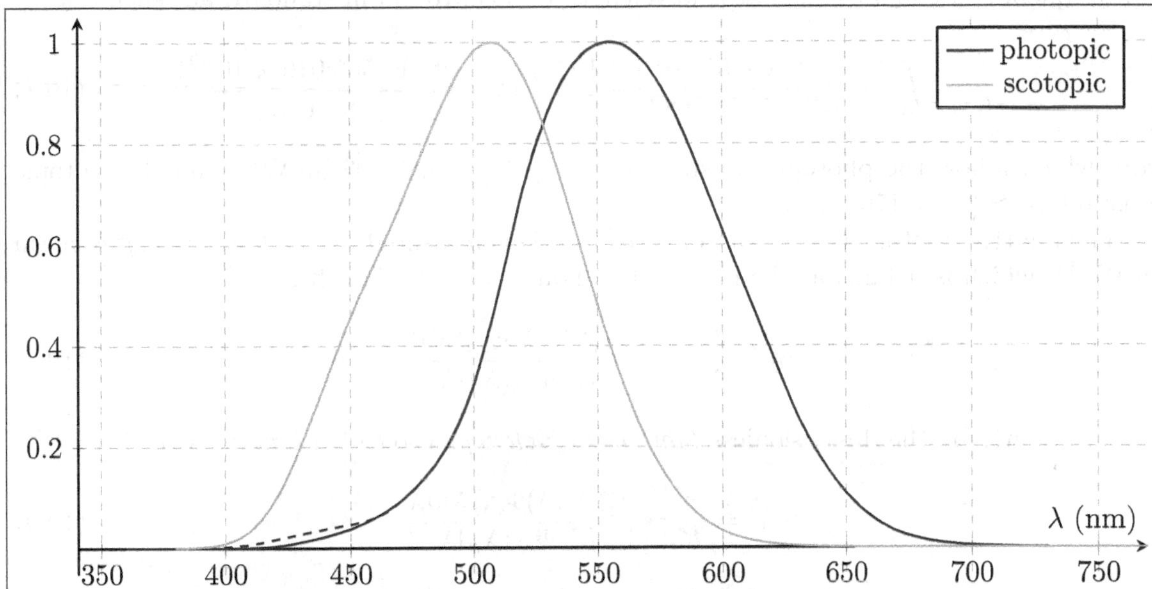

Figure 19.7: Luminous Efficiency Function: Plot of the photopic and scotopic luminosity functions, both standardized [CIE, 1931, CIE, 1951] (solid) and modified [Judd, 1951, Vos, 1978] (dashed).

In optics, *photometry* is the science of measuring *electromagnetic radiation* in terms of 420
visible light perceived by a human observer. As illustrated in *Table 19.1*, any quantity defined 687
in the field of *radiometry* can be converted into its photometric analog by integrating its 425
spectral distribution against the luminosity function.

Table 19.1: Photometric Quantities: Nomenclature of photometric quantities.

Quantity	Symbol	SI Unit
Luminous energy	Q_v	$\text{lm}\cdot\text{s} \equiv \text{T}$
Luminous exposure	H_v	$\text{T}\cdot\text{m}^{-2}$
Luminous energy density	w_v	$\text{T}\cdot\text{m}^{-3}$
Luminous flux/power	Φ_v	lm
Luminous intensity	I_v	$\text{lm}\cdot\text{sr}^{-1} \equiv \text{cd}$
Luminous exitance/emittance (emitted)	M_v	$\text{lm}\cdot\text{m}^{-2} \equiv \text{lx}$
Luminosity (emitted and reflected)	J_v / B_v	$\text{lm}\cdot\text{m}^{-2} \equiv \text{lx}$
Illuminance (incident)	E_v	$\text{lm}\cdot\text{m}^{-2} \equiv \text{lx}$
Luminance	L_v	$\text{lm}\cdot\text{m}^{-2}\cdot\text{sr}^{-1} \equiv \text{nt}$

Given a spectral power distribution $\Phi_{e\lambda}(\lambda)$, the corresponding *luminous flux* is consequently evaluated as

$$\Phi_v \triangleq K \int_0^\infty V(\lambda)\Phi_{e\lambda}(\lambda)\mathrm{d}\lambda \tag{19.5}$$

while *luminous intensity* is defined as

$$I_v \triangleq K \int_0^\infty V(\lambda)I_{e\lambda}(\lambda)\mathrm{d}\lambda \tag{19.6}$$

By definition, a lumen unit corresponds to a narrowband monochromatic light or Dirac
44 *delta function* $\Phi_{e\lambda}(\lambda) = \frac{\delta(\lambda - 555.016\times10^{-9})}{683}$ of radiant power $\frac{1}{683}$ watt (so that one candela unit
roughly corresponds to the luminous intensity of a "standard candle" of defined composition) at a frequency of 540 THz, i.e., at a wavelength of 555.016 nm in standard air, such that

45

$$\frac{1}{K} = \int_0^\infty V(\lambda)\frac{\delta(\lambda - 555.016\times10^{-9})}{683}\mathrm{d}\lambda \overset{(2.218)}{=} \frac{V(555.016\times10^{-9})}{683} \tag{19.7}$$

from which follow the photopic constant $K = \frac{683}{0.999997} = 683.002\ \mathrm{lm{\cdot}W^{-1}}$ and the scotopic constant $K \approx \frac{683}{0.4} \approx 1700\ \mathrm{lm{\cdot}W^{-1}}$.

The relative photometric impact of a given SPD is measured by the *luminous efficacy* (in $\mathrm{lm{\cdot}W^{-1}}$), which is defined as the ratio of luminous flux to radiant flux

$$\eta \triangleq \frac{\Phi_v}{\Phi_e} = \frac{K\int_0^\infty V(\lambda)\Phi_{e\lambda}(\lambda)\mathrm{d}\lambda}{\int_0^\infty \Phi_{e\lambda}(\lambda)\mathrm{d}\lambda} \tag{19.8}$$

or equivalently by the dimensionless *luminous efficiency*, also called *luminous coefficient*,

$$V \triangleq \frac{\eta}{K} = \frac{\int_0^\infty V(\lambda)\Phi_{e\lambda}(\lambda)\mathrm{d}\lambda}{\int_0^\infty \Phi_{e\lambda}(\lambda)\mathrm{d}\lambda} \tag{19.9}$$

whose respective maxima K and 100% are attained for an SPD described by a Dirac *delta*
44 *function* at a wavelength of 555 nm or 507 nm in the photopic and scotopic case, respectively.
In contrast, the *radiant efficiency*, also called *wall-plug efficiency*, is defined as the ratio of radiant flux to input electrical power, whose product with the luminous efficiency is then referred to as the *overall luminous efficiency* or *wall-plug luminous efficiency*. As illustrated
689 in *Figure 19.8*, a typical tungsten incandescent light bulb has a radiant efficiency of approx-
imatively 80% (the rest being lost by conduction), and a luminous efficacy of only 8–17 (the rest being mostly radiated in the infrared, i.e., as heat) against a maximum of about 95 for a blackbody at about 6600 K, whereas that of a fluorescent lamp and high-output white LED are in the ranges of 60–80 and 25–120, respectively.

Akin to radiance, *luminance* is then defined as

$$L_v(\vec{p},\hat{\omega}) \triangleq \frac{\mathrm{d}^2\Phi_v(\vec{p},\hat{\omega})}{\mathrm{d}A(\vec{p})_\perp \mathrm{d}\hat{\omega}} = \frac{\mathrm{d}^2\Phi_v(\vec{p},\hat{\omega})}{\mathrm{d}A(\vec{p})\langle\hat{n},\hat{\omega}\rangle\mathrm{d}\hat{\omega}} \tag{19.10}$$

689 for which representative values are given in *Table 19.2*.

681 At a given moment in time, the *photoreceptors* have a static contrast ratio of over 10^2
(or 6.5 f-stops), while the human eye as a whole may be able to sense contrast ratios of up to 10^3–10^5. Over time though, adjustments to the illumination level can accommodate luminance ranges of at most $10^8 \div 10^{-6} = 10^{14}$ (about 46.5 f-stops), while allowing the eye to adequately sense dynamic contrast ratios of about 10^9–10^{10}, a phenomenon known as
690 *adaptation*. As illustrated in *Figure 19.9*, the threshold level (in dB) at time t can be modeled

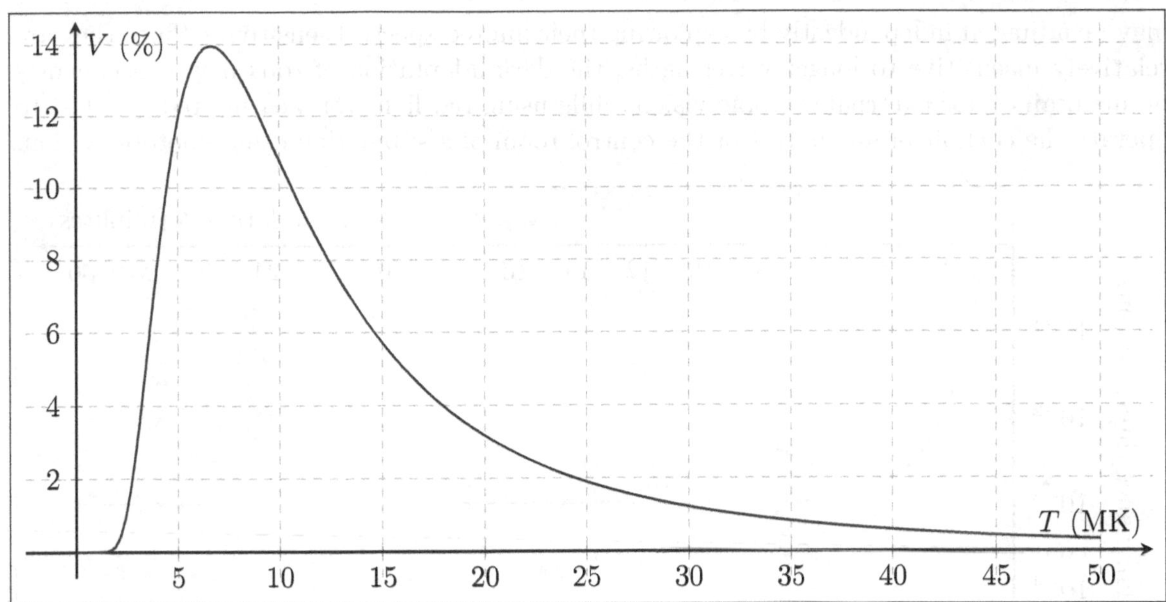

Figure 19.8: Luminous Efficiency: Plot of the luminous efficiency of a blackbody radiator at various temperatures.

Table 19.2: Luminance Values: Representative luminance values for various types of illumination.

Entity	Luminance
Sun at zenith	1–1.5 Gnt
Threshold of retinal lesion	100 Mnt
Sun at horizon	600 knt
Household lamp / light bulb	10–150 knt
Clear sky	7–8 knt
Lunar disk	2.5 knt
Cloudy sky	2 knt
Screen / monitor	50–300 nt
Mesopic/photopic threshold	3–5 nt
Phosphorescent substance	50 mnt
Scotopic/mesopic threshold	3–5 mnt
Night sky	1 mnt
Threshold of human vision	1 μnt

via an exponential decay with rate k between an initial level l_0 at time $t = 0$ and a limit level l_∞ at time $t = \infty$ [Aboshiha *et al.*, 2014]

$$l(t) = l_\infty + (l_0 - l_\infty)e^{-kt} \tag{19.11}$$

Initial *dark adaptation* via geometric dilation of the *iris* typically occurs in a couple of seconds, 681
and stabilization of the cone sensitivity as well as the chemical regeneration of bleached
rhodopsin photopigments in about 5–10 minutes, with the *rod-cone break* occurring after
about 7 minutes, whereas full adaptation of the rods may require 20–40 minutes (given good
blood flow circulation), depending on the luminance level of the pre-adaptation state. In
contrast, photobleaching of the rods is relatively instantaneous and full *light adaptation* of
the cones is achieved in only about 5 minutes. Because adaptation occurs in response to
the stimulation of each individual type of *photoreceptors*, the adaptation level of the latter 681

may be adjusted independently by exploiting their limited spectral sensitivity. Since they are relatively insensitive to longer wavelengths, the dark adaptation of rods may consequently be maintained for external scotopic vision while using red light (or wearing red goggles) to operate the cockpit of an aircraft or the control room of a submarine using photopic vision.

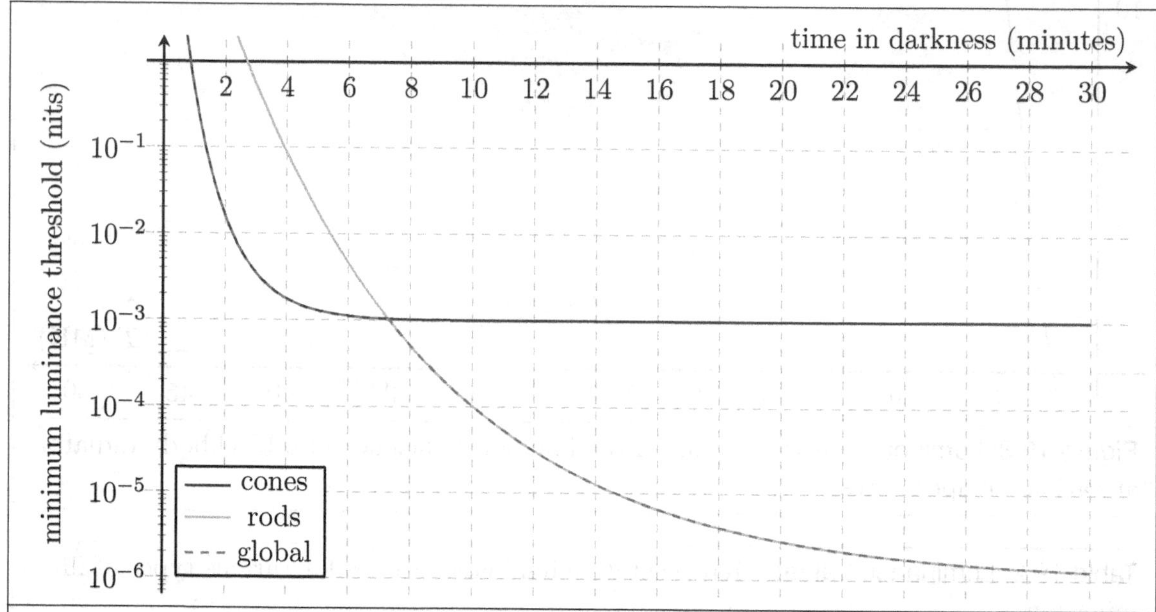

Figure 19.9: Adaptation: Illustration of the change in light sensitivity of the photoreceptors during dark adaptation.

19.2.8 Brightness

In psychophysics, a *just-noticeable difference* (*JND*), also called *difference limen*, refers to the minimal difference in stimulus that is perceivable, typically at a statistical rate of 50%. For
681 a given type of *photoreceptors*, the JND in luminance as a function of adapted background luminance L, commonly referred to as the *threshold versus intensity* (*TVI*) function, can be modeled by formulating its reciprocal, called flash *sensitivity*, as [Walraven and Valeton, 1984, Lamb, 2011]

$$s(L) = s_d \frac{e^{-\frac{L}{L_s}}}{1 + \frac{L}{L_d}} \tag{19.12}$$

where s_d is the dark-adapted sensitivity, and L_d and L_s are the transitional dark-to-light and
691 light-to-saturation luminance values, respectively. As illustrated in *Figure 19.10*, the curves are composed of four distinct sections. At low luminance levels, the nearly constant sensitivity is limited by the neural noise internal to the retina, or *dark light*. Instead, the dark-to-light transition is subject to the stimulus sufficiently exceeding the fluctuations of the background luminance, and can be modeled by the *square-root law*, also called the *de Vries–Rose law*,

$$\frac{\Delta L}{\sqrt{L}} = k \tag{19.13}$$

for a constant k. In contrast, the sensitivity at high luminance levels is impacted by the
681 saturation of the *photoreceptors*.

Defining *brightness* $B(L)$ as the subjective response (i.e., the magnitude of a non-physically measurable sensation) to the visual perception of an input luminance L, the

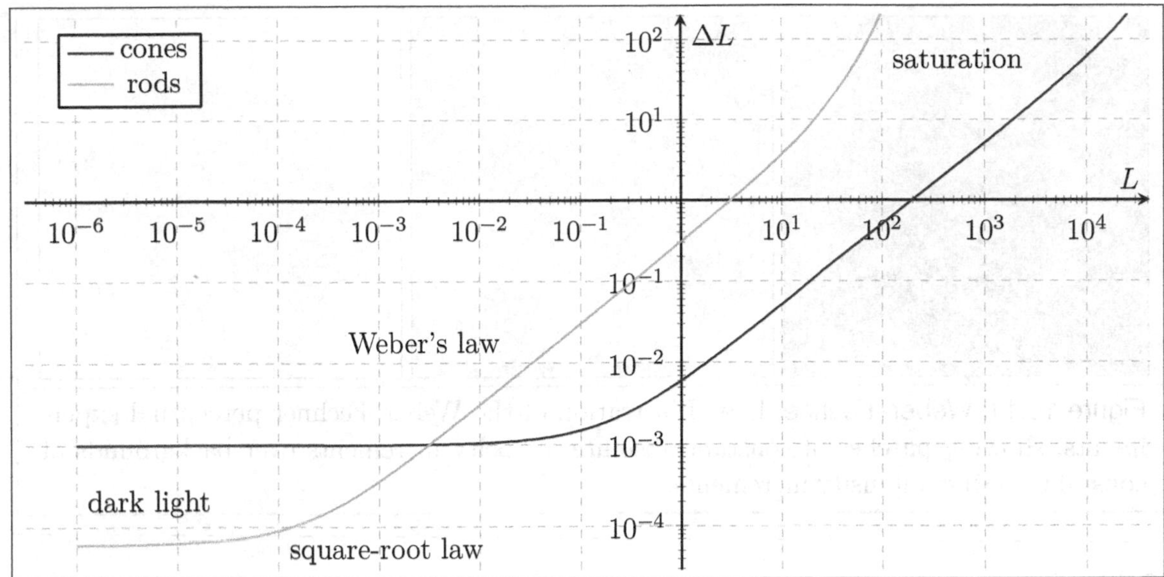

Figure 19.10: Threshold versus Intensity: Illustration of the minimum luminance increment threshold detectable by rods and cones as a function of background luminance.

variable JND in input luminance ΔL corresponds to the run necessary to achieve a constant JND rise in output brightness ΔB, such that the derivative of the response curve $B(L)$ is given as

$$\frac{\mathrm{d}B(L)}{\mathrm{d}L} \approx \frac{\Delta B}{\Delta L} \tag{19.14}$$

As illustrated in *Figure 19.11*, for luminance levels sufficiently far from the extremes, *Weber's* 692
law [Weber, 1846] states that the JND ΔL is proportional to the magnitude of the adapted luminance L, such that for some constant k, *Weber's fraction* reads

$$\frac{\Delta L}{L} = k \tag{19.15}$$

from which follows that the derivative of the response curve is

$$\mathrm{d}B(L) \approx \frac{\Delta B}{k} \frac{\mathrm{d}L}{L} \tag{19.16}$$

Solving the differential equation then yields *Fechner's law* [Fechner, 1907, §XVI], which states that the response to a luminance stimulus is proportional to its level (in dB)

$$B(L) \approx \frac{\Delta B}{k} (\ln(L) - \ln(L_0)) = \frac{\Delta B}{k} \ln\left(\frac{L}{L_0}\right) \tag{19.17}$$

given a reference luminance L_0 such that $B(L_0) = 0$.

As an alternative, the brightness response over a broader range of input luminances is better characterized by *Stevens's power law* [Stevens, 1957]

$$B(L) = kL^\alpha \tag{19.18}$$

where typically $\alpha \in [1/3, 1/2]$.

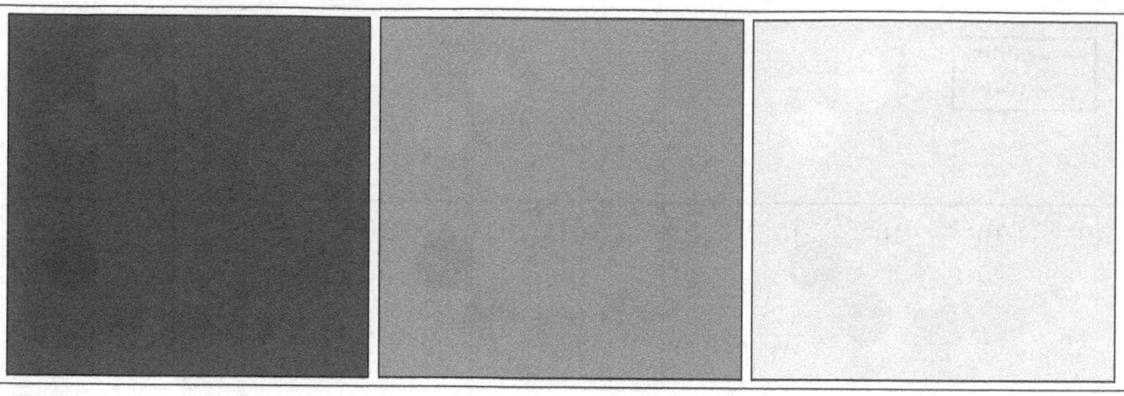

Figure 19.11: **Weber–Fechner Law:** Illustration of the Weber–Fechner perceptual experiments, showing patches of constant absolute intensity increments over backgrounds of constant relative intensity increments.

19.2.9 Retina

692 As illustrated in *Figure 19.12*, the vertebrate *retina* is a smooth multilayered structure organized into strata of neurons interconnected by synapses. In response to its synaptic input, each neuron may either be excited (i.e., depolarized) or inhibited (i.e., hyperpolarized). Complementing the action of the choroidal pigments, random scattering of stray light within the eyeball is further reduced by absorption from the outermost opaque layer, called *retinal pigment epithelium* (*RPE*).

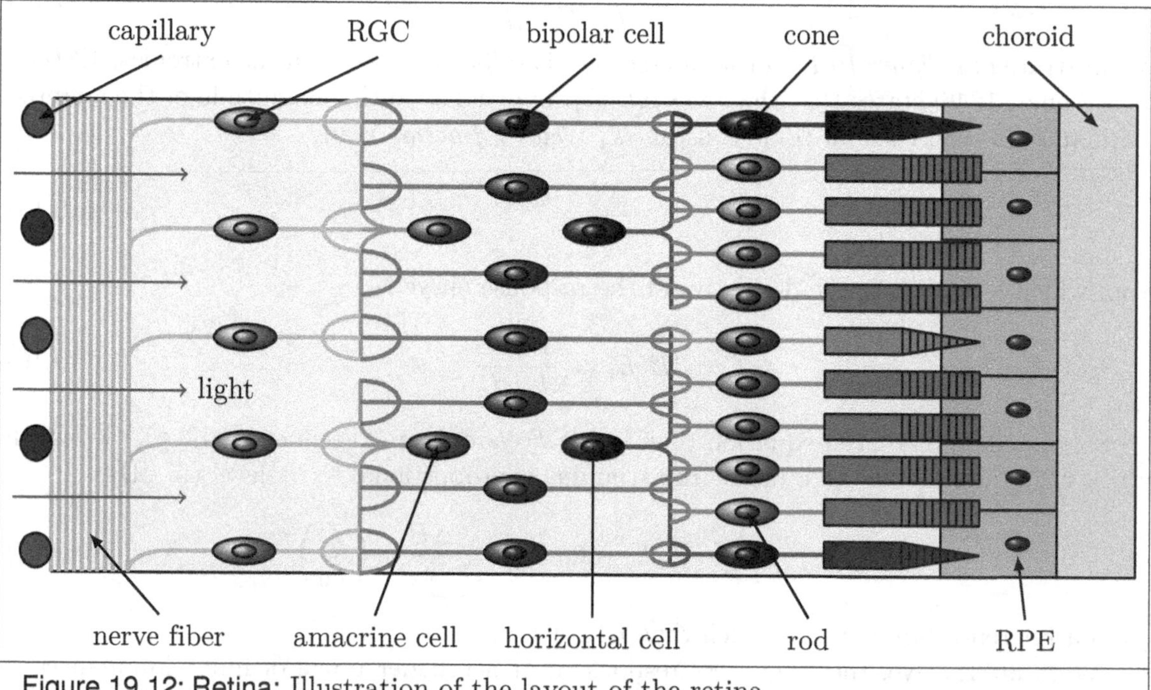

Figure 19.12: **Retina:** Illustration of the layout of the retina.

The layer below it is composed of the cone and rod cells distributed in an arrangement forming a so-called *retinal mosaic*, whose different regions are characterized by the angle subtended within the eye, so-called *visual angle*, or in case of a circular or spherical body,
693 *angular diameter*. As illustrated in *Figure 19.13*, the concentration of cones increases towards a region of the retina opposite to the lens known as the *macula lutea*, about 5.5 mm in diameter or a visual angle of 18° (about the visual angle between the stretched thumb and

pinky at arm's length), and reaches its peak within the *fovea centralis*, providing *central vision* with a much higher color discrimination ability than *peripheral vision*. The fovea is about 1.5 mm in diameter or 5°, and contains an average of about 147,000 cones per square millimeter. The central *foveal avascular zone* (*FAZ*) of about 0.5 mm or 1.66° (roughly the visual angle of the thumbnail at arm's length) receives most of its blood supply from the vessels in the underlying choroid rather than from capillaries on its surface, thereby reducing the absorption/scattering of light on its way to the *photoreceptors*. The central cone-shaped 681
depression of the fovea, whose inner neurons are displaced in the surrounding foveal rim, is called the *foveola*, of about 0.3–0.35 mm in diameter or 1° (about twice the angular diameter of the sun or moon), and is densely packed with a hexagonal arrangement of L and M type cones but a low concentration of S type cones, whose density is maximal on a ring approximately 1° around the center. While primates possess a single fovea, certain species of birds may have several (e.g., hawks are bifoviate), whereas cats, dogs and horses have a strip-shaped *visual streak* in place of the fovea. In humans, the average distance between the fovea and the lens is about 17 mm, and the line of sight between them, which lies a few horizontal degrees off the optical axis of the lens, is the *visual axis*. Although the foveola does not contain any rods, their concentration increases away from it and reaches its peak at an angle of about 18–20° off-center, while gradually decreasing towards the peripheral region of the retina. As a consequence, dim stars are better observed by gazing to their side (typically, opposite to the blind spot of the dominant eye), a technique known as *averted vision*.

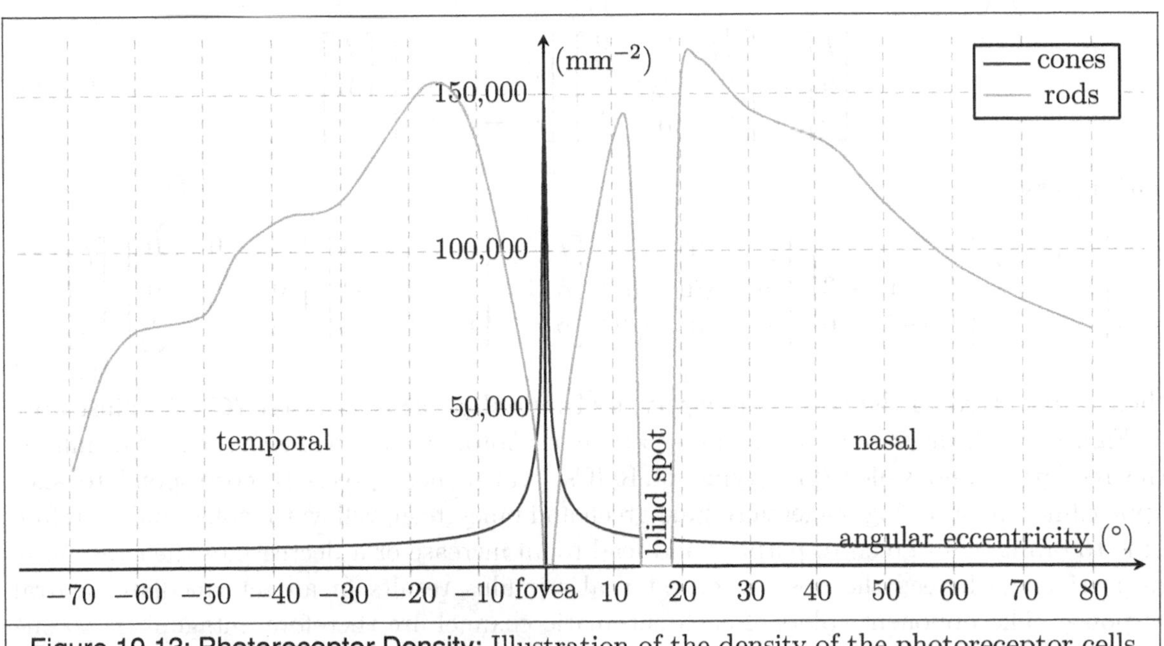

Figure 19.13: Photoreceptor Density: Illustration of the density of the photoreceptor cells along the horizontal meridian of the retina [Østerberg, 1935].

The rods and cones are locally interconnected by so-called *horizontal cells*. Upon photostimulation, a rod or cone hyperpolarizes and induces the hyperpolarization of a horizontal cell, which in turn causes the depolarization of the neighboring *photoreceptors* that it is 681
connected to, a phenomenon known as *lateral inhibition*.

The effective outputs of the *photoreceptors* are then transmitted to *bipolar cells*, each 681
having synaptic connections with either a single cone or several rods (thereby increasing their light-gathering ability by means of *spatial summation*), as well as with horizontal cells, a photoreceptor potentially feeding onto several bipolar cells. A bipolar cell can be one of two types, called on-center and off-center, respectively. In the absence of incident illumination, a

photoreceptor releases glutamate, which inhibits on-center bipolar cells and excites off-center bipolar cells, whereas the absorption of photons inhibits the photoreceptor, which reduces its release of glutamate, thereby exciting on-center bipolar cells and inhibiting off-center bipolar cells.

The output synapses of the rod bipolar cells are connected to *amacrine cells* via their dendritic trees, believed to complement the effect of lateral inhibition on the rod signals by feedback to the bipolar cells. When stimulated, the amacrine cells excite the cone on-center bipolar cells and inhibit the cone off-center bipolar cells, thereby routing the achromatic response at scotopic levels through the three chromatic channels used for photopic vision. Amacrine cells are additionally involved in the detection of directional motion, which is therefore more developed in peripheral than in central vision.

681 In order to reduce the redundancy in the *photoreceptors'* responses due to the overlap of their specific spectral sensitivities, the tristimulus signals at the output synapses of the cone bipolar cells are re-encoded by means of the so-called *opponent process* into the *opponent color space* [Machado *et al.*, 2009]

$$\begin{bmatrix} V \\ C_{YB} \\ C_{RG} \end{bmatrix} \triangleq \begin{bmatrix} 0.600 & 0.400 & 0.000 \\ 0.240 & 0.105 & -0.700 \\ 1.200 & -1.600 & 0.400 \end{bmatrix} \begin{bmatrix} L \\ M \\ S \end{bmatrix} \tag{19.19}$$

alternatively modeled by means of the *$L\alpha\beta$ color space*

$$\begin{bmatrix} L \\ \alpha \\ \beta \end{bmatrix} \triangleq \begin{bmatrix} \frac{1}{\sqrt{3}} & 0 & 0 \\ 0 & \frac{1}{\sqrt{6}} & 0 \\ 0 & 0 & \frac{1}{\sqrt{2}} \end{bmatrix} \begin{bmatrix} 1 & 1 & 1 \\ 1 & 1 & -2 \\ 1 & -1 & 0 \end{bmatrix} \begin{bmatrix} L \\ M \\ S \end{bmatrix} \tag{19.20}$$

with inverse

$$\begin{bmatrix} L \\ M \\ S \end{bmatrix} = \frac{1}{6} \begin{bmatrix} 2 & 1 & 3 \\ 2 & 1 & -3 \\ 2 & -2 & 0 \end{bmatrix} \begin{bmatrix} \sqrt{3} & 0 & 0 \\ 0 & \sqrt{6} & 0 \\ 0 & 0 & \sqrt{2} \end{bmatrix} \begin{bmatrix} L \\ \alpha \\ \beta \end{bmatrix} = \begin{bmatrix} 1 & 1 & 1 \\ 1 & 1 & -1 \\ 1 & -2 & 0 \end{bmatrix} \begin{bmatrix} \frac{1}{\sqrt{3}} & 0 & 0 \\ 0 & \frac{1}{\sqrt{6}} & 0 \\ 0 & 0 & \frac{1}{\sqrt{2}} \end{bmatrix} \begin{bmatrix} L \\ \alpha \\ \beta \end{bmatrix} \tag{19.21}$$

then transmitted to the corresponding type of *retinal ganglion cells* (*RGC*). As illustrated
695 in *Figure 19.14*, the stimulation of a given type of *photoreceptors* will either excite or inhibit
681 the red/green and yellow/blue types of RGCs (which more precisely correspond to axes approximately opposing magenta to blue-green and lime-green/yellow to violet, and therefore blue to orange and green to purple), and lead to an increase or a decrease of their response, respectively, whereas the absence of external stimulus results in an intermediate neutral response. The opponent colors of each chromatic channel are therefore antagonistic to one another, such that "red-green" or "yellow-blue" hues cannot normally be perceived, and are therefore referred to as *impossible colors*, while red, green, blue and yellow are generally considered to be the *unique hues*.

681 The set of all *photoreceptors* connected to an RGC via horizontal, bipolar and amacrine cells is known as its *receptive field*, the size of which determines the angular resolution of perceivable details, so-called *visual acuity*, measured in cycles per degree (of arc), or in reciprocal minute/second of arc. Visual acuity is then defined as twice the maximum number of discernible line-pairs/cycles per minute of arc, or equivalently as the reciprocal of the gap size between two successive lines expressed in minute of arc. It follows that an acuity of $1 = {}^{20}/_{20} = {}^{6}/_{6}$ corresponds to an optotype E (which contains 3 lines separated by 2 gaps, or 2.5 line-pairs/cycles) spanning an angle of view of 5 arcmin, with gaps of about 1.75 mm when observing a standard *Snellen chart* at a distance of 6 meters (or roughly

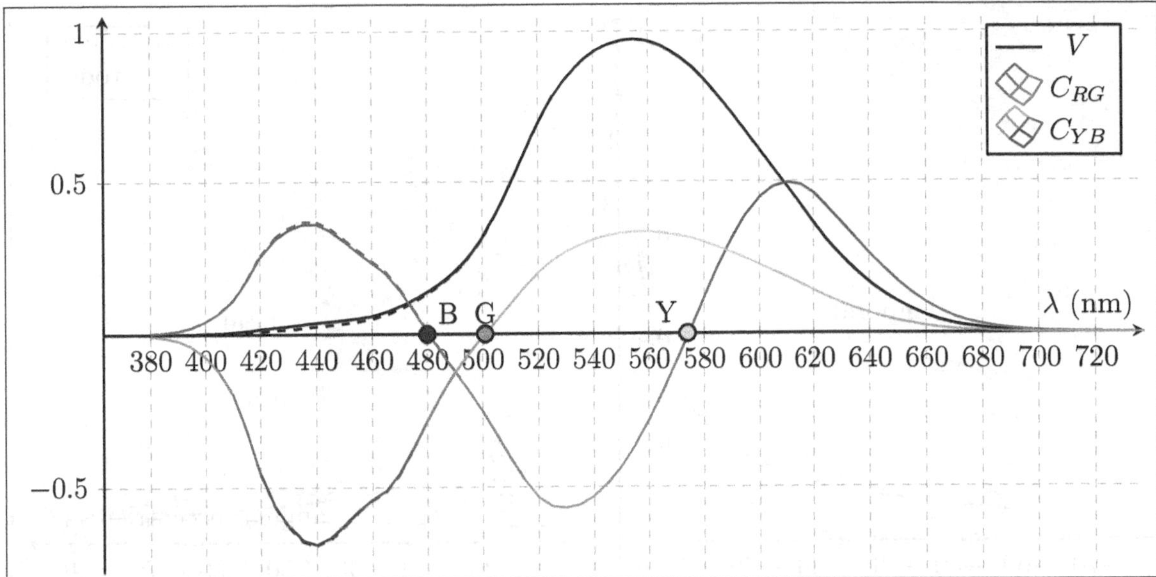

Figure 19.14: Opponent Process: Illustration of the spectral responses of the red-green and yellow-blue opponent color channels (dashed [Vos and Walraven, 1971] and solid [Smith and Pokorny, 1975]).

20 feet). While normal vision generally refers to an acuity no less than one, the average visual acuity of a young emmetropic human is about $^{20}/_{14}$ for photopic vision (whereas that of hawks is about $^{20}/_{2}$) and roughly $^{1}/_{2}$ for scotopic vision. Given that the angular span of a cone cell is roughly 0.4–0.5 arcmin, the theoretical upper bound of acuity is roughly $^{20}/_{8}$, which might be reached with an extremely constricted pupil (assuming no diffraction occurs), while spherical aberration due to an extremely dilated pupil may limit acuity to 1.5 arcmin in practice. Because the visual cortex analyzes the relative magnitude of neighboring signals (akin to the gradients of pixel intensities obtained across anti-aliased edges), the visual system is actually able to resolve spatial location with a 5–10 times increase in accuracy, so-called *hyperacuity*. The latter can be measured by the ability to detect an alignment offset between two line segments, then referred to as the *Vernier acuity*, whose upper limit may be as high as 8 arcsec (i.e., 0.13 arcmin).

The human eye counts about 1.2–1.3 million RGCs, yielding an average of about a 100
photoreceptors per RGC. The size of the receptive field varies greatly in different regions of 681
the retina, though, and that of foveal RGCs might count as few as a single cone, whereas the receptive field of RGCs at the extreme periphery of the retina generally consists of
several thousand *photoreceptors*. While this adaptive *retinal summation*, together with the 681
high density of L and M type cones, provides a very high visual acuity to central vision as
illustrated in *Figure 19.15*, that of S-type cones is lower and occurs at about 1° off-center, 696
whereas fine details of high spatial frequency cannot be resolved by peripheral vision, similarly so at scotopic illumination levels due to the spatial summation of the rods' output towards the rod bipolar cells.

An RGC may then be of one of two types, either on-center/off-surround or off-center/on-surround. An on-center RGC becomes excited upon stimulation of the center of its receptive field, and inhibited upon stimulation of its surround. On the contrary, an off-center RGC becomes excited upon stimulation of the surround of its receptive field, and inhibited upon stimulation of its center. As a result, both on-center and off-center RGCs yield a mild response upon stimulation of both their center and surround. This mechanism allows on-center RGCs
to act as a low-pass differential *reconstruction filter* with positive excitatory center and a 204

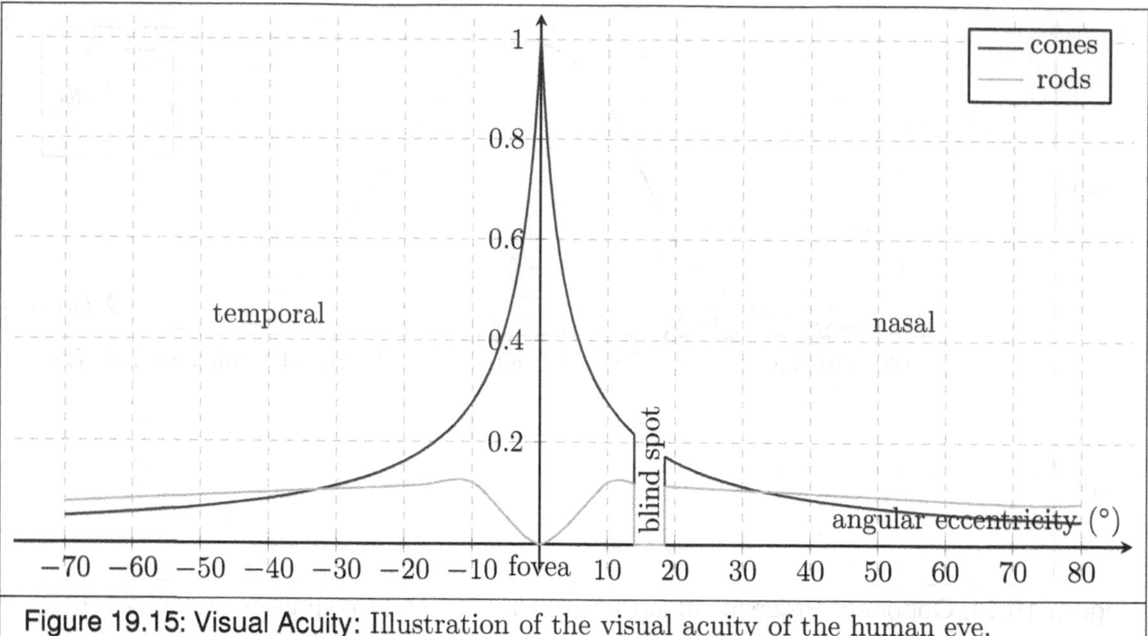

Figure 19.15: Visual Acuity: Illustration of the visual acuity of the human eye.

negative inhibitory surround, while off-center RGCs act as the opposite differential filter, with a negatively weighted center and a positively weighted surround. Together with lateral inhibition, the center-surround antagonism increases the perceived sharpness by enhancing the contrast in luminance along edges (whose spatial frequency is determined by the size of the receptive field) so as to facilitate their detection as well as the segmentation and classification by the brain of the objects contained in the visual field.

697 As illustrated in *Figure 19.16*, this mechanism is responsible for various optical illusions, such as the *Mach bands* (named after Ernst Mach), in which uniformly colored strips of various shades of gray appear to become brighter or darker near the edges with a darker or brighter strip, respectively. Other instances include the *Hermann grid illusion* [Hermann, 1870], in which dark spots seem to appear at the junctions of a light-gray grid superimposed onto a black background (most notably in the peripheral field but not within the foveal field when viewed at the intended distance due to the varying size of the receptive fields), and the *scintillating grid illusion*, in which white disks are added at the grid intersections, causing the illusory dark spots to appear and disappear, although lateral inhibition alone does not explain why both grid illusions vanish in the case of wavy, rather than straight, grid lines. Lateral inhibition is similarly involved in the sensitivity of the visual system to contrast as a function of angular frequency, so-called *contrast sensitivity function* (*CSF*) [Campbell and Robson, 1968], whose peak is at about 3–7 cycles per degree.

In addition to the input from rods and cones, a small fraction of RCGs (about 1–2% in humans) are themselves photoreceptors, so-called *intrinsically photosensitive retinal ganglion cells* (*ipRGCs*), which contain a *melanopsin photopigment* whose peak of spectral absorption lies around 470–490 nm. Their light detection ability is increased by temporal summation of the incident photons over a relatively longer period of time than rods and cones, thereby making them much slower to react to a light stimulus. While they are believed not to be involved in vision, the response of ipRGCs to incident light intensity has been shown to control the pupillary light reflex of mammals, and to act as a *zeitgeber* (i.e., German for "time-giver") regulating the physiological *entrainment* of their endogenous *circadian rhythm* to the 24-hour day/night cycle, as well as the secretion of melatonin hormone controlling sleep and wake cycles.

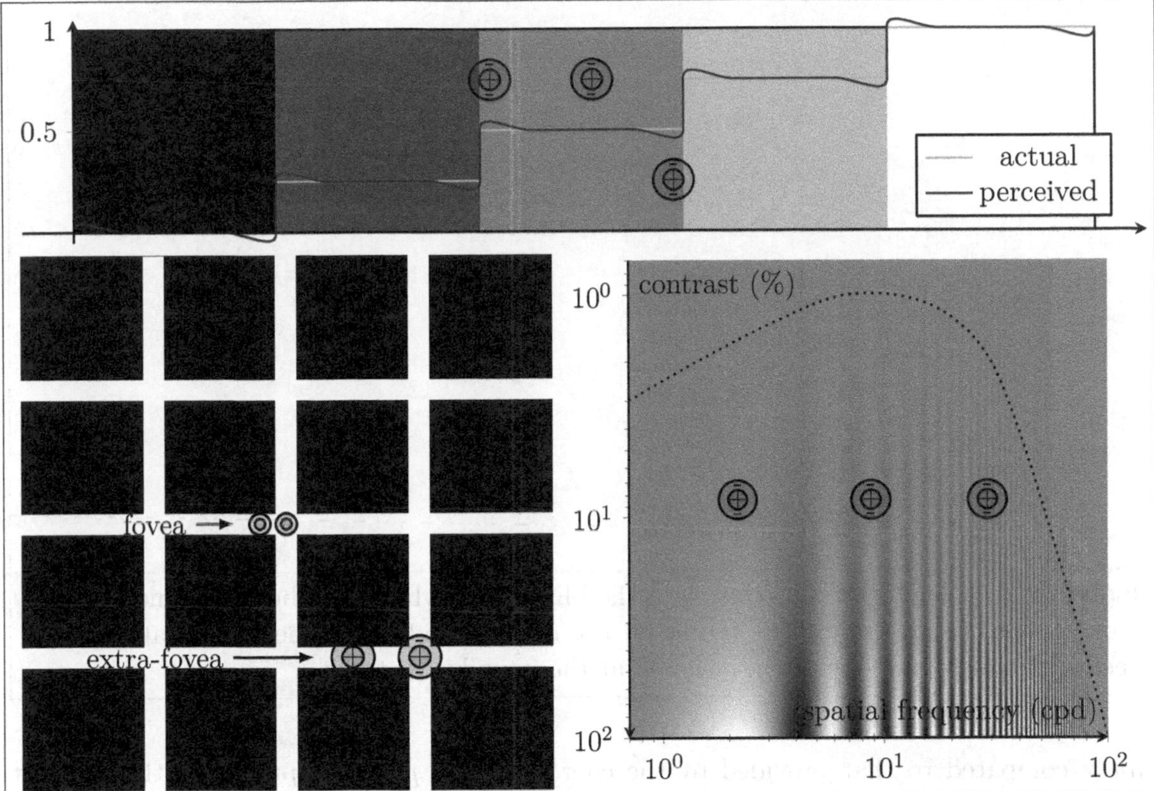

Figure 19.16: Lateral Inhibition: Illustration of the Mach bands (top) and Hermann grid [Hermann, 1870] (bottom left) optical illusions induced by lateral inhibition, as well as of the impact of the latter on contrast sensitivity [Campbell and Robson, 1968] (bottom right).

The signals from the retinal ganglion cells are then propagated through their 1.2 million individual axons, which form the innermost layer of the retina, and bundle into the *optic nerve*, about 10% of which being devoted to the fovea. The nerve fibers leave the eyeball at the point of entry of the central retinal artery, an oval-shaped region of the retina about 1.7 mm wide (5.5°) and 1.9 mm high (7.5°) called the *optic disc*, which is located about 3–4 mm nasal of the fovea (12–15°) and 1.5° downwards, and whose white-colored central pit is known as the *optic cup*. Because the optic disc does not contain any *photoreceptors*, it 681
forms a *blind spot* within the effectively perceivable *visual field*, which the visual system fills in with the surrounding information and the signals perceived by the other eye, a so-called *filling-in phenomenon* illustrated in *Figure 19.17*. 698

Due to the inverted structural arrangement of the vertebrate retina, light may only be detected by the *photoreceptors* once it has bypassed the neurons of the innermost layers, 681
as well as the capillary vessels supplying them. Because the location of the latter is static on the surface of the retina, the absorption of blue light by the red blood cells is readily counterbalanced by the chemical adaptation of the *photoreceptors*, although the rarer non- 681
absorptive white blood cells running through the capillaries can occasionally be perceived as quickly moving bright sprites when staring at a bright blue background such as the sky, a phenomenon known as the *blue field entoptic phenomenon* or as *Scheerer's phenomenon*. In contrast, the retina of cephalopods (e.g., squids and octopuses), which isn't an outgrowth of the brain as in vertebrates, exhibits a reversed structure, with the *photoreceptors* forming 681
the innermost layer and the RGCs and capillaries the outermost, thereby exhibiting no blind spot. However, it has been postulated that such an arrangement might yield a reduced blood

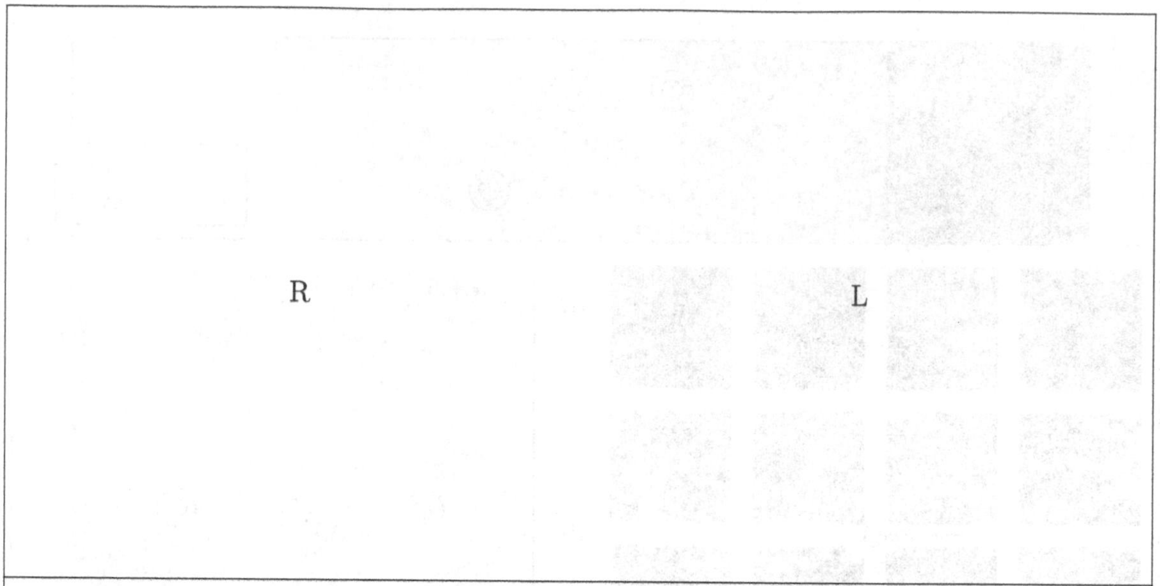

R L

Figure 19.17: Blind Spot: Illustration of the blind spot, which may be readily noticed by closing one eye and fixing the target on the opposite side with the other, causing the second target to disappear when viewed at the intended distance.

681 supply compared to that provided by the choroid to the *photoreceptors* and the pigment epithelium.

19.3 VISUAL SYSTEM

19.3.1 Visual Pathway

699 As illustrated in *Figure 19.18*, the signals from the *human eye* are transmitted through the
678 optic nerves to specific parts of the brain, which together form the *human visual system* (*HVS*). Signals from the ipRGCs reach the *suprachiasmatic nucleus* (*SCN*) of the hypothalamus (controlling the circadian rhythms) via the retinohypothalamic tract, as well as the *olivary pretectal nucleus* (*OPN*) (controlling the pupillary light reflex) and the *ventrolateral preoptic nucleus* (involved in the regulation of the melatonin hormone produced by the pineal gland).

Instead, the fibers of the image-forming RGCs from both eyes merge at the *optic chiasm* at the base of the hypothalamus, where half from each eye cross over and gather into the right and left *optic tracts* corresponding to the left and right visual fields, respectively. On each lobe of the brain, the signals then reach the *lateral geniculate nucleus* (*LGN*) in the thalamus, from which they travel along the *optic radiation* towards the *visual cortex* within the occipital lobe, where *visual perception* involves higher-level processing of the visual information, more than 50% of which being dedicated to the signals from the fovea.

19.3.2 Subjective Constancy

Rather than performing purely quantitative measurements of physical light intensities or absolute distances as exploited by many optical illusions, the main function of the human visual system as a whole is to reconstruct a 3-D representation of the scene from the 2-D image projected onto the retina (notably deceived by impossible objects [Browne, 2007], which are consistent at a local scale but not globally, such as the *impossible cube* (featured together with a *Necker cube* in Maurits Cornelis Escher's 1958 lithograph "Belvedere" [Tsuruno, 1997]),

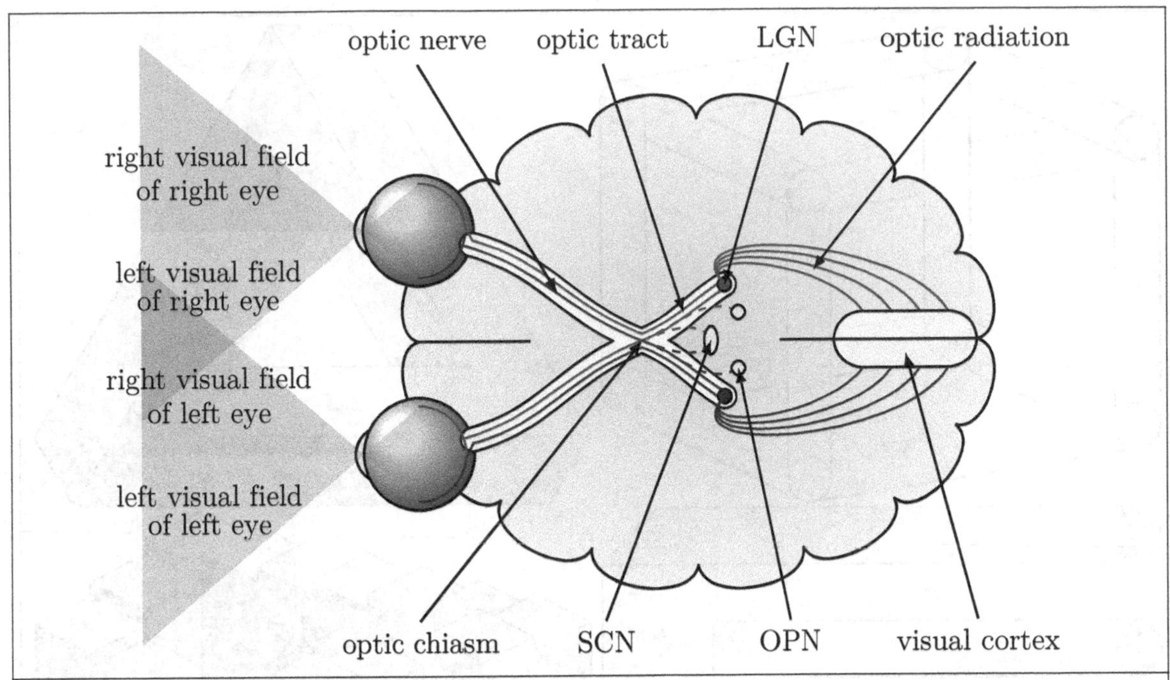

Figure 19.18: Visual Pathway: Illustration of the pathway followed by the visual signals from the eyes to the cerebral cortex, shown in top view.

the *impossible trident* [Schuster, 1964], the *Penrose triangle* and the *Penrose stairs* [Penrose and Penrose, 1958] illustrated in *Figure 19.19*), and to segment data from the visual field 700
into semantically meaningful information, thereby allowing cognitive interactions with the surrounding environment. While *physiology* is concerned with the biologic functions of the constitutive parts of living organisms, the study of sensation and perception is the focus of a branch of experimental psychology known as *psychophysics*.

Some of these high-level processes aim at maintaining the apparent characteristics of objects relatively constant under different viewing condition, a phenomenon known as *subjective constancy* or *perceptual constancy*. The latter may involve a comparative analysis of the various visual features such as colors, sizes and orientations of the objects in the visual field, either relative to one another, to the contextual environment or to expectations based on prior experience (e.g., the inference that an object occluding another is necessarily in front of it, a building facade is normally vertical and not horizontal as in the popular illusion, a room is cuboidal in shape unlike the *Ames room illusion* and a window is rectangular unlike the *Ames window illusion*).

Notably, *size constancy* allows the size of an object to be perceived consistently regardless of its position in space, relative to its surrounding and to its estimated distance. Various optical illusions exploit this characteristic of the visual system to deceive its judgment of size, such as the *Müller-Lyer illusion* [Müller-Lyer, 1889], the *Ebbinghaus illusion* (named after Hermann Ebbinghaus), the *Ponzo illusion* [Ponzo, 1910] and the *moon illusion* illustrated in *Figure 19.20*. Similarly, *shape constancy* allows the apparent shape of objects to be maintained 700
relatively constant regardless of their orientation (e.g., a closed or open rectangular door).

Additionally, *lightness constancy* allows the shade of an object to be perceived consistently regardless of the intensity of the light falling upon it, relative to the estimated illumination of its surrounding. As illustrated in *Figure 19.21*, optical illusions [Adelson, 2000] exploit- 701
ing this feature of the visual system to deceive it include the *simultaneous contrast illusion*, the *Cornsweet illusion* [Cornsweet, 1970] (which stimulates lateral inhibition to induce the

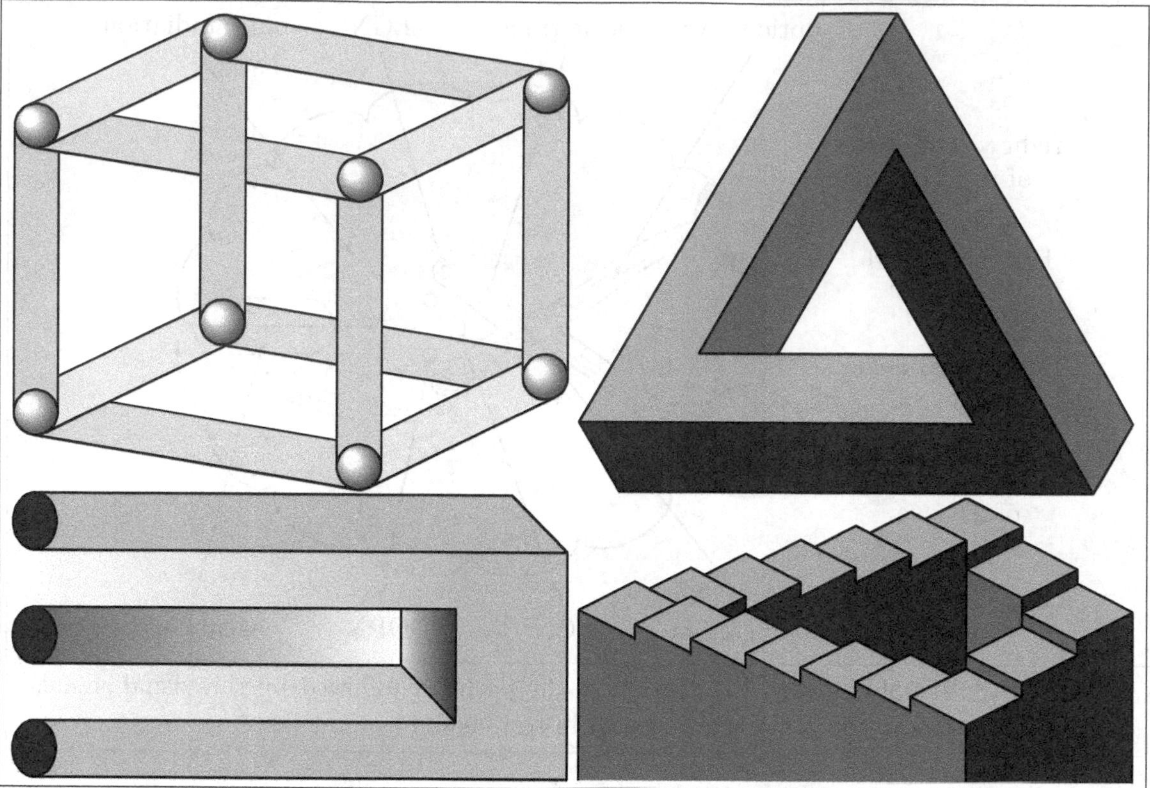

Figure 19.19: Impossible Objects: Illustration of Escher's impossible cube (top left), the impossible trident [Schuster, 1964] (bottom left) and the Penrose triangle and stairs [Penrose and Penrose, 1958] (top and bottom right, respectively).

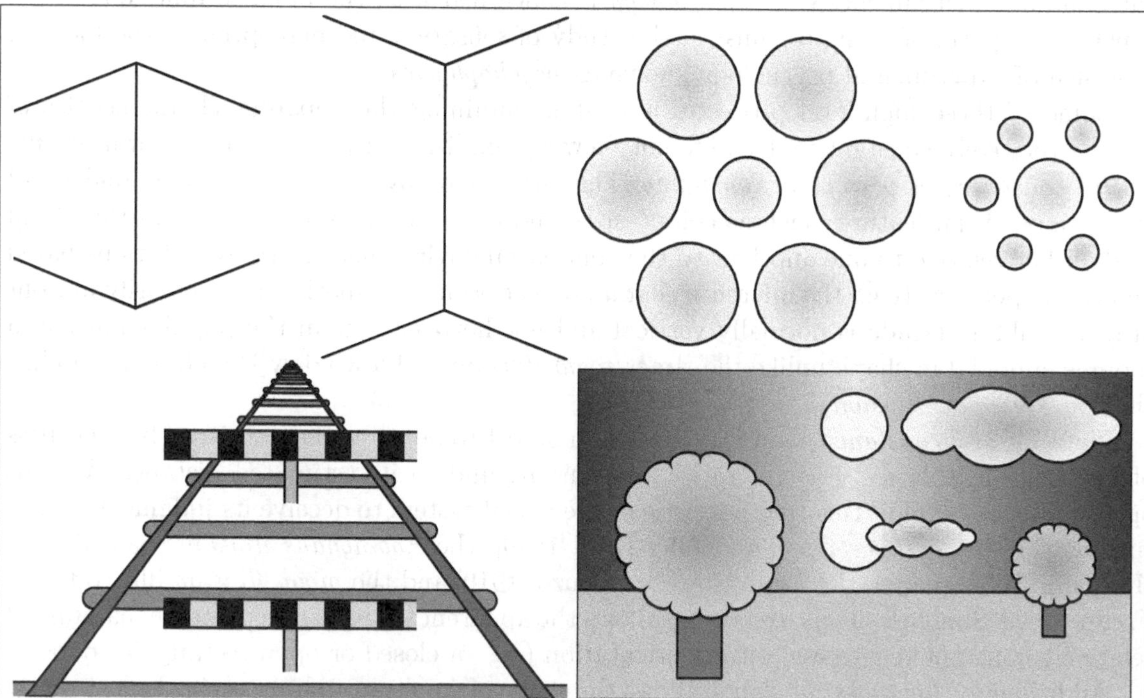

Figure 19.20: Size Constancy: Illustration of the Müller-Lyer [Müller-Lyer, 1889] (top left), Ebbinghaus (top right), Ponzo [Ponzo, 1910] (bottom left) and moon (bottom right) illusions where size constancy causes identical objects to be perceived as having different sizes.

perception of Mach bands), *White's illusion* [White, 1979], as well as the *checker-block illusion* [Adelson and Pentland, 1996] and *checker-shadow illusion*.[1] By the process of *chromatic adaptation*, *color constancy* similarly allows the apparent color of objects to be maintained 701
relatively constant under different non-neutral lighting conditions based on the color cast of the environment.

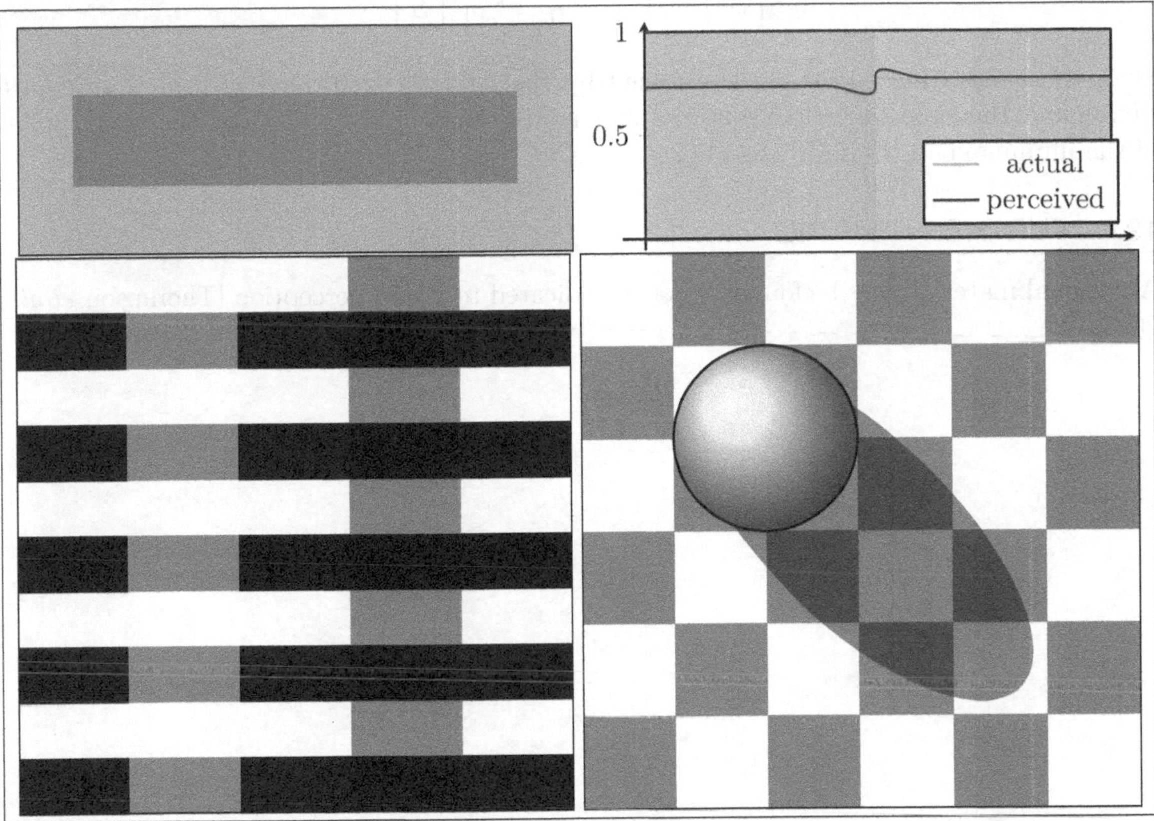

Figure 19.21: Lightness Constancy: Illustration of the simultaneous contrast (top left), Cornsweet [Cornsweet, 1970] (top right), White [White, 1979] (bottom left) and a 2-D adaptation of Adelson's checker-shadow (bottom right) illusions, in which objects of the same shade are perceived as having a different lightness.

19.3.3 Chromatic Adaptation

Besides the local adaptation of the retinal *photoreceptors* to a light stimulus, local ratios of 681
their overlapping spectral responses are computed in the primary visual cortex by specialized neurons called *double-opponent cells* (evaluating both color and spatial opponencies) in order to estimate the color cast of the incident illumination, assuming the spectral range of the latter is sufficiently broad. Human color vision then partially discounts the global effect of illumination on the perception of reflectance by means of *chromatic adaptation*.

The impact of two spatio-temporal adaptation states may be modeled by means of individual gains on the *LMS* responses of the three cone types 684

$$\begin{bmatrix} \frac{1}{L'_A} & 0 & 0 \\ 0 & \frac{1}{M'_A} & 0 \\ 0 & 0 & \frac{1}{S'_A} \end{bmatrix} \begin{bmatrix} L' \\ M' \\ S' \end{bmatrix} = \begin{bmatrix} \frac{1}{L_A} & 0 & 0 \\ 0 & \frac{1}{M_A} & 0 \\ 0 & 0 & \frac{1}{S_A} \end{bmatrix} \begin{bmatrix} L \\ M \\ S \end{bmatrix} \tag{19.22}$$

[1] `http://web.mit.edu/persci/people/adelson/checkershadow_illusion.html`.

thereby mapping the colors perceived in one adaptation state to those perceived in the other by means of the *von Kries chromatic adaptation transform* (*CAT*)

$$\begin{bmatrix} L' \\ M' \\ S' \end{bmatrix} = \begin{bmatrix} \frac{L'_A}{L_A} & 0 & 0 \\ 0 & \frac{M'_A}{M_A} & 0 \\ 0 & 0 & \frac{S'_A}{S_A} \end{bmatrix} \begin{bmatrix} L \\ M \\ S \end{bmatrix} \tag{19.23}$$

Shall the adaptation states be determined by the lighting conditions such as a *standard*
713 *illuminant*, the elements of the diagonal matrix are then readily defined by the white point
684 of the illuminant in the *LMS* color space.

19.4 FURTHER READING

Additional material may be found in books dedicated to visual perception [Thompson *et al.*, 2011].

CHAPTER 20

Color Science

TABLE OF CONTENTS

20.1 COLORIMETRY

Also known as *colorimetry*, *color science* is concerned with the physical measurement and
698 mathematical representation of the colors perceivable by the human *visual system*. Because
of the trichromatic nature of the latter, colors can be encoded as a triplet of values whose
704 semantics are defined by a relative *color model* such as *RGB*, *HSV & HSL* or *CMY*. Together
707 710 with the specification of basis vectors, called *color primaries*, the triplet then uniquely de-
711 termines the coordinates of the color in an absolute *color space* such as sRGB, *XYZ* or *Luv*
720 *& Lab* (even though the latter are arguably dependent on the specification of a white point).

20.2 RGB

20.2.1 From Spectrum

A series of experiments were conducted around 1930 in which human subjects were asked to carry observations through a circular screen filtering out light beyond the 2° angle of view of the cones in the fovea, and to match a monochromatic test color of variable wavelength with a mixture of three monochromatic primary colors of fixed wavelength but adjustable
704 intensities, as illustrated in *Figure 20.1*.

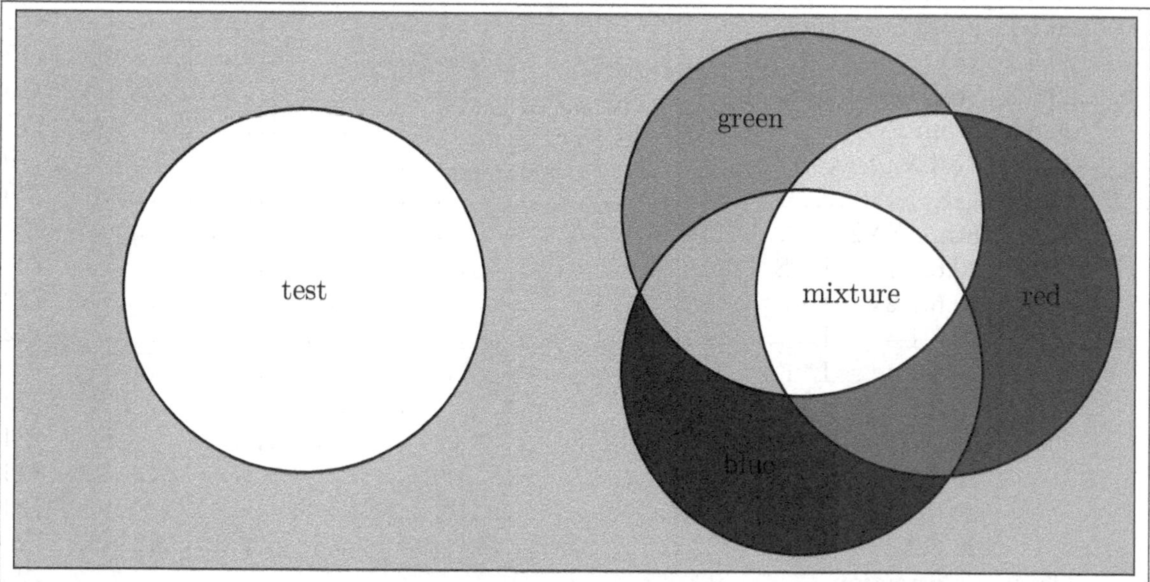

Figure 20.1: RGB Color Matching: Illustration of the color-matching experiments.

705 Because the positive span of the physical primaries illustrated in *Figure 20.2* represents a subset of the color space perceivable by a human with normal trichromatic vision, negative intensities were emulated by adding a positive intensity of the corresponding primary to the test color. In 1931, the results with primaries at 700 nm, 546.1 nm and 435.8 nm (the latter two corresponding to the monochromatic lines of a mercury vapor discharge lamp) were then standardized by the CIE [CIE, 1931] into the so-called red, green and blue *color-matching functions* $\overline{r}$, $\overline{g}$ and $\overline{b}$, normalized such that

$$\int_0^\infty \overline{r}(\lambda)\mathrm{d}\lambda = \int_0^\infty \overline{g}(\lambda)\mathrm{d}\lambda = \int_0^\infty \overline{b}(\lambda)\mathrm{d}\lambda \tag{20.1}$$

Given a polychromatic test color $I = \sum_{i=1}^{n} w_i I_i$ formed by the conical combination of n monochromatic lights with intensities I_i, the matching primaries were then empirically

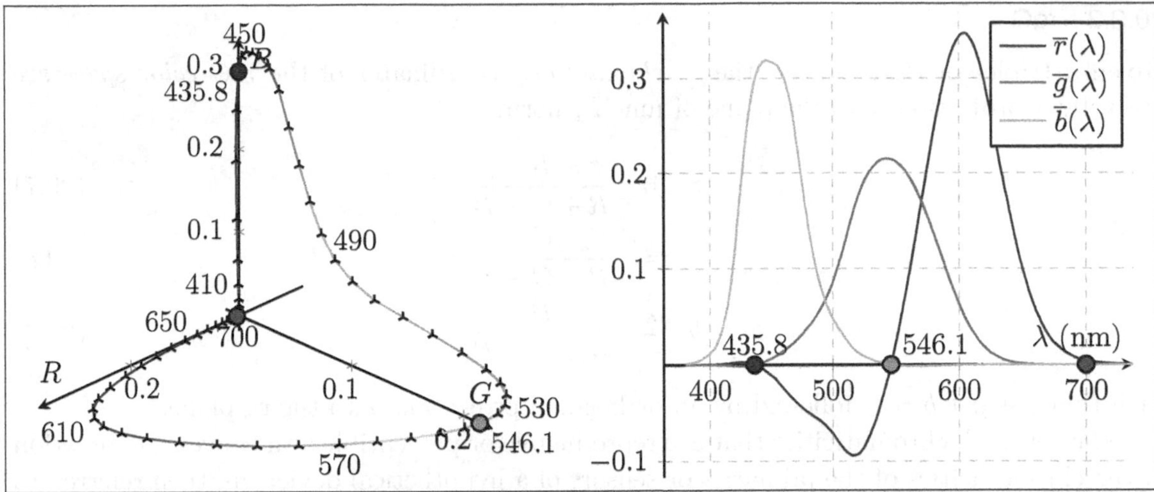

Figure 20.2: RGB Color Space: Illustration of the RGB physical primaries (left), and plot of the corresponding normalized color-matching functions [CIE, 1931] (right).

observed to be the identically weighted combination $[R, G, B] = \sum_{i=1}^{n} w_i[R_i, G_i, B_i]$ of the individual matching triplets, as stated by *Grassmann's law*. In the limit $n \to \infty$, the coordinates of a continuous spectral distribution I in the device-dependent *RGB color space* are then defined by the projection

$$R \triangleq \int_0^\infty I(\lambda)\overline{r}(\lambda)\mathrm{d}\lambda \tag{20.2}$$

$$G \triangleq \int_0^\infty I(\lambda)\overline{g}(\lambda)\mathrm{d}\lambda \tag{20.3}$$

$$B \triangleq \int_0^\infty I(\lambda)\overline{b}(\lambda)\mathrm{d}\lambda \tag{20.4}$$

Given the emission spectra of specific RGB primaries $r_e(\lambda)$, $g_e(\lambda)$ and $b_e(\lambda)$, the composite spectral distribution corresponding to a given RGB triplet is defined as the conical combination

$$I(\lambda) \triangleq R_e r_e(\lambda) + G_e g_e(\lambda) + B_e b_e(\lambda) \tag{20.5}$$

such that

$$\begin{aligned}
\begin{bmatrix} R \\ G \\ B \end{bmatrix} &= \begin{bmatrix} \int_0^\infty (R_e r_e(\lambda) + G_e g_e(\lambda) + B_e b_e(\lambda))\overline{r}(\lambda)\mathrm{d}\lambda \\ \int_0^\infty (R_e r_e(\lambda) + G_e g_e(\lambda) + B_e b_e(\lambda))\overline{g}(\lambda)\mathrm{d}\lambda \\ \int_0^\infty (R_e r_e(\lambda) + G_e g_e(\lambda) + B_e b_e(\lambda))\overline{b}(\lambda)\mathrm{d}\lambda \end{bmatrix} \\
&= \begin{bmatrix} \int_0^\infty r_e(\lambda)\overline{r}(\lambda)\mathrm{d}\lambda & \int_0^\infty g_e(\lambda)\overline{r}(\lambda)\mathrm{d}\lambda & \int_0^\infty b_e(\lambda)\overline{r}(\lambda)\mathrm{d}\lambda \\ \int_0^\infty r_e(\lambda)\overline{g}(\lambda)\mathrm{d}\lambda & \int_0^\infty g_e(\lambda)\overline{g}(\lambda)\mathrm{d}\lambda & \int_0^\infty b_e(\lambda)\overline{g}(\lambda)\mathrm{d}\lambda \\ \int_0^\infty r_e(\lambda)\overline{b}(\lambda)\mathrm{d}\lambda & \int_0^\infty g_e(\lambda)\overline{b}(\lambda)\mathrm{d}\lambda & \int_0^\infty b_e(\lambda)\overline{b}(\lambda)\mathrm{d}\lambda \end{bmatrix} \begin{bmatrix} R_e \\ G_e \\ B_e \end{bmatrix}
\end{aligned} \tag{20.6}$$

20.2.2 rgG

Given a triplet of RGB values, the *rg chromaticity* coordinates of the *rgG color space* are given by a projection onto the plane of unit L_1 norm

$$r \triangleq \frac{R}{R+G+B} \tag{20.7}$$

$$g \triangleq \frac{G}{R+G+B} \tag{20.8}$$

$$b \triangleq \frac{B}{R+G+B} \tag{20.9}$$

such that $r+g+b=1$, followed by an orthogonal projection onto the rg plane.

The set of all chromaticities that are reproducible or perceptible as a convex combination of the chromaticities of the primaries or sensors of a hypothetical device are then referred to as its *gamut*, while those that are not are conversely said to be "out of gamut." As illustrated
706 in *Figure 20.3*, the gamut of the chosen primaries corresponds to the *color triangle* formed by the monochromatic loci $[0,0]$ at 435.8 nm, $[0,1]$ at 546.1 nm and $[1,0]$ at 700 nm, with the
713 equal-energy *standard illuminant* E lying at its barycenter $[1/3, 1/3]$ due to the normalization of the color-matching functions.

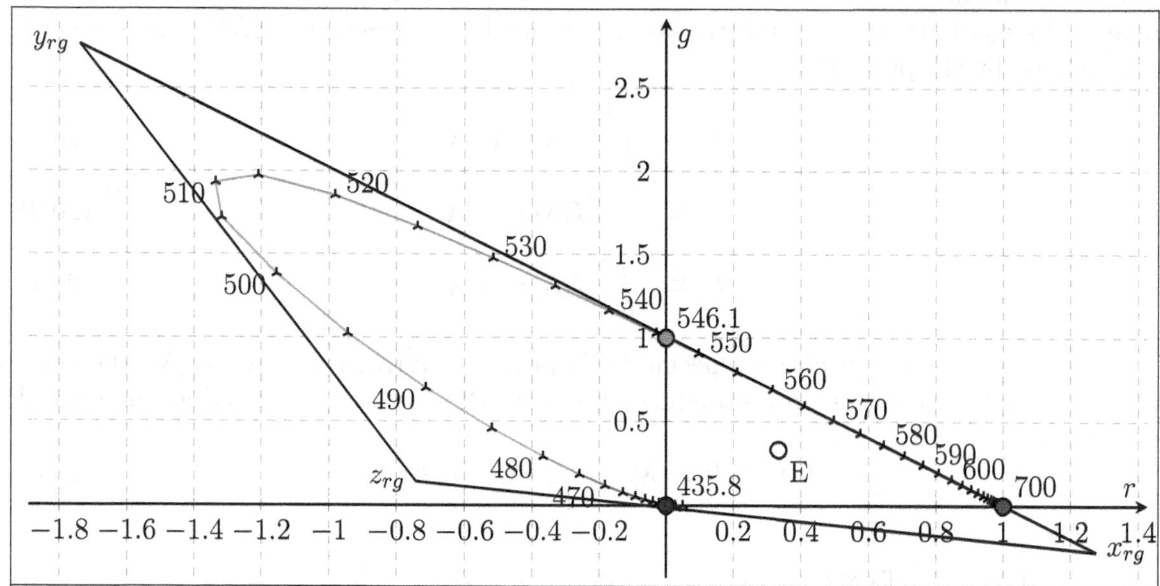

Figure 20.3: rgG Color Space: Illustration of the chromaticity diagram of the rgG color space [CIE, 1931].

Conversely, a triplet of rgG values can be converted into the RGB color space as

$$R = (R+G+B)r = \frac{G}{g}r \tag{20.10}$$

$$G = (R+G+B)g = \frac{G}{g}g \tag{20.11}$$

$$B = (R+G+B)b = \frac{G}{g}(1-r-g) \tag{20.12}$$

where $R+G+B = \frac{R}{r} = \frac{G}{g} = \frac{B}{b}$.

20.3 HSV & HSL

20.3.1 From RGB

As illustrated in *Figure 20.4*, a triplet of *RGB* values may be converted to a hexagonal 707
representation by means of an orthogonal projection onto a chromaticity plane perpendicular 704
to the black-white axis. The greatest coordinate $M \triangleq \max\{R, G, B\}$ determines whether the triplet lies in the rhombus with polar span $[-\pi/3, \pi/3]$, $[\pi/3, \pi]$ or $[\pi, -\pi/3]$, while the second greatest coordinate specifies the exact sextant. Together with the smallest coordinate $m \triangleq \min\{R, G, B\}$, the colorfulness is then measured by the *chroma*, $C \triangleq M - m$, while its *hue* $H \triangleq \frac{\pi}{3}H'$ is given as

$$H' \triangleq \begin{cases} 0 + \frac{G-B}{R-B} & \text{if } R > G \geq B \\ 2 - \frac{R-B}{G-B} & \text{if } G \geq R > B \\ 2 + \frac{B-R}{G-R} & \text{if } G > B \geq R \\ 4 - \frac{G-R}{B-R} & \text{if } B \geq G > R \\ 4 + \frac{R-G}{B-G} & \text{if } B > R \geq G \\ 6 - \frac{B-G}{R-G} & \text{if } R \geq B > G \end{cases} = \begin{cases} 2 + \frac{B-R}{C} & \text{if } M = G \\ 4 + \frac{R-G}{C} & \text{if } M = B \\ 6 + \frac{G-B}{C} \bmod 6 & \text{if } M = R \end{cases} \tag{20.13}$$

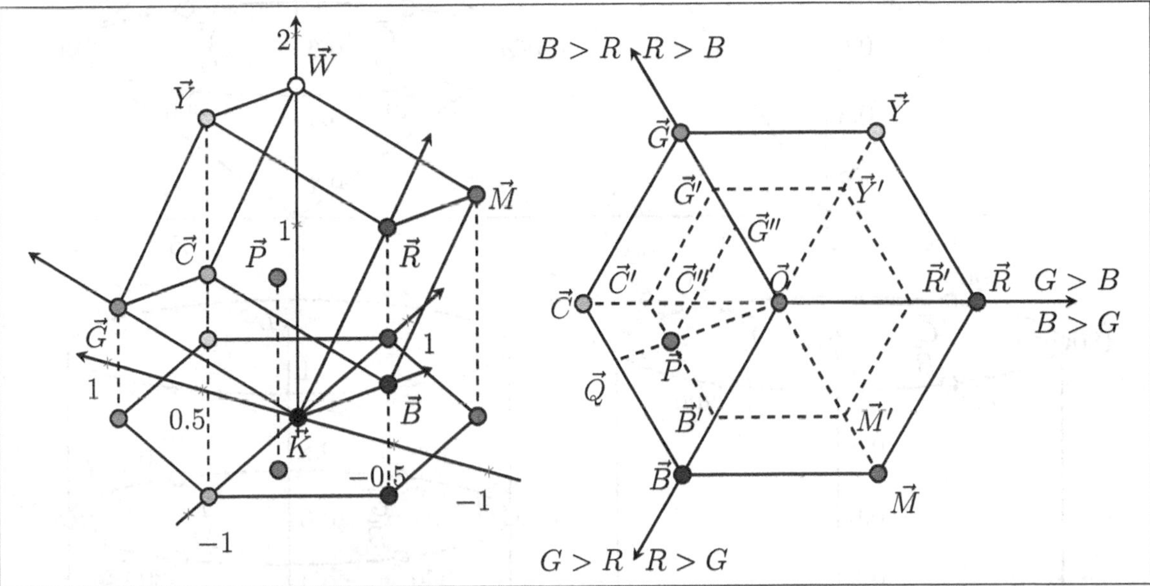

Figure 20.4: Hue and Chroma: Illustration of the hexagonal representation resulting from the orthogonal projection of an RGB triplet onto the chromaticity plane (left), and geometric interpretation of its chroma $C = \frac{d(\vec{O},\vec{P})}{d(\vec{O},\vec{Q})} = \frac{d(\vec{B}',\vec{C}')}{d(\vec{B},\vec{C})} = B - R$ (whose normalization effectively maps the hexagon to a circle) and hue $H = \pi/3(4 - t)$ where $t = \frac{d(\vec{B}',\vec{P})}{d(\vec{B}',\vec{C}')} = \frac{d(\vec{O},\vec{G}'')}{d(\vec{B},\vec{C})}\frac{d(\vec{B},\vec{C})}{d(\vec{B}',\vec{C}')} = \frac{d(\vec{C}'',\vec{G}'')}{d(\vec{C},\vec{G})}\frac{1}{C} = \frac{G-R}{B-R}$ (right).

As illustrated by the *color solids* shown in *Figure 20.5*, the value and saturation of the 708
HSV color space [Smith, 1978] are then defined as

$$V \triangleq M \tag{20.14}$$

708

$$S_V \triangleq \frac{C}{C_V} \stackrel{(20.18)}{=} \frac{M - m}{M} \tag{20.15}$$

while the lightness and saturation of the *HSL color space* [Joblove and Greenberg, 1978] are given by

708

$$L \triangleq \frac{M+m}{2} \tag{20.16}$$

$$S_L \triangleq \frac{C}{C_L} \overset{(20.19)}{=} \frac{M-m}{1-|M+m-1|} \tag{20.17}$$

where the normalization by the maximum achievable chroma

$$C_V \triangleq V \tag{20.18}$$

$$C_L \triangleq 1-|2L-1| = 2 \times \begin{cases} L & \text{if } L \in [0, 1/2] \\ 1-L & \text{if } L \in [1/2, 1] \end{cases} \tag{20.19}$$

at a given value/lightness effectively maps the cone/bicone into a cylinder.

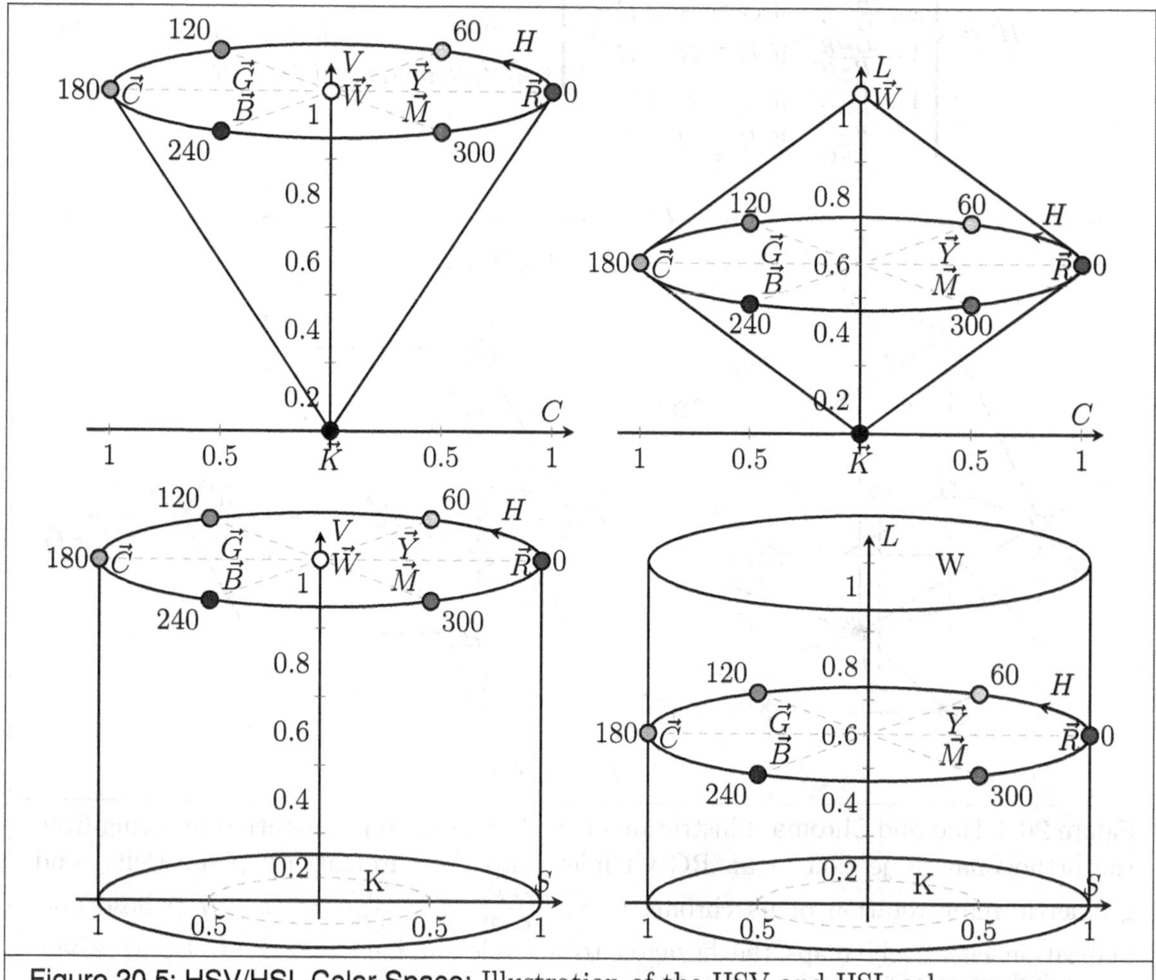

Figure 20.5: HSV/HSL Color Space: Illustration of the HSV and HSL color spaces.

704 Unlike their *RGB* counterpart, the HSV and HSL models allow for a more intuitive specification of colors, with those for which $S = C = 1$ (such that $V = 1$ or $L = 1/2$) being referred to as *saturated colors* (even though $S = 1$ is a necessary but not sufficient condition), whereas those for which $S = C = 0$ (with $V \in [0, 1]$ or $L \in [0, 1]$) are called *achromatic colors*. Given a saturated color of a certain hue, increasing its lightness is then said to yield different *tints* interpolating towards white, whereas decreasing its lightness is said to yield different *shades* interpolating towards black. In contrast, maintaining its lightness while decreasing its saturation is said to yield different *tones* interpolating towards gray.

20.3.2 To RGB

Given a hue value $H' \triangleq \frac{3}{\pi}H$, the full-chroma RGB triplet is defined by the back-projection 704
of the point from the periphery of the hexagon onto the edges of the RGB cube 704

$$[R', G', B'] \triangleq \begin{cases} [1, H'-0, 0] = [1, H'', 0] & \text{if } H' \in [0, 1] \\ [2-H', 1, 0] = [H'', 1, 0] & \text{if } H' \in [1, 2] \\ [0, 1, H'-2] = [0, 1, H''] & \text{if } H' \in [2, 3] \\ [0, 4-H', 1] = [0, H'', 1] & \text{if } H' \in [3, 4] \\ [H'-4, 0, 1] = [H'', 0, 1] & \text{if } H' \in [4, 5] \\ [1, 0, 6-H'] = [1, 0, H''] & \text{if } H' \in [5, 6] \end{cases} \tag{20.20}$$

where $H'' \triangleq 1 - |(H' \bmod 2) - 1|$. As illustrated in the resulting *color wheel* shown in
Figure 20.6, any pair of colors for which $\Delta H = k\pi, \forall k \in \mathbb{Z}$ are then referred to as *com-* 709
plementary colors (whose mixture is achromatic), with the *primary colors* being such that $H = k^2/3\pi$, while the secondary colors correspond to $H = \pi + k^2/3\pi$, and the *tertiary colors* to $H = 1/6\pi + k^1/3\pi$.

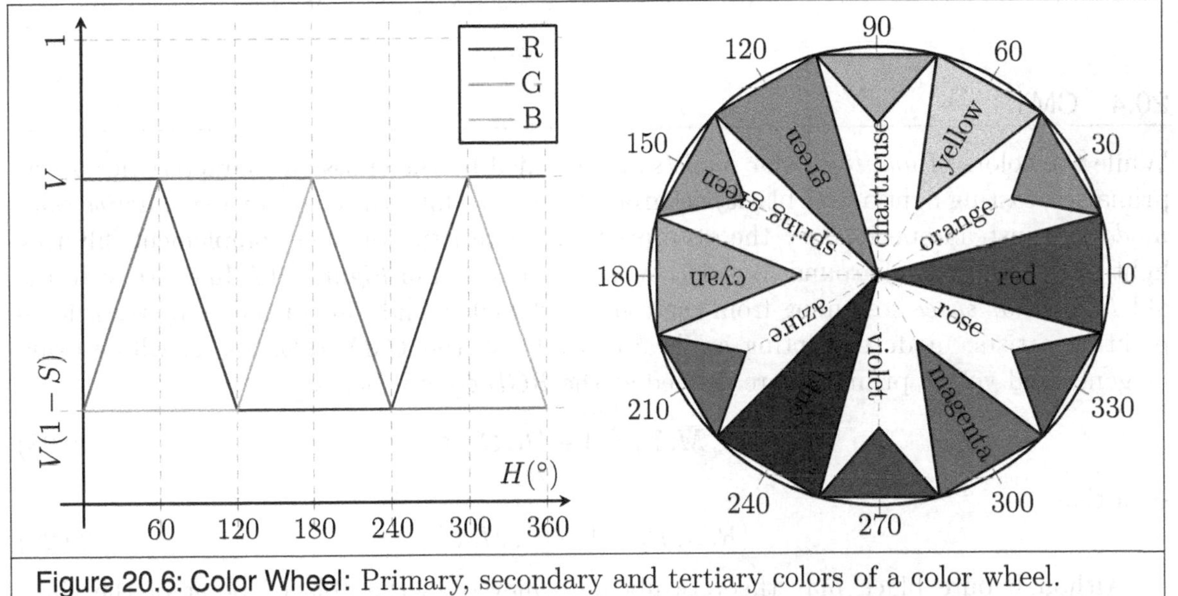

Figure 20.6: Color Wheel: Primary, secondary and tertiary colors of a color wheel.

Given an HSV or HSL triplet, the RGB coordinates are then obtained by scaling the 704
full-chroma RGB triplet by the actual chroma value, thereby displacing the point onto one 704
of the bottom three faces of the cube

$$[R, G, B] = m + C[R', G', B'] \tag{20.21}$$

and translating the result along the projection axis to the actual value/lightness by
component-wise scalar addition of the smallest coordinate $m = V - C \overset{(20.15)}{=} V(1 - S_V)$ 707
or $m = L - \frac{C}{2} \overset{(20.17)}{=} L - \frac{C_L S_L}{2}$, respectively, yielding 708

$$[R, G, B] = V - C(1 - [R', G', B']) \overset{(20.15)}{=} V(1 - S_V(1 - [R', G', B'])) \tag{20.22}$$ 707

$$[R, G, B] = L - C(1/2 - [R', G', B']) \overset{(20.17)}{=} L - C_L S_L(1/2 - [R', G', B']) \tag{20.23}$$ 708

20.3.3 Conversion

Given the value and saturation of an HSV triplet, the lightness and saturation of the corresponding HSL coordinates are given by

708 707 707
$$L \overset{(20.16)}{=} M - \frac{M-m}{2} \overset{(20.14)}{\underset{(20.15)}{=}} \left(1 - \frac{S_V}{2}\right) V \tag{20.24}$$

708 707 707
$$S_L \overset{(20.17)}{=} \frac{M-m}{1-|2M-(M-m)-1|} \overset{(20.14)}{\underset{(20.15)}{=}} \frac{S_V V}{1-|(2-S_V)V-1|} \tag{20.25}$$

Given the lightness and saturation of an HSL triplet, the value and saturation of the corresponding HSV coordinates are conversely given by

707 708 708
$$V \overset{(20.14)}{=} \frac{M+m}{2} + \frac{M-m}{2} \overset{(20.16)}{\underset{(20.17)}{=}} L + \frac{S_L C_L}{2} \tag{20.26}$$

707 708 708
$$S_V \overset{(20.15)}{=} \frac{2(M-m)}{(M+m)+(M-m)} \overset{(20.16)}{\underset{(20.17)}{=}} \frac{2S_L C_L}{2L + S_L C_L} \tag{20.27}$$

20.4 CMY

While the colors of *additive color models* are specified by the emission characteristics of the primaries, casting light onto a black background to yield white, the colors of a *subtractive color model* are instead specified by the absorption characteristics of their complement, filtering
711 light from a white background to yield black, as illustrated in *Figure 20.7*. In contrast to the old *RYB color space* stemming from the use of red, yellow and blue pigments by traditional painting artists, modern printing applications rely on the *CMY color space*, whose cyan,
704 magenta and yellow primaries are defined as the *RGB* complements

$$[C, M, Y] \triangleq 1 - [R, G, B] \tag{20.28}$$

such that

$$[R, G, B] = 1 - [C, M, Y] \tag{20.29}$$

Although pure black may theoretically be achieved as the "black" point of the three ink/dye primaries, this is hardly the case in practice due to the complex interaction of mixing and overlaying pigments. In order to also save on colored ink, actual printing devices use an additional key primary (named after the keyline used in black plates to outline colored art),
704 711 which absorbs all three *RGB* channels as illustrated in *Figure 20.8*. In theory, the effects of the colored and black inks are linearly combined to yield the RGB values

$$[R, G, B] = 1 - [C', M', Y'] - K \tag{20.30}$$

710
where $K \triangleq \min\{C, M, Y\} \overset{(20.28)}{=} 1 - \max\{R, G, B\}$, from which follows that the channels of the *CMYK color space* are given by

$$[C', M', Y'] = 1 - [R, G, B] - K = [C, M, Y] - K \tag{20.31}$$

However, in practice, the covering of the colors by one another corresponds to a non-linear relationship, which may be better described by

$$[R, G, B] = (1 - [C', M', Y'])(1 - K) \tag{20.32}$$

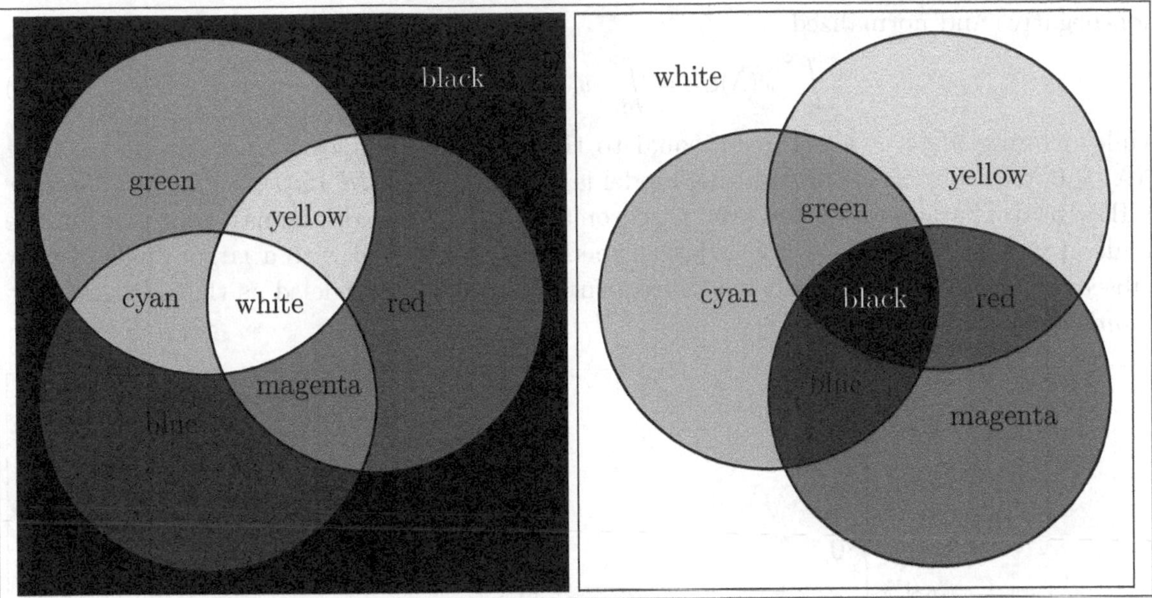

Figure 20.7: Additive/Subtractive Color Space: Illustration of the colors obtained by mixing the primaries of an additive (left) versus a subtractive (right) color space.

thus yielding

$$[C', M', Y'] = 1 - \frac{[R, G, B]}{1 - K} = \frac{[C, M, Y] - K}{1 - K} \tag{20.33}$$

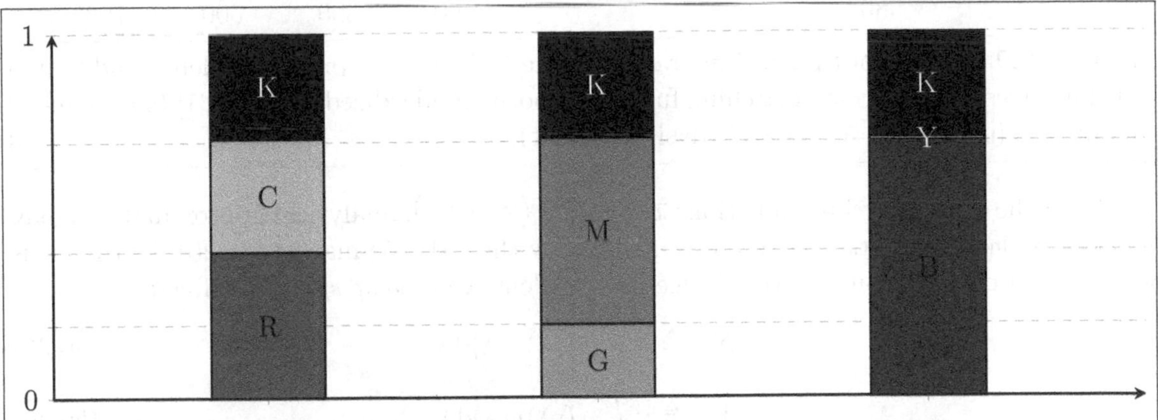

Figure 20.8: CMYK Color Space: Illustration of the correspondence between the RGB and CMYK color spaces.

In order to avoid the dotted artifacts resulting from half-toning, some ink-jet printers instead reproduce light cyan and light magenta by means of two additional primaries, yielding the *CcMmYK color space*.

20.5 XYZ

20.5.1 From Spectrum

Because there exists no triplet of physical monochromatic primaries whose gamut encompasses that of average human vision, the CIE devised a set of three virtual primaries, mathematically more saturated than pure physical monochromatic light as illustrated in *Figure 20.9*, such that the corresponding *color-matching functions* $\overline{x}$, $\overline{y}$ and $\overline{z}$ are everywhere non-negative and normalized

$$\int_0^\infty \overline{x}(\lambda)\mathrm{d}\lambda = \int_0^\infty \overline{y}(\lambda)\mathrm{d}\lambda = \int_0^\infty \overline{z}(\lambda)\mathrm{d}\lambda \tag{20.34}$$

while defining $\overline{y}(\lambda) = V(\lambda)$ to be equal to the standard luminosity function and setting $\overline{z}(\lambda) = 0, \forall\lambda > 650$ nm. The resulting model is known as the *CIE 1931 2° standard observer* [CIE, 1931], characterizing the average chromatic response of the human cones within the angle of view of the fovea, whereas later experiments conducted with a larger angle of view subsequently led to similar albeit less frequently used results modeled as the *CIE 1964 10° standard observer* [CIE, 1964].

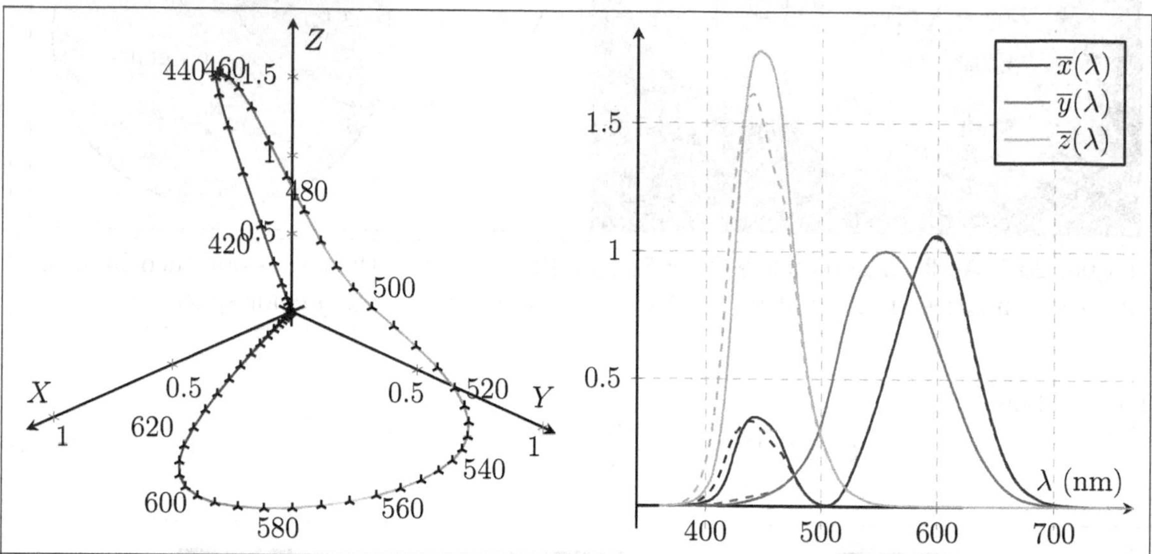

Figure 20.9: XYZ Color Space: Illustration of the XYZ virtual primaries (left), and plot of the corresponding color-matching functions, both standardized [CIE, 1931] (solid) and modified [Judd, 1951, Vos, 1978] (dashed) (right).

Given the color-matching functions $\overline{x}$, $\overline{y}$ and $\overline{z}$ (for which analytical approximations may be used in place of the tabulated data provided by the CIE [Wyman *et al.*, 2013]), the locus of a spectral distribution I in the device-independent *XYZ color space* is defined as

$$X \triangleq \int_0^\infty I(\lambda)\overline{x}(\lambda)\mathrm{d}\lambda \tag{20.35}$$

$$Y \triangleq \int_0^\infty I(\lambda)\overline{y}(\lambda)\mathrm{d}\lambda \tag{20.36}$$

$$Z \triangleq \int_0^\infty I(\lambda)\overline{z}(\lambda)\mathrm{d}\lambda \tag{20.37}$$

where Y corresponds to the *relative luminance* of a given spectral radiance. The set of all spectral distributions projects into a subset of the XYZ color space said to contain *real colors*, whereas XYZ triplets that do not correspond to any physically realizable light source are said to describe *imaginary colors*.

20.5.2 xyY

Based on the requirement that all three color-matching functions be positive, the rg chromaticities of the virtual XYZ primaries were designed such that their gamut tightly encompasses that of average human vision, delimited by the *spectral locus* of purely monochromatic light and the *purple line* corresponding to red-violet mixtures, as illustrated in *Figure 20.3*.
706 The line x_{rg}-y_{rg} of zero luminance, so-called *alychne*, was then defined by the

identity $\overline{y}(\lambda) = V(\lambda)$, and the constraint $\overline{z}(\lambda) = 0, \forall\lambda > 650$ nm induced the line x_{rg}-z_{rg} to be tangent to the spectral locus at this wavelength. The line y_{rg}-z_{rg} was finally specified by the additional requirement that the integral of the three color-matching functions be equal, therefore preserving the locus of the equal-energy *standard illuminant* E at the barycenter 713
$[1/3, 1/3]$ when transforming the triangle x_{rg}-y_{rg}-z_{rg} into the unit triangle with vertices $[0, 1]$, $[1, 0]$ and $[0, 0]$, as illustrated in *Figure 20.10*. 713

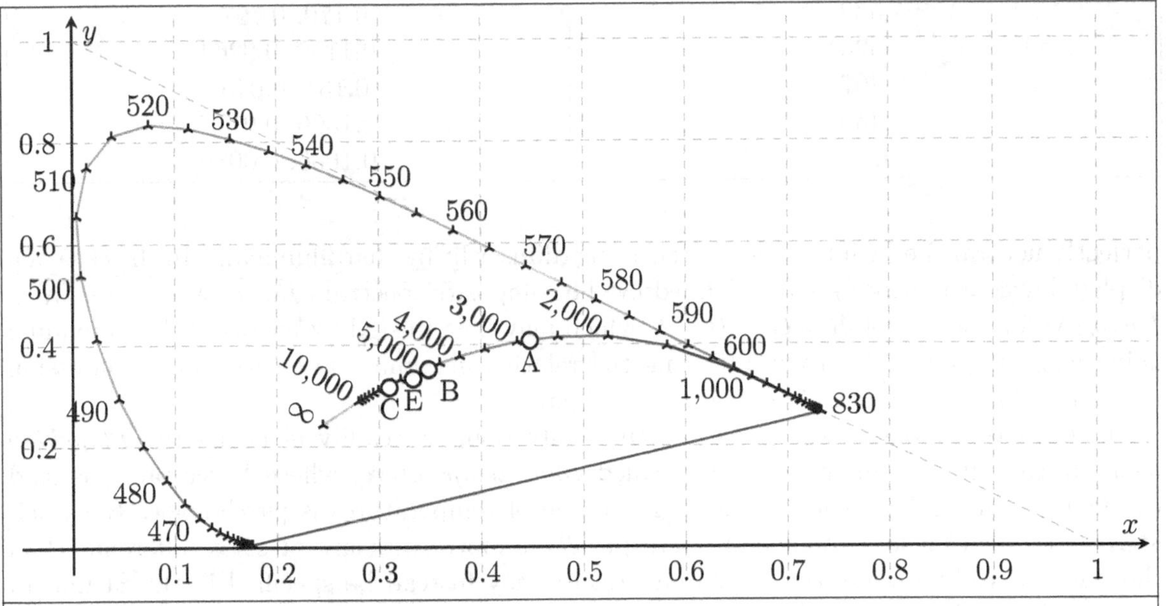

Figure 20.10: xyY Color Space: Illustration of the chromaticity diagram of the xyY color space [CIE, 1931].

Given a triplet of XYZ values, the *xy chromaticity* coordinates of the *xyY color space* are given by a projection onto the plane of unit L_1 norm

$$x \triangleq \frac{X}{X+Y+Z} \quad (20.38)$$

$$y \triangleq \frac{Y}{X+Y+Z} \quad (20.39)$$

$$z \triangleq \frac{Z}{X+Y+Z} \quad (20.40)$$

such that $x + y + z = 1$, followed by an orthogonal projection onto the xy plane. *Table 20.1* 714
illustrates the resulting coordinates of various sample *spectral colors*.

Conversely, a triplet of xyY values can be converted into the XYZ color space as

$$X = (X+Y+Z)x = \frac{Y}{y}x \quad (20.41)$$

$$Y = (X+Y+Z)y = \frac{Y}{y}y \quad (20.42)$$

$$Z = (X+Y+Z)z = \frac{Y}{y}(1-x-y) \quad (20.43)$$

where $X + Y + Z = \frac{X}{x} = \frac{Y}{y} = \frac{Z}{z}$.

20.5.3 Standard Illuminant

Given an illuminant, its locus in a given color space (such as the xy chromaticity diagram) is commonly referred to as the *white point*, as it corresponds to the color coordinates of a

Table 20.1: Spectral Locus: Chromaticities of purely monochromatic lights at various sample wavelengths.

Wavelength (nm)	CIE 1931 2° xy
700	0.7347, 0.2653
630	0.708, 0.292
546.1	0.2738, 0.7174
532	0.170, 0.797
525	0.1152, 0.8264
467	0.131, 0.046
450	0.1566, 0.0177
435.8	0.1666, 0.0089

perfectly neutral (i.e., white, or gray) reflecting diffuser lit by that illuminant. In the case of a display device, the white point is defined by the composite spectrum $Rw_r r_e(\lambda) + Gw_g g_e(\lambda) + Bw_b b_e(\lambda)$ for the triplet $R = G = B = 1$, which may be adjusted by means of the individual gains $w_{r|g|b} \in [0, 1]$, effectively adjusting the relative maximum intensities of the emission
704 spectra $r_e(\lambda)$, $g_e(\lambda)$ and $b_e(\lambda)$ of the *RGB* primaries.

427 In the case of *blackbody radiation*, the white point is readily given by the *Planckian locus* at the given temperature, then called *color temperature*, whose lower range is said to yield "warm" colors whereas the higher range of temperatures is psychologically associated with "cool" colors. As a more perceptually uniform measure of color difference than the physical Kelvin scale, the color temperature may instead be specified in the SI unit of reciprocal megakelvin MK^{-1}, commonly called microreciprocal degree or *mired*, as well as microreciprocal kelvin or *mirek*

$$M \triangleq \frac{10^6}{T} \tag{20.44}$$

The white point can alternatively be specified by means of a source of visible light with a spectral power distribution whose profile has been standardized by the CIE. Such *standard illuminants* are typically characterized by their *correlated color temperature* (*CCT*), which is the temperature of the point on the Planckian locus whose chromaticity is perceptually closest to that of the white point. After the definition of the illuminants, the scientific community revised the constant $\frac{hc}{k}$ in Planck's law, thereby necessitating the adjustments of the CCT values in order to maintain the identity

$$\left(\frac{hc}{k}\right)_{old} \frac{1}{CCT_{old}} = \left(\frac{hc}{k}\right)_{new} \frac{1}{CCT_{new}} \tag{20.45}$$

716 As illustrated in *Table 20.2*, illuminant A characterizes the SPD of a domestic incandescent
427 light source, described by Planck's law of *blackbody radiation*, with peak value around 560 nm. In contrast, illuminants B and C are daylight simulators obtained by applying liquid filters to illuminant A in order to approximate direct sunlight and indirect daylight, respectively. The latter have both been deprecated and replaced by the more accurate series of daylight illuminants D [CIE, 1964] at nominal CCT values of 5000, 5500, 6500 and 7500 K
715 illustrated in *Figure 20.11*, derived from measured SPDs of daylight, and defined as a linear combination

$$S(\lambda) = S_0(\lambda) + M_1 S_1(\lambda) + M_2 S_2(\lambda) \tag{20.46}$$

of three vector SPDs determined by principal component analysis (S_0 being the mean of all measured SPD samples, while S_1 and S_2 correspond to the yellow-blue and pink-green variations due to clouds or direct sunlight and to water vapor or haze, respectively). In turn, the weights are defined as

$$M_1 = \frac{-1.3515 - 1.7703x + 5.9114y}{0.0241 + 0.2562x - 0.7341y} \tag{20.47}$$

$$M_2 = \frac{0.03 - 31.4424x + 30.0717y}{0.0241 + 0.2562x - 0.7341y} \tag{20.48}$$

with the chromaticities corresponding to a given color temperature in milli reciprocal kelvin $m \triangleq \frac{10^3}{T}$ being given by

$$x = \begin{cases} 0.244063 + 0.09911m + 2.9678m^2 - 4.607m^3 & \text{if } T \in [4000, 7000] \text{ K} \\ 0.23704 + 0.24748m + 1.9018m^2 - 2.0064m^3 & \text{if } T \in [7000, 25000] \text{ K} \end{cases} \tag{20.49}$$

$$y = -0.275 + 2.87x - 3x^2 \tag{20.50}$$

In contrast, reference illuminant E has a constant SPD over the spectrum of visible wavelengths, such that its chromaticity coordinates lie at the barycenter $[x, y] = [1/3, 1/3]$, while the F series of illuminants [CIE, 2004] represents various types of fluorescent lighting, with F1 to F6 corresponding to standard lamps with semi-broadband emissions, while F7 to F9 and F10 to F12 correspond to broadband and three narrow-band emissions, respectively, as illustrated in *Figure 20.12.* 716

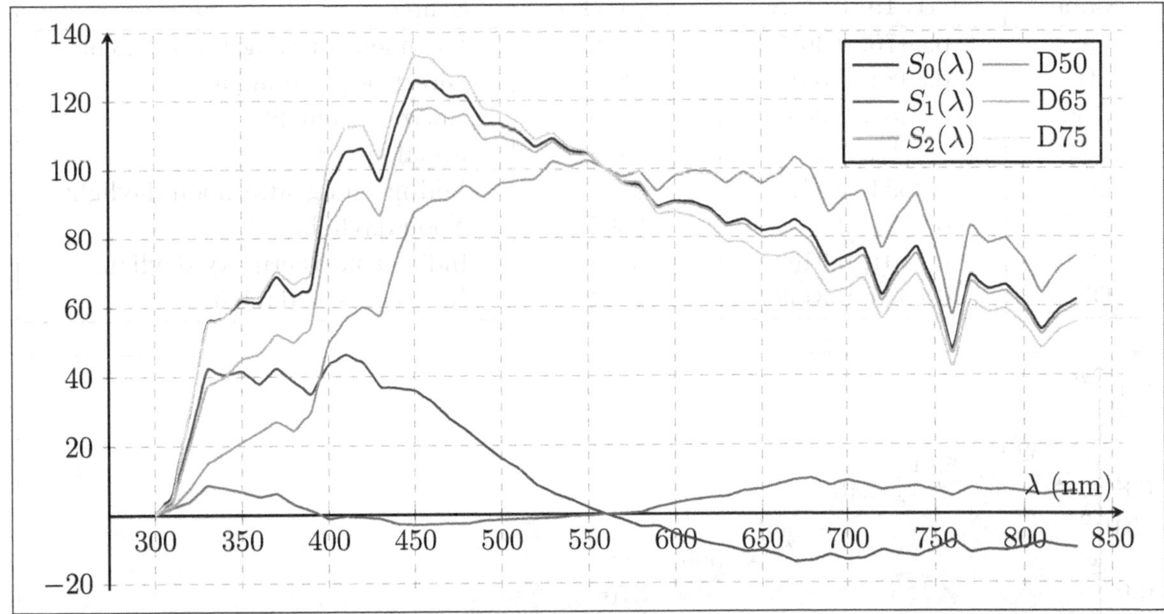

Figure 20.11: Daylight Illuminants: Plot of the normalized spectral distributions of the D series of standard illuminants [CIE, 1964].

Given a line joining a reference white point $\vec{p}_W$ to a polychromatic point $\vec{p}_P$, its intersection $\vec{p}_D$ with the spectral locus yields the so-called *dominant wavelength*, whereas the intersection on the opposite side of the white point yields the *complementary wavelength.* As illustrated in *Figure 20.13*, the *excitation purity* of $\vec{p}_P$ is then defined in terms of the distance 716
between the points as

$$p_e \triangleq \frac{d(\vec{p}_W, \vec{p}_P)}{d(\vec{p}_W, \vec{p}_D)} \tag{20.51}$$

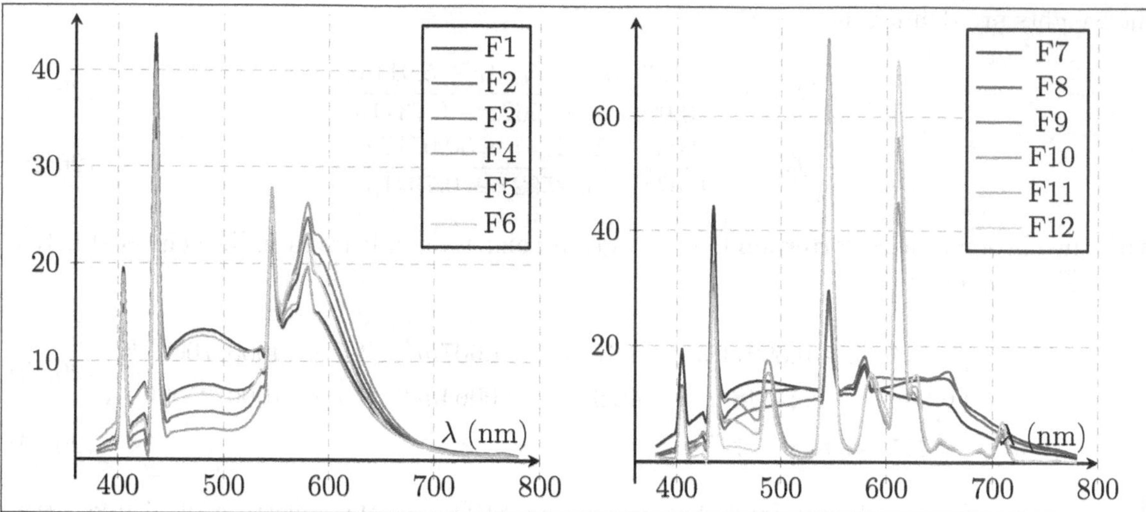

Figure 20.12: Fluorescent Illuminants: Plot of the spectral distributions of the F series of standard illuminants [CIE, 2004].

Table 20.2: Standard Illuminants: Chromaticities and color temperatures of various standard illuminants.

Name	CIE 1931 2° xy	CCT (K)	Source
A	0.4476, 0.4075	2856	Incandescent tungsten filament
B	0.3484, 0.3516	4874	Direct noon sunlight
D50	0.3457, 0.3585	5003	Horizon daylight
E	1/3, 1/3	5454	Equal energy
D55	0.3324, 0.3474	5503	Mid-morning/afternoon daylight
D65	0.3127, 0.3290	6504	Noon daylight
C	0.3101, 0.3162	6774	Indirect northern sky daylight
D75	0.2990, 0.3148	7504	Northern sky daylight

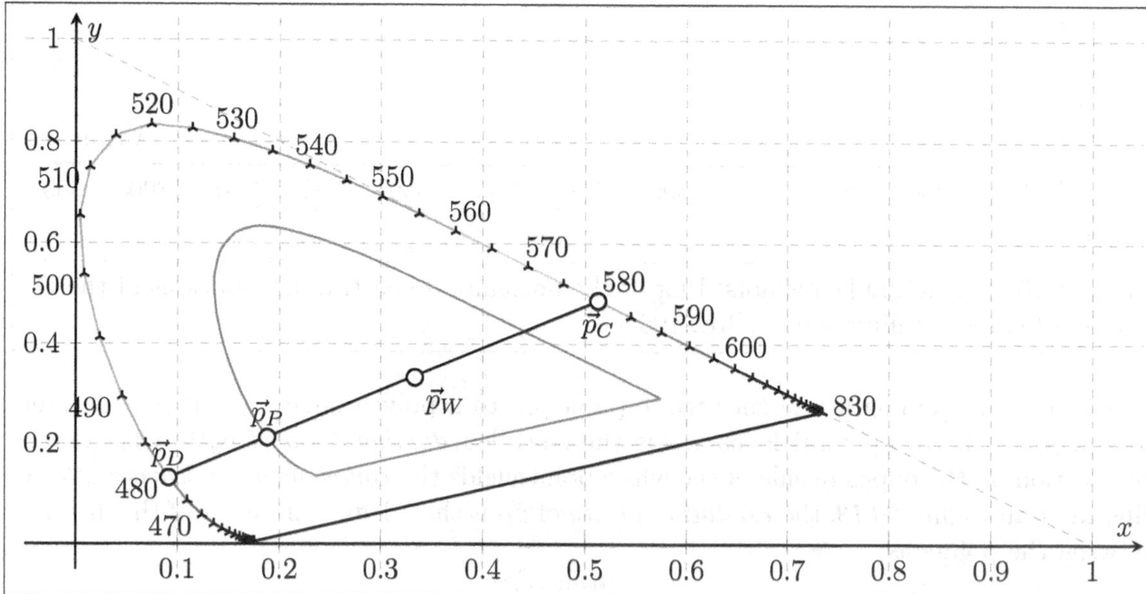

Figure 20.13: Wavelength and Purity: Illustration of the dominant and complementary wavelengths of a color point in the xy chromaticity diagram, and of its excitation purity as an isoline.

20.5.4 From RGB

Given the composite spectral distribution defined by the emission spectra of specific RGB 704
primaries $r_e(\lambda)$, $g_e(\lambda)$ and $b_e(\lambda)$ (such as those of a given LCD or LED display), and a
particular RGB triplet, the corresponding XYZ coordinates read 704

$$\begin{bmatrix} X \\ Y \\ Z \end{bmatrix} \overset{\substack{(20.35)\\(20.36)}}{\underset{\substack{(20.37)\\(20.5)}}{=}} \begin{bmatrix} \int_0^\infty (Rr_e(\lambda)+Gg_e(\lambda)+Bb_e(\lambda))\bar{x}(\lambda)\mathrm{d}\lambda \\ \int_0^\infty (Rr_e(\lambda)+Gg_e(\lambda)+Bb_e(\lambda))\bar{y}(\lambda)\mathrm{d}\lambda \\ \int_0^\infty (Rr_e(\lambda)+Gg_e(\lambda)+Bb_e(\lambda))\bar{z}(\lambda)\mathrm{d}\lambda \end{bmatrix}$$

712 712 712 705

$$= \begin{bmatrix} \int_0^\infty r_e(\lambda)\bar{x}(\lambda)\mathrm{d}\lambda & \int_0^\infty g_e(\lambda)\bar{x}(\lambda)\mathrm{d}\lambda & \int_0^\infty b_e(\lambda)\bar{x}(\lambda)\mathrm{d}\lambda \\ \int_0^\infty r_e(\lambda)\bar{y}(\lambda)\mathrm{d}\lambda & \int_0^\infty g_e(\lambda)\bar{y}(\lambda)\mathrm{d}\lambda & \int_0^\infty b_e(\lambda)\bar{y}(\lambda)\mathrm{d}\lambda \\ \int_0^\infty r_e(\lambda)\bar{z}(\lambda)\mathrm{d}\lambda & \int_0^\infty g_e(\lambda)\bar{z}(\lambda)\mathrm{d}\lambda & \int_0^\infty b_e(\lambda)\bar{z}(\lambda)\mathrm{d}\lambda \end{bmatrix} \begin{bmatrix} R \\ G \\ B \end{bmatrix} \quad (20.52)$$

Assuming that the RGB and XYZ color-matching functions can be linearly related by 704

$$\begin{aligned} \bar{x}(\lambda) &= X_R\bar{r}(\lambda)+X_G\bar{g}(\lambda)+X_B\bar{b}(\lambda) && (20.53) \\ \bar{y}(\lambda) &= Y_R\bar{r}(\lambda)+Y_G\bar{g}(\lambda)+Y_B\bar{b}(\lambda) && (20.54) \\ \bar{z}(\lambda) &= Z_R\bar{r}(\lambda)+Z_G\bar{g}(\lambda)+Z_B\bar{b}(\lambda) && (20.55) \end{aligned}$$

a triplet of RGB values may be alternatively converted to XYZ coordinates as 704

$$\begin{bmatrix} X \\ Y \\ Z \end{bmatrix} \overset{\substack{(20.35)\\(20.36)}}{\underset{(20.37)}{=}} \begin{bmatrix} \int_0^\infty I(\lambda)(X_R\bar{r}(\lambda)+X_G\bar{g}(\lambda)+X_B\bar{b}(\lambda))\mathrm{d}\lambda \\ \int_0^\infty I(\lambda)(Y_R\bar{r}(\lambda)+Y_G\bar{g}(\lambda)+Y_B\bar{b}(\lambda))\mathrm{d}\lambda \\ \int_0^\infty I(\lambda)(Z_R\bar{r}(\lambda)+Z_G\bar{g}(\lambda)+Z_B\bar{b}(\lambda))\mathrm{d}\lambda \end{bmatrix}$$

712 712 712

$$\overset{\substack{(20.2)\\(20.3)}}{\underset{(20.4)}{=}} \begin{bmatrix} X_RR+X_GG+X_BB \\ Y_RR+Y_GG+Y_BB \\ Z_RR+Z_GG+Z_BB \end{bmatrix} = M\begin{bmatrix} R \\ G \\ B \end{bmatrix} \quad (20.56)$$

705 705 705

where the matrix contains the XYZ coordinates of the RGB primaries 704

$$M \triangleq \begin{bmatrix} X_R & X_G & X_B \\ Y_R & Y_G & Y_B \\ Z_R & Z_G & Z_B \end{bmatrix} = \begin{bmatrix} C_Rx_R & C_Gx_G & C_Bx_B \\ C_Ry_R & C_Gy_G & C_By_B \\ C_Rz_R & C_Gz_G & C_Bz_B \end{bmatrix} = \begin{bmatrix} x_R & x_G & x_B \\ y_R & y_G & y_B \\ z_R & z_G & z_B \end{bmatrix} \begin{bmatrix} C_R & 0 & 0 \\ 0 & C_G & 0 \\ 0 & 0 & C_B \end{bmatrix} \quad (20.57)$$

with

$$\begin{aligned} C_R &\triangleq X_R+Y_R+Z_R = \frac{X_R}{x_R} = \frac{Y_R}{y_R} = \frac{Z_R}{z_R} && (20.58) \\ C_G &\triangleq X_G+Y_G+Z_G = \frac{X_G}{x_G} = \frac{Y_G}{y_G} = \frac{Z_G}{z_G} && (20.59) \\ C_B &\triangleq X_B+Y_B+Z_B = \frac{X_B}{x_B} = \frac{Y_B}{y_B} = \frac{Z_B}{z_B} && (20.60) \end{aligned}$$

Shall the relative luminance Y of the RGB primaries be unspecified, the chromaticities 704
x_W and y_W of the white point, whose luminance is arbitrarily defined as $Y_W = 1$, may instead
be used to evaluate its XYZ coordinates

$$\begin{bmatrix} X_W \\ Y_W \\ Z_W \end{bmatrix} \overset{\substack{(20.41)\\(20.42)}}{\underset{(20.43)}{=}} (X_W+Y_W+Z_W)\begin{bmatrix} x_W \\ y_W \\ z_W \end{bmatrix} = \frac{Y_W}{y_W}\begin{bmatrix} x_W \\ y_W \\ z_W \end{bmatrix} = \begin{bmatrix} \frac{x_W}{y_W} \\ 1 \\ \frac{z_W}{y_W} \end{bmatrix} \quad (20.61)$$

713 713 713

704 such that the coefficients can be computed from the RGB coordinates of the white point,
which are $[1, 1, 1]$ by definition, as the solution of the linear system

717
717

$$\begin{bmatrix} X_W \\ Y_W \\ Z_W \end{bmatrix} \underset{(20.57)}{\overset{(20.56)}{=}} \begin{bmatrix} x_R & x_G & x_B \\ y_R & y_G & y_B \\ z_R & z_G & z_B \end{bmatrix} \begin{bmatrix} C_R & 0 & 0 \\ 0 & C_G & 0 \\ 0 & 0 & C_B \end{bmatrix} \begin{bmatrix} 1 \\ 1 \\ 1 \end{bmatrix} = \begin{bmatrix} x_R & x_G & x_B \\ y_R & y_G & y_B \\ z_R & z_G & z_B \end{bmatrix} \begin{bmatrix} C_R \\ C_G \\ C_B \end{bmatrix} \tag{20.62}$$

719 As illustrated in *Figure 20.14*, the gamuts of the various RGB standards all encompass
704 different subsets of that of average human vision due to the convex horseshoe shape of the
latter. Notably, the *Adobe RGB color space* was designed to encompass most of the colors
710 achievable on $CMYK$ printers, and whose conversion matrix, computed from the specifica-
718 tions provided in *Table 20.3*, reads

$$M = \begin{bmatrix} 0.57667 & 0.18556 & 0.18823 \\ 0.29735 & 0.62736 & 0.07529 \\ 0.02703 & 0.07069 & 0.99134 \end{bmatrix} \tag{20.63}$$

while the *Adobe Wide Gamut RGB color space* has an even larger coverage, albeit at the cost of a low luminous efficiency of its red and blue primaries, and of potential *posterization* artifacts known as *color banding* due to color quantization by fixed-point representations of insufficient bit depth, so-called *color depth*, causing continuous gradients to appear as discrete bands of color. Instead, the conversion matrix for the *CIE RGB color space* is readily given as

$$M \approx \begin{bmatrix} 0.49 & 0.31 & 0.20 \\ 0.17697 & 0.81240 & 0.01063 \\ 0.00 & 0.01 & 0.99 \end{bmatrix} \tag{20.64}$$

possibly followed by a scaling with a factor of 5.65 in order to match the XYZ color-matching functions, while the conversion matrix for the *sRGB color space*, defined as an Internet standard for World Wide Web applications based on the primaries of a typical CRT monitor (while being referred to as the *scRGB color space* when extending the gamut by means of signed unnormalized triplets beyond the $[0, 1]$ range), instead reads

$$M = \begin{bmatrix} 0.4124 & 0.3576 & 0.1805 \\ 0.2126 & 0.7152 & 0.0722 \\ 0.0193 & 0.1192 & 0.9505 \end{bmatrix} \tag{20.65}$$

Table 20.3: RGB Primaries: Coverage of the human visual gamut, and specificied chromaticities of the primaries and white point for various RGB standards.

RGB	Gamut	x_R, y_R	x_G, y_G	x_B, y_B	x_W, y_W
Wide gamut RGB	77.6%	700 nm	525 nm	450 nm	D50
CIE RGB	–	700 nm	546.1 nm	435.8 nm	E
UHDTV	75.8%	630 nm	532 nm	467 nm	D65
SDTV-NTSC-1987	–	0.63, 0.34	0.31, 0.595	0.155, 0.07	D65
SDTV-PAL/SECAM	–	0.64, 0.33	0.29, 0.60	0.15, 0.06	D65
sRGB / HDTV	35.9%	0.64, 0.33	0.30, 0.60	0.15, 0.06	D65
Adobe RGB	52.1%	0.64, 0.33	0.21, 0.71	0.15, 0.06	D65
SDTV-NTSC-1953	–	0.67, 0.33	0.21, 0.71	0.14, 0.08	C

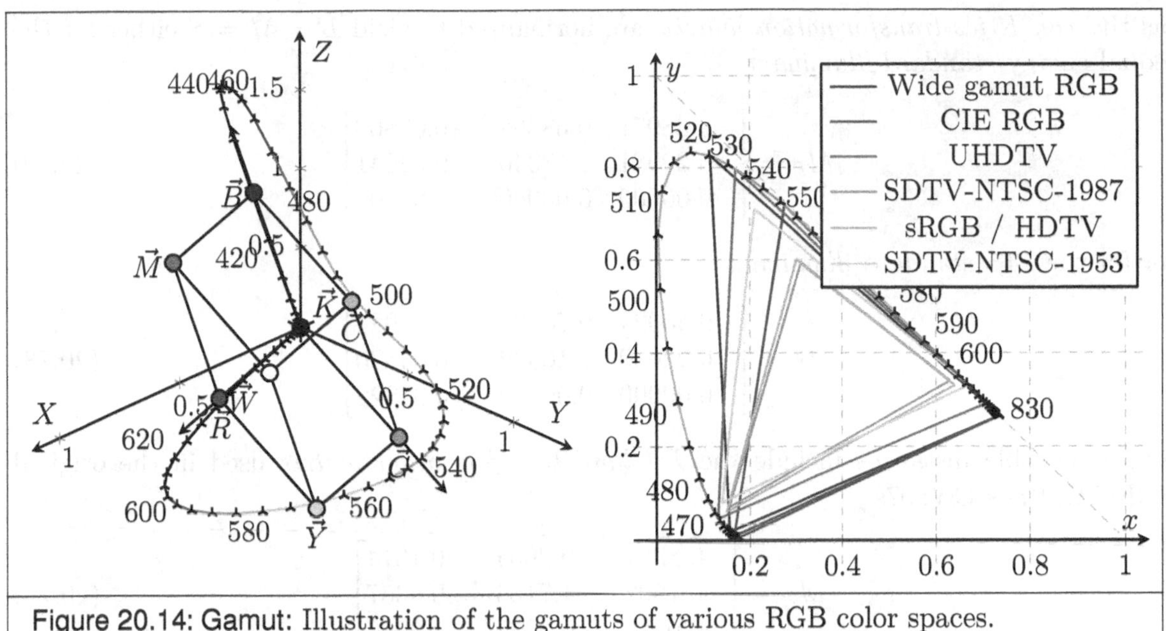

Figure 20.14: Gamut: Illustration of the gamuts of various RGB color spaces.

20.5.5 To LMS

Assuming that the *LMS* and XYZ color-matching functions can be linearly related by 684

$$\bar{l}(\lambda) = L_X\bar{x}(\lambda) + L_Y\bar{y}(\lambda) + L_Z\bar{z}(\lambda) \tag{20.66}$$
$$\bar{m}(\lambda) = M_X\bar{x}(\lambda) + M_Y\bar{y}(\lambda) + M_Z\bar{z}(\lambda) \tag{20.67}$$
$$\bar{s}(\lambda) = S_X\bar{x}(\lambda) + S_Y\bar{y}(\lambda) + S_Z\bar{z}(\lambda) \tag{20.68}$$

a triplet of XYZ values may be converted to *LMS* coordinates as 684

$$\begin{bmatrix} L \\ M \\ S \end{bmatrix} \overset{(19.1)(19.2)(19.3)}{=} \begin{bmatrix} \int_0^\infty I(\lambda)(L_X\bar{x}(\lambda) + L_Y\bar{y}(\lambda) + L_Z\bar{z}(\lambda))\mathrm{d}\lambda \\ \int_0^\infty I(\lambda)(M_X\bar{x}(\lambda) + M_Y\bar{y}(\lambda) + M_Z\bar{z}(\lambda))\mathrm{d}\lambda \\ \int_0^\infty I(\lambda)(S_X\bar{x}(\lambda) + S_Y\bar{y}(\lambda) + S_Z\bar{z}(\lambda))\mathrm{d}\lambda \end{bmatrix}$$

684 684 684

$$\overset{(20.35)(20.36)(20.37)}{=} \begin{bmatrix} L_XX + L_YY + L_ZZ \\ M_XX + M_YY + M_ZZ \\ S_XX + S_YY + S_ZZ \end{bmatrix} = M_T \begin{bmatrix} X \\ Y \\ Z \end{bmatrix} \tag{20.69}$$

712 712 712

Particular instances include the definition of the *LMS* tristimulus functions from the (modified) XYZ color-matching functions [Judd, 1951, Vos, 1978] via the *Vos–Walraven transformation matrix* [Vos and Walraven, 1971] 684

$$M_T = \begin{bmatrix} 0.1551646 & 0.5430763 & -0.0370161 \\ -0.1551646 & 0.4569237 & 0.0296946 \\ 0.0000000 & 0.0000000 & 0.0073215 \end{bmatrix} \tag{20.70}$$

or the *Smith–Pokorny transformation matrix* [Smith and Pokorny, 1975]

$$M_T = \begin{bmatrix} 0.15514 & 0.54312 & -0.03286 \\ -0.15514 & 0.45684 & 0.03286 \\ 0.00000 & 0.00000 & 0.00801 \end{bmatrix} \tag{20.71}$$

Instead, the sums of the rows of the *Hunt–Pointer–Estevez transformation matrix*, also known

as the *von Kries transformation matrix*, are normalized to yield $L = M = S$ either for the
713 equal-energy *standard illuminant*

$$M_T = \begin{bmatrix} 0.38971 & 0.68898 & -0.07868 \\ -0.22981 & 1.18340 & 0.04641 \\ 0.00000 & 0.00000 & 1.00000 \end{bmatrix} \tag{20.72}$$

713 or for the D65 *standard illuminant*

$$M_T = \begin{bmatrix} 0.40024 & 0.70760 & -0.08081 \\ -0.22630 & 1.16532 & 0.04570 \\ 0.00000 & 0.00000 & 0.91822 \end{bmatrix} \tag{20.73}$$

Other notable instances include the *Bradford transformation matrix* used in the original CIECAM97s's CAT97s

$$M_T = \begin{bmatrix} 0.8951 & 0.2664 & -0.1614 \\ -0.7502 & 1.7135 & 0.0367 \\ 0.0389 & -0.0685 & 1.0296 \end{bmatrix} \tag{20.74}$$

whose subsequent revision instead resorted to [Fairchild, 2001]

$$M_T = \begin{bmatrix} 0.8562 & 0.3372 & -0.1934 \\ -0.8360 & 1.8327 & 0.0033 \\ 0.0357 & -0.0469 & 1.0112 \end{bmatrix} \tag{20.75}$$

as well as the transformation matrix used in CIECAM02's CAT02 [Moroney *et al.*, 2002]

$$M_T = \begin{bmatrix} 0.7328 & 0.4296 & -0.1624 \\ -0.7036 & 1.6975 & 0.0061 \\ 0.0030 & 0.0136 & 0.9834 \end{bmatrix} \tag{20.76}$$

20.6 LUV & LAB

20.6.1 From XYZ

20.6.1.1 UCS

711 Given a triplet of XYZ values, the coordinates in the perceptually Uniform Chromaticity Scale, formally known as the *CIE 1960 UCS color space*, are defined as

$$U \triangleq \frac{2}{3}X \tag{20.77}$$

$$V \triangleq Y \tag{20.78}$$

$$W \triangleq \frac{-X + 3Y + Z}{2} \tag{20.79}$$

yielding the uv chromaticities

$$u \triangleq \frac{U}{U+V+W} = \frac{4X}{X+15Y+3Z} \underset{(20.43)}{\overset{(20.41)\,(20.42)}{=}} \frac{4x}{-2x+12y+3} \qquad (20.80)$$

713 713 713

$$v \triangleq \frac{V}{U+V+W} = \frac{6Y}{X+15Y+3Z} \underset{(20.43)}{\overset{(20.41)\,(20.42)}{=}} \frac{6y}{-2x+12y+3} \qquad (20.81)$$

713 713 713

$$w \triangleq \frac{W}{U+V+W} = \frac{-3X+9Y+3Z}{X+15Y+3Z} \underset{(20.43)}{\overset{(20.41)\,(20.42)}{=}} \frac{-6x+6y+3}{-2x+12y+3} \qquad (20.82)$$

713 713 713

such that $u+v+w=1$, followed by an orthogonal projection onto the uv plane. A specificity of the space is that the isothermal lines are perpendicular to the Planckian locus, thereby facilitating the calculation of correlated color temperatures, while mapping *MacAdam ellipses* [MacAdam, 1942] (which delimit the visual tolerance, or just-noticeable difference, to the chromaticity at their center) to nearly circular regions, as illustrated in *Figure 20.15.* 721

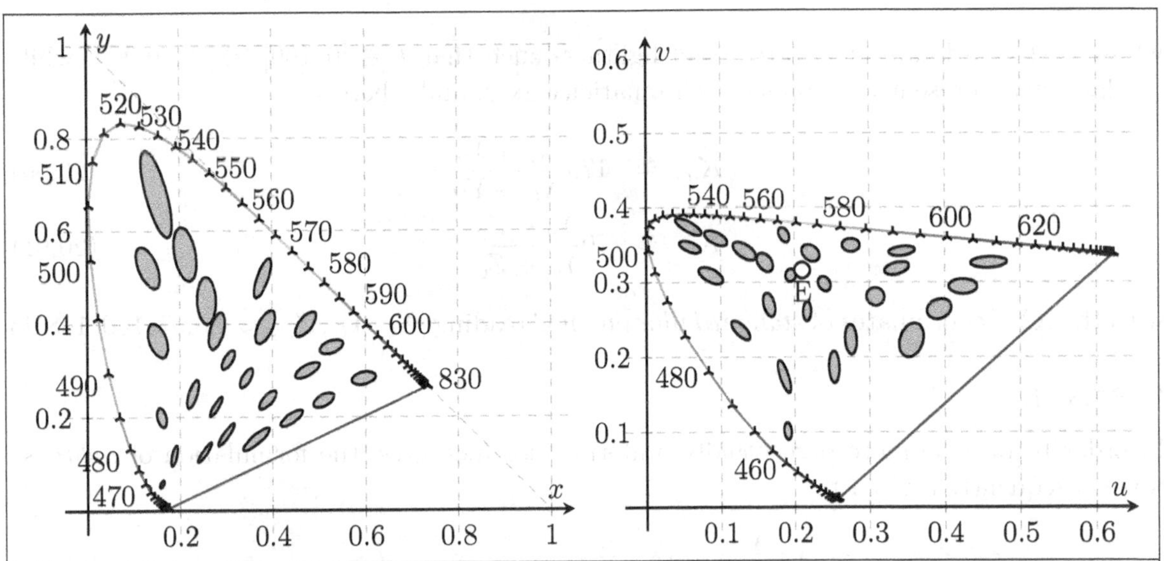

Figure 20.15: UCS Color Space: Illustration of the chromaticity diagram of the UCS color space (right), compared against the xy chromaticity space (left), shown with the radii of the MacAdam ellipses [MacAdam, 1942] increased by a factor 10.

Given the uv chromaticities $[u_n, v_n]$ of the neutral point, the *CIE 1964 UVW color space* is then defined as

$$U^* \triangleq 13W^*(u - u_n) \qquad (20.83)$$
$$V^* \triangleq 13W^*(v - v_n) \qquad (20.84)$$
$$W^* \triangleq 25\sqrt[3]{Y} - 17 \qquad (20.85)$$

whose third coordinate encodes lightness, while the first two encode chromaticity scaled by lightness to account for the increase/decrease of the latter with apparent saturation as per the *Helmholtz–Kohlrausch effect* (akin to the cone/bicone of the *HSV & HSL* color spaces), and by 707 a constant to match the chroma scale from the original Munsell color system. The white point being at the origin, the loci of constant saturation are given by constant values of $(U^*)^2 + (V^*)^2$, and the *color difference* (i.e., the difference in perceived sensation, or "Empfindung" in German) between two triplets is readily measured by their Euclidean distance

74

$$\Delta E \overset{(3.61)}{=} \sqrt{(\Delta U^*)^2 + (\Delta V^*)^2 + (\Delta W^*)^2} \tag{20.86}$$

20.6.1.2 Lab

711 Given the XYZ coordinates of the neutral point, the *Hunter Lab color space* is instead defined as an *Adams chromatic valence color space*

$$L \triangleq 100\sqrt{\frac{Y}{Y_n}} \tag{20.87}$$

$$a \triangleq K_a \frac{L}{100}\left(\frac{\frac{x}{x_n}}{\frac{y}{y_n}} - 1\right) = K_a \sqrt{\frac{Y}{Y_n}} \frac{\frac{y_n}{x_n}X - Y}{Y} = K_a \frac{\frac{X}{X_n} - \frac{Y}{Y_n}}{\sqrt{\frac{Y}{Y_n}}} \tag{20.88}$$

$$b \triangleq K_b \frac{L}{100}\left(1 - \frac{\frac{z}{z_n}}{\frac{y}{y_n}}\right) = K_b \sqrt{\frac{Y}{Y_n}} \frac{Y - \frac{y_n}{z_n}Z}{Y} = K_b \frac{\frac{Y}{Y_n} - \frac{Z}{Z_n}}{\sqrt{\frac{Y}{Y_n}}} \tag{20.89}$$

whose first coordinate is a correlate of lightness such that $L \in [0, 100], \forall Y \in [0, Y_n]$, while the last two represent the opponent chromaticity axes, and where

$$K_a \triangleq 175\frac{X_n + Y_n}{X_C + Y_C} \tag{20.90}$$

$$K_b \triangleq 70\frac{Y_n + Z_n}{Y_C + Z_C} \tag{20.91}$$

711 713 with the XYZ coordinates of *standard illuminant* C reading $[X_C, Y_C, Z_C] \approx [98.07, 100, 118.23]$.

20.6.1.3 L*

In order to provide more perceptually uniform color measures, the formulation of *lightness* was subsequently revised to

$$L^* \triangleq 116 f\left(\frac{Y}{Y_n}\right) - 16 \tag{20.92}$$

722

$$\overset{(20.94)}{=} \begin{cases} 116\sqrt[3]{\frac{Y}{Y_n}} - 16 & \text{if } \frac{Y}{Y_n} > \left(\frac{6}{29}\right)^3 \\ 116\left(\frac{1}{3}\left(\frac{29}{6}\right)^2 \frac{Y}{Y_n} + \frac{4}{29}\right) - 16 = \left(\frac{29}{3}\right)^3 \frac{Y}{Y_n} & \text{otherwise} \end{cases} \tag{20.93}$$

such that $L^* \in [0, 100], \forall Y \in [0, Y_n]$, and where the cube root function

$$f(t) \triangleq \begin{cases} \sqrt[3]{t} & \text{if } t > \left(\frac{6}{29}\right)^3 \\ \frac{1}{3}\left(\frac{29}{6}\right)^2 t + \frac{4}{29} & \text{otherwise} \end{cases} \tag{20.94}$$

is substituted by a linear polynomial of the form $f(t) = at + b, \forall t < t_0$ in order to avoid an infinite slope at $t = 0$, and to ensure that $L^* = 0$ when $Y = 0$. From the latter requirement it follows that

$$0 = 116f(0) - 16 = 116b - 16 \implies b = \frac{16}{116} = \frac{4}{29} \tag{20.95}$$

while ensuring the continuity of f at t_0 in both value and slope yields

$$f(t_0) = \sqrt[3]{t_0} = at_0 + b = \frac{t_0^{-\frac{2}{3}}}{3} t_0 + \frac{4}{29} = \frac{\sqrt[3]{t_0}}{3} + \frac{4}{29} = \frac{\frac{4}{29}}{1-\frac{1}{3}} = \frac{6}{29} \implies t_0 = \left(\frac{6}{29}\right)^3 \tag{20.96}$$

$$f'(t_0) = \frac{t_0^{-\frac{2}{3}}}{3} = a \implies a = \frac{\left(\left(\frac{6}{29}\right)^3\right)^{-\frac{2}{3}}}{3} = \frac{1}{3}\left(\frac{29}{6}\right)^2 \tag{20.97}$$

20.6.1.4 L*u*v*

The *CIE 1976 Luv color space* additionally defines the rescaled chromaticities $[u', v'] \triangleq [u, {}^3/_2 v]$. Given the rescaled chromaticities $[u'_n, v'_n]$ of the neutral point, the chromatic coordinates are then defined as

$$u^* \triangleq 13L^*(u' - u'_n) \tag{20.98}$$

$$v^* \triangleq 13L^*(v' - v'_n) \tag{20.99}$$

such that the color difference between two triplets is readily measured by their Euclidean distance

$$\Delta E \overset{(3.61)}{=} \sqrt{(\Delta L^*)^2 + (\Delta u^*)^2 + (\Delta v^*)^2} \tag{20.100}$$ 74

Akin to the first perceptually based HSV/HSL-like *Munsell color system*, the chroma and hue of the *CIE LCh$_{uv}$ color space* are, respectively, given by

$$C^*_{uv} \triangleq \sqrt{(u^*)^2 + (v^*)^2} \tag{20.101}$$

$$h_{uv} \triangleq \operatorname{arctan2}(v^*, u^*) \tag{20.102}$$

from which the saturation correlate is defined as

$$s_{uv} \triangleq \frac{C^*_{uv}}{L^*} = 13\sqrt{(u' - u'_n)^2 + (v' - v'_n)^2} \tag{20.103}$$

20.6.1.5 L*a*b*

Given the XYZ coordinates X_n, Y_n and Z_n of the neutral point, the chromatic coordinates 711
of the *CIE Lab color space* are instead defined as the color opponents

$$a^* \triangleq 500\left(f\left(\frac{X}{X_n}\right) - f\left(\frac{Y}{Y_n}\right)\right) \tag{20.104}$$

$$b^* \triangleq 200\left(f\left(\frac{Y}{Y_n}\right) - f\left(\frac{Z}{Z_n}\right)\right) \tag{20.105}$$

such that the color difference between two triplets is readily measured by their Euclidean distance

$$\Delta E \overset{(3.61)}{=} \sqrt{(\Delta L^*)^2 + (\Delta a^*)^2 + (\Delta b^*)^2} \tag{20.106}$$ 74

The chroma and hue of the *CIE LCh$_{ab}$ color space* are, respectively, given by

$$C^*_{ab} \triangleq \sqrt{(a^*)^2 + (b^*)^2} \tag{20.107}$$

$$h_{ab} \triangleq \operatorname{arctan2}(b^*, a^*) \tag{20.108}$$

from which the saturation correlate, although not officially defined by the CIE, may be analogously expressed as

$$s_{ab} \triangleq \frac{C^*_{ab}}{L^*} = \frac{\sqrt{(a^*)^2 + (b^*)^2}}{L^*} \tag{20.109}$$

20.6.2 To XYZ

20.6.2.1 L^*

Given the luminance of the neutral point Y_n, the conversion from lightness to luminance is defined as

722
$$Y \overset{(20.92)}{=} Y_n f^{-1}\left(\frac{L^*+16}{116}\right) \tag{20.110}$$

724
$$\overset{(20.112)}{=} Y_n \times \begin{cases} \left(\frac{L^*+16}{116}\right)^3 & \text{if } \frac{L^*+16}{116} > \frac{6}{29} \\ 3\left(\frac{6}{29}\right)^2\left(\frac{L^*+16}{116} - \frac{4}{29}\right) & \text{otherwise} \end{cases}$$

$$= Y_n \times \begin{cases} \left(\frac{L^*+16}{116}\right)^3 & \text{if } L^* > 8 \\ L^*\left(\frac{3}{29}\right)^3 & \text{otherwise} \end{cases} \tag{20.111}$$

where the inverse function reads

722
$$f^{-1}(t) \overset{(20.94)}{=} \begin{cases} t^3 & \text{if } t > \frac{6}{29} \\ 3\left(\frac{6}{29}\right)^2\left(t - \frac{4}{29}\right) & \text{otherwise} \end{cases} \tag{20.112}$$

20.6.2.2 $L^*u^*v^*$

723 Given the rescaled chromaticities $[u'_n, v'_n]$ of the neutral point, a triplet of $L^*u^*v^*$ coordinates may then be converted to the rescaled chromatic coordinates

723
$$u' \overset{(20.98)}{=} \frac{u^*}{13L^*} + u'_n \tag{20.113}$$

723
$$v' \overset{(20.99)}{=} \frac{v^*}{13L^*} + v'_n \tag{20.114}$$

720
720 to yield the uv chromaticities $[u, v] = [u', {}^2\!/\!{}_3 v']$. Exploiting the identity $V \overset{(20.78)}{=} Y$, the *UCS* coordinates are then given by

721
$$U \overset{(20.80)}{=} (U+V+W)u = \frac{V}{v}u \tag{20.115}$$

721
$$V \overset{(20.81)}{=} (U+V+W)v = \frac{V}{v}v \tag{20.116}$$

721
$$W \overset{(20.82)}{=} (U+V+W)w = \frac{V}{v}(1-u-v) \tag{20.117}$$

711 where $U+V+W = \frac{U}{u} = \frac{V}{v} = \frac{W}{w}$, from which follow the XYZ coordinates

720
$$X \overset{(20.77)}{=} \frac{3}{2}U = V\frac{3}{2}\frac{u}{v} = Y\frac{9u'}{4v'} \tag{20.118}$$

720
$$Z \overset{(20.79)}{=} \frac{3}{2}U - 3V + 2W = V\left(\frac{4-u}{2v} - 5\right) = Y\left(\frac{12-3u'}{4v'} - 5\right) \tag{20.119}$$

712 and their chromaticities in xyY space

713
$$x \overset{(20.38)}{=} \frac{3u}{2u-8v+4} = \frac{9u'}{6u'-16v'+12} \tag{20.120}$$

713
$$y \overset{(20.39)}{=} \frac{2v}{2u-8v+4} = \frac{4v'}{6u'-16v'+12} \tag{20.121}$$

20.6.2.3 L*a*b*

Given the XYZ coordinates X_n, Y_n and Z_n of the neutral point, a triplet of $L^*a^*b^*$ coordinates 711 723
may be converted to the XYZ coordinates 711

$$X \overset{(20.104)}{=} X_n f^{-1}\left(\frac{L^*+16}{116} + \frac{a^*}{500}\right) \tag{20.122}$$ 723

$$Z \overset{(20.105)}{=} Z_n f^{-1}\left(\frac{L^*+16}{116} - \frac{b^*}{200}\right) \tag{20.123}$$ 723

20.7 GAMMA CORRECTION

Due to the non-linear response of electron guns, the light intensity I displayed on old cathode ray tube (CRT) monitors was related to the input voltage V by a power law of the form

$$I \propto V^{\gamma} \tag{20.124}$$

with gamma exponent in the order of $\gamma \approx 2.2$. As illustrated in *Figure 20.16*, achieving 725
a linear response therefore entailed a priori correcting the input signal with the reciprocal
exponent $1/\gamma$ in order to cancel that of the device, a process known as *gamma correction*.
While the latter is typically applied to the individual components of RGB triplets normalized 704
to the range $[0, 1]$, signed color values may be similarly processed as

$$C' \triangleq \text{sgn}(C)|C|^{\frac{1}{\gamma}} \tag{20.125}$$

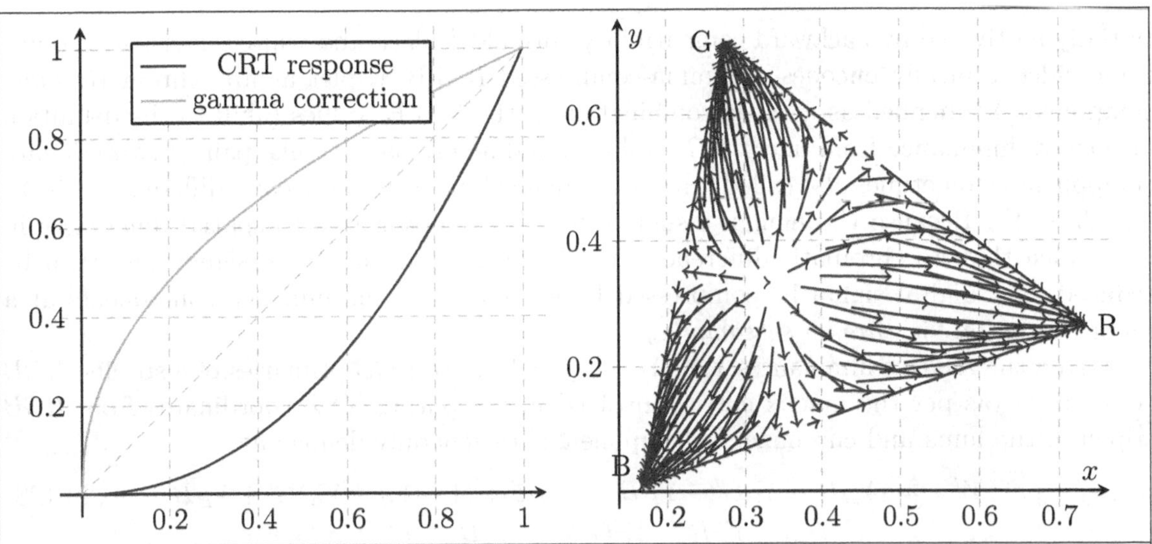

Figure 20.16: Gamma Correction: Illustration of the non-linear response of a CRT monitor and of the gamma-corrected signal obtained by a priori applying the inverse exponent in order to restore the linearity of the displayed values (left), and of the chromaticity shift due to inadequate gamma correction (right, drawn after [Glassner, 1994, Fig. 3.31]).

Because the non-linear mapping is independently applied to each individual color channel,
improper gamma correction generally leads to a shift in chromaticity of the input RGB 704
triplets, as illustrated in *Figure 20.16*. To this end, the actual gamma value of a specific device 725
can be calibrated by matching a gamma-corrected gray input value of a gamma calibration

chart with a black and white dither linearly averaged by the visual system into a reference gray intensity.

690 As the logarithmic perception of *brightness* by humans resembles a power law with an exponent of 1/3, gamma correction additionally allows for the compression and encoding
704 of normalized *RGB* triplets $\in [0,1]^3$ via a perceptually uniform linear distribution of the limited numerical precision of fixed-point representations (whereas floating-point representations intrinsically use a logarithmic distribution by means of their exponent), effectively
732 decreasing the lowest representable value and therefore increasing the *dynamic range*. To this end, the wide gamut and Adobe RGB standards specify the encoding of each color channel C corrected with a gamma value of $\gamma = \frac{563}{256} = 2.19921875$. In order to avoid an infinite slope at the origin, the sRGB standard instead emulates the compression with the latter exponent via the parameters $[a, b, p, t, t'] = [12.92, 0.055, 2.4, 0.0031308, 0.04045]$, while the ITU-R recommendations 709 and 2020 emulate an effective gamma value of 2.4 via $[a, b, p, t, t'] = [4.5, 0.099, 1/0.45, 0.018, 0.081]$, by means of the mapping

$$C' \triangleq \begin{cases} aC & \text{if } C \in [0,t] \\ (1+b)C^{\frac{1}{p}} - b & \text{if } C \in [t,1] \end{cases} \tag{20.126}$$

whose inverse gamma expansion to linear values is readily given as

$$C = \begin{cases} \frac{C'}{a} & \text{if } C' \in [0,t'] \\ \left(\frac{C'+b}{1+b}\right)^p & \text{if } C' \in [t',1] \end{cases} \tag{20.127}$$

20.8 LUMA & CHROMINANCE

20.8.1 YCC

Initially motivated by backward compatibility with older black-and-white television systems, color video typically encodes a gamma-compressed R'G'B' triplet as an achromatic *luma* component Y', defined as a linear combination of the R'G'B' values (akin to the definition
704 of relative luminance from linear *RGB* values), and a chromaticity-like pair of *chrominance* components (sometimes also called "chroma"), defined in terms of the color differences $B'-Y'$ and $R'-Y'$. Because the human visual system is more sensitive to spatial differences in luminance than to chromatic differences, the bandwidth of an analog signal may then be reduced or a digital signal be compressed by encoding the chrominance components at a lower resolution via *chroma subsampling*.

704 Given the relative luminances $Y_R + Y_G + Y_B = 1$ of the *RGB* primaries of a specific *RGB*
704 711 color space (as per the matrix entries involved in computing *XYZ* coordinates *from RGB*
717 triplets), the luma and chrominance components are generally defined as

$$Y' \triangleq Y_R R' + Y_G G' + Y_B B' = Y_R R' + (1 - Y_R - Y_B)G' + Y_B B' \tag{20.128}$$

$$U_B \triangleq S_B\left(B' - \frac{Y_R R' + Y_G G'}{Y_R + Y_G}\right) = S_B\frac{B' - Y'}{1 - Y_B} \tag{20.129}$$

$$V_R \triangleq S_R\left(R' - \frac{Y_G G' + Y_B B'}{Y_G + Y_B}\right) = S_R\frac{R' - Y'}{1 - Y_R} \tag{20.130}$$

such that $R' = G' = B' = c$ yields $[c, 0, 0]$, and with the scaling factors S_B and S_R such that $[Y', U_B, V_R] \in [0,1] \times [-S_B, S_B] \times [-S_R, S_R]$. Alternatively, the transformation may be written in matrix form as

$$\begin{bmatrix} Y' \\ U_B \\ V_R \end{bmatrix} = \begin{bmatrix} Y_R & 1 - Y_R - Y_B & Y_B \\ -S_B\frac{Y_R}{1-Y_B} & -S_B\frac{1-Y_R-Y_B}{1-Y_B} & S_B \\ S_R & -S_R\frac{1-Y_R-Y_B}{1-Y_R} & -S_R\frac{Y_B}{1-Y_R} \end{bmatrix} \begin{bmatrix} R' \\ G' \\ B' \end{bmatrix} \tag{20.131}$$

whose inverse is readily given as

$$\begin{bmatrix} R' \\ G' \\ B' \end{bmatrix} = \begin{bmatrix} 1 & 0 & \frac{1-Y_R}{S_R} \\ 1 & -\frac{Y_B}{Y_G}\frac{1-Y_B}{S_B} & -\frac{Y_R}{Y_G}\frac{1-Y_R}{S_R} \\ 1 & \frac{1-Y_B}{S_B} & 0 \end{bmatrix} \begin{bmatrix} Y' \\ U_B \\ V_R \end{bmatrix} \tag{20.132}$$

The International Telecommunication Union for Radiocommunication (*ITU-R*) (formerly Comité Consultatif International pour la Radio, or *CCIR*) then defined several standards for the *RGB* primaries, such as the Recommendation BT.470/BT.601 for *standard-definition* 704
television (*SDTV*), which prescribes the NTSC-1953 primaries $[Y_R, Y_B] = [0.299, 0.114]$. Instead, the Recommendation BT.709 for *high-definition television* (*HDTV*) prescribes the
sRGB primaries $[Y_R, Y_B] \overset{(20.65)}{=} [0.2126, 0.0722]$, and the Recommendation BT.2020 for 718
ultra-high-definition television (*UHDTV*) prescribes the corresponding primaries $[Y_R, Y_B] = [0.2627, 0.0593]$.

Regarding the scaling factors, the *YUV color space* (used in the PAL analog broadcast television system) defines $[S_R, S_B] \triangleq [0.615, 0.436]$, yielding the chromaticity plane illustrated
in *Figure 20.17*, while the *YDbDr color space* (used in the SECAM analog broadcast tele- 727
vision system) defines $[S_R, S_B] \triangleq [-4/3, 4/3]$. Instead, the *YPbPr color space* (used in analog component video) defines $[S_R, S_B] \triangleq [1/2, 1/2]$, whose components may then be converted to the *YCbCr color space* (used in digital image/video compression such as JPEG/MPEG-2 8-bit encoding) with the "studio swing" scale/offset $[Y'C_BC_R] \triangleq [16, 128, 128] + [219, 224, 224] \circ [Y'P_BP_R]$. The latter yields a range $[Y'C_BC_R] \in [16, 235] \times [16, 240] \times [16, 240]$ (in contrast to the "full swing" range $[0, 255]^3$) where the extra foot-/headroom of the luminance values accommodate transient signal content such as over-/undershoots from the *reconstruction fil-*
ter, while those of the chrominance channels are instead exploited by the *xvYCC color space* 204
to encode scRGB triplets for use by electronic devices supporting an extended gamut.

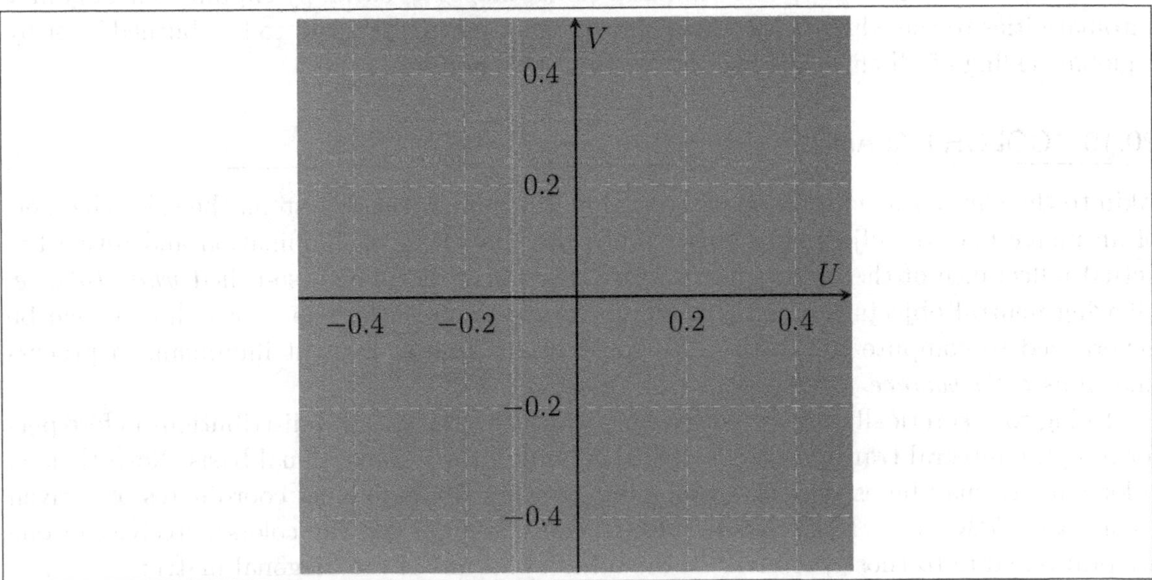

Figure 20.17: YUV Color Space: Illustration of the chrominance of the YUV color space, shown for $Y' = 1/2$ using the sRGB primaries.

20.8.2 YIQ & YCgCo

The YUV chromaticity plane may be rotated by 33° for conversion to the *YIQ color space* (used in the NTSC analog broadcast television system) so as to reduce the bandwidth of

Q compared to I by exploiting the lower sensitivity of the human eye to purple-green than orange-blue opponent pairs.

Instead, the luma and green & orange chrominances of the *YCgCo color space* (used in digital video compression such as H.264/MPEG-4 encoding) are defined to allow the lossless numerical conversion of colors via the forward and backward transformations

$$\begin{bmatrix} Y' \\ C_g \\ C_o \end{bmatrix} \triangleq \begin{bmatrix} 1/4 & 1/2 & 1/4 \\ -1/4 & 1/2 & -1/4 \\ 1/2 & 0 & -1/2 \end{bmatrix} \begin{bmatrix} R' \\ G' \\ B' \end{bmatrix} \tag{20.133}$$

$$\begin{bmatrix} R' \\ G' \\ B' \end{bmatrix} = \begin{bmatrix} 1 & -1 & 1 \\ 1 & 1 & 0 \\ 1 & -1 & -1 \end{bmatrix} \begin{bmatrix} Y' \\ C_g \\ C_o \end{bmatrix} \tag{20.134}$$

such that $[Y', C_g, C_o] \in [0, 1] \times [-1/2, 1/2] \times [-1/2, 1/2]$.

20.9 COLOR MANAGEMENT

Because the coordinates of a point in a color space only characterize a given color if the corresponding primaries of the space are known, the International Color Consortium (*ICC*) proposed to describe the color attributes of a calibrated input (e.g., an image scanner, digital camera or image editing software) or output (e.g., a monitor, screen or printer) device by means of an *ICC profile*. The latter specifies a mapping between the color space of the data (often assumed to be the sRGB standard if not explicitly provided) and a device-independent
711 *profile connection space* (*PCS*), such as the CIE Lab or *XYZ* color spaces, which serves as an intermediate space allowing any *color-matching module* to perform transformations between the color spaces of different devices. Because the gamuts of the input and output devices may differ, the conversion typically entails a *gamut mapping*, either by clipping out-of-gamut chromaticities to the edges of the gamut (yielding an image then said to be "burned"), or by a global scaling of all chromaticities about the white point.

20.10 COLOR BALANCE

701 Akin to the *chromatic adaptation* performed by the human visual system, the color channels of an image may be adjusted in order to abstract the effect of illumination and reveal the actual reflectance of the objects in the scene, thereby performing a so-called *white balance*, allowing neutral objects (i.e., gray or white) to appear as such. The approach can then be generalized to compute the colors that would result from a different illuminant, a process known as *color balance*.

Doing so theoretically requires operating directly on the spectral distributions before performing the integral transform projecting them into a three-dimensional basis. Nevertheless, color balance may be estimated by applying gains on the individual coordinates of a given
684 color space ABC (e.g., *LMS*, *XYZ* or *RGB*), thereby mapping the colors perceived in one
711
704 adaptation state to those perceived in the other by means of the diagonal matrix

$$\begin{bmatrix} A' \\ B' \\ C' \end{bmatrix} \triangleq \begin{bmatrix} \frac{A'_W}{A_W} & 0 & 0 \\ 0 & \frac{B'_W}{B_W} & 0 \\ 0 & 0 & \frac{C'_W}{C_W} \end{bmatrix} \begin{bmatrix} A \\ B \\ C \end{bmatrix} \tag{20.135}$$

The white point of the source illuminant $[A_W, B_W, C_W]$ can then be estimated from the color of an object presumed to be white or neutral gray. Alternatively, the retinex algorithm,
692 which aims at reproducing the combined adaptation of the *retina* and the cortex, estimates

the white point from the maximum value of each color channel in the image, assuming that each channel is fully reflected by some objects of the scene. For the purpose of white balance, the white point of the target illuminant may then be defined as $A'_W = B'_W = C'_W = 1$.

20.11 FURTHER READING

Additional material may be found in books dedicated to color science [Wyszecki and Stiles, 2000], digital color [Stone, 2002], color imaging [Reinhard *et al.*, 2008] and color appearance models [Fairchild, 2013].

CHAPTER 21

HDR Imaging

TABLE OF CONTENTS

21.1 DYNAMIC RANGE

The *contrast* of a luminous signal is a measure of the relative difference of its highest luminance value L_M (or possibly color ΔE) to its average or lowest luminance value L_m within a given field of view, and standard definitions include:

- *contrast ratio*: $$C_R \triangleq \frac{L_M}{L_m} \in [1, \infty] \tag{21.1}$$
- *Weber contrast*: $$C_W \triangleq \frac{L_M - L_m}{L_m} \in [0, \infty] \tag{21.2}$$
- *Michelson contrast*: $$C_M \triangleq \frac{L_M - L_m}{L_M + L_m} \in [0, 1] \tag{21.3}$$

732 where *Equation 21.2* assumes that L_m and L_M correspond to the background and foreground
692 luminances, respectively (as in *Figure 19.11*), while *Equation 21.3* corresponds to the ratio
732 of the peak-to-peak amplitude (or twice the peak amplitude) to twice the average value of a
symmetric wave signal. It then follows that the three definitions are interrelated by

$$C_R = 1 + C_W = \frac{1 + C_M}{1 - C_M} \tag{21.4}$$

Similarly, the *dynamic range* of a signal is a measure of the ratio of its maximum achievable (so-called peak) luminance value to its minimum achievable (so-called noise) luminance value, and standard definitions include:

- *contrast ratio*: $C_R : 1$ (21.5)
- *exposure range* (in stops): $\log_2(C_R)$ (21.6)
- *orders of magnitude*: $\log_{10}(C_R)$ (21.7)
- *signal to noise ratio* (*SNR*) (in dB): $10 \log_{10}(C_R)$ (21.8)

where C_R measures either the *static contrast ratio* achievable at a given moment in time (e.g., by an LCD panel modulating the transmission of a backlight, and/or by locally adjusting a back-light built as an array of LEDs), or the *dynamic contrast ratio* achievable over time (e.g., by modulating the overall intensity of the global backlight of an LCD screen).

678 The vast scope of luminance values that the *human eye* may experience in the real world
689 (as illustrated in *Table 19.2*) is then said to have a *high dynamic range* (*HDR*). In contrast,
actual devices for the acquisition, storage and display of luminance values typically span about two (e.g., high-quality paper print) to three (e.g., typical photographic films, CCD sensors or LCD displays) or even four (e.g., high-end CMOS sensors) orders of magnitude, and are consequently said to have a *low dynamic range* (*LDR*).

21.2 TONE MAPPING

In order to be processed by LDR devices, real-world HDR signals ought to be compressed to
732 a lower *dynamic range*, a technique known as *tone reproduction* (especially when aimed at
faithfully reproducing tones of brightness) or more generally as *tone mapping*. To this end, the most basic approach consists in linearly scaling the input values V by the reciprocal of the highest value V_M contained in the signal

$$V' \triangleq \frac{V}{V_M} \tag{21.9}$$

typically causing a loss of details due to the saturation of high values and/or to the subsequent quantization of low values for digital encoding.

Instead, the signal values may first be converted to *brightness*, either by means of a loga- 690
rithmic response in the spirit of the Weber–Fechner law, or by means of gamma compression
(with $\gamma \in [0,1]$) akin to Stevens's power law, via mapping functions of the form

$$T(t) \triangleq \ln(1+t) \tag{21.10}$$

$$T(t) \triangleq t^{\gamma} \tag{21.11}$$

As an alternative, compression may be carried by means of a *sigmoid function*, either re- 41
stricted to the positive range of input values, or logarithmically scaled so as to emulate the
S-shaped response of visual *photoreceptors* [Naka and Rushton, 1966a, Naka and Rushton, 681
1966b] and photographic films (whereas non-linear response curves are typically applied a
posteriori to the nearly linear output of digital sensors)

$$T(t) \triangleq S(t) \tag{21.12}$$

$$T(t) \triangleq \frac{1+S(\ln(t))}{2} \tag{21.13}$$

In both cases, the compressed and rescaled signal value V' becomes

$$V' \triangleq \frac{T(V \div V_a)}{T(V_M \div V_a)} \tag{21.14}$$

where the spatio-temporal average adaptation level to n input values V_i reads $V_a \triangleq T^{-1}\left(\frac{1}{n}\sum_{i=1}^{n} T(V_i)\right)$.

When solely applied to the luminance channel of a given *xyY* triplet so as to preserve its 712
chromaticity, the resulting LDR *XYZ* triplet is readily given as the input HDR triplet scaled 711
by the factor $c \triangleq \frac{Y'}{Y}$

$$X' \overset{(20.41)}{=} \frac{Y'}{y}x = \frac{cY}{y}x \overset{(20.41)}{=} cX \tag{21.15}$$
713 713

$$Y' \overset{(20.42)}{=} \frac{Y'}{y}y = \frac{cY}{y}y \overset{(20.42)}{=} cY \tag{21.16}$$
713 713

$$Z' \overset{(20.43)}{=} \frac{Y'}{y}(1-x-y) = \frac{cY}{y}(1-x-y) \overset{(20.43)}{=} cZ \tag{21.17}$$
713 713

Instead, the compression scheme may be applied to each individual channel of a given *LMS* 684
triplet in order to model the fact that the different types of visual *photoreceptors* tend to 681
adapt independently, thereby emulating *chromatic adaptation* phenomena. 701

While resorting to parameters that are spatially uniform across a given signal is generally
less computationally expensive, global operators inevitably cause a loss of detail in the case
of a very high *dynamic range*. Observing that human *visual perception* is more sensitive to 732 677
relative contrast than to absolute luminance (due to the local rather than global adaptation of the *photoreceptors*), local operators instead resort to spatially varying parameters 681
(such as the average adaptation level) tailored to the local spatio-temporal vicinity of each
sample value (such as the neighboring pixels of an image), the size of which then ought to
be adequately determined in order to avoid the appearance of haloing or ringing artifacts.
Under the hypothetical assumption of a truly comprehensive model of *visual perception*, an 677
ideal tone-mapping operator would then, in theory, quantitatively evaluate the *brightness* 690
perceived by a given observer in response to a real-world scene, and derive the corresponding input values necessary for a display device to induce a perceptually matching *brightness* 690
[Tumblin and Rushmeier, 1991, Tumblin and Rushmeier, 1993], as illustrated in *Figure 21.1*. 734

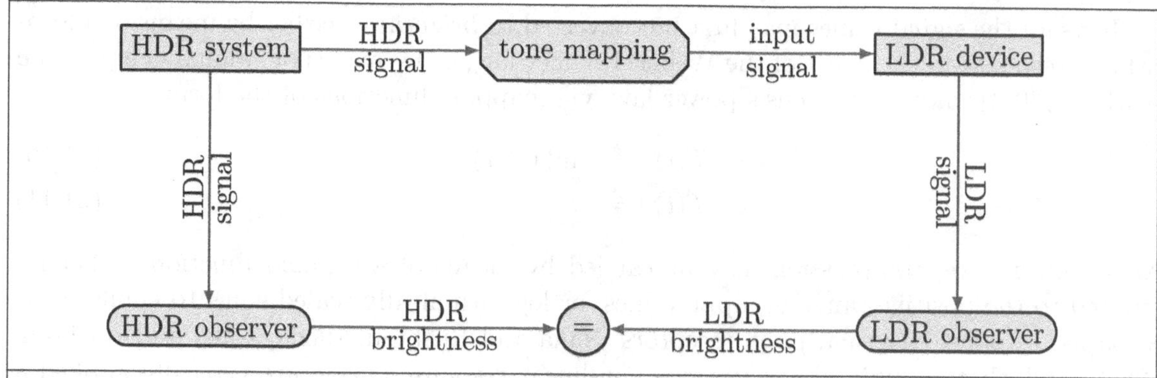

Figure 21.1: Tone Mapping: Illustration of a conceptually ideal, tone-mapping operator (drawn after [Tumblin and Rushmeier, 1991, Fig. 2a] and [Tumblin and Rushmeier, 1993, Fig. 1]).

732 For lack of such a theoretical model, a given (presumably low) *dynamic range* may instead
be optimally exploited by means of image processing techniques such as *histogram matching*,
129 treating the signal value as a *random variable*, which is mapped so as to yield a given target
132 133 *cumulative distribution* based on the properties of the *transformed probability density*. In
the case of a uniform target distribution, the technique is more specifically referred to as
histogram equalization, which consists in creating a histogram of the input values by dividing
their range into a fixed number of bins, the normalized histogram thus representing the
131 discretized *probability density* of the signal. According to the probability integral transform
rule, the corresponding CDF may then be applied to the input signal values in order to yield a uniform distribution, performing *dynamic range expansion* as a side effect by mapping the signal to the full LDR extent. Rather than operating globally on the entire signal, *adaptive histogram equalization* (*AHE*) instead creates a local histogram from the neighborhood of each input value. However, because doing so can occasionally overly exaggerate contrast, the histogram values are typically clipped to a predetermined threshold value (the excess being then optionally redistributed to neighboring or to all bins) before normalization, thereby limiting the slope of the resulting CDF, a technique known as *contrast-limited adaptive histogram equalization* (*CLAHE*).

21.3 FURTHER READING

Additional material may be found in books dedicated to HDR imaging [Reinhard *et al.*, 2005, Reinhard *et al.*, 2010] [Banterle *et al.*, 2011] and to HDR video [Myszkowski *et al.*, 2008].

Epilogue

CHAPTER 22

Conclusion

TABLE OF CONTENTS

22.1 VERIFICATION AND VALIDATION

Realism has been a long-standing goal in computer graphics, and the scientific advances made since the infancy of the field have allowed early, distinctively synthetic images [Newell and Blinn, 1977] to progressively reach an increasing degree of photo-realism [Nakamae and Tadamura, 1995, Slusallek, 1997, Purgathofer, 2003], to the point of becoming qualitatively indistinguishable from actual photographs. Despite those achievements, many open issues still stand on the way to physical realism, which, in contrast to photo-realism, aims for quantitative predictions [Wilkie *et al.*, 2009], and it may be argued that capturing and simulating physically accurate illumination [Debevec, 2004] still remain grand challenges for engineering.

738 As illustrated in *Figure 22.1*, industrial standards typically assess the quality of a simulation system via verification and validation (*V&V*), where *verification* evaluates the compliance of the system with the design specifications (thereby addressing what is colloquially known as "building the system right"), while *validation* assures the suitable accuracy of the designed system for a given application (which is colloquially known as "building the right system"). In essence, validation is therefore concerned with substantiating the conformity of the theoretical model to the real world, the source of their disparity lying in the *model uncertainty*. In practice, though, the real world may only be observed by means of experimental measurements, thereby introducing a potential source of error referred to as *experimental uncertainty*. Aside from trivial cases, the outcome predicted by a theoretical model might likewise only be determined by means of numerical simulation, and verification is thus concerned with identifying programming errors in software implementations (colloquially known as "computer bugs"), quantization errors due to the limited numerical precision of floating-point representations (e.g., round-off errors) and discretization errors due to approximate numerical schemes (e.g., truncation of infinite series, projection into a finite set of basis func-
36 tions, and discrete numerical integration and *root finding*), all of which being collectively referred to as *numerical uncertainty*. Similarly, theoretical models and their numerical implementation typically depend on a number of external parameters whose exact values might be unknown, and validating the predictions of the simulation system against experimentally measured observations is in turn subject to *parameter uncertainty*.

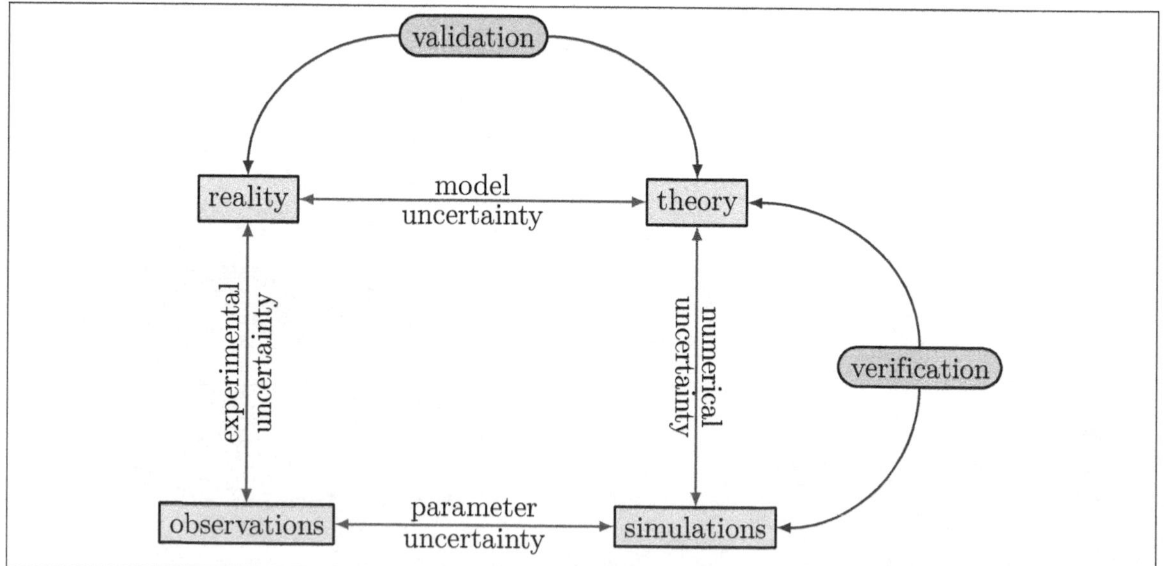

Figure 22.1: Verification and Validation: Illustration of the verification and validation cycle, and of the various types of uncertainty that it is prone to.

In the context of image synthesis, quality assessment entails verifying and validating

each individual component of a given predictive rendering system [Greenberg *et al.*, 1997],
including the goniometric evaluation of the spectral emittance of *light sources* and of the mi- 429
croscopic/mesoscopic material reflectance properties [Schregle and Wienold, 2004, Schregle,
2004, Ch. 7], the geometric evaluation of the macroscopic models, the radiometric evaluation
of the physically based *light transport* algorithms [Ulbricht *et al.*, 2005], as well as the pho- 563
tometric and colorimetric evaluation of the resulting sensorial/perceptual response [Bärz *et
al.*, 2010]. A so-defined V&V methodology may then not only be used to assess the quality
of a particular *light transport* algorithm, such as the *radiosity method* [Meyer *et al.*, 1986] or 563
cluster-based progressive hierarchical radiosity [Myszkowski and Kunii, 2000], but also serve 593
as a basis to evaluate complete rendering systems [Khodulev and Kopylov, 1996], such as the
Radiance lighting simulation software [Ward Larson, 1990, Ward Larson, 1994, Ward Larson
and Shakespeare, 1998, Ward Larson and Shakespeare, 2004].

To this end, systematic verification can be carried by means of a standard set of virtual
test scenes [Smits and Jensen, 2000] for which a closed-form solution is either obtained using
analytic methods [Szirmay-Kalos *et al.*, 2001], or for which a "ground-truth" solution has 575
been a priori computed using a "reference" numerical scheme. Similarly, validation may be
carried by means of standardized measurements of geometric models, luminaire emission and
surface reflectance for a given real-world environment [Drago and Myszkowski, 2001], and the 472
synthesized results compared either against a sparse set of discrete radiometric measurements (potentially allowing a denser set to be obtained by then defining a mapping of the pixel values from a photograph to actual luminance values [Karner and Prantl, 1996]) or directly against a dense array of measured data obtained from a calibrated CCD camera [Pattanaik *et al.*, 1997]. In both cases, the error ought to be quantified with respect to a given metric, and while pixel-to-pixel RMSE might be adequate for verification purposes, perceptual error metrics are generally better suited to the validation of rendering systems aimed at visual applications [Rushmeier *et al.*, 1995].

22.2 FURTHER READING

Additional material may be found in books dedicated to interactive computer graphics [Newman and Sproull, 1979, Foley and van Dam, 1982, Sung *et al.*, 2008] or to computer graphics overall [Watt, 1999, Foley *et al.*, 1994] [Foley *et al.*, 1990, Foley *et al.*, 1995, Hughes *et al.*, 2013] [Shirley, 2002, Shirley and Marschner, 2009, Marschner and Shirley, 2016] [Hearn and Baker, 1997, McConnell, 2005, Goldman, 2009, Kurachi, 2011, Gomes *et al.*, 2012, Gortler, 2012]. Additional material can also be found in primers dedicated to ray tracing [Glassner, 1989a, Suffern, 2007], in surveys dedicated to the ray-tracing literature [Speer, 1992] and in books dedicated to realistic ray tracing [Shirley, 2000, Shirley and Morley, 2003]. Additional material may finally be found in books dedicated to digital image synthesis [Glassner, 1994], in compendia dedicated to global illumination [Dutré, 2003] and in books dedicated to real-time rendering [Möller and Haines, 1999, Möller and Haines, 2002, Möller *et al.*, 2008] or to physically based rendering [Pharr and Humphreys, 2004, Pharr and Humphreys, 2010].

Appendices

APPENDIX A

Standard Units

TABLE OF CONTENTS

A.1 SI BASE UNITS

The Système International (SI) d'Unités is an internationally recognized standard system of
744 measurement units. As illustrated in *Table A.1*, the latter defines seven base units forming
a set of mutually independent dimensions, and from which other units are derived.

Table A.1: SI Base Units: Base units defined by the Système International d'Unités.

Unit	Symbol	Quantity
meter	m	length
kilogram	kg	mass
second	s	time
ampere	A	electric current
kelvin	K	temperature
candela	cd	luminous intensity
mole	mol	amount of substance

A.2 SI DERIVED UNITS

The International System of Units represents derived units as powers, products and quotients
744 744 of *SI base units*. As illustrated in *Table A.2*, various instances of derived units exist for which
a specific name and symbol have been defined.

Table A.2: SI Derived Units: Instances of named units derived from the SI base units (the latter portion of which are not officially part of the standard).

Unit	Symbol	Quantity	Equivalence
radian	rad	angle	$m{\cdot}m^{-1}$
steradian	sr	solid angle	$m^2{\cdot}m^{-2}$
hertz	Hz	frequency	s^{-1}
newton	N	force	$kg{\cdot}m{\cdot}s^{-2}$
pascal	Pa	pressure	$N{\cdot}m^{-2}$
joule	J	energy	N·m
watt	W	power	$J{\cdot}s^{-1}$
coulomb	C	electric charge	s·A
volt	V	electric voltage	$W{\cdot}A^{-1}$
farad	F	electric capacitance	$C{\cdot}V^{-1}$
lumen	lm	luminous flux	cd·sr
lux	lx	illuminance	$lm{\cdot}m^{-2}$
talbot	T	luminous energy	lm·s
nit	nt	luminance	$cd{\cdot}m^{-2}$
diopter	dpt	optical power	m^{-1}

A.3 NON-SI UNITS

744 For historical and/or cultural reasons, non-decimal multiples and fractions of *SI base units*
744 or *SI derived units* are commonly used in several scientific disciplines. As illustrated in
745 *Table A.3*, various instances of non-SI units exist for which a standard equivalence has been
defined.

Table A.3: Non-SI Units: Instances of non-SI units defined in terms of SI base or derived units.

Unit	Symbol	Quantity	Equivalence
foot	ft	length	0.3048 m
degree of arc	°	angle	$\pi/180$ rad
minute of arc	arcmin	angle	$1/60°$
second of arc	arcsec	angle	$1/60$ arcmin
standard atmosphere	atm	pressure	101325 Pa

A.4 METRIC PREFIXES

In the metric system, decimal multiples and fractions of the various units are defined by prepending the latter with one of the standard prefixes given in *Table A.4*. 745

Table A.4: Metric Prefixes: Standard prefixes defining decimal multiples and fractions of the various metric units.

Prefix	Symbol	Factor
yotta	Y	10^{24}
zetta	Z	10^{21}
exa	E	10^{18}
peta	P	10^{15}
tera	T	10^{12}
giga	G	10^{9}
mega	M	10^{6}
kilo	k	10^{3}
hecto	h	10^{2}
deca	da	10^{1}
—	—	10^{0}
deci	d	10^{-1}
centi	c	10^{-2}
milli	m	10^{-3}
micro	μ	10^{-6}
nano	n	10^{-9}
pico	p	10^{-12}
femto	f	10^{-15}
atto	a	10^{-18}
zepto	z	10^{-21}
yocto	y	10^{-24}

APPENDIX B

Numerical Data

TABLE OF CONTENTS

B.1 NUMERICAL CONSTANTS

748 As illustrated in *Table B.1*, mathematical constants are special numbers whose fixed numerical value may be used to define other mathematical or physical constants.

Table B.1: Mathematical Constants: Numerical value of various mathematical constants.

Constant	Symbol	Value
Archimedes's constant	π	$3.1415926535897932\ldots$
Euler's number	e	$2.7182818284590452\ldots$
golden ratio	φ	$(1+\sqrt{5}) \div 2$

Similarly, physical constants are universal quantities, and the numerical values of instances from which various other physical constants can be defined are readily provided in
748 *Table B.2.*

Table B.2: Physical Constants: Numerical value of various physical constants.

Constant	Symbol	Value	Unit
speed of light in vacuum	c	299792458	$\mathrm{m{\cdot}s^{-1}}$
vacuum permeability	μ_0	$4\pi \times 10^{-7}$	$\mathrm{N{\cdot}A^{-2}}$
Boltzmann's constant	k	$1.3806488\ldots \times 10^{-23}$	$\mathrm{J{\cdot}K^{-1}}$
Planck's constant	h	$6.62606957\ldots \times 10^{-34}$	$\mathrm{J{\cdot}s}$

B.2 REFRACTIVE INDICES

The refractive index $n(\lambda)$ of a particular transparent medium as a function of the wavelength λ of light (in the vacuum, and expressed in micrometers) is typically determined empirically by fitting n coefficients c_i of a predetermined equation to measured data.

To this end, *Cauchy's equation* reads

$$n(\lambda) = \sum_{i=0}^{n-1} \frac{c_i}{\lambda^{2i}} \tag{B.1}$$

which only models normal dispersion (i.e., a decreasing refractive index with increasing wavelength, as is the case in the visible range for most transparent materials such as air and glass) in the visible spectrum. As an alternative, the *Sellmeier equation* is expressed as a sum of absorption resonances of strengths c_i at wavelengths λ_i

$$n(\lambda)^2 - 1 = \sum_{i=0}^{n-1} c_i \frac{\lambda^2}{\lambda^2 - \lambda_i^2} \tag{B.2}$$

which additionally models anomalous dispersion (i.e., a refractive index increasing with wavelength, as is typically the case for X-rays) and is overall more accurate across the infrared, visible and ultraviolet spectrum.

B.2.1 Air

The refractive index of standard dry air (i.e., at a temperature of 15 °C, a pressure of 1 atm, 0 % humidity and with 450 ppm CO_2 content) is given by *Ciddor's equation* [Ciddor, 1996] as

$$n(\lambda) - 1 = \frac{0.05792105}{238.0185 - \lambda^{-2}} + \frac{0.00167917}{57.362 - \lambda^{-2}} \tag{B.3}$$

which may then be used to derive accurate results over a broad range of wavelengths and under extreme environmental conditions of temperature, pressure and humidity.

B.2.2 Glass

While *soda-lime glass* (used for windowpanes and commodity glassware) is composed of a mixture of materials, *fused silica* (also called *fused quartz*) is pure, thereby providing superior properties for optical devices in the ultraviolet range. In the visible range, *crown glass* exhibits a relatively low refractive index and dispersion, and is commonly used in optical lenses and *image-forming optical systems*, whereas *flint glass* exhibits a relatively high refractive index 647
and dispersion, thereby making it well suited for the manufacturing of plano-concave lenses that, combined together with a convex lens made of crown glass, form achromatic doublets used to correct chromatic aberration.

The optical dispersion of fused silica is given by the Sellmeier equation with coefficients [Bass, 1995b, Table 23]

$$n(\lambda)^2 - 1 = \frac{0.6961663\lambda^2}{\lambda^2 - 0.0684043^2} + \frac{0.4079426\lambda^2}{\lambda^2 - 0.1162414^2} + \frac{0.8974794\lambda^2}{\lambda^2 - 9.896161^2} \tag{B.4}$$

while that of borosilicate crown glass (BK7) reads

$$n(\lambda)^2 - 1 = \frac{1.03961212\lambda^2}{\lambda^2 - 0.00600069867} + \frac{0.231792344\lambda^2}{\lambda^2 - 0.0200179144} + \frac{1.01046945\lambda^2}{\lambda^2 - 103.560653} \tag{B.5}$$

and that of barium flint glass (BaF10) is given by

$$n(\lambda)^2 - 1 = \frac{1.5851495\lambda^2}{\lambda^2 - 0.00926681282} + \frac{0.143559385\lambda^2}{\lambda^2 - 0.0424489805} + \frac{1.08521269\lambda^2}{\lambda^2 - 105.613573} \tag{B.6}$$

B.2.3 Crystals

The optical dispersion of carbon diamond at room temperature is given by the Sellmeier equation with coefficients [Bass, 1995b, Table 22]

$$n(\lambda)^2 - 1 = \frac{4.3356\lambda^2}{\lambda^2 - 0.1060^2} + \frac{0.3306\lambda^2}{\lambda^2 - 0.1750^2} \tag{B.7}$$

Bibliography

[Aboshiha *et al.*, 2014] Jonathan Aboshiha, Vy Luong, Jill Cowing, Adam M. Dubis, James W. Bainbridge, Robin R. Ali, Andrew R. Webster, Anthony T. Moore, Frederick W. Fitzke, and Michel Michaelides. Dark-Adaptation Functions in Molecularly Confirmed Achromatopsia and the Implications for Assessment in Retinal Therapy Trials. *Investigative Ophthalmology & Visual Science*, 55(10):6340–6349, October 2014. 689

[Abramowitz and Stegun, 1972] Milton Abramowitz and Irene A. Stegun. *Handbook of Mathematical Functions with Formulas, Graphs, and Mathematical Tables.* U.S. Department of Commerce – National Bureau of Standards, 10th edition, December 1972. 64

[Adamson *et al.*, 2001] Andrew Adamson, Ken Bielenberg, James Hegedus, Lucia Modesto, Jonathan Gibbs, Vanitha Rangaraju, Rob Vogt, Scott Singer, Arnauld Lamorlette, Scott Peterson, Juan Buhler, Mark Wendell, and George Bruder. Shrek: The Story Behind the Screen. In *ACM SIGGRAPH Courses*, number 19. ACM Press, April 2001. 9

[Adelson and Pentland, 1996] Edward H. Adelson and Alex P. Pentland. The Perception of Shading and Reflectance. In David C. Knill and Whitman Richards, editors, *Perception as Bayesian Inference*, chapter 11, pages 409–423. Cambridge University Press, 1996. 701

[Adelson, 2000] Edward H. Adelson. Lightness Perception and Lightness Illusions. In M. Gazzaniga, editor, *The New Cognitive Neurosciences*, chapter 24, pages 339–351. MIT Press, 2nd edition, 2000. 699

[Adler, 1996] Joan Adler. Israel: Graphics and Visualization Education. *SIGGRAPH Computer Graphics*, 30(3):16–16, August 1996. 8

[Áfra, 2012] Attila T. Áfra. Incoherent Ray Tracing without Acceleration Structures. In *Eurographics Short Papers*, pages 97–100. Eurographics Association, 2012. 409

[Agate *et al.*, 1991] Mark Agate, Richard L. Grimsdale, and Paul F. Lister. The HERO Algorithm for Ray-Tracing Octrees. In *Proceedings of EGGH – The Eurographics Workshop on Graphics Hardware*, pages 61–73. Eurographics Association, 1991. 380

[Aitken *et al.*, 2004] Matt Aitken, Greg Butler, Dan Lemmon, Eric Saindon, Dana Peters, and Guy Williams. The Lord of the Rings: The Visual Effects that Brought Middle Earth to the Screen. In *ACM SIGGRAPH Courses*, number 10. ACM Press, 2004. 9

[Amanatides and Woo, 1987] John Amanatides and Andrew Chung How Woo. A Fast Voxel Traversal Algorithm for Ray Tracing. In *Proceedings of Eurographics – The Annual Conference of the European Association for Computer Graphics*, pages 3–10. Eurographics Association, 1987. 374, 391

[Ambarzumian, 1942] V. A. Ambarzumian. A New Method for Computing Light Scattering in Turbid Media. *Izvestiya Akademii Nauk SSSR*, 3:97–104, 1942. 485

[ANSI, 2010] ANSI. *Nomenclature and Definitions for Illuminating Engineering*, volume RP-16-10. Illuminating Engineering Society, 2010. 473, 474

[Appel, 1968] Arthur Appel. Some Techniques for Shading Machine Renderings of Solids. In *Proceedings of the AFIPS Spring Joint Computer Conference*, pages 37–45, April 1968. 5, 598

[Arnaldi *et al.*, 1987] Bruno Arnaldi, Thierry Priol, and Kadi Bouatouch. A New Space Subdivision Method for Ray Tracing CSG Modelled Scenes. *The Visual Computer*, 3(2):98–108, August 1987. 390

[Arvo and Kirk, 1987] James Richard Arvo and David Kirk. Fast Ray Tracing by Ray Classification. *SIGGRAPH Computer Graphics (Proceedings of SIGGRAPH – The ACM International Conference on Computer Graphics and Interactive Techniques)*, 21(4):55–64, August 1987. 411, 412

[Arvo and Kirk, 1988] James Richard Arvo and David Kirk. Fast Ray Tracing by Ray Classification. In Kenneth I. Joy, Charles W. Grant, Nelson L. Max, and Lansing Hatfield, editors, *Tutorial: Computer Graphics; Image Synthesis*, pages 196–205. Computer Science Press, 1988. 411

[Arvo and Kirk, 1989] James Richard Arvo and David Kirk. A Survey of Ray Tracing Acceleration Techniques. In Andrew S. Glassner, editor, *An Introduction to Ray Tracing*, chapter 6, pages 201–262. Academic Press, 1989. 359, 415

[Arvo and Kirk, 1990] James Richard Arvo and David Kirk. Particle Transport and Image Synthesis. *SIGGRAPH Computer Graphics (Proceedings of SIGGRAPH – The ACM International Conference on Computer Graphics and Interactive Techniques)*, 24(4):63–66, September 1990. 612, 614, 616

[Arvo, 1986] James Richard Arvo. Backward Ray Tracing. In *ACM SIGGRAPH Courses*, volume 12, pages 259–263. ACM Press, August 1986. 633

[Arvo, 1990a] James Richard Arvo. A Simple Method for Box-Sphere Intersection Testing. In Andrew S. Glassner, editor, *Graphics Gems I*, chapter V.8, pages 335–339. Academic Press, 1990. 369

[Arvo, 1990b] James Richard Arvo. Ray Tracing with Meta-Hierarchies. In *ACM SIGGRAPH Courses*, volume 24, pages 56–62. ACM Press, August 1990. 409

[Arvo, 1993] James Richard Arvo. Transfer Equations in Global Illumination. In *ACM SIGGRAPH Courses*. ACM Press, August 1993. 571

[Arvo, 1995a] James Richard Arvo. *Analytic Methods for Simulated Light Transport*. PhD thesis, Yale University, December 1995. 246, 247, 256, 257, 262, 584, 585

[Arvo, 1995b] James Richard Arvo. Applications of Irradiance Tensors to the Simulation of Non-Lambertian Phenomena. In *Proceedings of SIGGRAPH – The ACM International Conference on Computer Graphics and Interactive Techniques*, pages 335–342. ACM Press, 1995. 246, 247, 256, 262, 263, 501, 584, 585

[Arvo, 1995c] James Richard Arvo. Stratified Sampling of Spherical Triangles. In *Proceedings of SIGGRAPH – The ACM International Conference on Computer Graphics and Interactive Techniques*, pages 437–438. ACM Press, 1995. 257

[Asare *et al.*, 2002] Sampson D. Asare, Petros M. Mashwama, and Steve Cunningham. Building Computer Graphics Education in Developing African Countries. In *ACM SIGGRAPH Conference Abstracts and Applications*, pages 46–48. ACM Press, 2002. 8

[Ashdown, 1994] Ian Ashdown. *Radiosity: A Programmer's Perspective.* John Wiley & Sons, 1994. 596

[Ashikhmin and Premože, 2007] Michael Ashikhmin and Simon Premože. Distribution-Based BRDFs. Technical report, School of Computing, University of Utah, March 2007. 539, 542

[Ashikhmin and Shirley, 2000a] Michael Ashikhmin and Peter Schuyler Shirley. An Anisotropic Phong BRDF Model. *Journal of Graphics Tools (JGT)*, 5(2):25–32, February 2000. 520, 539, 556

[Ashikhmin and Shirley, 2000b] Michael Ashikhmin and Peter Schuyler Shirley. An Anisotropic Phong Light Reflection Model. Technical Report UUCS-00-014, School of Computing, University of Utah, 2000. 520, 539, 556

[Ashikhmin *et al.*, 2000] Michael Ashikhmin, Simon Premože, and Peter Schuyler Shirley. A Microfacet-Based BRDF Generator. In *Proceedings of SIGGRAPH – The ACM International Conference on Computer Graphics and Interactive Techniques*, pages 65–74. ACM Press, 2000. 532, 541, 542

[Ashikhmin *et al.*, 2001a] Michael Ashikhmin, Stephen Robert Marschner, Peter Schuyler Shirley, and Jos Stam. State of the Art in Modeling and Measuring of Surface Reflection. In *ACM SIGGRAPH Courses*, volume 10. ACM Press, 2001. 562

[Ashikhmin *et al.*, 2001b] Michael Ashikhmin, Simon Premože, Peter Schuyler Shirley, and Brian Edward Smits. A Variance Analysis of the Metropolis Light Transport Algorithm. *Computers & Graphics*, 25(2):287–294, April 2001. 622

[Bailey and Cunningham, 2005] Mike Bailey and Steve Cunningham. Computer Graphics in Education. *IEEE Computer Graphics and Applications*, 25(5):23–23, September 2005. 8

[Banterle *et al.*, 2011] Francesco Banterle, Alessandro Artusi, Kurt Debattista, and Alan Chalmers. *Advanced High Dynamic Range Imaging: Theory and Practice.* A. K. Peters/CRC Press, 2011. 734

[Barry and Goldman, 1988] Phillip J. Barry and Ronald N. Goldman. A Recursive Evaluation Algorithm for a Class of Catmull-Rom Splines. *SIGGRAPH Computer Graphics (Proceedings of SIGGRAPH – The ACM International Conference on Computer Graphics and Interactive Techniques)*, 22(4):199–204, June 1988. 349

[Bartz, 2003] Dirk Bartz. Virtual Endoscopy in Research and Clinical Practice. In *Eurographics State of the Art Reports.* Eurographics Association, 2003. 10

[Bärz *et al.*, 2010] Jakob Bärz, Niklas Henrich, and Stefan Müller. Validating Photometric and Colorimetric Consistency of Physically-Based Image Synthesis. In *Proceedings of CGIV – The European Conference on Colour in Graphics, Imaging, and Vision*, pages 148–154. Society for Imaging Science and Technology, June 2010. 739

[Bass, 1995a] Michael Bass. *Handbook of Optics – Volume I: Fundamentals, Techniques, and Design.* McGraw-Hill, 2nd edition, 1995. 437

[Bass, 1995b] Michael Bass. *Handbook of Optics – Volume II: Devices, Measurements, and Properties*. McGraw-Hill, 2nd edition, 1995. 437, 749

[Bass, 1995c] Michael Bass. *Handbook of Optics – Volume III: Classical Optics, Vision Optics, X-Ray Optics*. McGraw-Hill, 2nd edition, 1995. 437

[Bass, 1995d] Michael Bass. *Handbook of Optics – Volume IV: Fiber Optics and Nonlinear Optics*. McGraw-Hill, 2nd edition, 1995. 437

[Bauszat *et al.*, 2010] Pablo Bauszat, Martin Eisemann, and Marcus A. Magnor. The Minimal Bounding Volume Hierarchy. In *Proceedings of VMV – The Workshop on Vision, Modeling, and Visualization*, pages 227–234. Eurographics Association, 2010. 368

[Bayakovsky, 1996] Yuri M. Bayakovsky. Russia: Computer Graphics Education Takes off in the 1990s. *SIGGRAPH Computer Graphics*, 30(3):21–22, August 1996. 8

[Beckmann and Spizzichino, 1963] Petr Beckmann and André Spizzichino. *The Scattering of Electromagnetic Waves from Rough Surfaces*. Pergamon, March 1963. 511

[Beckmann, 1965] Petr Beckmann. Shadowing of Random Rough Surfaces. *IEEE Transactions on Antennas and Propagation*, 13(3):384–388, May 1965. 511

[Bekaert *et al.*, 2003] Philippe Bekaert, Philipp Slusallek, Ronald Cools, Vlastimil Havran, and Hans-Peter Seidel. A Custom Designed Density Estimation Method for Light Transport. Technical Report MPI-I-2003-4-004, Max-Planck-Institut für Informatik, April 2003. 637, 639, 641

[Bekaert, 1999] Philippe Bekaert. *Hierarchical and Stochastic Algorithms for Radiosity*. PhD thesis, Department of Computer Science, Katholieke Universiteit Leuven, December 1999. 157, 158

[Benthin *et al.*, 2002] Carsten Benthin, Tim Dahmen, Ingo Wald, and Philipp Slusallek. Interactive Headlight Simulation – A Case Study of Interactive Distributed Ray Tracing –. In *Proceedings of EGPGV – The Eurographics Symposium on Parallel Graphics and Visualization*, pages 83–88. Eurographics Association, 2002. 9

[Bentley and Friedman, 1979] Jon Louis Bentley and Jerome H. Friedman. Data Structures for Range Searching. *ACM Computing Surveys*, 11(4):397–409, December 1979. 357

[Bentley, 1975] Jon Louis Bentley. Multidimensional Binary Search Trees Used for Associative Searching. *Communications of the ACM*, 18(9):509–517, September 1975. 381

[Bikker, 2007] Jacco Bikker. Real-Time Ray Tracing through the Eyes of a Game Developer. In *Proceedings of RT – The IEEE Symposium on Interactive Ray Tracing*, pages 1–10. IEEE Computer Society, 2007. 9

[Bittner and Havran, 2009] Jiří Bittner and Vlastimil Havran. RDH: Ray Distribution Heuristics for Construction of Spatial Data Structures. In *Proceedings of SCCG – The Spring Conference on Computer Graphics*, pages 51–58. ACM Press, 2009. 400

[Bittner *et al.*, 2013] Jiří Bittner, Michal Hapala, and Vlastimil Havran. Fast Insertion-Based Optimization of Bounding Volume Hierarchies. *Computer Graphics Forum*, 32(1):85–100, February 2013. 400

[Blasi *et al.*, 1993] Philippe Blasi, Bertrand Le Saëc, and Christophe Schlick. A Rendering Algorithm for Discrete Volume Density Objects. *Computer Graphics Forum (Proceedings of Eurographics – The Annual Conference of the European Association for Computer Graphics)*, 12(3):201–210, August 1993. 453, 460

[Blinn, 1977] James Frederick Blinn. Models of Light Reflection for Computer Synthesized Pictures. *SIGGRAPH Computer Graphics (Proceedings of SIGGRAPH – The ACM International Conference on Computer Graphics and Interactive Techniques)*, 11(2):192–198, July 1977. 6, 511, 515, 534

[Blinn, 1978a] James Frederick Blinn. *Computer Display of Curved Surfaces.* PhD thesis, The University of Utah, 1978. 6

[Blinn, 1978b] James Frederick Blinn. Simulation of Wrinkled Surfaces. *SIGGRAPH Computer Graphics (Proceedings of SIGGRAPH – The ACM International Conference on Computer Graphics and Interactive Techniques)*, 12(3):286–292, August 1978. 6

[Blinn, 1982] James Frederick Blinn. Light Reflection Functions for Simulation of Clouds and Dusty Surfaces. *SIGGRAPH Computer Graphics (Proceedings of SIGGRAPH – The ACM International Conference on Computer Graphics and Interactive Techniques)*, 16(3):21–29, July 1982. 482

[Blinn, 2005] James Frederick Blinn. What Is a Pixel? *IEEE Computer Graphics and Applications*, 25(5):82–87, September 2005. 200

[Borgefors, 1986] Gunilla Borgefors. Distance Transformations in Digital Images. *Computer Vision, Graphics, and Image Processing*, 34(3):344–371, June 1986. 388

[Borshukov, 2003] George Borshukov. Measured BRDF in Film Production: Realistic Cloth Appearance for "The Matrix Reloaded". In *ACM SIGGRAPH Sketches*, pages 1–1. ACM Press, 2003. 473

[Boudet *et al.*, 2005] Antoine Boudet, Paul Pitot, David Pratmarty, and Mathias Paulin. Photon Splatting for Participating Media. In *Proceedings of GRAPHITE – The International Conference on Computer Graphics and Interactive Techniques in Australasia and Southeast Asia*, pages 197–204. ACM Press, 2005. 643

[Bouguer, 1729] Pierre Bouguer. *Essai d'Optique, sur la Gradation de la Lumière.* Claude Jombert, 1729. 463

[Bouguer, 1760] Pierre Bouguer. *Traité d'Optique sur la Gradation de la Lumière.* M. l'Abbé de la Caille, 1760. 505

[Bouville, 1985] Christian Bouville. Bounding Ellipsoids for Ray-Fractal Intersection. *SIGGRAPH Computer Graphics (Proceedings of SIGGRAPH – The ACM International Conference on Computer Graphics and Interactive Techniques)*, 19(3):45–52, July 1985. 359

[Bowmaker and Dartnall, 1980] J. K. Bowmaker and H. J. A. Dartnall. Visual Pigments of Rods and Cones in a Human Retina. *The Journal of Physiology*, 298(1):501–511, January 1980. 682

[Bredow *et al.*, 2007] Rob Bredow, David Schaub, Daniel Kramer, Matthew Hausman, Danny Dimian, and R. Stirling Duguid. Surf's Up: The Making of an Animated Documentary. In *ACM SIGGRAPH Courses*, number 12, pages 1–123. ACM Press, 2007. 9

[Bresenham, 1965] Jack E. Bresenham. Algorithm for Computer Control of a Digital Plotter. *IBM Systems Journal*, 4(1):25–30, March 1965. 4, 374

[Brodlie and Mumford, 1996] Ken W. Brodlie and A. M. Mumford. United Kingdom: Support Group Provides National Focus for Computer Graphics Education. *SIGGRAPH Computer Graphics*, 30(3):28–29, August 1996. 8

[Brown and Cunningham, 2007] Judy Brown and Steve Cunningham. A History of ACM SIGGRAPH. *Communications of the ACM*, 50(5):54–61, May 2007. 5

[Brown, 1980] Gary S. Brown. Shadowing by Non-Gaussian Random Surfaces. *IEEE Transactions on Antennas and Propagation*, 28(6):788–790, November 1980. 542

[Brown, 1992] Judith R. Brown. The Multifaceted Blackboard: Computer Graphics in Higher Education. *Interactive Learning through Visualization: The Impact of Computer Graphics in Education*, pages 103–113, 1992. 8

[Browne, 2007] Cameron Browne. Impossible Fractals. *Computers & Graphics*, 31(4):659–667, August 2007. 698

[Brunet and Navazo, 1996] Pere Brunet and Isabel Navazo. Spain: Computer Graphics Education Evolves with Curricula Structure. *SIGGRAPH Computer Graphics*, 30(3):23–24, August 1996. 8

[Brunetti, 1998] Gino Brunetti. Computer Graphics in the European 5th Framework Program for Research and Technological Development. *SIGGRAPH Computer Graphics*, 32(1):20–21, February 1998. 8

[Budge *et al.*, 2008] Brian C. Budge, Daniel Coming, Derek Norpchen, and Kenneth I. Joy. Accelerated Building and Ray Tracing of Restricted BSP Trees. In *Proceedings of RT – The IEEE Symposium on Interactive Ray Tracing*, pages 167–174. IEEE Computer Society, 2008. 386

[Cameron, 1996a] Gordon Cameron. Special Issue on Computer Graphics Around the World. *SIGGRAPH Computer Graphics*, 30(2), May 1996. 8

[Cameron, 1996b] Gordon Cameron. Special Issue on Computer Graphics Education. *SIGGRAPH Computer Graphics*, 30(3), August 1996. 8

[Campbell and Robson, 1968] Fergus W. Campbell and J. G. Robson. Application of Fourier Analysis to the Visibility of Gratings. *Journal of Physiology*, 197(3):551–566, August 1968. 696, 697

[Cassen *et al.*, 1995] T. Cassen, Kalpathi Raman Subramanian, and Zbigniew Michalewicz. Near-Optimal Construction of Partitioning Trees using Evolutionary Techniques. In *Proceedings of Graphics Interface – The Canadian Annual Conference on Computer Graphics, Interactive Systems, and Human-Computer Interaction*, pages 263–271. Canadian Human-Computer Communications Society, May 1995. 386

[Catmull and Rom, 1974] Edwin Earl Catmull and Raphael Rom. A Class of Local Interpolating Splines. *Computer Aided Geometric Design*, 74:317–326, 1974. 349

[Catmull, 1972] Edwin Earl Catmull. A System for Computer Generated Movies. In *Proceedings of the ACM Annual Conference*, volume 1, pages 422–431. ACM Press, 1972. 5

[Catmull, 1974] Edwin Earl Catmull. *A Subdivision Algorithm for Computer Display of Curved Surfaces.* PhD thesis, Department of Computer Science, University of Utah, December 1974. 5

[Cazals and Puech, 1997] Frédéric Cazals and Claude Puech. Bucket-Like Space Partitioning Data Structures with Applications to Ray-Tracing. In *Proceedings of SoCG – The Annual ACM Symposium on Computational Geometry*, pages 11–20. ACM Press, 1997. 410

[Cazals *et al.*, 1995] Frédéric Cazals, George Drettakis, and Claude Puech. Filtering, Clustering and Hierarchy Construction: a New Solution for Ray-Tracing Complex Scenes. *Computer Graphics Forum (Proceedings of Eurographics – The Annual Conference of the European Association for Computer Graphics)*, 14(3):371–382, August 1995. 410

[Cerezo *et al.*, 2005] Eva Cerezo, Frederic Pérez, Xavier Pueyo, Francisco José Serón, and François X. Sillion. A Survey on Participating Media Rendering Techniques. *The Visual Computer*, 21(5):303–328, June 2005. 470

[Chandrasekhar, 1960] Subrahmanyan Chandrasekhar. *Radiative Transfer.* Dover Publications, 1960. 457, 470

[Chang, 2001] Allen Yao-Hung Chang. A Survey of Geometric Data Structures for Ray Tracing. Technical Report TR-CIS-2001-06, Department of Computer and Information Science, Polytechnic University, October 2001. 415

[Charney and Scherson, 1990] Mark J. Charney and Isaac D. Scherson. Efficient Traversal of Well-Behaved Hierarchical Trees of Extents for Ray-Tracing Complex Scenes. *The Visual Computer*, 6(3):167–178, May 1990. 392, 406

[Chen *et al.*, 1991] Shenchang Eric Chen, Holly Edith Rushmeier, Gavin S. P. Miller, and Douglass Turner. A Progressive Multipass Method for Global Illumination. *SIGGRAPH Computer Graphics (Proceedings of SIGGRAPH – The ACM International Conference on Computer Graphics and Interactive Techniques)*, 25(4):165–174, July 1991. 634

[Chenais, 1996] Alain Chenais. France: Moving Fast to Keep Pace in an Ever-Changing Technological Environment. *SIGGRAPH Computer Graphics*, 30(2):5–16, May 1996. 8

[Christensen and Batali, 2004] Per Henrik Christensen and Dana Batali. An Irradiance Atlas for Global Illumination in Complex Production Scenes. In *Proceedings of EGSR – The Eurographics Symposium on Rendering*, pages 133–141. Eurographics Association, 2004. 640

[Christensen *et al.*, 1993] Per Henrik Christensen, David H. Salesin, and Tony D. DeRose. A Continuous Adjoint Formulation for Radiance Transport. In *Proceedings of EGWR – The Eurographics Workshop on Rendering Techniques*, pages 95–101. Springer-Verlag, 1993. 569

[Christensen *et al.*, 2006] Per Henrik Christensen, Julian Fong, David M. Laur, and Dana Batali. Ray Tracing for the Movie "Cars". In *Proceedings of RT – The IEEE Symposium on Interactive Ray Tracing*, pages 1–6. IEEE Computer Society, 2006. 9

[Christensen, 1997] Per Henrik Christensen. Global Illumination for Professional 3D Animation, Visualization, Special Effects. In *Proceedings of EGWR – The Eurographics Workshop on Rendering Techniques*, pages 321–326. Springer-Verlag, 1997. 564

[Christensen, 1999] Per Henrik Christensen. Faster Photon Map Global Illumination. *Journal of Graphics Tools (JGT)*, 4(3):1–10, November 1999. 640

[Christensen, 2003] Per Henrik Christensen. Adjoints and Importance in Rendering: An Overview. *IEEE Transactions on Visualization and Computer Graphics*, 9(3):329–340, July 2003. 569

[Chu and Churchill, 1955] Chiao-Min Chu and Stuart W. Churchill. Representation of the Angular Distribution of Radiation Scattered by a Spherical Particle. *Journal of the Optical Society of America*, 45(11):958–962, 1955. 458

[Ciddor, 1996] Philip E. Ciddor. Refractive Index of Air: New Equations for the Visible and Near Infrared. *Applied Optics*, 35(9):1566–1573, March 1996. 748

[CIE, 1931] CIE, editor. *Proceedings of the Commission Internationale de l'Éclairage*. Cambridge University Press, 1931. 686, 687, 704, 705, 706, 712, 713

[CIE, 1951] CIE, editor. *Proceedings of the Commission Internationale de l'Éclairage*, volume 1–3. Bureau Central de la CIE, 1951. 686, 687

[CIE, 1964] CIE, editor. *Proceedings of the Commission Internationale de l'Éclairage*, volume B. Bureau Central de la CIE, 1964. 712, 714, 715

[CIE, 2004] CIE. Publication 15. In *Colorimetry*. Bureau Central de la CIE, 3rd edition, 2004. 715, 716

[Clark, 1976a] James H. Clark. Hierarchical Geometric Models for Visible-Surface Algorithms. *SIGGRAPH Computer Graphics (Proceedings of SIGGRAPH – The ACM International Conference on Computer Graphics and Interactive Techniques)*, 10(2):267–267, July 1976. 360, 362

[Clark, 1976b] James H. Clark. Hierarchical Geometric Models for Visible Surface Algorithms. *Communications of the ACM*, 19(10):547–554, October 1976. 360, 362

[Claustres, 2000a] Luc Claustres. Modélisation de la Fonction de Distribution de la Réflectance Bidirectionnelle – Comparatif et Application à la Synthèse d'Image. Master's thesis, Institut de Recherche en Informatique de Toulouse, Université Paul Sabatier, June 2000. 561

[Claustres, 2000b] Luc Claustres. Modélisation de la Fonction de Distribution de la Réflectance Bidirectionnelle – Un Etat de l'Art. Technical Report 00-15-R, Institut de Recherche en Informatique de Toulouse, Université Paul Sabatier, June 2000. 561

[Cleary and Wyvill, 1988] John G. Cleary and Geoff Wyvill. Analysis of an Algorithm for Fast Ray Tracing using Uniform Space Subdivision. *The Visual Computer*, 4(2):65–83, 1988. 372, 374, 376

[Cline and Egbert, 2005] David Cline and Parris K. Egbert. A Practical Introduction to Metropolis Light Transport. Technical report, Brigham Young University, May 2005. 623

[Cline *et al.*, 2005] David Cline, Justin F. Talbot, and Parris K. Egbert. Energy Redistribution Path Tracing. *ACM Transactions on Graphics (Proceedings of SIGGRAPH – The ACM International Conference on Computer Graphics and Interactive Techniques)*, 24(3):1186–1195, July 2005. 623

[Cline *et al.*, 2006] David Cline, Kevin Steele, and Parris K. Egbert. Lightweight Bounding Volumes for Ray Tracing. *Journal of Graphics Tools (JGT)*, 11(4):61–71, 2006. 365

[Cline, 2007] David Cline. *Sampling Methods in Ray-Based Global Illumination.* PhD thesis, Department of Computer Science, Brigham Young University, December 2007. 365, 623

[Cohen and Sheffer, 1994] Daniel Cohen and Zvi Sheffer. Proximity Clouds – An Acceleration Technique for 3D Grid Traversal. *The Visual Computer*, 11(1):27–38, January 1994. 388, 390

[Cohen and Wallace, 1993] Michael F. Cohen and John R. Wallace. *Radiosity and Realistic Image Synthesis.* Academic Press, 1993. 596

[Cohen *et al.*, 2001] Elaine Cohen, Richard F. Riesenfeld, and Gershon Elber. *Geometric Modeling with Splines: An Introduction.* A. K. Peters, 2001. 354

[Cohen, 1994] Daniel Cohen. Voxel Traversal along a 3D Line. In Paul Seagrave Heckbert, editor, *Graphics Gems IV*, chapter V.3, pages 366–369. Academic Press, 1994. 374

[Coleman, 1968] W. A. Coleman. Mathematical Verification of a Certain Monte Carlo Sampling Technique and Applications of the Technique to Radiation Transport Problems. *Nuclear Science and Engineering*, 32:76–81, April 1968. 602

[Collins, 1995] Steven Collins. Adaptive Splatting for Specular to Diffuse Light Transport. In *Proceedings of EGWR – The Eurographics Workshop on Rendering Techniques*, pages 121–135. Springer-Verlag, 1995. 637

[Cook and Torrance, 1981] Robert L. Cook and Kenneth E. Torrance. A Reflectance Model for Computer Graphics. *SIGGRAPH Computer Graphics (Proceedings of SIGGRAPH – The ACM International Conference on Computer Graphics and Interactive Techniques)*, 15(3):307–316, August 1981. 492, 528, 534

[Cook and Torrance, 1982] Robert L. Cook and Kenneth E. Torrance. A Reflectance Model for Computer Graphics. *ACM Transactions on Graphics*, 1(1):7–24, January 1982. 492, 528, 534

[Cook *et al.*, 1984] Robert L. Cook, Thomas Porter, and Loren Carpenter. Distributed Ray Tracing. *SIGGRAPH Computer Graphics (Proceedings of SIGGRAPH – The ACM International Conference on Computer Graphics and Interactive Techniques)*, 18(3):137–145, July 1984. 7, 598

[Cook *et al.*, 1987] Robert L. Cook, Loren Carpenter, and Edwin Earl Catmull. The Reyes Image Rendering Architecture. *SIGGRAPH Computer Graphics (Proceedings of SIGGRAPH – The ACM International Conference on Computer Graphics and Interactive Techniques)*, 21(4):95–102, July 1987. 6

[Cook, 1981] Robert L. Cook. A Reflection Model for Realistic Image Synthesis. Master's thesis, Cornell University, 1981. 492, 528, 534

[Cook, 1984] Robert L. Cook. Shade Trees. *SIGGRAPH Computer Graphics (Proceedings of SIGGRAPH – The ACM International Conference on Computer Graphics and Interactive Techniques)*, 18(3):223–231, January 1984. 554

[Cook, 1986] Robert L. Cook. Stochastic Sampling in Computer Graphics. *ACM Transactions on Graphics*, 5(1):51–72, January 1986. 598

[Cook, 1988] Robert L. Cook. Stochastic Sampling in Computer Graphics. In Kenneth I. Joy, Charles W. Grant, Nelson L. Max, and Lansing Hatfield, editors, *Tutorial: Computer Graphics; Image Synthesis*, pages 283–304. Computer Science Press, 1988. 598

[Cook, 1989] Robert L. Cook. Stochastic Sampling and Distributed Ray Tracing. In Andrew S. Glassner, editor, *An Introduction to Ray Tracing*, chapter 5, pages 161–199. Academic Press, 1989. 7, 598

[Cornette and Shanks, 1992] William M. Cornette and Joseph G. Shanks. Physically Reasonable Analytic Expression for the Single-Scattering Phase Function. *Applied Optics*, 31(16):3152–3160, June 1992. 456

[Cornette and Shanks, 1995] William M. Cornette and Joseph G. Shanks. Physically Reasonable Analytic Expression for the Single-Scattering Phase Function: Errata. *Applied Optics*, 34(4):641–641, 1995. 456

[Cornsweet, 1970] Tom N. Cornsweet. *Visual Perception*. Academic Press, 1970. 699, 701

[Cosenza, 2008] Biagio Cosenza. A Survey on Exploiting Grids for Ray Tracing. In *Proceedings of the Italian Chapter of the Eurographics Conference*, pages 89–96. Eurographics Association, 2008. 369, 377

[Cottingham, 1996] Marion S. Cottingham. Australia: Universities Offer Diversity in Computer Graphics Curricula. *SIGGRAPH Computer Graphics*, 30(3):5–6, August 1996. 8

[Crow, 1977] Franklin C. Crow. The Aliasing Problem in Computer-Generated Shaded Images. *Communications of the ACM*, 20(11):799–805, November 1977. 6

[Crow, 1987] Franklin C. Crow. The Origins of the Teapot. *IEEE Computer Graphics and Applications*, 7(1):8–19, January 1987. 6

[Cychosz and Waggenspack, 1992] Joseph M. Cychosz and Warren N. Waggenspack, Jr. Intersecting a Ray with a Quadric Surface. In David Kirk, editor, *Graphics Gems III*, chapter VI.2, pages 275–283. Academic Press, 1992. 279

[Cychosz and Waggenspack, 1994] Joseph M. Cychosz and Warren N. Waggenspack, Jr. Intersecting a Ray with a Cylinder. In Paul Seagrave Heckbert, editor, *Graphics Gems IV*, chapter V.2, pages 356–365. Academic Press, 1994. 272

[Cychosz, 1990] Joseph M. Cychosz. Efficient Post-Concatenation of Transformation Matrices. In Andrew S. Glassner, editor, *Graphics Gems I*, chapter IX.9, pages 476–481. Academic Press, 1990. 119

[Cychosz, 1991] Joseph M. Cychosz. Intersecting a Ray with an Elliptical Torus. In James Richard Arvo, editor, *Graphics Gems II*, chapter V.2, pages 251–256. Academic Press, 1991. 291

[Cychosz, 1992] Joseph M. Cychosz. Use of Residency Masks and Object Space Partitioning to Eliminate Ray-Object Intersection Calculations. In David Kirk, editor, *Graphics Gems III*, chapter VI.3, pages 284–287. Academic Press, 1992. 391

[Dachsbacher *et al.*, 2014] Carsten Dachsbacher, Jaroslav Křivánek, Miloš Hašan, Adam Arbree, Bruce Jonathan Walter, and Jan Novák. Scalable Realistic Rendering with Many-Light Methods. *Computer Graphics Forum (Eurographics State of the Art Reports)*, 33(1):88–104, February 2014. 632

[Damez *et al.*, 2002] Cyrille Damez, Kirill Dmitriev, and Karol Myszkowski. Global Illumination for Interactive Applications and High-Quality Animations. In *Eurographics State of the Art Reports*. Eurographics Association, 2002. 644

[Damez *et al.*, 2003a] Cyrille Damez, Kirill Dmitriev, and Karol Myszkowski. State of the Art in Global Illumination for Interactive Applications and High-Quality Animations. *Computer Graphics Forum*, 22(1):55–77, March 2003. 644

[Damez *et al.*, 2003b] Cyrille Damez, Philipp Slusallek, Bruce Jonathan Walter, Karol Myszkowski, Ingo Wald, and Per Henrik Christensen. Global Illumination for Interactive Applications and High Quality Animations. In *ACM SIGGRAPH Courses*, number 27. ACM Press, 2003. 644

[Dammertz and Keller, 2008] Holger Dammertz and Alexander Keller. The Edge Volume Heuristic – Robust Triangle Subdivision for Improved BVH Performance. In *Proceedings of RT – The IEEE Symposium on Interactive Ray Tracing*, pages 155–158. IEEE Computer Society, August 2008. 392

[Dang *et al.*, 2002] Yumei Dang, Louis H. Kauffman, and Daniel J. Sandin. *Hypercomplex Iterations – Distance Estimation and Higher Dimensional Fractals.* World Scientific, 2002. 311

[Dartnall *et al.*, 1983] H. J. A. Dartnall, J. K. Bowmaker, and J. D. Mollon. Human Visual Pigments: Microspectrophotometric Results from the Eyes of Seven Persons. *Proceedings of the Royal Society of London*, 220(1218):115–130, November 1983. 682

[Davidovič *et al.*, 2010] Tomáš Davidovič, Jaroslav Křivánek, Miloš Hašan, Philipp Slusallek, and Kavita Bala. Combining Global and Local Virtual Lights for Detailed Glossy Illumination. *ACM Transactions on Graphics (Proceedings of SIGGRAPH Asia – The ACM Conference on Computer Graphics and Interactive Techniques in Asia)*, 29(6):143:1–143:8, December 2010. 631

[Davies, 1954a] H. Davies. The Reflection of Electromagnetic Waves from a Rough Surface. *Proceedings of the IEE – Part III: Radio and Communication Engineering*, 101(70):118, March 1954. 548

[Davies, 1954b] H. Davies. The Reflection of Electromagnetic Waves from a Rough Surface. *Proceedings of the IEE – Part IV: Institution Monographs*, 101(7):209–214, August 1954. 548

[de Berg *et al.*, 1991] Mark de Berg, Dan Halperin, Mark Overmars, Jack Snoeyink, and Marc van Kreveld. Efficient Ray Shooting and Hidden Surface Removal. In *Proceedings of SoCG – The Annual ACM Symposium on Computational Geometry*, pages 21–30. ACM Press, 1991. 413

[de Berg *et al.*, 1994] Mark de Berg, Dan Halperin, Mark Overmars, Jack Snoeyink, and Marc van Kreveld. Efficient Ray Shooting and Hidden Surface Removal. *Algorithmica*, 12(1):30–53, July 1994. 413

[de Berg, 1992] Mark de Berg. *Efficient Algorithms for Ray Shooting and Hidden Surface Removal.* PhD thesis, Rijksuniversiteit te Utrecht, 1992. 413

[Debevec *et al.*, 2003] Paul E. Debevec, Dan Lemmon, Gregory J. Ward Larson, Rod Bogart, and Frank Vitz. HDRI and Image-Based Lighting. In *ACM SIGGRAPH Courses*, number 19. ACM Press, 2003. 433

[Debevec, 1998] Paul E. Debevec. Rendering with Natural Light. In *ACM SIGGRAPH Electronic Theater*. ACM Press, 1998. 433

[Debevec, 2002] Paul E. Debevec. Image-Based Lighting. *IEEE Computer Graphics and Applications*, 22(2):26–34, March 2002. 433

[Debevec, 2004] Paul E. Debevec. Capturing and Simulating Physically Accurate Illumination in Computer Graphics. *The Bridge*, 34(4):28–36, 2004. 738

[Debevec, 2005] Paul E. Debevec. Image-Based Lighting. In *ACM SIGGRAPH Courses*. ACM Press, 2005. 433

[Devillers, 1988] Olivier Devillers. *Méthodes d'Optimisation du Tracé de Rayons*. PhD thesis, Université Paris Sud - Paris XI, June 1988. 388

[Devillers, 1989] Olivier Devillers. The Macro-Regions: An Efficient Space Subdivision Structure for Ray Tracing. In *Proceedings of Eurographics – The Annual Conference of the European Association for Computer Graphics*. Eurographics Association, 1989. 388

[Dietrich *et al.*, 2005] Andreas Dietrich, Carsten Colditz, Oliver Deussen, and Philipp Slusallek. Realistic and Interactive Visualization of High-Density Plant Ecosystems. In *Proceedings of EGNPH – The Eurographics Workshop on Natural Phenomena*, pages 73–81. Eurographics Association, 2005. 10

[Dietrich *et al.*, 2006] Andreas Dietrich, Ingo Wald, Holger Schmidt, Kristian Sons, and Philipp Slusallek. Realtime Ray Tracing for Advanced Visualization in the Aerospace Industry. In *Proceedings of the Paderborner Workshop on Augmented & Virtual Reality in der Produktentstehung*, June 2006. 9

[Dippé and Swensen, 1984] Mark A. Z. Dippé and John Swensen. An Adaptive Subdivision Algorithm and Parallel Architecture for Realistic Image Synthesis. *SIGGRAPH Computer Graphics (Proceedings of SIGGRAPH – The ACM International Conference on Computer Graphics and Interactive Techniques)*, 18(3):149–158, 1984. 376, 377, 387

[Djeu and Volchenok, 2008] Peter Djeu and Stan Volchenok. Using Annotated KD-Trees to Accelerate Shadow Ray Queries. Technical Report TR-08-36, Deptartment of Computer Sciences, The University of Texas at Austin, August 2008. 413

[Djeu *et al.*, 2009] Peter Djeu, Sean Keely, and Warren Andrew Hunt. Accelerating Shadow Rays using Volumetric Occluders and Modified KD-Tree Traversal. In *Proceedings of HPG – The Conference on High-Performance Graphics*, pages 69–76. Eurographics Association/ACM SIGGRAPH, 2009. 413

[Dodgson, 1992] Neil Anthony Dodgson. *Image Resampling*. PhD thesis, University of Cambridge, Wolfson College, August 1992. 208, 226

[Dodgson, 1997] Neil Anthony Dodgson. Quadratic Interpolation for Image Resampling. *IEEE Transactions on Image Processing*, 6(9):1322–1326, September 1997. 208, 226

[Dorsey and McMillan, 1998] Julie Dorsey and Leonard McMillan. Computer Graphics and Architecture: State of the Art and Outlook for the Future. *SIGGRAPH Computer Graphics*, 32(1):45–48, February 1998. 10

[Dorsey and Rushmeier, 2005] Julie Dorsey and Holly Edith Rushmeier. Digital Modeling of the Appearance of Materials. In *ACM SIGGRAPH Courses*. ACM Press, 2005. 561

[Dorsey *et al.*, 1991] Julie Dorsey, François X. Sillion, and Donald P. Greenberg. Design and Simulation of Opera Lighting and Projection Effects. *SIGGRAPH Computer Graphics (Proceedings of SIGGRAPH – The ACM International Conference on Computer Graphics and Interactive Techniques)*, 25(4):41–50, July 1991. 10

[Dorsey *et al.*, 2006] Julie Dorsey, Holly Edith Rushmeier, and François X. Sillion. Digital Modeling of the Appearance of Materials. In *ACM SIGGRAPH Courses*. ACM Press, 2006. 561

[Dorsey *et al.*, 2008] Julie Dorsey, Holly Edith Rushmeier, and François X. Sillion. *Digital Modeling of Material Appearance.* Morgan Kaufmann Publishers, 2008. 561

[Drago and Myszkowski, 2001] Frédéric Drago and Karol Myszkowski. Validation Proposal for Global Illumination and Rendering Techniques. *Computers & Graphics*, 25(3):511–518, June 2001. 739

[Dunn and Parberry, 2002] Fletcher Dunn and Ian Parberry. *3D Math Primer for Graphics and Game Development.* Wordware Publishing, 1st edition, 2002. 126

[Dunn and Parberry, 2011] Fletcher Dunn and Ian Parberry. *3D Math Primer for Graphics and Game Development.* A. K. Peters/CRC Press, 2nd edition, 2011. 126

[Dür, 2005] Arne Dür. On the Ward Model for Global Illumination. 2005. 537

[Dür, 2006] Arne Dür. An Improved Normalization for the Ward Reflectance Model. *Journal of Graphics Tools (JGT)*, 11(1):51–59, 2006. 537

[Dürer, 1525] Albrecht Dürer. *Underweysung der Messung, mit dem Zirckel und Richtscheyt, in Linien Ebnen und Gantzen Corporen.* Nüremberg, 1st edition, 1525. 598

[Dürer, 1538] Albrecht Dürer. *Underweysung der Messung, mit dem Zirckel und Richtscheyt, in Linien Ebnen und Gantzen Corporen.* Nüremberg, 2nd edition, 1538. 598

[Dutré *et al.*, 1993] Philip Dutré, Eric P. F. Lafortune, and Yves D. Willems. Monte Carlo Light Tracing with Direct Computation of Pixel Intensities. In *Proceedings of Compu-Graphics – The International Conference on Computational Graphics and Visualization Techniques*, pages 128–137, December 1993. 615

[Dutré *et al.*, 1994] Philip Dutré, Eric P. F. Lafortune, and Yves D. Willems. A Mathematical Framework for Global Illumination Algorithms. In *Proceedings of WSCG – The Winter School of Computer Graphics: The International Conference in Central Europe on Computer Graphics, Visualization and Computer Vision*, 1994. 565, 568

[Dutré *et al.*, 2002] Philip Dutré, Kavita Bala, and Philippe Bekaert. *Advanced Global Illumination.* A. K. Peters, 1st edition, 2002. 623, 644

[Dutré *et al.*, 2006] Philip Dutré, Kavita Bala, and Philippe Bekaert. *Advanced Global Illumination.* A. K. Peters, 2nd edition, August 2006. 623, 644

[Dutré, 1996] Philip Dutré. *Mathematical Frameworks and Monte Carlo Algorithms for Global Illumination in Computer Graphics.* PhD thesis, Department of Computer Science, Katholieke Universiteit Leuven, September 1996. 568, 615

[Dutré, 2003] Philip Dutré. Global Illumination Compendium. Department of Computer Science, Katholieke Universiteit Leuven, September 2003. 739

[Edwards *et al.*, 2006] David P. Edwards, Solomon Boulos, Jared M. Johnson, Peter Schuyler Shirley, Michael Ashikhmin, Michael M. Stark, and Christopher Wyman. The Halfway Vector Disk for BRDF Modeling. *ACM Transactions on Graphics*, 25(1):1–18, January 2006. 531

[Eisemann *et al.*, 2007] Martin Eisemann, Thorsten Grosch, Stefan Müller, and Marcus A. Magnor. Fast Ray/Axis-Aligned Bounding Box Overlap Tests using Ray Slopes. *Journal of Graphics Tools (JGT)*, 12(4):35–46, 2007. 301

[Eisemann *et al.*, 2008] Martin Eisemann, Christian Woizischke, and Marcus A. Magnor. Ray Tracing with the Single Slab Hierarchy. In *Proceedings of VMV – The Workshop on Vision, Modeling, and Visualization*, pages 373–381, October 2008. 366

[Eisemann *et al.*, 2011] Martin Eisemann, Pablo Bauszat, and Marcus A. Magnor. Implicit Object Space Partitioning: The No-Memory BVH. Technical Report 2011-12-16, Computer Graphics Lab, TU Braunschweig, December 2011. 365

[Eisemann *et al.*, 2012] Martin Eisemann, Pablo Bauszat, Stefan Guthe, and Marcus A. Magnor. Geometry Presorting for Implicit Object Space Partitioning. *Computer Graphics Forum (Proceedings of EGSR – The Eurographics Symposium on Rendering)*, 31(4):1445–1454, June 2012. 365

[Elek, 2010] Oskar Elek. Layered Materials in Real-Time Rendering. In *Proceedings of CESCG – The Central European Seminar on Computer Graphics*, April 2010. 558

[Encarnação and Felger, 1996] José L. Encarnação and Wolfgang Felger. Germany: Performance Indicators, Markets and Applications. *SIGGRAPH Computer Graphics*, 30(2):17–21, May 1996. 8

[Encarnação, 1994] José L. Encarnação. Computer Graphics Education in Germany. *SIGGRAPH Computer Graphics*, 28(3):193–197, August 1994. 8

[Endl and Sommer, 1994] Robert Endl and Manfred Sommer. Classification of Ray-Generators in Uniform Subdivisions and Octrees for Ray Tracing. *Computer Graphics Forum*, 13(1):3–19, February 1994. 374

[Engelhardt *et al.*, 2010] Thomas Engelhardt, Jan Novák, and Carsten Dachsbacher. Instant Multiple Scattering for Interactive Rendering of Heterogeneous Participating Media. Technical report, Karlsruhe Institut of Technology, December 2010. 632

[Engelhardt *et al.*, 2012] Thomas Engelhardt, Jan Novák, Thorsten-W. Schmidt, and Carsten Dachsbacher. Approximate Bias Compensation for Rendering Scenes with Heterogeneous Participating Media. *Computer Graphics Forum (Proceedings of Pacific Graphics – The Pacific Conference on Computer Graphics and Applications)*, 31(7):2145–2154, September 2012. 632

[Ernst and Greiner, 2007] Manfred Ernst and Günther Greiner. Early Split Clipping for Bounding Volume Hierarchies. In *Proceedings of RT – The IEEE Symposium on Interactive Ray Tracing*, pages 73–78. IEEE Computer Society, 2007. 392

[Ernst and Woop, 2011] Manfred Ernst and Sven Woop. Ray Tracing with Shared-Plane Bounding Volume Hierarchies. *Journal of Graphics Tools (JGT)*, 15(3):141–151, 2011. 365

[Es and İşler, 2007] Alphan Es and Veysi İşler. Accelerated Regular Grid Traversals using Extended Anisotropic Chessboard Distance Fields on a Parallel Stream Processor. *Journal of Parallel and Distributed Computing*, 67(11):1201–1217, November 2007. 389

[Es *et al.*, 2006] Alphan Es, Hacer Yalım Keleş, and Veysi İşler. Accelerated Volume Rendering with Homogeneous Region Encoding using Extended Anisotropic Chessboard Distance on GPU. In *Proceedings of EGPGV – The Eurographics Symposium on Parallel Graphics and Visualization*, pages 67–73. Eurographics Association, 2006. 389

[Ezquerra *et al.*, 1999] Norberto Ezquerra, Isabel Navazo, Tahia Infantes Morris, and Eva Monclus. Graphics, Vision, and Visualization in Medical Imaging: A State of the Art Report. In *Eurographics State of the Art Reports*. Eurographics Association, September 1999. 10

[Fabianowski and Dingliana, 2009] Bartosz Fabianowski and John Dingliana. Compact BVH Storage for Ray Tracing and Photon Mapping. In *Proceedings of Eurographics Ireland – The Irish Workshop on Computer Graphics*, pages 1–8. Eurographics Association, 2009. 365

[Fabianowski *et al.*, 2009] Bartosz Fabianowski, Colin Fowler, and John Dingliana. A Cost Metric for Scene-Interior Ray Origins. In *Eurographics Short Presentations*, pages 49–52. Eurographics Association, 2009. 400

[Fairchild, 2001] Mark D. Fairchild. A Revision of CIECAM97s for Practical Applications. *Color Research & Application*, 26(6):418–427, December 2001. 720

[Fairchild, 2013] Mark D. Fairchild. *Color Appearance Models.* John Wiley & Sons, 3rd edition, August 2013. 729

[Falcidieno, 1996] Bianca Falcidieno. Italy: An Explosion of Subdisciplines in Computer Graphics Education. *SIGGRAPH Computer Graphics*, 30(3):17–18, August 1996. 8

[Fan *et al.*, 2005] Shaohua Fan, Stephen Chenney, and Yu-Chi Lai. Metropolis Photon Sampling with Optional User Guidance. In *Proceedings of EGSR – The Eurographics Symposium on Rendering*, pages 127–138. Eurographics Association, 2005. 641

[Farin, 1996] Gerald Farin. *Curves and Surfaces for CAGD: A Practical Guide.* Academic Press, 4th edition, 1996. 354

[Farin, 2002] Gerald Farin. *Curves and Surfaces for CAGD: A Practical Guide.* Morgan Kaufmann Publishers, 5th edition, 2002. 354

[Favre and Löhner, 1994] Jean Favre and Rainald Löhner. Ray Tracing with a Space-Filling Finite Element Mesh. *International Journal for Numerical Methods in Engineering*, 37(20):3571–3580, October 1994. 387

[Fechner, 1907] Gustav Theodor Fechner. *Elemente der Psychophysik*, volume 2. Breitkopf & Härtel, 1907. 691

[Feltman *et al.*, 2012] Nicolas Feltman, Minjae Lee, and Kayvon Fatahalian. SRDH: Specializing BVH Construction and Traversal Order using Representative Shadow Ray Sets. In *Proceedings of HPG – The Conference on High-Performance Graphics*, pages 49–55. Eurographics Association/ACM SIGGRAPH, 2012. 400

[Filip and Haindl, 2009] Jiří Filip and Michal Haindl. Bidirectional Texture Function Modeling: A State of the Art Survey. *IEEE Transactions on Pattern Analysis and Machine Intelligence*, 31(11):1921–1940, November 2009. 473

[Fisher and Woo, 1994] Frederick Fisher and Andrew Chung How Woo. R.E versus N.H Specular Highlights. In Paul Seagrave Heckbert, editor, *Graphics Gems IV*, chapter VI.2, pages 388–400. Academic Press, 1994. 515

[Foley and Sugerman, 2005] Tim Foley and Jeremy Sugerman. KD-Tree Acceleration Structures for a GPU Raytracer. In *Proceedings of EGGH – The Eurographics Workshop on Graphics Hardware*, pages 15–22. Eurographics Association, 2005. 382

[Foley and van Dam, 1982] James D. Foley and Andries van Dam. *Fundamentals of Interactive Computer Graphics*. Addison-Wesley Longman Publishing, 1982. 739

[Foley *et al.*, 1990] James D. Foley, Andries van Dam, Steven K. Feiner, and John F. Hughes. *Computer Graphics: Principles and Practice*. Addison-Wesley Longman Publishing, 2nd edition, 1990. 739

[Foley *et al.*, 1994] James D. Foley, Andries van Dam, Steven K. Feiner, John F. Hughes, and Richard L. Phillips. *Introduction to Computer Graphics*. Addison-Wesley Longman Publishing, 1994. 739

[Foley *et al.*, 1995] James D. Foley, Andries van Dam, Steven K. Feiner, and John F. Hughes. *Computer Graphics: Principles and Practice – in C*. Addison-Wesley Longman Publishing, 2nd edition, 1995. 739

[Fóris *et al.*, 1996] Tibor Fóris, Gábor Márton, and László Szirmay-Kalos. Ray Shooting in Logarithmic Time. In *Proceedings of WSCG – The Winter School of Computer Graphics: The International Conference in Central Europe on Computer Graphics, Visualization and Computer Vision*, pages 84–90, February 1996. 412, 413

[Formella and Gill, 1995] Arno Formella and Christian Gill. Ray Tracing: A Quantitative Analysis and a New Practical Algorithm. *The Visual Computer*, 11(9):465–476, 1995. 360

[Fourier, 1808] Jean-Baptiste Joseph Fourier. Mémoire sur la Propagation de la Chaleur dans les Corps Solides. *Nouveau Bulletin des Sciences par la Société Philomatique de Paris*, 1(6):112–116, March 1808. 178

[Fourier, 1822] Jean-Baptiste Joseph Fourier. *Théorie Analytique de la Chaleur*. Didot, 1822. 178

[Fournier and Poulin, 1993] Alain Fournier and Pierre Poulin. A Ray Tracing Accelerator Based on a Hierarchy of 1D Sorted Lists. In *Proceedings of Graphics Interface – The Canadian Annual Conference on Computer Graphics, Interactive Systems, and Human-Computer Interaction*, pages 53–61. Canadian Human-Computer Communications Society, May 1993. 360

[Fowler, 1983] Bruce W. Fowler. Expansion of Mie-Theory Phase Functions in Series of Legendre Polynomials. *Journal of the Optical Society of America*, 73(1):19–22, January 1983. 458

[Friedrich *et al.*, 2006] Heiko Friedrich, Johannes Günther, Andreas Dietrich, Michael Scherbaum, Hans-Peter Seidel, and Philipp Slusallek. Exploring the Use of Ray Tracing for Future Games. In *Proceedings of Sandbox – The ACM SIGGRAPH Symposium on Videogames*, pages 41–50. ACM Press, 2006. 9

[Frisvad *et al.*, 2005] Jeppe Eliot Revall Frisvad, Niels Jørgen Christensen, and Peter Falster. Efficient Light Scattering through Thin Semi-Transparent Objects. In *Proceedings of GRAPHITE – The International Conference on Computer Graphics and Interactive Techniques in Australasia and Southeast Asia*, pages 135–138. ACM Press, 2005. 484

[Fuchs *et al.*, 1980] Henry Fuchs, Zvi M. Kedem, and Bruce Fountain Naylor. On Visible Surface Generation by a Priori Tree Structures. *SIGGRAPH Computer Graphics (Proceedings of SIGGRAPH – The ACM International Conference on Computer Graphics and Interactive Techniques)*, 14(3):124–133, July 1980. 385

[Fujimoto and Iwata, 1985] Akira Fujimoto and Kansei Iwata. Accelerated Ray Tracing. In *Proceedings of Computer Graphics Tokyo*, pages 41–65, 1985. 374, 380

[Fujimoto *et al.*, 1986] Akira Fujimoto, Takayuki Tanaka, and Kansei Iwata. ARTS: Accelerated Ray-Tracing System. *IEEE Computer Graphics and Applications*, 6(4):16–26, April 1986. 374, 380

[Fussell and Subramanian, 1988] Donald S. Fussell and Kalpathi Raman Subramanian. Fast Ray Tracing using K-D Trees. Technical Report TR-88-07, Department of Computer Sciences, The University of Texas at Austin, March 1988. 390, 395

[Gaboury, 2014] Jacob Gaboury. *Image Objects: An Archaeology of 3D Computer Graphics, 1965–1979.* PhD thesis, Department of Media, Culture and Communication, New York University, 2014. 4

[García *et al.*, 2012] Rubén Jesús García, Carlos Ureña, and Mateu Sbert. Description and Solution of an Unreported Intrinsic Bias in Photon Mapping Density Estimation with Constant Kernel. *Computer Graphics Forum*, 31(1):33–41, February 2012. 635

[Gassenbauer *et al.*, 2009] Václav Gassenbauer, Jaroslav Křivánek, and Kadi Bouatouch. Spatial Directional Radiance Caching. *Computer Graphics Forum (Proceedings of EGSR – The Eurographics Symposium on Rendering)*, 28(4):1189–1198, June 2009. 628

[Geisler-Moroder and Dür, 2010a] David Geisler-Moroder and Arne Dür. A New Ward BRDF Model with Bounded Albedo. *Computer Graphics Forum (Proceedings of EGSR – The Eurographics Symposium on Rendering)*, 29(4):1391–1398, June 2010. 538

[Geisler-Moroder and Dür, 2010b] David Geisler-Moroder and Arne Dür. Bounding the Albedo of the Ward Reflectance Model. Technical report, Department of Mathematics, University of Innsbruck, March 2010. 538

[Georgiades, 1992] Príamos Georgiades. Signed Distance from Point to Plane. In David Kirk, editor, *Graphics Gems III*, chapter V.3, pages 223–224. Academic Press, 1992. 247

[Georgiev and Slusallek, 2010] Iliyan Georgiev and Philipp Slusallek. Simple and Robust Iterative Importance Sampling of Virtual Point Lights. In *Eurographics Short Papers*, pages 57–60. Eurographics Association, 2010. 631

[Georgiev *et al.*, 2011] Iliyan Georgiev, Jaroslav Křivánek, and Philipp Slusallek. Bidirectional Light Transport with Vertex Merging. In *ACM SIGGRAPH Asia Sketches*, pages 27:1–27:2. ACM Press, 2011. 642

[Georgiev *et al.*, 2012a] Iliyan Georgiev, Jaroslav Křivánek, Tomáš Davidovič, and Philipp Slusallek. Light Transport Simulation with Vertex Connection and Merging. *ACM Transactions on Graphics (Proceedings of SIGGRAPH Asia – The ACM Conference on Computer Graphics and Interactive Techniques in Asia)*, 31(6):192:1–192:10, November 2012. 642

[Georgiev *et al.*, 2012b] Iliyan Georgiev, Jaroslav Křivánek, Stefan Popov, and Philipp Slusallek. Importance Caching for Complex Illumination. *Computer Graphics Forum (Proceedings of Eurographics – The Annual Conference of the European Association for Computer Graphics)*, 31(2pt3):701–710, May 2012. 631

[Georgiev, 2012] Iliyan Georgiev. Implementing Vertex Connection and Merging. Technical report, Department of Computer Science, Saarland University, November 2012. 642

[Georgiev, 2015] Iliyan Georgiev. *Path Sampling Techniques for Efficient Light Transport Simulation.* PhD thesis, Saarland University, June 2015. 631, 642

[Gigante, 1988] Michael Gigante. Accelerated Ray Tracing using Non-Uniform Grids. In *Proceedings of Ausgraph – The Australasian Conference on Computer Graphics*, pages 157–163, 1988. 376

[Glassner, 1984] Andrew S. Glassner. Space Subdivision for Fast Ray Tracing. *IEEE Computer Graphics and Applications*, 4(10):15–24, October 1984. 378, 380, 381

[Glassner, 1989a] Andrew S. Glassner. *An Introduction to Ray Tracing.* Academic Press, February 1989. 739

[Glassner, 1989b] Andrew S. Glassner. Surface Physics for Ray Tracing. In Andrew S. Glassner, editor, *An Introduction to Ray Tracing*, chapter 4, pages 121–160. Academic Press, 1989. 561

[Glassner, 1994] Andrew S. Glassner. *Principles of Digital Image Synthesis.* Morgan Kaufmann Publishers, 1994. 725, 739

[Glassner, 2000] Andrew S. Glassner. Soap Bubbles: Part 2. *IEEE Computer Graphics and Applications*, 20(6):99–109, November 2000. 561

[Goldman, 1990] Ronald N. Goldman. Matrices and Transformations. In Andrew S. Glassner, editor, *Graphics Gems I*, chapter IX.8, pages 472–475. Academic Press, 1990. 118

[Goldman, 1991a] Ronald N. Goldman. More Matrices and Transformations: Shear and Pseudo-Perspective. In James Richard Arvo, editor, *Graphics Gems II*, chapter VII.4, pages 338–341. Academic Press, 1991. 118

[Goldman, 1991b] Ronald N. Goldman. Recovering the Data from the Transformation Matrix. In James Richard Arvo, editor, *Graphics Gems II*, chapter VII.2, pages 324–331. Academic Press, 1991. 111

[Goldman, 2009] Ronald Goldman. *An Integrated Introduction to Computer Graphics and Geometric Modeling.* CRC Press, 2009. 739

[Goldsmith and Salmon, 1987] Jeffrey Goldsmith and John Salmon. Automatic Creation of Object Hierarchies for Ray Tracing. *IEEE Computer Graphics and Applications*, 7(5):14–20, May 1987. 361, 397

[Gomes *et al.*, 2012] Jonas Gomes, Luiz Velho, and Mario Costa Sousa. *Computer Graphics: Theory and Practice.* A. K. Peters/CRC Press, 2012. 739

[Gonzalez and Woods, 2002] Rafael C. Gonzalez and Richard E. Woods. *Digital Image Processing.* Prentice Hall, 2nd edition, 2002. 231

[Gonzalez and Woods, 2008] Rafael C. Gonzalez and Richard E. Woods. *Digital Image Processing.* Prentice Hall, 3rd edition, 2008. 231

[Goral *et al.*, 1984] Cindy M. Goral, Kenneth E. Torrance, Donald P. Greenberg, and Bennett Battaile. Modeling the Interaction of Light between Diffuse Surfaces. *SIGGRAPH Computer Graphics (Proceedings of SIGGRAPH – The ACM International Conference on Computer Graphics and Interactive Techniques)*, 18(3):213–222, July 1984. 7, 594

[Gortler, 2012] Steven J. Gortler. *Foundations of 3D Computer Graphics.* MIT Press, 2012. 739

[Gotsman, 1996] Craig Gotsman. Israel: State of the Art of Computer Graphics. *SIGGRAPH Computer Graphics*, 30(2):22–24, May 1996. 8

[Gouraud, 1971a] Henri Gouraud. *Computer Display of Curved Surfaces.* PhD thesis, Department of Computer Science, The University of Utah, June 1971. 5

[Gouraud, 1971b] Henri Gouraud. Continuous Shading of Curved Surfaces. *IEEE Transactions on Computers*, C-20(6):623–629, June 1971. 5

[Gradshteyn and Ryzhik, 2007] Izrail Solomonovich Gradshteyn and Iosif Moiseevich Ryzhik. *Table of Integrals, Series, and Products.* Academic Press, 7th edition, February 2007. 56, 64, 263

[Gradshteyn and Ryzhik, 2014] Izrail Solomonovich Gradshteyn and Iosif Moiseevich Ryzhik. *Table of Integrals, Series, and Products.* Academic Press, 8th edition, October 2014. 64

[Graf, 2010] Robert Graf. Rendering the Mandelbulb. In *ACM SIGGRAPH Dailies*, pages 28:1–28:1. ACM Press, 2010. 308

[Green and Hatch, 1995] Daniel Green and Don Hatch. Fast Polygon-Cube Intersection Testing. In Alan W. Paeth, editor, *Graphics Gems V*, chapter VII.2, pages 375–379. Academic Press, 1995. 369

[Green, 1969] R. Elliot Green. Computer Graphics in the United States. *Computer-Aided Design*, 1(3):33–38, January 1969. 8

[Greenberg *et al.*, 1997] Donald P. Greenberg, Kenneth E. Torrance, Peter Schuyler Shirley, James Richard Arvo, James A. Ferwerda, Sumanta N. Pattanaik, Eric P. F. Lafortune, Bruce Jonathan Walter, Sing-Choong Foo, and Ben Trumbore. A Framework for Realistic Image Synthesis. In *Proceedings of SIGGRAPH – The ACM International Conference on Computer Graphics and Interactive Techniques*, pages 477–494. ACM Press, August 1997. 739

[Greene, 1994] Ned Greene. Detecting Intersection of a Rectangular Solid and a Convex Polyhedron. In Paul Seagrave Heckbert, editor, *Graphics Gems IV*, chapter I.7, pages 74–82. Academic Press, 1994. 369

[Gribble and Parker, 2005] Christiaan Paul Gribble and Steven Gregory Parker. An Experimental Design for Determining the Effects of Illumination Models in Particle Visualization. In *Proceedings of APGV – The Symposium on Applied Perception in Graphics and Visualization*, Poster Session, pages 175–175. ACM Press, 2005. 564

[Gribble and Parker, 2006] Christiaan Paul Gribble and Steven Gregory Parker. Enhancing Interactive Particle Visualization with Advanced Shading Models. In *Proceedings of APGV – The Symposium on Applied Perception in Graphics and Visualization*, pages 111–118. ACM Press, 2006. 564

[Gröller and Purgathofer, 1995] Eduard Gröller and Werner Purgathofer. Coherence in Computer Graphics. Technical Report TR-186-2-95-04, Institute of Computer Graphics and Algorithms, Vienna University of Technology, March 1995. 357

[Gu *et al.*, 2007] Jinwei Gu, Ravi Ramamoorthi, Peter N. Belhumeur, and Shree K. Nayar. Dirty Glass: Rendering Contamination on Transparent Surfaces. In *Proceedings of EGSR – The Eurographics Symposium on Rendering*, pages 159–170. Eurographics Association, 2007. 559, 561

[Gutierrez *et al.*, 2007] Diego Gutierrez, Veronica Sundstedt, Fermin Gomez, and Alan Chalmers. Dust and Light: Predictive Virtual Archaeology. *Journal of Cultural Heritage*, 8(2):209–214, April 2007. 441

[Gutierrez *et al.*, 2008a] Diego Gutierrez, Srinivasa G. Narasimhan, Henrik Wann Jensen, and Wojciech Jarosz. Scattering. In *ACM SIGGRAPH Asia Courses*, pages 18:1–18:12. ACM Press, 2008. 470

[Gutierrez *et al.*, 2008b] Diego Gutierrez, Veronica Sundstedt, Fermin Gomez, and Alan Chalmers. Modeling Light Scattering for Virtual Heritage. *ACM Journal on Computing and Cultural Heritage*, 1(2):8:1–8:15, November 2008. 441

[Gutierrez *et al.*, 2009] Diego Gutierrez, Wojciech Jarosz, Craig Steven Donner, and Srinivasa G. Narasimhan. Scattering. In *ACM SIGGRAPH Courses*, pages 21:1–21:397. ACM Press, 2009. 470

[Haase and Meyer, 1992] Chet S. Haase and Gary W. Meyer. Modeling Pigmented Materials for Realistic Image Synthesis. *ACM Transactions on Graphics*, 11(4):305–335, October 1992. 479

[Hachisuka and Jensen, 2009] Toshiya Hachisuka and Henrik Wann Jensen. Stochastic Progressive Photon Mapping. *ACM Transactions on Graphics (Proceedings of SIGGRAPH Asia – The ACM Conference on Computer Graphics and Interactive Techniques in Asia)*, 28(5):141:1–141:8, December 2009. 638

[Hachisuka and Jensen, 2011] Toshiya Hachisuka and Henrik Wann Jensen. Robust Adaptive Photon Tracing using Photon Path Visibility. *ACM Transactions on Graphics*, 30(5):114:1–114:11, October 2011. 641

[Hachisuka *et al.*, 2008] Toshiya Hachisuka, Shinji Ogaki, and Henrik Wann Jensen. Progressive Photon Mapping. *ACM Transactions on Graphics (Proceedings of SIGGRAPH Asia – The ACM Conference on Computer Graphics and Interactive Techniques in Asia)*, 27(5):130:1–130:8, December 2008. 637

[Hachisuka *et al.*, 2010a] Toshiya Hachisuka, Wojciech Jarosz, and Henrik Wann Jensen. A Progressive Error Estimation Framework for Photon Density Estimation. *ACM Transactions on Graphics (Proceedings of SIGGRAPH Asia – The ACM Conference on Computer Graphics and Interactive Techniques in Asia)*, 29(6):144:1–144:12, December 2010. 638

[Hachisuka *et al.*, 2010b] Toshiya Hachisuka, Wojciech Jarosz, and Henrik Wann Jensen. An Error Estimation Framework for Photon Density Estimation. In *ACM SIGGRAPH Talks*, pages 3:1–3:1. ACM Press, 2010. 638

[Hachisuka *et al.*, 2012a] Toshiya Hachisuka, Wojciech Jarosz, Guillaume Bouchard, Per Henrik Christensen, Jeppe Eliot Revall Frisvad, Wenzel Alban Jakob, Henrik Wann Jensen, Michael Kaschalk, Claude Knaus, Andrew Selle, and Ben Spencer. State of the Art in Photon Density Estimation. In *ACM SIGGRAPH Courses*, pages 6:1–6:469. ACM Press, 2012. 643

[Hachisuka *et al.*, 2012b] Toshiya Hachisuka, Jacopo Pantaleoni, and Henrik Wann Jensen. A Path Space Extension for Robust Light Transport Simulation. *ACM Transactions on Graphics*, 31(6):191:1–191:10, November 2012. 642

[Hachisuka *et al.*, 2013] Toshiya Hachisuka, Wojciech Jarosz, Iliyan Georgiev, Anton S. Kaplanyan, Derek Nowrouzezahrai, and Ben Spencer. State of the Art in Photon Density Estimation. In *ACM SIGGRAPH Asia Courses*, pages 15:1–15:562. ACM Press, 2013. 643

[Hachisuka *et al.*, 2014] Toshiya Hachisuka, Anton S. Kaplanyan, and Carsten Dachsbacher. Multiplexed Metropolis Light Transport. *ACM Transactions on Graphics*, 33(4):100:1–100:10, July 2014. 623

[Hachisuka, 2011] Toshiya Hachisuka. *Robust Light Transport Simulation Using Progressive Density Estimation.* PhD thesis, University of California at San Diego, 2011. 637, 638, 641, 642

[Haines and Greenberg, 1986] Eric A. Haines and Donald P. Greenberg. The Light Buffer: A Shadow-Testing Accelerator. *IEEE Computer Graphics and Applications*, 6(9):6–16, September 1986. 410

[Haines, 1986] Eric A. Haines. The Light Buffer: A Ray Tracer Shadow Testing Accelerator. Master's thesis, Program of Computer Graphics, Cornell University, January 1986. 410

[Haines, 1987] Eric A. Haines. A Proposal for Standard Graphics Environments. *IEEE Computer Graphics and Applications*, 7(11):3–5, November 1987. 414

[Haines, 1991] Eric A. Haines. Efficiency Improvements for Hierarchy Traversal in Ray Tracing. In James Richard Arvo, editor, *Graphics Gems II*, chapter V.5, pages 267–272. Academic Press, 1991. 368

[Hall, 1986] Roy A. Hall. A Characterization of Illumination Models and Shading Techniques. *The Visual Computer*, 2(5):268–277, September 1986. 561

[Hall, 1989] Roy A. Hall. *Illumination and Color in Computer Generated Imagery.* Springer-Verlag, 1989. 561

[Hammersley and Handscomb, 1964] John Michael Hammersley and David Christopher Handscomb. *Monte Carlo Methods.* Methuen & Co., 1964. 172

[Hanrahan and Krueger, 1993] Patrick Hanrahan and Wolfgang Krueger. Reflection from Layered Surfaces Due to Subsurface Scattering. In *Proceedings of SIGGRAPH – The ACM International Conference on Computer Graphics and Interactive Techniques*, pages 165–174. ACM Press, 1993. 559, 561

[Hanrahan and Lawson, 1990] Patrick Hanrahan and Jim Lawson. A Language for Shading and Lighting Calculations. *SIGGRAPH Computer Graphics (Proceedings of SIGGRAPH – The ACM International Conference on Computer Graphics and Interactive Techniques)*, 24(4):289–298, August 1990. 7

[Hanrahan, 1989] Patrick Hanrahan. A Survey of Ray-Surface Intersection Algorithms. In Andrew S. Glassner, editor, *An Introduction to Ray Tracing*, chapter 3, pages 79–119. Academic Press, 1989. 304

[Hansmann, 1996] Werner Hansmann. Germany: Computer Graphics in Computer Science and Art Education. *SIGGRAPH Computer Graphics*, 30(3):14–15, August 1996. 8

[Hapala and Havran, 2011] Michal Hapala and Vlastimil Havran. Review: KD-Tree Traversal Algorithms for Ray Tracing. *Computer Graphics Forum*, 30(1):199–213, March 2011. 384

[Hapala *et al.*, 2011a] Michal Hapala, Tomáš Davidovič, Ingo Wald, Vlastimil Havran, and Philipp Slusallek. Efficient Stack-Less BVH Traversal for Ray Tracing. In *Proceedings of SCCG – The Spring Conference on Computer Graphics*, pages 7–12. ACM Press, 2011. 363

[Hapala *et al.*, 2011b] Michal Hapala, Ondřej Karlík, and Vlastimil Havran. When It Makes Sense to Use Uniform Grids for Ray Tracing. In *Proceedings of WSCG – The Winter School of Computer Graphics: The International Conference in Central Europe on Computer Graphics, Visualization and Computer Vision*, pages 193–200, 2011. Short Papers. 415

[Hapke, 1963] Bruce W. Hapke. A Theoretical Photometric Function for the Lunar Surface. *Journal of Geophysical Research*, 68(15):4571–4586, August 1963. 485

[Hapke, 1993] Bruce W. Hapke. *Theory of Reflectance and Emittance Spectroscopy*. Cambridge University Press, 1993. 485

[Happa *et al.*, 2010] Jassim Happa, Mark Mudge, Kurt Debattista, Alessandro Artusi, Alexandrino Gonçalves, and Alan Chalmers. Illuminating the Past: State of the Art. *Virtual Reality*, 14(3):155–182, September 2010. 10

[Hart *et al.*, 1989] John C. Hart, Daniel J. Sandin, and Louis H. Kauffman. Ray Tracing Deterministic 3-D Fractals. *SIGGRAPH Computer Graphics (Proceedings of SIGGRAPH – The ACM International Conference on Computer Graphics and Interactive Techniques)*, 23(3):289–296, July 1989. 308

[Hart, 1996] John C. Hart. Sphere Tracing: A Geometric Method for the Antialiased Ray Tracing of Implicit Surfaces. *The Visual Computer*, 12(10):527–545, December 1996. 306

[Hastings, 1970] W. Keith Hastings. Monte Carlo Sampling Methods using Markov Chains and Their Applications. *Biometrika*, 57(1):97–109, April 1970. 137

[Havran and Bittner, 1999] Vlastimil Havran and Jiří Bittner. Rectilinear BSP Trees for Preferred Ray Sets. In *Proceedings of SCCG – The Spring Conference on Computer Graphics*, pages 171–179, 1999. 400

[Havran and Bittner, 2002] Vlastimil Havran and Jiří Bittner. On Improving KD-Trees for Ray Shooting. *Journal of WSCG (Proceedings of WSCG – The Winter School of Computer Graphics: The International Conference in Central Europe on Computer Graphics, Visualization and Computer Vision)*, 10(1–3):209–216, February 2002. 369, 370, 399

[Havran and Bittner, 2006] Vlastimil Havran and Jiří Bittner. Efficient Sorting and Searching in Rendering Algorithms. In *Eurographics Tutorials*, pages 325–398. Eurographics Association, 2006. 415

[Havran and Bittner, 2007a] Vlastimil Havran and Jiří Bittner. Ray Tracing with Sparse Boxes. In *Proceedings of SCCG – The Spring Conference on Computer Graphics*, pages 49–54. ACM Press, 2007. 382

[Havran and Bittner, 2007b] Vlastimil Havran and Jiří Bittner. Stackless Ray Traversal for kD-Trees with Sparse Boxes. *Computer Graphics & Geometry*, 9(3):16–30, December 2007. 382

[Havran and Purgathofer, 2000] Vlastimil Havran and Werner Purgathofer. Comparison Methodology for Ray Shooting Algorithms. Technical Report TR-186-2-00-20, Institute of Computer Graphics and Algorithms, Vienna University of Technology, November 2000. 414

[Havran and Žára, 1997] Vlastimil Havran and Jiří Žára. Evaluation of BSP Properties for Ray-Tracing. In *Proceedings of SCCG – The Spring Conference on Computer Graphics*, pages 155–162, 1997. 414

[Havran *et al.*, 1997] Vlastimil Havran, Tomás Kopal, Jiří Bittner, and Jiří Žára. Fast Robust BSP Tree Traversal Algorithm for Ray Tracing. *Journal of Graphics Tools (JGT)*, 2(4):15–23, 1997. 383, 384

[Havran *et al.*, 1998] Vlastimil Havran, Jiří Bittner, and Jiří Žára. Ray Tracing with Rope Trees. In *Proceedings of SCCG – The Spring Conference on Computer Graphics*, pages 130–139, 1998. 383

[Havran *et al.*, 2000] Vlastimil Havran, Jan Přikryl, and Werner Purgathofer. Statistical Comparison of Ray-Shooting Efficiency Schemes. Technical Report TR-186-2-00-14, Institute of Computer Graphics and Algorithms, Vienna University of Technology, May 2000. 414

[Havran *et al.*, 2004] Vlastimil Havran, Jiří Bittner, and Hans-Peter Seidel. Ray Maps for Global Illumination. In *ACM SIGGRAPH Sketches*, pages 77–77. ACM Press, 2004. 636

[Havran *et al.*, 2005a] Vlastimil Havran, Jiří Bittner, Robert Herzog, and Hans-Peter Seidel. Ray Maps for Global Illumination. In *Proceedings of EGSR – The Eurographics Symposium on Rendering*, pages 43–54. Eurographics Association, 2005. 636

[Havran *et al.*, 2005b] Vlastimil Havran, Robert Herzog, and Hans-Peter Seidel. Fast Final Gathering via Reverse Photon Mapping. *Computer Graphics Forum (Proceedings of Eurographics – The Annual Conference of the European Association for Computer Graphics)*, 24(3):323–332, September 2005. 640

[Havran *et al.*, 2006] Vlastimil Havran, Robert Herzog, and Hans-Peter Seidel. On the Fast Construction of Spatial Hierarchies for Ray Tracing. In *Proceedings of RT – The IEEE Symposium on Interactive Ray Tracing*, pages 71–80. IEEE Computer Society, 2006. 366

[Havran, 1997a] Vlastimil Havran. Cache Sensitive Representation for the BSP Tree. In *Proceedings of CompuGraphics – The International Conference on Computational Graphics and Visualization Techniques*, pages 369–376. GRASP – Graphics Science Promotions & Publications, December 1997. 408, 409

[Havran, 1997b] Vlastimil Havran. Spatial Data Structures for Visibility Computation. Technical Report DC-PSR-97-xx, Department of Computer Science and Engineering, Faculty of Electrical Engineering, Czech Technical University, May 1997. Postgraduate Study Report. 415

[Havran, 1999] Vlastimil Havran. Analysis of Cache Sensitive Representation for Binary Space Partitioning Trees. *Informatica, Slovene Society Informatika*, 23(2):203–210, May 1999. 408, 409

[Havran, 2000] Vlastimil Havran. *Heuristic Ray Shooting Algorithms*. PhD thesis, Faculty of Electrical Engineering, Czech Technical University, November 2000. 383, 384, 400, 408, 409, 414

[Havran, 2007] Vlastimil Havran. About the Relation between Spatial Subdivisions and Object Hierarchies Used in Ray Tracing. In *Proceedings of SCCG – The Spring Conference on Computer Graphics*, pages 43–48. ACM Press, 2007. 357, 391, 392, 400

[Hašan *et al.*, 2009] Miloš Hašan, Jaroslav Křivánek, Bruce Jonathan Walter, and Kavita Bala. Virtual Spherical Lights for Many-Light Rendering of Glossy Scenes. *ACM Transactions on Graphics (Proceedings of SIGGRAPH Asia – The ACM Conference on Computer Graphics and Interactive Techniques in Asia)*, 28(5):143:1–143:6, December 2009. 631

[He *et al.*, 1991] Xiao Dong He, Kenneth E. Torrance, François X. Sillion, and Donald P. Greenberg. A Comprehensive Physical Model for Light Reflection. *SIGGRAPH Computer Graphics (Proceedings of SIGGRAPH – The ACM International Conference on Computer Graphics and Interactive Techniques)*, 25(4):175–186, July 1991. 547

[He *et al.*, 1992] Xiao Dong He, Patrick O. Heynen, Richard L. Phillips, Kenneth E. Torrance, David H. Salesin, and Donald P. Greenberg. A Fast and Accurate Light Reflection Model. *SIGGRAPH Computer Graphics (Proceedings of SIGGRAPH – The ACM International Conference on Computer Graphics and Interactive Techniques)*, 26(2):253–254, July 1992. 548

[He, 1993] Xiao Dong He. *Physically-Based Models for the Reflection, Transmission and Subsurface Scattering of Light by Smooth and Rough Surfaces, with Applications to Realistic Image Synthesis*. PhD thesis, Cornell University, January 1993. 547

[Hearn and Baker, 1997] Donald Hearn and M. Pauline Baker. *Computer Graphics, C Version*. Prentice Hall, 2nd edition, 1997. 739

[Heckbert, 1990] Paul Seagrave Heckbert. Adaptive Radiosity Textures for Bidirectional Ray Tracing. *SIGGRAPH Computer Graphics (Proceedings of SIGGRAPH – The ACM International Conference on Computer Graphics and Interactive Techniques)*, 24(4):145–154, August 1990. 571, 633

[Heckbert, 1992] Paul Seagrave Heckbert. Introduction to Global Illumination. In *ACM SIGGRAPH Courses*. ACM Press, 1992. 571

[Heidrich and Seidel, 1998] Wolfgang Heidrich and Hans-Peter Seidel. View-Independent Environment Maps. In *Proceedings of EGGH – The Eurographics Workshop on Graphics Hardware*, pages 39–45. Eurographics Association, 1998. 433, 675

[Heidrich, 2000] Wolfgang Heidrich. Interactive Display of Global Illumination Solutions for Non-Diffuse Environments – A Survey. In *Eurographics State of the Art Reports*. Eurographics Association, 2000. 644

[Heitz and d'Eon, 2014] Eric Heitz and Eugene d'Eon. Importance Sampling Microfacet-Based BSDFs using the Distribution of Visible Normals. *Computer Graphics Forum (Proceedings of EGSR – The Eurographics Symposium on Rendering)*, 33(4):103–112, July 2014. 532, 537

[Heitz *et al.*, 2013] Eric Heitz, Christophe Bourlier, and Nicolas Pinel. Correlation Effect between Transmitter and Receiver Azimuthal Directions on the Illumination Function from a Random Rough Surface. *Waves in Random and Complex Media*, 23(3):318–335, 2013. 546

[Heitz, 2014] Eric Heitz. Understanding the Masking-Shadowing Function in Microfacet-Based BRDFs. *Journal of Computer Graphics Techniques (JCGT)*, 3(2):32–91, 2014. 518, 534, 536, 537, 545

[Held, 1997] Martin Held. ERIT – A Collection of Efficient and Reliable Intersection Tests. *Journal of Graphics Tools (JGT)*, 2(4):25–44, 1997. 304

[Henderson, 1996] Michael Henderson. United States: Technology in Art Education. *SIGGRAPH Computer Graphics*, 30(3):30–30, August 1996. 8

[Henyey and Greenstein, 1941] Louis G. Henyey and Jesse Leonard Greenstein. Diffuse Radiation in the Galaxy. *Astrophysical Journal*, 93:70–83, 1941. 454

[Herbison-Evans, 1995] Don Herbison-Evans. Solving Quartics and Cubics for Graphics. In Alan W. Paeth, editor, *Graphics Gems V*, chapter I.1, pages 3–15. Academic Press, 1995. 32, 35

[Hermann, 1870] Ludimar Hermann. Eine Erscheinung simultanen Contrastes. *Archiv für die gesamte Physiologie des Menschen und der Tiere*, 3(1):13–15, December 1870. 696, 697

[Herzog and Seidel, 2007] Robert Herzog and Hans-Peter Seidel. Lighting Details Preserving Photon Density Estimation. In *Proceedings of Pacific Graphics – The Pacific Conference on Computer Graphics and Applications*, pages 407–410. IEEE Computer Society, 2007. 636

[Herzog *et al.*, 2007] Robert Herzog, Vlastimil Havran, Shinichi Kinuwaki, Karol Myszkowski, and Hans-Peter Seidel. Global Illumination using Photon Ray Splatting. *Computer Graphics Forum (Proceedings of Eurographics – The Annual Conference of the European Association for Computer Graphics)*, 26(3):503–513, September 2007. 636, 637

[Herzog, 2005] Robert Herzog. Advanced Density Estimation Techniques for Global Illumination. Master's thesis, MPI Informatik, Universität des Saarlandes, October 2005. 636, 640

[Hesterberg, 1988] Timothy Classen Hesterberg. *Advances in Importance Sampling.* PhD thesis, Department of Statistics, Stanford University, August 1988. 157

[Hesterberg, 1995] Timothy Classen Hesterberg. Weighted Average Importance Sampling and Defensive Mixture Distributions. *Technometrics*, 37(2):185–194, May 1995. 157

[Hey and Purgathofer, 2002] Heinrich Hey and Werner Purgathofer. Advanced Radiance Estimation for Photon Map Global Illumination. *Computer Graphics Forum (Proceedings of Eurographics – The Annual Conference of the European Association for Computer Graphics)*, 21(3):541–545, September 2002. 636

[Hiebert *et al.*, 2006] Brad Hiebert, Jubin Dave, Tae-Yong Kim, Ivan Neulander, Hans Rijpkema, and Will Telford. The Chronicles of Narnia: The Lion, the Crowds and Rhythm and Hues. In *ACM SIGGRAPH Courses*, number 11. ACM Press, 2006. 9

[Hill *et al.*, 2014] Stephen Hill, Stephen McAuley, Jonathan Dupuy, Yoshiharu Gotanda, Eric Heitz, Nathaniel Hoffman, Sébastien Lagarde, Anders Langlands, Ian Megibben, Farhez Rayani, and Charles de Rousiers. Physically Based Shading in Theory and Practice. In *ACM SIGGRAPH Courses*, pages 23:1–23:8. ACM Press, 2014. 473

[Hoffman and Preetham, 2002] Nathaniel Hoffman and Arcot J. Preetham. Rendering Outdoor Light Scattering in Real Time. ATI White Paper, 2002. 576

[Hoffman and Preetham, 2003] Nathaniel Hoffman and Arcot J. Preetham. Real-Time Light-Atmosphere Interactions for Outdoor Scenes. In Jeff Lander, editor, *Graphics Programming Methods*, chapter 3.11, pages 337–352. Charles River Media, 2003. 576

[Hoffman *et al.*, 2010] Nathaniel Hoffman, Yoshiharu Gotanda, Adam Martinez, and Ben Snow. Physically-Based Shading Models in Film and Game Production. In *ACM SIGGRAPH Courses*. ACM Press, 2010. 473

[Hofmann, 1990] Georg Rainer Hofmann. Who Invented Ray Tracing? *The Visual Computer*, 6(3):120–124, May 1990. 598

[Hook and Forward, 1995] David Geoffrey Hook and Kevin Forward. Using Kd-Trees to Guide Bounding Volume Hierarchies for Ray Tracing. *Australian Computer Journal*, 27(3):103–108, 1995. 392

[Hook, 1995] David Geoffrey Hook. Algorithms for Accelerating Ray Tracing. Master's thesis, Deptartment of Computer Engineering, University of Melbourne, May 1995. 392

[Horn *et al.*, 2007] Daniel Reiter Horn, Jeremy Sugerman, Mike Houston, and Patrick Hanrahan. Interactive K-D Tree GPU Raytracing. In *Proceedings of I3D – The ACM SIGGRAPH Symposium on Interactive 3D Graphics and Games*, pages 167–174. ACM Press, 2007. 408

[Hsiung and Thibadeau, 1992] Ping-Kang Hsiung and Robert Thibadeau. Accelerating ARTS. *The Visual Computer*, 8(3):181–190, March 1992. 377

[Hughes *et al.*, 2013] John F. Hughes, Andries van Dam, Morgan McGuire, David F. Sklar, James D. Foley, Steven K. Feiner, and Kurt Akeley. *Computer Graphics: Principles and Practice.* Addison-Wesley Publishing, 3rd edition, 2013. 739

[Hultquist, 1990] Jeff Hultquist. Intersection of a Ray with a Sphere. In Andrew S. Glassner, editor, *Graphics Gems I*, chapter VII.2, pages 388–389. Academic Press, 1990. 269

[Hunt and Mark, 2008a] Warren Andrew Hunt and William R. Mark. Adaptive Acceleration Structures in Perspective Space. In *Proceedings of RT – The IEEE Symposium on Interactive Ray Tracing*, pages 11–17. IEEE Computer Society, 2008. 412

[Hunt and Mark, 2008b] Warren Andrew Hunt and William R. Mark. Ray-Specialized Acceleration Structures for Ray Tracing. In *Proceedings of RT – The IEEE Symposium on Interactive Ray Tracing*, pages 3–10. IEEE Computer Society, 2008. 412

[Hunt *et al.*, 2006] Warren Andrew Hunt, William R. Mark, and Gordon Stoll. Fast KD-Tree Construction with an Adaptive Error-Bounded Heuristic. In *Proceedings of RT – The IEEE Symposium on Interactive Ray Tracing*, pages 81–88. IEEE Computer Society, 2006. 400, 403

[Hunt *et al.*, 2007] Warren Andrew Hunt, William R. Mark, and Donald S. Fussell. Fast and Lazy Build of Acceleration Structures from Scene Hierarchies. In *Proceedings of RT – The IEEE Symposium on Interactive Ray Tracing*, pages 47–54. IEEE Computer Society, 2007. 398, 406

[Hunt, 2008a] Warren Andrew Hunt. Corrections to the Surface Area Metric with Respect to Mail-Boxing. In *Proceedings of RT – The IEEE Symposium on Interactive Ray Tracing*, pages 77–80. IEEE Computer Society, 2008. 400

[Hunt, 2008b] Warren Andrew Hunt. *Data Structures and Algorithms for Real-Time Ray Tracing at the University of Texas at Austin.* PhD thesis, The University of Texas at Austin, December 2008. 398, 400, 403, 406, 412

[Hurley *et al.*, 2002] Jim Hurley, Alexander Kapustin, Alexander Reshetov, and Alexei Soupikov. Fast Ray Tracing for Modern General Purpose CPU. In *Proceedings of GraphiCon – The International Conference on Computer Graphics and Vision*, 2002. 398, 401, 403

[Hurst *et al.*, 1989a] Jan Hurst, Michael S. Mahoney, John T. Gilmore, Lawrence G. Roberts, and A. Robin Forrest. Retrospectives: The Early Years in Computer Graphics at MIT, Lincoln Lab and Harvard – Part 2. *SIGGRAPH Computer Graphics (ACM SIGGRAPH Panel Proceedings)*, 23(5):39–73, July 1989. 4

[Hurst *et al.*, 1989b] Jan Hurst, Michael S. Mahoney, Norman H. Taylor, Douglas T. Ross, and Robert M. Fano. Retrospectives: The Early Years in Computer Graphics at MIT, Lincoln Lab and Harvard – Part 1. *SIGGRAPH Computer Graphics (ACM SIGGRAPH Panel Proceedings)*, 23(5):19–38, July 1989. 4

[Inakage and Inakage, 1996] Masa Inakage and Hiroko Inakage. Japan: Computer Graphics Art and Design Education. *SIGGRAPH Computer Graphics*, 30(3):19–19, August 1996. 8

[Inanici, 2001] Mehlika N. Inanici. Application of the State-of-the-Art Computer Simulation and Visualization in Architectural Lighting Research. In *Proceedings of the International Building Performance Simulation Association Conference*, pages 1175–1182, 2001. 10

[Iones *et al.*, 1998] Andrei Iones, Sergey Zhukov, and Anton Krupkin. On Optimality of OBBs for Visibility Tests for Frustum Culling, Ray Shooting and Collision Detection. In *Proceedings of CGI – Computer Graphics International*, pages 256–263. IEEE Computer Society, 1998. 359

[Irvine, 1966] William M. Irvine. The Shadowing Effect in Diffuse Reflection. *Journal of Geophysical Research*, 71(12):2931–2937, 1966. 485

[Ishimaru, 1978] Akira Ishimaru. *Wave Propagation and Scattering in Random Media.* Academic Press, 1978. 461, 470

[Ize and Hansen, 2011] Thiago Ize and Charles D. Hansen. RTSAH Traversal Order for Occlusion Rays. *Computer Graphics Forum (Proceedings of Eurographics – The Annual Conference of the European Association for Computer Graphics)*, 30(2):297–305, April 2011. 400

[Ize *et al.*, 2007] Thiago Ize, Peter Schuyler Shirley, and Steven Gregory Parker. Grid Creation Strategies for Efficient Ray Tracing. In *Proceedings of RT – The IEEE Symposium on Interactive Ray Tracing*, pages 27–32. IEEE Computer Society, 2007. 372, 377

[Ize *et al.*, 2008] Thiago Ize, Ingo Wald, and Steven Gregory Parker. Ray Tracing with the BSP Tree. In *Proceedings of RT – The IEEE Symposium on Interactive Ray Tracing*, pages 159–166. IEEE Computer Society, 2008. 386, 387

[Ize, 2009] Thiago Ize. *Efficient Acceleration Structures for Ray Tracing Static and Dynamic Scenes.* PhD thesis, School of Computing, University of Utah, August 2009. 372, 377, 386, 387

[Jakob and Marschner, 2012a] Wenzel Alban Jakob and Stephen Robert Marschner. Manifold Exploration: A Markov Chain Monte Carlo Technique for Rendering Scenes with Difficult Specular Transport. *ACM Transactions on Graphics (Proceedings of SIGGRAPH – The ACM International Conference on Computer Graphics and Interactive Techniques)*, 31(4):58:1–58:13, July 2012. 623

[Jakob and Marschner, 2012b] Wenzel Alban Jakob and Stephen Robert Marschner. Manifold Exploration: A Markov Chain Monte Carlo Technique for Rendering Scenes with Difficult Specular Transport: Expanded Technical Report. Technical report, Department of Computer Science, Cornell University, May 2012. 623

[Jakob *et al.*, 2011] Wenzel Alban Jakob, Christian Regg, and Wojciech Jarosz. Progressive Expectation-Maximization for Hierarchical Volumetric Photon Mapping. *Computer Graphics Forum (Proceedings of EGSR – The Eurographics Symposium on Rendering)*, 30(4):1287–1297, June 2011. 643

[Jakob, 2013] Wenzel Alban Jakob. *Light Transport on Path-Space Manifolds.* PhD thesis, Cornell University, August 2013. 623

[Jansen, 1986] Frederik W. Jansen. Data Structures for Ray Tracing. In *Proceedings of the Workshop on Data Structures for Raster Graphics*, pages 57–73. Springer-Verlag, 1986. Eurographics Seminars. 383, 406

[Jarosz *et al.*, 2007] Wojciech Jarosz, Craig Steven Donner, Matthias Zwicker, and Henrik Wann Jensen. Radiance Caching for Participating Media. In *ACM SIGGRAPH Sketches.* ACM Press, 2007. 628

[Jarosz *et al.*, 2008a] Wojciech Jarosz, Craig Steven Donner, Matthias Zwicker, and Henrik Wann Jensen. Radiance Caching for Participating Media. *ACM Transactions on Graphics*, 27(1):7:1–7:11, March 2008. 628

[Jarosz *et al.*, 2008b] Wojciech Jarosz, Henrik Wann Jensen, and Craig Steven Donner. Advanced Global Illumination using Photon Mapping. In *ACM SIGGRAPH Courses*, pages 2:1–2:112. ACM Press, 2008. 643

[Jarosz *et al.*, 2008c] Wojciech Jarosz, Matthias Zwicker, and Henrik Wann Jensen. Irradiance Gradients in the Presence of Participating Media and Occlusions. *Computer Graphics Forum (Proceedings of EGSR – The Eurographics Symposium on Rendering)*, 27(4):1087–1096, June 2008. 626

[Jarosz *et al.*, 2008d] Wojciech Jarosz, Matthias Zwicker, and Henrik Wann Jensen. The Beam Radiance Estimate for Volumetric Photon Mapping. *Computer Graphics Forum (Proceedings of Eurographics – The Annual Conference of the European Association for Computer Graphics)*, 27(2):557–566, April 2008. 643

[Jarosz *et al.*, 2008e] Wojciech Jarosz, Matthias Zwicker, and Henrik Wann Jensen. The Beam Radiance Estimate for Volumetric Photon Mapping. In *ACM SIGGRAPH Courses*, pages 3:1–3:112. ACM Press, 2008. 643

[Jarosz *et al.*, 2011a] Wojciech Jarosz, Derek Nowrouzezahrai, Iman Sadeghi, and Henrik Wann Jensen. A Comprehensive Theory of Volumetric Radiance Estimation using Photon Points and Beams. *ACM Transactions on Graphics*, 30(1):5:1–5:19, February 2011. 643

[Jarosz *et al.*, 2011b] Wojciech Jarosz, Derek Nowrouzezahrai, Robert Thomas, Peter-Pike Sloan, and Matthias Zwicker. Progressive Photon Beams. *ACM Transactions on Graphics (Proceedings of SIGGRAPH Asia – The ACM Conference on Computer Graphics and Interactive Techniques in Asia)*, 30(6):181:1–181:12, December 2011. 643

[Jarosz *et al.*, 2012] Wojciech Jarosz, Volker Schönefeld, Leif P. Kobbelt, and Henrik Wann Jensen. Theory, Analysis and Applications of 2D Global Illumination. *ACM Transactions on Graphics*, 31(5):125:1–125:21, August 2012. 627, 635

[Jarosz, 2008] Wojciech Jarosz. *Efficient Monte Carlo Methods for Light Transport in Scattering Media.* PhD thesis, University of California at San Diego, 2008. 626, 628, 643

[Jensen and Christensen, 1995a] Henrik Wann Jensen and Niels Jørgen Christensen. Efficiently Rendering Shadows using the Photon Map. In *Proceedings of CompuGraphics – The International Conference on Computational Graphics and Visualization Techniques*, pages 285–291, 1995. 640

[Jensen and Christensen, 1995b] Henrik Wann Jensen and Niels Jørgen Christensen. Photon Maps in Bidirectional Monte Carlo Ray Tracing of Complex Objects. *Computers & Graphics*, 19(2):215–224, March 1995. 634, 637, 639

[Jensen and Christensen, 1998] Henrik Wann Jensen and Per Henrik Christensen. Efficient Simulation of Light Transport in Scenes with Participating Media using Photon Maps. In *Proceedings of SIGGRAPH – The ACM International Conference on Computer Graphics and Interactive Techniques*, pages 311–320. ACM Press, 1998. 643

[Jensen and Christensen, 2007] Henrik Wann Jensen and Per Henrik Christensen. High Quality Rendering using Ray Tracing and Photon Mapping. In *ACM SIGGRAPH Courses*. ACM Press, 2007. 643

[Jensen *et al.*, 2001a] Henrik Wann Jensen, James Richard Arvo, Marcos Fajardo, Patrick Hanrahan, Don P. Mitchell, Matthew M. Pharr, and Peter Schuyler Shirley. State of the Art in Monte Carlo Ray Tracing for Realistic Image Synthesis. In *ACM SIGGRAPH Courses*, number 29. ACM Press, 2001. 624

[Jensen *et al.*, 2001b] Henrik Wann Jensen, Per Henrik Christensen, and Frank Suykens. A Practical Guide to Global Illumination using Photon Mapping. In *ACM SIGGRAPH Courses*, number 38. ACM Press, 2001. 643

[Jensen *et al.*, 2002] Henrik Wann Jensen, Per Henrik Christensen, Toshiaki Kato, and Frank Suykens. A Practical Guide to Global Illumination using Photon Mapping. In *ACM SIGGRAPH Courses*, number 43. ACM Press, 2002. 643

[Jensen, 1995] Henrik Wann Jensen. Importance Driven Path Tracing using the Photon Map. In *Proceedings of EGWR – The Eurographics Workshop on Rendering Techniques*, pages 326–335. Springer-Verlag, 1995. 639

[Jensen, 1996a] Henrik Wann Jensen. Global Illumination using Photon Maps. In *Proceedings of EGWR – The Eurographics Workshop on Rendering Techniques*, pages 21–30. Springer-Verlag, 1996. 640

[Jensen, 1996b] Henrik Wann Jensen. Rendering Caustics on Non-Lambertian Surfaces. In *Proceedings of Graphics Interface – The Canadian Annual Conference on Computer Graphics, Interactive Systems, and Human-Computer Interaction*, pages 116–121. Canadian Human-Computer Communications Society, May 1996. 634, 635

[Jensen, 1997] Henrik Wann Jensen. Rendering Caustics on Non-Lambertian Surfaces. *Computer Graphics Forum*, 16(1):57–64, March 1997. 634, 635

[Jensen, 2001] Henrik Wann Jensen. *Realistic Image Synthesis using Photon Mapping.* A. K. Peters, 2001. 643

[Jensen, 2004] Henrik Wann Jensen. A Practical Guide to Global Illumination using Ray Tracing and Photon Mapping. In *ACM SIGGRAPH Courses.* ACM Press, 2004. 643

[Jevans and Wyvill, 1989] David Jevans and Brian Wyvill. Adaptive Voxel Subdivision for Ray Tracing. In *Proceedings of Graphics Interface – The Canadian Annual Conference on Computer Graphics, Interactive Systems, and Human-Computer Interaction*, pages 164–172. Canadian Human-Computer Communications Society, 1989. 377

[Joblove and Greenberg, 1978] George H. Joblove and Donald P. Greenberg. Color Spaces for Computer Graphics. *SIGGRAPH Computer Graphics (Proceedings of SIGGRAPH – The ACM International Conference on Computer Graphics and Interactive Techniques)*, 12(3):20–25, August 1978. 707

[Johnson *et al.*, 2011] Jared M. Johnson, Dylan Lacewell, Andrew Selle, and Wojciech Jarosz. Gaussian Quadrature for Photon Beams in Tangled. In *ACM SIGGRAPH Talks*, pages 54:1–54:1. ACM Press, 2011. 643

[Johnson, 2010] Charles S. Johnson. *Science for the Curious Photographer: An Introduction to the Science of Photography.* A. K. Peters, 2010. 675

[Jones and Lansdown, 1996] Huw Jones and John Lansdown. United Kingdom: Computer Graphics Work Covers the Full Spectrum. *SIGGRAPH Computer Graphics*, 30(2):45–48, May 1996. 8

[Judd, 1951] Deane B. Judd. Report of US Secretariat Committee on Colorimetry and Artificial Daylight. In *Proceedings of the Session of the CIE*, volume 1, page 11. Bureau Central de la CIE, 1951. 686, 687, 712, 719

[Kajiya, 1986] James T. Kajiya. The Rendering Equation. *SIGGRAPH Computer Graphics (Proceedings of SIGGRAPH – The ACM International Conference on Computer Graphics and Interactive Techniques)*, 20(4):143–150, August 1986. 7, 475, 565, 613

[Kalojanov and Slusallek, 2009] Javor Kalojanov and Philipp Slusallek. A Parallel Algorithm for Construction of Uniform Grids. In *Proceedings of HPG – The Conference on High-Performance Graphics*, pages 23–28. Eurographics Association/ACM SIGGRAPH, 2009. 377

[Kalos and Whitlock, 1986] Malvin H. Kalos and Paula A. Whitlock. *Monte Carlo Methods*, volume 1: Basics. Wiley-VCH, 1st edition, 1986. 172

[Kammaje and Mora, 2007] Ravi P. Kammaje and Benjamin Mora. A Study of Restricted BSP Trees for Ray Tracing. In *Proceedings of RT – The IEEE Symposium on Interactive Ray Tracing*, pages 55–62. IEEE Computer Society, 2007. 386, 387

[Kaplan, 1985] Michael R. Kaplan. Space-Tracing: A Constant Time Ray-Tracer. In *ACM SIGGRAPH Courses*, volume 11, pages 149–158. ACM Press, July 1985. State of the Art in Image Synthesis, Tutorial on the Uses of Spatial Coherence Ray Tracing. 382, 394

[Kaplan, 1987] Michael R. Kaplan. The Use of Spatial Coherence in Ray Tracing. In *Proceedings of Techniques for Computer Graphics*, pages 173–193, 1987. 382, 394

[Kaplanyan and Dachsbacher, 2013] Anton S. Kaplanyan and Carsten Dachsbacher. Adaptive Progressive Photon Mapping. *ACM Transactions on Graphics*, 32(2):16:1–16:13, April 2013. 638, 639, 643

[Karner and Prantl, 1996] Konrad F. Karner and Manfred Prantl. A Concept for Evaluating the Accuracy of Computer-Generated Images. In *Proceedings of SCCG – The Spring Conference on Computer Graphics*, 1996. 739

[Kay and Kajiya, 1986] Timothy L. Kay and James T. Kajiya. Ray Tracing Complex Scenes. *SIGGRAPH Computer Graphics (Proceedings of SIGGRAPH – The ACM International Conference on Computer Graphics and Interactive Techniques)*, 20(4):269 278, August 1986. 359, 408

[Kelemen and Szirmay-Kalos, 2001] Csaba Kelemen and László Szirmay-Kalos. A Microfacet Based Coupled Specular-Matte BRDF Model with Importance Sampling. In *Eurographics Short Presentations*. Eurographics Association, 2001. 535, 538, 557

[Kelemen *et al.*, 2002] Csaba Kelemen, László Szirmay-Kalos, György Antal, and Ferenc Csonka. A Simple and Robust Mutation Strategy for the Metropolis Light Transport Algorithm. *Computer Graphics Forum (Proceedings of Eurographics – The Annual Conference of the European Association for Computer Graphics)*, 21(3):531–540, September 2002. 623

[Keller and Wächter, 2011] Alexander Keller and Carsten Alexander Wächter. Efficient Ray Tracing without Auxiliary Acceleration Data Structure. In *High-Performance Graphics Posters*, 2011. 409

[Keller and Wald, 2000] Alexander Keller and Ingo Wald. Efficient Importance Sampling Techniques for the Photon Map. In *Proceedings of VMV – The Workshop on Vision, Modeling, and Visualization*, pages 271–280. Akademische Verlagsgesellschaft, 2000. 640, 641

[Keller *et al.*, 2015] Alexander Keller, Luca Fascione, Marcos Fajardo, Iliyan Georgiev, Per Henrik Christensen, Johannes Hanika, C. Eisenacher, and Greg Nichols. The Path Tracing Revolution in the Movie Industry. In *ACM SIGGRAPH Courses*, pages 24:1–24:7. ACM Press, 2015. 564

[Keller, 1997] Alexander Keller. Instant Radiosity. In *Proceedings of SIGGRAPH – The ACM International Conference on Computer Graphics and Interactive Techniques*, pages 49–56. ACM Press, 1997. 628

[Kensler and Shirley, 2006] Andrew E. Kensler and Peter Schuyler Shirley. Optimizing Ray-Triangle Intersection via Automated Search. In *Proceedings of RT – The IEEE Symposium on Interactive Ray Tracing*, pages 33–38. IEEE Computer Society, September 2006. 258

[Kensler, 2008] Andrew E. Kensler. Tree Rotations for Improving Bounding Volume Hierarchies. In *Proceedings of RT – The IEEE Symposium on Interactive Ray Tracing*, pages 73–76. IEEE Computer Society, 2008. 400

[Keys, 1981] Robert G. Keys. Cubic Convolution Interpolation for Digital Image Processing. *IEEE Transactions on Acoustics, Speech and Signal Processing*, 29(6):1153–1160, December 1981. 228

[Khodulev and Kopylov, 1996] Andrei B. Khodulev and Edward A. Kopylov. Physically-Accurate Lighting Simulation in Computer Graphics Software. In *Proceedings of GraphiCon – The International Conference on Computer Graphics and Vision*, volume 2, pages 111–119, July 1996. 739

[Kim *et al.*, 2002] Chang-Hun Kim, Myoung-Hee Kim, and Myung-Soo Kim. Computer Graphics in Korea. *SIGGRAPH Computer Graphics*, 36(3):22–26, August 2002. Computer Graphics around the World. 8

[Kim *et al.*, 2009a] Tae-Joon Kim, Bochang Moon, Duksu Kim, and Sung-Eui Yoon. RACBVHs: Random-Accessible Compressed Bounding Volume Hierarchies. In *ACM SIGGRAPH Posters*, pages 89:1–89:1. ACM Press, 2009. 365

[Kim *et al.*, 2009b] Tae-Joon Kim, Bochang Moon, Duksu Kim, and Sung-Eui Yoon. RACBVHs: Random-Accessible Compressed Bounding Volume Hierarchies. In *ACM SIGGRAPH Talks*, pages 46:1–46:1. ACM Press, 2009. 365

[Kim *et al.*, 2010] Tae-Joon Kim, Bochang Moon, Duksu Kim, and Sung-Eui Yoon. RACBVHs: Random-Accessible Compressed Bounding Volume Hierarchies. *IEEE Transactions on Visualization and Computer Graphics*, 16(2):273–286, March 2010. 365

[Kirk and Arvo, 1988] David Kirk and James Richard Arvo. The Ray Tracing Kernel. In *Proceedings of Ausgraph – The Australasian Conference on Computer Graphics*, pages 75–82, July 1988. 409

[Kirk and Arvo, 1991] David Kirk and James Richard Arvo. Improved Ray Tagging for Voxel-Based Ray Tracing. In James Richard Arvo, editor, *Graphics Gems II*, chapter V.4, pages 264–266. Academic Press, 1991. 391

[Kjelldahl and Jern, 1996] Lars Kjelldahl and Mikael Jern. Scandinavia: Computer Graphics Roots with Color Ink Jet Plotters. *SIGGRAPH Computer Graphics*, 30(2):37–40, May 1996. 8

[Kjelldahl, 1996] Lars Kjelldahl. Sweden: Survey of Computer Graphics and Visualization Education. *SIGGRAPH Computer Graphics*, 30(3):25–25, August 1996. 8

[Kjelldahl, 1999] Lars Kjelldahl. Computer Graphics in Scandanavia. *SIGGRAPH Computer Graphics*, 33(3):22–23, August 1999. Computer Graphics around the World. 8

[Klein *et al.*, 2003] Reinhard Klein, Jan Meseth, Gero Müller, Ralf Sarlette, Michael Guthe, and Ákos Balázs. RealReflect – Real-Time Visualization of Complex Reflectance Behaviour in Virtual Prototyping. In *Proceedings of Eurographics Industrial and Project Presentations.* Eurographics Association, 2003. 473

[Klein *et al.*, 2008] Jan Klein, Dirk Bartz, Ola Friman, Markus Hadwiger, Bernhard Preim, Felix Ritter, Anna Vilanova, and Gabriel Zachmann. Advanced Algorithms in Medical Computer Graphics. In *Eurographics State of the Art Reports*, pages 19–38. Eurographics Association, 2008. 10

[Klimaszewski and Sederberg, 1997] Krzysztof S. Klimaszewski and Thomas W. Sederberg. Faster Ray Tracing using Adaptive Grids. *IEEE Computer Graphics and Applications*, 17(1):42–51, January 1997. 372, 409

[Klimaszewski, 1994] Krzysztof S. Klimaszewski. *Faster Ray Tracing using Adaptive Grids and Area Sampling.* PhD thesis, Deptartment of Civil and Environmental Engineering, Brigham Young University, 1994. 372, 409

[Knaus and Zwicker, 2011] Claude Knaus and Matthias Zwicker. Progressive Photon Mapping: A Probabilistic Approach. *ACM Transactions on Graphics*, 30(3):25:1–25:13, May 2011. 638

[Kniss *et al.*, 2003a] Joe Michael Kniss, Simon Premože, Milan Ikits, Aaron Lefohn, and Charles D. Hansen. Closed-Form Approximations to the Volume Rendering Integral with Gaussian Transfer Functions. Technical Report UUCS-03-013, School of Computing, University of Utah, July 2003. 577

[Kniss *et al.*, 2003b] Joe Michael Kniss, Simon Premože, Milan Ikits, Aaron Lefohn, Charles D. Hansen, and Emil Praun. Gaussian Transfer Functions for Multifield Volume Visualization. In *Proceedings of Vis – The IEEE Conference on Visualization*, pages 497–504. IEEE Computer Society, October 2003. 577

[Kochanek and Bartels, 1984] Doris H. U. Kochanek and Richard H. Bartels. Interpolating Splines with Local Tension, Continuity, and Bias Control. *SIGGRAPH Computer Graphics (Proceedings of SIGGRAPH – The ACM International Conference on Computer Graphics and Interactive Techniques)*, 18(3):33–41, July 1984. 348

[Kollig and Keller, 2004] Thomas Kollig and Alexander Keller. Illumination in the Presence of Weak Singularities. In *Proceedings of the Conference on Monte Carlo and Quasi-Monte Carlo Methods*, pages 245–257, 2004. 630, 631

[Kroes *et al.*, 2012] Thomas Kroes, Frits H. Post, and Charl P. Botha. Exposure Render: An Interactive Photo-Realistic Volume Rendering Framework. *Public Library of Science (PLoS) ONE*, 7(7):1–10, July 2012. 441

[Krull, 1994] Fred N. Krull. The Origin of Computer Graphics Within General Motors. *IEEE Annals of the History of Computing*, 16(3):40–56, September 1994. 4

[Kubelka and Munk, 1931] Paul Kubelka and Franz Munk. Ein Beitrag zur Optik der Farbanstriche. *Zeitschrift für Technishen Physik*, 12(112):593–601, August 1931. 478

[Kubelka, 1948a] Paul Kubelka. Errata: New Contributions to the Optics of Intensely Light-Scattering Materials – Part I. *Journal of the Optical Society of America*, 38(12):1067–1067, 1948. 480

[Kubelka, 1948b] Paul Kubelka. New Contributions to the Optics of Intensely Light-Scattering Materials – Part I. *Journal of the Optical Society of America*, 38(5):448–457, 1948. 480

[Kubelka, 1954] Paul Kubelka. New Contributions to the Optics of Intensely Light-Scattering Materials – Part II: Nonhomogeneous Layers. *Journal of the Optical Society of America*, 44(4):330–334, 1954. 479, 481

[Kulla and Fajardo, 2011] Christopher Kulla and Marcos Fajardo. Importance Sampling of Area Lights in Participating Media. In *ACM SIGGRAPH Talks*, pages 55:1–55:1. ACM Press, 2011. 607

[Kulla and Fajardo, 2012] Christopher Kulla and Marcos Fajardo. Importance Sampling Techniques for Path Tracing in Participating Media. *Computer Graphics Forum (Proceedings of EGSR – The Eurographics Symposium on Rendering)*, 31(4):1519–1528, June 2012. 607

[Kunii *et al.*, 1996] Tosiyasu L. Kunii, Jianhua Ma, Runhe Huang, and Takao Maeda. Japan: Computer Graphics Research Activities. *SIGGRAPH Computer Graphics*, 30(2):28–31, May 1996. 8

[Kurachi, 2011] Noriko Kurachi. *The Magic of Computer Graphics*. A. K. Peters/CRC Press, 2011. 739

[Kurt and Edwards, 2009] Murat Kurt and David P. Edwards. A Survey of BRDF Models for Computer Graphics. *SIGGRAPH Computer Graphics*, 43(2):4:1–4:7, May 2009. 561

[Kurt *et al.*, 2010] Murat Kurt, László Szirmay-Kalos, and Jaroslav Křivánek. An Anisotropic BRDF Model for Fitting and Monte Carlo Rendering. *SIGGRAPH Computer Graphics*, 44(1):3:1–3:15, February 2010. 539

[Křivánek and Bubník, 2000] Jaroslav Křivánek and Vojtěch Bubník. Ray Tracing with BSP and Rope Trees. In *Proceedings of CESCG – The Central European Seminar on Computer Graphics*, 2000. 383

[Křivánek and Gautron, 2009] Jaroslav Křivánek and Pascal Gautron. *Practical Global Illumination with Irradiance Caching*. Synthesis Lectures on Computer Graphics and Animation. Morgan & Claypool Publishers, 2009. 627

[Křivánek and Žára, 2004] Jaroslav Křivánek and Jiří Žára. Radiance Caching for Fast Global Illumination with Arbitrary BRDFs. Workshop at Charles Technical University, 2004. 628

[Křivánek *et al.*, 2005a] Jaroslav Křivánek, Pascal Gautron, Kadi Bouatouch, and Sumanta N. Pattanaik. Improved Radiance Gradient Computation. In *Proceedings of SCCG – The Spring Conference on Computer Graphics*, pages 155–159. ACM Press, 2005. 628

[Křivánek *et al.*, 2005b] Jaroslav Křivánek, Pascal Gautron, Sumanta N. Pattanaik, and Kadi Bouatouch. Radiance Caching for Efficient Global Illumination Computation. *IEEE Transactions on Visualization and Computer Graphics*, 11(5):550–561, September 2005. 628

[Křivánek *et al.*, 2006] Jaroslav Křivánek, Kadi Bouatouch, Sumanta N. Pattanaik, and Jiří Žára. Making Radiance and Irradiance Caching Practical: Adaptive Caching and Neighbor Clamping. In *Proceedings of EGSR – The Eurographics Symposium on Rendering*, pages 127–138. Eurographics Association, 2006. 627, 628

[Křivánek *et al.*, 2008a] Jaroslav Křivánek, Kadi Bouatouch, Sumanta N. Pattanaik, and Jiří Žára. Making Radiance and Irradiance Caching Practical: Adaptive Caching and Neighbor Clamping. In *ACM SIGGRAPH Courses*, pages 77:1–77:12. ACM Press, 2008. 627, 628

[Křivánek *et al.*, 2008b] Jaroslav Křivánek, Pascal Gautron, Kadi Bouatouch, and Sumanta N. Pattanaik. Improved Radiance Gradient Computation. In *ACM SIGGRAPH Courses*, pages 76:1–76:5. ACM Press, 2008. 628

[Křivánek *et al.*, 2008c] Jaroslav Křivánek, Pascal Gautron, Sumanta N. Pattanaik, and Kadi Bouatouch. Radiance Caching for Efficient Global Illumination Computation. In *ACM SIGGRAPH Courses*, pages 75:1–75:19. ACM Press, 2008. 628

[Křivánek *et al.*, 2008d] Jaroslav Křivánek, Pascal Gautron, Gregory J. Ward Larson, Henrik Wann Jensen, Per Henrik Christensen, and Eric Tabellion. Practical Global Illumination with Irradiance Caching. In *ACM SIGGRAPH Courses*, pages 60:1–60:20. ACM Press, 2008. 627

[Křivánek *et al.*, 2010] Jaroslav Křivánek, Marcos Fajardo, Per Henrik Christensen, Eric Tabellion, Michael Bunnell, David Larsson, and Anton S. Kaplanyan. Global Illumination across Industries. In *ACM SIGGRAPH Courses*. ACM Press, 2010. 564

[Křivánek *et al.*, 2012] Jaroslav Křivánek, Miloš Hašan, Adam Arbree, Carsten Dachsbacher, Alexander Keller, and Bruce Jonathan Walter. Optimizing Realistic Rendering with Many-Light Methods. In *ACM SIGGRAPH Courses*, pages 7:1–7:217. ACM Press, 2012. 632

[Křivánek *et al.*, 2014] Jaroslav Křivánek, Iliyan Georgiev, Toshiya Hachisuka, Petr Vévoda, Martin Šik, Derek Nowrouzezahrai, and Wojciech Jarosz. Unifying Points, Beams, and Paths in Volumetric Light Transport Simulation. *ACM Transactions on Graphics*, 33(4):103:1–103:13, July 2014. 160, 643

[Křivánek, 2005] Jaroslav Křivánek. *Radiance Caching for Global Illumination Computation on Glossy Surfaces*. PhD thesis, Université de Rennes I & Czech Technical University in Prague, 2005. 628

[Lafortune and Willems, 1993] Eric P. F. Lafortune and Yves D. Willems. Bi-Directional Path Tracing. In *Proceedings of CompuGraphics – The International Conference on Computational Graphics and Visualization Techniques*, pages 145–153, December 1993. 618

[Lafortune and Willems, 1994a] Eric P. F. Lafortune and Yves D. Willems. A Theoretical Framework for Physically Based Rendering. *Computer Graphics Forum*, 13(2):97–107, May 1994. 565, 618

[Lafortune and Willems, 1994b] Eric P. F. Lafortune and Yves D. Willems. Using the Modified Phong Reflectance Model for Physically-Based Rendering. Technical Report CW197, Department of Computer Science, Katholieke Universiteit Leuven, November 1994. 500

[Lafortune and Willems, 1996] Eric P. F. Lafortune and Yves D. Willems. Rendering Participating Media with Bidirectional Path Tracing. In *Proceedings of EGWR – The Eurographics Workshop on Rendering Techniques*, pages 91–100. Springer-Verlag, 1996. 601, 621

[Lafortune *et al.*, 1997] Eric P. F. Lafortune, Sing-Choong Foo, Kenneth E. Torrance, and Donald P. Greenberg. Non-Linear Approximation of Reflectance Functions. In *Proceedings of SIGGRAPH – The ACM International Conference on Computer Graphics and Interactive Techniques*, pages 117–126. ACM Press, 1997. 502

[Lafortune, 1996] Eric P. F. Lafortune. *Mathematical Models and Monte Carlo Algorithms for Physically Based Rendering.* PhD thesis, Department of Computer Science, Katholieke Universiteit Leuven, February 1996. 565, 618

[Lagae and Dutré, 2008a] Ares Lagae and Philip Dutré. Accelerating Ray Tracing using Constrained Tetrahedralizations. *Computer Graphics Forum (Proceedings of EGSR – The Eurographics Symposium on Rendering)*, 27(4):1303–1312, June 2008. 387

[Lagae and Dutré, 2008b] Ares Lagae and Philip Dutré. Accelerating Ray Tracing using Constrained Tetrahedralizations. In *Proceedings of RT – The IEEE Symposium on Interactive Ray Tracing.* IEEE Computer Society, 2008. Poster Session. 387

[Lagae and Dutré, 2008c] Ares Lagae and Philip Dutré. Compact, Fast and Robust Grids for Ray Tracing. *Computer Graphics Forum (Proceedings of EGSR – The Eurographics Symposium on Rendering)*, 27(4):1235–1244, 2008. 369, 376

[Lagae and Dutré, 2008d] Ares Lagae and Philip Dutré. Compact, Fast and Robust Grids for Ray Tracing. In *ACM SIGGRAPH Talks*, pages 20:1–20:1. ACM Press, 2008. 369, 376

[Laine, 2010] Samuli Laine. Restart Trail for Stackless BVH Traversal. In *Proceedings of HPG – The Conference on High-Performance Graphics*, pages 107–111. Eurographics Association/ACM SIGGRAPH, 2010. 408

[Lamb, 2011] T. D. Lamb. Phototransduction: Adaptation in Rods. In Joseph C. Besharse and Dean Bok, editors, *The Retina and Its Disorders*, pages 596–599. Academic Press, April 2011. 690

[Lambert, 1760] Johann Heinrich Lambert. *Photometria: Sive de Mensura et Gradibus Luminis, Colorum et Umbrae.* Eberhard Klett, 1760. 463, 499

[Larsen and Christensen, 2003] Bent Dalgaard Larsen and Niels Jørgen Christensen. Optimizing Photon Mapping using Multiple Photon Maps for Irradiance Estimates. In *Proceedings of WSCG – The Winter School of Computer Graphics: The International Conference in Central Europe on Computer Graphics, Visualization and Computer Vision*, 2003. Poster Session. 635

[Larsson *et al.*, 2007] Thomas Larsson, Tomas Möller, and Eric Lengyel. On Faster Sphere-Box Overlap Testing. *Journal of Graphics Tools (JGT)*, 12(1):3–8, 2007. 369

[Larsson, 2008] Thomas Larsson. An Efficient Ellipsoid-OBB Intersection Test. *Journal of Graphics Tools (JGT)*, 13(1):31–43, 2008. 369

[Lastra *et al.*, 2002a] Miguel Lastra, Carlos Ureña, Jorge Revelles, and Rosana Montes Soldado. A Density Estimation Technique for Radiosity. In *Proceedings of SIACG – The Ibero-American Symposium in Computer Graphics*, pages 163–172. Eurographics Association, July 2002. 636

[Lastra *et al.*, 2002b] Miguel Lastra, Carlos Ureña, Jorge Revelles, and Rosana Montes Soldado. A Particle-Path Based Method for Monte-Carlo Density Estimation. In *Proceedings of EGWR – The Eurographics Workshop on Rendering Techniques*. Eurographics Association, 2002. Poster Session. 636

[Lavignotte and Paulin, 2002] Fabien Lavignotte and Mathias Paulin. A New Approach of Density Estimation for Global Illumination. In *Proceedings of WSCG – The Winter School of Computer Graphics: The International Conference in Central Europe on Computer Graphics, Visualization and Computer Vision*, pages 263–270, 2002. 636, 637

[Lazányi and Szirmay-Kalos, 2005] István Lazányi and László Szirmay-Kalos. Fresnel Term Approximations for Metals. In *Proceedings of WSCG – The Winter School of Computer Graphics: The International Conference in Central Europe on Computer Graphics, Visualization and Computer Vision*, pages 77–80, 2005. Short Papers. 492

[Leeson, 2003] William Leeson. Metropolis Density Estimation. In Jeff Lander, editor, *Graphics Programming Methods*, chapter 3.4, pages 261–270. Charles River Media, 2003. 641

[Lengyel, 2001] Eric Lengyel. *Mathematics for 3D Game Programming and Computer Graphics*. Charles River Media, 1st edition, 2001. 126

[Lengyel, 2004] Eric Lengyel. *Mathematics for 3D Game Programming and Computer Graphics*. Charles River Media, 2nd edition, 2004. 126

[Lengyel, 2011] Eric Lengyel. *Mathematics for 3D Game Programming and Computer Graphics*. Course Technology Press, 3rd edition, 2011. 126

[Lensch *et al.*, 2005] Hendrik Peter Asmus Lensch, Michael Goesele, Yung-Yu Chuang, Tim Hawkins, Stephen Robert Marschner, Wojciech Matusik, and Gero Müller. Realistic Materials in Computer Graphics. In *ACM SIGGRAPH Courses*. ACM Press, 2005. 474, 562

[Lensch *et al.*, 2007] Hendrik Peter Asmus Lensch, Michael Goesele, and Gero Müller. Capturing Reflectance – From Theory to Practice. In *Eurographics Tutorials*. Eurographics Association, 2007. 562

[Lensch, 2003] Hendrik Peter Asmus Lensch. *Efficient, Image-Based Appearance Acquisition of Real-World Objects*. PhD thesis, Max Planck Institute for Computer Science, Saarland University, 2003. 474

[Leppänen, 2007] Jaakko Leppänen. *Development of a New Monte Carlo Reactor Physics Code*. PhD thesis, Department of Engineering Physics and Mathematics, Helsinki University of Technology, June 2007. VTT Publications 640. 604

[Levi, 2009] Mark Levi. *The Mathematical Mechanic: Using Physical Reasoning to Solve Problems*. Princeton University Press, 2009. 505

[Levoy, 1990] Marc Levoy. Efficient Ray Tracing of Volume Data. *ACM Transactions on Graphics*, 9(3):245–261, July 1990. 591

[Lewis, 1994] Robert Ralph Lewis. Making Shaders More Physically Plausible. *Computer Graphics Forum*, 13(2):109–120, May 1994. 476, 500

[Li and Torrance, 2005a] Hongsong Li and Kenneth E. Torrance. A Practical, Comprehensive Light Reflection Model. Technical Report PCG-05-03, Program of Computer Graphics, Cornell University, April 2005. 548

[Li and Torrance, 2005b] Hongsong Li and Kenneth E. Torrance. Background Data for Validation of the He-Torrance Model. Technical Report PCG-05-02, Program of Computer Graphics, Cornell University, April 2005. 548

[Li, 2005] Hongsong Li. *Theoretical Framework and Physical Measurements of Surface and Subsurface Light Scattering from Material Surfaces.* PhD thesis, Cornell University, May 2005. 548

[Lin and Ching, 1996] Chyi-Cheng Lin and Yu-Tai Ching. An Efficient Volume-Rendering Algorithm with an Analytic Approach. *The Visual Computer*, 12(10):515–526, December 1996. 286

[Lindemann and Ropinski, 2011] Florian Lindemann and Timo Ropinski. About the Influence of Illumination Models on Image Comprehension in Direct Volume Rendering. *IEEE Transactions on Visualization and Computer Graphics*, 17(12):1922–1931, December 2011. 564

[Liu and Zheng, 2014] Xiao-Dan Liu and Chang-Wen Zheng. Adaptive Importance Photon Shooting Technique. *Computers & Graphics*, 38:158–166, February 2014. 641

[Liu *et al.*, 2004] Yong Kui Liu, Borut Žalik, and Hongji Yang. An Integer One-Pass Algorithm for Voxel Traversal. *Computer Graphics Forum*, 23(2):167–172, June 2004. 374

[Liu, 1994] Pingyu Liu. A New Phase Function Approximating to Mie Scattering for Radiative Transport Equations. *Physics in Medicine and Biology*, 39(6):1025–1036, June 1994. 451

[Löfstedt and Möller, 2005] Marta Löfstedt and Tomas Möller. An Evaluation Framework for Ray-Triangle Intersection Algorithms. *Journal of Graphics Tools (JGT)*, 10(2):13–26, 2005. 258

[Lommel, 1889] Eugene Lommel. Die Photometrie der Diffusen Zurückwerfung. *Bayerische Akademie der Wissenschaften München*, 272(2):473–502, 1889. Mathematisch-Physikalische Klasse 18: Sitzungsberichte. 486

[MacAdam, 1942] David Lewis MacAdam. Visual Sensitivities to Color Differences in Daylight. *Journal of the Optical Society of America*, 32(5):247–274, May 1942. 721

[MacDonald and Booth, 1990] J. David MacDonald and Kellogg S. Booth. Heuristics for Ray Tracing using Space Subdivision. *The Visual Computer*, 6(3):153–166, May 1990. 380, 398, 399

[MacDonald, 1988] J. David MacDonald. Space Subdivision Algorithms for Ray Tracing. Master's thesis, Department of Computer Science, University of Waterloo, 1988. 380, 398, 399

[Machado *et al.*, 2009] Gustavo M. Machado, Manuel M. Oliveira, and Leandro A. F. Fernandes. A Physiologically-Based Model for Simulation of Color Vision Deficiency. *IEEE Transactions on Visualization and Computer Graphics*, 15(6):1291–1298, November 2009. 694

[Machover, 1969] Carl Machover. Computer Graphics in the United States. In *Computer Graphics – Techniques and Applications*, pages 61–83. Springer-Verlag, 1969. 8

[Machover, 1978] Carl Machover. A Brief, Personal History of Computer Graphics. *Computer*, 11(11):38–45, November 1978. 4

[Machover, 1994] Carl Machover. Four Decades of Computer Graphics. *IEEE Computer Graphics and Applications*, 14(6):14–19, November 1994. 4

[Machover, 1996] Carl Machover. United States of America: State of the Art in Computer Graphics. *SIGGRAPH Computer Graphics*, 30(2):49–53, May 1996. 8

[Mahovsky and Wyvill, 2004] Jeffrey A. Mahovsky and Brian Wyvill. Fast Ray-Axis Aligned Bounding Box Overlap Tests with Plücker Coordinates. *Journal of Graphics Tools (JGT)*, 9(1):35–46, 2004. 301

[Mahovsky and Wyvill, 2006] Jeffrey A. Mahovsky and Brian Wyvill. Memory-Conserving Bounding Volume Hierarchies with Coherent Raytracing. *Computer Graphics Forum*, 25(2):173–182, June 2006. 365

[Mahovsky, 2005a] Jeffrey A. Mahovsky. Ray Tracing Bounding Volume Hierarchies with the Pluecker-AABB Test. Technical Report 2004-759-24, Department of Computer Science, University of Calgary, April 2005. 301, 363

[Mahovsky, 2005b] Jeffrey A. Mahovsky. *Ray Tracing with Reduced-Precision Bounding Volume Hierarchies.* PhD thesis, Department of Computer Science, University of Calgary, August 2005. 365

[Maillot, 1990] Patrick-Gilles Maillot. Using Quaternions for Coding 3D Transformations. In Andrew S. Glassner, editor, *Graphics Gems I*, chapter X.3, pages 498–515. Academic Press, 1990. 111

[Mair and Owen, 1993] Susan G. Mair and G. Scott Owen. Special Issue on Computer Graphics Education. *SIGGRAPH Computer Graphics*, 27(1), January 1993. 8

[Mandelbrot, 1975] Benoît B. Mandelbrot. *Les Objets Fractals: Forme, Hasard et Dimension.* Flammarion, 1975. 5

[Marcos, 1998] Adérito Fernandes Marcos. Computer Graphics as an Enabling Technology for Cooperative, Global Applications. *SIGGRAPH Computer Graphics*, 32(4):22–24, November 1998. 8

[Marlon, 2003] John Marlon. *Focus on Photon Mapping.* Premier Press, 2003. 643

[Marschner and Shirley, 2016] Stephen Robert Marschner and Peter Schuyler Shirley. *Fundamentals of Computer Graphics.* A. K. Peters/CRC Press, 4th edition, 2016. 739

[Márton and Szirmay-Kalos, 1995] Gábor Márton and László Szirmay-Kalos. On Average-Case Complexity of Ray Tracing Algorithms. In *Proceedings of WSCG – The Winter School of Computer Graphics: The International Conference in Central Europe on Computer Graphics, Visualization and Computer Vision*, pages 187–196, 1995. 414

[Márton, 1995a] Gábor Márton. Acceleration of Ray Tracing via Voronoi Diagrams. In Alan W. Paeth, editor, *Graphics Gems V*, chapter V.5, pages 268–284. Academic Press, 1995. 387

[Márton, 1995b] Gábor Márton. *Stochastic Analysis of Ray Tracing Algorithms.* PhD thesis, Department of Process Control, Technical University of Budapest, 1995. 414

[Massó and López, 2003] José Pascual Molina Massó and Pascual González López. Automatic Hybrid Hierarchy Creation: A Cost-Model Based Approach. *Computer Graphics Forum*, 22(1):5–13, March 2003. 410

[Matsumoto and Murakami, 1983] Hitoshi Matsumoto and Kouichi Murakami. Ray-Tracing with Octree Data Structure. In *Proceedings of the Information Processing Conference*, pages 1535–1536, 1983. (in Japanese). 378

[Max *et al.*, 1990] Nelson L. Max, Patrick Hanrahan, and Roger Crawfis. Area and Volume Coherence for Efficient Visualization of 3D Scalar Functions. *SIGGRAPH Computer Graphics (Proceedings of the ACM Workshop on Volume Visualization)*, 24(5):27–33, November 1990. 466

[Max *et al.*, 1992] Nelson L. Max, Roger Crawfis, and Dean Williams. Visualizing Wind Velocities by Advecting Cloud Textures. In *Proceedings of Vis – The IEEE Conference on Visualization*, pages 179–184. IEEE Computer Society, 1992. 576

[Max, 1995] Nelson L. Max. Optical Models for Direct Volume Rendering. *IEEE Transactions on Visualization and Computer Graphics*, 1(2):99–108, June 1995. 470, 590

[Maxwell *et al.*, 1973] J. R. Maxwell, J. Beard, S. Weiner, D. Ladd, and S. Ladd. Bidirectional Reflectance Model Validation and Utilization. Technical Report AFAL-TR-73-303, Infrared and Optics Division, Environmental Research Institute of Michigan, October 1973. 541

[McAuley *et al.*, 2012] Stephen McAuley, Stephen Hill, Nathaniel Hoffman, Yoshiharu Gotanda, Brian Edward Smits, Brent Burley, and Adam Martinez. Practical Physically-Based Shading in Film and Game Production. In *ACM SIGGRAPH Courses*, pages 10:1–10:7. ACM Press, 2012. 473

[McAuley *et al.*, 2013] Stephen McAuley, Stephen Hill, Adam Martinez, Ryusuke Villemin, Matt Pettineo, Dimitar Lazarov, David Neubelt, Brian Karis, Christophe Hery, Nathaniel Hoffman, and Hakan Zap Andersson. Physically Based Shading in Theory and Practice. In *ACM SIGGRAPH Courses*, pages 22:1–22:8. ACM Press, 2013. 473

[McConnell, 1996] Jeffrey J. McConnell. United States: Computer Graphics Education in Computer Science Undergoing a Transformation. *SIGGRAPH Computer Graphics*, 30(3):31–32, August 1996. 8

[McConnell, 2005] Jeffrey J. McConnell. *Computer Graphics: Theory into Practice.* Jones and Bartlett Publishers, 2005. 739

[Mehra and Kumar, 2008] Ravish Mehra and Subodh Kumar. Ray-Patch Intersection for Improving Rendering Quality of Per-Pixel Displacement Mapping. In *Proceedings of ICVGIP – The Indian Conference on Computer Vision, Graphics and Image Processing*, 2008. 264

[Meseth, 2006] Jan Meseth. *Towards Predictive Rendering in Virtual Reality.* PhD thesis, Mathematisch-Naturwissenschaftliche Fakultät der Rheinischen Friedrich-Wilhelms-Universität Bonn, October 2006. 473

[Metropolis *et al.*, 1953] Nicholas Metropolis, Arianna W. Rosenbluth, Marshall N. Rosenbluth, Augusta H. Teller, and Edward Teller. Equation of State Calculations by Fast Computing Machines. *The Journal of Chemical Physics*, 21:1087–1091, 1953. 137

[Meyer and Shimizu, 2005] Gary W. Meyer and Clement Shimizu. Computational Automotive Color Appearance. In *Proceedings of CAe – The Eurographics Workshop on Computational Aesthetics in Graphics, Visualization and Imaging*, pages 217–222. Eurographics Association, 2005. 473

[Meyer *et al.*, 1986] Gary W. Meyer, Holly Edith Rushmeier, Michael F. Cohen, Donald P. Greenberg, and Kenneth E. Torrance. An Experimental Evaluation of Computer Graphics Imagery. *ACM Transactions on Graphics*, 5(1):30–50, January 1986. 739

[Meyer *et al.*, 2005] Gary W. Meyer, Clement Shimizu, Alan Eggly, David Fischer, Jim King, and Allan Rodrigues. Computer Aided Design of Automotive Finishes. In *Proceedings of the Congress of the International Colour Association*, pages 685–688, 2005. 473

[Meyer, 2009] Gary W. Meyer. Computer Graphic Tools for Automotive Paint Engineering. In *Service Life Prediction of Polymeric Materials*, chapter 18, pages 273–282. Springer Publishing, 2009. 473

[Mie, 1908] Gustav Mie. Beiträge zur Optik trüber Medien, speziell kolloidaler Metallösungen. *Annalen der Physik*, 330(3):377–445, 1908. 457

[Mikkelsen, 2009] Morten S. Mikkelsen. Microfacet Based Bidirectional Reflectance Distribution Function. November 2009. 534

[Miller, 1988] Gavin S. P. Miller. From Wire-Frames to Furry Animals. In *Proceedings of Graphics Interface – The Canadian Annual Conference on Computer Graphics, Interactive Systems, and Human-Computer Interaction*, pages 138–145. Canadian Human-Computer Communications Society, 1988. 551

[Miller, 1994] Robert D. Miller. Computing the Area of a Spherical Polygon. In Paul Seagrave Heckbert, editor, *Graphics Gems IV*, chapter II.4, pages 132–137. Academic Press, 1994. 262

[Minnaert, 1941] Marcel Minnaert. The Reciprocity Principle in Lunar Photometry. *Astrophysical Journal*, 93:403–410, 1941. 500

[Mitchell and Netravali, 1988] Don P. Mitchell and Arun N. Netravali. Reconstruction Filters in Computer-Graphics. *SIGGRAPH Computer Graphics (Proceedings of SIGGRAPH – The ACM International Conference on Computer Graphics and Interactive Techniques)*, 22(4):221–228, June 1988. 230

[Modest, 2003] Michael F. Modest. *Radiative Heat Transfer*. Academic Press, 2nd edition, 2003. 470

[Möller and Haines, 1999] Tomas Möller and Eric A. Haines. *Real-Time Rendering*. A. K. Peters, 1st edition, 1999. 739

[Möller and Haines, 2002] Tomas Möller and Eric A. Haines. *Real-Time Rendering*. A. K. Peters, 2nd edition, 2002. 739

[Möller and Trumbore, 1997] Tomas Möller and Ben Trumbore. Fast, Minimum Storage Ray-Triangle Intersection. *Journal of Graphics Tools (JGT)*, 2(1):21–28, October 1997. 254

[Möller *et al.*, 2008] Tomas Möller, Eric A. Haines, and Nathaniel Hoffman. *Real-Time Rendering.* A. K. Peters, 3rd edition, 2008. 739

[Möller, 2001] Tomas Möller. Fast 3D Triangle-Box Overlap Testing. *Journal of Graphics Tools (JGT)*, 6(1):29–33, 2001. 369

[Mora, 2011] Benjamin Mora. Naive Ray-Tracing: A Divide-and-Conquer Approach. *ACM Transactions on Graphics*, 30(5):117:1–117:12, October 2011. 409

[Moroney *et al.*, 2002] Nathan Moroney, Mark D. Fairchild, Robert W. G. Hunt, Changjun Li, M. Ronnier Luo, and Todd Newman. The CIECAM02 Color Appearance Model. In *Proceedings of CIC – The Color and Imaging Conference*, pages 23–27. Society for Imaging Science and Technology, January 2002. 720

[Mudur *et al.*, 1999] Sudhir P. Mudur, S. Gopalsamy, Dinesh Shikhare, D. S. Dixit, B. S. Patwardhan, N. S. Nayak, and S. V. Shanbhag. Graphics Research at National Centre for Software Technology in India. *SIGGRAPH Computer Graphics*, 33(1):21–25, February 1999. Computer Graphics around the World. 8

[Müller and Fellner, 1999] Gordon Müller and Dieter W. Fellner. Hybrid Scene Structuring with Application to Ray Tracing. In *Proceedings of ICVC – The International Conference on Visual Computing*, pages 19–26, 1999. 405, 410

[Müller *et al.*, 2004] Gero Müller, Jan Meseth, Mirko Sattler, Ralf Sarlette, and Reinhard Klein. Acquisition, Synthesis and Rendering of Bidirectional Texture Functions. In *Eurographics State of the Art Reports*, pages 69–94. Eurographics Association, September 2004. 473

[Müller-Lyer, 1889] Franz Carl Müller-Lyer. Optische Urteilstäuschungen. *Archiv für Anatomie und Physiologie*, 2 – Supplement:263–270, 1889. 699, 700

[Musgrave, 1992] Forest Kenton Musgrave. A Panoramic Virtual Screen for Ray Tracing. In David Kirk, editor, *Graphics Gems III*, chapter VI.6, pages 288–294. Academic Press, 1992. 672

[Myszkowski and Kunii, 2000] Karol Myszkowski and Tosiyasu L. Kunii. A Case Study Towards Validation of Global Illumination Algorithms: Progressive Hierarchical Radiosity with Clustering. *The Visual Computer*, 16(5):271–288, 2000. 739

[Myszkowski *et al.*, 2008] Karol Myszkowski, Rafał K. Mantiuk, and Grzegorz Marek Krawczyk. *High Dynamic Range Video.* Morgan & Claypool Publishers, 2008. 734

[Naka and Rushton, 1966a] K. I. Naka and W. A. H. Rushton. S-Potentials from Colour Units in the Retina of Fish (Cyprinidae). *Journal of Physiology*, 185(3):536–555, August 1966. 733

[Naka and Rushton, 1966b] K. I. Naka and W. A. H. Rushton. S-Potentials from Luminosity Units in the Retina of Fish (Cyprinidae). *Journal of Physiology*, 185(3):587–599, August 1966. 733

[Nakamae and Tadamura, 1995] Eihachiro Nakamae and Katsumi Tadamura. Photorealism in Computer Graphics – Past and Present. *Computers & Graphics*, 19(1):119–130, 1995. 738

[Nakamae *et al.*, 1984] Eihachiro Nakamae, Makoto Nagao, and Norio Okino. Computer Graphics Research in Japanese Universities. *SIGGRAPH Computer Graphics (Proceedings of SIGGRAPH – The ACM International Conference on Computer Graphics and Interactive Techniques)*, 18(3):283–284, July 1984. Panel. 8

[Nakamae *et al.*, 1990] Eihachiro Nakamae, Kazufumi Kaneda, Takashi Okamoto, and Tomoyuki Nishita. A Lighting Model Aiming at Drive Simulators. *SIGGRAPH Computer Graphics (Proceedings of SIGGRAPH – The ACM International Conference on Computer Graphics and Interactive Techniques)*, 24(4):395–404, September 1990. 473

[Nakamaru and Ohno, 1997] Koji Nakamaru and Yoshio Ohno. Breadth-First Ray Tracing Utilizing Uniform Spatial Subdivision. *IEEE Transactions on Visualization and Computer Graphics*, 3(4):316–328, October 1997. 409

[Nayar and Oren, 1995] Shree K. Nayar and Michael Oren. Visual Appearance of Matte Surfaces. *Science*, 267(5201):1153–1156, February 1995. 549

[Naylor, 1996] Bruce Fountain Naylor. Constructing Good Partitioning Trees. In *Proceedings of Graphics Interface – The Canadian Annual Conference on Computer Graphics, Interactive Systems, and Human-Computer Interaction*, pages 181–191. Canadian Human-Computer Communications Society, 1996. 399

[Netto, 1998] Marcio Lobo Netto. Computer Graphics in Brazil. *SIGGRAPH Computer Graphics*, 32(2):23–23, May 1998. Computer Graphics around the World. 8

[Neumann and Neumann, 1989] László Neumann and Attila Neumann. Photosimulation: Interreflection with Arbitrary Reflectance Models and Illumination. *Computer Graphics Forum*, 8(1):21–34, May 1989. 558

[Neumann *et al.*, 1998a] László Neumann, Attila Neumann, and László Szirmay-Kalos. Analysis and Pumping of the Albedo Function. Technical Report TR-186-2-98-20, Institute of Computer Graphics, Vienna University of Technology, 1998. 477, 504

[Neumann *et al.*, 1998b] László Neumann, Attila Neumann, and László Szirmay-Kalos. New Simple Reflectance Models for Metals and Other Specular Materials. Technical Report TR-186-2-98-17, Department of Control Engineering and Information Technology, Technical University of Budapest, July 1998. 504

[Neumann *et al.*, 1999a] László Neumann, Attila Neumann, and László Szirmay-Kalos. Compact Metallic Reflectance Models. *Computer Graphics Forum (Proceedings of Eurographics – The Annual Conference of the European Association for Computer Graphics)*, 18(3):161–172, September 1999. 504

[Neumann *et al.*, 1999b] László Neumann, Attila Neumann, and László Szirmay-Kalos. Reflectance Models by Pumping up the Albedo Function. *Machine Graphics and Vision*, 8(1):3–17, 1999. 477, 504

[Newell and Blinn, 1977] Martin Edward Newell and James Frederick Blinn. The Progression of Realism in Computer Generated Images. In *Proceedings of SIGGRAPH – The ACM International Conference on Computer Graphics and Interactive Techniques*, pages 444–448. ACM Press, 1977. 738

[Newman and Sproull, 1979] William M. Newman and Robert F. Sproull. *Principles of Interactive Computer Graphics*. McGraw-Hill, 2nd edition, 1979. 739

[Ng and Trifonov, 2003] Kelvin Ng and Borislav Trifonov. Automatic Bounding Volume Hierarchy Generation using Stochastic Search Methods. In *Proceedings of the CPSC532D Mini-Workshop on Stochastic Search Algorithms*, pages 147–161. Department of Computer Science, University of British Columbia, April 2003. 361, 400

[Nicodemus *et al.*, 1977] Fred E. Nicodemus, Joseph C. Richmond, Jack J. Hsia, Irving W. Ginsberg, and Thomas Limperis. *Geometrical Considerations and Nomenclature for Reflectance.* U.S. Department of Commerce – National Bureau of Standards, October 1977. 473, 474

[Nielsen, 2003] Ralf Stokholm Nielsen. Real Time Rendering of Atmospheric Scattering Effects for Flight Simulators. Master's thesis, Department of Informatics and Mathematical Modeling, Technical University of Denmark, 2003. 441

[Nishita and Nakamae, 1985] Tomoyuki Nishita and Eihachiro Nakamae. Continuous Tone Representation of Three-Dimensional Objects Taking Account of Shadows and Interreflection. *SIGGRAPH Computer Graphics (Proceedings of SIGGRAPH – The ACM International Conference on Computer Graphics and Interactive Techniques)*, 19(3):23–30, July 1985. 584

[Nishita *et al.*, 1987] Tomoyuki Nishita, Yasuhiro Miyawaki, and Eihachiro Nakamae. A Shading Model for Atmospheric Scattering Considering Luminous Intensity Distribution of Light Sources. *SIGGRAPH Computer Graphics (Proceedings of SIGGRAPH – The ACM International Conference on Computer Graphics and Interactive Techniques)*, 21(4):303–310, August 1987. 452

[Novák *et al.*, 2012a] Jan Novák, Derek Nowrouzezahrai, Carsten Dachsbacher, and Wojciech Jarosz. Progressive Virtual Beam Lights. *Computer Graphics Forum (Proceedings of EGSR – The Eurographics Symposium on Rendering)*, 31(4):1407–1413, June 2012. 632

[Novák *et al.*, 2012b] Jan Novák, Derek Nowrouzezahrai, Carsten Dachsbacher, and Wojciech Jarosz. Virtual Ray Lights for Rendering Scenes with Participating Media. *ACM Transactions on Graphics (Proceedings of SIGGRAPH – The ACM International Conference on Computer Graphics and Interactive Techniques)*, 31(4):60:1–60:11, July 2012. 632

[Ochoa *et al.*, 2011] Carlos E. Ochoa, Myriam B. C. Aries, and Jan L. M. Hensen. State of the Art in Lighting Simulation for Building Science: A Literature Review. *Journal of Building Performance Simulation*, 5(4):209–233, January 2011. 10

[Ohta and Maekawa, 1987] Masataka Ohta and Mamoru Maekawa. Ray Coherence Theorem and Constant Time Ray Tracing Algorithm. In *Proceedings of CGI – Computer Graphics International*, pages 303–314. Springer-Verlag, 1987. 411

[Ooi *et al.*, 1987] Beng Chin Ooi, Ron Sacks-Davis, and Ken J. McDonnell. Spatial K-D-Tree: An Indexing Mechanism for Spatial Databases. In *Proceedings of COMPSAC – The IEEE International Computer Software and Applications Conference*, pages 433–438. IEEE Computer Society, 1987. 365

[Oren and Nayar, 1994] Michael Oren and Shree K. Nayar. Generalization of Lambert's Reflectance Model. In *Proceedings of SIGGRAPH – The ACM International Conference on Computer Graphics and Interactive Techniques*, pages 239–246. ACM Press, 1994. 549

[Østerberg, 1935] Gustav Østerberg. Topography of the Layer of Rods and Cones in the Human Retina. *Acta Ophthalmologica*, 6(1 – Supplement):11–97, 1935. 693

[Owen and Zhou, 2000] Art Owen and Yi Zhou. Safe and Effective Importance Sampling. *Journal of the American Statistical Association*, 95(449):135–143, March 2000. 157, 166

[Özgüç, 1996a] Bülent Özgüç. Turkey: A Report on Computer Graphics Education. *SIGGRAPH Computer Graphics*, 30(3):26–27, August 1996. 8

[Özgüç, 1996b] Bülent Özgüç. Turkey: State of the Art in Computer Graphics – the Turkish Scene. *SIGGRAPH Computer Graphics*, 30(2):41–44, May 1996. 8

[Paltashev, 1996] Timour Paltashev. Russia: Computer Graphics – Between the Past and the Future. *SIGGRAPH Computer Graphics*, 30(2):32–36, May 1996. 8

[Pan *et al.*, 2000] Zhigeng Pan, Pheng-ann Heng, and Rynson W. H. Lau. Computer Graphics in Hong Kong. *SIGGRAPH Computer Graphics*, 34(1):15–19, February 2000. Computer Graphics around the World. 8

[Parke, 1972] Frederick I. Parke. Computer Generated Animation of Faces. In *Proceedings of the ACM Annual Conference*, volume 1, pages 451–457. ACM Press, 1972. 5

[Parker *et al.*, 1998] Steven Gregory Parker, Peter Schuyler Shirley, Yarden Livnat, Charles D. Hansen, and Peter-Pike Sloan. Interactive Ray Tracing for Isosurface Rendering. In *Proceedings of Vis – The IEEE Conference on Visualization*, pages 233–238. IEEE Computer Society, 1998. 286

[Parker *et al.*, 1999] Steven Gregory Parker, Michael Parker, Yarden Livnat, Peter-Pike Sloan, Charles D. Hansen, and Peter Schuyler Shirley. Interactive Ray Tracing for Volume Visualization. *IEEE Transactions on Visualization and Computer Graphics*, 5(3):238–250, July 1999. 286

[Parker *et al.*, 2005] Steven Gregory Parker, Michael Parker, Yarden Livnat, Peter-Pike Sloan, Charles D. Hansen, and Peter Schuyler Shirley. Interactive Ray Tracing for Volume Visualization. In *ACM SIGGRAPH Courses*. ACM Press, 2005. 286

[Pattanaik and Bouatouch, 1995] Sumanta N. Pattanaik and Kadi Bouatouch. Interactive Walk-Through Using Particle Tracing. In *Proceedings of CGI – Computer Graphics International*, pages 57–69. Academic Press, 1995. 640

[Pattanaik and Mudur, 1992] Sumanta N. Pattanaik and Sudhir P. Mudur. Computation of Global Illumination by Monte Carlo Simulation of the Particle Model of Light. In *Proceedings of EGWR – The Eurographics Workshop on Rendering Techniques*, pages 71–83. Springer-Verlag, 1992. 634

[Pattanaik and Mudur, 1993a] Sumanta N. Pattanaik and Sudhir P. Mudur. Computation of Global Illumination in a Participating Medium by Monte Carlo Simulation. *The Journal of Visualization and Computer Animation*, 4(3):133–152, 1993. 600, 602, 643

[Pattanaik and Mudur, 1993b] Sumanta N. Pattanaik and Sudhir P. Mudur. Efficient Potential Equation Solutions for Global Illumination Computation. *Computers & Graphics*, 17(4):387–396, July 1993. 640

[Pattanaik and Mudur, 1993c] Sumanta N. Pattanaik and Sudhir P. Mudur. The Potential Equation and Importance in Illumination Computations. *Computer Graphics Forum*, 12(2):131–136, May 1993. 565

[Pattanaik and Mudur, 1995] Sumanta N. Pattanaik and Sudhir P. Mudur. Adjoint Equations and Random Walks for Illumination Computation. *ACM Transactions on Graphics*, 14(1):77–102, January 1995. 640

[Pattanaik *et al.*, 1997] Sumanta N. Pattanaik, James A. Ferwerda, Kenneth E. Torrance, and Donald P. Greenberg. Validation of Global Illumination Simulations through CCD Camera Measurements. In *Proceedings of CIC – The Color and Imaging Conference*, pages 250–253. Society for Imaging Science and Technology, 1997. 739

[Pattanaik, 1993a] Sumanta N. Pattanaik. *Computational Methods for Global Illumination and Visualisation of Complex 3D Environments.* PhD thesis, Birla Institute of Technology and Science, 1993. 565, 567, 634, 643

[Pattanaik, 1993b] Sumanta N. Pattanaik. The Mathematical Framework of Adjoint Equations for Illumination Computation. In *Proceedings of ICCG – The IFIP International Conference on Computer Graphics*, pages 123–138. North-Holland Publishing, 1993. 567

[Paulin, 2006] Mathias Paulin. Simulation Macroscopique des Effets de Surface. Ecole Pluridisciplinaire CNRS Couleur et Matériaux, March 2006. 561

[Pauly *et al.*, 2000] Mark Pauly, Thomas Kollig, and Alexander Keller. Metropolis Light Transport for Participating Media. In *Proceedings of EGWR – The Eurographics Workshop on Rendering Techniques*, pages 11–22. Springer-Verlag, 2000. 569, 602, 623

[Pauly, 1999] Mark Pauly. Robust Monte Carlo Methods for Photorealistic Rendering of Volumetric Effects. Master's thesis, Universität Kaiserslautern, October 1999. 623

[Pearce, 1991] Andrew Pearce. A Recursive Shadow Voxel Cache for Ray Tracing. In James Richard Arvo, editor, *Graphics Gems II*, chapter V.6, pages 273–274. Academic Press, 1991. 410

[Pegoraro and Parker, 2009] Vincent Pegoraro and Steven Gregory Parker. An Analytical Solution to Single Scattering in Homogeneous Participating Media. *Computer Graphics Forum (Proceedings of Eurographics – The Annual Conference of the European Association for Computer Graphics)*, 28(2):329–335, April 2009. 578

[Pegoraro and Slusallek, 2011] Vincent Pegoraro and Philipp Slusallek. On the Evaluation of the Complex-Valued Exponential Integral. *Journal of Graphics Tools (JGT)*, 15(3):183–198, 2011. 57

[Pegoraro *et al.*, 2010] Vincent Pegoraro, Mathias Schott, and Steven Gregory Parker. A Closed-Form Solution to Single Scattering for General Phase Functions and Light Distributions. *Computer Graphics Forum (Proceedings of EGSR – The Eurographics Symposium on Rendering)*, 29(4):1365–1374, June 2010. 459, 578, 579

[Pegoraro *et al.*, 2011] Vincent Pegoraro, Mathias Schott, and Philipp Slusallek. A Mathematical Framework for Efficient Closed-Form Single Scattering. In *Proceedings of Graphics Interface – The Canadian Annual Conference on Computer Graphics, Interactive Systems, and Human-Computer Interaction*, pages 151–158. Canadian Human-Computer Communications Society, 2011. 578, 582

[Pegoraro, 2009] Vincent Pegoraro. *Efficient Physically-Based Simulation of Light Transport in Participating Media.* PhD thesis, School of Computing, University of Utah, December 2009. 462, 578, 579

[Penrose and Penrose, 1958] Lionel S. Penrose and Roger Penrose. Impossible Objects: A Special Type of Visual Illusion. *British Journal of Psychology*, 49(1):31–33, February 1958. 699, 700

[Pérez *et al.*, 1997] Frederic Pérez, Xavier Pueyo, and François X. Sillion. Global Illumination Techniques for the Simulation of Participating Media. In *Proceedings of EGWR – The Eurographics Workshop on Rendering Techniques*, pages 309–320. Springer-Verlag, 1997. 470

[Perez Molina, 2014] Eduardo Perez Molina. The Technological Roots of Computer Graphics. *IEEE Annals of the History of Computing*, 36(3):30–41, July 2014. 4

[Perlin, 1985] Kenneth Perlin. An Image Synthesizer. *SIGGRAPH Computer Graphics (Proceedings of SIGGRAPH – The ACM International Conference on Computer Graphics and Interactive Techniques)*, 19(3):287–296, July 1985. 7

[Peter and Pietrek, 1998] Ingmar Peter and Georg Pietrek. Importance Driven Construction of Photon Maps. In *Proceedings of EGWR – The Eurographics Workshop on Rendering Techniques*, pages 269–280. Springer-Verlag, 1998. 640

[Pharr and Humphreys, 2004] Matthew M. Pharr and Greg Humphreys. *Physically Based Rendering: From Theory to Implementation.* Morgan Kaufmann Publishers, 1st edition, August 2004. 739

[Pharr and Humphreys, 2010] Matthew M. Pharr and Greg Humphreys. *Physically Based Rendering: From Theory to Implementation.* Morgan Kaufmann Publishers, 2nd edition, 2010. 408, 739

[Phong and Crow, 1975] Bùi Tuòng Phong and Franklin C. Crow. Improved Rendition of Polygonal Models of Curved Surfaces. In *Proceedings of the USA-Japan Computer Conference*, 1975. 5

[Phong, 1973] Bùi Tuòng Phong. *Illumination for Computer-Generated Images.* PhD thesis, The University of Utah, 1973. AAI7402100. 5, 500

[Phong, 1975] Bùi Tuòng Phong. Illumination for Computer Generated Pictures. *Communications of the ACM*, 18(6):311–317, June 1975. 5, 500

[Pique, 1990] Michael E. Pique. Rotation Tools. In Andrew S. Glassner, editor, *Graphics Gems I*, chapter IX.6, pages 465–469. Academic Press, 1990. 110

[Ponzo, 1910] Mario Ponzo. Intorno ad Alcune Illusioni nel Campo delle Sensazioni Tattili, Sull'Illusione di Aristotele e Fenomeni Analoghi. Italian Archives of Biology, 1910. 699, 700

[Popov *et al.*, 2006] Stefan Popov, Johannes Günther, Hans-Peter Seidel, and Philipp Slusallek. Experiences with Streaming Construction of SAH KD-Trees. In *Proceedings of RT – The IEEE Symposium on Interactive Ray Tracing*, pages 89–94. IEEE Computer Society, 2006. 401, 403

[Popov *et al.*, 2009] Stefan Popov, Iliyan Georgiev, Rossen Dimov, and Philipp Slusallek. Object Partitioning Considered Harmful: Space Subdivision for BVHs. In *Proceedings of HPG – The Conference on High-Performance Graphics*, pages 15–22. Eurographics Association/ACM SIGGRAPH, 2009. 362, 393

[Poulin and Fournier, 1990] Pierre Poulin and Alain Fournier. A Model for Anisotropic Reflection. *SIGGRAPH Computer Graphics (Proceedings of SIGGRAPH – The ACM International Conference on Computer Graphics and Interactive Techniques)*, 24(4):273–282, September 1990. 551, 553

[Pratt, 2001] William K. Pratt. *Digital Image Processing: PIKS Inside.* John Wiley & Sons, 3rd edition, 2001. 231

[Pratt, 2006] William K. Pratt. *Digital Image Processing: PIKS Scientific Inside.* John Wiley & Sons, 4th edition, 2006. 231

[Pratt, 2013] William K. Pratt. *Introduction to Digital Image Processing.* CRC Press, 2013. 231

[Premože, 2002] Simon Premože. Analytic Light Transport Approximations for Volumetric Materials. In *Proceedings of Pacific Graphics – The Pacific Conference on Computer Graphics and Applications*, pages 48–57. IEEE Computer Society, 2002. 478, 486

[Premože, 2003] Simon Premože. *Approximate Methods for Light Transport in Volumetric Materials.* PhD thesis, School of Computing, University of Utah, December 2003. 443, 470

[Press *et al.*, 1992] William H. Press, Saul A. Teukolsky, William T. Vetterling, and Brian P. Flannery. *Numerical Recipes in C: The Art of Scientific Computing.* Cambridge University Press, 2nd edition, 1992. 29, 32, 64

[Purgathofer, 2003] Werner Purgathofer. Open Issues in Photo-Realistic Rendering. *Computer Graphics Forum (Proceedings of Eurographics – The Annual Conference of the European Association for Computer Graphics)*, 22(3):222–222, September 2003. Invited Presentations. 738

[Raab *et al.*, 2006] Matthias Raab, Daniel Seibert, and Alexander Keller. Unbiased Global Illumination with Participating Media. *Monte Carlo and Quasi-Monte Carlo Methods*, 2:591–605, 2006. 601, 602, 621, 623, 632

[Raab *et al.*, 2007] Matthias Raab, Leonhard Grünschloß, Johannes Hanika, Manuel Finckh, and Alexander Keller. Benchmarking Ray Tracing for Realistic Light Transport Algorithms. 2007. 414

[Raible, 1990] Eric Raible. Matrix Orthogonalization. In Andrew S. Glassner, editor, *Graphics Gems I*, chapter IX.5, pages 464–464. Academic Press, 1990. 113

[Ramsey *et al.*, 2004] Shaun D. Ramsey, Kristin Potter, and Charles D. Hansen. Ray Bilinear Patch Intersections. *Journal of Graphics Tools (JGT)*, 9(3):41–47, 2004. 268

[Redner *et al.*, 1995] Richard A. Redner, Mark E. Lee, and Samuel P. Uselton. Smooth B-Spline Illumination Maps for Bidirectional Ray Tracing. *ACM Transactions on Graphics*, 14(4):337–362, October 1995. 633

[Reeves, 1983] William T. Reeves. Particle Systems — A Technique for Modeling a Class of Fuzzy Objects. *SIGGRAPH Computer Graphics (Proceedings of SIGGRAPH – The ACM International Conference on Computer Graphics and Interactive Techniques)*, 17(3):359–376, July 1983. 6

[Reinhard *et al.*, 1996] Erik Reinhard, Arjan J. F. Kok, and Frederik W. Jansen. Cost Prediction in Ray Tracing. In *Proceedings of EGWR – The Eurographics Workshop on Rendering Techniques*, pages 41–50. Springer-Verlag, 1996. 400

[Reinhard *et al.*, 2005] Erik Reinhard, Gregory J. Ward Larson, Sumanta N. Pattanaik, and Paul E. Debevec. *High Dynamic Range Imaging: Acquisition, Display, and Image-Based Lighting.* Morgan Kaufmann Publishers, 1st edition, 2005. 734

[Reinhard *et al.*, 2008] Erik Reinhard, Erum Arif Khan, Ahmet Oğuz Akyüz, and Garrett M. Johnson. *Color Imaging: Fundamentals and Applications.* A. K. Peters, 2008. 729

[Reinhard *et al.*, 2010] Erik Reinhard, Gregory J. Ward Larson, Sumanta N. Pattanaik, Paul E. Debevec, Wolfgang Heidrich, and Karol Myszkowski. *High Dynamic Range Imaging: Acquisition, Display, and Image-Based Lighting.* Morgan Kaufmann Publishers, 2nd edition, May 2010. 734

[Renner, 2009] Eric Renner. *Pinhole Photography: From Historic Technique to Digital Application.* Focal Press, 4th edition, 2009. 675

[Revelles *et al.*, 2000] Jorge Revelles, Carlos Ureña, and Miguel Lastra. An Efficient Parametric Algorithm for Octree Traversal. *Journal of WSCG (Proceedings of WSCG – The Winter School of Computer Graphics: The International Conference in Central Europe on Computer Graphics, Visualization and Computer Vision)*, 8(1–3), 2000. 380

[Riley *et al.*, 2004] Kirk Riley, David S. Ebert, Martin Kraus, Jerry Tessendorf, and Charles D. Hansen. Efficient Rendering of Atmospheric Phenomena. In *Proceedings of EGSR – The Eurographics Symposium on Rendering*, pages 375–386. Eurographics Association, 2004. 576

[Ritschel *et al.*, 2012] Tobias Ritschel, Carsten Dachsbacher, Thorsten Grosch, and Jan Kautz. The State of the Art in Interactive Global Illumination. *Computer Graphics Forum*, 31(1):160–188, February 2012. 644

[Ritter, 1990] Jack Ritter. An Efficient Bounding Sphere. In Andrew S. Glassner, editor, *Graphics Gems I*, chapter V.2, pages 301–303. Academic Press, 1990. 359

[Robertson, 1996] Philip K. Robertson. Australia: Services Dominated; Strong Advanced Applications and Software Industry. *SIGGRAPH Computer Graphics*, 30(2):5–7, May 1996. 8

[Rogers and Adams, 1989] David F. Rogers and J. Alan Adams. *Mathematical Elements for Computer Graphics.* McGraw-Hill, 2nd edition, 1989. 126

[Roth, 1982] Scott D. Roth. Ray Casting for Modeling Solids. *Computer Graphics and Image Processing*, 18(2):109–144, February 1982. 360, 363

[Rubin and Whitted, 1980] Steven M. Rubin and Turner Whitted. A 3-Dimensional Representation for Fast Rendering of Complex Scenes. *SIGGRAPH Computer Graphics (Proceedings of SIGGRAPH – The ACM International Conference on Computer Graphics and Interactive Techniques)*, 14(3):110–116, July 1980. 361

[Rushmeier *et al.*, 1995] Holly Edith Rushmeier, Gregory J. Ward Larson, Christine D. Piatko, Phil Sanders, and Bert Rust. Comparing Real and Synthetic Images: Some Ideas about Metrics. In *Proceedings of EGWR – The Eurographics Workshop on Rendering Techniques*, pages 213–222. Springer-Verlag, 1995. 739

[Rusinkiewicz, 1997] Szymon M. Rusinkiewicz. A Survey of BRDF Representation for Computer Graphics. Technical report, Department of Computer Science, Princeton University, 1997. 562

[Rusinkiewicz, 1998] Szymon M. Rusinkiewicz. A New Change of Variables for Efficient BRDF Representation. In *Proceedings of EGWR – The Eurographics Workshop on Rendering Techniques*. Springer-Verlag, June 1998. 523, 524

[Ryan, 2011] Daniel L. Ryan. *History of Computer Graphics*. DLR Associates Series. Author House, 2011. 10

[Sakas and Pommert, 1997] Georgios Sakas and Andreas Pommert. Advanced Applications of Volume Visualization Methods in Medicine. In *Eurographics State of the Art Reports*. Eurographics Association, 1997. 441

[Sakas *et al.*, 2009] Georgios Sakas, Grigorios Karangelis, and Andreas Pommert. Advanced Applications of Volume Visualization Methods in Medicine. In *Advanced Signal Processing: Theory and Implementation for Sonar, Radar, and Non-Invasive Medical Diagnostic Systems*, The Electrical Engineering & Applied Signal Processing Series, chapter 4, pages 147–219. Taylor & Francis/CRC Press, 2009. 441

[Salvaggio, 2009] Nanette L. Salvaggio. *Basic Photographic Materials and Processes*. Focal Press, 3rd edition, 2009. 675

[Samet and Webber, 1988a] Hanan Samet and Robert E. Webber. Hierarchical Data Structures and Algorithms for Computer Graphics – Part I: Fundamentals. *IEEE Computer Graphics and Applications*, 8(3):48–68, May 1988. 415

[Samet and Webber, 1988b] Hanan Samet and Robert E. Webber. Hierarchical Data Structures and Algorithms for Computer Graphics – Part II: Applications. *IEEE Computer Graphics and Applications*, 8(4):59–75, July 1988. 415

[Samet, 1989] Hanan Samet. Implementing Ray Tracing with Octrees and Neighbor Finding. *Computers & Graphics*, 13(4):445–460, 1989. 380

[Samet, 1990] Hanan Samet. *Applications of Spatial Data Structures: Computer Graphics, Image Processing, and GIS*. Addison-Wesley Longman Publishing, 1990. 415

[Saupe and Alexa, 2001] Dietmar Saupe and Marc Alexa. Computer Graphics in Germany. *SIGGRAPH Computer Graphics*, 35(3):14–21, August 2001. Computer Graphics around the World. 8

[Scherson and Caspary, 1987] Isaac D. Scherson and Elisha Caspary. Data Structures and the Time Complexity of Ray Tracing. *The Visual Computer*, 3(4):201–213, December 1987. 410

[Schjøth *et al.*, 2007a] Lars Schjøth, Ole Fogh Olsen, and Jon Sporring. Diffusion Based Photon Mapping. *Advances in Computer Graphics and Computer Vision (Proceedings of GRAPP – The International Conference on Computer Graphics Theory and Applications)*, 4:109–122, 2007. 637

[Schjøth *et al.*, 2007b] Lars Schjøth, Jeppe Eliot Revall Frisvad, Kenny Erleben, and Jon Sporring. Photon Differentials. In *Proceedings of GRAPHITE – The International Conference on Computer Graphics and Interactive Techniques in Australasia and Southeast Asia*, pages 179–186. ACM Press, 2007. 637

[Schjøth *et al.*, 2008] Lars Schjøth, Jon Sporring, and Ole Fogh Olsen. Diffusion Based Photon Mapping. *Computer Graphics Forum*, 27(8):2114–2127, December 2008. 637

[Schjøth, 2005] Lars Schjøth. Diffusion Based Photon Mapping. Master's thesis, IT University Copenhagen, November 2005. 637

[Schjøth, 2009] Lars Schjøth. *Anisotropic Density Estimation in Global Illumination – A Journey through Time and Space –*. PhD thesis, Department of Computer Science, University of Copenhagen, 2009. 637

[Schlick, 1993] Christophe Schlick. A Customizable Reflectance Model for Everyday Rendering. In *Proceedings of EGWR – The Eurographics Workshop on Rendering Techniques*, pages 73–83. Springer-Verlag, June 1993. 492, 518, 547, 555

[Schlick, 1994a] Christophe Schlick. A Survey of Shading and Reflectance Models. *Computer Graphics Forum*, 13(2):121–131, May 1994. 561

[Schlick, 1994b] Christophe Schlick. An Inexpensive BRDF Model for Physically-Based Rendering. *Computer Graphics Forum (Proceedings of Eurographics – The Annual Conference of the European Association for Computer Graphics)*, 13(3):233–246, August 1994. 492, 518, 547, 555

[Schmittler *et al.*, 2004] Jörg Schmittler, Tim Dahmen, Daniel Pohl, Christian Vogelgesang, and Philipp Slusallek. Ray Tracing for Current and Future Games. In *Proceedings of Jahrestagung der Gesellschaft für Informatik*, 2004. 9

[Schmittler *et al.*, 2005] Jörg Schmittler, Daniel Pohl, Tim Dahmen, Christian Vogelgesang, and Philipp Slusallek. Realtime Ray Tracing for Current and Future Games. In *ACM SIGGRAPH Courses*. ACM Press, 2005. 9

[Schneider and Eberly, 2002] Philip J. Schneider and David Eberly. *Geometric Tools for Computer Graphics*. Elsevier Science, 2002. 126

[Schregle and Wienold, 2004] Roland Schregle and Jan Wienold. Physical Validation of Global Illumination Methods: Measurement and Error Analysis. *Computer Graphics Forum*, 23(4):761–781, December 2004. 739

[Schregle *et al.*, 2013] Roland Schregle, Cornelia Denk, Philipp Slusallek, and Mashhuda Glencross. Grand Challenges: Material Models in the Automotive Industry. In *Proceedings of EGMAM – The Eurographics Workshop on Material Appearance Modeling*, pages 1–6. Eurographics Association, 2013. 473

[Schregle, 2003] Roland Schregle. Bias Compensation for Photon Maps. *Computer Graphics Forum*, 22(4):729–742, December 2003. 637

[Schregle, 2004] Roland Schregle. *Daylight Simulation with Photon Maps*. PhD thesis, Saarland University, 2004. 637, 739

[Schuster, 1964] D. H. Schuster. A New Ambiguous Figure: A Three-Stick Clevis. *American Journal of Psychology*, 77(4):673, December 1964. 699, 700

[Schwarze, 1990] Jochen Schwarze. Cubic and Quartic Roots. In Andrew S. Glassner, editor, *Graphics Gems I*, chapter VIII.1, pages 404–407. Academic Press, 1990. 31, 34

[Schwarzhaupt *et al.*, 2012] Jorge Schwarzhaupt, Henrik Wann Jensen, and Wojciech Jarosz. Practical Hessian-Based Error Control for Irradiance Caching. *ACM Transactions on Graphics*, 31(6):193:1–193:10, November 2012. 626, 627

[Seah and Lee, 1998] HockSoon Seah and Yong Tsui Lee. Computer Graphics in Singapore. *SIGGRAPH Computer Graphics*, 32(3):20–23, August 1998. Computer Graphics around the World. 8

[Segovia and Ernst, 2010] Benjamin Segovia and Manfred Ernst. Memory Efficient Ray Tracing with Hierarchical Mesh Quantization. In *Proceedings of Graphics Interface – The Canadian Annual Conference on Computer Graphics, Interactive Systems, and Human-Computer Interaction*, pages 153–160. Canadian Human-Computer Communications Society, 2010. 365

[Segovia *et al.*, 2006] Benjamin Segovia, Jean-Claude Iehl, Richard Mitanchey, and Bernard Péroche. Bidirectional Instant Radiosity. In *Proceedings of EGSR – The Eurographics Symposium on Rendering*, pages 389–397. Eurographics Association, 2006. 631

[Segovia *et al.*, 2007] Benjamin Segovia, Jean-Claude Iehl, and Bernard Péroche. Metropolis Instant Radiosity. *Computer Graphics Forum (Proceedings of Eurographics – The Annual Conference of the European Association for Computer Graphics)*, 26(3):425–434, September 2007. 631

[Segovia, 2007] Benjamin Segovia. *Interactive Light Transport with Virtual Point Lights.* PhD thesis, University of Lyon, October 2007. 631

[Segura and Feito, 2001] Rafael J. Segura and Francisco R. Feito. Algorithms to Test Ray-Triangle Intersection. Comparative Study. In *Proceedings of WSCG – The Winter School of Computer Graphics: The International Conference in Central Europe on Computer Graphics, Visualization and Computer Vision*, 2001. Short Paper. 258

[Shah *et al.*, 2007] Apurva Shah, Jun Han Cho, Athena Xenakis, and Stefan Gronsky. Anyone Can Cook — Inside Ratatouille's Kitchen. In *ACM SIGGRAPH Courses*, number 30. ACM Press, 2007. 9

[Shene, 1994] Ching-Kuang Shene. Computing the Intersection of a Line and a Cylinder. In Paul Seagrave Heckbert, editor, *Graphics Gems IV*, chapter V.1, pages 353–355. Academic Press, 1994. 272

[Shene, 1995] Ching-Kuang Shene. Computing the Intersection of a Line and a Cone. In Alan W. Paeth, editor, *Graphics Gems V*, chapter V.1, pages 227–231. Academic Press, 1995. 275

[Shevtsov *et al.*, 2007] Maxim Shevtsov, Alexei Soupikov, and Alexander Kapustin. Ray-Triangle Intersection Algorithm for Modern CPU Architectures. In *Proceedings of GraphiCon – The International Conference on Computer Graphics and Vision*, 2007. 391

[Shi and Pan, 1996a] Jiaoying Shi and Zhigeng Pan. China: Computer Graphics Education Available at Universities, Institutes and Training Centers. *SIGGRAPH Computer Graphics*, 30(3):7–9, August 1996. 8

[Shi and Pan, 1996b] Jiaoying Shi and Zhigeng Pan. China: Computer Graphics is Fastest Developing Computer Application. *SIGGRAPH Computer Graphics*, 30(2):11–14, May 1996. 8

[Shi and Pan, 2001] Jiaoying Shi and Zhigeng Pan. Computer Graphics in China: An Overview. *SIGGRAPH Computer Graphics*, 35(2):22–27, May 2001. Computer Graphics around the World. 8

[Shirley and Marschner, 2009] Peter Schuyler Shirley and Stephen Robert Marschner. *Fundamentals of Computer Graphics.* A. K. Peters, 3rd edition, 2009. 739

[Shirley and Morley, 2003] Peter Schuyler Shirley and R. Keith Morley. *Realistic Ray Tracing.* A. K. Peters, 2nd edition, 2003. 739

[Shirley and Wang, 1991] Peter Schuyler Shirley and Changyaw Allen Wang. Direct Lighting Calculation by Monte Carlo Integration. In *Proceedings of EGWR – The Eurographics Workshop on Rendering Techniques*, pages 54–59. Springer-Verlag, June 1991. 605, 606

[Shirley and Wang, 1992] Peter Schuyler Shirley and Changyaw Allen Wang. Distribution Ray Tracing: Theory and Practice. In *Proceedings of EGWR – The Eurographics Workshop on Rendering Techniques*, pages 33–44. Springer-Verlag, 1992. 608

[Shirley *et al.*, 1995] Peter Schuyler Shirley, Bretton Wade, Philip M. Hubbard, David Zareski, Bruce Jonathan Walter, and Donald P. Greenberg. Global Illumination via Density-Estimation. In *Proceedings of EGWR – The Eurographics Workshop on Rendering Techniques*, pages 219–230. Springer-Verlag, 1995. 634

[Shirley *et al.*, 1996] Peter Schuyler Shirley, Changyaw Allen Wang, and Kurt Zimmerman. Monte Carlo Techniques for Direct Lighting Calculations. *ACM Transactions on Graphics*, 15(1):1–36, January 1996. 604

[Shirley *et al.*, 1997] Peter Schuyler Shirley, Brian Edward Smits, Helen Hu, and Eric P. F. Lafortune. A Practitioners' Assessment of Light Reflection Models. In *Proceedings of Pacific Graphics – The Pacific Conference on Computer Graphics and Applications*, pages 40–49. IEEE Computer Society, October 1997. 555

[Shirley, 1990] Peter Schuyler Shirley. A Ray Tracing Method for Illumination Calculation in Diffuse-Specular Scenes. In *Proceedings of Graphics Interface – The Canadian Annual Conference on Computer Graphics, Interactive Systems, and Human-Computer Interaction*, pages 205–212. Canadian Human-Computer Communications Society, 1990. 634

[Shirley, 2000] Peter Schuyler Shirley. *Realistic Ray Tracing.* A. K. Peters, 1st edition, 2000. 739

[Shirley, 2002] Peter Schuyler Shirley. *Fundamentals of Computer Graphics.* A. K. Peters, 2nd edition, 2002. 739

[Shoemake, 1991] Ken Shoemake. Quaternions and 4x4 Matrices. In James Richard Arvo, editor, *Graphics Gems II*, chapter VII.6, pages 351–354. Academic Press, 1991. 113

[Shoemake, 1994] Ken Shoemake. Euler Angle Conversion. In Paul Seagrave Heckbert, editor, *Graphics Gems IV*, chapter III.5, pages 222–229. Academic Press, 1994. 108

[Siegel and Howell, 1981] Robert Siegel and John Reid Howell. *Thermal Radiation Heat Transfer.* Hemisphere Publishing Corporation, 4th edition, 1981. 470

[Sillion and Puech, 1994] François X. Sillion and Claude Puech. *Radiosity and Global Illumination.* Morgan Kaufmann Publishers, 1994. 596

[Sillion, 1996] François X. Sillion. France: Computer Graphics Education is Blossoming. *SIGGRAPH Computer Graphics*, 30(3):12–13, August 1996. 8

[Silverman, 1986] Bernard W. Silverman. *Density Estimation for Statistics and Data Analysis*, volume 26 of *Monographs on Statistics and Applied Probability.* Chapman & Hall/CRC Press, 1986. 172

[Simiakakis, 1995] George Simiakakis. *Accelerating Ray Tracing with Directional Subdivision and Parallel Processing.* PhD thesis, University of East Anglia, October 1995. 410

[Slater, 1992] Mel Slater. Tracing a Ray through Uniformly Subdivided N-Dimensional Space. *The Visual Computer*, 9(1):39–46, October 1992. 374

[Slavik, 1992] Pavel Slavik. Computer Graphics Education in Czechoslovakia. *SIGGRAPH Computer Graphics*, 26(1):74–75, January 1992. 8

[Slavik, 1996] Pavel Slavik. Computer Graphics Education in the Czech Republic. *SIGGRAPH Computer Graphics*, 30(1):22–23, February 1996. 8

[Slob, 2008] Jelmer J. Slob. State-of-the-Art Driving Simulators, a Literature Survey. Technical Report DCT 2008.107, Department of Mechanical Engineering, Eindhoven University of Technology, August 2008. 10

[Sloup, 2002] Jaroslav Sloup. A Survey of the Modelling and Rendering of the Earth's Atmosphere. In *Proceedings of SCCG – The Spring Conference on Computer Graphics*, pages 141–150. ACM Press, 2002. 448

[Slusallek, 1997] Philipp Slusallek. Photo-Realistic Rendering – Recent Trends and Developments –. In *Eurographics State of the Art Reports.* Eurographics Association, 1997. 738

[Smith and Pokorny, 1975] Vivianne C. Smith and Joel Pokorny. Spectral Sensitivity of the Foveal Cone Photopigments between 400 and 500 nm. *Vision Research*, 15(2):161–171, February 1975. 685, 695, 719

[Smith, 1967] Bruce G. Smith. Geometrical Shadowing of a Random Rough Surface. *IEEE Transactions on Antennas and Propagation*, 15(5):668–671, September 1967. 542

[Smith, 1978] Alvy Ray Smith. Color Gamut Transform Pairs. *SIGGRAPH Computer Graphics (Proceedings of SIGGRAPH – The ACM International Conference on Computer Graphics and Interactive Techniques)*, 12(3):12–19, August 1978. 707

[Smith, 1995] Alvy Ray Smith. A Pixel Is Not a Little Square, a Pixel Is Not a Little Square, a Pixel Is Not a Little Square! Technical Report 6, Microsoft Computer Graphics, June 1995. 200

[Smits and Jensen, 2000] Brian Edward Smits and Henrik Wann Jensen. Global Illumination Test Scenes. Technical Report UUCS-00-013, School of Computing, University of Utah, June 2000. 739

[Smits, 1998] Brian Edward Smits. Efficiency Issues for Ray Tracing. *Journal of Graphics Tools (JGT)*, 3(2):1–14, February 1998. 363

[Smits, 2005] Brian Edward Smits. Efficiency Issues for Ray Tracing. In *ACM SIGGRAPH Courses.* ACM Press, 2005. 363

[Smyk and Myszkowski, 2002] Mirosław Smyk and Karol Myszkowski. Quality Improvements for Indirect Illumination Interpolation. In *Proceedings of ICCVG – The International Conference on Computer Vision and Graphics*, pages 685–692, 2002. 627

[Snyder and Barr, 1987] John M. Snyder and Alan H. Barr. Ray Tracing Complex Models Containing Surface Tessellations. *SIGGRAPH Computer Graphics (Proceedings of SIGGRAPH – The ACM International Conference on Computer Graphics and Interactive Techniques)*, 21(4):119–128, August 1987. 374, 410

[Soupikov *et al.*, 2008] Alexei Soupikov, Maxim Shevtsov, and Alexander Kapustin. Improving Kd-Tree Quality at a Reasonable Construction Cost. In *Proceedings of RT – The IEEE Symposium on Interactive Ray Tracing*, pages 67–72. IEEE Computer Society, 2008. 369, 370, 385, 403

[Speer, 1992] L. Richard Speer. An Updated Cross-Indexed Guide to the Ray-Tracing Literature. *SIGGRAPH Computer Graphics*, 26(1):41–72, January 1992. 739

[Spencer and Jones, 2009a] Ben Spencer and Mark W. Jones. Hierarchical Photon Mapping. *IEEE Transactions on Visualization and Computer Graphics*, 15(1):49–61, January 2009. 640

[Spencer and Jones, 2009b] Ben Spencer and Mark W. Jones. Into the Blue: Better Caustics through Photon Relaxation. *Computer Graphics Forum (Proceedings of Eurographics – The Annual Conference of the European Association for Computer Graphics)*, 28(2):319–328, April 2009. 641

[Spencer and Jones, 2013] Ben Spencer and Mark W. Jones. Progressive Photon Relaxation. *ACM Transactions on Graphics*, 32(1):7:1–7:11, February 2013. 641

[Stam, 2001] Jos Stam. An Illumination Model for a Skin Layer Bounded by Rough Surfaces. In *Proceedings of EGWR – The Eurographics Workshop on Rendering Techniques*, pages 39–52. Eurographics Association/Springer-Verlag, 2001. 525

[Stanco *et al.*, 2011] Filippo Stanco, Sebastiano Battiato, and Giovanni Gallo. *Digital Imaging for Cultural Heritage Preservation: Analysis, Restoration, and Reconstruction of Ancient Artworks.* CRC Press, 2011. 10

[Stevens, 1957] Stanley S. Stevens. On the Psychophysical Law. *Psychological Review*, 64(3):153–181, May 1957. 691

[Stich *et al.*, 2009] Martin Stich, Heiko Friedrich, and Andreas Dietrich. Spatial Splits in Bounding Volume Hierarchies. In *Proceedings of HPG – The Conference on High-Performance Graphics*, pages 7–13. Eurographics Association/ACM SIGGRAPH, 2009. 392

[Stogryn, 1967] Alex Stogryn. Electromagnetic Scattering from Rough, Finitely Conducting Surfaces. *Radio Science*, 2(4):415–428, April 1967. 548

[Stone, 2002] Maureen C. Stone. *Field Guide to Digital Color.* A. K. Peters, 2002. 729

[Strutt, 1871a] John William Strutt. On the Light from the Sky, its Polarization and Colour. *Philosophical Magazine*, 41:107–120, 1871. 449

[Strutt, 1871b] John William Strutt. On the Scattering of Light by Small Particles. *Philosophical Magazine*, 41:447–454, 1871. 449

[Stürzlinger and Tobler, 1994] Wolfgang Stürzlinger and Robert F. Tobler. Two Optimization Methods for Raytracing. In *Proceedings of SCCG – The Spring Conference on Computer Graphics*, pages 104–107, June 1994. 365, 411, 413

[Subramanian and Fussell, 1990a] Kalpathi Raman Subramanian and Donald S. Fussell. A Cost Model for Ray Tracing Hierarchies. Technical Report TR-90-04, Department of Computer Sciences, The University of Texas at Austin, March 1990. 399

[Subramanian and Fussell, 1990b] Kalpathi Raman Subramanian and Donald S. Fussell. Factors Affecting Performance of Ray Tracing Hierarchies. Technical Report TR-90-21, Department of Computer Sciences, The University of Texas at Austin, July 1990. 392

[Subramanian and Fussell, 1991] Kalpathi Raman Subramanian and Donald S. Fussell. Automatic Termination Criteria for Ray Tracing Hierarchies. In *Proceedings of Graphics Interface – The Canadian Annual Conference on Computer Graphics, Interactive Systems, and Human-Computer Interaction*, pages 93–100. Canadian Human-Computer Communications Society, June 1991. 399

[Subramanian, 1987] Kalpathi Raman Subramanian. Fast Ray Tracing using K-D Trees. Master's thesis, Department of Computer Sciences, The University of Texas at Austin, December 1987. 390, 395

[Subramanian, 1990] Kalpathi Raman Subramanian. *Adapting Search Structures to Scene Characteristics for Ray Tracing.* PhD thesis, Department of Computer Sciences, The University of Texas at Austin, December 1990. 392, 399

[Suffern, 2007] Kevin Geoffrey Suffern. *Ray Tracing from the Ground Up.* A. K. Peters, 2007. 739

[Sundstedt *et al.*, 2005] Veronica Sundstedt, Diego Gutierrez, Fermin Gomez, and Alan Chalmers. Participating Media for High-Fidelity Cultural Heritage. In *Proceedings of VAST – The International Symposium on Virtual Reality, Archaeology and Cultural Heritage*, pages 83–90. Eurographics Association, 2005. 441

[Sung and Shirley, 1992] Kelvin Sung and Peter Schuyler Shirley. Ray Tracing with the BSP Tree. In David Kirk, editor, *Graphics Gems III*, chapter VI.1, pages 271–274. Academic Press, 1992. 381

[Sung *et al.*, 2008] Kelvin Sung, Peter Schuyler Shirley, and Steven Baer. *Essentials of Interactive Computer Graphics.* A. K. Peters, 2008. 739

[Sutherland, 1963a] Ivan Edward Sutherland. Sketchpad: A Man-Machine Graphical Communication System. In *Proceedings of the AFIPS Spring Joint Computer Conference*, pages 329–346, May 1963. 4

[Sutherland, 1963b] Ivan Edward Sutherland. *Sketchpad: A Man-Machine Graphical Communication System.* PhD thesis, Massachusetts Institute of Technology, January 1963. 4

[Sutherland, 1968] Ivan Edward Sutherland. A Head-Mounted Three Dimensional Display. In *Proceedings of the AFIPS Fall Joint Computer Conference*, pages 757–764, December 1968. 4

[Sutherland, 1998] Ivan Edward Sutherland. A Head-Mounted Three Dimensional Display. In *Seminal Graphics*, pages 295–302. ACM Press, 1998. 4

[Suykens and Willems, 2000] Frank Suykens and Yves D. Willems. Density Control for Photon Maps. In *Proceedings of EGWR – The Eurographics Workshop on Rendering Techniques*, pages 23–34. Springer-Verlag, 2000. 641

[Suzuki, 1997] Kaizo Suzuki. Meet the Multimedia Content Association of Japan. *SIGGRAPH Computer Graphics*, 31(4):18–19, November 1997. Computer Graphics around the World. 8

[Szécsi and Benedek, 2002] László Szécsi and Balázs Benedek. Improvements on the KD-Tree. In *Proceedings of the Hungarian Conference on Computer Graphics and Geometry (Elsõ Magyar Számítógépes Grafika és Geometria Konferencia)*, 2002. 400, 409

[Szécsi, 2003] László Szécsi. An Effective Implementation of the K-D Tree. In Jeff Lander, editor, *Graphics Programming Methods*, chapter 3.9, pages 315–326. Charles River Media, 2003. 381, 404

[Szirmay-Kalos and Antal, 2003] László Szirmay-Kalos and György Antal. Metropolis Sampling in Random Walk Global Illumination Algorithms. In Jeff Lander, editor, *Graphics Programming Methods*, chapter 3.3, pages 249–259. Charles River Media, 2003. 623

[Szirmay-Kalos and Márton, 1997] László Szirmay-Kalos and Gábor Márton. On the Limitations of Worst-Case Optimal Ray Shooting Algorithms. In *Proceedings of WSCG – The Winter School of Computer Graphics: The International Conference in Central Europe on Computer Graphics, Visualization and Computer Vision*, pages 562–571, 1997. 412, 414

[Szirmay-Kalos and Márton, 1998] László Szirmay-Kalos and Gábor Márton. Worst-Case versus Average Case Complexity of Ray-Shooting. *Computing*, 61(2):103–131, June 1998. 412, 413, 414

[Szirmay-Kalos *et al.*, 1999] László Szirmay-Kalos, Péter Dornbach, and Werner Purgathofer. On the Start-Up Bias Problem of Metropolis Sampling. In *Proceedings of WSCG – The Winter School of Computer Graphics: The International Conference in Central Europe on Computer Graphics, Visualization and Computer Vision*, 1999. 139, 622

[Szirmay-Kalos *et al.*, 2001] László Szirmay-Kalos, László Kovács, and Ali Mohamed Abbas. Testing Monte-Carlo Global Illumination Methods with Analytically Computable Scenes. *Journal of WSCG (Proceedings of WSCG – The Winter School of Computer Graphics: The International Conference in Central Europe on Computer Graphics, Visualization and Computer Vision)*, 9(1–3):419–430, February 2001. 586, 739

[Szirmay-Kalos *et al.*, 2002] László Szirmay-Kalos, Vlastimil Havran, Balázs Benedek, and László Szécsi. On the Efficiency of Ray-Shooting Acceleration Schemes. In *Proceedings of SCCG – The Spring Conference on Computer Graphics*, pages 97–106. ACM Press, 2002. 414

[Szirmay-Kalos *et al.*, 2010] László Szirmay-Kalos, Balázs Tóth, Milán Magdics, and Balázs Csébfalvi. Efficient Free Path Sampling in Inhomogeneous Media. In *Eurographics Posters*. Eurographics Association, 2010. 604

[Szirmay-Kalos *et al.*, 2011] László Szirmay-Kalos, Balázs Tóth, and Milán Magdics. Free Path Sampling in High Resolution Inhomogeneous Participating Media. *Computer Graphics Forum*, 30(1):85–97, March 2011. 603, 604

[Szirmay-Kalos, 1999] László Szirmay-Kalos. Monte-Carlo Global Illumination Methods – State of the Art and New Developments. In *Proceedings of SCCG – The Spring Conference on Computer Graphics*, pages 3–21, 1999. 623

[Szirmay-Kalos, 2000] László Szirmay-Kalos. Monte-Carlo Methods in Global Illumination. Institute of Computer Graphics, Vienna University of Technology, 2000. 623

[Tabellion and Lamorlette, 2004] Eric Tabellion and Arnauld Lamorlette. An Approximate Global Illumination System for Computer Generated Films. *ACM Transactions on Graphics (Proceedings of SIGGRAPH – The ACM International Conference on Computer Graphics and Interactive Techniques)*, 23(3):469–476, August 2004. 626, 627

[Tabellion and Lamorlette, 2008] Eric Tabellion and Arnauld Lamorlette. An Approximate Global Illumination System for Computer Generated Films. In *ACM SIGGRAPH Courses*, pages 74:1–74:8. ACM Press, 2008. 626, 627

[Tatarchuk *et al.*, 2006] Natalya Tatarchuk, Christopher Oat, Pedro V. Sander, Jason L. Mitchell, Carsten Wenzel, and Alex Evans. Advanced Real-Time Rendering in 3D Graphics and Games. In *ACM SIGGRAPH Courses*, number 26. ACM Press, 2006. 9

[Tatarchuk *et al.*, 2007] Natalya Tatarchuk, Johan Andersson, Shannon Drone, Nico Galoppo, Chris Green, Christopher Oat, Jason L. Mitchell, and Martin Mittring. Advanced Real-Time Rendering in 3D Graphics and Games. In *ACM SIGGRAPH Courses*, number 28. ACM Press, 2007. 9

[Tatarchuk *et al.*, 2008] Natalya Tatarchuk, Michael Boulton, Hao Chen, Dominic Filion, Xinguo Liu, Martin Mittring, Rob McNaughton, and Christopher Oat. Advances in Real-Time Rendering in 3D Graphics and Games. In *ACM SIGGRAPH Courses*. ACM Press, 2008. 9

[Tatarchuk, 2009] Natalya Tatarchuk. Advances in Real-Time Rendering in 3D Graphics and Games. In *ACM SIGGRAPH Courses*. ACM Press, 2009. 9

[Tatarchuk, 2011] Natalya Tatarchuk. Advances in Real-Time Rendering in 3D Graphics and Games. In *ACM SIGGRAPH Courses*. ACM Press, 2011. 9

[Teixeira, 1996] José Carlos Teixeira. Portugal: Network of Institutions Cooperate in Computer Graphics Education. *SIGGRAPH Computer Graphics*, 30(3):20–20, August 1996. 8

[Thompson *et al.*, 2011] William B. Thompson, Roland W. Fleming, Sarah Creem-Regehr, and Jeanine Kelly Stefanucci. *Visual Perception from a Computer Graphics Perspective*. A. K. Peters/CRC Press, 2011. 702

[Thompson, 1990] Kelvin Thompson. Matrix Identities. In Andrew S. Glassner, editor, *Graphics Gems I*, chapter IX.1, pages 453–454. Academic Press, 1990. 119

[Tinwell, 2014] Angela Tinwell. *The Uncanny Valley in Games and Animation*. A. K. Peters/CRC Press, December 2014. 8

[Tobler and Maierhofer, 2006] Robert F. Tobler and Stefan Maierhofer. Improved Illumination Estimation for Photon Maps in Architectural Scenes. In *Proceedings of WSCG – The Winter School of Computer Graphics: The International Conference in Central Europe on Computer Graphics, Visualization and Computer Vision*, pages 257–261, 2006. 636

[Torrance and Sparrow, 1966] Kenneth E. Torrance and Ephraim M. Sparrow. Off-Specular Peaks in the Directional Distribution of Reflected Thermal Radiation. *ASME Journal of Heat Transfer*, 88(2):223–230, 1966. 525, 534

[Torrance and Sparrow, 1967] Kenneth E. Torrance and Ephraim M. Sparrow. Theory for Off-Specular Reflection from Roughened Surfaces. *Journal of the Optical Society of America*, 57(9):1105–1114, September 1967. 525, 534, 535

[Trowbridge and Reitz, 1975] T. S. Trowbridge and Karl P. Reitz. Average Irregularity Representation of a Rough Surface for Ray Reflection. *Journal of the Optical Society of America*, 65(5):531–536, 1975. 513

[Trumbore, 1992] Ben Trumbore. Rectangular Bounding Volumes for Popular Primitives. In David Kirk, editor, *Graphics Gems III*, chapter VI.5, pages 295–300. Academic Press, 1992. 359

[Tsuruno, 1997] Sachiko Tsuruno. The Animation of M. C. Escher's Belvedere. In *ACM SIGGRAPH Visual Proceedings*, pages 237–237. ACM Press, 1997. 698

[Tumblin and Rushmeier, 1991] Jack John Erwin Tumblin and Holly Edith Rushmeier. Tone Reproduction for Realistic Computer Generated Images. Technical Report GIT-GVU-91-13, Georgia Institute of Technology, 1991. 733, 734

[Tumblin and Rushmeier, 1993] Jack John Erwin Tumblin and Holly Edith Rushmeier. Tone Reproduction for Realistic Images. *IEEE Computer Graphics and Applications*, 13(6):42–48, November 1993. 733, 734

[Turk, 1990] Greg Turk. Generating Random Points in Triangles. In Andrew S. Glassner, editor, *Graphics Gems I*, chapter I.5, pages 24–28. Academic Press, 1990. 255

[Turkowski, 1990a] Ken Turkowski. Filters for Common Resampling Tasks. In Andrew S. Glassner, editor, *Graphics Gems I*, chapter III.2, pages 147–165. Academic Press, 1990. 201

[Turkowski, 1990b] Ken Turkowski. Properties of Surface-Normal Transformations. In Andrew S. Glassner, editor, *Graphics Gems I*, chapter X.7, pages 539–547. Academic Press, 1990. 120

[Ulbricht *et al.*, 2005] Christiane Ulbricht, Alexander Wilkie, and Werner Purgathofer. Verification of Physically-Based Rendering Algorithms. In *Eurographics State of the Art Reports*, pages 95–112. Eurographics Association, 2005. 739

[Valle, 1996] Giorgio G. Valle. Italy: Double-digit Revenue Increase Marks 1995. *SIGGRAPH Computer Graphics*, 30(2):25–27, May 1996. 8

[van Antwerpen, 2010] Dietger G. van Antwerpen. Unbiased Physically Based Rendering on the GPU. Master's thesis, Department of Software Technology, Delft University of Technology, 2010. 624

[van Antwerpen, 2011] Dietger G. van Antwerpen. A Survey of Importance Sampling Applications in Unbiased Physically Based Rendering. April 2011. 624

[van de Hulst, 1957] Hendrik Christoffel van de Hulst. *Light Scattering by Small Particles.* Dover Publications, 1957. 470

[van de Hulst, 1980] Hendrik Christoffel van de Hulst. *Multiple Light Scattering: Tables, Formulas, and Applications.* Academic Press, 1980. 470

[van Verth and Bishop, 2004] James M. van Verth and Lars M. Bishop. *Essential Mathematics for Games and Interactive Applications: A Programmer's Guide.* Morgan Kaufmann Publishers, 1st edition, 2004. 126

[van Verth and Bishop, 2008] James M. van Verth and Lars M. Bishop. *Essential Mathematics for Games and Interactive Applications: A Programmer's Guide.* Morgan Kaufmann Publishers, 2nd edition, May 2008. 126

[van Verth and Bishop, 2015] James M. van Verth and Lars M. Bishop. *Essential Mathematics for Games and Interactive Applications.* A. K. Peters/CRC Press, 3rd edition, August 2015. 126

[Vanegas *et al.*, 2009] Carlos A. Vanegas, Daniel G. Aliaga, Peter Wonka, Pascal Müller, Paul Waddell, and Benjamin Watson. Modeling the Appearance and Behavior of Urban Spaces. In *Eurographics State of the Art Reports*, pages 1–16. Eurographics Association, 2009. 10

[Veach and Guibas, 1994] Eric Veach and Leonidas J. Guibas. Bidirectional Estimators for Light Transport. In *Proceedings of EGWR – The Eurographics Workshop on Rendering Techniques*, pages 147–162. Springer-Verlag, June 1994. 618

[Veach and Guibas, 1995] Eric Veach and Leonidas J. Guibas. Optimally Combining Sampling Techniques for Monte Carlo Rendering. In *Proceedings of SIGGRAPH – The ACM International Conference on Computer Graphics and Interactive Techniques*, pages 419–428. ACM Press, August 1995. 158, 608, 618

[Veach and Guibas, 1997] Eric Veach and Leonidas J. Guibas. Metropolis Light Transport. In *Proceedings of SIGGRAPH – The ACM International Conference on Computer Graphics and Interactive Techniques*, pages 65–76. ACM Press, 1997. 139, 621

[Veach, 1996] Eric Veach. Non-Symmetric Scattering in Light Transport Algorithms. In *Proceedings of EGWR – The Eurographics Workshop on Rendering Techniques*, pages 81–90. Springer-Verlag, 1996. 496, 569

[Veach, 1997] Eric Veach. *Robust Monte Carlo Methods for Light Transport Simulation.* PhD thesis, Department of Computer Science, Stanford University, December 1997. 139, 158, 166, 569, 608, 613, 618, 621

[Vidal *et al.*, 2004] Franck P. Vidal, Fernando Bello, Ken W. Brodlie, Nigel W. John, Derek Gould, Roger Phillips, and Nick J. Avis. Principles and Applications of Medical Virtual Environments. In *Eurographics State of the Art Reports.* Eurographics Association, 2004. 10

[Vince, 2005a] John A. Vince. *Geometry for Computer Graphics: Formulae, Examples and Proofs.* Springer-Verlag, 2005. 126

[Vince, 2005b] John A. Vince. *Mathematics for Computer Graphics.* Springer-Verlag, 2nd edition, 2005. 126

[Vince, 2007] John A. Vince. *Vector Analysis for Computer Graphics.* Springer-Verlag, 2007. 84

[Vince, 2008] John A. Vince. *Geometric Algebra for Computer Graphics.* Springer-Verlag, 2008. 126

[Vince, 2009] John A. Vince. *Geometric Algebra: An Algebraic System for Computer Games and Animation.* Springer Publishing, 2009. 126

[Vince, 2010] John A. Vince. *Mathematics for Computer Graphics.* Springer-Verlag, 3rd edition, 2010. 126

[Vince, 2011a] John A. Vince. *Quaternions for Computer Graphics.* Springer Publishing, 2011. 90

[Vince, 2011b] John A. Vince. *Rotation Transforms for Computer Graphics.* Springer Publishing, 2011. 115

[Vince, 2012] John A. Vince. *Matrix Transforms for Computer Games and Animation.* Springer Publishing, 2012. 124

[Vince, 2013a] John A. Vince. *Calculus for Computer Graphics.* Springer Publishing, 2013. 64

[Vince, 2013b] John A. Vince. *Mathematics for Computer Graphics.* Springer Publishing, 4th edition, 2013. 126

[Vinkler *et al.*, 2012] Marek Vinkler, Vlastimil Havran, and Jiří Sochor. Visibility Driven BVH Build up Algorithm for Ray Tracing. *Computers & Graphics*, 36(4):283–296, June 2012. 400

[Vlachos *et al.*, 2001] Alex Vlachos, Jörg Peters, Chas Boyd, and Jason L. Mitchell. Curved PN Triangles. In *Proceedings of I3D – The ACM SIGGRAPH Symposium on Interactive 3D Graphics and Games*, pages 159–166. ACM Press, 2001. 333, 334

[von Helmholtz, 1867] Hermann von Helmholtz. *Handbuch der Physiologischen Optik.* Leipzig, Leopold Voss, 1867. 444, 476

[von Seeliger, 1888] Hugo von Seeliger. *Zur Photometrie zerstreut reflektierender Substanzen.* Bayerische Akademie der Wissenschaften München, 1888. Mathematisch-Physikalische Klasse 18: Sitzungsberichte. 486

[Voorhies, 1992] Douglas Voorhies. Triangle-Cube Intersection. In David Kirk, editor, *Graphics Gems III*, chapter VII.2, pages 236–239. Academic Press, 1992. 369

[Vorba, 2011] Jiří Vorba. Bidirectional Photon Mapping. In *Proceedings of CESCG – The Central European Seminar on Computer Graphics*, 2011. 641

[Vos and Walraven, 1971] J. J. Vos and P. L. Walraven. On the Derivation of the Foveal Receptor Primaries. *Vision Research*, 11(8):799–818, August 1971. 685, 695, 719

[Vos, 1978] J. J. Vos. Colorimetric and Photometric Properties of a 2-Degree Fundamental Observer. *Color Research & Application*, 3(3):125–128, 1978. 686, 687, 712, 719

[Šrámek and Kaufman, 2000] Miloš Šrámek and Arie E. Kaufman. Fast Ray-Tracing of Rectilinear Volume Data Using Distance Transforms. *IEEE Transactions on Visualization and Computer Graphics*, 6(3):236–252, July 2000. 389, 390

[Šrámek, 1994a] Miloš Šrámek. Cubic Macro-Regions for Fast Voxel Traversal. *Machine Graphics and Vision (Proceedings of the Conference on Computer Graphics and Image Processing)*, 3(1/2):171–179, 1994. 388

[Šrámek, 1994b] Miloš Šrámek. Fast Surface Rendering from Raster Data by Voxel Traversal using Chessboard Distance. In *Proceedings of Vis – The IEEE Conference on Visualization*, pages 188–195. IEEE Computer Society, 1994. 388

[Šrámek, 1995] Miloš Šrámek. Comparison of Some Ray Generators for Ray Tracing Volumetric Data. In *Proceedings of WSCG – The Winter School of Computer Graphics: The International Conference in Central Europe on Computer Graphics, Visualization and Computer Vision*, volume 2, pages 466–475, February 1995. 388

[Šrámek, 1996] Miloš Šrámek. Fast Ray-Tracing of Rectilinear Volume Data. In *Proceedings of the Eurographics Workshop on Virtual Environments and Scientific Visualization*, pages 201–210. Eurographics Association, 1996. 388

[Wächter and Keller, 2006] Carsten Alexander Wächter and Alexander Keller. Instant Ray Tracing: The Bounding Interval Hierarchy. In *Proceedings of EGSR – The Eurographics Symposium on Rendering*, pages 139–149. Eurographics Association, 2006. 365

[Wächter and Keller, 2007] Carsten Alexander Wächter and Alexander Keller. Terminating Spatial Hierarchies by A Priori Bounding Memory. In *Proceedings of RT – The IEEE Symposium on Interactive Ray Tracing*, pages 41–46. IEEE Computer Society, 2007. 409

[Wacker *et al.*, 2005] Markus Wacker, Michael Keckeisen, Stefan Kimmerle, Wolfgang Straßer, Volker Luckas, Clemens Groß, Arnulph Fuhrmann, Mirko Sattler, Ralf Sarlette, and Reinhard Klein. Simulation and Visualisation of Virtual Textiles for Virtual Try-On. *Research Journal of Textile and Apparel*, 9(1):37–47, 2005. 473

[Wald and Havran, 2006] Ingo Wald and Vlastimil Havran. On Building Fast KD-Trees for Ray Tracing, and on Doing that in O(N log N). In *Proceedings of RT – The IEEE Symposium on Interactive Ray Tracing*, pages 61–69. IEEE Computer Society, 2006. 406

[Wald *et al.*, 2004] Ingo Wald, Johannes Günther, and Philipp Slusallek. Balancing Considered Harmful – Faster Photon Mapping using the Voxel Volume Heuristic –. *Computer Graphics Forum (Proceedings of Eurographics – The Annual Conference of the European Association for Computer Graphics)*, 23(3):595–603, September 2004. 635

[Wald *et al.*, 2006] Ingo Wald, Andreas Dietrich, Carsten Benthin, Alexander Efremov, Tim Dahmen, Johannes Günther, Vlastimil Havran, Hans-Peter Seidel, and Philipp Slusallek. Applying Ray Tracing for Virtual Reality and Industrial Design. In *Proceedings of RT – The IEEE Symposium on Interactive Ray Tracing*, pages 177–185. IEEE Computer Society, September 2006. 9

[Wald, 2007] Ingo Wald. On Fast Construction of SAH-Based Bounding Volume Hierarchies. In *Proceedings of RT – The IEEE Symposium on Interactive Ray Tracing*, pages 33–40. IEEE Computer Society, 2007. 361, 365, 401

[Walraven and Valeton, 1984] Jan Walraven and J. Mathé Valeton. Visual Adaptation and Response Saturation. In Andrea J. van Doorn, Wim A. van de Grind, and Jan J. Koenderink, editors, *Limits in Perception: Essays in Honour of Maarten A. Bouman*, chapter 14, pages 401–429. VNU Science Press, December 1984. 690

[Walter *et al.*, 1997] Bruce Jonathan Walter, Philip M. Hubbard, Peter Schuyler Shirley, and Donald P. Greenberg. Global Illumination using Local Linear Density Estimation. *ACM Transactions on Graphics*, 16(3):217–259, July 1997. 636

[Walter *et al.*, 2007] Bruce Jonathan Walter, Stephen Robert Marschner, Hongsong Li, and Kenneth E. Torrance. Microfacet Models for Refraction through Rough Surfaces. In *Proceedings of EGSR – The Eurographics Symposium on Rendering*, pages 195–206. Eurographics Association, 2007. 513, 525, 526, 528, 544, 546, 547

[Walter, 1998] Bruce Jonathan Walter. *Density Estimation Techniques for Global Illumination.* PhD thesis, Cornell University, 1998. 636

[Walter, 2005] Bruce Jonathan Walter. Notes on the Ward BRDF. Technical Report PCG-05-06, Program of Computer Graphics, Cornell University, April 2005. 516

[Walter, 2008] Bruce Jonathan Walter. Fast Agglomerative Clustering for Rendering. In *Proceedings of RT – The IEEE Symposium on Interactive Ray Tracing*, pages 81–86. IEEE Computer Society, August 2008. 361

[Wand and Jones, 1995] Matt P. Wand and M. Chris Jones. *Kernel Smoothing.* Chapman & Hall/CRC Press, 1995. 172

[Wang *et al.*, 2007] Ying Wang, Wei Zhang, Su Wu, and Yang Guo. Simulators for Driving Safety Study: A Literature Review. In *Proceedings of ICVR – The International Conference on Virtual Reality*, volume 4563, pages 584–593. Springer-Verlag, 2007. 10

[Wang, 1992] Changyaw Allen Wang. Physically Correct Direct Lighting for Distribution Ray Tracing. In David Kirk, editor, *Graphics Gems III*, chapter VI.7, pages 307–313. Academic Press, 1992. 605, 606

[Wang, 1994] Changyaw Allen Wang. *The Direct Lighting Computation in Global Illumination Methods.* PhD thesis, Indiana University, November 1994. 604

[Ward Larson and Heckbert, 1992] Gregory J. Ward Larson and Paul Seagrave Heckbert. Irradiance Gradients. In *Proceedings of EGWR – The Eurographics Workshop on Rendering Techniques.* Springer-Verlag, May 1992. 626

[Ward Larson and Heckbert, 2008] Gregory J. Ward Larson and Paul Seagrave Heckbert. Irradiance Gradients. In *ACM SIGGRAPH Courses*, pages 72:1–72:17. ACM Press, 2008. 626

[Ward Larson and Shakespeare, 1998] Gregory J. Ward Larson and Robert A. Shakespeare. *Rendering with Radiance: The Art and Science of Lighting Visualization.* Morgan Kaufmann Publishers, 1st edition, 1998. 739

[Ward Larson and Shakespeare, 2004] Gregory J. Ward Larson and Robert A. Shakespeare. *Rendering with Radiance: The Art and Science of Lighting Visualization.* Booksurge Llc, 2nd edition, 2004. 739

[Ward Larson *et al.*, 1988] Gregory J. Ward Larson, Francis M. Rubinstein, and Robert D. Clear. A Ray Tracing Solution for Diffuse Interreflection. *SIGGRAPH Computer Graphics (Proceedings of SIGGRAPH – The ACM International Conference on Computer Graphics and Interactive Techniques)*, 22(4):85–92, June 1988. 626

[Ward Larson, 1990] Gregory J. Ward Larson. Visualization. *Lighting Design and Application*, 20(6):4–5, 14–20, June 1990. 739

[Ward Larson, 1992] Gregory J. Ward Larson. Measuring and Modeling Anisotropic Reflection. *SIGGRAPH Computer Graphics (Proceedings of SIGGRAPH – The ACM International Conference on Computer Graphics and Interactive Techniques)*, 26(2):265–272, July 1992. 516, 537

[Ward Larson, 1994] Gregory J. Ward Larson. The RADIANCE Lighting Simulation and Rendering System. In *Proceedings of SIGGRAPH – The ACM International Conference on Computer Graphics and Interactive Techniques*, pages 459–472. ACM Press, 1994. 739

[Ward Larson, 1996] Gregory J. Ward Larson. Tools for Lighting Design and Analysis. In *ACM SIGGRAPH Courses*. ACM Press, 1996. 10

[Warn, 1983] David R. Warn. Lighting Controls for Synthetic Images. *SIGGRAPH Computer Graphics (Proceedings of SIGGRAPH – The ACM International Conference on Computer Graphics and Interactive Techniques)*, 17(3):13–21, July 1983. 432

[Watt, 1999] Alan H. Watt. *3D Computer Graphics*. Addison-Wesley Publishing, 3rd edition, June 1999. 739

[Weber, 1846] Ernst Heinrich Weber. Der Tastsinn und das Gemeingefühl. In Rudolph Wagner, editor, *Handwörterbuch der Physiologie III*, pages 481–588. Vieweg, 1846. 691

[Weghorst *et al.*, 1984] Hank Weghorst, Gary Hooper, and Donald P. Greenberg. Improved Computational Methods for Ray Tracing. *ACM Transactions on Graphics*, 3(1):52–69, January 1984. 358

[Weidlich and Wilkie, 2007] Andrea Weidlich and Alexander Wilkie. Arbitrarily Layered Micro-Facet Surfaces. In *Proceedings of GRAPHITE – The International Conference on Computer Graphics and Interactive Techniques in Australasia and Southeast Asia*, pages 171–178. ACM Press, 2007. 558, 559

[Weidlich and Wilkie, 2009] Andrea Weidlich and Alexander Wilkie. Exploring the Potential of Layered BRDF Models. In *ACM SIGGRAPH Asia Courses*, pages 7:1–7:58. ACM Press, 2009. 558

[Weidlich and Wilkie, 2011] Andrea Weidlich and Alexander Wilkie. Thinking in Layers – Modelling with Layered Surfaces. In *ACM SIGGRAPH Asia Courses*, pages 20:1–20:43. ACM Press, 2011. 558

[Welker, 2013] Cécile Welker. Early History of French CG. In *ACM SIGGRAPH Art Gallery*, volume 46, pages 376–385. ACM Press, August 2013. 8

[Wennberg, 1996] Teresa Wennberg. France: Our Shrinking Planet – a Birds Eye Perspective on Computer Graphics and Art Education. *SIGGRAPH Computer Graphics*, 30(3):10–11, August 1996. 8

[Westlund and Meyer, 2002] Harold Bruce Westlund and Gary W. Meyer. A BRDF Database Employing the Beard-Maxwell Reflection Model. In *Proceedings of Graphics Interface – The Canadian Annual Conference on Computer Graphics, Interactive Systems, and Human-Computer Interaction*. Canadian Human-Computer Communications Society, 2002. 541

[Weyrich *et al.*, 2008a] Tim Alexander Weyrich, Jason Lawrence, Hendrik Peter Asmus Lensch, Szymon M. Rusinkiewicz, and Todd Zickler. Principles of Appearance Acquisition and Representation. In *ACM SIGGRAPH Courses*, pages 80:1–80:119. ACM Press, 2008. 562

[Weyrich *et al.*, 2008b] Tim Alexander Weyrich, Jason Lawrence, Hendrik Peter Asmus Lensch, Szymon M. Rusinkiewicz, and Todd Zickler. Principles of Appearance Acquisition and Representation. *Foundations and Trends in Computer Graphics and Vision*, 4(2):75–191, 2008. 562

[Whang *et al.*, 1995] Kyu-Young Whang, Ju-Won Song, Ji-Woong Chang, Ji-Yun Kim, Wan-Sup Cho, Chong-Mok Park, and Il-Yeol Song. Octree-R: An Adaptive Octree for Efficient Ray Tracing. *IEEE Transactions on Visualization and Computer Graphics*, 1(4):343–349, December 1995. 378

[White, 1979] Michael White. A New Effect of Pattern on Perceived Lightness. *Perception*, 8(4):413–416, August 1979. 701

[Whitted, 1979] Turner Whitted. An Improved Illumination Model for Shaded Display. *SIGGRAPH Computer Graphics (Proceedings of SIGGRAPH – The ACM International Conference on Computer Graphics and Interactive Techniques)*, 13(2):14–14, August 1979. 6, 598

[Whitted, 1980] Turner Whitted. An Improved Illumination Model for Shaded Display. *Communications of the ACM*, 23(6):343–349, June 1980. 6, 598

[Wilkie and Weidlich, 2011] Alexander Wilkie and Andrea Weidlich. A Physically Plausible Model for Light Emission from Glowing Solid Objects. *Computer Graphics Forum (Proceedings of EGSR – The Eurographics Symposium on Rendering)*, 30(4):1269–1276, June 2011. 475

[Wilkie *et al.*, 1998] Alexander Wilkie, Robert F. Tobler, and Werner Purgathofer. Photon Radiosity Lightmaps for CSG Solids. In *Proceedings of CSG – The Conference on Set Theoretic Solid Modelling: Techniques and Applications*, 1998. 633

[Wilkie *et al.*, 2000] Alexander Wilkie, Robert F. Tobler, and Werner Purgathofer. Orientation Lightmaps for Photon Tracing in Complex Environments. In *Proceedings of CGI – Computer Graphics International*, pages 279–286. IEEE Computer Society, 2000. 633

[Wilkie *et al.*, 2001] Alexander Wilkie, Robert F. Tobler, and Werner Purgathofer. Orientation Lightmaps for Photon Tracing in Complex Environments. *The Visual Computer*, 17(5):318–327, June 2001. 633

[Wilkie *et al.*, 2009] Alexander Wilkie, Andrea Weidlich, Marcus A. Magnor, and Alan Chalmers. Predictive Rendering. In *ACM SIGGRAPH Asia Courses*, pages 12:1–12:428. ACM Press, 2009. 738

[Wilkie, 2001] Alexander Wilkie. *Photon Tracing for Complex Environments*. PhD thesis, Institute of Computer Graphics and Algorithms, Vienna University of Technology, April 2001. 633

[Williams and Max, 1992] Peter L. Williams and Nelson L. Max. A Volume Density Optical Model. In *Proceedings of the ACM Workshop on Volume Visualization*, pages 61–68. ACM Press, 1992. 465, 592

[Williams *et al.*, 1998] Peter L. Williams, Nelson L. Max, and Clifford M. Stein. A High Accuracy Volume Renderer for Unstructured Data. *IEEE Transactions on Visualization and Computer Graphics*, 4(1):37–54, January 1998. 592

[Williams *et al.*, 2005] Amy Williams, Steve Barrus, R. Keith Morley, and Peter Schuyler Shirley. An Efficient and Robust Ray-Box Intersection Algorithm. *Journal of Graphics Tools (JGT)*, 10(1):49–54, 2005. 301

[Wolfe, 1998a] Rosalee Wolfe. *Seminal Graphics: Pioneering Efforts that Shaped the Field.* ACM Press, December 1998. 4

[Wolfe, 1998b] Rosalee Wolfe. Seminole Graphics. *SIGGRAPH Computer Graphics*, 32(3):46–47, August 1998. 4

[Woo and Amanatides, 1990] Andrew Chung How Woo and John Amanatides. Voxel Occlusion Testing: A Shadow Determination Accelerator for Ray Tracing. In *Proceedings of Graphics Interface – The Canadian Annual Conference on Computer Graphics, Interactive Systems, and Human-Computer Interaction*, pages 213–220. Canadian Human-Computer Communications Society, 1990. 413

[Woo, 1989] Andrew Chung How Woo. Accelerators for Shadow Determination in Ray Tracing. Master's thesis, Department of Computer Science, University of Toronto, 1989. 413

[Woo, 1990] Andrew Chung How Woo. Fast Ray-Box Intersection. In Andrew S. Glassner, editor, *Graphics Gems I*, chapter VII.5, pages 395–396. Academic Press, 1990. 301

[Woodcock *et al.*, 1965] E. R. Woodcock, T. Murphy, P. Hemmings, and S. Longworth. Techniques Used in the GEM Code for Monte Carlo Neutronics Calculations in Reactors and Other Systems of Complex Geometry. In *Proceedings of the Conference on Applications of Computing Methods to Reactor Problems*, pages 557–579, 1965. Argonne National Laboratory Report ANL-7050. 602

[Woop *et al.*, 2006] Sven Woop, Gerd Marmitt, and Philipp Slusallek. B-KD Trees for Hardware Accelerated Ray Tracing of Dynamic Scenes. In *Proceedings of EGGH – The Eurographics Workshop on Graphics Hardware*, pages 67–77. Eurographics Association, 2006. 365

[Wrenninge and Bin Zafar, 2011] Magnus Wrenninge and Nafees Bin Zafar. Production Volume Rendering — Fundamentals. In *ACM SIGGRAPH Courses*. ACM Press, 2011. 441

[Wrenninge *et al.*, 2010] Magnus Wrenninge, Nafees Bin Zafar, Jeff Clifford, Gavin Graham, Devon Penney, Janne Kontkanen, Jerry Tessendorf, and Andrew Clinton. Volumetric Methods in Visual Effects. In *ACM SIGGRAPH Courses*. ACM Press, 2010. 441

[Wrenninge *et al.*, 2011] Magnus Wrenninge, Nafees Bin Zafar, Antoine Bouthors, Jerry Tessendorf, Victor Grant, Andrew Clinton, Ollie Harding, and Gavin Graham. Production Volume Rendering — Systems. In *ACM SIGGRAPH Courses*. ACM Press, 2011. 441

[Wrenninge, 2012] Magnus Wrenninge. *Production Volume Rendering: Design and Implementation.* A. K. Peters/CRC Press, 2012. 441

[Wu, 1992] Xiaolin Wu. A Linear-Time Simple Bounding Volume Algorithm. In David Kirk, editor, *Graphics Gems III*, chapter VI.6, pages 301–306. Academic Press, 1992. 359

[Wyman *et al.*, 2013] Christopher Wyman, Peter-Pike Sloan, and Peter Schuyler Shirley. Simple Analytic Approximations to the CIE XYZ Color Matching Functions. *Journal of Computer Graphics Techniques (JCGT)*, 2(2):1–11, 2013. 712

[Wyszecki and Stiles, 2000] Günther Wyszecki and Walter Stanley Stiles. *Color Science: Concepts and Methods, Quantitative Data and Formulae.* Wiley, 2nd edition, August 2000. 729

[Wyvill, 1990] Brian Wyvill. 3D Grid Hashing Function. In Andrew S. Glassner, editor, *Graphics Gems I*, chapter VI.1, pages 343–345. Academic Press, 1990. 376

[Yoon and Manocha, 2006] Sung-Eui Yoon and Dinesh Manocha. Cache-Efficient Layouts of Bounding Volume Hierarchies. *Computer Graphics Forum (Proceedings of Eurographics – The Annual Conference of the European Association for Computer Graphics)*, 25(3):507–516, September 2006. 409

[Yue *et al.*, 2010] Yonghao Yue, Kei Iwasaki, Bing-Yu Chen, Yoshinori Dobashi, and Tomoyuki Nishita. Unbiased, Adaptive Stochastic Sampling for Rendering Inhomogeneous Participating Media. *ACM Transactions on Graphics (Proceedings of SIGGRAPH Asia – The ACM Conference on Computer Graphics and Interactive Techniques in Asia)*, 29(6):177:1–177:8, December 2010. 604

[Yue *et al.*, 2011] Yonghao Yue, Kei Iwasaki, Bing-Yu Chen, Yoshinori Dobashi, and Tomoyuki Nishita. Toward Optimal Space Partitioning for Unbiased, Adaptive Free Path Sampling of Inhomogeneous Participating Media. *Computer Graphics Forum (Proceedings of Pacific Graphics – The Pacific Conference on Computer Graphics and Applications)*, 30(7):1911–1919, September 2011. 604

[Yuksel *et al.*, 2011] Cem Yuksel, Scott Schaefer, and John Keyser. Parameterization and Applications of Catmull-Rom Curves. *Computer-Aided Design*, 43(7):747–755, July 2011. 352

[Zhang *et al.*, 2011] Yingping Zhang, Dengming Zhu, Xianjie Qiu, and Zhaoqi Wang. Importance Sampling for Volumetric Illumination of Flames. *Computers & Graphics*, 35(2):312–319, April 2011. 429

[Zimmerman, 1995] Kurt Zimmerman. Direct Lighting Models for Ray Tracing Cylindrical Lamps. In Alan W. Paeth, editor, *Graphics Gems V*, chapter V.6, pages 285–289. Academic Press, 1995. 605, 606

[Zinke and Weber, 2006] Arno Zinke and Andreas Weber. Efficient Ray Based Global Illumination Using Photon Maps. In *Proceedings of VMV – The Workshop on Vision, Modeling, and Visualization*, pages 113–120, November 2006. 636

[Zsolnai and Szirmay-Kalos, 2013] Károly Zsolnai and László Szirmay-Kalos. Automatic Parameter Control for Metropolis Light Transport. In *Eurographics Short Papers*, pages 53–56. Eurographics Association, 2013. 623

[Zuffo, 1996] Marcelo Knörich Zuffo. Brazil: A Well Established Academic Community and a Fast Emerging Market. *SIGGRAPH Computer Graphics*, 30(2):8–10, May 1996. 8

[Zuiderveld *et al.*, 1992] Karel J. Zuiderveld, Anton H. J. Koning, and Max A. Viergever. Acceleration of Ray-Casting using 3-D Distance Transforms. In *Proceedings of the SPIE Conference on Visualization in Biomedical Computing*, volume 1808, pages 324–335. SPIE, September 1992. 388

[Zuniga and Uhlmann, 2006] Miguel R. Zuniga and Jeffrey K. Uhlmann. Ray Queries with Wide Object Isolation and the DE-Tree. *Journal of Graphics Tools (JGT)*, 11(3):27–45, 2006. 365, 366

Index